"Things worthwhile generally don't just happen. Luck is a fact, but should not be a factor. Good luck is what is left over after intelligence and effort have combined at their best. Negligence or indifference are usually reviewed from an unlucky seat. The law of cause and effect and causality both work the same with inexorable exactitudes. Luck is the residue of design."
--- Branch Rickey

"I don't care if I was a ditch-digger at a dollar a day, I'd want to do my job better than the fellow next to me. I'd want to be the best at whatever I do."
-- Branch Rickey

Julianne,
You're the reason I don't play the lottery or gamble. There's no way I would end up hitting the jackpot twice in one lifetime. I try to say it often, but in case there goes a day when I don't say it – Thank You for everything. I don't know what I did to deserve you, but I'm thankful for it.

Avery, Shay, McKenzie,
Watching you three grow up has been the single greatest joy of my life. And I know you've already asked – a million times. But the reason why I tell the three of you I love you so much is, so you'll never forget it. I love you. You're the best to happen to Mom and me, our entire world wrapped up into such tiny packages.

Cal,

I could write another book, 10,000 pages long, telling you what you meant to me or about all of our adventures or car rides. You were always more than a dog to me. You were my buddy, my sidekick, my traveling companion, my confidant. But more importantly, you always seemed to be there right when I needed you. I'm going to miss all the fun we had – the tricks we used to do early on (Cal, what does a hanging slider do? It just spins), the fetch in the backyard, watching you zoom around out there making impossible hairpin turns look easy. You were so impossibly good with our girls. When Shay was a toddler she adored being by you and you always let her. The snuggling with Avery on the couch. Letting little McKenzie tug on your tail. You were great, better than great.

The night Julie kneeled next to you and told you it was OK to let go, that you did your job, that you did a great job taking care of me. Over the last 13-plus years I thought I was the one taking care of you. But Julie was right. Somehow you ended of taking care of me. You always took care of me.

I'm going to miss you – every single day.

Author Bio: Joseph Werner provides further evidence that Jim Bouton was right when he wrote, "You spend your life gripping a baseball, and in the end it turns out that it was the other way around all the time."

As a lifelong Indians fan, Werner's lived and died multiple times over. First with the original revival of Cleveland baseball in the mid-1990s, then languishing through the lean years before having his life reinvigorated by their fantastically wonderful 2016 post-season run and continued success.

All along the way, though, he's heard two of the greatest radio voices in the game: Herb Score and Tom Hamilton. Despite his youth at the time, he proudly — and somewhat embarrassingly — remembers falling asleep with his arms clutched around a portable radio as Score made his last radio call during Game 7 of 1997 World Series.

Werner has been fortunate — and incredibly blessed — to have some of his work published and mentioned on several major media outlets, including: ESPN, The Athletic, Yahoo! Sports, Cleveland.com, The Baseball Research Journal, and Beyond the Box Score.

A Note from the Author: As I mentioned in every book, my continued goal is to provide the reader with the best product that I can. I want it to be something that not only is informative but also enjoyable to read. My hope is that I've achieved that goal with this year's Prospect Digest Handbook. Thank you for reading – as always.

I apologize about the delay in this year's edition.

I would just like to tip my hat to the following websites because without their invaluable data, none of this would have been possible:

> fangraphs.com
> baseballreference.com
> thebaseballcube.com
> claydavenport.com
> baseballprospectus.com
> MiLB.com (and their sometimes spotty TV Subscription)

Another special thank you goes out to Josh Stollings for his help on this year's cover.

I would like to thank you, the reader, once again. I enjoy hearing from you guys – be it before or after the book comes out. Please feel free to reach me at the following email address: JosephMWerner@yahoo.com. I absolutely love hearing everyone's thoughts/comments/concerns/feedback.

I'd also like to thank Michael Salfino. I appreciate you always championing my book – again. I'm forever indebted.

One final note: The book is a single-man operation. I'm the researcher, the scout, the writer, and – unfortunately – the proofreader / editor. I apologize in advance for typos, grammatical / punctuation errors.

All the best,

JOE

Table of Contents

The Top 300 Prospects	13
The Top 10 Prospects by Position	19
Ranking the Farm Systems	23
Organizational Analysis	29
Arizona Diamondbacks	31
Atlanta Braves	45
Baltimore Orioles	57
Boston Red Sox	73
Chicago Cubs	87
Chicago White Sox	101
Cincinnati Reds	115
Cleveland Guardians	129
Colorado Rockies	143
Detroit Tigers	157
Houston Astros	171
Kansas City Royals	185
Los Angeles Angels	199
Los Angeles Dodgers	211
Miami Marlins	225
Milwaukee Brewers	239
Minnesota Twins	253
New York Mets	267
New York Yankees	281
Oakland Athletics	295
Philadelphia Phillies	309
Pittsburgh Pirates	323
San Diego Padres	337
San Francisco Giants	351
Seattle Mariners	365
St. Louis Cardinals	379
Tampa Bay Rays	393
Texas Rangers	407
Toronto Blue Jays	421
Washington Nationals	435

The Top 300 Prospects

Ranking the Top 300 Prospects (1-100)

Rank	Player	Team	Age	POS
1	Jackson Chourio	Milwaukee Brewers	19	CF
2	Elly De La Cruz	Cincinnati Reds	21	SS
3	Gunnar Henderson	Baltimore Orioles	22	3B/SS
4	Corbin Carroll	Arizona Diamondbacks	22	CF
5	Jordan Walker	St. Louis Cardinals	21	3B/OF
6	James Wood	Washington Nationals	22	CF
7	Grayson Rodriguez	Baltimore Orioles	23	RHP
8	Eury Perez	Miami Marlins	20	RHP
9	Miguel Vargas	Los Angeles Dodgers	23	1B/3B/LF
10	Francisco Alvarez	New York Mets	21	C
11	Marcelo Mayer	Boston Red Sox	20	SS
12	Cam Collier	Cincinnati Reds	18	3B
13	Brett Baty	New York Mets	23	3B/LF
14	Anthony Volpe	New York Yankees	22	SS
15	Andrew Painter	Philadelphia Phillies	20	RHP
16	Jackson Holliday	Baltimore Orioles	19	SS
17	Jordan Lawlar	Arizona Diamondbacks	20	SS
18	Pete Crow-Armstrong	Chicago Cubs	21	CF
19	Termarr Johnson	Pittsburgh Pirates	19	2B/SS
20	Druw Jones	Arizona Diamondbacks	19	CF
21	Kyle Harrison	San Francisco Giants	21	LHP
22	Ezequiel Tovar	Colorado Rockies	21	SS
23	Jackson Merrill	San Diego Padres	20	SS
24	Diego Cartaya	Los Angeles Dodgers	21	C
25	Daniel Espino	Cleveland Guardians	22	RHP
26	Marco Luciano	San Francisco Giants	21	SS
27	Bobby Miller	Los Angeles Dodgers	24	RHP
28	Ricky Tiedemann	Toronto Blue Jays	20	LHP
29	Endy Rodriguez	Pittsburgh Pirates	23	C
30	George Valera	Cleveland Guardians	22	OF
31	Zac Veen	Colorado Rockies	21	RF
32	Evan Carter	Texas Rangers	20	CF
33	Tanner Bibee	Cleveland Guardians	24	RHP
34	Harry Ford	Seattle Mariners	20	C
35	Tink Hence	St. Louis Cardinals	20	RHP
36	Koudai Senga	New York Mets	30	RHP
37	Gavin Williams	Cleveland Guardians	23	RHP
38	Curtis Mead	Tampa Bay Rays	22	2B/3B
39	Brooks Lee	Minnesota Twins	22	SS
40	Jackson Jobe	Detroit Tigers	20	RHP
41	Shane Baz	Tampa Bay Rays	24	RHP
42	Mick Abel	Philadelphia Phillies	21	RHP
43	Brady House	Washington Nationals	20	SS
44	Taj Bradley	Tampa Bay Rays	22	RHP
45	Sal Frelick	Milwaukee Brewers	23	CF
46	Josh Jung	Texas Rangers	25	3B
47	Cade Cavalli	Washington Nationals	19	RHP
48	Tyler Soderstrom	Oakland Athletics	21	C/1B
49	Henry Davis	Pittsburgh Pirates	23	C
50	Jack Leiter	Texas Rangers	23	RHP
51	Edwin Arroyo	Cincinnati Reds	19	SS
52	Dalton Rushing	Los Angeles Dodgers	22	C
53	Alex Ramirez	New York Mets	20	CF
54	Samuel Zavala	San Diego Padres	18	CF
55	Edgar Quero	Los Angeles Angels	20	C
56	Kevin Alcantara	Chicago Cubs	20	CF
57	Jacob Berry	Miami Marlins	22	3B
58	Marco Raya	Minnesota Twins	20	RHP
59	Colson Montgomery	Chicago White Sox	21	SS
60	Logan O'Hoppe	Los Angeles Angels	23	C
61	Bo Naylor	Cleveland Guardians	23	C
62	Colt Keith	Detroit Tigers	21	2B/3B
63	Zach Neto	Los Angeles Angels	22	SS
64	Kevin Made	Chicago Cubs	20	SS
65	Mike Burrows	Pittsburgh Pirates	23	RHP
66	Emmanuel Rodriguez	Minnesota Twins	20	CF
67	Oswald Peraza	New York Yankees	23	SS
68	Brayan Rocchio	Cleveland Guardians	22	2B/SS
69	Jasson Dominguez	New York Yankees	20	CF
70	Royce Lewis	Minnesota Twins	24	SS
71	Ceddanne Rafaela	Boston Red Sox	22	SS/CF
72	Adael Amador	Colorado Rockies	20	SS
73	Noelvi Marte	Cincinnati Reds	21	SS
74	Triston Casas	Boston Red Sox	23	1B
75	Hunter Brown	Houston Astros	24	RHP
76	Kevin Parada	New York Mets	21	C
77	Nick Yorke	Boston Red Sox	21	2B
78	Masyn Winn	St. Louis Cardinals	21	SS
79	Max Meyer	Miami Marlins	24	RHP
80	Freddy Tarnok	Oakland Athletics	24	RHP
81	Brandon Pfaadt	Arizona Diamondbacks	24	RHP
82	Colton Cowser	Baltimore Orioles	23	OF
83	Quinn Priester	Pittsburgh Pirates	22	RHP
84	Cole Wilcox	Tampa Bay Rays	23	RHP
85	Carson Williams	Tampa Bay Rays	20	SS
86	Chase DeLauter	Cleveland Guardians	22	CF
87	Kyle Manzardo	Tampa Bay Rays	22	1B
88	James Triantos	Chicago Cubs	20	3B
89	Spencer Jones	New York Yankees	23	CF
90	Dylan Lesko	San Diego Padres	24	RHP
91	Jett Williams	New York Mets	19	SS
92	Gavin Cross	Kansas City Royals	22	CF
93	Jeferson Quero	Milwaukee Brewers	20	C
94	Brock Porter	Texas Rangers	24	RHP
95	Miguel Bleis	Boston Red Sox	19	CF
96	Jordy Vargas	Colorado Rockies	19	RHP
97	Aeverson Arteaga	San Francisco Giants	20	SS
98	Mitch Bratt	Texas Rangers	19	LHP
99	Joey Ortiz	Baltimore Orioles	24	SS
100	Gavin Stone	Los Angeles Dodgers	24	RHP

The 2023 Prospect Digest Handbook

Ranking the Top 300 Prospects (101-200)

Rank	Name	Team	Age	POS
101	DL Hall	Baltimore Orioles	24	LHP
102	Connor Norby	Baltimore Orioles	23	2B/LF
103	Jordan Westburg	Baltimore Orioles	24	IF
104	Matthew Lugo	Boston Red Sox	22	SS
105	Coby Mayo	Baltimore Orioles	21	3B
106	Michael Busch	Los Angeles Dodgers	25	2B/LF
107	Robert Hassell III	Washington Nationals	20	CF
108	Ken Waldichuk	Oakland Athletics	25	LHP
109	Austin Wells	New York Yankees	23	C
110	Elijah Green	Washington Nationals	19	CF
111	Jarlin Susana	Washington Nationals	19	RHP
112	Alec Burleson	St. Louis Cardinals	24	LF/RF
113	Jordan Wicks	Chicago Cubs	23	LHP
114	Matthew Liberatore	St. Louis Cardinals	23	LHP
115	Oscar Colas	Chicago White Sox	24	CF/RF
116	Benny Montgomery	Colorado Rockies	20	CF
117	Leonardo Bernal	St. Louis Cardinals	19	C
118	Joey Wiemer	Milwaukee Brewers	24	CF/RF
119	Drew Romo	Colorado Rockies	21	C
120	Luisangel Acuna	Texas Rangers	21	2B/SS
121	Jace Jung	Detroit Tigers	22	2B
122	Cole Young	Seattle Mariners	23	2B/SS
123	Daniel Susac	Oakland Athletics	22	C
124	Luis Ortiz	Pittsburgh Pirates	24	RHP
125	Drew Gilbert	Houston Astros	22	CF
126	Bryan Ramos	Chicago White Sox	21	3B
127	Bryce Miller	Seattle Mariners	24	RHP
128	Justyn-Henry Malloy	Detroit Tigers	23	3B/LF
129	Liover Peguero	Pittsburgh Pirates	22	SS
130	Chase Petty	Cincinnati Reds	20	RHP
131	Cade Horton	Chicago Cubs	26	RHP
132	Jared Jones	Pittsburgh Pirates	21	RHP
133	Nick Gonzales	Pittsburgh Pirates	24	2B/SS
134	Ty Madden	Detroit Tigers	23	RHP
135	Connor Prielipp	Minnesota Twins	25	LHP
136	Gabriel Hughes	Colorado Rockies	21	RHP
137	Zack Gelof	Oakland Athletics	23	2B/3B
138	Max Muncy	Oakland Athletics	20	SS
139	Yanquiel Fernandez	Colorado Rockies	20	RF
140	Reese Olson	Detroit Tigers	23	RHP
141	JR Ritchie	Atlanta Braves	20	RHP
142	Kumar Rocker	Texas Rangers	28	RHP
143	Owen Caissie	Chicago Cubs	20	LF/RF
144	Brice Turang	Milwaukee Brewers	23	IF/CF
145	Kyle Muller	Oakland Athletics	25	LHP
146	Bubba Chandler	Pittsburgh Pirates	20	RHP
147	Mike Siani	Cincinnati Reds	23	CF
148	Dax Fulton	Miami Marlins	21	LHP
149	Junior Caminero	Tampa Bay Rays	19	3B/SS
150	Ryan Pepiot	Los Angeles Dodgers	25	RHP
151	Garrett Mitchell	Milwaukee Brewers	24	CF
152	Mark Vientos	New York Mets	23	1B/3B/LF
153	Everson Pereira	New York Yankees	22	CF
154	Gabriel Arias	Cleveland Guardians	23	IF
155	Kahlil Watson	Miami Marlins	20	SS
156	Heston Kjerstad	Baltimore Orioles	24	RF
157	Brennen Davis	Chicago Cubs	23	OF
158	Wilmer Flores	Detroit Tigers	22	RHP
159	Mason Montgomery	Tampa Bay Rays	23	LHP
160	Dylan Beavers	Baltimore Orioles	21	OF
161	Yainer Diaz	Houston Astros	24	C/1B
162	Thomas Saggese	Texas Rangers	21	2B/3B
163	Yunior Severino	Minnesota Twins	23	2B/3B
164	Jose Salas	Minnesota Twins	20	SS
165	Cole Winn	Texas Rangers	23	RHP
166	Cole Phillips	Atlanta Braves	20	RHP
167	Justin Foscue	Texas Rangers	24	2B/3B
168	Bryan Mata	Boston Red Sox	24	RHP
169	Jhonkensy Noel	Cleveland Guardians	21	IF/OF
170	Angel Martinez	Cleveland Guardians	21	IF
171	Deyvison De Los Santos	Arizona Diamondbacks	20	1B/3B
172	Mikey Romero	Boston Red Sox	19	2B/SS
173	Frederick Bencosme	Baltimore Orioles	20	SS
174	Ben Brown	Chicago Cubs	26	RHP
175	Justin Crawford	Philadelphia Phillies	19	CF
176	Noah Schultz	Chicago White Sox	19	LHP
177	Alexander Canario	Chicago Cubs	23	OF
178	Brandon Barriera	Toronto Blue Jays	19	LHP
179	Blaze Jordan	Boston Red Sox	20	1B/3B
180	Sal Stewart	Cincinnati Reds	19	3B
181	C. Encarnacion-Strand	Cincinnati Reds	23	1B/3B
182	Axel Sanchez	Seattle Mariners	20	SS
183	Griff McGarry	Philadelphia Phillies	24	RHP
184	Addison Barger	Toronto Blue Jays	23	3B/SS
185	Esteury Ruiz	Oakland Athletics	24	OF
186	Connor Phillips	Cincinnati Reds	22	RHP
187	Cayden Wallace	Kansas City Royals	21	3B
188	Luis Matos	San Francisco Giants	21	CF
189	Robby Snelling	San Diego Padres	22	LHP
190	Cristian Mena	Chicago White Sox	20	RHP
191	Johan Rojas	Philadelphia Phillies	22	CF
192	Hao Yu Lee	Philadelphia Phillies	20	IF
193	Yosver Zulueta	Toronto Blue Jays	25	RHP
194	Gabriel Gonzalez	Seattle Mariners	19	RF
195	Jackson Ferris	Chicago Cubs	25	LHP
196	Carlos Jorge	Cincinnati Reds	19	2B/SS
197	Jake Bennett	Washington Nationals	21	LHP
198	Nelson Rada	Los Angeles Angels	17	CF
199	Willy Vasquez	Tampa Bay Rays	21	IF
200	Matt Mervis	Chicago Cubs	25	1B

Ranking the Top 300 Prospects (201-300)

Rank	Name	Team	Age	POS
201	Spencer Steer	Cincinnati Reds	19	IF
202	Ivan Herrera	St. Louis Cardinals	23	C
203	Jordan Diaz	Oakland Athletics	22	1B/2B/3B
204	Michael Arroyo	Seattle Mariners	21	SS
205	Angel Zerpa	Kansas City Royals	23	LHP
206	Cole Henry	Washington Nationals	23	RHP
207	Hunter Barco	Pittsburgh Pirates	23	LHP
208	Jorge Barrosa	Arizona Diamondbacks	22	CF
209	Jaime Melendez	Houston Astros	21	RHP
210	Blake Walston	Arizona Diamondbacks	22	LHP
211	Ryne Nelson	Arizona Diamondbacks	25	RHP
212	Chase Silseth	Los Angeles Angels	23	RHP
213	Ji-hwan Bae	Pittsburgh Pirates	23	IF/OF
214	Denzel Clarke	Oakland Athletics	23	OF
215	Henry Bolte	Oakland Athletics	19	OF
216	Owen White	Texas Rangers	23	RHP
217	Andy Pages	Los Angeles Dodgers	22	RF
218	Landon Sims	Arizona Diamondbacks	22	RHP
219	Yunior Garcia	Los Angeles Dodgers	21	1B/RF
220	Cristhian Vaquero	Washington Nationals	19	CF
221	Wilfred Veras	Chicago White Sox	20	1B/3B
222	Luis Perales	Boston Red Sox	20	RHP
223	Carter Jensen	Kansas City Royals	19	C
224	David Festa	Minnesota Twins	23	RHP
225	Gordon Graceffo	St. Louis Cardinals	23	RHP
226	Mason Auer	Tampa Bay Rays	22	CF
227	Max Wagner	Baltimore Orioles	21	3B
228	Eddinson Paulino	Boston Red Sox	20	IF/CF
229	Kerry Carpenter	Detroit Tigers	25	LF/RF
230	Maddux Bruns	Los Angeles Dodgers	21	LHP
231	Emerson Hancock	Seattle Mariners	24	RHP
232	Jordan Groshans	Miami Marlins	23	3B/SS
233	Jordan Beck	Colorado Rockies	22	LF/RF
234	Joe Perez	Houston Astros	23	3B
235	Eric Brown	Milwaukee Brewers	24	SS
236	Lawrence Butler	Oakland Athletics	22	OF
237	Trey Sweeney	New York Yankees	23	SS
238	Maikel Garcia	Kansas City Royals	23	SS
239	Tyler Gentry	Kansas City Royals	24	LF/RF
240	A.J. Vukovich	Arizona Diamondbacks	21	3B/LF
241	Korey Lee	Houston Astros	24	C
242	Sterlin Thompson	Colorado Rockies	22	3B/RF
243	Jacob Melton	Houston Astros	22	CF
244	Tyler Black	Milwaukee Brewers	22	2B/3B/CF
245	Asa Lacy	Kansas City Royals	24	LHP
246	S. Woods Richardson	Minnesota Twins	22	RHP
247	Logan Allen	Cleveland Guardians	24	LHP
248	Grant McCray	San Francisco Giants	23	CF
249	Jairo Pomares	San Francisco Giants	22	LF/RF
250	Thomas Harrington	Pittsburgh Pirates	25	RHP
251	Gabriel Martinez	Toronto Blue Jays	20	LF/RF
252	Tekoah Roby	Texas Rangers	21	RHP
253	Blade Tidwell	New York Mets	23	RHP
254	Jacob Miller	Miami Marlins	20	RHP
255	Owen Murphy	Atlanta Braves	19	RHP
256	Dahian Santos	Toronto Blue Jays	20	RHP
257	Hendry Mendez	Milwaukee Brewers	19	RF
258	Cristian Santana	Detroit Tigers	19	3B/SS
259	Jonathan Mejia	St. Louis Cardinals	21	SS
260	Edouard Julien	Minnesota Twins	24	2B
261	Jared Shuster	Atlanta Braves	24	LHP
262	Hayden Wesneski	Chicago Cubs	25	RHP
263	Braden Shewmake	Atlanta Braves	25	SS
264	Jaison Chourio	Cleveland Guardians	18	CF
265	Jacob Misiorowski	Milwaukee Brewers	26	RHP
266	Wikelman Gonzalez	Boston Red Sox	21	RHP
267	Ambioris Tavarez	Atlanta Braves	19	SS
268	Orelvis Martinez	Toronto Blue Jays	21	3B/SS
269	Lazaro Montes	Seattle Mariners	21	RF
270	Lonnie White Jr.	Pittsburgh Pirates	20	CF
271	Ryan Clifford	Houston Astros	19	1B/OF
272	Ariel Almonte	Cincinnati Reds	19	RF
273	Will Bednar	San Francisco Giants	25	RHP
274	Jose Rodriguez	Chicago White Sox	22	SS
275	Drey Jameson	Arizona Diamondbacks	25	RHP
276	Jadher Areinamo	Milwaukee Brewers	19	SS
277	Seth Johnson	Baltimore Orioles	24	RHP
278	Manuel Pena	Arizona Diamondbacks	19	2B/SS
279	Lyon Richardson	Cincinnati Reds	24	RHP
280	Ronny Mauricio	New York Mets	22	SS
281	William Bergolla	Philadelphia Phillies	21	2B/SS
282	Cooper Kinney	Tampa Bay Rays	22	2B/3B
283	Reggie Crawford	San Francisco Giants	22	LHP
284	Vaun Brown	San Francisco Giants	25	OF
285	Louie Varland	Minnesota Twins	25	RHP
286	Jordan Balazovic	Minnesota Twins	24	RHP
287	James Outman	Los Angeles Dodgers	26	OF
288	Jake Eder	Miami Marlins	20	LHP
289	Kendry Rojas	Toronto Blue Jays	20	RHP
290	Carson Whisenhunt	San Francisco Giants	24	LHP
291	Casey Schmitt	San Francisco Giants	24	3B/SS
292	Joey Estes	Oakland Athletics	21	RHP
293	Justin Campbell	Cleveland Guardians	23	RHP
294	Luke Little	Chicago Cubs	22	LHP
295	Justin Dirden	Houston Astros	25	OF
296	Aaron Zavala	Texas Rangers	23	RF
297	Ky Bush	Los Angeles Angels	23	RHP
298	Malcom Nunez	Pittsburgh Pirates	22	1B/3B
299	Warming Bernabel	Colorado Rockies	21	3B
300	Xavier Isaac	Tampa Bay Rays	19	1B

The Top 10 Prospects by Position

The Top 10 Prospects By Position

	Catchers	
1.	Francisco Alvarez	New York Mets
2.	Diego Cartaya	Los Angeles Dodgers
3.	Endy Rodriguez	Pittsburgh Pirates
4.	Harry Ford	Seattle Mariners
5.	Tyler Soderstrom	Oakland Athletics
6.	Henry Davis	Pittsburgh Pirates
7.	Dalton Rushing	Los Angeles Dodgers
8.	Edgar Quero	Los Angeles Angels
9.	Logan O'Hoppe	Los Angeles Angels
10.	Bo Naylor	Cleveland Guardians

	First Base	
1.	Miguel Vargas	Los Angeles Dodgers
2.	Tyler Soderstrom	Oakland Athletics
3.	Triston Casas	Boston Red Sox
4.	Kyle Manzardo	Tampa Bay Rays
5.	Mark Vientos	New York Mets
6.	Yainer Diaz	Houston Astros
7.	D. De Los Santos	Arizona Diamondbacks
8.	Blaze Jordan	Boston Red Sox
9.	C. Encarnacion-Strand	Cincinnati Reds
10.	Matt Mervis	Chicago Cubs

	Second Base	
1.	Termarr Johnson	Pittsburgh Pirates
2.	Curtis Mead	Tampa Bay Rays
3.	Colt Keith	Detroit Tigers
4.	Brayan Rocchio	Cleveland Guardians
5.	Nick Yorke	Boston Red Sox
6.	Connor Norby	Baltimore Orioles
7.	Jordan Westburg	Baltimore Orioles
8.	Michael Busch	Los Angeles Dodgers
9.	Luisangel Acuna	Texas Rangers
10.	Jace Jung	Detroit Tigers

	Third Base	
1.	Gunnar Henderson	Baltimore Orioles
2.	Jordan Walker	St. Louis Cardinals
3.	Miguel Vargas	Los Angeles Dodgers
4.	Cam Collier	Cincinnati Reds
5.	Brett Baty	New York Mets
6.	Curtis Mead	Tampa Bay Rays
7.	Josh Jung	Texas Rangers
8.	Jacob Berry	Miami Marlins
9.	Colt Keith	Detroit Tigers
10.	James Triantos	Chicago Cubs

	Shortstop	
1.	Elly De La Cruz	Cincinnati Reds
2.	Gunnar Henderson	Baltimore Orioles
3.	Marcelo Mayer	Boston Red Sox
4.	Anthony Volpe	New York Yankees
5.	Jackson Holliday	Baltimore Orioles
6.	Jordan Lawlar	Arizona Diamondbacks
7.	Termarr Johnson	Pittsburgh Pirates
8.	Ezequiel Tovar	Colorado Rockies
9.	Jackson Merrill	San Diego Padres
10.	Marco Luciano	San Francisco Giants

	Outfield	
1.	Jackson Chourio	Milwaukee Brewers
2.	Corbin Carroll	Arizona Diamondbacks
3.	Jordan Walker	St. Louis Cardinals
4.	James Wood	Washington Nationals
5.	Miguel Vargas	Los Angeles Dodgers
6.	Brett Baty	New York Mets
7.	Pete Crow-Armstrong	Chicago Cubs
8.	Druw Jones	Arizona Diamondbacks
9.	George Valera	Cleveland Guardians
10.	Zac Veen	Colorado Rockies

	Left-Handed Pitchers	
1.	Kyle Harrison	San Francisco Giants
2.	Ricky Tiedemann	Toronto Blue Jays
3.	Mitch Bratt	Texas Rangers
4.	DL Hall	Baltimore Orioles
5.	Ken Waldichuk	Oakland Athletics
6.	Jordan Wicks	Chicago Cubs
7.	Matthew Liberatore	St. Louis Cardinals
8.	Connor Prielipp	Minnesota Twins
9.	Kyle Muller	Oakland Athletics
10.	Dax Fulton	Miami Marlins

	Right-Handed Pitchers	
1.	Grayson Rodriguez	Baltimore Orioles
2.	Eury Perez	Miami Marlins
3.	Andrew Painter	Philadelphia Phillies
4.	Daniel Espino	Cleveland Guardians
5.	Bobby Miller	Los Angeles Dodgers
6.	Tanner Bibee	Cleveland Guardians
7.	Tink Hence	St. Louis Cardinals
8.	Koudai Senga	New York Mets
9.	Gavin Williams	Cleveland Guardians
10.	Jackson Jobe	Detroit Tigers

Ranking the 2023 Farm Systems

Ranking the 2023 Farm Systems

Rank	Team
#1	Baltimore Orioles
#2	Pittsburgh Pirates
#3	Cleveland Guardians
#4	Chicago Cubs
#5	Cincinnati Reds
#6	Arizona Diamondbacks
#7	Colorado Rockies
#8	Texas Rangers
#9	Los Angeles Dodgers
#10	Oakland Athletics
#11	New York Mets
#12	Tampa Bay Rays
#13	Boston Red Sox
#14	Milwaukee Brewers
#15	Washington Nationals
#16	Minnesota Twins
#17	St. Louis Cardinals
#18	Detroit Tigers
#19	Miami Marlins
#20	San Francisco Giants
#21	New York Yankees
#22	Toronto Blue Jays
#23	Philadelphia Phillies
#24	Seattle Mariners
#25	Los Angeles Angels
#26	Houston Astros
#27	San Diego Padres
#28	Kansas City Royals
#29	Chicago White Sox
#30	Atlanta Braves

#1 – Baltimore Orioles: Everyone knows about the big guns atop the club's farm system, guys like Gunnar Henderson, who barely held onto his rookie eligibility, Grayson Rodriguez, and Jackson Holliday, the top pick in last July's draft. But the Orioles' system is loaded with strong talent beyond the blue chippers. Slick fielding Joey Ortiz could be a solid cog on a contending team. Connor Norby and Jordan Westburg are also ready for extended looks in the big leagues. Deep on bats, but weak on arms beyond Rodriguez and – maybe – DL Hall and Tommy John surgery recipient Seth Johnson. Don't sleep on Heston Kjerstad either.

#2 – Pittsburgh Pirates: The Pirates' system is deep, geared towards high end athleticism, and own – arguably – the deepest collection of underrated arms in the minor leagues. High end bats like Termarr Johnson, who was one of the purest hitters in the draft last summer, Endy Rodriguez, who was pilfered from the Mets, and Henry Davis (don't buy into the overrated hype).

#3 – Cleveland Guardians: The organization quietly won 92 games last season when most pre-season projections had them finishing around the .500 mark. Cleveland top notch farm system is going to push the club into another World Series appearance, either through successful graduations or by fetching veterans off the trade market.

#4 – Chicago Cubs: The franchise got back to their World Series-winning roots by building a farm system around talented bats, like Pete Crow-Armstrong, Kevin Alcantara, Kevin Made, James Triantos, and – hopefully – Brennen Davis. The front office bet big on Cade Horton near the top of the draft. Very weak on arms – which can be bought at the big league level.

#5 – Cincinnati Reds: It's not just the Elly De La Cruz Show here. Cam Collier was the best available talent in the 2022 Draft. Edwin Arroyo is going to be one of the bigger breakout prospects in the game in 2023. The Reds have – somehow – cobbled together a top farm system despite quite a few swings-and-misses in the draft in recent years.

#6 – Arizona Diamondbacks: Elite talent and depth atop the club's farm system with the likes of Corbin Carroll, Jordan Lawlar, Druw Jones, and Brandon Pfaadt. There's some pretty good depth in the second and third tiers of their minor leagues. One guy to watch in the coming 18 months: former Mississippi State Bulldog Landon Sims.

#7 – Colorado Rockies: An underappreciated collection of young hitters as deep as any in the game – Ezequiel Tovar, Zac Veen, Adael Amador, Benny Montgomery, and Drew Romo, who seems to forever be underrated.

#8 – Texas Rangers: Diverse group of prospects with youngsters like Evan Carter, Luisangel Acuna, Thomas Saggese, and Mitch Bratt, who's one of the most underrated arms in the game, as well as former college alums like Josh Jung, the dynamic Vanderbilt duo of Jack Leiter and Kumar Rockers, and Justin Foscue.

#9 – Los Angeles Dodgers: Miguel Vargas seems like a lock to win one, or maybe multiple, batting titles. Diego Cartaya and Dalton Rushing add some insurance behind Will Smith. Bobby Miller is in line to be the next great Dodger grown ace. Lefty Maddux Bruns has as high of a ceiling as any arm in the system; he just can't find the strike zone.

#10 – Oakland Athletics: There's likely going to be a *wide* range of opinions on Oakland's farm system. But there's more talent than most realize. Freddy Tarnok is my guy. Combine the underrated right-hander with Ken Waldichuk and Oakland has the 40% of a solid big league rotation. Tyler Soderstrom is legit.

#11 – New York Mets: Limitless pocketbook and two Top 13 prospects. Jett Williams is a grinder.

#12 – Tampa Bay Rays: One of the lowest rankings I've had on their system in quite some time. Curtis Mead is a sweet-swinging infielder and made contend for a batting title or two. The trio of Shane Baz, Taj Bradley, and Cole Wilcox could be something to build around.

#13 – Boston Red Sox: Marcelo Mayer is going to be a star. Ceddanne Rafaela could be too. Triston Casas can't it lefties, and Nick Yorke needs to have a strong rebound season in 2023. Matthew Lugo would like get more publicity nationally is he wasn't playing in Mayer's shadow.

#14 – Milwaukee Brewers: Jackson Chourio. The End. Actually, there's more to that. Backstop Jeferson Quero could be a star.

#15 – Washington Nationals: James Wood is the type of player to build around. Elijah Green could be too, if he's making consistent contact – which he failed to do so in high school. Robert Hassell could be a solid complementary role, but he needs to hit southpaws. Cade Cavalli needs to stay healthy. Brady House is underrated now. Jarlin Susana has the best fastball in the minors, big upside.

#16 – Minnesota Twins: Brooks Lee, their top pick last July, should move quickly. Marco Raya is going to be *huge*, remember his name. Emmanuel Rodriguez could be a star or a bust, but there's a high ceiling here.

#17 – St. Louis Cardinals: Jordan Walker is going to be a star, Tink Hence *should* be too – if he can stay healthy. Masyn Winn, the talented, 100-mph throwing shortstop, really came into his own at the plate in 2022. Alec Burleson's the prototypical St. Louis Prospect that comes up and delivers league average or better production without missing a beat. Leonardo Bernal has massive power.

#18 – Detroit Tigers: Jackson Jobe was pretty good, but not great during his debut. Colt Keith is their only other Top 100 prospects. I've been writing for *years* about Reese Olson's potential, and now he's starting to gain some notoriety nationally. Lacks high end talent with the graduation of Spencer Torkelson and Riley Greene. Detroit's rebuilding, simply put, hasn't come to fruition.

#19 – Miami Marlins: Eury Perez was one of the most talked about pitching prospects last summer, showcasing elite potential, a power-based repertoire, and a strong feel for the strike zone. Jacob Berry, their top pick last summer, has the makings of an above-average big leaguer. Max Meyer's Tommy John surgery really impacts the club's plans for 2023.

#20 – San Francisco Giants: Three Top 100 Prospects – Kyle Harrison, Marco Luciano, and Aeverson Arteaga – and then not a lot beyond that.

#21 – New York Yankees: It's very top heavy with Anthony Volpe, Oswald Peraza (the presumed starting shortstop for 2023), Jasson Dominguez, Spencer Jones, and Austin Wells. Everson Pereira has the tools to be an impact player, but remains a project with plenty of risk. Trey Sweeney can pick it.

#22 – Toronto Blue Jays: It's the Ricky Tiedemann Show. Yosver Zulueta throws gas but is snake bitten.

#23 – Philadelphia Phillies: Andrew Painter and Mick Abel are quite the tandem, and Griff McGarry could be a stud, too, if he can continue to improve upon his strike-throwing ability. Very light on bats. And talent.

#24 - Seattle Mariners: Harry Ford is one of the game's best young catchers. Cole Young and Bryce Miller could be something too. That's it.

#25 – Los Angeles Angels: The farm system is improving, but it still sucks. Edgar Quero, Logan O'Hoppe, and Zach Neto are all ranked among the Top 65 prospects. Then there's a *large* gap.

#26 – Houston Astros: Clearly not the same system from just a few years ago.

#27 – San Diego Padres: Surprisingly, after deal away tons of high caliber talent, the Padres still sport three Top 100 prospects – Jackson Merrill, Samuel Zavala, and Dylan Lesko.

#28 – Kansas City Royals: All the club's top prospects have graduated, but they're *years* away from contending.

#29 – Chicago White Sox: Death, taxes, and a weak Chicago White Sox system.

#30 – Atlanta Braves: Atlanta went all in. And can you blame them?

Organizational Analysis

Arizona Diamondbacks

Top Prospects

Arizona Diamondbacks

1. Corbin Carroll, CF

Hit	Power	SB	Patience	Glove	Overall
60	55	60	60	55	70

Born: 08/21/00	Age: 22	Bats: L	Top Production Comp: Mookie Betts
Height: 5-10	Weight: 165	Throws: L	

Season	Team	Age	Level	PA	1B	2B	3B	HR	SB	CS	BB%	K%	AVG	OBP	SLG	ISO
2022	ARI	19	CPX	24	5	1	1	0	0	0	16.67%	25.00%	0.368	0.500	0.526	0.158
2022	ARI	19	A	208	39	9	4	9	24	4	12.98%	23.08%	0.351	0.447	0.603	0.253
2022	ARI	19	A+	130	19	8	2	3	13	1	12.31%	25.38%	0.288	0.385	0.477	0.189
2022	ARI	19	AA	97	14	0	0	4	2	1	10.31%	28.87%	0.212	0.299	0.353	0.141

Background: The opening round of the 2019 draft may prove to be one of the stronger ones in recent memory. The top overall pick, Adley Rutschman, is already a star and may be a perennial MVP candidate – barring injury. Bobby Witt Jr. became the fifth rookie *in baseball history* to slug 20 homeruns and swipe 30 bags in a season, joining Mike Trout, Devon White, Tommie Agee, and Mitchell Page. Andrew Vaughn posted a 111 OPS+ last season for the White Sox. Riley Greene, Nick Lodolo, and George Kirby turned in solid, sometimes impressive debuts. That doesn't even count Toronto ace Alek Manoah or current Top Prospects Josh Jung, Brett Baty, Daniel Espino, or Anthony Volpe. And then there's Corbin Carroll, who may be the best overall hitter among the entire group. A product of Seattle-based Lakeside School, Arizona drafted the pint-sized dynamo with the 16th overall pick that summer, signing him to a deal worth a hefty $3,745,500. The toolsy centerfielder has proven to be worth every penny – and so much more. Carroll turned in an impressive debut in 2019, splitting time between the stateside rookie league and Hillsboro, batting an aggregate .299/.409/.487 in 42 games. The 5-foot-10, 165-pound outfielder got off to a monster start in High-A two years ago, mashing .435/.552/.913 through a week of games before a shoulder injury forced him under the knife and knocked him out for the remainder of the year. Last season Carroll showed no ill effects as he moved through Double-A in dominant fashion and continued showcasing his five tools in Triple-A. The former prep star appeared in 32 games with the Diamondbacks as well, hitting .260/.330/.500. He finished his time in the minor leagues with an aggregate .307/.425/.611 with 22 doubles, eight triples, 24 homers, and 31 stolen bases. Per *Weighted Runs Created Plus*, his minor league production surpassed the league average mark by 57%.

Snippet from The 2022 Prospect Digest Handbook: He's a gamer, a ballplayer that does everything right and maximizes his ability to the Nth-degree. Plus speed that shows up out of the batter's box, on the base paths, and in center fielder.

Scouting Report: With respect to his work with Amarillo, consider the following:

> Since 2006, only five 21-year-old hitters tallied at least a 160 wRC+ in any Double-A league (min. 250 PA): Mookie Betts, Mike Moustakas, Austin Hays, Oswaldo Arcia, and – of course – Corbin Carroll.

Carroll can impact the game in every facet:

> He's a plus defensive centerfielder.
> He owns a plus hit tool and profiles as a consistent .300 big league hitter.
> He's going to be a consistent 20-homer threat.
> Plus speed.
> Above-average patience.

If there was one prospect that could ascend to the level of Mookie Betts, it's Corbin Carroll. He's going to be a .300/.360/.480-type big league hitter and a cornerstone for the Diamondbacks' franchise for *years* to come.

Ceiling: 6.5-win player
Risk: Moderate
MLB ETA: Debuted in 2022

2. Jordan Lawlar, SS

Hit	Power	SB	Patience	Glove	Overall
40/50	55	60	55	50	70

Born: 07/17/02	Age: 20	Bats: R	Top Production Comp: Hanley Ramirez
Height: 6-2	Weight: 190	Throws: R	

Season	Team	Age	Level	PA	1B	2B	3B	HR	SB	CS	BB%	K%	AVG	OBP	SLG	ISO
2022	ARI	19	CPX	24	5	1	1	0	0	0	16.67%	25.00%	0.368	0.500	0.526	0.158
2022	ARI	19	A	208	39	9	4	9	24	4	12.98%	23.08%	0.351	0.447	0.603	0.253
2022	ARI	19	A+	130	19	8	2	3	13	1	12.31%	25.38%	0.288	0.385	0.477	0.189
2022	ARI	19	AA	97	14	0	0	4	2	1	10.31%	28.87%	0.212	0.299	0.353	0.141

Background: The first time the Diamondbacks owned the sixth pick in the draft they selected Texas A&M ace Barret Loux, grabbing the right-hander directly ahead of Matt Harvey and several picks in front of Chris Sale. Loux, of course, washed out of the minor leagues just five years later. The second – and most recent – time Arizona had the sixth overall pick they made sure not to miss, drafting Jesuit

Arizona Diamondbacks

College Preparatory School of Dallas product Jordan Lawlar. Once named the *Jackie Robinson Perfect Game Player of the Year*, Lawlar put on a clinic of offensive prowess during his first full season in the minor leagues. The 6-foot-2, 190-pound infielder opened the year up with Visalia, but after mashing .351/.447/.603 through 44 games, the front office bumped him up to Hillsboro. And he continued to beat up the High-A competition (.288/.385/.478). So the player develop regime pushed the then-19-year-old burgeoning star up to the toughest minor league level, Double-A, for a 20-game cameo. Lawlar finished the year with an aggregate .303/.401/.509 with 18 doubles, seven triples, 16 homeruns, and 39 stolen bases. According to *Weighted Runs Created Plus*, his overall production smashed the league average mark by 38%. The front office sent the toolsy shortstop into the Arizona Fall League. And, of course, he passed with flying colors as he slugged .278/.469/.528.

Snippet from The 2022 Prospect Digest Handbook: Short, compact, quick swing with 20-homer potential as his body fills out. Lawlar seems to have a propensity to chase high fastballs. Patient approach; not afraid to take several pitches. He shows a willingness to take the ball the other way. Plus speed, as evidenced by his 6.45, 60-yard time. He's not as fluid as shortstop as his counterpart Marcelo Mayer, but should be no worse than solid average.

Scouting Report: With respect to his work in Low-A, his longest stint last season, consider the following:

> Since 2006, only eleven 19-year-old hitters tallied 160 wRC+ mark or greater in any Low-A league (min. 200 PA): Byron Buxton, Oscar Taveras, Javier Baez, Joey Gallo, Eloy Jimenez, Bo Bichette, Jarred Kelenic, Jaff Decker, Brennen Davis, James Wood, and – of course – Jordan Lawlar.

As expected, Lawlar's defense is fringy average, but it's decent enough to keep him at the most important position on the infield dirt. But when it comes to Lawlar it's not really about the leather, is it? Patient approach. Above-average hit tool *and* power *with* plus speed. Incredible bat speed with enough natural loft that Lawlar may eventually creep into 30-homer territory. He's entering his age-20 season with Double-A experience on his resume. He has a significant chance of claiming the big league club's shortstop gig some point late in 2023. Lawlar's profiling like a .280/.360/.460 hitter with average defense.

Ceiling: 6.0-win player
Risk: Moderate
MLB ETA: 2023/2024

3. Druw Jones, CF

Hit	Power	SB	Patience	Glove	Overall
55	50/60	70	50	70	70

Born: 11/28/03	Age: 19	Bats: R	Top Production Comp: N/A
Height: 6-4	Weight: 180	Throws: R	

Background: The legend of Druw Jones does not begin with Druw, nor does it begin with his 10-time Gold Glove winning father Andruw. No. The legend begins on the island of Curacao with Henry Jones. According to an article by Jennifer Frey in *The Washington Post* in October 1996, the elder Jones, a gifted centerfielder, is still bantered about in baseball circles. And legend has it, or at least according to a 2002 article in *ESPN the Magazine*, Henry fractured his foot from an acrobatic catch on the outfield wall and was told that he would miss six weeks. He was standing back in centerfield, the land of Joneses, less than two weeks later. Like Mutt Mantle did to Mickey, Henry molded Andruw into a dynamic, generational talent. One so gifted in the outfield that he would eventually become the greatest defensive centerfielder in history en route to winning those 10 Gold Gloves. Signed by the Braves for a paltry $46,000 in early July in 1996, Andruw would become just the second Curacaoan to sign with a big league franchise. The first, of course, was "Bam Bam" Hensley Meulens. Enter: Druw Jones, the next in line to don the family crown as a generational centerfielder. The youngest Jones, by the way, captured the *Perfect Game National Defensive Player of the Year* award in 2021. A product of Georgia-based Wesleyan High School, Druw slugged a scorching .570/.675/1.026 during his final amateur season, belting out seven doubles, three triples, and 13 homeruns. He also knocked in 39 RBIs and swiped 32 stolen bases. He also went 10-1 on the mound as well. Arizona happily selected the toolsy 6-foot-4, 180-pound outfielder with the second overall pick last July, signing him to a *massive* $8,189,400 deal. Prior to make his debut Jones underwent the knife to repair a torn posterior labrum in his left shoulder. He's expected to make a full recovery.

Scouting Report: Per the usual, my pre-draft analysis:

> "Tremendously gifted with the work ethic to match. Jones rocketed a ball to the opposite field (right field) during the Georgia State Championship game that posted an exit velocity of 106. He's a genuine five-tool player, much like his father was during his 10-year prime. The sound off of the younger Jones' bat is like an explosion. Simple, low maintenance swing. Plus power potential generated with natural loft and tremendous bat speed. Above-average hit tool. Above-average arm that's improved through a quick release from center field. Like Fernando Tatis Jr. and Vladimir Guerrero Jr., Jones will

Arizona Diamondbacks

forever be compared to his father. The young center fielder doesn't possess the sheer power of his old man, but he's more fleet of foot."

Ceiling: 6.0-win player
Risk: Moderate
MLB ETA: 2026

4. Brandon Pfaadt, RHP

FB	CB	SL	CH	Command	Overall
55	50	55/60	60	60	55

Born: 10/15/98	Age: 24	Bats: R	Top Production Comp: N/A
Height: 6-4	Weight: 220	Throws: R	

Season	Team	Age	Level	IP	TBF	K/9	K%	BB/9	BB%	K-BB%	ERA	FIP	xFIP	Pit/Bat
2021	ARI	22	A	40.1	160	12.72	35.63%	1.56	4.38%	31.25%	3.12	3.61	3.17	3.58
2021	ARI	22	A+	58.0	227	10.40	29.52%	2.17	6.17%	23.35%	2.48	3.67	4.39	3.69
2021	ARI	22	AA	33.1	142	9.72	25.35%	1.89	4.93%	20.42%	4.59	6.72	4.28	3.75
2022	ARI	23	AA	105.1	447	12.30	32.21%	1.62	4.25%	27.96%	4.53	4.22	3.63	3.74
2022	ARI	23	AAA	61.2	242	10.80	30.58%	2.04	5.79%	24.79%	2.63	4.18	4.42	3.69

Background: The Bellarmine University ace opened some eyes up during his strong debut showing two years ago. A fifth round pick in 2020, the 6-foot-4, 220-pound righty essentially moved from the Great Lakes Valley Conference and accrued some Double-A experience within a year. Pfaadt made 22 starts with Visalia, Hillsboro, and Amarillo that season, throwing 131.2 innings with a fantastical 160-to-28 strikeout-to-walk ratio and a solid 3.21 ERA. And you know what? The former Bellarmine Knight *continued* that level of dominance as he split the 2022 season between Amarillo and Reno. Pfaadt would average an otherworldly 11.7 strikeouts and a miniscule 1.8 walks per nine innings to go along with a 3.83 ERA and a 4.21 FIP. For his career, the big right-hander is averaging 11.4 strikeouts and 1.8 walks per nine innings with a 3.56 ERA.

Scouting Report: Not only did Pfaadt capture the minor league strikeout leader crown, his 218 punch outs were the most in minor league baseball since at least 2006, the first season in which *FanGraphs* data began. With respect to his work in Double-A in 2022, consider the following:

> Since 2006, since 2006 only two 23-year-old hurlers posted a strikeout percentage north of 30% in any Double-A league (min. 100 IP): Taylor Widener, a former Arizona farmhand, and Brandon Pfaadt.

The former Division II star owns one of the more underrated repertoires in all of the minor leagues. Pfaadt's fastball will sit comfortably in the 92- to 94-mph range and touch a few ticks higher on rare occasions. The above-average offering has some noticeable carry to it. His slider was wickedly unfair at points in the game and will oscillate between above-average and plus. And his changeup is one of the best in the minors. He'll also mix in a rare, get-me-over curveball a few times per start as well. What separates Pfaadt from similarly performing contemporaries is his ability to command his entire arsenal. He's not just a strike thrower, he's a *quality* strike thrower. At this point, just three years removed from Division II ball, Pfaadt is knocking loudly on the D-backs' door. And he just needs a chance to develop into a quality #3-type arm.

Ceiling: 3.5-win player
Risk: Moderate
MLB ETA: 2023

5. Deyvison De Los Santos, 1B/3B

Hit	Power	SB	Patience	Glove	Overall
45	50/60	35	50	45/50	50

Born: 06/21/03	Age: 20	Bats: R	Top Production Comp: N/A
Height: 6-1	Weight: 185	Throws: R	

Season	Team	Age	Level	PA	1B	2B	3B	HR	SB	CS	BB%	K%	AVG	OBP	SLG	ISO
2021	ARI	18	A	160	25	12	0	3	2	0	8.13%	26.88%	0.276	0.340	0.421	0.145
2021	ARI	18	CPX	95	16	4	2	5	1	1	13.68%	25.26%	0.329	0.421	0.610	0.280
2022	ARI	19	A	349	72	18	2	12	4	1	6.30%	24.07%	0.329	0.370	0.513	0.184
2022	ARI	19	A+	166	26	9	0	9	1	0	4.22%	32.53%	0.278	0.307	0.506	0.228
2022	ARI	19	AA	45	6	2	0	1	0	0	11.11%	20.00%	0.231	0.333	0.359	0.128

Background: Part of the club's 2019 international free agency class. Arizona signed the promising corner infielder for a modest – or *relatively* modest - $200,000. De Los Santos made his affiliated debut two years later – thanks to the pandemic. And he instantly became of the better low level hitters in the organization. The 6-foot-1, 185-pound first / third baseman slugged .295/.370/.489 in 62 games between the Complex League and Visalia. Last season the front office sent the then-19-year-old back to Low-A, but De Los Santos obliterated the competition through 78 games. He then moved into the Northwest League. That stinted lasted just over a month before he, too, was deemed ready for the minors' toughest challenge – Double-A. De Los Santos finished his second professional season with an aggregate .306/.348/.499 with 29 doubles, two triples, 22 homeruns, and five stolen bases (in six total attempts). Per *Weighted Runs Created Plus*, De Los Santos' overall production topped the league average mark by a solid 18%. The Dominican infielder owns a career .303/.355/.496 slash line.

Arizona Diamondbacks

Snippet from The 2022 Prospect Digest Handbook: An under-the-radar teenage hitter – at least for the time being. Good bat speed. Tremendous raw power – particularly to the opposite field. Despite never getting cheated at the plate, De Los Santos made a reasonable amount of contact, especially once he was promoted up to Low-A. In a year, we may be mentioned De Los Santos's name among the better prospects in baseball. Don't sleep on this kid.

Scouting Report: Despite a (A) second very solid season and (B) reaching Double-A during his age-19 season, De Los Santos remains one of the more underrated hitting prospects in the game. He's just beginning to tap into his plus power potential and should become a consistent 25- to 30-homer threat at full maturity. The young slugger has flirted with some problematic strikeout rates – or at least on the lower fringes – so that's something that will have to be monitored moving forward. He's a questionable defender at the hot corner, and if he can't show steady progress in the coming years a permanent move across the diamond is likely. Consider the following:

> Since 2006, only three 19-year-old hitters met the following criteria in any Low-A league (min. 300 PA): 117 to 127 wRC+, a 22% to 26% strikeout rate, and a 5.5% to 7.5% walk rate. Those three hitters: Javy Guerra, Angel Morales, and Deyvison De Los Santos.

If De Los Santos comes out swinging in 2023, he may be in position to make his big league debut late in the year.

Ceiling: 2.5-win player
Risk: Moderate
MLB ETA: 2023/2024

6. Jorge Barrosa, CF

Hit	Power	SB	Patience	Glove	Overall
50	40	60	50	70	45

Born: 02/17/01	Age: 22	Bats: B	Top Production Comp: Kevin Kiermaier
Height: 5-9	Weight: 165	Throws: L	

Season	Team	Age	Level	PA	1B	2B	3B	HR	SB	CS	BB%	K%	AVG	OBP	SLG	ISO
2021	ARI	20	A	163	38	8	0	3	9	4	4.29%	19.02%	0.333	0.389	0.449	0.116
2021	ARI	20	A+	272	37	18	3	4	20	7	8.09%	17.65%	0.256	0.332	0.405	0.149
2022	ARI	21	A+	43	8	3	0	1	4	1	4.65%	11.63%	0.300	0.349	0.450	0.150
2022	ARI	21	AA	510	76	30	2	12	22	11	12.75%	15.69%	0.276	0.374	0.438	0.161

Background: In baseball terms, 2017 seems like a lifetime ago. Royce Lewis beat out flame-throwing phenom Hunter Greene for the top overall pick in the midsummer draft. The Houston Astros captured the World Series trophy. Corey Kluber and Max Scherzer were named Cy Young Award winners for their respective leagues. And somewhere on the sports webpages, buried *deep*, was the announcement that the Diamondbacks signed a toolsy outfielder from Puerto Cabello, Venezuela for $415,000. The speedy switch-hitter has maintained an impressive level of consistency throughout his tenure in the Diamondbacks' organization. Barrosa batted a solid .279/.373/.389 during his professional debut in 2018. After a struggling a bit during his stint in short-season ball in 2019, the 5-foot-9, 165-pound centerfielder hit .285/.353/.422 as he split the 2021 season between Visalia and Hillsboro. And last season as he appeared in a career best 120 games (110 with Amarillo and 10 with Hillsboro), Barrosa put together a .279/.372/.439 slash line with career bests in doubles (33) and homeruns (13) to go along with two triples and 26 stolen bases. His production in Double-A topped the league average mark by 11%, according to *Weighted Runs Created Plus*.

Snippet from The 2022 Prospect Digest Handbook: Not overly big. Hell, he's small. But Barrosa started showing the type of pop that typically isn't associated with 5-foot-9, 165-pound, speedy center fielders. I'm not sure if it's a sustainable, repeatable skill – especially considering his groundball rates. Barrosa can run it down well in center field and he's tracking to be an above-average defender. If the power shows up continually in the field, he has a shot to – quietly – develop into a solid starting outfielder.

Scouting Report: Last season there were 12 qualified 21-year-old hitters in any Double-A league. Here's a ranking, based on *Weighted Runs Created Plus*, for those 12 hitters, which happens to feature some notable prospects:

1. George Valera (129 wRC+)
2. Anthony Volpe (122 wRC+)
3. Jordan Diaz (120 wRC+)
4. Malcom Nunez (116 wRC+)
5. Brayan Rocchio (114 wRC+)
6. Jorge Barrosa (111 wRC+)
7. Ronny Mauricio (104 wRC+)
8. Jose Rodriguez (103 wRC+)
9. Andy Pages (102 wRC+)
10. Jose Tena (91 wRC+)
11. Liover Peguero (88 wRC+)
12. Felix Valerio (78 wRC+)

Now let's take a look at how his numbers and peripherals stack up against his peers in recent history. Consider the following:

Arizona Diamondbacks

Since 2006, only two 21-year-old hitters posted a 105 to 115 wRC+ with a 14% to 17% strikeout rate and a double-digit walk rate in any Double-A league (min. 350 PA): Caleb Grindl and Jorge Barrosa.

One of the best defensive players at any position in the minor leagues, Barrosa's glove work and speed guarantees him at least a bench option at the big league level. He's a potential Gold Glove winner. But Barrosa value isn't just wrapped up into his spectacular outfield play either. Average hit tool with some added boost due to his speed. Barrosa's homerun output last year was *significantly* aided by the team's home park. With players like Myles Straw and Trent Grisham earning regular playing time – despite their offensive inefficiencies – Barrosa *certainly* has a spot in the big leagues. He has the potential to be a .260/.310/.390 hitter with plus defense.

Ceiling: 2.0-win player
Risk: Low to Moderate
MLB ETA: 2023

7. Blake Walston, LHP

FB	CB	SL	CH	Command	Overall
55	55	55	50	50	50

Born: 06/28/01	Age: 22	Bats: L	Top Production Comp: Matthew Liberatore
Height: 6-5	Weight: 175	Throws: L	

Season	Team	Age	Level	IP	TBF	K/9	K%	BB/9	BB%	K-BB%	ERA	FIP	xFIP	Pit/Bat
2021	ARI	20	A	43.1	180	12.46	33.33%	3.53	9.44%	23.89%	3.32	3.84	3.80	3.76
2021	ARI	20	A+	52.1	226	9.80	25.22%	2.75	7.08%	18.14%	4.13	5.76	4.88	3.82
2022	ARI	21	A+	17.2	73	13.75	36.99%	3.57	9.59%	27.40%	2.55	1.79	2.82	4.23
2022	ARI	21	AA	106.1	459	9.31	23.97%	3.30	8.50%	15.47%	5.16	4.86	4.70	3.82

Background: The 2019 draft was going to be a pivotal moment for the front office. It had the potential to be a franchise-altering draft class because the organization owned four first round selections and seven among the first 75 picks. After selecting future franchise cornerstone Corbin Carroll with their first pick, Arizona used their next five selections on pitchers – the first of which was on New Hanover High School ace Blake Walston. The 26th overall pick that summer, Walston breezed through his limited debut in the Arizona Summer and Northwest Leagues. And once minor league action returned following the lost 2020 season, the 6-foot-5, 175-pound southpaw continued to show promise as he blitzed through Low-A in eight starts and handled himself well in 11 games with Hillsboro. Last season Walston returned to High-A for additional seasoning, but after trouncing the opposition for four games the front office deemed him ready for the most important minor league test: Double-A. But the big southpaw got off to a terrible start as he allowed 20 earned runs over his first 14.2 innings of work. After that, though, Walston was able to right the ship – sans one 10-run clunker against the San Antonio Missions. The former first rounder finished the year with a career best 124.0 innings, recording a 137-to-46 strikeout-to-walk ratio to go along with a 4.79 ERA and a 4.42 FIP.

Snippet from The 2022 Prospect Digest Handbook: Two years ago I was postulating that Walston's low-90s heater would eventually creep up to the mid-90s, but that hasn't happened, though I still think it's a distinct possibility.

Scouting Report: Consider the following:

Since 2006, only five 21-year-old hurlers met the following criteria in any Double-A league (min. 100 IP): 23% to 25% strikeout percentage with a 7.5% to 9.5% walk percentage. Those five hitters: Edwin Diaz, Angel Rodon, Grant Holmes, Rony Garcia, and – of course – Blake Walston.

That uptick in heat *still* hasn't happened, and as he's entering his age-22 season it's becoming more and more unlikely. Walston's similar to Matthew Liberatore, St. Louis's young lefty prospect. Both own solid, deep arsenals without a true swing-and-miss offerings. Both command the strike zone well. And both blitzed through the low levels of the minor leagues. Walston features a 92-93 mph fastball, an above-average offering. His low-70s curveball and low-80s slider are both 55-grades with the former the better pitch. And his changeup his workable enough. Walston's more known for his lack of holes, rather than his ceiling. #4 / #5 type starter in the future. A solid first half of 2023 will likely put him in position for a late-season call up to Arizona.

Ceiling: 2.0-to 2.5-win player
Risk: Moderate
MLB ETA: 2023

Arizona Diamondbacks

8. Ryne Nelson, RHP

FB	CB	SL	CH	Command	Overall
60	55	60	50	50	50

Born: 02/01/98	Age: 25	Bats: R	Top Production Comp: Reynaldo Lopez
Height: 6-3	Weight: 184	Throws: R	

Season	Team	Age	Level	IP	TBF	K/9	K%	BB/9	BB%	K-BB%	ERA	FIP	xFIP	Pit/Bat
2021	ARI	23	A+	39.1	154	13.50	38.31%	3.20	9.09%	29.22%	2.52	3.27	3.99	4.07
2021	ARI	23	AA	77.0	316	12.16	32.91%	3.04	8.23%	24.68%	3.51	4.06	3.51	4.04
2022	ARI	24	AAA	136.0	593	8.47	21.59%	3.11	7.93%	13.66%	5.43	5.49	5.51	3.93

Background: The franchise has invested *heavily* in collegiate arms over the past couple of years. The front office snagged Drey Jameson, Ryne Nelson, and Tommy Henry in the first two rounds of the 2019 draft. The following year the organization selected Bryce Jarvis and Slade Cecconi in the opening rounds. And last season the team snagged Mississippi State flame-thrower Landon Sims in the first round and Nate Savino two rounds later. Nelson, the 56th overall pick four years ago, took a similar path to the big leagues as fellow draft-mate Drey Jameson. Nelson spilt time between Hillsboro and Amarillo two years ago, throwing 116.1 innings while averaging an impressive 12.6 K/9 and 3.1 BB/9 across 22 starts. Last season, Nelson started 26 games for the Reno Aces, posting a solid 128-to-47 strikeout-to-walk ratio in 136.0 innings. Arizona called him up in early September for a three-game cameo. And like Jameson, he was brilliant. Nelson tossed 18.1 innings across three starts, tallying a tidy 1.47 ERA with 16 whiffs and six free passes.

Snippet from The 2022 Prospect Digest Handbook: And the organization's player development has done a tremendous job crafting Nelson, a former reliever, into a viable starting pitching candidate. The organization has a strong collection of these types of arms, but they need to drag their development across the finish line.

Scouting Report: Consider the following:

Since 2006, there have been nine hurlers that met the following criteria during their age-24 season in any Triple-A league (min. 100 IP): 20.5% to 22.5% strikeout percentage and a 7% to 9% walk percentage. Those nine hurlers: Jeff Locke, Gavin Floyd, Jeff Niemann, Cody Martin, Chris Schwinden, Jerad Eickhoff, P.J. Walter, Drey Jameson, and – of course – Ryne Nelson.

The former collegiate reliever has really separated himself from the club's collection of high round, high octane hurlers in the system. Nelson still works exclusively from the stretch, but features a mid-rotation starter's repertoire. Mid-90s, plus fastball. Above-average, upper 70s, 12-6 bending curveball. A lethal mid-80s slider. And a rare, average-ish changeup. Nelson's fastball is lively, explosive, especially from his over-the-top release. But he's too reliant on the offering and needs to do a better job changing speeds. The former 2019 second round pick has #4-type potential. And beyond Pfaadt, he's the likeliest Arizona arm to reach his potential / ceiling. There may be more in the tank given his strictly relief background in college.

Ceiling: 2.0-win player
Risk: Low to Moderate
MLB ETA: Debuted in 2022

9. Landon Sims, RHP

FB	SL	CH	Command	Overall
65	70	N/A	50	50

Born: 01/03/01	Age: 22	Bats: R	Top Production Comp: N/A
Height: 6-2	Weight: 227	Throws: R	

Background: A product of South Forsyth High School, Sims combined with 2021 first rounder Will Bednar to form the backbone of Mississippi State's championship title run two years ago. The duo blanked the Vanderbilt Commodores on a combined one-hitter to capture the school's first ever championship. Sims, a two-sport star during his prep career, was featured on countless clips on the internet for his intimidating mound presence and plus-plus fastball-slider combination. A burly 6-foot-2, 227-pound right-hander, Sims began his collegiate career in dominating fashion with the pandemic the only thing capable of slowing him down. In 13.0 innings of work out of Mississippi State's pen, he struck out an impressive 23 and walked seven to go along with a 3.46 ERA. He followed it up with a crescendo of fireman brilliance in 2021. Making a career best 23 appearances, he averaged 16 strikeouts and just 2.4 walks per nine innings while tallying a 1.44 ERA. Last season the school converted the shutdown stopper into a full-time starting pitcher. And the results were magnificent – at least, momentarily. Sims posted a 27-to-2 strikeout-to-walk ratio in only 15.2 innings of work, along just two earned runs across his first three starts. After that, though, he would hit the disabled list with a wonky elbow, eventually succumbing to Tommy John surgery. Arizona took a calculated gamble and drafted him in the opening round, 34th overall, and signed him to a deal worth $2,347,050.

Arizona Diamondbacks

Scouting Report: My pre-draft write-up:

> "Mid- to upper-90s fastball that Sims commands exceptionally well to both sides of the plate. The borderline plus-plus offering has tremendous late life and it's practically unhittable up in the zone. He'll complement the offering with the class's top slider, unquestionably a plus-plus, elite breaking ball. He'll also mix in a reportedly average changeup (I didn't see one in 2022). Sims has the prototypical bulldog mentality and demeanor to be an elite big league closer a la Brian Wilson. And prior to the injury, he seemed to be on the precipice as a potential legitimate starting ace. Whichever team drafts the flame-throwing right-hander, the temptation to fast-track him to the big leagues (by putting him back in the bullpen) will be there. I wouldn't be shocked to see Washington or Houston take a gamble on him."

Ceiling: 2.5-win player
Risk: Moderate to High
MLB ETA: 2025

10. A.J. Vukovich, 3B/OF

Hit	Power	SB	Patience	Glove	Overall
40/45	50	55/40	45	50	50

Born: 07/20/01	Age: 21	Bats: R	Top Production Comp: N/A
Height: 6-5	Weight: 210	Throws: R	

Season	Team	Age	Level	PA	1B	2B	3B	HR	SB	CS	BB%	K%	AVG	OBP	SLG	ISO
2021	ARI	19	A	276	38	15	1	10	10	1	6.88%	27.90%	0.259	0.322	0.449	0.190
2021	ARI	19	A+	124	27	4	2	3	6	3	2.42%	22.58%	0.298	0.315	0.438	0.140
2022	ARI	20	A+	448	73	26	2	15	35	4	4.02%	23.44%	0.274	0.308	0.450	0.177
2022	ARI	20	AA	45	11	0	0	2	1	0	2.22%	28.89%	0.295	0.311	0.432	0.136

Background: The 2020 draft class will be interesting to look back on in a decade or so. Not only because it was limited to just five rounds, but also because all the potential prospects had very little updated data / scouting reports due to the pandemic. One thing is certain, though: Baltimore and Arizona had their eyes on a pair of high profile, high upside high school third baseman late in the draft that year. Baltimore would snag Colby Mayo with the second over pick in the fourth round, and Arizona would choose A.J. Vukovich 16 selections later. Both third basemen would eventually command the two highest bonuses handed out in the fourth round that summer, $1.75 million and $1.25 million, respectively. A product of East Troy High School, Vukovich turned in an impressive debut two years ago as he slugged .272/.320/.446 in 92 games between Visalia and Hillsboro. The front office brass sent their big fourth round investment back down to Hillsboro for a longer, more extended look in 2022. And the 6-foot-5, 210-pound infielder / part-time outfielder maintained status quo. Appearing in 106 games with the Hops, the Wisconsin-born Vukovich slugged .274/.308/.451 with 26 doubles, two triples, 15 homeruns, and 35 stolen bases (in only 39 total attempts). Vukovich's overall production in High-A, as measured by *Weighted Runs Created Plus*, topped the league average mark by 7%. He spent the final couple of weeks playing well in Double-A, going 13-for-44 with a pair of long balls.

Snippet from The 2022 Prospect Digest Handbook: A nice little developmental project that shows the basic skill set to man third base for a big league team. Average hit tool, power, and glove. He'll also work the count every now and then as well. He's entering is age-20 season with quite a bit of experience in High-A. A stop in Double-A at the end of 2022 isn't out of the question either.

Scouting Report: Consider the following:

> Since 2006, only two 20-year-old hitters met the following criteria in any High-A league (min. 350 PA): 102 to 112 wRC+, a sub-5.0% walk rate, and a 22% to 25% strikeout rate. Those two hitters: Alexfri Planez and A.J. Vukovich.

The young third baseman, who is now moonlighting as an outfielder, takes an aggressive approach at the plate. And while his K-rates haven't been an issue, his lack of patience at the plate has severely limited his offensive production in the minors thus far. Vukovich has breezed through the low levels and acquitted himself nicely in a brief debut in Double-A – at the age of 20 – and he's potentially positioned himself as a late season call up in 2023. Average hit tool, above-average power that he's *just* beginning to tap into. Solid glove at third base or in the outfield. There's some starting potential here. But the question is whether he can do enough to buoy his low walk rates.

Ceiling: 2.0-win player
Risk: Moderate
MLB ETA: 2023

Arizona Diamondbacks

11. Drey Jameson, RHP

FB	CB	SL	CH	Command	Overall
70	50	55	60	50	55

Born: 08/17/97	Age: 25	Bats: R	Top Production Comp: Nick Pivetta
Height: 6-0	Weight: 165	Throws: R	

Season	Team	Age	Level	IP	TBF	K/9	K%	BB/9	BB%	K-BB%	ERA	FIP	xFIP	Pit/Bat
2021	ARI	23	A+	64.1	270	10.77	28.52%	2.52	6.67%	21.85%	3.92	4.43	3.95	3.77
2021	ARI	23	AA	46.1	194	13.21	35.05%	3.50	9.28%	25.77%	4.08	3.65	3.23	3.72
2022	ARI	24	AA	18.2	71	11.09	32.39%	1.93	5.63%	26.76%	2.41	2.10	3.03	4.04
2022	ARI	24	AAA	114.0	514	8.61	21.21%	3.32	8.17%	13.04%	6.95	5.60	4.95	3.73

Background: After nabbing three straight high school prospects at the start of their 2019 draft, Arizona grabbed former Ball State University ace Drey Jameson with their fourth – and final – first round pick. Ball was one of the more dynamic strikeout artists during his two years with the MAC conference school, averaging an impossible 13.4 strikeouts every nine innings. The 6-foot, 165-pound right-hander opened up the 2021 season with Hillsboro in High-A. But after 13 solid games the front office bumped the former first rounder up to the minors' most difficult level, Double-A. And Jameson continued to dominate the competition across eight starts. He would finish the season with a whopping 145 punch outs and just 36 free passes across 110.2 innings of work. Last season Jameson returned to Amarillo for some additional seasoning – though it would last only four absurdly strong starts. The club would relent in early May and send him up to the final minor league stop: Triple-A. He would make another 22 appearances, though he was far more hittable than expected as he compiled an ERA near 7.00. Arizona promoted him up to the big leagues in mid-September. And he was *brilliant*. Making four starts against the Padres (1), Dodgers (1), and Giants (2), Jameson allowed just four earned runs in 24.1 innings, recording 24 punch outs and just seven walks.

Snippet from The 2022 Prospect Digest Handbook: Arizona's honed in on lean, hard-throwing collegiate hurlers in the draft the past couple of seasons (see: Bryce Jarvis, Slade Cecconi, Ryne Nelson), but Jameson has the best odds to succeed in a big league rotation.

Scouting Report: Consider the following:

> Since 2006, then have been 10 hurlers that met the following criteria during their age-24 season in any Triple-A league (min. 100 IP): Gavin Floyd, Philip Humber, Jeff Niemann, Cody Martin, Austin Voth, Chris Schwinden, Jerad Eickhoff, P.J. Walters, Ryne Nelson, and – of course – Drey Jameson.

A high quality arsenal that seems destined for a gig at the big league level. Jameson features a pair of plus offerings – a mid-90s heater and a tremendous changeup – to go along with an above-average, laterally darting mid-80s slider. Jameson will also mix in a rare, average curveball. The former Ball State hurler creates tremendous run on his two-seamer and he's one of the few minor league hurlers that throws two, visibly distinctive fastballs (two- and four-seamers). Jameson's more of a strike-thrower than a command guy, which is why he was smacked around in Triple-A. If the command ticks up, he's a surefire #3 / #4-type hurler. It just seems like he won't be able to fully tap into his potential, though. Obvious reliever risk. He's a tremendous athlete that fields his position exceptionally well.

Ceiling: 1.5- to 2.0-win player
Risk: Moderate
MLB ETA: Debuted in 2022

12. Manuel Pena, 2B/SS

Hit	Power	SB	Patience	Glove	Overall
50/55	40/50	40	50	45	50

Born: 12/05/03	Age: 19	Bats: L	Top Production Comp: N/A
Height: 6-1	Weight: 170	Throws: R	

Season	Team	Age	Level	PA	1B	2B	3B	HR	SB	CS	BB%	K%	AVG	OBP	SLG	ISO
2021	ARI	17	DSL	222	38	5	2	4	17	7	11.71%	20.72%	0.253	0.342	0.361	0.108
2022	ARI	18	CPX	128	23	3	3	4	4	1	7.81%	23.44%	0.284	0.336	0.466	0.181
2022	ARI	18	A	158	26	7	1	0	1	3	12.66%	25.95%	0.248	0.344	0.314	0.066

Background: One of the club's more notable international free agent signings two years ago. Arizona inked the lefty-hitting infielder to a $1.2 million pact, making him the only prospect signed by the D-backs that received a seven-figure bonus (as reported by MLB.com). A native of Santo Domingo, Dominican Republic, Pena stayed in his home country during his debut professional season. He batted a remarkably mediocre .253/.342/.361 with just 11 extra-base knocks in 57 games. Last summer, Pena made the leap to the stateside rookie league and his offense improved – significantly – as he slugged .285/.336/.466 in 32 games with the club's Complex League affiliate. The 6-foot-1, 170-pound middle infielder spent the last 2.5 months of the year as one of the youngest regulars at the Low-A level. He compiled an aggregate .265/.340/.383 with 10 doubles, four triples, four homeruns, and five stolen bases. Per *Weighted Runs Created Plus*, Pena's overall production was 5% below the league average – which was largely depressed by his abysmal showing with Visalia.

Arizona Diamondbacks

Scouting Report: A raw defender on either side of the keystone, though he's more likely to slide over to second as he matures. Pena has a smooth left-handed swing with above-average bat speed that's keyed towards launching extra-base hits. Pena's stint in Visalia started off in impressive fashion as he slugged .311/.380/.378 over his first 24 games. But his bat chilled in late August and he finished the year out on a 6-for-47 stint with the Rawhide. Ignoring his final 12 games, Pena's slash line is a rock solid .296/.355/.427 for the year. There's sneaky power brewing here. Pena's will be headed back to the Rawhide for the start of 2023, but he could spend a significant portion of the year in High-A. He could be one of the bigger breakouts in 2023.

Ceiling: 1.5- to 2.0-win player
Risk: Moderate
MLB ETA: 2025

13. Dominic Fletcher, CF

Hit	Power	SB	Patience	Glove	Overall
45	40	40	50	60	50

Born: 09/02/97	Age: 25	Bats: L	Top Production Comp: Michael A. Taylor
Height: 5-9	Weight: 185	Throws: L	

Season	Team	Age	Level	PA	1B	2B	3B	HR	SB	CS	BB%	K%	AVG	OBP	SLG	ISO
2021	ARI	23	AA	440	68	18	5	15	3	3	5.68%	24.77%	0.264	0.314	0.445	0.182
2022	ARI	24	AA	142	29	6	2	7	4	2	9.15%	17.61%	0.346	0.408	0.591	0.244
2022	ARI	24	AAA	449	77	29	8	5	5	6	9.35%	19.60%	0.301	0.368	0.452	0.152

Background: For just the fourth time in their history, the club added a University of Arkansas player to the fold during the midsummer draft. They grabbed the pint-sized centerfielder in the second round as part of their large haul in 2019. Fletcher was a three-year mainstay in the Razorbacks' lineup, leaving the SEC Conference school as a .298/.360/.497 hitter in 194 games. But here's the fascinating part: five years into his professional career, the 5-foot-9, 185-pound sparkplug is sporting a nearly identical career line, batting .296/.358/.467. Last season, though, was his finest to date. Spending time with Amarillo and Reno, Fletcher mashed .312/.378/.486 with career bests in doubles (35), triples (10), and stolen bases (nine) to go along with 12 dingers. According to *Weighted Runs Created Plus*, his overall production surpassed the league average threshold by 17%.

Scouting Report: Consider the following:

> Since 2006, only four 24-year-old hitters posted a 100 to 110 wRC+ with an 18% to 21% strikeout rate and an 8% to 11% walk rate in any Triple-A league (min. 350 PA): Mike Carp, Mark Mathias, Jaycob Brugman, and – of course – Dominic Fletcher.

Fletcher's not the typical small-ish centerfielder. He's lacking the stereotypical blazing speed and he's incredibly inefficient on the base paths. The former second round pick has swiped just 13 bags in his minor league career and he's been tossed out 12 times. Despite that, though, Fletcher's an incredibly gifted defender in centerfield, bordering on Gold Glove territory. Offensively speaking, he's more of a fourth or fifth outfielder type. Average hit tool, below average power, decent patience and contact rates. The glove is enough to push him into fringy starting territory on a non-contending team or a contender with loads of offensive threats already in place. He's going to be a .260/.320/.390 hitter.

Ceiling: 1.5- to 2.0-win player
Risk: Moderate
MLB ETA: 2023

14. Yu-Min Lin, LHP

FB	CB	SL	CU	CH	Command	Overall
50/55	55	50	50/55	60	50/55	45

Born: 07/12/03	Age: 19	Bats: L	Top Production Comp: N/A
Height: 5-11	Weight: 160	Throws: L	

Season	Team	Age	Level	IP	TBF	K/9	K%	BB/9	BB%	K-BB%	ERA	FIP	xFIP	Pit/Bat
2022	ARI	18	CPX	23.0	86	16.04	47.67%	2.35	6.98%	40.70%	2.35	1.74	2.06	2.20
2022	ARI	18	A	33.1	140	13.50	35.71%	4.32	11.43%	24.29%	2.97	3.46	3.71	4.15

Background: Well known on the international market for *years*. The slight-framed left-hander was rostered on the Chinese Taipei U12, U15, U18, and U23 squads for the Baseball World Cups. As noted on the World Baseball Softball Confederation (WBSC) website, the young southpaw was one of the youngest players on the U23 teams in 2021. Lin started two games against Cuba and Venezuela in the tourney, throwing 8.2 innings while recording 14 punch outs. Less than seven months after signing with Arizona, Lin was set loose on the Complex League opposition – a test he *easily* passed. And he continued his run of terror in seven starts with the Visalia Rawhide as well. The 5-foot-11, 160-pound southpaw finished his first professional season with a whopping 91 punch outs versus 22 free passes to go along with a tidy 2.72 ERA across just 56.1 innings of work. Lin sported a 2-2 win-loss record and an aggregate 2.76 FIP.

Arizona Diamondbacks

Scouting Report: A crafty southpaw that pitches like a 10-year vet. If the scouting reports are correct, Lin possesses as deep of an arsenal as there is in minor league baseball. Reports indicate he'll throw a fastball, curveball, slider, changeup, and a splitter. But that's not what I witnessed during a late-season Low-A start. Lin owns a sneaky low-90s fastball that teeters on the cusp of above-average. His changeup is lethal. He'll mix in a solid-average slider. And he'll throw a hard cutter with late movement – an offering that he'll feature to both lefties *and* righties. Lin's more of strike-thrower than quality strike-thrower at this point, but that's likely to improve in the coming years. He's

poised to move fast, and it wouldn't be shocking to him reach Double-A late in 2023.

Ceiling: 1.5-win player
Risk: Moderate
MLB ETA: 2024/2025

15. Slade Cecconi, RHP

FB	CB	SL	CH	Command	Overall
55	50	55	50	50	45

Born: 06/24/99	Age: 24	Bats: R	Top Production Comp: Jhoulys Chacin
Height: 6-4	Weight: 219	Throws: R	

Season	Team	Age	Level	IP	TBF	K/9	K%	BB/9	BB%	K-BB%	ERA	FIP	xFIP	Pit/Bat
2021	ARI	22	A+	59.0	248	9.61	25.40%	3.05	8.06%	17.34%	4.12	4.22	4.71	3.80
2022	ARI	23	AA	129.2	566	8.81	22.44%	2.22	5.65%	16.78%	4.37	4.98	4.85	3.68

Background: The D-backs opened up their COVID-limited, five-round 2020 draft class by selecting a pair of highly touted college arms. The organization nabbed Duke ace Bryce Jarvis with the 18th overall pick, and then swung back around and grabbed University of Miami hurler Slade Cecconi 15 selections later. Signed to a deal worth nearly $2.4 million, the front office assigned their big dollar investment straight up to High-A to begin his career. But after nine – mostly solid – starts with the Hops, Cecconi hit the disabled list with right elbow discomfort. The 6-foot-4, 219-pound hurler did make it back to the bump for three starts with the Salt River Rafters in the Arizona Fall League at the end of the year. Last season, Cecconi was sent straight into the fire of Double-A. And while he did make it out alive, the former Hurricane definitely looked a little toasty. He made 25 starts and one relief appearance for the Amarillo Sod Poodles, throwing 129.2 innings with 127 punch outs and just 32 free passes. He tallied a 4.37 ERA, a 4.98 FIP, and a 4.85 xFIP.

Snippet from The 2022 Prospect Digest Handbook: Cut from a similar cloth as fellow 2020 first rounder Bryce Jarvis with one exception: he lacks a second plus offering. The hard-throwing right-hander is another backend starting pitching option in the coming years.

Scouting Report: Consider the following:

> Since 2006, there have been nine 23-year-old hurlers that posted a 21.5% to 23.5% strikeout percentage with a 4.5% to 6.5% walk percentage in any Double-A league (min. 100 IP): Adam Conley, Austin Voth, Logan Verrett, Jesus Tinoco, Luis Cruz, Mike Wright, Scott Lewis, Taylor Dollard, and – of course – Slade Cecconi.

There was *considerable* more heft behind Cecconi's heater than what he showed in 2021. The former first rounder was working in the 91- to 94-mph range when I scouted him two years ago. Last season, though, he was *sitting* 94- to 96-mph and regularly touching 97 mph. His main secondary offering is a low- to mid-80s slider with late horizontal movement. He'll also mix in a low-70s, average curveball and an average straight changeup. Cecconi showed an uptick with his command as well. The former Hurricane would get in trouble when he wouldn't move away from the fastball, essentially becoming too predictable. There's backend starting material with some reliever risk as a fastball / slider seventh or eighth inning upside. He needs to develop a solid third offering.

Ceiling: 1.0- to 1.5-win player
Risk: Moderate
MLB ETA: 2023

16. Ivan Melendez, 1B/3B

Hit	Power	SB	Patience	Glove	Overall
45	60	30	55	45	45

Born: 01/24/00	Age: 23	Bats: R	Top Production Comp: N/A
Height: 6-3	Weight: 225	Throws: R	

Season	Team	Age	Level	PA	1B	2B	3B	HR	SB	CS	BB%	K%	AVG	OBP	SLG	ISO
2022	ARI	22	CPX	10	2	0	0	0	0	0	10.00%	50.00%	0.222	0.300	0.222	0.000
2022	ARI	22	A	106	11	3	1	3	0	0	9.43%	18.87%	0.207	0.349	0.368	0.161

Background: A product of Coronado High School, home to former Orioles righty Rocky Coppinger, Melendez spent his first two collegiate seasons at JuCo Odessa College – where he dominated during the shortened 2020 season (he batted .354 with four homeruns and 22 RBIs). The hulking first baseman transferred to the University of

Arizona Diamondbacks

Texas prior to his junior season. And the rest, as they say, is history. In 59 games for the Big 12 powerhouse in 2021, he slugged .319/.438/.603 with 13 doubles, three triples, and 13 homeruns. Production worthy enough for the Marlins to take a 16th round gamble on him. Undeterred by the disappointing draft position, Melendez headed back to the Longhorns for another season. And it was historic. In a career-best 67 games, the Texas-born basher belted out a school record – and national record since BBCOR bats were introduced in 2011 – 32 long balls. In total, college baseball's most potent bat slashed .387/.508/.863 with 18 doubles, two triples, and 32 homeruns. He finished the year with a strong 51-to-52 strikeout-to-walk ratio. Arizona snagged the hulkster in the second round, 43rd overall, and signed him to a deal worth $1.4 million. Melendez turned in a disappointing debut, hitting .206/.358/.351 in 29 games, most of which came in Low-A.

Scouting Report: Per the usual, my pre-draft write-up:

> "Consider the following:
>
> Since 2011, only two Division I hitters batted at least .350/.500/.700 in a season (min. 300 PA): Kyle Lewis, the 11th overall player drafted in 2011, and – of course – Ivan Melendez.
>
> Let's look at his production in a different way:
>
> Since 2011, there have been 17 Division I hitters that slugged 25 or more homeruns in a season. Melendez's strikeout rate, 15.8%, is the sixth lowest and his walk rate, 16.8%, is the fifth highest. In fact, only two of the 17 hitters posted a sub-16% strikeout rate and a walk rate north of 15%: Kris Bryant and – of course – Ivan Melendez.
>
> It was truly a historic season. The problem, of course, is that Melendez is old, at least in terms of amateur prospects are concerned. He's already 22. And he had some serious swing-and-miss issues during his first year at Texas, whiffing in more than 26% of his plate appearances. Plus power combined with a strong eye at the plate. The hit tool will likely prove to be a 45-grade once he enters the professional ranks. There's some Pete Alonso potential, but Melendez likely reaches about 80% of that value. It wouldn't be surprising to see a team take a second round gamble and sign him to a below-slot deal. He seems like an Oakland A's-type of draft pick."

Ceiling: 1.0- to 1.5-win player
Risk: Moderate
MLB ETA: 2025

17. Wilderd Patino, CF

Hit	Power	SB	Patience	Glove	Overall
45/50	40	70	45	50	45

Born: 07/18/01	Age: 21	Bats: R	Top Production Comp: N/A
Height: 6-1	Weight: 175	Throws: R	

Season	Team	Age	Level	PA	1B	2B	3B	HR	SB	CS	BB%	K%	AVG	OBP	SLG	ISO
2021	ARI	19	CPX	30	5	1	1	0	0	2	0.00%	30.00%	0.250	0.276	0.357	0.107
2021	ARI	19	A	132	20	2	1	2	6	3	3.79%	37.12%	0.210	0.288	0.294	0.084
2022	ARI	20	A+	80	15	5	0	1	13	2	5.00%	31.25%	0.288	0.342	0.397	0.110
2022	ARI	20	A	338	59	16	2	8	54	7	6.80%	24.85%	0.290	0.370	0.440	0.150

Background: Arizona's front office has quietly – or maybe not so quietly – collected a tremendous amount of talented outfield prospects over the past couple of years. Recent minor league graduates like Corbin Carroll or Alek Thomas or Daulton Varsho or Jake McCarthy. The front office now has Druw Jones, Jorge Barrosa, and Wilderd Patino stashed away in the minor leagues as well. Signed off the international free agency market in October 2017 – though it didn't happen without excitement: According to MLB.com, the Puerto Ordaz, Venezuela native originally had an agreement in place with the Rangers, but it was scratched due to an elbow issue. Patino, nonetheless, made his professional debut during his age-16 season and was dominating the stateside rookie league a year later. The toolsy 6-foot-1, 175-pound centerfielder lost the overwhelming majority of the 2021 season due to a calf issue. And even when he was healthy, he looked abhorrent. He batted .210/.288/.294 in 30 games with Visalia. Last season, though, Patino looked like his old self as he dominated the Low-A competition and looked rock solid in 19 games with Hillsboro. His season ended prematurely due to an undisclosed injury in mid-August. Patino finished the year with an aggregate .290/.365/.432 slash line with 21 doubles, two triples, nine homeruns, and a whopping 67 stolen bases (in only 76 total attempts). Per *Weighted Runs Created Plus*, his overall production surpassed the league average threshold by 11%.

Arizona Diamondbacks

Scouting Report: Consider the following:

> Since 2006, only three 20-year-old hitters met the following criteria in any Low-A league (min. 300 PA): 107 to 117 wRC+ with a 24% to 26% strikeout rate and a 6% to 8% walk rate. Those three hitters: Tim Anderson, Connor Lien, and Wilderd Patino.

Unlike fellow speedster Jorge Barrosa, Wilderd Patino's plus speed hasn't translated to exceptional defensive value. He's merely an average defender presently. Fringy walk rates. The hit tool can waver at times, leading to problematic contact issues. Doubles thump and enough pop to run into a dozen or so homeruns during the season. Patino's tracking like a part-timer / fourth outfielder. He's ticketed for a return to High-A and – likely – some time in Double-A late in the season as well.

Ceiling: 1.0- to 1.5-win player
Risk: Moderate
MLB ETA: 2024

18. Bryce Jarvis, RHP

FB	CB	SL	CH	Command	Overall
60	55	55	60	45	50

Born: 12/26/97	Age: 25	Bats: R	Top Production Comp: Vinnie Pestano
Height: 6-2	Weight: 195	Throws: R	

Season	Team	Age	Level	IP	TBF	K/9	K%	BB/9	BB%	K-BB%	ERA	FIP	xFIP	Pit/Bat
2021	ARI	23	A+	37.1	153	10.13	27.45%	3.13	8.50%	18.95%	3.62	4.17	4.46	3.75
2021	ARI	23	AA	35.0	152	10.29	26.32%	4.37	11.18%	15.13%	5.66	5.88	4.28	3.89
2022	ARI	24	AA	106.2	505	9.28	21.78%	5.06	11.88%	9.90%	8.27	6.87	5.44	3.84

Background: There were very few hurlers that got off to a better start to the 2020 season than Jarvis. The 6-foot-2, 195-pound righty was essentially unhittable during his four starts, tallying 40 punch outs against just two – TWO – free passes in 27.0 innings of work. But, unfortunately, the potentially special season was wrecked by the COVID pandemic. The Diamondbacks' brass, though, saw enough in the hard-throwing hurler and snagged him with the 18th overall pick that summer, selecting him between a pair of high ceiling prep hitters (Nick Yorke and Pete Crow-Armstrong). Jarvis would make his professional debut the following year, tallying just 16 starts due to an oblique-injury. He managed to work in 75.1 innings with 89 strikeouts and 30 free passes. Last year the former Duke ace put together one of the more odd seasons in recent memory. Jarvis compiled 110 strikeouts (9.3 K/9), 60 walks (5.1 BB/9), and a Frankenstein-esque 8.27 ERA. His true performance indicators weren't that much better either: 6.87 FIP and a 5.44 xFIP.

Snippet from The 2022 Prospect Digest Handbook: His command can be touch-and-go, which will ultimately limit his ceiling.

Scouting Report: Consider the following:

> Since 2006, there have been seven instances in which a 24-year-old hurlers posted a 21% to 23% strikeout percentage with an 11% to 13% walk percentage in any Double-A league (min. 100 IP): Alfred Gutierrez, Andrew Bailey, Garrett Williams, Jonnathan Aristil, Anthony Veneziano, Paxton Schultz, and Bryce Jarvis.

Everything about Jarvis screams future reliever. The funky, fast-paced mechanics. The power-based repertoire. The complete lack of command. The struggles as a starting pitcher, across parts of two seasons, in Double-A. Watching the former mid-first round selection is frustrating. On one pitch he'll dot an "I" with his fastball low-and-away, making it a nearly impossible pitch to hit. And then on the very next offering, another supposed low-and-away heater, he'll miss by three feet.

Ceiling: 1.0-win player
Risk: Moderate
MLB ETA: 2023

19. Blaze Alexander, IF

Hit	Power	SB	Patience	Glove	Overall
45	45	50	55	60	40

Born: 06/11/99	Age: 24	Bats: R	Top Production Comp: N/A
Height: 6-0	Weight: 160	Throws: R	

Season	Team	Age	Level	PA	1B	2B	3B	HR	SB	CS	BB%	K%	AVG	OBP	SLG	ISO
2019	ARI	20	A	406	67	12	4	7	14	4	10.34%	21.92%	0.262	0.355	0.382	0.120
2021	ARI	22	A+	389	45	16	3	10	17	4	11.31%	32.39%	0.218	0.316	0.372	0.153
2022	ARI	23	AA	363	60	17	3	17	10	6	9.09%	25.34%	0.306	0.388	0.539	0.233
2022	ARI	23	AAA	34	4	1	0	2	0	0	11.76%	23.53%	0.259	0.412	0.519	0.259

Background: Despite the club letting Matt McLain slip through their fingers as the 25th overall pick in 2018, the front office turned in a solid class as they added Jake McCarthy, who's quietly tallied nearly 3.0 wins above replacement in 123 career

Arizona Diamondbacks

games, and Alek Thomas, a consensus Top 100 prospect who debuted in the big leagues last season as a 22-year-old. But several rounds later the Diamondbacks' brass drafted IMG Academy star Blaze Alexander, handing him the fourth highest bonus in their entire class. The 6-foot, 160-pound infielder battled through an abysmal 2021 campaign in High-A, batting a paltry .218/.316/372 with 16 doubles, three triples, and 10 homeruns in 92 games with Hillsboro. But the former Bonus Baby rebounded last season as he put together his finest campaign to date. Appearing in 88 games with the Amarillo Sod Poodles, Alexander slugged .306/.388/.539 with 1 7doubles, three triples, and 17 homeruns. He also swiped 10 bags in 16 attempts. His overall production, according to *Weighted Runs Created Plus*, topped the league average mark by 35%. He spent the last several weeks in Triple-A.

Scouting Report: Consider the following:

Since 2006, only three 23-year-old hitters posted a 130 to 140 wRC+ with a 24% to 26% strikeout rate and an 8% to 12% walk rate in any Double-A league (min. 350 PA): Darick Hall, Corey Toups, and Blaze Alexander.

Despite the breakout campaign last season, it's not all roses and rainbows for the former 11th round pick. It's no coincidence that his offensive explosion happened to occur the same time that he spent half the season in Amarillo's bandbox. Alexander's destined for utility-dom. He's a plus defender at shortstop, but can handle second or third bases easily. 45-grade hit tool and matching power. He'll run a little bit.

Ceiling: 1.0-win player
Risk: Moderate
MLB ETA: 2023

20. Nate Savino, LHP

FB	SL	CH	Command	Overall
45	50	55	45	40

Born: 01/24/02	Age: 21	Bats: L	Top Production Comp: N/A
Height: 6-3	Weight: 210	Throws: L	

Background: A standout at Potomac Falls, Savino left the Virginia-based high school with a career 13-4 win-loss record, a sparkling 1.25 ERA, 220 punch outs, and 45 walks in only 112.1 innings of work. The COVID pandemic limited the 6-foot-3, 210-pound southpaw to just four games (three starts) during his true freshman season. Savino managed to squeeze in 10.2 innings with 10 strikeouts and five walks to go along with a 3.38 ERA. Still only 19-years-old during his sophomore season, the young lefty made a handful of relief appearances and 10 starts for the Cavaliers in 2021, posting a disappointing 34-to-16 strikeout-to-walk ratio in 54.2 innings of work. Savino finally put it all together during his final campaign for the ACC Conference powerhouse: 78.0 IP, 79 strikeouts, 32 walks, and a 3.69 ERA. Arizona selected him in the third round, 82nd overall, and signed him to a deal worth $700,000. He did not appear in an affiliated game after joining the organization.

Scouting Report: Long, lanky left-hander with a crossfire motion. Fringy average fastball that's not going to miss many bats in the professional ranks, even given his polished collegiate background. Mediocre slider. Above-average changeup. Savino's never been a pure command guy, so unless the velo ticks up or the command improves it's going to be a difficult road ahead.

Ceiling: 0.5- to 1.0-win player
Risk: Moderate
MLB ETA: 2025

Atlanta Braves

Top Prospects

Atlanta Braves

1. J.R. Ritchie, RHP

FB	CB	CH	Command	Overall
55/60	55/60	55	45/50	55

Born: 06/26/03	Age: 20	Bats: R	Top Production Comp: N/A
Height: 6-2	Weight: 185	Throws: R	

Season	Team	Age	Level	IP	TBF	K/9	K%	BB/9	BB%	K-BB%	ERA	FIP	xFIP	Pit/Bat
2022	ATL	19	A	10.0	38	9.00	26.32%	3.60	10.53%	15.79%	2.70	4.65	4.06	3.53

Background: Arms, especially high school arms, have an absurdly high attrition rate. Back in 2016, though, the Atlanta Braves selected teenage pitchers with their first three picks, nabbing Ian Anderson, Joey Wentz, and Kyle Muller – all coming off the board within the first 44 selections. And, surprisingly, all three young men would make it to the big leagues – with varying degrees of success. Six years later the reigning World Series champions took a similar path through the opening rounds of the draft. The Braves opened up their draft class by selecting two-way prospect Owen Murphy, who will eventually convert into a full time hurler, with the 20th overall pick. Fifteen selections later they grabbed Bainbridge High School ace J.R. Ritchie. And then circled back around to the prep ranks for right-hander Cole Phillips. Ritchie, the Washington Gatorade Player of the Year winner following his junior season, was nearly unhittable during his senior campaign with the Spartans: he batted .468 with four homeruns and struck out a whopping 74 batters – against just three free passes – in only 35.1 innings of work. Prior to the draft Ritchie was committed to UCLA. After signing with the club for nearly $2.4 million, Ritchie tossed 14.1 innings in the low levels, striking out 14 against five free passes. He surrendered just three earned runs.

Scouting Report: Quality three-pitch mix: a low- to mid-90s fastball, an upper 70s / low 80s curveball, and a promising changeup. Ritchie's heater will sit in the 92- to 93-mph range and will touch several ticks higher on occasion. There's considerable projection left on the offering as he begins to fill out, as well as his lack of pitching experience over his final two seasons with Bainbridge; he tossed fewer than 60 innings between his junior and senior campaigns. Ritchie reportedly throws two separate breaking balls – a curveball and a slider – but they appear to be one in the same, an above-average pitch that will flash plus at times. The 6-foot-2, 185-pound right-hander also throws a sneakily good changeup that is sure to garner a lot of whiffs in the professional ranks. It doesn't bend like Pedro Martinez's changeup, but it seemingly stops halfway to home plate for a bathroom break before easing its way into the catcher's glove. There's some #3-type upside here. Very, very savvy pick by the Braves.

Ceiling: 3.0-win player
Risk: Moderate
MLB ETA: 2025

2. Cole Phillips, RHP

FB	SL	CH	Command	Overall
70	60	55	45	55

Born: 05/26/03	Age: 20	Bats: R	Top Production Comp: N/A
Height: 6-3	Weight: 200	Throws: R	

Background: Cole Phillips, a 6-foot-3, 200-pound right-hander, was destined to become the next big, hard-throwing prospect to come out of Texas. It's practically what the state is known for. After committing to Baylor University as a sophomore, Phillips' big league potential seemed to be growing before reaching a bubbling crescendo throughout his senior year at Boerne High School. Through his first 23.1 innings of work, his punched out 42 hitters – 60% of the outs he recorded came via the whiff. And, according to a variety of reports, the wiry righty reached back touched a scorching 101 mph during a March 10th game against Corpus Christi Ray. A little more than two weeks later Phillips' world would come crashing down. In the midst of a perfect game, on a 1-2 pitch, Phillips tore the UCL in his coveted right elbow – an injury, of course, that necessitates Tommy John surgery. It should be noted, though, that the 18-year-old with a bulldog mentality stayed in the game to strike out the next hitter. On three straight sliders. Regardless of the injury, Atlanta drafted him in the second round, 57th overall, and signed him to a deal worth $1,497,500 – an agreement that saves the ball club $2,500. He did not appear in an affiliated game after joining the organization.

Scouting Report: Prior to the injury Phillips owned – arguably – the best arsenal in an admittedly weak class of hurlers. Plus, plus fastball that not only touched triple digits, but would regularly sit in the upper 90s. He complements the offering with a knee-buckling, almost unfair slider with plenty of late, hard tilt. He'll also mix a rare, underrated changeup with good fade that should serve him well in the professional ranks. Very wise gamble by the Braves who drafted an arm that could have been on par talent-wise with Andrew Painter, the 13th overall pick in 2021.

Ceiling: 3.5-win player
Risk: High
MLB ETA: 2025/2026

Atlanta Braves

3. Owen Murphy, RHP

FB	CB	SL	CH	Command	Overall
55	50	50/55	50	55	50

Born: 09/27/03	Age: 19	Bats: R	Top Production Comp: N/A
Height: 6-1	Weight: 190	Throws: R	

Background: Owen Murphy did a little bit of everything during his time at Riverside Brookfield High School: the prep athlete opened up his career as the starting quarterback as a freshman, starred at wide receiver the next year, and moved back to the QB spot the following season. On the diamond, he excelled at shortstop and on the mound for the Bulldogs. Murphy's baseball production *exploded* during the 2021 season as tallied a tidy 0.33 ERA with 97 punch outs in 42.1 innings of work to go along with a .453 batting average, six doubles, four triples, and nine homeruns at the plate. And, somehow, the mercurial two-way phenom raised the bar even high during his senior campaign. Murphy struck out 137 – against just four free passes – in 58.1 innings while tallying a nearly impossible 0.12 ERA. He also tossed an improbable four no-hitters during the season. At the dish, the 6-foot-1, 190-pound prospect batted .548 with 18 long balls and 75 RBIs. He easily captured the Illinois Gatorade Player of the Year. He left Riverside Brookfield as the school's record holder for season (.548) and career (.470) batting average, career RBIs (130), career homeruns (30), best season ERA (0.12), and career ERA (0.54). Atlanta selected Murphy in the opening round, 20th overall, and signed him to a deal worth $2,556,900. He appeared in five games between the Complex League and Low-A, throwing 12.0 innings with a 17-to-5 strikeout-to-walk ratio.

Scouting Report: Immediately after selecting Murphy in the opening round last July, the organization indicated that the infielder / right-hander could begin his professional career as a two-player. That lasted approximately one day before the front office reneged and told him the mound was his future. Murphy shows a quality four-pitch mix: low- to mid-90s fastball, a 12-6 bending, average curveball, a tightly wound slider that flashes above-average at times and a workable changeup. Murphy doesn't possess an elite arsenal. But it's deep enough. And he commands it – generally – well. There may be a little more in the tank in terms of velocity. Murphy looks like a #3/#4-type arm. Prior to the draft I had a second round grade on him.

Ceiling: 2.0-win player
Risk: Moderate
MLB ETA: 2025

4. Braden Shewmake, SS

Hit	Power	SB	Patience	Glove	Overall
40	45	40	45	60	50

Born: 11/19/97	Age: 25	Bats: L	Top Production Comp: Zack Cozart
Height: 6-4	Weight: 190	Throws: R	

Season	Team	Age	Level	PA	1B	2B	3B	HR	SB	CS	BB%	K%	AVG	OBP	SLG	ISO
2021	ATL	23	AA	344	45	14	3	12	4	2	4.94%	21.80%	0.228	0.271	0.401	0.173
2022	ATL	24	AAA	307	49	14	2	7	9	0	7.49%	18.57%	0.259	0.316	0.399	0.140

Background: Known for his sweet lefty swing and above-average glove-work throughout his tenure in College Station. Shewmake had the look, the *feel* as a fast moving, get-to-the-big-league-quickly type of player that could anchor the left side of an infield with good, not great value. He was as consistent as they come at the plate, hitting .323/.381/.487 in 188 games with the Aggies, with power (72 extra-base knocks) and speed (32 stolen bases). And he had the awards to back it up too, like: All-SEC First Team (2018), First Team All-American (2017), Freshman All-American (2017), and SEC Freshman of the Year (2017). Shewmake even spent two summers on Team USA's National squad. He was a surefire first rounder with a pedigree and a history of production. He was supposed to move quickly. And, on the onset, that's exactly what the 6-foot-4, 190-pound shortstop did. He ripped through the Low-A competition by hitting .318/.389/.473 through 51 games and Atlanta immediately shipped him up to Double-A, the true proving ground. But he struggled to the tune of .217/.289/.217 in 17 games. But still, though, in his first half season of pro ball Shewmake accrued time at the most trying level. Minor League Baseball would miss the entire following year due to COVID, so Shewmake was sent back to Double-A for another go round, a longer look at hurlers that will throw offspeed pitches where they want, when they want. And he was *miserable*. He batted a putrid .228/.271/.401 in 83 games with Mississippi. Atlanta pushed the aging prospect up to Triple-A at the start of 2022. And in an injury-shortened season, Shewmake hit .259/.316/.399 with 14 doubles, two triples, seven homeruns, and nine stolen bases. His overall production, as measured by *Weighted Runs Created Plus*, was 11% below the league average mark. Shewmake's campaign ended in early August courtesy of a leg injury after a gruesome collision with Travis Demeritte.

Snippet from The 2022 Prospect Digest Handbook: The truth is, he's probably somewhere in between. 45-grade bat. 50-grade power. He'll steal a base once or so a month. The above-average defense pushes him in to that low-end starting gig, which was my initial pre-draft thought.

Atlanta Braves

Scouting Report: Consider the following:

> Since 2006, only four 24-year-old hitters met the following criteria in any Triple-A league (min. 300 PA): 85 to 95 wRC+, 6.5% to 8.5% walk rate, and 17.5% to 20% strikeout rate. Those four hitters: Zack Cozart, Matt Reynolds, Scott Schebler, and – of course – Braden Shewmake.

Plus glove at the most important position on the infield, Shewmake's defense alone comes close to justifying giving me a shot at the starting gig – if there weren't better options available, which happens to the case in Atlanta. The hit tool has been a complete disappointment and the power hasn't shown up as consistently as expected either. Shewmake runs a little bit and will take the occasional walk. Like Cozart, Schebler, and Reynolds, Shewmake is likely to spend several years at the big league level, maybe even earning the a starting gig for a couple years in the right situation.

Ceiling: 1.5- to 2.0-win player
Risk: Low to Moderate
MLB ETA: 2023

5. Ambioris Tavarez, SS

Hit	Power	SB	Patience	Glove	Overall
50	40/55	50	50	55	50

Born: 11/12/03	Age: 19	Bats: R	Top Production Comp: N/A
Height: 6-0	Weight: 168	Throws: R	

Season	Team	Age	Level	PA	1B	2B	3B	HR	SB	CS	BB%	K%	AVG	OBP	SLG	ISO
2022	ATL	18	CPX	69	13	4	0	1	3	1	4.35%	40.58%	0.277	0.304	0.385	0.108

Background: One of the club's big international free agency expenditures two years ago, Atlanta signed the San Cristobal, Dominican Republic native to a hefty seven-figure bonus – $1.5 million, to be exact. As reported by MLB.com, the wiry middle infielder underwent the knife for thoracic outlet syndrome and wouldn't make his affiliated debut until early August last season. Tavarez was able to squeeze in 17 games with the club's Complex League team, hitting a respectable .277/.304/.385 with four doubles, one homerun, and three stolen bases.

Scouting Report: Quick and agile on defense, Tavarez should have no issues sticking at shortstop – as long as the arm hasn't degraded too much due to the thoracic outlet syndrome surgery. Lightning bat speed that projects for above-average power, especially once his 6-foot, 198-pound frame begins to fill out. Tavarez could be one of the bigger breakout prospects in 2023, not only in the Braves' system, but in all of baseball.

Ceiling: 2.5-win player
Risk: High
MLB ETA: 2026

6. Jared Shuster, LHP

FB	SL	CH	Command	Overall
50	50	70	55	45

Born: 08/03/98	Age: 24	Bats: L	Top Production Comp: Jason Vargas
Height: 6-3	Weight: 210	Throws: L	

Season	Team	Age	Level	IP	TBF	K/9	K%	BB/9	BB%	K-BB%	ERA	FIP	xFIP	Pit/Bat
2021	ATL	22	A+	58.1	235	11.26	31.06%	2.31	6.38%	24.68%	3.70	4.26	4.09	3.73
2021	ATL	22	AA	14.2	68	10.43	25.00%	3.07	7.35%	17.65%	7.36	6.54	4.53	3.69
2022	ATL	23	AA	90.2	353	10.52	30.03%	2.18	6.23%	23.80%	2.78	3.12	3.46	3.94
2022	ATL	23	AAA	48.2	201	7.21	19.40%	2.96	7.96%	11.44%	4.25	5.62	4.72	3.77

Background: It's readily apparent that the Braves' 2020 draft class is a win – a BIG win – thanks to the emergence of last year's National League Rookie of the Year runner-up Spencer Strider. And that doesn't even account for Bryce Elder's contributions either. Anything the front office gets from any of their remaining picks is simply icing on the cake. Atlanta drafted Shuster in the opening round, 25th overall, that year after a mostly frustrating career with the Demon Deacons of Wake Forest. But the front office gambled on his dominance in the Cape Cod in 2019, as well as his four-game showing with the ACC Conference squad in 2020. Shuster debuted with the club's High-A affiliate two years ago, but after 15 strong appearance he was bumped up to Double-A to close out his successful campaign. Last season the 6-foot-3, 210-pound southpaw made 25 starts and two relief appearances between his stints with Mississippi and Gwinnett, averaging 9.4 strikeouts and 2.5 walks per nine innings. He tallied an aggregate 3.29 ERA and a 3.99 FIP.

Snippet from The 2022 Prospect Digest Handbook: A bit of a unicorn, of sorts, in today's game. Shuster falls into the category of "crafty lefty". He's a low ceiling / high floor hurler. Extreme short-arm that adds much needed deception. He's reminiscent of former lefty reliever Ron Mahay, though Shuster looks to have the chops to start until the heater fades. One final note: prior to the draft, Shuster fastball was up into the mid-90s; last season it was down several ticks when I saw him.

Atlanta Braves

Scouting Report: Consider the following:

> Since 2006, only four 23-year-old hurlers posted a 29% to 31% strikeout percentage in any Double-A league (min. 75 IP): Bobby Miller, Andrew Abbott, Alexander Guillen, and – of course – Jared Shuster. Atlanta's young lefty owns the best walk percentage, 6.23%, among the group.

The mid-90s heat that Shuster was pumping during his final collegiate season is still nowhere to be found. Instead, he continues to operate in the 90- to 92-mph range but the average offering plays up considerably due to his plus-plus changeup. The offspeed offering shows *tremendous* velocity separation, roughly 13 or so mph in difference. It's arguably the finest in the minor leagues. He'll also mix in an average, horizontally darting slider as well. He's a command guy. And he *needs* to be a command guy to succeed. There's backend starting potential with the floor of a solid reliever.

Ceiling: 1.5- to 2.0-win player
Risk: Low to Moderate
MLB ETA: 2023

7. A.J. Smith-Shawver, RHP

FB	SL	CH	Command	Overall
60	55/60	45/50	35/45	45

Born: 11/20/02	Age: 20	Bats: R	Top Production Comp: N/A
Height: 6-3	Weight: 205	Throws: R	

Season	Team	Age	Level	IP	TBF	K/9	K%	BB/9	BB%	K-BB%	ERA	FIP	xFIP	Pit/Bat
2022	ATL	19	A	68.2	299	13.50	34.45%	5.11	13.04%	21.40%	5.11	3.53	3.84	3.99

Background: Texas-based Colleyville Heritage High School's produced an influx of minor league talent over the past couple years, including Alex Scherff, an over-slot fifth rounder by the Red Sox in 2017; Bobby Witt Jr., the second overall pick in 2019, and, most recently, A.J. Smith-Shawver. Taken by the Braves in the seventh round and handed a deal worth nearly $1 million two years ago, Smith-Shawver turned in a rollercoaster debut with the club's Complex League affiliate that summer, posting a 16-to-10 strikeout-to-walk ratio in 8.1 innings of work. Last season the Braves' brass bounced the 6-foot-3, 205-pound right-hander up to Augusta for his first crack at full season action. Smith-Shawver made 17 starts with the GreenJackets, averaging an impressive 13.5 punch outs and 5.1 free passes per nine innings. He finished the season with a 5.11 ERA, a significantly better 3.53 FIP, and a 3.84 xFIP.

Scouting Report: Consider the following:

> Since 2006, only three 19-year-old hurlers posted a strikeout percentage north of 33% with a walk percentage of at least 12% in any Low-A league (min. 50 IP): Tyler Glasnow, Ronan Kopp, and A.J. Smith-Shawver.

A two-sport star during his days at Colleyville Heritage High School, Smith-Shawver was dubbed "the best-kept secret in the state" by the school's football coach after leading the team to a big win over Midlothian. Unsurprisingly, the former star quarterback owns one of the best arms in the Braves' farm system with his fastball touching as high as 98 mph. But he commands the offering, as well as the rest of his arsenal, poorly. Smith-Shawver's slider has the potential to be a plus weapon, but inconsistency issues have made it unreliable at this point in his career. He'll also mix in a rare, fringy changeup. There's as much potential as any hurler still in Atlanta's farm system, but it's going to come down to developing command and a reliable third offering. His athleticism should allow his feel for the strike zone to improve in the coming years.

Ceiling: 2.0-win player
Risk: High
MLB ETA: 2024/2025

8. Blake Burkhalter, RHP

FB	CB	CH	Command	Overall
60	60	55	50	45

Born: 09/19/00	Age: 22	Bats: R	Top Production Comp: N/A
Height: 6-0	Weight: 204	Throws: R	

Background: Alabama-based Northview High School's had a few professional ballplayers walk through their hallowed halls, including a pair of former big leaguers in Gabe Gross, a first round pick by the Toronto Blue Jays in 2001, as well as Clint Robinson. Right-hander Blake Burkhalter could – potentially – become the third to join the list. A 6-foot, 204-pound reliever for the entirety of his collegiate career, Burkhalter made a brief, four-game cameo out of Auburn's bullpen during his COVID-shortened 2020 freshman season. He would finish the year with three walks, three strikeouts, and a 2.08 ERA in 4.1 innings of work. The scrappy hurler – with wavering control – dominated the SEC competition the following year as he posted a sparkling 1.71 ERA across 21.0 innings of work, striking out 30 and walking 16. He spent the ensuing summer playing for the Alexandria Aces in the Cal Ripken

Atlanta Braves

Collegiate Baseball League. He would throw another 16.0 innings, posting a dominating 30-to-4 strikeout-to-walk ratio. Finally moved into Auburn's closer's role, Burkhalter honed in on the strike zone like never before. In 46.1 innings, the hefty righty saved 16 games while posting an immaculate 71-to-7 strikeout-to-walk ratio. For those counting at home, that's 13.8 strikeouts and just 1.4 walks per nine innings. Atlanta selected him at the back of the second round, 76th overall, and signed him to a well-below slot deal worth $647,500, saving the club more than $200,000. He posted a 7-to-1 strikeout-to-walk ratio in 4.2 debut innings.

Scouting Report: With respect to his work as a pitcher during his sophomore season, consider the following:

> Since 2011, there have been a total of 106 instances in which a Division I hurler averaged at least 13 strikeouts per nine innings in a season (min. 40 IP). Of those 106 instances, only two pitchers – Nick Jones and Blake Burkhalter – averaged fewer than 1.5 walks per nine innings.

Burkhalter features a three-pitch mix: a mid-90s fastball, sitting in the 95- to 96-mph range, a power cutter in the upper 80s to low 90s, and a tumbling mid 80s changeup. Used only as a reliever for the past three years, it wouldn't be shocking to see the Braves convert the former Tiger into a starting pitcher – where he would have the ceiling as a #4-type arm. Despite it being an under-slot signing, it's incredibly savvy by the 2021 World Series Champs.

Ceiling: 1.5-win player
Risk: Moderate
MLB ETA: 2024/2025

9. Spencer Schwellenbach, SS/RHP

	FB	CU	CH	Control	Overall
	N/A	N/A	N/A	N/A	4

Born: 05/31/00	Age: 23	Bats: R	Top Production Comp: N/A
Height: 6-1	Weight: 200	Throws: R	

Background: A dynamic two-way player during his amateur days at the University of Nebraska, Schwellenbach captured the John Olerud Award after hitting .284/.403/.459 with 12 doubles, one triple, six long balls, and nine stolen bases as the team's shortstop and posting a barely-there 0.57 ERA with 34 punch outs, eight walks, and 10 saves as the their closer. Atlanta selected the part-time infielder / reliever in the second round two years ago, signing him to $997,500 deal as the 59th overall player chosen. Schwellenbach, a native of Saginaw, Michigan, immediately underwent Tommy John surgery and missed the entirety of the 2022 season. Reports indicate that he'll be back on the mound at the start of the 2023 season.

Scouting Report: Per the usual, here's what I wrote about Schwellenbach immediately after the 2021 draft:

> "A late-rising prospect because Schwellenbach was a virtual unknown on the mound prior to the 2021 season. The 6-foot-1, 200-pound right-hander features a mid-90s fastball, which averaged in excess of 2300 RPM. His plus slider sits in low- to mid-80s with wipeout movement that will miss plenty of bats and averaged more than 2500 RPM. Schwellenbach will mix in an incredibly underrated low 80s change with hard downward movement as well. As a hitter, Schwellenbach shows a 45-grade bat, tremendous on-base ability and decent power. Atlanta will likely look to stretch Schwellenbach out as a starting pitcher."

Fingers crossed that Schwellenbach doesn't have any setbacks in the coming months.

Ceiling: 2.0-win player
Risk: High
MLB ETA: 2024/2025

Atlanta Braves

10. Roddery Munoz, RHP

FB	SL	CH	Command	Overall
65	55/60	40	50/55	45

Born: 04/14/00	Age: 23	Bats: R	Top Production Comp: Brusdar Graterol
Height: 6-3	Weight: 210	Throws: R	

Season	Team	Age	Level	IP	TBF	K/9	K%	BB/9	BB%	K-BB%	ERA	FIP	xFIP	Pit/Bat
2021	ATL	21	A	29.2	129	10.01	25.58%	3.34	8.53%	17.05%	6.67	4.18	4.32	3.45
2022	ATL	22	A+	89.1	391	10.58	26.85%	3.73	9.46%	17.39%	4.03	3.93	3.85	3.89
2022	ATL	22	AA	11.0	52	11.45	26.92%	4.09	9.62%	17.31%	9.82	5.95	4.28	3.73

Background: What's better than one Munoz? Two, of course. Atlanta signed Roddery Munoz in mid-June, 2018 for the paltry sum of $30,000. Nearly one year to the day the organization swung back around and agreed to a deal with his twin brother, Rolddy. Roddery would appear in 10 games in the foreign rookie league the summer he signed his deal, posting a problematic 17-to-14 strikeout-to-walk ratio in 17.0 innings of work. So it wasn't shocking that he found himself back in the foreign rookie league for another do over the following year. While the results were improved – 9.7 K/9 and 4.2 BB/9 – they remained disappointing for a 19-year-old in the lowest levels of pro ball. Two years later, thanks to the lost COVID season, Munoz posted some interesting numbers in his limited stint with Augusta, averaging 10 K/9 and just 3.3 BB/9. And he was able to carry that momentum forward into 2023. The burly 6-foot-3, 210-pound right-hander made 19 starts with Rome and another three with Mississippi in his most successful season to date. He tossed a career best 100.1 innings, recording 119 punch outs, 42 free passes, and a 4.66 ERA.

Scouting Report: Consider the following:

> Since 2006, there have been eight 22-year-old hurlers that met the following criteria in a High-A season (min. 75 IP): 26% to 28% strikeout percentage with an 8.5% to 10.5% walk percentage. Those eight hurlers: Greg Holland, Rogelio Armenteros, Taylor Widener, Buddy Baumann, Victor Castaneda, Ryan Bergert, Mason Hickman, and Roddery Munoz.

Very, very good fastball / slider combination. Munoz attacks hitters with a mid- to upper-90s heater with plenty of late, explosive life. The type of fastball that avoids trouble even if it's over the heart of the plate. His slider sits in the 87- to 89-mph range and will touch the low 90s on occasion. It's hard with late, downward bite. He'll mix in a rare 89- to 91-mph changeup, but only because he's forced too. Atlanta currently has him stretching out as a starter, but the lack of a third option all but guarantees a trip to the bullpen. He's a strong candidate to develop a splitter / split-change. There's some Brusdar Graterol type bullpen potential here.

Ceiling: 1.5-win player
Risk: Moderate
MLB ETA: 2022

11. Victor Vodnik, RHP

FB	SL	CH	Command	Overall
65	50	55	40	45

Born: 10/09/99	Age: 23	Bats: R	Top Production Comp: Luke Jackson
Height: 6-0	Weight: 200	Throws: R	

Season	Team	Age	Level	IP	TBF	K/9	K%	BB/9	BB%	K-BB%	ERA	FIP	xFIP	Pit/Bat
2021	ATL	21	AA	33.2	150	10.96	27.33%	5.88	14.67%	12.67%	5.35	4.86	4.03	4.24
2022	ATL	22	AAA	27.2	121	10.73	27.27%	5.20	13.22%	14.05%	2.93	4.01	4.03	4.39

Background: Atlanta's 2018 draft class will always be remembered for their failure – or refusal – to come to terms with prep right-hander Carter Stewart, who was chosen with the eighth overall pick. Stewart would eventually sign with the Fukuoka Softbank Hawks of the Nippon Professional Baseball league – where he would team up with newly signed Mets ace Kodai Senga. The rest of the Braves' class has been large disappointments. Greyson Jenista, their second round pick, hasn't hit – at all. Tristan Beck, who was taken a round later, is now in the Giants' organization. And Trey Riley, who was selected in the fifth round, is coming off of a season in which he posted a 5.27 ERA and averaged more than seven walks per nine innings. With all of that disappointment and development failure it leaves Victor Vodnik, the club's 14th round pick, as the best player drafted and signed by the Braves that summer. After primarily working out of the pen, Atlanta started flirting with the idea to extend the hard-throwing right-hander in 2019 and they went all in in 2021. But after multiple stints on the disabled list two years ago, Vodnik was pushed back into a full-time relief role last season. He made 31 appearances between his time with Mississippi and Gwinnett, striking out 47 and walking 19 in 34.2 innings to go along with a 2.34 ERA.

Snippet from The 2022 Prospect Digest Handbook: The floor of a closer definitely exists. But the Braves seem content to groom him as a starter. There's legitimate mid-rotation caliber potential.

Scouting Report: Primarily a two-pitch pitcher now that he's transitioned back into a full-time reliever. Vodnik's heater sits consistently in the 95- to 98-mph range and has touched triple-digits in the past. It's explosive with a little bit of heft behind it. And he complements the plus

Atlanta Braves

fastball with an above-average changeup that hovers in the upper-80s / low-90s. He'll also mix in a rare, average-ish mid-80s slider, which lacks depth. Vodnik's command has never really taken a leap – or even a baby step forward – after regressing in 2021. There's still the ceiling as high leverage relief specialist, and he could be primed to help Atlanta once / if injuries strike in 2023.

Ceiling: 1.0- to 1.5-win player
Risk: Moderate
MLB ETA: 2023

12. Dylan Dodd, LHP

FB	CB	SL	CH	Command	Overall
50/55	45	50	55	50	45

Born: 06/06/98	Age: 24	Bats: L	Top Production Comp: Joe Saunders
Height: 6-3	Weight: 210	Throws: L	

Season	Team	Age	Level	IP	TBF	K/9	K%	BB/9	BB%	K-BB%	ERA	FIP	xFIP	Pit/Bat
2021	ATL	23	A	11.0	43	11.45	32.56%	2.45	6.98%	25.58%	4.91	2.25	3.11	3.79
2022	ATL	24	A+	89.0	369	9.20	24.66%	1.72	4.61%	20.05%	3.44	3.16	3.52	3.69
2022	ATL	24	AA	46.1	194	10.68	28.35%	2.53	6.70%	21.65%	3.11	2.89	3.87	3.98

Background: As part of the club's effort to conserve draft funds for the latter rounds for any potential top prospects that may fall through the cracks, Atlanta drafted Southeast Missouri State University southpaw Dylan Dodd In the third round, signing him to a *well* below-slot bonus worth just $122,500. The total savings was nearly half a million dollars, most of which went to securing the services of A.J. Smith-Shawver. Dodd was an effective, practically geriatric hurler during his final two seasons with the Redhawks. He would graduate from the Ohio Valley Conference School as (A) an elderly 23-years-old and (B) as the highest player drafted in the school history. Last season the 6-foot-3, 210-pound southpaw ripped through the High-A competition, continued his dominant roll through nine starts in Double-A, and made one final start in Triple-A. He finished the year with 153 punch outs, only 31 free passes and a tidy 3.36 ERA across 142.0 innings of work.

Snippet from The 2022 Prospect Digest Handbook: Dodd is tracking like a #6-type arm, maybe some type of relief floor.

Scouting Report: Consider the following:

> Since 2006, only eight 24-year-old hurlers met the following criteria in any Double-A league (min. 40 IP): 27.5% to 29.5% strikeout percentage and a 5.5% to 7.5% walk percentage. Those eight hurlers: Brandon Workman, Louis Coleman, Oneli Perez, Darius Vines, Matt Cooper, Chris Mobley, Jake Fishman, Nick Vincent, and Dylan Dodd.

Dodd's pretty simple to figure out – offspeed, offspeed, sneak in an average 92-mph fastball, offspeed, offspeed. The 6-foot-3 210-pound southpaw features three offspeed pitches: an average curveball, a slider that floats between average and above-average, and a fantastic, genuine swing-and-miss changeup. His success is predicated on changing speeds, which he does really well, and commanding the zone – something else he does really well. There's not a big margin for error – it's actually razor thin – but he could fill a role as a fifth or sixth starter.

Ceiling: 1.0- to 1.5-win player
Risk: Moderate
MLB ETA: 2023

13. Darius Vines, RHP

FB	SL	CH	Command	Overall
50	50	55	60	40

Born: 04/30/98	Age: 25	Bats: R	Top Production Comp: N/A
Height: 6-1	Weight: 190	Throws: R	

Season	Team	Age	Level	IP	TBF	K/9	K%	BB/9	BB%	K-BB%	ERA	FIP	xFIP	Pit/Bat
2021	ATL	23	A	36.0	143	12.00	33.57%	2.50	6.99%	26.57%	2.25	3.23	3.23	3.75
2021	ATL	23	A+	75.0	300	9.72	27.00%	2.28	6.33%	20.67%	3.24	4.45	4.16	3.64
2022	ATL	24	AA	107.0	445	10.68	28.54%	2.52	6.74%	21.80%	3.95	4.08	3.89	3.77
2022	ATL	24	AAA	33.2	143	7.75	20.28%	3.74	9.79%	10.49%	3.21	3.42	4.95	3.71

Background: Thrice-drafted throughout his amateur career. Vines was originally taken by the Houston Astros in the 32nd round coming out of St. Bonaventure High School in 2016, the same year the club added former top prospect and the forever snake-bitten right-hander Forrest Whitley. A year later the Cubs took a 27th round flier on the young right-hander after logging time at Oxnard College. And – finally – Atlanta selected him in the seventh round out of California State University, Bakersfield two years later. Vines split time between Augusta and Rome two years ago, posting a 129-to-29 strikeout-to-walk ratio in 111.0 innings to go along with a solid 2.92 ERA. Last season the California-born hurler began with Mississippi in the minors' toughest level, Double-A, but after 20 strong starts Atlanta bumped him up to Gwinnett. Vines finished with a career best 140.2 innings, averaging 10 strikeouts and just 2.8 walks per nine innings with an aggregate 3.77 ERA and a 3.92 FIP.

Scouting Report: Consider the following:

Atlanta Braves

Since 2006, only two 24-year-old hurlers posted a 27.5% to 29.5% strikeout percentage with a 6% to 8% walk percentage in any Double-A league (min. 100 IP): Jon Heasley and Darius Vines.

It's all about the changeup for Vines. The veteran minor leaguer shows complete trust in throwing his best pitch at any point in the count or doubling or even tripling up on the offering. Tremendous velocity separation with heavy sink and arm-side fade. Vines is one of the few command over control guys in the minor leagues, showing an uncanny ability to locate all four of his offerings where he wants. Average fastball that plays up due to the changeup. His command with the heater is among the best in the minors. Average, get-me-over slider. There's not a whole lot of upside here, but Vines could fill in for a spot start or so in a pinch.

Ceiling: 1.0-win player
Risk: Low to Moderate
MLB ETA: 2023

14. Diego Benitez, SS

	Hit	Power	SB	Patience	Glove	Overall
	20/50	20/55	50/40	50	50	45

Born: 11/19/04	Age: 18	Bats: R	Top Production Comp: N/A
Height: 6-1	Weight: 180	Throws: R	

Background: After handing shortstop Ambioris Tavarez $1.5 million two years ago, Atlanta signed another toolsy middle infielder last season, agreeing to terms on a $2.5 million pact with Diego Benitez. A native of Venezuela, the 6-foot-1, 180-pound shortstop was a consensus Top 10 prospect on the international market at the time of his signing. Hailing from Barquisimeto, Benitez made his affiliated debut months after joining the organization, appearing in 43 games with the club's foreign rookie league affiliate. He batted a disappointing .196/.363/.283 with just six doubles, two homeruns, and a trio of stolen bases in the hitter-friendly confines of the Dominican Summer League. His production, as measured by *Weighted Runs Created Plus*, was 8% below the league average.

Scouting Report: From a physical standpoint: Benitez is reminiscent of a young Carlos Correa, the almost-San-Francisco-Giant-turned-New-York-Met-turned-Minnesota-Twin. Beautiful swing with the potential to develop above-average thump at the plate. Benitez was lauded for his advanced approach at the plate, but after struggling – *mightily* – during his jaunt through the Dominican Summer League, that's no longer the case. Despite the struggles, Benitez is likely ticketed for the Complex League, maybe even Low-A at some point in 2023.

Ceiling: Too Soon to Tell
Risk: Too Soon to Tell
MLB ETA: Too Soon to Tell

15. Cal Conley, SS

	Hit	Power	SB	Patience	Glove	Overall
	40	50	60	50	45/50	40

Born: 07/17/99	Age: 23	Bats: B	Top Production Comp: N/A
Height: 5-10	Weight: 185	Throws: R	

Season	Team	Age	Level	PA	1B	2B	3B	HR	SB	CS	BB%	K%	AVG	OBP	SLG	ISO
2021	ATL	21	A	161	22	5	1	2	8	3	8.70%	20.50%	0.214	0.304	0.307	0.093
2022	ATL	22	A	349	50	10	6	10	23	7	7.16%	16.91%	0.246	0.307	0.414	0.168
2022	ATL	22	A+	199	29	10	1	6	13	1	9.55%	25.13%	0.260	0.337	0.429	0.169

Background: Conley's dad, Brian, spent a season each within the Cubs and Reds organizations in the mid- to late-90s. The elder Conley, who was twice drafted, was released from Cincinnati after just one year in the New York-Penn League. He would spend three seasons kicking around the Indy Leagues before hooking up with the Cubs for one more shot. Cal easily surpassed his dad's draft status by 12 rounds. A product of West Clermont High School, the switch-hitting shortstop transferred to Texas Tech after a quick jaunt with the Miami Hurricanes. After sitting out the 2019 season, Conley got off to a hot start with the Red Raiders in 2020, slugging a scorching .371/.444/.643 before COVID curtailed what could have been a spectacular season. But Conley continued to swing it during his final campaign with the Big-12 Conference school, mashing .329/.393/.587 with 13 doubles and 15 homeruns in 56 games. Atlanta snagged him in the fourth round, 126th overall, and signed him to a deal worth $422,500. The front office shipped him directly to Low-A for his first taste of pro ball. And, well, the results were a bit underwhelming as he put together a lowly .214/.304/.307. Unsurprisingly, he opened last season back up in Augusta and the results were improved: he batted .246/.307/.414. And he continued to hit after his promotion up to Rome as well. Conley finished the season with an aggregate .251/.318/.420 slash line with 20 doubles, seven triples, 16 homeruns, and 36 stolen bases. He appeared in 23 games with the Scottsdale Scorpions in the Arizona Fall League as well, hitting .267/.376/.465 in 101 trips to the dish.

Scouting Report: There's a lot of interesting ingredients to Conley's recipe. He shows surprising pop for a sub-6-foot infielder, particularly one that switch hits. He runs frequently *and* efficiently, posting an 80% success rate on the base paths. He's likely going to shift to the keystone, but the early returns on his defense suggest he's capable at playing a serviceable shortstop. Conley lacks a true standout tool, though, even if the

Atlanta Braves

speed grades out as plus. He's tracking as a potential super-sub of sorts, especially if the club experiments with him in the outfield in the coming years.

Ceiling: 1.0-win player
Risk: Moderate
MLB ETA: 2024

16. Drake Baldwin, C

Hit	Power	SB	Patience	Glove	Overall
45	55	30	50	50	40

Born: 03/28/01	Age: 22	Bats: L	Top Production Comp: N/A
Height: 6-0	Weight: 220	Throws: R	

Season	Team	Age	Level	PA	1B	2B	3B	HR	SB	CS	BB%	K%	AVG	OBP	SLG	ISO
2022	ATL	21	CPX	10	1	2	0	0	0	0	10.00%	30.00%	0.375	0.400	0.625	0.250
2022	ATL	21	A	101	17	3	0	0	1	0	17.82%	21.78%	0.247	0.396	0.284	0.037

Background: After nabbing four straight pitchers to open up their 2022 draft class, Atlanta selected Missouri State University backstop Drake Baldwin as their first hitter. A product of Madison West High School, Baldwin opened up his collegiate career without missing a beat, hitting .295/.377/.426 with five extra-base hits in 17 games before COVID prematurely curtailed the season. Baldwin continued to impress with the bat the following season for the Bears, mashing .291/.411/.446 with seven doubles, two triples, four homeruns, and three stolen bases in 43 games. And he continued to impress during his final season in the Missouri Valley Conference in 2022: he slugged .341/.448/.647 with career bests in doubles (14) and homeruns (19). Atlanta signed the lefty-swinging catcher to a deal worth $633,300. Baldwin batted .247/.396/.284 with three doubles in 21 games with Augusta.

Scouting Report: Consider the following:

> Between 2011 and 2021, only four Missouri Valley Conference hitters batted at least .330/.430/.630 in a season (min. 250 PA): Trever Adams, Chris O'Brien, Chris Serritella, and Casey Gillaspie.

Wide stance. The swing is a bit long. He finally developed above-average power during his final season at Missouri State University. Baldwin's strong and can take outside pitches the opposite way for homeruns. Solid eye at the plate with a track record of consistent contact rates. Baldwin could grow into a bat-first backup option.

Ceiling: 1.0-win player
Risk: Moderate
MLB ETA: 2024/2025

17. Alan Rangel, RHP

FB	CB	CH	Command	Overall
55	50	55	55	40

Born: 08/21/97	Age: 25	Bats: R	Top Production Comp: Keury Mella
Height: 6-2	Weight: 170	Throws: R	

Season	Team	Age	Level	IP	TBF	K/9	K%	BB/9	BB%	K-BB%	ERA	FIP	xFIP	Pit/Bat
2021	ATL	23	A+	70.2	293	12.10	32.42%	2.67	7.17%	25.26%	3.57	3.61	3.78	4.04
2021	ATL	23	AA	34.0	132	10.85	31.06%	1.32	3.79%	27.27%	4.50	2.58	3.09	4.09
2022	ATL	24	AA	114.2	511	10.91	27.20%	3.92	9.78%	17.42%	5.26	4.30	4.52	3.93

Background: There are several certainties in life, like death, taxes, and Alan Rangel being listed among the Braves' Top 20 prospects. Signed as an international free agent during the summer of 2014, Rangel has taken the slow, deliberate approach to climbing the minor league ladder. He spent two summers in the Gulf Coast League and another three full stints in the old South Atlantic League. But once minor league baseball returned from its COVID-induced absence, Rangel's pressed on the accelerator and quickly made up for lost time. He spent the 2021 season breezing through the High-A competition and spending the last several weeks of the year at the minors' true proving ground – Double-A. Last season Rangel returned to Mississippi for a longer look. And the results -- ignoring the bloated 5.26 ERA -- remain promising as he averaged 10.9 strikeouts and 3.9 walks per nine innings. He also made one single, disastrous start with Gwinnett.

Snippet from The 2022 Prospect Digest Handbook: Eerily similar to right-hander Keury Mella, who had the potential and repertoire but just never stood out.

Scouting Report: Consider the following:

> Since 2006, only two 24-year-old hurlers posted a 26% to 28% strikeout percentage with a 9% to 11% walk rate in any Double-A league (min. 100 IP): Alec Marsh and – of course – Mr. Perennial Top 20 Braves Prospect, Alan Rangel.

Atlanta Braves

Forever the enigma. Rangel has a spot-starter's arsenal, featuring a low-90s fastball that'll peak in the 94-mph range, an above-average mid-80s changeup, which is his go-to offering; and he's scrapped his average curveball for a stronger slider. The fastball's a little too hittable. The changeup's the type that's a problem if it's above the bottom third of the strike zone. And the slider won't miss too many bats.

Ceiling: 1.0-win player
Risk: Moderate
MLB ETA: 2023

18. Luke Waddell, 2B/SS

Hit	Power	SB	Patience	Glove	Overall
50	40	40	55	50	40

Born: 07/13/98	Age: 24	Bats: L	Top Production Comp: N/A
Height: 5-9	Weight: 180	Throws: R	

Background: After a bit of downturn within Georgia Tech's program to develop viable minor league prospects, the Yellow Jackets reemerged as a consistent pipeline to the professional ranks the past several years. Since 2018, the ACC Conference School churned out 15 players that were selected within the first 10 rounds. Two of those Top 10 Round picks were by the Braves in 2021 – Luke Waddell, taken in the fifth round, and Justyn-Henry Malloy, who was chosen a round later and then flipped to the Tigers for Joe Jimenez. Waddell, a pint-size infielder originally from Loveland, Ohio, was a consistent offensive threat during his four-year career with the Yellow Jackets, leaving the school as a career .308/.407/.432 hitter in 172 games. After joining the Braves' organization, Waddell was immediately pushed up to High-A for his debut and then eventually spent the final weeks in Double-A. He batted an aggregate .260/.324/.450 in 29 total games. Waddell spent the fall playing for the Peoria Javelinas and – of course – he continued to hit (.312/.394/.393). Last season Waddell returned to Double-A for an extended look. And prior to his year prematurely ending due to an injury, he hit .272/.364/.370 with 10 doubles, two homeruns, and three stolen bases in 41 games. His overall production, as measured by *Weighted Runs Created Plus*, was 1% *below* the league average threshold.

Scouting Report: An extreme bat-to-ball hitter, Waddell's only fanned 39 times in his 298 career plate appearances – or just over 13% of the time. He combines the strong contact rates with a patient approach. There's not a whole lot of power present or expected in the future. He's spent the majority of his brief professional career on the left side of second base, but he's more likely than not headed for the other side of the keystone. He's a grinder, which seems to be a reoccurring theme with a lot of the club's better infield prospects. He's likely headed for a super-sub role, nothing more, nothing less.

Ceiling: 1.0-win player
Risk: Moderate
MLB ETA: 2024

19. Jesse Franklin, OF

Hit	Power	SB	Patience	Glove	Overall
40	55/60	55	50	45	40

Born: 12/01/98	Age: 24	Bats: L	Top Production Comp: N/A
Height: 6-1	Weight: 215	Throws: L	

Season	Team	Age	Level	PA	1B	2B	3B	HR	SB	CS	BB%	K%	AVG	OBP	SLG	ISO
2021	ATL	22	A+	406	38	24	2	24	19	4	8.37%	28.33%	0.244	0.320	0.522	0.278

Background: Taken by the Mariners in the 38th round coming out of Seattle Preparatory School in 2017, Franklin, instead, attended the University of Michigan and quickly established himself as one of the team's best all-around players. He would eventually leave the School Up North with a .287/.385/.520 career slash line. The Braves would select him in the third round, 97th overall, and signed him to a deal worth $497,500. Atlanta would send the 6-foot-1, 215-pound outfielder directly up to High-A at the start of 2021. And the results were…mostly good. Franklin slugged .244/.320/.522 with 24 doubles, two triples, 24 homeruns, and 19 stolen bases. His production, according to *Weighted Runs Created Plus*, was 18% above the league average mark. So, of course, Atlanta sent the former third rounder up to Double-A, the true proving ground, for the 2022 season. But just 15 games into the year Franklin hit the disabled list and eventually underwent Tommy John surgery.

Scouting Report: There's very little new information to report on this he hit the DL just a few weeks into last year. Here's last year's scouting report:

> "The power is a legitimate, above-average and may even peak as a plus skill. The actual hit tool may never creep over a 40-grade, though. His value takes a hit if he can't stay in center field. And he likely shouldn't stay there, either. If the walk rates were above-average or better he could encroach on Gorman Thomas territory. And if I were smarter, I could work in professional baseball."

Atlanta Braves

His window to develop into a solid big leaguer was already small enough. Now after losing a season, it's shrunk considerably. Everything about him screams Quad-A.

Ceiling: 1.0-win player
Risk: Moderate
MLB ETA: 2024

20. Brandol Mezquita, OF

Hit	Power	SB	Patience	Glove	Overall
30/40	30/50	50	50	45	40

Born: 07/14/01	Age: 21	Bats: R	Top Production Comp: N/A
Height: 6-0	Weight: 170	Throws: R	

Season	Team	Age	Level	PA	1B	2B	3B	HR	SB	CS	BB%	K%	AVG	OBP	SLG	ISO
2021	ATL	19	CPX	171	32	8	2	3	15	4	11.11%	29.24%	0.308	0.402	0.452	0.144
2022	ATL	20	A+	66	10	0	1	0	0	1	9.09%	34.85%	0.193	0.273	0.228	0.035
2022	ATL	20	A	388	72	14	4	3	14	5	10.57%	26.03%	0.281	0.371	0.375	0.094

Background: Signed out of the Dominican Republic for $300,000 in late November 2017. Mezquita logged his first professional work a year later, appearing in 52 games with the club's foreign rookie league affiliate. The results were disappointing, at best, as he batted .212/.347/.327 in the hitter-friendly environment. The front office opted to send the then-17-year-old outfielder stateside the following season. The results were moderately improved: .246/.350/.280. After sitting out the 2020 season due to COVID (like every other minor leaguer), Mezquita popped back up in the Complex League as he put together his finest professional to date, slugging .308/.402/.452 with eight doubles, two triples, three homeruns, and 15 stolen bases in 43 games. Last season the Dominican outfielder appeared in 87 games with Augusta and another 17 contests with Rome, batting an aggregate .268/.357/.353 with 14 doubles, five triples, three homeruns, and 14 stolen bases (in 20 total attempts). His production, as measured by *Weighted Runs Created Plus*, topped the league average threshold by 3%.

Scouting Report: Consider the following:

> Since 2006, only four 20-year-old hitters met the following criteria in Low-A (min. 350 PA): 108 to 118 wRC+, a 9.5% to 11.5% walk rate, and a 25% to 28% strikeout percentage. Those four hitters: Bubba Starling, Eric Haase, Matt Helm, and Brandol Mezquita.

There's some serious power potential brewing in Mezquita's bat, but he hasn't even begun to scratch the surface of it during games. Mezquita's bounced between all three outfield positions. The problem is that his bat profiles better in centerfield and his glove belongs in a corner spot. Mezquita will work the count and take a frequent free pass. But there's some swing-and-miss to his game.

Ceiling: 0.5- to 1.0-win player
Risk: Moderate
MLB ETA: 2025

Baltimore Orioles

Top Prospects

Baltimore Orioles

1. Gunnar Henderson, 3B/SS

Hit	Power	SB	Patience	Glove	Overall
50/55	60	55	55	50	70

Born: 06/29/01	Age: 21	Bats: L	Top Production Comp: Kris Bryant
Height: 6-2	Weight: 210	Throws: R	

Season	Team	Age	Level	PA	1B	2B	3B	HR	SB	CS	BB%	K%	AVG	OBP	SLG	ISO
2021	BAL	20	A	157	24	11	1	8	5	1	8.92%	29.30%	0.312	0.369	0.574	0.262
2021	BAL	20	A+	289	28	16	3	9	11	1	13.84%	30.10%	0.230	0.343	0.432	0.202
2021	BAL	20	AA	17	2	1	0	0	0	0	11.76%	58.82%	0.200	0.294	0.267	0.067
2022	BAL	21	AA	208	27	11	3	8	12	2	19.71%	18.27%	0.312	0.452	0.573	0.261
2022	BAL	21	AAA	295	44	13	4	11	10	1	12.88%	26.44%	0.288	0.390	0.504	0.216

Background: The Baltimore Orioles hired current General Manager Mike Elias in mid-November 2018. Seven months later Elias would captain the most successful draft in recent memory – for any Major League franchise. The O's selected Oregon State University backstop Adley Rutschman with the first overall pick. Rutschman, of course, would go on to become a consensus Top 5 prospect for three consecutive seasons and quickly established himself as a one of the best young players in Major League Baseball during his debut campaign last season. Forty-one selections after the organization nabbed the former Beaver star, Baltimore circled back around and chose John T. Morgan Academy dynamo Gunnar Henderson – who quickly ascended towards the top of every top prospect list. The 6-foot-2, 210-pound shortstop / third baseman turned in a solid debut in the old Gulf Coast League, hitting .259/.331/.370 with five doubles, two triples, a dinger, and a pair of stolen bases in only 29 games. Two years later, after minor league action returned from its pandemic-induced absence, Henderson annihilated the Low-A competition to the tune of .312/.369/.575, made a brief stop in High-A, and closed out his breakout season with a five-game cameo in Double-A. That blitz through the mid-levels just set the tone for a massive 2022 season. Splitting time between Bowie and Norfolk, the former second rounder mashed .297/.416/.531 with 24 doubles, seven triples, 19 homeruns, and 22 stolen bases (in only 25 attempts). Per *Weighted Runs Created Plus*, Henderson's overall production blasted past the league average minimum by a whopping 53%. Baltimore called him up for his big league debut at the end of August. Henderson continued to impress as he batted .259/.348/.440 with 12 extra-base hits in 34 games.

Snippet from The 2022 Prospect Digest Handbook: The lefty-swinging infielder whiffed 29.3% of the time in Low-A, 30.1% in High-A, and a whopping 58.8% in 17 plate appearances in Double-A. That's red flag #1. Now here's red flag #2: he was *hapless* against southpaws as well, hitting a paltry .189/.293/.349 in 123 plate appearances.

Scouting Report: With regard to his longest stint at a minor league level last season, consider the following:

> Since 2006, only four 21-year-old hitters posted a 132 to 142 wRC+ mark in any Triple-A league (min. 275 PA): Wil Myers, Lastings Milledge, Dilson Herrera, and – of course – Gunnar Henderson.

Now let's address the two elephants in the room, shall we?

> #1. Strikeout Rates – Henderson took massive strides forward last season in terms of contact rates, posting a sub-20% whiff rate at the minors' toughest level (Double-A), though it did bloat to the 26% range in Triple-A and during his MLB debut.

> #2. Left-handers – Henderson batted a putrid .189/.293/.349 (.642 OPS) during his breakout 2021 campaign. Last season, he more or less maintained status quo, batting .208/.316/.354 (.670 OPS) against southpaws.

Henderson has every tool imaginable to be a transcendent superstar – hit tool, power, speed, patience, premium defensive position (either shortstop or the hot corner), but he's not going to achieve that level with those types of platoon splits.

Ceiling: 7.0-win player
Risk: Moderate to High
MLB ETA: Debuted in 2022

2. Grayson Rodriguez, RHP

FB	CB	SL	CU	CH	Control	Overall
70	50	60	55	70	60	70

Born: 11/16/99	Age: 23	Bats: R	Top Production Comp: Jose Fernandez
Height: 6-5	Weight: 220	Throws: R	

Season	Team	Age	Level	IP	TBF	K/9	K%	BB/9	BB%	K-BB%	ERA	FIP	xFIP	Pit/Bat
2021	BAL	21	A+	23.1	88	15.43	45.45%	1.93	5.68%	39.77%	1.54	2.48	2.47	3.75
2021	BAL	21	AA	79.2	310	13.67	39.03%	2.49	7.10%	31.94%	2.60	2.72	2.72	4.05
2022	BAL	22	AAA	69.2	271	12.53	35.79%	2.71	7.75%	28.04%	2.20	2.04	2.90	3.98

Background: Former Orioles GM Dan Duquette did a lot of good during his seven years in the captain's chair. The ball club placed second in the ultra-competitive AL East Division in his first season, though eventually losing in the ALDS to the hated Yankees. That year started a

Baltimore Orioles

stretch of five consecutive seasons of playing .500 or better ball. And while the front office wasn't without its sins during that time period, like signing one-dimensional slugger Chris Davis to a $161 million deal in January 2016, Duquette's tenure was, by and large, a success. But, perhaps, the best thing Duquette did for the organization could be found in his final draft class, leaving his eventual replacement, Mike Elias, with a head start on the organization's latest rebuild. That parting gift: Grayson Rodriguez, the 11th overall pick in the 2018 draft. A product of Central Heights High School, the 6-foot-5, 220-pound right-hander – almost immediately – established himself as one of the game's preeminent prospects. He would twirl 19.1 innings of dominance during his debut in the old Gulf Coast League, fanning 20 and walking seven to go along with a 1.40 ERA. The front office sent the fire-balling teenager up to the South Atlantic League in 2019, and Rodriguez simply overmatched the older competition as he fanned 129 against just 36 free passes in 94.0 innings of work. After minor league ball returned from its COVID-induced hiatus, Rodriguez was unearthly during his five-game cameo with Aberdeen and the franchise deemed the then-21-year-old ready for the toughest level – Double-A. And he put together a historic 18-start cameo with the Baysox of Bowie. He finished his second full season with a sparkling 2.36 ERA, averaging 14.1 strikeouts and just 2.4 walks per nine innings. Last season, in an injury-interrupted campaign, Rodriguez was limited to just 17 starts, 14 of which came in Triple-A, recording another absurd strikeout-to-walk ratio (109-to-28) in only 75.2 innings. A Grade 2 right lat strain knocked him out of action from early June through early September, essentially costing him the chance at his big league debut.

Snippet from The 2022 Prospect Digest Handbook: Throw in plus command and there's a recipe for an elite, premium ceiling. Four legitimate swing-and-miss, sit down on the bench offerings.

Scouting Report: Consider the following:

> Since 2006, only two 22-year-old hurlers met the following criteria in any Triple-A league (min. 60 IP): 34% to 37% strikeout percentage with a 6% to 9% walk percentage. Those two hurlers: former Braves top prospect Tommy Hanson and – of course – Grayson Rodriguez.

Rodriguez's repertoire is on the *short, short* list for best in the minor leagues – again. But what separates the budding ace from the rest of the pack is his ability to command the strike zone with each of his five offerings. The young right-hander, who likely wins a Cy Young award during his big league career, owns a pair of plus-plus offerings (mid- to upper-90s fastball and a fall-off-the-table changeup with Bugs Bunny action), a plus slider, an above-average cutter (which is a new addition to his attack), and a solid-average curveball. Elite ceiling.

Ceiling: 6.0-win player
Risk: Moderate
MLB ETA: 2023

3. Jackson Holliday, SS

Hit	Power	SB	Patience	Glove	Overall
60	50	55	50	50/55	70

Born: 12/04/03	Age: 19	Bats: L	Top Production Comp: N/A
Height: 6-1	Weight: 175	Throws: R	

Season	Team	Age	Level	PA	1B	2B	3B	HR	SB	CS	BB%	K%	AVG	OBP	SLG	ISO
2022	BAL	18	CPX	33	7	1	0	1	3	0	30.30%	6.06%	0.409	0.576	0.591	0.182
2022	BAL	18	A	57	6	4	0	0	1	1	26.32%	17.54%	0.238	0.439	0.333	0.095

Background: Oklahoma-based Stillwater High School hasn't produced a lot of future professional ballplayers during its history. But when a player *does* get drafted coming out of the prep school, the odds are pretty good that (A) he's going to make it to the big leagues and (B) he's probably going to fall somewhere on the Holliday family tree. Three of the school's six picks made the big leagues: seven-time All-Star and 2007 batting champ Matt Holliday (Jackson's old man), Brett Anderson, and Ryan Vilade. Likewise, two of the school's six picks are Hollidays. Along with Jackson's dad, the young shortstop's uncle Josh Holliday was the selected by the Twins coming out of high school – though he spurned the club's interest as a 14th round pick and opted to attend Oklahoma State University. Four years later the Blue Jays snagged him in the ninth round. But after two mediocre seasons in the low levels, Holliday called it quits. He would spend a couple years on his dad's coaching staff at Oklahoma State, would leave, and eventually return to take over the head coaching gig in 2012. Baseball runs deep in the Holliday family. And Jackson, a 6-foot-1, 175-pound lefty-swinging shortstop, is the next in line. Committed to Oklahoma State – where else would a Holliday go? – the young infielder was named the state's Gatorade Player of the Year following a tremendous senior campaign. He slugged .685/.749/1.392 with 17 homeruns and 79 RBIs. He also – quietly – set the National Federation of High Schools single season mark for hits in a season with 89. Baltimore selected Holliday atop the draft last season, signing the #1 overall pick to a deal worth $8,190,000. Jackson batted an impressive .297/.489/.422 between the Complex League and Delmarva.

Baltimore Orioles

Scouting Report: Per the usual, my pre-draft write-up:

"Beautiful left-handed swing that's going to spray line drives from foul line to foul line without too much bais. There's a chance the hit tool develops into a perennial .300 hitter during his peak in the professional ranks. Holliday isn't going to hit mammoth homeruns, but he should hit 20 dingers that leave the park in a hurry. Defensively, he has the chops to stay at the position. Smooth, quick, not flashy. He's a blue-collar shortstop that has a chance to grade out as above-average."

Ceiling: 6.0-win player
Risk: Moderate
MLB ETA: 2025/2026

4. Colton Cowser, OF

Hit	Power	SB	Patience	Glove	Overall
45	45	50	55	50	50

Born: 03/20/00	Age: 23	Bats: L	Top Production Comp: N/A
Height: 6-3	Weight: 195	Throws: R	

Season	Team	Age	Level	PA	1B	2B	3B	HR	SB	CS	BB%	K%	AVG	OBP	SLG	ISO
2021	BAL	21	CPX	25	7	3	0	1	3	2	12.00%	16.00%	0.500	0.560	0.773	0.273
2021	BAL	21	A	124	28	5	0	1	4	2	17.74%	15.32%	0.347	0.476	0.429	0.082
2022	BAL	22	A+	278	34	19	2	4	16	1	16.19%	28.42%	0.258	0.385	0.410	0.153
2022	BAL	22	AA	224	40	10	0	10	2	2	16.07%	25.45%	0.341	0.469	0.568	0.227
2022	BAL	22	AAA	124	11	7	0	5	0	0	10.48%	30.65%	0.219	0.339	0.429	0.210

Background: An offensive juggernaut during his two-plus seasons at Sam Houston State. Cowser left the Southland Conference-based school with a career .354/.460/.608 slash line. Baltimore drafted the former Bearkat bopper with the fifth overall pick two years ago, signing him to a well-below slot bonus worth $4.9 million, saving the ball club nearly $1.2 in draft monies. The 6-foot-3, 195-pound outfielder made the transition from the small Division I school into the minor leagues look like child's play as he mashed .375/.490/.492 during his 149-plate appearance debut two years ago. Last summer, Cowser, a native of Houston, Texas, blitzed through three stops along the minor league ladder, going from High-A to Double-A and then eventually settling in at Triple-A for the last month of the season. He finished his first full season in pro ball with an aggregate .278/.406/.469 triple slash line with 36 doubles, two triples, 19 homeruns, and 18 stolen bases (in only 21 total attempts). Per *Weighted Runs Created Plus*, Cowser's overall production topped the league average threshold by a whopping 42%.

Snippet from The 2022 Prospect Digest Handbook: Cowser doesn't project to hit from more than 10 or so homeruns during a full professional season. But he owns an above-average hit tool, enough speed to swipe 15 bags, and play a passable defense. He's low ceiling / high floor prospect and should be selected between picks 15 and 20.

Scouting Report: Consider the following:

> Since 2006, only three 22-year-old hitters posted a 118 to 128 wRC+ with a 26% to 30% strikeout rate and a double-digit walk rate in any High-A league (min. 275 PA): Marc Wik, Korry Howell, and – of course – Colton Cowser.

The sweet-swinging former early first round selection struggled *mightily* with contact issues throughout the duration of 2022, posting K-rate north of 25% in each of his three stops. Compounding the questions about his hit tool are the dramatic – and concerning – platoon splits that the lefty-swinging Cowser displayed. He batted a scorching .307/.432/.530 against righties but cobbled together a lowly .194/.329/.287 mark against lefties with a K-rate north of 33%. And don't buy into his power surge either. Cowser slugged more than half of his homeruns in 49 games in Double-A with the Bowie Baysox, who happen to have one of the most homer-friendly environments in the minor leagues. So just let's recap. In 2022, Cowser:

> #1. Struggled with contact issues.
> #2. Had significant troubles against southpaws.
> #3. Had a major power surge, though a portion of his career high thump
> #4. Can be attributed to friendly hitting environments.

Defensively speaking, he's better suited for a corner outfielder gig. There's some starting material here.

Ceiling: 2.5-win player
Risk: Moderate
MLB ETA: 2023

Baltimore Orioles

5. Joey Ortiz, SS

Hit	Power	SB	Patience	Glove	Overall
50	45	40	50	70	55

Born: 07/14/98	Age: 24	Bats: R	Top Production Comp: N/A
Height: 5-11	Weight: 175	Throws: R	

Season	Team	Age	Level	PA	1B	2B	3B	HR	SB	CS	BB%	K%	AVG	OBP	SLG	ISO
2021	BAL	22	A+	89	13	7	2	0	3	0	11.24%	20.22%	0.289	0.382	0.434	0.145
2021	BAL	22	AA	67	8	2	0	4	1	0	8.96%	20.90%	0.233	0.313	0.467	0.233
2022	BAL	23	AA	485	70	28	4	15	2	1	8.45%	16.70%	0.269	0.337	0.455	0.186
2022	BAL	23	AAA	115	23	7	2	4	6	1	7.83%	14.78%	0.346	0.400	0.567	0.221

Background: New Mexico State University is far from a traditional hotbed, historically speaking, but the school's provided a solid pipeline of talent over the past several years. Recent alums include: Nick Gonzales, the seventh overall pick three years ago; Kyle Bradish, Daniel Johnson, and – of course – Joey Ortiz. Taken in the fourth round, 108th overall, in 2019, Ortiz was productive hitter over first two seasons with the Aggies. But the 5-foot-11, 175-pound infielder had an offensive *explosion* during his junior campaign as he bashed .422/.474/.697 with 25 doubles, 10 triples, eight homeruns, and a dozen stolen bases. The California native looked miserable during his debut in the old New York-Penn League, hitting a scant .241/.345/.267 with just three extra-base knocks in 56 games. After minor league baseball returned from its COVID-induced hiatus, Ortiz's bat looked refreshed as he shredded the High-A competition. And just as he was settling in with Bowie in Double-A, a shoulder injury prematurely ended his campaign. Finally healthy last season, he made stops with the Baysox of Bowie and the Tides of Norfolk, hitting an aggregate .284/.349/.477 with 35 doubles, six triples, 19 homeruns, and eight stolen bases (in 10 total attempts). Per *Weighted Runs Created Plus*, his overall production topped the league average mark by 22%.

Scouting Report: Consider the following:

> Since 2006, only three 23-year-old hitters met the following criteria in any Double-A league (min. 350 PA): 110 to 120 wRC+, a 15.5% to 17.5% strikeout rate, and a 7.5% to 9.5% walk rate. Those three hitters: Dwight Smith Jr., Chad Tracy, and Joey Ortiz. Smith spent parts of four seasons in the big league, the last two with the Orioles of Baltimore. And Tracy was a promising power-hitting for a couple seasons early in his career before shifting to part-time duty.

A tremendous defender at the infield's premium position, Ortiz's leatherwork is good enough to make him a starter – even if he was a Mario Mendoza-type hitter. The offensive potential could push him up as an above-average regular. Plus-plus defender who has the potential to win a Gold Glove or two. Ortiz takes a strong contact-oriented approach at the plate, showing doubles power, a little bit of speed, and an average hit tool. There are a lot of similarities to Arizona's Nick Ahmed. There's an offensive ceiling of a .260/.320/.410 hitter.

Ceiling: 3.0-win player
Risk: Low to Moderate
MLB ETA: 2023

6. D.L. Hall, LHP

FB	CB	SL	CH	Command	Overall
70	60	60	70	30/40	60

Born: 09/19/98	Age: 24	Bats: L	Top Production Comp: Blake Snell
Height: 6-2	Weight: 195	Throws: L	

Season	Team	Age	Level	IP	TBF	K/9	K%	BB/9	BB%	K-BB%	ERA	FIP	xFIP	Pit/Bat
2021	BAL	22	AA	31.2	128	15.92	43.75%	4.55	12.50%	31.25%	3.13	3.33	2.33	4.12
2022	BAL	23	AAA	76.2	346	14.67	36.13%	5.75	14.16%	21.97%	4.70	3.94	3.60	4.27

Background: The hopes of the ball club's 2017 draft class are hinging on the erratic, yet oh-so-talented left arm of D.L. Hall. Taken with the 21st overall pick that summer, Hall blew the doors off the competition during his first full season in the minors in 2018, posting a 100-to-42 strikeout-to-walk ratio with a 2.10 ERA across 94.1 innings of work. His impressive strikeout ability shined brightly the next year in High-A, but his borderline concerning command issues blossomed into a full blown blunder as he walked 54 hitters in only 80.2 innings. After minor league baseball returned from its COVID-enforced vacation, Hall dealt with a stress reaction in the bone of his precious left elbow in 2021, limiting him to just 31.2 innings. Last season, Hall made a brief start with Aberdeen and another with Bowie before moving on up to Triple-A. He also squeezed in two separate stints in Baltimore as well. Overall, Hall tossed 84.1 minor league innings, striking out an impressive 137 against 50 free passes to go along with a 4.48 ERA and a 3.65 FIP. The well-built southpaw hurled another 13.2 innings in the Bigs as well, fanning 19 and walking six while surrendering nine earned runs.

Snippet from The 2022 Prospect Digest Handbook: Barring any setbacks from the stress reaction in his elbow, Hall could ascend to a mid-rotation arm – maybe even higher if the command ticks up closer to average.

Baltimore Orioles

Scouting Report: Consider the following:

> Since 2006, only two 23-year-olds posted a strikeout percentage north of 35% in any Triple-A league (min. 75 IP): Rays ace right-hander Tyler Glasnow and D.L. Hall.

Now the bad news:

> Glasnow, who's dealt with his own command issues, posted a walk percentage of 8.79%. Hall, on the other hand, finished his time in Triple-A with a hefty 14.16% walk percentage.

There aren't too many hurlers that could put their entire arsenal up against Grayson Rodriguez and come away the winner. But Hall's name is certainly on the short, *short* list. One of the best left-handed fastballs in the entire minor leagues; Hall's heater will operate in the 94- to 97-mph range and it will reach as high as 99 mph on occasion. It's plus-plus offering with late, riding life and some noticeable hop on the tail end. He backs up the offering with one of the best changeups I saw in 2022, adding another second plus-plus offering. His pair of breaking balls, curveball and slider, are both plus pitches. If Hall possessed 60-grade command, he'd be the best pitcher in Major League Baseball. If he had, above-average command, he'd be a Top 5 hurler. If he had average command, he'd be a lock for the Top 10. His 30-grade command may push him entirely out of a starting gig, though with the parent club completely out of contention he'll still get an extended look.

Ceiling: 4.5-win player
Risk: High
MLB ETA: Debuted in 2022

7. Connor Norby, 2B

Hit	Power	SB	Patience	Glove	Overall
55	50	40	50	45	55

Born: 06/08/00 **Age:** 23 **Bats:** R **Top Production Comp:** N/A
Height: 5-10 **Weight:** 187 **Throws:** R

Season	Team	Age	Level	PA	1B	2B	3B	HR	SB	CS	BB%	K%	AVG	OBP	SLG	ISO
2021	BAL	21	CPX	24	2	2	0	0	1	0	4.17%	29.17%	0.182	0.208	0.273	0.091
2021	BAL	21	A	126	20	4	1	3	5	3	16.67%	22.22%	0.283	0.413	0.434	0.152
2022	BAL	22	A+	209	27	7	2	8	6	3	8.61%	23.92%	0.237	0.311	0.425	0.188
2022	BAL	22	AA	296	42	14	2	17	10	2	11.49%	19.93%	0.298	0.389	0.571	0.274
2022	BAL	22	AAA	42	8	2	0	4	0	1	7.14%	11.90%	0.359	0.405	0.718	0.359

Background: There's a sub-theme that's surrounded each of Mike Elias's draft classes with the Orioles – college hitters. Beginning with his first class in 2019 through last summer, the franchise has owned a total of 17 selections among the first three rounds. Of those 17 picks, the front office has chosen a college hitter 14 times. The lone outliers: Gunnar Henderson, Jackson Holliday, and Nolan McLean. And the franchise started their 2021 draft class with five consecutive collegiate hitters, the second of which was East Carolina University infielder Connor Norby. Limited to just 105 plate appearances over his first two seasons with the Pirates, the 5-foot-10, 187-pound second baseman morphed into the American Athletic Conference's version of Ted Williams during his junior campaign. Norby posted a whopper of a slash line, .415/.484/.659, with a near one-to-one strikeout-to-walk ratio to go along with 15 doubles and 15 homeruns. After signing with the franchise for $1.7 million as the 41st overall pick two years ago, Norby was solid during his debut with Delmarva, batting .283/.413/.434 with eight extra-base knocks in only 26 games. Last season the second baseman / moonlighting left fielder struggled during his 48-game stint in High-A, hitting .237/.311/.425 with Aberdeen. His bat caught fire during his 64-game tenure with Bowie and continued to hit in a brief stint in Triple-A. When the dust finally settled Norby had compiled an aggregate .279/.360/.526 with 23 doubles, four triples, 29 homeruns, and 16 stolen bases (in 22 total attempts). Per *Weighted Runs Created Plus*, his overall production surpassed the league average mark by 37%.

Snippet from The 2022 Prospect Digest Handbook: He has the potential to be a fringy league average starter.

Scouting Report: Consider the following:

> Since 2006, only two 22-year-old hitters met the following criteria in any Double-A league (min. 275 PA): 152 to 162 wRC+, a double-digit walk rate, and an 18% to 21% strikeout rate. Those two hitters: M.J. Melendez and, of course, Connor Norby.

Norby's power has already surpassed my modest expectations. And it's now a repeatable, rock solid tool. The former ECU bopper got off to a solid start to the year, hitting .268/.344/.549 over his first 19 games with Aberdeen. But after going 3-for-14 over his next five games, the former second rounder hit the disabled list with an eye issue, an injury that knocked him out of action for a couple weeks. It would take him a couple weeks to get going again, but he didn't slow down for the remainder of the year. Not an overly patient hitter at the plate, Norby, though, is very selective. There's plus raw power, which he'll flash every once in a while when he really gets into one. Good looking swing. He

Baltimore Orioles

doesn't try to do too much with the ball either. He's a poor defender at the keystone, but he might be a candidate to bounce between the hot corner and left field. In terms of big league ceiling, think: .285/.345/.445.

Ceiling: 3.0- to 3.5-win player
Risk: Low to Moderate
MLB ETA: 2023

8. Jordan Westburg, IF

Hit	Power	SB	Patience	Glove	Overall
50	45/50	50	55	55	50

Born: 02/18/99 **Age:** 24 **Bats:** R **Top Production Comp:** N/A
Height: 6-3 **Weight:** 203 **Throws:** R

Season	Team	Age	Level	PA	1B	2B	3B	HR	SB	CS	BB%	K%	AVG	OBP	SLG	ISO
2021	BAL	22	A	91	17	5	1	3	5	1	13.19%	26.37%	0.366	0.484	0.592	0.225
2021	BAL	22	A+	285	43	16	2	8	9	4	12.28%	24.91%	0.286	0.389	0.469	0.183
2021	BAL	22	AA	130	14	6	2	4	3	0	10.77%	24.62%	0.232	0.323	0.429	0.196
2022	BAL	23	AA	209	22	14	0	9	3	0	12.44%	27.27%	0.247	0.344	0.473	0.225
2022	BAL	23	AAA	413	53	25	3	18	9	3	10.65%	21.79%	0.273	0.361	0.508	0.235

Background: SEC powerhouse Mississippi State University has churned out a *tremendous* amount of talent over the past four draft classes. Twenty-five Bulldogs have been drafted since 2019, including: five first round selections, two second round picks, and a pair of fourth rounders. One of those aforementioned first round picks is Jordan Westburg, who was taken near the back of the opening round, 30th overall, in the COVID-limit 2020 draft class. The 6-foot-3, 203-pound infielder turned in an impressive debut two years ago, slugging a rock solid .285/.389/.479 as he moved across three separate levels, including a semi-lengthy stint in Double-A. Westburg opened up last season back in Bowie, but after 47 games the front office pushed him up to the final minor league stop. He finished the year with an aggregate .265/.355/.496 slash line with 39 doubles, tied for the sixth most in the minors, three triples, 27 homeruns, and 12 stolen bases (in 15 attempts). Per *Weighted Runs Created Plus*, his overall production topped the league average threshold by 26%.

Snippet from The 2022 Prospect Digest Handbook: He looks like the prototypical low ceiling / high floor collegiate bat.

Scouting Report: Consider the following:

> Since 2006, only three 23-year-old hitters met the following criteria in any Triple-A league (min. 350 PA): 125 to 135 wRC+, 21% to 23% strikeout rate, and a double-digit walk rate. Those three hitters: Jon Singleton, Isan Diaz, and – of course – Jordan Westburg.

Westburg started the season off as cold as an iceberg, hitting a chilly .179/.304/.379 over his first 25 games, but he rebounded to slug .283/.367/.521 over his remaining 113 contests. An above-average defender at the most important position on the infield, as well as at second and third bases, Westburg also showed more thump than expected as well – particularly in Triple-A where Norfolk's ballpark was a neutral hitting ground. Westburg is tracking like a solid, league-average starter with the ceiling as a .270/.340/.425.

Ceiling: 2.5-win player
Risk: Moderate
MLB ETA: 2023

9. Coby Mayo, 3B

Hit	Power	SB	Patience	Glove	Overall
50	60	35	50	50	60

Born: 12/10/01 **Age:** 21 **Bats:** R **Top Production Comp:** Jay Bruce
Height: 6-5 **Weight:** 215 **Throws:** R

Season	Team	Age	Level	PA	1B	2B	3B	HR	SB	CS	BB%	K%	AVG	OBP	SLG	ISO
2021	BAL	19	CPX	84	14	6	0	3	6	0	13.10%	15.48%	0.324	0.429	0.535	0.211
2021	BAL	19	A	125	19	8	1	5	5	0	12.80%	20.80%	0.311	0.416	0.547	0.236
2022	BAL	20	AA	145	23	4	0	5	0	0	8.28%	34.48%	0.250	0.331	0.398	0.148
2022	BAL	20	A+	288	32	16	2	14	5	1	9.38%	21.53%	0.251	0.326	0.494	0.243

Background: Mike Elias's guidance in combination with the club perennially selecting near the top of the midsummer draft have helped restock the Orioles' once sagging farm system. Elias' 2019 class added Adley Rutschman, Gunnar Henderson, and the recently traded Darell Hernaiz. A year later the club added the likes of Heston Kjerstad, Jordan Westburg, and Coby Mayo. Taken with the 103rd overall pick that year, the front office signed the 6-foot-5, 215-pound third baseman to a hefty $1.75 million deal. Mayo turned in a solid debut showing two years ago, slugging .319/.426/.555 with 14 doubles, one triple, nine homeruns, and 11 stolen bases in only 53 games between the Complex League and Low-A. Last season, the Florida-born infielder continued to impress during his romp through High-A and Double-A as well. He slugged an

Baltimore Orioles

aggregate .247/.326/.456 with 20 doubles, two triples, 19 homeruns, and five stolen bases. His overall production, according to *Weighted Runs Created Plus*, topped the league average threshold by 10%. Mayo lost the entire month of July due to back spasms last summer.

Snippet from The 2022 Prospect Digest Handbook: Mayo owns the best power potential of any minor league hitter not named Adley Rutschman in the Orioles' farm system. I like him a lot. The ceiling is incredibly high. One of the most underrated prospects.

Scouting Report: Consider the following:

> Since 2006, only three 20-year-old hitters met the following criteria in a season in High-A (min. 275 PA): 113 to 123 wRC+, 20% to 23% strikeout rate, and an 8% to 11% walk rate. Those three hitters: Leody Taveras, Trey Michalczewski, and – of course – Coby Mayo.

Plus-plus raw power that he's just starting to pull into games. There isn't a ballpark in the world that can contain one of his prodigious blasts. Still not in love with the setup at the plate. The hulking 6-foot-5, 215-pound masher starts with a wide base at the plate. There's a lot of pre-swing movement, including shifting his weight entirely to back leg. But the swing is breathtakingly fast and short. If it weren't for a plethora of better defenders already in place, Mayo could stay at the hot corner. It wouldn't be shocking to see him wind up as a left or rightfielder. In terms of big league ceiling, think: .260/.330/.450.

Ceiling: 3.5- to 4.0-win player
Risk: Moderate to High
MLB ETA: 2024/2025

10. Heston Kjerstad, RF

Hit	Power	SB	Patience	Glove	Overall
55	60	30	50	55	55

Born: 02/12/99	Age: 24	Bats: L	Top Production Comp: N/A
Height: 6-3	Weight: 205	Throws: R	

Season	Team	Age	Level	PA	1B	2B	3B	HR	SB	CS	BB%	K%	AVG	OBP	SLG	ISO
2022	BAL	23	A	98	26	9	0	2	0	0	13.27%	17.35%	0.463	0.551	0.650	0.188
2022	BAL	23	A+	186	25	8	2	3	1	0	8.60%	25.27%	0.233	0.312	0.362	0.129

Background: The 2020 draft class marked the first time in four years that college hitters went back-to-back with the top two selections. Detroit led the mid-summer draft off by selecting Spencer Torkelson, the bashing Arizona State University star, with the #1 overall pick, and Baltimore followed it up with Arkansas masher Heston Kjerstad. Unfortunately, for the 6-foot-3, 205-pound outfielder, he wouldn't make his professional debut until nearly two years later due to myocarditis (heart inflammation) which was unknown heading into the draft. The former Razorback was medically cleared last season and appeared with the Delmarva Shorebirds in mid-June. And – amazingly – Kjerstad resembled the same type of power-hitting outfielder the Orioles drafted, despite the lengthy layoff. He shredded the Low-A competition for 22 games (.463/.551/.650) before slowing during a couple-month stint in High-A (.233/.312/.362). Kjerstad finished the year with an aggregate .309/.394/.457 with 17 doubles, two triples, five homeruns, and a stolen base. Per *Weighted Runs Created Plus*, his overall production topped the league mark by 35%. Baltimore sent the former #2 overall pick to the Arizona Fall League following the season. And he mashed. He slugged .357/.385/.622 with nine doubles, one triple, and five homeruns in 22 games with the Scottsdale Scorpions.

Scouting Report: One of the better feel good stories from the 2022 season. Not only did Kjerstad making it back from his extended absence, but he performed far better than expected. Not your typical power-hitting outfielder, Kjerstad showed a surprising willingness to consistently shoot the ball the other way. Plus power potential, particularly pull power, there's a solid chance he develops an above-average hit tool. Very similar swing as former All-Star Sean Casey. Kjerstad also showed a surprising amount of agility in right field as well. He's poised to be one of the bigger breakouts in 2023. After his strong AFL, it wouldn't be shocking to see the O's push him directly up to Double-A at the start of year.

Ceiling: 3.5-win player
Risk: Moderate to High
MLB ETA: 2024

Baltimore Orioles

11. Dylan Beavers, OF

Hit	Power	SB	Patience	Glove	Overall
50	55	40	50	50	50

Born: 08/11/01	Age: 21	Bats: L	Top Production Comp: N/A
Height: 6-4	Weight: 206	Throws: R	

Season	Team	Age	Level	PA	1B	2B	3B	HR	SB	CS	BB%	K%	AVG	OBP	SLG	ISO
2022	BAL	20	CPX	12	0	1	0	0	0	0	16.67%	16.67%	0.111	0.333	0.222	0.111
2022	BAL	20	A	77	14	7	2	0	6	1	15.58%	14.29%	0.359	0.468	0.531	0.172
2022	BAL	20	A+	16	4	0	0	0	0	0	12.50%	31.25%	0.286	0.375	0.286	0.000

Background: One of the younger draft-eligible prospects in the 2022 college draft class. Beavers, a well-built 6-foot-4, 206-pound outfielder, turned in a decent, COVID-shortened freshman season with the California Golden Bears in 2020, hitting .250/.333/.357 with one lone extra-base hit (a dinger) in 12 games. Beavers, a product of Mission College Prep, had a bit of a coming out party during his sophomore campaign for Head Coach Mike Neu. In 55 games for the Pac-12 conference school, the then-20-year-old slugger batted .303/.401/.630 with 11 doubles, two triples, 18 homeruns, and 10 stolen bases (in 12 total attempts). He split the ensuing summer between Team USA and the Cape Cod League. In nine games with the national club he batted a paltry .143/.333/.286 with a homerun. His eight games with the Cotuit Kettleers were slightly better: .233/.286/.300. Last season Beavers turned in another Beavers-like showing for the Bears. In a career-best 56 games, the California-born outfielder slugged .291/.427/.634 with 16 doubles, three triples, 17 homeruns, and seven stolen bases. Baltimore selected Beavers with the 33rd overall pick last July, signing him to a deal worth $2.2 million. The former California star batted .322/.438/.460 with eight doubles and two triples during his debut last season.

Scouting Report: Per the usual, my pre-draft write-up:

> "Consider the following:
>
> Since 2011, here's the list of Pac-12 hitters to bat between .280/.410/.575 and .310/.440/.650 in a season (250 PA): Chase Davis and Dylan Beavers.
>
> Like Tennessee's Jordan Beck, there's a little bit of a swing-and-miss approach to Dylan Beavers, though (A) it's not overly concerning and (B) Beavers' approach at the plate last season took major strides in working the count. Cal's young outfielder's walk rate jumped from 12.7% in 2021 to 18.8% in 2022. Above-average power. Average speed. Very simple, low maintenance swing that belies the 55-grade thump he's packing. League average starter potential, maybe a tick more."

Ceiling: 2.5-win player
Risk: Moderate
MLB ETA: 2025

12. Frederick Bencosme, IF

Hit	Power	SB	Patience	Glove	Overall
50/60	35/40	50/40	50	45/50	50

Born: 12/25/02	Age: 20	Bats: L	Top Production Comp: Ramon Urias
Height: 6-0	Weight: 02	Throws: R	

Season	Team	Age	Level	PA	1B	2B	3B	HR	SB	CS	BB%	K%	AVG	OBP	SLG	ISO
2021	BAL	18	DSL	158	32	6	4	2	10	3	6.96%	11.39%	0.310	0.365	0.451	0.141
2022	BAL	19	A	250	61	8	2	3	8	5	10.80%	12.40%	0.336	0.410	0.432	0.095
2022	BAL	19	A+	41	3	2	1	0	0	1	4.88%	21.95%	0.154	0.195	0.256	0.103

Background: Every now and then an international free agent goes largely unnoticed – for whatever reason – and ends up signing for the price of a five-yea-old used minivan. One of the best examples, of course, is lefty Framber Valdez, who joined the Astros for just $10,000 at the geriatric age of 21. Baltimore may have unearthed their version of Valdez. Sort of. Except he's a shortstop and joined the organization as a teenager. A native of Moca, Dominican Republic, Bencosme made his affiliated debut in his home country two years ago, leaving quite the impression. The lefty-swinging shortstop batted .310/.365/.451 with six doubles, four triples, two homeruns, and 10 stolen bases in only 44 games of work. But he was an 18-year-old, overlooked hitter performing well in a hitter friendly environment. There's *no way* he would continue at that level in 2022, right? Exactly. Kind of. Because he was actually *better* as he moved into the stateside leagues. Baltimore initially sent Bencosme to the Complex League at the start of the year. But after going 3-for-9 with a triple over two games, the front office deemed him ready for full season action. Bencosme promptly went 3-for-5 in his first fame with Delmarva. And he didn't stop hitting. The front office eventually moved him up to High-A the last few weeks of the year. Bencosme finished the year with an aggregate .311/.381/.412 with 10 doubles, four triples, three homeruns, and eight stolen bases (in 14 attempts). Per *Weighted Runs Created Plus*, Bencosme's overall production topped the league average mark by 24%.

Baltimore Orioles

Scouting Report: Just for fun, here's Bencosme's counting stats pro-rated for a full 162-game season: 22 doubles, nine triples, seven homeruns, and 18 stolen bases. With respect to his production with Delmarva, consider the following:

> Since 2006, only six 19-year-olds posted a 133 to 143 WRC+ with a K-rate between 10% - 14% in Low-A (min. 250 PA): Nolan Arenado, Gabriel Moreno, Albert Almora Jr., Xavier Edwards, Carlos Tocci, and Frederick Bencosme.

> For those counting at home:
> #1. Four players were consensus Top 100 prospects (Arenado, Moreno, Almora Jr., and Edwards)
> #2. Four players would spend time on a big league roster (Arenado, Moreno, Almora, and Tocci), and the fifth, Edwards, will likely debut in 2023.
> #3. Arenado is a future Hall of Famer. Moreno is one of the best young catchers in the league. Almora's big league career started impressively, but he's struggled in recent years.

Line drive hitter with good bat speed and will likely grow into 10- to 12-homeruns during a full season. Bencosme is a hit over power guy with extreme contact rates and a selective approach at the plate. Almost taking an Ichiro-like windup at the plate. Solid speed. The potential for a plus hit tool. Defensively, he's raw at shortstop and likely slides over to second base permanently.

Ceiling: 2.5-win player
Risk: Moderate
MLB ETA: 2023

13. Max Wagner, 3B

Hit	Power	SB	Patience	Glove	Overall
45/50	55/60	35	50	50	50

Born: 08/19/01	Age: 21	Bats: R	Top Production Comp: N/A
Height: 6-0	Weight: 215	Throws: R	

Season	Team	Age	Level	PA	1B	2B	3B	HR	SB	CS	BB%	K%	AVG	OBP	SLG	ISO
2022	BAL	20	A	62	7	2	2	1	0	0	14.52%	20.97%	0.250	0.403	0.438	0.188
2022	BAL	20	A+	19	3	0	0	0	1	0	0.00%	26.32%	0.167	0.158	0.167	0.000

Background: He earned the rare distinction of capturing the 2020 Wisconsin Gatorade Player of the Year – despite, you know, not actually playing a game thanks to the COVID shutdown. Nonetheless, Wagner wrapped up his time at Preble High School with a tremendous production line through three completed seasons: .457/.569/.731. After a brief – largely unsuccessful – jaunt through the Northwoods League following his senior year in high school, Wagner appeared in 35 games with Clemson during his first collegiate season – though the production was rather pitiful. In 99 plate appearances, the 6-foot, 215-pound third baseman batted a lowly .214/.305/.345 with five doubles and a pair of long balls. Wagner recaptured his high school glory during the ensuing summer with the Green Bay Booyah in the Northwoods League, batting .313/.485/.566 with five doubles, one triple, and six homeruns in 31 games. And he was able to carry that momentum into a breakout performance. In a career best 58 games, the hot swinging infielder slugged .370/.496/.852 with 15 doubles, one triple, and 27 homeruns – tied for the third best total in the nation. The Orioles drafted the Clemson star in the second round, 42nd overall, and signed him to a deal worth $1.9 million. He batted .243/.353/.386 during his debut.

Scouting Report: Per the usual, my pre-draft write-up:

> "Consider the following:
>
> Since 2011, only three Division I hitters met the following criteria in a season (min. 250 PA): hit at least .360/.480/.800 with a walk rate north of 17%. Those three hitters: Andrew Vaughn, former #3 overall pick, Sonny DiChiara, and – of course – Max Wagner.
>
> Wagner's massive production is largely limited to one stout showing with the Tigers in 2022. But it's one helluva production line. Above-average power and a lightning quick bat. Wagner consistently barreled up the baseball during his season. Throw in solid-average glove work at the corner, and Wagner could be a serviceable big league third baseman."

Ceiling: 2.0-win player
Risk: Moderate
MLB ETA: 2025

Baltimore Orioles

14. Seth Johnson, RHP

FB	CB	SL	CH	Command	Overall
60	55	60	45/50	45/50	50

Born: 09/19/98	Age: 24	Bats: R	Top Production Comp: N/A
Height: 6-1	Weight: 200	Throws: R	

Season	Team	Age	Level	IP	TBF	K/9	K%	BB/9	BB%	K-BB%	ERA	FIP	xFIP	Pit/Bat
2021	TBR	22	A	93.2	397	11.05	28.97%	3.17	8.31%	20.65%	2.88	3.71	3.71	3.96
2022	TBR	23	A+	27.0	110	13.67	37.27%	3.67	10.00%	27.27%	3.00	3.77	3.05	3.96

Background: There's a rule of thumb that most teams should abide by – *never* trade with the Tampa Bay Rays. Even savvy front offices like the Guardians have had the wool pulled over their eyes. But the Orioles-led by assistant General Manager Sig Mejdal, a former NASA engineer, decided to buck the trend. Not only did the Orioles get together with the Rays and Astros on a three-team deal last summer, but they acquired an injured Rays pitcher as the centerpiece of the deal. The specifics of the August 1st swap:

> Houston acquired veteran slugger – and longtime fan favorite and inspiration – Trey Mancini from the Orioles and minor leaguer Jayden Murray from the Rays.
>
> Tampa Bay acquired toolsy centerfielder Jose Siri from Houston.
>
> Baltimore acquired Seth Johnson from Tampa Bay and Chayce McDermott from the Astros.

Originally drafted by Tampa Bay near the end of the first round in 2019, Johnson surged from a relatively unknown player to the 40th overall pick in impressive fashion. The highest player taken in Campbell University until Zach Neto and Tom Harrington's names were called in the first round last summer, Johnson may have set the record for the highest ERA for any first round pick in history – he compiled a 4.61 ERA during his junior campaign with the Camels. But the often erratic right-hander honed in on the strike zone with sniper-like precision during his debut, walking just three hitters in 17.0 innings of work. And he continued to throw strikes and miss bats during his first full season in the minors as well, posting a dominating 115-to-33 strikeout-to-walk ratio in only 93.2 innings of work in Low-A two years ago. Last season, he continued to impress as he averaged 13.7 strikeouts and 3.7 walks per nine innings through seven High-A starts. He made his last start on May 20th, but wouldn't undergo Tommy John surgery until *after* the Orioles acquired him. He'll likely miss the majority of 2023 as well.

Snippet from The 2022 Prospect Digest Handbook: He's rawer than expected for a former college arm, though he made a late transition to pitching. There's solid backend starting caliber potential.

Scouting Report: In terms of stuff, the former JuCo shortstop was diabolically filthy in the starts leading up to his elbow woes. Johnson's heater was sitting – comfortably – at 96 mph and touching a tick higher on occasion. Both breaking balls took a step forward from his debut showing as well, with the curveball now an above-average, 12-6 bending hammer and his mid-80s slider was wicked. He kept his average changeup in his back pocket. Now the bad news: despite the premium octane gas, Johnson's fastball was a bit too hittable if he wasn't hitting his spots. There's some backend caliber potential with the floor as a setup man. Of course, that's assuming he shows no ill effects from the elbow surgery.

Ceiling: 2.0-win player
Risk: Moderate to High
MLB ETA: 2024

15. Samuel Basallo, C

Hit	Power	SB	Patience	Glove	Overall
45/50	50/60	30	50	40/45	45

Born: 08/13/04	Age: 18	Bats: L	Top Production Comp: N/A
Height: 6-3	Weight: 180	Throws: R	

Season	Team	Age	Level	PA	1B	2B	3B	HR	SB	CS	BB%	K%	AVG	OBP	SLG	ISO
2021	BAL	16	DSL	154	19	8	0	5	1	0	12.34%	20.78%	0.239	0.338	0.410	0.172
2022	BAL	17	CPX	180	33	5	0	6	1	0	8.33%	20.56%	0.278	0.350	0.424	0.146

Background: The Orioles' brass paid handsomely to convince the lefty-swinging teenager to join the organization - $1.3 million, to be exact. Officially joined the franchise in mid-January two years ago, Basallo made his debut a few months later in the foreign rookie leagues – where he would be one of the younger qualified hitters. The 6-foot-3, 180-pound backstop batted .239/.338/.410 with eight doubles and five homeruns in 41 games. The front office pushed the Santo Domingo, Dominican Republic native stateside to the Complex League for the 2022 season. And Basallo – quietly – put together a very solid showing. Appearing in 43 games, the lefty-swinging catcher slugged .279/.350/.424 with five doubles, six homeruns, and a stolen base. Per *Weighted Runs Created Plus*, his overall production topped the league average threshold by 16%.

Baltimore Orioles

Scouting Report: One of just four qualified 17-year-old hitters in the Complex Leagues last summer, Basallo's overall production, 116 wRC+, tied with San Diego's Roman Verdugo for tops among the group. Long and wiry with a bit of a soft body, Basallo's swing is geared toward jacking homeruns. Above-average bat speed. But theirs is some concern that he outgrows the catching position, so first base may be the only logical landing spot. He's very, *very* raw behind the plate as it stands, anyways. He could be primed for a big season with the bat in 2023.

Ceiling: 1.5-win player
Risk: Moderate
MLB ETA: 2026

16. Jud Fabian, OF

Hit	Power	SB	Patience	Glove	Overall
45/50	55/60	35	50	50	50

Born: 09/27/00	Age: 22	Bats: R	Top Production Comp: N/A
Height: 6-1	Weight: 195	Throws: L	

Season	Team	Age	Level	PA	1B	2B	3B	HR	SB	CS	BB%	K%	AVG	OBP	SLG	ISO
2022	BAL	21	CPX	17	4	1	0	0	1	0	35.29%	23.53%	0.500	0.647	0.600	0.100
2022	BAL	21	A	52	5	7	2	3	0	0	15.38%	17.31%	0.386	0.481	0.841	0.455
2022	BAL	21	A+	30	3	1	0	0	0	2	16.67%	26.67%	0.167	0.300	0.208	0.042

Background: The book on Jud Fabian is a well-known tome at this point: He starred at Trinity Catholic High School and enrolled early at the University of Florida to begin – what many thought – would be a dominant collegiate career. Fabian started the entire year as a true freshman with the Gators, despite: being just 18-years-old, playing for one of the top programs in the country, and cobbling together a mediocre .232/.353/.411. But things began to click the budding teenage phenom during his summer in the Cape Cod League: he hit a rock solid – and borderline impressive – .290/.350/.500 with eight doubles and six homeruns in 35 games. The best part? He was able to carry that momentum into breakout – albeit COVID-shortened – 2020 campaign in which he hit .294/.407/.603. And that's where the story turns for the worse. Beginning in 2021, Fabian began to sell out for more thump at the price of consistent contact. He would hit a lowly .249/.364/.560 with a punch out rate of nearly 30%. Still, though, the Red Sox took a second round gamble on the enigmatic, toolsy outfielder, but the sides failed to come to an agreement, so he headed back to the land of the Gators for his redshirt junior campaign. Fabian batted .239/.414/.598 with 10 doubles, one triple, 24 homeruns, and nine stolen bases in a career best 66 games. Fabian was drafted in the second round, 67th overall, and signed for $1,026,800. He batted .333/.455/.615 in 22 games during his debut.

Scouting Report: Per the usual, my pre-draft write-up:

> *"Consider the following:*
>
> > *#1. Since 2011, only 17 SEC hitters posted an OPS north of 1.000 in a season (min. 300 PA).*
> > *#2. Of those 17, two walked at least 20% of the time: Jonathan India and, of course, Jud Fabian.*
> > *#3. Looking at the same set of 17 hitters, only to struck out at least 20% of the time: Stephen Scott and, of course, Jud Fabian.*
>
> *Arguably the most polarizing hitter in this year's draft class. Depending upon the day Fabian looks like a surefire lock as a potential early first round pick. Other days he looks like an undrafted free agent. And batting average is certainly far from a reliable indicator, but when a collegiate prospect hits an aggregate .244 over his last 459 at bats has to mean something. The good news is that Fabian chewed down his bloated strikeout rate, going from 30% to 20%. He also maintained his phenomenal walk rates. The question is always going to come down to the hit tool. And I just don't see him making enough strides at this junction in his career to have a viable shot at the big leagues. Gambling on potential, though, is something some organization will do – just like when the Dodgers selected former Vanderbilt outfielder Jeren Kendall in the opening round in 2017."*

Ceiling: 2.0-win player
Risk: High
MLB ETA: 2025

Baltimore Orioles

17. Hudson Haskin, CF

Hit	Power	SB	Patience	Glove	Overall
50	40	55	50	50	45

Born: 12/31/98	Age: 24	Bats: R	Top Production Comp: N/A
Height: 6-2	Weight: 200	Throws: R	

Season	Team	Age	Level	PA	1B	2B	3B	HR	SB	CS	BB%	K%	AVG	OBP	SLG	ISO
2021	BAL	22	A	254	41	13	1	5	17	5	8.66%	23.62%	0.276	0.377	0.415	0.138
2021	BAL	22	A+	109	17	6	2	0	5	2	9.17%	16.51%	0.275	0.389	0.385	0.110
2022	BAL	23	AA	466	61	23	3	15	5	3	9.23%	21.67%	0.264	0.367	0.455	0.191

Background: The 2020 Draft was destined to be an absolute crapshoot – the pandemic wrecked the entire high school season and college ball was curtailed after a few weeks; the draft was limited to five rounds. But the Orioles – somehow – were able to hit on the majority of their selections. Heston Kjerstad looked impressive after missing a significant amount of time due to myocarditis. Jordan Westburg is knocking – loudly – on the big league club's door. Coby Mayo is one of the most underrated prospects in the game. Carter Baumler has shown glimpses in his return from Tommy John surgery. And then there's Hudson Haskin, the 39th overall pick that summer. A product of Tulane University, the 6-foot-2, 200-pound centerfielder left the Green Wave as a career .363/.457/.612 hitter across 73 games. Haskin turned in a solid debut the following season, batting an aggregate .276/.381/.406 between Delmarva and Aberdeen in 2021. Last season the former Tulane star squared off against the minors' toughest challenge, Double-A, and came out on the other side. Haskin slugged .264/.367/.455 with 23 doubles, three triples, 15 homeruns, and five stolen bases in 109 games with the Bowie Baysox. His overall production, as measured by *Weighted Runs Created Plus*, was 26% better the league average mark.

Snippet from The 2022 Prospect Digest Handbook: There's a lot of movement in Haskin's swing. Standing from nearly a perfect upright position, Haskin's take a massive stride to the ball – larger than nearly everyone I can think of – which causes a lot of movement in his head (north / south direction). He just "feels" like a fourth outfielder.

Scouting Report: Consider the following:

> Since 2006, only three 23-year-old hitters posted a 120 to 130 wRC+ with a 20% to 23% strikeout rate and an 8% to 10% walk rate in any Double-A league (min. 350 PA): Jared Oliva, Jason Vosler, and Hudson Haskin.

Not an overly athletic swing, Haskin's bat, nonetheless, continues to produce – even in the minors' most challenging league. The former Tulane outfielder does everything well without a true standout tool. Average bat, power, speed, glove, patience, contact rates. You name it, and its probably average. Still tracking like a fourth outfielder.

Ceiling: 1.0- to 1.5-win player
Risk: Moderate
MLB ETA: 2023

18. Drew Rom, LHP

FB	CB	SL	CH	Command	Overall
50	50	50	50	50	45

Born: 12/05/99	Age: 23	Bats: L	Top Production Comp: Stephen Gonsalves
Height: 6-2	Weight: 170	Throws: L	

Season	Team	Age	Level	IP	TBF	K/9	K%	BB/9	BB%	K-BB%	ERA	FIP	xFIP	Pit/Bat
2021	BAL	21	A+	67.2	275	9.71	26.55%	2.26	6.18%	20.36%	2.79	3.65	3.72	3.77
2021	BAL	21	AA	40.0	163	10.58	28.83%	2.03	5.52%	23.31%	3.83	3.94	3.09	4.05
2022	BAL	22	AA	82.1	366	11.04	27.60%	3.17	7.92%	19.67%	4.37	3.62	3.74	4.02
2022	BAL	22	AAA	37.2	165	10.27	26.06%	4.30	10.91%	15.15%	4.54	3.16	4.13	3.84

Background: The top crop of lefty pitching prospects heading into the 2023 season isn't overly strong. Beyond the likes of San Francisco's Kyle Harrison, Toronto's Ricky Tiedemann, and Baltimore's D.L. Hall, the overall ceiling is lacking. And, yet, Drew Rom, a lanky southpaw from Highland High School continues to fly under the radar. A fourth round pick all the way back in 2018, Rom has quietly moved through the minor leagues with assassin like precision. He spent the 2019 season dominating the old South Atlantic League. And once minor league ball returned from its pandemic absence, he breezed through High-A in 14 appearances, and maintained some promising peripherals during his first foray against the Double-A competition. Last season the front office sent the 6-foot-2, 170-pound southpaw back to Bowie for some extended seasoning. But after another solid 19 appearances, the club finally bumped him up to Triple-A. He finished the year with an impressive 144-to-47 strikeout-to-walk ratio in 120.0 innings of work. He tallied an aggregate 4.43 ERA and a 3.48 FIP. For his professional career, he's averaging 10.5 strikeouts and just 2.9 walks per nine innings to go along with a solid 3.41 ERA.

Snippet from The 2022 Prospect Digest Handbook: A crafty lefty, but not in the pejorative sense. It's clear to see that the young southpaw not only has the chops to pitch at the big league level, but he possesses the guile and smarts to match. Rom – for whatever reason – remains under-the-radar.

Baltimore Orioles

Scouting Report: Consider the following:

> Since 2006, only four 22-year-old hurlers posted a 6.5% to 9.5% walk percentage and a 26.5% to 28.5% strikeout percentage in any Double-A league (min. 75 IP): Stephen Gonsalves, Keyvius Sampson, Ronald Bolanos, and – of course – Drew Rom.

Rom looked less promising and more crafty during his first taste of Triple-A last season. Average fastball, curveball, slider, and changeup. But he changes speeds effectively, commands the zone well, changes arm angles on his heater, and never puts the ball in the same place twice during an at bat. Backend arm, low ceiling, safe floor.

Ceiling: 1.0- to 1.5-win player
Risk: Moderate
MLB ETA: 2023

19. Cade Povich, LHP

FB	CB	SL	CH	Command	Overall
45	50	50	55	50	40

Born: 04/12/00	Age: 23	Bats: L	Top Production Comp: N/A
Height: 6-3	Weight: 185	Throws: L	

Season	Team	Age	Level	IP	TBF	K/9	K%	BB/9	BB%	K-BB%	ERA	FIP	xFIP	Pit/Bat
2022	BAL	22	A+	12.0	42	11.25	35.71%	1.50	4.76%	30.95%	0.00	1.91	3.14	3.88
2022	MIN	22	A+	78.2	336	12.24	31.85%	2.97	7.74%	24.11%	4.46	3.36	3.31	3.93
2022	BAL	22	AA	23.1	103	10.03	25.24%	4.24	10.68%	14.56%	6.94	5.39	4.26	4.06

Background: The Orioles' front office put on a clinic on how to turn nothing into something. The club plucked veteran right-hander Jorge Lopéz off of waivers from the Kansas City Royals in August 2020. Baltimore kept Lopéz in their rotation for the entire 2021 season – despite mediocre results. Last season, though, they pushed him into the bullpen and he *blossomed* in an All-Star closer. He would throw 48.1 innings, recording a 54-to-17 strikeout-to-walk ratio with a tidy 1.68 ERA. The O's shipped him off at the peak of his value last August, acquiring Cade Povich, Juan Nunez, Juan Rojas, and Yennier Cano. Taken in the third round two years ago out of the University of Nebraska, Povich missed an impressive number of bats during his 18 starts in High-A, averaging 12.1 punch outs against just 2.8 walks per nine innings. Baltimore sent the 6-foot-3, 185-pound lefty up to the minors' toughest challenge, Double-A, for six final appearances. Povich finished the year with 148 strikeouts, 39 walks, and an aggregate 4.50 ERA across 114.0 innings of work.

Scouting Report: Consider the following:

> Since 2006, only four 22-year-old hurlers posted a strikeout percentage between 31.5% and 33.5% in any High-A league (min. 75 IP): Jose Arredondo, Wilmer Font, Spencer Arrighetti, and – of course – the recently acquired Cade Povich.

The 6-foot-3 and generously listed 185-pound southpaw is a generic, vanilla left-hander that relies heavily on command and guile because the arsenal doesn't leave much room for error. His fastball, which operates in the 91-mph range, has a little bit of life above the belt. He'll feature a pair of average breaking balls – a mid- to upper-70s curveball and low- to mid-80s slider that he'll vary his arm angle on to create more sweep. His best pitch is an 83-mph above-average changeup. Best case scenario is John Means, but Povich's command isn't quite of up to par.

Ceiling: 1.0-win player
Risk: Moderate
MLB ETA: 2023/2024

20. César Prieto, IF

Hit	Power	SB	Patience	Glove	Overall
45/50	40	30	45	50	40

Born: 05/10/99	Age: 24	Bats: L	Top Production Comp: N/A
Height: 5-9	Weight: 175	Throws: R	

Season	Team	Age	Level	PA	1B	2B	3B	HR	SB	CS	BB%	K%	AVG	OBP	SLG	ISO
2022	BAL	23	A+	105	20	6	0	7	3	1	4.76%	15.24%	0.340	0.381	0.619	0.278
2022	BAL	23	AA	389	68	22	0	4	2	5	3.86%	14.91%	0.255	0.296	0.348	0.092

Background: The Orioles paid out more than $6 million as part of their 2022 international free agent class. Cesar Prieto earned $650,000 of that bonus pool – which, as the *Baltimore Sun* pointed out, was the fourth largest bonus Mike Elias and Koby Perez, the senior director of international scouting, had ever given out to an international free agent. Hailing from Cienfuegos, Cuba, Prieto spent a couple years in the Cuban National Series before defecting, hitting an impressive .365/.426/.501 with 51 doubles, 16 triples, 17 homeruns, and 24 stolen bases in 247 career games. After joining the organization last January, Prieto made his debut

Baltimore Orioles

with the Aberdeen IronBirds a few months later. But after mashing .340/.381/.619 over 25 games, the front office pushed the lefty-swinging infielder up to the minors' toughest level, Double-A. And his offensive output declined dramatically. He batted .255/.296/.348 with six doubles and seven homeruns in 105 games with Bowie. His production in Double-A, according to *Weighted Runs Created Plus*, was 23% *below* the league average.

Scouting Report: Consider the following:

> Since 2006, only three 23-year-old hitters posted a 72 to 82 wRC+ with a sub-5% walk rate and a 14% to 16% strikeout rate in any Double-A league (min. 350 PA): Emmanuel Rivera, Brian Navarreto, and César Prieto.

Prieto's production at the start of his Double-A tenure was significantly better than you'd expect looking at his putrid final stat line. The 5-foot-9, 175-pound infielder batted a respectable .283/.325/.380 with 17 doubles and a pair of homeruns. But even during that stretch of solid production, his overall value was dragged down by a woefully poor walk rate. Prieto also showed some susceptibility to lefties as well. Average defender at shortstop or second and third bases, he's likely going to wind up on the right side of the keystone. Lacks a true standout tool.

Ceiling: 1.0-win player
Risk: Moderate
MLB ETA: 2023

Baltimore Orioles

Boston Red Sox

Top Prospects

Boston Red Sox

1. Marcelo Mayer, SS

Hit	Power	SB	Patience	Glove	Overall
50/60	40/50	60	55	50/55	70

Born: 12/12/02	Age: 19	Bats: L	Top Production Comp: Troy Tulowitzki
Height: 6-3	Weight: 188	Throws: R	

Season	Team	Age	Level	PA	1B	2B	3B	HR	SB	CS	BB%	K%	AVG	OBP	SLG	ISO
2021	BOS	18	CPX	107	17	4	1	3	7	1	14.02%	25.23%	0.275	0.377	0.440	0.165
2022	BOS	19	A	308	36	26	1	9	16	0	16.56%	25.32%	0.286	0.406	0.504	0.218
2022	BOS	19	A+	116	17	4	1	4	1	0	14.66%	25.00%	0.265	0.379	0.449	0.184

Background: The Red Sox have had a strong run of top notch play from their shortstops over the past couple of decades. John Valentin manned the most important position on the infield from 1992-96. He then gave way to a young Nomar Garciaparra, who captured the American League Rookie of the Year Award in 1997 and carried the team's offense for the better part of a decade. The offseason following Garciaparra's trade to the Cubs, the franchise signed Edgar Renteria, who handled the position for a year. Then the club tried all kinds of stopgaps for the next seven years, plugging the hole with the likes of Alex Gonzalez, Julio Lugo, Marco Scutaro, and Mike Aviles. Then – finally – the farm system churned out their next franchise cornerstone at the position – four-time All-Star Xander Bogaerts. But after an incredible 10-year run that saw Bogaerts win two World Series titles and five Silver Slugger awards, the historic franchise – in a penny pinching move – failed to re-sign the still-in-his-prime infielder, who departed for San Diego. For now it looks like the team will install their big dollar expenditure, Trevor Story, back to his normal position. That is until Marcelo Mayer is ready. Armed with the second highest pick in franchise history, the Red Sox were waiting with open arms as Mayer, the top prep hitter, fell into their laps at the fourth overall pick two years. (Note: the last time the club owned the fourth overall pick they chose Ken Brett in 1966.) Mayer, a product of Eastlake High School, turned in a solid debut in the Complex League that summer, hitting .275/.377/.440 with eight extra-base knocks in 26 games. Last season the lefty-swinging infielder quickly moved through Low-A in just 66 games before settling in nicely against the significantly older competition in High-A – despite dealing with a wrist injury that knocked him out of commission for a month, as well as a midseason back issue. Overall, the 6-foot-3, 188-pound Mayer slugged an aggregate .280/.399/.489 with 30 doubles, two triples, 13 homeruns, and 17 stolen bases (without getting caught). His overall production, as measured by *Weighted Runs Created Plus*, topped the league average mark by a stellar 43%.

Snippet from The 2022 Prospect Digest Handbook: He has surprisingly thump for his lean build. He adjusts to breaking balls well.

Scouting Report: Consider the following:

> Since 2006, only three 19-year-old hitters tallied a wRC+ of at least 145 with a 23% to 27% strikeout rate and a double-digit walk rate in any Low-A league (min. 300 PA): Miguel Sano, Orelvis Martinez, and – of course – Marcelo Mayer.

Mayer added noticeable bulk to his wiry frame over the past couple of years. Picture perfect swing with above-average bat speed. He's just beginning to tap into his 20-homerun power potential and should be a doubles machine for years to come. Above-average speed. Good patience at the plate. There's a little more-and-miss to his game than expected, but it shouldn't be a problem in the long term. Defensively, he should have no problems sticking at the position and may even sneak into a couple Gold Glove conversations. In terms of big league ceiling, think: .310/.390/.450.

Ceiling: 6.0-win player
Risk: Moderate
MLB ETA: 2024

2. Ceddanne Rafaela, SS/CF

Hit	Power	SB	Patience	Glove	Overall
55	50	60	40	60	55

Born: 09/18/00	Age: 22	Bats: R	Top Production Comp: Gerardo Parra
Height: 5-8	Weight: 152	Throws: R	

Season	Team	Age	Level	PA	1B	2B	3B	HR	SB	CS	BB%	K%	AVG	OBP	SLG	ISO
2021	BOS	20	A	432	60	20	9	10	23	3	5.79%	18.29%	0.251	0.305	0.424	0.173
2022	BOS	21	A+	209	35	17	4	9	14	2	4.78%	24.40%	0.330	0.368	0.594	0.264
2022	BOS	21	AA	313	46	15	6	12	14	5	5.11%	19.81%	0.278	0.324	0.500	0.222

Background: Tremendous job done by the ball club's scouting and development program. The organization unearthed the pint-sized dynamo from Willemstad, Curacao, and signed him for a paltry $10,000 as part of their 2017 international free agency class. Rafaela, who stands just 5-foot-8 and 152 pounds, made his professional debut with the club's foreign rookie league affiliate the following summer, hitting .271/.326/.379 in 54 contests. The part-time shortstop / centerfielder moved stateside in 2019, batting .244/.319/.409 in 41 games in the Gulf Coast League and another three in the New-York Penn League. After minor league action returned from its COVID hiatus in 2021, Rafaela moved into Low-A and continued to put up good, but not great production lines, cobbling together a .251/.305/.424 slash line with 20 doubles, nine triples, 10 homeruns, and 23 stolen bases in 102 games with Salem. Last season, though, Rafaela – finally – took that big step

Boston Red Sox

forward as he moved into High-A. He slugged a scorching .330/.368/.594 in 45 games with Greenville. And he continued to perform as he moved in the minors' most challenging level, Double-A, mashing .278/.324/.500. He slugged an aggregate .299/.342/.539 with career bests in doubles (32), triples (10), homeruns (21), and stolen bases (28). His production, per *Weighted Runs Created Plus*, topped the average by 34%.

Scouting Report: Consider the following:

> Since 2006, only three 21-year-old hitters met the following criteria in any Double-A league (min. 300 PA): 115 to 125 wRC+, a sub-7% walk rate, and an 18% to 22% strikeout rate. Those three hitters: Carlos Gonzalez, Ryan Mountcastle, and – of course – the pint-sized dynamo Ceddanne Rafaela. Gonzalez finished his lengthy big league career with a 111 wRC+ mark. And Mountcastle owns a 112 wRC+ through his first 324 big league games.

One of the best athletes in a farm loaded with tools. Boston has been bouncing the Curacao native between centerfield and the middle infielder the past couple of seasons. But wherever he plays, Rafaela has provided above-average defensive value. At the plate, he packs a surprising punch given his small frame size. Above-average speed, 25-homer thump. The lone knock thus far has been his walk abhorrence as he's found first base via the walk in fewer than 6% of his plate appearances since the start of 2021. Meaning: his offensive value is only going to go as far as his batting averages take him. Rafaela is projecting as a .270/.325/.450 hitter.

Ceiling: 3.0-win player
Risk: Moderate
MLB ETA: 2023

3. Triston Casas, 1B

Hit	Power	SB	Patience	Glove	Overall
45/55	55/60	45/30	60	45	60

Born: 01/15/00	Age: 23	Bats: L	Top Production Comp: N/A
Height: 6-4	Weight: 252	Throws: R	

Season	Team	Age	Level	PA	1B	2B	3B	HR	SB	CS	BB%	K%	AVG	OBP	SLG	ISO
2021	BOS	21	AA	329	51	12	2	13	6	3	14.89%	19.15%	0.284	0.395	0.484	0.200
2021	BOS	21	AAA	42	3	3	1	1	1	0	19.05%	19.05%	0.242	0.381	0.485	0.242
2022	BOS	22	AAA	317	40	20	1	11	0	0	14.51%	21.45%	0.273	0.382	0.481	0.208

Background: There's an ongoing theme that seems to surround the club's 2018 first round pick – loss of development time. Casas, the 26th overall pick that summer, appeared in just a pair of Gulf Coast League games during his debut before undergoing the knife to repair the ulnar collateral ligament in his right thumb, forcing him to miss the remainder of the year. He made it back for the start of the 2019 season and showed no ill side effects from the procedure as he mashed .256/.350/.480 with 26 doubles, five triples, and 20 homeruns in 120 games. COVID pushed minor league ball to the sidelines in 2020. Casas, like every other professional ballplayer, was impacted by the lockout two years ago, limiting him to just 86 games – though he managed to slug .279/.394/.484. Last season the hulking first baseman appeared in 72 games with Worcester, batting a Casas-like .273/.382/.481 with 20 doubles, one triple, and 11 homeruns. He also earned 95 plate appearances with Boston, hitting .197/.358/.408. He suffered a knee injury – of unknown severity – and was knocked out of winter ball.

Snippet from The 2022 Prospect Digest Handbook: All the ingredients to be an Anthony Rizzo-type cornerstone are sitting in the pot, the only thing from stopping it is the left-handed stove knob is broken. One more thought: Rizzo eventually learned how to handle lefties.

Scouting Report: Consider the following:

> Since 2006, just four 22-year-old hitters met the following criteria in a Triple-A season (min. 300 PA): 122 to 132 wRC+ total and a strikeout rate between 19% and 24%. Those four hitters: Clint Frazier, Arismendy Alcantara, Jarred Kelenic, and – of course – Triston Casas.

The lefty-swinging Casas continued the disturbing trend of struggling against fellow southpaws last season. His .216/.367/.250 slash line against them in 2022 comes on the heels of his disappointing showing in 2021 (.219/.289/.301) which – of course – followed his mediocre display in 2019 (.214/.317/.416). Oh, by the way, his MLB platoon splits – .193/.343/.474 (vs. RHP) and .211/.400/.211 (LHP) – only highlights his inability to drive the ball consistently against southpaws as well. Casas still hasn't fully tapped into his plus power potential, but there's 30-homer thump lurking in his bat. Elite walk rates. But his defense may ultimately relegate him to a Designated Hitter-only role, as well. Casas continues to be one of the more touted power hitters in the minors, but there are several large red flags that need to be addressed. At worst, he's going to do a lot of damage against right-handers. But his ultimate ceiling is limited due to his defense capabilities (and LHP platoon splits).

Ceiling: 4.0-win player
Risk: Moderate to High
MLB ETA: Debuted in 2022

Boston Red Sox

4. Nick Yorke, 2B

	Hit	Power	SB	Patience	Glove	Overall
	55/65	50/55	50	55	50/55	60

Born: 04/02/02	Age: 21	Bats: R	Top Production Comp: Whit Merrifield
Height: 6-0	Weight: 200	Throws: R	

Season	Team	Age	Level	PA	1B	2B	3B	HR	SB	CS	BB%	K%	AVG	OBP	SLG	ISO
2021	BOS	19	A	346	67	14	4	10	11	8	11.85%	13.58%	0.323	0.413	0.500	0.177
2021	BOS	19	A+	96	17	6	1	4	2	1	11.46%	22.92%	0.333	0.406	0.571	0.238
2022	BOS	20	A+	373	56	10	1	11	8	4	8.85%	25.20%	0.231	0.303	0.365	0.134

Background: There were very few, if any, hitters that were as consistently dominant – or impressive – over the course of the 2021 season than Nick Yorke. A product of Archbishop Mitty High School, Boston selected the prep-shortstop-turned-professional-second-baseman in the first round three years ago, 17th overall, and signed him to a deal worth $2.7 million. Pegged as a sweet-swinging middle infielder, Yorke easily surpassed all expectations during his phenomenal debut showing a year later. The 6-foot, 200-pound second baseman shredded the Low-A competition to the tune of .323/.413/.500 across 76 games and continued to mash in his 21-game cameo in High-A as well. He ultimately finished his debut campaign with a .325/.412/.516 slash line with 20 doubles, five triples, 14 homeruns, and 13 stolen bases. And, frankly, Yorke looked primed to continue his rapid ascension through the system's minor league chain entering 2022. But a variety of injuries dampened that momentum – and his production line. Appearing in just 80 games with the Greenville Drive, Yorke hit a disappointing .232/.303/.365 with 10 doubles, one triple, 11 homeruns, and eight stolen bases. Finally healthy at the end of the year, the California native regained his stroke in the Arizona Fall League, slugging .342/.424/.526 with eight doubles and pair of homeruns in just 19 games with the Scottsdale Scorpions.

Snippet from The 2022 Prospect Digest Handbook: Yorke has a chance for a plus (maybe even plus-plus) hit tool, average power, average speed, and a nose for first base that will only further pump up his value. There's really nothing to not like with the skill set. He plays above-average defense and may win a few Gold Gloves.

Scouting Report: Despite the significant downturn in production, Yorke seems primed for (A) significant playing time in the most challenging minor league level, Double-A, and (B) a tremendous bounce back campaign in 2023. Surprising power for a second baseman, Yorke and Marcelo Mayer could man the middle infielder for Boston for at least a decade. Plus hit tool, 20-homerun thump, a nose for first base, and positive defensive value. I'm still as high as ever on Yorke's potential. He could be a perennial .300/.370/.475-type hitter at the big league level.

Ceiling: 4.0-win player
Risk: Moderate to High
MLB ETA: 2023/2024

5. Miguel Bleis, CF

	Hit	Power	SB	Patience	Glove	Overall
	50/50	50/60	60	50	60	55

Born: 03/01/04	Age: 19	Bats: R	Top Production Comp: N/A
Height: 6-3	Weight: 170	Throws: R	

Season	Team	Age	Level	PA	1B	2B	3B	HR	SB	CS	BB%	K%	AVG	OBP	SLG	ISO
2021	BOS	17	DSL	136	19	6	1	4	7	4	8.82%	18.38%	0.252	0.331	0.420	0.168
2022	BOS	18	CPX	167	23	14	4	5	18	3	5.99%	26.95%	0.301	0.353	0.542	0.242

Background: The historic franchise handed Bleis a hefty $1.5 million early in 2021. A native of San Pedro de Macoris, Dominican Republic, Bleis would debut with the club's foreign rookie league affiliate a months later. He would bat a respectable .252/.331/.420 with six doubles, one triple, four homeruns, and seven stolen bases (in 11 attempts) in 36 games. Last season the club took the cautious approach and sent the young centerfielder stateside to the Complex Leagues. And the 6-foot-3, 170-pound teenager passed with flying colors. Bleis slugged .301/.353/.543 with 14 doubles, four triples, five homeruns, and 18 stolen bases (in 21 total attempts). His production, as measured by *Weighted Runs Created Plus*, topped the league mark by 41%.

Scouting Report: As quick of a bat as you'll see on any 18-year-old in the game nowadays. The bat speed combined with the natural loft in his swing should allow Bleis to slug 30 homeruns at full maturity. Above-average speed and the glove to match in centerfield. The lone pockmark on his otherwise phenomenal showing in 2022 was the bloated strikeout rate. Bleis may be one of the bigger prospects that pop in 2023.

Ceiling: 3.5-win player
Risk: Moderate
MLB ETA: 2025

Boston Red Sox

6. Matthew Lugo, SS

Hit	Power	SB	Patience	Glove	Overall
50/55	50	50	50	45/50	55

Born: 05/09/01	Age: 22	Bats: R	Top Production Comp: N/A
Height: 6-1	Weight: 187	Throws: R	

Season	Team	Age	Level	PA	1B	2B	3B	HR	SB	CS	BB%	K%	AVG	OBP	SLG	ISO
2021	BOS	20	A	469	85	21	3	4	15	4	8.10%	20.04%	0.270	0.338	0.364	0.093
2022	BOS	21	A+	512	81	25	10	18	20	7	6.84%	19.53%	0.288	0.344	0.500	0.212
2022	BOS	21	AA	12	0	1	0	0	0	0	0.00%	33.33%	0.083	0.083	0.167	0.083

Background: The nephew of future Hall of Famer Carlos Beltrán, so it's not shocking that the young shortstop graduated from his uncle's Baseball Academy in 2019. Boston drafted Lugo in the second round, 69th overall, and signed him to a deal worth $1.1 million. The young Puerto Rican turned in a solid, yet unremarkable debut in the Gulf Coast League that summer, hitting .257/.342/.331 with seven extra-base hits in 39 contests. Lugo moved into full season action with the Salem Red Sox in 2021, putting together another quietly solid campaign at the plate as he hit .270/.338/.364 with 21 doubles, three triples, four homeruns, and 15 stolen bases. Last season the young infielder continued his steady progress as he moved up the minor league ladder. Appearing in 114 games with the Greenville Drive, the former second rounder slugged .288/.344/.500 with career bests in doubles (25), triples (10), homeruns (18), and stolen bases (20). His overall production, as measured by *Weighted Runs Created Plus*, topped the league average threshold by 26%. He earned 12 plate appearances in Double-A too.

Snippet from The 2022 Prospect Digest Handbook: It's not a mixture for stardom, let alone superstardom, but he's still tracking as a low end starting shortstop. One more note: after struggling through his first 34 games (.216/.262/.269), he hit .296/.372/.408 over his remaining 71 contests. That should be the baseline as he moves into High-A in 2022.

Scouting Report: Consider the following:

> Since 2006, only five 21-year-old hitters met the following criteria in a High-A season (min. 350 PA): 120 to 130 wRC+, 17% to 22% strikeout rate, and a 6% to 8% walk rate. Those five hitters: Dylan Cozens, Blake Rutherford, Brandon Snyder, Jose Osuna, and – of course – Matthew Lugo, who's forever stuck in Marcelo Mayer's looming shadow.

Lugo continues to range from underappreciated to overlooked, but it's not difficult to do when one of the game's top shortstop prospects is in the same system. Lugo's hit tool has improved throughout his professional career to the point now that it projects to be an above-average skill at full maturity. The power continues to develop as well, going from below-average to average. And it should be noted that despite spending half of his time in Greenville's homer-friendly park, Lugo actually slugged more dingers on the road (8 to 10). The problem so far has been his lack of glove-work at shortstop, which has been surprising. He was abysmal at the position in 2022. Lugo is tracking like a bat-first starting shortstop, who may have to move away from the position anyway thanks to Mayer. Lugo remains one of the most underrated prospects in the game. He's the type that quietly carves out a very solid 10-year career. In terms of big league ceiling, think: .280/.340/.420.

Ceiling: 3.0- to 3.5-win player
Risk: Moderate
MLB ETA: 2023/2024

7. Bryan Mata, RHP

FB	SL	CH	Command	Overall
60	60	55	40/45	55

Born: 05/05/99	Age: 24	Bats: R	Top Production Comp: Yovani Gallardo
Height: 6-3	Weight: 238	Throws: R	

Season	Team	Age	Level	IP	TBF	K/9	K%	BB/9	BB%	K-BB%	ERA	FIP	xFIP	Pit/Bat
2022	BOS	23	AA	48.2	197	10.73	29.44%	4.25	11.68%	17.77%	1.85	3.58	3.56	3.96
2022	BOS	23	AAA	23.1	102	11.57	29.41%	5.79	14.71%	14.71%	3.47	3.12	3.90	4.37

Background: It wasn't too long ago that the young Venezuelan seemed poised to be a contributor for the Red Sox. He was 20-years-old, coming off of his finest professional season in which he dominated High-A for 10 starts and held his own for 11 more games in the minors' toughest level – Double-A. But in the baseball world, four years might as well be an eternity – especially when it comes to Mata. The burly 6-foot-3, 238-pound right-hander jumped from the Dominican Summer League straight into the old South Atlantic League without missing a beat in 2017. Boston sent the then-19-year-old youngster up to High-A the next season. And despite losing all feel for the strike zone – he averaged more than seven walks per nine innings – Mata somehow escaped the year with a respectable 3.50 ERA. Then his big breakout came in 2019. He returned to High-A, throwing more strikes, like he had early in his career, and breezed through 10 starts with a 1.76 ERA. And he continued throwing strikes (at least enough strikes) as well as missing bats in 11 starts in Double-A as a 20-year-old. COVID knocked out the 2020 campaign and his wonky elbow forced him under the knife at the start of the 2021 season. The Venezuelan right-hander finally made it back to the bump last season as he climbed his back from Low-A then onto High-A then onto Double-A before finally settling in for five final starts with Worcester. He finished the year with a 105-to-46 strikeout-to-walk ratio and a 2.49 ERA across 83.0 innings.

Boston Red Sox

Scouting Report: Mata faced two big questions while he was on the comeback trail last season:

1. Would the velocity / repertoire return to its pre-injury level?
2. What type of command / control would he have? Would it be the 50-grade feel for the zone that he showed in 2017 and 2019? Or would it be the disastrous, can't-hit-the-broadside-of-a-barn command that reared its ugly face in 2018?

The repertoire was spectacular – despite the long layoff in between starts. Mata's fastball was sitting *comfortably* in the 94-to 96-mph range and, according to reports, touched 101 mph during an extended spring training appearance. His 88- to 89-mph slider adds a second plus, swing-and-miss offering. And his upper 80s changeup is a third viable weapon in his arsenal. The command – as with many returning hurlers from Tommy John surgery – was a bit touch-and-go last season. Mata had stretches where he sparkled and others where he struggled. There's at least mid-rotation caliber potential, something along the lines of a #3 / #4 hurler – even if the command is a 45, which is where it'll likely land.

Ceiling: 3.0-win player
Risk: Moderate to High
MLB ETA: 2023

8. Mikey Romero, 2B/SS

Hit	Power	SB	Patience	Glove	Overall
55	40/45	50	50	50	50

Born: 01/12/04	Age: 19	Bats: L	Top Production Comp: N/A
Height: 6-1	Weight: 175	Throws: R	

Season	Team	Age	Level	PA	1B	2B	3B	HR	SB	CS	BB%	K%	AVG	OBP	SLG	ISO
2022	BOS	18	CPX	43	5	3	0	1	1	0	16.28%	9.30%	0.250	0.372	0.417	0.167
2022	BOS	18	A	44	8	4	3	0	1	0	2.27%	25.00%	0.349	0.364	0.581	0.233

Background: California-based Orange Lutheran High School's been home to several notable big leaguers throughout its history, including: Gerrit Cole, who was originally taken by the Yankees at the backend of the first round in 2008 but headed to UCLA after failing to come to terms; Cole Winn, the 15th overall pick in 2018; Garrett Mitchell, like Gerrit Cole was later drafted after an impressive college career; Jason Martin, and Brandon Mauerer. Hoping to add his name to the list of former Lancers to crack a big league lineup is shortstop Mikey Romero. Well known since his days on the U-12 Baseball World Cup in 2016, Romero, who would also play on the U-15 squad three years later, turned in a dominant senior showing last season. In 30 games for the prep school, the lefty-swinging middle infielder batted a scorching .372 (with a .419 OBP) while knocking in 26 and scoring 24 runs. Prior to the 2022 draft, Romero had changed his college commitment from the University of Arizona to SEC powerhouse Louisiana State University. The 6-foot-1, 175-pound shortstop made the decision when Wildcat head coach Jay Johnson left to take a job with the Tigers. Boston drafted Romero in the opening round, 24th overall, and signed a deal worth $2.3 million. He split his abbreviated debut between the Complex League and Salem, slugging an aggregate .304/.368/.506 with seven doubles, three triples, one homeruns, and a pair of stolen bases.

Scouting Report: Romero has the defensive chops to stick at shortstop, but the 6-foot-1, 175-pound infielder lacks the arm strength to make deep throws. A move to second base seems likely – and that's before considering that the club's top prospect – Marcelo Mayer – isn't moving away from the infield's most important position. Good bat but lacks current power, Romero projects to add 12- to 15 homeruns at his peak with plenty of doubles in the gaps.

Ceiling: 2.5-win player
Risk: Moderate
MLB ETA: 2025

9. Blaze Jordan, 1B/3B

Hit	Power	SB	Patience	Glove	Overall
50	50/60	35/30	50	45	50

Born: 12/19/02	Age: 20	Bats: R	Top Production Comp: N/A
Height: 6-2	Weight: 220	Throws: R	

Season	Team	Age	Level	PA	1B	2B	3B	HR	SB	CS	BB%	K%	AVG	OBP	SLG	ISO
2021	BOS	18	CPX	76	13	7	1	4	1	0	7.89%	17.11%	0.362	0.408	0.667	0.304
2021	BOS	18	A	38	6	1	0	2	0	0	5.26%	21.05%	0.250	0.289	0.444	0.194
2022	BOS	19	A	415	66	29	3	8	4	1	8.92%	16.14%	0.286	0.357	0.446	0.159
2022	BOS	19	A+	106	23	1	0	4	1	0	10.38%	25.47%	0.301	0.387	0.441	0.140

Background: One of the most ballyhooed third round prospects in recent memory or, perhaps, in history – at least in terms of baseball card collectors. Jordan's hype reached a fever pitch that rivaled that of Gregg Jefferies back in the 1980s. And, for the most part, he has quietly lived up to it – or at least a little bit, anyways. A product of DeSoto Central High School, Boston snagged the power-hitting corner infielder in the third round, 89th overall, and handed him a massive $1.75 million bonus. Jordan would make his debut the following season, hitting

Boston Red Sox

.324/.368/.591 in 28 games between the Complex League and Salem. The former Bonus Baby opened up last season back in Low-A, but after a successful 95-game stint he spent the remaining few weeks with Greenville. Jordan finished first full season in the Red Sox's organization with a stellar .289/.363/.445 slash line with 30 doubles, three triples, 12 homeruns, and five stolen bases (in six attempts). According to *Weighted Runs Created Plus,* his overall production topped the league mark by 24%.

Snippet from The 2022 Prospect Digest Handbook: Best case scenario is Nolan Gorman. Worst case: .290 OBP percentage with 25 homeruns. The outcomes are quite vast at this point.

Scouting Report: Well known for his prodigious power and mammoth homeruns. Jordan's production line last season lacked the type of homerun total that was expected. But – surprisingly – the hit tool and contact rates have been better than advertised. Average walk rates. Jordan's offensive profile plays well at either corner infield position, though he plays defense like a designated hitter. With regard to his work in Low-A last season, consider the following:

> Since 2006, only four 19-year-old hitters met the following criteria in a Low-A season (min. 350 PA): 117 to 127 wRC+, a 14% to 18% strikeout rate, and a 8% to 10% walk rate. Those four hitters: Kyle Tucker, Brett Lawrie, Forrest Wall, and – of course – Blaze Jordan.

Each time he digs in at the dish he has bad intentions. He's Bobby Dalbec with a better hit tool.

Ceiling: 2.5-win player
Risk: Moderate
MLB ETA: 2024/2025

10. Luis Perales, RHP

FB	CB	CH	Command	Overall
60	55	50/55	40/45	50

Born: 04/14/03	Age: 20	Bats: R	Top Production Comp: N/A
Height: 6-1	Weight: 160	Throws: R	

Season	Team	Age	Level	IP	TBF	K/9	K%	BB/9	BB%	K-BB%	ERA	FIP	xFIP	Pit/Bat
2022	BOS	19	CPX	25.0	94	12.24	36.17%	3.24	9.57%	26.60%	1.08	2.31	3.08	2.04
2022	BOS	19	A	10.2	52	13.50	30.77%	9.28	21.15%	9.62%	3.37	5.44	5.34	3.83

Background: Let me know if you've heard – or read – this before: the Red Sox quietly signed the promising youngster on a sub-$100,000 deal midsummer four years ago. A native of Guacara, Venezuela, his debut came to an abrupt end the following year as he dealt with an undisclosed injury. The official stat line: 2.0 innings pitched, one earned run, one walk, and three punch outs. So all things considered, last season proved to be the hard-throwing righty's "official" debut. Perales made nine appearances with the club's Complex League affiliate and another four brief outings in Low-A. He tossed a total of 35.2 innings, recording an impressive 50 punch outs against 20 free passes to go along with a sparkling 1.77 ERA and a 3.24 FIP.

Scouting Report: If it weren't for the facial hair, you'd assume that Perales was working for your local U15 traveling team. Then you watch unfurl one of the most explosive 95-mph heaters in the minor leagues and question everything you thought about the generously listed 6-foot-1 right-hander. Perales will mix in an above-average 12-6 curveball and a better than advertised changeup with the latter showing solid velocity separation and tumble. The young hurler, who will play the 2023 season as a 20-year-old, shows more poise and pitchability than most his age. There's some mid-rotation caliber potential. He's *definitely* a name to watch in 2023.

Ceiling: 2.5-win player
Risk: Moderate to High
MLB ETA: 2025

11. Eddinson Paulino, IF/CF

Hit	Power	SB	Patience	Glove	Overall
50	45/50	60/50	50	40/45	50

Born: 07/02/02	Age: 20	Bats: L	Top Production Comp: N/A
Height: 5-10	Weight: 155	Throws: R	

Season	Team	Age	Level	PA	1B	2B	3B	HR	SB	CS	BB%	K%	AVG	OBP	SLG	ISO
2021	BOS	18	CPX	133	18	16	4	0	5	2	11.28%	15.79%	0.336	0.436	0.549	0.212
2022	BOS	19	A	539	65	35	10	13	27	5	11.87%	19.48%	0.266	0.359	0.469	0.203

Background: The front office's track record at identifying under-the-radar, cost efficient (read: cheap) talent on the international market is highly underrated by most pundits. And Eddinson Paulino is just another example of the club's due diligence. Signed for just a smidgeon over $200,000 in early July 2019, the then-16-year old moved immediately into the Dominican Summer League for his debut. And he held his own, batting .287/.394/.380 with two doubles, four triples, and a pair of stolen

Boston Red Sox

bases. Paulino made the leap stateside to the Complex League two years later, raising the offensive bar even higher as he mashed .336/.436/.549 with 16 doubles and four triples in 36 games. Boston sent the lefty-swinging infielder / part-time centerfielder to Salem for his first crack at full season action last yer. And he did not disappoint, setting career highs in doubles (35), triples (10), homeruns (13), and stolen bases (27) while slugging .266/.359/.469. His production topped the league average threshold by 27%, according to *Weighted Runs Created Plus*.

Scouting Report: Paulino's 2022 season was – by all accounts – a smashing success as he squared off against the older competition in Low-A. But what makes it even more impressive is how his numbers look after his frigid start to the year. After batting .194/.268/.375 over the first month of the year, Paulino caught fire in early May and slugged .279/.375/.486 over his remaining 97 contests. The young Dominican infielder / outfielder went from hitting a total of ZERO homeruns over his first 71 professional games to belting out 13 last year. Patient approach with solid contact skills, Paulino has a gorgeous left-handed swing. Defensively, his glove work on the infield was pretty terrible last season, which may push him into a full-time outfielder.

Ceiling: 2.0-win player
Risk: Moderate
MLB ETA: 2025

12. Wikelman Gonzalez, RHP

FB	CB	CH	Command	Overall
60	60	55/60	40	50

Born: 03/25/02 **Age:** 21 **Bats:** R **Top Production Comp:** N/A
Height: 6-0 **Weight:** 200 **Throws:** R

Season	Team	Age	Level	IP	TBF	K/9	K%	BB/9	BB%	K-BB%	ERA	FIP	xFIP	Pit/Bat
2022	BOS	20	A	81.1	358	10.84	27.37%	5.31	13.41%	13.97%	4.54	3.86	4.51	4.16
2022	BOS	20	A+	17.0	70	12.18	32.86%	3.18	8.57%	24.29%	2.65	2.54	4.11	4.30

Background: A wiry right-hander out of Venezuela, it's difficult to imagine that the 6-foot, 200-pound hurler put on a tremendous amount of weight since joining the organization. But that's exactly what he did. He put on weight. And then more weight. And then just a little more weight. According to a report on *MassLive* by Christopher Smith (dated 04/28/2022), the once wispy hurler packed on 60 pounds. Must be a nice problem to have... After a successful jaunt through the Dominican Summer League, Gonzalez made the leap stateside following the return from the lost COVID season. And he blew the doors off the Low-A and Complex League competition by averaging 11.3 strikeouts and just 2.3 walks per nine innings across 11 starts and one relief appearance. Last season Gonzalez returned back to Low-A for additional seasoning before capping off the year with a four-game cameo with Greenville. He tossed a career best 98.1 innings of work, posting a 121-to-54 strikeout-to-walk ratio to go along with an aggregate 4.21 ERA. He finished the year with a 4-3 win-loss record.

Snippet from The 2022 Prospect Digest Handbook: If there was one arm brewing in the low levels that could match the arsenal and potential of top prospect Brayan Bello, its Wikelman Gonzalez. Bar none. And there's not even a debate. He's poised to be the club's biggest breakout minor leaguer and should be on the list for biggest breakout prospect in all of baseball. It wouldn't shock me to see Gonzalez as a consensus Top 100 pick within the next 12 to 18 months. Remember this kid's name. One more thought: I think there's some added velo in his right arm that's just waiting to be tapped. He's got some Jose Berrios aura about him.

Scouting Report: Consider the following:

> Since 2006, only six 20-year-old hurlers met the following criteria in a season in Low-A (min. 75 IP): 26.5% to 28.5% strikeout percentage with a walk percentage between 12% to 14%. Those six hurlers: Albert Abreu, Enny Romero, Ethan Martin, Bruce Pugh, Alexander Cornielle, and – of course – Wikelman Gonzalez.

If everything breaks just the right way, there's a shot that Gonzalez develops three plus offerings. He already has two in place – a mid-90s, riding fastball that simply overpowered the low levels of the minor leagues, and a knee-buckling low-80s curveball. His changeup, which already grades out as a 55, shows fade and tumble. The question with Gonzalez is centered on his ability – or inability – to control the strike zone. A bit of a silver lining: he finished the year on a high note, walking just eight over his final 28 innings. Mid-rotation caliber potential, definitely more if he can throw consistent strikes – particularly with his offspeed offerings.

Ceiling: 2.5-win player
Risk: High
MLB ETA: 2024/2025

Boston Red Sox

13. Nathan Hickey, C

Hit	Power	SB	Patience	Glove	Overall
40	55	30	60	45	45

Born: 11/23/99 | **Age:** 23 | **Bats:** L | **Top Production Comp:** N/A
Height: 6-0 | **Weight:** 210 | **Throws:** R |

Season	Team	Age	Level	PA	1B	2B	3B	HR	SB	CS	BB%	K%	AVG	OBP	SLG	ISO
2022	BOS	22	A	182	19	12	0	7	0	1	21.43%	21.43%	0.271	0.429	0.507	0.236
2022	BOS	22	A+	146	14	6	0	9	0	0	16.44%	26.71%	0.252	0.397	0.539	0.287

Background: A consistent offensive bat during his abbreviated two years at the University of Florida. Hickey earned a starting gig during his freshman season with the Gators, hitting an impressive .311/.439/.622 before the COVID pandemic prematurely ended the year. A lefty-swinging backstop, Hickey picked up right where he left off during his redshirt freshman campaign in 2021. He slugged .317/.435/.522 with 15 doubles, two triples, nine homeruns, and a stolen base. Boston drafted the Gator in the fifth round, 136th overall, signed him to an over-slot deal worth $1 million – the second highest bonus the organization handed to any of their 2021 picks. The Florida native struggled through his first – abbreviated – foray into the minor leagues that summer, hitting .214/.400/.286 in 11 games between the Complex League and Salem. Last summer, though, Hickey was able to get his feet underneath him and returned to mashing at the dish. Splitting time between Salem and Greenville, he slugged an aggregate .263/.415/.522 with 18 doubles and 16 homeruns. He finished the season with a strong 78-to-63 strikeout-to-walk ratio. According to *Weighted Runs Created Plus*, his overall production topped the league average mark by a massive 55%.

Snippet from The 2022 Prospect Digest Handbook: He could be a poor man's Yasmani Grandal at his peak with a poor man's Zack Collins floor.

Scouting Report: One of the best offensive performances by a minor league catcher in 2022. Hickey did what he's *always* done – hit for power and find a way to get on-base. Unlike a lot of the club's young middle infield prospects, not all of Hickey's offensive value is tied up in his bloated walk rates thanks in large part to his above-average power. And the lefty-swinging former Gator didn't show any concerning platoon splits in 2022 either, hitting .259/.429/.517 and .278/.350/.537 against righties and lefties. Crouched stance with a big, healthy cut. Good bat speed. Hickey nearly swings out of his helmet each time. Big time, light tower power. Defensively, he's a bat-first catcher.

Ceiling: 1.5-win player
Risk: Moderate
MLB ETA: 2024/2025

14. Cutter Coffey, IF

Hit	Power	SB	Patience	Glove	Overall
35/45	40/55	40	50	45/50	45

Born: 05/21/04 | **Age:** 19 | **Bats:** R | **Top Production Comp:** N/A
Height: 6-2 | **Weight:** 190 | **Throws:** R |

Season	Team	Age	Level	PA	1B	2B	3B	HR	SB	CS	BB%	K%	AVG	OBP	SLG	ISO
2022	BOS	18	CPX	40	3	1	0	0	1	0	17.50%	27.50%	0.125	0.300	0.156	0.031

Background: Drafting prep shortstop – and current top prospect – Marcelo Mayer with the fourth overall pick in the 2021 draft had little bearing on the club's 2022 draft plan. The Red Sox led off last July's draft by selecting a pair of high school shortstops with their top two picks: Mikey Romero, a lefty-swinging prospect out of Orange Lutheran High School, with the 24th overall pick, and then they snagged Cutter Coffey 16 selections later. A 6-foot-2, 190-pound infielder, Coffey once seemed destined to be a mound mainstay where he would come close to the mid-90s with his heater. But the Liberty High School star was a dynamic force in the middle of the club's lineup – particularly over his final two seasons. He batted .479/.564/.945 with five doubles, one triple, and nine homeruns in 21 games as a junior. And he followed that up with a stout .442/.581/1.021 slash line with 13 doubles, three triples, and 12 homeruns. Prior to signing with the Red Sox for $1,847,500, Coffey was part of a highly touted recruiting class for the University of Texas. He batted a disappointing .125/.300/.156 with one double in 40 plate appearances with the club's Florida Complex League affiliate.

Scouting Report: Stiff and robotic in the field, almost as if Coffey's planning his movements before he actually makes them. The former ace hurler has a plus arm and can make all the difficult throws, but likely heads over to second or third bases – regardless of whomever else is in the Red Sox's system. Above-average power. Coffee doesn't get cheated at the plate. Great bat speed, but the swing is a bit long at times and needs work to clean it up a bit. He figures to add some muscle to his lean, but strong frame as he fills out. There are some offensive similarities between former Red Sox first rounder Michael Chavis and Cutter Coffey. It wouldn't be shocking to see the club push him back to the mound if he struggles in the first two or three years.

Ceiling: 1.5-win player
Risk: Moderate
MLB ETA: 2026

Boston Red Sox

15. Gilberto Jimenez, CF/RF

Hit	Power	SB	Patience	Glove	Overall
40/50	35/45	50/60	45	40/55	45

Born: 07/08/00	Age: 22	Bats: B	Top Production Comp: N/A
Height: 5-11	Weight: 212	Throws: R	

Season	Team	Age	Level	PA	1B	2B	3B	HR	SB	CS	BB%	K%	AVG	OBP	SLG	ISO
2021	BOS	20	A	408	89	16	6	3	13	8	4.66%	21.08%	0.306	0.346	0.405	0.099
2022	BOS	21	A+	409	77	18	2	5	20	9	4.40%	24.45%	0.268	0.306	0.366	0.097

Background: One of my personal favorite prospects over the past several years. Boston signed the toolsy, enigmatic outfielder out of San Cristobal, Dominican Republic, for a paltry fee of $10,000. Jimenez was an offensive dynamo at the onset of his professional career. He ripped through the Dominican Summer League competition to the tune of .319/.384/.420 as a 17-year-old. And he shredded the New York-Penn League pitching by mashing .359/.393/.470 the following season. And Jimenez was receiving praise from far and wide on his potential as a table-setting sparkplug and his sheer athleticism. Following MiLB's return from their COVID hibernation, he moved into Low-A and his production remained solid as he batted .306/.346/.405 with 16 doubles, six triples, three homeruns, and 13 stolen bases (21 attempts). Last season the young outfielder continued his trek and entered High-A – though the results were quite disappointing. In a career best 99 games, the 5-foot-11, 212-pound athlete batted .268/.306/.366 with 18 doubles, two triples, five homeruns, and 20 stolen bases (in 29 total attempts). For the first time in his career, his numbers fell below the league average threshold (84 wRC+).

Snippet from The 2022 Prospect Digest Handbook: Raw, but plenty of intriguing talent and athleticism. He's an elite runner, though it hasn't translated to defensive value yet. But it will. He's showing some platoon splits, as expected given his inexperience as a switch-hitter, but that's going to improve too. My only question is whether he'll hit for enough power to push him into a full time gig. He's very much projection over production at this point.

Scouting Report: Jimenez remains one of the most intriguing athletes in the minor leagues, but that has yet to translate into premium production – at least over the past two seasons. Defensively, Jimenez's numbers are improving as a rightfielder, though his routes and numbers are still questionable in centerfielder. His athleticism is worth betting on. He could be a late-bloomer. If it's not time yet, it's very close for the organization to give up on the pipedream of Jimenez developing into a viable switch-hitter.

Ceiling: 1.5-win player
Risk: Moderate to High
MLB ETA: 2024

16. Brandon Walter, LHP

FB	SL	CH	Command	Overall
50	55	50	55	40

Born: 09/08/96	Age: 26	Bats: L	Top Comp: N/A
Height: 6-2	Weight: 200	Throws: L	

Season	Team	Age	Level	IP	TBF	K/9	K%	BB/9	BB%	K-BB%	ERA	FIP	xFIP	Pit/Bat
2021	BOS	24	A	31.0	127	13.35	36.22%	1.74	4.72%	31.50%	1.45	1.78	2.39	3.59
2021	BOS	24	A+	58.1	237	13.27	36.29%	2.16	5.91%	30.38%	3.70	3.13	2.58	3.89
2022	BOS	25	AA	50.0	196	12.24	34.69%	0.54	1.53%	33.16%	2.88	2.73	2.26	3.43

Background: A solid, yet unremarkable hurler during his time at the University of Delaware. The southpaw left the non-traditional baseball school as a 26th round pick in 2019 – the 797th overall player taken. Walter is also the last Delaware player to get drafted as well. The 6-foot-2, 200-pound left-hander averaged 9.8 strikeouts and 3.2 walks during his tenure with the Blue Hens, posting a 3.66 ERA and a 15-14 win-loss record. The New Castle, Delaware native turned in a strong debut showing against the younger, less experienced competition in the Gulf Coast League that summer, compiling a 39-to-8 strikeout-to-walk ratio in 33.1 innings of work. After losing a year to the COVID pandemic, Walter came back a geriatric 24-year-old, relegated to the Salem Red Sox's bullpen. Meaning: he had little shot at actually making good on his big league aspirations. Then he started shutting down the Low-A hitters and moved into Greenville's rotation in the second half of the year. And before anyone knew it, Walter averaged an impressive 13.3 strikeouts and just 2.0 walks per nine innings. Last season the front office brass pushed him up to the true proving ground, Double-A, and he continued to flummox the opposition across nine starts. So Boston continued to challenge him and sent him up to Triple-A. Two starts later his season prematurely ended. The cause: a neck injury. He finished the year with 57.2 innings, 75 punch outs, just seven walks, and a 3.59 ERA.

Scouting Report: Consider the following:

> Since 2006, only three 25-year-old hurlers struck out at least 33% and walked fewer than 7% of the hitters they faced in any Double-A league (min. 50 IP): Glenn Otto, Austen Williams, and Brandon Walter.

Funky low-slot slinger that creates deception and movement because of his release point. Velocity-wise, Walter's heater will sit in the 90- to 92-mph range but will sneak up on hitters, particularly up in the zone. It's heavier than the typical average heater and can be difficult to elevate.

Boston Red Sox

He'll mix in an above-average, darting slider and a solid changeup. He fills up the strike zone and effectively changes speeds, especially early in the count. Walter's better than the average depth option but there aren't a lot of big league clubs in baseball that can't run out a better option near the backend of their rotation either. He has the floor of a solid middle relief arm.

Ceiling: 1.0-win player
Risk: Low
MLB ETA: 2023

17. Roman Anthony, CF

Hit	Power	SB	Patience	Glove	Overall
45/50	45/50	35	50	50	45

Born: 05/13/04	Age: 19	Bats: L	Top Production Comp: N/A
Height: 6-3	Weight: 200	Throws: R	

Season	Team	Age	Level	PA	1B	2B	3B	HR	SB	CS	BB%	K%	AVG	OBP	SLG	ISO
2022	BOS	18	CPX	40	13	2	0	0	1	0	10.00%	10.00%	0.429	0.475	0.486	0.057
2022	BOS	18	A	43	5	2	0	0	0	0	11.63%	9.30%	0.189	0.279	0.243	0.054

Background: Marjory Stoneman-Douglas High School is home to several notable big leaguers: Mike Caruso, a second round pick by the Giants in 1996, finished third in the American League Rookie of the Year voting just two years later; Anthony Rizzo, of course, needs little introduction after slugging nearly 300 homeruns and earning almost $90 million in his 12-year big league career; Colton Welker, a fourth round pick by the Rockies in 2016, spent the majority of his early pro years among the club's Top 10 prospect lists; and Jesus Luzardo, a third rounder the same year, has battled some injuries but came into his own for the Marlins in 2022. And that list doesn't include burgeoning Orioles prospect Coby Mayo. Surprisingly, though, just two players – Caruso and David Christensen – were chosen ahead of Roman Anthony, the 79th overall pick last July. A long time commit to the University of Mississippi, the 6-foot-3, 200-pound center fielder batted a scorching .545/.622/.960 with 10 doubles, one triple, and 10 homeruns for the Eagles during his senior campaign, earning the Florida State Gatorade Player of the Year award as well. The Red Sox signed him to a well above-average deal worth $2.5 million, equivalent to late first round money. Anthony slugged .306/.374/.361 with four doubles in 20 games between the Complex League and Low-A.

Scouting Report: Lean, but strong, muscular. Average arm and speed, Anthony may eventually move away from center field as his wiry frame begins to fill out. Lefty-swinging hitter with a prototypical line-drive swing and doesn't project to hit more than 20 homeruns during his peak. Solid all around approach, but there doesn't seem to be a true standout offensive tool.

Ceiling: 1.0- to 1.5-win player
Risk: Moderate
MLB ETA: 2026

18. Brainer Bonaci, 2B/SS

Hit	Power	SB	Patience	Glove	Overall
45	40	60	60	55	40

Born: 07/09/02	Age: 20	Bats: B	Top Production Comp: N/A
Height: 5-10	Weight: 164	Throws: R	

Season	Team	Age	Level	PA	1B	2B	3B	HR	SB	CS	BB%	K%	AVG	OBP	SLG	ISO
2021	BOS	18	CPX	162	19	13	1	2	12	0	12.96%	22.84%	0.252	0.358	0.403	0.151
2021	BOS	18	A	52	7	3	1	0	0	0	5.77%	15.38%	0.224	0.269	0.327	0.102
2022	BOS	19	A	494	73	19	6	6	28	6	18.02%	18.02%	0.262	0.397	0.385	0.123

Background: The switch-hitting infielder cut his professional teeth as a baby-faced 16-year-old in the Dominican Summer League four years ago. And the results were quite impressive given his age: he batted .280/.356/.397 in 61 games that year. Bonaci, who joined the organization just few months prior to his debut, split the 2021 season between the Complex League and Low-A, hitting a completely mediocre .245/.336/.383 with 16 doubles, two triples, and two homeruns. Last season the former international top prospect returned to Salem for a longer look at full season pitching – with improved results. More than doubling his career total games in 2022, Bonaci batted .262/.397/.385 with 19 doubles, six triples, six homeruns, and 28 stolen bases (in 34 attempts). Per *Weighted Runs Created Plus*, his overall production topped the league average by 25%, the best mark of his young career.

Snippet from The 2022 Prospect Digest Handbook: First impression watching Bonaci in the Complex League last summer: he needs to get stronger. There were swings that were reminiscent of your kid brother grabbing the oversized lumber in a pickup game at the park. The swing, though, shows some potential as an above-average hit tool. It's good looking. I'm not sure how much power his 5-foot-10, 160-ish-pound frame will allow, but his above-average speed will compensate for some of that. There's some Erick Aybar vibes.

Boston Red Sox

Scouting Report: Consider the following:

> Since 2006, only six 19-year-olds posted a 120 to 130 wRC+ with a 16% to 20% strikeout rate in any Low-A league (min. 350 PA): Andrew McCutchen, Brett Lawrie, Blaze Jordan, Eddinson Paulino, Forrest Wall, and – of course – Brainer Bonaci.

Despite spending half of his time in the hitter-friendly confines of Salem's home park, Bonaci actually performed better on the road last season (.233/.372/.333 vs. .289/.418/.433). There's still not a lot of present power, though it's far better than what he previously showed, and he's likely not going to grow into anything more than 40-grade pop. Efficient on the base paths. And he continues to flash above-average leather at the keystone. A lot of his offensive value comes from his inflated walk rates – so he's going to have to compensate with better secondary skills as he progresses up the ladder. He's tracking like a utility infielder.

Ceiling: 1.0-win player
Risk: Moderate
MLB ETA: 2024/2025

19. Enmanuel Valdez, IF/OF

Hit	Power	SB	Patience	Glove	Overall
45	50	45	45	45	40

Born: 12/28/98	Age: 24	Bats: L	Top Production Comp: N/A
Height: 5-9	Weight: 191	Throws: R	

Season	Team	Age	Level	PA	1B	2B	3B	HR	SB	CS	BB%	K%	AVG	OBP	SLG	ISO
2021	HOU	22	A+	318	34	16	1	21	5	1	7.86%	21.07%	0.254	0.313	0.541	0.286
2021	HOU	22	AA	98	10	6	0	5	0	1	13.27%	22.45%	0.256	0.367	0.512	0.256
2022	HOU	23	AA	205	33	16	0	11	4	2	16.59%	22.93%	0.357	0.463	0.649	0.292
2022	HOU	23	AAA	173	26	10	1	10	1	1	6.36%	16.76%	0.296	0.347	0.560	0.264
2022	BOS	23	AAA	195	24	9	1	7	3	0	9.74%	24.62%	0.237	0.309	0.422	0.185

Background: The Red Sox said goodbye to longtime catcher Christian Vázquez last August, shipping the veteran to Houston for a pair of mediocre minor league vagabonds – Enmanuel Valdez and Wilyer Abreu. After struggling through the first four seasons of his professional career, Valdez emerged an improved hitter in 2021 following the COVID-imposed layoff. He spent time with Houston's High-A and Double-A affiliates that summer, hitting an aggregate .255/.326/.534 with career bests in doubles (22) and homeruns (26). Last season the lefty-swinging infielder / outfielder split time between Double-A and Triple-A between both organizations, slugging .296/.376/.542 while setting another round of career highs in doubles (35) and homeruns (28) to go along with two triples and eight stolen bases. Per *Weighted Runs Created Plus*, his overall production topped the league average threshold by 31%.

Snippet from The 2022 Prospect Digest Handbook: He's typically struggled against southpaws (though that wasn't the case last season). Low end utility guy. Unless he proves that he can hit outside of Asheville for extended periods of time.

Scouting Report: For the first time in his professional career, the lefty-swinging Valdez didn't struggle mightily against southpaws – though the platoon splits were still present. He slugged an impressive .309/.397/.598 against right-handers and batted 3261/.315/.388 against lefties. His offensive capabilities are his carrying tool, because his glove – at any position – has generally graded out as below-average. He might be a useful bench option, but certainly not on a contending team – which the Red Sox aren't projected to be in the next few seasons.

Ceiling: 1.0-win player
Risk: Moderate
MLB ETA: 2023

20. Dalton Rogers, LHP

FB	CB	SL	CH	Command	Overall
50	55	N/A	50	35/40	60

Born: 01/18/01	Age: 22	Bats: R	Top Production Comp: N/A
Height: 5-11	Weight: 172	Throws: L	

Background: The highest drafted pitcher out of the University of Southern Mississippi since Cleveland selected right-hander Nick Sandlin in the second round in 2018. Rogers, a small-ish left-hander, had an interesting run during his collegiate tenure. He was limited to just 8.1 innings during his freshman season at Southeastern Louisiana, walking (12) more than he struck out (11). The 5-foot-11, 172-pound southpaw transferred to Southern Mississippi and was forced to sit out the 2021 campaign – but he somehow found his way into the Cape Cod lead in between stops. He would throw 13.0 innings with the Cotuit Kettleers, posting a 21-to-14 strikeout-to-walk ratio. Last season Rogers worked out of the Golden Eagles' bullpen, throwing a career high 37.0 innings of work, averaging an impressive 13.9 strikeouts and a whopping 5.6 walks per nine innings. He also appeared – briefly – with the Kettleers, as well. Boston selected him in the third round, 99th overall, and signed him to a deal worth $447,500.

Boston Red Sox

Scouting Report: Despite the gaudy strikeout numbers, Rogers' arsenal is pretty mediocre outside of his above-average curveball. He'll feature a low-90s heater, a 50-grade changeup, and – of course – that big bending 11-5 curveball. Rogers' wildness lulled the opposition to sleep at times in college, but his command is a 35. Not overly big, there's not too much project left. He's a curious third round pick by the Sox.

Ceiling: 0.5-win player
Risk: Moderate
MLB ETA: 2025

Chicago Cubs

Top Prospects

Chicago Cubs

1. Pete Crow-Armstrong, CF

Hit	Power	SB	Patience	Glove	Overall
50/60	50/55	50	50	50	70

Born: 03/25/02	Age: 20	Bats: L	Top Production Comp: Ryan Braun
Height: 6-1	Weight: 180	Throws: L	

Season	Team	Age	Level	PA	1B	2B	3B	HR	SB	CS	BB%	K%	AVG	OBP	SLG	ISO
2021	NYM	19	A	32	8	2	0	0	2	3	21.88%	18.75%	0.417	0.563	0.500	0.083
2022	CHC	20	A	183	41	5	3	7	13	4	12.02%	18.03%	0.354	0.443	0.557	0.203
2022	CHC	20	A+	288	45	15	7	9	19	7	4.86%	23.96%	0.287	0.333	0.498	0.211

Background: Baseball is a romantic game. A game shared between fathers and sons, like Ken Griffey Sr. and Ken Griffey Jr. or Bobby and Barry Bonds, or brothers like Matty, Felipe, and Jesus Alou, or in place of absent fathers, mothers and sons, like the Alomars, who learned the game from their mother because their father, Sandy, was always on the road. Bloodlines run as deep as the game's history. But sometimes, though, those bloodlines briefly intersect with the game away from the diamond. Like, for instance, Pete Crow-Armstrong's mother, Ashley Crow, who starred in the childhood classic Little Big League as Billy Heywood's mother. (Also worth noting: Crow-Armstrong's father, Matthew John Armstrong, has worked in the film industry as well. Originally taken by the Mets in the middle of the first round three years ago, Crow-Armstrong got off to a scorching start to his career the following season as he bashed .417/.563/.500 before a torn right labrum issue knocked him out after just six contests. Despite sitting on the disabled list and accruing a week's worth of game's on his professional resume, the Cubs' front office honed in on the high upside outfielder during their fire sale two years ago as they looked to jumpstart their rebuild. The pried him away from the Mets for All-Star infielder Javier Baez, right-hander Trevor Williams, and cash. Last season, his first full campaign in the Cubs' farm system, Crow-Armstrong was extraordinary as he split time between Myrtle Beach and South Bend. He finished the year with an aggregate .312/.376/.520 slash line with 20 doubles, 10 triples, 16 homeruns, and 32 stolen bases (in 43 attempts). Per *Weighted Runs Created Plus*, his overall production surpassed the league average threshold by a whopping 44%.

Snippet from The 2022 Prospect Digest Handbook: Short, sweet stroke with gobs of bat speed. The simplicity of the swing reminds me of a young Joey Votto. I'm really impressed by his willingness to take outside pitches the opposite way. The sky could be the limit.

Scouting Report: Consider the following:

> Since 2006, only three hitters met the following criteria in any High-A league (min. 275 PA): 120 to 130 wRC+, a 23% to 25% strikeout rate, and a sub-7.0% walk rate. Those three hitters: Carlos Gonzalez, Thomas Saggese, and – of course – Pete Crow-Armstrong.

One of the purest hitters in the minor leagues, Crow-Armstrong's sweet lefty swing is geared towards future batting titles, line drives, and 25 homeruns. He grinds out at bats, making the opposition throw pitch after pitch. His walk rate plummeted during his extended stint in High-A last season, but it should hover near the league average, maybe a tick better, in coming years. No platoon splits, above-average power, plus speed, and a potential plus hit tool. Crow-Armstrong also was solid in centerfield last summer as well. In terms of big league ceiling, think: .310/.370/.490 with 25-homer / 25-stolen base potential.

Ceiling: 6.0-win player
Risk: Moderate
MLB ETA: 2024

2. Kevin Alcántara, CF

Hit	Power	SB	Patience	Glove	Overall
50/55	50/60	50/40	55	55	60

Born: 07/12/02	Age: 20	Bats: R	Top Production Comp: Matt Kemp
Height: 6-6	Weight: 188	Throws: R	

Season	Team	Age	Level	PA	1B	2B	3B	HR	SB	CS	BB%	K%	AVG	OBP	SLG	ISO
2021	CHC	18	CPX	107	19	3	5	4	3	0	12.15%	26.17%	0.337	0.415	0.609	0.272
2022	CHC	19	A	495	77	19	6	15	14	3	11.11%	24.85%	0.273	0.360	0.451	0.178

Background: I've written, ad nauseam, how the Cubs' World Series winning team was built upon the backs of young hitters, particularly power-hitters. The front office had the recipe for success, but they deviated in recent years as they targeted soft-tossing, crafty, low-ceiling / high-floor pitchers in the draft. Two years ago, though, the organization refocused their efforts on high upside hitters, acquiring the likes of Pete Crow-Armstrong, Alexander Canario, and Kevin Alcantara in various trades. Chicago sent three-time All-Star first baseman Anthony Rizzo to the Yankees in exchange for right-hander Alexander Vizcaíno and Alcantara. Last season the 6-foot-6, 188-pound centerfielder made the leap up to full season action for the first time in his career. And he shined – brightly. Appearing in 112 games with the Myrtle Beach Pelicans, the young Dominican prospect mashed .273/.360/.451 with 19 doubles, six triples, 15 homeruns, and 14 stolen bases. According to *Weighted Runs Created Plus*, his overall production topped the league average mark by an impressive 24%.

Chicago Cubs

Snippet from The 2022 Prospect Digest Handbook: He's the type of prospect where things appear to come quite easy for him. Very, very projectable. There's the potential for superstardom, but I'm hesitant to fully commit until he gets a year in Low-A, which will happen in 2022. He could be an impact player on both sides of the ball.

Scouting Report: Consider the following:

> Since 2006, only five 19-year-old hitters posted a 120 to 130 wRC+ in any Low-A league (min. 350 PA): Michael Burgess, Josh Morgan, Eddinson Paulino, Carson Williams, and – of course – Kevin Alcantara.

One of the more underrated prospects in the game. Alcántara owns a very loud, yet somewhat raw, toolkit. Plus-power potential. Above-average glove at a premium position. Above-average speed. The young centerfield takes a patient approach at the plate and, despite his massive frame, owns decent contact rates. Best power in the Cubs' system. Still believe there's superstar potential here. In terms of big league potential, think: .290/.370/.500 with 30-homer potential. A move to a corner outfield spot is a real possibility.

Ceiling: 4.0-win player
Risk: Moderate
MLB ETA: 2024/2025

3. Kevin Made, 3B/SS

Hit	Power	SB	Patience	Glove	Overall
50/55	50/55	40	30/40	60	60

Born: 09/10/02 **Age:** 20 **Bats:** R **Top Production Comp:** Jorge Polanco
Height: 5-10 **Weight:** 160 **Throws:** R

Season	Team	Age	Level	PA	1B	2B	3B	HR	SB	CS	BB%	K%	AVG	OBP	SLG	ISO
2021	CHC	18	A	243	47	13	3	1	2	0	2.47%	23.46%	0.272	0.296	0.366	0.094
2022	CHC	19	A	257	36	14	0	9	0	1	10.51%	19.07%	0.266	0.354	0.450	0.185
2022	CHC	19	A+	151	13	6	1	1	3	0	12.58%	20.53%	0.162	0.267	0.246	0.085

Background: High profile international free agent that joined the franchise for a massive $1.7 million in 2019. Made had to wait two years before making his debut. And despite making the leap from amateur pitching to Low-A hurlers as an 18-year-old in 2021, Made held his own in 58 games with Myrtle Beach. He batted .272/.296/.366 with 13 doubles, three triples, one homeruns, and a pair of stolen bases. Last season, after his solid – albeit short – debut in Low-A, the front office sent the 5-foot-10, 160-pound infielder back to the Pelicans for additional seasoning. And the results were certainly improved. Made slugged .266/.354/.451 with 14 doubles and nine dingers in only 57 games. The organization bumped the promising youngster up to High-A in late July, but Made promptly struggled as he hit a lowly .162/.267/.246. He finished the season with an aggregate .227/.322/.375 slash line with 20 doubles, one triple, 10 homeruns, and a trio of stolen bases. His overall production, which was dragged down considerably by his High-A work, was 4% below the league average mark. Made's start to the year was slowed significantly due to "elbow soreness", causing him to miss for a couple weeks.

Snippet from The 2022 Prospect Digest Handbook: It's reasonable to expect Made to show increased patience as he matures, after all it's not going to get any worse, but he's only going to go as far as his hit tool and power will take him.

Scouting Report: Consider the following:

> Since 2006, only three 19-year-old hitters posted a 118 to 128 wRC+ with an 18% to 20% strikeout rate and 9% to 12% walk rate in any Low-A league (min. 250 PA): Logan Morrison, Eddinson Paulino, and – of course – Kevin Made.

There aren't too many turnarounds like Made's approach at the plate from his first to second seasons. After walking just six times in 243 plate appearances (just 2.5% of the time), the Dominican shortstop walked 46 times in only 408 plate appearances between his stints with Myrtle Beach and South Bend (11.3% of the time). Some of the best bat speed in the minors, Made owns above-average power potential – despite being a wispy 160 pounds. If everything breaks the right way, he could have 55-grades on the bat and power. His defense is some of the best at the position in the minors. He could be a special player with a ceiling as a .280/.370/.480 hitter with Gold Glove defense. He could *pop* in a big way in 2023. Remember the name. +

Ceiling: 4.0-win player
Risk: Moderate
MLB ETA: 2024/2025

Chicago Cubs

4. James Triantos, 3B

	Hit	Power	SB	Patience	Glove	Overall
	50/55	50/60	50	50	50	55

Born: 01/29/03	Age: 20	Bats: R	Top Production Comp: N/A
Height: 6-1	Weight: 195	Throws: R	

Season	Team	Age	Level	PA	1B	2B	3B	HR	SB	CS	BB%	K%	AVG	OBP	SLG	ISO
2021	CHC	18	CPX	109	19	7	1	6	3	3	6.42%	16.51%	0.327	0.376	0.594	0.267
2022	CHC	19	A	504	92	19	6	7	20	3	7.74%	16.07%	0.272	0.335	0.386	0.114

Background: After drafting Kansas State University ace left-hander Jordan Wicks with the 21st overall pick, the front office circled back around and selected James Madison High School slugger James Triantos in the second round. Triantos signed with the club for nearly twice the recommended slot bonus that summer. The 6-foot-1, 195-pound infielder turned in a rock solid debut in the Complex League, mashing .327/.376/.594 with seven doubles, one triple, six homeruns, and a trio of stolen bases. Last summer the organization assigned him to Myrtle Beach. And the Virginia-born prospect responded well. In 113 games with the Pelicans, Triantos batted .272/.335/.386 with 19 doubles, six triples, seven homeruns, and 20 stolen bases (in 23 total attempts). Per *Weighted Runs Created Plus*, his overall production topped the league average production line by 2%.

Snippet from The 2022 Prospect Digest Handbook: The Cubs' front office hasn't been shy about praising the type and quality of contact Triantos makes as a professional hitter. And it's easy to see why, too. The swing is a beautiful mix of strength, explosiveness, and controlled chaos. He's going to be the biggest prospect riser in the 2022 season.

Scouting Report: Consider the following:

> Since 2006, only five 19-year-old hitters met the following criteria in any Low-A league (min. 350 PA): 97 to 107 wRC+, 6.5% to 8.5% walk percentage with a 14% to 18% strikeout rate. Those five hitters: Nick Gordon, Miguel Andujar, Jamie Westbrook, Edinson Rincon, and – of course James Triantos.

After having Triantos split time on both sides of the keystone during his debut, the front office pushed the former second rounder to the hot corner last season. Like a lot of the Cubs' Baby Bashers, he's still figuring out how to tap into his impressive power potential. Lighting quick bat that projects for at least an above-average hit tool and power. He's still learning the finer nuances at third base, but he should be at least an average defender. Triantos is poised to be one of the bigger breakouts in 2023.

Ceiling: 3.5-win player
Risk: Moderate
MLB ETA: 2024

5. Jordan Wicks, LHP

	FB	CB	SL	CH	Command	Overall
	55	50	55	70	60	55

Born: 09/01/99	Age: 23	Bats: L	Top Production Comp: Alex Wood
Height: 6-3	Weight: 220	Throws: L	

Season	Team	Age	Level	IP	TBF	K/9	K%	BB/9	BB%	K-BB%	ERA	FIP	xFIP	Pit/Bat
2022	CHC	22	A+	66.2	281	11.61	30.60%	2.30	6.05%	24.56%	3.65	2.78	2.95	3.94
2022	CHC	22	AA	28.0	121	11.25	28.93%	3.54	9.09%	19.83%	4.18	4.90	3.89	4.08

Background: The Cubs have dipped into the waters of the Kansas State baseball program via the midsummer draft just four times in their storied history. The first was all the way back in 1970 when the snagged second baseman William Huisman in the 13th round. The second time happened two years later with the selection of outfielder Bill Droege in the eighth round. Then the Wildcats experienced a 25-year Chicago draught before the organization grabbed the immortal Todd Fereday in the 36th round in 1997. And it took nearly that long before the Cubbies would select another KSU alum, though, this time it would be in the opening round. Taken with the 21st overall pick two years ago, Wicks was a consistent force atop the school's rotation as he averaged 10.2 strikeouts and just 2.6 walks per nine innings across 34 career starts. The 6-foot-3, 220-pound changeup artist would make four brief appearances with South Bend during his debut, fanning five and walking three in 7.0 innings of work. Last season, the southpaw returned to High-A for a longer look, but after (mostly) dominating for 16 starts, the front office deemed him ready to take on the minors' toughest test – Double-A. He would continue to miss bats at an impressive clip with the Smokies. Wicks would finish the year with 94.2 innings, posting a 121-to-28 strikeout-to-walk ratio with a 3.80 ERA.

Snippet from The 2022 Prospect Digest Handbook: Wicks looks like a backend starter, perhaps peaking as a #4 if everything breaks the right way. He could easily go the route of Tim Cate and Anthony Kay.

Chicago Cubs

Scouting Report: Consider the following:

> Since 2006, there have been eight 22-year-old hurlers that posted a 29.5% to 31.5% strikeout percentage with a 4% to 6% walk percentage in any High-A league (min. 50 IP): Eric Lauer, Tarik Skubal, Brandon Pfaadt, James McDonald, Jared Shuster, Ben Lively, Brett Conine, and Jordan Wicks.

I caught a couple of Wicks' starts throughout the year last season, and each time I came away thinking he was better than I originally thought. Low 90s, above-average fastball that he – generally – commands well. He'll mix in a rare, get-me-over curveball that has some shape and depth. He'll add and subtract on his above-average slider, morphing it from a more traditional cutter all the way down to a slurvy-type breaking ball. His plus-plus changeup is a game changer, one of the best offspeed pitches in the minor leagues. Wicks isn't your traditional crafty southpaw, though he does command the zone well. The ceiling isn't overly big as he's still tracking like a #4-type arm. But he's safe and likely to be with the Cubbies in 2023.

Ceiling: 2.5- to 3.0-win player
Risk: Low to Moderate
MLB ETA: 2023

6. Cade Horton, RHP

	FB	CB	SL	CH	Command	Overall
	60	N/A	70	45/50	50	60

Born: 08/20/01	**Age:** 22	**Bats:** R	**Top Production Comp:** N/A
Height: 6-2	**Weight:** 190	**Throws:** R	

Background: A highly touted two-way player coming out of Norman High School. *Perfect Game* and *Prep Baseball Report* ranked the infielder / right-hander as the second best prospect in the state of Oklahoma. Both outlets also ranked him as the 14th and 34th overall player in the country as well. On the gridiron the 6-foot-2, 190-pound quarterback passed for more than 3,000 yards and 26 touchdowns during his senior season, rushing for an additional 1,149 years and 15 TDs. The 2020 Oklahoma Gatorade Baseball Player of the Year committed to the University of Oklahoma as a two-sport athlete (he agreed to be a walk-on for the football team). But before his freshman baseball season could kickoff, Horton torn his UCL and missed the year rehabbing from the subsequent Tommy John surgery. Finally healthy in 2022, the hard-throwing right-hander made 14 appearances for the Sooners, 11 of which were starts, throwing 53.2 innings with 64 strikeouts and just 15 walks. He compiled a 4.86 ERA. Horton also batted .235/.323/.324 as the team's third baseman / shortstop. The Cubs took a surprising gamble on the righty in the opening round, 7th overall, and signed him to a deal worth $4.45 million, saving the club more than a million dollars – most of which went to their second pick (Jackson Ferris).

Scouting Report: My pre-draft write-up:

> *"Consider the following:*
>
> *Since 2015, only five Big 12 pitchers averaged between 10.25 and 11.5 K/9 and between 2.25 and 2.75 BB/9 in a season (min. 50 IP): Jordan Wicks, Jake Irvin, Micah Dallas, Kyle Tyler, and Cade Horton.*
>
> *Horton's season ended on a bittersweet note as he struck out 13 batters, a College World Series final record, in a loss to Ole Miss. Filthy arsenal highlighted by a mid- to upper-90s fastball and an 86- to 90-mph wicked slider, with the latter being his best pitch – a plus, plus offering. Horton will mix in a decent, reluctant changeup. He also did away with his curveball at some part in the latter half of the college season as well. The lack of a consistent third option and the recent Tommy John surgery are the only things keeping him away from being the first pitcher chosen in the 2022 draft. ELECTRIC."*

Ceiling: 4.0-win player
Risk: High
MLB ETA: 2025

Chicago Cubs

7. Owen Caissie, LF/RF

Hit	Power	SB	Patience	Glove	Overall
45	40/60	40/30	55	50	55

Born: 07/08/02	Age: 20	Bats: L	Top Production Comp: N/A
Height: 6-4	Weight: 190	Throws: R	

Season	Team	Age	Level	PA	1B	2B	3B	HR	SB	CS	BB%	K%	AVG	OBP	SLG	ISO
2021	CHC	18	CPX	136	24	7	1	6	1	2	19.12%	28.68%	0.349	0.478	0.596	0.248
2021	CHC	18	A	90	12	4	0	1	0	0	17.78%	31.11%	0.233	0.367	0.329	0.096
2022	CHC	19	A+	433	63	21	1	11	11	6	11.55%	28.64%	0.254	0.349	0.402	0.148

Background: Before the front office held their midseason Fire Sale in 2021, which featured the departures of the core of the club's 2016 World Series title (Anthony Rizzo, Javier Baez, and Kris Bryant), Chicago lit the tinder box with the Yu Darvish deal with San Diego in December of 2020. The North Siders packaged Darvish and Victor Caratini for veteran hurler Zach Davies, Ismael Mena, Reginald Preciado, Yeison Santana, and Owen Caissie. Drafted in the second round out of Burlington, Ontario-based Notre Dame High School, Caissie would make his professional debut in the Cubs' organization two years ago. He would split the year between the Complex League and Low-A, hitting a rock solid .302/.434/.489 between both stops, though the majority of the damage was done in the rookie league. Despite his lackluster showing in 22 games with Myrtle Beach in 2021, the front office aggressively shoved the 6-foot-4, 190-pound corner outfielder straight up to High-A. And Caissie acquitted himself nicely. Appearing in 105 games with the South Bend Cubs, he slugged .254/.349/.402 with 21 doubles, one triple, 11 homeruns, and 11 stolen bases (in 17 attempts). Per *Weighted Runs Created Plus*, his overall production surpassed the league average threshold by 13%. He also appeared in 16 games with the Mesa Solar Sox in the Arizona Fall League as well, batting .220/.270/.356 with five doubles and a dinger in 63 plate appearances.

Snippet from The 2022 Prospect Digest Handbook: Physically he reminds of a young Joey Gallo or Jason Botts. Big. Strong. Muscular. Caissie, like those counterparts, doesn't get cheated at the plate, never taking anything less than a massive hack. There's the potential to develop plus power, as well as turn into a Three True Outcomes-type hitter. He's the type of left-hander hitter that may show some platoon splits and eventually push him into platoon role.

Scouting Report: Consider the following:

> Since 2006, here's the list of 19-year-old hitters that posted a wRC+ total between 108 to 118 in any High-A league (min. 350 PA): Rafael Devers, Starlin Castro, Dylan Carlson, Orlando Arcia, Cristian Pache, Matt Dominguez, Daniel Fields, and Owen Caissie. Now the bad news: only two of those aforementioned hitters whiffed in more than 27% of their plate appearances – Daniel Fields and Owen Caissie.

Equipped with some of the best bat speed in the minor leagues, Caissie uncorks a vicious left-handed swing that projects – at least – 30 homeruns at maturity. The former second round will draw his fair share of walks, but it's going to come down to his ability to make consistent contact – he posted a whiff rate of nearly 29% in 2022. He's just scratching the surface of his prodigious power. The hulking 6-foot-4, 190-pounder is surprisingly nimble on the base paths and in the field, where he'll be no worse than an average defender.

Ceiling: 3.0- to 3.5-win player
Risk: Moderate to High
MLB ETA: 2024

8. Brennen Davis, OF

Hit	Power	SB	Patience	Glove	Overall
45	50/60	40	55	50	55

Born: 11/02/99	Age: 23	Bats: R	Top Production Comp: Cedric Mullins
Height: 6-4	Weight: 210	Throws: R	

Season	Team	Age	Level	PA	1B	2B	3B	HR	SB	CS	BB%	K%	AVG	OBP	SLG	ISO
2021	CHC	21	A+	32	5	2	0	2	2	0	9.38%	18.75%	0.321	0.406	0.607	0.286
2021	CHC	21	AA	316	34	20	0	13	6	4	11.39%	30.70%	0.252	0.367	0.474	0.222
2021	CHC	21	AAA	68	8	3	0	4	0	0	16.18%	22.06%	0.268	0.397	0.536	0.268
2022	CHC	22	AAA	174	17	6	0	4	0	1	13.22%	29.89%	0.191	0.322	0.319	0.128

Background: Everything came up aces for the former 2018 second round pick in 2021. Davis, who showed some offensive promise during his 50-game stint in Low-A in 2019, rocketed through three levels during his breakout two years ago, slugging .260/.375/.494 with 25 doubles, 19 homeruns, and eight stolen bases in 100 games of work split between South Bend, Tennessee, and Iowa. He was viewed as the face of the organization's rebuild, a potential above-average regular with plenty of tools that could lead the Cubs back to relevance. But everything that went well for Davis in 2021 went wrong last season. The front office sent the promising outfielder back to Iowa for additional seasoning. Davis started the year off frigid, going 0-for-10 across his first four games and batting a lowly .195/.286/.299 across his first 22 contests. He hit the disabled list in early May and eventually underwent a surgical procedure on his back that removed a "vascular formation that was impacting nerves and causing pain in his legs", according to report by Sahadev Sharma on *The Athletic*. Davis eventually made it back

Chicago Cubs

to Triple-A in late-August but continued to struggle at the plate. The franchise sent the former second rounder to the Arizona Fall League where his bat showed a heartbeat in five games with the Mesa Solar Sox, batting .278/.381/.667.

Snippet from The 2022 Prospect Digest Handbook: Blossoming power that could peak in the 30-homer territory.

Scouting Report: It was – in every sense of the word – a lost season for Davis. Nothing good came from it. And it remains to be seen as to how his nerve issue will impact him moving forward. The hit tool may never creep into average territory, and he's still learning how to fully tap into his plus-power potential. Davis has spent time in left and centerfields, but he's destined for the former. He's still a risky bet. And that's before considering he's reached 100 games just once in his career. He could very well end up as a fourth or fifth outfielder.

Ceiling: 3.0-win player
Risk: Moderate to High
MLB ETA: 2023

9. Ben Brown, RHP

FB	CB	SL	Command	Overall
60	50	55	55	50

Born: 09/09/99	Age: 23	Bats: R	Top Production Comp: Tyson Ross
Height: 6-6	Weight: 210	Throws: R	

Season	Team	Age	Level	IP	TBF	K/9	K%	BB/9	BB%	K-BB%	ERA	FIP	xFIP	Pit/Bat
2021	PHI	21	A+	12.0	54	10.50	25.93%	5.25	12.96%	12.96%	7.50	5.60	4.97	4.13
2022	PHI	22	A+	73.0	297	12.95	35.35%	2.84	7.74%	27.61%	3.08	3.14	3.13	3.94
2022	CHC	22	AA	31.0	137	12.77	32.12%	3.77	9.49%	22.63%	4.06	3.36	3.28	3.30

Background: Five years after originally trading for righty David Robertson near the deadline, the Phillies once again set their sights on the veteran reliever midway through the 2022 season. The price: former 33rd round pick Ben Brown. A product of Ward Melville High School, located in Setauket, New York, Brown lost a couple seasons of precious development time. First Tommy John surgery knocked him out of commission for the 2019 season then the pandemic kept him away from an affiliated mound the entire 2020 season. Then he would miss all but seven games in 2021. Finally healthy last season, the 6-foot-6, 210-pound right-hander quickly made up for lost time as he tossed 104.0 innings between the Phillies' High-A and Cubs' Double-A affiliates. He averaged an impressive 12.9 strikeouts and 3.1 walks per nine innings. He finished the year with an aggregate 3.37 ERA and a 3.20 FIP.

Scouting Report: Consider the following:

> Since 2006, only three 22-year-old hurlers posted a strikeout rate between 34.5% to 36.5% strikeout percentage in any High-A league (min. 70 IP): Dean Kremer, Nick Nastrini, and – of course – Ben Brown.

Brown owns the rare distinction, at least among viable starting pitching prospects, to not throw a changeup *or* split-change / splitter. Instead, the former late round flier features a fastball / slider / curveball combo. Easy, easy plus velocity on the explosive, late-lifed heater. His slider will flash plus on occasion, though it's rare. And he'll also throw a spike / knuckle-curveball as well. Brown commands the zone surprisingly well considering his lack of mound-time between 2019 and 2021 (he tossed just 29.2 affiliated innings). There's backend starting potential here with the floor of a seventh or eighth inning guy. In terms of ceiling, think: 9 K/9 and 3.2 BB/9 – if everything breaks the right way. The 2023 season will go a long way towards proving (A) he can stay healthy and (B) he can repeat his level of dominance.

Ceiling: 2.5-win player
Risk: Moderate
MLB ETA: 2023

10. Alexander Canario, OF

Hit	Power	SB	Patience	Glove	Overall
40/45	60	60	50	55	50

Born: 05/07/00	Age: 23	Bats: R	Top Production Comp: Michael Saunders
Height: 6-1	Weight: 165	Throws: R	

Season	Team	Age	Level	PA	1B	2B	3B	HR	SB	CS	BB%	K%	AVG	OBP	SLG	ISO
2021	SFG	21	A	274	30	14	3	9	15	3	12.04%	28.83%	0.235	0.325	0.433	0.197
2021	CHC	21	A+	182	22	6	1	9	6	5	5.49%	25.27%	0.224	0.264	0.429	0.206
2022	CHC	22	A+	100	12	6	0	7	3	0	10.00%	35.00%	0.281	0.360	0.584	0.303
2022	CHC	22	AA	350	33	18	2	24	17	3	10.29%	26.00%	0.248	0.329	0.552	0.303

Background: You've likely heard this before – at least a few times – but the Cubs acquired the promising, toolsy outfielder as part of their midseason fire sale two years ago. Chicago shipped off fan favorite Kris Bryant to the Giants of San Francisco for right-hander Caleb Kilian and Alexander Canario, the key to the deal. Signed out of Monte Cristi, Dominican Republic during the summer of 2016, Canario rocketed up

Chicago Cubs

prospect lists after a phenomenal showing in the old Northwest League in 2019 as he slugged .301/.365/.539 as a 19-year-old. But his prospect status took a significant hit during the 2021 season as he batted a lowly .230/.300/.431 between both organizations. Last season though, the 6-foot-1, 165-pound outfielder reemerged as an intriguing weapon. Splitting time between the club's High-A, Double-A, and Triple-A affiliates, Canario slugged .252/.343/.556 with career highs in doubles (26), homeruns (37), and stolen bases (23). Per *Weighted Runs Created Plus*, his overall production topped the league average mark by an impressive 33%.

Snippet from The 2022 Prospect Digest Handbook: The batted ball data is very good – his peak exit velocity was 109 mph – and the glove can play at any position in the outfield. The question is whether he's going to put it all together, have a season where it "clicks". He's shown glimpses of it. High risk / high reward lottery ticket.

Scouting Report: Consider the following:

> Since 2006, only three 22-year-old hitters met the following criteria in a Double-A season (min. 300 PA): 120 to 130 wRC+, a double-digit walk rate, and a 25% to 27% strikeout rate. Those three hitters: Isan Diaz, Troy Stokes, and Alexander Canario.

While the Tennessee Smokies' home ballpark will boost homeruns, Canario's prodigious homerun pace with the club's Double-A affiliate was more than just a favorable environment. He slugged 24 dingers in only 81 games (as well as 18 doubles and a pair of triples). However, the toolsy power-hitting outfielder, who can aptly handle all three outfield positions, still has some swing-and-miss issues to his game. Easy plus power. Solid patience at the plate. Great bat speed. Above-average glove and speed. It's going to come down to his hit tool. It's currently a 45-grade weapon, but if it jumps up to average he has the tools to be a franchise cornerstone. Currently tracking like a .250/.300/.500 hitter.

Ceiling: 2.5-win player
Risk: Moderate
MLB ETA: 2023/2024

11. Jackson Ferris, LHP

FB	CB	SL	CH	Command	Overall
60	60	50/55	55	50	50

Born: 01/15/04	Age: 19	Bats: L	Top Production Comp: N/A
Height: 6-4	Weight: 195	Throws: L	

Background: Following the trend of recent years, Florida-based IMG Academy didn't just boast one, but *two* potential first rounders heading into the 2022 MLB Draft. And that doesn't even include catcher Brady Neal. Overshadowed by tools-laden outfield Elijah Green, Jackson Ferris, nonetheless, might end up being the best prospect to graduate from the school's baseball program in 2022. Ferris, a lanky, projectable, 6-foot-4, 195-pound southpaw, turned a lot of heads during his phenomenal junior campaign. The Ole' Miss commit tossed 50.2 innings, recording 86 punch outs and just 13 free passes to go with a sparkling 0.55 ERA. But crowning achievement during his first year at IMG – he transferred following his sophomore season – was a dominant showing against Andrew Painter's Calvary Christian squad in which he tossed a one-hitter with 10 punch outs against the eventual 13th overall pick. It was Painter's only loss that year. And he picked up right where he left off in 2022. In one of his first starts of the year Ferris tossed another one-hit shutout and struck out 17 against George Jenkins. He would finish the year with another stellar stat line: 54.1 innings, 103 strikeouts, 16 walks, and a 1.03 ERA. He would go a perfect 16-0 during his two-year stint with IMG Academy. Chicago drafted Ferris in the second round, 47th overall, and signed him to an above-slot bonus worth a smidgeon over $3 million.

Scouting Report: My pre-draft write-up:

> "Polished beyond his years. Removing any injury risk from the equation, Ferris might be the safest prep arm to gamble on in the 2022 draft. Fluid mechanics that don't require a tremendous amount of effort. Quality strike-thrower – at times. Hides the ball well. And he throws three quality offerings, highlighted by a mid-90s fastball. He'll complement the plus-pitch with a dynamite upper-70s curveball and an above-average upper-80s changeup. He also showed a solid slider during the 2021 season. His poise and deep arsenal make him a potential quick-riser once he enters the minor leagues – if he can find a touch more consistency with the strike zone. Ferris doesn't have an elite ceiling, but he has the potential to be a quality mid-rotation caliber arm. There's some Max Fried-type potential. Mid-first round grade."

Ceiling: 2.5-win player
Risk: Moderate
MLB ETA: 2025/2026

Chicago Cubs

12. Matt Mervis, 1B

Hit	Power	SB	Patience	Glove	Overall
45	60	30	50	50	50

Born: 04/16/98	Age: 25	Bats: L	Top Production Comp: Bryan LaHair
Height: 6-4	Weight: 225	Throws: R	

Season	Team	Age	Level	PA	1B	2B	3B	HR	SB	CS	BB%	K%	AVG	OBP	SLG	ISO
2021	CHC	23	A	289	29	11	1	9	6	0	12.46%	22.84%	0.204	0.309	0.367	0.163
2022	CHC	24	A+	108	19	9	0	7	0	0	4.63%	24.07%	0.350	0.389	0.650	0.300
2022	CHC	24	AA	230	30	16	1	14	2	0	8.70%	20.00%	0.300	0.370	0.596	0.296
2022	CHC	24	AAA	240	31	15	1	15	0	0	10.42%	14.58%	0.297	0.383	0.593	0.297

Background: You'd be hard-pressed to find a more interesting backstory. So let's start at the beginning: Georgetown Preparatory High School. Mervis was a two-way star for the North Bethesda-based school, garnering some national publicity via *Perfect Game* at various points in his formidable teenage years. The Nationals would draft the kid next door in the 39th round – though they failed to sign him. Mervis, instead, packed his bags and headed south to Duke University. The 6-foot-4, 225-pound corner infielder / right-handed hurler only received 12 plate appearances over his first two seasons (as compared to nearly 50-innings on the bump). But his roles were reversed during his junior season with Blue Devils as he batted a solid .274/.358/.421 with eight doubles, one triples, and six homeruns. He would make just seven relief appearances as well, posting 8-to-5 strikeout-to-walk ratio in 8.1 innings of work. Mervis spent that summer starring for the Cotuit Kettleers in the vaunted Cape Cod League, slugging .325/.418/.571 while posting a 16-to-2 strikeout-to-walk ratio as a pitcher. Back at school, the burly prospect only made two brief relief appearances and hit .304/.458/.589 before COVID prematurely ended the year. He would eventually go undrafted in the five-round draft, but the Cubs swooped in and signed him to an undrafted deal. Mervis would make his debut with Myrtle Beach two years ago, hitting a dreadful .204/.309/.367 with 11 doubles, one triple, and nine homeruns in 69 games. At that point, it would have been fair to write off Mervis. He was old, undrafted, and looked abysmal against low level arms. Then 2022 happened. Mervis shredded the High-A competition, torched the arms of Double-A, and continued to swing a big stick in Triple-A. When the dust had finally settled, the hulking first baseman mashed .309/.379/.606 with 40 doubles, two triples, 36 homeruns, and a pair of stolen bases in 137 games. His overall production, per *Weighted Runs Created Plus*, passed the league average mark by a mindboggling 56%.

Scouting Report: Consider the following:

> There were 1,031 minor league hitters that received 300 or more plate appearances last season. Matt Mervis, the former undrafted Duke University two-way player, was the 10th most productive bat. Since 2006, only three 24-year-old hitters posted a 147 to 157 wRC+ with a 9% to 12% walk rate and a 13% to 16% strikeout rate in any Triple-A league (min. 200 PA): Matt LaPorta, Ronny Cedeno, and – of course – Matt Mervis.

I'm always leery of a prospect blitzing through multiple levels with tremendous production – let along ones that basically come out of nowhere. The book on Mervis hasn't been fully explored for weaknesses yet. There wasn't enough time in High-A, Double-A, or Triple-A to figure out and exploit his weaknesses. It's a red flag for me and one that – likely – means major regression is forthcoming. And that's *before* factoring in his age: he'll play 2023 as a 25-year-old. The lefty-swinging first baseman handled lefties and righties well, possesses plus power, and a solid glove. In terms of big league ceiling, think: .250/.330/.460. Real Bryan LaHair vibes going on here.

Ceiling: 2. 0- to 2.5-win player
Risk: Moderate
MLB ETA: 2023

13. Hayden Wesneski, RHP

FB	CU	SL	CH	Command	Overall
60	50	55	50	55	50

Born: 12/05/97	Age: 25	Bats: R	Top Production Comp: Jordan Lyles
Height: 6-3	Weight: 210	Throws: R	

Season	Team	Age	Level	IP	TBF	K/9	K%	BB/9	BB%	K-BB%	ERA	FIP	xFIP	Pit/Bat
2021	NYY	23	AA	83.0	344	9.98	26.74%	2.39	6.40%	20.35%	4.01	4.00	3.79	3.74
2021	NYY	23	AAA	11.0	46	9.82	26.09%	4.09	10.87%	15.22%	3.27	2.54	3.67	3.33
2022	NYY	24	AAA	89.2	371	8.33	22.37%	2.81	7.55%	14.82%	3.51	4.03	4.74	3.84
2022	CHC	24	AAA	20.2	86	10.02	26.74%	3.48	9.30%	17.44%	5.66	3.36	3.85	3.98

Background: A year after the Cubs and Yankees got together on a blockbuster deal involving three-time All-Star first baseman Anthony Rizzo, the two teams worked out another deadline deal last summer as well. This time, though, there were far less notable players involved. Chicago sent Twinsburg, Ohio, native Scott Effross, a late blooming, reliable reliever, for older minor league sensation Hayden Wesneski. Originally drafted by Tampa Bay in the 33rd round coming out of Cy-Fair High School, Wesneski opted to attend Sam Houston State University – where he developed into a reliable, strike-throwing starting pitcher. New York selected the 6-foot-3, 210-pound right-hander in the sixth round three years ago. Wesneski made his professional debut in 2021, blitzing through the three upper levels of the minor leagues, throwing 130.1 innings with 151 strikeouts against just 36 free passes. Last season, between both organizations' Triple affiliates, Wesneski averaged 8.6 K/9 and 2.9 BB/9 across 110.1 innings of work. He made six appearances for the Cubs down the stretch, throwing another 33.0

Chicago Cubs

innings with 33 punch outs and seven walks to go along with a sparkling 2.18 ERA. For his minor league career, he is averaging 9.6 strikeouts and just 2.6 walks per nine innings.

Snippet from The 2022 Prospect Digest Handbook: An intriguing pitcher with an intriguing arsenal, but it's not really about the entire arsenal. It's about his two separate fastballs. One is a Brandon Webb-esque bowling ball of an offering with tumble and fade like a changeup. I do think he could be a valuable two-pitch reliever just using both versions of his fastball.

Scouting Report: Consider the following:

> Since 2006, only three 24-year-old hurlers posted a 22% to 24% strikeout percentage with a 7% to 9% walk percentage in any Triple-A league (min. 100 IP): Jeff Locke, a former All-Star for the Pirates, Taylor Widener, and – of course – Hayden Wesneski.

Wesneski owns one of the more remarkable, intriguing fastballs in the minor leagues. He has two distinct fastball profiles: a hard, mid-90s four-seamer with a bit of riding life and his two-seamer owns some bowling ball type movement at a tick or two lower. Above-average low 80s slider with downward bite and a darting average, upper-80s cutter. I find his changeup interesting. There's not a significant velo difference between the offering and his fastballs, but there's some tumble and "hop" to it. Chicago did well in sending a solid, yet old and replaceable middle reliever for Wesneski, who profiles as a strike-throwing, backend starting pitcher.

Ceiling: 1.5- to 2.0-win player
Risk: Low to Moderate
MLB ETA: Debuted in 2022

14. Luke Little, LHP

FB	SL	CH	Command	Overall
70	55/60	50	35/40	50

Born: 08/30/00	Age: 22	Bats: L	Top Production Comp: N/A
Height: 6-8	Weight: 220	Throws: L	

Season	Team	Age	Level	IP	TBF	K/9	K%	BB/9	BB%	K-BB%	ERA	FIP	xFIP	Pit/Bat
2021	CHC	20	CPX	11.0	50	15.55	38.00%	4.09	10.00%	28.00%	4.91	4.92	4.56	2.14
2022	CHC	21	A	52.2	235	14.35	35.74%	5.47	13.62%	22.13%	2.91	2.76	3.37	4.03
2022	CHC	21	A+	13.0	50	11.77	34.00%	4.15	12.00%	22.00%	0.69	2.71	3.52	4.36

Background: Before former Tennessee Volunteer Ben Joyce electrified the social media-sphere with his triple-digit heater, there was Luke Little. A gargantuan left-hander out of San Jacinto College, the 6-foot-8, 220-pound behemoth set the internet ablaze with his plus-plus fastball. Little spent a year at the Houston, Texas-based JuCo, throwing 35.1 innings with a diabolical 69-to-36 strikeout-to-walk ratio and a tidy, barely-there 2.04 ERA. The North Carolina-born hurler would make his affiliated debut the following year, logging just five brief appearances in the Complex League, striking out 19 and walking five in 11.0 innings of work. Last season, Little quietly turned in a solid year as he split time between Myrtle Beach and South Bend. He would toss 65.2 innings, recording a whopper of a strike out total (101) to go along with a 38 free passes. He finished the year with a 2.47 ERA and a tidy 2.75 FIP.

Scouting Report: Consider the following:

> Since 2006, only three 21-year-old hurlers posted a 34.5% to 36.5% strikeout percentage with a walk percentage of at least 12% in any Low-A league (min. 50 IP): Dylan Cease, Alberto Tirado, and – of course – Luke Little.

The ironically named giant primarily works off of a two-pitch repertoire: a plus-plus fastball with a lot of natural movement due to his low arm slot, and an above-average horizontally darting slider that may climb into plus territory as he matures. Little will mix in a rare, average changeup. There's obvious reliever risk given (A) the command issues and (B) lack of depth in his arsenal. Little has become a better strike-thrower, but he's not a consistent *quality* strike-thrower. He's still only entering his age-22 season and owns a *massive* strikeout rate in his career, so he definitely has a puncher's chance moving forward.

Ceiling: 2.0-win player
Risk: Moderate to High
MLB ETA: 2025

Chicago Cubs

15. Miguel Amaya, C

Hit	Power	SB	Patience	Glove	Overall
40	50/55	30	60	50	45

Born: 03/09/99	Age: 24	Bats: R	Top Production Comp: Alex Avila
Height: 6-2	Weight: 230	Throws: R	

Season	Team	Age	Level	PA	1B	2B	3B	HR	SB	CS	BB%	K%	AVG	OBP	SLG	ISO
2018	CHC	19	A	479	71	21	2	12	1	0	10.44%	19.00%	0.256	0.349	0.403	0.147
2019	CHC	20	A+	410	45	24	0	11	2	0	13.17%	16.83%	0.235	0.351	0.402	0.167
2021	CHC	22	AA	106	12	4	0	1	2	0	19.81%	20.75%	0.215	0.406	0.304	0.089

Background: One of the longest tenured prospects in the Handbook. It's still difficult to believe that the former Consensus Top 100 prospect is only entering his age-24 season. Signed by the organization all the way back in 2015, Amaya began to open a lot of eyes when he batted a saber-friendly .256/.349/.403 with 21 doubles, two triples, and 12 homeruns as a 19-year-old in Low-A. His batting average slumped the following year with Myrtle Beach, but the secondary skills – namely a nose for first base and promising power – were still buoying his overall production. Things completely cratered for Amaya in Double-A in 2021, though, as he batted a lowly .215/.406/.304 and he eventually hit the operating table for Tommy John surgery, knocking him out for the remainder of the year and half of 2022. Finally healthy in July last season, Amaya made a two-week jaunt through the Complex League before moving back up to Double-A – where he hit surprisingly well. In 28 games with the Smokies, he slugged .278/.379/.485 with six doubles, one triple, and four homeruns.

Snippet from The 2022 Prospect Digest Handbook: There's such a dearth of catching at the big league level that Amaya should have no problem developing into a league average or better player – depending how the BABIP bounces.

Scouting Report: As much as anyone wants to believe that Amaya's found a viable hitting tool – as evidenced by his .278 batting average – there's no reason to believe that the light's bulbs actually come on for the no longer youthful backstop. His career BABIPs have consistently been in the .260 to .280 range. Last year it was .343 with Tennessee. And there's no change in the type of batted balls either. Above-average defender, above-average walk rates and power potential. It's still going to comes down to how lucky he's going to be. Last year, he was quite lucky. I'm not a betting man, but if I was I wouldn't bet on it to happen again. Still, though, catching at the big league level is atrocious so he'll get a shot to claim a gig. Big league ceiling: .240/.340/.420.

Ceiling: 1.5-win player
Risk: Moderate
MLB ETA: 2023

16. Cristian Hernandez, SS

Hit	Power	SB	Patience	Glove	Overall
40	40/55	50	50	50	45

Born: 12/13/03	Age: 19	Bats: R	Top Production Comp: N/A
Height: 6-2	Weight: 175	Throws: R	

Season	Team	Age	Level	PA	1B	2B	3B	HR	SB	CS	BB%	K%	AVG	OBP	SLG	ISO
2021	CHC	17	DSL	191	34	5	1	5	21	3	15.71%	20.42%	0.285	0.398	0.424	0.139
2022	CHC	18	CPX	175	33	4	1	3	6	3	7.43%	30.29%	0.261	0.320	0.357	0.096

Background: One of the more hyped prospects on the international scene two years ago. Chicago signed the top prospect for a hefty $3 million deal in January of 2021. The then-17-year-old would make his professional debut with the Cubs' foreign rookie league affiliate a few months later, batting a rock solid .285/.398/.424 with 11 extra-base knocks in 47 games. Somewhere around the midway point of that year Hernandez's baseball cards became one of the hottest tickets on the market. And that momentum continued into the offseason as well. Last year the front office sent the Bonus Baby up a notch and into the Complex League. But the numbers failed to live up to the hype. Appearing in 44 games, the 6-foot-2, 175-pound shortstop batted .261/.320/.357 with four doubles, one triple, three homeruns, and six stolen bases. Per *Weighted Runs Created Plus*, his production was 12% below the league average mark.

Snippet from The 2022 Prospect Digest Handbook: A very natural feel for hitting. Hernandez is big, wiry, and projectable. And the Dominican-born shortstop already owns average power with the potential to develop plus thump at a premium position. Despite being big for his age, the soon-to-be 18-year-old is incredibly smooth at shortstop as well.

Scouting Report: Things didn't go as planned for the international amateur superstar as he struggled (A) making consistent contact and (B) driving the ball with any type of authority. There's something going on with his swing because he's consistently getting under the ball and popping it up. Doesn't matter if it's in a game or batting practice. It's still incredibly early, but it's already difficult to imagine the Cubs' $3 million investment providing any great returns at the big league level without a major overhaul on the swing.

Ceiling: 1.5-win player
Risk: Moderate
MLB ETA: 2025/2026

Chicago Cubs

17. DJ Herz, LHP

FB	CB	SL	CH	Command	Overall
55	60	50	55	30/40	50

Born: 01/04/01	Age: 22	Bats: R	Top Production Comp: Sean Newcomb
Height: 6-2	Weight: 175	Throws: L	

Season	Team	Age	Level	IP	TBF	K/9	K%	BB/9	BB%	K-BB%	ERA	FIP	xFIP	Pit/Bat
2021	CHC	20	A+	16.0	64	14.63	40.63%	3.38	9.38%	31.25%	2.81	2.65	3.07	4.00
2022	CHC	21	A+	63.2	260	13.99	38.08%	5.23	14.23%	23.85%	2.26	2.82	3.20	4.52
2022	CHC	21	AA	31.2	158	11.94	26.58%	9.38	20.89%	5.70%	8.24	6.96	6.57	4.06

Background: While the Cubs' bountiful farm system is overflowing with a multitude of high upside bats, there are a couple intriguing, potentially high-ceiling arms brewing on the farm, as well. Like DJ Herz. Taken in the eighth round out of Terry Sanford High School in 2019, the Cubbies inked the lanky left-hander to a $500,000 over-slot bonus, the largest handed out to any player taken in the round that summer. Herz opened quite a few eyes during his first full season in pro ball two years ago as he recorded an impressive 131-to-44 strikeout-to-walk ratio in only 81.2 innings of work. Last season, Herz, who made three starts with South Bend to cap off his breakout campaign, returned back to High-A for a longer look. And despite battling some control demons, the 6-foot-2, 175-pound southpaw was incredibly dominant as he fanned 99 (against 37 free passes) in 63.2 innings. The Chicago front office bumped him up the true proving ground, Double-A, in late July for nine final starts. Herz finished the year with 95.1 innings, averaging 13.3 K/9 and a whopper of a walk total – 6.6 BB/9 – to go along with an 4.25 ERA.

Snippet from The 2022 Prospect Digest Handbook: Mechanically speaking, he's a hybrid between Chris Sale / MacKenzie Gore / Josh Hader. The young lefty trusts his change-of-pace as much as any young arm I can recall. He's a crossfire thrower and that needs to be cleaned up. There's some promising mid-rotation upside here.

Scouting Report: Consider the following:

> Since 2006, only two 21-year-old hurlers posted a strikeout rate north of 36% in any High-A league (min. 60 IP): Kansas City's Will Klein, who accomplished the feat in 2021, and DJ Herz, who reached the seemingly impossible plateau last year.

Herz's mechanics continue to be a nightmare. There's not a lot of hope that he develops any type of strike-throwing consistency without some mechanical cleanup work. The arsenal, though, remains as impressive as ever: above-average fastball, plus curveball combo backed up by a very strong changeup that's borderline plus, as well as a get-me-over slider. If the command can creep up into 40-grade territory, which is *far* from a certainty, there's some Sean Newcomb / mid- to late-career Francisco Liriano upside as a starter. Obvious reliever risk.

Ceiling: 2.0-win player
Risk: High
MLB ETA: 2024

18. Moisés Ballesteros, C

Hit	Power	SB	Patience	Glove	Overall
40/45	55	30	55	40/45	45

Born: 11/08/03	Age: 19	Bats: L	Top Production Comp: N/A
Height: 5-10	Weight: 215	Throws: R	

Season	Team	Age	Level	PA	1B	2B	3B	HR	SB	CS	BB%	K%	AVG	OBP	SLG	ISO
2021	CHC	17	DSL	187	28	10	0	3	6	1	16.58%	12.83%	0.266	0.396	0.390	0.123
2022	CHC	18	CPX	110	14	5	0	7	0	0	11.82%	17.27%	0.268	0.355	0.536	0.268
2022	CHC	18	A	129	17	7	0	3	0	1	13.95%	21.71%	0.248	0.349	0.394	0.147

Background: A part of the club's international free agency bounty in 2021, Ballesteros was stuck in the looming shadow of Cristian Hernandez. But the lefty-swinging catcher, who received a hefty $1.2 million bonus, has proven to be a better performer – at least two years into their respective careers. A native of Los Teques, Venezuela, Ballesteros made his organizational debut just a few months after signing his contract. He would hit an-OBP driven .266/.396/.390 with 10 doubles and three triples. The front office pushed the 5-foot-10, 215-pound catcher stateside to the Complex League and he began to tap into his impressive power potential as he slugged .268/.355/.536 in 32 games. Ballesteros spent the last month-and-a-half with the Pelicans of Myrtle Beach in Low-A. He would finish the year with a quietly solid .257/.352/.461 slash line with 12 doubles and 10 dingers. His overall production, as measured by *Weighted Runs Created Plus*, surpassed the league average mark by a 22% last season.

Scouting Report: Defensively, he's clearly a bat-first catcher as he struggled with the finer nuances at the position, including blocking, framing, and controlling the opposition's running game. Ballesteros is very similar to Miguel Amaya at the same level:

Name	Season	Team	Age	Level	PA	AVG	OBP	SLG	ISO	BB%	K%
Miguel Amaya	2018	CHC	19	A	479	0.256	0.349	0.403	0.147	10.44%	19.00%
Moises Ballesteros	2022	CHC	18	A	129	0.248	0.349	0.394	0.147	13.95%	21.71%

Chicago Cubs

Soft body lefty-swinging backstop owns plus raw power, which started to show up in games in Complex League and Low-A. His swing is a bit long and the hit tool doesn't project that well. Patient approach at the plate. He profiles as a low average, high OBP hitter with 15 to 20 homeruns in a full season. The defense may be the only thing that alters his rise to a solid lower-tier big league catcher.

Ceiling: 1.5-win player
Risk: Moderate
MLB ETA: 2024

19. Caleb Kilian, RHP

FB	CB	CU	CH	Command	Overall
55	55	50	N/A	40/45	40

Born: 06/02/97	Age: 26	Bats: R	Top Production Comp: Kendall Graveman
Height: 6-4	Weight: 180	Throws: R	

Season	Team	Age	Level	IP	TBF	K/9	K%	BB/9	BB%	K-BB%	ERA	FIP	xFIP	Pit/Bat
2021	SFG	24	A+	21.2	75	13.29	42.67%	0.42	1.33%	41.33%	1.25	1.16	2.18	3.84
2021	CHC	24	AA	15.2	64	9.19	25.00%	2.30	6.25%	18.75%	4.02	4.61	4.09	3.39
2021	SFG	24	AA	63.0	244	9.14	26.23%	1.14	3.28%	22.95%	2.43	2.37	3.13	3.61
2022	CHC	25	AAA	106.2	478	10.55	26.15%	4.98	12.34%	13.81%	4.22	3.76	4.15	4.05

Background: The 8th round of the 2019 draft is proving to be quite the fertile farmland for the Cubs. The front office selected prep southpaw DJ Herz and signed him to the round's largest bonus, $500,000. Sixteen picks earlier, though, the Giants grabbed Texas Tech University right-hander Caleb Killian, signing him to the fourth largest bonus in the round ($397,500). Just a little over two years later Chicago would acquire Kilian, along with outfielder Alexander Canario, as part of the Great Selloff. Kilian rocketed through his stints in High-A and Double-A in 2021, averaging 10.0 strikeouts and just 1.2 walks per nine innings cross 19 starts between both organizations. Last season, his first full one in the Cubs' organization, the 6-foot-4, 180-pound righty made 26 starts with Iowa, throwing 106.2 innings, 125 punch outs, and 59 walks. He finished the minor league season with a 4.22 ERA, 3.76 FIP, and a 4.15 xFIP. He also squeezed three big league starts in midway through the year, throwing 11.1 innings with nine strikeouts, 12 walks, and a bloated 10.32 ERA while going 0-2.

Snippet from The 2022 Prospect Digest Handbook: Kilian lacks a sit-'em-down type of secondary offering, but his strong feel for the strike zone helps compensate. These types of guys typically make successful relief arms, some graduating to high leverage outings, but it's not a strong profile for a starting pitcher. The Cubs are in full rebuild mode, so Kilian's likely to get a few opportunities to prove himself as a grab-the-ball-every-fifth-day type.

Scouting Report: Consider the following:

> Since 2006, six 25-year-old hurlers posted a 25% to 27% strikeout percentage with a double-digit walk percentage in any Triple-A league (min. 100 IP): Ethan Small, Ariel Pena, Pedro Avila, Deunte Heath, Enmanuel De Jesus, and – of course – Caleb Kilian.

From a fast-rising, strike-throwing machine to a dull, strike zone avoidance bore. Life came at Kilian fast last season and it left the former mid-round pick's head spinning. The big difference for Kilian last season was his lack of command. And when it comes to the upper minors and lacking a true out pitch, it's pretty pertinent that you can put them where you want them. Kilian didn't do that. His fastball hovers in the 93- to 94-mph range and will touch a couple ticks higher on occasion. It's an above-average offering. The curveball can be a beauty at times, but it's inconsistent. The cutter is average. He used to mix in a changeup, but seems to have completely scrapped it all together. He's now entering his age-26 season, coming off of a year plagued with command woes, so the ceiling is pretty limited. Just like his scouting report listed in last year's Handbook noted.

Ceiling: 1.0-win player
Risk: Low to Moderate
MLB ETA: Debuted in 2022

20. Pedro Ramírez, 2B/3B

Hit	Power	SB	Patience	Glove	Overall
50/55	35/40	40	50	50	40

Born: 04/01/04	Age: 19	Bats: B	Top Production Comp: N/A
Height: 5-9	Weight: 165	Throws: R	

Season	Team	Age	Level	PA	1B	2B	3B	HR	SB	CS	BB%	K%	AVG	OBP	SLG	ISO
2021	CHC	17	DSL	216	51	11	7	1	9	7	6.02%	9.26%	0.359	0.417	0.503	0.144
2022	CHC	18	CPX	163	30	9	5	4	11	4	10.43%	15.95%	0.329	0.399	0.541	0.212
2022	CHC	18	A	46	11	0	0	0	4	0	4.35%	13.04%	0.268	0.348	0.268	0.000

Background: Signed out of Temblador, Venezuela, in January of 2021. Ramirez, a pint-sized switch-hitting infielder, was an offensive dynamo during his debut in the Dominican Summer League two years ago, slugging a scorching .359/.417/.503 with 11

Chicago Cubs

doubles, three triples, one dinger, and nine stolen bases (in 16 attempts). Per *Weighted Runs Created Plus*, his overall production topped the league average mark by a whopping 55%. The organization's player development regime pushed the 5-foot-9, 165-pound second / third baseman to the Complex League at the start of 2022. And he continued to mash. Appearing in 43 games last season in the lowest stateside league, Ramírez bashed .329/.399/.541 with nine doubles, five triples, four homeruns, and 11 homeruns. His production surpassed the league average mark by 53%. Chicago bumped the baby basher up to Low-A for his final 10 games (.268/.348/.268).

Scouting Report: Consider the following:

> Since 2021, only three 18-year-old prospect posted a wRC+ mark of 150 or greater in the Complex / stateside rookie league (min. 150 PA): Juan Alonso (Los Angeles Dodgers), Carlos Jorge (Cincinnati), and – of course – Pedro Ramírez. All of whom accomplished the feat last season.

More of a hit tool over power guy, despite some impressive extra-base numbers over his first two seasons. Ramírez isn't an extreme contact hitter but he's not that far from one either. The young switch-hitter shows a slashing, inside-out swing from the left side of the batter's box. He's not likely to grow into much homerun power at full maturity. Solid glove at second; the bat doesn't profile as well at the hot corner. He's tracking like a utility guy.

Ceiling: 1.0-win player
Risk: Moderate
MLB ETA: 2025

Chicago White Sox

Top Prospects

Chicago White Sox

1. Colson Montgomery, SS

Hit	Power	SB	Patience	Glove	Overall
50	55	30	55	55	60

Born: 02/27/02	Age: 21	Bats: L	Top Production Comp: Dansby Swanson
Height: 6-4	Weight: 205	Throws: R	

Season	Team	Age	Level	PA	1B	2B	3B	HR	SB	CS	BB%	K%	AVG	OBP	SLG	ISO
2021	CHW	19	CPX	111	20	7	0	0	0	1	11.71%	19.82%	0.287	0.396	0.362	0.074
2022	CHW	20	A	205	38	12	1	4	0	1	12.68%	20.49%	0.324	0.424	0.476	0.153
2022	CHW	20	A+	164	24	4	1	5	1	0	15.85%	15.85%	0.258	0.387	0.417	0.159
2022	CHW	20	AA	52	4	1	0	2	0	0	3.85%	28.85%	0.146	0.192	0.292	0.146

Background: When the lefty-swinging shortstop was selected in the opening round two years ago it snapped a nine-year streak of the organization taking college or JuCo prospects in the first round. Before that the last high schooler to join the franchise as a first round pick was toolsy, albeit flawed, outfielder Courtney Hawkins – the 13th overall pick in 2012. Montgomery, a 6-foot-4, 205-pound shortstop, turned in a solid, sometimes impressive debut in the Complex League during his debut in 2021, hitting .287/.396/.362 while showing an advanced approach at the plate. And it proved to just be a harbinger of things to come in 2022. Beginning the year with the Kannapolis Cannon Ballers in the Carolina League (A-ball), Montgomery made quick work of the older competition, posting a scorching .324/.424/.477 slash line through 45 contests. The front office bumped their top prospect up to Winston-Salem (High-A) for another 37 games and he capped off a wildly successful first full season with a 14-game cameo in the minors' toughest level – Double-A. When the dust had finally cleared the Southridge High School product owned a .274/.381/.429 slash line with 17 doubles, two triples, 11 homeruns, and one stolen base – just for good measure. Per *Weighted Runs Created Plus*, his overall production topped the league average threshold by 25%.

Snippet from The 2022 Prospect Digest Handbook: Montgomery is surprisingly fluid in the field, showing some hands a strong arm to make difficult throws look easy. The swing is controlled violence, though it tends to get a little long at times. There's 25-homerun power lurking in the bat. He consistently saw a bevy of offspeed pitches during the showcases and showed no discernible red flags.

Scouting Report: Arguably the deepest everyday position among any Top 100 list, Montgomery's seemingly – almost frustratingly so – overlooked among his peers. But the lefty-swinging infielder showcased a little bit of everything during his phenomenal campaign in 2022 – despite playing against significantly older competition, including a 50-game on-base streak that extended through mid-July. With a swing reminiscent of a young Corey Seager, Montgomery showcases an average hit tool with matching contact rates and 50-grade power. The lone red flag: a slight, *slight* platoon split against lefties that which is hardly concerning. In terms of big league ceiling, think: .270/.340/.460.

Ceiling: 4.0-win player
Risk: Moderate
MLB ETA: 2023

2. Oscar Colás, CF/RF

Hit	Power	SB	Patience	Glove	Overall
50	60	30	45	50	55

Born: 09/17/98	Age: 24	Bats: L	Top Production Comp: Teoscar Hernandez
Height: 6-1	Weight: 220	Throws: L	

Season	Team	Age	Level	PA	1B	2B	3B	HR	SB	CS	BB%	K%	AVG	OBP	SLG	ISO
2022	CHW	23	A+	268	53	13	3	7	1	1	8.21%	20.15%	0.311	0.369	0.475	0.164
2022	CHW	23	AA	225	39	9	1	14	1	2	6.22%	24.00%	0.306	0.364	0.563	0.257
2022	CHW	23	AAA	33	8	2	0	2	1	1	6.06%	36.36%	0.387	0.424	0.645	0.258

Background: There are very few organizations, if any, that have had deeper roots to Cuban baseball than the White Sox. Cuban-born players to don the club's uniform include: Hall of Famer Minnie Minoso, Jose Abreu, Yoan Moncada, Luis Robert, Yasmani Grandal, Jose Contreras, Alexei Ramirez, Orlando Hernandez, Dayán Viciedo, Yolbert Sanchez, Norge Vera, Bryan Ramos, and Yoelqui Céspedes. The club's latest high profile import: first baseman / outfielder Oscar Colas, who took an interesting path to stateside ball. Born in La Habana, Cuba, Colas turned some heads as a 17-year-old mashing through the Cuban National Series in 2016-17, hitting .279/.370/.494 with nine extra-base hits in 23 games with the Avispas de Santiago de Cuba. After the year the government sent Colás, as well as lefty Liván Moinelo, to the Fukuoka SoftBank Hawks as part of a player development program. Colás would spend the next couple of years bouncing between both countries. In late January last season the Sox signed Colás to a deal worth $2.7 million after defecting from his home country. The then-23-year-old outfielder made up for any lost time during his stateside debut last season, splitting time between High-A, Double-A, and Triple-A as he slugged an aggregate .314/.371/.524 with 24 doubles, four triples, 23 homeruns, and a trio of stolen bases. Per *FanGraphs' Weighted Runs Created Plus*, his overall production topped the league average mark by 37%.

Chicago White Sox

Scouting Report: With regard to his production in Double-A, consider the following:

> Since 2006, only five 23-year-old hitters met the following criteria in a season (min. 200 PA): 135 to 145 wRC+, a 5% to 7% walk rate, and a strikeout rate of at least 20%. Those five hitters: Edwin Rios, Patrick Leonard, Jordan Patterson, Luis Barrera, and – of course – Oscar Colás.

A member of the 2022 Futures Game roster, Colas owns prodigious in-game and raw power. Broad shoulders wide enough to support a bridge, the Cuban outfielder handled lefties and righties equally well – though he did look uncomfortable against breaking balls from southpaws at times. He's currently splitting time between rightfield and centerfield – though his lumbering speed will keep him in a corner spot at the big league level. There's definitely going to be some swing-and-miss to his game and his walk rates will be subpar because he swings at everything, but there's legitimate big league middle of the lineup production brewing in his bat. Big league ceiling: .265/.325/.500.

Ceiling: 3.0-win player
Risk: Moderate
MLB ETA: 2023

3. Bryan Ramos, 3B

Hit	Power	SB	Patience	Glove	Overall
40/45	60	30	50	55	55

Born: 03/12/02 **Age:** 21 **Bats:** R **Top Production Comp:** Ryan McMahon
Height: 6-2 **Weight:** 225 **Throws:** R

Season	Team	Age	Level	PA	1B	2B	3B	HR	SB	CS	BB%	K%	AVG	OBP	SLG	ISO
2019	CHW	17	R	218	36	10	2	4	3	4	8.72%	20.18%	0.277	0.353	0.415	0.138
2021	CHW	19	A	504	63	23	6	13	13	4	10.12%	21.83%	0.244	0.345	0.415	0.172
2022	CHW	20	A+	433	69	16	1	19	1	0	9.24%	16.40%	0.275	0.350	0.471	0.196
2022	CHW	20	AA	86	12	3	0	3	0	1	5.81%	17.44%	0.225	0.279	0.375	0.150

Background: One of the club's larger acquisitions on the international market during the 2018 season. Ramos made his presence known in the Complex League during his debut – as a 17-year-old – a season later with a .277/.353/.415 slash line. After returning from the lost 2020 COVID season, the Cuban-born infielder spent the 2021 campaign with the Kannapolis Cannon Ballers in the Low-A East League with solid production for a teenager. He hit .244/.345/.415 with 23 doubles, six triples, 13 homeruns, and 13 stolen bases in 115 games. Last season the 6-foot-2, 225-pound third baseman mashed his way through 99 games in the South Atlantic League and spent the final few weeks in Birmingham in Double-A, the most challenging level for a prospect – at the ripe ol' age of 20. In total, Ramos batted .266/.338/.455 with 19 doubles, one triple, and a career best 22 dingers in 120 games. His overall production, as measured by *FanGraphs' Weighted Runs Created Plus*, topped the league average mark by 14%.

Snippet from The 2020 Prospect Digest Handbook: One of the highest ceilings in Chicago's farm system. Ramos, unlike a lot of the club's other better minor league at bats, takes a well-rounded approach to the plate: strong contact skills, above-average patience, average power with the potential to be above-average, and a smattering of speed. Throw in a solid glove at second or third bases, and Ramos could blossom into a Top 100 prospect. There's a lot of boom-bust potential here, but I'm betting bat speed and power potential.

Scouting Report: Consider the following:

> Since 2006, only four 20-year-old hitters met the following criteria in a High-A season (min. 400 PA): 117 to 127 wRC+, a 14% to 18% strikeout rate, and an 8% to 10% walk rate. Those four hitters: Ramon Flores, Alen Hanson, Blake DeWitt, and – of course – Bryan Ramos. Flores, Hanson, and DeWitt all logged parts of several seasons in the big leagues during their career.

Ramos added considerable bulk to his once wiry frame, now tipping the scales at 225 pounds, 30 pounds heavier than previously listed. So it's not surprising that the young infielder (A) who split the 2021 season between second and third bases has shifted over to the hot corner fully in 2022 and (B) saw a drastic decline in the stolen base and triples departments as well. Defensively, Ramos has the makings of an above-average – perhaps even borderline Gold Glove – third baseman. Offensively, the big swinging Cuban combines plus power potential and strong contact rates, a common trait among the club's better hitting prospects. Easy power to all fields. Ramos, with a simple flick of the wrist, took a Peter Van Loon offering to the opposite field for a dinger in late June. I'm not entirely sold on the bat completely, but the other tools all suggest a league average starter – bare minimum. Big League Ceiling: .250/.330/.440.

Ceiling: 3.0-win player
Risk: Moderate
MLB ETA: 2023

Chicago White Sox

4. Noah Schultz, LHP

FB	SL	CH	Command	Overall
60	55	50	50	55

Born: 08/05/03	Age: 19	Bats: L
Height: 6-9	Weight: 220	Throws: L

Top Production Comp: N/A

Background: Built like an All-NBA small forward, the 6-foot-9, 220-pound southpaw wasn't always destined to tower over his peers – or anyone else for that matter. The once-diminutive 8th grader grew six inches during the summer heading into his freshman season at Oswego East High School. And the Illinois native shot up another six inches just a few months later, taking his subpar velocity into premium, high octane territory. After a dominating junior campaign for the Wolves, Schultz would miss nearly his entire senior season as he dealt with a bout of mononucleosis. Chicago drafted the behemoth left-hander in the opening round of the 2022 draft, 26th overall, and signed him to a deal worth a hefty $2.8 million. Prior to joining the White Sox organization Schultz was committed to Vanderbilt University – a.k.a. Pitcher University.

Scouting Report: Lefties with premium velocity are typically worth their weight in gold, so it's not surprising to see the White Sox take a gamble on Schultz near the end of the opening round. And Schultz's velocity, which will top out in the upper 90s, plays up even further thanks to his enormous wingspan. The big southpaw complements the plus-plus fastball with a plus slider with hard, sharp horizontal bite. He'll also mix in a firm, average-ish changeup. He throws a surprising amount of strikes, especially considering his age and size, and he tends to hide the ball fairly well. Chicago hasn't done well drafting and developing pitchers, but Schultz has a chance to be very good.

Ceiling: 3.0-win player
Risk: Moderate to High
MLB ETA: 2026

5. Christian Mena, RHP

FB	CB	SL	CH	Command	Overall
50/55	60	50/60	N/A	40/50	50

Born: 12/21/02	Age: 20	Bats: R
Height: 6-2	Weight: 200	Throws: R

Top Production Comp: Reynaldo Lopez

Season	Team	Age	Level	IP	TBF	K/9	K%	BB/9	BB%	K-BB%	ERA	FIP	xFIP	Pit/Bat
2021	CHW	18	CPX	48.1	230	11.54	26.96%	3.91	9.13%	17.83%	7.82	5.42	4.46	1.96
2022	CHW	19	A	53.2	215	11.07	30.70%	2.52	6.98%	23.72%	2.68	2.77	3.30	3.68
2022	CHW	19	A+	40.2	179	10.40	26.26%	4.87	12.29%	13.97%	4.65	4.25	4.39	3.81
2022	CHW	19	AA	10.0	45	11.70	28.89%	0.90	2.22%	26.67%	6.30	2.58	3.51	3.33

Background: As noted by a bevy of reports on MLB.com, the organization made their largest pitching investment with Mena during the 2019 signing period. Three years later, that $250,000 bonus is proving to be quite a bargain. Mena made his professional debut two years ago in a largely successful campaign in the Complex League – despite what his 7.82 ERA would lead you to believe. The then-18-year-old hurler posted a dominating 62-to-21 strikeout-to-walk ratio in only 48.1 innings of work. Last season Mena started out in impressive fashion in the Low-A, averaging 11.1 strikeouts and just 2.5 walks per nine innings across 11 starts, then he held his own in 10 starts in the South Atlantic League (10.4 K/9 and 4.9 BB/9). He capped off the year with a three-game cameo with Birmingham in the Southern League. In total, Mena tossed 104.1 innings of work with 126 strikeouts and 38 walks per nine innings to go along with a 3.80 ERA.

Scouting Report: One of the most unheralded pitching prospects in the game – at least temporarily. Mena has everything you look for in a young arm: size (6-foot-2 and 200 pounds), athleticism, reasonable feel for the strike zone, at least one quality offspeed pitch (and in this instance two potentially plus breaking balls), and production against older competition. Mena's fastball will sit in the low 90s but has some giddy up high in the zone. Prior to the year his trademark offering was a hellacious 12-6 curveball, but the young Dominican hurler added a slider with late, hard bite – though it lacks consistency at this point. He'll mix in a below average / fringy changeup. He definitely seems to favor his newly found slider. Chicago hasn't been overly successful in developing young arms, particularly starting pitchers so Mena – who has all the ingredients for a Top 100 pitching prospect – will prove to be a solid litmus test. Mena has the potential to develop into a mid-rotation caliber arm, maybe more if his fastball adds a couple ticks.

Ceiling: 2.5-win player
Risk: Moderate
MLB ETA: 2023

Chicago White Sox

6. Wilfred Veras, 1B/3B

	Hit	Power	SB	Patience	Glove	Overall
	40/50	50/60	35/30	50	50	50

Born: 11/15/02	Age: 20	Bats: R	Top Production Comp: Jhonkensy Noel
Height: 6-2	Weight: 180	Throws: R	

Season	Team	Age	Level	PA	1B	2B	3B	HR	SB	CS	BB%	K%	AVG	OBP	SLG	ISO
2021	CHW	18	CPX	178	27	16	2	4	3	1	11.80%	23.60%	0.322	0.416	0.533	0.211
2022	CHW	19	A	433	67	19	2	17	5	0	6.24%	27.25%	0.266	0.319	0.454	0.188
2022	CHW	19	AA	48	6	3	0	3	0	0	6.25%	29.17%	0.267	0.313	0.533	0.267

Background: As pointed out as part of his report on MLB.com, Veras has some rather notable bloodlines in the sport. Notably: his father Wilton Veras spent parts of two years with the Boston Red Sox near the turn of the century; his uncle (Fernando Tatis) and cousins (Fernando Tatis Jr. and Elijah Tatis) are also somewhat baseball famous. Signed out of Santo Domingo, Dominican Republic, for $300,000 a couple years ago, the younger Veras mashed his way through an impressive professional debut in the Arizona Complex League two years ago, slugging .322/.416/.533 with 16 doubles, two triples, and a quartet of homeruns in 46 games. Last season, the 6-foot-2, 180-pound corner infielder moved his way into full season action. And he continued to hit. In 101 games with the Kannapolis Cannon Ballers, Veras batted .267/.319/.454 with 19 doubles, two triples, and 17 homeruns to go along with five stolen bases (in five attempts). The front office threw caution to the wind at the end of the year and bumped the teenager straight up to Double-A for the last three weeks of the year. Veras promptly hit a nearly identical .267/.313/.533.

Scouting Report: One of my sleeper picks to be a consensus Top 100 prospect by the end of 2023. Veras, who slugged 20 homeruns in only 113 games last season, has only begun to tap into his prodigious raw power. Really good rotation throughout his swing with the natural leverage to fully take advantage of his thump. There's some swing-and-miss to Veras's game, though it hasn't climbed into full blown red flag territory. Miscast as a third baseman, it's only a matter time before Veras permanently shifts across the diamond to first. As a bat-only prospect, there's little room for risk but don't sleep on Veras. It'll be interesting to see if the front office bounces Veras back down to High-A at the start of 2022 or if he'll start the year back up in Double-A.

Ceiling: 2.5-win player
Risk: Moderate to High
MLB ETA: 2024

7. Jose Rodriguez, SS

	Hit	Power	SB	Patience	Glove	Overall
	50/55	45	60	45	45	50

Born: 05/13/01	Age: 22	Bats: R	Top Production Comp: Jean Segura
Height: 5-11	Weight: 175	Throws: R	

Season	Team	Age	Level	PA	1B	2B	3B	HR	SB	CS	BB%	K%	AVG	OBP	SLG	ISO
2019	CHW	18	R	200	36	7	3	9	7	1	4.50%	22.50%	0.293	0.328	0.505	0.213
2021	CHW	20	A	361	60	22	4	9	20	5	5.82%	15.79%	0.283	0.328	0.452	0.170
2021	CHW	20	A+	126	33	4	1	5	10	5	3.97%	10.32%	0.361	0.381	0.538	0.176
2021	CHW	20	AA	14	2	1	0	0	0	1	0.00%	14.29%	0.214	0.214	0.286	0.071
2022	CHW	21	AA	484	85	21	6	11	40	10	7.85%	13.64%	0.280	0.340	0.430	0.150

Background: One of just two 21-year-olds to receive enough qualifying at bats in the Southern League in 2022. Rodriguez continued his rapid ascension towards the Sox's big league lineup. Signed out of Valverde, Dominican Republic in mid-February 2018, the young shortstop vaulted up the prospect charts after a stout showing in the Arizona Summer League during his second season as he slugged .293/.328/.505 with 19 extra-base hits in only 44 games. After a return from the lost 2020 season, Rodriguez rocketed through three stops along the minor league path, going from Low-A all the way to Double-A as a 20-year-old. Last season, the promising middle infielder squared off against the minors' toughest challenge for a longer look. And he came away victorious. In 104 games with the Birmingham Barons, Rodriguez batted .280/.340/.430 with 21 doubles, 11 homeruns, and career bests in triples (six) and stolen bases (40). Per *FanGraphs' Weighted Runs Created Plus*, his overall production was 3% better than the league average.

Snippet from The 2022 Prospect Digest Handbook: Incredible bat-to-ball skills that are offset by his abhorrence to take a free pass. Rodriguez has the makings of a solid big league shortstop. The bat could be a plus tool, which would match the speed. Throw in some surprising pop for a 5-foot-11, 175-pound middle infielder and the defensive chops to stay at the position, and that's a recipe for success.

Scouting Report: Consider the following:

> Since 2006, only four 20-year-old hitters posted a wRC+ total between 100 and 110 with a sub-15% strikeout rate and a walk rate between 6% and 9% in a Double-A season (min. 400 PA): Freddy Galvis, Albert Almora Jr., Kean Wong, and Jose Rodriguez.

Chicago White Sox

The power's been the most intriguing part of Rodriguez's toolkit – only because it was graded so lowly when he signed with the organization. It's not overly impressive, but it's enough to keep pitchers and defenses honest. Plus speed and a hit tool that can turn into a perennial .290 threat. Rodriguez has never been overly patient at the plate – his 7.9% walk rate in 2022 was a career high by a rather wide margin – so there's some skepticism that he'll be able to approach those marks in future years. Rodriguez has a lot of similar offensive tools / traits as longtime big league veteran Jean Segura, though the glove quite isn't up to that level. He plays shortstop with a pair of stone hands.

Ceiling: 1.5- to 2.0-win player
Risk: Moderate
MLB ETA: 2023

8. Sean Burke, RHP

FB	CB	SL	CH	Command	Overall
60	50	55/60	N/A	40/45	45

Born: 12/18/99	Age: 23	Bats: R	Top Production Comp: N/A
Height: 6-6	Weight: 230	Throws: R	

Season	Team	Age	Level	IP	TBF	K/9	K%	BB/9	BB%	K-BB%	ERA	FIP	xFIP	Pit/Bat
2021	CHW	21	A	14.0	62	12.86	32.26%	6.43	16.13%	16.13%	3.21	3.69	4.66	4.35
2022	CHW	22	A+	28.0	113	9.96	27.43%	3.86	10.62%	16.81%	2.89	4.23	4.53	3.54
2022	CHW	22	AA	73.0	317	12.21	31.23%	4.07	10.41%	20.82%	4.81	4.35	3.74	4.05
2022	CHW	22	AAA	7.0	36	9.00	19.40%	3.86	8.30%	11.10%	11.57	4.65	4.68	3.72

Background: The University of Maryland's become a bit of an interesting baseball school over the past couple of seasons, graduating nine players to pro ball since the start of 2018 – eight of whom, by the way, received six-figure bonuses. Chicago drafted Burke from the land of the Terrapins in the third round, 94th overall, two years ago, and handed him the third largest bonus in school history ($900,000). Essentially limited to just one college season courtesy of the COVID pandemic, Burke quickly made up for any lost time last season as the big right-hander made a jaunt through three levels of the minor leagues, going from Winston-Salem (High-A) all the way to Charlotte (Triple-A) in 2022. In total, the Massachusetts native made 27 appearances, 26 of them coming via the start, throwing 108.0 innings with 137 strikeouts (11.4 K/9), 48 free passes (4.0 BB/9), and a 4.75 ERA. Burke was a two-time Southern League Pitcher of the Week (6/05/2022 and 8/28/2022), as well as the Southern League Pitcher of the Month for August.

Snippet from The 2022 Prospect Digest Handbook: Easy above-average velocity that plays up even further given his big frame. He compliments it with a pair of breaking balls – an above-average curveball and an average slider – and a fringy average changeup that shows some arm-side run at times. Burke has a history of subpar command, though some of that can be attributed to his lack of development time; he missed his true freshman season recovering from Tommy John surgery. He's raw. There's reliever risk here.

Scouting Report: Even further removed from his 2019 Tommy John surgery. Burke is the type of pitcher that would be exceptionally successful in a pitching savvy organization like the Dodgers or the Guardians or the Mariners or the Rays. So it'll be interesting as to whether the White Sox can help the right-hander take the final step towards the club's rotation. The key: throwing his recently tuned slider more frequently. While the curveball has noticeable shape and downward bite, Burke's slider consistently missed bats and generated plenty of weak contact. Above-average fastball that was sitting 96 mph late in the year, Burke will also mix in a rare, almost non-existent changeup. Along with more slider usage, the command is another potential deal breaker. It's a firm 40 with hope that it eventually creeps into 45-grade territory. Still only entering his age-23 season, thanks to a late birthday, Burke likely has two years to show an improved feel for the strike zone before he drifts into a potential seventh or eighth innings relief role.

Ceiling: 1.5-win player
Risk: Moderate
MLB ETA: 2023

9. Lenyn Sosa, 2B/SS/3B

Hit	Power	SB	Patience	Glove	Overall
50	50	35	40	55	45

Born: 01/25/00	Age: 23	Bats: R	Top Production Comp: Luis Rengifo
Height: 6-0	Weight: 180	Throws: R	

Season	Team	Age	Level	PA	1B	2B	3B	HR	SB	CS	BB%	K%	AVG	OBP	SLG	ISO
2019	CHW	19	A	536	82	35	2	7	6	6	5.04%	19.03%	0.251	0.292	0.371	0.120
2021	CHW	21	A+	353	67	19	1	10	3	4	3.97%	21.81%	0.290	0.321	0.443	0.153
2021	CHW	21	AA	121	19	5	0	1	0	1	1.65%	23.14%	0.214	0.240	0.282	0.068
2022	CHW	22	AA	289	59	10	2	14	0	0	7.27%	13.84%	0.331	0.384	0.549	0.218
2022	CHW	22	AAA	247	46	12	0	9	3	4	7.29%	17.41%	0.296	0.352	0.469	0.173

Background: Coming off of an up-and-down 2021 year in which he (A) was a league average bat with Winston-Salem and (B) looked utterly overmatched during a 35-game stint in Double-A, it's unsurprising that Sosa found himself back with Birmingham to start last season. And he looked like the second coming of Nomar Garciaparra. Sosa slashed a scorching .331/.384/.549 in 62 games. The young Venezuelan infielder spent the remainder of the year yo-yoing between Triple-A and the big leagues. He would finish his fifth minor league season with an aggregate

Chicago White Sox

.315/.369/.511 with 22 doubles, two triples, and a career best 23 homeruns. Per *Weighted Runs Created Plus*, his overall production topped the league average mark by 31%.

Snippet from The 2022 Prospect Digest Handbook: Sosa (A) doesn't walk frequently, or ever, (B) flashes decent power, and (C) plays an up-the-middle position. Except he doesn't really showcase a true standout offensive tool – a la Leury Garcia.

Scouting Report: Cut from a similar cloth many of the top prospect bats in the system, Sosa still (A) doesn't swing-and-miss much, (B) walk all that frequently, and (C) flashes surprising pop for a smaller, up-the-middle hitter. Defensively, Sosa has the chops – maybe not the arm strength – to stay at shortstop. The problem, of course, is that he's locked in behind Tim Anderson and Yoan Moncada at the big league level and he falls behind Colson Montgomery, Bryan Ramos, and Jose Rodriguez on the prospect depth chart – all of whom are likely to see some time at the game's pinnacle level in 2023. He's best suited for a super-sub role on a contending team. Big League Line: .255/.300/.400.

Ceiling: 1.5-win player
Risk: Moderate
MLB ETA: 2023

10. Jonathan Cannon, RHP

FB	SL	CU	CH	Command	Overall
50	50	55/60	55	55	40

Born: 07/19/00	Age: 22	Bats: R	Top Production Comp: N/A
Height: 6-6	Weight: 213	Throws: R	

Background: For just the second team in franchise history the Chicago White Sox drafted a Georgia Bulldog. The first being former middle infielder Gordon Beckham, the eighth overall pick in 2008 who would make the big leagues less than a year later. The second, of course, is right-hander Jonathan Cannon. The 6-foot-6, 213-pound hurler spent his final two seasons in the Bulldogs' rotation, posting similar results. As a spry sophomore, Cannon averaged 8.1 strikeouts and just 1.8 walks per nine innings across 12 starts and one relief outing. And he followed that up by posting averages of 7.8 K/9 and 1.4 BB/9 in 78.1 innings of work as a junior. After the organization selected him in the third round, 101st overall, the two sides agreed to a deal worth $925,000. Cannon made four brief appearances in the low levels of the minors, throwing another 7.1 innings with four punch outs and three free passes.

Scouting Report: With regard to his work as a junior last season, consider the following:

> Since 2017, there are only seven instances in which a SEC hurler posted a walk rate below 1.5 BB/9 in a season (min. 75 IP): Casey Mize (who accomplished the feat twice), Chase Dollander, Garrett Stallings (twice), Sam Finnerty, and Jonathan Cannon. Now the bad news: Cannon owned the third lowest K-rate between Finnerty, who went undrafted last season after five years at Alabama, and Stallings, who first accomplished the spectacular walk rate as a freshman and later did so with a significantly improve K-rate.

Cannon's a phenomenally interesting pitcher. He's an extreme strike thrower that doesn't miss many bats – which would suggest a lackluster / mediocre repertoire. But there's a workable foundation in place. Cannon shows a 90- to 93-mph fastball, which he commands well. He'll throw his low 80s average curveball at any point in the count. He'll mix in above-average, hard-fading mid-80s changeup. His best offering, though, is an upper 80s / low 90s cutter / slider with plenty of late movement. Chicago will need Cannon to focus throwing his cutter / slider more frequently. Otherwise, he's going to have to pitch backwards because his fastball / curveball combo is going to prove to be too hittable.

Ceiling: 1.0- to 1.5-win player
Risk: Moderate
MLB ETA: 2024

11. Wes Kath, 3B

Hit	Power	SB	Patience	Glove	Overall
35/40	55	30	55	50	40

Born: 08/03/02	Age: 20	Bats: L	Top Production Comp: N/A
Height: 6-3	Weight: 200	Throws: R	

Season	Team	Age	Level	PA	1B	2B	3B	HR	SB	CS	BB%	K%	AVG	OBP	SLG	ISO
2021	CHW	18	CPX	115	17	0	2	3	1	0	6.96%	36.52%	0.212	0.287	0.337	0.125
2022	CHW	19	A	449	57	20	1	13	2	0	13.36%	32.96%	0.238	0.343	0.397	0.159
2022	CHW	19	AA	52	7	1	0	0	0	0	7.69%	44.23%	0.170	0.250	0.191	0.021

Background: After nabbing teenage shortstop Colson Montgomery in the first round two years ago, the front office dipped back into the prep ranks and grabbed Desert Mountain High School product Wes Kath in the second round. Unlike his 2021 high round counterpart, Kath struggled mightily during his first foray into professional ball, batting a disappointing .212/.287/.337 across 115 plate appearances in the Arizona Complex League. The good news for Kath: his performance improved last season as he moved into full season ball

Chicago White Sox

and he spent a couple weeks in Double-A. The bad news: his slash line with Kannapolis, .238/.343/.397, was still disappointing and his late-season promotion up to Double-A was nothing more than a courtesy. Per *Weighted Runs Created Plus*, Kath's production in the Carolina League was 9% better than the league average.

Snippet from The 2022 Prospect Digest Handbook: The swing can get a little long at times, but it's certainly not lacking in loft; Kath has the power potential to belt out 20 homeruns in a professional season. A little awkward on the defensive side of the game, he's lacking fluidity from other high school infielders, though the hands are soft enough. His arm is above-average and should have no issues moving over to third base.

Scouting Report: Consider the following:

> Since 2006, only four 19-year-old hitters posted a 105 to 115 wRC+ total with a strikeout rate north of 30% in a season in Low-A (min. 400 PA): Travis Demeritte, Kala'i Rosario, Brandon Howlett, and – of course – Wes Kath.

Expanding out the little study even further, the success rate for 19-year-old hitters sporting at least a 30% strikeout rate is quite limited. To date, only three have carved out successful big league careers: Joey Gallo, Max Stassi, and Robbie Grossman. Kath does offer up some important secondary skills, namely his ability to get on base via the walk and slug the long ball, but it's not likely going to be enough to compensate for the hole(s) in his swing.

Ceiling: 1.0-win player
Risk: Moderate
MLB ETA: 2025

12. Matthew Thompson, RHP

FB	CB	SL	CH	Command	Overall
55	55	45/50	45/50	45	40

Born: 08/11/00	Age: 22	Bats: R	Top Production Comp: N/A
Height: 6-3	Weight: 195	Throws: R	

Season	Team	Age	Level	IP	TBF	K/9	K%	BB/9	BB%	K-BB%	ERA	FIP	xFIP	Pit/Bat
2021	CHW	20	A	71.2	324	9.67	23.77%	4.77	11.73%	12.04%	5.90	4.85	4.89	3.92
2022	CHW	21	AA	25.1	112	11.01	27.68%	3.91	9.82%	17.86%	5.33	4.33	4.49	4.16
2022	CHW	21	A+	84.1	357	7.79	20.45%	3.09	8.12%	12.32%	4.70	5.28	4.83	3.58

Background: The wiry right-hander was part of a famous trio of arms at Cypress Ranch High School, teaming with fellow righties Ty Madden, who would go onto become the 32nd overall pick after a solid career at the University of Texas, and J.J. Goss, taken just 11 selections before the White Sox called Thompson's name in 2019. A 6-foot-3, 195-pound hurler, Thompson battled some command issues during his 19-game cameo in Low-A East two years, but the former second round pick showed an improved ability to hone in on the strike zone as he moved up to High-A – and eventually Double-A – in 2022. Making 18 starts with Winston-Salem and another seven starts with Birmingham, Thompson tossed a career best 109.2 innings, recording 104 strikeouts (8.5 K/9) and 40 free passes (3.3 BB/9) to go along with a 4.84 ERA.

Snippet from The 2022 Prospect Digest Handbook: Thompson's not the typical power-based young arm. He approaches at bats with a plan and a willingness to change speeds. The command – in general – needs to see an uptick.

Scouting Report: Thompson's arsenal didn't look as impressive as it did in 2021. The big righty's fastball was sitting in the mid-90s with relative ease during a late-season start in Double-A, but it was far too hittable and failed to miss many – if any – bats. The curveball remains an above-average offering, arguably his best overall pitch, but the slider has become almost unusable. Fringy average changeup in the low- to mid-80s. Frankly: there's nothing noteworthy about him as a prospect. He's instant pudding on a hot summer day when you're craving ice cream.

Ceiling: 1.0-win player
Risk: Moderate
MLB ETA: 2023/2024

Chicago White Sox

13. Jared Kelley, RHP

FB	SL	CH	Command	Overall
60	45/50	60	35	40

Born: 10/03/01   **Age:** 21   **Bats:** R   **Top Production Comp:** N/A
Height: 6-3   **Weight:** 245   **Throws:** R

Season	Team	Age	Level	IP	TBF	K/9	K%	BB/9	BB%	K-BB%	ERA	FIP	xFIP	Pit/Bat
2021	CHW	19	A	21.0	112	10.71	22.32%	9.43	19.64%	2.68%	6.86	5.64	6.25	4.52
2022	CHW	20	A	64.2	280	8.21	21.07%	5.57	14.29%	6.79%	3.34	5.13	4.94	3.79
2022	CHW	20	AA	12.0	48	9.00	25.00%	5.25	14.58%	10.42%	4.50	5.50	4.66	3.65

Background: Trivia Time: Who's the last high school pitcher the club drafted within the top five rounds that developed into anything tangible? Bonus points if you can name the year that player was drafted as well. The Answer: left-hander Gio Gonzalez, who was taken in the supplemental first round, 38th overall, all the way back in 2004 – nearly 20 years ago. Three of the past four years the front office has burned multiple early round selections on prep arms like Matthew Thompson (2019), Jared Kelly (2020), and most recently Noah Schultz (2022). Kelley, for his part, is the lesser of the three. A hard-throwing right-hander blessed with a borderline plus-plus heater, Kelley oft-times can be confused with Nuke LaLoosh of *Bull Durham* fame. And last season was much of the same. In 18 starts with Kannapolis and another trio in Birmingham, the hefty righty walked 47 in only 76.2 innings of work (5.5 BB/9) to go along with 71 punch outs and, somehow, a 3.52 ERA.

Snippet from The 2022 Prospect Digest Handbook: Thompson's not the typical power-based young arm. He approaches at bats with a plan and a willingness to change speeds. The command – in general – needs to see an uptick.

Scouting Report: Kelley continues to add noticeable heft to his large frame, an observation backed up by his bio stats showing his weight going from a large 230 pounds to a portly 245 pounds. Cut from a similar cloth as former White Sox legend Bobby Jenks, Kelley attacks hitters with a plus, mid-90s fastball, an average-ish cutter-like slider, and an exceptional, underappreciated changeup. Kelley's working an uphill – almost insurmountable – battle to remain in the club's starting rotation plans. His slider is a questionable third offering *and* he commands the strike zone as efficiently as a Captain Crunch would the United States Naval forces. He's strictly a reliever all the way.

Ceiling: 1.0-win player
Risk: Moderate
MLB ETA: 2025

14. Yoelquis Céspedes, CF

Hit	Power	SB	Patience	Glove	Overall
50	50	60	45	50	45

Born: 09/24/97   **Age:** 25   **Bats:** R   **Top Production Comp:** Late Career Austin Jackson
Height: 5-9   **Weight:** 209   **Throws:** R

Season	Team	Age	Level	PA	1B	2B	3B	HR	SB	CS	BB%	K%	AVG	OBP	SLG	ISO
2021	CHW	23	A+	199	25	17	0	7	10	2	6.53%	28.14%	0.278	0.355	0.494	0.216
2021	CHW	23	AA	100	22	3	2	1	8	4	3.00%	27.00%	0.298	0.340	0.404	0.106
2022	CHW	24	AA	512	71	29	1	17	33	12	5.66%	30.08%	0.258	0.332	0.437	0.179

Background: A reasonably large expenditure on the international market a few years ago, the White Sox agreed to a deal worth $2 million to secure the services of the Cuban outfielder. It was a gamble considering (A) Céspedes' mediocre performances in the Cuban National Series (though he was still a teenager and had logged several years of competition) and (B) his age. The diminutive center fielder wouldn't appear stateside until his age-23 season, essentially minimizing any type of developmental schedule. The Yara, Cuba, native turned in a solid debut in 2021, though more of the noteworthy work was done in High-A. Nonetheless, though, Céspedes batted an aggregate .285/.350/.463 with 20 doubles, two triples, eight homeruns, and 18 stolen bases in 74 games between Winston-Salem and Birmingham. The 5-foot-9, 209-pound speedster spent the entirety of last season squaring away against the minors' toughest challenge, Double-A, and came away with mediocre results. Appearing in 119 games with the Barons, Céspedes batted .258/.332/.437 with 29 doubles, one triple, 17 homeruns, and 33 stolen bases (in 45 total attempts). Per *Weighted Runs Created Plus*, his overall production, 103, was barely above the league average mark.

Snippet from The 2022 Prospect Digest Handbook: Natural loft and enough power to belt out 20 or so long balls in a season. The problem, of course, is that he walks about as often as a senior citizen coming off hip surgery and the strikeout rates are borderline red flag territory.

Scouting Report: Céspedes still swings from the heels, doesn't walk all that much (just 5.0% of the time last season), and sits down on strikeouts too frequently (30.1%). Throw in his age – he'll be 25 during the 2023 season – and it's a recipe for Quad-A / taxi squad status. The Cuban import does do a few things well, sometimes exceptionally well, including: showcase his plus speed on the base paths and can run down a lot of potential hits in the outfield.

Ceiling: 1.0-win player
Risk: Moderate
MLB ETA: 2023

Chicago White Sox

15. Norge Vera, RHP

FB	CB	SL	CH	Command	Overall
55	55	50	45	40	40

Born: 06/01/00	Age: 23	Bats: R	Top Production Comp: N/A
Height: 6-4	Weight: 215	Throws: R	

Season	Team	Age	Level	IP	TBF	K/9	K%	BB/9	BB%	K-BB%	ERA	FIP	xFIP	Pit/Bat
2021	CHW	21	DSL	19.0	69	16.11	49.28%	2.37	7.25%	42.03%	0.00	0.94	0.97	1.87
2022	CHW	22	A	24.0	99	13.13	35.35%	5.63	15.15%	20.20%	1.88	3.35	3.60	4.35
2022	CHW	22	A+	3.1	15	13.50	33.30%	10.80	26.70%	6.70%	8.10	4.26	4.70	4.53
2022	CHW	22	AA	8.0	40	13.50	30.00%	13.50	30.00%	0.00%	5.63	5.08	5.88	4.23

Background: The Sox inked the Cuban import to a hefty $1.5 million deal after defecting from his homeland while playing in the Canadian American Association of Professional Baseball. The big right-hander made his affiliated debut two years ago in the Dominican Summer League, throwing 19.0 innings with a whopping 34 punch outs and just five free passes. Last season, though, didn't go as planned – or as well. A Lat injury forced him to miss the opening months of the year and he wouldn't debut until a brief not-quite three-inning start with Kannapolis in early June. He would make a total of eight starts with the Cannon Ballers, miss a few weeks, and then pop up with Winston Salem for a pair of very short outings. Vera would cap off his injury-marred sophomore season with three starts with Birmingham – all three of which failed to get out of the third inning. In total, Vera would throw just 35.1 innings of work, recording a problematic 52-to-31 strikeout-to-walk ratio to go along with a surprising 3.31 ERA.

Scouting Report: If you were to sculpt an ideal pitcher's frame it'd look something like Vera – broad shoulders, muscular build, long limbs, athletic. Vera features a standard four-pitch mix: a low-90s fastball with an extra gear at times, an above-average, downward tilting curveball, an average-ish slider, and a below-average changeup that he clearly slows his body down when throwing it. Reports indicate he's touched triple digits at some point in his stateside career, but Vera was consistently sitting in the 90- to 92-mph range and touching 93 and 94 during his first start in Double-A. He's an enigma. And now he's entering his age-23 season with just a few dozen innings under his belt. There's a real concern for his lack of consistency already, which may simply be a result of little game play. He's tracking like a middle relief arm at this point.

Ceiling: 1.0-win player
Risk: Moderate
MLB ETA: 2023/2024

16. Peyton Pallette, LHP

FB	CB	CH	Command	Overall
60	60	50	50	45

Born: 05/09/01	Age: 22	Bats: R	Top Production Comp: N/A
Height: 6-1	Weight: 180	Throws: R	

Background: Benton High School boasts one notable big league alum: 2008 Cy Young Award winner and four-time All-Star Cliff Lee. The Marlins, back when they were known as the Florida Marlins, drafted the 6-foot-3, 205-pound lefty in the eighth round in 1997. Lee, instead, attended the University of Arkansas by way of Meridian Community College. And prior to 2022, Lee was the highest drafted former prep Panther. But Peyton Pallette changed that – despite a massive red flag. Recognized by *Perfect Game* as the second best right-hander in the state of Arkansas, Pallette, like Lee, would attend the land of the Razorbacks. The 6-foot-1, 180-pound right-hander made four brief relief appearances for the SEC Conference school during his freshman season before COVID prematurely ended the 2020 season. He would throw 5.2 innings, posting a 3-to-3 strikeout-to-walk ratio while saving one game. Pallette had a coming out party for head coach Dave Van Horn the following season: making 11 starts and four relief appearances, the hard-throwing hurler struck out 67 and walked 20 in 56.0 innings of work. Unfortunately for Pallette, he underwent Tommy John surgery in late January and missed the entirety of his junior campaign. Undeterred – and perhaps feeling lucky – the White Sox selected the righty in the second round, 62nd overall, and signed him to a deal worth $1.5 million.

Scouting Report: My pre-draft analysis:

> "Consider the following:
>
> Since 2015, only five SEC hurlers averaged between 10 K/9 and 11 K/9 with a walk rate between 3.1 BB/9 and 3.3 BB/9 in a season (min. 50 IP): TJ Sikkema, Carter Holton, Drew McDaniel, Drake Fellows, and – of course – Peyton Pallette.
>
> Prior to the injury Pallette showcased a standard three-pitch mix: fastball, curveball, and changeup. His heater, an above-average offering, sat in the 93-to 95-mph range but looked straight and lacks deception. His curveball, though, is among the best in the class, sitting in the low 80s with tremendous tilt, adding a much needed swing-and-miss offering to his

Chicago White Sox

repertoire. According to reports, he'll mix in an average changeup (though, I didn't see one on the game tape). Pallette looked like a backend arm with the high probability that his fastball / curveball combination makes him a decent backend relief arm."

Prior to the draft, I had a third / fourth round grade on Pallette.

Ceiling: 1.0-win player
Risk: Moderate to High
MLB ETA: 2024/2025

17. Luis Mieses, LF/RF

Hit	Power	SB	Patience	Glove	Overall
45	45/55	30	40	45	40

Born: 05/31/00	Age: 23	Bats: L	Top Production Comp: N/A
Height: 6-3	Weight: 232	Throws: L	

Season	Team	Age	Level	PA	1B	2B	3B	HR	SB	CS	BB%	K%	AVG	OBP	SLG	ISO
2018	CHW	18	R	204	30	10	2	2	3	0	1.96%	17.16%	0.226	0.236	0.328	0.103
2019	CHW	19	R	231	35	14	0	4	0	1	3.03%	19.91%	0.241	0.264	0.359	0.118
2021	CHW	21	A	225	43	12	1	6	0	0	5.78%	14.67%	0.305	0.347	0.463	0.158
2021	CHW	21	A+	234	22	19	2	9	0	1	4.70%	20.51%	0.236	0.278	0.464	0.227

Background: Coming off of his fifth full professional season in the White Sox's organization (not including the lost COVID season of 2020). Mieses continues to take the *slooooowwww* path of prospect development. After spending a year in the foreign rookie league and another two campaigns in both stateside rookie leagues, the sturdy Dominican outfielder split time between Low-A East and High-A East in 2021, hitting an aggregate .270/.312/.463. In an uncharacteristic move, the Sox had Mieses open up 2022 back in Winston-Salem. He responded by batting .281/.324/.448. The former international bonus baby would spend the final month or so squaring off against the Double-A competition. In total, he hit .284/.326/.447 with a career best 39 doubles to go along with a career-high tying 15 homeruns.

Snippet from The 2022 Prospect Digest Handbook: Mieses is another one of these Sox prospects that don't whiff or walk all that much. It's worked for Tim Anderson well enough. But Mieses isn't Tim Anderson. He hasn't flashed the type of power that corner outfielders are associated with. And his batted ball data, per *FanGraphs*, is mediocre: his average exit velocity was a run-of-the-mill 85 mph with a peak exit velocity of 106. There really isn't a true standout tool in place, nor does one project to be so either.

Scouting Report: It wasn't an overly rosy picture heading into last offseason and not much has changed a year later. Mieses loathes walking as much as anyone, but – again – the hit tool isn't enough to compensate and he's still not tapping into his above-average power potential. He added considerable bulk to his once lanky frame, gaining plenty of good weight over the past year, but the power hasn't developed as expected. Incredibly short swing, almost like Darryl Strawberry – just without the tools. He also struggled against lefties mightily last year too. Still, though, he's entering his age 23 season with a month of slightly better than league average production at Double-A on his resume.

Ceiling: 0.5- to 1.0-win player
Risk: Moderate
MLB ETA: 2023

18. Kohl Simas, RHP

FB	CB	SL	CH	Command	Overall
55	55	50	50	45	35

Born: 12/22/99	Age: 23	Bats: R	Top Production Comp: N/A
Height: 6-1	Weight: 210	Throws: R	

Season	Team	Age	Level	IP	TBF	K/9	K%	BB/9	BB%	K-BB%	ERA	FIP	xFIP	Pit/Bat
2021	CHW	21	A	18.0	66	11.50	34.85%	2.00	6.06%	28.79%	1.50	2.81	3.07	4.11
2022	CHW	22	A	61.2	254	11.09	29.92%	3.65	9.84%	20.08%	3.65	4.07	3.70	3.98

Background: The 1998 Sox were a disappointing team – despite having the fifth best offense in baseball that year. But the lineup, which featured the likes of Frank Thomas, Albert Belle, Magglio Ordonez, Robin Ventura, Ray Durham, and Mike Cameron wasn't enough to compensate for an abysmal pitching staff. The bullpen was fairly solid, centered around Bob Howry and Keith Foulke. Surprisingly enough, though, it was a 26-year-old middle reliever that led the club with 18 saves. That right-hander, Bill Simas, would spend a total of six years in the big leagues. Fast forward a couple decades and the two of Simas' sons would eventually make their way into professional baseball. Karson Simas, a middle infielder in the Red Sox organization, was handed $175,000 as a 25th round pick – though he hasn't hit well. And Kohl, a right-handed starter, took a $20,000 undrafted free agent deal in 2020 to join the White Sox. Last season, Kohl made a total of 22 appearances between Low-A and Double-A, throwing 68.0 innings with 82 punch outs and 29 free passes. He tallied a 4.24 ERA.

Scouting Report: The front office / player development engine governed Simas' workload after coming from back from a forearm strain in early July, an injury that knocked him out of action for four weeks. Once he returned he was allowed to throw more than 50 pitches just three times.

Chicago White Sox

The hefty right-hander features a standard four-pitch mix: a low 90s fastball, an above-average, 2-8 bending curveball, a 50-grade slider, and an average changeup. He's more of a strike-thrower rather than a command guy. There's not a lot of room for error with his arsenal. He looks more like a Quad-A / organizational depth guy.

Ceiling: 0.5- to 1.0-win player
Risk: Moderate
MLB ETA: 2024

19. D.J. Gladney, 1B/3B/RF

Hit	Power	SB	Patience	Glove	Overall
40	50/60	40	50	50	35

Born: 07/14/01	Age: 21	Bats: R	Top Production Comp: N/A
Height: 6-3	Weight: 195	Throws: R	

Season	Team	Age	Level	PA	1B	2B	3B	HR	SB	CS	BB%	K%	AVG	OBP	SLG	ISO
2019	CHW	17	R	220	38	5	2	8	1	0	4.55%	37.27%	0.264	0.309	0.428	0.164
2021	CHW	19	A	294	30	11	1	7	1	0	10.54%	42.18%	0.191	0.293	0.324	0.133
2022	CHW	20	A	460	60	17	4	18	10	1	9.57%	32.61%	0.243	0.322	0.437	0.194
2022	CHW	20	AA	58	8	2	0	1	1	0	1.72%	39.66%	0.193	0.207	0.281	0.088

Background: A 16th round pick that wasn't given an over slot signing. The Sox plucked the corner infielder / outfielder out of Illiana Christian High School four years ago as the 470th overall player taken. Gladney turned in a solid, leave average-ish debut in the Arizona Complex League that summer, hitting .264/.309/.428 in 50 games. The front office bumped the 6-foot-3, 195-pound teenager up to Low-A two years ago and the results were less than stellar. In 71 games with the Cannon Ballers, Gladney batted a lowly .191/.293/.324 with 11 doubles, one triple, and seven homeruns. So it wasn't surprising to see the former late round pick back with Kannapolis for a much needed do-over. This time, though, the results were significantly better. In 106 games with the club's Carolina League affiliate, Gladney batted .243/.322/.437 with 17 doubles, four triples, 17 homeruns, and 10 stolen bases (in 11 attempts). Per *Weighted Runs Created Plus*, his overall production was 9% better than the league average.

Scouting Report: An easy prospect to root for. Gladney wasn't highly touted coming out of high school – *Baseball America* had him as the 482nd rated prospect – but he gambled on himself. And there's something to be said about that. There's plus raw power brewing in his bat and it's beginning to show up in games as well. The problem – and it's been a problem since day one – is whether he can consistently make contact. He whiffed in more than 42% of his plate appearances two years ago, but chewed that number down to 32.6% in a repeat of Low-A. Quicker and more athletic than he looks. Gladney's the type of prospect that blooms late, like Ross Gload, and carves out a career as a solid platoon / bench option. There are probably better prospects in the system. But, again, he's easy to root for.

Ceiling: 0.5-win player
Risk: Moderate
MLB ETA: 2025

20. Andrew Dalquist, RHP

FB	CB	SL	CH	Command	Overall
55	55	50	50	35	35

Born: 11/13/00	Age: 21	Bats: R	Top Production Comp: N/A
Height: 6-1	Weight: 195	Throws: R	

Season	Team	Age	Level	IP	TBF	K/9	K%	BB/9	BB%	K-BB%	ERA	FIP	xFIP	Pit/Bat
2021	CHW	20	A	83.0	394	8.57	20.05%	6.07	14.21%	5.84%	4.99	4.54	5.94	4.07
2022	CHW	21	A+	90.2	415	6.85	16.63%	5.26	12.77%	3.86%	6.95	7.21	6.08	3.92
2022	CHW	21	AA	13.1	62	7.43	17.74%	7.43	17.74%	0.00%	3.38	5.61	6.06	3.84

Background: Redondo Union High School is far from a baseball hotbed, though the California-based school's alumnus includes All-Star and Silver Slugger Morgan Ensberg. Dalquist, a third round pick four years ago, became the second highest drafted player from the school, trailing only 1983 first rounder Wayne Wilson. Dalquist showed some promise during his first foray into full season action two years ago, averaging nearly a strikeout per inning – though he managed to walk a whopping 56 in 83.0 innings. Last season, completely undeterred by the young right-hander's control demons, the front office promoted him up to High-A to begin the year. And it was a repeat performance. In 22 starts with the Winston-Salem Dash, the 6-foot-1, 195-pound hurler posted a 69-to-53 strikeout-to-walk ratio in 90.2 innings of work. He also made four brief starts with the Barons at the end of the season as well, striking out 11 and walking 11 in 13.1 innings of work.

Snippet from The 2020 Prospect Digest Handbook: He still has the making of a #4/#5-type arm. But the command is definitely beyond concerning.

Chicago White Sox

Scouting Report: Consider the following:

> Since 2006, there have been 41 instances in which a 21-year-old hurler walked at least 11.5% of the hitters they faced in High-A season (min. 75 IP). Of those 41, only six posted a strikeout percentage between 15.5% and 17.5% -- Brandon Martinez, Bryan Hudson, Edgar Olmos, Mitch Brown, Nate Adcock, and Andrew Dalquist.

Regardless of the arsenal – and Dalquist's weaponry is enough to suggest there's a potential middle relief arm here at the big league level – the young righty's control (forget about command) is so poor that he's not likely to overcome the lack of strike-throwing ability. A lot of inconsistency in his mechanics, frequently spiking his fastball. Low 90s fastball, a smidge into above-average territory. His big bending, beautiful curveball will flash plus on occasion but it's a consistent above-average offering. Dalquist's slider, which was a 45-grade in 2021, improved a tick. And he'll mix in an average 84-mph changeup. Physically, he's far from maxed out and may find another gear on his 92- to 93-mph fastball. But, again, it comes down to his lack of strikes.

Ceiling: 0.5-win player
Risk: Moderate
MLB ETA: 2025

Cincinnati Reds Top Prospects

Cincinnati Reds

1. Elly De La Cruz, 3B/SS

Hit	Power	SB	Patience	Glove	Overall
45/55	60	60	50	50/55	70

Born: 01/11/02 **Age:** 21 **Bats:** B **Top Production Comp:** Trevor Story
Height: 6-5 **Weight:** 200 **Throws:** R

Season	Team	Age	Level	PA	1B	2B	3B	HR	SB	CS	BB%	K%	AVG	OBP	SLG	ISO
2021	CIN	19	CPX	55	9	6	2	3	2	0	7.27%	27.27%	0.400	0.455	0.780	0.380
2021	CIN	19	A	210	29	12	7	5	8	5	4.76%	30.95%	0.269	0.305	0.477	0.208
2022	CIN	20	A+	306	45	14	6	20	28	4	7.84%	30.72%	0.302	0.359	0.609	0.306
2022	CIN	20	AA	207	30	17	3	8	19	2	7.73%	30.92%	0.305	0.357	0.553	0.247

Background: Every season there's typically one player, usually a hitter, who separates himself from the rest of the pack, both in terms of production *and* excitement. Last season that hitter was Elly De La Cruz, a heralded signing off the international market during the summer of 2018. De La Cruz joined the organization for a paltry $65,000 – essentially the sum of a fully loaded family minivan. The 6-foot-5, 200-pound infielder turned in a decent, yet unremarkable debut showing in the Dominican Summer League in 2019, batting .285/.351/.382. But something happened during the lost COVID-season of 2020, something remarkable. De La Cruz emerged from the pandemic like Clark Kent from a phone booth. The Dominican dandy shredded the Complex League competition and flashed some intriguing tools during his 50-game stint with Daytona. He finished the year with a .296/.336/.539 slash line with 18 doubles, nine triples, eight homeruns, and 10 stolen bases. And while the production was impressive, it paled in comparison to what was waiting in 2022. The front office sent the toolsy infielder up to High-A at the start of the year, but after mashing .305/.360/.609, the franchise released him upon the competition awaiting in Double-A, the minor's toughest challenge. And Superman came out victorious. De La Cruz, who grew several inches and put on 40 pounds of good weight over the past couple of seasons, mashed an aggregate .304/.359/.586 with 31 doubles, nine triples, 28 homeruns, and 47 stolen bases (in 53 total attempts). Per *Weighted Runs Created Plus*, De La Cruz's overall production topped the league average mark by a massive 50%, the tenth best showing among all minor league hitters with more than 450 plate appearances.

Snippet from The 2022 Prospect Digest Handbook: The young Dominican is a premium athlete that's already providing value on both sides of the ball. The problem, though, is his already problematic swing-and-miss totals; he whiffed in 31.0% of his plate appearances in Low-A. But when he does connect, *watch out*. There's superstar potential with a high level of risk. One more thought: Tremendous bat speed with just a flick of the wrist.

Scouting Report: Consider the following:

> Since 2006, only five 20-year-old hitters posted at least a wRC+ of at least 160 in any High-A league (min. 300 PA): Christian Yelich, Corey Seager, Eric Hosmer, Harold Ramirez, and – of course – Elly De La Cruz.

For those counting at home:

> Yelich is a 2x batting champ, Gold Glove winner, 2x All-Star, and MVP.
> Seager is a former Rookie of the Year winner, 3x All-Star, and 2x Silver Slugger.
> Hosmer is a former Silver Slugger award winner and owns one All-Star appearance on his resume.
> Ramirez has quietly put together a solid .281/.320/.405 slash line in his big league career.

And now the bad news…

> De La Cruz's strikeout rate last season in High-A, 30.7%, was – *by far* – the worst mark among the group. In fact, it was 50% *higher* than the runner-up (Corey Seager).

De La Cruz fell just short of a seemingly unreachable plateau: 30 homeruns and 50 stolen bases. The offensive dynamo was just two homeruns and three stolen bases shy of the mark. Just for a reference point: only two big leaguers achieved the feat – Eric Davis, in 1987, and Barry Bonds, who accomplished it just three years later. Arguably the most exciting player not in the big leagues, De La Cruz is just scratching what seems like limitless potential. Long and lanky with plenty of quick-twitchy movements. Explosive bat speed. Plus power. Plus speed. The *potential* for him to develop into a borderline Gold Glove winner at the infield's most important position is present. He's the type of player that can become the face of the game in an instant. But his whiff rates continue to be concerning. It's likely going to improve as the maturation process plays out and the game slows down. In terms of big league ceiling, think: .290/.350/.550.

Ceiling: 7.0-win player
Risk: Moderate
MLB ETA: 2023

Cincinnati Reds

2. Cam Collier, 3B

Hit	Power	SB	Patience	Glove	Overall
55	60	50	60	50	70

Born: 11/20/04	Age: 18	Bats: L	Top Production Comp: N/A
Height: 6-2	Weight: 210	Throws: R	

Season	Team	Age	Level	PA	1B	2B	3B	HR	SB	CS	BB%	K%	AVG	OBP	SLG	ISO
2022	CIN	17	CPX	35	7	1	0	2	0	2	20.00%	17.14%	0.370	0.514	0.630	0.259

Background: Lou Collier beat the odds. The Astros took a 56th round flier on the former utility infielder / outfielder coming out of Vocational High School in 1991. Instead of joining the organization the 5-foot-10, 170-pound teenager headed to Kishwaukee College for a year before the Pirates took another late round flier on the Chicago-born prospect, nabbing him in the 31st round (875th overall). But here's the thing: Collier hit as soon as he stepped foot onto a professional diamond. And he'd hit at every stop along the minor league ladder, slashing .304/.356/.368 as a 19-year-old in the New York-Penn League all the way up to a .330/.393/.441 showing as a 23-year-old in Triple-A. In total, Collier would spend eight mostly non-descript years in the big leagues as a replacement level player. But he wasn't supposed to make it out of the lower minors. Not as a 31st round pick. Collier's kid, Cam, dwarfed his old man's draft status by 857 picks in the 2022 draft. And he did so as one of the class's youngest players. Originally slated for the 2023 draft, Collier reclassified after his stellar sophomore high school season at Mount Paran Christian School (he batted .434 with 13 homeruns and 19 stolen bases) and spent the 2022 season at JuCo Chipola College. The baby-faced 17-year-old, who remarkably was named on the preseason Golden Spikes Watch List, more than held his own: .333/.419/.537 with 12 doubles, eight homeruns, and five stolen bases. He also made 10 relief appearances for the squad as well, posting a 16-to-5 strikeout-to-walk ratio in 11.1 innings of work. Prior to joining Chipola he had committed to the University of Louisville. Cincinnati selected him with the 18th overall pick, signing him to a deal worth $5 million, well above the recommended $3.69 million slot. He hit the ground running, slugging .370/.514/.630 in nine Complex League games.

Scouting Report: My pre-draft scouting report:

> "Confident. And a lot of fun to watch during each at bat. Collier shows an advanced approach at the plate with patience that belies his age – especially considering his level of competition as a 17-year-old. He shows an incredible willingness to let pitcher's pitches pass and wait for mistakes. Short bat to the zone. Plus power potential with the possibility the hit tool climbs into a perennial .280 threat. The lefty-swinging Collier also shows the ability to hang in against tough left-handed pitching. He made a lot of mechanical adjustments from mid-2021 to last year, holding his hands lower, tighter to his body and a more pronounced crouch. Soft hands on defense. And his long term position is likely going to be third base as he continues to add bulk to his lean frame. Collier's one of my favorite prep prospects in the class – enough so, that I might make him the top pick – especially if he takes a discount."

Ceiling: 6.0-win player
Risk: Moderate
MLB ETA: 2025

3. Edwin Arroyo, SS

Hit	Power	SB	Patience	Glove	Overall
55	50/55	55	50	50	60

Born: 08/25/03	Age: 19	Bats: B	Top Production Comp: N/A
Height: 6-0	Weight: 175	Throws: R	

Season	Team	Age	Level	PA	1B	2B	3B	HR	SB	CS	BB%	K%	AVG	OBP	SLG	ISO
2021	SEA	17	CPX	86	11	2	0	2	4	1	11.63%	30.23%	0.211	0.337	0.324	0.113
2022	SEA	18	A	410	76	19	7	13	21	4	8.54%	21.95%	0.316	0.385	0.514	0.198
2022	CIN	18	A	109	12	6	3	1	4	2	8.26%	28.44%	0.227	0.303	0.381	0.155

Background: Viewed as the second best prospect the ball club received from the Mariners in the Luis Castillo swap last summer. Arroyo is confidently making a strong argument as the club's top return piece. Originally taken by the Mariners in the second round of the 2021 draft, Arroyo looked abysmal during his abbreviated debut in the Complex League that summer, hitting a lowly .211/.337/.324 with just a pair of doubles and dingers in 21 games. Undeterred by his lackadaisical initial showing, the front office sent the former early round pick up to Low-A at the start of last season. And he blossomed. Appearing in 87 games with the Modesto Nuts, the 6-foot, 175-pound shortstop batted .316/.385/.514 with 19 doubles, seven triples, 13 homeruns, and 21 stolen bases. His numbers took a noticeable step backwards during his brief tenure with the Daytona Tortugas as he batted a lowly .227/.303/.381. He finished the year with an aggregate .293/.366/.480 with 25 doubles, 10 triples, 14 homeruns, and 27 stolen bases (in 33 total attempts). Per *Weighted Runs Created Plus*, his overall production topped the league average mark by 20%.

Cincinnati Reds

Snippet from The 2022 Prospect Digest Handbook: Arroyo's a potentially premium athlete – as evidenced by his work on the mound as an amateur southpaw. The swing from the left side looks more complete than from the right side. I just don't know if he's going to (A) hit or (B) hit for any type of meaningful power.

Scouting Report: One of the more uniquely talented ballplayers in the minor leagues, Arroyo is an ambidextrous thrower and was quite the amateur southpaw – despite playing shortstop as a right-handed thrower. Very quietly Arroyo had one of the better breakout seasons in 2022, though it was clouded by his struggles in the Reds' farm system. It's likely just the result of a young prospect, barely into pro ball, changing organizations and looking to make a good first impression. So let's take a look at his extended stint in Modesto, a heavily slanted pitcher-friendly ballpark. Consider the following:

> Since 2006, only two 18-year-old hitters posted a 125 to 135 wRC+ mark in any Low-A league (min. 350 PA): Jake Bauers, the failed former consensus top prospect, and Edwin Arroyo.

Arroyo has quietly become one of the better shortstop prospects in the minor leagues and most haven't realized it yet. Better than expected power from one of the youngest players in the 2021 draft class. He showed a solid feel on both sides of the batter's box. The left-handed swing looks better, more powerful than his debut. Low, squat stance. A big breakout is coming in 2023. He's the second best shortstop prospect in the Reds' system, which is saying something nowadays.

Ceiling: 4.0-win player
Risk: Moderate
MLB ETA: 2024/2025

4. Noelvi Marte, SS

Hit	Power	SB	Patience	Glove	Overall
50/55	50/55	60	55	50	55

Born: 10/16/01	Age: 21	Bats: R	Top Production Comp: Gleyber Torres
Height: 6-1	Weight: 181	Throws: R	

Season	Team	Age	Level	PA	1B	2B	3B	HR	SB	CS	BB%	K%	AVG	OBP	SLG	ISO
2021	SEA	19	A	478	69	24	2	17	23	7	12.13%	22.18%	0.271	0.368	0.462	0.191
2021	SEA	19	A+	33	5	4	0	0	1	0	6.06%	33.33%	0.290	0.333	0.419	0.129
2022	SEA	20	A+	394	60	19	0	15	13	6	10.66%	21.32%	0.275	0.363	0.462	0.187
2022	CIN	20	A+	126	23	4	0	4	10	3	13.49%	18.25%	0.292	0.397	0.443	0.151

Background: While the Reds' impressive farm system would stand near the top of baseball just based on their homegrown talent, not *all* of the club's bounty has been drafted or signed off the international free agent market. Like Noelvi Marte. Part of the massive talent package the front office received from the Mariners for ace right-hander Luis Castillo. Marte, who was acquired along with Edwin Arroyo, Andrew Moore, and Levi Stoudt, originally signed with Seattle during the summer of 2018 for a massive $1.55 million. The 6-foot-1, 181-pound shortstop manhandled the Dominican Summer League in 2019. And he continued to impress in Low-A two years later, batting .271/.368/.463 with the Modesto Nuts. Last season, between both organizations' High-A affiliates, Marte mashed .279/.371/.458 with 23 doubles, 19 homeruns, and 23 stolen bases (in 32 total attempts). Per *Weighted Runs Created Plus*, his production topped the league average mark by 31%.

Snippet from The 2022 Prospect Digest Handbook: He looks like a potential All-Star at his peak.

Scouting Report: Consider the following:

> Since 2006, only two 20-year-old hitters posted a 125 to 135 wRC+ with a 19.5% to 21.5% strikeout percentage with a 9.5% to 11.5% walk percentage in any High-A league (min. 350 PA): Jeter Downs and Noelvi Marte.

Not nearly the type of impact player that Elly De La Cruz is – or will be at the Major League level – Marte, nonetheless, owns a high upside ceiling. Loose, quick swing with plus bat speed and the chance to grow into an above-average hit tool. Strong contact and walk rates. Above-average power potential – even though he spent a lot of 2022 in Everett's homer-inducing ballpark. He's never going to be confused with Ozzie Smith, but he has the chops to stay at the position. In terms of big league ceiling, think: .280/.350/.440.

Ceiling: 3.5-win player
Risk: Moderate
MLB ETA: 2023/2024

Cincinnati Reds

5. Chase Petty, RHP

FB	CB	SL	CH	Command	Overall
60	55	55	50/55	45/50	55

Born: 04/04/03	Age: 20	Bats: R	Top Production Comp: N/A
Height: 6-1	Weight: 190	Throws: R	

Season	Team	Age	Level	IP	TBF	K/9	K%	BB/9	BB%	K-BB%	ERA	FIP	xFIP	Pit/Bat
2022	CIN	19	A	67.2	275	8.38	22.91%	3.19	8.73%	14.18%	3.06	3.90	3.77	3.59
2022	CIN	19	A+	30.2	130	9.68	25.38%	2.05	5.38%	20.00%	4.40	3.35	3.79	3.40

Background: Owner of one of the best fastballs in the entire 2021 draft class. Petty, who once touched as high as 102 mph with his heater, was snagged by the Twins near the backend of the first round two years ago. The 6-foot-1, 190-pound righty signed for a hefty $2.5 million as the 26th overall pick that summer. Petty would make just a pair of appearances with Minnesota's Complex League affiliate, throwing 5.0 innings with six punch outs and a free pass. And that was entirety of Chase Petty's career with the Twinkies. The franchise would ship their most recent first rounder off to the Reds for veteran right-hander Sonny Gray and minor league reliever Francis Peguero. For all intents and purposes, Petty's *real* professional debut happened in Cincinnati's system last summer. He would make 25 appearances, 20 of which were starts, between Daytona and Dayton, throwing 98.1 innings with 96 strikeouts and 31 free passes. He finished the season with an aggregate 3.48 ERA and a 3.73 FIP.

Snippet from The 2022 Prospect Digest Handbook: There's been a lot of talk about his mechanics, but they're clean, fluid, and repeatable. The arm action is a little long in the back, a la Daniel Espino. Barring injury, Petty has a chance to be a solid mid-rotation arm – something along the line of a healthy Nate Eovaldi.

Scouting Report: Consider the following:

> Since 2006, only eight 19-year-old hurlers posted a 22% to 24% strikeout percentage with a 7.5% to 9.5% walk percentage in any Low-A league (min. 60 IP): Jack Flaherty, Matthew Liberatore, Michael Fulmer, Michael Morales, Paul Demny, Hildemaro Requena, Victor Juarez, and Chase Petty.

After touching as high as 102 mph during his amateur career, Petty's fastball has nestled in at the 94-to- 95-mph range in the professional ranks. But he's far more polished than the typical flame-throwing high schooler. He was very poised during his first full season in the minor leagues, showing a solid aptitude to pitching as he consistently changed speeds and moved the ball around. Petty shows a lot of trust / faith in his above-average, mid-80s slider, which flashes plus on occasion. He has no qualms about starting a batter off with one, or multiple, breaking balls. His changeup, though, is what surprised me the most. There's not a whole lot of velocity separation, just seven or so miles-per-hour, but there's a lot of arm-side fade through heavy pronation and it will flash plus as well. A year after prognosticating that the former first rounder would be a mid-rotation, he's still tracking as such. Ironically, there's some Sonny Gray upside for Petty.

Ceiling: 3.0-win player
Risk: Moderate
MLB ETA: 2024/2025

6. Michael Siani, CF

Hit	Power	SB	Patience	Glove	Overall
40	40	60	55	70	50

Born: 07/16/99	Age: 23	Bats: L	Top Production Comp: Kevin Pillar
Height: 6-1	Weight: 188	Throws: L	

Season	Team	Age	Level	PA	1B	2B	3B	HR	SB	CS	BB%	K%	AVG	OBP	SLG	ISO
2021	CIN	21	A+	408	53	13	4	6	30	10	12.25%	25.25%	0.216	0.321	0.327	0.111
2022	CIN	22	AA	531	77	19	7	12	49	12	12.05%	16.95%	0.252	0.351	0.404	0.151
2022	CIN	22	AAA	38	7	0	0	2	3	0	2.63%	13.16%	0.250	0.263	0.417	0.167

Background: The Reds must have liked what they saw heading into the 2018 Draft because they handed Siani $2 million as the 109th overall player taken that summer. That fourth round bonus has only been surpassed just once since then – the Rangers signed projected first rounder Brock Porter to a hefty $3.7 million deal last summer. Ironically, enough, Porter was *also* taken with the 109th overall pick. A gifted defender in centerfield, Siani put an abysmal showing in High-A in 2021 firmly in the rearview mirror last season. Appearing in 121 games with the Lookouts of Chattanooga, the 6-foot-1, 188-pound former Bonus Baby batted a respectable .252/.351/.404 with 19 doubles, seven triples, 12 homeruns, and 49 stolen bases (in 61 total attempts). Siani's overall production with the club's Double-A affiliate topped the league average mark by 2%, according to *Weighted Runs Created Plus*. He also made a quick eight-game through Triple-A and he spent another nine games with the Reds as well.

Snippet from The 2022 Prospect Digest Handbook: He has the tools to be an average or better big league center fielder, but he lacks the consistently. It's like his baseball development is going through puberty and he's still trying to find out who he actually is.

Cincinnati Reds

Scouting Report: Consider the following:

> Since 2006, only four 22-year-old hitters met the following criteria in a Double-A season (min. 350 PA: 97 to 107 wRC+, 16% to 18% strikeout rate, and a double-digit walk rate. Those four hitters: Tyler Saladino, David Cooper, Maikel Garcia, and – of course – Mike Siani, the former fourth rounder.

Always a contender for the best defensive player in the minor leagues, the 2022 season further cemented Siani's ability to take hits and runs away from the opposition. Clay Davenport's defensive metrics had him as a +21 defender; *Baseball Prospectus* had him at 2.8 *Fielding Runs Above Average*, as well. The question entering last season was whether or not he would hit enough to elicit any type of starting gig because his offense was beyond atrocious in High-A. Below-average hit tool and power. Plus speed that he utilizes incredibly well on the base paths and the outfield (obviously). There's always been starting potential and now that his bat has a bit of pulse he's one step closer. In terms of big league ceiling, think: .250/.310/.390.

Ceiling: 2.5-win player
Risk: Low to Moderate
MLB ETA: Debuted in 2022

7. Sal Stewart, 3B

Hit	Power	SB	Patience	Glove	Overall
50	65	30	50	45/50	50

Born: 12/07/03	Age: 19	Bats: R	Top Production Comp: N/A
Height: 6-3	Weight: 215	Throws: R	

Background: Westminster Christian High School went nearly 30 years in between first round selections. Alex Rodriguez, of course, was famously selected atop the 1993 draft and would go on to slug nearly 700 homeruns and tally 117.6 wins above replacement during his 22-year big league career. Twenty-nine years later the Cincinnati Reds cast their net into the school's baseball pond and fished out another infield prospect: Sal Stewart. A hulking 6-foot-3, 215-pound third baseman, Stewart was a dynamic force in the Warriors' lineup throughout his four-year career, earning a spot on *USA Today*'s HSSA Baseball Team. Stewart batted a scorching .514/.670/1.081 during the 2022 season, belting out 13 doubles, one triple, and nine homeruns. According to the *Miami Herald*, he finished his career as a .488/.621/1.621 hitter with 31 doubles, three triples, and 30 homeruns to go along with 95 runs batted in. Stewart, the 32nd overall pick last July, was committed to SEC powerhouse Vanderbilt University. Cincinnati signed the slugging infielder to a deal worth $2.1 million. He batted .292/.393/.458 in eight Complex League games.

Scouting Report: At 6-foot-3 and 215 pounds, Stewart's already pushing the size for a typical third baseman. And he hasn't even begun to fill out. Above-average arm strength. A bit robotic in the field. It wouldn't be surprising to see him slide across the diamond to first base. Big, *big* time power potential – arguably the best raw thump in the entire draft class. When Stewart connects it's like an explosion. Really, really good looking swing – especially considering that power is Stewart's main asset. Impressive speed and explosion throughout his rotation. It wouldn't be overly shocking to see Stewart consistently post better-than-average contact rates. There's definitely some Triston Casas-type potential here. Very, very savvy pick by the Cincinnati Reds front office.

Ceiling: 2.5-win player
Risk: Moderate
MLB ETA: 2025/2026

8. Christian Encarnacion-Strand, 1B/3B

Hit	Power	SB	Patience	Glove	Overall
50	50	35	50	55	50

Born: 12/01/99	Age: 23	Bats: R	Top Production Comp: Mitch Moreland
Height: 6-0	Weight: 224	Throws: R	

Season	Team	Age	Level	PA	1B	2B	3B	HR	SB	CS	BB%	K%	AVG	OBP	SLG	ISO
2021	MIN	21	A	92	26	2	2	4	2	0	5.43%	28.26%	0.391	0.424	0.598	0.207
2022	MIN	22	A+	330	41	23	3	20	7	1	9.09%	25.76%	0.296	0.370	0.599	0.303
2022	MIN	22	AA	60	10	2	1	5	1	1	6.67%	23.33%	0.333	0.400	0.685	0.352
2022	CIN	22	AA	148	28	6	1	7	0	0	4.05%	25.68%	0.309	0.351	0.522	0.213

Background: After watching years and years *and* years of minor league baseball, one of my favorite quips involves former prospect Jarrod Saltalamacchia. His nickname, at least according to his bio on Baseball Reference, is Salty. But he was also known as "Pits", because his 14-letter last name extended from arm pit to arm around the back of his jersey. But that's nothing compared to Christian Encarnacion-Strand, who's surname extends a total of 18 characters. Does that now make him "Super Pits"? Taken out of Oklahoma State University in the fourth round two years ago, Encarnacion-Strand was a force at the plate during his lone season with the Cowboys as he mashed .361/.442/.661 with 17 doubles, three triples, and 15 homeruns. And the former JuCo-turned-Division-I star continued to batter the competition during his 22-game

Cincinnati Reds

debut with Minnesota's Low-A affiliate as well: he hit .391/.424/.598. Last season was much the same for the corner infielder: he shredded High-A and looked almost Ruthian during his first two weeks in Double-A. Cincinnati acquired Encarnacion-Strand, along with Spencer Steer and Steve Hajjar in early August for veteran right-hander Tyler Mahle. The former fourth rounder spent the rest of the year doing what he seemingly always does: hit. He would finish the year with an aggregate .304/.368/.587 with 31 doubles, five triples, 32 homeruns, and eight stolen bases (in ten attempts). Per *Weighted Runs Created Plus*, his overall production topped the league average mark by a mindboggling 52%.

Scouting Report: Consider the following:

> Since 2006, only two 22-year-old hitters met the following criteria in any High-A league (min. 300 PA): at least a 159 wRC+ and a strikeout rate between 24% and 28%. Those two hitters: former minor league saber-slanted darling Kala Ka'aihue and, of course, Christian Encarnacion-Strand.

When watching Encarnacion-Strand play with such dominance, one name immediately jumps to mind. Consider the following:

Season	Name	Level	Age	Level	PA	AVG	OBP	SLG	BB%	K%
2010	Paul Goldschmidt	A+	22	A+	599	0.314	0.384	0.606	9.50%	26.90%
2022	Christian Encarnacion-Strand	A+	22	A+	330	0.296	0.370	0.599	9.09%	25.76%

Impressive power to all fields, Encarnacion-Strand has been a dynamic slugger during his brief career, combining his plus-power with a remarkably solid hit tool. Is he the second coming of Paul Goldschmidt? No. But could he be 75% of the future Hall of Famer? It certainly looks like it. Defensively, he's fringy at the hot corner but could put it off if he reaches his offensive ceiling to help compensate. Otherwise, he'll move across the diamond. The lone knock of hyphenated hulk: he struggled against lefties (.206/.263/.411 vs. .344/.409/.659). Obvious platoon risk here, but there's definite big league value to be extracted from thumping bat.

Ceiling: 2.5-win player
Risk: Moderate
MLB ETA: 2023

9. Connor Phillips, RHP

FB	CB	SL	CH	Command	Overall
60	50	50/55	50	40/45	55

Born: 05/04/01	Age: 22	Bats: R	Top Production Comp: N/A
Height: 6-2	Weight: 190	Throws: R	

Season	Team	Age	Level	IP	TBF	K/9	K%	BB/9	BB%	K-BB%	ERA	FIP	xFIP	Pit/Bat
2021	SEA	20	A	72.0	322	13.00	32.30%	5.50	13.66%	18.63%	4.75	3.52	4.56	4.03
2022	CIN	21	A+	64.0	256	12.66	35.16%	4.50	12.50%	22.66%	2.95	3.51	3.36	4.14
2022	CIN	21	AA	45.2	217	11.82	27.65%	6.70	15.67%	11.98%	4.93	4.11	5.06	4.47

Background: A few weeks before last season officially kicked off the Reds and Mariners got together on a rather large trade. The specifics: Cincinnati dealt away former All-Star Eugenio Suarez and Jesse Winker in exchange for Brandon Williamson, Justin Dunn, Jake Fraley, and a Player To Be Named Later. A little more than two weeks later the Redlegs' front office decided that final piece of the deal would be right-hander Connor Phillips. A 2020 second round pick out of McLennan Community College, the 6-foot-2, 190-pound hurler turned in a rollercoaster debut in the Mariners' organization two years ago. Spending the majority of the year with the club's Low-A affiliate, Phillips tossed 76.0 innings of work, recording a whopper of a strike total (111) while dealing with some problematic control issues (46 free passes). Last season, his first in Cincy's organization, the former early round pick split time between Dayton and Chattanooga, averaging 12.3 strikeouts and 5.4 walks per nine innings across 24 starts. He finished the year with an aggregate 3.78 ERA across a career best 109.2 innings.

Snippet from The 2022 Prospect Digest Handbook: Phillips fits the mold of the new Seattle pitcher: he throws gas and a couple solid breaking balls. He doesn't have a firm grip on the strike zone. And I'm not hopeful that the command bumps past a 45. There's definite reliever risk.

Scouting Report: Consider the following:

> Since 2006, only two 21-year-old hurlers posted a strikeout percentage between 34% to 36% with a walk percentage between 10% and 12% in any High-A league (min. 60 IP): Matt Moore, who would go on to develop into a *consensus Top 2 prospect in baseball*, and – of course – Connor Phillips, the former Player To Be Named Later.

Phillips has the floor of a backend reliever just built off of his fastball / slider combo, which he is *heavily* reliant on. He'll run his heater upwards of 97 mph, though it sits more in the 95-mph range the majority of the time. The slider is *definitely* better than what I saw in 2021, generating all kinds of awkward swings during his stint in High-A. The curveball shows some serious depth and fantastic shape, it's arguably as good as the slider, though he tends to keep it in his back pocket. He flashed an average changeup two years ago, though he was reluctant to throw it during the games I saw. You could make the argument – and a rather convincing one – that he's one of the better starting pitching prospects most

Cincinnati Reds

people haven't quite discovered. Just like former Red Tyler Mahle, who I wrote extensively about over the years. Obvious reliever risk due to command issues. But he's already logged nearly half of a season in Double-A before his age-22 season. Maybe 85% of a healthy Tyler Glasnow.

Ceiling: 3.0-win player
Risk: Moderate to High
MLB ETA: 2022

10. Carlos Jorge, 2B/SS

Hit	Power	SB	Patience	Glove	Overall
35/45	60	55	50	55	55

Born: 09/22/03	Age: 19	Bats: L	Top Production Comp: N/A
Height: 5-10	Weight: 160	Throws: R	

Season	Team	Age	Level	PA	1B	2B	3B	HR	SB	CS	BB%	K%	AVG	OBP	SLG	ISO
2021	CIN	17	DSL	188	34	8	10	3	27	5	12.77%	17.02%	0.346	0.436	0.579	0.233
2022	CIN	18	CPX	154	15	7	2	7	27	4	16.23%	26.62%	0.261	0.405	0.529	0.269

Background: Another part of the club's bounty off the international market in January of 2021. A few months later, the Puerto Plata, Dominican Republic native morphed into one of the most explosive bats in the foreign rookie leagues. He mashed .346/.436/.579 with eight doubles, 10 triples, three homeruns, and 27 stolen bases (in 32 total attempts). Last season the front office pushed the 5-foot-10, 160-pound dynamo up to the Complex League. And he continued to surpass expectations. Appearing in 42 games in the stateside rookie league, the lefty-swinging middle infielder slugged .261/.405/.529 with seven doubles, two triples, seven homeruns, and swiped another 27 stolen bases (in only 31 total attempts). Per *Weighted Runs Created Plus*, his overall production passed the league average threshold by a massive 51%. For his career, Jorge is sporting .309/.422/.558 with 15 doubles, 12 triples, 10 homeruns, and 54 stolen bases.

Scouting Report: Jorge packs an incredible punch at the plate with the type of natural power that shouldn't be found in a 5-foot-10, 160-pound frame. The Dominican youngster has always shown a knack for pop, even when it looked like he could barely get the bat around in time as an amateur. There's obvious risk here given his propensity to swing-and-miss and the hit tool is a bit unrefined. But there's a chance to have plus power on the right-side of the keystone and that doesn't happen too often. There's some potential stardom developing here. He's one to remember over the next couple of years. He could pop in a very big way.

Ceiling: 3.5-win player
Risk: High
MLB ETA: 2025

11. Spencer Steer, IF

Hit	Power	SB	Patience	Glove	Overall
50	50	35	50	55	50

Born: 12/07/97	Age: 25	Bats: R	Top Production Comp: Brian Anderson
Height: 5-11	Weight: 185	Throws: R	

Season	Team	Age	Level	PA	1B	2B	3B	HR	SB	CS	BB%	K%	AVG	OBP	SLG	ISO
2021	MIN	23	A+	208	28	7	1	10	4	4	16.83%	15.38%	0.274	0.409	0.506	0.232
2021	MIN	23	AA	280	33	11	2	14	4	4	7.14%	26.07%	0.241	0.304	0.470	0.229
2022	MIN	24	AA	156	20	13	1	8	1	3	8.97%	14.74%	0.307	0.385	0.591	0.285
2022	CIN	24	AAA	104	17	7	0	3	1	0	8.65%	22.12%	0.293	0.375	0.467	0.174
2022	MIN	24	AAA	232	25	10	1	12	2	0	12.07%	18.53%	0.242	0.345	0.485	0.242

Background: The former 3rd round pick out of the University of Oregon has quietly become the soup du jour of the Reds' farm system this offseason. A solid, line-drive oriented hitter during his time with the Pac-12 powerhouse, Steer, the 90th overall player taken in 2019, turned in a solid debut that summer as well, hitting .280/.385/.424 with 18 doubles, three triples, four homeruns, and five stolen bases in 64 games between the old Appalachian and Midwest Leagues. Minnesota was able to get the 5-foot-11, 185-pound infield vagabond to tap into his power potential two years later. Steer would slug 18 doubles, three triples, and 24 homeruns during his time with Minnesota's High-A and Double-A affiliates. The former Duck carried that momentum in the 2022 season as well. He bashed his way through a 35-game stint in Double-A and he continued mashing during his 23-game stint with Louisville. But the Twins, always in search of good pitching and riding Steer's surging prospect status, packaged him with Christian Encarnacion-Strand, and Steve Hajjar for the always underrated right-hander Tyler Mahle last August. Steer finished his minor league campaign with an aggregate .274/.364/.515 with 30 doubles, two triples, 23 homeruns, and four stolen bases. His overall production between both organizations' minor league affiliates topped the league average by 27%. Cincinnati called him up in early September, but for the first time in his professional career he struggled. He batted a lowly .211/.306/.326 in 108 trips to the plate.

Scouting Report: Consider the following:

> Since 2006, only three 24-year-old hitters met the following criteria in any Triple-A league (min. 300 PA): 115 to 125 wRC+, an 18.5% to 20.5% strikeout rate, and a 9% to 13% walk rate. Those three hitters: Kyle Isbel, Tim Federowicz, and – of course – Spencer Steer.

Cincinnati Reds

There may not be a prospect that has rocketed up the prospect charts as much as Steer over the past 12 to 16 months. Steer's reached the point where he's likely overrated – believe it or not. Average hit tool, average power, average speed, above-average glove. It's a toolkit that screams low-end starting potential, maybe more if he's slugging 20 homeruns. Poor man's Jake Cronenworth. In terms of big league ceiling, think: .265/.335/.420.

Ceiling: 2.0-win player
Risk: Low to Moderate
MLB ETA: Debuted in 2022

12. Ariel Almonte, RF

Hit	Power	SB	Patience	Glove	Overall
35/50	40/55	50/40	50	55	55

Born: 12/01/03	Age: 19	Bats: L	Top Production Comp: N/A
Height: 6-1	Weight: 170	Throws: L	

Season	Team	Age	Level	PA	1B	2B	3B	HR	SB	CS	BB%	K%	AVG	OBP	SLG	ISO
2021	CIN	17	DSL	196	30	9	1	5	15	6	13.27%	26.53%	0.278	0.398	0.438	0.160
2022	CIN	18	CPX	164	23	11	0	6	1	0	12.80%	29.88%	0.286	0.390	0.493	0.207

Background: One of the crown jewels the club signed off the international market two years ago. The Redlegs signed the 6-foot-1, 170-pound outfielder to a hefty $1.85 million deal in mid-January 2021. A few months later the wiry rightfielder immediately started mashing as he squared off against the Dominican Summer League: he batted .278/.398/.438 with nine doubles, one triple, five homeruns, and 15 stolen bases (in 21 attempts) in only 48 games of action. Last season the club took the cautious route and sent the teenager up to the Complex Leagues. And Almonte posted a similar slash line with some additional thump. He slugged .286/.390/.493 with 11 doubles, six homeruns, and a stolen base – just for good measure. Per *Weighted Runs Created Plus*, his overall production topped the league average by a whopping 41%.

Snippet from The 2022 Prospect Digest Handbook: Raw, but the toolsy. They just need to be polished and cleaned up a bit. Almonte's lower mechanics need cleaned up as he's not utilizing his legs much – or at all. The young Dominican struggled a bit with consistently making contact, but his foundation is strong enough to push him stateside to the Complex League for the start of 2022.

Scouting Report: Despite the added thump in 2022, Almonte continued to showcase some concerning swing-and-miss numbers as he whiffed in nearly 30% of his plate appearances. But Almonte owns the type of bat speed you bet on. You might not bet the house on it, but you might be willing to bet a garage. There's a lot of risk here that he winds up taking the Austin Hendrick path. There are literally only two outcomes at this point: franchise cornerstone or low level flameout. Don't expect anything else in between.

Ceiling: 3.0-win player
Risk: Extreme
MLB ETA: 2025

13. Lyon Richardson, RHP

FB	CB	SL	CH	Command	Overall
60	55	55	55	40	50

Born: 01/18/00	Age: 23	Bats: R	Top Production Comp: N/A
Height: 6-2	Weight: 192	Throws: R	

Season	Team	Age	Level	IP	TBF	K/9	K%	BB/9	BB%	K-BB%	ERA	FIP	xFIP	Pit/Bat
2018	CIN	18	R	29.0	139	7.45	17.27%	4.97	11.51%	5.76%	7.14	5.54	5.51	3.82
2019	CIN	19	A	112.2	497	8.47	21.33%	2.64	6.64%	14.69%	4.15	3.76	3.65	3.78
2021	CIN	21	A+	76.0	346	10.78	26.30%	4.50	10.98%	15.32%	5.09	4.69	4.44	3.79

Background: Always a bit of favorite of mine in the Reds' farm system. Richardson, a former second round pick out of Jensen Beach High School, missed the entirety of 2022 recovering from Tommy John surgery, though he did make it back to the Instructional Leagues following the season. The 6-foot-2, 192-pound right-hander last toed the rubber for the Dayton Dragons in High-A in 2021, throwing just 76.0 innings with an impressive 91 strikeouts against 38 free passes. He finished the year with a 5.09 ERA, a 4.69 FIP, and a 4.44 xFIP.

Scouting Report: With nothing new to report on, here's Richardson's scouting report following the 2021 season:

> *"Consider the following:*
>
> *Since 2006, only three 21-year-old hurlers posted a 25.5% to 27.5% strikeout percentage with a walk percentage between 10% and 12% in High-A (min. 75 IP): Luis Pena, Jose Almonte, and Lyon Richardson.*
>
> *Richardson's an interesting arm. When you sit and watch the arsenal, ignoring everything else, it's easy to come away impressed. His fastball was sitting in the 95- to 96-mph range; his loopy curveball tumbles off of the side of a table; his*

Cincinnati Reds

slider flashed plus fairly regularly; and his changeup is significantly underrated. One plus pitch (the heater) and the remaining three are either above-average (CB and CH) or project to be above-average (SL). But Richardson certainly has his flaws: he struggles commanding the zone, frequently deals with bouts of wildness, and runs hot-and-cold. Richardson's overall production was torpedoed by an awful three-game stint in July (he coughed up 13 ER in 9.0 IP). Otherwise, he posted a 4.15 ERA. He's tracking like a multi-inning reliever. But he's only entering his age-22 season, so there's plenty of time to harness his repertoire. One more final thought: he seemed to scrap his curveball later in the year."

Ceiling: 2.0-win player
Risk: Moderate to High
MLB ETA: 2024/2025

14. Matt McLain, SS

Hit	Power	SB	Patience	Glove	Overall
45	55	60	55	50	45

Born: 08/06/99	Age: 23	Bats: R	Top Production Comp: N/A
Height: 5-11	Weight: 180	Throws: R	

Season	Team	Age	Level	PA	1B	2B	3B	HR	SB	CS	BB%	K%	AVG	OBP	SLG	ISO
2021	CIN	21	A+	119	18	6	0	3	10	2	14.29%	20.17%	0.273	0.387	0.424	0.152
2022	CIN	22	AA	452	43	21	5	17	27	3	15.49%	28.10%	0.232	0.363	0.453	0.221

Background: The talented middle infielder took a sizeable gamble after not signing with Arizona after the club used the 25th overall pick on him coming out of high school in 2018. At first, it looked like a grave miscalculation on McLain's part as he batted a lowly .203/.276/.355 during his freshman season. But after rebounding – *significantly* – over his final two campaigns, the Reds swooped in and selected him with the 17th overall pick, signing him to a *massive* $4,625,000 bonus. The franchise immediately placed the 5-foot-11, 180-pound infielder on the fast track to the big leagues as they sent him directly into High-A. And McLain handled the transition from the Pac-12 to the minor leagues with aplomb as he batted .273/.387/.424. Last season the Reds continued to challenge the former Bruin and sent him directly into the fires of Double-A – though he struggled for the first time since his freshman season. He batted .232/.363/.453 with 21 doubles, five triples, 17 homeruns, and 27 stolen bases (in only 30 attempts). His overall production, as measured by *Weighted Runs Created Plus*, topped the league average mark by 16%. McLain spent the fall – mostly struggling – with the Glendale Desert Dogs, hitting a paltry .190/.340/.317 with just five extra-base knocks in 23 games.

Snippet from The 2022 Prospect Digest Handbook: McLain is an advanced college bat without a true standout. There's a little bit of thump, enough to belt out eight to 12 homeruns in a full season. He runs well. And he profiles as a .270/.280-type hitter. In a college class lacking premium bats, McLain's likely to hear his name in the opening half of the draft, though he's a high floor/low ceiling type prospect.

Scouting Report: Consider the following:

> Since 2006, only three 22-year-old hitters posted a 110 to 120 wRC+ with a 26% to 30% strikeout percentage and a double-digit walk rate in any Double-A league (min. 350 PA): Brett Phillips, Jai Miller, and – of course – Matt McLain.

The year started off well enough for McLain during his first foray into the fires of Double-A, hitting .282/.374/.671 over his first 24 contests, but the league figured him out and he failed to adjust. He would cobble together a lowly .217/.360/.388 over his remaining 70 contests – not including his vapid appearance in the Arizona Fall League. McLain was more known for his high floor and lack of red flags heading into the draft, but he struggled – significantly – with contact issues last summer, posting a K-rate north of 28%. There's plenty of bat speed and patience at the plate, but the hit tool is lagging significantly. He does get the benefit of the doubt, at least a little bit, since he essentially moved from the Pac-12 straight into Double-A with just a month of High-A in between. Defensively, he flashed the leather that was on par with the bat. He's a lock to move over to second base at this point because he doesn't have the chops to stick on the other side of the keystone.

Ceiling: 1.5-win player
Risk: Moderate
MLB ETA: 2023/2024

Cincinnati Reds

15. Brandon Williamson, LHP

	FB	CB	SL	CH	Command	Overall
	60	55	55	50	50	45

Born: 04/02/98	Age: 25	Bats: R	Top Production Comp: Roenis Elías
Height: 6-6	Weight: 210	Throws: L	

Season	Team	Age	Level	IP	TBF	K/9	K%	BB/9	BB%	K-BB%	ERA	FIP	xFIP	Pit/Bat
2021	SEA	23	A+	31.0	124	17.13	47.58%	2.90	8.06%	39.52%	3.19	3.11	2.09	4.26
2021	SEA	23	AA	67.1	285	12.56	32.98%	3.07	8.07%	24.91%	3.48	3.24	3.84	3.99
2022	CIN	24	AA	67.1	298	9.89	24.83%	5.35	13.42%	11.41%	4.14	4.35	5.25	4.09
2022	CIN	24	AAA	55.1	256	7.97	19.14%	6.02	14.45%	4.69%	4.07	4.90	6.29	3.90

Background: A part of the club's return from the Eugenio Suarez and Jesse Winker deal with Seattle. The Mariners targeted the Texas Christian University southpaw in the second round four years ago. The 6-foot-6, 210-pound lefty was incredibly dominant during his brief debut in the old Northwest League that summer, and he continued his run of impressive performances during his first full season two years ago. He finished the 2021 campaign with 98.1 innings, recording a downright fanciful 153-to-33 strikeout-to-walk ratio between his time with Seattle's High-A and Double-A affiliates. Last season, his first full in the Redlegs' organization, Williamson split time between Chattanooga and Louisville as he tossed 122.2 innings with 123 strikeouts and 77 walks. He finished the year with an aggregate 4.11 ERA and a 4.60 FIP. For his career, he's averaging 11.5 strikeouts and 4.4 walks per nine innings to go along with a 3.69 ERA.

Snippet from The 2022 Prospect Digest Handbook: Lefties with three above-average pitches (and a fourth average one) with solid command don't exactly grow on trees. There's some #4-type upside. Maybe more if everything breaks the right way.

Scouting Report: Velocity alone, Williamson's fastball is solid, yet unremarkable. But hitters consistently had trouble timing up the 93 mph heater. And even when they did, the offering just seemed to miss the fat part of the bat thanks to a little hop on the tail end. Williamson owns two above-average breaking balls: a horizontally shifting slider that's going to be hell on lefties, and a big bending 11-to-5 curveball. He'll also mix in a rare average changeup as well. His command, which was never a strong skill, all but evaporated last season. The fastball command, in particular, was egregious. There's some backend starting potential, but he's already entering his age-25 season so he'll need to find the strike zone. And fast.

Ceiling: 1.0- to 1.5-win player
Risk: Moderate
MLB ETA: 2023

16. Logan Tanner, C

	Hit	Power	SB	Patience	Glove	Overall
	40/45	50/55	30	50	55	45

Born: 11/10/00	Age: 22	Bats: R	Top Production Comp: N/A
Height: 6-0	Weight: 215	Throws: R	

Background: Not dissimilar from a lot of the prospects with bloodlines in this year's draft class, Tanner's mother, Dalenah, lettered in softball at the University of Southern Mississippi and his father, Brandon, was a hurler at the same school. A two-way player throughout his prep career at George County High School, Tanner' squads captured two South State Championships, as well making an appearance in the 2018 Mississippi High School Activities Association Championship Game. A Second-Team All-American, according to *Perfect Game*, Tanner's college career got off to a solid start, batting .268/.388/.439 in 14 games before the pandemic forced the season to a premature end. The 6-foot, 215-pound backstop turned in a quietly strong showing during his sophomore season with the Bulldogs, slugging .287/.383/.525 with 13 doubles and 15 homeruns to go along with a solid 48-to-39 strikeout-to-walk ratio. This season Tanner saw a modest dip in the power department as he hit .285/.387/.425 with just eight doubles and seven homeruns in 55 games for the SEC Conference powerhouse. The Reds drafted Stewart in the second round, 55th overall, and signed him to a deal worth a smidgeon over a million dollars. He batted a lowly .200/.329/.300 in 17 low level games.

Scouting Report: Consider the following:

> Since 2011, only three SEC hitters met the following criteria in a season (min. 225 PA): hit between .275/.375/.410 and .300/.400/.440 with a double-digit walk rate and a strikeout rate between 16% and 20%. Those three hitters: Jordan Thompson, Jake Ring, and – of course – Logan Tanner.

Tanner looked prime for a massive offensive season entering his junior year with the Bulldogs, but he actually regressed. And it looks like he's made some mechanic tweaks to his stance between his sophomore and junior campaigns. Most notably: he's holding his hands higher and the bat head droops behind his back this year. 45-grade hit tool. There's above-average power potential, but it's still largely untapped. But he compensates for any offensive shortcomings with added value behind the plate. There's the potential recipe for a Jake Rogers-type career path.

Cincinnati Reds

Ceiling: 1.0- to 1.5-win player
Risk: Moderate
MLB ETA: 2025

17. Justin Boyd, OF

Hit	Power	SB	Patience	Glove	Overall
40/45	50/55	30	50	55	45

Born: 03/30/01	Age: 22	Bats: R	Top Production Comp: N/A
Height: 6-0	Weight: 201	Throws: R	

Background: Attended the aptly named Legend High School, Boyd was – well – a legend during his prep career. *Prep Baseball Report* ranked the slugging infielder / outfielder as the second best prospect in the state of Colorado and among the Top 200 nationally. Boyd was named All-League and All-State during his junior season after batting .478 with nine doubles and seven homeruns. And he followed that up with a .487/.604/.948 slash line with six homeruns during his final season. And, perhaps, as a bit of foreshadowing, Boyd played for the Reds team during the 2018 Area Code Games, as well. After sitting out the 2020 COVID-shortened season, Boyd moonlighted as a first baseman and outfielder in a part-time gig the following year at Oregon State University. And he took advantage of the 83 trips to the plate he made, batting .301/.395/.411 with four doubles, two triples, and a stolen base. Last season, with regular playing, Boyd ripped through the Pac-12 competition all year long, slugging a robust .373/.490/.577 with 14 doubles, four triples, nine homeruns, and 24 stolen bases (in 31 total attempts). The Reds – remember them from above? – selected the outfielder in the second round, 73rd overall and signed him to a below-slot deal worth $847,500. He batted .203/.277/.270 in 83 plate appearances during his debut between the Complex League and Low-A.

Scouting Report: Consider the following:

> Since 2011, only five Division I hitters batted at least .370/.480/.570 with a walk rate north of 15% in a season (min. 300 PA): Adley Rutschman, Kyle Lewis, James Ramsey, Ivan Melendez, and – of course – Justin Boyd. It should noted that Rutschman, Lewis, and Ramsey were all first rounders. Melendez and Boyd were both taken in the second round last July.

Patient approach with speed to burn. Boyd's approach at the plate is reminiscent of a young little leaguer: hands far from his body, held high, with the bat close to perpendicular to the ground. But it works for the former Beaver star. Great bat speed, but he's not likely going to hit for nearly the type of power he showcased during his final season at Oregon State. He's tracking like a fourth outfielder.

Ceiling: 1.0- to 1.5-win player
Risk: Moderate
MLB ETA: 2025

18. Jay Allen, CF

Hit	Power	SB	Patience	Glove	Overall
35/40	35/50	55	50	50/55	40

Born: 11/22/02	Age: 20	Bats: R	Top Production Comp: N/A
Height: 6-2	Weight: 190	Throws: R	

Season	Team	Age	Level	PA	1B	2B	3B	HR	SB	CS	BB%	K%	AVG	OBP	SLG	ISO
2021	CIN	18	CPX	75	13	3	1	3	14	1	10.67%	16.00%	0.328	0.440	0.557	0.230
2022	CIN	19	A	299	36	13	2	3	31	6	13.38%	24.41%	0.224	0.359	0.332	0.108
2022	CIN	19	A+	84	14	1	2	0	12	4	4.76%	22.62%	0.230	0.301	0.297	0.068

Background: The club's draft gurus squeezed in just one high school player among the team's first nine selections in the 2021 draft. The lone holdout: Jay Allen, a centerfielder out of John Carroll Catholic High School. Taken with the 30th overall pick that summer, the Reds signed the toolsy prepster to a deal worth a smidgeon less than $2.4 million. And it looked like the 6-foot-2, 190-pound outfielder was going to be the absolute steal of the draft as well as he mashed .328/.440/.557 with three doubles, a triple, three homeruns, and 14 stolen bases (in only 15 attempts). But Allen wasn't able to carry that momentum in his 2022 campaign. In 93 games with Daytona and Dayton, most of which came with the former, the former first rounder batted a lowly .225/.347/.324 with just 14 doubles, four triples, three triples, and 43 stolen bases (in 53 total attempts). Per *Weighted Runs Created Plus*, his overall production was 1% *below* the league average mark.

Snippet from The 2022 Prospect Digest Handbook: He has an inconsistent hitch in his swing that needs to be cleaned up.

Cincinnati Reds

Scouting Report: Consider the following:

Since 2006, only three 19-year-old hitters met the following criteria in a Low-A season (min. 275 PA): 102 to 112 wRC+ with a 23.5% to 25.5% strikeout rate with a walk rate north of 12%. Those three hitters: Grant Lavigne, Joe Rizzo, and Jay Allen.

The contact rates aren't the problem, per se. The issue, though, is the *quality* of contact. And it's only exacerbated by his early debut success. The Reds have expended a lot of draft capital, as well as actual capital, in young, high upside bats in recent years – like Austin Hendrick, Rece Hinds, and Tyler Callihan with little to show. And Allen already has taken a couple unfortunate steps down the same path.

Ceiling: 1.0-win player
Risk: Moderate
MLB ETA: 2025

19. Andrew Abbott, LHP

FB	CB	SL	CH	Command	Overall
60	55	55	50	50	45

Born: 06/01/99	Age: 24	Bats: L	Top Production Comp: N/A
Height: 6-0	Weight: 180	Throws: L	

Season	Team	Age	Level	IP	TBF	K/9	K%	BB/9	BB%	K-BB%	ERA	FIP	xFIP	Pit/Bat
2021	CIN	22	A	11.0	49	15.55	38.78%	3.27	8.16%	30.61%	4.91	4.07	2.71	3.88
2022	CIN	23	A+	27.0	103	13.33	38.83%	2.33	6.80%	32.04%	0.67	1.89	2.43	4.04
2022	CIN	23	AA	91.0	386	11.77	30.83%	4.05	10.62%	20.21%	4.75	3.48	3.67	4.03

Background: The Reds haven't dipped into the waters at the University of Virginia too frequently, especially when it comes to early round selections. In fact, Cincinnati has taken former Cavaliers just twice in the top two rounds of the draft. The first: back in 2014 the club used the 19th overall pick on surging right-hander Nick Howard, who had the look *and* feel of a fast-moving, mid-rotation caliber arm, but battled the yips as soon as he toed a professional mound. The second: Andrew Abbott, the average-sized southpaw who was taken midway through the second round two years ago. A member of the school's pitching staff for parts of four seasons, the 6-foot, 180-pound lefty made six brief appearances during his debut that summer, posting an absurd 22-to-4 strikeout-to-walk ratio in only 13.0 innings of work. Last season, the front office took the aggressive approach and sent Abbott straight up to High-A. But after stringing together a nearly perfect 0.67 ERA across 27.0 innings, Abbott proved himself ready for the toughest minor league challenge: Double-A. And despite a few speedbumps along the way, the former Cavalier toughed out 20 starts with the Lookouts of Chattanooga. He finished the year with 159 punch outs against 48 free passes with an aggregate 3.81 ERA in 118 innings of work. He finished the year with a 3.12 xFIP.

Snippet from The 2022 Prospect Digest Handbook: As long as Abbott continues to pound the zone with the same regularity, he has the potential move quickly and settle in as a #4-type arm.

Scouting Report: Consider the following:

Since 2006, only two 23-year-old hurlers posted a 30% to 32% strikeout percentage with a 9% to 12% walk percentage in any Double-A league (min. 75 IP): Ken Waldichuk and Andrew Abbott.

Abbott already was entering pro ball with the deck stacked against him, despite his second round draft status. He was old, lacked projection, and had just one year of starting on his collegiate resume. But he quickly made up for any lost time as he blitzed through High-A and reached an age-appropriate level early in 2022. The arsenal is lacking: the fastball sits at 93 mph; his curveball is a vanilla breaking ball; his cutter / slider is mediocre; and his changeup isn't the type to miss many bats. Backend potential, especially with the 45-grade command.

Ceiling: 1.0-win player
Risk: Moderate
MLB ETA: 2023

20. Bryce Hubbart, LHP

FB	CB	SL	CH	Command	Overall
50	55	55	45/50	50	40

Born: 06/28/01	Age: 22	Bats: L	Top Production Comp: N/A
Height: 6-1	Weight: 181	Throws: L	

Background: Highly touted as a senior at Windermere High School. The talented southpaw capped off his prep career in fashion, twirling a 0.73 ERA across 57.2 innings with a whopping 96 punch outs. *Perfect Game* ranked the 6-foot-1, 181-pound hurler as the 43rd best overall player in the state of Florida, the fourth best southpaw. Hubbart was able

Cincinnati Reds

to squeeze in seven appearances at Florida State University, three of which were starts, during the abbreviated 2020 season. His breakout would come the following season as he moved into the Seminoles' rotation full time: he would throw 71.0 innings, averaging 11.9 strikeouts and 3.7 walks per nine innings to go along with a 3.80 ERA. And after a ridiculously dominant jaunt through the Cape Cod League with Brewster, Hubbart raised the bar during his final season in college. He tossed 76.0 innings, recording a rock solid 96-to-21 strikeout-to-walk ratio and a 3.32 ERA. Cincinnati selected the Seminole ace in the third round, 94th overall, and signed him to a deal slightly more than $500,000. He would throw another 7.1 low-level innings during his professional debut, fanning 12 and walking six to go along with a 1.23 ERA.

Scouting Report: Consider the following:

> Since 2011, here's the list of ACC hurlers that averaged at least 11 strikeouts and fewer than 2.75 walks per nine innings in a season (min. 75 IP): Marcus Stroman, Danny Hultzen, Reid Detmers, Andrew Abbott, Parker Messick (twice), and – of course – Bryce Hubbart.

A soft-tossing lefty that, unfortunately, really doesn't have a place in today's high octane, supercharged fastball world. Hubbart's fastball works in the upper 80s and will peak at 92-mph. He features a pair of above-average breaking balls; an upper 70s curveball and a low 80s slider. He'll also mix in a fringy changeup, rarely. The command is so-so. There's just not a high ceiling *or* floor.

Ceiling: 0.5- to 1.0-win player
Risk: Moderate
MLB ETA: 2025

Cleveland Guardians

Top Prospects

Cleveland Guardians

1. Daniel Espino, RHP

FB	CB	SL	CH	Command	Overall
70	60	70	50	60	70

Born: 01/05/01	Age: 22	Bats: R	Top Production Comp: Jose Fernandez
Height: 6-2	Weight: 225	Throws: R	

Season	Team	Age	Level	IP	TBF	K/9	K%	BB/9	BB%	K-BB%	ERA	FIP	xFIP	Pit/Bat
2021	CLE	20	A	42.2	180	13.50	35.56%	4.85	12.78%	22.78%	3.37	3.20	3.29	4.00
2021	CLE	20	A+	49.0	195	16.16	45.13%	2.94	8.21%	36.92%	4.04	3.08	2.41	4.05
2022	CLE	21	AA	18.1	68	17.18	51.47%	1.96	5.88%	45.59%	2.45	3.09	1.52	4.03

Background: Throughout the history of the draft, extending all the way back to 1965, there's never been a high school right-handed pitcher picked with the top overall selection. More than a few have come close, going with the second overall pick – J.R. Richard, one of the game's greatest "What Ifs", the underrated Bill Gullickson, Josh Beckett, Jameson Taillon, Tyler Kolek (one of the biggest busts in history), and Hunter Greene. But, again, no teenage right-hander as gone atop the draft. There was a time during his junior season at Georgia Premier Academy that Espino *looked* like a true 1 / 1 candidate. Social media was *exploding* with viral clips of triple-digits fastballs and wickedly devastating breaking balls. But even after an equally dominant senior season, Espino tumbled in the draft. He didn't go #1. Or even among the Top 5. He continued to free fall past the tenth pick, beyond the 20th. And, finally, the team formerly known as the Indians sat with arms wide open with the 24th pick ended his lengthy waiting. With the exception of the Orioles (Adley Rutschman); the Royals (Bobby Witt Jr.), Blue Jays (Alek Manoah), Diamondbacks (Corbin Carroll), and Mariners (George Kirby), all the teams that passed on him have to be re-evaluating their reports. The 6-foot-2, 225-pound right-hander made quick work of the competition during his debut, posting a 34-to-10 strikeout-to-walk ratio in nine brief outings. But nothing could have prepared the baseball world for what was waiting in 2021. After returning from the COVID-induced hiatus, Espino averaged a whopping 14.9 strikeouts and 3.8 walks per nine innings across 20 starts with Lynchburg and Lake County. And the 2022 season started off in an even more impressive fashion – he posted an almost unbelievable 35-to-4 strikeout-to-walk ratio in only 18.1 innings of work. For those counting at home: he averaged 17.2 strikeouts and just 2.0 walks per nine innings. Unfortunately for fans, the organization, and especially Espino, the dominant righty originally hit the disabled list with a knee injury, but a wonky right shoulder kept him on the shelf the remainder of the year.

Snippet from The 2022 Prospect Digest Handbook: Insanely talented. Espino owns one of the best arsenals in the game. There's bonafide ace potential, but he'll need a third option uptick to get there.

Scouting Report: The season lasted just four starts before he hit the disabled list, but Espino was as dominant as I've seen any minor league hurler over the past decade or so. His fastball wasn't just electric, it was *nuclear*. The type of plus-plus offering that hitters could sit on it and still miss it by a country mile. The curveball will flash plus at times. And his slider adds a second plus-plus offering to his repertoire. Solid-average changeup. Espino's command showed tremendous improvement as well, moving from average to plus during his limited showings. You could make the argument that his ceiling is higher than any pitcher in the minor leagues. Missing significant time to a shoulder issue is a major red flag. The sky's the limit as long as he can stay on the mound. If it weren't for the injuries, Espino would have likely played a factor for the Guardians coming down the stretch.

Ceiling: 6.0-win player
Risk: Moderate to High
MLB ETA: 2023/2024

2. George Valera, LF/RF

Hit	Power	SB	Patience	Glove	Overall
45/55	55/65	50	70	55	60

Born: 11/13/00	Age: 22	Bats: L	Top Production Comp: Cliff Floyd
Height: 6-0	Weight: 195	Throws: L	

Season	Team	Age	Level	PA	1B	2B	3B	HR	SB	CS	BB%	K%	AVG	OBP	SLG	ISO
2021	CLE	20	A+	263	29	2	4	16	10	5	20.91%	22.05%	0.256	0.430	0.548	0.291
2021	CLE	20	AA	100	17	3	0	3	1	0	11.00%	30.00%	0.267	0.340	0.407	0.140
2022	CLE	21	AA	387	52	17	3	15	2	4	13.44%	25.84%	0.264	0.367	0.470	0.206
2022	CLE	21	AAA	179	17	8	0	9	0	0	12.29%	25.14%	0.221	0.324	0.448	0.227

Background: Cleveland's 2016 draft class will go down as one of the greatest in franchise history. While the books on Will Benson and Nolan Jones, the club's top two selections, are far from written, the front office somehow unearthed three quality big league starting pitchers in the mid- to late-rounds of the draft. Aaron Civale, the forever underappreciated hurler, was a third round selection out of Northeastern University. Shane Bieber, a product of UC Santa Barbara, fell to them a round later. And Ball State hurler Zach Plesac, who can't quite seem to get out of his own way at the big league level, was the 362nd overall pick that summer. It was a franchise altering class. One year later the Chris Antonetti-led regime may have pulled off the seemingly impossible task again. This time, though, on the international free agency market. As part of the 2017-18 signing period, the organization added the likes of Jose Tena, Alexfri Planez, Jhonkensy Noel, Brayan Rocchio, and George Valera with the latter two potential franchise cornerstones. Originally born in Queens, New York, Valera moved to the Dominican Republic as a young teenager, allowing him to cash in on his potential as potent, middle-of-the-lineup thumper. He would sign with the club eventually known as the Guardians for $1.3 million on July 2, 2017. And it wouldn't take long for the 6-foot, 195-pound outfielder to

Cleveland Guardians

establish himself as one of the system's – and game's – best prospects. After a brief debut in the Arizona Summer League in 2018, Valera put together a saber-slanted showing in the New York-Penn League the following summer, batting .236/.356/.446 with seven doubles, one triple, eight homeruns, and six stolen bases (in eight attempts) in only 46 games of work. The New York native, with the rest of minor league baseball, would sit out the 2020 season as the pandemic raged on. And when he returned, Valera looked like a masher on a mission. Appearing in just 86 games between Lake County and Akron, he slugged an aggregate .260/.405/.505 with five doubles, four triples, 19 homeruns, and 11 stolen bases. Last season he continued his assault on minor league arms as he quickly passed the Double-A test by hitting .264/.367/.470 in 90 games with the RubberDucks. He would spend the last few weeks battling the Triple-A competition. Valera finished the year with a combined .250/.353/.463 slash line with career highs in doubles (25) and homeruns (24) to go along with three triples and a pair of stolen bases. Per *Weighted Runs Created Plus*, his overall production topped the league average mark by 21%.

Snippet from The 2022 Prospect Digest Handbook: He hits laser beams as well and as hard as any prospect. Valera has the makings of the best homegrown everyday player since Francisco Lindor.

Scouting Report: Consider the following:

> Since 2006, only three 21-year-old hitters met the following criteria in any Double-A league (min. 350 PA): 125 to 135 wRC+, a 24% to 28% strikeout rate, and a double-digit walk rate. Those three hitters: Josh Lowe, Jordan Schafer, and – of course – George Valera.

Well over a decade ago, the Guardians' farm system boasted a young power-hitting outfielder by the name of Nick Weglarz, a former third round pick out of a Canadian High School. Weglarz had the *look* of a future potent big league bat – solid hit tool, above-average power with a 60-grade on his future power, and he drew walks by the gobs. He battled some injuries and never quite took the final step forward. George Valera is at the point in his career when Weglarz eventually stumbled. The young Dominican outfielder has the *look* of a future big league bopper – plus-plus raw power that's just beginning to show up in games, a solid hit tool, and a surprisingly above-average glove in either corner outfield spot. Watching Valera at bats are a fun, a bit of a spectacle. Long and wiry, but strong. He has a bit of a bat waggle as he's progressing through his mechanics, a little bit of Gary Sheffield. What separates Valera from the pack is his ability to adjust mid-pitch. His recognition is off the charts. He's struggled with middling batting averages throughout his career, but it wouldn't be shocking to see him grow into a .270/.380/.500-type hitter at the big league level. He's a natural pull hitter, so he may be exploited by good pitching / offspeed low and away.

Ceiling: 6.0-win player
Risk: Moderate
MLB ETA: 2023

3. Tanner Bibee, RHP

FB	CB	SL	CH	Command	Overall
60	50	60	70	55	60

Born: 03/05/99	Age: 24	Bats: R	Top Production Comp: Aaron Nola
Height: 6-2	Weight: 205	Throws: R	

Season	Team	Age	Level	IP	TBF	K/9	K%	BB/9	BB%	K-BB%	ERA	FIP	xFIP	Pit/Bat
2022	CLE	23	A+	59.0	231	13.12	37.23%	1.98	5.63%	31.60%	2.59	3.04	2.55	3.82
2022	CLE	23	AA	73.2	285	9.90	28.42%	1.71	4.91%	23.51%	1.83	2.61	3.67	3.99

Background: The Guardians front office, analytics gurus, and scouting department have seemingly done the improbable – again. They unearthed a competent future big league arm beyond the first few opening rounds of the draft. Following in the footsteps of Shane Bieber, Aaron Civale, Zach Plesac, Xzavion Curry, Hunter Gaddis, among many others. But, perhaps, the most astonishing footnote to the Bibee story is his lackadaisical senior campaign at Cal State Fullerton. The 6-foot-2, 205-pound right-hander averaged just 6.7 strikeouts and 2.1 walks per nine innings across 14 starts and a pair of relief appearances. But Bibee was rejuvenated as he made his professional debut last season. Splitting time between Lake County and Akron, the club's High-A and Double-A affiliates, the former Titan tossed 132.2 innings with an impeccably dominant 167-to-27 strikeout-to-walk ratio to go along with a sparkling 2.17 ERA and a 2.80 FIP. He averaged 11.3 strikeouts and just 1.8 walks per nine innings last year.

Scouting Report: Consider the following:

> Since 2006, only four 23-year-old hurlers posted a 27% to 30% strikeout percentage with a 4% to 6% walk percentage in any Double-A league (min. 70 IP): Alex Faedo, former Cleveland top prospect Justus Sheffield, Jarod Plummer, and – of course – Tanner Bibee.

There were points last season that Bibee looked like a man among boys, simply overpowering, outthinking, and outperforming the competition by such a wide margin that it was almost unfair. The former Cal State Fullerton hurler not only pounds the strike zone with high regularity, but he consistently throws quality strikes. Here's the thing: Bibee made 25 starts between the Captains and RubberDucks in 2022; he never walked

Cleveland Guardians

more than two hitters in any of those games. And he walked one or fewer batters 16 times. The 6-foot-2, 205-pound right-hander, though, isn't the typical soft-tossing, finesse artist either. Plus fastball that sits, like clockwork, in the 94- to 96-mph range. Average curveball, plus upper 80s slider. But his changeup is a real differentiator. It's phenomenal. One of the best in professional baseball. Tremendous velocity separation, usually between 12- to 13-mph slower than his heater. Bibee throws it with exceptional arm speed and conviction. He had no qualms about doubling – or even tripling – up on the pitch and Double-A hitters still couldn't figure it out. It almost seems crazy, but there's some Aaron Nola type potential here.

Ceiling: 5.0-win player
Risk: Moderate
MLB ETA: 2023

4. Gavin Williams, RHP

FB	CB	SL	CH	Command	Overall
70	60	50/55	55	50	60

Born: 07/26/99	Age: 22	Bats: L	Top Production Comp: Luis Castillo
Height: 6-6	Weight: 238	Throws: R	

Season	Team	Age	Level	IP	TBF	K/9	K%	BB/9	BB%	K-BB%	ERA	FIP	xFIP	Pit/Bat
2022	CLE	22	A+	45.0	168	13.40	39.88%	2.80	8.33%	31.55%	1.40	1.64	2.43	4.20
2022	CLE	22	AA	70.0	282	10.54	29.08%	3.34	9.22%	19.86%	2.31	4.03	4.13	4.19

Background: The Guardians have been universally praised for their pitching development program over the past several seasons, sending the likes of Shane Bieber, Triston McKenzie, Aaron Civale, Zach Plesac, Cal Quantrill, Sam Hentges, Trevor Stephan, James Karinchak, and Emmanuel Clase up to the big leagues. Some were drafted, others were acquired via trade and, yet, some found in the Rule 5 Draft (like the underappreciated Trevor Stephan). Cleveland is not only adept at identifying pitching talent, but their incredibly efficient at developing it as well. So it's no surprise that their first pick in the 2021 draft has shot up every prospect list in the world as he dominated during his first full year in the professional ranks. A product of East Carolina University, the once erratic reliever blossomed during his final season with the Pirates as he averaged 14.4 strikeouts and just 2.3 walks per nine innings with a sparkling 1.88 ERA across 12 starts and three relief appearances. After signing for $2.25 million two years ago, Williams would have to wait until 2022 to make his debut. And, boy, was it worth the wait. The 6-foot-6, 238-pound right-hander allowed three runs in his second professional start. It would be seven starts and 36.1 innings before he allowed another three runs total. He would make nine starts in High-A and another 16 in Double-A, throwing an aggregate 115.0 innings, averaging a whopping 11.7 punch outs and 3.1 walks per nine innings. He finished the year with a sparkling 1.96 ERA.

Snippet from The 2022 Prospect Digest Handbook: Williams showed a surprising amount of strikes during his final season with ECU. And even though he's now in his fourth collegiate season, he's still only 21. There's some reliever risk, but also some mid-rotation caliber potential.

Scouting Report: Consider the following:

> Since 2006, only two 22-year-old hurlers posted a 28% to 30% strikeout percentage with an 8% to 10% walk percentage in any Double-A league (min. 70 IP): Touki Toussaint and Gavin Williams.

Owner of a deep, well-rounded arsenal highlighted by a true-70 grade fastball that operates in the 96- to 98-mph range. Williams, though, is far from a one trick pony. The former ECU ace is adept at moving the ball around, changing speeds, and commanding all four quadrants of the strike zone. Plus mid-70s curveball. An upper-80s slider that flashes above-average on occasion. And a sneakily good changeup that will generate a surprising amount of swings-and-misses. Williams' numbers / performance continue to be impressive, but the Guardians limited his workload considerably last season. The big righty threw five or fewer innings in 16 of his 25 appearances. There's #2/ #3-type potential brewing here, a slight uptick from my report heading into the draft – though the reliever risk has evaporated. Big league ceiling: 10 K/9 and 3.3 BB/9.

Ceiling: 4.5-win player
Risk: Moderate
MLB ETA: 2023

5. Bo Naylor, C

Hit	Power	SB	Patience	Glove	Overall
35/45	45	50/40	50	60	60

Born: 02/21/00	Age: 23	Bats: L	Top Production Comp: Russell Martin
Height: 6-0	Weight: 205	Throws: R	

Season	Team	Age	Level	PA	1B	2B	3B	HR	SB	CS	BB%	K%	AVG	OBP	SLG	ISO
2021	CLE	21	AA	356	35	13	1	10	10	0	10.39%	31.46%	0.188	0.280	0.332	0.144
2022	CLE	22	AA	220	26	12	2	6	11	3	20.45%	20.91%	0.271	0.427	0.471	0.200
2022	CLE	22	AAA	290	32	14	2	15	9	1	12.76%	25.86%	0.257	0.366	0.514	0.257

Background: Like a rising phoenix from the ashes of the catching prospect scrap heap, Bo Naylor's prospect status – and future big league career – reemerged after phenomenal showing in 2022. Taken with the 29th overall pick out of St. Joan

Cleveland Guardians

of Arc Catholic High School in 2018, the lefty-swinging backstop quickly established himself as a solid second tier prospect at the position. He moved quickly through the Arizona Summer League during his debut, hitting .274/.381/.402 in 33 games. And he handled the old Midwest League the following season as well, batting .243/.313/.421 as a 19-year-old at the most demanding position – both in terms of physicality and mental – on the diamond. The Guardians, a normally conservative organization, pushed their former first rounder up to Double-A at the start of 2021, bypassing High-A altogether. And the squat 6-foot, 205-pound catcher was *abysmal*. Appearing in 87 games with the RubberDucks, Naylor cobbled together a paltry .189/.280/.332 showing with just 24 extra-base knocks. Last season, as a shock to no one, the front office sent the then-22-year-old back down to Double-A for another crack at the minors' most important test. He put together a career-best showing: he mashed .271/.427/.471 in 52 games. And Naylor continued to batter the competition as he moved up to Triple-A as well. He finished his minor league season with an aggregate .263/.392/.496 with personal bests in doubles (26), homeruns (21), and stolen bases (20). His overall production, as measured by *Weighted Runs Created Plus*, surpassed the league average mark by a stellar 39%. Cleveland called him up for a quick five-game cameo at the end of the year (he went 0-for-8) and even made their playoff roster as well.

Snippet from The 2022 Prospect Digest Handbook: It's not unheard of for a 21-year-old prospect to step into Double-A, struggle as much as Naylor did in 2021, and eventually carve out of a successful big league career. But it is exceptionally rare. The notable guys to do so include Cedric Hunter, Marwin Gonzalez, and Austin Hedges. The differentiating factor between those three and Naylor: swing-and-miss rates. Naylor posted a 31% K-rate last season, more than 50% higher than any of the three. The most troubling aspect about Naylor's disastrous 2021 campaign: he showed no signs of month-to-month progress. He's still a quality receiver behind the dish: *Baseball Prospectus* has him at +5.6 Framing Runs and Clay Davenport's metrics have him +4 overall on defense. He's still young enough to rebound, but it's likely going to come down to his ability to make consistent contact – which he *was* doing *prior* to 2021.

Scouting Report: Consider the following:

> Since 2006, only three 22-year-old hitters posted a 125 to 135 wRC+ with a double-digit walk rate and a 25% to 29% strikeout rate in any Triple-A league (min. 275 PA): Yoan Moncada, Mark Vientos, and – of course – Bo Naylor. For those counting at home: Moncada's been a streaky, rollercoaster-type hitter at the big league level, but sports a career .253/.334/.425 slash line, and Vientos is one of the Mets' best hitting prospects.

When it comes to Naylor, the conversation is always going to start with his work behind the plate, not at the plate. So let's start there. Simply put, he's an elite defender *and* strong pitch-framer – the best of both worlds for a backstop. It wouldn't be surprising to see him earn a Gold Glove or two at the big league level. Now the bat… Naylor's one of the more patient, grind-it-out bats in the minor leagues. He was able to tone down the swing-and-miss issues in his return to Double-A, but they popped back up again with Columbus (25.9% K-rate). His above-average raw power started to show up more consistently in games last season. The above-average speed continues to be an unexpected bonus. In terms of big league ceiling, think: .245/.330/.430 with 15 homeruns, six to eight stolen bases and tremendous defensive value.

Ceiling: 4.0-win player
Risk: Moderate
MLB ETA: 2023

6. Brayan Rocchio, 2B/SS

Hit	Power	SB	Patience	Glove	Overall
55	50	55	45	60	55

Born: 01/13/01	Age: 22	Bats: B	Top Production Comp: N/A
Height: 5-10	Weight: 170	Throws: R	

Season	Team	Age	Level	PA	1B	2B	3B	HR	SB	CS	BB%	K%	AVG	OBP	SLG	ISO
2021	CLE	20	A+	288	45	13	1	9	14	6	6.94%	22.57%	0.265	0.337	0.428	0.163
2021	CLE	20	AA	203	31	13	4	6	7	4	6.40%	20.20%	0.293	0.360	0.505	0.212
2022	CLE	21	AA	432	64	21	1	13	12	6	9.72%	18.75%	0.265	0.349	0.432	0.166
2022	CLE	21	AAA	152	21	6	0	5	2	3	7.89%	13.82%	0.234	0.298	0.387	0.153

Background: The Robin to George Valera's Batman – or maybe it'll end up being the other way around. Rocchio was part of the club's massive international free agency heist during the 2017-18 signing period. Though, to be fair, Rocchio's $125,000 bonus should provide a far superior return on investment (as compared to the seven-figure sum Valera commanded). The switch-hitting middle infielder turned in a dynamite debut showing in 2018, slugging a scorching .335/.390/.442 in 60 games between the foreign and stateside rookie leagues. The front office pushed the then-18-year-old Venezuelan into the old New York-Penn League, but he seemingly left his swing in the Arizona Summer League as he batted a mediocre .250/.310/.373. Following the return of minor league ball from its COVID-induced vacation, Rocchio mashed his way through High-A and breezed through 44 games in at the minors' toughest level – Double-A. He finished the year with an aggregate .277/.346/.460 with 26 doubles, five triples, 15 homeruns, and 21 stolen bases. Last season, the organization sent the promising youngster back down to Akron for some additional seasoning. But after hitting a solid .265/.349/.432 through 99 games, he was deemed ready for the final minor league stop. Rocchio finished the year with an aggregate .257/.336/.420 with career bests in doubles (27) and homeruns (18) to go along with 14 stolen bases. His overall production, as measured by *Weighted Runs Created Plus*, topped the league average mark by 6%.

Cleveland Guardians

Snippet from The 2022 Prospect Digest Handbook: One of the club's biggest risers up the prospect charts in 2021. Beyond Valera, Rocchio represent the highest ceiling bat in the entire farm system. He's not a lock of superstardom, but he could be a perennial All-Star.

Scouting Report: Consider the following:

> Since 2006, only four 21-year-old hitters met the following criteria in a Double-A season (min. 350 PA): 110 to 120 wRC+, a 17% to 20% strikeout rate, and a 7% to 10% walk rate. Those four hitters: Ian Stewart, Ryan Kalish, Chris Marrero, and – of course – Brayan Rocchio.

A gifted defender that may earn a Gold Glove or two on either side of the keystone. Rocchio packs considerable more thump than his generously listed 5-foot-10, 170-pound frame would suggest. The young switch-hitter uncorks a hellacious swing with premium bat speed on either side of the batter's box. There's a chance for at least an above-average hit tool, maybe even plus, with average power and strong value with the glove. Rocchio's the type of player that does everything well without truly standing out. He could really pop like Andres Gimenez.

Ceiling: 3.5-win player
Risk: Moderate
MLB ETA: 2023

7. Chase DeLauter, CF

Hit	Power	SB	Patience	Glove	Overall
55	55/60	55	50	50	55

Born: 10/08/01	Age: 21	Bats: L	Top Production Comp: N/A
Height: 6-4	Weight: 235	Throws: L	

Background: The list of notable sports alumni from Hedgesville High School is short: QJ Peterson, who starred at VMI, has played European pro basketball since 2017, and Gale Catlett, the former University of Cincinnati and West Virginia University basketball coach. Chase DeLauter is about to become the biggest athlete to come out Hedgesville. A three-sport phenom during his prep career, DeLauter, who starred on the court and the gridiron, was spectacular during his junior campaign for the Eagles. He hit a scorching .500 and was practically unhittable on the mound, posting a 1.95 ERA with 64 punch outs. DeLauter followed that up with an even better showing during his senior campaign – en route to winning the West Virginia Gatorade Player of the Year. He bashed .606 with 21 doubles, eight homeruns, and 52 RBIs. He also posted a 0.82 ERA with a 9-2 win-loss record. And DeLauter didn't stop hitting once he stepped foot on James Madison University's campus. In the COVID-shortened 2020 season, the 6-foot-4, 235-pound centerfielder slugged .382/.455/.559 with seven doubles, one triple, one homerun, and seven stolen bases (in eight attempts) in only 16 games. *Collegiate Baseball* named him a Freshman All-American. DeLauter upped the ante even further during his follow up redshirt season, hitting .386/.508/.723 with 12 doubles, two triples, six homeruns, and seven stolen bases in 26 games. The West Virginian spent that summer dominating the Cape Cod League competition to the tune of .298/.397/.589 with seven doubles, one triple, and nine homeruns in 34 games for the New Orleans Firebirds. Last season – despite a foot injury that prematurely ended his junior campaign – DeLauter batted .437/.576/.828 with eight doubles, one triple, eight homeruns, and 10 stolen bases (in 11 attempts). Cleveland selected DeLauter in the opening round, 17th overall, and signed him to a deal worth $3.75 million. He did not appear in a professional game.

Scouting Report: Per the usual, my pre-draft write-up:

> "Consider the following:
>
>> Since 2011, only three Division I hitters posted a .400/.550/.800 slash line in a season (min. 100): Erik Ostberg, Michael Carico, and – of course – Chase DeLauter.
>
> The level of competition in the Colonial Athletic Association isn't exactly equivalent to the SEC – so some of DeLauter's career .402/.520/.715 slash line has to be discounted. Except that the toolsy center fielder was among the best offensive performers in the Cape Cod League in 2021. Well rounded offensive performer with the rare potential to be a five-tool contributor in the professional ranks. Above-average hit tool, plus power potential, speed, defense, arm. DeLauter hits all the checkboxes. A swing taken out of the Will Clark handbook, DeLauter's could be the second college hitter off the board – after Brooks Lee. The Chicago Cubs and Minnesota Twins seem like ideal landing spots."

Ceiling: 3.5-win player
Risk: Moderate
MLB ETA: 2024/2025

Cleveland Guardians

8. Gabriel Arias, 3B/SS

Hit	Power	SB	Patience	Glove	Overall
50	50	40	45	50	50

Born: 02/27/00	Age: 23	Bats: R	Top Production Comp: Amed Rosario
Height: 6-1	Weight: 217	Throws: R	

Season	Team	Age	Level	PA	1B	2B	3B	HR	SB	CS	BB%	K%	AVG	OBP	SLG	ISO
2021	CLE	21	AAA	483	79	29	3	13	5	1	8.07%	22.77%	0.284	0.348	0.454	0.170
2022	CLE	22	AAA	323	47	9	0	13	5	1	7.74%	24.15%	0.240	0.310	0.406	0.167

Background: Two years removed from the deal with the Padres, it's clear that the Guardians are winners. The franchise sent veteran right-hander Mike Clevinger, outfielder Greg Allen, and minor league hurler Matt Waldron to San Diego for righty Cal Quantrill, underrated slugger Josh Naylor, who's become an emotional leader on the team, Owen Miller, Austin Hedges, Joey Cantillo, and Gabriel Arias. Originally signed by the Padres for just under $2 million, Arias was one of the more pleasant surprises in the Cleveland farm system two years ago as he mashed .284/.348/.454 with 29 doubles, three triples, 13 homeruns, and five stolen bases in 115 games in Triple-A as a 21-year-old. And with his prospect status arrow surging upwards, the 6-foot-1, 217-pound infielder missed more than a month due to a fractured hand, which required surgery, and hardly resembled the same hitter at the plate as he batted a mediocre .240/.310/.406 with nine doubles and 13 homeruns in 77 games with the Clippers. Per *Weighted Runs Created Plus*, his overall production was 11% *below* the league average mark. Arias also made a couple trips to the big leagues as well, hitting a paltry .192/.321/.319 in 57 plate appearances.

Snippet from The 2022 Prospect Digest Handbook: As with a lot of prospects last season, especially ones that bypassed an entire level, there was an adjustment period (e.g. slow start) for Arias. He batted a putrid .196/.318/.299 over his first 31 games. But beginning on June 12th through the rest of the season, the 6-foot-1, 217-pound infielder slugged an impressive .313/.359/.505 with 27 doubles, three triples, and 10 homeruns. He has always shown an advanced feel at the plate, but last season he displayed a more patient approach as well, something that he's only hinted at in the past. There's 20-homer thump brewing in the bat.

Scouting Report: Consider the following:

> Since 2006, only a pair of 22-year-old hitters met the following criteria in any Triple-A league (min. 300 PA): 85 to 95 wRC+, 23% to 25% strikeout rate, and a 6% to 9% walk rate. Those two hitters: Reid Brignac and Gabriel Arias. For those that don't remember, Brignac was four-time consensus Top 100 prospect during his minor league career and finished his nine-year big league career with .219/.264/.309 slash line as a utility guy.

Just like the previous season, Arias started 2022 as frigid as a Cleveland winter, hitting a lowly .180/.249/.317 over his first 46 games between Triple-A, his rehab assignment, and the big leagues. But he batted an impressive .288/.366/.458 over his remaining 42 games with Columbus. When Arias is bad, he's *really* bad. And when he's good, he's a quality player that can help any team. Cleveland needs to unlock the reason as to why he starts the year off so slowly. It feels like Arias is undervalued at this point, thanks in large part to his injury-riddled 2022. I'm still a believer in the bat, power, and speed. There's some Amed Rosario-type ceiling, something along the lines of .275/.315/.430 with 15 homeruns.

Ceiling: 2.5-win player
Risk: Moderate
MLB ETA: Debuted in 2022

9. Jhonkensy Noel, 1B/3B/RF

Hit	Power	SB	Patience	Glove	Overall
50	60	30	45	45/50	50

Born: 07/15/01	Age: 21	Bats: R	Top Production Comp: N/A
Height: 6-3	Weight: 250	Throws: R	

Season	Team	Age	Level	PA	1B	2B	3B	HR	SB	CS	BB%	K%	AVG	OBP	SLG	ISO
2021	CLE	19	A	162	37	10	1	11	2	1	4.32%	16.67%	0.393	0.426	0.693	0.300
2021	CLE	19	A+	111	17	3	0	8	3	1	8.11%	27.93%	0.280	0.351	0.550	0.270
2022	CLE	20	A+	252	22	9	0	19	1	0	7.14%	31.75%	0.219	0.286	0.509	0.289
2022	CLE	20	AA	278	27	16	2	13	2	0	10.79%	22.66%	0.242	0.338	0.488	0.246
2022	CLE	20	AAA	18	2	1	0	0	0	0	5.56%	38.89%	0.176	0.222	0.235	0.059

Background: During the 1990s, the John Hart-led regime dealt away a *tremendous* amount of high-end caliber talent, particularly young power hitters. Guys like Jeremy Burnitz or Richie Sexson or Brian Giles or Sean Casey. But the one guy that the front office did hold onto was Russell Branyan. Owning true 80-grade power and the author of mammoth moonshots, Russell the Muscle was a man well ahead of his time with low batting averages, high OBPs, and massive thump. Jhonkensy Noel turned in a Russell Branyan-esque season in 2022. Added as part of the same international free agent class as Brayan Rocchio, Jose Tena, and George Valera, Noel was one of the system's biggest surprises in 2021. The 6-foot-2, 250-pound corner infielder / outfielder mashed .340/.390/.615 with 14 doubles, one triple, and 19 homeruns in only 70 games between the Complex League, Low-A, and High-A. Last season, Noel made extended stops with Lake County and Akron and capped the year off with a brief tour of Triple-A. His numbers, though, declined as he batted .229/.310/.489 with 26 doubles, two triples, 32 homeruns, and a surprising trio of stolen bases. Per *Weighted Runs Created Plus*, his overall production topped the league average mark by a solid 14%.

Cleveland Guardians

Snippet from The 2022 Prospect Digest Handbook: In the running for the single most underrated prospect in baseball entering the 2022 season. He might own some of the best pure raw power in the game; it's on the same level of Franmil Reyes. Defensively, he's still seeing significant time at the hot corner, but once he fills out he's all but destined to slide over to first base.

Scouting Report: Consider the following:

Name	Season	Level	Age	PA	AVG	OBP	SLG	BB%	K%
Anthony Rizzo	2010	AA	20	467	0.263	0.334	0.481	9.64%	21.41%
Jhonkensy Noel	2022	AA	20	278	0.242	0.338	0.488	10.79%	22.66%

Noel had an interesting 2022 season, to say the least. The husky corner infielder / outfielder struggled with his contact rates during his time with Lake County, whiffing in nearly 32% of his plate appearance. And, almost inexplicably, the Dominican bopper made far better, more consistent contact during his time in Double-A, the minors' toughest level. Noel remains one of the better breaking ball hitters in the minor leagues. But his setup is odd, lacking a typical load. His thump is enough of a carrying rate that he could start with a 40-grade hit tool. I do think the hit tool creeps up close to 50-grade territory. And I'm still firmly on the Jhonkensy Noel bandwagon.

Ceiling: 2.5-win player
Risk: Moderate
MLB ETA: 2023/2024

10. Angel Martinez, 2B/SS

Hit	Power	SB	Patience	Glove	Overall
50	50	50	50	55	50

Born: 01/27/02	Age: 21	Bats: B	Top Production Comp: N/A
Height: 6-0	Weight: 165	Throws: R	

Season	Team	Age	Level	PA	1B	2B	3B	HR	SB	CS	BB%	K%	AVG	OBP	SLG	ISO
2021	CLE	19	A	424	58	20	6	7	13	6	10.14%	20.75%	0.241	0.319	0.382	0.141
2022	CLE	20	A+	331	51	17	3	10	10	6	12.08%	17.52%	0.288	0.384	0.477	0.189
2022	CLE	20	AA	103	10	6	1	3	2	1	11.65%	17.48%	0.244	0.356	0.451	0.207

Background: Former big leaguer Sandy Martinez was a grinder, a baseball lifer that (A) was once a Top 100 prospect according to *Baseball America*, (B) spent parts of 15 seasons in the minor leagues, yet only tallied 880 games (or an average of just 59 games a season, and (C) appeared in 218 big league games across parts of eight seasons (or just 27 games per year). One of Sandy's sons, Angel, has developed into a significantly superior prospect. A switch-hitting 6-foot, 186-pound middle infielder out of Santo Domingo, Martinez turned in an impressive professional debut in his home country in 2019, slugging .306/.402/.428 with a perfectly even 29-to-29 strikeout-to-walk ratio in 56 games. The front office sent the then-19-year up to Low-A in 2021 – though the bat didn't perform nearly as well as he batted .241/.319/.382 with 20 doubles, six triples, seven homeruns, and 13 stolen bases (in 19 attempts). Last season, though, Martinez regained his offensive prowess with some added thump. He mashed an aggregate .278/.378/.471 with career bests in doubles (23) and homeruns (13) to go along with four triples, and 12 stolen bases (in 19 attempts). Per *Weighted Runs Created Plus*, his overall production topped the league average mark by an impressive 35%. Following the season, Martinez appeared in 21 games with Peoria Javelinas, hitting .260/.341/.343 with just two extra-base knocks (both of them homeruns) in 85 plate appearances.

Snippet from The 2022 Prospect Digest Handbook: He could be one of the bigger breakouts in the G-Men's system in 2022.

Scouting Report: Consider the following:

> Since 2006, only three 20-year-old hitters met the following criteria in any High-A league (min. 300 PA): 135 to 145 wRC+, a 16% to 19% strikeout rate, and a double-digit walk rate. Those three hitters: Joc Pederson, Lars Anderson, and – of course – Angel Martinez.

A power-hitting outfielder, a power-hitting first baseman, and...a middle infielder. Martinez shows a short, lightning quick stroke at the plate, allowing him to give the inside pitch a surprising jolt and just as easily shoot the outside offering to the opposite field. Strong bat to ball skills, average power, and above-average speed (though he's not overly efficient on the base paths). Defensively, the Guardians are loaded at the shortstop position, but he's an above-average defender on either side of the keystone. Even after his breakout campaign, Martinez remains one of the more underrated prospects in the minor leagues. There's the floor as a solid backup infielder with the ceiling as a league average starter, maybe a touch higher.

Ceiling: 2.5-win player
Risk: Moderate
MLB ETA: 2023/2024

Cleveland Guardians

11. Logan Allen, LHP

FB	CU	SL	CH	Command	Overall
50	55	55	60	55	60

Born: 09/05/98	Age: 24	Bats: L	Top Production Comp: Joey Lucchesi
Height: 6-0	Weight: 190	Throws: R	

Season	Team	Age	Level	IP	TBF	K/9	K%	BB/9	BB%	K-BB%	ERA	FIP	xFIP	Pit/Bat
2021	CLE	22	A+	51.1	200	11.75	33.50%	2.28	6.50%	27.00%	1.58	2.80	3.17	3.80
2021	CLE	22	AA	60.0	231	11.40	32.90%	1.95	5.63%	27.27%	2.85	3.73	3.54	4.04
2022	CLE	23	AA	73.0	292	12.82	35.62%	2.71	7.53%	28.08%	3.33	3.15	2.85	3.93
2022	CLE	23	AAA	59.2	270	11.01	27.04%	4.37	10.74%	16.30%	6.49	4.36	4.45	3.94

Background: For just the fourth time in franchise history, the Guardians went fishing in the waters at Florida International University as they selected southpaw Logan Allen in the second round three years ago. Allen, the 56th overall player taken that summer, was remarkably consistent during his tenure with the Panthers, leaving the school with a career 3.33 ERA, 246 punch outs, and just 47 free passes in 183.2 innings of work. The 6-foot, 190-pound left-hander would make his professional debut two years ago, moving quickly through High-A and settling in for a dozen appearances at the game's most challenging minor league level – Double-A. He finished his first pro season by averaging 11.6 strikeouts and just 2.1 walks per nine innings. Last season, the front office sent the promising hurler back down to Akron for some additional seasoning. But after continued dominance across 13 starts, he was eventually promoted up to the final minor league stop – though his command backed up and his ERA bloated like a dead whale. He finished his sophomore season with an impressive 177-to-51 strikeout-to-walk ratio, a 4.75 ERA, and a 3.70 FIP in 132.2 innings of work. He averaged 12.0 K/9 and 3.5 BB/9.

Scouting Report: Consider the following:

> Since 2006, only four 23-year-old hurlers met the following criteria in any Triple-A league (min. 50 IP): 26% to 28% strikeout percentage with a 9.5% to 11.5% walk percentage. Those four hurlers: Mike Foltynewicz, Allen Webster, Jacob Rhame, and – of course – Logan Allen.

The crafty type that relies on a strong feel for the strike zone and a bevy of quality secondary offerings. Allen's fastball operates in the 90- to 92-mph range and he loves to elevate it to try and close out at bats. His cutter and slider are both sweeping, horizontally darting breaking balls – each above-average. Like Tanner Bibee, Allen's changeup is a difference maker. It lacks a whole lot of velocity separation as it sits in the 85-mph range, but it generates a lot of swings-and-misses. Unlike a lot of the club's other top hurlers, like Daniel Espino, Tanner Bibee, and Gavin Williams, Allen's ceiling is limited, but he *does* have a high floor. He should be a competent backend starter.

Ceiling: 1.5- to 2.0-win player
Risk: Low to Moderate
MLB ETA: 2023

12. Jaison Chourio, CF

Hit	Power	SB	Patience	Glove	Overall
30/55	30/55	50	50	55	55

Born: 05/19/05	Age: 18	Bats: B	Top Production Comp: N/A
Height: 6-1	Weight: 162	Throws: R	

Season	Team	Age	Level	PA	1B	2B	3B	HR	SB	CS	BB%	K%	AVG	OBP	SLG	ISO
2022	CLE	17	DSL	175	26	7	3	1	14	4	22.86%	12.57%	0.280	0.446	0.402	0.121

Background: Milwaukee hit an absolute homerun when the organization signed Jackson Chourio to a $1.9 million in 2019. Just two years later the former shortstop turned outfielder has vaulted all the way to one of the game's premier prospects. Cleveland's hoping for similar results with Chourio's younger brother, Jaison. The 6-foot-1, 162-pound switch-hitting outfielder inked a deal with the Guardians for $1.2 million in January 2021. The younger Chourio made his anticipated professional debut last summer in the Dominican Summer League, hitting an impressive .280/.446/.402 with seven doubles, three triples, one homerun, and 14 stolen bases (in 18 total attempts). Per *Weighted Runs Created Plus*, his overall production topped the league average mark by a stellar 40%.

Scouting Report: Long limbed with a body type like NBA future Hall of Famer Kevin Durant, the younger Chourio has *plenty* of room to add to his potentially explosive frame. Above-average runner with the skills and instincts to remain in centerfield. Chourio has the potential to develop above-average power and a matching hit tool – though he's years away from maturity in both regards. He could be a someone to watch in the coming years.

Ceiling: 3.0-win player
Risk: Extreme
MLB ETA: 2026

Cleveland Guardians

13. Justin Campbell, RHP

FB	CB	SL	CH	Command	Overall
55	55	55	50	55	50

Born: 02/14/01	Age: 22	Bats: L	Top Production Comp: N/A
Height: 6-7	Weight: 219	Throws: R	

Background: California-based Simi Valley High School has a pretty lengthy track record of sending players to the professional ranks. The list of big leaguers includes: Jeff Weaver, Jered Weaver, Scott Radinsky, Tim Laker, and Red Barrett. The prep school's also produced three third round picks (Radinsky, Nick Barnese, and Jonathan Meyer), a fourth rounder (Bryan Anderson), and a fifth rounder (Bob Skube). Campbell, who was originally drafted by the Astros in the 18th round in 2019, significantly improved his draft stock over the past three seasons at Oklahoma State University. The big, hard-throwing right-hander was in the midst of a strong true freshman season before COVID prematurely ended it, throwing 20.1 innings with 22 strikeouts and six walks. Campbell continued to impress over the course of a full season the following year, posting a 102-to-27 strikeout-to-walk ratio in 84.0 innings of work. He spent the summer playing for the Stripes squad for Team USA, tossing another 6.0 innings with seven punch outs and a free pass. Last season Campbell's production – once again – took another step forward as he posted the best peripherals of his three-year career: he averaged 12.5 strikeouts and just 2.2 walks per nine innings. He finished the year with a 3.82 ERA. Cleveland selected the big righty in the opening round last summer, 37th overall, and signed him to a deal worth $1.7 million. He did not make his debut last season.

Scouting Report: Per the usual, my pre-draft write-up:

> "Consider the following:
>
> Since 2015, only four Division I hurlers averaged at least 12 strikeouts and between 2.0 and 2.5 walks per nine innings in a season (min. 100 IP): Logan Gilbert, Cooper Hjerpe, Drew Thorpe, and Justin Campbell.
>
> Not only is the big righty a consistent strike-thrower, but he throws a surprising number of quality strikes – surprising for a 6-foot-7 hurler. Campbell's fastball isn't overpowering, sitting in the low 90s, but it plays up given his 6-foot-7 frame size. There's also more in the tank as well. It wouldn't be surprising to see him consistently throwing in the mid-90s if he goes to the right organization – like Cleveland or Seattle. Above-average curveball, an above-average, workable slider, and a solid changeup. Campbell looks like a potential backend starting pitcher. At this point in his career, he's a better prospect than Giants gigantic right-hander Sean Hjelle, a second round pick in 2018. Relatively high floor."

Ceiling: 1.5- to 2.0-win player
Risk: Moderate
MLB ETA: 2023

14. Will Brennan, OF

Hit	Power	SB	Patience	Glove	Overall
55	40	40	50	50	45

Born: 02/02/98	Age: 25	Bats: L	Top Production Comp: Ben Francisco
Height: 6-0	Weight: 200	Throws: L	

Season	Team	Age	Level	PA	1B	2B	3B	HR	SB	CS	BB%	K%	AVG	OBP	SLG	ISO
2021	CLE	23	A+	269	42	22	1	4	13	4	9.29%	15.99%	0.290	0.368	0.441	0.151
2021	CLE	23	AA	177	34	6	0	2	2	2	10.17%	16.38%	0.280	0.369	0.360	0.080
2022	CLE	24	AA	157	25	12	1	4	5	2	10.83%	10.19%	0.311	0.382	0.504	0.193
2022	CLE	24	AAA	433	84	28	3	9	15	1	7.62%	12.24%	0.316	0.367	0.471	0.155

Background: While the club's 2019 draft class is highlighted by the supremely talented Daniel Espino – and rightfully so – Cleveland added several complementary prospects during the midsummer showcase, including: Hunter Gaddis, Xzavion Curry, and outfielder Will Brennan. An eighth round pick out of Kansas State University, Brennan has been a consistent source of production throughout the tenure of his minor league career. The 6-foot, 200-pound outfielder batted .306/.386/.438 in 31 games in rookie ball during his debut (but struggled in the old New York-Penn League). And then once minor league ball returned to action from its COVID-induced vacation, Brennan maintained his level of consistency by hitting .286/.369/.410 with 28 doubles, one triple, six homeruns, and 15 stolen bases between stints with Lake County and Akron. Last season, the former Wildcat did what he's always done – hit. He put together a career best .314/.371/.479 slash line with personal highs in doubles (40), homeruns (13), and stolen bases (20) while tying his previous best of four triples. Per *Weighted Runs Created Plus*, his overall production topped the league average mark by 27%. Cleveland called him up down the stretch as well. And, of course, he mashed to the tune of .357/.400/.500 in 11 games while cracking their playoff roster.

Cleveland Guardians

Scouting Report: Consider the following:

Since 2006, only five 24-year-old hitters posted a 117 to 127 wRC+ with a sub-14.0% strikeout rate in any Triple-A league (min. 350 PA): Ben Francisco, Rob Refsnyder, Chris Getz, José Pirela, and – of course – Will Brennan. Francisco was a league average bat for the duration of his seven-year big league career, including parts of three seasons in Cleveland. Refsnyder owns an 88 wRC+ in his big league career. Getz was a light-hitting utility guy in his career. And the same can be said for Pirela as well.

An average glove in any of the three outfield spots, Brennan owns an above-average hit tool, doubles power, solid speed, and a high-contact, grind-it-out approach at the plate. He's destined to be a quality backup outfielder for the better part of a decade. In terms of big league production, think: .255/.330/.400.

Ceiling: 1.5-win player
Risk: Low to Moderate
MLB ETA: Debuted in 2022

15. Cody Morris, RHP

FB	CB	SL	CH	Command	Overall
60	55	50	50/55	50	50

Born: 11/04/96	Age: 26	Bats: R	Top Production Comp: Michael Wacha
Height: 6-4	Weight: 205	Throws: R	

Season	Team	Age	Level	IP	TBF	K/9	K%	BB/9	BB%	K-BB%	ERA	FIP	xFIP	Pit/Bat
2021	CLE	24	AA	20.0	80	13.05	36.25%	3.15	8.75%	27.50%	1.35	2.62	3.14	4.18
2021	CLE	24	AAA	36.2	144	12.76	36.11%	2.95	8.33%	27.78%	1.72	1.86	3.06	4.15
2022	CLE	25	AAA	15.1	58	17.61	51.72%	3.52	10.34%	41.38%	2.35	2.46	1.85	4.41

Background: Now five years removed for their 2018 draft, it's safe to say that the Guardians class is an easy win. The organization added the likes of Steven Kwan, who finished third in the 2022 AL Rookie of the Year award and captured a Gold Glove, quality setup man Nick Sandlin, and Bo Naylor, one of the game's top catching prospects. And that doesn't include Bryan Lavastida, Richie Palacios, and – of course – right-hander Cody Morris, forever one of my favorite pitching prospects. The big 6-foot-4, 205-pound right-hander has been banged up for a lot of his amateur and professional career, dealing with Tommy John surgery, a wonky right shoulder, and some upper back issues. And 2022 was much the same. Morris started the year on the 60-day disabled list and – eventually – made it back to the mound in mid-July. After a trio of rehab appearances in the Complex League, the organization pushed the hard-throwing hurler up to Triple-A for six brief appearances. They eventually called him up in early September for the stretch run. He would throw 23.2 – mostly quality – innings with the Guardians, averaging 8.7 strikeouts and 4.6 walks per nine innings to go along with a dazzling 2.28 ERA, a 4.34 FIP, and a 4.19 xFIP.

Snippet from The 2022 Prospect Digest Handbook: One of my favorite arms in the entire minor leagues. Despite throwing just 150.0 minor league innings, Morris is nearing big league-readiness. He's a strike-thrower, but seems prone to bouts of wildness.

Scouting Report: If you catch Morris on the right day, you'd swear his ceiling would be something close to 80% to 85% of Corbin Burnes. A plus, mid-90s fastball, a cutter that flashes plus at times, an above-average curveball and changeup. And he'll throw some quality strikes as well. The problem with Morris, though, is his ability – or inability – to stay on the mound for extended periods of time. He's thrown fewer than 90 innings in each of his three full professional seasons. The Guardians had Morris start a handful of games down the stretch, but the big league club is chock full of starting pitchers, including: Shane Bieber, Cal Quantrill, Triston McKenzie, Zach Plesac, Aaron Civale. That doesn't include the likes of Tanner Bibee, Gavin Williams, Logan Allen, and Xzavion Curry. And – potentially – Daniel Espino. So Morris and his spotty health track record seem like an ideal fit for a multi-inning relief role.

Ceiling: 2.0-win player
Risk: High
MLB ETA: Debuted in 2022

16. Juan Brito, 2B

Hit	Power	SB	Patience	Glove	Overall
50/55	45	55	55	50	45

Born: 09/24/01	Age: 21	Bats: B	Top Production Comp: N/A
Height: 5-11	Weight: 162	Throws: R	

Season	Team	Age	Level	PA	1B	2B	3B	HR	SB	CS	BB%	K%	AVG	OBP	SLG	ISO
2019	COL	17	R	140	28	4	3	3	12	3	11.43%	10.71%	0.328	0.403	0.491	0.164
2021	COL	19	CPX	109	20	3	0	3	5	4	13.76%	19.27%	0.295	0.406	0.432	0.136
2022	COL	20	A	497	69	29	6	11	17	9	15.69%	14.29%	0.286	0.407	0.470	0.184

Background: Unheralded – or maybe, less heralded – signing off the international free agency market during the 2018 summer by the Rockies, Brito quietly developed into a solid little prospect. Better yet: maybe pundits

Cleveland Guardians

and analysts are just starting to notice. The Dominican-born middle infielder looked quite comfortable against the foreign rookie league pitching during his debut, batting .328/.403/.491 as a spry 17-year-old in 2019. His next season, which came after the lost year of COVID, Brito maintained status quo as he squared off against the stateside rookie league pitching, hitting .296/.406/.432. And last season, the now-20-year-old second baseman continued to perform as he moved into full season action in Low-A. In 107 games with the Fresno Grizzlies, the Santo Domingo native slugged .286/.407/.470 with 29 doubles, six triples, 11 homeruns, and 17 stolen bases (though he was thrown out eight times). Per *Weighted Runs Created Plus*, his numbers topped the average mark by 30%. Cleveland acquired Brito for former top prospect Nolan Jones.

Scouting Report: Consider the following:

> Last season Brito's 130 wRC+ tied for the seventh best showing in the California League. And only three players – Edgar Quero, Harry Ford, and Edwin Arroyo – were younger.

Now let's take a look at his performance relative to his peers. Consider the following:

> Since 2006, fifty-three 20-year-olds have posted a 125 to 135 wRC+ mark in any Low-A league (min. 350 PA). Only one of those players, Juan Brito, did so with more walks than strikeouts. Among those aforementioned 53, only six hitters posted a sub-16% strikeout rate and a double-digit walk rate: Luis Valbuena, Dan Vogelbach, Domonic Brown, Dom Nunez, Corban Joseph, and – of course – Juan Brito. The first five, by the way, spent at least a few years in the big leagues.

Another one of these extreme contact hitters. Brito was as consistent as they come in 2022: he hit against lefties (.283/.379/.424) and righties (.285/.414/.477) equally well, as well as at home (.295/.425/.495) and on the road (.275/.385/.430). And just for fun, here are his monthly OPS totals from April to August: .742, .910, .810, .974, 1.014. Very athletic without a true standout tool. Brito is solid at the keystone, flashes 45-grade power, and above-average speed. The hit tool may climb into above-average territory. Simple approach at the plate: see ball, hit ball. There's not enough to project as an eventual starter, but the foundation and groundwork as a solid bench option are certainly in place. Second base-only certainly limits his ceiling.

Ceiling: 1.5-win player
Risk: Moderate
MLB ETA: 2024/2025

17. Xzavion Curry, RHP

FB	CB	SL	CH	Command	Overall
55	55	55	50	50	45

Born: 07/27/98	Age: 24	Bats: R	Top Production Comp: Eli Morgan
Height: 6-0	Weight: 190	Throws: R	

Season	Team	Age	Level	IP	TBF	K/9	K%	BB/9	BB%	K-BB%	ERA	FIP	xFIP	Pit/Bat
2021	CLE	22	A	25.1	94	13.50	40.43%	1.42	4.26%	36.17%	1.07	2.08	2.90	3.93
2021	CLE	22	A+	67.2	270	10.64	29.63%	1.60	4.44%	25.19%	2.66	3.99	3.91	3.82
2022	CLE	23	AA	69.0	282	10.43	28.37%	2.48	6.74%	21.63%	3.65	3.75	3.96	4.02
2022	CLE	23	AAA	53.0	230	9.17	23.48%	3.91	10.00%	13.48%	4.58	4.98	4.96	3.90

Background: Oh, you know, just one of the seemingly countless arms the front office identified and developed as mid- to late-round draft picks. Cleveland selected the Georgia Tech hurler in the seventh round, 220th overall, four years ago. Curry wouldn't make his professional debut until the 2021 season, thanks to the COVID pandemic. But the undersized, at least in terms of the baseball world, right-hander quickly made up for lost time as soon as he toed a minor league rubber. The 6-foot, 190-pound hurler made stops at three separate levels that summer, throwing 97.2 innings with 123 strikeouts and just 16 free passes to go along with a sparkling 2.30 ERA. Last season the former Yellow Jacket split time between the RubberDucks and Clippers, throwing a career best 122.0 innings with 134 punch outs and 42 free passes. He finished the minor league season with an aggregate 4.06 ERA and a 4.28 FIP. Cleveland called up the former seventh rounder for two separate spot-starts against the Tigers and Mariners, throwing another 9.1 innings with three strikeouts and six walks. For his minor league career, he's averaging 10.5 K/9 and just 2.4 BB/9 with a 3.28 ERA.

Snippet from The 2022 Prospect Digest Handbook: A very intriguing, Cleveland-like pitching prospect. Curry hits a lot of the organizational check boxes: he consistently throws pitcher's pitches, hurls a heavy, riding fastball that he elevates with regularity, and can spin an above-average breaking ball. In all reality, there's not a whole lot of separation between Curry and, say, Eli Morgan. But you can never discount the organization's ability to maximize a pitcher's potential.

Cleveland Guardians

Scouting Report: Consider the following:

> Since 2006, ten 23-year-old hurlers posted a 22.5% to 24.5% strikeout percentage and a 9% to 11% walk percentage in any Triple-A league (min. 50 IP): Dylan Cease, Matt Harvey, Corbin Burnes, Brandon Bielak, Cody Martin, Rafael Montero, Scott Barnes, Edgmar Escalona, Jose Ascanio, and Xzavion Curry.

There aren't too many 92-mph fastballs that have the riding life that Curry's heater continually shows. It's more explosive than expected and he *loves* to elevate the offering any chance he can get. Above-average curveball and slider, both of which are spin-rate monsters averaging more than 2400 RPMs. He'll also mix a solid average, upper 80s changeup. Curry's high arm angle adds deception and blends his breaking balls well with his fastball. Just as I remarked in last year's Handbook, Curry continues to give off major Eli Morgan production vibes and that still remains true following his 2022 campaign.

Ceiling: 1.0- to 1.5-win player
Risk: Moderate
MLB ETA: Debuted in 2022

18. Parker Messick, LHP

FB	CB	SL	CH	Command	Overall
50	50	50/55	55	55	45

Born: 10/26/00	Age: 22	Bats: L	Top Production Comp: N/A
Height: 6-0	Weight: 225	Throws: L	

Background: It might not be the equivalent of the Gatorade Player of the Year Award, but the hefty lefty captured a notable award following his junior season at Plant City High School. The Hillsborough County Commission named the 6-foot, 225-pound former two-way star as The Wade Boggs Athletic Achievement Award winner in 2018. The southpaw punched out 45 and tallied a 1.58 ERA while hitting .298 and four homeruns. And he followed that with an even better showing during his senior campaign with the Raiders as he posted a 1.06 ERA while winning 11 games and struck out an impressive 125 hitters – production worthy of being named Mr. Florida Baseball. Messick made six relief appearances during his freshman season at Florida State University, allowing just one earned run (on a dinger) with 19 punch outs and just a pair of walks in 11.2 innings. The Seminoles' coaching staff transitioned the promising youngster into the rotation the following season. And he blossomed. In 16 starts for the ACC Conference school, Messick posted a 3.10 ERA while averaging 12.6 strikeouts and just 2.3 walks per nine innings in 90.0 innings. Last season Messick upped the production level into another stratosphere. In 16 starts, the Florida-born left-hander struck out 144, the fifth highest total in the country, against just 18 free passes in 98.2 innings of work. The Cleveland Guardians drafted him in the second round, 54th overall, and signed him to a deal worth $1.3 million. He did not make his professional debut last summer.

Scouting Report: Consider the following:

> Since 2015, only three Division I hurlers struck out at least 13 and walked fewer than 2.5 hitters per nine innings in a season (min. 90 IP): Logan Gilbert, Cooper Hjerpe, and – of course – Parker Messick. Among the aforementioned trio, here's the list of players to average less than 2.0 walks per nine innings: Parker Messick.

Not only did Messick finish fifth in the country in strikeouts, he finished 11th in strikeout-to-walk ratio as well. Herky, jerky southpaw with some deception thrown into his solid four-pitch mix. Messick features an average low 90s fastball that's quicker than the velocity would suggest. He'll complement it with an above-average changeup, a slider that will flash 55, and a mid-70s curveball. The changeup is, by far, his best offering, showing plenty of arm side run. Messick's arsenal plays up due to his strong feel for the strike zone. Cleveland does well in developing these type of pitchers (see: Aaron Civale, Josh Tomlin), so Messick seems to have landed in the ideal spot. Backend arm unless the velocity climbs two or three miles-per-hour.

Ceiling: 1.5-win player
Risk: Moderate
MLB ETA: 2025

Cleveland Guardians

19. Angel Genao, SS

Hit	Power	SB	Patience	Glove	Overall
40/50	30/40	40	50	50	40

Born: 05/19/03	**Age:** 19	**Bats:** B	**Top Production Comp:** N/A
Height: 5-9	**Weight:** 150	**Throws:** R	

Season	Team	Age	Level	PA	1B	2B	3B	HR	SB	CS	BB%	K%	AVG	OBP	SLG	ISO
2021	CLE	17	DSL	192	31	4	4	1	16	0	20.31%	15.10%	0.265	0.422	0.364	0.099
2022	CLE	18	CPX	171	39	6	1	2	6	3	9.36%	23.39%	0.322	0.394	0.416	0.094
2022	CLE	18	A	33	4	1	0	0	0	1	12.12%	15.15%	0.179	0.303	0.214	0.036

Background: It's probably difficult to believe, but the ball club cornered the market on a couple of high profile middle infielders on the international market in January of 2021, signing Fran Alduey and Angel Genao to seven-figure deals. While the early returns on Alduey are mixed, at best, Genao, who signed for $1.175 million, turned in a solid debut in the Dominican Summer League two years ago as he batted .265/.422/.364 with four doubles, four triples, one homeruns, and 16 stolen bases. Last season, the front office took the cautious approach and sent the switch-hitting Dominican infielder up to the Complex League. He responded with a hefty .322/.394/.416 slash line with six doubles, one triple, two homeruns, and half-a-dozen stolen bases. His overall production, per *Weighted Runs Created Plus*, topped the league average mark by 27%. He spent the last three weeks of the season battling – and mostly struggling – in Low-A.

Scouting Report: Very animated at the plate with his head shaking and nodding on pitch calls. Genao owns some of the system's best bat speed, but needs to get stronger to drive the ball more consistently. Solid contact rates and approach at the plate. Average glove around the diamond (second and third bases, as well as shortstop). He's not overly big – 5-foot-9, 150-pounds – but there's some room for growth. He could be one of the club's next waves of middle infield prospects.

Ceiling: 1.0-win player
Risk: Moderate
MLB ETA: 2026

20. Joe Lampe, CF

Hit	Power	SB	Patience	Glove	Overall
55	40/45	55	45	55	45

Born: 12/05/00	**Age:** 22	**Bats:** L	**Top Production Comp:** N/A
Height: 6-1	**Weight:** 185	**Throws:** R	

Background: A product of Casa Grande High School, home to former big league slugger Jonny Gomes, Lampe spent his freshman collegiate season with Santa Rosa Junior College – where he torched the competition by batting a white hot .424/.477/.687 with seven doubles, eight triples, one homeruns, and 17 stolen bases in only 20 games. The 6-foot-1, 185-pound speed demon transferred to Arizona State – where he didn't miss a beat. The lefty-swinging centerfielder hit a rock solid .294/.383/.461 with 13 doubles, four triples, three homeruns, and six stolen bases – though it took 11 attempts. Lampe spent the ensuing summer playing for the Bourne Braves in the vaunted Cape Cod League. Playing alongside fellow top prospects Reggie Crawford, Tanner Schobel, Jake Bennett, Lampe batted .269/.416/.296 with just one double and one triple in 32 games. The Sun Devil did, however, continue to display his keen eye at the plate, walking 21 times and whiffing 22 times. Last season the California native picked right up where he left off: in a career high 57 games, he slugged .340/.394/.590 with 22 doubles, three triples, 12 homeruns, and 17 stolen bases (in 20 attempts). The Guardians selected the former JuCo star in the third round, 92nd overall, and signed him to an above-slot deal worth $800,000.

Scouting Report: Consider the following:

> Since 2011, only three Pac-12 hitters batted at least .330/.380/.580 with a sub-12.0% strikeout rate in a season (min. 250 PA): Andrew Vaughn, Cameron Cannon, and – of course – Joe Lampe.

Perhaps predictably so, but Lampe falls into the Steven Kwan mold. He has a knack for consistently making contact. And in today's game that's becoming increasingly uncommon, a trait of yesteryear. Lampe fanned in just 11% of his plate appearances over his two years with the Sun Devils. Plus-speed. The defensive chops to stay in centerfield. The deciding factor between fourth or fifth outfielderdom and a starting gig will come down to his ability to consistently drive the ball – which he started to do during his final stint in college.

Ceiling: 1.0-win player
Risk: Moderate
MLB ETA: 2025/2026

Colorado Rockies

Top Prospects

Colorado Rockies

1. Ezequiel Tovar, SS

Hit	Power	SB	Patience	Glove	Overall
55	50	60	50	70	70

Born: 08/01/01	Age: 21	Bats: B	Top Production Comp: Bo Bichette
Height: 6-0	Weight: 162	Throws: R	

Season	Team	Age	Level	PA	1B	2B	3B	HR	SB	CS	BB%	K%	AVG	OBP	SLG	ISO
2021	COL	19	A	326	57	21	3	11	21	4	4.29%	11.66%	0.309	0.346	0.510	0.201
2021	COL	19	A+	143	19	9	0	4	3	2	2.10%	13.29%	0.239	0.266	0.396	0.157
2022	COL	20	AA	295	53	15	3	13	17	3	8.47%	21.69%	0.318	0.386	0.545	0.227
2022	COL	20	AAA	23	6	0	0	1	0	0	8.70%	8.70%	0.333	0.391	0.476	0.143

Background: For the better part of two decades the Rockies ran out a premier shortstop as part of their everyday lineup, beginning with Troy Tulowitzki's rookie year in 2006 all the way through Trevor Story's departure from the club following 2021. It was the most stable, consistent aspect for Colorado during that time. But it – finally – ended in 2022 as the franchise looked to veteran Jose Iglesias as a stopgap. A role, by the way, that he filled well enough, hitting .292/.328/.380 in 118 games. Almost like clockwork, though, Colorado's farm system churned out another potential franchise cornerstone at the infield's preeminent position. Enter: Ezequiel Tovar. Signed out of Maracay, Venezuela, for $800,000 in 2017, Tovar's offense turned the corner as he moved into full-season action two years ago as he slugged an aggregate .287/.322/.475 with 30 doubles, three triples, 15 homeruns, and 24 stolen bases. And he took his production line to another level in 2022 as he put together his finest professional season to date – despite missing nearly three months of action due to a groin injury. In 77 minor league contests, most of which were spent with the Yard Goats in the Eastern League, the 6-foot, 162-pound infielder mashed .319/.387/.540 with 15 doubles, three triples, 14 homeruns, and 17 stolen bases (in only 20 attempts). His overall production with Hartford, according to *Weighted Runs Created Plus,* topped the league average threshold by 53%. Colorado called up their burgeoning star in late September for a nine-game cameo (.212/.257/.333).

Snippet from The 2022 Prospect Digest Handbook: Still one of my favorite prospects in all of baseball. And this year he was raw – just less raw. He's in the conversation as one of the best defensive shortstops in the minor leagues. It's likely an argument between Tovar and Oakland's Nick Allen. Either way, Colorado's defensive wizard is an elite defender. Per Clay Davenport's defensive metrics, he saved 12 runs more than the average in only 64 games with Fresno. That's otherworldly. And last year his offense decided to lurch forward as well. His production is going to be capped by subpar walk rates, but he doesn't swing-and-miss much, shows some thump, and runs well.

Scouting Report: Consider the following:

> Since 2006, only six 20-year-old hitters posted a wRC+ north of 150 in a season in any Double-A league (min. 250 PA): Oscar Tovar, Xander Bogaerts, Rafael Devers, Maikel Franco, Dilson Herrera, and – of course – Ezequiel Tovar.

A tremendous defender that likely wins a couple Gold Gloves during his future big league career. Tovar's offense continues to take gargantuan strides forward as he moves quickly through the Rockies' system. He's now sporting a 55-grade bat, 50-grade power, plus speed, and a plus glove. It's a recipe for a perennial All-Star. But he's added a new weapon to his arsenal: the normally free-swinging shortstop is now walking at the highest clip since his debut season in the Dominican Summer League. Really good looking swing with incredible bat speed. He could be one of the game's brighter stars and should settle in as a franchise cornerstone in Colorado for the next decade. Big league ceiling: .290/.340/.460.

Ceiling: 6.0-win player
Risk: Moderate
MLB ETA: Debuted in 2022

2. Zac Veen, RF

Hit	Power	SB	Patience	Glove	Overall
50/55	50/60	60	60	55	60

Born: 12/12/01	Age: 21	Bats: L	Top Production Comp: Bobby Abreu
Height: 6-4	Weight: 190	Throws: R	

Season	Team	Age	Level	PA	1B	2B	3B	HR	SB	CS	BB%	K%	AVG	OBP	SLG	ISO
2021	COL	19	A	479	74	27	4	15	36	17	13.36%	26.30%	0.301	0.399	0.501	0.201
2022	COL	20	A+	400	59	19	3	11	50	4	12.50%	22.50%	0.269	0.368	0.439	0.170
2022	COL	20	AA	141	17	4	0	1	5	5	9.93%	29.79%	0.177	0.262	0.234	0.056

Background: Colorado may not have the best collection of young hitting prospects in the game, but they certainly *deserve* to be in the conversation. The club's farm system sports the likes of: Ezequiel Tovar, Drew Romo, Benny Montgomery, Adael Amador, Yanquiel Fernandez, and – of course – Zac Veen. The ninth overall pick in 2020, sandwiched between the selections of Robert Hassell and Reid Detmers, Veen put on an offensive showcase during his debut in Low-A West the following season as he slugged a scorching .301/.399/.501 with gobs of extra-base thump and speed to burn. Last season, the 6-foot-4, 190-pound rightfielder handled the promotion up to High-A with aplomb, hitting .269/.368/.439 with 19 doubles, three triples, 11 homeruns, and an eye-catching 50 stolen bases (in only 54 attempts). The front office sent their young outfielder up to the true testing grounds, Double-A, but it proved a little too much for the former top pick. He hit a lowly .177/.262/.234 in 34 games with the Hartford Yard Goats. Veen did regain his stroke in the Arizona Fall League as he put together – arguably – the most dominant performance by any prospect, slugging .409/.500/.546 over his 12 contests.

Colorado Rockies

Snippet from The 2022 Prospect Digest Handbook: A supremely gifted ballplayer whose numbers get even better if his slow start to the year is ignored; he batted .317/.406/.526 from May 21st through the end of the year.

Scouting Report: Consider the following:

> Since 2006, only four 20-year-old hitters met the following criteria in a High-A season (min. 350 PA): 120 to 130 wRC+, a double-digit walk rate, and a strikeout rate between 20% and 24%. Those four hitters: Noelvi Marte, Michael Saunders, Taylor Trammell, and Zac Veen.

Interestingly enough, right-handed hurlers created more issues for Veen in 2022 than southpaws (.236/.330/.389 vs. .280/.380/.366). The former first round pick might be the best base stealer in the minor leagues and likely belongs on a short list for top base stealer at any level. Plus speed. And he's just tapping into his above-average power potential. Very wiry and thin, Veen is far from maxing out physically. There's plus raw power already. Throw in plus glovework in right field and Veen, like some of his farm system counterparts, looks like a potential star. Definite Bobby Abreu vibes going on. Big league ceiling: .280/.370/.475.

Ceiling: 5.0-win player
Risk: Moderate
MLB ETA: 2023/2024

3. Adael Amador, SS

Hit	Power	SB	Patience	Glove	Overall
50/55	45/50	60	55	50	55

Born: 09/11/03	Age: 20	Bats: B	Top Production Comp: N/A
Height: 6-0	Weight: 160	Throws: R	

Season	Team	Age	Level	PA	1B	2B	3B	HR	SB	CS	BB%	K%	AVG	OBP	SLG	ISO
2021	COL	18	CPX	200	34	10	1	4	10	7	13.50%	14.50%	0.299	0.394	0.445	0.146
2022	COL	19	A	555	92	24	0	15	26	12	15.68%	12.07%	0.292	0.415	0.445	0.154

Background: Recognized as one of the top available free agents on the international market in 2019. Amador, a Santiago, Dominican Republic native, was swayed to join the Rockies' rebuilding efforts for a small $1.5 million fee.

The 6-foot, 160-pound middle infielder would have to wait another two years before making his highly anticipated debut. But his performance lived up to those expectations. Appearing in 47 games with the club's Arizona Complex League affiliate, Amador batted a rock solid .299/.394/.445 with 10 doubles, one triple, four homeruns, and 10 stolen bases. His overall production, according to *Weighted Runs Created Plus*, topped the league average mark by 22%. Last season the young shortstop continued to impress as he moved into the California League. Amador, only 19-years-old in 2022, slugged .292/.415/.445 with 24 doubles, 15 homeruns, and 26 stolen bases (in 38 total attempts). He finished his first taste of full season action with a 128 wRC+ total.

Snippet from The 2022 Prospect Digest Handbook: His swing looks more natural from the right-side, more loft. He's more open as a left-handed hitter – it's a short, compact, slashing type of swing a la Johnny Damon.

Scouting Report: Consider the following:

> Since 2006, only three 19-year-olds posted a 123 to 133 wRC+ mark with a sub-15% strikeout rate in any Low-A league (min. 400 PA): Manuel Margot, Jorge Polanco, and – of course – Adael Amador. For those counting at home: Margot, once a consensus Top 25 Prospect, is a career .254/.308/.386 hitter in 689 big league games and Jorge Polanco owns a career 111 wRC+ mark in 752 games with the Twins.

Part of the "new breed" of prospects that's becoming more en vogue, simply put, Amador doesn't swing-and-miss all that much, posting a swinging strike percentage of just 6.94% and a 12.1% strikeout rate. Unlike a lot of extreme bat-to-ball, contact-based hitters, he packs a punch as well, showcasing average power to go along with plus speed and a great eye at the plate. Average defender. Two years ago Amador looked like two different hitters at the plate – a left- *and* right-handed version. Last season, though, there was more consistently. Quick bat with a natural line drive feel. It's eerily reminiscent to former All-Star second baseman Luis Castillo – with more pop. He's going to be one of the bigger breakout players in 2023.

Ceiling: 3.5-win player
Risk: Moderate
MLB ETA: 2024

Colorado Rockies

4. Jordy Vargas, RHP

FB	CB	CH	Command	Overall
60	60	50	45/50	60

Born: 11/06/03	Age: 19	Bats: R	Top Production Comp: N/A
Height: 6-3	Weight: 153	Throws: R	

Season	Team	Age	Level	IP	TBF	K/9	K%	BB/9	BB%	K-BB%	ERA	FIP	xFIP	Pit/Bat
2021	COL	17	DSL	34.2	142	11.94	32.39%	4.15	11.27%	21.13%	1.30	2.55	3.12	2.06
2022	COL	18	A	24.2	104	8.76	23.08%	4.74	12.50%	10.58%	3.65	6.66	5.76	4.28
2022	COL	18	CPX	26.2	99	13.50	40.40%	1.35	4.04%	36.36%	2.36	1.93	2.76	1.97

Background: Vargas's old man, Yorkis Perez, spent nine seasons in the big leagues, bouncing between six teams (Cubs, Marlins, Mets, Phillies, Astros, and Orioles) and was the prototypical replacement level player. The former left-handed reliever accrued just 0.7 Wins Above Replacement (*Baseball Reference*) and had four seasons of negative production against five positive. Colorado signed Vargas, a native of Moca, Dominican Republic, in January of 2021 for a cool half million dollars. A thin, wiry right-hander built in the Triston McKenzie mold, Vargas made his professional debut in the foreign rookie leagues a few months after signing. He would make 11 mostly dominant appearances, throwing 34.2 innings with 46 strikeouts and just 16 free passes to go along with a sparkling 1.30 ERA. Last season the front office took the cautious approach and bumped the teenager up to the Complex League. But after seven strong outings – five of his seven earned runs allowed were in one disastrous start – he was sent to full season ball. Vargas would finish the season with 51.1 total innings of work, averaging a fantastic 11.2 strikeouts and just 3.0 walks per nine innings. He tallied an aggregate 2.98 ERA.

Scouting Report: Consider the following:

> Since 2006, there have been only sixty-five 18-year-old hurlers to make at least one appearance in Low-A. That's fewer than four per season, by the way. But, incredibly so, there were a whopping twenty-two 18-year-old hurlers that tossed at least one inning at the level in 2022.

One of my favorite pitching prospects in the entire minor leagues. If he can avoid the dreaded injury nexus, Vargas could be one of the best pitching prospects in the game. The wiry righty owns one of the loosest, easy flowing arms in the game. Plus fastball. Plus curveball. Average change that may see an uptick with some more fine tuning. Years ago Anderson Espinoza was the heir apparent to the Crown of the Top MiLB pitching prospect. Then injury after injury robbed him of a lot development time. Vargas has that type of potential.

Ceiling: 4.0-win player
Risk: Moderate to High
MLB ETA: 2024/2025

5. Benny Montgomery, CF

Hit	Power	SB	Patience	Glove	Overall
45	45/55	65	50	50/55	55

Born: 09/09/02	Age: 20	Bats: R	Top Production Comp: N/A
Height: 6-4	Weight: 200	Throws: R	

Season	Team	Age	Level	PA	1B	2B	3B	HR	SB	CS	BB%	K%	AVG	OBP	SLG	ISO
2021	COL	18	CPX	52	15	0	1	0	5	1	9.62%	17.31%	0.340	0.404	0.383	0.043
2022	COL	19	CPX	22	4	1	1	0	0	0	0.00%	27.27%	0.273	0.273	0.409	0.136
2022	COL	19	A	264	44	20	3	6	9	1	7.95%	26.89%	0.313	0.394	0.502	0.189

Background: After selecting prep outfielder Zac Veen with the ninth overall pick in the 2020 draft, the Rockies went back to the high school ranks and selected Benny Montgomery with the eighth overall pick a year later. A product of Red Land High School, home to former Phillies great Greg Gross, Montgomery shredded the Arizona Complex League competition during his abbreviated 14-game debut two years ago, batting .340/.404/.383 with one triple and five stolen bases. Last season, Montgomery opened the year up with Fresno, but managed to log only 56 contests due to a combination of a lingering quad issue and an "undisclosed" injury. The former prep star mashed an impressive .313/.394/.502 with 20 doubles, three triples, six homeruns, and nine stolen bases with the Fresno Grizzlies. Per *Weighted Runs Created Plus*, his overall production topped the league average mark by a solid 32%.

Snippet from The 2022 Prospect Digest Handbook: Speed to burn. Montgomery's been clocked at a 6.45-second 60-yard dash. And he has an arm to match: he's been clocked as high as 96 mph as well. The question with Montgomery isn't athleticism or tools, it's whether he's going to hit enough in the professional ranks. Above-average or better bat speed. But…Montgomery's developed a timing hitch with his hands that might make him vulnerable to mid-level minor league breaking balls. He's long and gangly, like Hunter Pence.

Scouting Report: Just for fun, here's here are Montgomery's numbers with the Grizzlies prorated for a full 162-game season: 58 doubles, nine triples, 17 homeruns, and 26 stolen bases. Yeah, that'll play. Now let's look at how his numbers stack up against his peers in recent history. Consider the following:

Colorado Rockies

Since 2006, only three 19-year-old hitters met the following criteria in a season in Low-A (min. 250 PA): 127 to 137 wRC+, 26% to 28% strikeout rate, and a 6% to 8% walk rate. Those three hitters: Austin Riley, Moises Gomez, and Benny Montgomery.

A full year into his pro ball career, Montgomery is still showing a tremendous amount of pre-swing hand movement. And despite a borderline concerning strikeout rate last season, 26.9%, the young outfielder hit. And he hit well. One of the tools-iest outfield prospects in the minor leagues, Montgomery projects for average power – maybe a half grade higher if everything clicks the right way – with plus-plus speed, solid patience, and a playable glove in centerfield. I'm still not entirely sold on the bat – and likely won't feel comfortable till he hits in Double-A – but there's plenty of potential.

Ceiling: 3.0-win player
Risk: Moderate
MLB ETA: 2024/2025

6. Drew Romo, C

	Hit	Power	SB	Patience	Glove	Overall
	50/55	40/45	60/45	50	60	55

Born: 08/29/01	Age: 21	Bats: B	Top Production Comp: Paul Lo Duca
Height: 6-1	Weight: 205	Throws: R	

Season	Team	Age	Level	PA	1B	2B	3B	HR	SB	CS	BB%	K%	AVG	OBP	SLG	ISO
2021	COL	19	A	339	73	17	2	6	23	6	5.60%	14.75%	0.314	0.345	0.439	0.125

Background: Even after the graduation of Orioles' franchise cornerstone Adley Rutschman, the catching position in the minor leagues is incredibly deep and plenty talented. Francisco Alvarez is going to be star. Diego Cartaya headlines a bountiful Dodgers farm system. A resurgent Bo Naylor re-established his value in 2022. Then there's Henry Davis, Endy Rodriguez, Kevin Parada, Logan O'Hoppe, and the supremely underrated Edgar Quero. A bit lost in the shuffle – or at least so it seems – is the Rockies' Drew Romo. The 35th overall pick three years ago and the fourth backstop drafted that year, Romo made his debut the following season. Despite missing the 2020 season (thanks to COVID), the switch-hitting backstop hit and didn't stop the entire year. He would finish with a .314/.345/.439 slash line in 79 games with Fresno. Last season, the front office bounced him up Spokane, their High-A affiliate, but the former first rounder struggled a bit. He batted .254/.321/.372 with just 19 doubles, five triples, and five homeruns – though he did steal 18 bases in 21 attempts. His overall production, per *Weighted Runs Created Plus*, was 5% *below* the league average mark.

Snippet from The 2022 Prospect Digest Handbook: Romo has the quiet potential to develop into one of the better catching prospects in baseball. A sweet-swinging switch-hitter with strong contact skills and a line drive approach to shoot balls from foul line to foul line.

Scouting Report: Consider the following:

Since 2006, only four 20-year-old hitters met the following criteria in a High-A season (min. 400 PA): 90 to 100 wRC+, 7.5% to 9.5% walk rate, and a 17% to 21% strikeout rate. Those four hitters: Dustin Peterson, John Drennen, Nick Noonan, and Drew Romo.

Romo's production line can be split into two separate seasons, a pre- *and* a post-injury stat lines. Pre-injury he batted .280/.348/.408. But after hitting the disabled list for three weeks and returning in mid-August he hit a lowly .165/.228/.247. Bet heavily on the former. Great looking line-driving hitting swing. Short, fast. It's going to pepper balls from foul line to foul line. He's probably not going to be a star – unless the hit tool climbs into plus territory – but he should be an above-average bat for 10 years. In terms of big league ceiling: .270/.340/.420. The defense may push him into All-Star territory.

Ceiling: 3.0-win player
Risk: Moderate
MLB ETA: 2024

7. Gabriel Hughes, RHP

	FB	SL	CH	Command	Overall
	60	55	50/55	45	55

Born: 08/22/01	Age: 21	Bats: R	Top Production Comp: N/A
Height: 6-4	Weight: 220	Throws: R	

Background: A product of Rocky Mountain High School, Hughes was an unstoppable force during his final two prep seasons in Idaho as he captured back-to-back Gatorade State Player of the

Colorado Rockies

Year awards. During his junior season in 2018, the burly right-hander / first baseman batted .461 and posted a 7-1 win-loss record to go along with a sparkling 1.85 ERA . And Hughes followed that up with .365 batting average and seven homeruns in the field and won seven games and posted a tidy 0.95 ERA. Hughes' collegiate career got off to a fast start during his freshman season at Gonzaga, posting a 0.77 ERA through four relief appearances and one start in 2020 before COVID prematurely ended the year. And he continued to impress – as a 19-year-old – during his first full season with the Bulldogs the following year: in 61.1 innings, he averaged 9.8 strikeouts and 4.4 walks per nine innings to go along with a 3.23 ERA. He spent the summer working out of Team USA's Stripes' rotation, making three brief starts. In 2022 Hughes improved his ability to (A) miss bats and (B) limit troublesome free passes as he vaulted up the prospect charts. In a career best 15 starts, the big 6-foot-4, 220-pound righty struck out 138 and walked 37 in 98.0 innings of work. Colorado selected him in the first round, 10th overall, and signed him to a deal worth $4 million. Hughes would make one brief, three-inning start with Fresno, striking out and walking one.

Scouting Report: Per the usual, my pre-draft write-up:

> "Consider the following:
>
> Since 2015, only four Division I pitchers struck out at least 12.5 hitters and walk between 3.3 and 3.6 batters per nine innings (min. 90 IP): Zack Thompson, Dominic Hamel, Hurston Waldrep, and – of course – Gabriel Hughes.
>
> Hughes' fastball consistently sits in the 94- to 96-mph range, easily making it a plus offering. He'll complement the heater with an above-average upper 70s to low-80s slider and a quietly solid low 80s changeup that shows tremendous velocity separation. Despite being the top arm in the collegiate class, Hughes' ceiling isn't elite. Mid-rotation caliber potential. Seattle, with their version of Cleveland's pitching development program, looks like a logical landing place, but he likely won't be available. Look for a team like Colorado, Detroit, or the Angels to snag Hughes."

Ceiling: 3.0-win player
Risk: Moderate
MLB ETA: 2024

8. Yanquiel Fernandez, RF

Hit	Power	SB	Patience	Glove	Overall
50	55/60	35	50	55	55

Born: 01/01/03	Age: 20	Bats: R	Top Production Comp: N/A
Height: 6-2	Weight: 198	Throws: R	

Season	Team	Age	Level	PA	1B	2B	3B	HR	SB	CS	BB%	K%	AVG	OBP	SLG	ISO
2021	COL	18	DSL	202	36	17	0	6	0	0	10.89%	12.87%	0.333	0.406	0.531	0.198
2022	COL	19	A	523	76	33	5	21	5	1	7.46%	21.80%	0.284	0.340	0.507	0.223

Background: Two years ago the Rockies' Low-A affiliate, the Fresno Grizzlies, sported a trio of teenage phenoms in Zac Veen, Ezequiel Tovar, and Drew Romo. This season the California League club featured *another* trio of top teenage hitting prospects: Yanquiel Fernandez, Benny Montgomery, and Adael Amador. Born on New Year's Day in Havana, Cuba, in 2003, the Rockies' brass inked the 6-foot-2, 198-pound corner outfielder to a deal worth slightly less than $300,000 in 2019. Two years later he would make his anticipated debut in the Dominican Summer League, mashing to the tune of .333/.406/.531 with 17 doubles and six homeruns in 54 games. Last season, the organization aggressively sent the then-19-year-old straight up to Low-A. And he continued to hit. In 112 games with Fresno, the Cuban import batted .284/.340/.507 with 33 doubles, five triples, 21 homeruns, and five stolen bases. Per *Weighted Runs Created Plus*, his overall production topped the league average mark by 12%.

Scouting Report: Consider the following:

> Since 2006, only three 19-year-old hitters met the following criteria in a season in Low-A (min. 400 PA): 107 to 117 wRC+, a walk rate between 6.5% and 8.5%, and a strikeout rate between 20% and 24%. Those three hitters: Dilson Herrera, Jack Suwinski, and – of course – Yanquiel Fernandez.

Perhaps, unsurprisingly, Fernandez got off to a bit of slow start to the 2022 season. He hit a lowly .200/.304/.300 over the first couple of weeks. After that he got his feet underneath him and slugged .303/.353/.542 the remainder of the season. Fernandez shows an intriguing toolkit not highlighted by a lot of the club's other top young bats. It's a power-oriented approach with little speed. The early returns on defense are phenomenal. He doesn't show any platoon splits, did a lot of damage in a pitcher-friendly ballpark, and made consistent contact. Broad shoulder with a bit of swagger that borderlines on cockiness. Beautiful left-handed swing, not quite picture-esque like a Darryl Strawberry or Ken Griffey Jr. But it's beautiful nonetheless. Plus-raw power that may eventually grow into 30 homeruns in a season. Easy power – flick of the wrist type stuff.

Colorado Rockies

Ceiling: 3.0-win player
Risk: Moderate
MLB ETA: 2024/2025

9. Jordan Beck, LF/RF

Hit	Power	SB	Patience	Glove	Overall
45	60	35	45	55	50

Born: 04/19/01	Age: 22	Bats: R	Top Production Comp: N/A
Height: 6-3	Weight: 225	Throws: R	

Season	Team	Age	Level	PA	1B	2B	3B	HR	SB	CS	BB%	K%	AVG	OBP	SLG	ISO
2022	COL	21	CPX	57	9	5	0	1	0	0	14.04%	19.30%	0.306	0.404	0.469	0.163
2022	COL	21	A	52	7	2	0	2	0	0	25.00%	17.31%	0.282	0.462	0.487	0.205

Background: Starred on the basketball court and the baseball diamond during his prep career at Hazel Green High School. Beck led the hoop's team to the state semifinals in 2018 during his All-State career. And the 6-foot-3, 225-pound first baseman / outfielder batted .500 with 16 doubles, 13 homeruns, 52 RBIs, and 60 runs scored during his senior campaign en route to earning the Super 10 Player of the Year award. The Red Sox took a late round flier on Beck following the season, selecting him in the 14th round of the 2019 draft. After bypassing the opportunity to join the historic organization, Beck headed to the University of Tennessee – where he immediately made an impact for the SEC powerhouse. In 16 games during the COVID-shortened 2020 season, the Alabama-born prospect batted .275/.396/.475 with five doubles and one homerun. Beck turned in a solid, at times phenomenal, campaign during his 2021 season: In 67 games with the Volunteers he hit .271/.336/.523 with 16 doubles, two triples, 15 homeruns, and eight stolen bases. He spent the summer with the Harwich Mariners in the Cape Cod League, batting .267/.377/.400 in 27 games. Last year Beck continued to make strides in his performance for the nearly perfectly built Tennessee Volunteers: in 66 games he slugged .298/.391/.595 with 15 doubles, three triples, 18 homeruns, and six stolen bases. Colorado selected him in the opening round, 38th overall, and signed him to a deal worth $2.2 million. The Alabama native split his debut between the Complex League and Low-A , hitting an aggregate .296/.431/.477 in 26 games.

Scouting Report: Per the usual, my pre-draft write-up:

> "The whiff rate isn't a red flag, per se, but it isn't going to leave anyone warm and fuzzy. And he's made modest – at best – improvements over the past two seasons with Tennessee. He fanned in nearly 21% of his plate appearances in 2021 and he posted a nearly identical mark [in 2022]. 45-grade hit tool. 60-grade power. Average-ish eye at the plate. Good speed and glove to match. Consider the following:
>
>> Since 2011, only four SEC hitters batted between .280/.375/.575 and .310/.425/.625 in a season (min. 275 PA): Greg Deichmann, Chad Spanberger, Andre Lipcius, and – of course – Jordan Beck. Deichmann was a second rounder by the Athletics in 2017; Spanberger was a sixth rounder by the Brewers the same season; and Lipcius, a former Volunteer, was a third rounder by the Tigers in 2019.
>
> Upright stance with a bit of an intimidating presence at the plate, Beck has a surprisingly short swing – especially given his size. Big time power that no ballpark can contain when he fully gets into one. It's going to come down to the hit tool. If he makes enough contact, Beck looks like a low end middle-of-the-lineup thumper. If not, he's got Quad-A written all over him."

Ceiling: 2.0-win player
Risk: Moderate
MLB ETA: 2024/2025

10. Sterlin Thompson, 3B/RF

Hit	Power	SB	Patience	Glove	Overall
50	50	50	50	50	50

Born: 06/26/01	Age: 22	Bats: L	Top Production Comp: N/A
Height: 6-4	Weight: 200	Throws: R	

Season	Team	Age	Level	PA	1B	2B	3B	HR	SB	CS	BB%	K%	AVG	OBP	SLG	ISO
2022	COL	21	CPX	61	11	3	0	1	1	0	3.28%	26.23%	0.273	0.328	0.382	0.109
2022	COL	21	A	50	11	4	0	1	2	0	6.00%	24.00%	0.348	0.380	0.500	0.152

Background: Thompson's tenure at North Marion High School lasted a single season (2020), but he's going to become the most successful professional player to walk through the school's hallowed halls. Ranked as the 55th best prospect by *Perfect Game*, Thompson made an immediate impact during his freshman season at the University of Florida. Primarily used as a right fielder, the 6-foot-4, 200-pounder batted an impressive .301/.396/.470 in 2021, belting out 10 doubles, three triples, and five homeruns in 55 games for the SEC conference powerhouse. After shredding the Florida Collegiate Summer League to the tune of .391/.482/.609, Thompson continued

Colorado Rockies

to swing a hot bat during his sophomore season with the Gators. In 66 games for head coach Kevin O'Sullivan, Thompson slugged .354/.443/.563 and set career highs in doubles (16), homeruns (11), and stolen bases (10). The Rockies selected the young Gator in the opening round, 31st overall, and signed him to a deal worth $2,430,500. Thompson split his debut between the Complex League and Fresno, hitting an aggregate .307/.351/.436 with seven doubles, two homeruns, and 10 stolen bases in 26 games.

Scouting Report: Per the usual, my pre-draft write-up:

> "Consider the following:
>
> > Since 2011, only four SEC hitters batted at least .340/.430/.550 with a sub-16% strikeout rate and a walk rate between 11% and 13% in a season (min. 300 PA): Austin Martin, Wyatt Langford, Jacob Gonzalez, and – of course – Sterlin Thompson.
>
> Very simple, low maintenance swing with impressive bat speed. Thompson's power grades out as average, maybe a tick better, but when he turns on the inside pitch he can give it a surprising jolt. He's going to spray line drives from gap to gap. Solid-average speed and patience. Florida experimented with having the former prep-shortstop-turned-collegiate-right-fielder at the keystone last season. Obviously, the bat plays significantly better on the infield, as opposed to a corner outfield position. Lacks a difference-making tool."

Ceiling: 2.0-win player
Risk: Moderate
MLB ETA: 2024/2025

11. Warming Bernabel, 3B

Hit	Power	SB	Patience	Glove	Overall
50/55	45/50	55	50	50	50

Born: 06/06/02 **Age**: 21 **Bats**: R **Top Production Comp**: N/A
Height: 6-0 **Weight**: 180 **Throws**: R

Season	Team	Age	Level	PA	1B	2B	3B	HR	SB	CS	BB%	K%	AVG	OBP	SLG	ISO
2021	COL	19	CPX	86	21	5	0	6	5	1	5.81%	13.95%	0.432	0.453	0.743	0.311
2021	COL	19	A	94	10	6	0	1	4	1	7.45%	14.89%	0.205	0.287	0.313	0.108
2022	COL	20	A	300	54	19	0	10	21	6	9.67%	13.00%	0.317	0.390	0.504	0.187
2022	COL	20	A+	109	21	7	0	4	2	2	1.83%	15.60%	0.305	0.315	0.486	0.181

Background: Another of the international free agent success stories the Rockies can add to their growing list. The front office inked the Dominican-born third baseman for $900,000 in the 2018. A native of Bani, Bernabel has been on the slow and steady trek thus fall into his professional career. The 6-foot, 180-pounder spent his first season struggling against the DSL pitching, cobbling together a disappointing .250/.320/.387 slash line in 2019. He, like every other minor leaguer, missed the entire next season as minor league ball was placed on the inactive list courtesy of COVID. Then, when he returned to action in 2021, he split time between the Complex League and Fresno, dominating the former (.432/.454/.743) and struggling in the latter (.205/.287/.313). So it's not a surprise that Bernabel found himself back in Low-A for a re-do. This time, though, he proved up to the task. Bernabel slugged .317/.390/.504 in 65 games and he continued to hit in a late-season promotion up to Spokane. The former bonus baby batted an aggregate .313/.370/.499 adding 26 doubles, 14 homeruns, and 23 stolen bases (in 31 attempts). Following the season Bernabel struggled – *mightily* – in the Arizona Fall League, hitting a lowly .081/.079/.162 in 38 plate appearances.

Scouting Report: Consider the following:

> Since 2006, only three 20-year-old prospects posted a 125 to 135 wRC+ with a sub-15% strikeout rate and a walk rate between 9% and 11% in Low-A (min. 250 PA): Vaughn Grissom, Atlanta's impressive rookie, Mat Gamel, and – of course – Warming Bernabel.

Not overly big by any stretch of the imagination, particularly for a corner infielder. Simple line drive approach kicked off with a *massive* leg kick he employs as a timing mechanism. Above-average speed. Solid, but not spectacular glove at third base. The swing can get away from him at times, leading to longer, slower approaches. He's currently a bat over power guy. He also makes consistent contact, which we've seen from a number of the club's better hitting prospects. There's a wide range of outcomes here, but the hit tool has to carry him because the power and glove won't. Potential fringy starting option in a couple years.

Ceiling: 1.5- to 2.0-win player
Risk: Moderate
MLB ETA: 2024

Colorado Rockies

12. Nolan Jones, 3B/RF

Hit	Power	SB	Patience	Glove	Overall
45	50	40/35	55	50	50

Born: 05/07/98	Age: 25	Bats: L	Top Production Comp: Jay Bruce
Height: 6-4	Weight: 195	Throws: R	

Season	Team	Age	Level	PA	1B	2B	3B	HR	SB	CS	BB%	K%	AVG	OBP	SLG	ISO
2021	CLE	23	AAA	407	42	25	1	13	10	2	14.50%	29.98%	0.238	0.356	0.431	0.194
2022	CLE	24	AAA	248	38	11	1	9	4	1	12.50%	25.81%	0.276	0.368	0.463	0.187

Background: The team formerly known as the Indians opened up their 2016 draft class with a pair of high upside high school bats. The organization used the 14th overall pick on Georgia-born, supremely athletic outfielder Will Benson and circled back around and grabbed Pennsylvania native Nolan Jones with the 55th overall pick. Both Benson and Jones would make their big league debuts in 2022. And a few months later the front office would ship out the former high round picks to different organizations. Benson to Cincinnati. Jones to Colorado. The Rockies sent infielder Juan Brito eastward to complete the one-for-one swap. Jones, a lefty-swinging third baseman / corner outfielder, struggled through his first stint in Triple-A two years ago, hitting a disappointing .238/.356/.431 with 25 doubles, one triple, and 13 homeruns. Last season, though, the former second rounder recaptured his previous offensive prowess as he slugged .276/.368/.463 with 11 doubles, one triple, nine homeruns, and four stolen bases (in five attempts). Per *Weighted Runs Created Plus*, his overall production surpassed the league average mark by 22%. Jones nearly exhausted his rookie eligibility with Cleveland in July and August. He batted a mediocre .244/.309/.372 in 28 games, belting out five doubles and a pair of dingers.

Snippet from The 2022 Prospect Digest Handbook: He's still a dark horse candidate for a breakout at the big league level in 2022. Big league line: .260/.360/.450.

Scouting Report: Consider the following:

> Since 2006, only three 24-year-old hitters met the following criteria in any Triple-A league (min. 225 PA): 117 to 127 wRC+, a double-digit walk rate, and a 25% to 27% strikeout rate. Those three hitters: A.J. Reed, J.J. Bleday, and – of course – Nolan Jones.

It doesn't bode well that Reed and Bleday are both disappointing early round picks. Jones handled lefties decently last season, the second consecutive year he's done so. But his swing-and-miss rates are still borderline concerning. Jones has never really tapped into his plus raw power, so maybe the Rockies can unlock it. He's probably better suited for first base rather than a corner outfield spot.

Ceiling: 1.5-win player
Risk: Moderate
MLB ETA: 2022

13. Dyan Jorge, SS

Hit	Power	SB	Patience	Glove	Overall
45	40/50	50/45	45	55	45

Born: 03/18/03	Age: 20	Bats: R	Top Production Comp: N/A
Height: 6-3	Weight: 170	Throws: R	

Background: The Rockies' system is chock full of notable international free agents, guys like – Ezequiel Tovar or Jordy Vargas or Adael Amador or Yanquiel Fernandez or Warming Bernabel. But it's Jorge, a 6-foot-3, 170- shortstop, that garnered the largest international bonus in team history. A native of La Habana, Cuba, Jorge signed him the rebuilding organization in early 2022 for a hefty $2.8 million. Last season the front office took the cautious approach and assigned him to the their Dominican Summer League affiliate. Jorge would appear in 53 games, slugging .320/.402/.452 with 13 doubles, one triple, four homeruns, and 13 stolen bases. His overall production, per *Weighted Runs Created Plus*, topped the league average production by 34%.

Scouting Report: The production is solid, though far from spectacular given (A) his age and (B) history on Cuba's teenage national teams. Tall and wiry, Jorge should – easily – add strength and weight to his projectable frame. Nice, easy right-handed swing with good torque through the torso. Jorge projects to have a 45-grade bat, average power, and a potential 55-grade glove. It's nearly a lock the club sends him directly to Low-A, bypassing the stateside rookie league. There's going to be some swing-and-miss issues, maybe starting as early as the 2023 season.

Ceiling: 1.5-win player
Risk: Moderate
MLB ETA: 2024

Colorado Rockies

14. Victor Juarez, RHP

	FB	CB	SL	CH	Command	Overall
	50/55	55	50	55	50	45

Born: 06/19/03	**Age:** 20	**Bats:** R	**Top Production Comp:** N/A
Height: 6-0	**Weight:** 173	**Throws:** R	

Season	Team	Age	Level	IP	TBF	K/9	K%	BB/9	BB%	K-BB%	ERA	FIP	xFIP	Pit/Bat
2021	COL	18	DSL	26.2	98	11.47	34.69%	2.02	6.12%	28.57%	0.67	1.97	2.35	1.94
2021	COL	18	CPX	10.0	44	11.70	29.55%	0.90	2.27%	27.27%	6.30	5.07	3.88	1.73
2022	COL	19	A	103.0	434	8.74	23.04%	2.88	7.60%	15.44%	4.98	5.24	4.85	3.84

Background: Let me know if you've heard this one before – because if you haven't, well, you're not paying close enough attention. Colorado signed the 16-year-old hurler fresh off the international free agency market, handing the Mexican-born youngster a hefty $500,000 in early 2019. And like so many of his peers that signed at the same time, Juarez wouldn't make his debut until two years later due to the COVID shutdown. Despite his age – he was 18 at the time – Colorado sent the righty down to the foreign rookie leagues to make his debut. And he dominated, posting a 34-to-6 strikeout-to-walk ratio in 26.2 innings of work. He spent the last few weeks of the year in the Complex League. Last season the front office took the training wheels off and shipped him directly into the Low-A, where he would make 21 starts with Grizzlies. Juarez would throw 103.0 innings, posting an impressively solid 100-to-33 strikeout-to-walk ratio. He would finish the year with a 4.98 ERA, a 5.24 FIP, and a 4.85 xFIP.

Scouting Report: Consider the following:

> Since 2006, there have been 154 hurlers to throw at least 100 innings in Low-A during their age-19 seasons. Of those 154, only four posted a 22% to 24% strikeout rate with a 6.5% to 8.5% walk rate. Those four hurlers: Jarrod Parker, Michael Fulmer, Aneury Rodriguez, and – of course – Victor Juarez. A few things to note: Parker, Fulmer, and Rodriguez all saw time at the big league level. Both Parker and Fulmer were consensus Top 100 prospects at various points in their careers.

The slight-framed right-hander did something I don't think I've ever seen to start of his June 11th game: he opened the game with two straight changeups then proceeded to throw changeups four of his next five pitches. Juarez is incredibly advanced for a 19-year-old, showing more than the typical willingness to mix in his secondary offerings. Average fastball and slider combo. But his curveball and changeup are both above-average with the latter showing solid improvement. His curveball is a beautiful 12-6 breaking ball that plays up when he's spotting his heater in the upper half of the zone. His changeup shows some solid downward tumble. There also may be an additional gear on the fastball in the coming years. Loose arm, smooth mechanics. Juarez is tracking like a fourth or fifth starter, but Colorado hasn't quite figured out to unlock the key to developing consistent pitching either.

Ceiling: 1.5-win player
Risk: Moderate
MLB ETA: 2024

15. McCade Brown, RHP

	FB	CB	SL	CH	Command	Overall
	60	60	60	45	50	50

Born: 05/15/00	**Age:** 22	**Bats:** R	**Top Production Comp:** N/A
Height: 6-6	**Weight:** 225	**Throws:** R	

Season	Team	Age	Level	IP	TBF	K/9	K%	BB/9	BB%	K-BB%	ERA	FIP	xFIP	Pit/Bat
2022	COL	21	A	89.2	380	11.84	31.05%	2.31	6.05%	25.00%	5.22	3.87	3.73	3.79

Background: Indiana University's typically been a solid baseball school – though they did finish near the bottom of the Conference standings last season – but they've had a difficult time converting that on-field success into professional success. Indiana's churned out just two players chosen in the opening three rounds of the draft since 2015: Matt Gorski, a second rounder in 2019, and McCade Brown, a third rounder two years ago. Limited to just 6.2 innings over his first two years with the Hoosiers courtesy of (A) a back issue during his freshman season and (B) the pandemic, Brown put together an intriguing – sometimes frustrating – junior campaign in 2021. Making 12 starts, the 6-foot-6, 225-pound right-hander struck out a whopping 97 hitters in only 61.0 innings of work. Of course, he also walked 43 during the same time. Brown spent the entirety of last season with the Grizzlies in Low-A. He would toss 89.2 innings of work, fanning 118 and zeroing in on the strike zone with an undiscovered talent by walking just 23. He finished the year with a 5.22 ERA, 3.87 FIP, and 3.73 xFIP.

Snippet from The 2022 Prospect Digest Handbook: Brown was basically an unknown heading into the 2021 season; a back injury limited him to less than three innings as a freshman and he made just four brief appearances during the COVID-shortened 2020 season. There's more growth here than the typical 21-year-old college arm.

Colorado Rockies

Scouting Report: Consider the following:

Since 2006, only two 21-year-old hurlers posted a strikeout percentage north of 30% *and* a sub-7% walk percentage in any Low-A league (min. 75 IP): Eric Surkamp, who accomplished the feat in 2009, and McCade Brown.

Brown's the type of arm that would flourish in an organization like the Dodgers or Rays or Guardians. The hard-throwing right-hander has a lot interesting / promising pieces to work with. Three plus offerings: a mid-90s fastball, a biting (and improved) slider, and a big 12-6 curveball. His below-average changeup is the lone pockmark. Not only does Brown have an impressive repertoire, but he's loose and very athletic. His command also picked up as he's throwing more consistent quality strikes. Brown needs to improve his sequencing. He's too fastball reliant when he's behind in the count / full count. Relief floor.

Ceiling: 1.5-win player
Risk: Moderate
MLB ETA: 2024

16. Jackson Cox, RHP

FB	CB	CH	Command	Overall
55	60	50	45	45

Born: 09/25/03	Age: 19	Bats: R	Top Production Comp: N/A
Height: 6-1	Weight: 185	Throws: R	

Background: It's doesn't seem that long ago that the Rockies were willing to go all in on hard-throwing, talented high school hurlers early in the draft – easily the riskiest group of prospects to build around. And that's not factoring in the club's Mile High altitude. The front office selected Ryan Castellani in the second round of the 2014 draft. A year later the NL West club grabbed enigmatic, supremely gifted right-hander Mike Nikorak with the 27th overall pick and would draft Peter Lambert 17 picks later. And, of course, their crescendo of missed opportunities came in 2016 when they called Riley Pint's name with the fourth overall pick in an admittedly overall weak first round. Since then, though, the Rockies have shied away from young impressionable arms in the opening parts of the draft. That is…until last season when they selected 18-year-old righty Jackson Cox in the second round, 50th overall. The Toutle Lake High School product inked a deal with the organization for $1.8 million – roughly a quarter million dollars above the recommended slot bonus value. Prior to the draft, the young hurler was committed to the University of Oregon.

Scouting Report: Far from physically imposing, Cox is listed – perhaps generously – at 6-foot-1 and 185-pounds. The young righty will feature a standard three-pitch mix: an above-average low- to mid-90s fastball that sits in the 93 mph range and will touch upwards of 96 at times. His true calling card though is a plus, upper 70s / low 80s curveball with good depth – though he's inconsistent with it. He'll also mix in an average changeup too. Cox is tracking like a backend arm. The command is less than impressive.

Ceiling: 1.5-win player
Risk: Moderate
MLB ETA: 2025

17. Jaden Hill, RHP

FB	SL	CH	Command	Overall
60	55	80	45	45

Born: 12/22/99	Age: 23	Bats: R	Top Production Comp: N/A
Height: 6-4	Weight: 234	Throws: R	

Season	Team	Age	Level	IP	TBF	K/9	K%	BB/9	BB%	K-BB%	ERA	FIP	xFIP	Pit/Bat
2022	COL	22	CPX	10.1	45	9.58	24.44%	3.48	8.89%	15.56%	3.48	3.58	4.70	1.84

Background: An organization that typically isn't known for taking health-based risks. But the Rockies did so in the second round two years ago, selecting the supremely talented, enigmatic, and oft-injured right-hander. Hill's past injuries include: surgery on his collarbone due to a football injury in high school, a UCL injury during his freshman season at LSU, and – of course – the Tommy John repair his howling elbow required during his junior campaign with the Tigers. Over parts of three separate college seasons, not including the 2020 COVID year, Hill logged exactly 50.1 innings of work. But Colorado's front office came calling, waving more than $1.6 million in bonus money to convince the hard-throwing right-hander to join the organization. Last season the 6-foot-4, 234-pound behemoth finally got back on the mound in mid-July. He would make it through the remainder of the year, throwing 17.2 innings with 25 strikeouts and just six walks split between the Complex and California Leagues. He finished the year with a 3.06 ERA.

Snippet from The 2022 Prospect Digest Handbook: At his best – which was not often in 2021 – Hill will flash a dominant plus fastball, an above-average tightly spun slider, and the best changeup in the entire draft class. The control's been mediocre throughout his three abbreviated

Colorado Rockies

collegiate years with the command slightly worse. It's easy to see Hill and dream upon a bonafide frontline ace. But there's a lot of Dillon Tate to his projection.

Scouting Report: Tree trunk legs that would lead you to believe he was a veteran NFL running back. Despite all the injuries, Hill came out of the chute firing seeds. Explosive plus fastball, late biting above-average slider, and an elite, almost-Devin Williams-esque changeup. If Williams' change-of-pace is the 1A standard, Hill's offering is 1B. But Hill has to answer several important questions in the next 12 to 18 months: #1. Can he stay healthy? #2. Can he take the ball every fifth, or even *sixth* day? #3. Can he command the zone? There's obvious risk that he (A) flames out or (B) becomes a reliever. I'm betting on the latter.

Ceiling: 1.5-win player
Risk: Moderate to High
MLB ETA: 2024

18. Ryan Rolison, LHP

FB	CB	SL	CH	Command	Overall
N/A	N/A	N/A	N/A	N/A	45

Born: 07/11/97	Age: 25	Bats: R	Top Production Comp: N/A
Height: 6-2	Weight: 213	Throws: L	

Season	Team	Age	Level	IP	TBF	K/9	K%	BB/9	BB%	K-BB%	ERA	FIP	xFIP	Pit/Bat
2018	COL	20	R	29.0	109	10.55	31.19%	2.48	7.34%	23.85%	1.86	3.71	3.35	3.58
2019	COL	21	A	14.2	53	8.59	26.42%	1.23	3.77%	22.64%	0.61	1.99	3.13	3.64
2019	COL	21	A+	116.1	509	9.13	23.18%	2.94	7.47%	15.72%	4.87	5.12	4.05	3.65
2021	COL	23	AA	14.2	57	12.27	35.09%	1.23	3.51%	31.58%	3.07	2.29	2.90	3.84
2021	COL	23	AAA	45.2	202	8.87	22.28%	3.15	7.92%	14.36%	5.91	5.20	5.37	3.75

Background: Rolison's had a rough go of it the past couple of years. He missed more than two months due to appendicitis surgery and *then* missed the entirety of the 2022 courtesy of left shoulder surgery. The former first rounder looked to be on the precipice of making his big league debut not too long ago, but that's obviously become murkier – to say the least. For his career, the former Mississippi ace is averaging an impressive 9.4 strikeouts and just 2.7 walks per nine innings to go along with a 4.35 ERA.

Scouting Report: Lacking any type of updates due to his health, here's Rolison's Scouting Report from 2022:

> "Not only a consistent strike-thrower, but a consistent quality strike-thrower. Rolison has a quality four-pitch mix showcased by an above-average low-90s fastball and a plus-curveball. He'll also mix in a slider and a changeup – both of them earning 50 grades. Unfortunately, though, Rolison and Colorado are – and have always been – a poor match. I still think he ends up a quality mid-rotation arm – though it's likely not going to be with the Rockies."

Ceiling: 1.5-win player
Risk: High
MLB ETA: 2022

19. Joe Rock, LHP

FB	SL	CH	Command	Overall
55	55/60	50	45	50

Born: 07/29/00	Age: 22	Bats: L	Top Production Comp: N/A
Height: 6-6	Weight: 200	Throws: L	

Season	Team	Age	Level	IP	TBF	K/9	K%	BB/9	BB%	K-BB%	ERA	FIP	xFIP	Pit/Bat
2022	COL	21	A+	107.2	454	9.11	24.01%	3.76	9.91%	14.10%	4.43	4.21	4.42	3.79

Background: Trivia Part I: Name the most successful pitcher drafted by the Colorado Rockies in the first round. Answer Part I: Jake Westbrook, of course, who was the 21st overall pick in the 1996 draft. Trivia Part II: Name the most successful second round pitcher drafted by the organization. Answer Part II: Aaron Cook. While the Rockies have hit on several notable draft picks – like Troy Tulowitzki or Nolan Arenado or Trevor Story or Todd Helton – the franchise has *notoriously* struggled in drafting and developing arms. But the front office took a gamble on one of the more intriguing, quickly rising arms in the 2021 draft out of Ohio University – far from a baseball hotbed. After the club selected him in the second round, Rock made a quartet of brief appearances in the Arizona Complex League, posting an 11-to-1 strikeout-to-walk ratio. Last season the front office had him bypass Low-A and pushed him directly into High-A. He would make 20 starts with Spokane, averaging 9.1 strikeouts and 3.8 walks per nine innings. He made another pair of starts with the Yard Goats to cap off his first full season in pro ball.

Colorado Rockies

Scouting Report: Consider the following:

> Since 2006, here's the list of 21-year-old hurlers to post a 23% to 25% strikeout rate with a walk rate between 9% and 11% in any High-A season (min. 100 IP): Sam Hentges, Chris Anderson, Pedro Avila, David Bromberg, Conner Nurse, Bruce Pugh, and Joe Rock.

Watching Rock pitch and it's easy to see why the Rockies burned a second round pick on him. A lot of arms and legs. Above-average fastball that sits in the 92- to 94-mph range. A slider that shows terrific horizontal sweeping action, hovering in the mid-80s but peaking several ticks higher. He'll also mix in a quietly solid mid-80s changeup, an average offering. The former Ohio University ace works low, low, low – which is aided by his low three-quarter arm slot. Long arm action that won't allow his below-average command jump into 50-grade territory. Backend option that could succeed in a Sam Hentges-type relief role.

Ceiling: 1.0- to 1.5-win player
Risk: Moderate
MLB ETA: 2023/2024

20. Carson Palmquist, LHP

FB	SL	CH	Command	Overall
45	55	55	45	40

Born: 10/17/00	Age: 22	Bats: L	Top Production Comp: N/A
Height: 6-3	Weight: 185	Throws: L	

Background: The lanky 6-foot-3, 185-pound left-hander put together, perhaps, the greatest run of dominance over his final two seasons at Riverdale High School. Palmquist, a native of Fort Myers, Florida, did not allow an earned run in either his junior *or* senior seasons for the Raiders. And the pinnacle came during his final prep campaign as he punched out 106 hitters in only 60.2 innings of work. In other words: more than 58% of the outs he recorded came via the strikeout. After going undrafted, Palmquist, one of the country's better teenage left-handers, stayed close to home and attended the University of Miami – where he confounded hitters. Working out of the Canes' bullpen as a true freshman, he posted a 15-to-5 strikeout-to-walk ratio in 11.2 innings of work. The following year, 2021, Palmquist worked as the school's closer, saving 14 games while averaging an absurd 15.1 strikeouts and just 1.6 walks per nine innings. He made another five relief appearances for Team USA that summer as well, tossing five innings with seven whiffs and just one free pass. Last season, finally, Palmquist was converted into a fulltime starting pitcher. And he blossomed. In 84.0 innings of work, spread across 16 starts, the big lefty tallied a 2.89 ERA with 118 strikeouts and just 32 free passes. Colorado selected him in the third round, 88th overall, and signed him to an above-slot deal worth $775,000. He tossed one inning in the Complex League, striking out one and walking a pair.

Scouting Report: With respect to his work during his sophomore season, consider the following:

> Since 2015, only 13 Division I pitchers have averaged at least 15 strikeouts per nine innings in a season (min. 40 IP). Of those 13, only one – Carson Palmquist – posted a sub-2.0 walk rate.

Now let's take a look at his junior year:

> Since 2015, only two (2) ACC Conference pitchers posted a strikeout rate north of 12 K/9 with a walk rate between 3.2 BB/9 and 3.6 BB/9 in a season (min. 75 IP): Griffin Roberts, 2018 first rounder by the Cardinals, and – of course – Carson Palmquist.

Low three-quarter slot slinger almost to the point of becoming a sidearm delivery. Palmquist is a pitcher taken directly from yesteryear. He sports an upper 80s / very low 90s fastball, a fringy average offering with some arm side run thanks to the arm slot. A solid above-average change with a touch of deception and solid velocity separation. And an above-average breaking ball – it was tabbed a curveball in high school but now referred to as a slider. It'll sit in the upper 70s with good movement. Everything about him screams future reliever. And that's before considering the organization he's headed to.

Ceiling: 1.0-win player
Risk: Moderate
MLB ETA: 2024/2025

Detroit Tigers

Top Prospects

Detroit Tigers

1. Jackson Jobe, RHP

FB	CB	SL	CH	Command	Overall
60	55	70	60	45/50	60

Born: 07/30/02	Age: 20	Bats: R	Top Production Comp: Zack Wheeler
Height: 6-2	Weight: 190	Throws: R	

Season	Team	Age	Level	IP	TBF	K/9	K%	BB/9	BB%	K-BB%	ERA	FIP	xFIP	Pit/Bat
2022	DET	19	A	61.2	270	10.36	26.30%	3.65	9.26%	17.04%	4.52	5.21	3.98	3.73
2022	DET	19	A+	15.2	63	5.74	15.87%	2.87	7.94%	7.94%	1.15	5.02	4.78	3.48

Background: At one point in the not so distant past, it seemed like the Tigers had one priority in the opening round of the July draft – right-handed pitchers. From 2013 through 2018, the club owned eight first round selections. Dave Dombrowski and his successor, Al Avila, used six of those picks on righties – Jonathon Crawford, Corey Knebel, Beau Burrows, Matt Manning, Alex Faedo, and Casey Mize. The next two drafts, however, the front office went in a completely different direction, snagging toolsy prep centerfielder Riley Greene and college masher Spencer Torkelson in the first rounds. But some habits prove to be too hard to quit – like taking right-handed hurlers. So the franchise doubled in the opening round in 2021, selecting Jackson Jobe, who was touted as a potential 1 / 1 guy heading into the draft, and University of Texas fireballer Ty Madden. A product of Heritage Hall School, Jobe would eventually agree to a massive $6.9 million deal with the Tigers after being picked with the third overall pick. Detroit held the teenage phenom out for the remainder of the year. Last season, though, the 6-foot-2, 190-pound righty made the most of his first crack at professional ball. Beginning his pro career with the Lakeland Flying Tigers, Jobe made 18 starts with the club's Florida State League affiliate, posting a 71-to-25 strikeout-to-walk ratio in only 61.2 innings of work. The front office would bump the farm system's top hurler up to the Midwest League in late August for another three contests. Jobe would finish the year with 77.1 innings of work, averaging 9.4 strikeouts and 3.5 walks per nine innings.

Snippet from The 2022 Prospect Digest Handbook: Barring any injury concerns that come along with a young arm, Jobe has the potential to slide into the front of a rotation

Scouting Report: Consider the following:

> Since 2006, there have been five hurlers that met the following criteria during their age-19 season in Low-A (min. 60 IP): 25.5% to 27.5% strikeout percentage with an 8.5% to 10.5% walk percentage. Those five hurlers: Michael Kopech, Trevor Cahill, Sam Hentges, Randall Delgado, and – of course – Jackson Jobe.

There are very few hurlers – at any age – in the minor leagues that can match Jobe's arsenal *or* his spin rate. During his last start of the year the hard-throwing right-hander was pumping 95- to 97-mph with relative ease. His curveball is – firmly – an above-average offering. His slider is like a gift from Steve Carlton or Bob Gibson. And his changeup – which ranks as his third best option – is among the best in the minor leagues. Jobe, like a lot of young fireballers, lacks a strong feel for the strike zone, but shows the athleticism and flexibility that allows it to project to average. If the command can creep up into above-average territory, the sky's the limit for the former third overall pick.

Ceiling: 4.5-win player
Risk: Moderate
MLB ETA: 2024/2025

2. Colt Keith, 2B/3B

Hit	Power	SB	Patience	Glove	Overall
60	55	30	55	50	60

Born: 08/14/01	Age: 20	Bats: L	Top Production Comp: Jeff McNeil
Height: 6-3	Weight: 211	Throws: R	

Season	Team	Age	Level	PA	1B	2B	3B	HR	SB	CS	BB%	K%	AVG	OBP	SLG	ISO
2021	DET	19	CPX	10	4	1	0	0	0	0	30.00%	0.00%	0.714	0.800	0.857	0.143
2021	DET	19	A	181	37	6	3	1	4	1	16.57%	21.55%	0.320	0.436	0.422	0.102
2021	DET	19	A+	76	8	1	1	1	0	0	10.53%	35.53%	0.162	0.250	0.250	0.088
2022	DET	20	A+	216	32	14	3	9	4	0	10.19%	19.44%	0.301	0.370	0.544	0.244

Background: In what quickly became known as the Spencer Torkelson draft, the front office quietly put together a stout class – despite COVID limiting the draft to just five rounds. Detroit added backstop Dillon Dingler in the second round and lefty-swinging infielder Colt Keith with their final selection. Taken with the 132nd overall pick, Keith wouldn't make his professional debut until the following season. And he quickly made up for lost time. Splitting time between Lakeland and West Michigan – as well as a couple brief rehab stints in the Complex League – the Biloxi High School product hit an aggregate .286/.396/.393 with eight doubles, five triples, two homeruns, and a quartet of stolen bases in only 65 games of work. Last season, in an injury-marred campaign that limited him to just 48 games, Keith slugged a red hot .301/.370/.544 with 14 doubles, three triples, nine homeruns, and four stolen bases. Per *Weighted Runs Created Plus*, his overall production topped the league average mark by a whopping 50%. After missing the final four months of the year, Keith made his way to the Arizona Fall League with the Salt River Rafters where he – almost amazingly – slugged .344/.463/.541 in 80 plate appearances.

Detroit Tigers

Snippet from The 2022 Prospect Digest Handbook: The former fifth round pick has the makings of a professional hitter, the infamous label slapped onto sweet-swinging players with little pop. He sprays line drives all over the diamond with little bias. Very patient approach, which is often lacking in young players making their debuts directly in Low-A. Throw in a solid-average glove and Keith has the makings of a decent little prospect. Cut from the Colin Moran mold, though. No platoon splits.

Scouting Report: Consider the following:

Since 2006, only three 20-year-old hitters posted a 145 to 155 wRC+ with a strikeout rate between 19% to 22% with a walk rate between 9% and 12% in a High-A season (min. 200 PA): Anthony Alford, Clint Frazier, and – of course – Colt Keith.

Keith went from a line-driving hitter during his first pro season to a legitimate power-hitting bat – albeit one in a smallish sample size. Keith got stronger, began elevating the ball more frequently, and he was able to maintain his similar approach from at bat to at bat. Really good looking, silky smooth swing. Keith shoots the ball all over the diamond without regard. If everything clicks just right – which is a long shot – there's some Justin Turner / Jeff McNeil upside.

Ceiling: 4.0-win player
Risk: Moderate
MLB ETA: 2023/2024

3. Jace Jung, 2B

Hit	Power	SB	Patience	Glove	Overall
55	50	40	55	50	55

Born: 10/04/00	Age: 22	Bats: L	Top Production Comp: N/A
Height: 6-0	Weight: 205	Throws: R	

Season	Team	Age	Level	PA	1B	2B	3B	HR	SB	CS	BB%	K%	AVG	OBP	SLG	ISO
2022	DET	21	A+	134	17	6	1	1	0	0	18.66%	20.90%	0.231	0.373	0.333	0.102

Background: It has to be difficult growing up with an older brother who (A) is a former Big 12 Freshman of the Year and (B) Freshman All-American, and (C) All-American, and (D) Team USA alumnus, and (E) the eighth the overall pick in the 2019 MLB Draft. Unless, of course, that person is Jace Jung, who has practically gone toe-to-toe with his older brother Josh Jung, a top prospect in the Rangers' organization. After a solid, COVID-limited true freshman campaign in 2020, the younger Jung, who batted .264/.438/.604 for the Red Raiders, had a massive breakout during his follow up campaign for Head Coach Tim Tadlock. In 56 games for the Big 12 conference school, the lefty-swinging second / third baseman slugged .337/.462/.697 with 10 doubles, one triple, and 21 homeruns. He finished the year with a sparkling 45-to-49 strikeout-to-walk ratio. And then the awards started rolling in:

Consensus All-American including First Team Honors by *Collegiate Baseball Newspaper*, the NCBWA, *Perfect Game*, and the *College Baseball Foundation*; Big 12 Player of the Year; Unanimous All-Big 12 First Team

The younger Jung also earned a spot on Team USA's roster, the first Red Raider to do so since his older brother. He would bat a solid .267/.371/.400 for the national squad in 11 games, belting out a double and a dinger. The Texas Tech star maintained status quo during his phenomenal 2022 season as well. In a career best 61 games, Jung batted a scorching .335/.481/.612 with a career best 18 doubles, one triple, and 14 homeruns. He also went a perfect 5-for-5 in the stolen base department as well. Like the previous year, Jung walked more times than he whiffed (59 to 42). Detroit selected the second / third baseman with the 12th overall pick last July, handing him to a deal worth $4,590,300. After signing, Jung appeared in 30 games in High-A with West Michigan, batting .232/.373/.333 with six doubles, one triple, and a dinger. Per *Weighted Runs Created Plus*, his overall production was 6% better than the league average mark.

Scouting Report: Per the usual, my pre-draft write up on the 12th overall pick:

"Consider the following:

Since 2011, there are only seven instances in which a Big 12 hitter met the following criteria in a season (min. 250 PA): bat at least .300/.450/.600 with more walks than strikeouts: Ivan Melendez (Texas, 2022), Grant Little (Texas Tech, 2018), Jaxx Groshans (Kansas, 2019), Josh Jung (Texas Tech, 2018 and 2019), and Jace Jung (2021 and 2022).

Detroit Tigers

Expanding it out a bit, consider the following:

Since 2011, only six players met the aforementioned criteria in two separate seasons for any conference in Division 1 baseball: Kyle Schwarber, Adley Rutschman, D.J. Peterson, Tyler Locklear, Josh Jung, and – of course – Jace Jung. For those counting at home Schwarber was the 4th overall pick in 2014; Rutschman was the top pick in 2019; Peterson was the 12th pick in 2013; Locklear, a projected early round pick in 2022; Josh Jung, the 8th overall pick in 2019; and – of course – Jace Jung.

Starting from an abnormal, almost Kevin Youkilis / Cal Ripken Jr.-type hand setup, Jung holds his hands high and lets the bat almost rest at a 45-degree drop away from him. And it creates an odd approach to the zone as well, never really straightening the bat head at any point. It's a peculiar swing, but it's short and lightning quick. Jung has above-average power potential, a little bit of footspeed, and he's had no trouble with better college-age competition. The ceiling is higher if he can stick to second base. Ben Zobrist-type offensive performer."

Ceiling: 3.0-win player
Risk: Moderate
MLB ETA: 2024

4. Justyn-Henry Malloy, 3B/LF

Hit	Power	SB	Patience	Glove	Overall
50/55	50/60	30	60	45/50	55

Born: 0219/00	Age: 23	Bats: R	Top Production Comp: N/A
Height: 6-2	Weight: 212	Throws: R	

Season	Team	Age	Level	PA	1B	2B	3B	HR	SB	CS	BB%	K%	AVG	OBP	SLG	ISO
2021	ATL	21	A	147	23	5	0	5	4	2	16.33%	20.41%	0.270	0.388	0.434	0.164
2022	ATL	22	A+	320	54	16	0	10	3	0	14.69%	22.81%	0.304	0.409	0.479	0.175
2022	ATL	22	AA	238	34	11	0	6	0	0	18.07%	25.21%	0.268	0.403	0.421	0.153
2022	ATL	22	AAA	33	5	1	0	1	2	0	21.21%	15.15%	0.280	0.424	0.440	0.160

Background: As the draft approaches every season, the inevitable stories pop up on how a player bet on himself by forgoing an earlier opportunity to play pro ball and is projected to be taken significantly higher. Ace Gerrit Cole famously bypassed the Yankees' offer as the 28th overall pick coming out of high school in 2008 and went #1 overall three years later. Jack Leiter's strong commitment to Vanderbilt forced teams away from taking him early in the first round as well. The stories are abundant. But not quite like Justyn-Henry Malloy. Highly touted coming out of St. Joseph Regional High School, Malloy attended – arguably – the top baseball program in the entire country: Vanderbilt University. Except he didn't see the field in 2019. And he didn't see the field again in 2020, though it's hard to say just how much COVID impacted that. But either way, though, through two seasons in college he made only 61 trips to the plate *and* he looked terrible during that time as well. So he transferred to Georgia Tech, morphed into a dominant force by mashing .308/.436/.558, and was drafted by the Braves in the sixth round two years ago. The part-time third baseman / corner outfielder continued to hit during his extended debut in Low-A, batting .271/.388/.434. And he *continued* to hit – again, throughout the entirety of 2022. Spending time at High-A, Double-A, and (briefly) Triple-A, the 6-foot-2, 212-pound prospect slugged .289/.408/.454 with 28 doubles, 17 homeruns, and five stolen bases. His overall production, per *Weighted Runs Created Plus*, topped the league average mark by 36%. Detroit acquired the burgeoning big leaguer, as well as minor league veteran reliever Jake Higginbotham, for All-Star reliever Joe Jimenez.

Scouting Report: Consider the following:

Since 2006, only four 22-year-old hitters met the following criteria in a Double-A season (min. 200 PA): 120 to 130 wRC+, at least a 14% walk rate, and a strikeout rate between 23% to 27%. Those four hitters: Brett Jackson, Isan Diaz, Canaan Smith-Njigba, and – of course – Justyn-Henry Malloy.

Malloy takes a saber-slanted approach at the plate, walking at an elite clip in his minor league career, mashing mammoth homeruns, and – of course – there's a bit of swing-and-miss to his game as well (he fanned in more than a quarter of his plate appearances in Double-A last season). But here's the interesting tidbit: when he swings, he doesn't miss frequently. Despite a K-rate north of 25% in Double-A, he had a swinging strike percentage of just 9.7%. Plus power potential that's just beginning to show up in games. And the hit tool may develop into an above-average weapon in the coming years. There's *a lot* to like on Malloy. And he's just beginning to scratch the surface of his talent. And if Malloy's taught us anything, never – *ever* – bet against him.

Ceiling: 3.0-win player
Risk: Moderate
MLB ETA: 2023

Detroit Tigers

5. Ty Madden, RHP

	FB	CB	CU	CH	Command	Overall
	60	60	50	50	55	55

Born: 02/21/00	Age: 23	Bats: R	Top Production Comp: Lance Lynn
Height: 6-3	Weight: 215	Throws: R	

Season	Team	Age	Level	IP	TBF	K/9	K%	BB/9	BB%	K-BB%	ERA	FIP	xFIP	Pit/Bat
2022	DET	22	AA	35.2	142	12.36	34.51%	3.03	8.45%	26.06%	2.78	3.86	2.81	4.25
2022	DET	22	A+	87.0	359	8.69	23.40%	2.69	7.24%	16.16%	3.10	4.15	4.35	3.77

Background: Heading into the 2021 draft there were some whispers that Ty Madden, the Texas-born right-hander missing plenty of bats with Longhorns, might be a potential Top 10 selection. He was – and is – the prototypical Detroit Tigers pitching prospect – big, right-handed, hard-throwing – and likely would have only caused a few ripples in the media if the front office used the third overall pick on the big hurler. And it seemed almost impossible that Madden, who averaged 10.8 strikeout per nine innings during his junior campaign, would be available when the ballclub from Motown came up for a second selection. But he was. And Detroit didn't hesitate to snag him with the 32nd overall pick. Madden, who signed for $2.5 million, made his professional debut last summer, opening the year up in West Michigan, but quickly got promoted up to Double-A by early August. The former University of Texas ace finished his freshman professional season with 122.2 innings, racking up 133 strikeouts and just 38 free passes to go along with an aggregate 3.01 ERA.

Snippet from The 2020 Prospect Digest Handbook: If his changeup fails to materialize – or if the command/control regresses – he's a dominant relief arm. But if everything clicks [Madden] looks like a #2/#3-type starting pitcher.

Scouting Report: Madden attacks hitters with a solid four-pitch mix – fastball, curveball, cutter, and changeup. But unlike a lot of pitchers equipped with a mid-90s fastball, the big right-hander relies heavily on his quality secondary offerings, particularly his plus curveball and improved upper 80s changeup. Madden continues to throw quality strikes, which wasn't the case early in his collegiate career. A year after the draft, the 6-foot-2, 215-pound hurler still has the makings a #3-type arm. He's just one step closer to accomplishing it.

Ceiling: 3.0-win player
Risk: Moderate
MLB ETA: 2024

7. Reese Olson, RHP

	FB	SL	CH	Command	Overall
	55	60	60	50	55

Born: 07/31/99	Age: 23	Bats: R	Top Production Comp: Jake Odorizzi
Height: 6-1	Weight: 160	Throws: R	

Season	Team	Age	Level	IP	TBF	K/9	K%	BB/9	BB%	K-BB%	ERA	FIP	xFIP	Pit/Bat
2019	MIL	19	A	94.2	425	7.99	19.76%	4.47	11.06%	8.71%	4.66	4.45	4.26	4.09
2021	MIL	21	A+	69.0	294	10.30	26.87%	4.57	11.90%	14.97%	4.30	4.16	4.51	4.15
2021	DET	21	A+	11.0	41	11.45	34.15%	1.64	4.88%	29.27%	0.00	1.77	2.93	4.20
2021	DET	21	AA	24.2	104	7.66	20.19%	5.11	13.46%	6.73%	4.74	4.04	4.98	3.74
2022	DET	22	AA	119.2	508	12.64	33.07%	2.86	7.48%	25.59%	4.14	3.31	3.08	4.00

Background: It was the kind of deal that the Brewers don't make very often, particularly under the captainship of former GM David Stearns. But the Tigers definitely pulled one over on the Brew Crew's savvy front office. A day before the trade deadline two years ago, Detroit sent lefty reliever – and former consensus Top 100 prospect – Daniel Norris to Milwaukee for right-hander Reese Olson. Drafted in the 13th round out of North Hall High School in 2018, Reese put together one of the best Double-A showings in 2022. After capping off his 2021 campaign with a five-game cameo in Erie, the 6-foot-1, 160-pound righty made 25 starts (and one relief appearance) with the SeaWolves, throwing a career best 119.2 innings of work, striking out an impressive 168 and walking 38. He trailed Double-A leader Kai-Wei Teng by one punch out and tied for the seventh most in the minor leagues. Olson set the SeaWolves' single season strikeout record as well, passing Seth Etherton.

Snippet from The 2020 Prospect Digest Handbook: One of my favorite arms in the minors. You don't have to squint too hard to see a viable big league starting pitcher, and one, who may eke his was into a Top 100 prospect list at some time. He's entering his age-22 season with Double-A experience. Don't sleep on this guy.

Scouting Report: Consider the following comparison:

Season	Name	Team	Level	Age	IP	K/9	BB/9	K/BB	K%	BB%	K-BB%
2011	Matt Moore	TB	AA	22	102.1	11.52	2.46	4.68	32.75%	7.00%	25.75%
2022	Reese Olson	DET	AA	22	119.2	12.64	2.86	4.42	33.07%	7.48%	25.59%

That 2011 season by Moore, of course, was the one that vaulted him up as one of the top few prospects in the minor leagues – *Baseball America* ranked him #1, as did *MLB.com*, and *Baseball Prospectus* had the big lefty listed as #2 overall. Olson arsenal's three-pitches deep, each

Detroit Tigers

having at least a 55-grade. Olson's fastball sits in the 93 – to 95-mph range. He'll feature a plus slider that shows an equal blend of sweep and downward bite. And the young right-hander also possesses one of the best changeups in the minors as well, throwing in the 87- to 89-mph range with plenty of sink and fade. Olson showed an above-average curveball in prior years, but it looks like he may have scrapped it all together. The former late rounder Bonus Baby has battled command issues throughout the early parts of his career, but he was able to hone in on the strike zone with significantly improved command in 2022. There's legitimate #3 / #4-type potential here. Olson's one of the few starting pitching prospects – and potential big leaguer – that can pitch backward – despite possessing a mid-90s fastball.

Ceiling: 3.0-win player
Risk: Moderate
MLB ETA: 2022/2023

7. Wilmer Flores, RHP

FB	CB	SL/CU	CH	Command	Overall
55	60	50	60	55	55

Born: 02/20/01	Age: 21	Bats: R	Top Production Comp: N/A
Height: 6-4	Weight: 225	Throws: R	

Season	Team	Age	Level	IP	TBF	K/9	K%	BB/9	BB%	K-BB%	ERA	FIP	xFIP	Pit/Bat
2021	DET	20	CPX	13.0	57	12.46	31.58%	1.38	3.51%	28.07%	4.85	2.53	3.07	1.79
2021	DET	20	A	53.0	224	12.23	32.14%	3.74	9.82%	22.32%	3.40	2.80	3.21	3.91
2022	DET	21	A+	19.2	77	16.02	45.45%	0.92	2.60%	42.86%	1.83	1.86	1.27	3.84
2022	DET	21	AA	83.2	345	10.22	27.54%	2.26	6.09%	21.45%	3.01	3.50	3.53	3.72

Background: Arguably the best undrafted free agent signing following the five-round, COVID limited draft three years ago. Detroit unearthed the talented and underrated right-hander after less than a dozen innings at Arizona Western College. Since then Flores has rocketed through the low levels of the minor leagues and shot up prospect charts. The burly right-hander made a trio of brief appearances in the Complex League to begin his career in 2021, and spent the remainder of his debut dominating the Low-A Southeast League competition. Last season, the Venezuelan-born right-hander zipped through six appearances with West Michigan and continued to confound the competition at Double-A, the minors' toughest challenge. Flores would end his sophomore campaign with 103.1 innings of work, recording a whopping 130 strikeouts against just 23 free passes. He tallied an aggregate 2.79 ERA.

Snippet from The 2020 Prospect Digest Handbook: He's one of the guys I'm really looking forward to scouting in 2022.

Scouting Report: Consider the following:

> Since 2006, only four 21-year-old pitchers posted a strikeout percentage between 26% and 29% with a sub-8% walk percentage in a season in Double-A (min. 75 IP): Matt Manning, Brett Cecil, Logan Allen, and – of course – Wilmer Flores, the 2020 undrafted free agent.

Two years later and it's hard to fathom why more teams weren't in on Flores. The well-built right-hander features a solid four-pitch mix. He locates his fastball, which was sitting in the 93- to 95-mph range in a late season contest against Bowie, incredibly well and appears to cut it in on lefties at times as well. His best secondary pitch is a big bending, 12-6 curveball that he'll add and subtract on, throwing it anywhere from the low 70s to 80 mph. He'll lean heavily on his slider / cutter. There's a little bit of a wrinkle to it, but it generated a lot of awkward swings. Reports indicate he'll mix in below-average changeup, but I didn't personally see one. There's #4-type upside here thanks to his command and three solid pitches.

Ceiling: 2.5- to 3.0-win player
Risk: Moderate
MLB ETA: 2023

8. Kerry Carpenter, LF/RF

Hit	Power	SB	Patience	Glove	Overall
45	55	35	45	50	50

Born: 09/02/97	Age: 25	Bats: L	Top Production Comp: Randal Grichuk
Height: 6-2	Weight: 220	Throws: R	

Season	Team	Age	Level	PA	1B	2B	3B	HR	SB	CS	BB%	K%	AVG	OBP	SLG	ISO
2019	DET	21	R	191	23	16	3	9	6	0	11.52%	9.42%	0.319	0.408	0.625	0.306
2019	DET	21	A-	18	3	0	0	0	1	0	0.00%	16.67%	0.167	0.167	0.167	0.000
2021	DET	23	AA	461	69	24	1	15	5	6	6.29%	20.39%	0.262	0.319	0.433	0.171
2022	DET	24	AA	262	35	16	0	22	1	3	6.11%	27.48%	0.304	0.359	0.646	0.342
2022	DET	24	AAA	138	19	11	1	8	2	7	12.32%	12.32%	0.331	0.420	0.644	0.314

Background: Let's play a game, OK? The practically unknown Kerry Carpenter spent the opening few months in Class AA, the most difficult challenge for a minor leaguer, at the start of 2022. Where did his overall production rank (min. 250 PA)? Fourth best. He spent the next two months playing for the Toledo Mudhens. Where did his overall production rank at that level (min. 100 PA)? Fifth. Eventually the Tigers

Detroit Tigers

called him up in mid-August for the remainder of the year. Where did Carpenter's production rank among all MLB rookies (min. 100 PA)? Tenth. Needless to say, it was quite the breakout campaign for the former Virginia Tech Hokie. Taken all the way back in the 19th round in 2019, Detroit coaxed the lefty-swinging corner outfielder to sign for a paltry $125,000. Carpenter, a former JuCo transplant, ripped through the Gulf Coast League and appeared for a cup of coffee in short season ball. Then…he disappeared thanks to the lost COVID season. Detroit challenged him in 2021, sending him directly up to Double-A. And you know what? He handled himself well, batting .262/.319/.433 with 24 doubles, one triple, and 15 homeruns. The front office kept him back down in Double-A to begin last season. And he mashed. He mashed in Triple-A. And he kept on hitting in the big leagues. Carpenter slugged an aggregate .313/.380/.645 with 27 doubles, one triple, 30 homeruns, and three stolen bases in the minor leagues. And he hit .252/.310/.485 with four doubles, one triple, and six homeruns with the Tigers.

Scouting Report: A tremendous find by the Tigers' scouting department, unearthing a gritty, potential league average starting outfielder all the way back in the draft. Carpenter has a simple setup at the plate, little movement, quiet. He unleashes an uppercut swing and doesn't complete a normal follow though, in the traditional sense. But the power is undeniable. It's legitimate 25- to 30-homer thump, at any level. He's not going to walk very frequently, and there's some swing-and-miss to his game, but the defense is passable enough in either corner outfield spot. He also doesn't show any platoon splits either. His showing as a rookie, .252/.310/.485, seems like a reasonable baseline moving forward. Very Randal Grichuk-esque type potential.

Ceiling: 2.0-win player
Risk: Moderate
MLB ETA: Debuted in 2022

9. Cristian Santana, 3B/SS

Hit	Power	SB	Patience	Glove	Overall
45/45	50/55	50/40	50	40/45	50

Born: 11/25/03	Age: 19	Bats: R	Top Production Comp: N/A
Height: 6-0	Weight: 165	Throws: R	

Season	Team	Age	Level	PA	1B	2B	3B	HR	SB	CS	BB%	K%	AVG	OBP	SLG	ISO
2021	DET	17	DSL	216	23	12	2	9	12	7	13.89%	21.30%	0.269	0.421	0.520	0.251
2022	DET	18	A	340	35	13	0	9	10	5	15.88%	25.88%	0.215	0.379	0.366	0.151

Background: The front office pulled out all the stops – and then some – to sign the Dominican infielder in early 2021, handing the 17-year-old a *hefty* $2.95 million – a club record. Detroit sent the 6-foot, 165-pound teenager to the Dominican Summer League a few months later to begin his debut, where he showed gobs of promise. In 54 games, Santana batted .269/.421/.521 with 12 doubles, two triples, nine homeruns, and 12 stolen bases (in 19 total attempts). Last season the front office sent the then-18-year-old straight up to the Florida State League. In 80 games with the Flying Tigers of Lakeland, Santana batted a saber-friendly .215/.379/.366 with 13 doubles, nine homeruns, and 10 stolen bases. Despite the poor Mario Mendoza-esque batting average, Santana's overall production topped the league average mark by 23%, according to *Weighted Runs Created Plus*.

Snippet from The 2022 Prospect Digest Handbook: Short, quick, compact swing with above-average power potential. Santana showed a bit too much swing-and-miss during his debut, fanning in more than 21% of his plate appearances. But after a strong showing as a 17-year-old, Santana's all but punched his ticket to the states for 2022.

Scouting Report: Consider the following:

> Since 2006, only six 18-year-old hitters posted a wRC+ total between 118 to 128 in a season in Low-A (min. 300 PA): Ozzie Albies, Willy Adames, Gary Sanchez, Jomar Reyes, T.J. White, and Cristian Santana. Of those six players Santana's strikeout rate, 25.9%, was only lower than Gary Sanchez (27.1%) and T.J. White (27.2%). Santana's batting average, .215, was – by far – the worst in the group. The runner up, Sanchez, batted .256.

Santana was particularly awful during five weeks of the season, hitting .149/.289/.284 – which is to be expected given (A) his previous level of competition and (B) his age. He promptly disappeared from the Flying Tigers' lineup and popped back up in Low-A on June 9th. From that point through the remainder of the year he batted .241/.412/.398. His production during that point? A scorching 45% better than the league average. Santana's interesting because a lot, *a lot* of his value is tied to his impeccable patience at the plate (he walked in nearly 16% of his plate appearances in 2022). He already shows average power and projects to be a perennial 20-homer threat. Solid speed. His glove is underwhelming. So there's a lot riding on his bat. The ingredients to be a superlative player are clearly in place, but they're being swirled around like a tornado. If they land in place, watch out… He could be a sleeper pick to be a Top 100 Prospect by the end of 2023.

Ceiling: 2.0-win player
Risk: Moderate
MLB ETA: 2025

Detroit Tigers

10. Parker Meadows, CF

Hit	Power	SB	Patience	Glove	Overall
45	55	55	50	50	50

Born: 11/02/99	Age: 23	Bats: L	Top Production Comp: N/A
Height: 6-5	Weight: 205	Throws: R	

Season	Team	Age	Level	PA	1B	2B	3B	HR	SB	CS	BB%	K%	AVG	OBP	SLG	ISO
2018	DET	18	A-	21	5	1	0	0	0	0	9.52%	28.57%	0.316	0.381	0.368	0.053
2018	DET	18	R	85	14	2	1	4	3	1	9.41%	29.41%	0.284	0.376	0.500	0.216
2019	DET	19	A	504	74	15	2	7	14	8	9.33%	22.42%	0.221	0.296	0.312	0.090
2021	DET	21	A	12	2	1	0	0	0	0	0.00%	25.00%	0.273	0.333	0.364	0.091
2021	DET	21	A+	408	49	15	2	8	9	8	9.07%	24.26%	0.208	0.290	0.330	0.121
2022	DET	22	A+	67	5	4	1	4	0	0	5.97%	26.87%	0.230	0.288	0.525	0.295
2022	DET	22	AA	489	74	21	6	16	17	2	10.63%	18.40%	0.275	0.354	0.466	0.191

Background: Let's play a game. How many players from the second round of the 2018 draft class made it to the big leagues by the end of the 2022 season? The answer: eight. Just eight of the 35 players taken in the second round have accrued big league experience on their pro resumes. Question #2: Who are the three most valuable players from the second round (in terms of bWAR)? The answer: Ryan Jeffers (1.9 bWAR), Alek Thomas (1.5), and Nick Sandlin (1.5). The point: It takes a *long* time – longer than many likely understand – for even a high round pick to make their way through the minors and establish themselves as a viable big leaguer. Now let's talk about Parker Meadows. The first selection in the second round that year, Meadows, the younger brother of Tigers outfielder Austin Meadows, looked solid during his professional debut as he hit .290/.377/.476 between brief stints in the Gulf Coast and New York-Penn Leagues. And then things went south – for quite a while. The lefty-swinging outfielder batted an abysmal .221/.296/.312 in Low-A in 2019. He followed that up with an aggregate .210/.292/.331 slash line in 2021, most of which occurred in High-A. Meadows opened last season back up in High-A, but would earn a promotion up to the minors' toughest challenge, Double-A, just two weeks later. In 113 games with the West Michigan Whitecaps, the 6-foot-5, 205-pound prospect slugged an impressive .275/.354/.466 with 21 doubles, six triples, 16 homeruns, and 17 stolen bases (in 19 total attempts). His overall production in Double-A, per *Weighted Runs Created Plus*, topped the league average mark by 23%.

Snippet from The 2020 Prospect Digest Handbook: Peripheral-wise, there's little in terms of red flags: power, speed, patience, not overly large strikeout rates. He's just…not living up to the billing.

Scouting Report: Consider the following:

> Since 2006, only four 22-year-old hitters met the following criteria in a season in Double-A (min. 400 PA): 118 to 128 wRC+, a sub-20.0% strikeout rate, and a double-digit walk rate. Those four hitters: Kurt Suzuki, Robbie Grossman, Tyler Nevin, and – of course – Parker Meadows.

The tools were always in place for Meadows – speed, above-average power, solid contact rates, defense, no major platoon issues (surprisingly). Except now, though, Meadows is actually barreling up the baseball. He's not likely going to be a star – though, again, the tools are there – but Meadows' resurgent 2022 season all but guarantees him several looks at the big league level. There's plenty of skepticism, but one more similar season and Meadows could be a fringy average starter.

Ceiling: 1.5- to 2.0-win player
Risk: Moderate to High
MLB ETA: 2023

11. Izaac Pacheco, SS

Hit	Power	SB	Patience	Glove	Overall
40/45	45/55	50/40	50	55	45

Born: 11/18/02	Age: 02	Bats: L	Top Production Comp: Nolan Jones
Height: 6-4	Weight: 225	Throws: R	

Season	Team	Age	Level	PA	1B	2B	3B	HR	SB	CS	BB%	K%	AVG	OBP	SLG	ISO
2021	DET	18	CPX	125	17	4	2	1	1	0	14.40%	34.40%	0.226	0.339	0.330	0.104
2022	DET	19	A	371	57	21	2	8	12	4	10.24%	21.56%	0.267	0.342	0.415	0.148
2022	DET	19	A+	73	6	2	0	3	0	1	12.33%	23.29%	0.183	0.274	0.367	0.183

Background: The early returns on the club's 2021 draft class are incredibly favorable. Jackson Jobe, their first pick, is one of the better young hurlers in the minor leagues and sits atop Detroit's farm system. Their second pick, right-hander Ty Madden, blitzed through High-A and he spent more than a month in Double-A during his first season in the minor leagues. And Izaac Pacheco, the third overall pick in the second round, quietly turned in a strong showing in Low-A after an abysmal debut in the Complex League. A well-built, lefty-swinging infielder, Pacheco looked completely overmatched in pro ball after the club selected him 39th overall two years ago, cobbling together a lowly .226/.339/.330 slash line with a whiff rate approaching 35%. His 88-game stint with Lakeland was more indicative of his true talent level. Splitting time between shortstop and the hot corner, Pacheco hit .267/.342/.415 with 21 doubles, two triples, eight homeruns, and 12 stolen

Detroit Tigers

bases. His production with the Flying Tigers, according to *Weighted Runs Created Plus*, topped the league average mark by 16%. The front office bumped him up to the Midwest League in early August – though the initial test proved to be a bit too much for the teenager.

Snippet from The 2022 Prospect Digest Handbook: owns a great looking swing, a quasi-picture-esque lefty one, but I think he's going to show some massive platoon splits, especially once southpaws start pounding him low-and-away with soft stuff.

Scouting Report: Pacheco not only was one of just nine qualified 19-year-old hitters in the Florida State League, but he was the most productive hitter among the group. While he cut his swing-and-miss issues down considerably, the Friendswood High School product was still showing some strong red flags. As mentioned in last year's Handbook, Pacheco proved to be inept against left-handed pitching, batting a putrid .205/.271/.296 against them with a near 30% strikeout rate in 2021. And the initial results on his glove work suggest he's a capable third baseman moonlighting as a shortstop. Pacheco is still learning how to tap into his above-average power potential and he's not likely to swipe double-digit steals as he continues to fill out. There's some Nolan Jones feel to him.

Ceiling: 1.5-win player
Risk: Moderate
MLB ETA: 2024

12. Peyton Graham, IF

Hit	Power	SB	Patience	Glove	Overall
45	50	55	45	50	45

Born: 01/26/01	Age: 22	Bats: R	Top Production Comp: Chad Pinder
Height: 6-3	Weight: 185	Throws: R	

Season	Team	Age	Level	PA	1B	2B	3B	HR	SB	CS	BB%	K%	AVG	OBP	SLG	ISO
2022	DET	21	A	113	20	5	1	1	7	1	8.85%	25.66%	0.270	0.345	0.370	0.100

Background: Waxahachie High School has some deep roots to the game of baseball: seven players have walked through the school's hallowed halls and would eventually grace the fields of big league ballparks. But it's been a *long, long* time since a former Wolf appeared in a big league game – 64 years to be exact. Peyton Graham, part of the school's 2019 graduating class, could help break that drought. A member of the Texas High School Baseball Coaches All-Star Game (Class 6A) as a senior, Graham got off to an explosive start to his collegiate career in 2020, slugging a scorching .358/.457/.612 in 18 games before COVID prematurely wrecked the year. The 6-foot-3, 185-pound infielder saw a modest decline in production the following year as he batted .288/.400/.502 with 11 doubles, one triple, 11 homeruns, and seven stolen bases (in 10 total attempts). Graham spent the summer playing for the Yarmouth-Dennis Red Sox in the Cape Cod League, hitting a mediocre .247/.367/.370 in 20 games. Last season, though, Graham rediscovered his stroke during his junior campaign with the Oklahoma Sooners. In a career best 67 games, he slugged .335/.417/.640 with career highs in doubles (17), triples (four), homeruns (20), and stolen bases (34). Detroit selected Graham in the second round, 51st overall, and signed him to a deal worth $1.8 million. He appeared in 27 games in Low-A after joining the organization, hitting .270/.345/.370 with five doubles, one triple, and one homerun. He also swiped seven bags in eight total attempts.

Scouting Report: Per the usual, my pre-draft write up on the 12th overall pick:

> *"Consider the following:*
>
> *Since 2011, only three Division I hitters batted at least .325/.410/.625 with a strikeout percentage between 20% and 22% in a season (min. 300 PA): Trevor Larnach, the Minnesota Twins' first round pick in 2018; Connor Owings, a late, late round pick by the Arizona Diamondbacks in 2016; and – of course – Peyton Graham.*
>
> *Tall and lanky with plenty of room to add strength and weight. Graham has a slow, stiff, robotic leg kick he employees as a timing mechanism that he uses inconsistently, alternating with a slide step at times. Long arms, but generates good bat speed. Above-average power potential, but there's going to be some swing-and-miss to his game in the professional ranks. 45-grade hit tool. He's likely going to have to slide away from shortstop. There's some Chad Pinder-type potential here. Back end of the first round / opening second round grade."*

Ceiling: 1.5-win player
Risk: Moderate
MLB ETA: 2024

Detroit Tigers

13. Wenceel Perez, 2B

Hit	Power	SB	Patience	Glove	Overall
50	45	55	50	50	45

Born: 10/30/99	Age: 23	Bats: B	Top Production Comp: N/A
Height: 5-11	Weight: 203	Throws: R	

Season	Team	Age	Level	PA	1B	2B	3B	HR	SB	CS	BB%	K%	AVG	OBP	SLG	ISO
2019	DET	19	A	516	82	16	6	3	21	13	8.72%	16.86%	0.233	0.299	0.314	0.081
2021	DET	21	A	107	20	5	1	1	9	1	11.21%	19.63%	0.293	0.383	0.402	0.109
2021	DET	21	A+	369	59	13	6	3	13	1	8.40%	17.34%	0.245	0.313	0.348	0.103
2022	DET	22	A+	236	32	13	5	9	13	1	11.44%	16.10%	0.286	0.364	0.529	0.243
2022	DET	22	AA	171	26	10	5	5	5	4	8.77%	13.45%	0.307	0.374	0.540	0.233

Background: A relatively large international free agent in 2016, at least in terms of how the organization typically approached the market. Detroit signed the switch-hitting infielder to a deal worth $550,000 in 2016. For the first two seasons Perez looked like a solid prospect. He hit a respectable .314/.387/.358 in 61 games in the Dominican Summer League in 2017. And he followed that up with a surprising .312/.363/.429 slash line with 12 doubles, three triples, and three homeruns as he hopped, skipped, and jumped his way from the Gulf Coast League to the New York-Penn League and then the Midwest League. Then things took a downward turn. Perez struggled in his full-season return to A-ball in 2019, hitting a lowly .233/.299/.314 in 124 games. After the lost 2020 season of COVID, Perez – perhaps, surprisingly – found himself back in Low-A for a third time to open the 2021 campaign – where he eventually regained his lost stroke (.294/.383/.402). The front office bumped him up to High-A where he looked...underwhelming. Needless to say, Perez's prospect luster lacked any type of shine at that point. Detroit kept the switch-hitting second baseman back with West Michigan for the first half of 2022. And his offensive production exploded as he slugged .286/.364/.529. He continued to mash in Double-A as well, batting .307/.374/.540 in 39 games with Erie. In total, the still-only-22-year-old prospect mashed .295/.369/.534 with 23 doubles, two triples, 14 homeruns, and 18 stolen bases. His overall production, per *Weighted Runs Created Plus*, topped the league average mark by a stellar 43%.

Scouting Report: Consider the following:

> Since 2006, only eight 22-year-old hitters met the following criteria in High-A in a season (min. 225 PA): 140 to 150 wRC+, 14% to 18% strikeout rate, 10 to 13% walk rate. Those eight hitters: Kyle Seager, Brad Miller, Chase d'Arnaud, Ryan Lavarnway, James Darnell, Tim Kennelly, Tristan Peters, and Wenceel Perez.

Ignoring the past couple of terrible campaigns that Perez limped through, his 2022 production line – a well-rounded showing, by the way – would have him firmly among the second tier of second base prospects in the game. He hit for average and for power. He ran well and efficiently. And he played a solid second base. At the beginning of his career Perez looked like a bat / speed over power type of prospect but he developed legitimate 45, maybe even 50-grade thump over the past year or so. Really, really good bat speed and impressive torque in his torso through the swing. Perez looked like a minor league vagabond heading into the year – and one that wasn't long for a professional career – but he's put himself in place for at least a utility role. Maybe more.

Ceiling: 1.0-win player
Risk: Moderate
MLB ETA: 2023

14. Roberto Campos, OF

Hit	Power	SB	Patience	Glove	Overall
40/45	40/60	40/30	50	40/45	45

Born: 07/14/03	Age: 20	Bats: R	Top Production Comp: Franmil Reyes
Height: 6-2	Weight: 200	Throws: R	

Season	Team	Age	Level	PA	1B	2B	3B	HR	SB	CS	BB%	K%	AVG	OBP	SLG	ISO
2021	DET	18	CPX	155	18	5	0	8	3	0	10.97%	26.45%	0.228	0.316	0.441	0.213
2022	DET	19	A	448	68	26	5	5	7	3	8.93%	21.65%	0.258	0.326	0.385	0.127

Background: Former General Manager Al Avila reached deep down into the vast pocketbook of Illitch family and handed a practically unknown Cuban outfield prospect a then-franchise record $2.85 million in 2019. And then radio silence. Campos wouldn't make his professional debut, thanks in large part to the COVID pandemic, for a couple yars. The well-built outfielder, of course, belted a massive 400-foot homerun in his first professional at bat in the Florida Complex League in 2021. The La Habana, Cuba, native spent the remainder of the year hitting a disappointing .228/.316/.441 with five doubles and eight homeruns in 39 games. Last season, despite the poor showing, the front office sent their big international free agent expenditure up to the Florida State League. And the numbers were...improved. In 112 games with the Flying Tigers, the 6-foot-2, 200-pound outfielder batted .258/.326/.385 with 26 doubles, five triples, five homeruns, and seven stolen bases (in 10 attempts). His overall production, per *Weighted Runs Created Plus*, was 3% better than the league average showing.

Detroit Tigers

Snippet from The 2022 Prospect Digest Handbook: Fast bat and does not get cheated; there's always going to be a swing-and-miss element to Campos' game. There's some potential as a lower end, power-oriented outfielder, but he's quite raw. I'm not overly optimistic that he remains in center field, either.

Scouting Report: There's nothing statistically notable about Campos' production in 2022 beyond his youth. Campos is a big, strong kid that's already physically maxed out, but there's 70-grade raw power in his well-built frame. And he's only showing 40-grade pop in games at this point. There was an early-April spring game where Campos was jammed and still had enough strength to belt it over the rightfield fence. He's very, very raw and still quite a project. But there's some Franmil Reyes-type potential here.

Ceiling: 1.5-win player
Risk: Moderate
MLB ETA: 2025

15. Manuel Sequera, SS

Hit	Power	SB	Patience	Glove	Overall
35/45	50/55	30	40/45	45/50	45

Born: 09/28/02	Age: 20	Bats: R	Top Production Comp:
Height: 6-1	Weight: 170	Throws: R	

Season	Team	Age	Level	PA	1B	2B	3B	HR	SB	CS	BB%	K%	AVG	OBP	SLG	ISO
2021	DET	18	CPX	194	19	12	0	11	1	1	7.73%	29.38%	0.246	0.314	0.509	0.263
2022	DET	19	A	491	58	28	1	19	4	5	4.07%	22.40%	0.232	0.279	0.422	0.190

Background: Signed by the club out of Barquisimeto, Venezuela, for a sizeable $750,000 bonus a couple years ago. The player development engine sent the wiry teenager to the Complex League to begin his professional career two years ago. Sequera responded by posting a power-driven .246/.314/.509 slash line in 46 contests. The club bounced him up to Lakeland for the 2022 campaign. And the results were similar. In 116 games with the Flying Tigers, the 6-foot-1, 170-pound shortstop slugged .232/.279/.422 with an impressive number of extra-base knocks – 28 doubles, one triple, and 19 homeruns. Per *Weighted Runs Created Plus*, his overall production was 3% below the league average mark. Not bad work for an 18-year-old.

Scouting Report: Consider the following:

> Since 2006, only four 19-year-old hitters posted a wRC+ between 92 and 102 with a sub-6% walk rate and a strikeout rate between 20% and 24% in Low-A in a season (min. 400 PA): Adrian Marin, Randy Ventura, Hector Gomez, and – of course – Manuel Sequera.

Sequera showed some concerning swing-and-miss issues during his debut in the Complex League two years ago, posting a whiff rate just under 30%, but – surprisingly – he was able to chew that down significantly as he moved into full season ball, despite his free swinging tendencies. There's no mistaking what Sequera intends to do in each at bat – go yard. Loads of loft in his swing, quick bat. And, perhaps, the largest silver lining to his league average season? Major improvement in the second half of the year. Sequera began the campaign by hitting an icy .214/.252/.389 over his first 63 games, but he mashed .254/.311/.463 over his remaining 53 contests. The hit tool is going to be the career-defining trait. If it's somewhere between a 45- and 50-grade, he'll be a starter at the big league level. Otherwise, he could contend with Mike Hessman's minor league homerun record. Defensively, an eventual move to third base is almost guaranteed.

Ceiling: 1.5-win player
Risk: Moderate to High
MLB ETA: 2025

16. Joey Wentz, LHP

FB	CB	CU	CH	Command	Overall
55	55	45	55	45	40

Born: 10/06/97	Age: 25	Bats: L	Top Production Comp: Logan Allen
Height: 6-5	Weight: 220	Throws: L	

Season	Team	Age	Level	IP	TBF	K/9	K%	BB/9	BB%	K-BB%	ERA	FIP	xFIP	Pit/Bat
2018	ATL	20	A+	67.0	266	7.12	19.92%	3.22	9.02%	10.90%	2.28	3.64	3.91	4.07
2019	DET	21	AA	25.2	98	12.97	37.76%	1.40	4.08%	33.67%	2.10	2.27	1.86	4.57
2019	ATL	21	AA	103.0	436	8.74	22.94%	3.93	10.32%	12.61%	4.72	4.40	4.08	3.97
2021	DET	23	A	18.2	84	11.57	28.57%	3.86	9.52%	19.05%	6.75	6.00	4.14	4.10
2021	DET	23	AA	53.1	233	9.79	24.89%	5.57	14.16%	10.73%	3.71	4.96	5.17	4.27
2022	DET	24	AAA	48.1	196	9.87	27.04%	3.72	10.20%	16.84%	3.17	4.23	4.09	4.22

Background: Part of the Braves' vaunted trio of high school hurlers that were selected within the top 44 picks of the 2016 draft – though Wentz was the last one to crack a big league pitching staff. And that happened outside of Atlanta. Detroit acquired the left-hander at the deadline four years ago as part of the return for veteran Shane Greene. Wentz, now a full-fledged minor league veteran of six seasons, had a yo-yo type of 2022 season

Detroit Tigers

with a bevy of highs – he made his Major League debut in mid-May – and lows (he missed two full months dealing with a wonky shoulder), and everything in between as he bounced between Triple-A and Detroit, as well as a brief rehab stint in the Midwest League. The big lefty tossed 53.1 minor league innings, recording a 57-to-22 strikeout-to-walk ratio. And he hurled another 32.2 innings with the Tigers, averaging a completely mediocre 7.4 strikeouts and just 3.6 walks per nine innings.

Snippet from The 2020 Prospect Digest Handbook: He still hasn't distinguished himself from a backend starting pitcher or an up-and-down arm. There's a lot of Logan Allen vibes going on here.

Scouting Report: The book on Wentz is pretty well written at this point. Solid four-pitch mix: 93- to 94-mph above-average fastball, a mid- to upper-70s curveball that he doesn't throw nearly as often as he should; a below-average cutter that ranges from the mid-80s to 90 mph; and a very good changeup. The problems for Wentz are also well known: He hasn't topped 100 innings since 2019, had Tommy John surgery, and – of course – the doozy, he lacks solid command. The former high round pick is now entering his age-25 season and he's staring down Logan Allen territory pretty squarely in the eyes.

Ceiling: 1.0-win player
Risk: Low to Moderate
MLB ETA: Debuted in 2022

17. Dillon Dingler, C

Hit	Power	SB	Patience	Glove	Overall
40	50	30	50	55	40

Born: 09/17/98	Age: 24	Bats: R	Top Production Comp: Eric Haase
Height: 6-3	Weight: 210	Throws: R	

Season	Team	Age	Level	PA	1B	2B	3B	HR	SB	CS	BB%	K%	AVG	OBP	SLG	ISO
2021	DET	22	A	12	3	1	0	0	0	0	0.00%	25.00%	0.333	0.333	0.417	0.083
2021	DET	22	A+	141	20	6	1	8	0	0	9.22%	25.53%	0.287	0.376	0.549	0.262
2021	DET	22	AA	208	28	3	3	4	1	0	4.33%	29.81%	0.202	0.264	0.314	0.112
2022	DET	23	AA	448	53	22	3	14	1	0	10.04%	31.92%	0.238	0.333	0.419	0.181

Background: The Ohio State Buckeyes are well known for their propensity to churn out high end caliber football talent year after year. And, likewise, the Big 10 University – as well my alma mater – isn't exactly known as a premium baseball hotbed. The Buckeyes, believe it or not, have produced just seven players taken in the opening two rounds of the draft in their history. And Dingler, the 38th overall player taken three years ago, was the school's highest drafted player in a decade and just the fourth Buckeye taken in the top two rounds since the late 1980s. A sturdy, well-built, defensive-minded backstop, Dingler opened some eyes during his first year in pro ball in 2021. The Massillon, Ohio native ripped through the High-A pitching for a couple weeks and was promoted up to Double-A, the most important test for a prospect, by mid-June. But he struggled to hit his weight over the remainder of the season, which was sandwiched around a three-week stint on the DL. Unsurprisingly, the former second round pick found himself back in Class AA for do over. The results, though, were only modestly improved. Appearing in 107 games with the SeaWolves, the 6-foot-3, 210-pound backstop batted .238/.333/.419 with 22 doubles, three triples, 14 homeruns, and – just for good measure – a single, solitary stolen base. Per *Weighted Runs Created Plus*, Dingler's overall production was 7% better than the league average mark.

Snippet from The 2020 Prospect Digest Handbook: Dingler basically went from college ball to the minors' toughest challenge, Double-A, with only a few weeks of game play in between. There's 20-homer potential with above-average defense. The hit tool will be hard pressed to post .250+ batting averages. But there's certainly everyday production here.

Scouting Report: When it comes to offensive approach, Detroit almost has a predisposed requisite for their catchers. 40-grade bat, above-average power, average-ish patience, swing-and-miss issues. Eric Haase fits this to a tee. Jake Rogers, once the top catching prospect in their system, is cut from a similar mold. And now, too, does Dillon Dingler. During his first foray into Double-A two years ago, his borderline K-rates blossomed into full blown red flag territory, and that continued in his return to the level in 2022. He's now entering his age-24 season, sporting a .226/.312/.384 slash line in 157 Double-A games in his career. But the dearth of talent at the position in the big leagues almost guarantees him at least a backup role without further improvement.

Ceiling: 1.0-win player
Risk: Low to Moderate
MLB ETA: 2023

Detroit Tigers

18. Dylan Smith, RHP

FB	CB	SL	CH	Command	Overall
50	55	55	50	50+	40

Born: 05/28/00	Age: 23	Bats: R	Top Production Comp: N/A
Height: 6-2	Weight: 180	Throws: R	

Season	Team	Age	Level	IP	TBF	K/9	K%	BB/9	BB%	K-BB%	ERA	FIP	xFIP	Pit/Bat
2022	DET	22	A+	83.1	349	9.29	24.64%	2.27	6.02%	18.62%	4.00	3.29	3.51	3.76

Background: A late-blooming college prospect. Smith limped through a disappointing first season at the University of Alabama, posting a bloated 6.48 ERA across 13 relief appearances. His sophomore season started out in similar fashion – he tallied a 5.68 ERA in three relief outings and a start – before COVID prematurely ended the year. But things clicked for the 6-foot-2, 180-pound right-hander during the 2021 season. A full time starting pitcher for the first time, Smith made 16 starts, throwing 98.1 innings with 113 strikeouts against just 20 free passes. Detroit snagged the late-rising prospect in the third round, 74th overall, and signed him to a hefty $1.1 million deal. The former Crimson Tide ace made his professional debut last season, spending the entire year with West Michigan – sans a two game rehab stint with Lakeland as he was coming back from "arm fatigue." Smith tossed 88.1 innings, recording 89 punch outs against just 21 free passes to go along with a 3.77 ERA.

Snippet from The 2020 Prospect Digest Handbook: There's not a lot of room for error for Smith, so there's some reliever risk with backend upside.

Scouting Report: Consider the following:

> Since 2006, there have been twelve 22-year-old hurlers to post a 23.5% to 25.5% strikeout percentage with a 5% to 7% walk percentage in a season in High-A (min. 75 IP): Adbert Alzolay, Drew Smyly, Eli Morgan, Matt Barnes, Josh Sborz, Brendan White, Daniel Meadows, Glenn Sparkman, Jhonny Nunez, Tyson Miller, and Dylan Smith.

There's really nothing spectacular about Smith's arsenal. It's not bad, per se, but it simply lacks a noteworthy component. His fastball, an average offering, sits in the 92- to 93-mph range and may touch a tick or two higher a few times a game. His above-average slider is his best offering. He'll mix in an above-average curveball with some downward bite. And his changeup shows a bit of fade. He's caught in a no man's land of sorts – his command isn't great but it's more than your average strike-thrower. He looks like organizational depth at this point.

Ceiling: 1.0-win player
Risk: Moderate
MLB ETA: 2024

19. Abel Bastidas, IF

Hit	Power	SB	Patience	Glove	Overall
35/50	35/45	50	50	50/55	40

Born: 11/24/03	Age: 19	Bats: B	Top Production Comp: N/A
Height: 6-2	Weight: 165	Throws: R	

Season	Team	Age	Level	PA	1B	2B	3B	HR	SB	CS	BB%	K%	AVG	OBP	SLG	ISO
2021	DET	17	DSL	219	25	4	3	2	12	5	15.98%	21.00%	0.188	0.324	0.276	0.088
2022	DET	18	CPX	180	25	10	2	3	4	6	13.33%	18.33%	0.260	0.361	0.409	0.149

Background: Mid-January 2021, the front office decided to bet heavily on a pair of 17-year-old infielders, Cristian Santana and Abel Bastidas, handing the young duo more than $4 million in bonuses. Bastidas, a wiry switch-hitting infielder, looked completely abysmal during his debut in the foreign rookie league that summer, hitting a paltry .188/.324/.276 with just four doubles, three triples, and two homeruns in 54 games. His overall production in the notoriously hitter friendly league was 18% below the league average, per *Weighted Runs Created Plus*. Despite the struggles the Tigers sent the then-18-year-old hitter to the Complex League last summer. And the results – perhaps surprisingly – were significantly improved. In 44 games, the defensive vagabond batted .260/.361/.409 with 10 doubles, two triples, three homeruns, and four stolen bases (in six attempts). This time his overall production was 18% better than the league average threshold.

Scouting Report: Pure projection at this point. Bastidas flashes a lot of interesting offensive traits at this point in his career. His hit tool projects to be average as he matures. He flashes more pop at this point in his career than you'd expect. He'll run, though not overly efficiently. And the defensive metrics are just as favorable. He's very reminiscent of a young Matthew Lugo, a second round pick by the Red Sox in 2019. It wouldn't be shocking to see his ceiling creeping up towards league average status.

Ceiling: 1.0-win player
Risk: Moderate
MLB ETA: 2025

Detroit Tigers

20. Keider Montero, RHP

FB	CB	SL	CH	Command	Overall
50	55	50/55	45	50	40

Born: 07/06/00	Age: 22	Bats: R	Top Comp: N/A
Height: 6-1	Weight: 145	Throws: R	

Season	Team	Age	Level	IP	TBF	K/9	K%	BB/9	BB%	K-BB%	ERA	FIP	xFIP	Pit/Bat
2018	DET	17	R	46.1	204	7.77	19.61%	3.11	7.84%	11.76%	2.14	3.76	3.76	1.67
2019	DET	18	A-	24.2	91	9.49	28.57%	1.82	5.49%	23.08%	2.55	2.96	2.33	4.85
2019	DET	18	R	23.0	100	9.00	23.00%	4.30	11.00%	12.00%	1.57	2.94	3.42	1.85
2021	DET	20	A+	61.1	290	8.66	20.34%	2.79	6.55%	13.79%	5.28	4.44	4.67	3.61
2022	DET	21	A+	103.2	447	8.77	22.60%	3.21	8.28%	14.32%	4.51	4.43	4.19	3.87

Background: Montero was one of the more unheralded international free agent signings in 2017. And after spending two years in the Dominican Summer League to begin his career, Montero's quietly been fast-tracked ever since. He split his age-18 season between the Gulf Coast and New York-Penn Leagues in 2019. Bypassed Low-A entirely all together and popped up in High-A when minor league baseball returned to action in 2021. Last year, though, the front office sent the young Venezuelan back down to West Michigan for a bit more seasoning. In a career best 25 starts, Montero eclipsed the 100-inning threshold (a first, as well), while averaging 8.8 strikeouts and 3.2 walks per nine innings. He compiled a 4.51 ERA, a 4.43 FIP, and a 4.19 xFIP.

Scouting Report: Consider the following:

> Since 2006, there have been nine 21-year-old hurlers to post a 21% to 24% strikeout percentage with a 7.5% to 9.5% walk percentage in a season in High-A (min. 100 IP): Zack Britton, Kodi Medeiros, Brett Kennedy, Evan Anundsen, Luis Lugo, Ronald Bolanos, Tommy Romero, Jonathan Barrett, and – of course – Keider Montero.

Very similar arsenal – without the refinement – as Dylan Smith. Montero sports an average-ish 93 mph fastball – which he relies heavily on. He'll mix in a pair of breaking balls: a curveball with beautiful 12-6 shape and a power slider that generates some awkward swings. The slider flashes above-average at times and it's the type of offering that a pitching savvy organization would have him focus on, but Detroit hasn't proven to be that type of organization, at least not yet. He'll also mix in a below-average changeup.

Ceiling: 1.0-win player
Risk: Moderate
MLB ETA: 2024

Houston Astros

Top Prospects

Houston Astros

1. Hunter Brown, RHP

FB	CB	SL	CH	Command	Overall
60	65	60	N/A	45	60

Born: 08/29/98	Age: 24	Bats: R	Top Production Comp: Tyler Glasnow
Height: 6-2	Weight: 212	Throws: R	

Season	Team	Age	Level	IP	TBF	K/9	K%	BB/9	BB%	K-BB%	ERA	FIP	xFIP	Pit/Bat
2021	HOU	22	AA	49.1	217	13.86	35.02%	5.29	13.36%	21.66%	4.20	3.86	3.33	4.24
2021	HOU	22	AAA	51.0	216	9.71	25.46%	3.71	9.72%	15.74%	3.88	4.60	4.59	3.86
2022	HOU	23	AAA	106.0	426	11.38	31.46%	3.82	10.56%	20.89%	2.55	3.27	3.59	4.19

Background: As difficult as it may be for some to admit, but the Astros are nearing the tail end of their incredibly dominant, drama filled dynasty run – unless the front office somehow outmaneuvers the rest of baseball. *For years* the farm system was a lifeline to the big league club which continued to breathe life into their run of six-straight American League Championship appearances and two World Series crowns. But that pipeline of youth is going to slow to a drip in the coming years. The Houston Astros have gotten every ounce of talent that it could ring out of the system – though there are a few standouts that will likely make a lasting impact in the coming years. Like Hunter Brown. A fifth round pick out of Wayne State University, home to veteran reliever Anthony Bass, Brown rocketed through the Astros' farm system with very few speedbumps. The former Warriors ace made a brief 12-game, 23.2-inning debut with Tri-City in 2019. And once minor league baseball returned from its COVID-imposed break, Brown jumped straight into Double-A and closed out the year with 11 appearances in Triple-A. The 6-foot-2, 212-pound wickedly talented right-hander finished his first full season with 100.1 innings of work, striking out 131 and walking 50 to go along with an aggregate 4.04 ERA. Last season the hard-throwing hurler was able to hone in on the strike zone for the first extended period since high school during his time with Sugar Land. He averaged 11.4 strikeouts and 3.8 walks per nine innings to go along with a sparkling 2.55 ERA, a 3.27 FIP, and a 3.59 xFIP. Houston called up their top prospect in early September for the stretch run. And he was magnificent. He posted a 22-to-7 strikeout-to-walk ratio while surrendering only a pair of earned runs in 20.1 innings.

Snippet from The 2022 Prospect Digest Handbook: Brown not only owns the best arsenal in the Houston system, but he's among the most lethal hurlers in all of minor league baseball. There's obvious reliever risk given his propensity for handing out walks. Boom-bust. Reliever or Front half of a rotation caliber starting pitcher.

Scouting Report: Consider the following:

> Since 2006, only two 23-year-old hurlers posted a strikeout percentage of at least 30% with a walk percentage been 8% and 11% in a season in Triple-A (min. 75 IP): Tyler Glasnow and Hunter Brown.

Two pitches into each outing and it is crystal clear that Brown's arsenal belongs near the top – or atop – a contender's rotation. It's filthy. It's deep. Often times it almost looks unfair for those unfortunate souls that dig in against him. Plus fastball sitting in the mid-90s with late, explosive action – particularly up in the zone. A hard, late tilting low-90s slider with vertical movement. It's a second plus offering, a true swing-and-miss pitch. His curveball can be hellacious, a hammer like it was gifted from Thor. At its best, it's a *third* plus offering. But it's inconsistent and he'll struggle finishing it at times. He'll also mix in a rare – *very rare* – split finger fastball, utilizing it as a changeup (note: I've never seen it across multiple seasons, but *Baseball Savant* showed that he threw it just seven times during his debut with Houston). Brown's fastball command up-ticked last season. Now, though, it's all about finding a spot in the Astros' crowded rotation.

Ceiling: 4.0-win player
Risk: Moderate to High
MLB ETA: Debuted in 2022

2. Drew Gilbert, CF

Hit	Power	SB	Patience	Glove	Overall
55	50	55	55	55	55

Born: 09/27/00	Age: 22	Bats: L	Top Production Comp: N/A
Height: 5-9	Weight: 185	Throws: L	

Background: A legend coming out of Stillwater High School, the 5-foot-9, 185-pound center fielder / pitching ace did a little bit of everything for the Ponies – including leading them to the Minnesota state title as a junior. During that epic championship performance, the little left-hander dazzled Minnetonka for seven shutout innings, racking up 15 punch outs. Gilbert was practically unhittable during his senior campaign as well, surrendering one earned run in 49 innings to go along with 97 strikeouts. He also batted a scorching .370 with 16 RBIs and eight stolen bases. After a little flirtation from the Red Sox in the late rounds, the Minnesota-born prospect packed his bags and headed to the land of the Volunteers – where he would become a key cog in one of the best collegiate teams in history. As a two-way player his first two seasons, Gilbert's performance was filled with highs and lows: he battled control / command issues as a part-time reliever and hit a mediocre .274/.341/.437 as a center fielder during his sophomore season. Last season, though, the pint-sized dynamo focused solely on hitting. And he put together a record performance. In 58 games for the SEC Conference powerhouse, Gilbert slugged .362/.455/.673 with career highs in doubles (21), triples (four), homeruns (11), and RBIs (70). He

Houston Astros

also swiped four bags (in six attempts). Houston snagged him in the opening round, 28th overall, and signed him to a deal worth $2,497,500. He appeared in just 10 games between the Complex League and Low-A, hitting .313/.405/.531 with three extra-base hits.

Scouting Report: Per the usual, my pre-draft write-up:

> "Consider the following:
>
>> Since 2011, only three SEC hitters have batted at least .360/.450/.650 in a season (min. 225 PA): Brent Rooker, Sonny DiChiara, and – of course – Drew Gilbert.
>
> So let's expand that a bit. Consider the following:
>
>> Since 2011, only two Division hitters batted at least .360/.450/.650 with a strikeout and walk rate between 12% and 14% in a season (min. 225 PA): Hunter Dozier and – of course – Drew Gilbert.
>
> Likely the strongest arm among any non-pitching prospect coming out of the collegiate class, Gilbert's fastball in high school reached upwards of 97 mph. Cut from a similar cloth as consensus Top 20 big league prospect Corbin Carroll, Gilbert packs a wallop in a deceivingly strong frame. He's pure muscle and athleticism. Above-average hit tool, lightning quick bat, and does not get cheated. Above-average hit tool, good patience, 50-grade power with maybe a little more in the tank, and above-average speed. Gilbert could be the complete package. Gritty. Gamer."

Ceiling: 3.0-win player
Risk: Moderate
MLB ETA: 2024

3. Yainer Diaz, C/1B

Hit	Power	SB	Patience	Glove	Overall
55	50	30	45	50	50

Born: 09/21/98	Age: 23	Bats: R	Top Production Comp: N/A
Height: 6-0	Weight: 195	Throws: R	

Season	Team	Age	Level	PA	1B	2B	3B	HR	SB	CS	BB%	K%	AVG	OBP	SLG	ISO
2021	CLE	22	A	258	50	19	1	5	1	1	5.81%	16.28%	0.314	0.357	0.464	0.151
2021	HOU	22	A	49	8	2	0	1	1	0	0.00%	8.16%	0.229	0.224	0.333	0.104
2021	HOU	22	A+	105	23	4	0	11	2	0	7.62%	16.19%	0.396	0.438	0.781	0.385
2022	HOU	23	AA	267	52	13	3	9	1	0	7.87%	14.98%	0.316	0.367	0.504	0.189
2022	HOU	23	AAA	219	33	9	1	16	1	0	5.94%	17.81%	0.294	0.342	0.587	0.294

Background: The Cleveland Guardians own a nearly spotless track record when it comes to trading. Sure, the occasional stinker of a deal slips through the organization's fingers, but – by and large – their unheralded front office is incredibly astute when it comes to evaluating their own talent. Yainer Diaz may prove to be one of the deals that haunt the franchise. Acquired along with the "Spin Doctor" Phil Maton for offensive deficient defensive wizard Myles Straw near the trade deadline two years ago, Diaz rocketed up prospect charts with his phenomenal showing between both organizations that season. He batted an aggregate .324/.362/.527 as he spent time between Low-A and High-A. And last season the young Dominican backstop was *even better*. Splitting time between Corpus Christi and Sugar Land, the 6-foot, 195-pound catcher / part-time first baseman mashed .306/.356/.542 with 22 doubles, four triples, 25 homeruns, and a pair of stolen bases. Per *Weighted Runs Created Plus*, Diaz's overall production topped the league average threshold by an impressive 21%.

Snippet from The 2022 Prospect Digest Handbook: He doesn't walk all that often, but he doesn't strikeout all that often either. Solid average power. He shows a knack for squaring the ball up. And he controls the opposition's running game relatively well too. The problem, of course, is his lack of experience against meaningful competition.

Scouting Report: Diaz answered the most important question facing him last season – how will he handle more advanced pitching. The answer: with aplomb. Consider the following:

> Since 2006, only five 23-year-old hitters met the following criteria in Double-A (min. 250 PA): 115 to 125 wRC+, 14% to 16% strikeout rate and a 7% to 9% walk rate. Those five hitters: A.J. Pollock, Jake Goebbert, Miguel Negron, Jared James, and – of course – former Guardians farmhand Yainer Diaz.

Houston continued the trend of bouncing Diaz between catcher and first base last season in an effort to keep his potentially potent bat in the lineup. High contact approach, despite his blossoming power. He's not going to ever be mistaken for Mike Hargrove or Kevin Youkilis at the plate. But there's a solid chance he develops into a .280/.335/.430-type hitter.

Houston Astros

Ceiling: 2.5-win player
Risk: Moderate
MLB ETA: Debuted in 2022

4. Jaime Melendez, RHP

FB	CB	CH	Command	Overall
55	60	55	30/40	

Born: 09/26/01	Age: 21	Bats: L	Top Production Comp: Cristian Javier
Height: 5-8	Weight: 190	Throws: R	

Season	Team	Age	Level	IP	TBF	K/9	K%	BB/9	BB%	K-BB%	ERA	FIP	xFIP	Pit/Bat
2021	HOU	19	A	18.1	68	18.65	55.88%	2.45	7.35%	48.53%	0.49	1.36	1.31	4.62
2021	HOU	19	A+	32.0	155	11.53	26.45%	6.75	15.48%	10.97%	4.78	4.45	5.48	3.64
2022	HOU	20	AA	73.2	326	12.95	32.52%	6.23	15.64%	16.87%	5.01	4.40	4.25	4.34

Background: Much of the talk surrounding electric sub-21-year-old arms in Double-A last season was centered on Miami's burgeoning ace Eury Perez, 19, and San Francisco's Kyle Harrison, 20. And deservedly so. But lost in the discussion was Houston's talented – yet diminutive – right-hander Jaime Melendez. Signed out of Puebla, Mexico for a $195,000 in 2019, the 5-foot-8, 190-pound youngster rocketed through three levels during his first full season in pro ball two years later. Melendez shredded the Low-A East competition for six appearances, continued to miss a promising number of bats during his 11-game cameo with Asheville, and settled in nicely for three brief outings with Corpus Christi. Last season the now-20-year-old righty spent the entirety of the year with Corpus Christi, throwing a career high 73.2 innings of work, averaging 12.95 strikeouts and a whopping 6.2 walks per nine innings. He finished the year with a 5.01 ERA, 4.40 FIP, and a 4.25 xFIP.

Scouting Report: Consider the following:

> Since 2006, there have been 35 hurlers that tossed at least 70 innings in Double-A during their age-20 season. Melendez's strikeout rate, 12.95 K/9, and his strikeout percentage, 32.52%, rank as the second best total.

Now the bad news...

> His walk rate, 6.23 BB/9, and walk percentage, 15.64%, are the worst among the aforementioned group.

Firing from a high, over the top release, Melendez's low 90s fastball is particularly effective in the upper half the zone, where he typically lives. His 12-6 curveball is especially effective with his high-spin heater. The young right-hander also owns an above-average changeup as well. There are a lot of parallels with Cristian Javier – though Melendez's command is a full grade worse than the young Astros starter.

Ceiling: 3.0-win player
Risk: High
MLB ETA: 2023

5. Joe Perez, 3B

Hit	Power	SB	Patience	Glove	Overall
50/55	50	35	50	45	50

Born: 08/12/99	Age: 23	Bats: R	Top Production Comp: N/A
Height: 6-2	Weight: 198	Throws: R	

Season	Team	Age	Level	PA	1B	2B	3B	HR	SB	CS	BB%	K%	AVG	OBP	SLG	ISO
2021	HOU	21	A	59	9	4	0	2	0	2	15.25%	22.03%	0.300	0.407	0.500	0.200
2021	HOU	21	A+	109	16	11	0	8	1	1	9.17%	19.27%	0.354	0.413	0.707	0.354
2021	HOU	21	AA	307	48	19	0	8	2	1	7.82%	26.06%	0.267	0.322	0.420	0.153
2022	HOU	22	AA	284	46	16	0	6	3	0	9.15%	24.65%	0.265	0.335	0.397	0.132
2022	HOU	22	AAA	35	12	1	0	1	0	0	17.14%	17.14%	0.483	0.571	0.621	0.138

Background: A striking number of the Astros' 2017 draft class have already accrued big league time – 12 of the club's 42 picks have debuted in the bigs. But it's a class light on stardom *or* production. Chas McCormick and Josh Rojas, both hovering in the 3.5 WAR range, top the list. Beyond that there's Jake Meyer (1.7) and a bunch of disappointing stat lines. Perez, the club's second pick that year, has *technically* spent time in the big leagues, earning just one at bat. But his struggles to stay on the field, yet again, have continued to chew into valuable development time. The 53rd overall pick six years ago, Perez, who signed for a hefty $1.6 million, underwent Tommy John right around draft time. And he would make his abbreviated debut in the Gulf Coast League the following year, appearing in just four games in the stateside rookie league. The former two-way prep star was abysmal the following season, 2019, hitting an atrocious .188/.246/.365 in 50 games with Tri-City. But things seemed to click for the former Bonus Baby the in 2021 as he slugged .291/.354/.495 in 106 games between Fayetteville, Asheville, and Corpus Christi. Last season, though, Perez's production took a noticeable step back – particularly in the power department. Hampered by an oblique injury, the Archbishop McCarthy High School product hit .265/.335/.397 in 64 games in his return to Corpus Christi. But he was scorching hot during his eight game cameo in Triple-A, going 14-for-29 with a double and a dinger.

Houston Astros

Snippet from The 2022 Prospect Digest Handbook: I'm a believer in the bat. In terms of ceiling, think along the lines: .270/.340/.470.

Scouting Report: I've been one of Perez's biggest supporters throughout the years, through the good *and* bad production lines. So let's continue to take a deep dive into his production. His bat was frigid during the month of April, hitting just .196/.281/.275 over his first 13 games. Then he hit the disabled list for nearly two full months. Once he returned, Perez batted .282/.348/.427 over his remaining 51 games in Double-A and .306/.378/.451 throughout the rest of the year. There's average power, average patience, and the hit tool has a chance to be above-average. I still think there's a chance to be a .270/.340/.430-type hitter (the power may not uptick as I once expected). Perez is a good buy low option, both in terms of future big league employment as well as those that speculate on baseball cards.

Ceiling: 2.0-win player
Risk: Moderate
MLB ETA: Debuted in 2022

6. Korey Lee, C

Hit	Power	SB	Patience	Glove	Overall
45	45	35	50	60	50

Born: 07/25/98	Age: 24	Bats: R	Top Production Comp: James McCann
Height: 6-2	Weight: 210	Throws: R	

Season	Team	Age	Level	PA	1B	2B	3B	HR	SB	CS	BB%	K%	AVG	OBP	SLG	ISO
2021	HOU	22	A+	121	28	5	0	3	1	0	9.92%	19.83%	0.330	0.397	0.459	0.128
2021	HOU	22	AA	203	29	9	1	8	3	1	8.37%	17.24%	0.254	0.320	0.443	0.189
2021	HOU	22	AAA	38	4	4	0	0	0	0	5.26%	23.68%	0.229	0.263	0.343	0.114
2022	HOU	23	AAA	446	49	20	2	25	12	1	8.07%	28.48%	0.238	0.307	0.483	0.245

Background: The franchise's track record of selecting backstops in the first round is spotty at best. Just two of their 10 selections have turned into meaningful big leaguers (Craig Biggio and Jason Castro) while the others have generally been a disappointment. But the jury's still out on their latest first round catching expenditure. Taken with the 32nd overall pick out of the University of California, Berkley four years ago, Lee left the Golden Bears after a tremendous junior campaign when he slugged a robust .337/.416/.619 with 12 doubles and 15 homeruns. And after signing with the organization quickly, Lee squeezed in a full season of work with Tri-City during his debut, hitting .268/.359/.371 in 64 games of work. Once minor league baseball returned from their COVID-induced layoff, the 6-foot-2, 210-pound catcher got off to a roaring start in High-A, moved quickly through Double-A, and settled in at Triple-A for the final week-plus of the year. He finished the season with an aggregate .277/.340/.438 slash line. And it seemed that Lee was positioning himself for a prime spot on the club's big league roster entering 2022. But his bat was as cold as an Ohio April to begin the year and dragged down his overall production. He hit .238/.307/.483 with 20 doubles, two triples, 25 homeruns, and 12 stolen bases in 104 games with Sugar Land. He spent the month of July in the Astros' lineup, hitting .160/.192/.240 in limited action.

Snippet from The 2022 Prospect Digest Handbook: The bar for catcher production is fairly low at the big league level, so Lee's still tracking as a potential starting option within the next year or two.

Scouting Report: Consider the following:

> Since 2006, just three hitters met the following criteria in Triple-A (min. 350 PA): 85 to 95 wRC+ with a strikeout rate between 26% and 30%. Those three hitters: Anthony Alford, a consensus Top 100 prospect several times early in his career; Willy Garcia, and – of course – Korey Lee.

Lee was particularly chilly during the first two months of the minor league season as he batted .203/.256/.387 over his first 40 games. But he caught fire in June (.271/.340/.482) and batted a rock solid .256/.335/.546 over the remainder of his minor league season. The former Golden Bear started selling out for more power in 2022, leading to a precipitous rise in his K-rate. Lee's tracking like a defensive specialist with low batting average, average power, and near Gold Glove defense. In terms of big league production, think .240/.300/.430.

Ceiling: 2.0-win player
Risk: Moderate
MLB ETA: Debuted in 2022

Houston Astros

7. Ryan Clifford, 1B/LF/RF

Hit	Power	SB	Patience	Glove	Overall
40/50	40/60	35/30	60	50	50

Born: 07/20/03	**Age:** 19	**Bats:** L	**Top Production Comp:** N/A
Height: 6-3	**Weight:** 200	**Throws:** L	

Season	Team	Age	Level	PA	1B	2B	3B	HR	SB	CS	BB%	K%	AVG	OBP	SLG	ISO
2022	HOU	18	CPX	50	4	3	0	1	2	0	24.00%	32.00%	0.222	0.440	0.389	0.167
2022	HOU	18	A	51	8	2	0	1	0	0	19.61%	29.41%	0.268	0.412	0.390	0.122

Background: It's not very often that an 11th round draft pick, fresh from high school will crack a club's Top 20 prospect list – let alone the defending World Champs. But Clifford isn't exactly the prototypical 11th round pick either. A member of Team USA squads since his preteen days, Clifford was a dominant standout during his time with Crossroads FLEX High School. The first baseman / corner outfielder mashed his way into a commitment with collegiate – and SEC – powerhouse Vanderbilt University. But the Astros were able to sway the hulking slugger away from the prime time lights of the SEC for pro ball with a hefty $1,256,530 deal. The North Carolina native began his career slowly, hitting .222/.440/.389 during his brief stint in the Complex Leagues, before finding his footing with Fayetteville. Clifford would finish the year with an aggregate .247/.426/.390 slash line with five doubles, two homeruns, and pair of stolen bases. Per *Weighted Runs Created Plus*, his overall production topped the league average mark by an impressive 39%.

Scouting Report: Big, hulking middle-of-the-lineup thumper, Clifford, simply, does not get cheated. The swing is a bit long. And there's a solid chance he turns into a dead pull hitter. But it's easy to see why he commanded such a large bonus. He could develop into a 50-grade bat, 60-grade power, and be an OBP monster. He's raw, though, and he's going to need time to figure it out.

Ceiling: 2.5-win player
Risk: High
MLB ETA: 2025

8. Jacob Melton, CF

Hit	Power	SB	Patience	Glove	Overall
50	55	55	50	50	50

Born: 09/07/00	**Age:** 22	**Bats:** L	**Top Production Comp:** N/A
Height: 6-3	**Weight:** 208	**Throws:** L	

Season	Team	Age	Level	PA	1B	2B	3B	HR	SB	CS	BB%	K%	AVG	OBP	SLG	ISO
2022	HOU	21	CPX	17	0	0	0	0	1	0	0.00%	35.29%	0.000	0.000	0.000	0.000
2022	HOU	21	A	86	13	6	0	4	4	2	12.79%	23.26%	0.324	0.424	0.577	0.254

Background: Here's a little tidbit to consider: South Medford High School has had three former players graduate into professional baseball – Jeff Barry, Steve Bechler, and Andy Larkin. The interesting part: all three have spent some time in the big leagues. Enter: Jacob Melton, a member of the Class of 2018 from the Oregon-based school. Melton shredded the competition during his senior year with the Panthers, batting a scorching .513 with eight dingers and a whopping 33 stolen bases. The dynamic center fielder spent his first season in college with JuCo Linn-Benton – which provided little in terms of competition. In 42 games with the Roadrunners, Melton slugged .365/.436/.617 with 14 doubles, seven triples, and three homeruns. The native Oregonian would transfer to Pac-12 powerhouse Oregon State – though he barely saw the field in the COVID-shortened 2020 season. Handed the starting gig after the 2021 season began, Melton slashed a scorching .404/.466/.697 with five doubles, three triples, six homeruns, and eight stolen bases before season-ending shoulder surgery knocked him out in April. Finally healthy, he made the best of his first full season of Division I action in 2022. Playing in a career best 63 games, the 6-foot-3, 208-pound tools-laden center fielder slugged .360/.424/.671 with 22 doubles, four triples, and 17 homeruns. He also swiped 21 bags in 22 total attempts. For his career at OSU, Melton stolen 29 bases and was caught just twice. Houston selected him in the second round, 64th overall, and signed him a deal worth $1 million. Melton appeared in 23 games between the Complex League and Fayetteville, hitting an aggregate .261/.353/.466 with 10 extra-base hits and five stolen bases (in seven total attempts).

Scouting Report: Per the usual, my pre-draft write-up:

> "Consider the following:
>
> Since 2011, only three Pac-12 hitters batted at least .350/.415/.660 in a season (min. 275 PA): Spencer Torkelson, Jacob Berry, and – of course – Jacob Melton. Melton, by the way, owns the lowest walk rate among the trio, at 8.8%. Torkelson's was 14.2% and Berry tallied an 11.1%.
>
> Melton did everything well during his brief time on the field for Oregon State: he hit for average and power, ran well and efficiently, and played an up-the-middle position well. The lone knock on the dynamic OSU Beaver: he's

Houston Astros

completed four years of college, but he's just 21-years-old thanks to a later birthday. Dead pull-hitter with phenomenal bat speed. Surprisingly patient, particularly on low offspeed pitches, given his average-ish walk rate. Sees a lot of pitches. Melton needs to improve his ability to use the entire field. Low end starting material who likely demolishes the low levels of the minor leagues."

Ceiling: 1.5- to 2.0-win player
Risk: Moderate
MLB ETA: 2024

9. Justin Dirden, OF

Hit	Power	SB	Patience	Glove	Overall
50	55	40	50	55	50

Born: 07/16/97	Age: 25	Bats: L	Top Production Comp: Corey Dickerson
Height: 6-3	Weight: 209	Throws: R	

Season	Team	Age	Level	PA	1B	2B	3B	HR	SB	CS	BB%	K%	AVG	OBP	SLG	ISO
2021	HOU	23	A	249	25	15	3	11	8	1	16.06%	29.72%	0.267	0.402	0.535	0.267
2021	HOU	23	A+	101	14	3	3	4	2	3	11.88%	25.74%	0.289	0.386	0.542	0.253
2022	HOU	24	AA	407	56	32	5	20	7	2	10.07%	23.10%	0.324	0.411	0.616	0.292
2022	HOU	24	AAA	142	19	8	0	4	5	1	7.04%	28.17%	0.242	0.305	0.398	0.156

Background: The 2020 draft class provided an abundance of opportunity for savvy organizations, allowing clubs to sign an *unlimited* amount of undrafted prospects for the rather paltry sum of $20,000. The five-round limited draft greatly affected fifth year seniors – like Justin Dirden. A product of SE Missouri State courtesy of Jefferson Junior College, which in turn was courtesy of East Carolina. Dirden, a Missouri native, was an absolute force to be reckoned with during his first season with the Redhawks, mashing a Ruthian .340/.437/.665 with 19 doubles, one triple, 16 homeruns, and nine stolen bases in only 57 games. And his 2020 season started off even better. He slugged an otherworldly .414/.471/.900 with three doubles, two triples, and nine homeruns in only 17 games. He continued to produce at well above-average levels since joining Houston's system as well, hitting .274/.397/.537 in 82 games between Fayettevlile and Asheville two years ago. And last season was much the same. In 124 games between Corpus Christi and Sugar Land, the 6-foot-3, 209-pound outfielder mashed .302/.384/.558 with 40 doubles, five triples, 24 homeruns, and 12 stolen bases. Per *Weighted Runs Created Plus*, his overall production topped the league average mark by an impressive 35%. Not bad for an undrafted, fifth year senior.

Scouting Report: Consider the following:

> Since 2006, only six 24-year-old hitters posted a wRC+ north of 150 with a strikeout rate between 21% and 25% in Double-A (min. 350 PA): Russ Canzler, Ryan Goleski, Fernando Perez, Corey Brown, Taylor Jones, and Justin Dirden.

Evan Gattis is kind of the unofficial poster boy for older, surging power bats. And while there are several similarities between the duo, Dirden's strikeout rate is leaps and bounds worse than Gattis' during his minor league stint. Miscast as a centerfield, though he'll provide positive value at either corner outfield spot, Dirden is fairly toolsy, showing solid speed, a 50-grade bat, above-average power, and decent patience at the plate. On a rebuilding team, Dirden would likely be handed a spot in the lower third of a lineup to see what he can do. On the Astros, well, that's not likely to happen. There's some lower end starting potential here. Ceiling: .250/.310/.450.

Ceiling: 1.5- to 2.0-win player
Risk: Moderate
MLB ETA: 2023

10. Miguel Ullola, RHP

FB	CB	SL	CH	Command	Overall
65	55/60	60	N/A	30/40	60

Born: 06/19/02	Age: 21	Bats: R	Top Production Comp: Cristian Javier
Height: 6-1	Weight: 184	Throws: R	

Background: Tell me if you've heard this story before: Houston took a gamble on an older international prospect and said prospect is showing serious potential. Enter: Miguel Ullola. A native of Puerto Plata, Dominican Republic, the Astros signed the wiry right-hander to a deal worth $75,000 in mid-January two years ago. The 6-foot-1, 184-pound hurler made just 10 appearances between the club's Dominican Summer League and Florida Complex League affiliates a few months later, throwing just 24.1 innings with 38 punch outs and 21 free passes to go along with a 4.07 ERA. Last season Houston sent the hard-throwing youngster to Fayetteville. And Ullola showcased an impressive ability to miss bats as well as the strike zone. He averaged a staggering 15.0 strikeouts and a whopping 6.9 walks per nine innings. He finished the year with a – shocking – 3.25 ERA, 3.64 FIP, and a 3.92 xFIP.

Houston Astros

Scouting Report: Consider the following:

> Since 2006, only six 20-year-old hurlers have posted a strikeout percentage north of 33% in any Low-A league (min. 70 IP): Matt Moore, Seth Corry, Pedro Avila, Max Lazar, Juan Carela, and – of course – Miguel Ullola.

Now the fun starts...

> #1. Of those six hurlers, only one has posted a strikeout percentage of at least 34.5% - Miguel Ullola.
> #2. Here's the list of hurlers at any age, in any level, that posted a strikeout rate of at least 38% in any year since 2006: Grayson Rodriguez (AA), Cristian Javier (AA), MacKenzie Gore (A+), Tyler Glasnow (AAA), Ryan Murphy (A), Joe Boyle (A+), Dahian Santos (A), Anthony Slama (A+), Darwin De Leon (R), Will Klein (A+), and Miguel Ullola (A)
> #3. Ullola struck out an incredible 38.3% of the hitters he faced.

There's the potential for an *elite* arsenal with three plus offerings: a mid-90s, explosive, riding fastball; a hellacious curveball, and a wickedly darting slider. The problem, of course, is whether Ullola can find the strike zone with any type of consistency. He's still only entering his age-21 season and barely has a year-and-a-half of pro ball under his belt. He could have the highest ceiling of any arm in the system if everything clicks.

Ceiling: 3.5-win player
Risk: Extreme
MLB ETA: 2025

11. Forrest Whitley, RHP

FB	CB	SL	CU	CH	Control	Overall
60	60	60	N/A	60	30/40	50

Born: 09/15/97	Age: 25	Bats: R	Top Production Comp: N/A
Height: 6-7	Weight: 238	Throws: R	

Season	Team	Age	Level	IP	TBF	K/9	K%	BB/9	BB%	K-BB%	ERA	FIP	xFIP	Pit/Bat
2018	HOU	20	AA	26.1	108	11.62	31.48%	3.76	10.19%	21.30%	3.76	3.34	3.71	4.31
2019	HOU	21	AA	22.2	103	14.29	34.95%	7.54	18.45%	16.50%	5.56	4.33	3.93	4.51
2019	HOU	21	AAA	24.1	119	10.73	24.37%	5.55	12.61%	11.76%	12.21	8.07	5.57	4.14
2022	HOU	24	AAA	33.0	158	9.82	22.78%	6.82	15.82%	6.96%	7.09	4.92	6.09	3.99

Background: From meteoric rise to supernova flameout. It wasn't supposed to happen like this, at least in the beginning. But now, though, Whitley's projected big league stardom has dwindled down to a candle light flicker. So let's just count the ways injuries and a bad decision disrupted his once promising career. Taken with the 17th overall pick in 2016, the former Florida State University commit chewed through the Gulf Coast and Appalachian League competition and immediately established himself as one of the best young arms in baseball. And that just set the stage for his brilliant 2017 campaign. Whitley would looked unhittable during his 12-game cameo in Low-A, continued to dominate with Buies Creek for another seven games, and he posted an absurd 26-to-4 strikeout-to-walk ratio in only 14.2 innings in Double-A, the minors' toughest challenge. Then things started to unravel for the budding ace. Prior to the 2018 season, the 6-foot-7, 238-pound righty got popped for banned stimulant was subsequently suspended for 50 games – for which he took full responsibility, claiming it was an unknown substance given to him by a friend. Once he got back to the mound an oblique issue knocked him out of action for more than a month. And when it was all said and done, the club's prized pitching prospect was limited to just eight starts and just 26.1 innings. Still, though, Whitley looked poised to play a key role for Houston at some point in the 2019 season but a wonky shoulder issue – eventually termed "fatigue" – knocked him out of for two months midway through the year. He would toss just 59.2 innings. The 2020 season, of course, was a wash due to COVID. Then two years ago Tommy John surgery knocked him out for the entire campaign. Last season, after a few rehab appearances, Whitley finally made it back to Triple-A – though the results were a mixed bag. He would fan 36 and walk 25 in only 33.0 innings of work. He tallied a 7.09 ERA with Sugar Land.

Scouting Report: From a pure "stuff" standpoint, Whitley still possesses an elite, front-of-the-rotation caliber arsenal. His heater was hovering in the mid-90s with tremendous life as it was exploding past bats. His curveball is a genuine Uncle Charlie – a knee-buckling 12-6 bender. His slider and changeup add a third *and* a fourth plus pitch. The problem, of course, is two-fold: Can he stay healthy and can he regain is once promising feel for the strike zone? There's still a chance he develops into a viable big league starter, but at this point he just seems like he's going to deal with injuries every year.

Ceiling: 2.5-win player
Risk: Extremely High
MLB ETA: 2023

Houston Astros

12. Colin Barber, OF

Hit	Power	SB	Patience	Glove	Overall
40/50	45/50	40	55	50	45

Born: 12/04/00	**Age:** 22	**Bats:** L	**Top Production Comp:** Preston Tucker
Height: 6-0	**Weight:** 194	**Throws:** L	

Season	Team	Age	Level	PA	1B	2B	3B	HR	SB	CS	BB%	K%	AVG	OBP	SLG	ISO
2021	HOU	20	A+	53	5	1	0	3	1	1	16.98%	41.51%	0.214	0.365	0.452	0.238
2022	HOU	21	A+	260	47	10	1	7	7	4	11.54%	21.92%	0.298	0.408	0.450	0.151

Background: The club went well beyond the assigned slot value when they handed Barber, their fourth round pick in 2019, a seven-figure bonus – the largest deal for any player taken in the round that year. And the early returns looked like the club made a wise investment. The 6-foot, 194-pound outfielder batted .263/.387/.394 in 28 games in the Gulf Coast League. Once minor league baseball returned to action from its COVID-induced break, Barber was pushed directly up to High-A but an injured shoulder forced him under the knife after just 16 games. So it's not surprising the former Bonus Baby was sent back to Asheville for an extended look at High-A pitching. And, once again, injury forced the former fourth rounder to miss roughly a month of action. The Pleasant Valley High School product batted an impressive .298/.408/.450 in 63 games with the Tourists, belting out 10 doubles, one triple, and seven homeruns to go along with seven stolen bases (in 11 total attempts). His overall production, as measured by *Weighted Runs Created Plus*, topped the league average mark by an impressive 39%.

Snippet from The 2022 Prospect Digest Handbook: The swing is short, compact, and quick, but it doesn't lend itself to a ton of over-the-fence thump. He's likely going to return to High-A following his recovery from should surgery in 2022.

Scouting Report: Consider the following:

> Since 2006, three 21-year-old hitters met the following criteria in a season in High-A (min. 250 PA): 135 to 145 wRC+, 20% to 24% strikeout rate, and a 9% to 12% walk rate. Those three hitters: Anthony Santander, Kirk Nieuwenhuis, and – of course – Colin Barber. Santander, by the way, has been a league average bat during his big league career. And Nieuwenhuis spent parts of his six seasons in the bigs, sporting a 92 wRC+.

And now the bad news: Asheville's home field, McCormick Field, is a *notorious* bandbox and easily the best hitting environment in any of the High-A leagues. Barber *clearly* benefited from the favorable confines as well. He slugged .379/.459/.603 in 33 home games and he posted a .205/.343/.268 slash line in 33 away games. *Plus*, he continued to show very concerning platoon splits (.315/.388/.472 vs. RHP and .220/.435/.350 vs. LHP). He's consistently posted above-average production marks, though it's largely built upon his bloated walk rates. He's also dangerously close to be labeled injury prone as well.

Ceiling: 1.5-win player
Risk: Moderate
MLB ETA: 2024

13. Andrew Taylor, RHP

FB	CB	SL	CH	Command	Overall
55/60	N/A	50	50	50	45

Born: 09/23/01	**Age:** 21	**Bats:** R	**Top Production Comp:** N/A
Height: 6-5	**Weight:** 190	**Throws:** R	

Background: Believe it or not, the last time Central Michigan University had a player chosen before the third round was all the way back in 1986 when the Oakland Athletics called right-hander Kevin Tapani's name with the 40th overall pick. Tapani would go onto a long, successful – and underrated – 13-year career spent mostly with the Twins and Cubs, winning a total of 143 games and earning more than $34 million. Houston is hoping that fellow righty Andrew Taylor can amount to similar success. A four-year letter winner during his career at Caledonia High School, the big hurler made two starts and a trio of relief appearances during his COVID-abbreviated freshman season at Central Michigan University in 2020, throwing 16.2 innings while compiling a tidy 2.16 ERA with 10 strikeouts and a quartet of walks. Taylor spent the next season dominating atop the Chippewa's rotation – as a baby-faced 19-year-old. He would throw 94.1 innings of work, averaging 11.9 strikeouts and just 2.3 walks per nine innings to go along with a sparkling 1.81 ERA. He made another pair of brief starts with the Bourne Braves that summer in the Cape Cod League, posting an 11-to-3 strikeout-to-walk ratio in seven innings. Last season, the 6-foot-5, 190-pound prospect raised the bar even further as he posted a career best 13.5 K/9 in 84.0 innings. He walked just 27 and tallied a 3.43 ERA en route to winning eight games for the Mid-American Conference School. Houston selected him in the second round, 80th overall, and signed him to an $807,200 – the recommended slot bonus.

Houston Astros

Scouting Report: Consider the following:

> Since 2015, there have been 15 instances in which a Division I pitcher averaged at least 13.5 strikeouts per nine innings in a season (min. 75 IP). Of those 15, just six posted a walk rate between 2.5 and 3.0 BB/9: Will Bednar, Ethan Small, Noah Song, Nicholas Sinacola, Andrew Abbott, and Andrew Taylor.

Not only is Taylor young for a third-year college hurler, he has additional projection given his long, wiry 6-foot-5 frame. The former Chippewa ace works in the low 90s and generally commands his fastball well. He'll mix in a pair of breaking balls: a curveball and slider – though I only saw the low-80s slider. He'll also mix in a low-80s running changeup. Long arm action that likely gets cleaned up within a year of entering Houston's organization. The Astros have a recent track record of pumping out high strikeout minor league arms, and Taylor's poised to become the next one. He's a big contender to be throwing 94- to 96-mph consistently by end of 2023. There's definite helium here.

Ceiling: 1.5-win player
Risk: Moderate
MLB ETA: 2024/2025

14. Luis Baez, OF

	Hit	Power	SB	Patience	Glove	Overall
	35/45	50/60	35/30	45	45	45

Born: 01/11/04	Age: 19	Bats: R	Top Production Comp: N/A
Height: 6-1	Weight: 205	Throws: R	

Background: In terms of signing free agents off the international market, Baez was practically a geriatric when the club offered him a massive bonus four days past his 18th birthday. Houston and Baez's representation agreed to a deal worth $1.3 million. (Note: Houston's had luck signing older prospects like Cristian Javier and Jose Urquidy, who immediately come to mind.) A native of Bani, Dominican Republic, Baez shredded the DSL competition in 2022 during his professional debut, mashing .305/.351/.552 with 19 doubles, two triples, and nine homeruns. Per *Weighted Runs Created Plus*, his production topped the average mark by 33%.

Scouting Report: In a system completely depleted by high upside offensive players, Baez represents one of the club's best chances as a legitimate power-hitting outfielder. Average bat speed and there's already questions about the hit tool, having punched out in more than a quarter of his plate appearances last summer. Below-average speed which won't translate well to defensive value. He's not expected to walk much either. There's definite risk here, but he'll go as far as the actual hit tool carries him.

Ceiling: 1.5-win player
Risk: Moderate to High
MLB ETA: 2026

15. Misael Tamarez, RHP

	FB	SL	CH	Command	Overall
	60	55	45	45	40

Born: 01/16/00	Age: 23	Bats: R	Top Production Comp: N/A
Height: 6-1	Weight: 206	Throws: R	

Season	Team	Age	Level	IP	TBF	K/9	K%	BB/9	BB%	K-BB%	ERA	FIP	xFIP	Pit/Bat
2021	HOU	21	A	43.0	188	13.40	34.04%	5.86	14.89%	19.15%	3.98	4.14	4.33	4.18
2021	HOU	21	A+	33.2	137	10.43	28.47%	2.67	7.30%	21.17%	3.48	3.88	4.91	3.92
2022	HOU	22	AA	103.1	431	10.63	28.31%	4.79	12.76%	15.55%	4.62	5.34	4.76	4.13
2022	HOU	22	AAA	18.0	72	10.00	27.78%	7.50	20.83%	6.94%	2.50	5.58	6.16	4.11

Background: There are very few clubs that can sift through the weeds and find underappreciated talent as well as the Astros. And Misael Tamarez is just another example. A native of San Pedro de Macoris, Dominican Republic, the organization signed the hard-throwing righty for the paltry sum of $15,000 in early March 2019. Since then the 6-foot-1, 206-pound hurler rocketed through the club's farm system – particularly after minor league baseball returned to regular action in 2021. Last season Tamarez made 24 appearances, 19 of which were starts, with the Corpus Christi Hooks, throwing 103.1 innings with 122 strikeouts and 55 free passes. He made another four starts with the Sugar Land Space Cowboys. When the dust finally settled Tamarez finished the year with a career best 121.1 innings of work to go along with an aggregate 4.30 ERA. His 142 strikeouts (another career best) ranked as the 43rd best total among all qualified minor league arms.

Snippet from The 2022 Prospect Digest Handbook: Tamarez needs to develop a consistent third option otherwise he's going to get pushed into a relief role.

Houston Astros

Scouting Report: Consider the following:

Since 2006, only three 22-year-old hurlers posted a strikeout percentage between 27.5% and 29.5% in any Double-A league (min. 100 IP): Marcus Stroman, Lewis Thorpe, and – of course – Misael Tamarez. The big differentiator, of course, is Tamarez's feel for the strike zone – or lack thereof. His walk percentage, 12.8%, was nearly double that of the other duo's.

Another one of the hard-throwing youngsters that the club has had tremendous success churning out in recent years. Tamarez's true calling card is his explosive, riding 96 mph fastball. He complements the plus offering with an interesting slider. The breaking ball, thrown with good velocity, lacks a lot of depth but hitters generally didn't square it up. He'll also mix in a firm changeup that shows some dive to it. There's backend starting material here. But, again, he looks like he's best suited for a relief role in the next year or two.

Ceiling: 1.0- to 1.5-win player
Risk: Moderate
MLB ETA: 2023

16. J.C. Correa, C/2B/3B

Hit	Power	SB	Patience	Glove	Overall
55	40	30	50	30/45	45

Born: 09/15/98	Age: 24	Bats: R	Top Production Comp: N/A
Height: 6-0	Weight: 200	Throws: R	

Season	Team	Age	Level	PA	1B	2B	3B	HR	SB	CS	BB%	K%	AVG	OBP	SLG	ISO
2021	HOU	22	A	255	42	19	2	5	7	7	10.98%	11.76%	0.306	0.392	0.477	0.171
2021	HOU	22	A+	193	41	13	0	4	3	2	3.63%	15.03%	0.314	0.337	0.449	0.135
2022	HOU	23	A+	453	87	29	1	8	1	2	8.17%	7.95%	0.309	0.364	0.446	0.136

Background: Correa has the rare distinction of being drafted *twice* by the Astros. Houston first took a late, 33rd round gamble on him coming out of Alvin Community College. The former fulltime infielder opted, instead, to transfer to Lamar University. And Correa made the transition from JuCo to the Southland Conference with aplomb, bashing .332/.381/.529 with 14 doubles and 10 homeruns in 53 games for the Cardinals. His production would tank at the start of the next season, 2020, as he batted a disappointing .245/.317/.321 through 14 games before COVID prematurely ended the year. Still, though, the Astros took a 38th round flier on Correa, eventually convincing him to join the club as the 1,156th overall player taken. The 6-foot, 200-pound infield vagabond began his professional career with Fayetteville two years ago, hitting an impressive .306/.392/.478 through 56 games. And his numbers hovered in similar territory as he spent the second half of the year in High-A (.314/.337/.449). Last season, with his prospect status improving and his defensive home still unknown, the front office gambled – once again – on Correa's potential. They opted to keep him back in Asheville and shift him from the infield to behind the dish. He continued to hit (.309/.364/.446) in 105 games, 65 of which were as a catcher, though the results behind the dish weren't nearly as impressive.

Scouting Report: Let's talk about the glove work first. The results were – quite predictably – pretty terrible. He managed to throw out just 15% of would-be base thieves and, according to Clay Davenport's metrics, he was a -14 behind the dish. But, again, he was a fulltime infielder since his college days. Offensively, Correa showcases an above-average hit tool, double powers, and extreme bat-to-ball skills. The former late rounder punched out in fewer than 8% of his plate appearances in 2022. If he continues to make progress behind the plate, Correa could be a hit-tool first backup at the big league level. Consider the following:

Since 2006, only five 23-year-old hitters posted a 115 to 125 wRC+ mark with a sub-10% strikeout rate in any High-A league (min. 350 PA): Willians Astudillo, Paul Janish, Cole Figueroa, Matt Miller, and – of course – the newly converted catcher J.C. Correa.

Ceiling: 1.0- to 1.5-win player
Risk: Moderate
MLB ETA: 2024

17. Spencer Arrighetti, RHP

FB	CB	SL	CH	Command	Overall
55	55	55	45	40	40

Born: 01/02/01	Age: 23	Bats: R	Top Production Comp: N/A
Height: 6-2	Weight: 186	Throws: R	

Season	Team	Age	Level	IP	TBF	K/9	K%	BB/9	BB%	K-BB%	ERA	FIP	xFIP	Pit/Bat
2022	HOU	22	A+	85.2	393	13.03	31.55%	4.83	11.70%	19.85%	5.04	3.53	3.99	4.06
2022	HOU	22	AA	21.0	81	12.00	34.57%	3.86	11.11%	23.46%	3.43	4.23	4.12	4.49

Background: A two-time First Team All-District pitcher during his tenure at Cinco Ranch High School, Arrighetti spent his freshman season working out of Texas Christian University's bullpen – where the results were mostly mixed. The 6-foot-2,

Houston Astros

186-pound right-hander posted a 19-to-11 strikeout-to-walk ratio in 17.0 innings of work for the Horned Frogs. Following the season, the former high school All-State award winner transferred to Navarro Junior College for a year. Though his season's workload would be limited by the COVID pandemic, Arrighetti managed to make four stats, winning and losing a pair. Prior to his junior campaign, the New Mexico native transferred to Louisiana-Lafayette and immediately moved atop the Ragin' Cajuns rotation. He tossed a collegiate career best 83.2 innings, striking out 91 and walking just 29 to go along with a 3.12 ERA. Houston selected him in the sixth round, 178th overall, and signed him to a deal worth slightly less than $150,000. Arrighetti would make six brief appearances between the Complex League and Low-A during his debut, posting a dominating 22-to-2 strikeout-to-walk ratio in only 13.2 innings of work. Which helped set the stage for his 2022 season. Making 22 appearances with Asheville and another five with Corpus Christi, Arrighetti averaged an impressive 12.8 strikeouts and 4.6 walks per nine innings. He finished the year with an aggregate 4.73 ERA to go along with seven wins and six losses.

Scouting Report: Consider the following:

> Since 2006, only five 22-year-old hurlers posted a strikeout percentage north of 30% with a walk percentage between 10.5% to 12.5% in High-A (min. 75 IP): Wilmer Font, Oliver Ortega, Nick Nastrini, Daniel Palencia, and – of course – Spencer Arrighetti.

Technically, Arrighetti owns a four-pitch mix. But in all reality it's three solid offerings and one that should likely be scrapped all together. Low- to mid-90s fastball, low- to mid-80s slider, and upper 70 12-6 bending curveball – all of which are either above-average or project to be above-average. His changeup, though, is terrible. It's straight, lacks deception *and* noticeable velocity separation. Arrighetti's command is subpar. There's backend starting potential here, but it's going to come down to his ability to throw consistent strikes. He's tracking like a reliever unless something pops – either added velocity or command.

Ceiling: 1.0-win player
Risk: Moderate
MLB ETA: 2023

18. Pedro Leon, IF/CF

Hit	Power	SB	Patience	Glove	Overall
40	50	60	60	55	40

Born: 05/28/98	Age: 25	Bats: R	Top Production Comp: N/A
Height: 5-10	Weight: 170	Throws: R	

Season	Team	Age	Level	PA	1B	2B	3B	HR	SB	CS	BB%	K%	AVG	OBP	SLG	ISO
2021	HOU	23	AA	217	29	7	1	9	13	8	11.52%	30.88%	0.249	0.359	0.443	0.195
2021	HOU	23	AAA	75	6	2	0	0	4	2	18.67%	30.67%	0.131	0.293	0.164	0.033
2022	HOU	24	AAA	504	47	27	3	17	38	18	14.09%	28.77%	0.228	0.365	0.431	0.203

Background: The franchise didn't hold back when it came to signing Leon on the international market two years ago, handing the Cuban import a hefty $4 million deal. A native of La Habana, Leon was a potent offensive weapon during his two seasons in the Cuban National Series between 2017 and 2019, hitting an aggregate .369/.420/.678 in 67 games with the Huracanes de Mayabeque. But that firepower didn't translate during his rollercoaster stateside debut in 2021. He batted .220/.339/.369 with nine doubles, one triple, nine homeruns, and 18 stolen bases in 72 games between the Complex League, Corpus Christi, and Sugar Land. But his production improved – slightly – during his stint with the Glendale Desert Dogs in the Arizona Fall League, batting .257/.381/.343. Last season, Leon's bat – once again – limped through a disappointing campaign. Appearing in 115 games with the Space Cowboys, the 5-foot-10, 170-pound infielder / outfielder cobbled together a .228/.365/.431 slash line, belting out 27 doubles, three triples, and 17 homeruns to go along with 38 stolen bases (in 56 total attempts). As measured by *Weighted Runs Created Plus*, his overall production topped the league average mark by 3%.

Snippet from The 2022 Prospect Digest Handbook: If you're into speculating on prospect baseball cards, here's one I'd be buying.

Scouting Report: To be frank, if the Astros' farm system wasn't in complete shambles and strip mined from years of incredible development, Leon would have completely fallen off the club's Top 20 list. And just like last season, depending how the season is viewed, you'll either walk away convinced there's no meaningful big league value will be extracted or further cement your views as a Leon apologist (which I *was*).

Part I – The Skeptic: Leon's production is abysmal and somehow managed to be in the league average territory. But his complementary skills (average power and above-average speed) simply don't compensate for a 40-grade hit tool.

Part II – The Apologist: While it's true that Leon's numbers were terrible, an early season slump sank his overall production. After beginning the season with a .250/.378/.441 in 17 games, the Cuban's bat froze. He hit just .216/.367/.448 over his next 51 games. But after that he batted .291/.390/.500 through the first of September. Then he went cold and finished the year out on a .167/.323/.308 line. When he's good, he's good. But when he's bad, he's bad.

Houston Astros

The truth is simple, though: he's going to be 25-years-old, can run into 15 or so homeruns in a season, but doesn't utilize his speed efficiently on the base paths. He can play centerfield well, but not enough to compensate for a low batting average. Leon is not long for professional baseball at this point.

Ceiling: 1.0-win player
Risk: Moderate
MLB ETA: 2023

19. Alex Santos II, RHP

FB	CB	SL/CU	CH	Command	Overall
55	55	50	45	40/45	40

Born: 02/10/02	Age: 21	Bats: R	Top Production Comp: N/A
Height: 6-4	Weight: 194	Throws: R	

Season	Team	Age	Level	IP	TBF	K/9	K%	BB/9	BB%	K-BB%	ERA	FIP	xFIP	Pit/Bat
2021	HOU	19	A	41.2	183	10.37	26.23%	6.48	16.39%	9.84%	3.46	4.53	5.50	4.09
2022	HOU	20	A	82.2	362	11.32	28.73%	4.03	10.22%	18.51%	5.99	5.07	4.02	4.09

Background: After handing over a bevy of draft picks as part of the organization's punishment for sign stealing, Houston made the Mount St. Michael High School ace their first selection in the 2020 draft. Standing a solid 6-foot-4 and 194-pounds, the New York native signed with the club for a hefty $1.25 million as the 72nd overall pick. Santos would make his professional debut the following season, making seven starts and five relief appearances with Fayetteville, averaging 10.4 strikeouts and 6.5 walks per nine innings. Unsurprisingly, Santos made a return to the Woodpeckers for some additional seasoning – or at least, in hopes that he can hone in on the strike zone with a little more consistency. Which he did. In 23 appearances, 14 of which were starts, Santos posted an impressive 104-to-37 strikeout-to-walk ratio in 82.2 innings of work. He finished the year with a 5.99 ERA, 5.07 FIP, and a 4.02 xFIP.

Snippet from The 2022 Prospect Digest Handbook: Santos is certainly a name to watch in the coming years.

Scouting Report: Consider the following:

> Since 2006, only two 20-year-old hurlers posted a 27.5% to 29.5% strikeout percentage with a 9% to 11% walk percentage in Low-A (min. 75 IP): Luis Pena and Alex Santos II.

Santos made significant progress slimming down his problematic walk rates last season, but his command – at best – is a 40-grade skill. Above-average fastball with two solid breaking balls and a subpar changeup. Santos continued to miss an impressive amount of bats in his return to Fayetteville. The New York native is still only entering his age-21 season, but he's already heading down the path of a future reliever unless the command upticks in the next year or two.

Ceiling: 1.0-win player
Risk: Moderate
MLB ETA: 2025

20. Michael Knorr, RHP

FB	CB	SL	CH	Command	Overall
60	55	50	N/A	45	60

Born: 05/12/00	Age: 23	Bats: R	Top Production Comp: N/A
Height: 6-5	Weight: 245	Throws: R	

Background: Coastal Carolina returned to prominence during their phenomenal 2022 season, winning 39 games against just 20 losses. And the Sun Belt Conference School churned a pair of high round draft picks as well, making it the first time since 1983 that two Chanticleers were drafted within the first three rounds (Mickey Brantley and John Rigos). Last season, of course, the Brewers selected shortstop Eric Brown Jr. in the opening round and the Astros followed up with their pick of Michael Knorr two rounds later. Knorr, the 103rd overall player taken last July, turned in a phenomenal campaign in his lone season at Coastal. A transplant after spending three years at Cal State Fullerton, Knorr averaged an impressive 11.2 strikeouts and just 1.7 walks per nine innings to go along with a perfect 5-0 record and a 3.39 ERA. He signed with Houston for $487,500.

Scouting Report: Consider the following:

> Since 2017, only two Sun Belt Conference hurlers averaged at least 11 strikeouts and fewer than 2.0 walks per nine innings in a season (min. 60 IP): Jeremy Lee and Michael Knorr.

Knorr's velocity took a dramatic leap forward between his final season at Cal State Fullerton and his first year at Coastal Carolina. The big 6-foot-5, 245-pound right-hander was previously sitting in the upper-80s / low-90s but was touching the upper 90s a year later. He'll also mix in

Houston Astros

an average slider and an above-average changeup (note: I did not see the changeup). There's the making of a backend starter, especially if he's throwing consistent strikes. He's likely to move quickly through the lower levels.

Ceiling: 1.0-win player
Risk: Moderate
MLB ETA: 2024/2025

Kansas City Royals

Top Prospects

Kansas City Royals

1. Gavin Cross, CF

Hit	Power	SB	Patience	Glove	Overall
55	55	55	50	50	55

Born: 02/13/01	Age: 22	Bats: L	Top Production Comp: N/A
Height: 6-3	Weight: 210	Throws: L	

Season	Team	Age	Level	PA	1B	2B	3B	HR	SB	CS	BB%	K%	AVG	OBP	SLG	ISO
2022	KCR	21	CPX	12	2	2	0	1	0	0	16.67%	16.67%	0.500	0.583	1.000	0.500
2022	KCR	21	A	123	15	5	2	7	4	2	17.89%	25.20%	0.293	0.423	0.596	0.303

Background: Continuing the trend of 2022 Top Draft Prospects with strong bloodlines to professional baseball, Cross's father, Adam, squeezed in three minor league seasons in the mid-1990s with the San Diego Padres and Atlanta Braves. The elder Cross was speedy infielder with doubles power and little offensive upside. Gavin Cross, on the other hand, is a potential five-tool outfielder and a potential Top 5 pick heading into the 2022 Draft. A product of Tennessee High, where he set the state record for stolen bases with 40 during his junior season, Cross got off to a tremendous start to his collegiate career – until COVID prematurely cut the season short. He would slug .369/.409/.385 in 16 games with the Hokies. The next season, 2021, the 6-foot-3, 210-pound outfielder added a new dimension to his offensive repertoire: power. And he was nearly unstoppable. In 57 games, Cross batted .345/.415/.621 with 13 doubles, five triples, and 11 homeruns. He also swiped nine bags in 13 attempts. He spent part of the ensuing summer leading Team USA's collegiate squad in batting average (.455) and slugging percentage (.879) while tying for the team lead with four homeruns. Last season Cross continued to dominate the competition, slugging .328/.411/.660 with career bests in doubles (14), triples (eight), homeruns (17), and stolen bases (12). Kansas City selected him in the first round, ninth overall, and signed him to a deal worth $5,200,400. Cross mashed .312/.437/.633 with seven doubles, two triples, eight homeruns, and four stolen bases in 29 games during his debut – all but three coming with the Fireflies of Columbia.

Scouting Report: Per the usual, my pre-draft write-up:

> *"Consider the following:*
>
> > *Since 2011, five ACC hitters met the following criteria in a season (min. 250 PA): bat at least .320/.400/.650 with a double-digit walk rate and a strikeout rate between 13% and 15%. Those five hitters: Brendan McKay, James Ramsey, Drew Ellis, Tanner Schobel, and – of course – Gavin Cross.*
>
> *Virginia Tech doesn't exactly have a strong track record of producing big league talent, the best being Joe Saunders and Chad Pinder. And the ACC Conference School has produced just one first round pick – Joe Saunders – since 1989. Cross has solid power to all fields, but his nitro zone is down and in. He should be able to handle tough lefties. Strong ability to adjust mid-pitch for offspeed offerings and still barrel up the ball. Watching game tape from 2022, it's amazing how many of his dingers were off of offspeed pitches. Above-average speed. Decent glove if he stays in center. Very sound prospect. The Guardians won't have a shot at drafting him, but he's a very typical Cleveland prospect. Pittsburgh and Miami seem like logical landing spots."*

Ceiling: 3.5-win player
Risk: Moderate
MLB ETA: 2024

2. Cayden Wallace, 3B

Hit	Power	SB	Patience	Glove	Overall
50	50/60	40	50	50	50

Born: 08/07/01	Age: 21	Bats: R	Top Production Comp: N/A
Height: 6-1	Weight: 205	Throws: R	

Season	Team	Age	Level	PA	1B	2B	3B	HR	SB	CS	BB%	K%	AVG	OBP	SLG	ISO
2022	KCR	20	CPX	10	1	1	0	0	0	0	30.00%	10.00%	0.286	0.500	0.429	0.143
2022	KCR	20	A	122	20	7	3	2	8	1	9.84%	18.03%	0.294	0.369	0.468	0.174

Background: Heading into the 2022 MLB Draft, only one former Greenbrier High School product has trekked a road into professional baseball: Paxton Wallace, who's seeing some time in the low levels of the Angels organization. Paxton happens to be the older brother of Cayden, one of the nation's best bats in this year's draft class. A dynamic middle-of-the-lineup force during his prep career, the younger Wallace brother batted .514 with six dingers as a junior. And, despite playing in eight games before the pandemic-imposed shutdown, he was named Arkansas Gatorade Player of the Year. Wallace put together a rock solid showing as a true freshman for the Razorbacks, hitting .279/.369/.500 with 11 doubles and 14 homeruns in 60 games for the SEC conference squad. He spent the summer handling the Cape Cod League pitching with aplomb, batting .290/.352/.468 with five doubles and a pair of homeruns in 18 games with the Bourne Braves. Last season, the young sophomore set career bests in nearly every offensive category,

Kansas City Royals

including: batting average (.298), on-base percentage (.387), slugging percentage (.553), doubles (20), triples (one), homeruns (16), stolen bases (12), and RBIs (60). Kansas City snagged him in the second round, 49th overall, and signed him to a deal worth $1,697,500. Wallace slugged .294/.369/.468 with seven doubles, three triples, two homeruns, and eight stolen bases in 27 games with Columbia.

Scouting Report: Per the usual, my pre-draft write-up:

> *"Consider the following:*
>
> *Since 2011, only six SEC hitters posted an OPS total between .920 and .960 with a strikeout rate between 15% and 20% and a walk rate north of 11% in a season (min. 275 PA): Dominique Thompson-Williams, Tyler Keenan, Ryan Tella, Max Kuhn, Sikes Orvis, and – of course – Cayden Wallace.*
>
> *Wallace made some mechanical tweaks between his solid freshman and standout sophomore seasons with the Razorbacks. He's standing more upright, with his hands lower and closer to his body. Despite slugging a career best 16 homeruns in 2022, Wallace is just beginning to scratch the surface of his prodigious homerun power. Solid base runner. Plus-power potential. Average hit tool. Wallace is a young college bat for his class, so there's some added projection. He looks like a back-of-the-first round type talent Oakland (#19), Toronto (#23), and Milwaukee (#27) seem like ideal landing spots."*

Ceiling: 2.5-win player
Risk: Moderate
MLB ETA: 2024/2025

3. Ángel Zerpa, LHP

FB	SL	CH	Command	Overall
55	55	60	50	50

Born: 09/27/99	Age: 23	Bats: L	Top Production Comp: Drew Smyly
Height: 6-0	Weight: 220	Throws: L	

Season	Team	Age	Level	IP	TBF	K/9	K%	BB/9	BB%	K-BB%	ERA	FIP	xFIP	Pit/Bat
2021	KCR	21	A+	41.2	167	11.45	31.74%	1.73	4.79%	26.95%	2.59	2.57	3.00	3.78
2021	KCR	21	AA	45.1	200	10.72	27.00%	3.77	9.50%	17.50%	5.96	4.43	3.71	4.01
2022	KCR	22	AA	64.0	278	9.70	24.82%	2.95	7.55%	17.27%	4.36	4.15	4.19	3.81

Background: During the 2016 summer, the Royals could have invested $10,000 in limitless ways – upgrade a concession stand or two, or maybe use the funds towards a fan appreciation night. Instead the front office did the wise thing: they convinced a stocky southpaw from Valle de la Pascua, Venezuela to join the organization. A small pittance, even by standards several decades ago, Zerpa dominated the foreign rookie league the following summer, tallying a tidy 1.84 ERA in 63.2 innings – though he barely missed any bats (39 punch outs). The team pushed him stateside and Zerpa continued to hold his own and saw a modest uptick in his strikeout rate as well. The next season, 2019, Zerpa continued his slow trek through the minor leagues as he moved up to the Appalachian and Pioneer Leagues and – once again – he saw a jump in his whiff numbers as he averaged a career best 8.9 strikeouts per nine innings. Then the club unleashed him on full-season action in 2021. And Zerpa blitzed through High-A, Double-A, Triple-A, and he managed to squeeze in a brief 5.0-inning start in The Show. Last season, despite missing more than a month due to a knee injury, the 6-foot, 220-pound southpaw recorded a 69-to-25 strikeout-to-walk ratio in 71.2 innings between Northwest Arkansas and Omaha. He tossed another 11.0 innings with Kansas City, striking out and walking a trio.

Snippet from The 2022 Prospect Digest Handbook: There's definite #4-type potential here – something along the line of a Drew Smyly.

Scouting Report: Consider the following:

> *Since 2006, there have eleven 22-year-old hurlers that posted a 24% to 26% strikeout percentage with 6.5% to 8.5% walk percentage in any Double-A league (min. 60 IP): Alex Cobb, Anibal Sanchez, Brian Moran, Brian Shaffer, Fernando Hernandez, Jackson Kowar, Juan Gutierrez, Luke Jackson, Mitch Talbot, Trevor Stephan, and Ángel Zerpa.*

Low three-quarter slinger that unfurls a 93- to 95-mph fastball that plays up do to his release point. He'll complement the plus offering with a pair of above-average offspeed pitches: a mid-80s, horizontally darting slider and a mid-80s, firm changeup. Zerpa's ability to command the strike zone with all three pitches makes him the safest bet in the Royals' system to reach their potential. #4-top ceiling.

Ceiling: 2.0-win player
Risk: Low to Moderate
MLB ETA: Debuted in 2021

Kansas City Royals

4. Carter Jensen, C

	Hit	Power	SB	Patience	Glove	Overall
	40/45	40/50	40/35	60	55	45

Born: 07/03/03	Age: 19	Bats: L	Top Production Comp: N/A
Height: 6-1	Weight: 210	Throws: R	

Season	Team	Age	Level	PA	1B	2B	3B	HR	SB	CS	BB%	K%	AVG	OBP	SLG	ISO
2021	KCR	17	CPX	65	12	1	1	1	4	0	15.38%	29.23%	0.273	0.385	0.382	0.109
2022	KCR	18	A	485	52	24	2	11	8	6	17.11%	21.24%	0.226	0.363	0.382	0.155

Background: Jensen and right-hander Ben Kudrna were supposed to be roommates at Louisiana State University. Instead, they joined the same organization, just 35 picks apart, and spent the entirety of 2022 playing for the Fireflies of Columbia. The 78th overall pick two years ago, Kansas City signed the lefty-swinging teenage backstop to a deal worth slightly more than $1 million. Jensen, who happened to grow up a stone's throw from Kauffman Stadium, turned in an impressive debut in the Complex League as he slugged .281/.388/.404 with four extra-base hits in 19 games. Last season, though, was a completely different story. Appearing in 113 games with the club's Low-A affiliate, the 6-foot-1, 210-pound backstop batted a lowly .227/.363/.382 with 24 doubles, two triples, 11 homeruns, and eight stolen bases (in 14 total attempts). As measured by *Weighted Runs Created Plus*, his overall production last season topped the league average mark by a surprising 13% -- thanks in large part due to his bloated walk rate (17.1%) and thump.

Snippet from The 2022 Prospect Digest Handbook: Big time uppercut from the lefty-swinging backstop, who projects to have above-average power at full maturation. Jensen loads up by shifting his entire weight on his back leg before uncoiling his swing – almost a little Ichiro-esque. Defensively, he shows a solid-average arm that plays up because of his accuracy. There's some Mitch Moreland-type upside with the bat. One more positive note: he's only entering his age-18 season.

Scouting Report: Consider the following:

> Since 2006, only four 18-year-old hitters posted a 108 to 118 wRC+ mark with a strikeout rate between 20% to 22% in any Low-A league (min. 350 PA): Gleyber Torres, Wendell Rijo, Jeisson Rosario, and – of course – Carter Jensen.

The problem with viewing Jensen's overall production (113 wRC+) just in terms of *Weighted Runs Created Plus* is that it hides the fact that he actually didn't really hit that well and a lot of his production came from his swollen walk rates. BUT…on the other hand, Jensen made some important adjustments over the season's final months leaving plenty of hope for a bright future. The lefty-swinging backstop batted a putrid .166/.284/.325 over his first 47 games. Beginning on June 12th through the remainder of the year – a span of 66 games – he batted .272/.417/.424 with 17 doubles, one triple, and five homeruns. If Jensen can repeat his second half, he'll be one of the ten best catching prospects in the game within a year. A lot of risk here, though.

Ceiling: 2.5-win player
Risk: Moderate to High
MLB ETA: 2025

5. Maikel Garcia, SS

	Hit	Power	SB	Patience	Glove	Overall
	55	40	55	50	50	50

Born: 03/03/00	Age: 23	Bats: R	Top Production Comp: N/A
Height: 6-0	Weight: 145	Throws: R	

Season	Team	Age	Level	PA	1B	2B	3B	HR	SB	CS	BB%	K%	AVG	OBP	SLG	ISO
2021	KCR	21	A	237	42	13	3	1	24	3	16.03%	13.92%	0.303	0.409	0.415	0.113
2021	KCR	21	A+	243	46	8	4	3	11	3	9.88%	16.46%	0.281	0.351	0.396	0.115
2022	KCR	22	AA	369	65	24	1	4	27	3	11.11%	16.26%	0.291	0.369	0.409	0.118
2022	KCR	22	AAA	186	28	10	0	7	12	5	9.14%	22.58%	0.274	0.341	0.463	0.189

Background: One of the more under-the-radar prospects in the entire Kansas City farm system. Garcia, a cousin of former Royal Alcides Escobar, struggled through his first two seasons in pro ball as he barely hit his weight in the Dominican Summer League in 2017 *and* during his stateside debut the following year. But the 6-foot, 145-pound infielder quietly pieced together a solid showing in the old Appalachian League in 2019 as he batted .286/.353/.373 with 13 extra-base hits in 55 games. After minor league ball returned from its COVID-induced hiatus, Garcia continued to hit as he moved through Low-A and later on into High-A in 2021. He finished the season with an aggregate .291/.380/.405 slash line with 21 doubles, seven triples, four homeruns, and 35 stolen bases (in 41 total attempts). Last season Garcia continued his blitz through the system as he appeared in 78 games with Northwest Arkansas, another 40 in Omaha, and he squeezed in nine games with the parent company. The 6-foot, 145-pound shortstop slugged .285/.359/.427 with career bests in doubles (34), homeruns (11), and stolen bases (39) during his minor league tenure. Per *Weighted Runs Created Plus*, his overall production topped the league average mark by 6%. Garcia went 7-for-22 during his big league debut as well.

Kansas City Royals

Scouting Report: Consider the following:

> Since 2006, there have been three 22-year-old hitters that posted a 100 to 110 wRC+ with a 10% to 12% walk rate and a 14% to 18% strikeout rate in any Double-A league (min. 350 PA): Tucker Barnhart, David Cooper, and – of course – Maikel Garcia.

Garcia falls into the fringy starting caliber tier of shortstop prospects. Above-average hit tool, below-average power, above-average speed, and a solid glove at a premium infield position. Scouting reports tend to favor Garcia's defensive abilities, but he's typically graded out as average-ish. He has the potential to be a .275/.330/.400 hitter. He could be a key cog, a mainstay on rebuilding team – like the Royals. But the organization likely won't be hard-pressed to find a suitable replacement.

Ceiling: 2.0-win player
Risk: Moderate
MLB ETA: Debuted in 2022

6. Tyler Gentry, LF/RF

Hit	Power	SB	Patience	Glove	Overall
50	55	55	50	55	50

Born: 02/01/99	Age: 24	Bats: R	Top Production Comp: Kole Calhoun
Height: 6-2	Weight: 210	Throws: R	

Season	Team	Age	Level	PA	1B	2B	3B	HR	SB	CS	BB%	K%	AVG	OBP	SLG	ISO
2021	KCR	22	A+	186	22	10	0	6	4	0	15.59%	29.57%	0.259	0.395	0.449	0.190
2022	KCR	23	A+	152	31	6	1	5	2	2	13.16%	25.66%	0.336	0.434	0.516	0.180
2022	KCR	23	AA	331	56	16	0	16	8	4	12.08%	19.94%	0.321	0.417	0.555	0.234

Background: The Royals, under the captainship of Dayton Moore, put an emphasis on pitching, termed the "currency of baseball." So it's not surprising that the club used only two of their six picks in the COVID-limited 2020 draft on hitters. They selected Baylor shortstop Nick Loftin with their second first round pick and then swung back around and grabbed Alabama outfielder Tyler Gentry two rounds later. Taken with the 76th overall pick that summer, Gentry spent his freshman season at baseball hotbed Walters State Community College, hitting .379 with 32 extra-base hits in only 64 games. And the 6-foot-2, 210-pound outfielder immediately made an impact after transferring to the Tide. He slugged .310/.378/.552 in 2019, and got off to a scorching start the following year (.429/.554/.750) before COVID prematurely ended it. Gentry made his professional debut two years ago, hitting a respectable .259/.395/.449 in 44 games with Quad Cities. Last season, the former SEC masher upped the production level to a new stratosphere as he split time with Quad Cities and Northwest Arkansas. He batted an aggregate .326/.422/.542 with 22 doubles, one triple, 21 homeruns, and 10 stolen bases (in 16 attempts). Per *Weighted Runs Created Plus*, his overall production topped the league average mark by a whopping 52%.

Scouting Report: Consider the following:

> Since 2006, only three 23-year-old hitters met the following criteria in a season in Double-A (min. 300 PA): 140 to 150 wRC+, a 19% to 21% strikeout rate, and a double-digit walk rate. Those three hitters: Jason Donald, Darnell Sweeney, and Tyler Gentry.

One of the top performing bats since entering the minor leagues two years ago, Gentry has (A) handled aggressive assignments by the club without missing a beat and (B) managed to improve his once problematic swing-and-miss rate at each stop along the way. Broad-shouldered with above-average in-game power and an average hit tool. Gentry possesses some Kole Calhoun-type offensive potential – .260/.340/.440 with 20 homeruns. The former centerfielder will add some value on the defensive side of the ball, as well.

Ceiling: 2.0-win player
Risk: Moderate
MLB ETA: 2023

7. Asa Lacy, LHP

FB	CB	SL	CH	Command	Overall
60	60	60	60	40/45	60

Born: 06/02/99	Age: 24	Bats: L	Top Production Comp: N/A
Height: 6-4	Weight: 215	Throws: L	

Season	Team	Age	Level	IP	TBF	K/9	K%	BB/9	BB%	K-BB%	ERA	FIP	xFIP	Pit/Bat
2021	KCR	22	A+	52.0	237	13.67	33.33%	7.10	17.30%	16.03%	5.19	4.81	4.70	4.15
2022	KCR	23	AA	20.0	105	11.25	23.81%	12.60	26.67%	-2.86%	11.25	7.96	8.14	4.15

Background: After spending the majority of his freshman season in the Aggies' bullpen, Lacy established himself as one of college's preeminent hurlers in 2019 as he averaged an impressive 13.2 strikeouts and 4.4

Kansas City Royals

walks per nine innings across 15 starts. Lacy, who's always battled some command demons, seemed to have figured it out during the 2020 COVID-abbreviated season, though, as he posted an immaculate 46-to-8 strikeout-to-walk ratio in 24.0 innings of work. The Royals, an organization driven by acquiring young pitching, saw enough of the 6-foot-4, 215-pound southpaw and decided he was worthy of the fourth overall pick that summer, drafting him ahead of several notable collegiate arms like: Emerson Hancock, Reid Detmers, and Garrett Crochet. But almost immediately things seemed to be off with the enigmatic left-hander. During his debut showing the former Texas A&M ace lost all feel for the strike zone *and* his season prematurely ended in late July courtesy of a barking left shoulder. He would finish his disappointment campaign with 79 strikeouts and a whopping 41 walks in only 52.0 innings of work. Kansas City sent him to the Arizona Fall League in hopes of getting him some additional innings, but the results were largely the same: 7.2 IP, 15, and 6 walks. With a renewal of hope eternal at the start of every season, Lacy's 2022 season was actually *worse* than the year before. Just two starts into the time with the Northwest Arkansas Naturals, the big lefty hit the disabled list for two months thanks to a back issue. He would make four – largely – disastrous outings in the Complex League before being shuffled back up to Double-A in mid-July. The front office would limit his outings to two or fewer innings, but it didn't matter. He was a train wreck. Lacy finished his sophomore season in Double-A with more walks (25) than innings pitched (20). Not to mention an 11.25 ERA.

Snippet from The 2022 Prospect Digest Handbook: Lacy seems to have it all. Except a grasp on the strike zone.

Scouting Report: The year actually started off a decent footing, at least in terms of Lacy's previous strike-throwing issues. He walked "only" five hitters across 9.2 innings. But after he hit the disabled list all hell broke loose for the former first rounder. Lacy's command – if you're being generous – is a 20 on the 20-80 scouting scale. The fastball command is particularly alarming. He's *consistently* missing to away to the first base side of the plate and any inside offerings barely cross the halfway point on the plate. Meaning: there's some serious mechanical flaws going on that's inhibiting him from working the other way of the dish. Plus fastball sitting in the 94- to 97-mph range. Plus mid- to upper-80s slider. Plus changeup. He was showing a plus curveball in previous years, but seems to have scrapped the bender last year. It's still an elite arsenal, which is why I'm not ready to jump off the Lacy Bandwagon, but the organization is clearly doing him no favors. I'd love to what he could do in Tampa or Cleveland or Los Angeles or Seattle.

Ceiling: 4.0-win player
Risk: Extreme
MLB ETA: 2023/2024

8. Ben Kudrna, RHP

FB	CB	SL	CH	Command	Overall
55	45/50	50	55	45/50	50

Born: 01/30/03	Age: 20	Bats: R	Top Production Comp: N/A
Height: 6-3	Weight: 175	Throws: R	

Season	Team	Age	Level	IP	TBF	K/9	K%	BB/9	BB%	K-BB%	ERA	FIP	xFIP	Pit/Bat
2022	KCR	19	A	72.1	311	7.59	19.61%	3.98	10.29%	9.32%	3.48	4.29	5.02	3.83

Background: Part of the club's plan in selecting prep lefty Frank Mozzicato with the seventh overall pick was to spread the significant savings around – or in a best case scenario, to another highly touted prospect that slipped during the draft. The club ended up saving $1,884,900 with the Mozzicato signing and turned around and signed Ben Kudrna to a deal that went $1,267,700 beyond the recommended slot value. Kudrna, who was one of two local boys snagged by the Royals that year, made his debut with the Columbia Fireflies last summer. Making 17 starts for the club's Low-A affiliate, the 6-foot-3, 175-pound righty tossed 72.1 innings while averaging 7.6 strikeouts and 4.0 walks per nine innings. He finished the year with a 3.48 ERA, 4.29 FIP, and a 5.02 xFIP.

Snippet from The 2022 Prospect Digest Handbook: It's easy to see why the club went well beyond the slot value to sign him. The more I watch, the more I like.

Scouting Report: Consider the following:

> Since 2006, there have been ten 19-year-old hurlers that posted an 18.5% to 20.5% strikeout percentage with a 9.5% to 11.5% walk percentage in any Low-A league (min. 70 IP): Max Fried, Zach Davis, Genesis Cabrera, Junior Fernandez, Reese Olson, Ricardo Sanchez, Carlos Perez, Robinson Ortiz, Zach Phillips, and – of course – Ben Kudrna.

Being a local kid, the Royals had plenty of looks on the teenage right-hander over the years. Heading into the draft, Kudrna was sporting a fastball, slider, changeup mix. But he's added a fringy curveball during the offseason. The fastball didn't look as lively, though he generally commands it well. His slider is average, but he seems to prefer the newer breaking ball. And his changeup is – arguably – his best offering. He's athletic enough and lives around the zone enough to project his command as average in the coming years.

Ceiling: 1.5- to 2.0-win player
Risk: Moderate
MLB ETA: 2025

Kansas City Royals

9. Nick Loftin, IF/OF

Hit	Power	SB	Patience	Glove	Overall
50	40	55	50	50	45

Born: 09/25/98	**Age:** 24	**Bats:** R	**Top Production Comp:** Alberto Callaspo	
Height: 6-1	**Weight:** 180	**Throws:** R		

Season	Team	Age	Level	PA	1B	2B	3B	HR	SB	CS	BB%	K%	AVG	OBP	SLG	ISO
2021	KCR	22	A+	410	66	22	5	10	11	2	10.24%	14.63%	0.289	0.373	0.463	0.174
2022	KCR	23	AA	425	68	17	1	12	24	4	10.59%	13.41%	0.270	0.354	0.421	0.152
2022	KCR	23	AAA	168	21	7	0	5	5	2	5.95%	24.40%	0.216	0.280	0.359	0.144

Background: The Royals opened up their 2020, COVID-limited draft class by selecting a pair of notable collegiate players – Asa Lacy, who was taken with the fourth overall pick, and Nick Loftin, who was chosen 28 picks later. A consistent star at Baylor University during his three-year tenure, Loftin left the Big 12 school as a .311/.370/.479 hitter in 122 games, belting out 34 doubles, five triples, and 14 stolen bases during that time. After signing with Kansas City for an even $3 million, the 6-foot-1, 180-pound infielder / outfielder turned in a quietly solid debut with Quad Cities two years ago as he batted .289/.374/.464 with 22 doubles, five triples, 10 homeruns, and 11 stolen bases (in only 13 total attempts). Last season the front office sent the Texas-born first rounder into the fires of Double-A, and he came out a little singed but ultimately passed the minors' most important test. He hit a league average .270/.354/.421 in 90 games with Northwest Arkansas. The front office brass bounced Loftin up to Omaha in early August for the remainder of the season. Loftin finished his sophomore professional season with an aggregate .254/.333/.403 with career bests in doubles (24), homeruns (17), and stolen bases (29). His overall production, according to *Weighted Runs Created Plus*, was 9% below the league average mark – thanks to his struggles in Triple-A.

Snippet from The 2022 Prospect Digest Handbook: There's an interesting speed/power blend built into a middle-infielder's role. Loftin's a throwback player in a lot of ways by making consistent hard contact. Defensively, he could stay at either middle infielder spot, but the club had him experiment at the hot corner – where his bat doesn't profile nearly as well. He could be a low end starting option in 18 months.

Scouting Report: Consider the following:

> Since 2006, there have been seven 23-year-old hitters that met the following criteria in a season in Double-A (min. 350 PA): 95 to 105 wRC+, 11% to 15% strikeout rate, and a 9% to 12% walk rate. Those seven hitters: Rafael Ortega, Brad Emaus, Mike Baxter, Jamie Hoffman, Evan Frey, Stephen Alemais, and – of course – Nick Loftin.

For the first time in his career, Loftin struggled with contact issues – at least for him – during his 38-game tenure in Triple-A, so it's not surprising that his numbers tanked. Kansas City continues to bounce him around the diamond, as well as having him spend time at second and third bases, shortstop and – for the first time – he played left and center fields. He still profiles as a low end starting option, but his versatility, contact skills, and speed are best suited for a super-sub role which he already seemed destined for. He's going to be a .260/.330/.400 hitter at the game's pinnacle level, running into enough fat fastballs to slug eight- to 10-homeruns.

Ceiling: 1.5-win player
Risk: Low to Moderate
MLB ETA: 2023

10. Frank Mozzicato, LHP

FB	CB	CH	Command	Overall
50	65	50	35/45	45

Born: 06/09/03	**Age:** 20	**Bats:** L	**Top Production Comp:** N/A
Height: 6-3	**Weight:** 175	**Throws:** L	

Season	Team	Age	Level	IP	TBF	K/9	K%	BB/9	BB%	K-BB%	ERA	FIP	xFIP	Pit/Bat
2022	KCR	19	A	69.0	306	11.61	29.08%	6.65	16.67%	12.42%	4.30	4.74	4.36	4.21

Background: The Royals' selection of the East Catholic High School left-hander has to be near the top for biggest draft surprises – certainly in recent memory, and maybe of all time. Not entirely an unknown commodity heading into the 2021 draft, but *definitely* not one that was supposed to hear his name called at the opening of the first round. The Royals, though, fell in love with the lanky left-hander's curveball and snagged him with the eighth overall pick that summer, signing him to a well below-slot deal worth $3,547,500 – bonus money equivalent to somewhere around the 16th or 17th slot. Mozzicato rocketed up the organization's draft chart after a spectacular senior season as he *averaged* nearly 22 punch outs per nine innings. The 6-foot-3, 175-pound southpaw would make his highly anticipated debut with the Columbia Fireflies last season. He would make 19 starts with the organization's Low-A affiliate, throwing 69.0 innings with 89 strikeouts and 51 walks. He finished the year with a 4.30 ERA, a 4.74 FIP, and a 4.36 xFIP.

Snippet from The 2022 Prospect Digest Handbook: There's some sneaky upside here, reminiscent of a young Cole Hamels, though the trademark offspeed pitches differ (changeup vs. curveball).

Kansas City Royals

Scouting Report: Consider the following:

> Since 2006, there have been ten 19-year-old hurlers that met the following criteria in any Low-A league (min. 60 IP): 28% to 30% strikeouts percentage with a walk percentage north of 14%. Those 10 hurlers: Ken Giles, Hector Santiago, Aiden McIntyre, Andrew Lee, R.J. Freure, Tony Locey, Carlos Jimenez, Deylen Miley, Ryan Cardona, and – of course – Frank Mozzicato, the surprise early first round pick.

Spinning a plus curveball is an inherent ability. It can't be taught. You can either do it, or you can't. And Frank Mozzicato can. Beyond that ability, though, he remains raw, a work in progress. His fastball, an average offering, was sitting in the upper 80s / low 90s during a late season start. His changeup, which he's surprisingly reliant upon, is a solid average pitch. Mozzicato shows an impressive willingness to change speeds, but he seems to reserve his best offering – that gorgeous deuce – only to put hitters away when he's ahead in the count with two strikes. It's imperative for Mozzicato and his future big league aspirations, that he can consistently throw the bender for strikes – when he's ahead *and* behind in the count. 35-grade command that likely creeps into 45-grade territory. Kansas City left themselves open for a lot of criticism when they selected the prep southpaw – especially with the likes of Benny Montgomery, Brady House, Harry Ford, and Andrew Painter still on the board. And right now, Mozzicato's done nothing to dispel that criticism.

Ceiling: 1.5-win player
Risk: Moderate
MLB ETA: 2025

11. Drew Waters, OF

Hit	Power	SB	Patience	Glove	Overall
45	40/45	50	50	55	45

Born: 12/30/98	Age: 23	Bats: B	Top Production Comp: Drew Stubbs
Height: 6-2	Weight: 185	Throws: R	

Season	Team	Age	Level	PA	1B	2B	3B	HR	SB	CS	BB%	K%	AVG	OBP	SLG	ISO
2021	ATL	22	AAA	459	63	22	1	11	28	9	10.24%	30.94%	0.240	0.329	0.381	0.141
2022	ATL	23	AAA	210	32	7	3	5	5	1	7.62%	27.14%	0.246	0.305	0.393	0.147
2022	KCR	23	AAA	143	22	5	2	7	13	0	13.99%	28.67%	0.295	0.399	0.541	0.246

Background: At the onset of his hiring as the club's General Manager, Dayton Moore had a penchant for acquiring former or current Braves prospects, which made sense because he spent more than a decade in Atlanta. And in a bit of ironic poetry one of the club's final moves prior to Moore's release was acquiring a former top prospect from the Braves system that had fallen on hard times in the upper minors. The specifics of the July 11th deal: Kansas City agreed to send the 35th overall pick to Atlanta in exchange for outfielder Drew Waters, right-hander Andrew Hoffman, and corner infielder C.J. Alexander. Once considered a consensus Top 100 prospect, Waters, who was originally drafted in the second round of the 2017 draft class, has struggled to regain his once illustrious prospect status since minor league action returned from its COVID hiatus. The 6-foot-2, 185-pound centerfielder batted a mediocre .240/.329/.381 with 22 doubles, one triple, 11 homeruns, and 28 stolen bases (in 37 attempts) during his second stint in Triple-A two years ago. Last season, splitting between both organizations' Triple-A affiliates (plus a three-game rehab assignment in High-A), Waters hit .269/.345/.460 with 13 doubles, five triples, and a career best 13 homeruns. He also swiped 18 bags in only 19 attempts. Per *Weighted Runs Created Plus*, his overall production topped the league average mark by 13%. Kansas City called him up to The Show at the end of August. He promptly slugged .240/.324/.479 with 12 extra-base knocks in only 32 games.

Snippet from The 2020 Prospect Digest Handbook: Waters is giving off some major Drew Stubbs vibes. But for that happen, though, he's going to have to show more power and cut down on his 56% groundball rate.

Scouting Report: Maybe all he needed was a change of scenery? Sure, but it's doubtful. Waters went from hitting .246/.305/.393 in 49 games in Triple-A with the Braves' affiliate to slugging .295/.399/.541 in 31 games with KC's top minor league team. And that doesn't include his successful debut in the big leagues either. In all actuality, though, it's likely just luck. Waters hasn't been able to solve his swing-and-miss issues, but he owns enough power and speed to help buoy his value. He's likely to get a couple extended cracks at the club's starting centerfield gig as they rebuild / re-tool. Fringy, low-end starting caliber potential.

Ceiling: 1.5-win player
Risk: Moderate
MLB ETA: 2022

Kansas City Royals

12. Luca Tresh, C

Hit	Power	SB	Patience	Glove	Overall
40	55	30	55	45/50	45

Born: 01/11/00	Age: 23	Bats: R	Top Production Comp: N/A
Height: 6-0	Weight: 193	Throws: R	

Season	Team	Age	Level	PA	1B	2B	3B	HR	SB	CS	BB%	K%	AVG	OBP	SLG	ISO
2021	KCR	21	CPX	19	3	3	0	1	0	0	5.26%	21.05%	0.389	0.421	0.722	0.333
2021	KCR	21	A	39	4	1	0	0	0	0	10.26%	28.21%	0.143	0.231	0.171	0.029
2022	KCR	22	A+	347	52	15	1	14	3	3	11.82%	24.50%	0.273	0.360	0.470	0.197
2022	KCR	22	AA	106	14	4	0	5	1	0	12.26%	23.58%	0.253	0.358	0.462	0.209

Background: The Royals scouting department did their due diligence on the little-used backstop out of North Carolina State. And they were right. Locked behind eventually first rounder Patrick Bailey during his first two seasons, Tresh finally got a stranglehold on the Wolfpack's catching duties in 2021. And the results were a mixed bag. The 6-foot, 193-pound Florida native batted a disappointing .231/.310/.476 but slugged nine doubles, a triple, and 15 homeruns in 56 games. Kansas City took a 17th round flier on Tresh, signing the 499th overall pick to a deal worth $423,000. It was the largest bonus handed out in the 17th round that summer and it's the equivalent to an early fifth round pick. After a brief jaunt through the lower levels two years ago, the front office deemed the power-hitting, questionable hit-tooled backstop ready for High-A. And he was. Tresh bashed .273/.360/.470 in 80 games with Quad Cities. And he continued hitting in a 24-game cameo in Double-A, the minors' toughest test. Tresh finished his first full season with an aggregate .269/.360/.468 slash line with 19 doubles, one triple, 19 homeruns, and four stolen bases. His production topped the league average mark by 25%, per to *Weighted Runs Created Plus*.

Scouting Report: Consider the following:

> Since 2006, only two 22-year-old hitters posted a 125 to 135 wRC+ with a 10% to 13% walk rate and a 23.5% to 25.5% strikeout rate in any High-A league (min. 300 PA): Peyton Wilson, the Royals' second round pick in 2021, and Luca Tresh, the former 17th round pick the same year.

An offensive-minded backstop that relies heavily upon his ability / skill to give the ball a jolt, Tresh is a slightly below-average defender. The power, though, is above-average teetering on plus. Tresh has a potential Three True Outcomes slant to his offensive game, walking more than 10% of the time to go along with mid-20% strikeout rates. He's as valuable as long as he bashing the baseball on regular basis.

Ceiling: 1.0- to 1.5-win player
Risk: Moderate
MLB ETA: 2024

13. Peyton Wilson, 2B/CF

Hit	Power	SB	Patience	Glove	Overall
50	50	60	50	45/50	45

Born: 11/01/99	Age: 23	Bats: B	Top Production Comp: N/A
Height: 5-9	Weight: 180	Throws: R	

Season	Team	Age	Level	PA	1B	2B	3B	HR	SB	CS	BB%	K%	AVG	OBP	SLG	ISO
2021	KCR	21	A	46	5	3	1	0	5	0	8.70%	21.74%	0.231	0.326	0.359	0.128
2022	KCR	22	A+	390	58	16	3	14	23	2	10.51%	24.87%	0.268	0.359	0.456	0.188

Background: The younger brother of former Alabama quarterback John Parker Wilson, an undrafted free agent of the Atlanta Falcons, Peyton Wilson, nonetheless, was able to separate himself from one of the most prolific passer's in the Tide's history. The Royals selected the pint-sized second baseman / centerfielder in the second round of the 2021 draft, 66th overall, and signed him to a deal worth a smidgeon north of $1 million. Wilson left the SEC-based school as a .295/.360/.457 hitter in 70 career games. The 5-foot-9, 180-pound infielder / outfielder hopped straight into High-A in 2022 after a very brief debut the year before. Appearing in 88 games with the Quad Cities River Bandits, Wilson batted .268/.359/.456 with 16 doubles, three triples, 14 homeruns, and 23 stolen bases (in 25 total attempts). Per *Weighted Runs Created Plus*, his overall production topped the league average mark by 28%.

Snippet from The 2022 Prospect Digest Handbook: A good, not great collegiate bat during his first full season of action. Wilson did everything well without owning a true standout tool other than defensive versatility. The diminutive infielder/former backstop looks like a super sub if everything breaks the right way. But he doesn't figure to walk much, so the hit tool is going to have to carry him.

Scouting Report: Consider the following:

> Since 2006, only five 22-year-old hitters posted a 123 to 133 wRC+ with a double-digit walk rate and a 24% to 26% K-rate in any High-A league (min. 350 PA): Kyle Kubitza, Ryan Casteel, Eric Jagielo, Joe DeCarlo, and Peyton Wilson.

Kansas City Royals

Wilson got off to frigid start to the year, hitting a lowly .178/.257/.307 over his first 27 games. After that, though, he batted an impressive .305/.401/.519 over his remaining 61 contests. Kansas City continued Wilson's experiment in centerfield last season, and the results were decent. If he can continue the momentum moving into Double-A, Wilson may be able to carve out a low end starting gig.

Ceiling: 1.0- to 1.5-win player
Risk: Moderate
MLB ETA: 2023/2024

14. T.J. Sikkema, LHP

FB	SL	CH	Command	Overall
45	55	55	55	40

| **Born:** 07/25/98 | **Age:** 24 | **Bats:** L | **Top Production Comp:** N/A |
| **Height:** 6-0 | **Weight:** 221 | **Throws:** L | |

Season	Team	Age	Level	IP	TBF	K/9	K%	BB/9	BB%	K-BB%	ERA	FIP	xFIP	Pit/Bat
2019	NYY	20	A-	10.2	40	10.97	32.50%	0.84	2.50%	30.00%	0.84	1.53	2.09	3.68
2022	NYY	23	A+	36.1	142	13.38	38.03%	2.23	6.34%	31.69%	2.48	3.00	2.82	3.99
2022	KCR	23	AA	32.2	155	7.99	18.71%	4.13	9.68%	9.03%	7.44	6.02	5.07	3.61

Background: Let's start from the beginning – sort of. Sikkema began his collegiate career as a multi-inning reliever / rare spot-starter for the Missouri Tigers. He would eventually transition into the school's rotation in 2018, and he missed a lot of bats and threw a ton of strikes. That summer he shredded the Cape Cod League lumber to the tune of 23 strikeouts, eight walks, and a 1.72 ERA in 31.1 innings with the Falmouth Commodores. And, believe it or not, Sikkema posted an even better ERA (1.32) across 88.2 innings during his junior campaign. The Yankees grabbed the portly left-hander in the opening round, 38th overall, and let him loose on the old New York-Penn League as he allowed one earned run with 13 strikeouts and just one walk in 10.2 innings of work. Then the pandemic hit and he was forced to miss the 2020 season. Then lat and shoulder injuries kept him on the sidelines for the entirety of 2021. New York sent the once promising southpaw up to High-A for the start of last season. And the 6-foot, 221-pound hurler dominated in 11 brief appearances with the Hudson Valley Renegades, recording a 54-to-9 strikeout-to-walk in 36.1 innings. Kansas City acquired him, along with Beck Way, at the end of July for veteran outfielder Andrew Benintendi. The Royals promptly pushed Sikkema straight into the fires of Double-A. And he was *torched*: 7.44 ERA, 29 K, 15 BB, 32.2 IP.

Scouting Report: The very essence of a Royals pitching prospect. Sikkema was destined to throw for the organization at some point in his professional career. Soft-tossing, crafty left-hander with a below-average 89- to 90-mph fastball, an above-average sweeping slider, and a 55-grade changeup. Sikkema's the Tim Tebow of minor league hurlers with an arm action long enough to scratch the middle of back during his throwing motion. Like several of the club's "top" pitching prospects, Sikkema is a future bullpen candidate – but he's going to make millions of dollars as a lefty specialist. He held left-handers to a .101/.244/.130 mark last season.

Ceiling: 1.0-win player
Risk: Low to Moderate
MLB ETA: 2023/2024

15. Diego Hernandez, CF

Hit	Power	SB	Patience	Glove	Overall
45	40	60	50	50/55	40

| **Born:** 11/21/00 | **Age:** 22 | **Bats:** L | **Top Production Comp:** N/A |
| **Height:** 6-0 | **Weight:** 150 | **Throws:** L | |

Season	Team	Age	Level	PA	1B	2B	3B	HR	SB	CS	BB%	K%	AVG	OBP	SLG	ISO
2021	KCR	20	A	310	61	9	2	1	34	10	10.32%	21.29%	0.274	0.355	0.335	0.060
2022	KCR	21	A+	371	64	17	4	7	27	8	7.28%	19.41%	0.279	0.343	0.418	0.139
2022	KCR	21	AA	141	31	4	0	2	13	4	8.51%	19.86%	0.298	0.357	0.379	0.081

Background: The biggest international free agent the club signed in 2017 – at least in terms of signing bonus. Kansas City inked the Santo Domingo native to a deal worth $200,000. The 6-foot, 150-pound outfielder would make his professional debut the following summer as he appeared in just 10 games in his home country with the club's rookie league affiliate. He did manage to bat .325/.391/.375 with a triple in 40 at bats. Kansas City bounced the toolsy centerfielder stateside the following year and he put together a decent slash line (.278/.319/.330) in 42 games. After minor league baseball returned to action following its COVID-imposed hiatus, Hernandez spent the majority of 2021 mired in mediocrity with the Fireflies of Columbia. He hit .274/.355/.335 with nine doubles, two triples, one homerun, and 34 stolen bases (in 44 attempts). Truth be told, Hernandez was tracking like a fifth outfielder – at best – at that point in his career. But the young Dominican outfielder morphed into a more consistent, viable threat at the dish last season. Appearing in 115 total games between Quad Cities and Northwest Arkansas, Hernandez slashed .284/.347/.408 with career bests in doubles (21), triples (four), homeruns (nine), and stolen bases (40). Per *Weighted Runs Created Plus*, his overall production topped the league average mark by 7%.

Kansas City Royals

Scouting Report: Consider the following:

> Since 2006, only two 21-year-old hitters met the following criteria in any High-A league (min. 350 PA): 108 to 118 wRC+, 18.5% to 20.5% strikeout rate with a 6.5% to 8.5% walk rate. Those two hitters: Jake Cave and Diego Hernandez.

Once a well above-average defender in the outfield, Hernandez's leather-work has quietly regressed over the past couple years as his body's matured. And his defensive value is somewhere between average and below-average in centerfield. One of the largest developments for him last season, beyond the addition of a little bit of pop, is his work against fellow lefties – which has typically been a black hole for him in the past. Average-ish peripherals, Hernandez's thump has crept up from a 30- to a 40-grade. It's still below-average but he can at least reach the warning track nowadays. Pull hitter that tends to hit off of his front foot frequently. Plus speed. Hernandez is now tracking like a fourth outfielder.

Ceiling: 1.0-win player
Risk: Moderate
MLB ETA: 2024

16. Noah Cameron, LHP

FB	CB	CH	Command	Overall
50	50/55	60	55	40

Born: 06/17/99	Age: 23	Bats: L	Top Production Comp: N/A
Height: 6-3	Weight: 220	Throws: L	

Season	Team	Age	Level	IP	TBF	K/9	K%	BB/9	BB%	K-BB%	ERA	FIP	xFIP	Pit/Bat
2022	KCR	22	A	29.0	116	12.10	33.62%	2.79	7.76%	25.86%	3.72	3.43	2.95	3.94
2022	KCR	22	A+	31.0	128	15.39	41.41%	2.03	5.47%	35.94%	3.48	1.77	2.12	4.17

Background: The 2020 season, which was cut short by the COVID pandemic, prematurely curtailed a seemingly endless number of potentially special seasons. Take, for example, University of Central Arkansas southpaw Noah Cameron. A stocky 6-foot-3, 220-pound hurler from Missouri, Cameron was nearly unhittable during his four-game campaign with the Bears, posting a 31-to-2 strikeout-to-walk ratio in 28.0 innings. But things went from bad to worse for the budding collegiate ace. A wonky elbow would eventually force him to undergo Tommy John surgery and he would miss the entirety of 2021. Still, though, the Royals took a seventh round flier on Cameron and – eventually – convinced him to join the organization for $197,500. The former Central Arkansas ace made his return to the mound – as well as his professional debut – last season, making 19 starts between the Complex League, Columbia, and Quad Cities. He tossed 65.2 innings, posting an absurdly dominant 99-to-16 strikeout-to-walk ratio to go along with an aggregate 3.56 ERA. A shoulder injury forced him out for the entire month of July.

Scouting Report: The initial returns on the club's modest investment are already proving to be better than expected. However, like a lot of the club's other top pitching prospects, Cameron's ceiling is limited with a high floor. A crafty left-hander with an average fastball and curveball combination, Cameron's main go-to offering his is plus changeup. His deuce shows late bite, so it wouldn't be surprising to see hitters struggle to square it up. Above-average command, which extends back to his collegiate days, he didn't show any negative signs from his extended layoff. Cameron owns a #5-type ceiling as long as he can fill the zone up and successfully change speeds.

Ceiling: 1.0-win player
Risk: Moderate
MLB ETA: 2024

17. Ben Hernandez, RHP

FB	CB	CH	Command	Overall
50	55	60	35/40	40

Born: 07/01/01	Age: 21	Bats: R	Top Production Comp: N/A
Height: 6-2	Weight: 205	Throws: R	

Season	Team	Age	Level	IP	TBF	K/9	K%	BB/9	BB%	K-BB%	ERA	FIP	xFIP	Pit/Bat
2021	KCR	19	A	31.1	139	8.90	22.30%	4.88	12.23%	10.07%	4.31	4.84	5.05	3.93
2022	KCR	20	A	77.0	350	8.30	20.29%	4.68	11.43%	8.86%	5.38	5.09	5.01	3.91

Background: The only high school player the front office selected during their five-round, COVID-limited 2020 draft class. Hernandez starred at Chicago-based De La Salle Institute as he became just the fourth player in school history to get drafted. The 6-foot-2, 205-pound right-hander, who signed for $1.45 million, would make his debut the following summer with the Fireflies of Columbia. An undisclosed injury limited the former second rounder to just 35.1 innings spread across 12 brief starts. So it's not surprising that the organization bounced Hernandez back down to Columbia for another crack at Low-A – though the results were remarkably similar. Hernandez averaged 8.3 strikeouts and 4.7 walks per nine innings across 23 starts (77 IP). He finished with a 5.38 ERA, a 5.09 FIP, and a 5.01 xFIP.

Kansas City Royals

Snippet from The 2022 Prospect Digest Handbook: Hernandez is quite raw, often battling control/command issues and was prone to bouts of wildness during his abbreviate debut. There's a lot to like here. And Kansas City has proven that they can develop arms well. I wouldn't be shocked to see him among the club's best prospects in a year.

Scouting Report: Consider the following:

> Since 2006, only four 20-year-old hurlers posted a 19.5% to 21.5% strikeout percentage with a 10.5% to 12.5% walk percentage in any Low-A league (min. 75 IP): Justin Steele, Edgar Olmos, Luis Morel, and Ben Hernandez.

Not only did Hernandez fail to ascend to one of the club's best prospects, as I postulated prior to last season, but his once plus fastball lost considerable oompf. Once touching as high as 98 mph, according to reports, Hernandez's fastball was operating in the 89- to 91-mph range during a late season start I scouted. The former second round has a weird, inconsistent arm slot that not only makes it difficult to throw strikes, but I think it's holding his velocity back as well. It's a low, slinging motion that he – sometimes – short-arms. His curveball is still an above-average hammer, the changeup is still plus. But he's 35-command guy with an average-ish fastball. Not a recipe for long term success.

Ceiling: 1.0-win player
Risk: Moderate
MLB ETA: 2025

18. Beck Way, RHP

FB	CB	SL	CH	Command	Overall
50	40	50	50	50	40

Born: 08/06/99	Age: 23	Bats: R	Top Production Comp: N/A
Height: 6-4	Weight: 200	Throws: R	

Season	Team	Age	Level	IP	TBF	K/9	K%	BB/9	BB%	K-BB%	ERA	FIP	xFIP	Pit/Bat
2021	NYY	21	A	47.0	195	10.34	27.69%	5.55	14.87%	12.82%	2.68	4.29	4.44	3.91
2021	NYY	21	A+	16.1	75	15.98	38.67%	4.96	12.00%	26.67%	7.71	4.62	3.14	4.15
2022	NYY	22	A+	72.1	290	9.95	27.59%	3.24	8.97%	18.62%	3.73	4.31	3.80	3.87
2022	KCR	22	A+	35.2	153	11.86	30.72%	4.29	11.11%	19.61%	3.79	3.15	3.92	3.95

Background: The front office brass played the game perfectly. They bought low on Andrew Benintendi, the former seventh overall pick who was coming off of a disappointing 2019 season and a horrific 14-game stint in 2020. The cost: Franchy Cordero, Khalil Lee, Luis De La Rosa, and Grant Gambell. Roughly 17 months later Kansas City turned around and dealt a resurgent Andrew Benintendi for Chandler Champlain, T.J. Sikkema, and Beck Way. The kicker: Boston and New York paid a combined $6.07 million of Benintendi's $15.1 million salary. And one more final note: Benintendi bolted the Yankees for significantly greener pastures of Chicago, signing with the White Sox for a five-year, $75 million deal – the largest in team history. New York selected Beck in the fourth round of the 2020 MLB draft out of Northwest Florida State College, a JuCo. Way would make his debut the following season, throwing 63.1 innings between the Yankees' Low-A and High-A affiliates, recording an 83-to-38 strikeout-to-walk ratio. Last season, splitting time between both organizations' High-A affiliates, Way struck out 127 and walked 43 in a career best 108.0 innings pitched. He finished the year with an aggregate 3.75 ERA and a 3.92 FIP.

Scouting Report: Average across the board. Way's a boring pitching prospect without a notable offering. Various reports indicated that the former fourth round pick would be pumping mid-90s heat, but that was hardly the case during the two starts I scouted as his fastball failed to miss many bats and looked average. His main weapon is an average slider. And he'll mix in an average changeup. It also looked like he was working on a cutter of sorts, but it's raw and – well – not good. It's distinctive from his slider in shape and velo (and the catcher uses a different sign). It's bad. The Royals seem to be collecting just mediocre pitching prospects. And Beck's the epitome.

Ceiling: 1.0-win player
Risk: Moderate
MLB ETA: 2024

19. Alec Marsh, RHP

FB	CB	SL	CH	Command	Overall
50	60	50	55	40	40

Born: 05/14/98	Age: 25	Bats: R	Top Production Comp: N/A
Height: 6-2	Weight: 220	Throws: R	

Season	Team	Age	Level	IP	TBF	K/9	K%	BB/9	BB%	K-BB%	ERA	FIP	xFIP	Pit/Bat
2021	KCR	23	AA	25.1	106	14.92	39.62%	4.62	12.26%	27.36%	4.97	3.87	3.15	4.16
2022	KCR	24	AA	114.1	536	11.57	27.43%	4.25	10.07%	17.35%	7.32	5.83	4.75	3.90
2022	KCR	24	AAA	10.0	43	8.10	20.93%	4.50	11.63%	9.30%	1.80	4.81	5.66	3.81

Background: After a bit of disappointing first season at Arizona State University, Marsh developed into a mediocre prospect during his sophomore season in 2018 as he posted a 64-to-31 strikeout-to-walk ratio in 71.2 innings. But his domination in the Cape Cod League that summer opened *a lot* of eyes: he struck out 20 and walked just six in 11.1 innings with the Yarmouth-Dennis Red Sox. Marsh wouldn't be able to repeat that level of production during his junior campaign – but he did turn in his finest collegiate season, averaging 8.8 strikeouts and 3.2 walks per nine innings across 16 starts and one relief appearance. Kansas City would take the hard-throwing Sun Devil in the second round four years ago, 70th overall, and signed him to a deal worth just $904,300. Marsh squeezed in 33.1 innings of dominance in the Pioneer League that summer, but was forced to miss the entire 2020 season due to the pandemic. Then we would lose the majority of 2021 due to a bicep issue. So the fact that the 6-foot-2, 220-pound right-hander was (A) able to log 124.1 innings and (B) make the 2022 Futures Team squad is a win in itself. Marsh finished with 156 punch outs, 59 walks, and a bloated 6.88 ERA in 27 starts between Double-A and Triple-A.

Snippet from The 2022 Prospect Digest Handbook: He was a typical power-pitcher's build – big, burly, barrel-chested. Great pickoff move. There's obvious reliever risk due to the 40-grade command – and that was before the loss of 2021. He's a name to watch though.

Scouting Report: Consider the following:

> Since 2006, only two 24-year-old hurlers posted a 26.5% to 28.5% strikeout percentage with a 9% to 11% walk percentage in any Double-A league (min. 100 IP): Alan Rangel and Alec Marsh.

It's a backend starter's arsenal: a 91- to 94-mph fastball, an upper-70s plus curveball, an average slider, and an above-average, tumbling changeup. The problem, of course, is his 40-grade command – which hasn't improved since entering pro ball. Marsh may get a crack at a fifth spot in a rotation, but he's going to end up as a middle relief option.

Ceiling: 0.5- to 1.0-win player
Risk: Moderate
MLB ETA: 2023

20. Mason Barnett, RHP

FB	CB	SL	CH	Command	Overall
55	50/55	55	N/A	40	40

Born: 11/07/00	Age: 22	Bats: R	Top Production Comp: N/A
Height: 6-0	Weight: 218	Throws: R	

Background: The 6-foot, 218-pound right-hander was a stout two-way performer during his time at Cartersville High School. Barnett was named as the 2017 All-County Pitcher of the Year after his junior campaign, and then captured the 2018 All-County Hitter of the Year award as a senior. Barnett was able to squeeze in six appearances with the Auburn Tigers as a true freshman, despite the pandemic prematurely ending the year. He posted an absurd 16-to-3 strikeout-to-walk ratio in only 7.2 innings of work. Barnett split time between the SEC Conference School's rotation and bullpen in 2021, making six starts and 10 relief appearances, throwing 40.0 innings with 43 punch outs and 21 free passes to go along with a 5.40 ERA. The Georgia native spent the summer with the Brewster Whitecaps, averaging 10.4 strikeouts and just 2.7 walks per nine innings. His final campaign with the Tigers, though, was a rollercoaster of mixed results: he tossed a career best 63.2 innings and averaged a phenomenal 11.7 K/9 but continued to battle command / control demons (4.5 BB/9). Kansas City selected him in the third round, 87th overall, and signed him to a deal worth $697,500. Mason twirled 8.0 innings during his debut, fanning 12 and walking one. He did not allow an earned run.

Scouting Report: Low- to mid-90s fastball. Big bending, beauty of a curveball that flashes above-average at times. A 55-grade horizontally-darting slider with late movement that avoids the fat part of the bat. He'll also mix in a changeup, though I didn't see one. His curveball is very reminiscent of Guardians lights out, wacky reliever James Karinchak. The problem for Barnett is that everything about him screams future reliever: max effort hurler, below-average command, stocky build. Kansas City will give him a couple years to carve out a spot in the rotation, but he's ultimately going to slide into a relief role. He does have a history – albeit a brief one – of throwing more strikes in relief.

Ceiling: 0.5- to 1.0-win player
Risk: Moderate
MLB ETA: 2025

Kansas City Royals

Los Angeles Angels

Top Prospects

Los Angeles Angels

1. Edgar Quero, C

Hit	Power	SB	Patience	Glove	Overall
55	60	50/40	60	50/55	65

Born: 04/06/03	Age: 19	Bats: B	Top Production Comp: Francisco Alvarez
Height: 5-11	Weight: 170	Throws: R	

Season	Team	Age	Level	PA	1B	2B	3B	HR	SB	CS	BB%	K%	AVG	OBP	SLG	ISO
2021	LAA	18	CPX	116	9	8	1	4	1	1	19.83%	24.14%	0.253	0.440	0.506	0.253
2021	LAA	18	A	42	4	2	0	1	1	0	11.90%	38.10%	0.206	0.310	0.353	0.147
2022	LAA	19	A	515	75	35	2	17	12	5	14.17%	17.67%	0.312	0.435	0.530	0.218

Background: The Angels have invested serious chunks of money on the international free agency market in recent history, but one of the club's small bonuses handed out two years ago is making the largest impact. A native of Cienfuegos, Cuba, Quero agreed to join the Halos' organization for $200,000 prior to the start of the 2021 season. And he's been a revelation ever since. The 5-foot-11, 170-pound backstop ripped through the Arizona Complex League during his professional debut that summer, hitting .256/.440/.506 with 13 extra-base knocks, before earning a late-season promotion up to Inland Empire. The front office kept the then-19-year-old catcher back in Low-A for a full-season crack at the league's pitching. And he dominated. Quero mashed .312/.435/.530 with 35 doubles, two triples, 17 homeruns, and 12 stolen bases. Per *Weighted Runs Created Plus*, his overall production topped the league average mark by 50%.

Snippet from The 2022 Prospect Digest Handbook: Another of the club's better prospects that simply didn't get in a ton of playing in 2021. Really like the swing from both sides of the plate. Above-average bat speed, natural loft to belt out 15 to 20 homeruns. And, perhaps most importantly, Quero shows a strong ability to work the count and doesn't give away at bats. He's a good athlete and shows a bit of speed on the base paths as well. He's the type of athlete that would be able to move to second or third bases without much trouble.

Scouting Report: Consider the following:

> Since 2006, only four 19-year-old hitters posted at a wRC+ total between 145 and 155 with a sub-20% strikeout rate in a season in Low-A (min. 400 PA): Luis Arraez, Alek Thomas, Alen Hanson, and – of course – Edgar Quero.

At this point it's probably easier to list what the young phenom *can't do*. And, well, there's nothing on the list. Quero's a (A) switch-hitter with no platoon splits, (B) hits for average, (C) hits for power, (D) runs well – especially for a catcher, (E) works the count, (F) gets on base, and (G) plays strong defense. He may eventually creep into the same of talent as Francisco Alvarez, Endy Rodriguez, and Diego Cartaya. Incredible bat speed, among the best in the system, with easy plus power. He's going to be a consensus Top 10 prospect within in a year. The Angels haven't had a dominant bat behind the dish since Mike Napoli. Now the system has two premium options in Quero and Logan O'Hoppe.

Ceiling: 4.0-win player
Risk: Moderate
MLB ETA: 2024/2025

2. Logan O'Hoppe, C

Hit	Power	SB	Patience	Glove	Overall
50	55	30	45	55	60

Born: 02/09/00	Age: 22	Bats: R	Top Production Comp: J.T. Realmuto
Height: 6-2	Weight: 185	Throws: R	

Season	Team	Age	Level	PA	1B	2B	3B	HR	SB	CS	BB%	K%	AVG	OBP	SLG	ISO
2019	PHI	19	A-	177	16	12	2	5	3	0	6.78%	27.68%	0.216	0.266	0.407	0.191
2021	PHI	21	A+	358	54	17	2	13	6	3	8.38%	17.60%	0.270	0.335	0.459	0.189
2021	PHI	21	AA	57	12	1	0	3	0	0	1.75%	15.79%	0.296	0.333	0.481	0.185
2021	PHI	21	AAA	23	2	1	0	1	0	0	8.70%	17.39%	0.190	0.261	0.381	0.190
2022	PHI	22	AA	316	45	11	1	15	6	2	12.97%	16.46%	0.275	0.392	0.496	0.221
2022	LAA	22	AA	131	16	3	0	11	1	2	22.14%	16.79%	0.306	0.473	0.673	0.367

Background: It was one of the more intriguing – almost out of nowhere – deals at the deadline last summer with the Angels agreeing to send struggling former top prospect Brandon Marsh to the Phillies for prospect Logan O'Hoppe. And the initial results look promising for both organizations. Marsh, a 2016 second round pick, benefitted from a change of scenery as he slugged .288/.319/.455 in 41 games in Philadelphia and he stayed hot during the club's deep playoff run. And O'Hoppe looked Ruthian in his month-long stint with the Angels' Double-A club and briefly made his Major League debut. The 6-foot-2, 185-pound backstop, who was a 23rd round pick by the Phillies in 2018, hit an aggregate .283/.416/.544 with 14 doubles, one triple, 26 homeruns, and – surprisingly – seven stolen bases. His overall production with both club's Double-A affiliates was a whopping 59% better than the league average, per *Weighted Runs Created Plus*.

Snippet from The 2022 Prospect Digest Handbook: One of the most underrated catching prospects in the minor leagues. O'Hoppe offers up some interesting, tantalizing potential as a power-oriented backstop who won't kill a team on defense. And, perhaps, the best news: he makes consistent contact. I think there's 20- to 25-homer pop brewing in the bat.

Los Angeles Angels

Scouting Report: Just how good was O'Hoppe's bat last season? His 159 wRC+ ranked second among all qualified Double-A bats (trailing only Mets top prospect Brett Baty) and the sixth best production line in all of the minors' (among hitter with at least 300 PA). Despite his late round draft status, O'Hoppe has always flashed tremendous offensive potential and it – finally – came to fruition last summer. An absolute grinder on both sides of the ball, O'Hoppe has the makings of a potential All-Star caliber backstop. And he's shown a new plus skill: working the count thanks to his improved eye. Great looking swing with impressive bat speed, O'Hoppe stands tall but crouches as the pitcher begins his approach towards the plate. Defensively, he may win a Gold Glove or two. In terms of upside, think .270/.340/.480.

Ceiling: 4.0-win player
Risk: Moderate
MLB ETA: Debuted in 2022

3. Zach Neto, SS

Hit	Power	SB	Patience	Glove	Overall
55	50	50	50	50	60

Born: 01/31/01	Age: 22	Bats: R	Top Production Comp: Jung Ho Kang
Height: 6-0	Weight: 185	Throws: R	

Season	Team	Age	Level	PA	1B	2B	3B	HR	SB	CS	BB%	K%	AVG	OBP	SLG	ISO
2022	LAA	21	A+	31	3	0	1	1	1	0	12.90%	12.90%	0.200	0.355	0.400	0.200
2022	LAA	21	AA	136	26	9	0	4	4	2	5.88%	21.32%	0.320	0.382	0.492	0.172

Background: Miami Coral Park Senior High School has a surprisingly long list of famous alums, including ballplayers Jose Canseco, Ozzie Canseco, Orestes Destrade, Steve Foucault, Pete Gonzalez, Luis Montanez, Sean Rodriguez, and Eric Soderholm. And that's not including other celebrities like Pedro Gomez, the beloved ESPN reporter who passed away in 2021; Elsa Murano, the 23rd President of Texas A&M; Alex Marvez, former President of the Pro Football Writers of America; Steven Reinemund, the former Chairman of the Board and CEO of Pepsico; and – of course – Mr. World Wide, Pitbull. Zach Neto, a 6-foot, 190-pound, was a phenomenal two-way player during his time at Miami Coral Park Senior High School, earning: All-District Team nominations three times, Second Team All-American as a junior, HSBN Senior All-Star Game MVP, and 2019 Senior All-Star Public Team. After a bit of a slow start to his collegiate career, Neto, who earned just six plate appearances and a brief start on the mound, had a massive breakout campaign for the Campbell Fighting Camels during his sophomore season. In 44 games, the young shortstop / right-handed reliever batted .405/.488/.746 with 17 doubles, three triples, 12 homeruns, and 12 stolen bases while posting a 3.43 ERA in 21.0 innings of work. Neto moved into the Cape Cod League that summer and continued to rake, slugging .304/.439/.587 against some of the best collegiate arms. Last season the redshirt sophomore continued to manhandle the competition to the tune of .407/.514/.769 with career bests in doubles (23), homeruns (15), and stolen bases (19). He also made four relief appearances for the Big South Conference squad, striking out eight and walking three in 4.2 innings of work. The Halos selected Neto in the opening round, 13th overall, and signed him to a deal worth $3.5 million. Los Angeles briefly sent their first rounder to High-A, but after seven games they bumped him up to the minors' toughest challenge – Double-A – for the remainder of the season. The former Camel star slugged an aggregate .299/.377/.476 with nine doubles, one triple, five homeruns and five stolen bases.

Scouting Report: Per the usual, here's Neto's pre-draft write-up:

> "Consider the following:
>
> Since 2011, here's the list of Division I hitters to bat at least .400/.500/.700 with a 2-to-1 walk-to-strikeout ratio in a season (min. 250 PA): Adley Rutschman, the first overall pick in 2019; Andrew Vaughn, the third overall pick the same year; and – of course – Zach Neto, the Campbell University star.
>
> One of the largest knocks on Neto is his level of competition: the Big South Conference will never be confused with the likes of the SEC or Big 12 or ACC or Pac 21. So Neto's statistical domination with the Fighting Camels will always be viewed with some level of skepticism. Except that he dominated the Cape Cod League by slugging .304/.439/.587 with a one-to-one strikeout-to-walk ratio. Neto's leg kick is a cross between late-career Darryl Strawberry and Sadaharu Oh. It's a massive leg kick, almost like he's going through a pitcher's windup, not reading himself to hit. Neto has a chance for an above-average hit tool, 50-grade pop, speed, and the defensive chops to stick at shortstop."

Ceiling: 4.0-win player
Risk: Moderate
MLB ETA: 2024

Los Angeles Angels

4. Nelson Rada, CF

Hit	Power	SB	Patience	Glove	Overall
40/50	30/55	55	50	50/55	55

Born: 08/24/05	Age: 17	Bats: L	Top Production Comp: N/A
Height: 5-10	Weight: 160	Throws: R	

Season	Team	Age	Level	PA	1B	2B	3B	HR	SB	CS	BB%	K%	AVG	OBP	SLG	ISO
2022	LAA	16	DSL	206	35	12	3	1	27	6	12.62%	12.62%	0.311	0.446	0.439	0.128

Background: Like a lot of the other up-the-middle Top 20 prospects in the Angels' farm system, Rada was handed a hefty seven-figure bonus off the international free agency scene – nearly $2 million, to be precise. A native of Valencia, Venezuela, Rada turned in an impressive showing in the foreign rookie leagues last summer, slugging .311/.446/.439 with 12 doubles, three triples, one homeruns, and 27 stolen bases (in 33 total attempts). His overall production, per *Weighted Runs Created*, his overall production topped the Dominican Summer League average by a whopping 48%. Oh, by the way, he was just 16-years-old, among the youngest prospects in any level of the game.

Scouting Report: Consider the following:

> Since 2006, there have been eighty-eight 16-year-old hitters that earned at least 200 plate appearances in any foreign rookie leagues. Of those 88, Nelson Rada's overall production, 148 wRC+, ranks as the sixth best. The five hitters that topped Rada's production line – Alexander Mojica, Rayne Santana, Eguy Rosario, Moises Gomez, and Michael De La Cruz – all had a worse contact rate than Rada.

Really good looking swing, particularly from a baby-faced 16-year-old. There's a lot of maturity in his mechanics, very controlled with great rotation. Rada – clearly – is still a project / lottery ticket at this point. But there's a lot, *a lot* of potential to turn into an impact hitter in the coming years. Great bat speed with natural loft that projects for above-average pop. He made consistent contact during his stint in the DSL and – more importantly – his production wasn't solely based on high walk rates (which is common for the level). Don't be surprised if he pops up as a Top 100 prospect in two years.

Ceiling: 3.0-win player
Risk: High
MLB ETA: 2025

5. Chase Silseth, RHP

FB	CB	SL	SF	Command	Overall
60	45/50	55	60	55	50

Born: 05/18/00	Age: 23	Bats: R	Top Production Comp: Early Career Kevin Gausman
Height: 6-0	Weight: 217	Throws: R	

Season	Team	Age	Level	IP	TBF	K/9	K%	BB/9	BB%	K-BB%	ERA	FIP	xFIP	Pit/Bat
2022	LAA	22	AA	83.0	320	11.93	34.38%	2.93	8.44%	25.94%	2.28	3.78	3.26	3.92

Background: The list of viable big leaguers the organization has drafted since 2013 is fairly small: Sean Newcomb (2014), David Fletcher (2015), Taylor Ward (2015), Jared Walsh (2015), former top prospect Brandon Marsh (2016), Griffin Canning (2017), and Reid Detmers (2020). And if the 2015 draft class is ignored, the franchise's lack of big leaguers stings like stubbed toe. But for all the front office(s) shortcomings, the ball club not only unearthed a viable pitching prospect in Chase Silseth, but they did so in latter parts of the 2021 draft with a pitcher that was rather abysmal during his collegiate career. Mainly a relief option during his freshman season with the Tennessee Volunteers, Silseth posted a 4.35 ERA in 20.2 innings of work, recording a stout 24-to-6 strikeout-to-walk ratio. The 6-foot, 217-pound right-hander would transfer to the College of Southern Nevada and then eventually on to the University of Arizona – where he would spend his final amateur season in the Wildcats' rotation posting a 5.55 ERA with solid peripherals (9.7 K/9 and 2.7 BB/9) in 18 starts. Los Angeles would draft him in the 11th round, 321st overall, and sign him to a deal worth $485,000. Then after a quick debut in the Complex League, the organization promptly bumped him up to Rocket City for two brief starts. Five more starts in Double-A in 2022 and – somehow? – Silseth was up in the big leagues shutting out the Oakland A's for six innings. He would yo-yo between the minors' toughest level, AA, and the game's pinnacle level, MLB, for the remainder of the year. Silseth would throw 83.0 innings with Rocket City, averaging 11.9 strikeouts and just 2.9 walks per nine innings. He tossed another 28.2 innings of work with the Angels, recording a 24-to-12 strikeout-to-walk ratio.

Scouting Report: Consider the following:

> Since 2006, only four 22-year-old hurlers have posted a strikeout rate north of 33% in any Double-A league in one season (min. 75 IP): Clay Buchholz, Jose De Leon, Reese Olson, and – of course – 2021 11th round pick Chase Silseth.

A vastly superior arsenal than you'd expect given his late round draft status, Silseth attacks hitters with a plus mid-90s fastball, reaching as high as 97 mph a few times during his final start of the year. He backs that up with a trio of offspeed pitches. He'll throw a rare upper 70s curveball that is fringy average with good appeal but minor league hitters didn't miss it much. He'll rely on his above-average, mid-80s slider and a plus

Los Angeles Angels

splitter (which is often listed as a changeup). The split-finger offering shows tremendous dive and tumble. The best part: he can throw the plus offering for strikes. LA let Silseth get his feet wet in the big leagues – just a year removed from pitching in college – so he'll likely get a longer look in 2023. There's backend potential with a very high floor as a fastball / splitter combo guy in high leverage relief outings.

Ceiling: 2.0-win player
Risk: Low to Moderate
MLB ETA: Debuted in 2022

6. Ky Bush, LHP

FB	CB	SL	CH	Command	Overall
55	50	60	N/A	50	50

Born: 11/12/99	Age: 23	Bats: L	Top Production Comp: Daniel Norris
Height: 6-6	Weight: 240	Throws: L	

Season	Team	Age	Level	IP	TBF	K/9	K%	BB/9	BB%	K-BB%	ERA	FIP	xFIP	Pit/Bat
2021	LAA	21	A+	12.0	54	15.00	37.04%	3.75	9.26%	27.78%	4.50	2.15	2.67	3.94
2022	LAA	22	AA	103.0	427	8.83	23.65%	2.53	6.79%	16.86%	3.67	4.29	4.13	3.76

Background: After the front office selected hard-throwing Miami University of Ohio ace Sam Bachman in the opening round two years ago, the front office grabbed Saint Mary's College of California lefty Ky Bush in the second round, 45th overall. And just like they did with Bachman – as well as Chase Silseth – Bush was almost immediately pushed directly in Double-A, the true proving ground. The big 6-foot-6, 240-pound southpaw, who made five brief – mostly dominant – starts in High-A West during his debut, spent the entirety of last season twirling strong start after strong start with the Trash Pandas. He would average nearly a punch out per inning (8.8 K/9) with a strong feel for the strike zone (2.5 BB/9). He would finish his first full season in the minor leagues with a 3.67 ERA, 4.29 FIP, and a 4.13 xFIP.

Snippet from The 2022 Prospect Digest Handbook: A plus fastball / slider combo that tends to be death on both left- and right-handers. Bush, according to reports, mixes in a pair of 45-grade offerings in his curveball and changeup – though I didn't see any prior to the draft. He'll need the development of one of the two to at least tick up to average, but there's a lot to like in the Angels' second round pick. He could move quickly in the next 12 to 18 months.

Scouting Report: Consider the following:

> Since 2006, only seven 22-year-old hurlers posted a 22.5% to 24.5% strikeout percentage with a 6% to 8% walk percentage in a season in Double-A (min. 100 IP): Corbin Martin, Brett Kennedy, Nick Tropeano, Robert Dugger, Vladimir Gutierrez, Juan Gutierrez, and – of course – Ky Bush.

The prototypical polished college lefty. Bush fills the zone up with plenty of strikes, shows a well-rounded arsenal mixed with a bit of guile and guts. Bush's fastball seemed to take a small step backward in his first year in the professional ranks, now sitting comfortably in the 91- to 93-mph range. His curveball has ticked up to fringy average at this point, though he struggled locating in the bottom half of the zone in the start I scouted. His slider remains a veritable out pitch. And his changeup has crept up into average territory, though it's straight but still misses the fat part of the bat. Bush looks like a solid #4 / #5 option, something along the lines of early career Daniel Norris.

Ceiling: 1.5- to 2.0-win player
Risk: Moderate
MLB ETA: 2023

7. Kyren Paris, 2B/SS

Hit	Power	SB	Patience	Glove	Overall
40/45	50	60	55	50	50

Born: 11/11/01	Age: 21	Bats: R	Top Production Comp: Josh Rojas
Height: 6-0	Weight: 180	Throws: R	

Season	Team	Age	Level	PA	1B	2B	3B	HR	SB	CS	BB%	K%	AVG	OBP	SLG	ISO
2021	LAA	19	A	136	16	5	6	2	16	4	19.85%	30.15%	0.274	0.434	0.491	0.217
2021	LAA	19	A+	55	8	2	1	1	4	0	3.64%	36.36%	0.231	0.273	0.365	0.135
2022	LAA	20	A+	392	44	18	5	8	28	4	12.50%	29.85%	0.229	0.345	0.387	0.159
2022	LAA	20	AA	51	9	2	0	3	5	0	19.61%	27.45%	0.359	0.510	0.641	0.282

Background: The Angels' front office opened up their 2019 draft class with a pair of shortstops – N.C. State star Will Wilson and Freedom High School product Kyren Paris – before ripping off fourteen straight pitching selections. A little more than six months later Wilson was used as a sweetener to convince the Giants to take on Zack Cozart's $12.7 million deal – thus leaving Paris as the highest player in their class. The 55th overall player taken that year, Paris was limited to just a trio of games in the rookie leagues during his debut. And his 2020 season was KO'd thanks to COVID, so – by and large – his true debut wouldn't happen until the following year. Paris ripped through A-ball for a month before hitting the DL, returned to Inland Empire 2.5 months later where he continued to hit. And he would eventually spend the last several weeks in High-A. Last season, though, didn't go as well. Opening the year back up in High-A, the 6-foot, 180-

Los Angeles Angels

pound infielder started the year as cold as a woolly mammoth's toe nails, hitting a frigid .176/.306/.290 over his first 49 contests. But he seemed to right the ship in late June and got hotter as the season came to end, batting an impressive .291/.407/.517 over his remaining 58 games – 14 of which were with Rocket City in the Southern League. He finished the year with an aggregate .241/.363/.417 slash line, belting out 20 doubles, five triples, 12 homeruns, and 33 stolen bases (in 37 total attempts). His overall production, according to *Weighted Runs Created Plus*, was a surprising 20% better than the league average mark.

Snippet from The 2020 Prospect Digest Handbook: The swing looks improved and he's utilizing his lower half much more efficiently now. Plus speed. Developing power that looks like a potential average tool. The long red flag for Paris: there's a little too much swing-and-miss to his game, even in a couple short sample sizes. He's whiffed in 68 of his 219 total plate appearances – roughly 27% of the time. There's a utility floor with some Jazz Chisholm-type ceiling.

Scouting Report: Not only is Paris one of the better athletes in the Angels' system, but he's also one of the more intriguing prospects as well. The problem, though, is that the track record is too short and pockmarked with inconsistencies. He wouldn't make his debut – more or less – until two years after he was drafted. Then a broken tibia limited him to just 40 games in 2021. And, now, he looked abysmal for the first few months of 2022 before looking like a budding minor league superstar late in the year. He's a plus runner with great instincts. He's miscast as a shortstop, but has graded out well enough at the keystone. The bat speed is tremendous. There's sneaky thump in his maturing, still wiry frame. But the hit tool is still quite raw, leading to lengthy bouts of poor production and swollen strikeout rates. Paris is still only entering his age-21 season – which is hard to believe – and has a couple weeks of Double-A on his resume. The range of outcomes is still fairly enormous at this point, but there's some starting potential here.

Ceiling: 2.0-win player
Risk: Moderate to High
MLB ETA: 2024

8. Adrian Placencia, 2B/SS

Hit	Power	SB	Patience	Glove	Overall
40/45	50	60	50	50	50

Born: 06/02/03	Age: 20	Bats: B	Top Production Comp: N/A
Height: 5-11	Weight: 155	Throws: R	

Season	Team	Age	Level	PA	1B	2B	3B	HR	SB	CS	BB%	K%	AVG	OBP	SLG	ISO
2021	LAA	18	CPX	175	14	3	3	5	4	2	16.00%	28.00%	0.175	0.326	0.343	0.168
2022	LAA	19	A	469	59	23	2	13	21	8	16.20%	30.28%	0.254	0.387	0.427	0.173

Background: Part of the bounty the club hauled in off the international scene during the 2019-20 signing period. Placencia received a hefty $1.1 million bonus. The diminutive switch-hitting middle infielder would make his affiliated debut two years ago in the Arizona Complex League – though, the results were abysmal. The Los Alcarrizos, Dominican Republic native hit a putrid .175/.326/.343 with just 11 extra-base knocks in 43 games. Needless to say, the initial return on vestment was lacking. Then 2022 happened. Undeterred by Placencia swinging a wet noodle during his debut, the front office aggressively challenged the teenage prospect by sending him up to the California League. And he shined. In 104 games with Inland Empire, the 5-foot-11, 155-pound infielder slugged .254/.387/.427 with 23 doubles, two triples, 13 homeruns, and 21 stolen bases (in 29 attempts). His overall production, according to *Weighted Runs Created Plus*, was 16% better than the league average – an improvement of 32 percentage points over his weak debut.

Scouting Report: Consider the following:

> Since 2006, only three 19-year-old hitters posted a 110 to 120 wRC+ total with a 28% to 32% strikeout rate and a double-digit walk rate in a season in Low-A (min. 400 PA): Robbie Grossman, Jackson Frazier (formerly known as Clint Frazier), and – of course – Adrian Placencia. Just for those counting at home: Frazier owns a career 105 wRC+ and Grossman owns a career 103 wRC+ mark.

Great bat control and shows an incredible willingness to shoot the outside pitch the other way *and* he has no qualms about turning on the inside pitch. Good bat speed, especially for a smaller player. The swing can get a little long at times. And he's already showing some swing-and-miss issues: he whiffed 30% of the time in 2022. I'm betting on the bat control and suspect his K-rates will decline in the coming years. Plus speed. Solid glove at the keystone, where he'll eventually shift permanently. Really interesting pieces here. If he puts it all together, he could be a massive breakout candidate in the next year or two.

Ceiling: 2.0-win player
Risk: Moderate to High
MLB ETA: 2024/2025

Los Angeles Angels

9. Sam Bachman, RHP

FB	SL	CH	Command	Overall
55/60	60	50	45	45

Born: 09/30/99   **Age:** 23   **Bats:** R   **Top Production Comp:** Nate Pearson
Height: 6-1   **Weight:** 235   **Throws:** R

Season	Team	Age	Level	IP	TBF	K/9	K%	BB/9	BB%	K-BB%	ERA	FIP	xFIP	Pit/Bat
2021	LAA	21	A+	14.1	58	9.42	25.86%	2.51	6.90%	18.97%	3.77	3.84	3.70	3.55
2022	LAA	22	AA	43.2	193	6.18	15.54%	5.15	12.95%	2.59%	3.92	5.32	5.33	3.66

Background: One of the biggest risers in the 2021 draft class. Everything about Bachman typified a potential Angels draft pick: (A) he pitched, (B) he was a college prospect (C) he threw hard, (D) he could have a quick track to the big leagues, and – oh year – (E) he pitched. So it wasn't surprising when the Angels, who are *always* in search of any type of pitching (particularly in the Mike Trout era), selected the former RedHawk ace with the ninth overall pick two years ago. And just like a few of his 2021 draft counterparts, he spent the year in Double-A in 2022 – though it was plagued with an extended stay on the disabled list and some mediocre production. Bachman would make just 12 starts for the Trash Pandas, throwing 43.2 innings with 30 strikeouts and 25 free passes. He finished the year with a 3.92 ERA, 5.32 FIP, and 5.33 xFIP.

Snippet from The 2022 Prospect Digest Handbook: An explosive, plus-plus fastball that can touch as high as 101 mph. Bachman compliments the offering with a deadly plus slider. He'll also mix in a solid-average changeup. Bachman has a high floor/high ceiling. He has legitimate #2-type potential, though the changeup will need to see an uptick. Similar to Toronto's Nate Pearson.

Scouting Report: The book on Bachman was quite simple: he'd come in and blow the doors off the competition with his plus-plus, triple-digit fastball. Except that's not what he did or what he showed in 2022. Bachman's fastball sat in the 93- to 94- mph range and touched 95 with noticeable effort. His slider looked plus still. And his changeup was a 50-grade hit or miss offering. Based on his work in 2022 alone, Bachman looked like a potential backend reliever. He did lose a lot of developmental time due to injury, so 2023 will go a long way towards determining his future. One more final thought: the command seemed to really leave him at points.

Ceiling: 1.5-win player
Risk: Moderate
MLB ETA: 2023

10. Werner Blakely, 3B/SS

Hit	Power	SB	Patience	Glove	Overall
40/45	40/55	60	55	45	45

Born: 02/21/02   **Age:** 21   **Bats:** L   **Top Production Comp:** N/A
Height: 6-3   **Weight:** 185   **Throws:** R

Season	Team	Age	Level	PA	1B	2B	3B	HR	SB	CS	BB%	K%	AVG	OBP	SLG	ISO
2021	LAA	19	CPX	186	18	6	0	3	15	2	17.74%	37.10%	0.182	0.339	0.284	0.101
2022	LAA	20	A	235	34	13	2	5	24	2	19.15%	29.79%	0.295	0.447	0.470	0.175

Background: A product of Detroit Edison High School, the Halos selected Blakely in the fourth round in 2020, 111th overall, and signed him to a deal worth $900,000 – the fifth largest bonus in the round. And he promptly flopped during his debut in the Complex League two years ago, hitting a lackluster .182/.339/.284 with six doubles and three homeruns in 44 games. But things seemed to click for the lefty-swinging third baseman / shortstop because he was a revelation for Inland Empire last year. While injuries sapped a lot of his game time – he appeared in just 55 contests – Blakely slugged a scorching .295/.447/.470 with 13 doubles, two triples, five homeruns, and 24 stolen bases (in 26 total attempts). His overall production, according to *Weighted Runs Created Plus*, was a whopping 45% above the league average – a 66-percentage point improvement from his debut showing.

Scouting Report: Consider the following:

> Since 2006, only four 20-year-old hitters posted a 140 to 150 wRC+ with a walk rate north of 15% and a strikeout rate north of 24% in Low-A (min. 225 PA): Nolan Jones, Anthony Alford, Drew Robinson, and Werner Blakely.

Formerly committed to Auburn University, Blakely is long and wiry with plenty of room to fill out. Offensively, he takes *massive* cuts, nearly swinging out of his shoes at times. The swing is long, but fast. He hasn't tapped into his above-average, maybe even plus, power potential yet. But it's definitely in there. Like a few of the club's other better hitting prospects, Blakely, too, has some massive swing-and-miss issues; he K'd in 29.8% of the time last year. Great eye at the plate. Plus speed. Very good athlete. Defensively, he's an outfielder masquerading as a third baseman / shortstop. Very high risk, but the tools are undeniable.

Ceiling: 1.5-win player
Risk: Moderate
MLB ETA: 2024/2025

Los Angeles Angels

11. Denzer Guzman, SS

	Hit	Power	SB	Patience	Glove	Overall
	40/50	35/45	50/40	50	50	50

Born: 02/08/04	Age: 19	Bats: R	Top Production Comp: N/A
Height: 6-1	Weight: 180	Throws: R	

Season	Team	Age	Level	PA	1B	2B	3B	HR	SB	CS	BB%	K%	AVG	OBP	SLG	ISO
2021	LAA	17	DSL	164	16	10	1	3	11	7	12.20%	14.63%	0.213	0.311	0.362	0.149
2022	LAA	18	CPX	211	38	11	3	3	3	1	7.11%	20.85%	0.286	0.341	0.422	0.135
2022	LAA	18	A	23	3	0	0	0	1	0	26.09%	43.48%	0.176	0.391	0.176	0.000

Background: Another one of the club's high profile free agent signings on the international scene. The front office handed the wiry teenager a hefty $2 million a couple years ago. Guzman, a 6-foot-1, 180-pound shortstop, made his professional debut in the Dominican Summer League a few months later. And he promptly looked overmatched, hitting a paltry .213/.311/.362 in 44 games. Undeterred by his previous struggles (sense a theme here?), the organization continued to challenge its young infielder and sent him up to the Arizona Complex League. This time, though, Guzman showed significantly more promise with the bat. In 52 contests, the Dominican Republic native batted .286/.341/.422 with 11 doubles, three triples, three homeruns, and – you guessed it – three stolen bases. His overall production, according to *Weighted Runs Created Plus*, was 9% above the league average threshold.

Scouting Report: As with any young prospect, Guzman has matured noticeably since first signing with the organization. From a physical projection standpoint, there's still quite a bit of ways to go. The teenage shortstop still has to get stronger, but projects to have close to 50-grade power at full maturity. He's lacking a true standout tool, but makes up for it with a well-rounded feel to his game.

Ceiling: 1.5-win player
Risk: Moderate
MLB ETA: 2025

12. Ben Joyce, RHP

	FB	SL	CH	Command	Overall
	80	55	45/50	50	45

Born: 09/17/00	Age: 22	Bats: R	Top Production Comp: N/A
Height: 6-5	Weight: 225	Throws: R	

Season	Team	Age	Level	IP	TBF	K/9	K%	BB/9	BB%	K-BB%	ERA	FIP	xFIP	Pit/Bat
2022	LAA	21	AA	13.0	57	13.85	35.09%	2.77	7.02%	28.07%	2.08	2.12	3.59	3.95

Background: There were very few – if any – pitchers that dominated social media like Ben Joyce in 2022. Or in any year for that matter. Joyce, of course, was gifted by the baseball gods with a breathtakingly explosive, almost Nolan Ryan-esque fastball. But that's only a piece of his story. The 6-foot-5, 225-pound fire-bolt slinging right-hander, who touched triple digits in high school, attended Walters State Community College following his graduation from Farragut High School. But things didn't exactly go as planned. Joyce missed the first year courtesy of a stress fracture in his right elbow. Finally healthy, the big righty made five starts for the JuCo Senators, throwing 20.2 innings with 35 strikeouts and 14 walks to go along with an unexpectedly high 4.79 ERA. Joyce would transfer to the land of the Volunteers after the year, but would miss his first season in the SEC thanks to another major elbow issue. This time it was Tommy John surgery. Back to full health for the 2022 season, Joyce captured the attention of much of the nation as he lit up radar gun after radar gun through his redshirt junior campaign. Making 27 appearances for the SEC powerhouse, he posted a fantastic 53-to-14 strikeout-to-walk ratio in 32.1 innings of work. The Angels drafted him in the third round, 89th overall, and signed him to an above-slot bonus worth $997,500. Los Angeles immediately pushed him directly into Double-A. He made 13 appearances out of the Trash Pandas' bullpen, posting a 20-to-4 strikeout-to-walk in 13.0 innings of work.

Scouting Report: A generational fastball that belongs in the same class as a Steve Dalkowski or a Bob Feller or a Nolan Ryan or an Aroldis Chapman. It's an 80-grade offering. Joyce's offering consistently touches 103 mph and topped out at 105.5 mph, the fastest recorded pitch in college baseball history. His primary go-to secondary offering is an upper 80s slider, an above-average pitch that plays up due to the speed. He'll also mix in a rare 90 mph changeup. Talent was never the question. The ability to stay on the mound year after year is, however. Joyce feels like a streaking meteor. And the Angels are hoping that they can catch lightning in a bottle.

Ceiling: 1.5-win player
Risk: Moderate to High
MLB ETA: 2023

Los Angeles Angels

13. Landon Marceaux, RHP

FB	CB	SL	CH	Command	Overall
50	55	55	55	50	40

Born: 10/08/99	Age: 23	Bats: R	Top Production Comp: N/A
Height: 6-0	Weight: 199	Throws: R	

Season	Team	Age	Level	IP	TBF	K/9	K%	BB/9	BB%	K-BB%	ERA	FIP	xFIP	Pit/Bat
2022	LAA	22	A+	85.0	329	7.31	20.97%	1.48	4.26%	16.72%	2.65	3.33	3.67	3.33

Background: Trivia Time: The Angels' franchise selected just five players from Louisiana State University. Of those five, who put together the most successful career? Shortstop Mike Miley, the 10th overall pick in 1974, who tallied a -0.9 Wins Above Replacement total. Needless to say, as long as Marceaux cracks the club's pitching staff he has a chance to be the most successful LSU product in Angels history. Taken in the third round, 80th overall, two years ago, the 6-foot, 199-pound right-hander began last season in High-A with Tri-City. In 16 starts with the Dust Devils, Marceaux averaged 7.3 strikeouts and just 1.5 walks per nine innings in 85.0 innings. The former Tiger made two final starts with the Rocket City Trash Pandas in Double-A to cap off his first full season in pro ball.

Snippet from The 2020 Prospect Digest Handbook: It's all about the offspeed, baby! Had his heater been two ticks higher Marceaux would've been a lock as a mid- to late-first rounder. Alas, it's not.

Scouting Report: Landon Marceaux is what he is. And what exactly is he? A pitcher cut from the mold of hurlers two or three decades before his time. Upper 80s to low 90s fastball – clearly a fringy average offering. But he complements – or supplements – that offering with three above-average secondary weapons: curveball, slider, and changeup. He's not going to miss many bats, but as long as he can limit walks like he did with Tri-City, Marceaux has a chance to be a #5 arm. I wouldn't bet too much money on that happening, though.

Ceiling: 1.0-win player
Risk: Low to Moderate
MLB ETA: 2023/2024

14. Jeremiah Jackson, IF

Hit	Power	SB	Patience	Glove	Overall
40	50	50	50	50	40

Born: 03/26/00	Age: 23	Bats: R	Top Production Comp: Zach Walters
Height: 6-0	Weight: 165	Throws: R	

Season	Team	Age	Level	PA	1B	2B	3B	HR	SB	CS	BB%	K%	AVG	OBP	SLG	ISO
2019	LAA	19	R	291	29	14	2	23	5	1	8.25%	32.99%	0.266	0.333	0.605	0.340
2021	LAA	21	A	196	19	14	3	8	11	3	12.24%	33.16%	0.263	0.352	0.527	0.263
2022	LAA	22	AA	351	36	16	0	14	7	4	10.83%	21.94%	0.215	0.308	0.404	0.189

Background: The Angels' 2018 draft class laid the blueprint for their 2019 approach. And, truthfully, it's quite simple. Use the organization's first two selections on high ceiling, up-the-middle prospects, then bombard their pitching deprived farm system with as many arms as possible, just hoping they can get something to stick. Los Angeles opened their June draft by taking – and spending *big* on – Green Hope High Schooler Jordyn Adams with the 17th overall pick. Forty selections later the front office dipped their toes back into the prep ranks and chose power-hitting middle infielder Jeremiah Jackson. A product of St. Luke's Episcopal School, Jackson's first three years in pro ball were – by and large – quite productive. He batted .254/.314/.491 between the rookie league and Orem during his debut (though the majority of the damage was done with the former). Then he bashed a Pioneer League record 23 dingers a year later en route to hitting .266/.333/.606. And he managed to slug .264/.352/.527 in 45 games in an injury interrupted campaign with Inland Empire two years ago. Despite the limited exposure to full season pitching, the front office decided to throw caution to the wind and *aggressively* promoted the free-swinging Jackson straight up to Double-A for the 2022 season. It pretty much went as expected. Limited to just 87 games, thanks to injuries, the 6-foot, 185-pound infielder hit .215/.308/.404 with 16 doubles, 14 homeruns, and seven stolen bases. His overall production, per *Weighted Runs Created Plus*, was 14% below the league average threshold.

Snippet from The 2020 Prospect Digest Handbook: He's intriguing the same way that 2014 first rounder Jake Gatewood was – a middle infielder with plus-power potential and a questionable hit tool. The power and speed can be dreamed upon. But he's going to have to keep the strikeouts in check – or at least make sure they don't increase in the coming years.

Scouting Report: It wasn't all doom-and-gloom for the former second rounder in 2022. Jackson was able to chew some precious – and much needed – percentage points away from his typical 30% strikeout rate, gobbling it down to an impressive 21.9% -- despite bypassing an entire level. There's probably not enough here to start – unless the hit tool ticks up a bit – but Jackson could be a power-oriented bench option for the Halos in a couple years.

Ceiling: 1.0-win player
Risk: Moderate
MLB ETA: 2023

Los Angeles Angels

15. Alejandro Hidalgo, RHP

	FB	CB	SL	CH	Command	Overall
	50/55	50	45	60	45/50	40

Born: 05/22/03	Age: 20	Bats: R	Top Production Comp: Victor Arano
Height: 6-1	Weight: 160	Throws: R	

Season	Team	Age	Level	IP	TBF	K/9	K%	BB/9	BB%	K-BB%	ERA	FIP	xFIP	Pit/Bat
2021	LAA	18	CPX	27.0	118	10.33	26.27%	3.00	7.63%	18.64%	4.67	6.17	4.95	2.29
2022	LAA	19	A	39.0	175	13.38	33.14%	4.38	10.86%	22.29%	4.62	3.94	4.32	4.18

Background: In the grand scheme of things the $30,000 Hidalgo received from the organization is *a lot* of money. In baseball terms, though, it pales in comparison to the bonuses received by nearly every other player in the Angels' entire Top 20 Prospect List. A native of Maracay, Venezuela, the wiry right-hander posted some intriguing peripherals during his professional debut in the Complex League two years ago, averaging 10.3 strikeouts and 3.0 walks per nine innings in seven brief appearances. The front office bounced the 6-foot-1, 160-pound hurler up to Low-A for his first taste of full season ball in 2022. And he sparkled in 10 very brief outings before an undisclosed injury knocked him out in mid-June for the remainder of the year. Hidalgo struck out an impressive 58 and walked 19 in 39.0 innings of work.

Scouting Report: An interesting low level prospect that already has a brief history of missing plenty of bats thanks to his pitchability and outstanding changeup. Hidalgo attacks hitters with a low-90s above-average fastball from a high arm slot, which adds a little bit of deceptive funk on all of his offerings. His curveball has 12-6 downward movement and nice shape, but it lacks consistent swing-and-miss potential. He also showed a very raw – unreported – slider as well. Barring the severity of his undisclosed injury, Hidalgo is the type of prospect that should have a relatively high hit rate when it comes to making the big leagues, but it's likely going to be in middle relief role.

Ceiling: 1.0-win player
Risk: Moderate
MLB ETA: 2024/2025

16. Arol Vera, 2B/SS

	Hit	Power	SB	Patience	Glove	Overall
	35/40	40/45	55	50	55	40

Born: 09/12/02	Age: 20	Bats: B	Top Production Comp: N/A
Height: 6-2	Weight: 170	Throws: R	

Season	Team	Age	Level	PA	1B	2B	3B	HR	SB	CS	BB%	K%	AVG	OBP	SLG	ISO
2021	LAA	18	CPX	164	27	16	3	0	2	2	7.32%	23.78%	0.317	0.384	0.469	0.152
2021	LAA	18	A	90	23	0	0	0	9	2	6.67%	22.22%	0.280	0.344	0.280	0.000
2022	LAA	19	A	551	77	16	4	4	19	7	9.62%	27.04%	0.207	0.291	0.281	0.074

Background: The franchise went all in on the switch-hitting middle infielder during the 2019-20 signing period, handing him a hefty $2 million bonus to convince him to join the organization. And, despite a COVID-delayed start to his career, Vera looked every bit the top prospect that prognosticators thought he was (present company included). The Venezuelan-born prospect torched the Complex League with a .317/.384/.469 line through 38 games before earning a three-week trial in Low-A. It *looked* like the front office hit *big* with their high-profile signing. Vera showcased a potential five-tool approach. One, by the way, that could fast-track him to the big leagues. Then 2022 happened. Vera was sent back to Inland Empire to begin his sophomore campaign. But it really never got on track. He hit .183/.247/.281 in April and never recovered. He finished the season with a putrid .207/.291/.281 line, adding 16 doubles, four triples, four homeruns, and 19 stolen bases. His production, per *Weighted Runs Created Plus*, was a whopping 46% *below* the league average threshold.

Snippet from The 2020 Prospect Digest Handbook: Vera is poised to be one of the bigger breakout prospects in 2022.

Scouting Report: Consider the following:

> Since 2006, only six 19-year-old players have posted a sub-60 wRC+ mark in a season in Low-A (min. 400 PA): Hernan Perez, Luis Marte, Jose Castro, Quentin Holmes, Justin Twine, and – of course – Arol Vera. For those keeping track at home: surprisingly enough, at least to me, two of the six eventually cracked a big league lineup (Perez and Marte) with the former carving out a lengthy career at the game's pinnacle level.

Vera didn't hit at home or on the road. He didn't hit left-handed or right-handed pitching. He didn't hit in April, May, June, July, August, *or* September. He, simply, didn't hit – at all, at any time. Vera just did not look comfortable at the plate. The bat speed is still intact, but he just looked lost at times. He's made considerable changes to his stance since first signing with the team, holding his hands lower and a closer, smaller base. He's still young enough where a strong bounce back performance will realign his ceiling to previous levels, but the production was so poor in 2022 that it makes any type of noticeable improvement less likely.

Ceiling: 1.0-win player
Risk: Moderate
MLB ETA: 2024/2025

Los Angeles Angels

17. Coleman Crow, RHP

FB	CB	SL	CH	Command	Overall
50	50	55	N/A	50/55	40

Born: 12/30/00	Age: 22	Bats: R	Top Production Comp: N/A
Height: 6-0	Weight: 175	Throws: R	

Season	Team	Age	Level	IP	TBF	K/9	K%	BB/9	BB%	K-BB%	ERA	FIP	xFIP	Pit/Bat
2021	LAA	20	A	62.1	287	8.95	21.60%	4.19	10.10%	11.50%	4.19	5.29	5.37	3.68
2022	LAA	21	AA	128.0	554	9.00	23.10%	2.46	6.32%	16.79%	4.85	4.64	4.17	3.60

Background: Since the Mike Trout draft, the Angels farm system has been bereft of both talent *and* depth. But quietly over the past couple years the front office has added some promising depth, particularly in the latter parts of the draft – which is exactly where the Halos selected right-hander Coleman Crow. A product of Pike County High School, Crow earned a hefty $317,500 bonus as the 841st player taken in 2019. The bonus, by the way, was the largest one handed out to any player taken in the 28th round that year. The 6-foot, 175-pound right-hander wouldn't make his debut until two years later, popping up with Inland Empire for 13 appearances (three relief appearance, 10 starts). He finished the year with solid peripherals (9.0 K/9 and 4.2 BB/9) across 62.1 innings of work. But it was his dominance in the Arizona Fall League that year that turned a lot of heads. Splitting time between Glendale Desert Dogs' rotation and pen, Crow posted a 20-to-2 strikeout-to-walk ratio in 17.0 innings. So the organization decided to aggressively challenge their late round bonus baby and sent him directly the minors' ultimate proving ground – AA. And he proved to be more than ready. Throwing a career best 128.0 innings, Crow struck out 128 and walked just 35 with the Trash Pandas. He finished the year with a 4.85 ERA, 4.64 FIP, and 4.17 xFIP.

Scouting Report: Consider the following:

> Since 2006, only six 21-year-old hurlers met the following criteria in a Double-A season (min. 100 IP): 22% to 24% strikeout percentage with a walk percentage between 5.5% and 7.5%. Those six hurlers: German Marquez, Zach Davies, Zach Lee, Ronald Herrera, Juan Pablo Oramas, and – of course – Coleman Crow.

Maxed out physically, despite just coming off of his age-21 season. Crow's slight 6-foot, 175-pound frame doesn't portend itself to significant muscle gain. His fastball, an average offering, sits in the 90- to 91-mph range consistently. He'll mix in an average 12-6 breaking curveball. But his bread-and-butter offering is a tightly spun, above-average slider which sits in the mid-80s. He'll change a hitter's look at the pitch by occasionally dropping his arm slot a touch as well. Reports indicate that he'll also work in an average changeup, but I didn't see one. There's nothing extraordinary about Crow's arsenal, but he could carve out a role as #6 / middle relief arm in the coming years. One more interesting fact: Crow was particularly good during his first 12 games, posting a 2.82 ERA with 65 Ks and 15 BBs in 67 innings. Likewise, he was particularly awful over his final 12 contests, tallying a 7.08 ERA with 61 Ks and 20 BBs in 61.0 IP.

Ceiling: 1.0-win player
Risk: Moderate
MLB ETA: 2023

18. Randy De Jesus, OF

Hit	Power	SB	Patience	Glove	Overall
40/45	40/55	30	50	50	40

Born: 02/13/05	Age: 18	Bats: R	Top Production Comp: N/A
Height: 6-4	Weight: 201	Throws: R	

Season	Team	Age	Level	PA	1B	2B	3B	HR	SB	CS	BB%	K%	AVG	OBP	SLG	ISO
2022	LAA	17	DSL	210	29	13	1	7	5	3	9.52%	21.43%	0.272	0.362	0.467	0.196

Background: Last offseason the Angels went all in on a couple of hitters on the amateur free agent market, handing outfielders Nelson Rada and Randy De Jesus nearly $3 million. De Jesus, who received a $1.2 million bonus, looked comfortable squaring off against the hitter-friendly arms of the Dominican Summer League during his debut in 2022. Appearing in 52 games, the Dominican-born prospect slugged .272/.362/.467 with 13 doubles, one triple, seven homeruns, and five stolen bases (in eight total attempts). According to *Weighted Runs Created Plus*, his overall production topped the league average mark by 23%.

Scouting Report: Very robotic swing with a pronounced load. With that being said, De Jesus shows a quick bat and projects to have above-average power. There's going to be some contact questions he's going to have to answer – though he managed to just whiff on 21% of his plate appearances last summer. He saw a handful of games in centerfield, but he's destined for a fulltime gig as a corner outfielder. He's going to be large when he's done maturing. It wouldn't be surprising to see LA send him up to Low-A at some point in 2023.

Ceiling: 1.0-win player
Risk: Moderate
MLB ETA: 2026

Los Angeles Angels

19. Livan Soto, IF

Hit	Power	SB	Patience	Glove	Overall
35/40	40/45	55	50	55	40

Born: 06/22/00 | **Age:** 23 | **Bats:** L | **Top Production Comp:** N/A
Height: 6-0 | **Weight:** 160 | **Throws:** R |

Season	Team	Age	Level	PA	1B	2B	3B	HR	SB	CS	BB%	K%	AVG	OBP	SLG	ISO
2021	LAA	21	A+	406	49	14	8	7	14	5	9.61%	24.38%	0.217	0.293	0.358	0.142
2021	LAA	21	AA	44	8	1	0	0	0	0	6.82%	25.00%	0.225	0.295	0.250	0.025
2022	LAA	22	AA	543	104	17	1	6	18	8	13.08%	18.78%	0.281	0.379	0.362	0.081

Background: Baseball's a funny game, isn't it? Soto, a left-swinging infielder from Valencia, Venezuela, has been pretty abysmal at the plate for the overwhelming majority of his career. He posted a .586 OPS in the Gulf Coast as a 17-year-old during his professional debut. He performed better as he moved in the Pioneer League the following season, hitting .291/.385/.349. But he was swinging a wet noodle in 2019 (.220/.304/.256), missed all of 2020 due to the lost COVID year, and picked up right where he left off in 2021 (.218/.293/.348). Entering last season he was (A) 21-years-old, (B) hadn't hit well in three years, and (C) looked like he had no shot of playing in the big leagues anytime in the near – or distant – future. Then…he began to hit – at the minors' toughest level. Soto was sent up to Double-A, a "true proving ground", in 2022 and responded with an above-average .281/.379/.362 slash line. And then he capped off his career year with a month-long stint in the big leagues, as well, where he promptly hit .400/.414/.582 in 59 plate appearances. Just like everyone thought.

Scouting Report: Despite the offensive breakout last season, Soto is still destined for future utility-dom – even if everything breaks just the right way. He runs well, though he's not overly efficient. He can play any position on the infield. He typically has a nose for first base. But lacks any type of meaningful power. Soto's the type of guy to help round out a team's bench. Nothing more. But there's value in that too.

Ceiling: 0.5- to 1.0-win player
Risk: Low to Moderate
MLB ETA: Debuted in 2022

20. Mason Albright, LHP

FB	CB	SL	CH	Command	Overall
45	55	50	55	50/55	35

Born: 11/26/02 | **Age:** 19 | **Bats:** L | **Top Production Comp:** N/A
Height: 6-0 | **Weight:** 190 | **Throws:** L |

Season	Team	Age	Level	IP	TBF	K/9	K%	BB/9	BB%	K-BB%	ERA	FIP	xFIP	Pit/Bat
2022	LAA	19	A	48.0	238	9.94	22.27%	4.31	9.66%	12.61%	9.00	6.88	5.24	3.96

Background: Another one of those late round bonus babies unearthed by the club that's made his way onto their Top 20 list. Los Angeles selected Albright, a 6-foot, 190-pound southpaw, in the 12th round two years ago. They quickly handed him $1.2 million – equivalent to second round money. Not bad as the 351st overall player drafted that year. The Frederick, Maryland, native made a brief – albeit dominant – debut in the Arizona Complex League that summer, throwing eight innings across three starts while fanning eight and walking a pair. Last season, though, didn't go so well for the young millionaire. Albright opened his first full season in professional ball in Low-A, making 12 starts but hit the disabled list for two months before making three limited appearances at the end of the year in High-A. Including his two rehab appearances, Albright tossed just 55.0 innings, averaging 9.7 strikeouts and 4.6 walks per nine innings to go along with a horrific looking 8.67 ERA.

Snippet from The 2020 Prospect Digest Handbook: Kudos to the Angles for going above-and-beyond on locking up the young left-hander. But it's a risky investment. Not only because he's a young arm – which should go without saying – but Albright's arm action is ugly. And potentially career limiting. It's long and stiff. And I think it's going to make him susceptible to right-handers in the future. The fastball velocity is fringy average, and I'm not sure how much more is left in the take in terms of projection. He can spin an above-average deuce. But it's his changeup that should be a difference maker.

Scouting Report: The arm action is still *looooong* and ugly. Albright's fastball is still below-average, too hittable. Velocity-wise it'll sit in the 91 mph range but he lacks the command to even make it a *"sneaky"* 91. Above-average curveball – still – and he's added an average-ish slider. The changeup remains his best weapon, though he seemed to shy away from it. The command is still lacking – by a wide margin. One more final thought: the arm action likely has a lot to do with his inability to throw strikes. It just seems like a wasted investment at this point.

Ceiling: 0.5-win player
Risk: Moderate
MLB ETA: 2025

Los Angeles Dodgers

Top Prospects

Los Angeles Dodgers

1. Miguel Vargas, 1B/3B/LF

Hit	Power	SB	Patience	Glove	Overall
65	50/60	50/40	50	45/50	70

Born: 11/17/99	Age: 22	Bats: R	Top Production Comp: Jose Ramirez
Height: 6-3	Weight: 205	Throws: R	

Season	Team	Age	Level	PA	1B	2B	3B	HR	SB	CS	BB%	K%	AVG	OBP	SLG	ISO
2021	LAD	21	A+	172	30	11	1	7	4	0	5.23%	18.60%	0.314	0.366	0.532	0.218
2021	LAD	21	AA	370	72	16	1	16	7	1	9.73%	15.41%	0.321	0.386	0.523	0.202
2022	LAD	22	AAA	520	80	32	4	17	16	5	13.65%	14.62%	0.304	0.404	0.511	0.208

Background: There was a lot of talk – especially coming from me – on the impressive bloodlines in a lot of the top prospects in the MLB Draft last summer. The sons of Matt Holliday, Andruw Jones, Carl Crawford, and Lou Collier played prominent roles throughout the opening day of the draft. But there were lesser-known family ties to the game as well, like Brooks Lee, whose father happens to captain the ship at Cal Poly, or Jace Jung and Daniel Susac, both of whom have notable big league brothers. Miguel Vargas's ties to the game fall somewhere in between. Vargas' father, Lazaro, led the Cuban Serie Nacional in hits during the 1983-84 season and was eventually named the league's Most Valuable Player. The elder Vargas also spent some time on Cuba's Olympic squads as well, including the Gold Medal-winning 1996 team. The younger Vargas is already proving to be the superior ballplayer. Signed for only $300,000 after defecting from his home country, the 6-foot-3, 205-pound corner infielder / outfielder immediately started impacting the club's prospect rankings. He mashed .330/.404/.465 with 15 doubles, three triples, and a pair of homeruns in 53 low level games during his debut in 2018. A year later he was bashing his way through Low-A and High-A to the tune of .308/.380/.440. And he continued battering the competition in 2021 as he split time between Great Lakes and Tulsa, slugging .319/.380/.526. Last season Vargas appeared in 113 games with the Oklahoma City Dodgers, compiling an impressive .304/.404/.511 slash line with 32 doubles, four triples, 17 homeruns, and 16 stolen bases (in 21 total attempts). Per *Weighted Runs Created Plus*, his overall production topped the league average mark by 29%. Vargas also made 18 appearances with the big league club, going 8-for-47 with a double, a long ball, and a stolen base. He slashed .170/.200/.255 during that time.

Snippet from The 2022 Prospect Digest Handbook: One of the more talented hitters in the minor leagues. Vargas possesses the rare ability to hit for power and consistently make contact.

Scouting Report: Consider the following:

> Since 2006, only three 22-year-old hitters posted a 125 to 135 wRC+ with a double-digit walk rate and a 12% to 16% strikeout rate in any Triple-A league (min. 350 PA): Jesse Winker, Chris Young, and – of course – Miguel Vargas. For those counting at home: Winker owns a 126 wRC+ career mark through 549 games and Young finished his career with a 95 wRC+.

Possessing one of the best hit tools in the minor leagues, Vargas has yet to fully tap into his plus power potential – but it's coming, especially in the Dodgers' hitting school. Tall and lanky with *plenty* of room to fill out. Vargas has the potential to win multiple batting titles in his big league career. He consistently barrels up the ball. Plus bat speed. And he improved his pitch selection in 2022, which was already impressive. Defensively, he plays third base and left field like a first baseman. He's going to be a .315/.380/.500 hitter.

Ceiling: 6.0-win player
Risk: Moderate
MLB ETA: Debuted in 2022

2. Diego Cartaya, C

Hit	Power	SB	Patience	Glove	Overall
50	60	30	60	55	60

Born: 09/07/01	Age: 21	Bats: R	Top Production Comp: Jorge Posada
Height: 6-3	Weight: 219	Throws: R	

Season	Team	Age	Level	PA	1B	2B	3B	HR	SB	CS	BB%	K%	AVG	OBP	SLG	ISO
2021	LAD	19	A	137	18	6	0	10	0	0	13.14%	27.01%	0.298	0.409	0.614	0.316
2022	LAD	20	A	163	15	9	1	9	0	0	14.11%	26.99%	0.260	0.405	0.550	0.290
2022	LAD	20	A+	282	32	13	0	13	0	0	14.18%	26.60%	0.251	0.379	0.476	0.225

Background: The Dodgers' history book is littered with the achievements of two of the greatest catchers in history. Roy Campanella was *the* preeminent catcher during the peak of his career as he captured three MVP awards and was named to eight straight All-Star games before his career was tragically cut short. He was so good that Ty Cobb once remarked, "Campanella will be remembered longer than any catcher in baseball history." Four decades later the club's farm system churned out a former 62nd round pick that would eventually go on to become the game's best power-hitting backstop in history. Mike Piazza captured the National League Rookie of the Year in 1993, the second of five consecutive Dodgers to earn the award, and was named to 12 All-Star teams. Dodgers' catching greatness isn't just limited to the pair of Hall of Famers either, though. Mike Scioscia was a two-time All-Star and earned more than 26 wins above replacement in his 13-year

Los Angeles Dodgers

career, all of which were spent in a Dodgers uniform. Lefty-swinging John Roseboro was a five-time All-Star and captured two Gold Glove awards- though he's largely remembered for something else. Steve Yeager, Paul Lo Duca, Russell Martin (who quietly assembled a borderline Hall of Fame career), and current Dodger Will Smith all have been stout performers as well. Diego Cartaya is poised to become the next notable Dodgers backstop, maybe even more. Signed off the international scene during the 2018 signing period, the front office brass handed the power-hitting backstop a massive $2.5 million deal. And almost immediately Cartaya proved to be worth every single penny. A native of Maracay, Venezuela, the 6-foot-3, 219-pound catcher slugged .281/.343/.432 during his debut in 2019 – most of the time coming in the Arizona Summer League. Once minor league action returned from its pandemic-induced absence, Cartaya mashed his way through an injury-shortened campaign in Rancho Cucamonga, slugging .298/.409/.614 with six doubles and 10 homeruns in only 31 games. Last season, the promising youngster appeared in a career-best 95 games (two third of them coming in High-A) while setting personal highs in doubles (22) and homeruns (22) en route to slugging .254/.389/.503. According to *Weighted Runs Created Plus*, his overall production surpassed the league average threshold by an impressive 39%.

Snippet from The 2022 Prospect Digest Handbook: As high of a ceiling as any hitter – read: not ballplayer – in the minor leagues, Cartaya put his talents on full display during his abbreviated 2021 campaign: He showed plus power, plus patience, and a decent hit tool. The lone knock on an otherwise superb, albeit shortened, season: his 27.0% K-rate.

Scouting Report: Consider the following:

> Since 2006, only three 20-year-old hitters met the following criteria in any High-A league (min. 275 PA): 133 to 143 wRC+ with a 24% to 28% strikeout rate. Those three hitters: Ryan McMahon, Khalil Lee, and – of course – Diego Cartaya.

Cartaya's never going to be confused with Johnny Bench or Yadier Molina behind the dish, but he's solid enough where he's likely to remain at the spot, though his bat – *clearly* – plays at any power-hitting position. As much raw power as any hitter in the Dodgers' system. Little unnecessary movement during his setup at the plate, Cartaya does a tremendous job keeping his hands inside the ball. He looks like a young Juan Gonzalez throughout his swing. Plus bat speed, plus in-game power with plus-plus raw power. He's going to be a .280/.350/.500 big league hitter – assuming he can stay healthy.

Ceiling: 5.5-win player
Risk: Moderate
MLB ETA: 2024

3. Bobby Miller, RHP

FB	CB	SL	CH	Command	Overall
60	55	60	55	55	60

Born: 04/05/99	Age: 24	Bats: L	Top Production Comp: Walker Buehler
Height: 6-5	Weight: 220	Throws: R	

Season	Team	Age	Level	IP	TBF	K/9	K%	BB/9	BB%	K-BB%	ERA	FIP	xFIP	Pit/Bat
2021	LAD	22	A+	47.0	188	10.72	29.79%	2.11	5.85%	23.94%	1.91	2.81	3.71	4.20
2022	LAD	23	AA	91.0	384	11.57	30.47%	3.07	8.07%	22.40%	4.45	3.45	3.47	4.11
2022	LAD	23	AAA	21.1	85	11.81	32.94%	2.53	7.06%	25.88%	3.38	4.65	3.64	3.89

Background: The club opened up their COVID-limited 2020 draft class with three straight college hurlers, nabbing University of Louisville ace Bobby Miller with the 29th overall pick, East Tennessee righty Landon Knack with the 60th selection, and then grabbing Texas Tech flamethrower Clayton Beeter six picks later. Miller was magnificent during his limited junior campaign for Head Coach Dan McDonnell, posting an impressive 34-to-9 strikeout-to-walk ratio in only 23.1 innings. The hard-throwing right-hander would make his affiliated debut in 2021, making 14 appearances with Great Lakes and three starts with Tulsa. He finished the season with 70 punch outs and 13 free passes in 56.1 innings during his injury-interrupted campaign. Last season, Miller made 24 appearances, 23 of which were starts, between Tulsa and Oklahoma City, averaging 11.6 punch outs and just 3.0 walks per nine innings. He finished his sophomore professional season with a 4.25 ERA and a 3.68 FIP.

Snippet from The 2022 Prospect Digest Handbook: The Dodgers brought Miller along slowly last season, limiting him to four or fewer innings until early July. But despite their best efforts, the hard-throwing right-hander would eventually hit the disabled list for roughly six weeks with an undisclosed injury. The former Louisville hurler commands the zone well. And has the potential to be a front-of-the-rotation caliber arm.

Scouting Report: Consider the following:

> Since 2006, only three 23-year-old hurlers met the following criteria in any Double-A league (min. 75 IP): 29% to 32% strikeout percentage with a 7% to 9% walk percentage. Those three hurlers: Taylor Widener, Alexander Guillen, and – of course – Bobby Miller.

Los Angeles Dodgers

An intense, intimidating mound presence with the arsenal to front a big league rotation. The formerly erratic collegiate hurler landed in an ideal spot due to the Dodgers' pitching development success. At his best, the 6-foot-5, broad-shouldered right-hander will show two borderline plus-plus offerings (fastball and slider), an above-average changeup, and a sneaky – albeit rare – curveball. Miller's command had a tendency to waver at points during his amateur days, but he's been locked in on not only throwing strikes, but quality strikes since joining the organization – which isn't a coincidence. There's a lot of similarities between the former Louisville ace and Walker Buehler. Fast, efficient worker. Miller just needs to take that final step towards ace-dom.

Ceiling: 5.0-win player
Risk: Moderate
MLB ETA: 2023

4. Dalton Rushing, C

Hit	Power	SB	Patience	Glove	Overall
45/50	55	20	50	50	55

Born: 02/21/01	Age: 22	Bats: L	Top Production Comp: N/A
Height: 6-1	Weight: 220	Throws: R	

Season	Team	Age	Level	PA	1B	2B	3B	HR	SB	CS	BB%	K%	AVG	OBP	SLG	ISO
2022	LAD	21	A	128	23	11	0	8	1	0	16.41%	16.41%	0.424	0.539	0.778	0.354

Background: An unknown – at least to the casual fan – heading into the 2022 season. Of course, locked into a backup role behind the eventual top pick in the 2021 draft will have that effect. But Rushing, a lefty-swinging backstop, patiently waited for his opportunity for a full time starting gig. And he capitalized on it. After seeing limited time as Henry Davis's backup during his freshman and sophomore seasons, Rushing got his first taste of regular action as a member of the Bourne Braves during the summer of 2021. He responded by slugging .314/.401/.542 with nine doubles and six homeruns in 34 games. And he carried that momentum into his breakout junior campaign. In 64 games for the Cardinals, the 6-foot-1, 220-pound catcher mashed .310/.470/.686 with 16 doubles, 23 homeruns, and four stolen bases. He finished the year with an impeccable 58-to-50 strikeout-to-walk ratio as well. The Dodgers selected Rushing in the second round, 40th overall, and signed him to a deal worth $1,956,890. Then he promptly shredded the Low-A pitching to the tune of .424/.539/.778 with 11 doubles and eight homeruns in only 28 games.

Scouting Report: My pre-draft write-up:

> "Consider the following:
>
>> Since 2011, only four Division I hitters met the following criteria in a season (min. 275 PA): bat at least .300/.450/.675 with a walk rate north of 15% and a strikeout rate between 18% and 22%. Those four hitters: Jonathan India, the 2021 National League Rookie of the Year and fifth overall pick in 2018; Brent Rooker, the 35th overall pick in 2017; Austin Listi (met the criteria as a 23-year-old); and Dalton Rushing.
>
> Rushing continues to play the shadow to other backstops. This time, though, it's catchers in the 2022 draft class. Above-average patience at the plate, solid contact skills, and above-average thump. He also controls the opposition's running game incredibly well. Starts from a wide, open stance. Good bat speed. He's going to face shifts (for as long as they're legal). There's more projection left for someone his age, thanks to his lack of playing time the first few years in college."

Ceiling: 3.0-win player
Risk: Moderate
MLB ETA: 2025

5. Gavin Stone, RHP

FB	SL	CH	Command	Overall
55	50	60	55	50

Born: 10/15/98	Age: 24	Bats: R	Top Production Comp: Tyler Anderson
Height: 6-1	Weight: 175	Throws: R	

Season	Team	Age	Level	IP	TBF	K/9	K%	BB/9	BB%	K-BB%	ERA	FIP	xFIP	Pit/Bat
2021	LAD	22	A	70.0	295	12.99	34.24%	2.57	6.78%	27.46%	3.73	3.17	3.29	3.83
2021	LAD	22	A+	21.0	83	15.86	44.58%	2.14	6.02%	38.55%	3.86	2.20	1.57	3.99
2022	LAD	23	A+	25.0	100	10.08	28.00%	2.16	6.00%	22.00%	1.44	2.60	2.98	3.49
2022	LAD	23	AA	73.1	303	13.13	35.31%	3.68	9.90%	25.41%	1.60	2.24	2.90	3.96
2022	LAD	23	AAA	23.1	93	12.73	35.48%	3.09	8.60%	26.88%	1.16	2.87	3.79	3.72

Background: The club used their final selection in the COVID-capped five-round 2020 draft on Gavin Stone. The 6-foot-1, 175-pound right-hander was nearly unhittable during his final two seasons at the University of Central Arkansas as he tallied an impeccable 1.44 ERA over 75 innings, recording an 89-

Los Angeles Dodgers

to-17 strikeout-to-walk ratio for the Southland Conference squad. Stone opened up the 2021 season with the Rancho Cucamonga Quakes, but after a dominant 18-game tenure, the front office bumped him up to Great Lakes for five final starts. The former Bear struck out 138 and walked just 25 across 91.0 innings. Last season, Stone's performance harkened back to his collegiate days as he tallied a shimmering 1.48 ERA across 25 starts and one relief appearance with Great Lakes, Tulsa, and Oklahoma City. He averaged 12.4 strikeouts and just 3.3 walk per nine innings. For his career, Stone is averaging 12.9 K/9 and 2.9 BB/9 in 212.2 innings of work.

Snippet from The 2022 Prospect Digest Handbook: Stone does a lot things that older pitching prospects showcase in the lower levels that lead to gaudy strikeout numbers and overall production: he commands the strike zone, throws several pitches for strikes, and can throw offspeed strikes early in the count. Everything plays up, though, due to his ability to consistently throw quality strikes.

Scouting Report: The former University of Central Arkansas ace paced the minor leagues in ERA last season – by a wide margin, by nearly half-of-a-run. Stone takes a simplistic approach to pitching: change speeds, fill up the strike zone with quality offerings, and own a spectacular changeup. The slight-framed right-hander's fastball operates in the 91- to 94 mph range. His average-ish slider hovers around 86- to 87-mph. And, of course, there's his mid-80s change as well. Stone fits it that Tony Gonsolin, Tyler Anderson, Ross Stripling mold that the organization seems to utilize / develop exceptionally well.

Ceiling: 3.0-win player
Risk: Low to Moderate
MLB ETA: 2023

6. Michael Busch, 2B

Hit	Power	SB	Patience	Glove	Overall
45	60	35	60	50	55

Born: 11/09/97	Age: 25	Bats: L	Top Production Comp: Brian Dozier
Height: 6-1	Weight: 210	Throws: R	

Season	Team	Age	Level	PA	1B	2B	3B	HR	SB	CS	BB%	K%	AVG	OBP	SLG	ISO
2021	LAD	23	AA	495	61	27	1	20	2	3	14.14%	26.06%	0.267	0.386	0.484	0.218
2022	LAD	24	AA	137	16	6	0	11	1	0	17.52%	26.28%	0.306	0.445	0.667	0.361
2022	LAD	24	AAA	504	65	32	0	21	3	2	9.92%	25.99%	0.266	0.343	0.480	0.214

Background: The Dodgers' 2019 draft class may eventually end up proving to be a miss by a traditionally exceptionally savvy team. Their first pick, Kody Hoese, has been an utter disaster at the plate throughout the duration of his career. Jimmy Lewis, the behemoth right-hander out of Lake Travis High School who was taken in the second round, just posted an 8.28 ERA in 25.0 innings last season. Brandon Lewis, their fourth rounder, just batted .209/.271/.438 in his first stint in Double-A. So the success of the club's entire class hangs on the shoulders of Jimmy Lewis, who lacks a reliable third offering, and Michael Busch. Taken six selections after Kody Hoese, Busch was a man without a position during his collegiate days but was a consistent force at the dish during his sophomore and junior campaigns. After a brief jaunt through the rookie league and Low-A during his debut, the front office aggressively challenged the former first rounder and sent him directly to the fires of Double-A. And he came out relatively unscathed as he mashed .267/.386/.484 with 27 doubles, one triple, and 20 homeruns in 107 games. Last season, the front office brass sent the lefty-swinging second baseman / left fielder back to Double-A for some more seasoning, but after mashing for six weeks he was eventually bumped up to Triple-A for the remainder of the year. Busch batted an aggregated .274/.365/.516 with 38 doubles and 32 homeruns. His overall production, according to *Weighted Runs Created Plus*, topped the league average mark by 18%.

Snippet from The 2022 Prospect Digest Handbook: There's above-average starting material – a la Brian Dozier – but he needs to prove he can handle southpaws first.

Scouting Report: Consider the following:

> Since 2006, only three 24-year-old hitters posted a 97 to 107 wRC+ with a 25% to 27% strikeout rate and a 9% to 11% walk rate in any Triple-A league (min. 350 PA): Josh Bell, the former Orioles prospect and not the current Guardians first baseman, Eric Wood, and Michael Busch.

The good news is that Busch put his horrific showing against lefties in 2021 (.198/.355/.354) behind him as he batted a respectable .258/.352/.477 against southpaws in 2022. Plus power potential that even Oklahoma City's homer-suppressing ballpark couldn't slow him down as he belted out a career best 32 dingers. Nose for first base. 45-grade hit tool that'll constantly register consistent batting averages in the .240- to .250-range. Big league ceiling: .245/.340/.460. He seems primed to be the big league club's next version of Max Muncy.

Ceiling: 3.0 to 3.5-win player
Risk: Moderate
MLB ETA: 2023

Los Angeles Dodgers

7. Ryan Pepiot, RHP

FB	SL	CH	Command	Overall
55	50	70	45	50

Born: 08/21/97	Age: 25	Bats: R	Top Production Comp: Tony Gonsolin
Height: 6-3	Weight: 215	Throws: R	

Season	Team	Age	Level	IP	TBF	K/9	K%	BB/9	BB%	K-BB%	ERA	FIP	xFIP	Pit/Bat
2021	LAD	23	AA	59.2	233	12.22	34.76%	3.92	11.16%	23.61%	2.87	3.75	4.07	4.00
2021	LAD	23	AAA	41.2	202	9.94	22.77%	4.54	10.40%	12.38%	7.13	7.12	5.79	3.88
2022	LAD	24	AAA	91.1	369	11.23	30.89%	3.55	9.76%	21.14%	2.56	4.29	4.51	3.98

Background: Perceived as the – underrated – darling of the club's always bountiful farm system since entering the organization as a third round pick in 2019. The former Butler University ace with sometimes problematic command continued to miss bats – and the strike zone – during his brief debut that summer as well, posting a 31-to-13 strikeout-to-walk ratio in 23.1 innings between the old Arizona Summer and Midwest Leagues. After minor league action returned from the lost 2020 COVID season, Los Angeles sent the promising – still erratic – right-hander straight in the fires of Double-A. And he was a revelation – or at least close to one. Pepiot struck out 81 and walked 26 in 59.2 innings of work with Tulsa. But his command was like a fleeting dream during a second half promotion up to Oklahoma City as he walked 21 (with 46 punch outs) in only 41.2 innings of work. Pepiot spent the entirety of last season yo-yoing between Oklahoma City and big leagues as he was promoted and demoted six separate times. He finished the minor league season with 91.1 innings of work, averaging 11.2 strikeouts and just 3.5 walks per nine innings. And while his 3.47 ERA with the Dodgers *appeared* swell, he managed to walk 27 in only 36.1 innings.

Snippet from The 2022 Prospect Digest Handbook: Watching Pepiot dominate with his fastball / changeup combo, and it's easy to dream upon a #4-type arm. But his lack of third quality option – especially lack of an option he trusts – almost dooms him to a future role as a relief ace. White Sox ace Lucas Giolito has mainly lived off of his tremendous FB/CH combination, but he also shows above-average command.

Scouting Report: Consider the following:

> Since 2006, only three 24-year-old hurlers posted a 28% to 32% strikeout percentage with a 9% to 11% walk percentage in any Triple-A league (min. 75 IP): Kolby Allard, Brock Burke, and Ryan Pepiot.

Nothing's really changed since 2021. Pepiot's fastball sits in the low- to mid-90s with above-average spin (2400 RPM) that helps it up in the zone. And his change is – arguably – the finest in professional baseball. It's up there right alongside Lucas Giolito, it's that good. His slider hovers in the 50-grade range. His command continues to waver at points, sometimes pitch-to-pitch. Pepiot has Tony Gonsolin-type production potential, but he needs to learn how to consistently throw quality strikes.

Ceiling: 2.5- to 3.0-win player
Risk: Moderate
MLB ETA: 2023

8. Andy Pages, RF

Hit	Power	SB	Patience	Glove	Overall
35/40	60	35	55	55	50

Born: 12/08/00	Age: 22	Bats: R	Top Production Comp: Franmil Reyes
Height: 6-1	Weight: 212	Throws: R	

Season	Team	Age	Level	PA	1B	2B	3B	HR	SB	CS	BB%	K%	AVG	OBP	SLG	ISO
2021	LAD	20	A+	538	59	25	1	31	6	3	14.31%	24.54%	0.265	0.394	0.539	0.274
2022	LAD	21	AA	571	57	29	3	26	6	3	10.86%	24.52%	0.236	0.336	0.468	0.232

Background: In terms of the baseball card market, there wasn't a showing that turned more heads in 2021 than Pages' breakout campaign with the Great Lakes Loons. And while some of his cards still command a premium, the market on Pages is – clearly – cooling. Signed out of La Habana, Cuba for $300,000 in 2017, Pages turned in a batting average-deficient debut showing the following summer as he hit .229/.392/.464 with nine doubles and ten homeruns in 52 games between the foreign and stateside rookie leagues. The 6-foot-1, 212-pound rightfielder, however, came roaring back in 2019 as he feasted off the Pioneer League pitching to the tune of .298/.398/.651 with 43 extra-base knocks in only 63 games with Ogden. The club bounced him up to High-A at the start of 2021. And he flourished. Appearing in 120 games with the Loons of Great Lakes, the Cuban outfielder batted .265/.394/.539 with 25 doubles and 31 dingers. Last season, though, Pages' hit tool vanished as he squared off against the toughest minor league level – Double-A. He batted .236/.336/.468 with 29 doubles, three triples, 26 homeruns, and six stolen bases. His overall production topped the league average mark by 2%, according to *Weighted Runs Created Plus*. His offense rebounded during his 22-game stint in the Arizona Fall League, hitting .296/.398/.506 with Glendale.

Snippet from The 2022 Prospect Digest Handbook: Off the charts power thanks to his lightning fast hands. The problem for Pages, however, is his massive swing-and-miss totals; he whiffed in slightly more than 28% of his plate appearances last season. A large, untimely leg kick is clearly causing timing issues as he's struggling to get his foot back down. It's a pretty safe bet that the Dodgers' player development guys are going to eliminate it – or at least quiet it a bit. Mike Stanton type power but the hit tool needs to take several leaps forward.

Los Angeles Dodgers

Scouting Report: Consider the following:

> Since 2006, three 21-year-old hitters met the following criteria in any Double-A league (min. 350 PA): 97 to 107 wRC+, a 9% to 12% walk rate and a 23% to 26% strikeout rate. Those three hitters: Jonathan Villar, Yorman Rodriguez, and Andy Pages.

The year started off on the right foot for Pages as he slugged an impressive .316/.435/.509 over the first couple of weeks. But after that, though, he hit .222/.318/.455 over his remaining 119 games. Pages owns some of the best power in the minor leagues, but it's going to come down to whether the hit tool performs. And it didn't last year in Double-A and it didn't in either rookie ball league either. Offspeed stuff gives him fits, like Jarred Kelenic. And he can't get on top of high, hard offerings either. He's very pitchable. But he can bang middle-middle stuff.

Ceiling: 2.5-win player
Risk: Moderate to High
MLB ETA: 2023/2024

9. Yunior Garcia, 1B/RF

Hit	Power	SB	Patience	Glove	Overall
50/55	45/55	35	50	50	50

Born: 07/29/01	Age: 21	Bats: R	Top Production Comp: N/A
Height: 6-0	Weight: 198	Throws: R	

Season	Team	Age	Level	PA	1B	2B	3B	HR	SB	CS	BB%	K%	AVG	OBP	SLG	ISO
2021	LAD	19	CPX	124	23	5	1	4	2	0	8.06%	23.39%	0.300	0.371	0.473	0.173
2022	LAD	20	A	377	60	28	1	13	2	0	8.75%	19.89%	0.305	0.383	0.512	0.207
2022	LAD	20	A+	34	5	0	0	0	0	0	0.00%	35.29%	0.152	0.147	0.152	0.000

Background: An under-the-radar signing during the summer of 2017. The front office quietly handed the promising first baseman / outfielder a $300,000 deal, the max the organization was allowed to spend due to their big expenditures a few years prior. Garcia looked *completely overwhelmed* during his first two years in pro ball, hitting .226/.319/.411 as a 16-year-old in the Dominican Summer League and .236/.253/.403 in the Arizona Summer League a year later. The front office brass decided to keep the then-19-year-old in the Complex League in 2021 and – finally – his bat showed some promising signs of life: he slugged .300/.371/.473 with five doubles, one triple, and four homeruns in 31 games. And Garcia, who measures in at 6-feet and 198 pounds, continued that momentum towards his breakout with Rancho Cucamonga in 2022. Appearing in 98 games with the Quakes, the Bani, Dominican Republic native mashed .305/.383/.512 with 28 doubles, one triple, 13 homeruns, and – just for good measure – a pair of stolen bases. As measured by *Weighted Runs Created Plus*, his overall production surpassed the league average mark by 30%. Garcia appeared in 10 games with the Loons to cap off his wildly successful campaign.

Scouting Report: Consider the following:

> Since 2006, seven 20-year-old hitters met the following criteria in a season in any Low-A league (min. 350 PA): 125 to 135 wRC+, an 8% to 10% walk rate, and an 18% to 22% strikeout rate. Those seven hitters: Christian Vazquez, Daz Cameron, Thomas Neal, Adam Hall, Aderlin Rodriguez, Chris Bostick, and Yunior Garcia.

Betting big on Garcia means betting on his plus bat speed. The young Dominican first baseman (and part-time right-fielder) is still beginning to tap into his offensive ceiling, including above-average thump. There's some Josh Bell level of offensive potential with Garcia. The Dodgers are going to send him back to High-A at the start of the year, but an extended stint in Double-A isn't out of the question either. Breakout candidate. There's a .280/.340/.440 type ceiling, but it's risky at this point. It's a long shot, but he could be a Top 100 prospect within a year.

Ceiling: 2.5-win player
Risk: Moderate to High
MLB ETA: 2024/2025

10. Maddux Bruns, LHP

FB	CB	SL	CH	Command	Overall
60	60	60	50	45/50	60

Born: 06/20/02	Age: 21	Bats: L	Top Production Comp: Max Fried
Height: 6-2	Weight: 205	Throws: L	

Season	Team	Age	Level	IP	TBF	K/9	K%	BB/9	BB%	K-BB%	ERA	FIP	xFIP	Pit/Bat
2022	LAD	20	A	44.1	216	13.60	31.02%	9.14	20.83%	10.19%	5.68	5.01	5.77	3.80

Background: For the first time since Clayton Kershaw's selection in the opening round in 2006, the Dodgers of Los Angeles opted for a teenage southpaw in the first round of the draft. Less than two years later after his joining the organization, Kershaw was starring for the Dodgers on what would become the first steps of a historic, Hall of Fame career. Maddux John Bruns, who was named after Greg Maddux and John Smoltz, isn't embarking on the same meteoric rise through the minor leagues. Taken

Los Angeles Dodgers

with the 29th overall pick two years ago – and the only selection the organization owned among the Top 100 picks – Bruns dominated the competition at Alabama-based UMS-Wright Prep. But the club's $2.4 million investment hardly resembled the same hurler since donning a professional uniform. Bruns showed some yips during his abbreviated debut in the Complex League, posting a 5-to-7 strikeout-to-walk ratio in five innings of work. And what was hoped to be a minor speed bump in loss of command, proved to a Grand Canyon-esque roadblock. Last season, in 21 starts with Rancho Cucamonga, Bruns averaged 13.6 strikeouts and a historically poor 9.1 walks per nine innings.

Snippet from The 2022 Prospect Digest Handbook: There's some Max Fried-type potential brewing in his left arm.

Scouting Report: You could make the argument – and a rather *strong* argument – that Bruns owns the best repertoire in the entire Dodgers' farm system. And that's saying something given some of the high octane arms the club's stashed away in the minor leagues. Explosive, late-lifed fastball that's difficult to get on top of, even if a hitter is sitting on it. A wickedly unfair snap-dragon of curveball, like it was betrothed to him from Clayton Kershaw, who was handed down the secret from Sandy Koufax. His slider adds a *third* plus offering. And his changeup may eventually creep into above-average territory. But the elephant in the room is whether Bruns can hit the broadside of a barn, let along throw strikes consistently. If Bobby Miller's baseball ceiling is the equivalent to a million dollar mansion, then Bruns' house is in the same neighborhood – it just needs a little TLC. And strikes. Lots of strikes.

Ceiling: 4.0-win player
Risk: Extreme
MLB ETA: 2025/2026

11. James Outman, OF

Hit	Power	SB	Patience	Glove	Overall
45	55	55	55	50	50

Born: 05/14/97 **Age:** 26 **Bats:** L **Top Production Comp:** Josh Willingham
Height: 6-3 **Weight:** 215 **Throws:** R

Season	Team	Age	Level	PA	1B	2B	3B	HR	SB	CS	BB%	K%	AVG	OBP	SLG	ISO
2021	LAD	24	A+	304	33	12	8	9	21	2	14.80%	28.95%	0.250	0.385	0.472	0.222
2021	LAD	24	AA	187	29	9	1	9	2	2	9.63%	27.27%	0.289	0.369	0.518	0.229
2022	LAD	25	AA	307	43	17	1	16	7	3	12.38%	28.99%	0.295	0.394	0.552	0.257
2022	LAD	25	AAA	252	27	14	6	15	6	1	12.70%	25.00%	0.292	0.390	0.627	0.335

Background: One of the most productive minor leagues bats over the past two seasons. Outman has forced the Dodgers – as well as outsiders – to take notice, despite his advancing age. Taken as part of the club's now disastrous 2018 draft class, Outman, the 224th player selected that summer, was a bit of a surprise pick given his lackluster showing at Sacramento State. He left the school as a .249/.359/.482 career hitter in 147 games for the Western Athletic Conference squad. Despite the mediocre production lines, the front office brass saw something lurking deep *and* they were able to unlock it – rather quickly, too. After a decent debut showing in the Pioneer League, Outman struggled *mightily* during his jaunt thorough the old Midwest League in 2019, batting a lowly .226/.322/.407 with 15 doubles, four triples, 19 homeruns, and 20 stolen bases. But something happened once minor league action returned after the lost 2020 season. Something career altering. Outman slugged an aggregate .266/.379/.490 with 21 doubles, nine triples, 18 homeruns, and 23 stolen bases between his time with Great Lakes and Tulsa. And he raised his production another level last season. In 125 games with Tulsa and Oklahoma City, the 6-foot-3, 215-pound outfielder bashed .294/.393/.586 with career bests in doubles (31) and homeruns (31) to go along with seven triples and 13 stolen bases. Per *Weighted Runs Created Plus*, his overall production topped the league average mark by an impressive 41%. Los Angeles called him for a four-game cameo in late July / early August. Outman promptly went 6-for-13 with two doubles and a dinger.

Scouting Report: Consider the following:

> Since 2006, only four 25-year-old hitters met the following criteria in any Triple-A league (min. 250 PA): 140 to 150 wRC+, 24% to 26% strikeout rate, and a double-digit walk rate. Those four hitters: Jorge Soler, Drew Ellis, David Villar, and – of course – James Outman.

Every couple of years or so an older prospect with a history of production – unexpectedly – forces his way into a big league lineup and produces. Guys like Justin Turner or Jeff McNeil or Ty France, all of whom wouldn't become big league regulars until their age-26 season. Outman has all the tools to follow in their footsteps as an unheralded, late blossoming regular – if he can make enough contact. Above-average power and speed, solid defense, and strong walk rates. Below-average hit tool. But Outman has enough secondary skills to keep him as a low end regular. In terms of big league ceiling, think: .245/.330/.440.

Ceiling: 1.5- to 2.0-win player
Risk: Moderate
MLB ETA: Debuted in 2022

Los Angeles Dodgers

12. Nick Nastrini, RHP

FB	CB	SL	CH	Command	Overall
60	55	55	55	40/45	45

Born: 02/18/00	Age: 23	Bats: R	Top Production Comp: N/A
Height: 6-2	Weight: 215	Throws: R	

Season	Team	Age	Level	IP	TBF	K/9	K%	BB/9	BB%	K-BB%	ERA	FIP	xFIP	Pit/Bat
2021	LAD	21	A	13.0	55	20.77	54.55%	4.85	12.73%	41.82%	2.08	3.69	2.13	4.31
2022	LAD	22	A+	86.1	364	13.24	34.89%	4.07	10.71%	24.18%	3.86	3.88	3.39	4.06
2022	LAD	22	AA	30.1	118	12.46	35.59%	4.75	13.56%	22.03%	4.15	4.81	3.87	4.19

Background: The 6-foot-3, 215-pound right-hander had a rollercoaster of a career at UCLA. The California-born right-hander was practically unhittable during brief freshman season with the Bruins in 2019, posting a 28-to-7 strikeout-to-walk ratio in 19.2 innings to go along with a sparkling 1.37 ERA. A year later he made four mediocre starts before the pandemic forced a premature end to the year. Nastrini struck out 19 and walked 10 in 15.2 innings of work. So that checks off the good (2019) and the mediocre (2020). That means his 2021 was the bad (2021). Nastrini finished his collegiate career with a 6.89 ERA across 31.1 innings with 48 punch outs and a worrisome 38 free passes. The loss of command, though, didn't stop the Dodgers from snagging the enigmatic right-hander in the fourth round two years ago, though. And he immediately became a force to be reckoned with. Nastrini posted a ridiculous 32-to-7 strikeout-to-walk ratio in 14.0 innings – which only proved to be a harbinger of things to come in 2022. Making 27 starts last season (21 with Great Lakes and six with Tulsa), the former Bruin tossed 116.2 innings of work, recording 169 punch outs, 55 walks, and a 3.93 ERA. He finished the season with an aggregate 4.12 FIP.

Scouting Report: Consider the following:

> Since 2006, only four 22-year-old hurlers posted a strikeout percentage of at least 33% in any High-A league (min. 75 IP): Dean Kremer, Kai-Wei Teng, Ignacio Feliz, and Nick Nastrini.

Definite big league starter's arsenal; the former fourth rounder owns four above-average or better offerings. Nastrini's plus fastball sits in the 95- to 96 mph range with life upstairs. Both breaking balls are above-average with the nod to the curveball as the better of the two options, though he will struggle throwing it consistently for strikes. He'll also mix in an above-average, mid-80s changeup, which is thrown with tremendous arm speed. While his command has taken several important strides forward, it's still in 40-grade territory at times. It wavers. At points in the season Nastrini locked in on the strike zone and was utterly dominant (he posted a 109-to-26 strikeout-to-walk ratio in 76 innings between June 3 and August 30). Beyond on that widow he walked 29 in 40 innings.

Ceiling: 1.5-win player
Risk: Moderate
MLB ETA: 2023

13. Eddys Leonard, SS

Hit	Power	SB	Patience	Glove	Overall
45	50	50	50	40/45	45

Born: 11/10/00	Age: 22	Bats: R	Top Production Comp: N/A
Height: 5-11	Weight: 195	Throws: R	

Season	Team	Age	Level	PA	1B	2B	3B	HR	SB	CS	BB%	K%	AVG	OBP	SLG	ISO
2021	LAD	20	A	308	42	19	2	14	6	2	11.04%	24.03%	0.295	0.399	0.544	0.249
2021	LAD	20	A+	184	29	10	2	8	3	1	9.24%	22.83%	0.299	0.375	0.530	0.232
2022	LAD	21	A+	566	80	32	4	15	4	4	7.95%	21.02%	0.264	0.348	0.435	0.171

Background: An under-the-radar signing from Santo Domingo during the summer of 2017. Leonard would make his debut with a Dodgers affiliate the following year as he appeared in 45 games in his home country. The batting average-deprived output was largely buoyed by his bloated walk rates. The 5-foot-11, 195-pound infielder moved stateside in 2019 and quickly breezed through the Arizona Summer League and enjoyed a quick jaunt in the Pioneer League. He even squeezed in an appearance with Great Lakes near the end of the year. Leonard had his true coming out party two years ago as he mashed his way through Low-A and continued slugging in a second half promotion up to High-A. He finished the season with an aggregate .297/.390/.539 slash line with 29 doubles, four triples, and 22 homeruns in 107 games. Last season the front office – in a surprising move – sent the slugging shortstop back down to High-A for a longer look. His production backed up a bit as he finished the year with a .264/.348/.436 mark with 32 doubles, four triples, 15 homeruns, and a quartet of stolen bases. His overall production, according to *Weighted Runs Created Plus*, topped the league average mark by 19%.

Snippet from The 2022 Prospect Digest Handbook: Last season, though, he cut down his batted ball rates and began driving the ball more consistently, with more authority. There are some mechanical tweaks in his swing that are still required. For example, his back foot has a tendency to disengage from the ground.

Los Angeles Dodgers

Scouting Report: Consider the following:

> Since 2006, only three 21-year-old hitters posted a 115 to 125 wRC+ mark with a 7% to 9% walk rate and a 20% to 22% strikeout rate in any High-A league (min. 350 PA): Xavier Paul, Brad Harman, and Eddys Leonard.

Coming off of his stupendous showing in 2021, Leonard looked poised to spend a significant portion of 2022 in Double-A, but that never materialized for the streaky infielder. Leonard plays defense like he brings a sieve out to shortstop. And his regression with the bat doesn't allow for his offense to carry the position. Average bat speed. Average foot speed. Average-ish power. There's just not a tool – both present or projecting in the future – to paves a way to everyday duties.

Ceiling: 1.5-win player
Risk: Moderate
MLB ETA: 2024

14. Jorbit Vivas, 2B/3B

Hit	Power	SB	Patience	Glove	Overall
50/55	40	40	50	50	45

Born: 03/09/01	Age: 22	Bats: L	Top Production Comp: Omar Infante
Height: 5-10	Weight: 171	Throws: R	

Season	Team	Age	Level	PA	1B	2B	3B	HR	SB	CS	BB%	K%	AVG	OBP	SLG	ISO
2021	LAD	20	A	375	65	20	4	13	5	3	7.20%	11.20%	0.311	0.389	0.515	0.204
2021	LAD	20	A+	102	20	6	0	1	3	1	12.75%	12.75%	0.318	0.422	0.424	0.106
2022	LAD	21	A+	570	93	19	7	10	2	1	11.05%	10.18%	0.269	0.374	0.401	0.132

Background: Signed off the international market for $300,000 during the summer of 2017. Vivas looked dreadful during his debut in the Dominican Summer League the following year, hitting a lowly .222/.350/.296 with just 11 doubles and a triple in 51 games. But the lefty-swinging infielder was a remade prospect during his showing in 2019 as he dominated the Arizona Summer League for 30 games and looked comfortable against the older competition in the Pioneer League. He finished the year with an aggregate .327/.410/.472 in 54 total games. Vivas continued to produce as he moved into Low-A and – eventually – High-A, posting an impressive .312/.396/.496. Last season Vivas's production continued to march onward. Appearing in 128 games with the Great Lakes Loons, the 5-foot-10, 171-pound second / third baseman cobbled together a mediocre .267/.374/.401 with 19 doubles, seven triples, and 10 homeruns. Per *Weighted Runs Created Plus*, his overall production topped the league average mark by an impressive 20%.

Snippet from The 2022 Prospect Digest Handbook: One of the more underrated prospects in the system, as well as in all of baseball. A throwback to ballplayers of yesteryear, Vivas is an extreme contact hitter, posting an aggregate K-rate of just 11.5% last season. The walk rates will never inflate his OBP, but he's a patient hitter and won't chase frequently. He profiles better at the keystone, but may hit enough to justify keep him at the hot corner as he matures.

Scouting Report: Consider the following:

> Since 2006, six 21-year-old hitters posted a 115 to 125 wRC+ with a sub-13% strikeout rate in any High-A league (min. 350 PA): Andrelton Simmons, Steven Kwan, Ben Revere, Willie Cabrera, Steve Lombardozzi, and Jorbit Vivas. For those counting at home: with the exception of Vivas, Cabrera is the only player not to make it to the big leagues.

An extreme contact hitter that's grown into more power than originally expected – though it's still a below-average skill. The Dodgers continue to bounce Vivas between the keystone and hot corner, though the bat plays far better at the former. Southpaws have given the lefty-swinging prospect fits throughout his career and 2022 was no different as he hit .222/.357/.333 against them (compared to .285/.380/.423 vs. RHP). Utility man in the making.

Ceiling: 1.5-win player
Risk: Moderate
MLB ETA: 2024

Los Angeles Dodgers

15. Alex Freeland, IF

Hit	Power	SB	Patience	Glove	Overall
45/50	50	45	55	50	45

Born: 08/24/01	Age: 21	Bats: B	Top Production Comp: N/A
Height: 6-2	Weight: 200	Throws: R	

Season	Team	Age	Level	PA	1B	2B	3B	HR	SB	CS	BB%	K%	AVG	OBP	SLG	ISO
2022	LAD	20	A	36	6	1	0	3	2	0	5.56%	30.56%	0.313	0.389	0.625	0.313

Background: Highly touted coming out of Mariner High School in 2019, *Perfect Game* listed the former prep star as the 27th best incoming freshman on their Top 500 list. Freeland left the Cape Coral-based high school as a .323 hitter in 92 career games. The 6-foot-2, 200-pound infielder stepped into the heart of Central Florida's lineup as a true freshman without missing a beat as he batted a rock solid .288/.402/.429 with 10 doubles and seven dingers in 60 games. Freeland earned a trip to the prestigious Cape Cod League that summer – though the results were mediocre (.242/.383/.288). Freeland picked up right where he left off as a sophomore for the Knights as he slugged .282/.419/.570 with eight doubles, 11 homeruns, and six stolen bases (in just seven total attempts). LA selected the pesky sophomore in the third round, 105th overall, and signed him to a deal worth $580,200. Freeland appeared in eight games with the Quakes of Rancho Cucamonga, hitting .313/.389/.625 with a double, three homeruns, and two stolen bases.

Scouting Report: A tremendous value pick by the Dodgers last season. A wiry twitchy infielder with a nose for first base and some intriguing power potential for an up-the-middle player. Good bat to ball skills, patient approach, and he'll grind out at bats. He can really turn on the inside hard stuff. This guy's a gamer. He'll find a spot in the big leagues.

Ceiling: 1.5-win player
Risk: Moderate
MLB ETA: 2025

16. Jose Ramos, OF

Hit	Power	SB	Patience	Glove	Overall
35/40	60	30	50	50	45

Born: 01/01/01	Age: 22	Bats: R	Top Production Comp: N/A
Height: 6-1	Weight: 200	Throws: R	

Season	Team	Age	Level	PA	1B	2B	3B	HR	SB	CS	BB%	K%	AVG	OBP	SLG	ISO
2021	LAD	20	CPX	68	14	6	0	3	1	0	10.29%	20.59%	0.383	0.456	0.633	0.250
2021	LAD	20	A	220	32	18	3	8	1	4	7.27%	25.91%	0.313	0.377	0.559	0.246
2022	LAD	21	A+	407	46	19	3	19	2	0	9.58%	32.68%	0.240	0.322	0.467	0.227
2022	LAD	21	A	138	19	3	3	6	2	0	13.04%	26.09%	0.277	0.391	0.518	0.241

Background: The Dodgers have never been shy about spending – and spending BIG – on the international market, be it on the likes of Yasiel Puig or Yaisel Sierra or teenage phenoms like Diego Cartaya. But it's an organization that also does its due diligence. Say, like, Jose Ramos, who joined the organization five years ago for the price of new family car – $30,000. After a solid debut showing in the Dominican Summer League, Ramos blitzed through the rookie leagues in dominant fashion in 2021, slugging .383/.456/.633 in 15 games – though he *was* 20-years-old. The front office – finally – relented and sent Ramos with his scorching stick up to Low-A. And he continued to swing it as he batted .313/.377/.559 in 47 games. Ramos opened up last season back with Rancho Cucamonga, where he continued to mash (.277/.391/.518). He spent the season's final four months getting comfortable with the Loons in High-A. Ramos finished the year with an aggregate .249/.339/.479 with 22 doubles, six triples, 25 homeruns, and four stolen bases. His overall production, according to *Weighted Runs Created Plus*, topped the league average mark by 20%. Los Angeles sent him to the Arizona Fall League after the season. And he…continued to hit as he batted .275/.326/.463 with Glendale.

Snippet from The 2022 Prospect Digest Handbook: is going to be a boom-or-bust type of hitter: he's either going to make enough consistent contact to become an All-Star or his K-rates are going to bloat and he's going to flame out. I don't see it ended any other way.

Scouting Report: Consider the following:

> Since 2006, only four 21-year-old hitters met the following criteria in any High-A league (min. 350 PA): 112 to 122 wRC+ with an 8% to 11% walk rate and a strikeout rate north of 31%. Those four hitters: Billy Rowell, Jairo Pomares, Brandon Howlett, and – of course – Jose Ramos.

Boom. Bust. No other option. And it's not surprising that his all-or-nothing approach was exposed in High-A as he set a career worst 32.7% strikeout rate at the level. Fantastic bat speed, but the swing is long and he can't / won't make any adjusts on offspeed offerings. If you hang it, he'll bang it. But if you can keep things soft low and way, he'll go away. He plays a solid centerfielder.

Ceiling: 1.0- to 1.5-win player
Risk: Moderate to High
MLB ETA: 2023

Los Angeles Dodgers

17. Landon Knack, RHP

FB	CB	SL	CH	Command	Overall
50	50	50	55	50	40

Born: 07/15/97	Age: 25	Bats: L	Top Production Comp: Joe Blanton
Height: 6-2	Weight: 220	Throws: R	

Season	Team	Age	Level	IP	TBF	K/9	K%	BB/9	BB%	K-BB%	ERA	FIP	xFIP	Pit/Bat
2021	LAD	23	A+	39.2	154	12.48	35.71%	1.13	3.25%	32.47%	2.50	2.33	2.86	3.87
2021	LAD	23	AA	22.2	92	10.72	29.35%	1.19	3.26%	26.09%	4.37	5.20	3.64	3.82
2022	LAD	24	AA	64.2	282	11.13	28.37%	3.76	9.57%	18.79%	5.01	4.24	4.16	3.93

Background: Not exactly bloodlines, per se, but Knack has some family times at the big league level. His brother-in-law, Will Craig, was a former first round pick by the Pirates and had a couple cups of big league coffee on his resume. Knack spent two seasons at Walters State Community College before transferring to East Tennessee State. But once he stepped foot on the Buccaneers' campus, he flourished as the club's best hurler. And he was nothing short of magnificent during his COVID-abbreviated 2020 season: he tossed 25 innings and recorded a mind-boggling 50-to-1 strikeout-to-walk ratio. Los Angeles selected Knack in the second round, 60th overall, and signed him a team-friendly $712,500 deal. Knack maintained his absurd level of dominance during his debut season in 2021 as well, averaging 11.8 strikeouts and just 1.2 walks per nine innings during his time with Great Lakes and Tulsa. Last season the hard-throwing right-hander got off to a delayed start, courtesy of a soft tissue issue, and he would miss a month of action during the year as well. Beyond those bumps and bruises, the 6-foot-2, 220-pound former Buccaneer was able to log 64.2 innings with Tulsa, posting an 80-to-27 strikeout-to-walk ratio.

Snippet from The 2022 Prospect Digest Handbook: One of the most, in not *the most*, consistent strike-throwing machine in the minor leagues. Knack fills up the zone with quality pitches at will. And when he does miss, it's often on purpose as a chase offering. Rick Porcello-type potential.

Scouting Report: During a midseason start that I scouted, Knack's entire repertoire was *considerably* worse than the previous season. His fastball was sitting in the 90- to 91-mph range. His curveball was loopier. His slider lacked bite. And his changeup floated. The entire arsenal downgraded at least an entire grade. Even the command backed up. Knack's now entering his age-25 season and he resembles Joe Blanton, both in terms of physique and soft-tossing repertoire. A late-career Joe Blanton.

Ceiling: 1.0-win player
Risk: Low to Moderate
MLB ETA: 2023

18. Josue De Paula, OF

Hit	Power	SB	Patience	Glove	Overall
40/50	30/55	50/40	50	50	45

Born: 05/24/05	Age: 18	Bats: L	Top Production Comp: N/A
Height: 6-3	Weight: 185	Throws: L	

Season	Team	Age	Level	PA	1B	2B	3B	HR	SB	CS	BB%	K%	AVG	OBP	SLG	ISO
2022	LAD	17	DSL	223	45	13	2	5	16	6	14.35%	13.90%	0.349	0.448	0.522	0.172

Background: Signed off the international market last January for an undisclosed bonus (there aren't any reports indicating the cost, to the best of my knowledge). De Paula, who was born in Brooklyn, New York, was one of the most dynamic bats in the Dominican Summer League in 2022. Appearing in a 53 games, the 6-foot-3, 185-pound outfielder mashed .349/.448/.522 with 13 doubles, two triples, five homeruns, and 16 stolen bases (in 22 total attempts). Per *Weighted Runs Created Plus*, his overall production topped the league average threshold by 61%.

Scouting Report: Consider the following:

> Last season there were 255 qualified hitters in the Dominican Summer League. De Paula's 161 wRC+ ranked as 10th best mark. Only five other 17-year-old hitters topped that total: Aron Estrada (178 wRC+), Reylin Perez (176 wRC+), Carlos Sanchez (169 wRC+), Enmanuel Tejeda (162 wRC+), and Lazaro Montes (162 wRC+).

Long and projectable, De Paula made quick work of the inferior pitching in the foreign rookie league last summer. A lot of the league's top performance's tend be inflated – *significantly* – by bloated walk rates. Perez, Sanchez, and Tejeda all walked more than 20% of the time. And while De Paula found first base via the free pass 14% of the time, it's less of a concern. Lightning fast hands, De Paula didn't have any issues getting around on inside hard stuff. Great bat speed and loft which should allow him to grow into above-average power. It wouldn't be surprising to see De Paula rank among the team's Top 5 prospects by the end of 2023. Breakout candidate.

Ceiling: 1.0- to 1.5-win player
Risk: Moderate to High
MLB ETA: 2026

Los Angeles Dodgers

19. Yeiner Fernandez, C/2B

	Hit	Power	SB	Patience	Glove	Overall
	50/55	40	35	50	50	40

Born: 09/19/02	Age: 20	Bats: R	Top Production Comp: N/A
Height: 5-9	Weight: 170	Throws: R	

Season	Team	Age	Level	PA	1B	2B	3B	HR	SB	CS	BB%	K%	AVG	OBP	SLG	ISO
2021	LAD	18	CPX	157	31	11	1	2	1	3	6.37%	17.20%	0.319	0.382	0.454	0.135
2021	LAD	18	A	34	14	1	0	1	0	0	5.88%	8.82%	0.516	0.559	0.645	0.129
2022	LAD	19	A	423	78	16	2	10	3	2	10.87%	13.00%	0.292	0.383	0.430	0.138

Background: The Dodgers signed the Barquisimeto, Venezuela, native to a deal worth slightly less than three-quarters of a million dollars three years ago. The 5-foot-9, 170-pound catcher / second baseman made his professional debut two years ago. And he left *quite* the impression. Bypassing the foreign rookie league and heading straight in the Complex Leagues, Fernandez went 2-for-5 in his first professional game and he continued to mash during the rest of season – including a seven-game cameo in Rancho Cucamonga. He finished the first pro season with a .355/.414/.488 line with 12 doubles, one triple, and three homeruns. He spent the entirety of last season battling the pitching in Low-A, often times coming away as the victor. Appearing in 89 games with the Quakes, Fernandez slugged .292/.383/.430 with 16 doubles, two triples, 10 homeruns, and a trio of stolen bases. His overall production, as measured by *Weighted Runs Created Plus*, topped the league average threshold by 14%. For his career, he's sporting a .312/.393/.449 mark through 131 games.

Scouting Report: Consider the following:

> Since 2006, only a pair of 19-year-old hitters posted a 110 to 120 wRC+ with a 12% to 16% strikeout rate and an 8% to 11% walk rate in any Low-A league (min. 350 PA): Jose Pirela and Yeiner Fernandez.

The Dodgers are taking a page out of Austin Barnes' book, who – in turn – took a page out Craig Biggio's book, as Fernandez spent time behind the dish *and* at the keystone last season. Not overly big and lacks a ton of physical projection, Fernandez takes a solid approach at the plate that results in *a lot* of contact and plenty of free passes. There's not a lot of hope for added power down the line without reworking his swing to create more loft.

Ceiling: 1.0-win player
Risk: Moderate
MLB ETA: 2025

20. Rayne Doncon, 2B/SS

	Hit	Power	SB	Patience	Glove	Overall
	40/45	50/60	40	50	45/50	40

Born: 09/22/03	Age: 19	Bats: R	Top Production Comp: N/A
Height: 6-2	Weight: 176	Throws: R	

Season	Team	Age	Level	PA	1B	2B	3B	HR	SB	CS	BB%	K%	AVG	OBP	SLG	ISO
2021	LAD	17	DSL	119	19	4	2	3	7	1	13.45%	23.53%	0.283	0.387	0.455	0.172
2022	LAD	18	CPX	215	25	16	1	9	6	2	6.98%	17.67%	0.256	0.307	0.482	0.226
2022	LAD	18	A	43	7	0	0	3	0	0	6.98%	11.63%	0.250	0.302	0.475	0.225

Background: Not too make anyone – especially myself – feel exceptionally old, but the young Dominican middle infielder was born the same year that the Dodgers selected former All-Star right-hander Chad Billingsley in the opening round – 2003. Los Angeles signed the 6-foot-2, 176-pound middle infielder for slightly less than $500,000 at the end of January two years ago. Doncon, a native of San Pedro de Macoris, Dominican Republic, made his organizational debut a few months later as he stayed in his home country with the club's foreign rookie league affiliate. Doncon batted a rock solid .283/.387/.455 with four doubles, a pair of triples, three homeruns, and seven stolen bases in only 31 games. Last season, the front office sent the International Bonus Baby stateside into the Complex League. He responded by hitting .256/.307/.482 with 26 extra-base knocks in 51 games. He spent the last couple of weeks maintaining an eerily similar slash line in Low-A (.250/.302/.475). Per *Weighted Runs Created Plus*, Doncon's overall production topped the league average mark by 7%.

Scouting Report: Wide-based stance with a big leg kick to get things moving. Doncon's long limbed and has *plenty* of room to fill out on his 6-foot-2, 176-pound frame. He makes more contact than expected based on his swing. It's violent and can get long at times. There's impressive raw power already present, and it projects to be a plus in-game tool at full maturity. Doncon didn't punch out that frequently, but there wasn't a lot of consistent quality contact either. Pitch recognition seemed to be an issue. Bat first infielder that only goes as far as the hit tool carries him in the coming years.

Ceiling: 1.0-win player
Risk: Moderate
MLB ETA: 2026

Miami Marlins

Top Prospects

Miami Marlins

1. Eury Perez, RHP

FB	CB	SL	CH	Command	Overall
70	60	60	65	55	70

Born: 04/15/03   **Age:** 20   **Bats:** R   **Top Production Comp:** Jose Fernandez
Height: 6-8   **Weight:** 200   **Throws:** R

Season	Team	Age	Level	IP	TBF	K/9	K%	BB/9	BB%	K-BB%	ERA	FIP	xFIP	Pit/Bat
2021	MIA	18	A	56.0	222	13.18	36.94%	3.38	9.46%	27.48%	1.61	2.73	3.33	4.20
2021	MIA	18	A+	22.0	83	10.64	31.33%	2.05	6.02%	25.30%	2.86	5.32	4.04	4.08
2022	MIA	19	AA	75.0	311	12.72	34.08%	3.00	8.04%	26.05%	4.08	3.52	3.52	3.99

Background: A lot of things haven't gone right during the Marlins' latest rebuild cycle. Their draft classes have – typically – been uninspiring, at best. Southpaw Trevor Rogers is the only notable big leaguer from their 2017 class. The club's first four picks a year later have been utterly disappointing – Connor Scott, who's not even with the organization anymore, Osiris Johnson, Will Banfield, and Tristan Pompey. Armed with the fourth overall pick a year later, Miami opted to take Vanderbilt slugger J.J. Bleday over Riley Greene, CJ Adams, Nick Lodolo, Alek Manoah, Brett Baty, and Corbin Carroll. Their 2021 first rounder Max Meyer, the third overall pick, just underwent Tommy John surgery in early August. And if *that* wasn't bad enough, the front office swung-and-missed mightily when they dealt away Giancarlo Stanton (even though it was really a straight up salary dump), J.T. Relamuto, and Christian Yelich. (Note: they did hit big on the Marcell Ozuna deal with St. Louis, which brought Sandy Alcantara, last season's Cy Young winner, and Zac Gallen; and Jazz Chisholm for Gallen looks like a rare win-win too.) But there's one thing that the franchise's farm system has going for it – Eury Perez. Not exactly unheralded on the international free agency market in 2019, Perez, though, was *clearly* underrated by all of baseball – especially consider that Miami inked the 6-foot-8, 200-pound right-hander to a relatively modest $200,000 deal. Since then the lanky right-hander has added several inches and a couple dozen pounds to his still growing frame, taking his vast potential along for the ride as well. The Dominican was figuratively – and almost *literally* – unhittable during his debut in 2021 as his split time between Jupiter and Beloit. Perez would throw 78.0 innings with a whopping 108 strikeouts and only 26 free passes to go along with a Bob Gibson-esque 1.96 ERA. Last season he was just as dominant. This time, though, it came against the challenging Double-A competition. In 17 starts with the Pensacola Blue Wahoos, the young righty averaged an impressive 12.7 strikeouts against just 3.0 walks per nine innings. His season was interrupted as a "minor right should injury" forced him out of action for six weeks late in the year.

Snippet from The 2022 Prospect Digest Handbook: Combine his age, frame size, and impressive repertoire with his ability to consistently throw *quality* strikes, and it's not unreasonable to think that Perez has a puncher's chance to develop into the minors' top pitching prospect – as long as he can navigate through the injury nexus.

Scouting Report: Consider the following:

> Since 2006, there have been only nine 19-year-old hurlers to throw at least 50 innings in any Double-A league. Here's how Perez's production stacks up against his peers:
>
> Strikeout Percentage (34.08%): 1st
> Strikeout-to-Walk Percentage (26.05%): 1st
> Strikeout Rate (12.72 K/9): 1st
> Strikeout-to-Walk Rate (4.24): 2nd

There are certain pitchers that just have "it" -- that undeniable mix of talent, youth, and production that doesn't come along to often – or rarely. Eury Perez, the former underrated international free agent, has IT. And then some. The big right-hander combines arguably the best repertoire in the minor leagues with a strong feel for the strike zone *and* the guile / willingness to change speeds. Perez's heater, a borderline plus-plus offering, sits *comfortably* in the mid- to upper-90s that just screams late life from the moment it leaves his hand. He'll feature two different breaking balls: a plus curveball and a newly added plus slider that will often look like a hard, impossibly difficult to hit cutter. And if that wasn't enough, the young right-hander features a deadly, almost unfairly wicked changeup with plenty of arm side fade. Perez is on the short list of top pitching in the game – unequivocally. The only thing that might derail him – rob fans of the joy of watching him dominate – is any unfortunate injuries to his precious right elbow or shoulder.

Ceiling: 6.0-win player
Risk: Moderate
MLB ETA: 2023

Miami Marlins

2. Jacob Berry, 3B

	Hit	Power	SB	Patience	Glove	Overall
	50/55	50/60	30	55	45	60

Born: 05/05/01	Age: 22	Bats: B	Top Production Comp: N/A
Height: 6-0	Weight: 212	Throws: R	

Season	Team	Age	Level	PA	1B	2B	3B	HR	SB	CS	BB%	K%	AVG	OBP	SLG	ISO
2022	MIA	21	CPX	18	2	0	0	0	0	0	5.56%	33.33%	0.125	0.222	0.125	0.000
2022	MIA	21	A	148	23	7	0	3	1	1	8.78%	15.54%	0.264	0.358	0.392	0.128

Background: Falling in similar company as a lot of the other top prospects in the 2021 draft class, Berry's father – Perry – has strong ties to professional baseball. The elder Berry, a former middle infielder, was a late round draft pick by the California Angels coming out of high school – though he would eventually attend the University of Louisiana at Lafayette. Three years later the Astros called his name in the fourth round in 1990. His professional career would span four mostly disappointing seasons in the low minors. The younger Berry figures to handle the transition to the pro game significantly better. A powerfully built 6-foot, 212-pound third baseman / right fielder, Berry was a tremendous force in the middle of Arizona's lineup during his true freshman season: in 63 games, he slugged .352/.439/.676 with 19 doubles, five triples, and 17 dingers. He spent the following summer starring for Team USA, putting together a jaw-dropping .387/.475/.871 triple-slash line as he tied for the team lead in doubles (three) and homeruns (four). Prior to the 2022 season, Berry followed former Arizona head coach Jay Johnson to LSU where – of course – he would continue to rake. In 53 games with the Tigers, the 21-year-old switch-hitter batted .370/.464/.630 with nine doubles and 15 homeruns. Miami made him the sixth overall pick last July, signing him to a deal worth an even $6 million. After a four-game jaunt through the Complex League, Berry appeared in 33 games with the Hammerheads, hitting .264/.358/.392 with seven doubles and three homeruns. His overall production, per *Weighted Runs Created Plus*, topped the league average production mark by 18% -- a solid debut for the former collegiate slugger.

Scouting Report: Per the usual, my pre-draft write-up:

> "Consider the following:
>
> Since 2011, only five players have batted at least .350/.425/.650 in a Pac-12 season (min. 250 PA): Spencer Torkelson, Andrew Vaughn, Adley Rutschman, Cameron Cannon, and – of course – Jacob Berry, who accomplished the feat as a freshman (though, to be fair, he was a 20-year-old freshman).
>
> Let's continue:
>
> Since 2011, here's the list of SEC hitters to post a .360/.450/.600 slash line with more walks than strikeouts and a sub-12.0% K-rate in a season (min. 225 PA): Andrew Benintendi, Austin Martin, and Jacob Berry.
>
> Regardless of the mini-study, Berry's statistical comps are littered with early first round picks (sans Cannon, who was a second rounder). Cody Bellinger from the left side and a hulking middle-of-the-lineup thumper from the right side. Berry's contact rates took huge strides between his freshman and sophomore seasons, chopping his K-rate down from 19% to 8%. Patient approach. Above-average power, but he hasn't quite fully tapped into his 30- to 35-homer thump. He's too lumbering to play third, so he's likely headed towards the outfield or first base full time. Ryan Braun without the speed. If he provided defensive value, he'd be a lock as the #1 – though he's still in conversation."

Ceiling: 4.0-win player
Risk: Moderate
MLB ETA: 2024

3. Max Meyer, RHP

	FB	SL	CH	Command	Overall
	60	70	55/60	55	60

Born: 03/12/99	Age: 24	Bats: L	Top Production Comp: Walker Buehler
Height: 6-0	Weight: 196	Throws: R	

Season	Team	Age	Level	IP	TBF	K/9	K%	BB/9	BB%	K-BB%	ERA	FIP	xFIP	Pit/Bat
2021	MIA	22	AA	101.0	416	10.07	27.16%	3.56	9.62%	17.55%	2.41	3.34	3.61	3.57
2021	MIA	22	AAA	10.0	38	15.30	44.74%	1.80	5.26%	39.47%	0.90	1.86	1.98	3.97
2022	MIA	23	AAA	58.0	229	10.09	28.38%	2.95	8.30%	20.09%	3.72	3.47	3.72	3.96

Background: The early part of the 2021 first round looked to be absolutely loaded with the likes of Spencer Torkelson, who was one of the most damaging college bats in recent memory, Heston Kjerstad, an under-slot signing with a

Miami Marlins

long track record of SEC success, and – of course – Max Meyer, the fast-rising reliever-turned-Minnesota-ace, with the third overall pick. Asa Lacy, the dominant southpaw from Texas A&M, and Austin Martin. But each member of the quintet has hit a few roadblocks or obstacles during their young, once promising careers. Torkelson was abysmal during his extended debut in Detroit last season, hitting a hugely disappointing .203/.285/.319 in more than 400 plate appearances. Kjerstad's battled medical issues that kept him seeing a ballfield from 2020 through the beginning of last season. Lacy walked 42 hitters in only 28.0 innings last season. Martin was dealt from Toronto to Minnesota roughly a year after the draft and he's coming off of a .241/.367/.316 showing in Double-A. And, of course, there's Max Meyer, the slider-snapping strikeout artist who dominated Triple-A but dealt with a couple DL stints before succumbing to Tommy John surgery in early August – an injury that will likely knock him out through the majority of 2023. Wonky elbow notwithstanding, Meyer finished his 2022 minor league campaign with 65 strikeouts and only 19 walks in 58.0 innings with Jacksonville. He made two disastrous starts with the Marlins as well.

Snippet from The 2022 Prospect Digest Handbook:. There's a strong #2 vibe to his potential with a non-zero chance he ascends to ace-dom.

Scouting Report: Pre-elbow injury, Meyer owned – perhaps – the best fastball / slider combo among all starting pitchers in the minor leagues. His heater, a plus offering, sits in the mid-90s and would touch a few ticks high on occasion. It's particularly difficult above the belt and in on hitters' hands. His slider, of course, is the real story – a hard, biting upper 80s breaking ball that nearly perfectly mirrors the spin on his four-seamer, which only adds to its wickedness. Meyer will seemingly alter the break on the pitch, something opting for a tighter, more traditional slider. Other times, it'll show more downward tilt – a la a power curveball. And, yet, other times it looks more like a hard cutter. Either way, though, they're all one in the same. Meyer will also feature a rare – too rare, in fact – changeup that flashes plus at times. The former college reliever-turned-starter needs to throw it more often, particularly once he carves out a spot in the Marlins' rotation – assuming there aren't any setbacks in his recovery. A Sandy Alcantara / Max Meyer one-two punch atop a rotation would be lethal.

Ceiling: 4.0-win player
Risk: Moderate to High
MLB ETA: Debuted in 2022

4. Dax Fulton, LHP

FB	CB	SL	CH	Command	Overall
60	55	55	45/50	50	50

Born: 10/16/01 **Age:** 21 **Bats:** L **Top Production Comp:** N/A
Height: 6-7 **Weight:** 225 **Throws:** L

Season	Team	Age	Level	IP	TBF	K/9	K%	BB/9	BB%	K-BB%	ERA	FIP	xFIP	Pit/Bat
2021	MIA	19	A	58.2	251	10.12	26.29%	4.60	11.95%	14.34%	4.30	3.85	4.01	4.04
2021	MIA	19	A+	19.2	86	8.24	20.93%	3.66	9.30%	11.63%	5.49	5.45	4.55	3.98
2022	MIA	20	A+	97.1	423	11.10	28.37%	3.24	8.27%	20.09%	4.07	3.08	3.31	3.92
2022	MIA	20	AA	21.0	80	12.86	37.50%	3.00	8.75%	28.75%	2.57	3.11	2.55	4.14

Background: After selecting University of Minnesota ace Max Meyer with the third overall pick three years ago, the front office brass followed that up with five consecutive pitching picks. Two of those picks – Kyle Nicolas and Kyle Hurt – are no longer with the organization. The second of those selections was used on prep left-hander Dax Fulton. Standing a gargantuan 6-foot-7, 225 pounds, Fulton was one the larger surprises in the farm system two years ago. The Mustang High School product would split his debut season between Low-A and High-A, averaging 9.7 strikeouts and 4.4 walks per nine innings across 19 starts and one relief appearance. And last season was much the same for the big lefty – except better. Fulton began the season back in High-A. He would make 20 starts with the Beloit Sky Carp, throwing 97.1 innings with 120 strikeouts and only 35 walks. Miami bumped him up to the minors' toughest level, Double-A, in late August for four – mostly dominant starts.

Snippet from The 2022 Prospect Digest Handbook: Fulton's young enough that it's likely just him wearing down during his first full season in pro ball. If that assumption's correct, that's a lot of intrigue here. Command and changeup need to show an uptick, though.

Scouting Report: Consider the following:

> Since 2006, only 20-year-old hurlers posted a 27.5% to 29.5% strikeout rate with a walk rate between 7.5% to 9.5% in High-A (min. 75 IP): Tekoah Roby and Dax Fulton, both of whom accomplished the feat in 2022.

A tremendous value pick in the opening parts of the second round. Fulton showcases a standard four-pitch mix: a mid-90s, plus fastball, an above-average, sometimes slurvy curveball, a new above-average slider, and a workable, sometimes decent changeup. Fulton, in spite of his big frame, consistently throws strikes – though he will deal with random bouts of wildness. There's a lot to like about Fulton as a pitching prospect, but he's not an *elite* prospect. He's tracking like a #3 /#4 hurler during his peak.

Ceiling: 2.5- to 3.0-win player
Risk: Moderate
MLB ETA: 2023/2024

Miami Marlins

5. Kahlil Watson, SS

	Hit	Power	SB	Patience	Glove	Overall
	40/55	40/55	60	50	45/55	60

Born: 04/16/03	Age: 20	Bats: L	Top Production Comp: N/A
Height: 5-9	Weight: 178	Throws: R	

Season	Team	Age	Level	PA	1B	2B	3B	HR	SB	CS	BB%	K%	AVG	OBP	SLG	ISO
2021	MIA	18	CPX	42	8	3	2	0	4	1	19.05%	16.67%	0.394	0.524	0.606	0.212
2022	MIA	19	CPX	18	0	2	0	1	0	0	27.78%	27.78%	0.273	0.500	0.727	0.455
2022	MIA	19	A	358	45	16	5	9	16	3	7.54%	35.47%	0.231	0.296	0.395	0.164

Background: Going back to their first draft class in 1992, the Marlins have selected just two shortstops in the opening round – Josh Booty, fifth overall pick in 1994, and – of course – Kahlil Watson, the 16th player taken two years ago. A product of Wake Forest High School, Watson was an offensive dynamo during his abbreviated debut in the Florida Complex League, mashing .394/.524/.606 with three doubles, triples, four stolen bases, and more walks than strikeouts (8-to-7) in nine games. Things seemed to be clicking not only for Watson, but also the organization's new front office. But for all the promise the lefty-swinging shortstop showed in 2021, his production and behavior on the field was on the opposite end of the spectrum. The former prep star started 2022 right where he left off, slugging .294/.338/.603 over the first month, but his numbers cooled considerably over the next two months (.190/.247/.276). And then *The Incident* happened. Watson swung-and-missed following a questionable check-swing strike. On his way back to the dugout the young prospect appeared to mimic a shotgun shooting towards the offending umpire. He was promptly suspended for a several weeks. He would make it back to Jupiter at the end of the month and batted a respectable .256/.347/.454 over his remaining 22 games. Watson finished the season with an aggregate .231/.296/.395 slash line, belting out 16 doubles, five triples, nine homeruns, and 16 stolen bases.

Snippet from The 2022 Prospect Digest Handbook: Love the swing. Does. Not. Get. Cheated. Watson unfurls some impressive power potential despite a modest frame size. He may have some swing-and-miss issues in the professional ranks – at least initially. Phenomenal bat speed combined with a patient approach at the plate. There's some Brandon Phillips-type offensive potential here.

Scouting Report: The success rate for similarly performing 19-year-old hitters is terrible. Consider the following:

> Since 2006, only five 19-year-old hitters posted a 90 to 100 wRC+ with a strikeout rate north of 32% in Low-A (min. 300 PA): Cristian Santana, Jhailyn Ortiz, Ryan Spikes, Eduardo Garcia, and – of course – Khalil Watson.

The swing-and-miss issues that I suspected were on the horizon came into fruition last season as he whiffed in 35.5% of his plate appearances. He's a tremendous athlete, the type that *could* become a key piece as a franchise cornerstone – behavior notwithstanding. Not to excuse Watson's incident, but he's young, clearly has maturity issues, and was mired in an awful two-month stint. The April, July, August, and September production is where the true talent lies. I'd bet on a big bounce back. Watson's the type of athlete that can be a valuable big league with a 40-grade hit tool.

Ceiling: 3.0-win player
Risk: Moderate to High
MLB ETA: 2025

6. Jordan Groshans, 3B/SS

	Hit	Power	SB	Patience	Glove	Overall
	50/55	50/55	30	55	50	50

Born: 10/10/99	Age: 23	Bats: R	Top Production Comp: Nick Castellanos
Height: 6-3	Weight: 205	Throws: R	

Season	Team	Age	Level	PA	1B	2B	3B	HR	SB	CS	BB%	K%	AVG	OBP	SLG	ISO
2021	TOR	21	AA	316	51	23	0	7	0	0	10.76%	19.30%	0.291	0.367	0.450	0.158
2022	TOR	22	AAA	279	51	8	0	1	2	0	12.54%	16.49%	0.250	0.348	0.296	0.046
2022	MIA	22	AAA	133	25	7	0	2	1	0	14.29%	14.29%	0.301	0.398	0.416	0.115

Background: The Marlins' 2018 draft was particularly abysmal. Connor Scott, the 13th overall pick, hasn't hit well and he's no longer with the organization. Infielder Osiris Johnson is coming off of his best professional season, hitting .238/.299/.322 – most of which occurred during his *third* stint in Low-A. Will Banfield is a career .207/.262/.336 in 309 career minor league games. And Tristan Pompey, their third round pick, played Indy Ball in 2022. Last summer, though, the front office dipped their toes back into the 2018 draft and traded for oft-injured, though always promising infielder Jordan Groshans from the Toronto Blue Jays in exchange for Anthony Bass, Zach Pop, and Edward Duran, the Player To Be Named Later. The 12th overall pick five years ago, Groshans finally reach the 100-game threshold in a season last year – despite getting a late start. Between both organizations' Triple-A affiliates, the shortstop / third baseman batted .263/.359/.331 with just 16 doubles and three homeruns. He also appeared In 17 games with the Marlins down the stretch as well, hitting as empty .262/.308/.312 in 65 plate appearances.

Miami Marlins

Snippet from The 2022 Prospect Digest Handbook: Groshans hasn't started tapping into his above-average power, but it's coming. Regardless of his defensive ability, he's not going to stick at shortstop as long as Bo Bichette is around, so third base is his for the taking.

Scouting Report: Despite the loss of considerable development time, Groshans, who was limited to just 98 games between 2019 and 2021, *always* hit and flashed promising power potential. Until last season, that is. The former first rounder started off like a bat out of hell, hitting .350/.449/.425 over his first 24 Triple-A games. But a two month funk wrecked his overall numbers. I'm still a big believer in the hit tool and feel that there's 20-homer pop brewing in the bat, but I'm not sure the Marlins are the organization to coax it out of him. Very short, direct swing with fast hands. Defensively, he plays a passable left side of the infield, though third base is his likely landing spot. In terms of big league ceiling, think: .280/.340/.430.

Ceiling: 2.0-win player
Risk: Moderate
MLB ETA: Debuted 2022

7. Jacob Miller, RHP

FB	CB	SL	CH	Command	Overall
60	60	55	45/50	50	50

Born: 08/10/03	Age: 19	Bats: R	Top Production Comp: N/A
Height: 6-2	Weight: 180	Throws: R	

Background: The population of Baltimore, Ohio, is the equivalent of a large high school – roughly just 3,000 people live in the small mid-state city. So it's no surprise that the only high school in town, Liberty Union, hasn't (A) produced whole lot of athletes in its history and (B) it's home to the Ohio Gatorade Player of the Year. On the radar for big time college programs since his early teenage years, the 6-foot-2, 180-pound right-hander committed to the University of Louisville before he even entered high school. It turned out that there was little chance the hard-throwing youngster would attend the collegiate powerhouse. Miller shot up draft charts during his dominating junior campaign with the Lions, throwing just 60 innings of high school ball but racking up a whopping 143 strikeouts to go along with a 0.70 ERA. And he was just as dominant during his final campaign with Liberty Union as well: he went 9-1 with a 133 punch outs in just 57 innings of work – or roughly 78% of the outs he registered were on strikeouts. Miami selected him in the second round, 46th overall, and signed him to a deal worth just a smidgeon under $1.7 million. Miller would throw 5.2 innings during his debut, posting a 6-to-2 strikeout-to-walk ratio in the Complex League and Low-A.

Scouting Report: My pre-draft write-up:

> "A lot of pitching-specialized training focuses on moving fast towards home plate, building up and taking advantage of momentum. Miller bucks that trend from the windup, moving slowly with strength before exploding through his finish. Mid-90s fastball, sitting in the 94- to 95-mph range. Very good, plus low-80s curveball. Above-average mid-80s slider. And a sneakily good changeup that may creep into above-average territory with some tweaking and fine-tuning. Cold weather teenage pitchers – especially from Ohio – are always a gamble, but Miller is built sturdily with a deep, potentially potent repertoire. He's reminiscent of a high school Jordan Balazovic."

Ceiling: 2.0-win player
Risk: Moderate
MLB ETA: 2025

8. Jake Eder, LHP

FB	SL	CH	Command	Overall
55	55	50	45	50

Born: 10/09/98	Age: 24	Bats: L	Top Production Comp: Jarrod Washburn
Height: 6-4	Weight: 215	Throws: L	

Season	Team	Age	Level	IP	TBF	K/9	K%	BB/9	BB%	K-BB%	ERA	FIP	xFIP	Pit/Bat
2021	MIA	22	AA	71.1	287	12.49	34.49%	3.41	9.41%	25.09%	1.77	2.48	3.18	3.87

Background: More than two years removed from their 2020 draft class, it's evident that the Marlins knocked it out of the park – despite two of the class's most promising arms succumbing to Tommy John surgery. Max Meyer, Dax Fulton, and Jake Eder, their first, second, and fifth picks, rank among the club's Top 8 prospects. Zach McCambley could be a useful bullpen piece in the near future. Kyle Nicolas was dealt to Pittsburgh as part of the booty for Jacob Stallings. And their last pick, Kyle Hurt, was part of the package that brought Dylan Floro to the Fish. Eder, the 104th player taken that year, turned in one of the most impressive debuts for the entire draft class – regardless of organization. The former Vanderbilt hurler jumped straight into Double-A the following season and was practically unhittable across 71.1 innings before succumbing to Tommy John surgery.

Miami Marlins

Scouting Report: All reports indicate he's on target to return in 2023. Here's his pre-injury scouting report:

> *"A fairly solid three-pitch repertoire highlighted by a 92- to 94-mph fastball. He'll complement the above-average offering with a slurvy slider, a second above-average offering. He'll also mix in a solid average changeup. Eder is more of a strike-thrower than a pure command guy and he's susceptible to bouts of wildness from time-to-time. With the recent Tommy John surgery, he will miss the entire 2022 season."*

Ceiling: 2.0-win player
Risk: Moderate to High
MLB ETA: 2023/2024

9. Yiddi Cappe, SS

Hit	Power	SB	Patience	Glove	Overall
40/45	40/45	50/40	45	50	50

Born: 09/17/02	**Age:** 20	**Bats:** R	**Top Production Comp:** Adeiny Hechavarria
Height: 6-3	**Weight:** 175	**Throws:** R	

Season	Team	Age	Level	PA	1B	2B	3B	HR	SB	CS	BB%	K%	AVG	OBP	SLG	ISO
2021	MIA	18	DSL	216	31	17	1	2	9	8	8.80%	16.20%	0.270	0.329	0.402	0.132
2022	MIA	19	CPX	132	23	7	0	6	6	4	6.82%	14.39%	0.305	0.364	0.517	0.212
2022	MIA	19	A	167	35	5	1	3	7	1	3.59%	13.17%	0.278	0.299	0.380	0.101

Background: Led by new front office czar Kim Ng, the Marlins went all in – both figuratively and literally – when they signed the young Cuban shortstop two years ago, handing him a massive $3.5 million deal on the international scene. A few months later Cappe, a native of La Habana, was squaring off against the hitter-friendly arms of the Dominican Summer League, batting a solid – yet uninspiring – .270/.329/.402 with 17 doubles, one triple, two homeruns, and nine stolen bases (in 17 total attempts). His overall production during his debut, according to *Weighted Runs Created Plus*, was just 3% better than the league average. Last year the front office took the predictable approach and sent the 6-foot-3, 175-pound middle infielder to the stateside rookie league. And Cappe mashed. He slugged .305/.364/.517 with seven doubles, six homeruns, and six stolen bases. The organization bumped him up to Low-A in late July. He would bat a respectable .279/.299/.380 in 37 games with Jupiter. His overall production with the Hammerheads was 9% *below* the league average mark.

Snippet from The 2022 Prospect Digest Handbook: Not only was he old for someone considered a top prospect in the Dominican Summer League, but his production was lackluster – at best. Long limbs and wiry, Cappe's bat looked slow and long. And it's clear he needs to add quite a bit of strength to be competitive in the coming years. Truthfully, I think it's already clear that the Marlins overextended themselves – quite a bit – by signing him to a big $3.5 million.

Scouting Report: It was nice little bounce back year for the former Bonus Baby – though future projection remains modest, at best. Cappe moved into the Complex League and did exactly what an older-ish prospect should do against low level arms: hit. But the Cuban import remains raw, an unfinished prospect. He shows solid speed, but runs haphazardly / inefficiently on the base paths. He makes consistent contact, but doesn't consistently barrel up the ball. And defensively his glove has been average. Two years into his pro career and Cappe has shown a few flashes, but nothing to indicate more than a fringe average regular is lurking deep within.

Ceiling: 1.5- to 2.0-win player
Risk: Moderate
MLB ETA: 2025

10. Ian Lewis, 2B/3B

Hit	Power	SB	Patience	Glove	Overall
40/55	40/45	60	45	50/60	45

Born: 02/04/03	**Age:** 20	**Bats:** B	**Top Production Comp:** N/A
Height: 5-10	**Weight:** 177	**Throws:** R	

Season	Team	Age	Level	PA	1B	2B	3B	HR	SB	CS	BB%	K%	AVG	OBP	SLG	ISO
2021	MIA	18	CPX	161	27	10	5	3	9	4	6.83%	14.91%	0.302	0.354	0.497	0.195
2022	MIA	19	A	213	37	7	3	2	16	1	10.33%	21.13%	0.265	0.347	0.368	0.103

Background: Another one of the club's aggressive, big dollar international free agency deals. Miami signed the slick-fielding infielder from Nassau, Bahamas, for $950,000 in 2019. Like other members of the signing class, Lewis would be held out of professional action until the 2021 season. But he proved to be worth the wait. Appearing in 43 games with the club's Florida Complex League affiliate, the 5-foot-10, 177-pound infielder slugged .302/.354/.497 with 10 doubles, five triples, three homeruns, and nine stolen bases. Unsurprisingly, the front office bumped the young prospect up to Low-A for the 2022 season. After missing the opening month of the year due to a personal issue in the Bahamas, Lewis joined in mid-May but the stay barely lasted two months. An injury on a swing in mid-

Miami Marlins

July knocked him out of the remainder of the season. In all, Lewis put together a mediocre season with Jupiter, hitting .265/.347/.368 with seven doubles, three triples, two homeruns, and 16 stolen bases (in only 17 total attempts). Per *Weighted Runs Created Plus*, Lewis' overall production topped the league average mark by 6%.

Snippet from The 2022 Prospect Digest Handbook: Lewis is blessed with plus-plus speed that's easy to see on the base paths as well as in his agility and fluidity on defense. Offensively, he's already showing more thump than his 5-foot-10, 177-pound frame would suggest. Lewis isn't going to walk very frequently, but there's a chance for an above-average hit tool, 15 homeruns, and 25 stolen bases. Like a lot of the club's young players, he needs to get stronger though.

Scouting Report: Consider the following:

> Since 2006, only three 19-year-old hitters met the following criteria in a season in Low-A (min. 200 PA): 100 to 110 wRC+, 9.5% to 10.5% walk rate and a strikeout rate between 19% and 23%. Those three hitters: Tyler Wade, Bryan Ramos, and – of course – Ian Lewis.

Another one of the Marlins' infield prospects who remain low level wild cards. Lewis has an intriguing foundation in place: he's a plus runner, a silky smooth defender, enough pop to keep pitchers and defenses honest, and some promising ability as a switch-hitter. The question, of course, like every other toolsy, projectable youngster is whether he'll put it all together.

Ceiling: 1.5-win player
Risk: Moderate
MLB ETA: 2024/2025

11. Joe Mack, C

Hit	Power	SB	Patience	Glove	Overall
30/40	40/55	30	60	50	45

Born: 12/27/02 **Age:** 20 **Bats:** L **Top Production Comp:** N/A
Height: 6-1 **Weight:** 201 **Throws:** R

Season	Team	Age	Level	PA	1B	2B	3B	HR	SB	CS	BB%	K%	AVG	OBP	SLG	ISO
2021	MIA	18	CPX	75	5	1	0	1	0	1	26.67%	29.33%	0.132	0.373	0.208	0.075
2022	MIA	19	CPX	31	6	0	0	2	0	0	12.90%	22.58%	0.296	0.387	0.519	0.222
2022	MIA	19	A	152	20	4	1	3	0	0	19.08%	26.32%	0.231	0.382	0.355	0.124

Background: The Marlins attacked two up-the-middle prep prospects in the first round of the 2021 draft, first nabbing mercurial shortstop Kahlil Watson with the 16th overall pick and then selecting backstop Joe Mack 15 picks later. A product of Williamsville East High School, Mack looked abysmal during his abbreviated debut in the Florida Complex League that summer, hitting a paltry .132/.373/.208 in 75 plate appearances. Last season was another struggle for the former first rounder. Mack's start to the year was delayed and he wouldn't make his first appearance with Jupiter until Mid-May. But after just four games the lefty-swinging backstop hit the disabled list for a lengthy stay courtesy of a severe hamstring issue. He would make it back to Low-A in late July but would struggle with the bat over his final 31 contests. Mack hit a disappointing .231/.382/.355 with four doubles, one triple, and three homeruns in 152 plate appearances. His overall production, per *Weighted Runs Created Plus*, topped the league average mark by 20% thanks in large part to his bloated 19.1% walk rate. Miami sent Mack to the Arizona Fall League for some additional at bats, but the results were largely the same; he batted .230/.347/.459 in 18 games with the Mesa Solar Sox.

Snippet from The 2022 Prospect Digest Handbook: Mack showcases plus bat speed at the plate that combines with a natural loft to generate easy above-average power – though he looks to be a bit too pull happy. Mack starts his hands from a high position, above his ears, which causes for a lot of pre-pitch movement to get into position.

Scouting Report: Thick lower half, like a running back, Mack struggled against breaking balls during his stint in the Arizona Fall League. The swing looks pretty good, but it's going to come down to pitch recognition. There's a chance for better than average power. And he's showing enough behind the dish to stay there. Mack has the feel of a three true outcomes hitter, though he's several years away.

Ceiling: 1.5-win player
Risk: Moderate
MLB ETA: 2025

Miami Marlins

12. Cody Morissette, 2B/3B

Hit	Power	SB	Patience	Glove	Overall
45/55	50	40	50	50	45

Born: 01/16/00	Age: 23	Bats: L	Top Production Comp: N/A
Height: 6-0	Weight: 175	Throws: R	

Season	Team	Age	Level	PA	1B	2B	3B	HR	SB	CS	BB%	K%	AVG	OBP	SLG	ISO
2021	MIA	21	A	159	18	8	1	1	0	2	12.58%	23.90%	0.204	0.308	0.299	0.095
2022	MIA	22	A+	379	48	17	0	13	4	1	8.71%	23.75%	0.232	0.311	0.399	0.167

Background: The last time the Marlins went fishing in the Boston College pond they were able to pull out an underrated right-hander by the name of Michael King, who became a key cog in the Yankees' bullpen the past couple of seasons. The ball club's most recent draft pick from the ACC Conference School hasn't quite lived up to his – nor the front office's – expectations. A sweet swinging infield vagabond throughout his three-year tenure at BC, Morissette left the school as a career .337/.400/.507 hitter when Miami called his name in the second round, 52nd overall, two years ago. After quickly signing, the 6-foot, 175-pound former Eagle was able to get an extended look at the Low-A competition – though the results were, simply, disappointing. Morissette cobbled together a lowly .204/.308/.299 showing in 35 games with Jupiter. Unconcerned with the lack of production, the front office brass sent the 2021 second rounder straight up to High-A to begin last season. And, unfortunately, the results were hardly improved. In an injury-interrupted sophomore campaign, Morissette hit .232/.311/.399 with 17 doubles, and 13 homeruns. His overall production, as measured by *Weighted Runs Created Plus*, was 2% below the league average.

Snippet from The 2022 Prospect Digest Handbook: A bat first infielder without a true home. Morissette's bounced between shortstop, and second and third bases throughout his collegiate career. 45-grade power. Not a lot of speed. Morissette's a well-rounded player without a red flag or a dominant standout tool. He profiles more as a second baseman in the professional ranks.

Scouting Report: At first blush, it looks like a repeat of his disappointing debut season. But after an adjustment period at the start of the year, Morissette slugged a healthy .250/.322/.476 from May 7th through July 3rd before hitting the disabled list with a hand injury, which eventually forced him out of action for roughly a month. When he did make it back in mid-August he failed to drive the ball with the same type of authority. If you're shopping in the prospect bargain bin, Morissette's the exact type of prospect to bet on. He's been aggressively shoved through the low levels, dealt with a hand injury that clearly impacted his late season production, and has lengthy college track record of success. The hit tool may never creep beyond average, but the power has been better than expected – especially considering Beloit's run / homerun suppressive environment.

Ceiling: 1.5-win player
Risk: Moderate
MLB ETA: 2023/2024

13. Xavier Edwards, IF

Hit	Power	SB	Patience	Glove	Overall
55/60	30	60	50	55	45

Born: 08/09/99	Age: 23	Bats: B	Top Production Comp: Dee Strange-Gordon
Height: 5-10	Weight: 175	Throws: R	

Season	Team	Age	Level	PA	1B	2B	3B	HR	SB	CS	BB%	K%	AVG	OBP	SLG	ISO
2019	SDP	19	A	344	85	13	4	1	20	9	8.72%	10.17%	0.336	0.392	0.414	0.078
2019	SDP	19	A+	217	50	5	4	0	14	2	6.45%	8.76%	0.301	0.349	0.367	0.066
2021	TBR	21	AA	337	72	13	3	0	19	11	10.68%	12.46%	0.302	0.377	0.368	0.065
2022	TBR	22	AAA	400	61	19	1	5	7	4	10.75%	18.75%	0.246	0.328	0.350	0.103

Background: It's *exactly* the type of deal a club like the Marlins should make. In mid-November Miami acquired Xavier Edwards, a former first round pick and consensus Top 100 Prospect, and reliever JT Chargois from the Rays in exchange for Marcus Johnson and Santiago Suarez, a couple of low level lottery ticket hurlers. Edwards, who is now with his third organization, was superlative during his first three professional seasons. The switch-hitting infielder batted .346/.453/.409 during his dynamic professional debut, then with the Padres. He followed that up with an aggregate .322/.376/.396 slash line between San Diego's Low-A and High-A affiliates. Then in 2021 he moved into the true testing ground, Double-AA, in his first year in the Rays' organization. He promptly hit .302/.377/.368. Last season, though, Edwards stumbled a bit during his Triple-A debut as he batted .246/.328/.350 with 19 doubles, one triple, five homeruns, and seven stolen bases (in 11 attempts). Per *Weighted Runs Created Plus*, his numbers were 16% *below* the average mark – easily the lowest mark of his career.

Snippet from The 2022 Prospect Digest Handbook: A unicorn of sorts, at least in today's game. Edwards takes a slashing, high contact approach at the plate with above-average speed and a strong glove up the middle. The red flag, though, remains unchanged: he's slugged just one dinger in 247 career minor league games. And his near 50% groundball rate doesn't offer up much in terms of future power projection.

Miami Marlins

Scouting Report: Consider the following:

> Since 2006, just four 22-year-old hitters met the following criteria in a Triple-A season (min. 350 PA): 80 to 90 wRC+ and 16% to 20% strikeout rate. Those four hitters: Billy Hamilton, Ryan Vilade, Neil Walker, and Xavier Edwards.

At this point, Xavier Edwards is what Xavier Edwards has always been: a solid defensive player at multiple infield positions with a high contact approach at the plate. And, of course, Lays BBQ Chips pack more of a punch than Edwards' bat. He's an above-average runner, but hasn't run as frequently or efficiently the past two years as earlier in his career. There's not a whole lot that separates Edwards' bat from former Marlins All-Star Dee Strange-Gordon's bat. The big differentiator, though, comes down to speed. If he's hitting .280-ish with solid walk rates, he's an everyday regular. And I think that happens. Eventually.

Ceiling: 1.5-win player
Risk: Low to Moderate
MLB ETA: 2023

14. Karson Milbrandt, RHP

FB	CB	SL	CH	Command	Overall
60	50	50/55	50	50	45

Born: 04/21/04	Age: 19	Bats: R	Top Production Comp: N/A
Height: 6-2	Weight: 190	Throws: R	

Background: Missouri-based Liberty High School went nearly 50 years between producing draft picks, last graduating a professional ball player directly from the prep ranks all the way back in 1977 when the Houston Astros selected left-hander Kevin Houston in the third round, 66th overall. Fast forward to last July and the Marlins of Miami drafted right-hander Karson Milbrandt, also in the third round, with the 85th overall pick, handing him a whopping $1,497,500 – the largest bonus handed out to a player taken in the round, by roughly half-a-million dollars. Committed to Pitcher University – a.k.a. Vanderbilt University – prior to the draft, Milbandt starred on both sides of the ball for Liberty during his senior season. As a pitcher, the 6-foot-3, 200-pound senior struck out 91 and tallied a tidy 1.66 ERA in only 50.2 innings of work. At the plate, he batted an even .400. Milbrandt was eventually recognized as the Missouri Gatorade Player of the Year. He made one brief start in Low-A during his debut, throwing two innings with one strikeout, one walk, and two earned runs.

Scouting Report: Milbrandt's arsenal is headlined by a low- to mid-90s fastball that projects to sit consistently in the mid-90s at full maturation. The lanky right-hander will mix in a pair of average, albeit raw, breaking balls with the slider showing more promise as a professional offering. He'll also showcase a solid-average changeup. There's quite a bit of projection left for the two-way star. There's close to league average potential, but he needs to improve one of the breaking balls and trust the changeup more often. I had a second round grade on the young right-hander heading into the draft.

Ceiling: 1.5-win player
Risk: Moderate
MLB ETA: 2025

15. Sixto Sanchez, RHP

FB	CU	SL	CH	Command	Overall
N/A	N/A	N/A	N/A	N/A	60

Born: 07/29/98	Age: 23	Bats: R	Top Production Comp: N/A
Height: 6-0	Weight: 234	Throws: R	

Background: The franchise was entering an important offseason following the 2017 season. The club was coming off of a surprising second place finish in the beleaguered National League East Division, though their 77-85 record was more indicative of their true level of play. But the roster had a surprising amount of young talent, including: Giancarlo Stanton, Christian Yelich, J.T. Realmuto, Marcell Ozuna, Dee Strange-Gordon, and – to a lesser extent – Justin Bour. The front office – or more likely than not, ownership – decided the funds weren't available to resign the young core (beyond Stanton and his bloated contract) *or* add enough complementary pieces (e.g. pitching) to make a serious run at the postseason. So it was decided to blow the whole thing up and start from scratch. And with so many attractive, young hitters on the roster, it was assumed that their rebuild effort would be greatly accelerated. They basically gave Stanton away, which was their only *real* option since only a small number of club's could absorb his massive deal. Miami has *nothing* to show for their return in the Yelich deal with Milwaukee – Lewis Brinson owns a.198/.246/.328 slash line in 357 big league games; Isan Diaz, surprisingly, has been even worse (.185/.275/.287); Monte Harrison has appeared in just 50 big league games and he's now entering his age-27 season; and Jordan Yamamoto, who showed the most big league promise spent last season in the Mets' organization. Miami did incredibly well in the Marcell Ozuna swap with St. Louis, adding Sandy Alcantara, the newly crown Cy Young winner, and Zac Gallen (who would be later flipped for Jazz Chisholm). The Marlins held onto Bour for half a season too long and basically got nothing

Miami Marlins

for him. And, of course, there's the J.T. Realmuto trade with the Phillies. The brass sent the All-Star backstop to Philly for a trio of prospects – Jorge Alfaro, who's no longer with the organization, Will Stewart, who drifted into minor league obscurity, and Sixto Sanchez, the centerpiece of the deal – despite arm issues. At first glance, the deal *looked* like it would work out for the Marlins as Sanchez dominated High-A and Double-A in 2019. And he posted a solid 3.46 ERA across seven big league starts the in 2021. Since then, though, it's been arm injury after arm injury. His latest: a surgical procedure for right shoulder: arthroscopic bursectomy.

Snippet from The 2022 Prospect Digest Handbook: Beyond the new injury, there's something else that should be addressed: Heading into the 2020 season Sanchez's weight was listed as a svelte 185 pounds. Now, he's tipping the scales 234 pounds. That's not a great sign.

Scouting Report: At this point, it's difficult to imagine Sanchez developing into any meaningful. The Marlins have to hope that they catch lightning in a bottle for a year. Anything more than that seems unlikely.

Ceiling: 2.0-win player
Risk: Extremely High
MLB ETA: Debuted in 2020

16. Antony Peguero, OF

Hit	Power	SB	Patience	Glove	Overall
40/50	50/55	50/35	50	50	40

Born: 06/14/05	Age: 18	Bats: R	Top Production Comp: N/A
Height: 6-0	Weight: 175	Throws: R	

Season	Team	Age	Level	PA	1B	2B	3B	HR	SB	CS	BB%	K%	AVG	OBP	SLG	ISO
2022	MIA	17	DSL	217	40	10	1	5	7	6	5.99%	16.13%	0.286	0.355	0.423	0.138

Background: Signed out of Santo Domingo Este, Dominican Republic last January for a sizeable deal worth more than half of a million dollars. The 6-foot, 175-pound outfielder would make his professional debut just a few months later. Staying in his home country, Peguero batted a respectable .286/.355/.423 with 10 doubles, one triple, five homeruns, and seven stolen bases (though it took 13 total attempts). Per *Weighted Runs Created Plus*, his overall production in the most hitter-friendly professional environment was 12% better than the league average mark.

Scouting Report: Unlike a lot of the top offensive performances typically associated in the Dominican Summer League, Peguero's average-ish walk rate (6.0% BB%), didn't artificially inflate his production. Long and wiry with a very short bat path to the strike zone. Peguero possesses impressive power potential for a young teenager. It wouldn't be shocking to see him spend a good portion of 2023 in Low-A.

Ceiling: 1.0-win player
Risk: Moderate
MLB ETA: 2026

17. Nasim Nunez, SS

Hit	Power	SB	Patience	Glove	Overall
45	25	80	60	50	40

Born: 08/18/00	Age: 22	Bats: B	Top Production Comp: N/A
Height: 5-9	Weight: 158	Throws: R	

Season	Team	Age	Level	PA	1B	2B	3B	HR	SB	CS	BB%	K%	AVG	OBP	SLG	ISO
2019	MIA	18	R	214	31	5	1	0	28	2	15.89%	20.09%	0.211	0.340	0.251	0.040
2021	MIA	20	A	228	43	2	1	0	33	10	15.35%	20.18%	0.243	0.366	0.265	0.021
2022	MIA	21	A+	378	58	11	3	2	49	11	18.78%	27.25%	0.247	0.390	0.323	0.077
2022	MIA	21	AA	171	31	6	0	0	21	5	14.04%	21.05%	0.261	0.371	0.303	0.042

Background: The second round of the 2019 draft saw shortstops come off the board with four of the first five selections. The last of those picks was Nasim Nunez, a slight-framed, twitchy, switch-hitter from Suwanee, Georgia. A product of Collins Hill High School, Nunez struggled through a disappointing debut in the Gulf Coast League, hitting a scrawny .211/.340/.251. Once minor league ball returned to action from its COVID-imposed vacation, Nunez moved up to Low-A Southeast in 2021. And his numbers, while still underwhelming, showed improvement. He batted .243/.366/.265 in 52 games with the Hammerheads. Last season, the front office bumped the wiry middle infielder up to High-A. And, once again, Nunez's number quietly lurched forward. He hit .247/.390/.323 with 11 doubles, three triples, two homeruns, and 49 stolen bases. Nunez spent the second half of the year squaring off against the tough pitching of Double-A. And he held his own, batting .261/.371/.303. Nunez would finish the year with an aggregate .251/.384/.317 with 17 doubles, three triples, two homeruns, and 70 stolen bases (in 86 total attempts).

Miami Marlins

Scouting Report: Consider the following:

> Since 2006, only three 21-year-old hitters posted a 107 to 117 wRC+ with a walk rate north of 15% in any High-A league (min. 350 PA): John Whittleman, Beamer Weems, and – of course – Nasim Nunez, who, by the way, owned the worst K-rate, 27.2%, by a *wide margin*.

Nunez does two things really, *really* well:

> #1. Run. The young shortstop is a plus runner. His 70 stolen bases tied with Omar De Los Santos and David Hamilton as the third best mark in all of the minor leagues.
> #2. Walk. A lot of Nunez's production is tied into his patient approach at the plate. Not only does he avoid making outs, but it allows him to capitalize upon his lethal swiftness.

Nunez does two things average / mediocrely:

> #1. He plays a passable – not great, not bad – shortstop.
> #2. The hit tool will hover somewhere in the 45- to fringy, 50-grade range.

Nunez does one thing poorly, almost as poorly as any player in the minor leagues:

> #1. He just doesn't hit for any type of power.

Best case: he's an infield version of Terrace Gore.

Ceiling: 1.0-win player
Risk: Low to Moderate
MLB ETA: 2024

18. Yoffry Solano, SS

Hit	Power	SB	Patience	Glove	Overall
35/50	20/50	50	50	50	45

Born: 11/04/04	Age: 18	Bats: R	Top Production Comp: N/A
Height: 5-10	Weight: 155	Throws: R	

Season	Team	Age	Level	PA	1B	2B	3B	HR	SB	CS	BB%	K%	AVG	OBP	SLG	ISO
2022	MIA	17	DSL	117	27	4	2	0	4	2	8.55%	16.24%	0.320	0.393	0.398	0.078

Background: It was far from the organization's splashiest international free agent acquisition – particularly when compared to years past – but the Marlins quietly added Solano as the top prospect in last season's class. A wiry infielder out of Nizao, Dominican Republic, the Fish signed the teenage infielder to a deal worth $750,000. Solano spent his affiliated debut in the Dominican Summer League, hitting .320/.393/.398 with four doubles, two triples, and a quartet of stolen bases (in six tries). His overall production, as measured by *Weighted Runs Created Plus*, topped the league average mark by 20%.

Scouting Report: Quality signing by the front office brass. Solano handled the move into professional ball with aplomb last season, showing everything you'd expect as an upper tier international free agent. Thin and wiry, Solano will eventually grow into average power as he fills out. Good looking swing from the right side from an upright stance. He'll need to continue to refine the mechanics from the lefty's batter's box. Defensively, he looks like a solid defender.

Ceiling: 1.5-win player
Risk: High
MLB ETA: 2025

Miami Marlins

19. Zach McCambley, RHP

FB	CB	CH	Command	Overall
55	60	50	45	40

Born: 05/04/99	Age: 24	Bats: L	Top Production Comp: Jason Frasor
Height: 6-2	Weight: 220	Throws: R	

Season	Team	Age	Level	IP	TBF	K/9	K%	BB/9	BB%	K-BB%	ERA	FIP	xFIP	Pit/Bat
2021	MIA	22	A+	57.0	231	11.53	31.60%	0.95	2.60%	29.00%	3.79	3.96	3.17	3.83
2021	MIA	22	AA	40.0	178	10.58	26.40%	4.50	11.24%	15.17%	5.18	6.58	5.02	4.01
2022	MIA	23	AA	94.0	421	9.67	23.99%	4.98	12.35%	11.64%	5.65	5.14	4.83	3.97

Background: The Marlins ran the table on pitchers in the COVID-limited 2020 draft by using all six of their selections on arms, five of which were college arms. McCambley, a product of Coastal Carolina University, was the club's third round pick that year, 75th overall. The 6-foot-2, 220-pound right-hander shot through High-A in only 11 starts during his debut two years ago, posting an unbelievable 73-to-6 strikeout-to-walk ratio in only 57.0 innings of work. McCambley continued to miss an above-average amount of bats with a major regression in command in nine late-season starts with Pensacola following a promotion. Last season the former Chanticleer found himself back in Double-A for an extended crack at the minors' toughest level – though the results continued to backup. In 19 starts with the Blue Wahoos, he averaged 9.7 strikeouts and 5.0 walks per nine innings. He would miss the remaining several weeks of the season due to an undisclosed injury.

Snippet from The 2022 Prospect Digest Handbook: Definite reliever risk.

Scouting Report: McCambley was never really a true "command" guy, per se. Sure, he's had stints where he would throw strikes with a higher frequency, but the bouts of wildness would almost always follow. Last season was one of those times where the wildness came roaring back. Above-average fastball that didn't really miss too many bats. McCambley's bread-and-butter pitch is a power curveball that he'll vary the break, tilt, and velocity on. He'll mix in a solid-average changeup. It's a backend starter's toolkit, but – again – the command almost assuredly pushes him into some type of middle relief role. Fastball command really needs to improve. He missed too frequently on the fat part of the plate.

Ceiling: 1.0-win player
Risk: Moderate
MLB ETA: 2023

20. Victor Mesa Jr., CF

Hit	Power	SB	Patience	Glove	Overall
40/45	35/40	50	50	55	40

Born: 09/08/01	Age: 21	Bats: L	Top Production Comp: N/A
Height: 6-0	Weight: 195	Throws: L	

Season	Team	Age	Level	PA	1B	2B	3B	HR	SB	CS	BB%	K%	AVG	OBP	SLG	ISO
2019	MIA	17	R	207	36	9	4	1	7	4	11.59%	14.01%	0.284	0.366	0.398	0.114
2021	MIA	19	A	474	77	21	11	5	12	5	6.96%	21.52%	0.266	0.316	0.402	0.136
2022	MIA	20	A+	525	78	26	3	5	10	4	10.10%	19.05%	0.243	0.323	0.346	0.102

Background: It's hard to believe, but it's been four-plus years already. But back in mid-October 2018, the Marlins opened up their typically tightly wound purse strings and doled out a bunch of money for a pair of Cuban brothers: Victor Victor Mesa and his younger brother, Victor Mesa Jr. And as it turns out the massive $5 million sum that was allotted toward older brother (Victor Victor) would turn little, if any, return on investment. However, the $1 million deal with Mesa Jr. has proved to be a significantly better use of funds. A native of La Habana, Cuba, Mesa Jr. quietly turned in a solid debut in the stateside rookie league in 2019 as he batted 284/.366/.398 in 47 games with the club's Gulf Coast League affiliate. Once MiLB returned to work in 2021, the wiry centerfielder moved into Low-A Southeast with little downturn in production – despite being just 19 years old at the time. He hit .266/.317/.402 with 21 doubles, 11 triples, five homeruns, and 12 stolen bases in 112 games. Last season Mesa Jr. continued his one-stop-per-year approach on the development ladder, moving up to High-A. In a career best 121 games with the Beloit Sky Carp, the 6-foot, 195-pound outfielder cobbled together a .244/.323/.346 slash line with 26 doubles, three triples, five homeruns, and 10 stolen bases (in 14 total attempts). Per *Weighted Runs Created Plus*, his overall production was 11% below the league average threshold.

Snippet from The 2020 Prospect Digest Handbook: He's going to go as far as the batting averages will take him. Above-average speed, below-average power that project to eventually get to a 40-grade, won't walk a ton, and a good, maybe even borderline great, glove in center field.

Scouting Report: Consider the following:

> Since 2006, only four 20-year-old hitters met the following criteria in High-A (min. 350 PA): 85 to 95 wRC+, 18% to 22% strikeout rate, and a 9% to 11% walk rate. Those four hitters: Nick Noonan, Carlos Rodriguez, Luis Carpio, and – of course – Victor Mesa Jr.

Miami Marlins

A glove-first centerfielder, Mesa Jr. continued to showcase borderline Gold Glove caliber defense in centerfield. Not a plus runner, the Cuban import relies heavily on natural baseball instincts and route running to track down potential hits. Offensively speaking, there's not a whole lot of hope stored up in his bat. Below-average power, below-average hit tool. In past years Mesa Jr. would be tracking as a fifth outfielder. Now, though, he's likely going to be destined for Quad-A-dom.

Ceiling: 1.0-win player
Risk: Moderate
MLB ETA: 2024

Milwaukee Brewers

Top Prospects

Milwaukee Brewers

1. Jackson Chourio, CF

Hit	Power	SB	Patience	Glove	Overall
55	60	60	50	70	80

Born: 03/11/04 **Age:** 19 **Bats:** R **Top Production Comp:** Julio Rodriguez
Height: 6-1 **Weight:** 165 **Throws:** R

Season	Team	Age	Level	PA	1B	2B	3B	HR	SB	CS	BB%	K%	AVG	OBP	SLG	ISO
2021	MIL	17	DSL	189	34	7	1	5	8	3	12.17%	14.81%	0.296	0.386	0.447	0.151
2022	MIL	18	A	271	41	23	5	12	10	2	7.01%	28.04%	0.324	0.373	0.600	0.276
2022	MIL	18	A+	142	18	6	0	8	4	1	7.75%	21.83%	0.252	0.317	0.488	0.236
2022	MIL	18	AA	26	1	1	0	0	2	1	7.69%	42.31%	0.087	0.154	0.130	0.043

Background: It was a move that garnered a few waves of national publicity at that time, but not much beyond that. MLB.com revised their international free agency tracker and noted that, according to their ranking, the 18th best prospect on the international scene signed with the Brewers. Reviewing The Brew, the club's dedicated *FanSided* site, relayed the information, also listing in there that *Baseball America* ranked him as the 15th best prospect still available. Barely a year after that fateful January 2021 day, it's abundantly clear that Jackson Chourio (A) was – unequivocally – the best available prospect on the international market and (B) is – unequivocally – the best prospect in all of baseball. After signing for $1.8 million, Chourio spent that summer squaring off against the Dominican Summer League competition, hitting an impressive .296/.386/.447 with seven doubles, one triple, five homeruns, and eight stolen bases (in 11 attempts). Per *Weighted Runs Created Plus*, his overall production topped the league average mark by 31%. Production that up-ticked his prospect needle and made some heads turn, but *nothing* could have predicted the offensive explosion awaiting Chourio in 2022. Opening the season up with the Carolina Mudcats in Low-A, the toolsy 6-foot-1, 165-pound centerfielder mashed a scorching .324/.373/.600 with 23 doubles, five triples, 12 homeruns, and 10 stolen bases in 12 total attempts. The front office brass moved him up to High-A in late July and the Maracaibo, Venezuela native continued to produce, batting .252/.317/.488 in 31 games. Chourio would spend the season's final week squaring off against the toughest competition in the minor leagues, Double-A, at the ripe ol' age of 18. He would finish the year with an unbelievable .288/.342/.538 slash line, belting out 30 doubles, five triples, and 20 homeruns to go along with 16 stolen bases (in 20 attempts). His overall production, per *Weighted Runs Created Plus*, topped the league average mark by 36%.

Scouting Report: Just for fun, consider the following:

> Since 2006, only four 18-year-old hitters appearance in at least one Double-A game: Bryce Harper, Fernando Tatis Jr., Fernando Martinez, and – of course – Jackson Chourio. Harper is already a two-time MVP and trekking towards the Hall of Fame. Tatis Jr. looked to be the face of his generation and signed a massive 14-year, $340 million before getting popped for a PED suspension. And Martinez, a perennial consensus Top 100 prospect for multiple years, never really figured it out at the big league level.

Now let's see how Chourio's production in Low-A stacks up against his peers in recent peers. Consider the following:

> Since 2006, here's the eight best 18-year-old hitters in any Low-A league (min. 250 PA) by wRC+:
> #1. Giancarlo Stanton (169 wRC+), #2. Bryce Harper (164), #3. Jackson Chourio (160), #4. Wander Franco (155), #5. Fernando Tatis Jr. (154), #6. Vladimir Guerrero Jr. (151), Freddie Freeman (150), and #8 Carlos Correa (148).

The sky is – literally – the limit for Chourio. Just one full season into his professional career and his production is among the best over the past 17 minor league seasons. Among the best bat speed in the minors. And he's *just beginning* to tap into his plus power that may eventually climb in 40-homer territory. There was an at bat against Oakland prospect Jorge Juan, a notable flamethrower, in late August. Chourio gets caught on his front foot, almost lunging at a Juan breaking ball. A mortal hitter pops it up to shallow leftfield. Chourio knocks it out of the park. Plus speed. He plays centerfield like Willie Mays or "Shoeless" Joe Jackson – his glove is the place where triples go to die. He's breathtaking as a prospect, a perennial MVP candidate. He's going to put a peak season together in which he slugs .320/.400/.650. One more note: this is the highest I've rated a player in nine *Prospect Digest Handbooks*.

Ceiling: 9.0-win player
Risk: Moderate
MLB ETA: 2023

Milwaukee Brewers

2. Sal Frelick, CF

Hit	Power	SB	Patience	Glove	Overall
60	40	60	50	55	55

Born: 04/19/00	Age: 23	Bats: L	Top Production Comp: Steven Kwan
Height: 5-9	Weight: 175	Throws: R	

Season	Team	Age	Level	PA	1B	2B	3B	HR	SB	CS	BB%	K%	AVG	OBP	SLG	ISO
2021	MIL	21	CPX	17	5	1	1	0	3	0	11.76%	11.76%	0.467	0.529	0.667	0.200
2021	MIL	21	A	81	23	6	1	1	6	2	11.11%	12.35%	0.437	0.494	0.592	0.155
2021	MIL	21	A+	71	7	1	1	3	0		14.08%	18.31%	0.167	0.296	0.267	0.100
2022	MIL	22	A+	92	15	5	1	2	6	3	14.13%	15.22%	0.291	0.391	0.456	0.165
2022	MIL	22	AA	253	51	12	3	5	9	2	7.91%	13.04%	0.317	0.380	0.464	0.147
2022	MIL	22	AAA	217	52	11	2	4	9	3	8.76%	7.37%	0.365	0.435	0.508	0.143

Background: Maybe David Stearns, the recently departed General Manager of the Brewers, knows something we all don't – especially when it comes to first round picks in the summer draft. During his tenure as GM with franchise, the former wunderkind owned nine (9) first round draft selections (2016-2022). He used seven of those selections on college players and six of those aforementioned picks on hitters. Here's the list of his first round draft choices:

- 2016: Corey Ray (5th overall)
- 2017: Keston Hiura (9th)
- 2017: Tristen Lutz (34th)
- 2018: Brice Turang (21st)
- 2019: Ethan Small (28th)
- 2020: Garrett Mitchell (20th)
- 2021: Sal Frelick (15th)
- 2021: Tyler Black (33rd)
- 2022: Eric Brown (27th)

The Brewers fell in love with Frelick during the 2021 draft process, using the 15th overall pick and signing him to a slightly above-slot bonus of $4 million after a phenomenal tenure at Boston College. Frelick, a hard-nosed centerfielder, left the ACC Conference squad as a .345/.435/.521 hitter. And he stepped right into the professional ranks without missing a beat two years ago as well, batting .329/.414/.466 between the Complex League, Low-A, and High-A. The 2022 season was much the same, as well. Spending time between Wisconsin, Biloxi, and Nashville, the 5-foot-9, 175-pound dynamo slugged an aggregate .331/.403/.480 with 28 doubles, six triples, 11 homeruns, and 24 stolen bases in 32 total attempts. Per *Weighted Runs Created Plus*, his overall production topped the league average mark by a stellar 37%.

Snippet from The 2022 Prospect Digest Handbook: He's another low ceiling, high floor prospect that has the ceiling of a .280/.340/.400-type hitter with solid defense.

Scouting Report: Double-A remains – and will always be – the true testing ground for prospects. It's the ultimate make-it-or-break-it level. Pitchers throw offspeed for strikes more frequently, in any count. And hitters consistently hit offspeed pitches, in any count. So let's take a look at how Frelick's production stacks up against his peers at that level. Consider the following:

> Since 2006, only three 22-year-old hitters met the following criteria in any Double-A league (min. 250 PA): 118 to 128 wRC+, sub-15% strikeout rate, and a walk rate between 7% and 9%. Those three hitters: Max Schrock, Jose Pirela, and Sal Frelick.

Above-average defense in centerfielder that may contend for a few Gold Gloves in his career. Frelick's similar to the Guardians' Steven Kwan. As long as the batting average (i.e. the hit tool) hovers near .300, he's going to be incredibly valuable. Plus speed. Below-average power. Frelick's an absolute gamer, a grinder that will get every ounce out of his talent. In terms of big league ceiling, think: .300/.350/.410.

Ceiling: 4.0-win player
Risk: Moderate
MLB ETA: 2023

3. Jeferson Quero, C

Hit	Power	SB	Patience	Glove	Overall
55	40/55	50/35	50	55	60

Born: 10/08/02	Age: 20	Bats: R	Top Production Comp: Willson Contreras
Height: 5-10	Weight: 165	Throws: R	

Season	Team	Age	Level	PA	1B	2B	3B	HR	SB	CS	BB%	K%	AVG	OBP	SLG	ISO
2021	MIL	18	CPX	83	13	5	1	2	4	3	14.46%	12.05%	0.309	0.434	0.500	0.191
2022	MIL	19	A	320	54	18	1	6	10	2	8.75%	19.06%	0.278	0.345	0.412	0.134
2022	MIL	19	A+	85	17	4	1	4	0	0	2.35%	17.65%	0.313	0.329	0.530	0.217

Background: Two years before signing wunderkind Jackson Chourio from Valenzuela on the free agency market, the Brewers quietly signed one of the better catching prospects from the same country. Living less than five hours away from his

Milwaukee Brewers

fellow countryman, Quero, a native of Barquisimeto, joined the Brewers' organization for $200,000 four years ago. And he's quietly – and *consistently* – shown tremendous offensive promise at each step of his minor league journey. Debuting with the club's Complex League affiliate in 2021, the 5-foot-10, 165-pound backstop slugged a hearty .309/.434/.500 with eight extra-base hits in only 23 games. Last season, the young Venezuelan blitzed through Low-A in only 75 games and continued to mash in his 20-game cameo with Wisconsin in High-A. Quero would finish his first full professional season with a .286/.342/.439 triple-slash line, belting out 22 doubles, two triples, and 10 homeruns to go along with 10 stolen bases (in only 12 attempts). Per *Weighted Runs Created Plus*, his overall production topped the league average mark by 16%. Milwaukee sent the young catcher to the Arizona Fall League following his successful regular season, but he struggled in limited action, batting .222/.346/.333 in 15 games with the Glendale Desert Dogs.

Snippet from The 2022 Prospect Digest Handbook: He did show an interesting bat-first approach at the plate during his debut last season, shooting the ball from gap-to-gap without much bias. He also walked more times (12) then he whiffed (10). Defensively, he looked to be an above-average defender in limited action while throwing out roughly one-third of would-be base thieves.

Scouting Report: The youngest player on the Glendale Desert Dogs during his stint in the Arizona Fall League, Quero has quietly – and arguably – the most underrated catching prospect in the minor leagues. He looks like a potential plus defender behind the plate *and* one that can control the opposition's running game. He tossed out 31% of would-be base stealers during the regular season and caught 11 of the 24 would-be base thieves in the Fall League. Offensively, there's even more to like. From a statistical standpoint, Quero dealt with a bit of an adjustment period at the start of the year, hitting a disappointing .229/.295/.329 over his first 36 games. After that, though, his bat caught fire and he mashed .322/.371/.507 over his remaining 59 games. He's a contact oriented hitter that shows intriguing power potential that may peak in the 25-homer territory. And despite strong contact numbers Quero doesn't get cheated at the plate. Pull power, great bat speed. Midway through 2023, Quero will be a consensus Top 100 prospect.

Ceiling: 3.5-win player
Risk: Moderate
MLB ETA: 2024

4. Joey Wiemer, OF

Hit	Power	SB	Patience	Glove	Overall
45	55	60	55	65	65

Born: 02/11/99	Age: 24	Bats: R	Top Production Comp: Hunter Pence
Height: 6-5	Weight: 215	Throws: R	

Season	Team	Age	Level	PA	1B	2B	3B	HR	SB	CS	BB%	K%	AVG	OBP	SLG	ISO
2021	MIL	22	A	320	48	11	2	13	22	4	14.06%	21.56%	0.276	0.391	0.478	0.201
2021	MIL	22	A+	152	22	7	0	14	8	2	11.84%	23.68%	0.336	0.428	0.719	0.383
2022	MIL	23	AA	374	46	19	1	15	25	1	9.09%	30.21%	0.243	0.321	0.440	0.198
2022	MIL	23	AAA	174	21	15	1	6	6	2	12.07%	19.54%	0.287	0.368	0.520	0.233

Background: The front office brass dipped into a pair of non-traditional Ohio baseball schools to make a pair of early rounds picks in 2020 and 2021. Two years ago the Milwaukee Brain Trust used a late first round pick on Ty Black, a product of Dayton-based Wright State University. And, of course, the previous year the organization plucked toolsy outfielder Joey Wiemer out of the University of Cincinnati in the fourth round. Weimer, an athletic 6-foot-4, 215-pound rightfielder / part-time centerfielder, made his professional debut in 2021, easily surpassing the High-A test before absolutely torching the Double-A competition for 34 games. Wiemer would finish the campaign with an aggregate .296/.403/.556 with 18 doubles, two triples, 27 homeruns, and 30 stolen bases (in 36 total attempts). And his bat remained hot as he moved into the Arizona Fall League that year as well, slugging .467/.568/.667 in nine games with the Salt River Rafters. Needless to say, but Wiemer's prospect status was boiling as the 2022 season kicked off. And, for the most part, he lived up to the hype. The former Bearcat started the year off back in Double-A with Biloxi, batting .243/.321/.440 with 35 extra-base hits. And just like the previous year, he manhandled the competition after his promotion. This time, though, mashing .287/.368/.520 in 43 games with the Nashville Sounds. Wiemer finished the year with an aggregate .256/.336/.465 production line, to go along with 34 doubles, two triples, 21 homeruns, and 31 stolen bases. His overall production, per *Weighted Runs Created Plus*, was 9% above the league average status.

Snippet from The 2022 Prospect Digest Handbook: With another strong showing in High-A / Double-A and Wiemer, The former Cincinnati nobody, could easily find himself on the brink of Top 100 prospect stardom.

Scouting Report: Beyond the club's obvious top prospect, Jackson Chourio, Wiemer is *easily* the most toolsy prospect brewing in their farm system. The former Bearcat, who slugged just 12 homeruns in his college career, continued to showcase his above-average power and speed combination. The hit tool still has some questions – and his 30% whiff rate in his extended look in Double-A further raised those concerns – but the potential is evident. Elite defender in rightfield. Patience. Power. Speed. If the hit tool hovers in the 50-grade territory, he's going to be a borderline All-Star contributor year-in-and-year-out. He could go one of two routes: Hunter Pence or Bradley Zimmer. There's .250/.330/.430-type potential with Gold Glove defense in rightfield.

Milwaukee Brewers

Ceiling: 3.5-win player
Risk: Moderate to High
MLB ETA: 2023

5. Brice Turang, IF/CF

Hit	Power	SB	Patience	Glove	Overall
45	40	60	60	50	50

Born: 11/21/99	Age: 23	Bats: L	Top Production Comp: Daniel Robertson
Height: 6-0	Weight: 173	Throws: R	

Season	Team	Age	Level	PA	1B	2B	3B	HR	SB	CS	BB%	K%	AVG	OBP	SLG	ISO
2019	MIL	19	A	357	68	13	4	2	21	4	13.73%	15.13%	0.287	0.384	0.376	0.089
2019	MIL	19	A+	207	25	6	2	1	9	1	16.43%	22.71%	0.200	0.338	0.276	0.076
2021	MIL	21	AA	320	54	14	3	5	11	7	8.75%	15.00%	0.264	0.329	0.385	0.122
2021	MIL	21	AAA	176	27	7	0	1	9	2	18.18%	19.89%	0.245	0.381	0.315	0.070
2022	MIL	22	AAA	603	113	24	2	13	34	2	10.78%	19.57%	0.286	0.360	0.412	0.126

Background: It seems, at least to me, that Turang has been around forever at this point. And in a lot of way, he *has* been around forever. Turang was one of the more well-known prospects heading into the 2018 draft thanks in part to years spent playing on some of the country's best amateur teams growing up. He had the look, the feel, of being a potential prep prospect that could move rather quickly through the minor leagues. A prospect that didn't own any elite tools, but one that didn't really have a lot of flaws either. The Santiago High School product reached Triple-A two years ago as a grinder-type 21-year-old, batting a league average-ish .245/.381/.315 in 44 games with the Nashville Sounds. Again, production that's serviceable, but it's not standout in any way. The lefty-swinging infielder / part-time centerfielder returned back to the level for a more extended look in 2022. And the results, while improved, lacked any eye-catching notoriety. In a career-best 131 games, the 6-foot, 173-pound prospect batted .286/.360/.412 with 24 doubles, two triples, 13 homeruns, and 34 stolen bases (in 36 total attempts). Per *Weighted Runs Created Plus*, his overall production topped the league average mark by 8%. .

Snippet from The 2022 Prospect Digest Handbook: A grinder at the plate that sniffs out first base via a walk with a high frequency. Turang continued his trend of improved flyball rates, posting a career-low 38.5% groundball rate during his extended stint in Double-A. He's speedy, owns an above-average glove, and generally does things well without a lot of flare. There's definite big league value here. Big ceiling: something along the lines of .270/.340/.380.

Scouting Report: At this point, Turang may be one of the more known commodities developing in the minor leagues. He continues to be a high contact, high walk rate offensive player. But he began driving the ball with more authority last season – which is particularly surprising because the Sounds' home ballpark – especially when it comes to homeruns – is one of the more suppressive hitting environments in the minor leagues. He hit more dingers at home (four) last season, than he had in any previous season. Consider the following:

> Since 2006, only a pair of 22-year-old hitters met the following criteria in Triple-A (min. 350 PA): 103 to 113 wRC+, 18% to 21% strikeout rate, and a walk rate between 10% and 12%. Those two hitters: Daniel Robertson and Brice Turang. Robertson, by the way, was a consensus Top 100 prospect and batted .262/.382/.415 during his best Major League season.

The former first rounder spent time at second and third bases, shortstop, and – for the first time in his career – centerfield last season. Milwaukee is already grooming him for a utility role and having someone that can play three up the middle positions is valuable. He's going to be a .270/.340/.380-type hitter.

Ceiling: 2.0- to 2.5-win player
Risk: Low
MLB ETA: 2023

6. Garrett Mitchell, CF

Hit	Power	SB	Patience	Glove	Overall
45	45	60	50	55	50

Born: 09/04/98	Age: 24	Bats: L	Top Production Comp: Dexter Fowler
Height: 6-3	Weight: 215	Throws: R	

Season	Team	Age	Level	PA	1B	2B	3B	HR	SB	CS	BB%	K%	AVG	OBP	SLG	ISO
2021	MIL	22	A+	120	21	5	2	5	12	1	23.33%	25.00%	0.359	0.508	0.620	0.261
2021	MIL	22	AA	148	20	1	0	3	5	1	12.16%	27.70%	0.186	0.291	0.264	0.078
2022	MIL	23	AA	187	31	9	2	4	7	1	8.56%	27.81%	0.277	0.353	0.428	0.151
2022	MIL	23	AAA	85	18	6	0	1	9	0	11.76%	21.18%	0.342	0.435	0.466	0.123

Background: The 2020 and 2021 drafts marked just the second time the club drafted college outfielders in the opening round in back-to-back years. The first time it happened: 1995-1996 when the Brew Crew selected former fan favorite Geoff Jenkins and Chad Green with the ninth and eighth overall picks. One of the best bats in college over his final two seasons, Mitchell was one of the biggest breakout stars in 2019 as he

Milwaukee Brewers

mashed .349/.418/.566 for UCLA and he followed that up with a .355/.425/.484 slash line in his COVID-abbreviated junior campaign. The 6-foot-3, 215-pound centerfielder started his professional career off in similar fashion in 2021, slugging .359/.508/.620 in 29 games with Wisconsin – though his numbers came crashing back to earth upon his promotion up to Double-A. Last season, in another injury-marred campaign, Mitchell batted an aggregate .287/.377/.426 with 16 doubles, two triples, five homeruns, and 17 stolen bases (in 18 attempts) in 68 minor league games. And he acquitted himself nicely in 28 games in Milwaukee, hitting .312/.373/.459 with three doubles, two homeruns, and a perfect eight-for-eight in the stolen base department.

Snippet from The 2022 Prospect Digest Handbook: He's not going to be a star, but he could be a solid contributing player on a championship caliber squad. In terms of big league ceiling: think Trent Grisham, something along the lines of .250/.330/.430.

Scouting Report: For the second consecutive season, the former first rounder missed considerable time due to injury. The latest ailment: a barking oblique that forced him out of action for nearly two full months. Mitchell, perhaps more than any Top 150 prospect, had questions to answer after his dreadful performance in Double-A at the end of the 2021 season. And, for the most part, he showed a solid – if unremarkable – bounce back year in the minors' toughest proving ground. The former UCLA Bruin is showing signs of some concerning swing-and-miss issues – he whiffed nearly 28% of the time in Double-A last season and fanned a whopping 41.2% of his plate appearances in the big leagues. But he's toolsy with plus speed, an above-average glove, and enough pop to keep pitchers / defenses honest. The lefty-swinging centerfielder also allayed platoon split concerns last season as well. The hit tool – or lack thereof – is the only thing keeping him from stardom. In terms of big league ceiling (over a full year), think: .245/.320/.430.

Ceiling: 2.5-win player
Risk: Moderate
MLB ETA: Debuted in 2022

7. Eric Brown, SS

Hit	Power	SB	Patience	Glove	Overall
50	45	60	55	55	50

Born: 12/19/00 **Age:** 22 **Bats:** R
Height: 5-10 **Weight:** 190 **Throws:** R
Top Production Comp: N/A

Season	Team	Age	Level	PA	1B	2B	3B	HR	SB	CS	BB%	K%	AVG	OBP	SLG	ISO
2022	MIL	21	CPX	17	1	3	0	0	4	0	23.53%	23.53%	0.308	0.471	0.538	0.231
2022	MIL	21	A	100	14	4	1	3	15	2	11.00%	17.00%	0.262	0.370	0.440	0.179

Background: The talented shortstop was able to live up to the hype entering his senior season at Parkway High School in 2019, batting a red hot .523 with seven doubles, six triples, and six homeruns while knocking in 36 runs. That production earned Brown a bevy of awards and recognition, including the All-District 1-5A MVP. *Perfect Game* ranked him as the 85th best shortstop in the nation; the second best shortstop in Louisiana; and 10th overall best prospect in the state. Splitting time between second and third bases during his freshman season at Coastal Carolina, Brown put together a mediocre offensive debut, hitting .259/.377/.310 with a trio of doubles before COVID prematurely ended the year. Brown followed that up with a breakout campaign for the Chanticleers during his sophomore season, slugging .294/.413/.513 with 12 doubles, one triple, nine homeruns, and 11 stolen bases. And he was able to continue showcasing his offensive potential during the summer with the Cotuit Kettleers in the Cape Cod League (.282/.375/.436) as well. Last season the 5-foot-10, 190-pound shortstop turned in his best performance to date for Coastal Carolina. Appearing in a career best 57 games, Brown set personnel bests in average (.330), on-base percentage (.460), slugging percentage (.544), doubles (19), triples (two), and stolen bases (12). He also banged out seven homeruns, two off from his previous high. Milwaukee drafted the Coastal Carolina star in the opening round, 27th overall, and signed him to a deal worth a smidgeon over $2 million. Brown made four starts in the Complex League before moving up to Low-A for another 23 contests. He batted an aggregate .268/.385/.454 with seven doubles, one triple, three homeruns, and 19 stolen bases.

Scouting Report: Per the usual, my pre-draft write-up:

> "Consider the following:
>
> Since 2011, only five Sun Belt Conference hitters met the following criteria in a season (min. 250 PA): hit at least .325/.450/.525 with a walk rate north of 14% and a strikeout rate between 8% and 12%. Those five players: Zach George, Mike Martinez, Matt Sanders, Billy Cooke, and – of course – Eric Brown.
>
> Another one of these extreme contact hitters that is becoming more en vogue nowadays. Good patience at the plate. Average hit tool. 45-grade power and a little bit of speed. Brown's stance is a bit peculiar, starting with his hands held high, at the top of his head. As he gets his bat in position he points the bat head almost directly at the pitcher. Brown doesn't have a lot of offensive upside, but his above-average defense could make him a low end starting option."

Milwaukee Brewers

Just to note: I had Brown as a late second / early third round grade.

Ceiling: 2.0-win player
Risk: Moderate
MLB ETA: 2024/2025

8. Tyler Black, 2B/3B/CF

Hit	Power	SB	Patience	Glove	Overall
50/55	40	50	60	50	50

Born: 07/26/00	Age: 22	Bats: L	Top Production Comp: N/A
Height: 6-2	Weight: 190	Throws: R	

Season	Team	Age	Level	PA	1B	2B	3B	HR	SB	CS	BB%	K%	AVG	OBP	SLG	ISO
2021	MIL	20	A	103	14	4	0	0	3	2	19.42%	28.16%	0.222	0.388	0.272	0.049
2021	MIL	20	CPX	12	2	0	0	1	2	0	50.00%	16.67%	0.500	0.750	1.000	0.500
2022	MIL	21	A+	283	44	13	4	4	13	6	15.90%	15.55%	0.281	0.406	0.424	0.143

Background: Wright State University's produced just a pair of first round picks in their history, coming nearly 30 years apart. Back in 1993, the "Alex Rodriguez Draft Class", the Angels selected southpaw Brian Anderson two picks after the former high school phenom. Twenty-eight years later the Brewers called out Tyler Black's name in the first round. The former Raider star went 33rd overall and signed for $2 million, approximately $200,000 below the recommended slot bonus. A stout bat throughout his two-plus years at the Horizon Conference School, the lefty-swinging second baseman, who sported a .353/.468/.612 slash line in college, struggled – *mightily* – during his brief 23-game debut in Low-A East two years ago; he batted a lowly .222/.388/.272. Unconcerned about his initial struggles in pro ball, the front office sent the 6-foot-2, 190-pound infielder up to Wisconsin in 2022. Black slugged .281/.406/.424 with 13 doubles, four triples, four homeruns, and 13 stolen bases (in 19 attempts). His season prematurely ended in late July courtesy of a broken left scapula. His overall production, per *Weighted Runs Created Plus*, was 37% above the league average mark. Finally healthy – at least, temporarily – Black spent the fall playing with the Glendale Desert Dogs, hitting .279/.413/.377 in 17 games. Unfortunately for the snake-bitten top prospect, Black broke his left thumb near the end of Fall Ball, a result from sliding into second base.

Snippet from The 2022 Prospect Digest Handbook: Above-average, perhaps even peaking with a plus-hit tool. Solid-average power. Can run a little bit. Tremendous bat-to-ball skills. Great eye. Add it all up and Black is one of the more underrated prospects in the draft class. He feels like A Tampa Bay or Oakland-type prospect.

Scouting Report: Consider the following:

> Since 2006, only two 21-year-old hitters posted a 132 to 142 wRC+ with a 14% to 17% strikeout rate and a walk rate north of 14% in High-A (min. 275 PA): Yonny Hernandez and Tyler Black.

Ignoring his knack for injuring the left side of his body, Black's cut from a similar cloth as current Brewers manager Craig Counsell: wiry, big leg kick, scrappy. Black shows a short, quick path to the ball, but doesn't project to hit for much power – though it's more than Counsell showed during his lengthy big league career. Decent glove, good not great. He profiles as a low end starting option. One more thought: He handles lefties and righties equally well. If he can stay healthy, he could be a strong candidate for a late-season call up in 2023.

Ceiling: 2.0-win player
Risk: Moderate
MLB ETA: 2023/2024

9. Hendry Mendez, RF

Hit	Power	SB	Patience	Glove	Overall
40/55	35/45	45/40	55	50	50

Born: 11/07/03	Age: 19	Bats: L	Top Production Comp: N/A
Height: 6-2	Weight: 175	Throws: L	

Season	Team	Age	Level	PA	1B	2B	3B	HR	SB	CS	BB%	K%	AVG	OBP	SLG	ISO
2021	MIL	17	DSL	64	9	5	1	1	0	0	10.94%	3.13%	0.296	0.391	0.481	0.185
2021	MIL	17	CPX	74	15	4	2	0	3	1	13.51%	13.51%	0.333	0.425	0.460	0.127
2022	MIL	18	A	446	75	11	1	5	7	8	13.90%	15.70%	0.244	0.357	0.318	0.074

Background: Signed out of Santo Domingo, Dominican Republic, prior to the start of the 2021 season. The Brewers sent him to their Dominican rookie league affiliate that summer, but Mendez's stay lasted a mere few weeks. The 6-foot-2, 175-pound corner outfielder batted .296/.391/.482 while striking out just two times in 64 plate appearances. He would spend the rest of the summer mashing in the Arizona Complex League (.333/.425/.460). Last season, to the utter surprise of no one, Mendez made the move up to full season action – despite being only 18-years-old. As expected, the results were mixed. He batted a respectable .244/.357/.318 with 11 doubles, one triple, five

The 2023 Prospect Digest Handbook

Milwaukee Brewers

homeruns, and seven stolen bases (in a whopping 15 attempts). His overall production, per *Weighted Runs Created Plus*, was 2% below the league average threshold.

Scouting Report: Consider the following:

> Since 2006, only 67 hitters made at least 350 trips to the plate in Low-A during their age-18 season. Of those aforementioned 67, only 23 of them posted a strikeout rate below 17%. And, finally of those 23 only five posted a double-digit walk rate. Those five hitters are: Mike Trout, Carlos Correa, Jurickson Profar, Jon Singleton, and – of course – Hendry Mendez.

Now to be fair Mendez's production level was – *literally* – two-thirds of anyone in the group. But the peripherals are certainly intriguing. Mendez struggled throughout the entire year – except for a scorching July. Starting from a slightly open stance, Mendez owns some of the best bat speed in the Brewers' system. His extreme contact approach doesn't lend itself to a whole lot of projection. But there's a chance for a 55-grade hit tool. Very raw, but he's the type of prospect that could put it all together quickly and shoot through the farm system.

Ceiling: 2.0-win player
Risk: Moderate
MLB ETA: 2025

10. Jacob Misiorowski, RHP

FB	SL	CH	Command	Overall
70/80	60	N/A	40	55

Born: 04/03/02	Age: 21	Bats: R	Top Production Comp: N/A
Height: 6-7	Weight: 190	Throws: R	

Background: The Milwaukee Brewers are no strangers to JuCo Crowder College. The NL Central Division team unearthed hard-throwing left-hander Aaron Ashby in the fourth round from the Missouri-based junior college in 2018, making him the highest drafted Roughrider in school history. That is…until Milwaukee called for flame-throwing right-hander Jacob Misiorowski's name last July. Standing a wispy 6-foot-7 and 190 pounds, Misiorowski teamed with fellow Grain Valley High Schooler Mason Rogers to capture Missouri All-State honors during their respective junior seasons. The big right-hander tossed a pair of no-hitters that year, compiling a 1.48 ERA with nine wins (against two losses) and 67 strikeouts in 47 innings of work. Misiorowski, who missed all of his senior year due to the COVID pandemic, changed his commitment from Oregon State University to JuCo Crowder College. After redshirting in the 2021 season, Misiorowski made 15 starts for the Roughriders last year, striking out 136, walking 45, and tallying a 2.72 ERA in 76.0 innings of work. The Brewers selected him in the second round, 63rd overall, and signed him to a deal worth 2.35 million – roughly double the recommended slot bonus value. The big righty, though, had a disastrous – albeit incredibly short – debut last summer. He walked seven in only 1.2 innings of work.

Scouting Report: Misiorowski opened as many eyes as anyone during the Draft Combine last summer. According to MLB.com's Jim Callis, the hard-throwing right-hander not only topped out at 100.7 mph, but his cumulative fastball velocity, 99.8 mph, was the highest among all participants. Callis also noted that his fastball peaked at 2,816 rpm and averaged 2,688 rpm, also best among the group. Misiorowski complements the plus-plus offering with upper 80s / low 90s hellacious slider. Milwaukee will need to work with him on developing a third offering – any type of third offering – or he could be headed down the path of Jeremy Jeffress. He's a lottery ticket that not only needs a third pitch, but he'll have to throw strikes far more frequently as well.

Ceiling: 3.0-win player
Risk: High
MLB ETA: 2025

11. Jadher Areinamo, IF

Hit	Power	SB	Patience	Glove	Overall
				55	

Born: 11/28/03	Age: 19	Bats: R	Top Production Comp: N/A
Height: 5-10	Weight: 160	Throws: R	

Season	Team	Age	Level	PA	1B	2B	3B	HR	SB	CS	BB%	K%	AVG	OBP	SLG	ISO
2021	MIL	17	DSL	175	33	7	2	0	5	4	9.71%	12.57%	0.276	0.366	0.349	0.072
2022	MIL	18	CPX	149	27	10	3	1	4	4	12.75%	12.75%	0.323	0.416	0.472	0.150
2022	MIL	18	A	110	27	2	0	0	2	1	8.18%	12.73%	0.299	0.373	0.320	0.021
2022	MIL	18	A+	26	1	1	0	0	0	0	0.00%	30.77%	0.077	0.077	0.115	0.038

Background: An under-the-radar signing out of Maracay, Venezuela, two years ago. The 5-foot-10, 160-pound infielder made his professional debut a few months after joining the organization. He hit a respectable .276/.366/.349 with seven doubles, a pair of triples, and five stolen

Milwaukee Brewers

bases (in nine attempts) in 44 games with the club's Dominican Summer League affiliate. Last season, after appearing in seven games in High-A at the start of the year, the front office sent the wiry infielder to the Complex League and he flourished. Appearing in 34 games in the stateside rookie league, Areinamo mashed .323/.416/.472 with 10 doubles, three triples, one triple, and four stolen bases. Areinamo spent the last several weeks holding his own in Low-A. He finished the year with an aggregate .288/.368/.376 with 13 doubles, three triples, one homerun, and six stolen bases. Per *Weighted Runs Created Plus*, his overall production topped the league average mark by 10%.

Scouting Report: One of the few prospects in the club's system that has a chance to develop a plus-hit tool. The power barely registers on the 20-80 scouting scale, but there's a chance he could develop into a league average shortstop, maybe more if the glove work continues to grade out above-average. There's the floor of a solid backup utility option.

Ceiling: 2.0-win player
Risk: Moderate to High
MLB ETA: 2025

12. Robert Moore, 2B/SS

Hit	Power	SB	Patience	Glove	Overall
45/50	45	40	55	60	50

Born: 03/31/02	Age: 21	Bats: B	Top Production Comp: N/A
Height: 5-9	Weight: 170	Throws: R	

Season	Team	Age	Level	PA	1B	2B	3B	HR	SB	CS	BB%	K%	AVG	OBP	SLG	ISO
2022	MIL	20	CPX	13	0	1	0	0	0	0	7.69%	7.69%	0.091	0.231	0.182	0.091
2022	MIL	20	A	125	18	8	0	3	6	2	10.40%	22.40%	0.264	0.352	0.418	0.155

Background: The theme of bloodlines was reoccurring throughout the early parts of the 2022 Draft. Guys like Jackson Holliday, Druw Jones, and Cam Collier all immediately come to mind. But there isn't a lineage quite like Robert Moore, whose father, Dayton, was the World Series winning president of the Kansas City Royals. The younger Moore, though, already has a reputation to stand on his own. One of the country's top prospects coming out of Shawnee Mission East High School, Moore was ranked by *Perfect Game* as the number one player in the state of Kansas and the 20th best player in the nation. And, of course, he was an early enrollee at the University of Arkansas – where he would earn a starting gig as an 18-year-old during the shortened pandemic season. After batting .318/.403/.444 as a true freshman, the switch-hitting middle infielder slugged a rock solid .283/.384/.558 with 10 doubles, three triples, 16 homeruns, and six stolen bases during his sophomore campaign with the Razorbacks. He spent the summer playing with the STARS squad on Team USA's national roster, hitting .351/.415/.378 with one double in 11 games. Simply put: Moore was poised for a big, *big* junior campaign in the SEC. But it never materialized. In a career best 65 games last season, the silky smooth defender hit a disappointing .232/.374/.427 with 19 doubles, two triples, eight homeruns, and five stolen bases. Milwaukee took a calculated gamble on Moore last summer, selecting him in the second round, 72nd overall. They signed him to a deal worth $800,000. Moore, like Eric Brown, appeared in four games in the Complex League before capping his season off with a couple weeks in Low-A. Moore batted an aggregate .248/.343/.392 with 12 extra-base knocks.

Scouting Report: "Consider the following:

> Since 2011, there have been just five Division I hitters that posted a sub-.240 batting average with a walk rate north of 12% and strikeout below 15% in a season (min. 275 PA): Cal Raleigh, Matt Duce, Stephen McGee, Alex Perez, and – of course – Robert Moore. Interestingly enough, all five of the aforementioned players would eventually be drafted by the big leagues teams: Raleigh, who's blossoming into a serviceable big league catcher, was taken by the Mariners in the third round in 2018; Duce was a ninth round pick by the Cardinals in 2018; the Dodgers snagged McGee in the ninth round in 2013; and Perez was a 23rd round pick by the Twins in 2015.

An absolute grinder, a gamer, a dirt bag. Moore's an offensive sparkplug waiting to happen. The problem, of course, is that not only did his offense fail to take a step forward, but it regressed so much it's a bit shocking he was drafted in the second round. Plus defender. Solid looking swing with an average bat. 50-grade power and speed. He's well rounded without a true standout offensive weapon. He has youth on his side; had he not enrolled early, Moore would be entering his junior season at Arkansas."

Ceiling: 1.5- to 2.0-win player
Risk: Moderate to High
MLB ETA: 2024/2025

Milwaukee Brewers

13. Freddy Zamora, SS

Hit	Power	SB	Patience	Glove	Overall
50	40	55	55	55	45

Born: 11/01/98	Age: 24	Bats: R	Top Production Comp: Yunel Escobar
Height: 6-1	Weight: 190	Throws: R	

Season	Team	Age	Level	PA	1B	2B	3B	HR	SB	CS	BB%	K%	AVG	OBP	SLG	ISO
2021	MIL	22	A	321	58	13	1	5	9	5	14.02%	17.76%	0.287	0.396	0.399	0.112
2021	MIL	22	A+	92	17	9	0	1	1	0	13.04%	20.65%	0.342	0.435	0.494	0.152
2022	MIL	23	AA	100	14	4	0	1	4	0	5.00%	22.00%	0.209	0.270	0.286	0.077

Background: There was — perhaps — no player that put together a better debut showing in the Brewers' organization in 2021 than Zamora. A stout performer on both sides of the ball during his freshman and sophomore seasons at the University of Miami, Zamora would miss the entire 2020 campaign recovering from a left knee ACL injury – which came at an ideal time due to COVID wiping out the majority of the year. Milwaukee took a calculated gamble on the recovering shortstop, nabbing the Nicaraguan native in the second round, 53rd overall. Less than a year later it looked like another brilliant move by one of baseball's savviest organizations. Zamora ripped through Low-A in 70 games and caught fire during his 22-game cameo in High-A, finishing his debut professional season with an aggregate .300/.404/.421 with 22 doubles, one triple, six homeruns, and 10 stolen bases (in 15 attempts). Needless to say, but Zamora's prospect status was quickly ascending – especially consider his defensive contributions. And then injury struck. Moving up to the minors' toughest challenge, Double-A, last season, Zamora's bat never really got going as he batted a lowly .209/.270/.286 with four doubles and one homerun in 24 games. He hit the disabled list in mid-May with an ailing left shoulder that knocked him out for the remainder of the year.

Snippet from The 2022 Prospect Digest Handbook: There's a chance for three above-average or better tools: bat, speed, and glove. Zamora doesn't project for much power, but may reach 10 or so homeruns in a season. There's legitimate starting potential here. And it's another example of the Brewers' savvy drafting / developing. I'm a really big fan. A strong showing in AA in 2022 may put him in position for a late-season call up.

Scouting Report: Ignoring the left shoulder injury momentarily, Zamora was already tasked with a difficult test – moving up to Double-A with just 22 games of experience in High-A. And, predictably so, he struggled. But there's plenty of hope for optimism, though: like his plate discipline. Even going back to his freshman season at Miami, Zamora's *always* been a patient, work-the-count type of hitter. He walked in 11% of his plate appearances as a Hurricane and he walked in nearly 14% of his trips to the plate as a professional. Last season, though, it was down to 5%. While it's expected to see *some* regression as he faces much better pitching competition in Double-A, it's also so far of an outlier that it's highly likely it dramatically improves next season. I'd bet on a significant bounce back. He has the ceiling of a .260/.335/.390 hitter.

Ceiling: 1.5-win player
Risk: Moderate
MLB ETA: 2024

14. Ethan Small, LHP

FB	SL	CH	Command	Overall
50	50	60	40	45

Born: 02/14/97	Age: 26	Bats: L	Top Production Comp: Wade Miley
Height: 6-4	Weight: 215	Throws: L	

Season	Team	Age	Level	IP	TBF	K/9	K%	BB/9	BB%	K-BB%	ERA	FIP	xFIP	Pit/Bat
2019	MIL	22	A	18.0	68	15.50	45.59%	2.00	5.88%	39.71%	1.00	0.67	1.35	4.47
2021	MIL	24	AA	41.1	164	14.59	40.85%	4.57	12.80%	28.05%	1.96	2.14	2.96	4.10
2021	MIL	24	AAA	35.0	147	6.17	16.33%	5.40	14.29%	2.04%	2.06	4.99	5.86	4.03
2022	MIL	25	AAA	103.0	446	9.96	25.56%	5.07	13.00%	12.56%	4.46	4.11	4.64	3.94

Background: Not only was Small a prolific strikeout artist during his three-year career at Mississippi State, but his senior season established the wiry southpaw as his generation's elite swing-and-miss hurler. The former Bulldog ace averaged a whopping 14.8 strikeouts per nine innings in 2019, the highest K-rate among all hurlers with at least 100 innings in a season since 2011. The college-oriented Brewers selected him in the opening round, 28th overall, that summer with designs of quickly pushing the polished lefty through the minor leagues. And after a dominant debut that summer – he posted 36-to-4 strikeout-to-walk ratio in only 21.0 innings – Small rocketed through the minors' toughest challenge, Double-A, once baseball returned from its COVID-induced absence. He would cap off his 2021 campaign in style, posting a 2.06 ERA in nine Triple-A starts. Last season Small made 27 appearances with the Nashville Sounds, throwing a career best 103 innings while averaging 10 strikeouts and a whopping 5.1 walks per nine innings. He made two brief starts with the Brew Crew throughout the season as well. One disastrous May outing against the Cubs and two months later an equally disastrous game versus the Twins.

Snippet from The 2022 Prospect Digest Handbook: His changeup is an elite offering, generating tons of weak contact and swings-and-misses. It's the type of pitch that's tough to hit, even if the opposition is sitting on it. It looks like he's scrapped his curveball for a more tradition slider, showing pretty solid horizontal movement. Small has consistently posted lower-than-expected, even miniscule, ERAs. He looks like a potential backend starting option.

Milwaukee Brewers

Scouting Report: Consider the following:

> Since 2006, only four 25-year-old hurlers posted a strikeout percentage between 24.5% and 26.5% with a walk percentage north of 12% in Triple-A (min. 100 IP): Ariel Pena, Deunte Heath, Caleb Kilian, and Ethan Small.

The very definition of all arms and legs, Small forever remains an interesting pitcher. His fastball, an average offering, generates more swings-and-misses than expected, particularly up in the zone, where he loves to locate it – especially when he's ahead in the count. His bread-and-butter offering is an easy plus changeup, showing phenomenal velo separation that is a true game changer. He'll also mix in an underrated slider that he should throw more frequently. Small's always shown elite strikeout rates – even extending back to his early college days – but his command has completely backed up in the professional ranks. He's now entering his age-26 season and lefties – historically speaking – have found command later in their career (or so the wives' tale goes) so the window for a productive big league career hasn't completely closed.

Ceiling: 1.5-win player
Risk: Moderate to High
MLB ETA: Debuted in 2022

15. Luis Lara, CF

Hit	Power	SB	Patience	Glove	Overall
N/A	N/A	N/A	N/A	N/A	N/A

Born: 11/17/04 **Age:** 18 **Bats:** B **Top Production Comp:** N/A
Height: 5-9 **Weight:** 155 **Throws:** R

Season	Team	Age	Level	PA	1B	2B	3B	HR	SB	CS	BB%	K%	AVG	OBP	SLG	ISO
2022	MIL	17	DSL	229	35	11	4	2	7	7	9.17%	12.23%	0.260	0.341	0.385	0.125

Background: The same few teams continually pop up for their success on the international free agency market, clubs like the Dodgers or the Guardians or Braves immediately come to mind. But the Brewers have added several quality prospects on the international free agency market in recent years, including: Jackson Chourio, Hendry Mendez, Carlos Rodriguez, Luis Castillo, and – of course – Luis Lara, one of their prized signings last season. Agreeing to join the organization for a reportedly seven-figure bonus last January, Lara, a native of San Felipe, Venezuela, spent his professional debut in the foreign rookie league. In 58 games with the club's Dominican Summer League affiliate, the diminutive centerfielder – who's listed at just 5-foot-9 and 155 pounds, batted a respectable .255/.341/.385 with 11 doubles, four triples, two homeruns, and seven stolen bases (in 14 total attempts). His overall production was 1% *below* the league average mark, according to *Weighted Runs Created Plus*.

Scouting Report: To the best of my knowledge, there's no game tape available on Lara. But reports indicated a smooth stroke with promising bat speed. The small centerfielder showed promising bat-to-ball skills during his debut in the Dominican Summer League last year, fanning just 12.2% of the time. While he showed a little bit of pop, the question is whether his 5-foot-9, 155-pound frame is going to project for more thunder in the coming years. He's likely ticketed for the Complex Leagues for 2023.

Ceiling: Too Soon to Tell
Risk: Too Soon to Tell
MLB ETA: N/A

16. Eduardo Garcia, SS

Hit	Power	SB	Patience	Glove	Overall
40	50	45	45	45/55	45

Born: 07/10/02 **Age:** 19 **Bats:** R **Top Production Comp:** Orlando Arcia
Height: 6-2 **Weight:** 160 **Throws:** R

Season	Team	Age	Level	PA	1B	2B	3B	HR	SB	CS	BB%	K%	AVG	OBP	SLG	ISO
2021	MIL	18	CPX	136	13	10	3	3	2	2	6.62%	29.41%	0.238	0.316	0.443	0.205
2021	MIL	18	A	42	7	4	0	0	1	0	14.29%	30.95%	0.333	0.452	0.455	0.121
2022	MIL	19	A	372	65	13	3	10	14	2	5.11%	32.80%	0.262	0.309	0.403	0.141
2022	MIL	19	A+	108	18	3	0	5	1	0	0.00%	37.04%	0.248	0.269	0.419	0.171

Background: One of the more highly touted prospects on the international scene in 2018, the Brewers handed the young Venezuelan shortstop a seven-figure bonus. He would make his debut in the Dominican Summer League the following year. And despite appearing in just 10 games, the 6-foot-2, 160-pound infielder looked comfortable squaring off against the older competition; he batted .313/.450/.469 as a 16-year-old. Two years ago as minor league baseball returned from its COVID-induced hiatus, Garcia spent the majority of the year in the Complex League – though, with mixed results. He hit .268/.354/.470 with 16 doubles, three triples, four homeruns, and a trio of stolen bases including his 10-game stint in Low-A. Unsurprisingly, the ball club sent Garcia back to the Carolina Mudcats for an extended look at full season pitching. He would put together a .262/.309/.404 slash line in 85 games before moving up to Wisconsin for the final five weeks of the year. He finished with an aggregate .259/.300/.407 mark with 16 doubles, three triples, 15 homeruns, and 15 stolen bases. Per *Weighted Runs Created Plus*, his overall production was 5% *below* the league average mark.

Milwaukee Brewers

Snippet from The 2022 Prospect Digest Handbook: The teenage shortstop was pegged for his defensive prowess as a free agent – which he's lived up to the billing as a smooth defender – so anything he contributes with the bat is a positive. And it's been *a lot*. Surprising pop. But there's too much swing-and-miss going on with him at the plate. He fanned in more than 29% of his appearances with the Gold team last year. If Garcia chews his problematic K-rate down to the lower 20% range, he's going to be a competent starter.

Scouting Report: Despite his reputation as a stalwart on the defensive side of the ball, metrics weren't too kind to him last season. Per Clay Davenport's numbers, Garcia posted a -13 at shortstop during his time with Carolina. On top of the step backwards with the glove, the former Bonus Baby continued to show concerning swing-and-miss numbers, fanning in roughly a third of his Low-A plate appearances. Average power with speed. Garcia has plenty of developmental time on his side to improve on the areas of concern.

Ceiling: 1.5-win player
Risk: Moderate to High
MLB ETA: 2024/2025

17. Carlos Rodriguez, RHP

FB	CB	SL	CH	Command	Overall
55	50	50	55	50	45

Born: 11/27/01	Age: 21	Bats: R	Top Production Comp: Adrian Houser
Height: 6-0	Weight: 180	Throws: R	

Season	Team	Age	Level	IP	TBF	K/9	K%	BB/9	BB%	K-BB%	ERA	FIP	xFIP	Pit/Bat
2022	MIL	20	A	71.1	287	10.60	29.27%	3.41	9.41%	19.86%	3.53	4.20	4.14	4.07
2022	MIL	20	A+	36.1	141	11.15	31.91%	3.22	9.22%	22.70%	1.98	2.24	3.55	4.06

Background: Last season the Brewers had a remarkably solid rotation, featuring the likes of Corbin Burnes, Brandon Woodruff, Eric Lauer, Aaron Ashby, Adrian Houser, and Freddy Peralta. But here's what makes the club success so interesting – all of the homegrown arms (Burnes, Woodruff, and Ashby) were drafted after the fourth round, and the remaining (Lauer, Houser, and Peralta) were acquired via trade. And the front office may have unearthed another mid-round pitching gem under the direction of former czar David Stearns, as well. Taken in the sixth round, 177th overall two years ago, out of burgeoning baseball hot bed Florida SouthWestern State College, Rodriguez turned in a dominant debut showing in 2022. The 6-foot, 180-pound right-hander, who's a native of Rivas, Nicaragua, made a total of 26 appearances between Carolina and Wisconsin, throwing 107.2 innings with 129 strikeouts and 40 free passes to go along with a 3.01 ERA.

Scouting Report: Consider the following:

> Since 2006, only five 21-year-old hurlers posted a 28% to 30% strikeout percentage with an 8.5% to 10.5% walk percentage in any Low-A league (min. 70 IP): Alex Santos II, Keyvius Sampson, Eddie Morlan, Cristian Hernandez, and – of course – Carlos Rodriguez.

Not overly big, at least in terms of professional athletes, Rodriguez doesn't offer up a whole lot of future projection – if any. But there's plenty of present value to like. The young righty, who's only entering his age-21 season, owns a solid, well-rounded four-pitch mix: an above-average low 90s fastball, a slider that looked better than reports indicated, a rare curveball (which wasn't listed on any report), and a really good changeup. None of the offerings are standalone swing-and-miss pitches, but the young hurler changes speeds indiscriminately and consistently works around the plate. There's some backend starting potential and Milwaukee generally gets the most out of these types too.

Ceiling: 1.0- to 1.5-win player
Risk: Moderate
MLB ETA: 2024

18. Robert Gasser, LHP

FB	CB	SL	CH	Command	Overall
50	50	55	50	50	40

Born: 05/31/99	Age: 24	Bats: L	Top Production Comp: N/A
Height: 6-1	Weight: 190	Throws: L	

Season	Team	Age	Level	IP	TBF	K/9	K%	BB/9	BB%	K-BB%	ERA	FIP	xFIP	Pit/Bat
2021	SDP	22	A	14.0	51	8.36	25.49%	1.29	3.92%	21.57%	1.29	3.73	4.13	3.75
2022	SDP	23	A+	90.1	377	11.46	30.50%	2.79	7.43%	23.08%	4.18	3.22	3.40	3.93
2022	MIL	23	AA	20.1	83	11.51	31.33%	3.54	9.64%	21.69%	2.21	3.78	3.99	3.83
2022	MIL	23	AAA	26.1	119	10.59	26.05%	5.47	13.45%	12.61%	4.44	3.58	4.97	3.86

Background: Part of the quartet of players the club received in the Josh Hader swap with the Padres. Gasser, who was acquired along with Dinelson Lamet, Esteury Ruiz, and Taylor Rogers, parlayed his lone full season as a college starting hurler into a second round selection. Originally attending the University of New Mexico, the 6-foot-1, 190-pound southpaw transferred to San Joaquin Delta College for a season before packing his bags – once again – to make the move to the University of Houston. And after a brief COVID-induced 2020 season working out of the Cougars' bullpen, Gasser shined brightly during his fourth college season. He would make 14 starts, throwing 85.2 innings

Milwaukee Brewers

while averaging 11.0 strikeouts and just 2.6 walks per nine innings. After the Friars added him in the second round two years ago, Gasser dominated the Low-A competition for 14.0 innings to cap off his wildly successful year. Last year Gasser rocketed through the minors' top three levels between both organizations, throwing an aggregate 137.0 innings with 172 punch outs and 52 walks to go along with a 3.94 ERA.

Snippet from The 2022 Prospect Digest Handbook: Funky lefty that short-arms the ball. Gasser's sneaky heater shows some solid arm side action. It's currently a 55-grade offering, but I'm not optimistic on its future and expect it to downgrade to a 50 due to the rigors of pro ball.

Scouting Report: One of Gasser's main selling points was his increased velocity heading into the draft two years ago. But as I noted in *The 2022 Prospect Digest Handbook*, I remained quite skeptical that the slight-framed, generously listed 6-foot-1, 190-pound southpaw would be able to maintain the bump in velo over the course of a full professional season. And he didn't. During his final start of the year against the Memphis Redbirds, the southpaw's fastball hovered in the 89-mh range and kissed 92 mph with some noticeable effort. The University of Houston product, though, succeeds on his low arm slot, riding life, and a lot of horizontal movement on his offspeed offerings. The break on his mid-80s slider, easily his best pitch, will morph from sweeping movement to more of a cut-fastball look. Either version, though, breaks a lot of right-handed sticks. His curveball is essentially the same pitch, but it is five miles-per-hour slower. He'll also mix in a solid average changeup. Gasser's repertoire doesn't leave a lot of room for error, but his offspeed mix and moxie give him a puncher's chance at the #5-spot in the Brewers' rotation in the coming years. At worst, he could be a very effective reliever.

Ceiling: 1.0-win player
Risk: Low to Moderate
MLB ETA: 2023

19. Felix Valerio, 2B

Hit	Power	SB	Patience	Glove	Overall
40/45	45	60	55	50	40

Born: 12/26/00	Age: 21	Bats: R	Top Production Comp: N/A
Height: 5-7	Weight: 165	Throws: R	

Season	Team	Age	Level	PA	1B	2B	3B	HR	SB	CS	BB%	K%	AVG	OBP	SLG	ISO
2021	MIL	20	A	377	64	24	3	6	27	8	14.32%	13.00%	0.314	0.430	0.469	0.155
2021	MIL	20	A+	134	9	13	0	5	4	1	11.19%	16.42%	0.229	0.321	0.466	0.237
2022	MIL	21	AA	480	67	14	2	12	30	9	10.00%	16.67%	0.228	0.313	0.357	0.129

Background: Like so many of the club's other moves under David Stearns, the Brewers played this one to perfection. The front office brass shipped off toolsy, hit tool-deficient outfielder Keon Broxton – who was just two years removed from a 20/20 season – and minor leaguer Adam Hill in exchange for reliever Bobby Wahl and a then-17-year-old Dominican Summer League prospect by the name of Felix Valerio in 2019. Less than three years later Valerio, a diminutive infielder, was earning valuable development time at the game's harshest level – Double-A. A native of Bonao, Dominican Republic, Valerio made the transition to the stateside rookie leagues during his first year in Milwaukee's organization, hitting a respectable .306/.376/.389 in 41 games. He – like every other minor leaguer – would miss the following season due to the COVID closure. But the 5-foot-7, 165-pound second baseman made up for any lost development time in 2021. Valerio would torch Low-A (he slugged .314/.430/.469) for 85 games and spent the last remaining weeks in High-A. And despite his struggles with Wisconsin to close out the year, the front office aggressively shoved the young infielder straight up to Double-A to begin the 2022 season. And, of course, Valerio's campaign was filled with plenty of ups-and-downs. He would finish the season with a disappointing .228/.313/.357 slash line, adding 14 doubles, two triples, 12 homeruns, and 30 stolen bases (in 39 total attempts).

Scouting Report: Consider the following:

> Since 2006, three 21-year-old hitters met the following criteria in Double-A (min. 400 PA): 73 to 83 wRC+ with a sub-20% strikeout rate and an 8% to 11% walk rate. Those three: Carlos Rivero, Marcus Lemon, and Felix Valerio.

Valerio has an intriguing toolkit wrapped up in his 5-foot-7, 165-pound frame. He runs well, plays solid defense (which took a few steps forward in 2022), and flashes surprising pop. But his success moving forward is going to be tied – almost single handedly – to the actual hit tool. While he earns a pass at his struggles last season due to his limited exposure in High-A, it's important to point out that he *struggled* in his month-long cameo with Wisconsin to close out 2021. Valerio did bat .258/.329/.452 through his first 64 contests before bottoming out over the remaining 49 games (.182/.288/.212). If the hit tool bounces back, which I'm expecting it to, he's tracking like a low end starter / bench option.

Ceiling: 1.0-win player
Risk: Moderate
MLB ETA: 2023/2024

Milwaukee Brewers

20. Luis Castillo, LF/RF

Hit	Power	SB	Patience	Glove	Overall
45/50	40/50	35	50	50	40

Born: 11/11/03   **Age:** 19   **Bats:** L   **Top Production Comp:** N/A
Height: 5-11   **Weight:** 175   **Throws:** L

Season	Team	Age	Level	PA	1B	2B	3B	HR	SB	CS	BB%	K%	AVG	OBP	SLG	ISO
2021	MIL	17	DSL	156	28	7	0	0	3	1	9.62%	15.38%	0.252	0.327	0.302	0.050
2022	MIL	18	CPX	137	21	9	2	3	1	0	12.41%	20.44%	0.297	0.387	0.483	0.186
2022	MIL	18	A	113	20	2	0	3	4	2	9.73%	22.12%	0.250	0.336	0.360	0.110

Background: Signed out of the Dominican Republic in January of 2021, Castillo, a short-framed corner outfielder, would make his professional debut just months later in his home country's affiliated rookie league – though the results were clearly lacking. The 5-foot-11, 175-pound left / right-fielder batted a lowly .252/.327/.302 with just seven doubles in 43 games. Undeterred by his lack of offensive punch, the front office sent the young teenager stateside to the Complex Leagues. And Castillo's bat showed some signs of life. Appearing in 33 games in the lowest stateside league, he slugged .297/.387/.483. He looked competent during his 28-game cameo with Carolina last in the year as well, batting .250/.336/.360. He finished the season with an aggregate .275/.364/.427 slash line with 11 doubles, two triples, six homeruns, and five stolen bases (in seven attempts) in only 61 games.

Scouting Report: Just for fun, here's Castillo's numbers pro-rated for a full 162-game season: 29 doubles, five triples, 16 homeruns, and 13 stolen bases. Not too shabby. After not showing any type of thump during his debut, Castillo's average power potential started to pop up in games last season. Solid approach at the plate, a little bit of speed. It's a decent foundation to start out. Not a whole lot of physical projection remains for Castillo, though.

Ceiling: 1.0-win player
Risk: Moderate
MLB ETA: 2025

Minnesota Twins Top Prospects

Minnesota Twins

1. Brooks Lee, SS

Hit	Power	SB	Patience	Glove	Overall
60	50/55	35	55	55	60

Born: 02/14/01	Age: 22	Bats: B	Top Production Comp: N/A
Height: 6-2	Weight: 205	Throws: R	

Season	Team	Age	Level	PA	1B	2B	3B	HR	SB	CS	BB%	K%	AVG	OBP	SLG	ISO
2022	MIN	21	CPX	17	4	2	0	0	0	0	0.00%	0.00%	0.353	0.353	0.471	0.118
2022	MIN	21	A+	114	20	4	0	4	0	2	14.04%	15.79%	0.289	0.395	0.454	0.165

Background: Despite a few notable alumni – like Ozzie Smith or Mike Krukow or Mitch Haniger – Cal Poly San Luis Obispo is far from a baseball hotbed. The Big West Conference school has produced just one player taken before the third round since 2015 (Spencer Howard). In normal circumstances it would have been a bit odd for Brooks Lee, a likely top prospect in the 2019 draft, to withdraw his name from consideration due to his unusually strong commitment to the Mustangs, but this wasn't exactly a normal circumstance. Lee's father, Harry, just happened to be the Head Coach of Cal Poly's baseball team – and an alumnus of the school. A tremendous athlete since entering San Luis Obispo High School, Lee, a switch-hitting shortstop, was limited to just a pair of contests during his freshman collegiate season – courtesy of a combination of injury (hyper-extended knee) and a pandemic. But after torching the Northwoods League competition that summer, Lee continued to swing a hot bat during breakout follow up season in 2021. In 55 games, the California native posted a whopper of a slash line, .342/.384/.626, with plenty of extra-base firepower: 27 doubles, three triples, and 10 homers. And he didn't stop hitting that summer as he split time between Team USA's national squad (.306/.342/.444) and the Cape Cod League (.405/.432/.667). Last season Lee continued to do what he's always done: hit. In a career best 58 games, he slugged .357/.462/.664 with 25 doubles, one triple, and 15 homeruns. He also swiped three stolen bases in four total attempts. Minnesota selected him in the first round, 8th overall, and signed him to a big $5,675,000 million deal. Lee split his debut between the Complex League, Cedar Rapids, and Wichita, hitting an impressive .303/.389/.451 with six doubles and four homeruns in 139 plate appearances.

Scouting Report: Per the usual, here's my pre-draft write-up:

> "Consider the following:
>
> Since 2011, only nine Division I hitters batted at least .350/.450/.650 with at least a 1.5 walk-to-strikeout ratio and a walk rate north of 15% in season (min. 275 PA): Andrew Benintendi, Nick Gonzales, Seth Beer, James Ramsey, Peyton Burdick, Jameson Fisher, Tyler Locklear, Chase Chambers, and Brooks Lee.
>
> Lee will have no issues sticking at the most important infield position. Explosive, agile, quick. He may not contend for an annual Gold Glove, but he's going to provide value on the defensive side of the ball. Offensively speaking, he's a tough at bat, fighting off pitcher's pitches and capitalizing on mistakes. More power from the right side and more of a slashing approach from the left. Great bat speed. Great baseball instincts. He may have the highest floor among all prospects in 2022 draft."

Ceiling: 4.5-win player
Risk: Moderate
MLB ETA: 2024

2. Marco Raya, RHP

FB	CB	SL	CH	Command	Overall
60	60	60	55	50/55	60

Born: 08/07/02	Age: 20	Bats: R	Top Production Comp: Lance McCullers Jr.
Height: 6-1	Weight: 170	Throws: R	

Season	Team	Age	Level	IP	TBF	K/9	K%	BB/9	BB%	K-BB%	ERA	FIP	xFIP	Pit/Bat
2022	MIN	19	A	65.0	263	10.52	28.90%	3.18	8.75%	20.15%	3.05	3.98	3.45	3.71

Background: For a team that's generally viewed as a well-run organization, the Twins have had some real stinker draft classes in recent years. Take, for example, their 2020 class. Limited to just five rounds due to the COVID-pandemic, Minnesota owned a quartet of picks: #27, #59, #128, and #158. Their first pick, former UNC bopper Aaron Sabato, has failed to his weight in two seasons in pro ball – *literally*. Former Tennessee outfielder Alerick Soularie, their second selection, has *barely* hit Sabato's 230-pound weight. And their final pick, Hawaiian outfielder Kala'i Rosario, whiffed 136 times in only 419 plate appearances in Low-A last season. That leaves the success of the franchise's entire draft class resting solely on the slight framed shoulders of Marco Raya. A product of United South High School, Raya was only one of the team's 2020 Draft Class that didn't debut in 2021; a wonky shoulder forced him to sit out the entire year. Finally healthy in 2022, Raya made 17 starts and a pair of relief appearances with the Fort Myers Mighty Mussels, throwing 65.0 innings with an impressive 76-to-23 strikeout-to-walk ratio. He finished his debut showing with a 3.05 ERA, a 3.98 FIP, and a 3.45 xFIP.

Minnesota Twins

Scouting Report: Consider the following:

> Since 2006, only six 19-year-old hurlers posted a 28% to 30% strikeout percentage with a 7.5% to 9.5% walk percentage in any Low-A league (min. 50 IP): Hunter Harvey, Joey Wentz, Tyler Robertson, Benino Pruneda, and – of course – Marco Raya.

Immediately blown away with Raya's combination of poise, pitchability, command, and deep repertoire. It isn't hyperbole: Marco Raya may be one of the most underrated pitching prospects in the minor leagues entering 2023. The wiry right-hander was sitting 94- to 95-mph during a late season start last year, showing strong command with his plus heater. But that's not even half the story. Raya features a pair of plus breaking balls: a low 80s, Jose Berrios-like curveball and mid-80s, horizontally darting slider. Again, that's not the entire story either because the young right-hander with just over 60 innings of professional experience features an upper-80s, above-average changeup. Raya has several questions that he'll need to address in the coming years, all of which surround holding up to the rigors of starting and maintaining velocity. But there's a very high ceiling here, without question. He's going to shoot up a lot of prospect lists by midway 2023. And he's one of my favorite prospects heading into the year. Don't. Sleep. On. Him.

Ceiling: 4.0-win player
Risk: Moderate
MLB ETA: 2024/2025

3. Emmanuel Rodriguez, CF

Hit	Power	SB	Patience	Glove	Overall
45/55	60	55/40	80	45/50	60

Born: 02/28/03	Age: 20	Bats: L	Top Production Comp: N/A
Height: 5-10	Weight: 210	Throws: L	

Season	Team	Age	Level	PA	1B	2B	3B	HR	SB	CS	BB%	K%	AVG	OBP	SLG	ISO
2021	MIN	18	CPX	153	10	5	2	10	9	4	15.03%	36.60%	0.214	0.346	0.524	0.310
2022	MIN	19	A	199	20	5	3	9	11	5	28.64%	26.13%	0.272	0.492	0.551	0.279

Background: Touted as the "next Eddie Rosario" at the time of his signing. The ball club inked the Santiago, Dominican Republic native to massive free agency deal in early July 2019, handing the international free agent a hefty $2.5 million bonus to join the American League Central Division franchise. Rodriguez would have to wait a while before making his professional debut, though, thanks in large part due to the COVID pandemic. Two years ago the front office brain trust sent the 5-foot-10, 210-pound outfielder to the Complex League – though the results were mediocre, at best, as he batted a .214/.346/.524 while posting a whiff rate of nearly 37%. Last season, Rodriguez was in the midst of a massive breakout before a torn meniscus in early June forced him to miss the remainder of 2022. The injury occurred as he was sliding into third base feet-first on June 8th. He finished the year with a .272/.493/.552 slash line with five doubles, three triples, nine homeruns, and 11 stolen bases (in 16 attempts). Per *Weighted Runs Created Plus*, his overall production crushed the league average threshold by an unfathomable 96%.

Scouting Report: Consider the following:

> Since 2006, there have been 638 instances in which a 19-year-old received 175 plate appearances or more in any Low-A league. Emmanuel Rodriguez's 196 wRC+ ranks as the greatest total among the group. And just for comparison's sake, here's the top five 19-year-old hitters (in descending order):
>
> #1. Emmanuel Rodriguez (196 wRC+)
> #2. Oscar Taveras (190 wRC+)
> #3. Jarred Kelenic (181 wRC+)
> #4. Byron Buxton (176 wRC+)
> #5. Javier Baez (170 wRC+)

Needless to say, but Rodriguez was in rarified company after just a couple months in Low-A. The toolsy centerfielder owns incredible offensive potential, showcasing present plus in-game power, above-average speed, and plus-plus patience at the plate. Rodriguez, by the way, owns the highest walk rate among all 19-year-old hitters with at least 175 PA in Low-A since 2006. Smooth, easy left-handed swing that should allow for his borderline red flag strikeout numbers to decline in the coming years. Rodriguez also plays with a bit of swagger, a touch of cockiness – which is good. He could pop in a large way in 2023.

Ceiling: 4.5-win player
Risk: Moderate to High
MLB ETA: 2024/2025

Minnesota Twins

4. Royce Lewis, SS

Hit	Power	SB	Patience	Glove	Overall
40/55	45/55	55	50	50	60

Born: 06/05/99	Age: 24	Bats: R	Top Production Comp: Chris Taylor
Height: 6-2	Weight: 200	Throws: R	

Season	Team	Age	Level	PA	1B	2B	3B	HR	SB	CS	BB%	K%	AVG	OBP	SLG	ISO
2019	MIN	20	A+	418	61	17	3	10	16	8	6.46%	21.53%	0.238	0.289	0.376	0.138
2019	MIN	20	AA	148	19	9	1	2	6	2	7.43%	22.30%	0.231	0.291	0.358	0.127
2022	MIN	23	AAA	153	23	12	1	5	12	2	11.76%	20.92%	0.313	0.405	0.534	0.221

Background: At the onset of his career, Lewis seemed destined for superstardom. The JSerra Catholic High School product went atop the 2017 draft, ahead of Hunter Greene, who had already donned the cover of Sports Illustrated; ahead of Golden Spikes Award winning Brendan McKay; and ahead of Braves young ace Kyle Wright, who tallied 21 wins last season. And Lewis immediately hit the ground running as soon as he joined the Twins' organization, hitting an aggregate .279/.381/.407 between the old Gulf Coast and Midwest Leagues. Minnesota sent their prized prospect back to Low-A to begin the 2018, but after torching the competition to the tune of .315/.368/.485, the front office bumped him to High-A. And he held his own as a 19-year-old (.255/.327/.377). Then the wheels started to come off the Lewis Express. The 6-foot-2, 200-pound shortstop looked abysmal during his return to Fort Myers (.238/.290/.376) and he was completely overwhelmed during his surprising promotion up to the minors' toughest level – Double-A (.231/.291/.358). Lewis, like all minor leaguers, would lose the 2020 due to the COVID pandemic. But then he would miss the entire 2021 season recovering from a torn ACL surgery. Finally healthy, at least temporarily, he returned to action in early April as the St. Paul Saints penciled him in as their #2 hitter. The former top pick turned back the clock to better times and immediately started hitting, putting together an impressive .310/.430/.563 through 24 games before Minnesota promoted him up to the big leagues. And he continued to hit for a couple weeks before being sent back down in mid-May. By the end of the month, though, he had hit the disabled list and eventually underwent a second ACL surgery. The former prep star hit .313/.405/.534 with St. Paul in 34 games.

Snippet from The 2020 Prospect Digest Handbook: The problem isn't necessarily his swing, per se. It's this massive leg kick that's creating issues. Sometimes he's late getting his foot down. Sometimes it seems as if his weight is leaning too forward. It's just…bad. Lewis possesses the intangibles that made him the top pick in the draft. I think he needs to alter his lower half, rather than the whole swing.

Scouting Report: As part of The 2020 Prospect Digest Handbook, I noted that Lewis' massive leg kick was creating timing issues at the plate as he often failed to get his front foot down in time to begin his swing. Fast forward a few seasons and Lewis has eliminated the leg kick in favor of a more traditional stride. Last season – at least before the major injury – was a major success for the former first rounder as he showed an improved ability to consistently barrel up the baseball. Above-average pop. Solid patience and contact rates. His glove looked decent enough to stay at shortstop, but a second ACL issue may force him to the hot corner or an outfield position. Regardless of the position, he's still profiling as an impact bat at the game's pinnacle level. He looks to be a .280/.350/.450 type hitter. I don't think a move to first base should be taken off the table either. The club has to find a way to keep him healthy and his bat in the lineup.

Ceiling: 4.0-win player
Risk: Moderate to High
MLB ETA: Debuted in 2022

5. Connor Prielipp, LHP

FB	SL	CH	Command	Overall
55	70	55	55	55

Born: 01/10/01	Age: 21	Bats: L	Top Production Comp: N/A
Height: 6-2	Weight: 210	Throws: L	

Background: A product of Wisconsin-based Tomah High School. Prielipp was nearly unhittable – both literally and figuratively – during his final two seasons with the Timberwolves. The well-built left-hander hurled 52 innings during his junior campaign – with the opposition failing to score in 51 of those frames. He would finish his third high school season with a laughably low 0.27 ERA with a whopping 97 punch outs. For those counting at home: he allowed one earned run, the result of the lone extra-base hit he surrendered that year. Prielipp, a projected top pick in the 2019 draft, captured the Wisconsin Gatorade Player of the Year after an equally dominant showing during his senior season: He posted a "bloated" 0.85 ERA across 49 innings of work while racking up a mind-boggling 118 strikeouts (against just five free passes). Again, for those counting at home, 80.2% of the outs accumulated during his mound work came via the punch out. The Red Sox took a late round flier on the lethal lefty, though he would eventually head to the University of Alabama. A year later – as a true freshman – he was named the Tides' Opening Day starter. He was magnificent across four starts, posting a 35-to-6 strikeout-to-walk ratio without surrendering a run – earned or unearned – in 21.0 innings of work. After that, though, COVID prematurely forced the end of what promised to be a dominating campaign. Prielipp came back strong for a trio of games during the 2021 season, fanning 12 and walking one in seven innings, before he succumbed to Tommy John surgery. Finally healthy, Prielipp chose not to pitch during the 2022 season, opting, instead, to throw bullpens for Major League clubs. He would finish his

Minnesota Twins

collegiate career with a 0.96 ERA, averaging 15.1 strikeouts and 2.3 walks per nine innings. Minnesota would select him in the second round, 48th overall, and signed him to a deal worth $1,825,000.

Scouting Report: My pre-draft write-up:

> "Prior to the injury, Prielipp showed an above-average, low 90s fastball, sitting in the 92 mph range and touching a tick higher. He complements the 55-grade offering with an elite mid-80s slider, arguably the best in this year's class – a genuine swing-and-miss offering. He'll also mix in a low 80s changeup. Even going back to his days at Tomah High School, Prielipp always had a knack for making consistent pitcher's pitches, showcasing an above-average – maybe even plus – ability to command the strike zone. There's some Reid Detmers feel to Prielipp. He won't be an ace, but he could be a very competent mid-rotation caliber arm – assuming the arm won't give him any issues in the future."

Prior to the draft, I had a first round grade on the southpaw.

Ceiling: 3.0-win player
Risk: Moderate
MLB ETA: 2024/2025

6. Yunior Severino, 2B/3B

Hit	Power	SB	Patience	Glove	Overall
50	50	35	50	45	50

Born: 10/03/99	Age: 23	Bats: B	Top Production Comp: Eduardo Escobar
Height: 6-1	Weight: 189	Throws: R	

Season	Team	Age	Level	PA	1B	2B	3B	HR	SB	CS	BB%	K%	AVG	OBP	SLG	ISO
2021	MIN	21	A	268	33	17	1	5	2	0	11.94%	27.99%	0.245	0.347	0.393	0.148
2021	MIN	21	A+	157	27	12	1	3	1	0	12.74%	31.85%	0.321	0.414	0.493	0.172
2022	MIN	22	A+	191	23	9	2	11	0	0	13.09%	22.51%	0.283	0.398	0.572	0.289
2022	MIN	22	AA	160	23	8	0	8	0	1	8.75%	30.00%	0.273	0.338	0.497	0.224

Background: Severino was inadvertently caught in the Braves' international free agency scandal several years back and granted another tour on the market. The Twins stepped in and signed the Dominican infielder to large $2.5 million deal in late 2017. Severino's remained one of the more consistent offensive threats in the minor leagues throughout his career. The 6-foot-1, 189-pound second / third baseman split time between Fort Myers and Cedar Rapids two years ago, hitting an aggregate .273/.372/.430 with 29 doubles, two triples, eight homeruns, and a trio of stolen bases. Last season, after appearing in 35 High-A games, Severino returned to work with Cedar Rapids for additional seasoning. He responded with the best half-season of his career, slugging .283/.398/.572 across 46 games, and the front office deemed him ready for the minors' most challenging test: Double-A. And he maintained his breakout performance as well, hitting .273/.338/.497 in 37 contests with the Surge. Severino finished the year with an aggregate .278/.370/.536 slash line with 17 doubles, two triples, and a career best 19 dingers. His overall production topped the league average mark by 39%, according to *Weighted Runs Created Plus*.

Snippet from The 2022 Prospect Digest Handbook: There's the potential to develop 20-homer pop, but he needs to elevate the ball more frequently. Solid patience, but not enough to compensate for some bloated swing-and-miss tendencies. He's raw defensively, though likely better suited for third base. He could be a solid complementary player, something like a young Eduardo Escobar.

Scouting Report: Severino managed to turn his career high in doubles in 2021 into a career best in long balls last season, despite missing two months due to a thumb contusion at the start of the year. Prorating his output, the young Dominican infielder was on pace for 37 taters over a 162-game schedule. Severino still isn't elevating the ball with a higher frequency, so it'll be interesting to see if he can repeat that level of thump in 2023. His strikeout rates tend to fluctuate from red flag to non-concerning. Average defense, but he's better suited for the hot corner as opposed to the keystone. He's still tracking like a .255/.310/.440 hitter.

Ceiling: 2.5-win player
Risk: Moderate
MLB ETA: 2023

Minnesota Twins

7. Jose Salas, SS

Hit	Power	SB	Patience	Glove	Overall
45/55	40/45	50/40	50	45/50	50

Born: 04/26/03   **Age:** 20   **Bats:** B   **Top Production Comp:** Asdrubal Cabera
Height: 6-2   **Weight:** 191   **Throws:** R

Season	Team	Age	Level	PA	1B	2B	3B	HR	SB	CS	BB%	K%	AVG	OBP	SLG	ISO
2021	MIA	18	CPX	107	23	10	0	1	8	5	10.28%	21.50%	0.370	0.458	0.511	0.141
2021	MIA	18	A	123	22	4	0	1	6	0	8.94%	22.76%	0.250	0.333	0.315	0.065
2022	MIA	19	A	257	38	13	3	5	15	1	8.95%	21.01%	0.267	0.355	0.421	0.154
2022	MIA	19	A+	217	32	7	1	4	18	0	9.22%	18.89%	0.230	0.319	0.340	0.110

Background: The Marlins chose the young shortstop to be the Crown Jewel of their 2019 International Free Agency Class, handing Salas a hefty bonus worth $2.8 million. Due to the 2020 COVID season, the 6-foot-2, 191-pound middle infielder wouldn't make his highly anticipated debut until two years later. But it was worth the wait. Salas smashed the Florida Complex League, slugging .370/.458/.511 through 28 games. And he continued to perform well at the plate during his late-season promotion up to Low-A (.250/.333/.315). Last season, the front office sent their prized Bonus Baby back down to Low-A for an extended look. Salas responded with another promising showing, batting .267/.356/.421 through 61 contests. Miami bumped him up to Beloit at the end of June. He would hit a lowly .230/.319/.340 against the significantly older competition. Salas finished the year with an aggregate .250/.339/.384 with 20 doubles, four triples, nine homeruns, and 33 stolen bases (in 34 total attempts). His production, per *Weighted Runs Created Plus*, topped the league average threshold by 7%. Minnesota acquired Salas, along with veteran right-hander Pablo López and minor league Bryon Chourio, for batting champion Luis Arraez this offseason.

Snippet from The 2022 Prospect Digest Handbook: Salas did everything the organization expected during his debut last season: he was dominating in the Complex League and didn't look too overmatched as an 18-year-old in Low-A. He ran and fielded well. And he flashed gap-to-gap pop. Above-average bat speed and showed some promise on turning on low-90s fastballs. Salas didn't show a ton of homerun thump during his debut – he belted out just a pair of long balls – but there's 50-grade power brewing in his stick.

Scouting Report: With respect to his production with Jupiter, consider the following:

> Since 2006, only three 19-year-old hitters posted a 118 to 128 wRC+ with an 8% to 10% walk rate and a 19% to 23% strikeout rate in Low-A (min. 250 PA): Nick Franklin, a former consensus Top 100 prospect in the Mariners' system, Cal Mitchell, and – of course – Jose Salas.

Not quite an elite shortstop prospect, but Salas remains on the outer fringes of the conversation. His overall toolkit isn't defined by a true standout tool, but rather for its lack of flaws. Salas has a shot to develop an above-average hit tool thanks to his quick bat and above-average bat speed. Plus runner. Average defender. And there's double-digit homer thump lurking around the corner as well. An extended look at Double-A as a 20-year-old in 2023 isn't out of the question either.

Ceiling: 2.5-win player
Risk: Moderate
MLB ETA: 2024

8. David Festa, RHP

FB	SL	CH	Command	Overall
60	60	55	50	50

Born: 03/08/00   **Age:** 23   **Bats:** R   **Top Production Comp:** Hunter Harvey
Height: 6-6   **Weight:** 185   **Throws:** R

Season	Team	Age	Level	IP	TBF	K/9	K%	BB/9	BB%	K-BB%	ERA	FIP	xFIP	Pit/Bat
2022	MIN	22	A	24.0	88	12.38	37.50%	2.25	6.82%	30.68%	1.50	2.19	2.72	4.06
2022	MIN	22	A+	79.2	325	8.47	23.08%	3.16	8.62%	14.46%	2.71	3.66	4.06	3.76

Background: After taking a couple of talented high school kids in the opening round two years ago, the front office ripped off 18 four-year college players over their remaining 19 picks. Festa, the club's 13th round pick who received a run-of-the-mill $125,000 bonus as the 399th player taken, was a three-year member of Seton Hall's rotation. The big 6-foot-6, 185-pound right-hander mostly turned in mixed results for the Pirates. He was good, but not great during his freshman season. He got hit pretty hard during his follow up sophomore campaign during the COVID-abbreviated 2020 season. But his work as junior fell somewhere in between as he averaged 8.4 strikeouts and 4.1 walks per nine innings. Festa opened last season up on a tear as he shredded Low-A lumber across five starts before settling in for the long haul with Cedar Rapids. The New Jersey-born behemoth finished the year with 103.2 innings, recording 108 punch outs against only 34 free passes to go along with an aggregate 2.43 ERA.

Minnesota Twins

Scouting Report: Consider the following:

> Since 2006, eleven 22-year-old hurlers posted a 22% to 24% strikeout percentage with a 7.5% to 9.5% walk percentage in any High-A league (min. 75 IP): Deck McGuire, Mat Bowman, Thomas Hatch, Juan Sosa, Camilo Vazquez, Henry Hirsch, Kyle Johnston, Michael Peoples, Taylor Siemens, Domingo Gonzalez, and David Festa.

Festa's stint in the Florida State League lasted all of five starts, spanning 24.0 innings. His first game was on April 9th and moved up to High-A in mid-May. But the big 6-foot-6, 185-pound right-hander with tons of moving arms and legs clearly left an impression on the opposition. Florida State managers named his plus slider as the league's best breaking ball, which is saying something. Combine that mid-80s offering with mid- to high-90s heat and an above-average changeup, and it's clear that the Twins unearthed a potential big league starter in the late rounds of the draft. Festa's more of a strike-thrower than a command guy, but there's a #4-type ceiling here.

Ceiling: 2.5-win player
Risk: Moderate
MLB ETA: 2023/2024

9. Simeon Woods Richardson, RHP

FB	CB	SL	CH	Command	Overall
50	55	50	60	55	50

Born: 09/27/00 **Age:** 22 **Bats:** R **Top Production Comp:** Kyle Gibson
Height: 6-3 **Weight:** 210 **Throws:** R

Season	Team	Age	Level	IP	TBF	K/9	K%	BB/9	BB%	K-BB%	ERA	FIP	xFIP	Pit/Bat
2021	TOR	20	AA	45.1	202	13.30	33.17%	5.16	12.87%	20.30%	5.76	3.78	4.08	4.07
2022	MIN	21	AAA	36.2	139	9.33	27.34%	2.45	7.19%	20.14%	2.21	2.96	3.83	3.97
2022	MIN	21	AA	70.2	287	9.81	26.83%	3.31	9.06%	17.77%	3.06	3.55	4.56	3.92

Background: The promising right-hander's been passed around like a bad side dish at Thanksgiving throughout his young career. Taken by the Mets in the second round of the 2018 draft as part of the same class that added Jarred Kelenic to the fold, Woods Richardson's stay in the Big Apple lasted barely a year before he was packaged along with Anthony Kay for veteran hurler Marcus Stroman. Nearly two years to the day Toronto shipped the 6-foot-3, 210-pound righty to Minnesota as part of the package for another veteran hurler – José Berríos. And, for the most part, Woods Richardson has moved from stop to stop without showing a significant downturn in production – sans his 2021 campaign where he battled control / command demons. Last season, though, the Sugar Land, Texas native regained his previous strike-throwing ability as he posted – arguably – his finest season to date. Making 16 appearances with Wichita and another seven starts with St. Paul, Woods Richardson tossed a career best 107.1 innings, averaging 9.6 strikeouts and 3.0 walks per nine innings. He finished the minor league season with a sparkling 2.77 ERA. He capped the year with one big league start against the Tigers, throwing five innings and allowing a pair of earned runs.

Snippet from The 2022 Prospect Digest Handbook: The promising youngster has always shown a solid feel for the strike zone, so the Twins were wise to bet on the past, as opposed to the present. There's #3/#4-type potential, assuming the command bounces back.

Scouting Report: Consider the following:

> Since 2006, only three 21-year-old hurlers met the following criteria in any Double-A league (min. 70 IP): 26% to 28% strikeout percentage with an 8% to 10% walk percentage. Those three hurlers: Tommy Hanson, Tyler Clippard, and Simeon Woods Richardson, the oft-traded right-hander.

There's usually a reason – or at least a driving factor – as to why a consensus Top 100 prospect would get traded multiple times in such a short span (see: Andy Marte). And Richardson's loss of velocity *has* to be the culprit. Coming out of high school, Woods Richardson would regularly touch the mid-90s with the heater. Now, though, his fastball is sitting in the 89- to 91-mph. He succeeds with guile, above-average command, and three solid or better secondary weapons. His changeup shows arm side run and fade with solid velocity separation, making it a plus offering. He'll mix in a curveball and slider with the former being the better option. The Twins have indicated that they'll work with their promising right-hander to regain the lost mph this offseason. At worst, he's a backend starter with the ceiling as a #3.

Ceiling: 1.5- to 2.0-win player
Risk: Moderate
MLB ETA: Debuted in 2022

Minnesota Twins

10. Edouard Julien, 2B

Hit	Power	SB	Patience	Glove	Overall
60	45	50	60	35/45	50

Born: 04/30/99	Age: 24	Bats: L	Top Production Comp: Cord Phelps
Height: 6-2	Weight: 195	Throws: R	

Season	Team	Age	Level	PA	1B	2B	3B	HR	SB	CS	BB%	K%	AVG	OBP	SLG	ISO
2021	MIN	22	A	204	28	12	1	3	21	2	24.51%	26.47%	0.299	0.490	0.456	0.156
2021	MIN	22	A+	310	30	16	0	15	13	3	19.35%	29.03%	0.247	0.397	0.494	0.247
2022	MIN	23	AA	508	81	19	3	17	19	7	19.29%	24.61%	0.300	0.441	0.490	0.190

Background: The Twins' 2019 draft class will forever be known for their gigantic swing-and-miss on shortstop Keoni Cavaco. Taken with the 13th overall pick and signed to a hefty $4 million bonus, Cavaco owns a disappointing .224/.276/.346 career slash line. The team selected Cavaco just ahead of the likes of Corbin Carroll and George Kirby. The emergence of Edouard Julien helps ease the disappointment in their top pick. Taken in the 18th round, 539th overall, and signed to a well above-slot bonus worth nearly $500,000, Julien essentially made the leap from the SEC in 2019 to Fort Myers in 2021 without missing a beat. He would slug an aggregate .267/.434/.480 between his time with the Mighty Mussels and the Cedar Rapids Kernels. Last season the front office sent the lefty-swinging infielder straight into the fire of Double-A and Julian walked away smelling like roses, not like burnt ash. Appearing in 113 games with the Surge, Julian slugged a career best .300/.441/.490 with 19 doubles, three triple, 17 homeruns, and 19 stolen bases (in 26 total attempts). His overall production, per *Weighted Runs Created Plus*, smashed the league average threshold by 44%. He also continued his dominance in the Arizona Fall League, hitting .400/.563/.686 in 21 games with Glendale.

Scouting Report: Consider the following:

> Since 2006, only five 23-year-old hitters posted a 140 to 150 wRC+ with a 22% to 26% strikeout rate in any Double-A league (min. 350 PA): Casey Gillaspie, Kala Ka'aihue, Joe Benson, Kyle Kubitza, and – of course – Edouard Julien. It's certainly worth pointing out that:
> (A) each member of the group had bloated walk rates and all but Benson walked in more than 14% of their plate appearances during the time frame listed above and
> (B) the first four members of the aforementioned group never developed into tangible big league bats, despite their minor league performances.

Julien played defense like a sieve was attached his hand, posting some well below-average metrics at the keystone. And the bat may not even be enough to compensate for the negative value that he may bring to the table. It wouldn't be surprising to see him man first base or designated hitter in the coming year because the defense is that bad. Offensively speaking, Julien takes a well-rounded approach at the dish, showcasing an above-average hit tool, 45-grade power, a smattering of speed, and an incredibly patient approach at the plate. He did struggle against southpaws last season (.210/.373/.276), but performed well enough against them during his debut (.244/.409/.422) to suggest it shouldn't be an ongoing issue as he continues to accrue plate appearances. He could be a .280/.360/.415 hitter in the right big league environment, but there's more risk here than most realize. He feels like a poor man's Max Muncy.

Ceiling: 2.0-win player
Risk: Moderate to High
MLB ETA: 2023

11. Louie Varland, RHP

FB	CU	SL	CH	Command	Overall
60	50	55	50	50	50

Born: 12/09/97	Age: 25	Bats: L	Top Production Comp: Zach Plesac
Height: 6-1	Weight: 205	Throws: R	

Season	Team	Age	Level	IP	TBF	K/9	K%	BB/9	BB%	K-BB%	ERA	FIP	xFIP	Pit/Bat
2021	MIN	23	A	47.1	200	14.45	38.00%	3.04	8.00%	30.00%	2.09	2.34	2.64	3.96
2021	MIN	23	A+	55.2	221	10.67	29.86%	2.26	6.33%	23.53%	2.10	3.20	4.02	3.74
2022	MIN	24	AA	105.0	450	10.20	26.44%	3.34	8.67%	17.78%	3.34	4.40	4.30	3.81
2022	MIN	24	AAA	21.1	84	11.39	32.14%	1.27	3.57%	28.57%	1.69	2.29	3.38	3.99

Background: The Twins have done a solid job finding intriguing prospects in the late rounds of the draft in recent years. David Festa was a 13th round pick out of Seton Hall a couple years ago. And four years ago they unearthed a *pair* of overlooked college players in the 15th and 18th rounds: right-hander Louie Varland and infielder Edouard Julien. Taken with the 449th overall pick out of Concordia University in 2019, Varland was particularly strong during his junior campaign for the Golden Bears, averaging 11.1 strikeouts and just 2.3 walks per innings across 12 appearances. After a brief jaunt through the low minor league levels that summer, Varland reappeared in Low-A at the start of 2021. He would make 10 appearances with the Mighty Mussels before moving up to Cedar Rapids in the second half. The 6-foot-1, 205-pound southpaw tossed 103.0 innings that season, posting a dominant 142-to-30 strikeout-to-walk ratio with an aggregate 2.10 ERA. And that was the arrival of the former Concordia ace. Last season Varland torched the lumber of Double-A hitters, breezed through four starts with St.

Minnesota Twins

Paul, and continued to perform in five big league starts with the Twins. He finished the minor league season with 126.1 innings, 146 punch outs, and 42 walks. He tossed another 26 frames in the big leagues, recording an impressive 21-to-6 strikeout-to-walk ratio.

Scouting Report: Consider the following:

> Since 2006, only two 24-year-old hurlers posted a 25.5% to 27.5% strikeout percentage with a 7.5% to 9.5% walk percentage in any Double-A league (min. 100 IP): Corey Kluber, the two-time Cy Young Award winner, and – of course – Louie Varland.

Varland attacks hitters with a solid four-pitch mix. His plus fastball sits in the mid-90s and touched several ticks higher on occasion. His mid-80s slider can be difficult for both left- and right-handed hitters, particularly when he's locating it down and in on lefties / away and low on righties. He'll mix in an average upper 80s cutter that climbs into the low 90s and a decent changeup. Varland command the zone well, particularly with his fastball. Backend starting material, something along the lines of healthy Zach Plesac.

Ceiling: 1.5- to 2.0-win player
Risk: Low to Moderate
MLB ETA: Debuted in 2022

12. Jordan Balazovic, RHP

FB	CB	SL	CH	Command	Overall
60	50	55	55	40	50

Born: 09/17/98	Age: 23	Bats: R	Top Production Comp: N/A
Height: 6-5	Weight: 215	Throws: R	

Season	Team	Age	Level	IP	TBF	K/9	K%	BB/9	BB%	K-BB%	ERA	FIP	xFIP	Pit/Bat
2021	MIN	22	AA	97.0	429	9.46	23.78%	3.53	8.86%	14.92%	3.62	3.91	4.28	3.90
2022	MIN	23	AAA	70.2	343	9.68	22.16%	4.46	10.20%	11.95%	7.39	6.61	4.54	4.09

Background: Two years ago the former 2016 fifth round pick battled a back injury and would miss the opening two months of the season. Balazovic would eventually make his affiliated season debut in early June and quietly put together another strong showing in the minors' toughest level, Double-A. The Canadian hurler still managed to log a career-best 97.0 innings while averaging 9.5 strikeouts and 3.5 walks per nine innings. Last season started out in a similar fashion but it certainly didn't *finish* the year in a similar way. Balazovic suffered a left knee strain and hit the disabled list in early April. He wouldn't make it back to the mound until early May. And then the real disaster happened. Balazovic lasted just 3.2 innings against the Iowa Cubs in his first Triple-A start. Then the Columbus Clippers lit him up, the Omaha Storm Chasers took more than a few swings, and the Indianapolis Indians joined in on the fun. It continued through the majority of the year as well. And before anyone realized it the former consensus Top 100 prospect tallied an incredible 7.68 ERA across 72.2 innings.

Snippet from The 2022 Prospect Digest Handbook: There's some genuine #2-type potential. And I think the command actually creeps into above-average territory at some point as well.

Scouting Report: Even if you add up Balazovic's ERA from 2019 and 2021, it *still wouldn't equal* his disastrous showing last season. But it's not all doom-and-gloom for the young right-hander. Consider the following:

> #1. His strikeout percentage, 22.2%, was still in the general neighborhood from the previous year (23.8) – despite moving up a level.
> #2. He finished the season on a high note, posting a 3.55 ERA with a 38-to-15 strikeout-to-walk ratio over his final 33.0 innings (spanning eight appearances).
> #3. His xFIP, 4.54, was significantly better than his actual ERA (7.39).

Balazovic's fastball still showed some heft behind it, but it didn't have enough riding life to consistently miss bats if he wasn't locating well – which was most of the season. Even during his good stretch he was leaving to many heaters middle-middle. The slider would flash plus at times, showing tight, hard bite, but more often than not he struggled finishing it. The same could be said for his curveball, which is typically an above-average offering. The once-promising hurler also seemed to move shy away from throwing what was his best pitch: changeup. Mechanically, he looked to be stiffer than in years past and he really struggled with missing high in the zone. The ingredients are still in place for Balazovic to become a competent big league starter, but he needs to recapture some past performances before that happens. A more pitching-savvy organization may be able to coax more out of Balazovic. This will be an interesting litmus test for the Twins.

Ceiling: 2.0-win player
Risk: Moderate to High
MLB ETA: 2023

Minnesota Twins

13. Matt Canterino, RHP

FB	CB	SL	CH	Command	Overall
55	55	60	60	55	50

Born: 12/14/97	Age: 25	Bats: R	Top Production Comp: Rich Harden
Height: 6-2	Weight: 222	Throws: R	

Season	Team	Age	Level	IP	TBF	K/9	K%	BB/9	BB%	K-BB%	ERA	FIP	xFIP	Pit/Bat
2021	MIN	23	A+	21.0	78	18.43	55.13%	1.71	5.13%	50.00%	0.86	0.87	1.12	4.17
2022	MIN	24	AA	34.1	144	13.11	34.72%	5.77	15.28%	19.44%	1.83	3.15	4.74	3.99

Background: There may be fewer things more certain than death and taxes, but *nothing* is more certain than former Rice hurlers dealing with a litany of injuries in the professional ranks. And Matt Canterino's inability to stay healthy only strengthens any – and all – personal biases I have against the Texas-based school. After the Twins (foolishly) selected the former Owl in the second round in 2019, Canterino hit the disabled list *multiple times* during his first full season in the minor leagues two years later, dealing with several injuries that were termed as right-elbow strains. But when he was on the bump, the 6-foot-2, 222-pound right-hander was *electric* – through 23.0 innings of work he *averaged* an impossible 17.6 strikeouts and nearly impossible 1.6 walks per nine innings. And, almost like clockwork, Canterino hit the disabled list last season with – drumroll please – a severe elbow injury. This time, though, he eventually had to undergo Tommy John surgery, essentially knocking him out for the majority of 2022 and (likely) 2023. Canterino finished last year with 54 punch outs and 23 walks in 37.0 innings. He's averaging 13.8 strikeouts and 3.7 walks per nine innings in his abbreviated professional career.

Snippet from The 2022 Prospect Digest Handbook: I scouted two of Canterino's six appearances. He was as dominant – if not more dominant – than any other minor league hurler I saw in 2021. Canterino showed the talent to slide into the upper part of rotation. But I think the injuries are going to be a constant in his career.

Scouting Report: You could make a reasonable argument that Canterino's arsenal belongs on the short list for best in the minor leagues – at least when he's healthy, which hasn't been often (or hardly ever). Prior to his latest elbow issue, the 6-foot-2, 222-pound right-hander was sitting, consistently, in the mid-90s with his heater. The plus-offering showed late life and an innate difficulty to be driven. He shows two above-average or better breaking balls, a low 80s curveball and a mid-80s slider. But his changeup, when it's on, may be the best in the minor leagues. The plus-plus offering features nearly 17 mph of velocity difference from his fastball and fall-off-the-table tumble. Clearly, the jury is still out on whether Canterino make throw 50 innings in a professional season, let alone make it through a complete season, but fingers remain firmly crossed that the Tommy John surgery can correct whatever lingering issues he's had over the past couple of years.

Ceiling: 3.0-win player
Risk: Extremely High
MLB ETA: 2024

14. Austin Martin, SS/CF

Hit	Power	SB	Patience	Glove	Overall
55/60	40/45	50	65	45/55	60

Born: 03/23/99	Age: 24	Bats: R	Top Production Comp: Brandon Belt
Height: 6-0	Weight: 185	Throws: R	

Season	Team	Age	Level	PA	1B	2B	3B	HR	SB	CS	BB%	K%	AVG	OBP	SLG	ISO
2021	TOR	22	AA	250	41	10	2	2	9	3	14.80%	21.20%	0.281	0.424	0.383	0.102
2021	MIN	22	AA	168	23	8	0	3	5	1	13.69%	17.86%	0.254	0.399	0.381	0.127
2022	MIN	23	AA	406	63	13	3	2	34	5	11.58%	13.30%	0.241	0.367	0.315	0.074

Background: Faced with the potential of losing All-Star righty Jose Berrios after the 2022 season, the Minnesota brass opted to maximize his trade value and deal him at the deadline two years ago. The specifics of the swap are simple: The Twins would send their former first round selection north of the border for former collegiate star Austin Martin and right-hander Simeon Woods Richardson. Drafted by Toronto with the fifth overall pick and signed to the second largest bonus in 2020, Martin left SEC powerhouse Vanderbilt University as a .368/.474/.532 hitter but has failed – *massively* – to live up to the lofty expectations that comes along with $7 million. At the onset of the 2021 season, the Blue Jays had the former Commodore star bypass the low levels of the minor leagues and sent him directly into Double-A, the true proving grounds for prospects. He batted an OBP-driven .281/.424/.383 with New Hampshire before the trade. After acquiring the shortstop / centerfielder, Minnesota sent him to their Double-A affiliate, the Wichita Wind Surge, but the results declined precipitously. He would finish his debut showing with an aggregate .270/.414/.382. Last season, in an injury-interrupted campaign, Martin returned to the level but the numbers failed to improve. He batted a disappointing .241/.367/.315 with just 13 doubles, three triples, two homeruns, and 34 stolen bases. His overall production, according to *Weighted Runs Created Plus*, was 11% blow the league average mark. Martin did recapture his collegiate glory in the Arizona Fall League as he slugged .374/.454/.482 in 21 games with Glendale.

Snippet from The 2022 Prospect Digest Handbook: Martin may never be a star. But he's going to be a very good player on a championship caliber team.

Minnesota Twins

Scouting Report: Consider the following:

> Since 2006, only three 23-year-old hitters met the following criteria in a Double-A season (min. 350 PA): 85 to 95 wRC+, an 8% to 12% walk rate, and a 12% to 16% strikeout rate. Those three hitters: Beau Mills, Andy Dirks, and – of course – former Vandy star Austin Martin.

Even though Martin's debut showing in 2021 was plagued with doubters and a bevy of disappointment, it's important to remember that he left college, stepped into the most difficult level of the minor leagues, and still managed to top the league average production line by 28%. But last season was the *true* disappointment. Martin was so abysmal at shortstop that it's actually difficult to believe he ever played the position before in his life. On the offensive side of the game, the 6-foot, 185-pound prospect made consistent contact, but it wasn't consistent quality contact. His power, which was average during his collegiate days, has regressed to well below-average just two years later. The best case scenario now is that Martin turns into a batting average-driving low end regular who is likely better suited coming off the bench.

Ceiling: 1.5-win player
Risk: Moderate
MLB ETA: 2023

15. Yasser Mercedes, CF

Hit	Power	SB	Patience	Glove	Overall
40/55	50	50	50	50	40

Born: 11/16/04	Age: 18	Bats: R	Top Production Comp: N/A
Height: 6-2	Weight: 175	Throws: R	

Season	Team	Age	Level	PA	1B	2B	3B	HR	SB	CS	BB%	K%	AVG	OBP	SLG	ISO
2022	MIN	17	DSL	176	35	13	3	4	30	5	10.23%	19.89%	0.355	0.420	0.555	0.200

Background: The Twins were willing to go big to sign MLB Pipeline's 14th best prospect on the international market last summer, signing the 6-foot-2, 175-pound outfielder to a hefty $1.7 million pact. A little more than five months after joining the American League Central Division organization, Mercedes was debuting with the club's Dominican Summer League affiliate. The Puerto Rican-born centerfielder was an offensive dynamo, bashing the competition to the tune of .355/.421/.555 with 13 doubles, three triples, four homeruns, and 30 stolen bases (in only 35 total attempts). Mercedes' overall production, as measured by *Weighted Runs Created Plus*, topped the Dominican Summer League average by a staggering 55%.

Scouting Report: One of the most explosive 17-year-old bats in the foreign rookie league last season, Mercedes did a little bit – or a lot of bit – of everything last summer. He hit for average and power, ran frequently and efficiently, and played an up-the-middle position. Smooth right-handed stroke with gobs of bat speed. It wouldn't be surprising to see the Twins now-18-year-old stateside and into Low-A at some point in 2023. It wouldn't be shocking to see him rank among the club's best prospects within a year.

Ceiling: 1.5-win player
Risk: Moderate
MLB ETA: 2026

16. Noah Miller, SS

Hit	Power	SB	Patience	Glove	Overall
30/45	30	60	55	60	45

Born: 11/12/02	Age: 20	Bats: B	Top Production Comp: Nick Allen
Height: 6-0	Weight: 190	Throws: R	

Season	Team	Age	Level	PA	1B	2B	3B	HR	SB	CS	BB%	K%	AVG	OBP	SLG	ISO
2021	MIN	18	CPX	96	14	3	1	2	1	1	9.38%	27.08%	0.238	0.316	0.369	0.131
2022	MIN	19	A	469	63	12	4	2	23	7	16.20%	23.45%	0.211	0.348	0.279	0.068

Background: The Twins – like the rest of baseball, seemingly – have focused on high ceiling prep shortstops in the opening round of the draft over the past decade or so. The club's brass selected five high school shortstops in the first round over the past 12 draft classes – though the results have been mixed. The wins: Nick Gordon and Royce Lewis, regardless of his ongoing health / injuries. The misses: Levi Michael, Keoni Cavaco. The To Be Determined: Noah Miller. Taken with their second first rounder two years ago, Miller, who was the 36th overall pick, turned in a disappointing debut showing in the Complex League that summer, hitting a paltry .238/.316/.369. Last season, the front office sent the youngster up to Low-A as an aggressive challenge. And the results were...mixed. Miller looked overwhelmed at the dish, hitting .212/.348/.279 with 12 doubles, four triples, two homeruns, and 23 stolen bases (in 30 attempts). His overall production was 8% *below* the league average threshold. Miller comes from solid bloodlines: his older brother, Owen, was dealt by the Guardians to the Brewers this past offseason.

Snippet from The 2022 Prospect Digest Handbook: He reminds me of a young Cole Tucker. Miller profiles as a low ceiling / high floor type of prospect.

Minnesota Twins

Scouting Report: Consider the following:

> Since 2006, only two 19-year-old hitters met the following criteria in a Low-A season (min. 350 PA): 87 to 97 wRC+, 22.5% to 24.5%, and a walk rate north of 12%. Those two hitters: Frederick Parejo and – of course – Noah Miller.

After an abysmal start to the year, Miller's bat caught fire in May as he slugged .341/.453/.511, but immediately chilled after the month and he batted .171/.308/.212 over his remaining 71 games. Heading into the draft Miller was touted for his advanced approach at the plate, but his hit tool has failed – enormously – to live up to expectations. And he was never projected to hit for a ton of power, so there's not a real shocker that he belted out just 18 extra-base hits in 108 games. But his defense was nothing short of spectacular during his first full season in the minors – so much so that it may carry him up to the big leagues as a bench option regardless of the bat. Best case scenario: Oakland's Nick Allen, who was a defensive wizard and a terrible hitter until his third year in the minor leagues.

Ceiling: 1.5-win player
Risk: Moderate
MLB ETA: 2025

17. Tanner Schobel, 2B/SS

Hit	Power	SB	Patience	Glove	Overall
50	45	40	50	50	45

Born: 06/04/01	Age: 22	Bats: R	Top Production Comp: N/A
Height: 5-10	Weight: 170	Throws: R	

Season	Team	Age	Level	PA	1B	2B	3B	HR	SB	CS	BB%	K%	AVG	OBP	SLG	ISO
2022	MIN	21	CPX	16	2	1	0	0	1	0	6.25%	18.75%	0.200	0.250	0.267	0.067
2022	MIN	21	A	120	20	3	0	1	6	1	15.00%	19.17%	0.242	0.367	0.303	0.061

Background: The son of a two notable athletes. Schobel's father, David, played golf and rugby at the Air Force Academy and his mother, Shea, was a Junior Olympic swimmer. Unsurprisingly, he was a standout prep player at Walsingham Academy during his prep days, earning a bevy of awards and recognitions, including: Two-Time State Champion, Four-Time All-State, Three-Time First Team All-TCIS, and Two-Time VISAA DII Player of the Year. Schobel wouldn't make his collegiate debut until the 2021 season, but he showed little signs of struggling with the transition to the ACC Conference. In 52 games with the Hokies of Virginia Tech, the 5-foot-10, 170-pound middle infielder batted a respectable .279/.359/.441 with 10 doubles, one triple, and seven homeruns. And Schobel, a native of Panama City, Florida, handled himself well in the Cape Cod League that summer too, hitting .302/.378/.465 in 29 games with the Bourne Braves. Schobel combined with fellow 2022 high draft pick Gavin Cross to lead the squad to a phenomenal 45-14 record during their respective final collegiate campaigns. The second baseman / shortstop slugged a scorching .362/.445/.689 with 18 doubles, one triple, and 19 homeruns. He also swiped seven bags in eight attempts. Minnesota drafted in the back of the second round, 68th overall, and signed him to a deal worth $1,002,000. He batted .237/.353/.298 in 32 games in his professional debut.

Scouting Report: Per the usual, here's my pre-draft write-up:

> "Consider the following:
>
> Since 2011, only four ACC hitters have batted at least .340/.440/.675 in a season (min. 275 PA): Seth Beer, the Diamondbacks' first round pick in 2018; Drew Ellis, a second round pick by the Diamondbacks in 2017; Kevin Parada, the 11th overall selection by the Mets last July; and, of course, Tanner Schobel, the lone middle infielder in the group of sluggers.
>
> Patient approach at the plate that isn't afraid to make pitchers work. Simple efficient, low maintenance swing. Schobel doesn't project to hit for the same type of thump he showed with the Hokies during his final season – though he should settle in with a stat line in the neighborhood of .275/.330/.400 with 12 homeruns and a handful of stolen bases. Schobel's strength is his lack of weaknesses. He'll shoot the ball the other way, turn on the inside pitch, and really grind out at bats. Defensively, he's likely to slide over to the right side of the keystone."

Ceiling: 1.5-win player
Risk: Moderate
MLB ETA: 2024/2025

Minnesota Twins

18. Ronny Henriquez, RHP

FB	SL	CH	Command	Overall
55	55	55	55	40

Born: 06/20/00	Age: 23	Bats: R	Top Production Comp: Carlos Torres
Height: 5-10	Weight: 155	Throws: R	

Season	Team	Age	Level	IP	TBF	K/9	K%	BB/9	BB%	K-BB%	ERA	FIP	xFIP	Pit/Bat
2021	TEX	21	A+	24.0	96	10.13	28.13%	3.00	8.33%	19.79%	3.75	3.85	4.46	3.70
2021	TEX	21	AA	69.2	291	10.08	26.80%	2.20	5.84%	20.96%	5.04	4.86	4.02	3.85
2022	MIN	22	AAA	95.1	412	10.01	25.73%	3.12	8.01%	17.72%	5.66	5.07	4.02	3.94

Background: The Twins' brass was busy heading into last year. On March 12th, Minnesota dealt former Silver Slugger Mitch Garver to the Rangers for infielder Isiah Kiner-Falefa and right-hander Ronny Henriquez. The very next day the Twins turned around and dealt Kiner-Falefa, third baseman Josh Donaldson, and backstop Ben Rortvedt to the Yankees for Gary Sanchez and Gio Urshela. Signed by the Rangers out of the Dominican Republic midsummer 2017, Henriquez was one of Texas' more pleasant surprises during his stout showing in 2021. The wiry hurler averaged 10.1 strikeouts and 2.4 walks per nine innings across 21 appearances in High-A and Double-A. Last season, his first in the Twins' organization, Henriquez made 24 appearances in St. Paul (14 starts and 10 relief appearances), recording another Henriquez-like 106-to-33 strikeout-to-walk ratio in a career best 95.1 innings. He made three multi-inning relief appearances in Minnesota at the end of the year, allowing three earned runs in 11.2 innings, fanning nine and walking three.

Snippet from The 2022 Prospect Digest Handbook: Henriquez is going to have to continue to fight the good fight when it comes to answering the bell on whether he can withstand the rigors of grabbing the ball every day. There's #4/#5-type ceiling with a solid relief floor.

Scouting Report: Consider the following:

> Since 2006, only four 22-year-old hurlers posted a 23% to 27% strikeout percentage with a 7% to 9% walk percentage in any Triple-A league (min. 75 IP): Zac Gallen, Genesis Cabrera, Matthew Liberatore, and – of course – Ronny Henriquez.

The Dominican right-handed has been underrated for his entire career, despite continually posting impressive peripherals against older competition. The slight-framed right-hander owns three above-average or better offerings: a low- to mid-90's fastball, a mid-80s slider, and a mid- to upper-80s changeup. Henriquez takes a slider-heavy approach to pitching, throwing the above-average breaking ball more frequently than his heater. He finally topped the 100-inning threshold for the first time last season, but he's likely best suited for the role Minnesota deployed him in last season – a multi-inning relief specialist.

Ceiling: 1.0-win player
Risk: Low to Moderate
MLB ETA: Debuted in 2022

19. Matt Wallner, LF/RF

Hit	Power	SB	Patience	Glove	Overall
45	60	30	50	40	40

Born: 12/12/97	Age: 25	Bats: L	Top Production Comp: Daniel Palka
Height: 6-5	Weight: 220	Throws: R	

Season	Team	Age	Level	PA	1B	2B	3B	HR	SB	CS	BB%	K%	AVG	OBP	SLG	ISO
2021	MIN	23	A+	294	37	14	2	15	0	1	9.52%	33.33%	0.264	0.350	0.508	0.244
2022	MIN	24	AAA	229	21	17	3	6	1	0	15.28%	27.51%	0.247	0.376	0.463	0.216
2022	MIN	24	AA	342	43	15	1	21	8	5	18.13%	31.29%	0.299	0.436	0.597	0.299

Background: If you don't succeed, try, try again. The Twins originally drafted the hulking corner outfielder coming out of Forest Lake High School in the late rounds of the 2016 draft. And the front office circled back around and selected him with the 39th overall pick three years later after a stellar career at Southern Mississippi University. Wallner left the Conference USA team with a career .337/.461/.652 slash line. The 6-foot-5, 220-pound corner outfielder continued to bash during his debut in the organization, slugging .258/.357/.452 in the old Appalachian and Midwest Leagues. Wallner maintained status quo during his injury-riddled 2021 campaign as he moved up to High-A. Last season, the former first rounder – finally – moved into the upper minors, quietly putting together his finest showing to date. Splitting time between Wichita and St. Paul. Waller mashed .277/.412/.542 with career highs in doubles (32), triples (four), homeruns (27), and stolen bases (nine). Per *Weighted Runs Created Plus*, his overall production level topped the league average threshold by 44%. The Twins called him in mid-September and he hit .228/.323/.386 in 18 big league contests.

Snippet from The 2022 Prospect Digest Handbook: Here are the facts: above-average power, decent patience, below-average – perhaps even – unplayable glove in the outfield. I expect him to eventually shift into a full time designated hitter role. He shows no platoon splits. But he's a one dimensional hitter that provides one dimensional value.

Minnesota Twins

Scouting Report: Consider the following:

> Since 2006, only two 24-year-old hitters have met the following criteria in a Double-A season (min. 300 PA): 142 to 152 wRC+ with at least a 28.5% K-rate. Those two hitters: Daniel Palka, who's a .218/.310/.413 career big league hitter, and – of course – Matt Wallner.

After spending his first two professional seasons as a one dimensional (power) prospect, Wallner quietly added a secondary skill to help widen his big league appeal. Namely, his ability to get on first base via the walk. The former Southern Mississippi standout also showed improved routes and aptitude in the outfield as well. With that being said, Wallner's big league ceiling is limited to a low-end power-oriented bat.

Ceiling: 1.0-win player
Risk: Low to Moderate
MLB ETA: 2023

20. Misael Urbina, CF

Hit	Power	SB	Patience	Glove	Overall
40/45	50/55	50/40	50	55	40

Born: 04/26/02	Age: 21	Bats: R	Top Production Comp: N/A
Height: 6-0	Weight: 190	Throws: R	

Season	Team	Age	Level	PA	1B	2B	3B	HR	SB	CS	BB%	K%	AVG	OBP	SLG	ISO
2021	MIN	19	A	439	49	12	4	5	16	6	12.30%	18.68%	0.191	0.299	0.286	0.095
2022	MIN	20	A	217	25	16	1	5	9	4	10.60%	23.50%	0.246	0.323	0.419	0.173

Background: The ball club went all in on the toolsy outfielder during the summer of 2018, handing the young Venezuelan a hefty deal worth $2.75 million, making it one of the largest given out by the Twins on the international market. And the immediate returns on their big investment looked promising as Urbina batted a rock solid .279/.383/.443 in the Dominican Summer League in 2019. But once minor league ball returned to action in 2021, the 6-foot, 190-pound outfielder *really* struggled with Fort Myers in 2021, batting a putrid .191/.299/.286 with just 21 extra-base knocks in 439 plate appearances. So, unsurprisingly, Urbina found himself back in Fort Myers for another crack at re-establishing his lost prospect luster. The results were significantly improved, but lacked overall. Urbina batted .246/.323/.419 with 16 doubles, one triple, five homeruns, and nine stolen bases. His overall production, as measured by *Weighted Runs Created Plus*, topped the league average mark by 9%.

Scouting Report: As reported by MLB.com, Urbina missed the opening few months of the season due to visa issues and then he spent a couple weeks in the Complex League getting back up to speed. Ignoring the average-ish slash line for a moment or two. Urbina's peripheral and secondary skills are quite solid: average power with a chance to climb into above-average territory, solid walk and contact rates, and an above-average glove in centerfield. The hit tool is just…lagging. The Twins will likely never get the return they were looking for on their initial investment, but Urbina may develop into a good bench option in the coming years.

Ceiling: 1.0-win player
Risk: Moderate
MLB ETA: 2025

New York Mets

Top Prospects

New York Mets

1. Francisco Alvarez, C

	Hit	Power	SB	Patience	Glove	Overall
	50/60	55	35	55	50	70

Born: 11/19/01 **Age:** 21 **Bats:** R
Height: 5-11 **Weight:** 233 **Throws:** R
Top Production Comp: Jorge Posada

Season	Team	Age	Level	PA	1B	2B	3B	HR	SB	CS	BB%	K%	AVG	OBP	SLG	ISO
2021	NYM	19	A	67	13	5	0	2	2	2	22.39%	10.45%	0.417	0.567	0.646	0.229
2021	NYM	19	A+	333	33	13	1	22	6	3	12.01%	24.62%	0.247	0.351	0.538	0.290
2022	NYM	20	AA	296	36	16	0	18	0	0	12.16%	23.99%	0.277	0.368	0.553	0.277
2022	NYM	20	AAA	199	22	6	0	9	0	0	17.09%	26.13%	0.234	0.382	0.443	0.209

Background: The 2018-19 international free agency class may go down as one of the best in recent seasons. Notable prospects include: Marco Luciano, Diego Cartaya, Noelvi Marte, Orelvis Martinez, Jairo Pomares, Kevin Alcantara, Malcom Nunez, and – of course – a young Venezuelan backstop by the name of Francisco Alvarez, who narrowly cracked the Top 10 list by several major publications at that time. New York signed the stocky catcher to a massive $2.3 million deal. And immediately Alvarez (A) proved that the bonus was a significant bargain *and* (B) established himself as one of the best catching prospects in the minor leagues. The 5-foot-11, 233-pound backstop blitzed through his debut in the Gulf Coast League by slugging .462/.548/.846 in seven games and continued to mash during his extended look in the old Appalachian League as well, batting .282/.378/.443 – at the age of 17. Once minor league baseball returned from its COVID-induced absence, Alvarez shredded the Low-A competition to the tune of .417/.567/.646 over 15 games before earning a trip up to High-A for the remainder of the year. The then-19-year-old finished the season with a .272/.388/.554 slash line. Last season Alvarez continued his barrage on minor league arms as he moved through Double-A, Triple-A, and even squeezed in five games with the Mets as well. Alvarez finished the year with an aggregate .260/.374/.511 minor league slash line with career bests in doubles (22) and homeruns (27). His production, per *Weighted Runs Created Plus*, topped the league average mark by 36%. He went 2-for-12 with a double and a dinger in his 14-plate appearance cameo in the Bigs as well.

Snippet from The 2022 Prospect Digest Handbook: Above-average thump that could creep into plus territory in a couple years. Solid contact skills. Above-average patience at the plate. Not a terrible runner. Elite production against significantly older competition. And a solid enough glove so that he can stay behind the dish. After starting slowly in High-A last season – he batted .218/.342/.452 over his first 39 games – Alvarez slugged .271/.359/.606 over his remaining 45 contests. Elite prospect that closed the gap on Adley Rutschman's status as the best in baseball.

Scouting Report: Consider the following:

> Since 2006, there have been just nine 20-year-old hitters that posted a 140 to 150 wRC+ mark in any Double-A league (min. 250 PA): Cody Bellinger, Joey Gallo, Miguel Sano, Dylan Carlson, Colby Rasmus, Riley Greene, Jon Singleton, Drew Waters, and – of course – Francisco Alvarez, the lone backstop among the group.

With Metropolitan fans screaming in frustration due to the offensive punchless duo of Tomás Nido and James McCann, who's been *incredibly* disappointing after signing a massive free agency deal two years ago, the calls for Alvarez to take over the reins have grown audibly and virtually loud, but…

> Since 1940, there have been only seven 21-year-old rookie backstops that appeared in at least 75 big league games: Gary Carter, Darrell Porter, Bill Freehan, John Ellis, Dave Roberts, Jerry Grote (former Mets great who accomplished the feat with Houston), and Álex Trevino. The feat hasn't been accomplished since 1979, by the way.

Alvarez has the makings of a middle-of-the-lineup thumper, showcasing above-average power and projecting for 35 or so dingers at his peak. Plus patience at the plate. His strikeout rates have ballooned up the past two seasons, going from low-20% early in his career to slightly above the mid-20%. But there's little concern that the swing-and-miss issues will be a problem in the coming years given the demand of his position and level of competition. For example, over his remaining 80 plate appearances in Double-A, Alvarez fanned just 12 times – or 15% of the time. In terms

of big league ceiling, think: .285/.380/.500 with 30 to 35 homeruns.

Ceiling: 6.0-win player
Risk: Moderate
MLB ETA: Debuted in 2022

New York Mets

2. Brett Baty, 3B/LF

Hit	Power	SB	Patience	Glove	Overall
55	55/60	35	60	50	70

Born: 11/13/99	Age: 23	Bats: L	Top Production Comp: Ryan Zimmerman
Height: 6-3	Weight: 210	Throws: R	

Season	Team	Age	Level	PA	1B	2B	3B	HR	SB	CS	BB%	K%	AVG	OBP	SLG	ISO
2021	NYM	21	A+	209	34	14	1	7	4	3	11.48%	25.36%	0.309	0.397	0.514	0.204
2021	NYM	21	AA	176	28	8	0	5	2	0	12.50%	25.57%	0.272	0.364	0.424	0.152
2022	NYM	22	AA	394	65	22	0	19	2	3	11.68%	24.87%	0.312	0.406	0.544	0.232
2022	NYM	22	AAA	26	8	0	0	0	0	1	11.54%	23.08%	0.364	0.462	0.364	0.000

Background: In the not too distant past the Twins' farm system sported arguably the top two prospects in baseball – dynamic, tools-laden centerfielder Byron Buxton and power-hitting third baseman Miguel Sano. It was a rarity that one system could contain that much *potential* big league value wrapped up in their top two minor leaguers. The prospect statuses of the Mets' dynamic duo of Francisco Alvarez and Brett Baty certainly rivals that of Minnesota's from years past. New York selected Baty in the opening round, 12th overall, just one selection after the Blue Jays snagged budding ace Alek Manoah. The young third baseman, who was on the older side for a prep player that year, showed some offensive prowess during his debut between the Gulf Coast, Appalachian, and New York-Penn Leagues that summer, hitting a power-oriented .234/.368/.452 in 51 games. And after minor league action returned to normal following its COVID absence, Baty shredded the High-A and Double-A competition two years ago, slugging .292/.382/.473 with 22 doubles, one triple, 12 homeruns, and six stolen bases in only 91 games. Last season the lefty-swinging top prospect appeared in 95 minor league games, most of which were with Binghamton, mashing .315/.410/.533 with 22 doubles and a career high 19 homeruns. His overall production, according to *Weighted Runs Created* Plus, topped the league average threshold by a staggering 58%. He also batted a paltry .184/.244/.342 in 11 games with the Metropolitans as well.

Snippet from The 2022 Prospect Digest Handbook: Baty still hasn't tapped into his plus-raw power. And unlike a lot of power-hitting, lefty-swinging prospects, Baty doesn't show any platoon concerns. He has to potential to elevate his production to the superstar stratus.

Scouting Report: Consider the following:

> Since 2006, only three 22-year-old hitters sported a 155 to 165 wRC+ with a 9% to 12% walk rate in any Double-A league (min. 350 PA): Daulton Varsho, who's quietly become one of the better, more underrated big leaguers over the past two seasons, Dylan Cozens, and – of course – Brett Baty.

Baty continued adding to his impressive resume as he torched the toughest level in the minor leagues – Double-A. He still hasn't fully tapped into his plus-power potential, but it's coming, in a large way. The baby-faced prospect has plenty of room on his lean frame to fill out as he continues to mature. Gorgeous left-handed swing with enough power to slug homeruns off his front foot during mid-pitch adjustments. What makes Baty so effective is his willingness to take the outside pitch the other way. There's superstar status, and it wouldn't be surprising to see him carve out a better career than presumed top prospect Francisco Alvarez (due to the rigors of catching). There's the potential to develop into a perennial .300/.380/.500-type hitter.

Ceiling: 6.0-win player
Risk: Moderate
MLB ETA: Debuted in 2022

3. Kodai Senga, RHP

FB	CB	SL	FO/SP	Control	Overall
65	55	60	70	50	60

Born: 01/30/93	Age: 30	Bats: L	Top Production Comp: N/A
Height: 6-0	Weight: 178	Throws: R	

Background: Even with the history of high profile Nippon Professional Baseball players defecting to the Major Leagues, the arrival – and press – of Kodai Senga rivals those of Yu Darvish, Shohei Ohtani, Hideki Matsui, Hideo Nomo, Daisuke Matsuzaka, Seiya Suzuki, and Ichiro. A supremely gifted, triple-digit touching fire-baller, Senga left an indelible mark on the NPB throughout his eleven-year career. Drafted as a developmental prospect by the Fukuoka Softbank Hawks as a 17-year-old in 2020, the 6-foot, 178-pound right-hander would make his professional debut two seasons later, setting in motion a streak of dominance that saw him post four sub-2.00 ERA campaigns and 10 seasons in which he finished with an ERA below 3.00. Senga burst onto the seen as a baby-faced 19-year-old in 2012, posting a sparkling 1.68 ERA across 112.2 innings – though his peripherals were mediocre, at best, as he averaged a lowly 6.7 strikeouts and just 4.5 walks per nine innings. But his strikeout rate exploded the following season as he was shifted to the Hawks' pen: he posted an 87-to-26 strikeout-to-walk ratio in 58.1 innings of work. His season would come to a premature end due to a "left flank" injury. Senga returned to the bullpen the following season, continuing his dominance by averaging 11.2 strikeouts and 1.8 walks per nine innings. But, once again, he dealt with an injury that prematurely curtailed his season. A right shoulder issue knocked him out of commission in mid-June. Senga continued to deal with a right shoulder issues in 2015, as well, though he was able to break the 100-inning threshold for the

New York Mets

first time since 2015. The wiry hurler was able to shed the injury woes over the next several seasons, logging at least 121.0 innings of work between 2016 and 2020 while averaging more than a strikeout per inning to go along with some wavering command issues. A left ankle issue put a temporary pause on his newly found ironman streak two years ago, limiting him to just 84.2 innings. In his final campaign for the Hawks, Senga averaged 9.8 strikeouts and 3.1 walks per nine innings while winning 11 games and tallying a 1.94 ERA in 144.0 innings of work. New York signed the Japanese ace to a five-year, $75 million in mid-December. Senga would leave the NPB with numerous accolades, including: three-time All-Star, five-time Japan Series Champion, two-time Mitsui Golden Glove winner, two-time strikeout leader, and the 2020 Pacific League ERA champion.

Scouting Report: Working consistently in the 94- to 96-mph range, Senga's fastball famous reached 102 mph during the 2017 World Baseball Classic. But his most famous offering is termed the "Ghost Fork", a ruthlessly diving forkball that shows ungodly tumble and is nearly impossible to hit when he's ahead in the count. He'll also mix in a plus slider and an above-average curveball. Senga is the front-runner to capture the National League Rookie of the Year award. He's has the makings of a #3-type starting pitcher with the potential to average 10.5 strikeouts and 3.3 walks per nine innings. The question, though, is whether his past injury woes will chew into his playing time. One more thing to watch: NPB's baseball is slightly smaller than MLB's ball, so there may be an adjustment period with his Ghost Fork.

Ceiling: 4.0-win player
Risk: Low to Moderate
MLB ETA: 2023

4. Alex Ramirez, OF

Hit	Power	SB	Patience	Glove	Overall
55	40/55	55	50	40/55	60

Born: 01/13/03 **Age:** 20 **Bats:** R
Height: 6-3 **Weight:** 170 **Throws:** R
Top Production Comp: Andrew McCutchen

Season	Team	Age	Level	PA	1B	2B	3B	HR	SB	CS	BB%	K%	AVG	OBP	SLG	ISO
2021	NYM	18	A	334	54	15	4	5	16	7	6.89%	31.14%	0.258	0.326	0.384	0.126
2022	NYM	19	A	306	52	13	6	6	17	9	9.15%	22.22%	0.284	0.359	0.443	0.159
2022	NYM	19	A+	246	40	17	1	5	4	7	6.50%	21.95%	0.278	0.329	0.427	0.150

Background: Aggressively pursued by the club on the international market three years ago. New York convinced the toolsy outfielder to sign with the ball club for a hefty $2.1 million in early July 2019. Ramirez, a native of Santo Domingo, wouldn't make his debut until the 2021 season – in large part due to the pandemic. Still, though, the Mets' brass had no qualms about sending the then-18-year-old outfielder straight into Low-A without any prior professional experience. Ramirez responded by batting a respectable .258/.326/.384 with 15 doubles, four triples, five homeruns, and 16 stolen bases. Last season, in a bit of an atypical move, the player development engine sent the young prospect back down to Low-A for additional seasoning. This time, though, Ramirez's talents were on full display as he slugged .284/.360/.443 with 13 doubles, six triples, six homeruns, and 17 stolen bases. He spent the second half of the season performing well in High-A (.278/.329/.427). Ramirez finished the year with an aggregate .281/.346/.436 line with 30 doubles, seven triples, 11 homeruns, and 21 stolen bases – though he was thrown out 16 times. Per *Weighted Runs Created Plus*, his production topped the average threshold by a rock solid 19%.

Snippet from The 2022 Prospect Digest Handbook: Ronny Mauricio has long been lauded as the best bat speed in the system – until Ramirez came along. The swing is long, but it's ferocious and there's a little Gary Sheffield bat waggle in there too. And he does not get cheated. The K-rate is going to have to improve as he matures, but there's a lot of potential with his premium athleticism.

Scouting Report: Consider the following:

> Since 2006, only four 19-year-old hitters met the following criteria in a High-A season (min. 225 PA): 100 to 110 wRC+, 5% to 8% walk rate, and a 20% to 24% strikeout rate. Those four hitters: Eguy Rosario, Anthony Gose, Wendell Rijo, and – of course – Alex Ramirez.

Arguably the most athletic player in the entire Mets' system. There's superstar potential brewing in the supremely gifted outfielder. Whether everything comes together just right is to be determined. He could be one of the larger breakout candidates in 2023. He's raw, but the tools are too good to ignore. Plus bat speed, above-average speed, plus-power potential. And despite squaring off against significantly older competition, Ramirez made serious strides in chewing down his strikeout rate to a solid 22.1% last season. With the ball club in a "win now" mode, it wouldn't be surprising to see teams seek him as the centerpiece of a mid-season deal as soon as 2023. Do not sleep on him. Big time potential.

Ceiling: 4.0-win player
Risk: Moderate
MLB ETA: 2024/2025

New York Mets

5. Kevin Parada, C

	Hit	Power	SB	Patience	Glove	Overall
	50	60	30	45	50	55

Born: 08/03/01	Age: 21	Bats: R	Top Production Comp: N/A
Height: 6-1	Weight: 197	Throws: R	

Season	Team	Age	Level	PA	1B	2B	3B	HR	SB	CS	BB%	K%	AVG	OBP	SLG	ISO
2022	NYM	20	CPX	14	1	2	0	0	0	0	14.29%	7.14%	0.273	0.429	0.455	0.182
2022	NYM	20	A	41	6	1	0	1	0	1	24.39%	29.27%	0.276	0.463	0.414	0.138

Background: Georgia Tech's churned out an impressive amount of high end talent throughout the years, sending the likes of Kevin Brown, Mark Teixeira, Nomar Garciaparra, Charlie Blackmon, and Jay Payton to the big leagues. But the ACC conference school's catching pipeline is even more impressive: Jason Varitek, a twice-drafted first rounder (1993 and 1994), made three All-Star appearances and earned a Gold Glove; Matt Wieters, the fifth overall pick in 2007, is a four-time All-Star and two-time Gold Glove winner; and, Joey Bart, the second overall pick in 2018, is still trying to find his way in the big leagues. The next big Yellow Jacket catching prospect to hear his name called in the opening round: Kevin Parada. A product of Loyola High School, Parada, who was a three-year letter winner, got off to an impressive start to his collegiate career: in 52 games with the ACC powerhouse, the 6-foot-1, 197-pound backstop slugged .318/.379/.550 with 20 doubles, two triples, and nine homeruns. The California native spent the ensuing summer splitting time with Team USA (.400/.500/.520 in 10 games) and the Chatham Anglers in the Cape Cod League (.250/.344/.321 in nine games). Last season Parada, the consensus top catching prospect in the draft class, continued his assault on the opposition. In 60 games he slugged a scorching .361/.453/.709 with 10 homeruns, one triple, and 26 homeruns – the sixth best total among all Division I hitters. New York drafted him in the opening round, 11th overall, and signed him to a deal worth $5,019,753. The 6-foot-1, 197-pound backstop split time between the Complex League and St. Lucie, hitting .275/.455/.425 with three doubles and a homerun in 13 games.

Scouting Report: Per the usual, my pre-draft write-up:

> "Consider the following:
>
> Since 2011, only six Division I hitters slugged at least .350/.450/.700 with a strikeout rate between 8% and 12% in a season (min. 275 PA): Andrew Benintendi, Nick Gonzales, Kody Hoese, D.J. Peterson, Tyler Locklear, and – of course – Kevin Parada, who – by the way – owned the lowest walk rate among the group (9.86%). Benintendi was the seventh overall pick in 2015; Gonzales was the seventh player chosen in 2020; Kody Hoese was nabbed by the Dodgers in the latter part of the 2019 first round; and Peterson was 12th pick in 2013. Locklear will be an early round pick in 2022.
>
> In a similar vein as fellow top prospect Jace Jung, Parada has an interesting – perhaps, odd – timing mechanism at the start of his stance. He tilts the bat nearly straight down his back and nearly covers his face with his lead arm. As the pitcher moves through the windup he'll get in a move traditional stance. Big time power potential. Solid contact rates. And the ability to drive solid offspeed pitches. Parada doesn't walk a whole lot, but he should hover around the 7% mark in the professional ranks. In terms of big league ceiling, think: .260/.320/.460 with 20 homeruns."

Ceiling: 3.5-win player
Risk: Moderate
MLB ETA: 2024

6. Jett Williams, SS

	Hit	Power	SB	Patience	Glove	Overall
	55	45/50	60	50	55	55

Born: 11/03/03	Age: 19	Bats: R	Top Production Comp: N/A
Height: 5-8	Weight: 175	Throws: R	

Season	Team	Age	Level	PA	1B	2B	3B	HR	SB	CS	BB%	K%	AVG	OBP	SLG	ISO
2022	NYM	18	CPX	41	5	1	1	1	6	0	9.76%	14.63%	0.250	0.366	0.438	0.188

Background: Rockwall-Heath High School doesn't have a particularly lengthy track record of sending prospects into the professional ranks. Just three players – former big league right-hander Jake Thompson (a second round pick by the Tigers in 2012), Canaan Smith-Njigba (a fourth round pick by the Yankees in 2017), and Cole Stilwell (a 38th round pick by the Astros in 2018) – have been drafted out of the Texas-based prep school. Another pair of hurlers – Tyler Ivey and Drew VerHagen – would graduate from Rockwall-Heath, go onto to successful college careers, and become early round selections. Jett Williams, a diminutive pint-sized shortstop, easily surpassed the club's most notable alums draft statuses. Standing just 5-foot-8 and 175-pounds, Williams was an offensive dynamo during his four-year prep career. After batting .310 as a true-freshman, the middle infielder slugged .346/.460/.519 with a trio of triples and a dinger as

New York Mets

a sophomore. He followed that up with a stellar junior campaign: .347/.514/.723 with five doubles, nine triples, five homeruns, and 15 stolen bases. Williams batted a scorching .427 during his final season for the Hawks, who won 35 games and lost just six times. Originally committed to Texas A&M, Williams de-committed and pledged his allegiance to Mississippi State University. New York selected him in the first round, 14th overall, and signed him to a deal worth $3.9 million. He appeared in 10 Complex League games, hitting .250/.366/.438.

Scouting Report: My pre-draft write-up:

> "Small in stature but strong. Quick and agile on defense with enough arm to stay at the position. Williams has the potential to be a borderline Gold Glove winner at either side of the keystone – if he's moved as a professional. Lightning quick bat with surprising pop for a sub-6-foot hitter. Williams has some Nick Madrigal potential as a hitter: strong, borderline incredible bat-to-ball skills with plus speed. He's going to be a doubles machine that will run into 15 or so homeruns at peak maturity. Bulldog. Gamer."

Ceiling: 3.5-win player
Risk: Moderate
MLB ETA: 2026

7. Mark Vientos, 1B/3B/LF

Hit	Power	SB	Patience	Glove	Overall
45	60	35	50	45	50

Born: 12/11/99	Age: 23	Bats: R	Top Production Comp: Wil Myers
Height: 6-4	Weight: 220	Throws: R	

Season	Team	Age	Level	PA	1B	2B	3B	HR	SB	CS	BB%	K%	AVG	OBP	SLG	ISO
2021	NYM	21	AA	306	39	16	0	22	0	1	8.50%	28.43%	0.281	0.346	0.580	0.299
2021	NYM	21	AAA	43	5	2	0	3	0	1	16.28%	30.23%	0.278	0.395	0.583	0.306
2022	NYM	22	AAA	427	65	16	1	24	0	2	10.30%	28.57%	0.280	0.358	0.519	0.238

Background: Always a bridesmaid, but never the bride. Vientos has been locked behind a litany of the system's top prospects throughout the years, including current guys like Francisco Alvarez, Brett Baty, and Alex Ramirez or past notables like Pete Crow-Armstrong, Andres Gimenez, Pete Alonso, Amed Rosario, and Dominic Smith. But Vientos, a second round pick by the club all the way back in 2017, has continued to plod along the minor league ladder, meticulously climbing each rung, step by step, showing progress all along the way. Vientos' breakout season came two years ago as he mashed .281/.352/.581 with 18 doubles and a career best 25 homeruns in only 83 games between Binghamton and Syracuse. Last season the corner infielder appeared in 101 games with the club's Triple-A affiliate, slugging .280/.358/.519 with 16 doubles, one triple (which tied a career best), and 24 homeruns. His overall production, as measured by *Weighted Runs Created Plus*, topped the league average threshold by 29%. Like Alvarez and Baty, Vientos appeared in a handful of games of the big league club, going 6-for-36 with a double and a homeruns in 16 games.

Snippet from The 2022 Prospect Digest Handbook: Boom-bust potential and there likely isn't a level in between.

Scouting Report: Consider the following:

> Since 2006, only two 22-year-old hitters posted a 125 to 135 wRC+ with a 27% to 30% strikeout rate, and a double-digit walk rate in any Triple-A league (min. 350 PA): Yoan Moncada and – of course – Mark Vientos. Moncada owns a career .253/.334/.425 slash line in 643 big league games.

A more contact oriented hitter during the early parts of his minor league career, Vientos has traded consistent contact for more power the past couple of seasons. He's been on pace for 43 homeruns every 162 games since the start of 2021, but has whiffed in nearly 29% of his plate appearances during the same period. Fringy-average defense at the hot corner, so his eventual home may be a combination of first base / designated hitter / leftfield in the coming years. Vientos is profiling like a .250/.320/.460-type hitter.

Ceiling: 2.5-win player
Risk: Moderate
MLB ETA: Debuted in 2022

New York Mets

8. Blade Tidwell, RHP

FB	CB	SL	CH	Command	Overall
60	50	55	50	50	50

Born: 06/08/01	Age: 22	Bats: R	Top Production Comp: N/A
Height: 6-4	Weight: 207	Throws: R	

Background: Tidwell famously teamed with Ryan Weathers, the seventh overall pick in the 2018 draft, to give the Loretto Mustangs a lethal one-two punch atop their vaunted rotation for a couple of seasons. And while the hard-throwing right-hander's watched his former teammate earn an extended look with the Padres, Tidwell continued to make his case as any early round pick in 2022. A star on both sides of the ball during his prep career, Tidwell earned a bevy of awards and recognition throughout his teenage years, including: 2019 Tennessee Class A Mr. baseball, 2020 Most Valuable Pitcher at the *Perfect Game* 18U *Battle of the Southeast*, and 2020 *Perfect Game* Preseason All-America and All-Southeast Region Selection. The outlet named the big hurler as the 22nd best right-hander in the nation, and the third overall player in the state. COVID, though, prematurely ended his senior campaign after just one game. After going undrafted, Tidwell packed his bags and headed to SEC powerhouse Tennessee – which is hardly Plan B. The 6-foot-4, 207-pound hurler made 18 starts for the Volunteers in 2021, throwing 98.2 innings with 90 strikeouts and 34 walks to go along with a 3.74 ERA. The big righty made a trio of brief appearances for the Stars squad on Team USA, tossing an additional seven innings with nine strikeouts and four walks. Last season began on a bit of a sour note for Tidwell: he missed the opening month-and-a-half dealing with right shoulder soreness and then made a couple of short relief outings once he did make it back to action for the nation's top team. Tidwell would eventually make four relief appearances and nine starts for the Volunteers, posting a dominating 51-to-11 strikeout-to-walk ratio in 39.0 innings of work. He finished his sophomore season with a 3.00 ERA. New York snagged him in the second round last July, 52nd overall, and signed him to a deal worth $1.85 million. He struck out 11 and walked 7 during his 9.1-inning debut.

Scouting Report: Pre-draft write-up:

> "Despite being a draft-eligible sophomore, Tidwell's already 21-years-old – the typical age of a junior. The right-hander's arsenal is highlighted by a mid- to upper-90s heater with plenty of explosive, late life. He'll complement the plus offering with a trio of offspeed pitches: an average upper-70s curveball, a 55-grade mid-80s slider, and an upper-80s changeup. Tidwell's command took a step forward during the 2022 season, particularly late in the year. There's some mid-rotation caliber upside with the floor of a dominant backend reliever. The early season shoulder woes, though, are concerning and would likely push him down into a second round grade if I were interested in drafting him.

Ceiling: 2.0-win player
Risk: Moderate
MLB ETA: 2024/2025

9. Ronny Mauricio, SS

Hit	Power	SB	Patience	Glove	Overall
40	55	50	40	50	50

Born: 04/04/01	Age: 22	Bats: B	Top Production Comp: Ian Desmond
Height: 6-3	Weight: 166	Throws: R	

Season	Team	Age	Level	PA	1B	2B	3B	HR	SB	CS	BB%	K%	AVG	OBP	SLG	ISO
2021	NYM	20	A+	420	57	14	5	19	9	7	5.71%	24.05%	0.242	0.290	0.449	0.207
2021	NYM	20	AA	33	8	1	0	1	2	0	6.06%	33.33%	0.323	0.364	0.452	0.129
2022	NYM	21	AA	541	78	26	2	26	20	11	4.44%	23.11%	0.259	0.296	0.472	0.212

Background: Another of the club's high profile, big dollar free agent signings off the international market. New York signed the toolsy, lightning quick bat of Mauricio for a massive $2.1 million. And the club, like they do with a lot of their top youngsters, instantly placed Mauricio on the fast-track to the big leagues. The switch-hitting shortstop spent time in the Appalachian League as a 17-year-old, logged a full season in the old South Atlantic League a year later, and reached Double-A during his age-20 season. Last season, the then-21-year-old San Pedro de Macoris, Dominican Republic native registered a full stint with Binghamton. Appearing in a career best 123 games, Mauricio slugged .259/.296/.472 with career bests in doubles (26), homeruns (26), and stolen bases (20) to go along with a pair of three-baggers. Per *Weighted Runs Created Plus*, his overall production topped the league average mark by just 4%. For his minor league career, Mauricio is sporting a .261/.300/.424 slash line through 404 games spanning four seasons.

Snippet from The 2022 Prospect Digest Handbook: Mauricio's lack of patience at the plate severely limits his offensive ceiling. And it ultimately cost him a place among the Top 100 prospects this year.

New York Mets

Scouting Report: Consider the following:

Since 2006, just five 21-year-old hitters posted a 100 to 110 wRC+ with a sub-6.0% walk rate in any Double-A league (min. 350 PA): Dustin Fowler, Leury Garcia, Josh Vitters, Edinson Rincon, and Ronny Mauricio.

The question has never really been about the tools, but rather is Mauricio (A) willing to walk enough to compliment his value or (B) hit enough to compensate his lack of patience? To this point the answer has been a resounding no and no. Known for his plus-bat speed, the Dominican infielder owns above-average in-game power, above-average speed, a 40-grade hit tool, and enough leather to stick at the infield's most premium position. But the ceiling remains severely limited due to his terrible approach at the plate.

Since 2015, there have been 136 instances in which a qualified hitter walked 5.5% of the time or fewer in a season. Barely 41% of those instances did the hitter post a league average or better offensive season (100 wRC+ or better).

Mauricio's tracking like a .260/.310/.440 type hitter, but the hit tool has to creep up at least another half-grade for that to happen.

Ceiling: 2.0-win player
Risk: Moderate to High
MLB ETA: 2023

10. Nick Morabito, CF

Hit	Power	SB	Patience	Glove	Overall
50	45/50	50	50	50	50

Born: 05/07/03	Age: 20	Bats: R	Top Production Comp: N/A
Height: 5-11	Weight: 185	Throws: R	

Background: An interesting little tidbit: Only one former Gonzaga College High School player appeared in a Major League game – right-hander Tom Cantwell, who played a handful of games with the Cincinnati Reds all the way back in 1909 and 1910. And Cantwell, for those that may find it interesting, had two outings at the end of his first season in which he squared off against John McGraw's vaunted New York Giants club and the other coming against Zack Wheat's Brooklyn Superbas. Gonzaga College High School went nearly two full decades between draft picks, last sending first baseman Victor Hamisevicz into the Montreal Expos' system in 2003. Fast forward 19 years and outfielder Nick Morabito heard his name called at the back of the second round by the New York Mets. The District of Columbia Gatorade Player of the Year in 2022, Morabito capped off his amateur career by slugging .545/.644/1.119 with 10 doubles, six triples, and 12 homeruns. The Mets signed him to a deal worth an even $1 million, roughly $125,000 above the recommended slot bonus. He struggled during his brief debut in the Complex League, though, hitting .091/.167/.136 with just one double in 24 plate appearances.

Scouting Report: Morabito has some solid bloodlines into the game of baseball. Brian, his father, played college ball at James Madison University. And his personal hitting coach, Uncle John, spent a year in the White Sox's organization after being drafted in the 36th round in 1987. Very simple, easy to maintain swing. Morabito holds his hands close to his body, fully relaxed, before the pitcher begins his motion. Really good looking swing that's long through the zone and should allow him to continue to spray the ball all over the field. Solid pop, plus runner. He was a shortstop in high school, but likely shifts over to the keystone or center field.

Ceiling: 1.5- to 2.0-win player
Risk: Moderate
MLB ETA: 2026

11. Calvin Ziegler, RHP

FB	SL	CH	Command	Overall
60	55	45/50	30/40	45

Born: 10/03/02	Age: 20	Bats: R	Top Production Comp: N/A
Height: 6-0	Weight: 214	Throws: R	

Season	Team	Age	Level	IP	TBF	K/9	K%	BB/9	BB%	K-BB%	ERA	FIP	xFIP	Pit/Bat
2022	NYM	19	A	46.2	199	13.50	35.18%	6.75	17.59%	17.59%	4.44	3.80	4.36	4.31

Background: The front office opened up 2021 draft by selecting pitchers with their first three selections and five of their first six. Ziegler, the 46th overall pick, became the organization's de facto top selection after the team failed to sign Vanderbilt ace Kumar Rocker. Standing 6-foot and tipping the scales at a portly 214 pounds, Ziegler made his professional debut last season with the St. Lucie Mets. Making 16 starts and throwing 46.2 innings, the Canadian-born righty struck out a mindboggling 70 and walked an equally mindboggling 35 – or an average of 13.5 strikeouts and 6.8 walks per nine innings. He finished his first professional season with a 4.44 ERA, 3.80 FIP, and a 4.36 xFIP.

New York Mets

Snippet from The 2022 Prospect Digest Handbook: Ziegler is maxed out from a physical standpoint, but he's a high upside arm with the potential to be a #4-type starting pitcher. The changeup will need to be fine-tuned.

Scouting Report: Consider the following:

> Since 2006, only three 19-year-old hurlers struck out at least 34% and walked at least 14% of the hitters they faced in Low-A (min. 40 IP): Mick Abel, Ronan Kopp, and – of course – Calvin Ziegler.

Thick lower half that suggests he could squat a Buick. Really promising youngster with a power-based arsenal. Featuring a mid-90s, plus heater, a plus power curveball, and a better than advertised average, mid-80s straight changeup. The command is currently a 30 and projects to be a 40 at peak. Mechanically, he's a throwback to power pitchers from yesteryear, almost a drop-and-drive hurler. If the command takes some leaps forward, Ziegler could be one of the major surprises in 2023. But of his 16 brief appearances with St. Lucie last season, the hard-throwing righty walked one or fewer hitters just six times and two or fewer hitters nine times. He only had one game where he pitched more than four innings. Obvious reliever risk here, of course.

Ceiling: 3.0-win player
Risk: High
MLB ETA: 2025

12. Matt Allan, RHP

FB	CB	CH	Command	Overall
N/A	N/A	N/A	N/A	55

Born: 04/17/01	Age: 21	Bats: R	Top Production Comp: N/A
Height: 6-3	Weight: 225	Throws: R	

Background: There likely isn't a more snake-bitten prospect in the minor leagues than Matt Allan. Widely regarded as one of the top prospects entering the 2019 draft class, Allen's strong commitment to the University of Florida scared teams away from using a first or second round pick on the fireballing Seminole High School product. But the Mets – as they often do – took a third round gamble on the 6-foot-3, 225-pound right-hander and signed him to a massive $2.5 million as the 89th overall pick. And Allan showcased all his promise during his limited debut with the club's lower level affiliates that summer, posting a 14-to-5 strikeout-to-walk ratio in 10.1 innings of work. But then the pandemic happened, forcing him to work at the organization's training site. Then he hurt his expensive right elbow and eventually underwent the knife for Tommy John surgery in early 2021. And *then* he had a follow up surgery to transpose the ulnar collateral nerve, which knocked him out for the entirety of the 2022 season. He's expected to be at full health for 2023.

Scouting Report: With nothing new to report on his 2019, here's my analysis prior to the draft:

> "The owner of two plus- to plus-plus pitches. Allen attacks hitters with a lethal fastball/curveball combination that was – simply – too overpowering for his current peers. The fastball sits in the mid-90s, touching 96 mph on several occasions, and his knee-buckling curveball hovers in the 79- to 81-mph range. Allen generates the premium velocity without much effort and – generally – commands the zone well. His third offering, an upper-80s changeup, profiles no worse than average. Allen has the build and arsenal to suggest a #2-type ceiling."

Ceiling: 3.0-win player
Risk: Extremely High
MLB ETA: 2022

13. Joel Diaz, RHP

FB	CB	CH	Command	Overall
60	50/55	50	45/50	45

Born: 02/26/04	Age: 19	Bats: R	Top Production Comp: Rafael Montero
Height: 6-2	Weight: 208	Throws: R	

Season	Team	Age	Level	IP	TBF	K/9	K%	BB/9	BB%	K-BB%	ERA	FIP	xFIP	Pit/Bat
2021	NYM	17	DSL	49.1	192	11.31	32.29%	1.64	4.69%	27.60%	0.55	2.25	2.77	1.90
2022	NYM	18	A	55.1	247	8.30	20.65%	4.07	10.12%	10.53%	5.86	4.79	4.44	3.83

Background: A number of the club's current or recent top prospects plucked from the international scene have been hitters. But the Mets may have unearthed an underappreciated prospect in Joel Diaz. Signed out of San Cristobal, Dominican Republic two years ago, Diaz turned in a phenomenal debut showing in the foreign rookie league that summer. He allowed only three earned runs in 50.1 innings of work to go along with a dominating 63-to-9 strikeout-to-walk ratio. Last season – unsurprisingly – the front office had Diaz bypass the Complex League and sent him directly up to Low-A. He would make 16 appearances, 10 of which were starts, throwing 55.1 innings with 51 strikeouts and 25 free passes. He compiled an unsightly 5.86 ERA, a 4.79 FIP, and a 4.44 xFIP.

New York Mets

Scouting Report: Consider the following:

> Since 2005, there's been just forty-one 18-year-old hurlers to throw at least 50 innings in Low-A. Of those 41 instances, nine of them posted a strikeout percentage between 19% and 22%. Of those nine, only two posted a walk percentage between 9% and 11%: Jairo Heredia and Joel Diaz.

A young, very projectable, baby-faced right-hander. Diaz will unfurl a mid-90s fastball that projects to be a plus offering at maturity. His 12-6 bending curveball is an interesting breaking ball, showing phenomenal shape but has the appearance of floating at times. When it's right, it'll flash above-average. And it certainly got its fair share of awkward looks from hitters. His changeup is another intriguing offspeed pitch. It's not bad, and sometimes flashes, but it has ways to go. Very good velocity separation, though. The command is better than most 18-year-olds and should be in the average range at its peak.

Ceiling: 1.5-win player
Risk: Moderate
MLB ETA: 2025

14. Mike Vasil, RHP

FB	CB	SL	CH	Command	Overall
60	60	50	50	45	45

Born: 03/19/00	Age: 23	Bats: L	Top Production Comp: N/A
Height: 6-4	Weight: 244	Throws: R	

Season	Team	Age	Level	IP	TBF	K/9	K%	BB/9	BB%	K-BB%	ERA	FIP	xFIP	Pit/Bat
2022	NYM	22	A	37.0	147	9.49	26.53%	2.68	7.48%	19.05%	2.19	2.66	3.22	3.81
2022	NYM	22	A+	33.1	140	11.88	31.43%	4.05	10.71%	20.71%	5.13	3.72	3.48	4.26

Background: It isn't too often the University of Virginia would (A) insert a true freshman into their regular starting rotation and (B) stick with that true freshman despite some disappointing peripherals and overall lackluster performance. But that's exactly what the ACC powerhouse did when it came to Mike Vasil, a hefty left-hander out of Boston, Massachusetts. He posted a 5.93 ERA while averaging 6.2 strikeouts and 3.4 walks per nine innings across 12 starts and one relief appearance. Vasil took a massive step forward during his COVID-shortened 2020 campaign, but his junior year production fell somewhere in between. He finished his collegiate time by tallying a 4.52 ERA, 73 punch outs and 18 walks in a career best 81.2 innings of work. New York selected him in the eighth round two years ago, 232nd overall, and signed him to a deal worth $181,200. Vasil opened the year up with St. Lucie and moved up to Brooklyn after just eight starts. But he hit the disabled list in late June with an undisclosed elbow woe and wouldn't make it back until late August. He finished his first full year in professional ball with 71.1 innings, averaging 10.7 strikeouts and 3.3 walks per nine innings. He made six appearances with Peoria in the Arizona Fall League as well, striking out 18 and walking nine in 15.1 innings of work.

Scouting Report: Despite owning one of the better fastballs in the Mets' system, Vasil shows an aptitude for changing speeds early and frequently, particularly when he's ahead in the count. The former Virginia hurler will sit 94- to 96-mph with his fastball. His curveball – when it's on – is an absolute 12-6 hammer. He'll also mix in a 50-grade slider and changeup with the latter being the better third option. Vasil has a couple things going against him, namely: lack of track record, an elbow injury that sidelined him a couple months last season, and he's more of a strike-thrower than a command guy. Meaning: there's reliever risk here. But he's the best of the bunch of second tier pitching prospects the Mets have to offer. Jason Frasor vibes, for real.

Ceiling: 1.5-win player
Risk: Moderate
MLB ETA: 2024

15. José Butto, RHP

FB	CB	CH	Command	Overall
50	50	60	50	40

Born: 03/19/98	Age: 25	Bats: R	Top Production Comp: N/A
Height: 6-1	Weight: 202	Throws: R	

Season	Team	Age	Level	IP	TBF	K/9	K%	BB/9	BB%	K-BB%	ERA	FIP	xFIP	Pit/Bat
2021	NYM	23	A+	58.1	239	9.26	25.10%	2.31	6.28%	18.83%	4.32	5.03	4.38	3.94
2021	NYM	23	AA	40.1	167	11.16	29.94%	2.01	5.39%	24.55%	3.12	4.01	3.48	3.83
2022	NYM	24	AA	92.1	397	10.53	27.20%	3.41	8.82%	18.39%	4.00	4.48	4.17	3.91
2022	NYM	24	AAA	36.2	143	7.36	20.98%	2.21	6.29%	14.69%	2.45	3.83	4.62	3.90

Background: Butto's already exceeded any – and *every* – expectation that's been placed on him. An elderly prospect signed off the international market in 2017, Butto joined the organization at the geriatric age of 19. And while expectations for a 19-year-old off the international mark are modest, at best, Butto cracked the Mets' pitching staff – albeit however briefly – for one start in 2022. It was disastrous, sure, but he *wasn't supposed* to make it that far. He would toss just four innings against the eventual National League Champion Phillies, allowing seven earned runs on nine hits and two walks. He tossed another 129.0 innings between his stints with Binghamton and Syracuse, averaging 9.6

New York Mets

strikeouts and 3.1 walks per nine innings. For his five-year minor league career, the righty owns a 3.44 ERA with 453 strikeouts and 130 walks in 450.1 innings of work.

Snippet from The 2022 Prospect Digest Handbook: Butto could be a solid middle relief arm relying solely on his fastball/changeup combo.

Scouting Report: Consider the following:

> Since 2006, only six 24-year-old hurlers met the following criteria in a Double-A season (min. 75 IP): 26% to 28% strikeout percentage with an 8% to 10% walk percentage. Those six hurlers: Devin Sweet, Michael Kelly, Louie Varland, Alan Rangel, Carlos Guevara, and José Butto.

Better than your typical up-and-down arm, but not good enough to hold down a starting gig for an extended period. Butto's fastball will sit in the 92- to 93-mph range and touch a tick or so higher. Velocity-wise it's borderline above-average, but it just doesn't miss enough bats to push it into that territory. His curveball is the very definition of average. But his change, well, that's a real difference maker. He throws strikes, generally keeps his team in the game. There are worse options as a sixth or seventh starter.

Ceiling: 1.0-win player
Risk: Low to Moderate
MLB ETA: Debuted in 2022

16. Wyatt Young, 2B/SS

Hit	Power	SB	Patience	Glove	Overall
55	40	40	60	45	40

Born: 12/05/99	Age: 23	Bats: L	Top Production Comp: N/A
Height: 5-7	Weight: 185	Throws: R	

Season	Team	Age	Level	PA	1B	2B	3B	HR	SB	CS	BB%	K%	AVG	OBP	SLG	ISO
2021	NYM	21	CPX	101	25	8	1	0	4	2	8.91%	20.79%	0.370	0.426	0.478	0.109
2022	NYM	22	A+	18	3	0	0	0	0	1	16.67%	11.11%	0.214	0.389	0.214	0.000
2022	NYM	22	AA	434	66	20	4	6	5	2	12.90%	20.51%	0.257	0.353	0.380	0.123
2022	NYM	22	AAA	84	21	3	0	1	2	0	13.10%	15.48%	0.352	0.446	0.437	0.085

Background: A consistent bat throughout his three-year tenure at Pepperdine. The lefty-swinging middle infielder opened up his career with the Waves with a .315/.351/.366 slash line as a true freshman and spent the ensuing summer ripping through the Cape Cod League for the Yarmouth-Dennis Red Sox (.339/.416/.446). His numbers took a slight downturn during the COVID-shortened 2020 season, .299/.373/.299, but he rebounded during his junior campaign and several career highs including average (.332), on-base percentage (.405), slugging percentage (.442) doubles (12), homeruns (three), and stolen bases (six). New York snagged the undersized prospect in the 15th round two years ago, 442nd overall, and signed him to a deal worth $125,000. Young promptly did what Young has *always* done – hit. He shredded the Complex League competition to the tune of .370/.426/.478 through 26 games. Last season the 5-foot-7, 185-pound infielder opened the year up in High-A, but after five game got sent directly up to Triple-A – where he promptly caught fire. He was eventually sent to Double-A for the remainder of the season in early May. He batted a respectable .270/.369/.383 with 23 doubles, four triples, seven homeruns, and seven stolen bases (in 10 total attempts) in 122 games. His overall production, per *Weighted Runs Created Plus*, topped the league average threshold by 11%. Not too shabby as a late round pick out of a non-traditional baseball school.

Scouting Report: Consider the following:

> Since 2006, only three 22-year-old hitters met the following criteria in a Double-A season (min. 350 PA): 100 to 110 wRC+, at least an 11% walk rate, and an 18% to 22% strikeout rate. Those three hitters: Dorssys Paulino, Livan Soto, and – of course – Wyatt Young.

Young doesn't offer up a whole lot of offensive upside beyond his above-average hit tool and plus patience at the plate. Beyond that, though, there is not enough complementary tools to carry him to a meaningful spot in a big league lineup. The lefty-swinging infielder did show a modest platoon split last season (.277/.383/.399 vs. RHP and .248/.315/.327 vs. LHP), so that'll have to be monitored. The glove was spotty at the keystone as well. Still, though, for the initial investment of a 15th round pick and a little over a hundred grand, the Mets have to be quite pleased that Wyatt's already accrued Double-A success in one year.

Ceiling: 1.0-win player
Risk: Moderate
MLB ETA: 2023

17. William Lugo, 3B/SS

Hit	Power	SB	Patience	Glove	Overall
40	50/55	30	50	45	40

Born: 01/02/02	Age: 21	Bats: R	Top Production Comp: N/A
Height: 6-2	Weight: 230	Throws: R	

Season	Team	Age	Level	PA	1B	2B	3B	HR	SB	CS	BB%	K%	AVG	OBP	SLG	ISO
2021	NYM	19	CPX	183	22	6	0	6	5	1	12.57%	28.42%	0.218	0.328	0.372	0.154
2022	NYM	20	A+	121	17	7	0	4	0	0	10.74%	22.31%	0.267	0.347	0.448	0.181
2022	NYM	20	A	357	52	18	2	10	0	0	10.36%	25.21%	0.261	0.347	0.427	0.166

Background: Signed out of the Dominican Republic in late August five years ago, the Mets handed the hefty infielder a bonus worth $475,000. And New York, a team that has traditionally challenged their recent high profile international free agents with aggressive assignments, sent the 6-foot-2, 230-pound man-child to the Gulf Coast League for his professional debut in 2019. The results were…horrific. Lugo batted a paltry .158/.280/.219 in 176 trips to the plate. And his numbers in the Complex League following the COVID layoff were hardly any better: he "hit" a lowly .218/.328/.372 in 46 games. But for some reason, Lugo emerged at the start of the 2022 season as a changed hitter. He put together a significantly improved slash line during his extended stint with St. Lucie (.261/.347/.427) and continued hitting once he moved up to High-A. Overall, Lugo finished his breakout campaign with a respectable .263/.347/.432 slash line, belting out 25 doubles, two triples, and 14 homeruns. His yearly production, according to *Weighted Runs Created Plus*, topped the league average by 21%.

Scouting Report: Consider the following statistical comparison:

Name	Season	Age	PA	AVG	OBP	SLG	OPS	ISO	BB%	K%	wRC+
Will Middlebrooks	2009	20	427	0.265	0.349	0.404	0.753	0.139	11.24%	28.81%	117.85
William Lugo	2022	20	357	0.261	0.347	0.427	0.774	0.166	10.36%	25.21%	122.47

Resurrected from the prospect scrap heap, Lugo showed some promising offensive potential despite playing half of his time in either a neutral hitting environment (St. Lucie) or a pitcher-friendly environment (Brooklyn). Lugo got off to a slow start to the season, hitting .217/.277/.383 over the first month of the season, but responded by slugging .269/.359/.446 the remainder of the way. Everything about Lugo screams future Quad-A slugger, but the arrow is definitely pointing upward.

Ceiling: 1.0-win player
Risk: Moderate
MLB ETA: 2025

18. Christian Scott, RHP

FB	SL	CH	Command	Overall
55	55	50/55	50	40

Born: 06/15/99	Age: 24	Bats: R	Top Production Comp: N/A
Height: 6-4	Weight: 207	Throws: R	

Season	Team	Age	Level	IP	TBF	K/9	K%	BB/9	BB%	K-BB%	ERA	FIP	xFIP	Pit/Bat
2022	NYM	23	A	37.1	165	12.54	31.52%	2.89	7.27%	24.24%	4.82	2.72	3.11	3.88
2022	NYM	23	A+	21.1	96	10.55	26.04%	4.22	10.42%	15.63%	3.80	2.86	3.90	3.93

Background: The New York Mets' 2021 draft class has the possibility to be forever known as the Kumar Rocker Draft, or perhaps as the lack of Kumar Rocker due to their insistence on a lower signing bonus based on medicals. But the front office quietly assembled a strong class without their first round pick. Calvin Ziegler, Dominic Hamel, Mike Vasil, Wyatt Young, and – of course – Christian Scott all rank among the club's Top 20 List. Scott, their fifth round pick that year out of the University of Florida, spent the majority of his career working out of the Gators' bullpen. He would leave the SEC powerhouse with 55 appearances, only five of them coming via the start, while averaging 8.3 strikeouts and 2.5 walks per nine innings. Last season the 6-foot-4, 207-pound right-hander split time between the Mets' Low-A and High-A affiliates' bullpen and rotation, throwing 58.2 innings with a whopping 77 strikeouts and only 22 walks to go along with a 4.45 ERA.

Scouting Report: More projection than the typical hurler coming out of college thanks to his bullpen relegation. The Mets seem content on stretching out the lanky right-hander. He threw multiple innings in all but one of his appearances, and lasted into the fourth inning eight times. Scott's fastball reportedly touched the upper 90s in shorter stints, but he would generally work several ticks lower throughout the 2022 season. He'll complement the above-average offering with a potential swing-and-miss slider. And his changeup was noticeably better than preseason reports indicated, flashing above-average a few times during an outing I scouted. There's a high probability that he eventually ends up back in a multi-inning relief role but, for now, he's tracking like a spot-starter.

Ceiling: 1.0-win player
Risk: Moderate
MLB ETA: 2024

New York Mets

19. Dominic Hamel, RHP

FB	CB	SL	CH	Command	Overall
55	50	55	50	45	40

Born: 03/02/99	Age: 24	Bats: R	Top Production Comp: N/A
Height: 6-2	Weight: 237	Throws: R	

Season	Team	Age	Level	IP	TBF	K/9	K%	BB/9	BB%	K-BB%	ERA	FIP	xFIP	Pit/Bat
2022	NYM	23	A	63.1	267	10.09	26.59%	4.12	10.86%	15.73%	3.84	3.96	4.05	3.90
2022	NYM	23	A+	55.2	223	11.96	33.18%	4.04	11.21%	21.97%	2.59	2.45	3.76	3.96

Background: Prior to the 2021 draft, the Mets have selected just four Dallas Baptist University products in the mid-summer draft: Jordan Martinson (2019, 11th round), Matt Duce (2017, 14th round), Joe Shaw (2015, 12th round), and Ricky Sparks (2006, 30th round). But the club opened up their pocketbooks and signed Hamel to a deal worth slightly more than $750,000 two years ago when they made him their third round pick – which, in turn, made Hamel the sixth highest drafted Patriot in school history. A 22-year-old senior in 2021, Hamel posted an impressive 136-to-34 strikeout-to-walk ratio in 91.2 innings of work for the Missouri Valley conference School, tallying a 13-2 win-loss record to go along with a 4.22 ERA. Last season, the 6-foot-2, 237-pound righty split time between the Mets' Low-A and High-A affiliates, throwing 119.0 innings of work, averaging an impressive 11.0 strikeouts and 4.1 walks per nine innings. He tallied a 3.25 ERA.

Snippet from The 2022 Prospect Digest Handbook: Hamel's the type of pitcher that would excel in Cleveland's farm system, so it'll be interesting to see how the Mets develop the third round pick. There's some sneaky mid-rotation upside.

Scouting Report: The fastball velocity downgraded noticeably from his final college season to last year, going from the low 90s into the upper 80s. During a mid-season start with Brooklyn, Hamel's heater was hovering in the 88-89 mph range and kissing 90 mph on occasion. His low 70s curveball shows beautiful shape, but the velocity allows hitters to adjust mid-pitch as it humps up out of his hand. Above-average low 80s slider. And an upper 70s vanilla changeup. Hamel's never been a command guy, even going back to his college days, and the velocity just isn't there to compensate for his lack of strike-throwing ability. He looks like an org-guy unless he can find another gear on his fastball.

Ceiling: 0.5- to 1.0-win player
Risk: Moderate
MLB ETA: 2024

20. Javier Atencio, LHP

FB	CB	CH	Command	Overall
55	55	45/50	35	35

Born: 11/26/01	Age: 21	Bats: L	Top Production Comp: N/A
Height: 6-0	Weight: 195	Throws: L	

Season	Team	Age	Level	IP	TBF	K/9	K%	BB/9	BB%	K-BB%	ERA	FIP	xFIP	Pit/Bat
2021	NYM	19	DSL	48.0	187	14.25	40.64%	3.56	10.16%	30.48%	2.44	2.21	2.29	2.26
2022	NYM	20	A	39.2	169	10.89	28.40%	5.22	13.61%	14.79%	2.27	3.32	4.40	4.26

Background: Signed out of Ocumare del Tuy, Venezuela, in early July five years ago. Atencio made his pro debut the following summer with the Mets' foreign rookie league affiliate. He would throw 36.0 innings, recording 25 strikeouts and 16 walks to go along with a 4.75 ERA. Once baseball returned from its COVID absence, Atencio spent the 2021 season back in the Dominican Summer League for another refresher. And this time his production was absurd. He averaged a whopping 14.3 strikeouts and 3.6 walks per nine innings across 14 starts and one relief appearance. Finally convinced by his development, the front office sent the 6-foot, 195-pound southpaw up to St. Lucie to begin the 2022 season. And he was *dominant*. Atencio opened the year up with a strong start against Dunedin and allowed just one run across his first 14 innings. An undisclosed injury would force him out of action midseason. He would finish the year with a 48-to-23 strikeout-to-walk ratio in 39.2 innings with the club's Low-A affiliate.

Scouting Report: A low level lottery ticket that owns an intriguing 93-mph fastball that caused more than a few late / awkward swings with St. Lucie last season. The above-average offering showed some late explosion and hop, particularly up in the zone. He'll mix in a wicked above-average, big bending curveball and a fringy changeup that projects to average at maturity. Atencio racked up some gaudy strikeout numbers last season, averaging 10.9 K/9, but his command has ways to go. He's tracking like a reliever.

Ceiling: 0.5-win player
Risk: Moderate
MLB ETA: 2026

New York Yankees Top Prospects

New York Yankees

1. Anthony Volpe, SS

	Hit	Power	SB	Patience	Glove	Overall
	55/60	60	60	55	60	70

Born: 04/28/01 **Age:** 22 **Bats:** R **Top Production Comp:** Trevor Story
Height: 5-11 **Weight:** 180 **Throws:** R

Season	Team	Age	Level	PA	1B	2B	3B	HR	SB	CS	BB%	K%	AVG	OBP	SLG	ISO
2021	NYY	20	A	257	25	18	5	12	21	5	19.84%	16.73%	0.302	0.455	0.623	0.322
2021	NYY	20	A+	256	28	17	1	15	12	4	10.55%	22.66%	0.286	0.391	0.587	0.300
2022	NYY	21	AA	497	53	31	4	18	44	6	11.47%	17.71%	0.251	0.348	0.472	0.220
2022	NYY	21	AAA	99	13	4	1	3	6	1	8.08%	30.30%	0.236	0.313	0.404	0.169

Background: There is a well-known photo that pops up rather frequently on the internet, sometimes on forums, other times on terribly written websites, and fairly frequently on random social media sites. It's shot of two kids, one tall and one smaller, on the backlot ballfields of yesteryear. They're not looking at the camera, but eyes diverted to someplace else, midstride each holding a bat. Black and white image. They're in high school with their entire lives in front of them – lives destined for baseball stardom and the golden walls of Cooperstown enshrinement. It's Ozzie Smith, the Wizard of Oz, and Eddie Murray, the switch-hitting consistency that lead to 3,000 hits and 500 homeruns. And they just happened to go to the same high school, at the exact same time. In a perfect world – though it's, admittedly, likely never going to happen – but maybe a similar photo will pop up of a pair of Delbarton seniors, Class of 2019. The New Jersey-based prep school featured a pair of eventual first round picks: ace right-hander Jack Leiter, who would have gone in the opening round that summer if not for his unbreakable commitment to Vanderbilt University, and middle infielder Anthony Volpe, who was taken by the Yankees of New York with the 30th overall pick. The 5-foot-11, 180-pound shortstop looked otherworldly during his meteoric rise in 2021 as he bashed .294/.423/.604 with 35 doubles, six triples, 27 homeruns, and 33 stolen bases. Volpe quickly unseated hyped outfielder Jasson Dominguez as the club's top prospect, a nearly unthinkable task just months earlier. Last season the New Jersey-born infielder set his sights on the upper minors, spending 110 games with Somerset and another 22 contests with Scranton / Wilkes-Barre. Volpe finished the season with an aggregate .249/.342/.460 slash line with 35 doubles, five triples, 21 homeruns, and a new career high in stolen bases (50). As measured by *Weighted Runs Created Plus*, his overall production line topped the league average threshold by 17%.

Snippet from The 2022 Prospect Digest Handbook: Needless to say, it was a season for the ages for Volpe.

Scouting Report: Consider the following:

> Since 2006, only a pair of 20-year-old bats met the following criteria in a Double-A season (min. 350 PA): 117 to 127 wRC+, a 10% to 13% walk rate, and a 16.5% to 18.5% strikeout rate. Those two hitters: former Top 100 prospect Chris Lubanski, who happened to never make it to The Show, and Anthony Volpe.

Volpe's been a slow starter a few times through his young career:

> In 2021, he batted .229/.359/.409 over his first 22 games in Low-A. He then slugged .369/.536/.825 over his remaining 32 contests in the level. Last season he hit .181/.299/.348 over his first 37 games in Double-A, and then mashed .285/.373/.532 over his final 73 games with Somerset. And he finished the year by hitting .236/.313/.405 in 22 games in Triple-A.

It's an adjustment period -- nothing more and nothing less. It's not overly surprising that Volpe continues to showcase above-average power potential with the likely step into plus-power territory in the coming years. He's continually posted sky high fly ball rates in his career, including: a 57% in Double-A and 52.5% in Triple-A last season. The New Jersey native looks noticeably bulkier than his listed 180 pounds, but that added weight / strength didn't limit impact on his defensive ability. Lightning quick bat, above-average speed, the potential to win a couple Gold Gloves. There's not a lot that Volpe can't do. In terms of big league ceiling, think: .280/.360/.500.

Ceiling: 6.0-win player
Risk: Moderate
MLB ETA: 2023

New York Yankees

2. Oswald Peraza, SS

Hit	Power	SB	Patience	Glove	Overall
50	50	55	45	50	55

Born: 06/15/00	Age: 23	Bats: R	Top Production Comp: Asdrubal Cabrera
Height: 6-0	Weight: 165	Throws: R	

Season	Team	Age	Level	PA	1B	2B	3B	HR	SB	CS	BB%	K%	AVG	OBP	SLG	ISO
2021	NYY	21	A+	127	19	10	0	5	16	1	9.45%	18.90%	0.306	0.386	0.532	0.225
2021	NYY	21	AA	353	66	16	2	12	20	8	6.52%	23.23%	0.294	0.348	0.466	0.172
2021	NYY	21	AAA	31	7	0	0	1	2	1	6.45%	16.13%	0.286	0.323	0.393	0.107
2022	NYY	22	AAA	429	65	16	0	19	33	5	7.93%	23.31%	0.259	0.329	0.448	0.189

Background: Little did the front office know that when they signed the Venezuelan teen to a $175,000 deal in 2016, that he would provide some insurance for the club's struggling shortstop during their American League Championship push six years later. But that's exactly how things played out for Peraza and the Yankees. A native of Barquisimeto, Peraza began his professional career as a light-hitting speedster but emerged a dynamic offensive threat following the 2020 COVID lost season. Measuring a wiry 6-foot and 165 pounds, Peraza opened up the 2021 campaign with Hudson Valley, but stayed only a few weeks before moving onto Double-A and then eventually Triple-A. He would finish his breakout season with a remarkable .297/.356/.477 slash line with career highs in doubles (26), homeruns (18), and stolen bases (38). Last season, before helping the Yankees down the stretch and eventually in the playoffs, Peraza continued his offensive assault on minor league pitching during his extended stay in Scranton / Wilkes-Barre. He would appear in 99 games with the RailRiders, slugging .259/.329/.448 with 16 doubles, 19 homeruns, and 33 stolen bases (in only 38 total attempts). Per *Weighted Runs Created Plus*, his overall production topped the league average mark by 6%. He mashed .306/.404/.429 in 18 games for the Yanks in September, as well.

Snippet from The 2022 Prospect Digest Handbook: I don't think he's going to be a perennial 20-plus-homerun threat, but he could settle in somewhere between 15 and 18 dingers a year. Average to slightly better-than-average glove.

Scouting Report: Consider the following:

> Since 2006, only two 22-year-old hitters met the following criteria in a season in any Triple-A league (min. 350 PA): 100 to 110 wRC+, 22.5% to 24.5% strikeout rate and a 7% to 9% walk rate. Those two hitters: Jonathan Villar and Oswald Peraza. Villar's spent the past decade in the big leagues, bouncing between Houston, Milwaukee, Baltimore, Miami, Toronto, New York, Chicago, and Los Angeles while compiling a .255/.322/.397 slash line in more than 1,000 big league games.

After driving up his fly ball rate during his breakout campaign two years ago, Peraza continued to push his fly ball numbers even higher in 2022, posting a career high 41.9% mark. Average-ish walk and punch out rates. Peraza may never crest over into above-average power, but he won't knock any cheap dingers out of the park either. Last year began slowly for the young middle infielder as he batted a lowly .194/.262/.333 over his first 33 games. But beginning on May 25th through the end of his stay in Scranton / Wilkes-Barre, Peraza bashed .292/.362/.506 while launching 15 of his 19 homeruns. Plus speed, above-average hit tool, and a solid enough glove to stick at shortstop; Peraza has the tools and production potential to spend the next decade quietly manning the brightest spot on the diamond in the hottest city in America. In terms of big league ceiling, think: .280/.340/.450 hitter. Whether Volpe or Peraza wind up as the starting shortstop is a whole different discussion.

Ceiling: 3.5-win player
Risk: Moderate
MLB ETA: Debuted in 2022

3. Jasson Dominguez, CF

Hit	Power	SB	Patience	Glove	Overall
50	50/60	60/40	50	50	55

Born: 02/07/03	Age: 19	Bats: B	Top Production Comp: Tyler O'Neill
Height: 5-10	Weight: 190	Throws: R	

Season	Team	Age	Level	PA	1B	2B	3B	HR	SB	CS	BB%	K%	AVG	OBP	SLG	ISO
2021	NYY	18	CPX	27	4	0	0	0	2	0	22.22%	22.22%	0.200	0.407	0.200	0.000
2021	NYY	18	A	214	33	9	1	5	7	3	9.81%	31.31%	0.258	0.346	0.398	0.140
2022	NYY	19	A	324	45	17	2	9	19	6	14.20%	27.47%	0.265	0.373	0.440	0.175
2022	NYY	19	A+	184	32	6	4	6	17	1	12.50%	18.48%	0.306	0.397	0.510	0.204
2022	NYY	19	AA	22	0	0	1	1	1	0	13.64%	22.73%	0.105	0.227	0.368	0.263

Background: Sometimes a perfect storm is created, developing a completely unreasonable, irrational environment. Enter: Jasson Dominguez, who became the eye of the surging sports card storm. The environment was ripe for a tornado of epic proportions. He (A) was a massive international free agent, agreeing to a deal worth more than $5 million, (B) joining the most historical franchise in baseball history, (C) a product of the New York media hype machine, (D) built like a brick shithouse, and (E) entering his professional career at the peak of the unsustainable sports card bubble. One of his cards sold for nearly $500,000. It was *impossible* for Dominguez to live up to that level of hype. No one outside of Babe Ruth could. So as the air on the Dominguez hype bubble continues to deflate, he's become an underappreciated top

New York Yankees

prospect, which seemed almost impossible a year ago. After hitting a disappointing .258/.346/.398 in 50 games in Low-A in 2021, Dominguez returned back to Tampa for a second lease on life. And he capitalized. The stocky centerfielder batted .266/.374/.440 in 75 games before moving onto Hudson Valley. After a successful 40-game tour through High-A Dominguez capped the year off with a five-game cameo in Double-A. The young Dominican outfielder batted an aggregate .273/.376/.461 with 23 doubles, seven triples, 16 homers, and 37 stolen bases. His production topped the average threshold by 35%, according to *Weighted Runs Created Plus*. Following the season, Dominguez struggled through his first stint in the Arizona Fall League, hitting .159/.250/.217 in 20 games with the Mesa Solar Sox.

Snippet from The 2022 Prospect Digest Handbook: There's superstar potential, but he does need to tone the swing down and I definitely expect him to slide over into a corner outfield position at some point in the next few years.

Scouting Report: Consider the following:

>Since 2006, only three 19-year-old hitters met the following criteria in a Low-A season (min. 300 PA): 130 to 140 wRC+, a double-digit walk rate, and a 26% to 30% strikeout rate. Those three hitters: Zac Veen, a current consensus Top 100 Prospect, Kevin Padlo, and – of course – Jasson Dominguez.

Dominguez began the year as chilly as a December Lake Erie, hitting .209/.253/.314 over his first 20 games. After that, though, he bashed .296/.410/.520 over his remaining 105 games. Dominguez is built like a Division I running back, but runs incredibly well for his girth. With that being said, he's still likely going to slide over to a corner outfield position in the coming as years due to lack of positive defensive value. Patient approach at the plate, though he can be vulnerable to breaking balls in the dirt. Fantastic bat speed that create an audible explosion when he meets the ball. I may have been a bit overaggressive when I stated superstar potential last year, but there's the potential to be a very good big league stick in the next two or three years.

Ceiling: 3.5-win player
Risk: Moderate
MLB ETA: 2024

4. Spencer Jones, CF

Hit	Power	SB	Patience	Glove	Overall
55	55/60	50	50	50	55

Born: 05/14/01	Age: 22	Bats: L	Top Production Comp: N/A
Height: 6-7	Weight: 225	Throws: L	

Season	Team	Age	Level	PA	1B	2B	3B	HR	SB	CS	BB%	K%	AVG	OBP	SLG	ISO
2022	NYY	21	CPX	11	3	1	0	1	2	0	9.09%	18.18%	0.500	0.545	0.900	0.400
2022	NYY	21	A	95	19	5	0	3	10	0	10.53%	18.95%	0.325	0.411	0.494	0.169

Background: Three years after the Philadelphia Phillies selected Mickey Moniak atop the 2016 draft La Costa Canyon High School produced another draft pick – though he was far less notable, at least at the time. The Angels selected Spencer Jones, a gangly, toolsy outfielder, in the 31st round, 931st overall, though the two sides failed to come to an agreement. Jones, a massive 6-foot-7, 225-pound hulk, took the collegiate route, heading to one of the best programs in the nation – Vanderbilt University. The California native got off to a less than impressive start to his collegiate career in 2020, batting a paltry .206/.333/.324 in 14 games before the pandemic forced a premature end to the year. During the ensuing summer the former high school hurler hit the disabled list and would eventually succumb to Tommy John surgery – an injury that would limit him to just 34 games during his sophomore season. Jones, though, would make the best of the situation as he batted .274/.346/.421 with five doubles, three homeruns, and a quartet of stolen bases. That summer he starred with the Brewster Whitecaps in the vaunted Cape Cod League, slugging .312/.424/.481 with four doubles, three homeruns, and six stolen bases in 25 games. And that proved to be a harbinger of things to come. In a career best 61 games for head coach Tim Corbin, Jones morphed into one of college baseball's most feared sluggers as he mashed .370/.460/.644 with 21 doubles, three triples, 12 homeruns, and 14 stolen bases (in 15 total attempts). The Yankees selected the massive outfielder in the opening round, 25th overall, and signed him to a deal worth $2,880,800. After a three game jaunt through the Complex League, Jones appeared in 22 contests with Tampa, mashing .325/.411/.494 with five doubles, three homeruns, and 10 stolen bases (in 10 attempts).

Scouting Report: Consider the following:

>Since 2011, only six SEC hitters have batted at least .360/.450/.630 in a season (min. 250 PA): Pete Alonso, Andrew Benintendi, Brent Rooker, Mason Katz, Sonny DiChiara, Dominic Keegan, and – of course Spencer Jones. Only one of those hitters, Jones, whiffed in more than 20% of his plate appearances.

New York Yankees

The – unfair – Aaron Judge comparison has been predictably thrown around as soon as the Yankees drafted the 6-foot-7 outfielder from Vanderbilt. And, unfortunately, it's likely going to stick around for the foreseeable future. Due to the pandemic and Tommy John surgery and recovery process, Jones projects more than the typical third year, polished college hitter. The tools are readily apparent: above-average power, above-average speed, and a solid approach at the plate. Good looking swing, but it tends to be long, leading to some concerning swing-and-miss tendencies. Pitchers seemed to have a lot of success living on the outer part of the plate.

Ceiling: 3.5-win player
Risk: Moderate
MLB ETA: 2025

5. Austin Wells, C

Hit	Power	SB	Patience	Glove	Overall
45	55	30	50	40/45	45

Born: 07/12/99	Age: 23	Bats: L	Top Production Comp: Yasmani Grandal
Height: 6-2	Weight: 220	Throws: R	

Season	Team	Age	Level	PA	1B	2B	3B	HR	SB	CS	BB%	K%	AVG	OBP	SLG	ISO
2021	NYY	21	A	299	31	17	4	9	11	0	17.06%	20.74%	0.258	0.398	0.479	0.220
2021	NYY	21	A+	170	26	6	1	7	5	0	11.76%	32.35%	0.274	0.376	0.473	0.199
2022	NYY	22	A+	121	19	7	0	6	9	0	15.70%	22.31%	0.323	0.429	0.576	0.253
2022	NYY	22	A	34	2	2	0	2	0	0	23.53%	14.71%	0.231	0.412	0.538	0.308
2022	NYY	22	AA	247	34	8	1	12	7	0	11.74%	23.48%	0.261	0.360	0.479	0.218

Background: Throughout their long, storied history the ball club's selected just five catchers in the first round of the draft: (should be Hall of Famer) Thurman Munson, Dave Parrish, Jon Poterson, Anthony Siegler, and – the latest – Austin Wells. A dynamic bat during his abbreviated two-year career at the University of Arizona, Wells left the Pac-12 School as a .357/.476/.560 hitter when the club drafted him with the 28th overall pick three years ago. The lefty-swinging backstop earned a hefty $2.5 million deal for his potential. Wells would make his professional debut in 2021 as he batted a rock solid .264/.390/.476 with 23 doubles, five triples, 16 homeruns, and 16 stolen bases (without getting caught) in 103 games between Tampa and Hudson Valley. And he continued to rake in the Arizona Fall League as well, hitting .344/.456/.578 in 18 games with Surprise. Last season a groin injury limited the former Wildcat star to just 92 games (including nine rehab games with Tampa). But the injury didn't slow the powerful catcher as he slugged .277/.385/.512 with most of the time spent in Double-A, the true proving ground.

Snippet from The 2022 Prospect Digest Handbook: Unless Wells' defensive production makes a complete reversal it's going to be difficult to not push him to first base or a full time designated hitter.

Scouting Report: If a great defensive catcher is referred to as a brick wall, Wells' work behind the dish was like spaghetti strainer two years ago. But, surprisingly, he *did* make a complete reversal on the defensive side of the ball during his follow up campaign last season. He nearly doubled his caught stealing rate (13% to 25%) *and*, according to Clay Davenport's metrics, he was a net +6 in 2023. *Baseball Prospectus*' numbers also show Wells' framing as a positive asset as well. Offensively speaking, that's the easy part: he mashes. Above-average power, incredibly patient – all wrapped up into a left-handed swing. He's likely going to border on a Three True Outcome performance at the big league level, something along the lines of .240/.350/.450. He's now entering his age-23 season and knocking – loudly – on New York's door. Gamer.

Ceiling: 3.0-win player
Risk: Moderate
MLB ETA: 2024

6. Everson Pereira, CF

Hit	Power	SB	Patience	Glove	Overall
40/45	55	55	50	45	50

Born: 04/10/01	Age: 22	Bats: R	Top Production Comp: N/A
Height: 6-0	Weight: 191	Throws: R	

Season	Team	Age	Level	PA	1B	2B	3B	HR	SB	CS	BB%	K%	AVG	OBP	SLG	ISO
2021	NYY	20	A	83	15	5	1	5	4	1	12.05%	25.30%	0.361	0.446	0.667	0.306
2021	NYY	20	A+	127	11	3	0	14	5	2	11.81%	29.92%	0.259	0.354	0.676	0.417
2022	NYY	21	A+	325	51	13	6	9	19	5	10.46%	26.77%	0.274	0.354	0.455	0.181
2022	NYY	21	AA	123	20	4	3	5	2	2	7.32%	30.08%	0.283	0.341	0.504	0.221

Background: One of the club's prized international free agents from a few years back, Pereira hit the grounding running on Day One and he's only been slowed by a nasty outfield collision four years ago. Otherwise, the youngster marches onward. After missing all but 17 games following the crash with the outfield wall in 2019, Pereira re-established his top prospect status during minor league's return from their COVID absence as he slugged .303/.398/.686 in only 49 games between the Complex League, Low-A, and High-A. Last season the 6-foot, 191-pound centerfielder opened the year back up with Hudson Valley for 73 games before moving up to the minors' toughest challenge, Double-A, for the remainder of the year. The former Bonus Baby hit an aggregate .277/.350/.469 with 17 doubles, nine triples, 14 homeruns, and a career best 21 stolen bases (in 30 total attempts). His production line surpassed the league average mark by 22%, per *Weighted Runs Created Plus*.

New York Yankees

Snippet from The 2022 Prospect Digest Handbook: He's never been a groundball hitter, so the power could very well be legitimate. Above-average batted ball data (89 mph average exit velocity with a peak of 108 mph). Good patience. Above-average speed. The lone pock mark is his swing-and-miss rate (29.9% in High-A) is fully in red flag territory. He's a bit miscast as a center fielder, but can fake it for the time being. The K-rates make him risky, but he's only entering his age-21 season.

Scouting Report: Consider the following:

> Since 2006, only three 21-year-old hitters posted a 115 to 125 wRC+ with a strikeout rate between 26% and 28% in any High-A league (min. 300 PA): Bobby Borchering, Mike McDade, and Everson Pereira, who owned the best walk rate among the trio.

As noted in last year's Handbook, Pereira was miscast as a centerfielder and he made it *blatantly* obviously that his future is likely in a corner spot in 2022. Pereira is toolsy, flashing an impressive power / speed combo but he remains raw. He's willing to walk, but his swing-and-miss issues aren't going away any time soon either. Fast hands and can really turn on the inside hard stuff. The ingredients to become a solid average big leaguer are present, but who knows how long it needs to bake, though.

Ceiling: 2.5-win player
Risk: Moderate to High
MLB ETA: 2024

7. Trey Sweeney, SS

Hit	Power	SB	Patience	Glove	Overall
40/45	50	55/40	55	60	50

Born: 04/24/00	Age: 22	Bats: L	Top Comp: N/A
Height: 6-4	Weight: 200	Throws: R	

Season	Team	Age	Level	PA	1B	2B	3B	HR	SB	CS	BB%	K%	AVG	OBP	SLG	ISO
2021	NYY	21	A	129	13	4	4	6	3	1	13.95%	22.48%	0.245	0.357	0.518	0.273
2022	NYY	22	A+	458	58	18	4	14	29	2	12.88%	23.58%	0.241	0.350	0.415	0.174
2022	NYY	22	AA	50	7	1	0	2	2	1	14.00%	20.00%	0.233	0.340	0.395	0.163

Background: For the first time since 2014 and just the second time since 1973 the New York Yankees selected a ballplayer in the summer draft out of Eastern Illinois University in 2021. The lefty-swinging middle-infielder showed consistent, steady progress during his three-year tenure with the Ohio Valley Conference squad, leaving the school as a career .328/.437/.517 hitter with 22 doubles, two triples, 17 homeruns, and seven stolen bases in 117 games. After the Yanks selected him with the 20th overall pick in 2021, Sweeney, who agreed to join the historic franchise for an even $3 million, batted a respectable .246/.357/.518 with four doubles, four triples, six homeruns, and a trio of stolen bases in 30 games with Tampa. Last season, despite his lack of premium opposition in college as well as just logging 30 games in Low-A, the front office sent the Kentucky-born infielder straight up to High-A. And he maintained status quo – at least, for the most part. He batted .241/.350/.415 with 18 doubles, four triples, 14 homeruns, and 29 stolen bases. His overall production with Hudson Valley, per *Weighted Runs Created Plus*, topped the league average mark by 12%. He capped off his first full year as pro with an 11-game stint in Double-A.

Snippet from The 2022 Prospect Digest Handbook: The swing is intriguing: plus bat speed, natural loft, and 15- to 20-homerun power potential. He's likely going to move from short, so he's a man without a position. Sweeney looks like a project, but he could develop into a Hunter Dozier-type.

Scouting Report: Consider the following:

> Since 2006, eight 22-year-old hitters met the following criteria in a High-A season (min. 350 PA): 107 to 117 wRC+, a 22% to 25% whiff rate, and a walk rate of at least 11%. Those eight hitters: Lucas Duda, Riley Adams, Michael Burgess, Mike Papi, Derrick Loveless, Max George, Blake Perkins, and – of course – Trey Sweeney.

Sweeney's glove work far surpassed any modest expectations that were placed on him heading into the draft two years ago. He was downright dazzling on defense. According to Clay Davenport's metrics he was +10 with Hudson Valley and +2 in only 11 games with Somerset. The hit tool is still going to hover somewhere between the 40- and 45-grade, but he shows enough secondary skills (like average power and patience) to help round out a potential starting shortstop resume. He also handled both lefties and righties without showing any concerning platoon splits. He likely won't get a chance to establish himself in New York, so it won't be surprising to see him dangled on the trade block some time in 2023.

Ceiling: 2.0-win player
Risk: Moderate
MLB ETA: 2023/2024

New York Yankees

8. Clayton Beeter, RHP

	FB	CB	SL	CH	Command	Overall
	55	60	60	N/A	50	50

Born: 10/09/98	Age: 23	Bats: R	Top Production Comp: James Karinchak
Height: 6-2	Weight: 220	Throws: R	

Season	Team	Age	Level	IP	TBF	K/9	K%	BB/9	BB%	K-BB%	ERA	FIP	xFIP	Pit/Bat
2021	LAD	22	A+	37.1	151	13.26	36.42%	3.62	9.93%	26.49%	3.13	3.24	3.41	4.12
2021	LAD	22	AA	15.0	62	13.80	37.10%	4.20	11.29%	25.81%	4.20	3.95	3.28	4.19
2022	LAD	23	AA	51.2	244	15.33	36.07%	6.10	14.34%	21.72%	5.75	5.07	4.11	3.81
2022	NYY	23	AA	25.1	104	14.57	39.42%	3.91	10.58%	28.85%	2.13	1.99	2.70	4.13

Background: Last August 2nd closed out one of worst – and, perhaps, saddest – chapters in Yankee history. It marked the end of the Joey Gallo Saga. Going out with a whimper, not a bang, the former 2012 first round pick stumbled through 140 games in New York, cobbling together a .159/.291/.368 slash line with 11 doubles, one triple, 25 homeruns, and a whole lot of boos and frustrated fans. Brian Cashman and Co. turned Gallo's reputation – and not his recent production – into right-hander Clayton Beeter. A product of Texas Tech, the Dodgers drafted the hard-throwing strikeout artist in the second round, 66th overall, three years ago. The 6-foot-2, 220-pound hurler made his professional debut the following spring as he annihilated the Low-A hitters for 23 appearances and recorded an impressive 23-to-7 strikeout-to-walk ratio in 15.0 Double-A innings. Beeter spent the entirety of last season with both organizations' Double-A affiliates, throwing 77.0 innings while averaging a whopping 15.1 strikeouts and 5.4 walks per nine innings to go along with a 4.56 ERA.

Snippet from The 2022 Prospect Digest Handbook: Possesses some of the best pure "stuff" in the entire organization – which is saying something given the Dodgers' lengthy history of pitching development success. There's definite reliever risk, and it remains to be seen whether Beeter can turnover a lineup without a changeup, but the Dodgers develop arms as well as any club.

Scouting Report: Beeter's heater was less fearsome than in previous years. Typically sitting in the mid-90s, the former second rounder was working more in the 92 mph range and reaching back for a few extra clicks when needed – which is a bit of a worrisome given his injury history (Tommy John surgery and a second procedure on his elbow). Combine that along with his lack of heavy workload two years into his professional career, and the hard-throwing righty may be staring down a relief path in the coming years. Last season the Dodgers had Beeter shelve his slider in favor of his filthy curveball. But it appears the Yankees took the restraints off and opened his arsenal back up. Above-average fastball, plus curveball, plus slider. He'll also mix in a *rare* changeup, though I've yet to see it across two seasons. Beeter's an interesting prospect because he just pumps breaking ball after breaking ball, regardless of the count or situation. Curveball shows more 12-6 break and the slider has more horizontal movement. Beeter *really* struggled commanding the strike zone in LA, but seemed to settle considerably in New York. There's #4-type potential with a high probability that he moves into a James Karinchak role.

Ceiling: 1.5- to 2.0-win player
Risk: Moderate to High
MLB ETA: 2023

9. Yoendrys Gomez, RHP

	FB	CB	SL	CH	Command	Overall
	60	50	55	45/50	45/50	50

Born: 10/15/99	Age: 23	Bats: R	Top Production Comp: N/A
Height: 6-3	Weight: 175	Throws: R	

Season	Team	Age	Level	IP	TBF	K/9	K%	BB/9	BB%	K-BB%	ERA	FIP	xFIP	Pit/Bat
2021	NYY	21	A	23.2	96	11.03	30.21%	3.42	9.38%	20.83%	3.42	4.27	3.84	4.24
2022	NYY	22	A+	28.0	113	8.68	23.89%	3.86	10.62%	13.27%	1.93	3.23	4.77	4.23
2022	NYY	22	AA	16.1	68	10.47	27.94%	3.31	8.82%	19.12%	3.86	3.17	4.46	4.12

Background: One of the ball club's more unheralded signings on the international market over the past several seasons. New York signed the 6-foot-3, 175-pound right-hander to a deal worth just $50,000 in early July 2016. Gomez, a native of Nirgua, Venezuela, made his affiliated debut the following summer as he spent time in the foreign and stateside rookie leagues. He spent the next two seasons toiling away in the low levels, including another stint through the Dominican Summer League. And after the minor leagues returned from its COVID absence, Gomez began the 2021 on a high note, averaging 11.0 strikeouts and just 3.4 walks per nine innings through nine brief starts with Tampa. However, his season ended in late July when he was placed on the COVID list – or at least that's what was reported. Reports last February stated he underwent the knife to repair his precious right elbow – a.k.a. Tommy John surgery. Gomez made his way back to the bump in early June for a quick start in the Complex League. He moved on to Hudson Valley for 10 starts before wrapping it up with a four-game cameo with Somerset. He finished his comeback tour with 47.0 innings, recording 49 strikeouts, 18 free passes, and an aggregate 2.49 ERA.

Snippet from The 2022 Prospect Digest Handbook: He's going to have to start making up for lost time in 2022.

Scouting Report: The good news for Gomez (and the Yankees) is that the fastball came back to his pre-injury level. It's explosive and he had no problem missing bats with the plus offering. His slider remains a legitimate lethal weapon that should probably be outlawed in most states. His

New York Yankees

changeup was inconsistent but – rarely – flashed its pre-injury movement and velocity separation. He should have no issues regaining the pitch's consistency as he moves further away from the TJ surgery. Curveball looked good. Gomez is now entering his age-23 season and has yet to throw more than 56.1 innings in any of his five minor league campaigns. If all goes well Gomez should be on target for about 100 innings in 2023, most of which would be spent in Double-A and Triple-A. A late season call up is not out of the question either.

Ceiling: 1.5-win player
Risk: Moderate to High
MLB ETA: 2024

10. Will Warren, RHP

FB	CB	SL	CH	Command	Overall
60	50	55	50	50	45

Born: 06/16/99	Age: 24	Bats: R	Top Production Comp: N/A
Height: 6-2	Weight: 175	Throws: R	

Season	Team	Age	Level	IP	TBF	K/9	K%	BB/9	BB%	K-BB%	ERA	FIP	xFIP	Pit/Bat
2022	NYY	23	A+	35.0	140	10.80	30.00%	2.31	6.43%	23.57%	3.60	2.94	2.84	4.12
2022	NYY	23	AA	94.0	402	7.95	20.65%	3.16	8.21%	12.44%	4.02	4.03	4.21	3.76

Background: For just the second time in club history the Yankees dipped into the ranks at Southeastern Louisiana University and called out a name during the draft. The name: Will Warren, a 6-foot-2, 175-pound right-hander that became the highest drafted Lion in four years. Taken with the 243rd overall pick two years ago, Warren sparkled during his final two seasons at SE Louisiana. And he kept that momentum going during his debut season in 2022 – despite New York's aggressive development plan. Warren didn't throw an affiliated pitch two years ago, but he made the leap directly into High-A without missing a beat. Across eight starts with Hudson Valley, the wiry righty sported a 42-to-9 strikeout-to-walk ratio in 35.0 innings. And that's all it took for the brass to be convinced he was ready for the most challenging minor league level – Double-A. He would make another 18 starts with Somerset, fanning 83 and walking 33 in 94.0 innings. Warren finished the season by averaging 8.7 strikeouts and just 2.9 walks per nine innings to go along with a 3.91 ERA.

Scouting Report: A significantly better arsenal than you'd expect coming for an older-ish college player taken in the mid-rounds of draft. Warren's fastball will show a bit of life as it typically sits in the 94- to 95-mph range, making it a plus offering. His go-to secondary offering is a wipeout, Frisbee-esque slider that sits in the mid-80s. He'll also mix in a big bending, 12-6 curveball (high-70s), and a mid- to upper-80s change with some surprising fade. Solid command, but nothing that's going to allow the repertoire to take another leap forward. There's backend starting material, but it's never going to happen in New York. He's either staring down a relief role or a trade.

Ceiling: 1.0- to 1.5-win player
Risk: Moderate
MLB ETA: 2023

11. Randy Vasquez, RHP

FB	CB	SL	CH	Command	Overall
60	60	50	50	50	45

Born: 11/03/98	Age: 24	Bats: R	Top Production Comp: N/A
Height: 6-0	Weight: 165	Throws: R	

Season	Team	Age	Level	IP	TBF	K/9	K%	BB/9	BB%	K-BB%	ERA	FIP	xFIP	Pit/Bat
2021	NYY	22	A	50.0	212	10.44	27.36%	4.14	10.85%	16.51%	2.34	3.56	3.95	3.98
2021	NYY	22	A+	36.0	145	13.25	36.55%	2.00	5.52%	31.03%	1.75	1.49	2.15	3.61
2021	NYY	22	AA	21.1	97	8.02	19.59%	2.95	7.22%	12.37%	4.22	4.08	4.40	3.59
2022	NYY	23	AA	115.1	496	9.36	24.19%	3.20	8.27%	15.93%	3.90	3.90	4.10	3.90

Background: The odds were stacked against Vasquez from the very beginning. Possessing an undersized 6-foot, 165-pound frame, the Dominican Republic native didn't sign a professional contract until the elderly age of 19-years-old. And, even then, it was for just $10,000 - which, at that point, Vasquez is just signing for hopes-and-dreams and nothing more. Fast forward a handful of seasons, the Navarette native's quietly knocking on the historic franchise's big league door. Vasquez had a breakout season two years ago as he returned from the lost COVID season, spending time with Tampa, Hudson Valley, and Somerset. He tossed a career best 107.1 innings, recording an impressive 130-to-38 strikeout-to-walk ratio across 21 starts and a pair of relief appearances. Last season, after making four starts with the Patriots, the front office bounced the wiry righty back down to the minors' toughest level, Double-A, for a longer look. And he more than held his own. Making a career best 25 starts, Vasquez struck out 120 and walked 41 in 115.1 innings. He finished the year with a 3.90 ERA, a matching 3.90 FIP, and a 4.10 xFIP.

New York Yankees

Scouting Report: Consider the following:

> Since 2006, eleven 23-year-old hurlers met the following criteria in a Double-A season (min. 100 IP): 23% to 25% strikeout percentage with a 7.5% to 9.5% walk percentage. Those eleven hurlers: James McDonald, Eli Morgan, Anthony Ranaudo, Ariel Pena, Austin Gomber, David Parkinson, George Kontos, Jorge Alcala, Nabil Crismatt, Carmen Mlodzinski, and Randy Vasquez.

Similar to Will Warren there's definite big league value to be extracted from Vasquez's right arm, but whether or not that comes with the Yankees – and their large payroll – is an entirely different question. Plus fastball sitting in the 94- to 95-mph range. Average upper 80s slider, same with the changeup. His best offspeed offering – and, perhaps, his best pitch in general – is a sweeping power curveball sitting 82- to 84-mph that bores in on lefties and dives away from right-handers. Average control / command. There's #4 / #5-type potential here. But, again, he'd likely get the opportunity on a rebuilding team like Orioles or Pirates.

Ceiling: 1.0- to 1.5-win player
Risk: Moderate
MLB ETA: 2023

12. Drew Thorpe, RHP

FB	SL	CH	Command	Overall
50	50/55	65	50	45

Born: 10/01/00	Age: 22	Bats: L	Top Production Comp: N/A
Height: 6-4	Weight: 190	Throws: R	

Background: Cal Poly is far from a baseball powerhouse. Prior to the 2022 season, the Big West Conference School was home to just five players taken before the third round since 1988. But right-hander Drew Thorpe teamed with shortstop extraordinaire Brooks Lee to give the squad a pair of high round picks last July. Limited to just four – mostly dominant – starts prior to the COVID shutdown in 2020, Thorpe, a true freshman that season, posted a dominant 31-to-7 strikeout-to-walk ratio in 28.0 innings of work for the Mustangs. The following year the 6-foot-4, 190-pound right-hander continued to show plenty of promise on the mound as he averaged 10.4 strikeouts and 3.8 walks per nine innings across 15 starts and one relief appearance. Thorpe spent time with Team USA and the Yarmouth-Dennis Red Sox that summer. He made three brief appearances for the national squad, fanning 11 and walking just a pair in 8.0 innings of work. The well-traveled Mustang made two dominant starts in the Cape as well, posting a 9-to-3 strikeout-to-walk ratio in 10.0 innings of work. Last season, Thorpe was – simply – one of the most dominant hurlers at the college level. In 15 starts he struck out 149 and walked just 25 in 104.2 innings of work. He compiled a 2.32 ERA while going 10-1. The Yankees selected him in the second round, 61st overall, and signed him for $1,187,600 – roughly the recommended slot bonus.

Scouting Report: Consider the following:

> Since 2015, only three Division I hurlers averaged at least 12.5 strikeouts and between 2.0 and 2.2 walks per nine innings in a season (min. 100 IP): Logan Gilbert, Cooper Hjerpe, and – of course – Drew Thorpe.

Extreme short-arm hurler cut from the same cloth as Lucas Giolito. Thorpe, like Giolito, features a fantastically devastating changeup that's become a genuine swing-and-miss offering. He'll complement the borderline plus-plus offering with a low-90s, average fastball and a slider that may creep into above-average territory as he refines it in the professional ranks. Thorpe has the potential to develop into a solid backend starting option.

Ceiling: 1.0- to 1.5-win player
Risk: Moderate
MLB ETA: 2025

13. Brendan Beck, RHP

FB	CB	SL	CH	Command	Overall
55/60	55	55	55	50	45

Born: 10/06/98	Age: 24	Bats: R	Top Production Comp: N/A
Height: 6-2	Weight: 205	Throws: R	

Background: Prior to the 2022 draft, the Beck brothers, Tristan and Brendan, represented the last two times the Yankees selected a Stanford University prospect. (Note: that changed last summer with the selection of shortstop Brett Barrera, who was taken in the eighth round.) The younger Beck turned in a solid career with the Cardinal, leaving the school with a career 3.11 ERA across 289.1 innings while averaging 9.0 strikeouts and just 2.1 walks per nine innings. The Yankees grabbed the 6-foot-

New York Yankees

2, 205-pound polished right-hander in the second round two years ago, signing the 55th overall pick to a deal just a smidgeon over a million dollars. Unfortunately for Beck and the Yankees, the college ace's elbow started barking and eventually required Tommy John surgery, knocking him out for the entire 2022 season.

Scouting Report: Nothing new to report since Beck hasn't thrown an affiliated / professional pitch in his career. Here's last year's scouting report:

> "Consider the following:
>
> Between 2011 and 2020, there were only ten Division I hurlers that averaged at least 11.5 K/9 and less than 2.5 BB/9 in a season (min. 100 IP): Trevor Bauer, Logan Gilbert, Danny Hultzen, Casey Mize, David Peterson, Nick Sandlin, Adam Scott, Alek Manoah, and Reid Detmers.
>
> An accomplished pitcher cut from a similar cloth as former first rounder Clarke Schmidt. Beck attacks hitters with a lively low-90s fastball that topped 96 mph in a game against Vanderbilt. He throws three above-average offspeed offerings as well: a low-80s slider, a mid-70s curveball, and an underrated, fading changeup. Throw in Beck's propensity for...uh hmmm...throwing strikes, and it's a recipe for some backend starting value. It's a fantastic little under-slot signing by the Yankees."

Ceiling: 1.5-win player
Risk: High
MLB ETA: 2025

14. Roderick Arias, SS

Hit	Power	SB	Patience	Glove	Overall
20/50	40/55	50	50	55	45

Born: 09/09/04	Age: 18	Bats: B	Top Production Comp: N/A
Height: 6-2	Weight: 178	Throws: R	

Season	Team	Age	Level	PA	1B	2B	3B	HR	SB	CS	BB%	K%	AVG	OBP	SLG	ISO
2022	NYY	17	DSL	140	10	6	2	3	10	2	20.00%	32.86%	0.194	0.379	0.370	0.176

Background: Just three years after signing Jasson Dominguez to a massive $5.1 million deal on the international market, the team that used to be known for their limitless spending circled back around and handed Roderick Arias, who was viewed as the top prospect in the class, a hefty $4 million pact last summer. The San Pedro de Macoris, Dominican Republic native made his debut a few months later with the club's foreign rookie league affiliate – though the results were disappointing. He batted a lowly .194/.379/.370 with six doubles, two triples, three homeruns, and 10 stolen bases (in 12 total attempts). Per *Weighted Runs Created Plus*, his overall production still managed to top the league average threshold by a surprising 13%.

Scouting Report: Ignoring the results – at least momentarily – and it's easy to see how Arias would command such a strong bonus on the open market. He plays an up-the-middle position with enough twitch and fluidity to stick at the spot as he matures; he's projectable with speed and power and plenty of bat speed. But the early results were beyond abysmal. He swung-and-missed way too frequently and the bat was nearly not as advanced as originally projected. The swing is quick, but long. The young switch-hitter was significantly better against righties (.243/.440/.473) and lefties (.080/.207/.120). It's doubtful the front office sends their big investment back to the Dominican Summer League, so he's likely moving stateside into the Complex League.

Ceiling: 1.5-win player
Risk: High
MLB ETA: 2026

15. Luis Serna, RHP

FB	CB	SL	CH	Command	Overall
50/55	55	50/55	N/A	50	40

Born: 07/20/04	Age: 18	Bats: R	Top Production Comp: N/A
Height: 5-11	Weight: 162	Throws: R	

Season	Team	Age	Level	IP	TBF	K/9	K%	BB/9	BB%	K-BB%	ERA	FIP	xFIP	Pit/Bat
2021	NYY	16	DSL	40.0	168	10.35	27.38%	3.83	10.12%	17.26%	2.25	3.23	3.62	1.98
2022	NYY	17	CPX	41.1	174	12.19	32.18%	3.70	9.77%	22.41%	1.96	2.86	3.55	2.05

Background: It didn't take long for the Yankees to get the teenage right-hander suited up and on a minor league mound. New York signed the youngster on May 11th, 2021. Two months to the day he was assigned to the Dominican Summer League for his debut. The 5-foot-11, 162-pound right-hander made 12 appearances, 11 of which were starts, for the organization's foreign rookie league affiliate, throwing 40.0 innings with 46 strikeouts and 17 walks to go along with a 2.25 ERA. Last season the front office took the

New York Yankees

cautious approach with the then-17-year-old and sent him to the Complex League. And, once again, Serna shined – brightly. In 10 starts and one relief appearance, he averaged 12.2 K/9 and 3.7 BB/9 in 41.1 innings of work. He finished the year with a 1.96 ERA, 2.86 FIP, and 3.55 xFIP.

Scouting Report: One of the more interesting low level arms in New York's system. Serna already shows an advanced aptitude for the mound. Four-pitch arsenal: an average fastball; an above-average 12-6 bending curveball, a solid-average slider that projects as a 55-grade; and he reportedly throws an average changeup (though I didn't see one). Serna's not overly big – in fact, he's on the smaller side – so he'll have to continually compensate for the lack of size (and maybe velocity). He's a name to watching as he's heads in Low-A competition early in 2023.

Ceiling: 1.5-win player
Risk: High
MLB ETA: 2026

16. Estevan Florial, CF

Hit	Power	SB	Patience	Glove	Overall
20/50	40/55	50	50	55	45

Born: 11/25/97	Age: 25	Bats: L	Top Production Comp: N/A
Height: 6-1	Weight: 195	Throws: R	

Season	Team	Age	Level	PA	1B	2B	3B	HR	SB	CS	BB%	K%	AVG	OBP	SLG	ISO
2021	NYY	23	AA	39	2	2	0	4	0	1	10.26%	23.08%	0.229	0.308	0.629	0.400
2021	NYY	23	AAA	362	37	17	1	13	13	7	11.60%	30.94%	0.218	0.315	0.404	0.186
2022	NYY	24	AAA	461	66	31	2	15	39	10	11.71%	30.37%	0.283	0.368	0.481	0.199

Background: As the sports card world continues to pump hot air into a nearly full capacity party balloon, Florial should serve as yet another cautionary tale on high profile, super-hyped prospects simply not living up to the unrealistic expectations. Back in 2019 Florial *exploded* – almost out of nowhere – to become the *IT* prospect that season. You couldn't turn around without an unfair comparisons being bandied about as he mashed .298/.372/.479 with 23 doubles, seven triples, 13 homeruns, and 23 steals between his time with Tampa and Charleston. Then things started to go sideways for the young Dominican centerfielder. He was limited to just 75 games in High-A the following season as he struggled at the dish, batting a mediocre .255/.354/.361. New York sent him back down to High-A for a do-over in 2019, but the results got worse: he strung together a lowly .237/.297/.383 slash line in another shortened campaign. The 2021 season brought no change in the disappointment as he hit .219/.314/.427 between Somerset and Scranton / Wilkes-Barre. But – finally – Florial's bat emerged during his-age 24-season. Appearing in 101 games with the RailRiders, he slugged .283/.368/.481 with 31 doubles, two triples, 15 homeruns, and a career best 39 stolen bases (in 49 attempts). His overall production topped the league average mark by 24%, as measured by *Weighted Runs Created Plus*. Florial also appeared in 17 big league games as well, hitting a lowly .097/.200/.097.

Scouting Report: Consider the following:

> Since 2006, only two 24-year-old hitters posted a 120 to 130 wRC+ mark with a strikeout rate between 27% to 32% in any Triple-A league (min. 350 PA): Jai Miller and Estevan Florial.

As nice as the production line is, it's important to point out that Florial remains a deathly flawed prospect – even as he's entering his mid-20s. The death knell, and it's *always* been the death knell, is an underwhelming hit tool that's plagued by red flag poppin' strikeout rates. He has a history of struggling against southpaws as well. Average power, above-average speed, and a glove that can handle the position. There's just not enough here to stand on its own as a starter. But he's probably going to continue to get the occasional call up to fill in during an injury crunch.

Ceiling: 1.0-win player
Risk: Moderate
MLB ETA: Debuted in 2020

17. Antonio Gomez, C

Hit	Power	SB	Patience	Glove	Overall
40/45	40/45	30	50	60	40

Born: 11/13/01	Age: 21	Bats: R	Top Production Comp: N/A
Height: 6-2	Weight: 210	Throws: R	

Season	Team	Age	Level	PA	1B	2B	3B	HR	SB	CS	BB%	K%	AVG	OBP	SLG	ISO
2021	NYY	19	CPX	113	18	8	1	2	4	0	14.16%	27.43%	0.305	0.416	0.474	0.168
2021	NYY	19	A	71	8	2	0	2	1	0	14.08%	25.35%	0.197	0.310	0.328	0.131
2022	NYY	20	A	370	62	10	2	8	1	3	9.46%	27.03%	0.252	0.332	0.369	0.117

Background: The front office has invested a lot of early round draft capital into catching over the past several seasons. Former University of Arizona standout Austin Wells was taken with the 28th overall pick in 2020. Two years before that they selected high schooler Anthony Siegler with the 23rd overall pick, and then circled back around and grabbed JuCo slugger Josh Breaux in the second round. And that's not including any high profile international free agents – like Antonio Gomez. The 6-foot-2, 210-pound prospect signed with

New York Yankees

the Yankees for a hefty $600,000 bonus in early July 2018 – though he wouldn't make his affiliated debut until the following summer. Then 17-years-old, it took Gomez just one fantastical Dominican Summer League game (3-for-6 with a double) before the front office was convinced he was ready for the Gulf Coast League. He finished the year with an aggregate .289/.351/.442 showing in 15 games. Once minor league action returned from its COVID vacation, Gomez was sent to the Complex League, but quickly earned a promotion up to Tampa where he would struggle mightily (.197/.310/.328). To the shock of no one, New York sent the young backstop back down to Low-A for a do-over. This time, though, the results were better. Appearing in 89 games with the Tampa Yankees, Gomez hit .252/.332/.369 with 10 doubles, two triples, eight homeruns, and one stolen base (though it took four attempts). His overall production topped the league average mark by 3%, according to *Weighted Runs Created Plus*.

Scouting Report: Consider the following:

> Since 2006, three 20-year-old hitters posted a 98 to 108 wRC+ with an 8% to 11% walk rate and a 25% to 29% strikeout rate in any Low-A league. Those three hitters: Kellin Deglan, Greg Burns, and – of course – Antonio Gomez.

A defensive-minded catcher that's still learning the offensive intricacies of the game. Gomez has consistently graded out between an above-average to plus-defender behind the dish. *Baseball Prospectus'* Catcher Framing Metrics also show him to be well above-average in that facet of the game as well. While his true-calling card maybe with the glove and his ability to work with pitchers, Gomez isn't completely inept with the bat either. The young Venezuelan shows a decent bat and enough power to keep pitchers and defenses honest. And he projects to hit 12 to 15 homeruns in a full season. There's some swing-and-miss to his game, but it's not overly concerning / career damning at this point. He's tracking like a solid backup at the big league level.

Ceiling: 1.0-win player
Risk: Moderate
MLB ETA: 2025

18. Luis Gil, RHP

FB	SL	CH	Command	Overall
70	60	55	35	45

Born: 06/03/98	Age: 25	Bats: R	Top Production Comp: Bryan Abreu
Height: 6-2	Weight: 185	Throws: R	

Season	Team	Age	Level	IP	TBF	K/9	K%	BB/9	BB%	K-BB%	ERA	FIP	xFIP	Pit/Bat
2021	NYY	23	AA	30.2	130	14.67	38.46%	3.82	10.00%	28.46%	2.64	2.37	3.37	4.24
2021	NYY	23	AAA	48.2	212	12.39	31.60%	5.92	15.09%	16.51%	4.81	4.64	4.45	4.01
2022	NYY	24	AAA	21.2	103	12.88	30.10%	6.23	14.56%	15.53%	7.89	6.32	4.78	4.34

Background: Brian Cashman is likely going to wind up in the Hall of Fame, barring any damning revelations. Under his captainship, which is now in its fourth decade, the Yankees have captured four World Series titles, frequent playoff appearances, and numerous pennants. While Cashman's had one of baseball's largest pocketbooks – if not *the* largest – to work with, he's proven to be a savvy trader. Take, for example, the club's acquisition of right-hander Luis Gil. An underrated international free agent signing in early 2015, New York acquired the banged up right-hander from the Twins in exchange for vagabond outfielder Jake Cave, who owns a subpar .235/.297/.411 slash line in 335 big league games. As for Gil, well, he's developed into one of the minors most lethal (and erratic) strikeout artists throughout his six-year professional career. Last season started out like any other year for the hard-throwing right-hander: he struck out a ton of guys (12.9 K/9) and walked a ton of guys (6.2 BB/9) across six starts with Scranton / Wilkes-Barre. And he squeezed in one not-so-great start against the White Sox. But his right elbow started barking in mid-May and he eventually underwent Tommy John surgery and missed the remainder of the year.

Snippet from The 2022 Prospect Digest Handbook: You'll be hard-pressed to find a hurler that (A) generates the velocity and explosion that Gil's fastball has and (B) does it with as little effort as he does. There's definite upper-rotation caliber potential here, but the command has to at least get to a 45-grade.

Scouting Report: Prior to the injury, Gil was to busy showing off one of the best repertoires in the minor leagues. Highlighted by a plus-plus mid- to upper-90s fastball with explosive, late life. His upper-80s slider can be otherworldly when he's throwing it for strikes. And he'll mix an above-average low-90s changeup. After dealing with a shoulder issue earlier in his career, Gil's now added an elbow procedure to his medical resume. By the time he returns to the mound he'll be 26-years-old with 35-grade command. He's headed to a bullpen role where he could be New York's version of Bryan Abreu.

Ceiling: 1.0- to 1.5-win player
Risk: High
MLB ETA: Debuted in 2021

New York Yankees

19. Indigo Diaz, RHP

FB	CB	CH	Command	Overall
65	50	55	40/45	40

Born: 10/14/98	Age: 24	Bats: R	Top Production Comp: N/A
Height: 6-5	Weight: 250	Throws: R	

Season	Team	Age	Level	IP	TBF	K/9	K%	BB/9	BB%	K-BB%	ERA	FIP	xFIP	Pit/Bat
2019	ATL	20	R	10.1	42	13.06	35.71%	1.74	4.76%	30.95%	3.48	1.47	2.04	1.93
2021	ATL	22	A+	27.0	102	18.00	52.94%	2.33	6.86%	46.08%	1.00	0.65	1.61	4.19
2021	ATL	22	AA	18.0	73	14.50	39.73%	4.50	12.33%	27.40%	1.50	2.57	3.37	4.11
2022	ATL	23	AA	49.2	213	11.42	29.58%	5.62	14.55%	15.02%	3.08	4.27	5.37	4.08

Background: There were few, if any, pitchers that popped quite like Diaz did in 2021, going from a 27th round afterthought to averaging more than 16 strikeouts per nine innings between High-A and Double-A just two years later. POP! The Braves unearthed the strikeout artist after a rollercoaster season at Michigan State University. The burly reliever posted a 51-to-29 strikeout-to-walk ratio in 44.0 innings of work across 25 games, 19 of which were bullpen appearances. As soon as Diaz donned a Braves affiliate jersey he shredded the competition. The 6-foot-5, 250-pound righty struck out 15 and walked just a pair in 10.1 innings in the Gulf Coast League during his debut. And that provide to be just the appetizer to the 2021 main course. Diaz split the season between Rome and Mississippi, averaging an unfathomable 16.6 strikeouts and just 3.2 walks per nine innings. The front office sent the hard-throwing right-hander back to Mississippi for additional seasoning. He would make a career best 49 appearances, throwing 49.2 innings with 63 whiffs and 31 free passes. He finished the year with a 3.08 ERA, a 4.27 FIP, and a 5.37 xFIP. For his career, Diaz is averaging 13.8 strikeouts and 4.2 walks every nine innings. The Yankees acquired Diaz, along with Caleb Durbin, this offseason for lefty reliever Lucas Luetge.

Snippet from The 2022 Prospect Digest Handbook: Hitters looked very, very uncomfortable squaring off against the behemoth right-hander. He's the type of guy that will shine bright, but burnout quickly – unfortunately.

Scouting Report: Heavy mid-90s fastball that particularly difficult when he's elevating it above the belt – which is often. Diaz complements the plus offering with his average-ish curveball. But, surprisingly, the hefty righty added a viable third option: an upper-80s changeup, which actually grades out better than his breaking ball. Diaz is going to inevitably log several years of innings at the big league level before all is said and done. But he's going to be supernova, burning brightly before burning out.

Ceiling: 1.0-win player
Risk: Moderate
MLB ETA: 2023

20. Trystan Vrieling, RHP

FB	CB	SL	CH	Command	Overall
55	55	55	N/A	40	40

Born: 10/02/00	Age: 22	Bats: R	Top Production Comp: N/A
Height: 6-4	Weight: 200	Throws: R	

Background: During last July's draft New York started down the collegiate route and never looked back as they stuck to all four-year or junior college players. The third of those players chosen was Trystan Vrieling, a 6-foot-4, 200-pound right-hander out of Gonzaga University. A product of Kamiakin High School, Vrieling left his prep career on a high note as he tallied a 0.56 ERA with 63 punch outs in 55.0 innings of work. But the big righty stumbled early in his collegiate career as he walked (8) more than he struck out (5) during the COVID-capped 2020 season. He spent the following year mostly working out of the Bulldogs' bullpen, throwing 48.2 innings while averaging 12.2 K/9 and 3.5 BB/9. After a successful jaunt through the Cape Cod League that summer, Vrieling transitioned into a full time starter as junior. And the results were largely mixed. In a career best 80.2 innings, he struck out a bunch (107), walked a bunch (46), and tallied the highest ERA of his career (4.91). The Yankees selected him in the third round, 100th overall, and singed him to a deal worth $608,900.

Scouting Report: Vrieling's fastball sits in the 92- to 94-mph range. He'll mix in a pair of above-average breaking balls: a low 80s curveball and a mid- to upper-80s slider / cutter with the latter flashing plus at times. Reports indicate he'll also throw a rare below-average changeup (though I didn't see one). In terms of arsenal, the slider / cutter is going to be the important pitch for Vrieling. His control / command regressed as he moved into the rotation. He looks like an organizational arm at this point – unless the player development engine can unlock some more velocity or some type of command consistency.

Ceiling: 0.5- to 1.0-win player
Risk: Moderate
MLB ETA: 2025

Oakland Athletics

Top Prospects

Oakland Athletics

1. Tyler Soderstrom, C/1B

Hit	Power	SB	Patience	Glove	Overall
50/55	60	30	50	45	60

Born: 11/24/01	Age: 21	Bats: L	Top Production Comp: Paul Konerko
Height: 6-2	Weight: 200	Throws: R	

Season	Team	Age	Level	PA	1B	2B	3B	HR	SB	CS	BB%	K%	AVG	OBP	SLG	ISO
2021	OAK	19	A	254	35	20	1	12	2	1	10.63%	24.02%	0.306	0.390	0.568	0.261
2022	OAK	20	A+	371	45	19	3	20	0	0	7.82%	26.68%	0.260	0.323	0.513	0.254
2022	OAK	20	AA	147	26	1	2	8	0	1	6.80%	22.45%	0.278	0.327	0.496	0.218
2022	OAK	20	AAA	38	9	1	0	1	0	0	2.63%	34.21%	0.297	0.316	0.405	0.108

Background: The opening round of the 1993 draft proved to be loaded with a bevy of eventual big league superstars like Alex Rodriguez, Billy Wagner, Torii Hunter, Derek Lee, Chris Carpenter, and Jason Varitek. And there were several notable prospects that turned in long, productive big league careers too, such as Trot Nixon, Brian Anderson, Jamey Wright, and Darren Dreifort (who earned a higher bonus than A-Rod, by the way). But Tyler Soderstrom's dad, Steve, only earned a brief, three-game cup of big league coffee – despite being the sixth overall pick. The younger Soderstrom, though, is proving to be a significantly superior prospect – despite hearing his name called 20 selections later. A product of Turlock High School, home to the Bulldogs, Soderstrom ripped through the Low-A competition during his injury-abbreviated debut in 2021. He would mash .306/.390/.568 with 20 doubles, one triple, and 12 homeruns in only 57 games. His overall production with Stockton that year topped the league average threshold by a whopping 45%, per *Weighted Runs Created Plus*. And that, truly, proved to be a harbinger of things to come. Oakland bumped their prized youngster up to High-A to begin the 2022 season, but after hitting .260/.323/.513 through 89 games, the front office deemed him ready for the minors' toughest challenge – Double-A. And he was. Soderstrom's stint with Midland lasted just 36 games before moving on to Triple-A for a nine-game cameo with Las Vegas. Overall, the 6-foot-2, 200-pound catcher / first baseman slugged .267/.324/.501 with 21 doubles, five homeruns, and 29 stolen bases. His overall production topped the league average mark by 16%. And his 29 dingers tied for the 19th highest total among all minor league bats.

Snippet from The 2022 Prospect Digest Handbook: It's concerning – needless to say – that a 19-year-old missed considerable time with a back injury, so hopefully that doesn't impact his future greatly. Defensively, he's a first baseman feigning the ability to play catcher. In terms of offensive upside, think .300/.380/.540.

Scouting Report: With regard to his longest stint last season (High-A), consider the following:

> Since 2006, only three 20-year-old hitters posted a wRC+ between 120 and 130 with a 6% to 9% walk rate and a strikeout rate north of 25% in High-A (min. 350 PA): Tyler O'Neill (who's been a well above average big league hitter in his career), Brewers prospect Mario Feliciano, and – of course – Tyler Soderstrom.

If Billy Beane himself created a young prospect he might resemble something like Soderstrom. Tall, lean, muscular, lefty-swinging part-time catcher and first baseman. Strong bloodlines. Tremendous raw power, something close to plus-plus. Soderstrom might have the fastest bat in the minor leagues. It's explosive. It's the type that can barrel up elite velocity with ease. Last season the former Bonus Baby struggled against southpaws for the first time in his professional career, though it's not a long term concern. Soderstrom is still posing as a catcher, at least part time, but his eventual full time position will be first base. He's a genuine middle-of-the-lineup, future cornerstone bat in the making. In terms of big league ceiling, think: .280/.340/.500. If his defense at the bag hovers around league average, he has a chance to be a perennial All-Star caliber player.

Ceiling: 4.0-win player
Risk: Moderate
MLB ETA: 2023

2. Freddy Tarnok, RHP

FB	CB	SL	CH	Command	Overall
60	60	55	50	45/50	55

Born: 11/24/98	Age: 24	Bats: R	Top Production Comp: Lance McCullers Jr.
Height: 6-3	Weight: 185	Throws: R	

Season	Team	Age	Level	IP	TBF	K/9	K%	BB/9	BB%	K-BB%	ERA	FIP	xFIP	Pit/Bat
2021	ATL	22	A+	28.1	118	15.25	40.68%	4.13	11.02%	29.66%	4.76	4.72	3.72	4.21
2021	ATL	22	AA	45.0	181	12.20	33.70%	3.00	8.29%	25.41%	2.60	2.27	3.45	4.20
2022	ATL	23	AA	62.2	270	10.77	27.78%	3.88	10.00%	17.78%	4.31	4.28	4.68	4.23
2022	ATL	23	AAA	44.0	186	10.02	26.34%	3.48	9.14%	17.20%	3.68	4.64	4.38	4.56

Background: After dangling the club's last big trade chip on the market for seemingly forever, Oakland's brass – finally – found a deal they liked. It just took two other organizations to get it done. In mid-December the A's, Braves, and Brewers got together on a massive nine-player swap. The actual specifics of the deal are as follows: Atlanta acquired Gold Glove-winning backstop Sean Murphy; Milwaukee acquired William Contreras, Joel Payamps, and Justin Yeager; and Oakland received Freddy Tarnok, Royber Salinas, Kyle Muller, Manny Pina, and Esteury Ruiz. Tarnok, a wiry 6-foot-3, 185-pound right-hander, is the best among the large quantity of players Oakland received. Originally taken in the

Oakland Athletics

third round of the 2017 draft, Tarnok quietly put together a breakout – albeit abbreviated – campaign in 2021. He averaged 13.4 strikeouts and 3.4 walks per nine innings across 16 appearances between the organization's High-A and Double-A affiliates. Last season the Florida-born hurler split time between Double-A and Triple-A, throwing a career best 106.2 innings with 124 punch outs and 44 free passes to go along with a 4.05 ERA and a 4.43 FIP. Tarnok made one brief appearance against the New York Metropolitans as well.

Snippet from The 2022 Prospect Digest Handbook: Steady progress for the young right-hander, so much so, that he may have one of the more underrated repertoire / ceiling's among all minor league arms. When he was drafted Tarnok showed a solid feel for the strike zone with a couple pitches that projected to be 55-grade offerings. Last season Tarnok's weaponry was blowing the doors off the competition. There's legitimate #2/#3-type potential here. If you're not on the bandwagon yet, it's probably too late. The lone red flag: he's only surpassed 80 innings once his professional career (2019, 106.0 IP).

Scouting Report: Consider the following:

> Since 2006, only four 23-year-old hurlers posted a 25.5% to 27.5% strikeout percentage with an 8% to 10% walk percentage in any Triple-A league (min. 40 IP): Cade Cavalli, Zack Littell, Allen Webster, and Freddy Tarnok.

Tarnok remains (A) one of my favorite pitching prospects in all the minor leagues *and* (B) one of the most underrated prospects in all the minors, as well. A repertoire that screams mid-rotation, maybe even a true #2, potential. Tarnok hurls a borderline plus-plus fastball, hovering in the 96- to 97-mph range. His curveball is an absolute 12-6 hammer, adding a second true swing-and-miss pitch. Mid-80s above-average slider. And a workably decent changeup. The command wavers between a 45- and 50-grade skill. It's mind blowing that Tarnok isn't a consensus Top 100 prospect. Barring any injury concerns, he's going to be able to slide right into Oakland's #3 spot in the rotation. Love, love, love Tarnok and his underrated, underappreciated potential.

Ceiling: 3.5-win player
Risk: Moderate
MLB ETA: 2022

3. Ken Waldichuk, LHP

FB	CB	SL	CH	Command	Overall
60	50	55	50	45	55

Born: 01/08/98	Age: 25	Bats: L	Top Production Comp: Nick Pivetta
Height: 6-4	Weight: 220	Throws: L	

Season	Team	Age	Level	IP	TBF	K/9	K%	BB/9	BB%	K-BB%	ERA	FIP	xFIP	Pit/Bat
2021	NYY	23	A+	30.2	113	16.14	48.67%	3.82	11.50%	37.17%	0.00	1.45	2.59	4.29
2021	NYY	23	AA	79.1	340	12.25	31.76%	4.31	11.18%	20.59%	4.20	4.59	4.02	4.07
2022	NYY	24	AA	28.2	112	14.44	41.07%	3.14	8.93%	32.14%	1.26	2.26	2.44	3.97
2022	NYY	24	AAA	47.2	206	13.22	33.98%	4.34	11.17%	22.82%	3.59	3.82	3.92	4.19
2022	OAK	24	AAA	18.2	79	10.12	26.58%	1.45	3.80%	22.78%	3.37	4.34	4.20	4.08

Background: As part of the club's continued rebuilding efforts, the front office dealt away right-hander Frankie Montas, one of their largest remaining trade chips, in early August last summer. It ended up being a two-for-four deal with the Yankees as Oakland acquired pitchers Ken Waldichuk, Luis Medina, J.P. Sears, and infielder Cooper Bowman in exchange for Lou Trivino and Montas. Originally drafted in the fifth round in 2019 out of Saint Mary's College of California, which has quietly become a haven for pitching prospects, Waldichuk turned in – arguably – the most dominant debut in the entire class. He would make 10 brief starts for New York's Appalachian League affiliate, posting an absurd 49-to-7 strikeout-to-walk ratio in only 29.1 innings of work. Once baseball returned from its COVID absence, Waldichuk shredded High-A hitters across seven unhittable starts (30.2 IP, 0.00 ERA, 55 K, and 13 BB) and settled in comfortably for 16 more appearances in the minors' toughest level – Double-A. Last season the 6-foot-4, 220-pound southpaw made six more starts in AA and another 11 in Triple-A before settling in Oakland for seven late-season guest appearances. Waldichuk finished his minor league season with 95.0 innings, 137 strikeouts, just 36 walks and a 2.84 ERA. He would throw another 34.2 innings in the big leagues, averaging 8.6 strikeouts and 2.6 walks nine innings.

Snippet from The 2022 Prospect Digest Handbook: There's some funk in his delivery that causes some inconsistencies with his release point. He's going to have one helluva time trying to crack New York's rotation, though.

Scouting Report: Consider the following:

> Since 2006, only four 24-year-old hurlers posted a strikeout percentage north of 30% and a walk percentage between 8% and 11% in Triple-A (min. 60 IP): Adbert Alzolay, Jackson Kowar, Ryan Pepiot, and Ken Waldichuk.

There's long arm actions. And then there's Ken Waldichuk's looooong arm action. It's brutal to watch and it's never going to allow the hard-throwing left-hander's command to spill over into average territory. But it does allow for some deception. Waldichuk will run his heater upwards of 96 mph with some extra giddy up above the belt. His go-to offspeed pitch is an above-average slider that's particularly filthy for

Oakland Athletics

right-handers when he's locating down and in. He'll vary the break and velocity on the offering, throwing it anywhere between 79 mph and 84 mph. What makes the offering so potent is that its spin mirrors that of his fastball. Waldichuk will also mix in a solid average changeup and a rare curveball. He has a serious propensity for missing bats, but his 45-grade command will keep him from ascending towards the front of a rotation. He should be a lock for Oakland's #3 / #4 spot for the next four or five years.

Ceiling: 3.0- to 3.5-win player
Risk: Moderate
MLB ETA: Debuted in 2022

4. Daniel Susac, C

Hit	Power	SB	Patience	Glove	Overall
50	50	30	45	50	55

Born: 05/14/01	Age: 22	Bats: R	Top Production Comp: N/A
Height: 6-4	Weight: 218	Throws: R	

Season	Team	Age	Level	PA	1B	2B	3B	HR	SB	CS	BB%	K%	AVG	OBP	SLG	ISO
2022	OAK	21	A	107	20	7	0	1	0	0	6.54%	23.36%	0.286	0.346	0.388	0.102

Background: Taking a page out of the Jung Brothers' playbook, Susac's following in *his brother's* footsteps as a top prospect. Originally a product out of Jesuit High School – home to Andrew Susac (of course), Lars Anderson, and J.P. Howell – the young backstop was a standout two-sport athlete during his teenage years, starring on the diamond and the gridiron for the California-based school. A 6-foot-4, 218-pound prospect, Susac was an offensive dynamo during his freshman season at the University of Arizona, slugging a scorching .335/.393/.591 with 24 doubles, one triple, and 12 homeruns in 61 games for the Pac-12 powerhouse. He spent the ensuing summer playing for Team USA, compiling .273/.273/.318 slash line in nine games (including seven starts). Last season the Wildcat's star upped the ante even further. In a career best 64 games, Susac batted .366/.430/.582 with 19 doubles, two triples, and 12 homeruns – earning him a bevy of awards, including:

> #1. *Perfect Game* Second Team All-American
> #2. *NCBWA* Second Team All-American
> #3. *ACBA* First Team West All-Region
> #4. *Coral Cables NCAA* Regional All-Tournament Team
> #5. *Collegiate Baseball* Second Team All-American
> #6. Pac-12 All-Conference
> #7. Golden Spike Award Semifinalist
> #8. Dick Howser Trophy Semifinalist

Oakland selected the star catcher in the opening round, 19th overall, and signed him to a deal worth a $3,531,200 – the recommended slot bonus. Once signed, Susac did a two-game cameo in the Complex League before spending the rest of the season in Low-A. He would hit a rock solid .286/.346/.388 in 25 games with the Stockton Ports.

Scouting Report: Per the usual, my pre-draft write-up:

> *"Consider the following:*
>
> *Since 2011, only two Pac-12 hitters posted a .360/.425/.575 slash line with a single-digit walk rate in a season (min. 275 PA): J.J. Matijevic and – of course – Andrew Susac.*
>
> *Plenty of natural loft and strength to jolt 20 homeruns a year in the professional ranks. The problem with Susac is that his swing tends to get a bit long at times. He loves the ball low, so he can elevate it. He may struggle with pitches at the top of the zone. Solid defensive contributor who can help control the run game. Susac doesn't figure to be a star at the big league level, he but should have no problem carving out a lengthy career as a better than average backstop."*

Ceiling: 3.0-win player
Risk: Moderate
MLB ETA: 2024

Oakland Athletics

5. Zack Gelof, 3B

Hit	Power	SB	Patience	Glove	Overall
55	45/50	50	55	45/50	55

Born: 10/19/99	Age: 23	Bats: R	Top Production Comp: Chris Taylor
Height: 6-3	Weight: 205	Throws: R	

Season	Team	Age	Level	PA	1B	2B	3B	HR	SB	CS	BB%	K%	AVG	OBP	SLG	ISO
2021	OAK	21	A	145	21	8	1	7	11	2	13.10%	24.83%	0.298	0.393	0.548	0.250
2021	OAK	21	AAA	13	6	1	0	0	0	0	7.69%	15.38%	0.583	0.615	0.667	0.083
2022	OAK	22	AA	402	65	16	2	13	9	2	11.69%	27.36%	0.271	0.356	0.438	0.167
2022	OAK	22	AAA	38	3	1	0	5	1	0	7.89%	28.95%	0.257	0.316	0.714	0.457

Background: The Oakland franchise went nearly three full decades in between selecting college-aged third baseman in the second round. All the way back in 1992 the A's, captained by Sandy Alderson, drafted Long Beach slugger Jason Giambi, then a third baseman, with the 58th overall pick. Giambi, of course, would go to have a borderline Hall of Fame career – though one not without drama. Twenty-nine years later, under the guidance of David Forst, the ball club snagged University of Virginia star Zack Gelof with the 60th overall pick. A career .316/.396/.478 hitter over three seasons with the Cavaliers, Gelof not only established himself as one of the better value picks in the 2021 draft, but also one of the better college bats as well. The young third baseman mashed .298/.393/.548 with eight doubles, one triple, and seven homeruns in just 32 games with the Stockton Ports during professional debut. And his performance last season only further solidified his status as a prospect. Opening the year up in Double-A, the minors' toughest challenge and just 36 total games removed from college competition, Gelof slugged a rock solid .271/.356/.438 with 16 doubles, two triples, 13 homeruns, and nine stolen bases (in 11 total attempts). His production with the RockHounds, according to *Weighted Runs Created Plus*, topped the league average mark by 5%. The former second rounder spent the last handful of games (successfully) squaring off against Triple-A pitching. Gelof appeared in 19 games with the Mesa Solar Sox in the Arizona Fall League following the season, hitting a meager .211/.296/.324.

Snippet from The 2022 Prospect Digest Handbook: The Athletics have a history of developing these type of under-the-radar players and tapping into more power than expected.

Scouting Report: Consider the following:

> Since 2006, only two 22-year-old hitters posted a 100 to 110 wRC+ with a 10.5% to 12.5% walk percentage and a strikeout percentage north of 25% in Double-A (min. 350 PA): John Tolisano and Zack Gelof.

So there are two stories to Gelof's first full season in professional ball: #1 pre-torn labrum in his left shoulder and #2 post-torn labrum in his left shoulder – an injury suffered during a dive attempt in late May. And, as expected, the pre-injury production is *significantly* better than the post-injury production. From Opening Day through May 26th, the second / third baseman slugged .316/.372/.458. But after he returned to action on July 15th through the rest of the year, he hit a meager .235/.339/.466. Gelof hasn't fully tapped into his power just yet, but there's some sneaky raw thump. He has a knack for first base, shows an above-average hit tool, and runs well. He's still rough around the edges on the defensive side of things, but should be serviceable with some fine tuning. In terms of big league ceiling, think .290/.355/.440.

Ceiling: 3.0-win player
Risk: Moderate
MLB ETA: 2023

6. Max Muncy, SS

Hit	Power	SB	Patience	Glove	Overall
35/45	50/55	50	50	50	55

Born: 08/25/02	Age: 20	Bats: R	Top Production Comp: N/A
Height: 6-1	Weight: 180	Throws: R	

Season	Team	Age	Level	PA	1B	2B	3B	HR	SB	CS	BB%	K%	AVG	OBP	SLG	ISO
2021	OAK	18	CPX	34	4	0	0	0	1	0	8.82%	35.29%	0.129	0.206	0.129	0.000
2022	OAK	19	A	365	37	16	1	16	6	5	13.97%	29.86%	0.230	0.352	0.447	0.217
2022	OAK	19	A+	190	21	12	2	3	13	3	9.47%	31.58%	0.226	0.305	0.375	0.149

Background: Unbelievably – or, perhaps not, due to the nature of the organization – but the Athletics have selected just five high school shortstops in the first round in the franchise's storied history: Chet Lemon, who would go on to have a borderline Hall of Fame career, in 1972; Juan Bustbad, who was taken directly in front of Andy Van Slyke, with the fifth overall pick in 1979; Addison Russell and Daniel Robertson, both drafted in 2012; and – of course – Max Muncy. Not to be confused with Oakland's 2012 fifth round pick that happens to share the same name *and* birthdate, the A's snagged the promising prep player in the opening round, 25th overall, out of Thousand Oaks High School two years ago. Muncy would appear in 11 Complex League games that summer, compiling a lowly .129/.206/.129 slash line. Last season, despite the lack of experience, the front office pushed the former *Bonus Baby* up to Stockton to begin the year. Muncy responded with a .230/.325/.447 slash line in 81 games. He was promoted up to High-A in late July for his final 41 games of the year (.226/.305/.375). The 6-foot-1, 180-pound infielder hit an aggregate .229/.336/.422 with 28 doubles, three triples, 19 homers, and 19 stolen bases. His production, per *Weighted Runs Created Plus*, topped the league average threshold by 1%.

Oakland Athletics

Snippet from The 2022 Prospect Digest Handbook: A natural born shortstop who (A) should have no problem sticking at the position and (B) shows a little bit of flair for the dramatic. Strong arm, but not elite. He'll make all the throws – accurately. Surprising pop for a wiry, thin-framed middle infielder. He projects to add some strength as he matures. Muncy shows a willingness to shoot the ball to the opposite field with his in-and-out swing and approach at the plate. He's not going to be a star, but he should settle in nicely at the big league level.

Scouting Report: Consider the following:

> Since 2006, only four 19-year-old hitters met the following criteria in Low-A (min. 350 PA): 100 to 110 wRC+, a walk rate north of 12%, and a strikeout rate above 28%. Those four hitters: Wes Kath, Brandon Howlett, Maikol Escotto, and – of course – Max Muncy.

Muncy ticks off quite a few of the important checkboxes. Not only does he play a premium defensive position, but he also *projects* to remain at that spot. He shows an advanced approach at the plate. The former Thousand Oaks star packs a surprising punch. And he runs better than most. The problem, however, is quite clear: will the former first rounder make enough consistent contact to take advantage of his well-rounded toolkit? In short: Yes, it's just going to take time. Muncy shows a simple approach at the plate, short quick swing with good torque. And despite the gaudy strikeout rate hovering in the 30% range, he displayed promising ability to (A) lay off of offspeed pitches out of the zone and (B) adjust mid-pitch on secondary offerings. There's a lot of similar offensive traits as Orioles standout rookie Gunnar Henderson. Muncy has a .245/.330/.450-type offensive ceiling with solid defense.

Ceiling: 3.0-win player
Risk: Moderate
MLB ETA: 2024

7. Kyle Muller, LHP

FB	CB	SL	CH	Command	Overall
55	55	55	50	50	50

Born: 10/07/97 **Age:** 25 **Bats:** R **Top Production Comp:** Sean Newcomb
Height: 6-7 **Weight:** 250 **Throws:** L

Season	Team	Age	Level	IP	TBF	K/9	K%	BB/9	BB%	K-BB%	ERA	FIP	xFIP	Pit/Bat
2021	ATL	23	AAA	79.2	345	10.51	26.96%	4.74	12.17%	14.78%	3.39	4.12	4.30	4.10
2022	ATL	24	AAA	134.2	542	10.63	29.34%	2.67	7.38%	21.96%	3.41	3.52	3.49	3.89

Background: A part of the multitude of players Oakland received in the three-team deal that involved Gold Glove-winning backstop Sean Murphy going to Atlanta. Muller was part of the Braves' trio of high schoolers selected atop the 2016 draft class, falling behind Ian Anderson and Joey Wentz. The 6-foot-7, 250-pound southpaw has been a mainstay among some publications Top 100 Prospect Lists since entering pro ball. Muller spent last season bouncing between the Gwinnett Stripers (Triple-A) and Atlanta. He tossed 134.2 innings in the minor leagues, recording an impressive 159-to-40 strikeout-to-walk ratio to go along with a 3.41 ERA. He made three big league starts spread across the length of the season as well, throwing another 12.1 innings with 12 punch outs and eight free passes. For his minor league career, he's averaging 9.8 punch outs and 3.8 walks per nine innings with a 3.18 ERA.

Snippet from The 2022 Prospect Digest Handbook: Muller has a chance to be a viable league average starting pitcher. But there's a lot more in the tank he can somehow figure out how to get his walk rate under 4.0 BB/9.

Scouting Report: Consider the following:

> Since 2006, only two 24-yer-old hurlers posted a strikeout percentage between 27% and 31% with a walk percentage between 6% and 9% in any Triple-A league (min. 100 IP): J.P. Howell and Kyle Muller.

Muller's rookie eligibility remained intact – by one single inning. Seemingly always a work in progress, the big lefty's command improved by leaps-and-bounds during his sixth professional season, going from a 40-grade skill all the way up to average. Equally important, as well, is the progress his changeup, which was always lagging, showed as well. Above-average fastball, curveball, and slider. It's the foundation for a league average hurler, maybe a tick better if he can chew up 200 or more innings in a season.

Ceiling: 2.5-win player
Risk: Moderate
MLB ETA: Debuted in 2021

Oakland Athletics

8. Esteury Ruiz, OF

	Hit	Power	SB	Patience	Glove	Overall
	50	45	70	50	50	50

Born: 02/15/99	Age: 24	Bats: R	Top Production Comp: Chone Figgins
Height: 6-0	Weight: 169	Throws: R	

Season	Team	Age	Level	PA	1B	2B	3B	HR	SB	CS	BB%	K%	AVG	OBP	SLG	ISO
2021	SDP	22	AA	353	49	16	2	10	36	7	7.93%	20.68%	0.249	0.328	0.411	0.162
2022	SDP	23	AA	232	34	17	2	9	37	5	13.79%	17.24%	0.344	0.474	0.611	0.267
2022	SDP	23	AAA	142	25	6	0	4	23	4	14.08%	17.61%	0.315	0.457	0.477	0.162
2022	MIL	23	AAA	167	35	10	0	3	25	5	8.38%	17.37%	0.329	0.402	0.459	0.130

Background: It was the most criticized move near the trade deadline last summer – especially for an organization with playoff aspirations. But the Brewers shipped off four-time All-Star closer Josh Hader, theoretically still in his prime, to the Padres for fellow veteran lefty reliever Taylor Rogers, 2021 second rounder Robert Gasser, outfielder Esteury Ruiz, and right-hander Dinelson Lamet, who was claimed off waiver by the Rockies just four days after the big deal. A native of Azua, Dominican Republic, Ruiz began his professional career in impressive fashion, slugging .313/.378/.512 in the foreign rookie league in 2016 and promptly following that up with a .350/.395/.602 slash line in the Arizona Summer League the following season. The 6-foot, 169-pound former infielder / outfielder continued to show offensive promise as he moved into the Midwest League in 2018, batting a respectable .253/.324/.403 as a 19-year-old. From there, though, Ruiz struggled over his next few seasons in the Padres' organization as he moved up to High-A and Double-A. Last season, though, the young Dominican prospect – now 23-years-old – rediscovered whatever magic he showed in early parts of his career. Splitting time between Double-A and Triple-A in both organizations, Ruiz mashed an aggregate .332/.447/.526 with career highs in doubles (33), homeruns (16), and stolen bases (85). His overall production, as measured by *Weighted Runs Created Plus*, was a whopping 56% better than league average threshold. He also split time at the big league level as well, batting a lowly .171/.194/.257 in 17 games with Milwaukee and San Diego. Oakland acquired Ruiz as part of the Sean Murphy swap with the Brewers and Braves this offseason.

Snippet from The 2022 Prospect Digest Handbook: That's what Esteury Ruiz is – a stat-sheeting stuffing infielder / outfielder. Ruiz has an impressive toolkit – or at least, an interesting one. His versatility adds a bit of value, some hope that he carves out a big league bench option.

Scouting Report: Consider the following:

> Since 2006, only four 23-year-old hitters posted a 135 to 145 wRC+ with a strikeout rate between 16% and 19% and a double-digit walk rate (min. 300 PA): Joey Votto, Shin-Soo Choo, Marcus Semien, and – of course – Esteury Ruiz. Four those counting at home: Votto owns a career 146 wRC+ and should eventually get into the Hall of Fame; Choo finished his career with a 123 wRC+ mark, and Semien, owner of a massive new deal from the Rangers, has topped the league average mark by 9%.

The minor league leader in stolen bases by a wide margin (he swiped 14 more than runner up Luis Valdez), Ruiz is – clearly – a plus-plus runner. But he complements his speed with a solid approach at the plate, including a willingness to get on base via the walk and his concerning strikeout rates earlier in his career continue to move further in the rearview mirror. There's not a lot of homerun potential – or projection – at this point. In terms of big league upside, think: .270/.330/.415 with 25 stolen bases.

Ceiling: 2.0-win player
Risk: Low to Moderate
MLB ETA: Debuted in 2022

9. Jordan Diaz, 1B/2B/3B

	Hit	Power	SB	Patience	Glove	Overall
	55	50	30	45	45/50	50

Born: 08/13/00	Age: 22	Bats: R	Top Production Comp: N/A
Height: 5-10	Weight: 175	Throws: R	

Season	Team	Age	Level	PA	1B	2B	3B	HR	SB	CS	BB%	K%	AVG	OBP	SLG	ISO
2021	OAK	20	A+	365	58	24	1	13	2	3	6.85%	15.89%	0.288	0.337	0.483	0.195
2022	OAK	21	AA	407	80	26	0	15	0	0	5.41%	14.99%	0.319	0.361	0.507	0.187
2022	OAK	21	AAA	120	26	8	1	4	0	0	5.00%	12.50%	0.348	0.383	0.545	0.196

Background: Not only did Diaz put together one of the best – if not *the best* – season in Oakland's farm system in 2022, but his production ranks among the game's best prospects as well. A slow, methodically moving trek through the first four years of his professional career, Diaz spent parts of three seasons in the foreign and stateside rookie leagues. He would spend the entirety of 2019 squaring off against the New York-Penn League, hitting a mediocre .264/.307/.430 in 70 games with the Vermont Lake Monsters. And after minor league baseball returned from its COVID-induced absence, the 5-foot-10, 175-pound corner infielder / outfielder turn in his best performance to date in High-A two years ago, slugging .288/.337/.484 with 24 doubles, one triple, and 13 homeruns in just 90 games with the Lansing Lugnuts. But nothing would have suggested that the Monteria, Colombia, native was on the precipice of an

Oakland Athletics

offensive explosion. In 120 combined games with Midland and Las Vegas, Diaz mashed an aggregate .326/.366/.515 with career highs in doubles (34) and homeruns (19). His production for the year, according to *Weighted Runs Created Plus*, topped the league average by 22%

Snippet from The 2022 Prospect Digest Handbook: Oakland tends to get a ton of value out of their fringy hitting prospects, so it wouldn't be surprising to look up and see Diaz as a competent big league bat in a couple years.

Scouting Report: Consider the following:

> Since 2006, only two 21-year-old hitters posted a 115 to 125 wRC+ with a 4.5% to 6.5% walk rate and a 14% to 18% strikeout rate in Double-A (min. 350 PA): Randal Grichuk and Jordan Diaz.

It's almost too easy to slap the "*Professional Hitter*" label on Diaz, but it fits oh-so-well. Despite being underrated for his entire professional career – some of that due to size or lack of projection or position or defensive shortcomings – but Diaz has been a remarkably consistent bat at each stop along the way. Good bat speed, but not great. Average power, but not noteworthy. But he shows an incredible knack of consistently putting the ball in play. The front office continues to explore a defensive landing spot for him but he profiles as a .270/.330/.400-type bat.

Ceiling: 2.0-win player
Risk: Low to Moderate
MLB ETA: Debuted in 2022

10. Denzel Clarke, OF

Hit	Power	SB	Patience	Glove	Overall
35/40	60	60	60	55	55

Born: 05/01/00	Age: 23	Bats: R	Top Production Comp: N/A
Height: 6-5	Weight: 220	Throws: R	

Season	Team	Age	Level	PA	1B	2B	3B	HR	SB	CS	BB%	K%	AVG	OBP	SLG	ISO
2022	OAK	22	A	193	23	14	2	7	14	2	14.51%	29.02%	0.295	0.420	0.545	0.250
2022	OAK	22	A+	218	20	9	2	8	16	1	12.84%	36.24%	0.209	0.317	0.406	0.198

Background: Oozing the tantalizing combination of speed, power, explosive tendencies, and strength, it's no wonder Clarke's family tree is sprinkled with several premium athletes. His mother, Donna, competed in the women's heptathlon at the 1984 Summer Olympics at the age of 19. His uncle, Kevin Smellie, was a running back for the Toronto Argonauts in the Canadian Football League. His cousin, Gavin Smellie, participated in the Summer Olympics a decade ago. And, then, of course, his other cousins spent last season on the Guardians' playoff roster – Josh and Bo Naylor. A fourth round pick out of California State University, Northridge, home to the Matadors, two years ago, Clark opened up his first full season in pro ball with the Stockton Ports in Low-A. But after mashing .295/.420/.545 with 23 extra-base hits in only 42 games, the front office bumped him up a level. And his production dropped – precipitously. He would cobble together a lowly .209/.317/.406 slash line in 51 games with the Lugnuts of Lansing. He would finish the year with an aggregate .248/.365/.469 line with 23 doubles, four triples, 15 homeruns, and 30 stolen bases (in only 33 attempts).

Snippet from The 2022 Prospect Digest Handbook: There's some poor man's Danny Tartabull-type potential here. If you speculate on prospect cards, Clarke maybe a penny stock to tuck away for a few years.

Scouting Report: The knock on Clarke – like a lot of other A's prospects – is whether he's going to make enough contact to take full advantage of his raw ability. If he does make enough contact, the ceiling's as high as any in the system. If he doesn't, well, you know how it'll turn out. Easy power – the type only superstar sluggers possess. The kind that drives balls 450 feet the other way with a flick of the wrist. Incredible bat speed. Plus speed. Plus patience at the plate. Above-average glove in any outfield spot. The odds are long on this lottery ticket, but sometimes they payoff.

Ceiling: 3.0-win player
Risk: High
MLB ETA: 2024

11. Henry Bolte, OF

Hit	Power	SB	Patience	Glove	Overall
40/45	55	70	50	55	55

Born: 08/04/03	Age: 19	Bats: R	Top Production Comp: N/A
Height: 6-3	Weight: 195	Throws: R	

Season	Team	Age	Level	PA	1B	2B	3B	HR	SB	CS	BB%	K%	AVG	OBP	SLG	ISO
2022	OAK	18	CPX	39	7	0	0	0	0	1	12.82%	48.72%	0.212	0.333	0.212	0.000

Background: For a warm weather school that boasts the likes of famous alumni like Jim Harbaugh, Jeremy Lin, Davante Adams, and 1920 Olympic Gold Medalist Dink Templeton,

Oakland Athletics

Palto Alto's baseball presence has been pretty sparse. Just seven draft picks have graduated from the California-based prep school, most notably Joc Pederson and B.J. Boyd, a 2012 fourth round pick by the Oakland A's who also happens to be the school's most recent MLB selection. Boyd, by the way, is also the highest drafted player in school history as well. Until Henry Bolte heard his name on draft day. A well-built 6-foot-3, 195-pound outfielder, Bolte starred for the Vikings during his final amateur season, helping the squad capture its first CCS (Central Coast Section) championship. The trophy was secured on Bolte's game-winning dash around the bases against the San Benito Haybalers. He finished his senior campaign in style, batting .441 with a .577 on-base percentage with double-digit homeruns and more than 40 stolen bases. Oakland drafted Bolte in the second round, 56th overall, and signed him to a deal worth $2 million – roughly $650,000 above the recommended slot bonus. Bolte appeared in 11 games with the Athletics' Complex League affiliate, hitting a paltry .212/.333/.212 with 19 punch outs in only 39 plate appearances. He was committed to the University of Texas.

Scouting Report: Per the usual, my pre-draft write-up:

> "A tremendous athlete disguised as a baseball player – at least for the time being. Bolte, a multi-sport star during his high school career, showcases plus-plus speed, above-average power potential, and all the tools required to be an above-average big leaguer. He's just raw and the swing is too mechanical. Bolte looked fooled by offspeed pitches at various points during his senior season as well. He's very reminiscent of a young Bradley Zimmer. Bolte looks like a mid-second round grade with some added risk due to the rawness of his toolkit. Wouldn't be surprised to see a team like the Reds or Athletics take a flier on the talented young outfielder."

Ceiling: 3.0-win player
Risk: High
MLB ETA: 2025

12. Lawrence Butler, 1B/OF

Hit	Power	SB	Patience	Glove	Overall
40/45	55/60	55/45	55	55	50

Born: 07/10/00	Age: 22	Bats: L	Top Production Comp: N/A
Height: 6-3	Weight: 210	Throws: R	

Season	Team	Age	Level	PA	1B	2B	3B	HR	SB	CS	BB%	K%	AVG	OBP	SLG	ISO
2021	OAK	20	A	396	47	20	4	17	26	4	13.89%	33.08%	0.263	0.364	0.499	0.236
2021	OAK	20	A+	54	11	4	0	2	3	1	7.41%	27.78%	0.340	0.389	0.540	0.200
2022	OAK	21	A+	333	46	19	3	11	13	5	12.01%	31.53%	0.270	0.357	0.468	0.198

Background: The club's 2018 draft class hasn't produced a whole lot of big league value – just slightly more than half a win above replacement in the form of Alfonso Rivas, who did so in the Cubs' lineup, and Jonah Bride. Otherwise, they missed on their first round gamble (sort of), Kyler Murray, who chose to play quarterback in the NFL. Their second round pick, Jameson Hannah, is now with the Rockies. And the disappointment just continues down the line. Except – maybe – for Lawrence Butler, the club's sixth round pick that summer. After struggling – *mightily* – through his first two seasons in pro ball, Butler looked renewed during his 2021 campaign as he hit .273/.367/.504 between Stockton and Lansing. Last season, in an arm-injury-interrupted year, Butler slugged .270/.357/.468 with 19 doubles, three triples, 11 homeruns, and 13 stolen bases (in only 18 attempts). His overall production with the Lugnuts, according to *Weighted Runs Created Plus*, topped the league average mark by a rock solid 29%. Following the season, he appeared in 19 games with the Mesa Solar Sox in the Arizona Fall League, batting .241/.389/.444 with six extra-base hits.

Snippet from The 2022 Prospect Digest Handbook: Butler's cut from the Three True Outcomes mold: he walked nearly 14% of the time in Low-A, whiffed in slightly more than a third of the time, and was on pace for a 30-homer season. Butler's always swung-and-missed way too much, but last season's tally marks a career low.

Scouting Report: Consider the following:

> Since 2006, there have been forty-one 21-year-old hitters that posted a 125 to 135 wRC+ in any High-A league (min. 300 PA). Here's the list of those that topped a 30% strikeout rate: Lawrence Butler. Chris Davis, the former Orioles star, was a close second at 29.4%.

At first blush it looks like Butler had a tremendously effective offensive season in High-A. He hit well, walked plenty, continued to show progress with improved contact rates, and swiped double-digit bags. But let's add some important context:

> Butler spent half of his time in an extremely hitter-friendly environment (Lansing's home field). Per *Baseball America's* park factors, the ballpark had a 127 PF for runs, 122 PF for homeruns. And his actual numbers showed a noticeable split as well. He batted .279/.384/.483 at home and .252/.318/.432 on the road.

Oakland Athletics

Butler is more athletic than his 6-foot-3, 210-pound frame would suggest. There's still some starting caliber potential here. But the 2023 season will go a long way in determining if he's going to make enough contact as he entered Double-A.

Ceiling: 2.0-win player
Risk: Moderate
MLB ETA: 2024

13. Joey Estes, RHP

FB	SL	CH	Command	Overall
60	50	50	55	50

Born: 10/08/01	Age: 21	Bats: R	Top Production Comp: N/A
Height: 6-2	Weight: 190	Throws: R	

Season	Team	Age	Level	IP	TBF	K/9	K%	BB/9	BB%	K-BB%	ERA	FIP	xFIP	Pit/Bat
2019	ATL	17	R	10.0	46	7.20	17.39%	6.30	15.22%	2.17%	8.10	4.01	5.18	1.89
2021	ATL	19	A	99.0	396	11.55	32.07%	2.64	7.32%	24.75%	2.91	3.30	3.78	3.85
2022	OAK	20	A+	91.0	387	9.10	23.77%	2.97	7.75%	16.02%	4.55	5.18	4.42	3.78

Background: The Athletics left little doubt as to whether they were in full rebuild mode or not last spring following the owners implanted Lockout. In a matter of four days Oakland dealt away core club members Chris Bassitt, Matt Olson, and Matt Chapman – the last two being the largest deals. General Manager David Forst shipped Olson to the reigning World Champion Atlanta Braves to become Freddie Freeman's replacement for a quartet of prospects: backstop Shea Langeliers, Cristian Pache, Ryan Cusick, and lesser-known Joey Estes. A 16th round pick coming out of Paraclete High School in 2019, Estes, who signed for a well above bonus of $497,500, limped through an abbreviate debut in the Gulf Coast League as he posted an 8-to-7 strikeout-to-walk ratio in 10.0 innings of work. But once he returned from the lost COVID season, the 6-foot-2, 190-pound right-hander morphed into one of the better hurlers in the low levels. He would make 20 starts with the Augusta GreenJackets, the Braves' Low-A affiliate, two years ago, throwing 99.0 innings with a bevy of strikeouts (127) and few free passes (29). Then, poof, he disappeared from Atlanta's farm system and reappeared as a potential key cog in Oakland's future resurgence. Making 20 starts for the Lansing Lugnuts last season, the hard-throwing righty averaged an impressive 9.1 strikeouts and just 3.0 walks per nine innings.

Snippet from The 2022 Prospect Digest Handbook: The production has him on track for a league average starter, but he needs to continue developing his offspeed. But 19-year-old hurlers with big time strikeout rates combined with a strong feel for the strike zone are in short supply. Don't sleep on this kid either.

Scouting Report: Consider the following:

> Since 2006, nine 20-year-old pitchers posted a 23% to 25% strikeout percentage with a 7% to 9% walk percentage in High-A (min. 75 IP): Danny Duffy, Jake Thompson, Brandon Erbe, Dan Cortes, Eric Hurley, Johnny Barbato, Troy Patton, Jesse Biddle, and – of course – Joey Estes, the former 16th round pick.

Equipped with long, curly, luxurious locks of flowing hair, Estes attacks hitters with a three-pitch mix: a plus fastball, which sits in the mid-90s, an average slider, and a 50-grade changeup. Neither of his offspeed pitches project to be swing-and-miss offerings at any point in the immediate future. The slider is loopy and lacks both hard bite and late movement – one of which being essential to get big league hitters out consistently. His changeup is straight and misses the fat part of the bat most of the time. Estes continues to succeed due to his above-average command and pitchability. Despite his blasé secondary offerings, he shows extraordinary confidence in them – which is typically half the battle. He's entering his age-21 season and likely ticketed for a full season in Double-A, which bodes well for his big league prospects. But at least one secondary option needs to uptick to help him stay at the big league level.

Ceiling: 2.0-win player
Risk: High
MLB ETA: 2023/2024

14. Jeff Criswell, RHP

FB	CB	SL	CH	Command	Overall
55	50	55	60	45	45

Born: 03/10/99	Age: 24	Bats: R	Top Production Comp: Jakob Junis
Height: 6-4	Weight: 225	Throws: R	

Season	Team	Age	Level	IP	TBF	K/9	K%	BB/9	BB%	K-BB%	ERA	FIP	xFIP	Pit/Bat
2021	OAK	22	A+	12.0	50	9.00	24.00%	3.00	8.00%	16.00%	4.50	4.11	4.20	3.68
2022	OAK	23	A+	50.0	205	10.44	28.29%	3.24	8.78%	19.51%	3.78	4.24	3.66	4.00
2022	OAK	23	AA	57.2	252	8.90	22.62%	3.75	9.52%	13.10%	4.21	4.38	5.17	3.56
2022	OAK	23	AAA	10.2	42	3.37	9.52%	2.53	7.14%	2.38%	4.22	3.95	7.37	3.67

Background: The Oakland A's have established a rather lengthy, strong pipeline to the University of Michigan – particularly over the past several reasons. U of M's baseball program churned out 15 draft picks since 2019. Oakland has made four of those selections (as well as 12

Oakland Athletics

total picks in their history). The club's earliest selection from the Wolverine's program was former All-Star and 1994 American League ERA leader Steve Ontiveros, who was taken in second round, 54th overall, all the way back in 1982. Nearly four decades later the A's would make Jeff Criswell the second earliest Wolverine drafted in their history. The 58th overall pick three years ago, Criswell, who signed with the team for $1 million, was limited to just five brief starts during his pro debut with Lansing in 2021 – courtesy of an undisclosed injury. Last season, though, the 6-foot-4, 225-pound right-hander quickly made up for any lost developmental time as he skipped-and-hopped from High-A to Double-A and then on to Triple-A. He would throw a total of 118.1 innings, recording a solid 119 strikeouts, 45 walks, and a 4.03 ERA.

Snippet from The 2022 Prospect Digest Handbook: His slider, though, is a game changer in terms of a second viable "out" pitch. Criswell has never been mistaken for Daulton Jefferies or his ability to command the strike zone like an artist with a paintbrush. And like a lot of the club's other top arms, He's quickly advancing in age. He's now entering his age-23 season with just 12.0 minor league innings on his resume. He needs to prove he can take the ball every fifth day and throw quality strikes. Otherwise, he's heading down the path of a reliever.

Scouting Report: Consider the following:

> Since 2006, there have twenty-nine different 23-year-old hurlers that posted a 21.5% to 23.5% strikeout percentage with an 8.5% to 10.5% walk percentage in any Double-A league (min. 50 IP). Of those 29 aforementioned hurlers, the most notable include Felipe Paulino, James McDonald, Parker Bridwell, Sam LeCure, Tanner Houck, Tyler Beede, Wade Miley, Emerson Hancock, and – of course – Jeff Criswell.

While Criswell's arsenal isn't overpowering, the big 6-foot-4, 225-pound right-hander owns a deep repertoire. Highlighted by a heavy low 90s heater, Criswell mixes in a pair of breaking balls – a beautiful 12-6 bending curveball and a legitimate swing-and-miss slider. But his best offspeed weapon is a tumbling changeup that shows tremendous velocity separation. The command can be spotty at times, but Criswell is knocking at the club's big league door and should settle in nicely as a #4-type arm.

Ceiling: 1.5-win player
Risk: Low to Moderate
MLB ETA: 2023

15. Darell Hernaiz, IF

Hit	Power	SB	Patience	Glove	Overall
40/45	35/45	55	50	55	45

Born: 08/03/01 **Age:** 21 **Bats:** R **Top Production Comp:** N/A
Height: 6-1 **Weight:** 170 **Throws:** R

Season	Team	Age	Level	PA	1B	2B	3B	HR	SB	CS	BB%	K%	AVG	OBP	SLG	ISO
2021	BAL	19	A	410	85	12	0	6	22	6	6.83%	17.07%	0.277	0.333	0.358	0.081
2022	BAL	20	A	138	21	7	2	6	9	0	5.80%	15.94%	0.283	0.341	0.512	0.228
2022	BAL	20	A+	255	48	13	3	5	22	3	8.63%	16.86%	0.305	0.376	0.456	0.150
2022	BAL	20	AA	59	4	1	0	1	1	1	8.47%	27.12%	0.113	0.186	0.189	0.075

Background: The front office played the rebuilding game perfectly. Two years ago, Oakland purchased the contract of right-hander Cole Irvin from the Philadelphia Phillies. After back-to-back seasons of chewing up innings at a league average pace the franchise flipped the 29-year-old right-hander to the Orioles for infield prospect Darell Hernaiz. The son of a former minor league vagabond, Hernaiz was grabbed by Baltimore in the fifth round of the 2019 draft. After a solid debut season in rookie ball, Hernaiz held his own as a teenager in Low-A two years ago, batting .277/.333/.358 with 18 extra-base knocks in only 94 games with Delmarva. Last season, though, he started growing into more thump as he split the year between Delmarva, Aberdeen, and Bowie. He slugged a rock solid .273/.341/.438 with 21 doubles, five triples, 12 homeruns, and 32 stolen bases (in only 36 total attempts). Per *Weighted Runs Created Plus*, his overall production topped the league average mark by 12%.

Snippet from The 2022 Prospect Digest Handbook: Hernaiz owns the basic building blocks for a low end starting middle infielder at the big league level. But the bat needs to uptick to average or better for him to get there. Hernaiz is only entering his age-20 season, so plenty of time of his side.

Scouting Report: Consider the following:

> Since 2006, there have been five 20-year-old hitters that met the following criteria in any High-A league (min. 250 PA): 122 to 132 wRC+ with a 15% to 18% strikeout rate and a 7% to 10% walk rate. Those five hitters: Nick Allen, Ryan Vilade, Bryan Ramos, Edinson Rincon, and Darell Hernaiz.

Oakland Athletics

Hernaiz continued his path towards a low end starter / strong backup infielder in 2022. The former fifth round grew into more power and continued to run and field well. His initial struggles in Double-A (he hit .113/.186/.189 in 59 plate appearances) really impacted the over line. Definitely a solid move by the front office brass.

Ceiling: 1.5-win player
Risk: Moderate
MLB ETA: 2024

16. Clark Elliot, OF

Hit	Power	SB	Patience	Glove	Overall
50	50	50	55	50	45

Born: 09/29/00	Age: 22	Bats: L	Top Production Comp: N/A
Height: 6-0	Weight: 185	Throws: R	

Background: The University of Michigan has transformed its program from a draft afterthought into a prominent pipeline of big league talent under recently departed Head Coach Erik Bakich. After churning out of total of three players to be taken in the opening three rounds of the draft from 2000 to 2018, the Wolverines' program belched out a staggering eight players taken in the opening three rounds since 2019. The latest: outfielder Elliott Clark. A product of Barrington High School, home to former All-Star catcher Dan Wilson, Elliott looked a bit unprepared during his – admittedly brief – 2020 season as he batted .245/.369/.340 in 15 games before the pandemic forced a premature end to the year. The 6-foot, 183-pound corner outfielder took several leaps forward during his sophomore season in Ann Arbor, hitting a respectable .270/.403/.428 with nine doubles, five homeruns, and eight stolen bases. Elliott spent the ensuing summer playing for the Hyannis Harbor Hawks in the vaunted Cape Cod. And he took full advantage of the opportunity to showcase his talents. In 24 games he slugged a scorching .344/.464/.478 with four doubles, one triple, two homeruns, and seven stolen bases against some of the best amateur pitching talent in the county. And he was able to carry that momentum into his tremendous junior campaign for the Wolverines as well. In a career best 61 games, Elliot bashed .337/.460/.630 with career highs doubles (17), triples (3), homeruns (16), and stolen bases (19). Oakland selected the dynamic outfielder in the second round, 69th overall, and signed him to a deal worth $900,000, saving the club a little less than $80,000.

Scouting Report: Consider the following:

> Since 2011, only six (6) Division I hitters batted at least .330/.450/.620 with a walk rate north of 15% and a strikeout rate between 17% and 19% in a season (min. 275 PA): Jonathan India, Brent Rooker, Chase Strumpf, Luke Reynolds, Aaron Westlake, and – of course – Clark Elliott.

Tracking like a fourth or fifth outfielder before his breakout with Hyannis two summers ago. Elliott morphed into a completely different type of offensive threat between his sophomore and junior seasons. Silky smooth left-handed swing that generates solid power, especially when he pulls the ball. Above-average speed. He's miscast as a corner outfielder and will likely see some time in center at some point during his career with the Oakland Organization. He's tracking like a .265/.335/.420-type hitter.

Ceiling: 1.5-win player
Risk: Moderate
MLB ETA: 2024/2025

17. Luis Medina, RHP

FB	CB	CH	Command	Overall
80	60	55/60	35/45	45

Born: 05/03/99	Age: 24	Bats: R	Top Production Comp: Albert Abreu
Height: 6-1	Weight: 175	Throws: R	

Season	Team	Age	Level	IP	TBF	K/9	K%	BB/9	BB%	K-BB%	ERA	FIP	xFIP	Pit/Bat
2021	NYY	22	A+	32.2	133	13.78	37.59%	5.23	14.29%	23.31%	2.76	4.22	3.71	4.05
2021	NYY	22	AA	73.2	318	10.14	26.10%	5.01	12.89%	13.21%	3.67	4.25	4.21	3.99
2022	NYY	23	AA	72.0	307	10.13	26.38%	5.00	13.03%	13.36%	3.38	3.85	4.39	4.08
2022	OAK	23	AA	20.2	114	11.32	22.81%	9.58	19.30%	3.51%	11.76	6.47	5.51	4.02

Background: Oakland's plan of action on their rebuild had a pretty clear objective: defense and young arms. Shea Langeliers and Crisian Pache are elite defenders and Kevin Smith can certainly pick it as well. And the list of acquired arms includes: J.T. Ginn, Ryan Cusick, Joey Estes, Gunnar Hoglund, J.P. Sears, Ken Waldichuk, and – of course – Luis Medina. Signed out of Nagua, Dominican Republic all the way back in 2015, Medina's been on the slow-and-steady approach through the minor leagues. He spent parts of three seasons in rookie ball, and then another couple years making his way up to Double-A. Last season, the hard-throwing right-hander made a career best 24 starts between both organizations Double-A affiliates, throwing 92.2 innings with 107 strikeouts and a whopping 62 free passes. He finished the year with a 5.24 ERA, a number – more or less – in line with his career mark.

Oakland Athletics

Snippet from The 2020 Prospect Digest Handbook: There are pitchers in baseball that throw as hard, maybe even a mile-per-hour or two harder, but I've yet to see a pitcher that throws as hard with as little effort as Medina.

Scouting Report: On the days that Medina's working around the strike zone, there are very few hurlers – at any level – that can match the quality of his arsenal. When things are right Medina's repertoire suggests a potential no-hitter each time he toes the rubber. The problem, of course, is that things rarely click for the mercurial right-hander – particularly after the trade to Oakland. In his 24 total appearances, Medina walked at least three hitters 12 times and failed to pitch past five innings. The immediate – and *appropriate* – comparison is Houston's Bryan Abreu, who could go toe-to-toe with Medina's weaponry and failed to find the strike zone with any type of consistency until 2022. Then…BAM!...Abreu was lights out, particularly in the playoffs for the World Champs (11.1 IP, 19K, 4BB, 0.00 ERA). There's no way that Medina heads down a different path. He's going to be magnificent coming out of Oakland's pen in two years. Plus-plus fastball, plus curveball, and his changeup showed *tremendous* promise, uptick from below average to borderline plus.

Ceiling: 1.5-win player
Risk: Moderate
MLB ETA: 2022

18. Gunnar Hoglund, RHP

FB	CB	SL	CH	Command	Overall
N/A	N/A	N/A	N/A	N/A	50

Born: 12/17/99	Age: 23	Bats: L	Top Production Comp: N/A
Height: 6-4	Weight: 220	Throws: R	

Background: Oakland clearly has an affinity for talented, albeit injured / injury prone, former 2018 first round picks that spurned professional ball and took the collegiate route through Mississippi. The rebuilding franchise first acquired J.T. Ginn, the 30th overall pick in 2018, from the Mets as part of the return for the underrated Chris Bassitt on March 12, 2022. Ginn, of course, had Tommy John surgery to correct his ailing right elbow during his final season with Mississippi State University. Four days later the A's traded All-Star Matt Chapman to the Blue Jays for a package that included Gunnar Hoglund. The ace of the University of Mississippi's squad, Hoglund, who was originally taken six picks after Ginn and stood atop the University of Mississippi's rotation, underwent the knife for Tommy John surgery in mid-July 2021. He would eventually make it back to the mound in late July last season. After three brief starts in the low minors, the 6-foot-4, 220-pound right-hander hit the disabled list – again – with a biceps injury.

Scouting Report: Since there's virtually no new information available on Hoglund, here's my most recent scouting report heading into the 2021 draft:

> "Ignoring the injury momentarily, consider the following:
>
> Between 2011 and 2020, only three SEC starting pitchers averaged at least 12 strikeouts and fewer than three walks per innings in a season (min. 50 IP): Casey Mize, Ethan Small, and Mason Hickman.
>
> Obviously, Hoglund's abbreviated 2021 season places him among the group. Prior to the injury, Hoglund, according to reports, showcased a low 90s fastball, an above-average slider and changeup, and a decent curveball. He had the look and production to go within the Top 15 picks of the draft before the elbow issues, but a team in the latter part of the 20s will likely take a gamble."

Ceiling: 2.0-win player
Risk: High
MLB ETA: 2024

19. J.T. Ginn, RHP

FB	CB	SL	CH	Command	Overall
55	N/A	55	50	45	45

Born: 05/20/99	Age: 24	Bats: R	Top Production Comp: Jarrod Parker
Height: 6-2	Weight: 200	Throws: R	

Season	Team	Age	Level	IP	TBF	K/9	K%	BB/9	BB%	K-BB%	ERA	FIP	xFIP	Pit/Bat
2021	NYM	22	A	38.2	148	8.15	23.65%	2.33	6.76%	16.89%	2.56	3.93	3.78	3.63
2021	NYM	22	A+	53.1	222	7.76	20.72%	2.03	5.41%	15.32%	3.38	3.00	3.90	3.53
2022	OAK	23	AA	35.1	162	10.44	25.31%	3.57	8.64%	16.67%	6.11	4.07	4.10	3.64

Background: At first glance it looks like Ginn committed a grave sin coming out of high school. The promising right-hander, armed with a strong commitment to Mississippi State University, failed to come to terms with the Los Angeles Dodgers after they selected him with the 30th overall pick. But Ginn, a 6-foot-2, 200-pound right-hander, began to blossom into one of college baseball's best starting pitchers during his freshman season with the Bulldogs as he averaged 10.9 strikeouts and 2.0 walks across 17 starts. Then an aching elbow forced him under the knife, limiting him to just three innings of work during his follow up campaign. Undeterred, the Mets came calling in the second round that summer, signing him to a massive $2.9 million deal as the 52nd overall pick. So, despite being chosen 16 picks later *and* a serious elbow injury, Ginn got more money taking the college route. Ginn would make it back to the mound two years ago, making 18 starts between the Mets' Low-A and High-A affiliates, averaging a mediocre 7.9 strikeouts and 2.2 walks per nine innings. Oakland acquired the former college ace as part of the return for Chris Bassitt following the lockout last offseason. Forearm tightness, or so it was dubbed, limited him to just 10 starts in Double-A in 2022: 35.1 IP, 41 K, 14 BB, and a 6.11 ERA. Ginn would throwing another 16 innings with the Mesa Solar Sox in the Arizona Fall League, posting a 14-to-4 strikeout-to-walk ratio.

Snippet from The 2022 Prospect Digest Handbook: A bit disappointed. At least based on the reports on how he looked prior to undergoing the knife. Ginn, reportedly, was touching as 97 mph with his heater. But last season he was sitting 92, 93 mph and took some noticeable effort to get up to 94.

Scouting Report: When working out of the windup, Ginn's one of the slowest hurlers I've seen since Rafael Betancourt. It's a methodical approach to the plate, like molasses dripping down a fence pole in the middle of winter. Ginn throws a solid, if unremarkable, four-pitch mix. A low-90s fastball that tops out in the 94 mph, an above-average offering. A pair of breaking balls: a curveball, and a 55-grade slider. (Note: his backstop repeatedly called for the curveball, but he didn't throw it.) Decent, workable changeup. While Ginn has the draft pedigree (twice), and a high level of successful (at least for one year) in college, he looks like backend starting option – at best. He lacks a true out pitch.

Ceiling: 1.5-win player
Risk: Moderate
MLB ETA: 2023

20. Ryan Cusick, RHP

FB	CB	SL	CH	Command	Overall
70	N/A	50/55	50	45	45

Born: 11/12/99	Age: 23	Bats: R	Top Production Comp: N/A
Height: 6-6	Weight: 235	Throws: R	

Season	Team	Age	Level	IP	TBF	K/9	K%	BB/9	BB%	K-BB%	ERA	FIP	xFIP	Pit/Bat
2021	ATL	21	A	16.1	67	18.73	50.75%	2.20	5.97%	44.78%	2.76	1.53	1.23	4.61
2022	OAK	22	AA	41.0	200	9.44	21.50%	6.59	15.00%	6.50%	7.02	5.20	5.67	3.97

Background: A significant part of the quartet of prospects that rebuilding A's acquired from the Matt Olson deal with the Braves last offseason – or, at least, after the owners imposed lockout. Atlanta snagged the hard-throwing, hellacious curveball spinning right-hander in the first round, 24th overall, in the 2021 draft after a largely up-and-down career at Wake Forest University. The 6-foot-6, 235-pound hurler struggled through a disappointing freshman season with the Demon Deacons in 2019, posting an unsightly 6.44 ERA and mediocre peripherals (7.5 K/9 and 4.0 BB/9) across 65.2 innings of work. Things seemed to click for the then-19-year-old righty that summer in the Cape Cod League as he posted an impressive 33-to-7 strikeout-to-walk ratio in 35.2 innings of work with the Bourne Braves. But, unfortunately, Cusick's strike-throwing momentum faded at the start of the 2020 campaign. The Connecticut native walked a whopping 18 hitters (against an equally whopping 43 strikeouts) in only 22.1 innings before COVID prematurely ended the year. His junior campaign with the Deacons was a mixture of his first two: he averaged an impressive 13.9 K/9, but managed to hand out 32 free passes in 70 innings. Last season an oblique injury limited Cusick to just 41.0 Double-A innings with the Midland RockHounds. He proved his strikeout potential was viable against the competition, averaging more than a punch out per inning. And, likewise, he showed his lack of touch for the strike zone, walking 30 in 41.0 innings. Cusick would throw another 23.0 innings with the Mesa Solar Sox in the Arizona Fall League as well, recording a 24-to-13 strikeout-to-walk ratio.

Snippet from The 2022 Prospect Digest Handbook: The question – of course – is whether he can consistently find the strike zone enough in the professional ranks. There's some real concern about whether he winds up in the bullpen as a two-pitch power arm. There's some risk, but a team with limited [or multiple] picks would likely be willing to gamble late in the opening round."

Scouting Report: Prior to turning pro, Cusick's heater had reportedly touched as high as 102 mph. Last season, in longer stints with shorter rest periods, his fastball was sitting in the mid-90s and touching a couple ticks higher on occasion. It's a plus-plus pitch with a lot of life up in the zone. The big right-hander has previously thrown an above-average curveball, but seems to have scrapped it in favor of a hard, mid-80s slider – which flashes above-average. He'll also mix in an average changeup. Cusick's still young enough to overcome some control demons (let alone command issues), but his slack of a quality second offering will likely force him into a relief role in the future.

Ceiling: 1.5-win player
Risk: Moderate
MLB ETA: 2024

Philadelphia Phillies

Top Prospects

Philadelphia Phillies

1. Andrew Painter, RHP

FB	CB	SL	CH	Command	Overall
70	50	60	55/60	60	70

Born: 04/10/03 **Age:** 20 **Bats:** R **Top Production Comp:** Justin Verlander
Height: 6-7 **Weight:** 215 **Throws:** R

Season	Team	Age	Level	IP	TBF	K/9	K%	BB/9	BB%	K-BB%	ERA	FIP	xFIP	Pit/Bat
2022	PHI	19	AA	28.1	109	11.75	33.94%	0.64	1.83%	32.11%	2.54	2.60	2.98	3.79
2022	PHI	19	A+	36.2	143	12.03	34.27%	1.72	4.90%	29.37%	0.98	2.35	3.22	3.54
2022	PHI	19	A	38.2	149	16.06	46.31%	3.72	10.74%	35.57%	1.40	1.27	1.83	3.76

Background: Who's the best homegrown pitching prospect in Phillies history? Surprisingly, the list is a rather short one. Grover Cleveland Alexander certainly belongs at the top. "Old Pete" was nabbed by the club from Syracuse as part of the Rule 5 draft in 1910 and he would go to tally nearly 120 wins above replacement in his legendary career. Robin Roberts signed as an amateur free agent in mid-October 1961 and he, too, would go onto a Hall of Fame career. The same could be said for Fergie Jenkins – though he was famously dealt to the Cubs early in his big league career. Cole Hamels and his fabulous changeup and sparkling command should be mentioned. As does Chris Short and Aaron Nola. There are likely others, but you get the general gist. Someday, injuries notwithstanding, Andrew Painter may find his name apart of the conversation – even if it is only a courtesy mention, a tip of the hat. The Phillies' top pick in 2021, Painter would wait longer than expected to hear his name called with the 13th overall selection. Five pitchers would go ahead him – three college hurlers (Vanderbilt teammates Jack Leiter and Kumar Rocker, as well as Sam Bachman) and a pair of prep stars (Jackson Jobe and Frank Mozzicato). But it's Painter, a massive 6-foot-7, 215-foot right-hander, who shined the brightest. The Calvary Christian High School product was practically unhittable during his limited debut in the Complex League two years ago, posting a 12-to-0 strikeout-to-walk ratio in only six innings of work. And that level of dominance – practically unheard for a teenage arm – continued as he rolled over hitter after hitter in 2022. Painter shredded the Low-A competition, annihilated the opposition at High-A, and looked like the second coming of Bob Gibson during his five-game cameo in Double-A. He finished the year with 103.2 innings of work, striking out a mindboggling 155 and walked only 25 to go along with a sparkling 1.56 ERA.

Snippet from The 2022 Prospect Digest Handbook: It's almost sacrilege to say it, but he's reminiscent of young Justin Verlander in some ways.

Scouting Report: Painter has a lot of elite traits:

> #1. Plus-plus fastball, sitting easily in the mid- to upper-90s.
> #2. Command of his plus-plus fastball.
> #3. A wickedly unfair low- to mid-80s slider.
> #4. Command of his wickedly unfair slider.
> #5. A tremendously underrated changeup.
> #6. Command of his tremendously underrated changeup.
> #7. A willingness to mix speeds and throw his offspeed offerings in any count.
> #8. Athletic with a quick pickoff move.

With a little more seasoning on his changeup, Painter will – unquestionably – own three plus offerings backed up by a rare, solid-average curveball that could climb into above-average territory if he focused more heavily on it. Painter's two breaking balls are especially effective due to their different movements – the slider is more of horizontally darting / sweeping pitch and his curveball is more traditional with downward bite. There's a lot of luck that goes into navigating through the injury nexus, but Painter has the makings of a true, genuine ace.

Ceiling: 6.0-win player
Risk: Moderate
MLB ETA: 2023

2. Mick Abel, RHP

FB	CB	SL	CH	Command	Overall
70	N/A	60	55	45	60

Born: 08/18/01 **Age:** 21 **Bats:** R **Top Comp:** Zack Wheeler
Height: 6-5 **Weight:** 190 **Throws:** R

Season	Team	Age	Level	IP	TBF	K/9	K%	BB/9	BB%	K-BB%	ERA	FIP	xFIP	Pit/Bat
2021	PHI	19	A	44.2	189	13.30	34.92%	5.44	14.29%	20.63%	4.43	4.52	4.11	4.38
2022	PHI	20	A+	85.1	372	10.86	27.69%	4.01	10.22%	17.47%	4.01	3.71	4.34	3.93
2022	PHI	20	AA	23.0	99	10.57	27.27%	4.70	12.12%	15.15%	3.52	5.72	4.85	3.94

Background: There's aren't too many farm systems in baseball where Abel wouldn't rank as the top young arm in the organization. Unfortunately for him – but fortunately for Phillies fans – Philadelphia happens to be one of the select few where he ranks as the second best pitching prospect. The 15th overall player selected in 2020, sandwiched between Justin Foscue and Ed Howard, Abel made a smooth transition into the professional ranks during his debut a year later. In an injury-shortened campaign, the 6-foot-5, 190-pound right-hander made 14 brief starts with the Clearwater Threshers, averaging an impressive 13.3 strikeouts and a bloated 5.4 walks per nine innings. Undeterred about some command blips, the front office sent their former first rounder up to Jersey Shore and – surprisingly – Abel was able to

Philadelphia Phillies

dial in his control quite a bit. He posted a 103-to-38 strikeout-to-walk ratio in 85.1 innings of work. Abel capped off his 2022 season with a five-game cameo with Reading, averaging 10.6 strikeouts and 4.7 walks per nine innings. He finished the year with an aggregate 3.90 ERA.

Snippet from The 2022 Prospect Digest Handbook: The shoulder issue, which was termed as tendonitis, is concerning. Assuming it won't hamper him in the coming seasons, Abel looks like a viable mid-rotation caliber arm – unless the command ticks up. One final note: he trusts his breaking ball more than most teenagers.

Scouting Report: Consider the following:

> Since 2006, only six 20-year-old hurlers posted a 26% to 29% strikeout percentage and a walk percentage between 9% and 11% in High-A (min. 75 IP): Ian Anderson, Josh Hader, Caleb Ferguson, Aaron Kurcz, Jared Jones, and – of course – Mick Abel.

Perhaps unfairly, but the dynamic duo of Andrew Painter and Mick Abel will *forever* be linked and compared to each other. Taken in the opening round in back-to-back drafts, each talented hurler features similar repertoires: plus-plus fastball, plus slider, above-average changeup, and a rare curveball (I did not witness Abel's reported deuce). The big differentiator, though, is Abel's wavering command / control. The 6-foot-5, 190-pound right-hander has a little bit of late arm side run on his heater, particularly when he's locating it in on righties / away from lefties due to his lower-ish three-quarter arm slot. His heater, by the way, touched 99 mph several times during a late-season start.

Ceiling: 5.0-win player
Risk: Moderate to High
MLB ETA: 2024

3. Justin Crawford, CF

Hit	Power	SB	Patience	Glove	Overall
50/55	30/45	70	55	70	60

Born: 01/13/04	**Age:** 19	**Bats:** L	**Top Production Comp:** N/A
Height: 6-3	**Weight:** 175	**Throws:** R	

Background: There was a point very early in his career that former Tampa Bay Ray, Boston Red Sox, and Los Angeles Dodgers All-Star outfielder Carl Crawford was tracking as a potential Hall of Fame talent. Using *Baseball Reference's* Stathead, there are 179 total players to accrue 30 wins above replacement through their age-28 season. Of those 179, 94 of them would go onto Hall of Fame careers – or roughly 52.5%. Crawford battled injuries and stopped being great after his age-28 season. But during his prime the four-time All-Star outfielder was a force in all facets of the game: he could hit, mash the occasional homerun, run like the wind, and play defense like a multiple Gold Glove-winning left fielder. And like a lot of the other top prep prospects in last year's class, Crawford's son, Justin, is showing tremendous potential. The teenage outfielder's school, Bishop Gorman, produced several notable players including: All-Star Joey Gallo, 1995 AL Rookie of the Year Marty Cordova, and Yankees catching prospect Austin Wells. The younger Crawford became the highest drafted player in the school's history. Standing a muscular, yet lean, 6-foot-3 and 170 pounds, Crawford was an absolute wrecking ball at the plate during his final two prep seasons: in 2021, he slugged .492/.536/.746 and followed that up with an even better showing as a senior, mashing .503/.562/.816 with five homeruns, 52 RBI, and 60 runs scored. Philadelphia selected him in the opening round last July, 17th overall, and signed him to a deal worth $3,894,000. Crawford split his debut between the Complex League and Low-A, hitting .241/.333/.276 with one triple and 10 stolen bases in 16 games. Prior to the draft, Crawford committed to baseball powerhouse Louisiana State University.

Scouting Report: Per the usual, my pre-draft write-up:

> "Blessed with his father's speed, Crawford's one of the class's top runners. His nonstop motor out of the box will turn plenty of singles into doubles and doubles into triples. He shows good bat-to-ball skills and a patient approach at the plate, making him an ideal candidate to hit at the top of a lineup. The swing needs some fine tuning and he doesn't barrel the ball quite as frequently as many of the other top high school hitters in the class. He doesn't have a ton of present power, but could develop into a 15-home run perennial threat. There's some work to do be done, but he has the potential to develop into an above-average big leaguer. Some teams that could look to draft him in the first round include: the Marlins (sixth overall), the Mets (picks 11 and 14), and Padres (15)."

Ceiling: 3.5-win player
Risk: Moderate
MLB ETA: 2025

Philadelphia Phillies

4. Griff McGarry, RHP

FB	CB	SL	CH	Command	Overall
70	55	60	55	45	60

Born: 06/08/99 | **Age:** 24 | **Bats:** R | **Top Production Comp:** N/A
Height: 6-2 | **Weight:** 190 | **Throws:** R |

Season	Team	Age	Level	IP	TBF	K/9	K%	BB/9	BB%	K-BB%	ERA	FIP	xFIP	Pit/Bat
2021	PHI	22	A	11.0	46	18.00	47.83%	5.73	15.22%	32.61%	3.27	1.71	2.21	4.17
2021	PHI	22	A+	13.1	54	14.18	38.89%	4.73	12.96%	25.93%	2.70	2.19	3.85	4.15
2022	PHI	23	A+	46.2	195	15.81	42.05%	4.63	12.31%	29.74%	3.86	3.62	2.99	4.14
2022	PHI	23	AA	32.2	132	10.74	29.55%	5.51	15.15%	14.39%	2.20	3.63	4.37	4.23

Background: With an arsenal that screams ace caliber hurler and the command that's reminiscent of Steve Dalkowski, the famed flame-throwing southpaw in the late 1950's and early 60s, McGarry turned in one of the most complete *and* dominant outings during the College World Series two years ago. Squaring off against SEC powerhouse Mississippi State, the mercurial Virginia right-hander blanked the Bulldogs across seven innings (he lasted one out into the eighth frame) with eight punch outs and two walks. It was masterfully brilliant, a must watch performance. And, frankly, it was exactly how McGarry's rollercoaster career *should* have gone. The 6-foot-2, 190-pound right-hander, though, was plagued by control demons so badly that the word "command" didn't even enter into his lexicon. He finished his four-year career with the Cavaliers with 131 walks (and 186 strikeouts) in 134 innings of work. But it was that performance against Mississippi State, with the game's lights shining brightest, that inevitably convinced a team to take a mid-round gamble on the control-less, fireballing hurler. Philadelphia signed McGarry to a deal worth $322,500 after selecting him in the fifth round, 145th overall, two years ago. During his 24.1-inning cameo with Clearwater and Jersey Shore, McGarry showed an improved – albeit still poor – feel for the strike zone during his debut, averaging 15.9 strikeouts and 5.2 walks per nine innings. Last season was much the same. McGarry opened the year back up with the BlueClaws, but eventually moved onto the Fightin' Phils and IronPigs of Lehigh Valley. He would throw 87.1 innings – by far the most since his high school days – recording a whopping 130 strikeouts and 53 free passes to go along with an aggregate 3.71 ERA.

Snippet from The 2022 Prospect Digest Handbook: Absurdly talented. So much so, in fact, if his command was even a 45 he'd be a lock for a Top 10 or Top 15 selection. McGarry's fastball is explosive with late riding life, sitting – almost effortless – in the mid-90s and touching 97 mph with regularity. His slider is an 83- to 84-mph lethal swing-and-miss pitch. And he'll mix in a surprisingly solid mid-80s changeup. The problem, of course, is for four years McGarry couldn't hit the broadside of a barn. 45-grade command puts him as a #3/#4-type arm because that's how good the arsenal is. I'd take a third round flier on him and hope to harness the lightning oozing from his right arm. The Royals took Josh Staumont in the second round in 2015 and developed him into a late-inning arm – which could be a nice fallback for McGarry.

Scouting Report: In the recently released documentary *Facing Nolan*, there's a brief snippet of former Hall of Famers (or would be Hall of Famers like Pete Rose) describing Nolan Ryan as "conveniently wild". Griff McGarry is the opposite. He's inconveniently wild – so much so, in fact, that onlookers have to be wary of hitters getting comfortable in the box. But it *definitely* plays to McGarry's advantage. Unfurling an explosive, high octane mid- to upper-90s fastball that approaches triple-digits, the former Virginia hurler complements the borderline plus-plus offering with a hellacious, wickedly unfair mid-80s sweeping slider. He'll also mix in a firm, mid-80s changeup and an upper-70s / low-80s above-average 12-6 bending deuce. McGarry throws all kinds of lightning. And, again, if he had 45-grade command he's be a legitimate #3-type starting pitcher. Philadelphia had him working in short relief late the year – perhaps as an effort to get him ready for a potential stretch run. He's likely headed for some type of relief career, but I'd still run him out every fifth day for at least the next two years.

Ceiling: 3.5-win player
Risk: High
MLB ETA: 2023/2024

5. Johan Rojas, CF

Hit	Power	SB	Patience	Glove	Overall
40/45	45/50	60	50	70	55

Born: 08/14/00 | **Age:** 22 | **Bats:** R | **Top Production Comp:** Tyrone Taylor
Height: 6-1 | **Weight:** 165 | **Throws:** R |

Season	Team	Age	Level	PA	1B	2B	3B	HR	SB	CS	BB%	K%	AVG	OBP	SLG	ISO
2021	PHI	20	A	351	50	15	3	7	25	6	7.41%	19.66%	0.240	0.305	0.374	0.134
2021	PHI	20	A+	74	15	3	1	3	8	3	9.46%	10.81%	0.344	0.419	0.563	0.219
2022	PHI	21	A+	292	44	12	2	3	33	1	7.19%	18.84%	0.230	0.287	0.325	0.094
2022	PHI	21	AA	264	44	8	5	4	29	4	7.95%	16.67%	0.260	0.333	0.387	0.128

Background: In a system where its quality has become heavily slanted toward high octane, fire-bolt slinging arms, Rojas' athleticism and underrated potential stands out among Philly's everyday prospects. Signed out of San Francisco de Macoris, Dominican Republic early in 2018, Rojas' paltry contract agreement – just $10,000 – hardly qualifies as a bonus in the world of baseball. But the 6-foot-1, 165-pound outfielder hit the ground running, hitting .321/.376/.421 in 68 games in the foreign rookie league. Rojas continued his onslaught against hurlers in the Gulf Coast League the following season before settling in for an extended stint in the former New York-Penn League. Two years ago the toolsy centerfielder hit an aggregate .263/.329/.417 between stints with Clearwater and Jersey Shore. And he looked primed for a massive breakout in

Philadelphia Phillies

2022 – except it never really happened. Rojas was completely abysmal during the season's first two months before righting the proverbial ship in early June. He would cobble together an aggregate .244/.309/.354 with 20 doubles, seven triples, seven homeruns, and an impressive 62 stolen bases in only 75 total attempts. Per *Weighted Runs Created Plus*, his yearly production was 17% *below* the league average mark.

Snippet from The 2022 Prospect Digest Handbook: After an absolutely abysmal start the year in which he batted an awful .184/.231/.281 through his first 26 games, Rojas' production *exploded*. He slugged a scorching .296/.368/.476.

Scouting Report: For the second consecutive season Rojas looked completely and utterly useless at the beginning of the season – though it was for a significantly longer period in 2022. Rojas batted a putrid .191/.256/.255 over his first 41 games with the BlueClaws. After that, though, he hit .276/.325/.419 over his remaining 29 games in High-A. At some point, though, Rojas has got to figure out a way to put it all together or he's going to head down the Tyrone Taylor career path. On paper the Phillies' young outfielder has the makings of a dynamic table setter: plus-plus speed, an elite glove in centerfield, and 30 doubles and 15 to 20-homer thump. It's the Devon White toolkit. He's only entering his age-22 season and he's already spent half a year in Double-A – where he was a league average bat. The glove is enough to earn a spot in the lineup. The bat has the potential to make his an above-average regular.

Ceiling: 3.0-win player
Risk: Moderate to High
MLB ETA: 2023

6. Hao Yu Lee, IF

Hit	Power	SB	Patience	Glove	Overall
55	45/55	30	50	50	50

Born: 02/03/03	Age: 20	Bats: R	Top Production Comp: N/A
Height: 5-10	Weight: 190	Throws: R	

Season	Team	Age	Level	PA	1B	2B	3B	HR	SB	CS	BB%	K%	AVG	OBP	SLG	ISO
2021	PHI	18	CPX	25	3	2	2	1	0	0	12.00%	20.00%	0.364	0.440	0.773	0.409
2022	PHI	19	A	302	54	11	1	7	10	7	11.92%	18.87%	0.283	0.384	0.415	0.132
2022	PHI	19	A+	40	4	3	1	1	3	0	12.50%	22.50%	0.257	0.350	0.486	0.229

Background: Arguably the best high school hitter from Taiwan in recent years. Lee had been on the Phillies' radar for several years before agreeing to join the National League Champions two years ago, earning a bonus in the $600,000 neighborhood. Due to his late signing – he officially joined the franchise in June of 2021 – the 5-foot-10, 190-pound infielder was only relegated to a brief, albeit dominant, debut in the Complex League. The New Taipei native mashed .364/.440/.773 with two doubles, two triples, and one homerun in only nine games. Needless to say, Lee made quite the impression during his limited field work. Last season, the club pushed the then-19-year-old prospect up to Low-A. And he continued to show plenty of promise with the bat. He slugged .283/.384/.415 with 11 doubles, one triple, seven homeruns, and 10 stolen bases (in 17 total attempts) in 68 games. His overall production, as measured by *Weighted Runs Created Plus*, topped the league average mark by 31%. He spent the final few weeks of the season with Jersey Shore, hitting .257/.350/.486 in nine games. Lee missed nearly two full months in the middle of the year due to an undisclosed injury.

Scouting Report: Consider the following:

> Since 2006, only two 19-year-old hitters met the following criteria in Low-A (min. 300 PA): 125 to 135 wRC+, 10% to 13% walk rate, and a 18% to 20% strikeout percentage. Those two hitters: Eddinson Paulino and Hao Yu Lee.

Renowned for his prodigious power during his amateur days in Taiwan, Lee's thump has translated fairly well into the professional ranks and projects for at least average and it may climb into above-average territory. The defensive vagabond showed a well-rounded approach at the dish, making solid contact and consistently working the count. Simple, low maintenance swing. Good bat speed. Defensively, he's bounced around between shortstop and second and third bases with the latter likely his final landing spot. There's definite starting potential here. One more final note: his numbers before the DL stint (.283/.385/.472) suggest there's more in the tank. He may be primed to be one of the minors' bigger breakouts in 2023.

Ceiling: 2.5-win player
Risk: Moderate
MLB ETA: 2024/2025

Philadelphia Phillies

7. William Bergolla, 2B/SS

	Hit	Power	SB	Patience	Glove	Overall
	40/55	30/45	50	50	50	50

Born: 10/20/04   **Age:** 18   **Bats:** L   **Top Production Comp:** N/A
Height: 5-11   **Weight:** 165   **Throws:** R

Season	Team	Age	Level	PA	1B	2B	3B	HR	SB	CS	BB%	K%	AVG	OBP	SLG	ISO
2022	PHI	17	DSL	83	24	3	0	0	2	3	13.25%	3.61%	0.380	0.470	0.423	0.042

Background: A highly touted and sought after free agent on the international market last offseason, Bergolla's father, who goes by the same name, appeared in the 2005 Future Game and appeared to be on the precipice of a long big league career as a low end starter / utility infielder. But his time in the bigs was limited to just two short stints in Cincinnati, tallying only 17 games. The elder Bergolla batted a lowly .132/.132/.132 in 38 plate appearances. As for the younger Bergolla, well, Philadelphia rolled out the red carpet and opened their wallet to convince the lefty-swinging middle infielder to join the organization – ultimately agreeing to a deal worth a smidgeon over $2 million last January. He appeared in just 24 games in the Dominican Summer League last season, hitting a scorching .380/.470/.423 with three doubles and a pair of stolen bases (in five attempts). Per *Weighted Runs Created Plus*, his overall production was a staggering 80% better than the league average mark.

Scouting Report: It's not surprisingly that Bergolla shows an advanced feel on both sides of the ball given his baseball bloodlines / heritage. At the dish, the 5-foot-11, 165-pound infielder shows a simple swing geared towards line drives and gap shots – some of which will grow some legs and climb over the outfield fence as he continues to get stronger. His swing is a bit too long at present day, but hasn't inhibited his production due to the level of competition. Defensively, he should have no trouble sticking at the position. It wouldn't be shocking to see the Phillies, who are normally aggressive with their athletic youngsters, push him to Low-A start of the year.

Ceiling: 2.0-win player
Risk: Moderate to High
MLB ETA: 2025

8. Rickardo Perez, C

	Hit	Power	SB	Patience	Glove	Overall
	55	20/45	30	50	40/50	45

Born: 12/04/03   **Age:** 19   **Bats:** L   **Top Production Comp:** N/A
Height: 5-10   **Weight:** 172   **Throws:** R

Season	Team	Age	Level	PA	1B	2B	3B	HR	SB	CS	BB%	K%	AVG	OBP	SLG	ISO
2021	PHI	17	DSL	146	28	3	0	0	3	1	15.07%	10.27%	0.256	0.370	0.281	0.025
2022	PHI	18	CPX	93	27	1	0	1	0	1	7.53%	13.98%	0.349	0.387	0.398	0.048

Background: One of the ball club's crown jewels from their international signing class two years ago. Philadelphia signed the teenage backstop to a seven-figure bonus. Perez, a native of Valencia, Valenzuela, turned in a decent little debut with the club's foreign rookie league affiliate, hitting .256/.370/.281 with a trio of doubles in 146 trips to the plate. Last season the front office bumped their young catcher up to the stateside rookie leagues. And Perez morphed into a batting title-contending dynamo. In 30 games Perez mashed .349/.387/.398 with one double and a dinger. His overall production, according to *Weighted Runs Created Plus*, topped the league average mark by 21%.

Snippet from The 2022 Prospect Digest Handbook: And despite the underwhelming professional debut showing Perez showed a willingness to work the count, make consistent contact, and threw out more than one-third of the potential base thieves. There is no available tape on Perez, but next summer the Phillies may aggressively push him stateside.

Scouting Report: Perez finished tied with the fifth highest average in the Complex Leagues last summer (min. 90 PA). A hit tool over power player at this point in his career, Perez had little trouble hanging with the more advanced rookie league pitching in 2022, showing a consistent ability to make solid contact. His current power is a 20 as he's slugged just five extra-base hits in 73 games. He projects for doubles / gap power with 10 homeruns. Defensively, he's raw and – of course – projectable.

Ceiling: 1.5-win player
Risk: Moderate
MLB ETA: 202

Philadelphia Phillies

9. Erik Miller, LHP

FB	CB	CH	Command	Overall
65	60	50	40	45

Born: 02/13/98	Age: 25	Bats: L	Top Production Comp: Justin Wilson
Height: 6-5	Weight: 240	Throws: L	

Season	Team	Age	Level	IP	TBF	K/9	K%	BB/9	BB%	K-BB%	ERA	FIP	xFIP	Pit/Bat
2022	PHI	24	AA	36.1	146	10.90	30.14%	4.21	11.64%	18.49%	2.23	2.56	3.80	4.13
2022	PHI	24	AAA	12.0	65	13.50	27.69%	10.50	21.54%	6.15%	7.50	8.59	7.15	4.22

Background: Looking back at the Phillies' recent draft classes, it's not overly surprising to see that the same organization that took a mid-round flier – or a calculated gamble – on Griff McGarry in 2021, used a similar tact a few years earlier. Erik Miller, perhaps Griff McGarry O.G., was a talented, enigmatic starter during his three-year career at Stanford University. The big 6-foot-5, 240-pound southpaw initially showed a strong feel for the strike zone – he walked just 21 in 61.2 innings as a true freshman – but displayed an increasingly slippery touch for throwing strikes as his career progressed. He averaged 4.3 walks per nine innings as a sophomore and then finished his third season sporting a 5.0 BB/9 rate. That's not including his time in the Cape Cod League during the 2018 summer when he walked 15 hitters in only 23.2 innings of work. But Miller seemed to regain his command during his debut in 2019, posting an impressive 52-to-15 strikeout-to-walk ratio in 36.0 innings. But, alas, that proved to be fleeting. In an injury-interrupted 2021 season Miller walked 11 in 12.2 innings. Last season, the former fourth rounder was relegated to shorter outings. He finished the year with 62 whiffs, 31 walks, and a 3.54 ERA in 48.1 innings.

Snippet from The 2022 Prospect Digest Handbook: Raw. Wild. Aging.

Scouting Report: A full time starter throughout his amateur and professional career heading into last season. Everything about Miller screamed future reliever, though. The power arsenal, aggressive fastball-heavy approach, and – of course – the lackluster, wavering feel for the strike zone. So it's not surprising that the organization finally relented to destiny and moved him to the pen last year. Miller's approach for each at bat is pretty simple. If the hitter's right-handed, it's fastball, fastball, fastball, maybe a rare changeup. If the hitter's left-handed, it's get ahead with the fastball, curveball, curveball, finish him off with a high fastball. Borderline plus fastball that touched as high as 98 mph during his shortened stints. Hellacious curveball (most reports call it a slider, but it's definitely signaled by the backstop as a deuce and slower, more shapely than a slider). There's late-inning, high leverage potential in his left arm, but he needs his command to uptick half a grade.

Ceiling: 1.0- to 1.5-win player
Risk: Moderate
MLB ETA: 2023

10. Simon Muzziotti, CF

Hit	Power	SB	Patience	Glove	Overall
50	40	50	50	50	40

Born: 12/27/98	Age: 24	Bats: L	Top Production Comp: N/A
Height: 6-1	Weight: 175	Throws: L	

Season	Team	Age	Level	PA	1B	2B	3B	HR	SB	CS	BB%	K%	AVG	OBP	SLG	ISO
2021	PHI	22	AA	18	3	2	0	0	0	0	5.56%	11.11%	0.313	0.353	0.438	0.125
2021	PHI	22	AAA	32	5	0	0	0	2	0	15.63%	12.50%	0.200	0.333	0.200	0.000
2022	PHI	23	AA	165	23	5	4	5	7	3	11.52%	18.79%	0.259	0.339	0.455	0.196
2022	PHI	23	AAA	18	5	0	0	1	0	0	11.11%	16.67%	0.313	0.389	0.313	0.000

Background: Originally signed by the Boston Red Sox for $300,000 all the way back in 2015, Muzziotti's stint with the organization lasted 17 games before Major League Baseball declared him a free agent, ruling that the club broke signing rules. So the Phillies swooped in and handed the toolsy centerfielder a hefty $750,000. Since then, the 6-foot-1, 175-pound Muzziotti has maintained a solid level of consistency as he's hopped, skipped, and jumped through the minor leagues. And despite his 2022 season being pockmarked by two severe injuries, Muzziotti turned in another Muzziotti-type campaign. He batted .249/.330/.414 with five doubles, four triples, five homeruns, and eight stolen bases in 46 games between Clearwater (2 games), Reading (38), and Lehigh Valley (5). He also spent a few weeks with the Phillies at the start of the season, going 1-for-7 with a pair of punch outs. Muzziotti missed several weeks midseason courtesy of a pesky hamstring injury, which knocked him out of commission for roughly six weeks. His 2022 ended prematurely thanks to a partially torn right patellar tendon.

Scouting Report: A solid, well rounded ballplayer in every facet of the game without a true weakness *or* a standout tool. Average hit tool, glove, approach at the plate, speed, and doubles power. A decade ago Muzziotti would be destined for a five-year career as a fourth outfielder. In today's game, though, he's going to be clawing for the final spot on the Phillies' roster.

Ceiling: 1.0-win player
Risk: Low
MLB ETA: Debuted in 2022

Philadelphia Phillies

11. Hans Crouse, RHP

FB	CB	SL	CH	Command	Overall
50	50	50	55	45	40

Born: 09/15/98	Age: 24	Bats: L	Top Production Comp: N/A
Height: 6-4	Weight: 180	Throws: R	

Season	Team	Age	Level	IP	TBF	K/9	K%	BB/9	BB%	K-BB%	ERA	FIP	xFIP	Pit/Bat
2021	PHI	22	AA	29.2	122	11.53	31.15%	3.64	9.84%	21.31%	2.73	3.68	4.33	4.12
2021	TEX	22	AA	51.0	195	9.53	27.69%	3.35	9.74%	17.95%	3.35	3.87	4.62	4.15
2022	PHI	23	AAA	12.1	63	9.49	20.63%	4.38	9.52%	11.11%	13.14	4.97	6.08	3.92

Background: Trivia Time: In terms of present day WAR, name the top two most valuable players taken in the second round of the 2017 draft. The Answer: Daulton Varsho (6.7) and Griffin Canning (2.5). Beyond that, though, 21 other players have made their respective big league debut. Only four of them tallying a positive WAR total. It's really difficult to pin down baseball talent – even with batted ball data and spin rates and high tech devices and algorithms that Neil Armstrong would have only dreamed about while he was standing on the moon. Enter: Hans Crouse. A second round pick by the Rangers that year, Philadelphia acquired the former Bonus Baby, along with Kyle Gibson and Ian Kennedy in exchange for prospects Spencer Howard, Kevin Gowdy, and Josh Gessner near the trade deadline two years ago. And it *looked* like Crouse was emerging as a dominant young arm at the time. He would finish the 2021 season with 98 punch outs, 34 walks, and a 3.28 ERA across 85.0 innings between both organizations. That didn't include a brief two-game cameo in Philly either. And the 6-foot-4, 180-pound righty seemed well positioned to play a potentially large role for the Phillies as 2022 crept closer. But Crouse's season was essentially over just as it starter. Severe right biceps tendonitis knocked him out of action from April 20th through September 10th, limiting him to just 12.1 mostly miserable innings. He tallied a 13.14 ERA with 13 strikeouts and six free passes.

Snippet from The 2022 Prospect Digest Handbook: Twenty-two-year-old pitchers with (A) three above-average pitches and (B) success at Double-A are pretty rare. Crouse works exclusively from the stretch, which is becoming more en vogue these days. His fastball, during a late season Double-A start, was sitting in the 92-94 mph range and peaked at 95. His slider shows some hard, sweeping cutter-like movement. And his upper 80s changeup is deceiving, an equalizer. He throws plenty of strikes and may eventually see an uptick in command, going from average to above-average. Crouse has some #3/#4-type upside.

Scouting Report: Slow worker, like the pitching equivalent of Mike Hargrove, the Human Rain Delay. Crouse's fastball lacked the same visual zip that he's shown in past season – some of which is to be expected given his lost season / extended stint on the disabled list. Average curveball. The slider downgraded from a 55 to 50. But his changeup, his true bread-and-butter, still looked as good as it was. A year ago he looked like he could be a backend starting pitcher. Now, though, he's tracking more like a future Quad-A type arm.

Ceiling: 1.0-win player
Risk: Moderate
MLB ETA: Debuted in 2021

12. Alex McFarlane, RHP

FB	SL	CH	Command	Overall
60	60	55	35/40	40

Born: 06/09/01	Age: 22	Bats: R	Top Production Comp: N/A
Height: 6-4	Weight: 205	Throws: R	

Background: The Cardinals took a late round flier on the broad-shouldered right-hander coming out of Habersham Central High School, McFarlane, of course, bypassed the opportunity to join the storied franchise and opted to attend the University of Miami. But the hard-throwing hurler's career with the Hurricane's was pockmarked with command / control issues but highlighted with a pair of stints with the Chatham Anglers in the vaunted Cape Cod League. McFarlane left the school with a 4.35 ERA, 120 strikeouts, and 44 walks in 91.0 innings of work – most of which was spent working out of the ACC Conference School's bullpen. Philadelphia took McFarlane in the fourth round, 122nd overall, and signed him to a deal worth $572,500. He appeared in three games with the Clearwater Threshers in Low-A, striking out 12 and walking three in eight innings.

Scouting Report: McFarlane hits a few of the important checkboxes for modern day hurlers: he's massive yet athletic, strong but lean; he throws hard with his fastball sitting in the mid- to upper-90s; he features a dominant offspeed offering; he's projectable despite spending three full seasons in college; and – of course – he's squared off against tough competition, both in the ACC and in the Cape. Now the bad news: he can't throw strikes consistently. Philly has a tendency to take mid-round gambles on projectable, albeit raw JuCo or older hurlers, and McFarlane is the latest. There's definite starting caliber potential here with two plus pitches (fastball and a mid-80s wipeout slider) and a third offering that's incredibly promising (an upper 80s, fading / diving changeup). It's going to come down to his ability to throw strikes.

Ceiling: 1.0-win player
Risk: Moderate
MLB ETA: 2025

Philadelphia Phillies

13. Gabriel Rincones Jr., OF

Hit	Power	SB	Patience	Glove	Overall
45	55	30	55	45	40

Born: 03/03/0	Age: 22	Bats: L	Top Production Comp: N/A
Height: 6-4	Weight: 225	Throws: R	

Background: There's a really great piece on *Phillies Nation* by Ty Daubert that tells the story – or stories – of Gabriel Rincones Jr. And to sum up Daubert's fine work: Rincones Jr. comes from some baseball bloodlines – his father, Gabriel Sr., spent a summer with the Mariners Rookie Ball team in 1997. Junior grew up in Scotland, moved to Venezuela to live with relatives to compete against better players, and eventually landed at H.B. Plant High School in Tampa, Florida. The 6-foot-4, 225-pound lefty-swinging outfielder spent some time at St. Petersburg College, where he would eventually be drafted as a late-round flier by the Padres in 2021. Instead of jumping at the chance to realize his lifelong dream, Rincones Jr. transferred to Florida Atlantic University. And he mashed. A lot. In 58 games with the Owls, he bashed .346/.451/.658 with 17 doubles, 19 homeruns, and a pair of stolen bases. Philadelphia drafted him in the third round, 93rd overall, and signed him to a slightly below slot deal worth $627,500.

Scouting Report: Consider the following:

Since 2011, only eight (8) Division I hitters met the following criteria in a season (min. 275 PA): bat at least .340/.440/.640 with a walk rate north of 14% and a strikeout rate between 16% and 19%. Those eight hitters are: Jonathan India, J.J. Bleday, Brent Rooker, Luke Reynolds, Dominic Keegan, Aaron Westlake, Heath Quinn, and – of course – Gabriel Rincones Jr.

Tremendous makeup. An absolute gamer. Rincones showcases above-average power with a solid approach at the plate. The lefty-swinging outfielder, of course, didn't face elite competition in Conference USA, so he'll need to prove himself early in the minors. 45-grade hit tool. Not enough speed to play centerfield. There's some fourth / fifth outfielder-type potential here.

Ceiling: 1.0-win player
Risk: Moderate
MLB ETA: 2025

14. Jordan Viars, LF/RF

Hit	Power	SB	Patience	Glove	Overall
35/45	40/55	30	50	50	40

Born: 07/18/03	Age: 19	Bats: L	Top Production Comp: N/A
Height: 6-4	Weight: 215	Throws: L	

Season	Team	Age	Level	PA	1B	2B	3B	HR	SB	CS	BB%	K%	AVG	OBP	SLG	ISO
2021	PHI	17	CPX	64	8	1	0	3	2	0	17.19%	18.75%	0.255	0.406	0.468	0.213
2022	PHI	18	CPX	179	28	6	1	2	5	0	9.50%	22.35%	0.240	0.330	0.331	0.091
2022	PHI	18	A	28	5	0	0	0	0	0	7.14%	32.14%	0.208	0.286	0.208	0.000

Background: The Phillies went above slot to convince their 2021 third round pick to bypass his commitment to the University of Arkansas. Viars' price point was just a smidgeon under three-quarters of a million dollars. The Rick Reedy High School product turned in a solid, sometimes impressive debut in the Complex League two years ago, slugging .255/.406/.468 with one double, three homeruns, and a pair of stolen bases. Last season, Philadelphia took the uncharacteristically cautious approach and sent their young corner outfielder back down to the Complex League for further seasoning. And they clearly knew – or saw – something no one else did. Viars cobbled together a disappointing .240/.330/.331 in 44 contests. He spent the final week-plus of the year with Clearwater, going 5-for-24.

Snippet from The 2022 Prospect Digest Handbook: Big time raw power, though he didn't flash much in-game pop during his debut, Viars has 25-homer potential. He's shown a willingness to work the count and an ability to shoot the ball the other way. Above-average bat speed.

Scouting Report: Consider the following:

Since 2006, only five 18-year-old hitters posted an 85 to 95 wRC+ with an 8.5% to 9.5% walk rate and a 21.5% to 23.5% strikeout rate in stateside rookie leagues (min. 175 PA): Cory Scammell, Angel Reyes, Joseph Miranda, Andres Chaparro, and – of course – Jordan Viars.

Philadelphia Phillies

The left-handed Viars *really* struggled against southpaws last season, hitting .100/.263/.167 in 38 plate appearances (vs. .276/.354/.362 against RHP). On top of that, the young corner outfielder hasn't even scratched the surface of his power potential. He's significantly more raw than the initial impression following his debut.

Ceiling: 1.0-win player
Risk: Moderate
MLB ETA: 2025

15. Noah Skirrow, RHP

	FB	SL	CH	Command	Overall
	50	55	50	50	40

Born: 07/21/98	Age: 24	Bats: R	Top Production Comp: N/A
Height: 6-3	Weight: 215	Throws: R	

Season	Team	Age	Level	IP	TBF	K/9	K%	BB/9	BB%	K-BB%	ERA	FIP	xFIP	Pit/Bat
2021	PHI	22	A+	31.1	136	11.49	29.41%	4.60	11.76%	17.65%	3.73	3.86	4.74	3.93
2021	PHI	22	AA	23.2	111	6.85	16.22%	3.42	8.11%	8.11%	5.70	5.88	6.05	3.78
2022	PHI	23	AA	98.2	433	10.49	26.56%	2.92	7.39%	19.17%	4.65	3.53	4.01	3.82
2022	PHI	23	AAA	21.0	82	7.71	21.95%	3.86	10.98%	10.98%	3.00	4.94	4.65	4.09

Background: Caught up in the numbers game as part of the COVID-limited 2020 draft class. The Phillies swooped in and signed the Liberty University ace to an undrafted free agent contract three years ago. And since then, the 6-foot-3, 215-pound right-hander has blitzed through the club's minor league system. A strikeout artist with problematic command during his first two seasons in college, Skirrow's strikeout rate plummeted to a career low 7.8 K/9 as his walk rate, which showed improvement as sophomore, regressed mightily (5.1 BB/9). Since joining the organization, though, Skirrow has showed continued improvement in his strike-throwing ability while maintaining impressive swing-and-miss numbers. He tossed 58.0 innings during his debut in 2021, striking out 60 and walking 27. And last season he was utterly brilliant during his 21-game cameo with the Reading Fightin' Phillies: he would punch out 115 and walked 32 in only 98.2 innings of work. He made another four solid starts with Lehigh Valley to cap off his second professional season.

Scouting Report: Consider the following:

> Since 2006, only five 23-year-old hurlers posted a 25.6% to 27.5% strikeout percentage with a 6.5% to 8.5% walk percentage in Double-A (min. 90 IP): Brandon Woodruff, Luis Ortiz, Michael Mercado, Brett Kerry, and Noah Skirrow, the former undrafted free agent.

Had Skirrow's production not cratered during his disappointing – and shortened junior campaign – at Liberty, he likely would have been ticketed as a fourth round flier. Low-90s fastball that touched 94 mph late in the season. His bread-and-butter offering, though, is an above-average, sweeping mid-80s slider. He'll also mix in a quality average changeup, hovering in the 84 mph range. The change-of-pace has some nice fade, but lacks a whole lot of velocity separation. Skirrow's already exceeded expectations and has a chance to be a solid up-and-down arm / spot starter / multi-inning reliever.

Ceiling: 1.0-win player
Risk: Moderate
MLB ETA: 2023

16. Francisco Morales, RHP

	FB	SL	CH	Command	Overall
	60	60	N/A	40	40

Born: 10/27/99	Age: 23	Bats: R	Top Production Comp: Kyle Crick
Height: 6-4	Weight: 185	Throws: R	

Season	Team	Age	Level	IP	TBF	K/9	K%	BB/9	BB%	K-BB%	ERA	FIP	xFIP	Pit/Bat
2021	PHI	21	AA	83.0	390	11.93	28.21%	6.51	15.38%	12.82%	6.94	5.01	4.86	3.93
2022	PHI	22	AA	30.1	116	16.02	46.55%	5.04	14.66%	31.90%	1.48	1.63	2.76	4.21
2022	PHI	22	AAA	20.2	113	6.97	14.16%	12.19	24.78%	-10.62%	9.58	6.80	8.33	3.98

Background: With a quote ripped out of the pages of every stoner's high school yearbook, Morales' 2022 season was "a wild and strange journey". A native of San Juan de los Morros, Venezuela, the fire-bolt slinging right-handed with a penchant for handing out free passes began the year off in Double-A, working out the bullpen for the first time in his career. And it was a revelation for the 6-foot-4, 185-pound hurler as he struck out 28, walked just six, and allowed one earned run through 16.1 innings of work. So it made sense that the Phillies, in their constant search for quality relief arms, called Morales up in mid-May and he was brilliant – at least in his first game. He struck out three and walked one in a pair of innings against the Mariners. He would make one more appearance against the Dodgers four days later but his newly found / improved command all but deserted him as he walked three in one inning. Back down to the minors for more seasoning – though he was sent to Triple-A. Except he couldn't throw strikes – again. He posted a 12-to-17 strikeout-to-walk ratio in only 10 innings of work. The front office bumped him back down to Reading and the results were much better (2.57 ERA) but he still walked 11 in only 14.0 innings of work.

Philadelphia Phillies

He was recalled back up to Philadelphia for one more disastrous outing against the Braves before being relegated back to Lehigh Valley for the remainder of the year. Morales finished his minor league journey last season with a 4.76 ERA across 51.0 innings with 70 strikeouts and walked 45. He tossed another 5.0 innings with the Phillies, tallying a 3-to-6 strikeout to walk ratio. Morales appeared in nine games with the Surprise Saguaros in the Arizona Fall League, fanning 17 and – of course – handing out way too many free passes (seven) in 10.2 innings of work.

Snippet from The 2022 Prospect Digest Handbook: The big righty attacks hitters with a hyper-focused two-pitch mix: a mid-90s fastball with riding life and a knee-buckling slider with 12-6 break. He'll – *rarely* – mix in a rare, underdeveloped changeup as well. Along with lacking a consistent third offering, Morales lack of command almost immediately pushes him into some type of future relief role – unless he seems a major uptick in the next year or two.

Scouting Report: On the right days – those outings where Morales is pounding the strike zone with his wicked fastball / slider combo – the big Venezuelan hurler looks practically unhittable. His fastball, sitting in the mid-90s, and his 12-6 bending breaking ball roughly 10 mph slower simply overpowers hitters. But those days just don't happen too frequently. The command is – maybe – a 35 on average. He'll continue to get opportunities in the upper minors, both in the Phillies' organization and beyond, for as long as he's throwing 95 mph. If the velo dips slightly, those opportunities are going to stop as long as the command is as spotty as Lenny Dykstra's investment career.

Ceiling: 1.0-win player
Risk: Moderate to High
MLB ETA: Debuted in 2022

17. Ethan Wilson, LF/RF

Hit	Power	SB	Patience	Glove	Overall
35/40	35/40	55	45	50	40

Born: 11/07/99	Age: 23	Bats: L	Top Production Comp: N/A
Height: 6-1	Weight: 210	Throws: L	

Season	Team	Age	Level	PA	1B	2B	3B	HR	SB	CS	BB%	K%	AVG	OBP	SLG	ISO
2021	PHI	21	A	117	14	4	2	3	2	2	8.55%	21.37%	0.215	0.282	0.374	0.159
2022	PHI	22	A+	458	72	20	2	7	25	7	6.11%	20.31%	0.238	0.290	0.344	0.106
2022	PHI	22	AA	78	12	2	0	1	1	2	6.41%	26.92%	0.214	0.286	0.286	0.071

Background: The University of South Alabama is far from a baseball hotbed. But from the mid-1980s through the early-2000s the school *quietly* churned out a surprising number of notable big leaguers, including Luis Gonzalez and his 354 career homeruns; All-Star centerfielder Lance Johnson; right-hander Jon Lieber, who made the 2001 NL All-Star squad; post-season hero David Freese; speedy centerfielder Juan Pierre; Silver Slugger Adam Lind; and former Phillie fan favorite Marlon Anderson. But over the previous decade-and-a-half, the Jaguars' program has produced just two notable draft picks: Travis Swaggerty, the 10th overall pick in 2018, and Ethan Wilson, Philadelphia's second round pick two years ago. After signing with the organization for just over $1.5 million, Wilson looked abysmal during his debut in with the Clearwater Threshers, hitting just .215/.282/.374 in 30 games. Unfortunately last season was much the same for the 6-foot-1, 210-pound outfielder. In 112 games with Jersey Shore and another 18 with Reading, the former high round pick hit an aggregate .235/.290/.336 with 22 doubles, two triples, eight homeruns, and 26 stolen bases (in 35 total attempts). Per *Weighted Runs Created Plus*, his overall production was a whopping 29% *below* league average mark.

Snippet from The 2022 Prospect Digest Handbook: Short and stocky, but not quite the typical power associated from a corner outfielder position. Wilson makes a uniform look good though. Not in love with the swing, it's a bit long and his toe tap might cause some timing issues in the professional ranks. Wilson looks like a tweener: the tools aren't enough to scream big league left fielder and his lack of positional versatility keeps him from a fourth outfielder role.

Scouting Report: It was an over-draft at the time and Wilson confirmed that during his disappointing debut and he only further solidified it during his disastrous showing in 2022. The hit tool is worse than expected. His power is in line with a soft-hitting utility infielder, let alone a corner outfielder. The speed is above-average but that hasn't translated into any meaningful value on the defensive side of the ball. He's now entering his age-23 season with 653 career minor league plate appearances on his resume, sporting an atrocious .231/.288/.344 slash line. Consider the following:

> Since 2006, there have been thirty 22-year-old hitters that posted a wRC+ between 68 and 78 in a High-A season (min. 350 PA). None of those players would go on to any notable big league career.

It was a poor pick by the organization at the time. And nothing has since then, either.

Ceiling: 0.5- to 1.0-win player
Risk: Moderate
MLB ETA: 2024/2025

18. Carlos De La Cruz, 1B/OF

Hit	Power	SB	Patience	Glove	Overall
40	50/60	35	45	50	40

Born: 10/06/99 | **Age:** 23 | **Bats:** R | **Top Production Comp:** N/A
Height: 6-8 | **Weight:** 210 | **Throws:** R |

Background: An under-the-radar type signing on the international market near the end of the 2017 season. De La Cruz opened some eyes during his impressive, albeit strikeout plagued, debut in the Gulf Coast League the following summer as he slugged .284/.345/.459 with eight doubles and six dingers in 43 games. But whatever prospect momentum De La Cruz was building all but disappeared during his abysmal showing with Lakewood in 2019. He batted a putrid .220/.271/.327 in 117 games. After minor league ball returned from its COVID-induced absence in 2021, De La Cruz battled ineffectiveness and injury while cobbling together a .181/.291/.299. And it was pretty easy to continue to ignore the massive first baseman / outfielder at that point. But the 6-foot-8, 201 pound hulkster rebounded during surprisingly strong 2022 campaign. De La Cruz slugged .266/.344/.463 in 64 games with Jersey Shore, continued to mash in his 38-game cameo with Reading, and didn't miss a beat in his stint in the Arizona Fall League either (.307/.368/.516).

Scouting Report: One of the biggest everyday players at any level of professional baseball, De La Cruz stands an imposing 6-foot-8, and Shawn Bradley-esque 210 pounds. The New York-born infielder / outfielder's shaved some percentage points off of his problematic strikeout rate as he fanned in 29.8% of his plate appearances – easily the best mark of his career. Promising power potential that he hasn't quite fully tapped into. Breaking balls, particularly low in the zone, give him fits. But his rebound last season – and continued performance in the Arizona Fall League – has him tracking as a Quad-A / fifth outfielder.

Ceiling: 0.5- to 1.0-win player
Risk: Moderate
MLB ETA: 2023

19. Gunner Mayer, RHP

FB	CB	CH	Command	Overall
50/55	50	55/60	35/45	40

Born: 07/27/00 | **Age:** 22 | **Bats:** R | **Top Production Comp:** N/A
Height: 6-6 | **Weight:** 190 | **Throws:** R |

Season	Team	Age	Level	IP	TBF	K/9	K%	BB/9	BB%	K-BB%	ERA	FIP	xFIP	Pit/Bat
2021	PHI	20	A	23.1	125	12.73	26.40%	8.49	17.60%	8.80%	10.03	7.23	5.75	4.11
2022	PHI	21	A	48.2	208	12.39	32.21%	4.81	12.50%	19.71%	5.18	5.10	3.77	3.81

Background: Stockton-based San Joaquin Delta College is most known for producing former two-time All-Star reliever "Everyday" Eddie Guardado. Beyond that, though, former big league alumnus has been sparse. And the junior college's pipeline to the minor leagues has all but dried up in recent years as well. So much so, in fact, that the school's last two draft picks were four years ago when the Phillies and Twins called the names of Gunner Mayer and Zack Mathis in the fifth and 38th rounds. The 150th overall pick in 2019, Mayer received the highest bonus in school history, agreeing to join the Phillies' organization for a hefty $600,000 contract. Mayer missed the majority of his first full season in pro ball, tossing just over 26 innings between Clearwater and the Complex League, averaging 13 strikeouts and 7.5 walks per nine innings. Last season was much the same for the big right-hander. In another injury-marred campaign, Mayer made 12 starts and a pair of relief appearances with the Threshers, posting a 67-to-26 strikeout-to-walk ratio in 48.2 innings of work.

Scouting Report: A potential diamond in the rough. Mayer has more projection than the typical hurler his age. The 6-foot-6, 190-pound right-hander was a full-time reliever during his stint in college, throwing jut 37.2 innings across 25 appearances. Combine that with his lack of time on a professional mound and the big righty may find an extra gear on his low-90s heater. Big 12-6 curveball, an average offering. But his changeup is a firm 55-grade and may climb into plus territory. The organization seems content on stretching out the former reliever. If he can stay healthy in 2023, he may be poised for a big year.

Ceiling: 1.0-win player
Risk: Moderate to High
MLB ETA: 2024/2025

Philadelphia Phillies

20. Cristian Hernandez, RHP

	FB	CB	SL	CH	Command	Overall
	45	50	50	50	60	35

Born: 09/23/00	Age: 22	Bats: R	Top Production Comp: N/A
Height: 6-3	Weight: 180	Throws: R	

Season	Team	Age	Level	IP	TBF	K/9	K%	BB/9	BB%	K-BB%	ERA	FIP	xFIP	Pit/Bat
2021	PHI	20	A	70.2	301	10.95	28.57%	3.69	9.63%	18.94%	3.69	4.79	4.18	3.71
2022	PHI	21	A+	74.2	323	8.08	20.74%	2.29	5.88%	14.86%	4.70	4.05	4.77	3.59

Background: Signed during the 2017 season out of Cumana, Venezuela, Hernandez, a wiry right-hander, would wait another season before debuting in with the organization's Dominican Summer League affiliate. He would throw 63.0 innings during his first stint in pro ball, averaging a solid 7.0 strikeouts and just 1.4 walks per nine innings. Hernandez would miss the 2019 and the 2020 seasons and then pop with the Clearwater Threshers two years ago. But the 6-foot-3, 180-pound hurler wasn't able to shake the injury bug, though, missing roughly six weeks of action towards the middle of the year. Last season, despite the limited development time, Hernandez spent the entire campaign with the Jersey Shore BlueClaws, throwing 74.2 innings with an impeccable 67-to-19 strikeout-to-walk ratio. He finished the year with a 4.70 ERA, 4.05 FIP, and a 4.77 xFIP. Hernandez appeared in eight games (one start and seven relief appearances) with the Surprise Saguaros in the Arizona Fall League, striking out 11, walking just one, and surrendering one earned run in 11.0 innings of work.

Scouting Report: Consider the following:

Since 2006, there have been eighteen 21-year-old hurlers that met the following criteria in a season in High-A (min. 70 IP): 20% to 22% strikeout percentage and a 5% to 7% walk rate. Those eighteen hurlers: Alex Cobb, Johnny Cueto, Miguel Almonte, Mitch Keller, Zack Littell, Brooks Pounders, Scott Diamond, Bobby Bundy, Chih-Wei Hu, Daryl Thompson, Dylan Owen, Ian Krol, Jesus Castillo, Jose Rodriguez, Tim Cate, Tony Santillan, Yennsy Diaz, and – of course – Cristian Hernandez, Philadelphia's underrated hurler.

Hernandez's production last season is puts him in a group that's littered with future big leaguers. Guys like Alex Cobb, Johnny Cueto, Miguel Almonte, Mitch Keller, Zack Littell, Brooks Pounders, Scott Diamond, Chih-Wei Hu, Daryl Thompson, Ian Krol, Jose Rodriguez, Tony Santillan, and Yennsy Diaz. Removing Hernandez from the equation, slightly higher than 76% of similarly performing 21-year-old hurlers in High-A would go onto the big leagues. Hernandez is a throwback from yesteryear, a soft-tossing right-hander with guile and pitchability. His fastball sits in the 88- to 90-mph range. He'll mix in a pair of similar breaking balls: an upper 70s slider and a mid-70s curveball with the former showing a 2-8 break and the latter a 12-6 bite. His changeup sits in the low 80s. It wouldn't be surprising to see Hernandez carve out a brief year career as a multi-inning, command oriented reliever. Nothing more though.

Ceiling: 0.5-win player
Risk: Low to Moderate
MLB ETA: 2023/2024

Pittsburgh Pirates Top Prospects

Pittsburgh Pirates

1. Termarr Johnson, 2B/SS

Hit	Power	SB	Patience	Glove	Overall
60/70	50/60	50/40	55	55	70

Born: 06/11/04	**Age:** 19	**Bats:** L	**Top Production Comp:** N/A
Height: 5-7	**Weight:** 175	**Throws:** R	

Season	Team	Age	Level	PA	1B	2B	3B	HR	SB	CS	BB%	K%	AVG	OBP	SLG	ISO
2022	PIT	18	CPX	29	1	2	0	0	2	0	20.69%	27.59%	0.130	0.310	0.217	0.087
2022	PIT	18	A	53	6	4	0	1	4	1	18.87%	24.53%	0.275	0.396	0.450	0.175

Background: Benjamin Elijah Mays High School, located in Atlanta, Georgia, has churned out an impressive collection of athletes and celebrities throughout the years, including: NBA shooting guard / small forward Gerald Wilkins, NFL players Tyrell Adams, Natrez Patrick and Reggie Wilkes, former Atlanta Mayor Andre Dickens, and – easily the most famous – singer / actress Rozonda Thomas, a.k.a. Chili from TLC. Middle infielder Termarr Johnson is slated to become the best baseball player to come from the school's hallowed halls. A mighty mite that's well known on the baseball circuits, the 5-foot-7, 175-pound lefty-swinging infielder has already put together an impressive resume: he slugged a scorching .375/.483/.542 with a trio of extra-base knocks on Team USA's U15 Gold Medal-winning squad in 2019. Two years later he finished third at the All-Star High School Homerun Derby, trailing only Jared Jones (committed to LSU) and Sal Stewart (committed to Vanderbilt). Johnson, who committed to Arizona State University, led Benjamin Elijah Mays to the state playoffs, though they fell to North Oconee in the first round. Pittsburgh happily snagged the offensive dynamo in the opening round, 4th overall, and signed him to a deal worth $7,219,000 – the third highest bonus given out last July. Johnson appeared in 23 games between the Complex League and Bradenton, hitting an aggregate .222/.366/.365.

Scouting Report: Per the usual, my pre-draft write-up:

> "Advanced approach at the plate, well beyond his years. Johnson combines a patient approach with tremendous bat-to-ball skills, and the potential to slug 25 homeruns in the professional ranks. He's the most well-rounded high school bat I've seen since writing about prep prospects. Silky smooth swing, strong wrists just flick the ball around the diamond. Average speed and arm, but he moves well with plus agility and a quick release to compensate. He's tabbed to slide over to second base. There's a little bit of Joe Morgan here, though minus the speed."

Ceiling: 6.0-win player
Risk: Moderate
MLB ETA: 2025/2026

2. Endy Rodriguez, C

Hit	Power	SB	Patience	Glove	Overall
55	55/60	35	55	50	60

Born: 05/26/00	**Age:** 23	**Bats:** B	**Top Production Comp:** Jorge Posada
Height: 6-0	**Weight:** 170	**Throws:** R	

Season	Team	Age	Level	PA	1B	2B	3B	HR	SB	CS	BB%	K%	AVG	OBP	SLG	ISO
2021	PIT	21	A	434	65	25	6	15	2	0	11.52%	17.74%	0.294	0.380	0.512	0.218
2022	PIT	22	A+	370	54	23	3	16	3	3	11.35%	20.81%	0.302	0.392	0.544	0.242
2022	PIT	22	AA	138	20	14	0	8	1	0	13.04%	15.22%	0.356	0.442	0.678	0.322
2022	PIT	22	AAA	23	6	2	1	1	0	0	0.00%	13.04%	0.455	0.435	0.773	0.318

Background: The Pirates, Mets, and Padres got together for a good, old fashioned three-team deal in mid-January two years ago. The details of the trade: the Padres received Joe Musgrove; the Mets acquired Joey Lucchesi, and the Pirates were handed David Bednar, Omar Cruz, Drake Fellows, Hudson Head, and Endy Rodriguez. The sole prospect / player New York dealt away in the trade, Rodriguez has blossomed into one of the better catching prospects in the minor leagues. Pittsburgh sent the Santiago, Dominican Republic native to their Low-A affiliate months after acquiring him. And Rodriguez did what he's always done: hit. He batted a rock solid .294/.380/.512 with 25 doubles, six triples, 15 homeruns, and a pair of stolen based in only 98 games. Then they let him loose on the rest of the minor leagues in 2022. Rodriguez dominated the High-A competition to the tune of .302/.392/.544, looked Ruthian during his 31-game cameo in Double-A (.356/.442/.678), and promptly went 10-for-22 in his six-game cameo with Indianapolis. The 6-foot, 170-pound backstop finished his second season in Pittsburgh's farm system with an aggregate .323/.407/.590 with 39 doubles, four triples, 25 homeruns, and – just for good measure – four stolen bases. His overall production, according to *Weighted Runs Created Plus*, surpassed the league average mark by a massive 66%.

Snippet from The 2022 Prospect Digest Handbook: Rodriguez is an interesting low level bat-first backstop. There's some sleeper starting potential here, but he needs to show some improved performance behind the dish as well. The Pirates may look to accelerate his develop arc in 2022. Double-A isn't out of the question.

Pittsburgh Pirates

Scouting Report: Consider the following:

> Since 2006, only three 22-year-old hitters posted a 145 to 155 wRC+ with a double-digit walk rate and a 19% to 23% strikeout rate in any High-A league (min. 350 PA): Tyler Flowers, Kyle Parker, and Endy Rodriguez. His 166 wRC+ wRC+ total was the fifth highest mark in the minor leagues among all hitters with at least 250 plate appearances. FYI: there were 1,251 players that met that criteria.

An average pitch-framer with improving defense that's bumped up from slightly below-average to better than average; Rodriguez was an absolute force to be reckoned with at the plate. Above-average hit tool *and* power, strong contact *and* walk rates, and enough leather and mobility to stick behind the dish. Oh, yeah, he's a switch-hitter as well. Not only is Rodriguez a good breaking ball hitter, but he hits good breaking balls – consistently. Very natural hitter with an easy swing that generates a ton of power. In terms of big league ceiling, think: .290/.340/460.

Ceiling: 5.0-win player
Risk: Moderate
MLB ETA: 2023

3. Henry Davis, C

Hit	Power	SB	Patience	Glove	Overall
50	60	40/35	50	50	60

Born: 09/21/99 **Age:** 23 **Bats:** R **Top Production Comp:** J.T. Realmuto
Height: 6-2 **Weight:** 210 **Throws:** R

Season	Team	Age	Level	PA	1B	2B	3B	HR	SB	CS	BB%	K%	AVG	OBP	SLG	ISO
2021	PIT	21	A+	24	2	0	1	2	1	0	16.67%	33.33%	0.263	0.375	0.684	0.421
2022	PIT	22	A	15	2	1	0	1	1	0	6.67%	13.33%	0.364	0.467	0.727	0.364
2022	PIT	22	A+	100	19	3	1	5	5	1	8.00%	18.00%	0.341	0.450	0.585	0.244
2022	PIT	22	AA	136	12	8	0	4	3	1	8.82%	22.06%	0.207	0.324	0.379	0.172

Background: Despite most remembering the club's massive swing-and-miss atop the 2002 when they selected Ball State ace Bryan Bullington, the Pirates have generally done well when they've been equipped with the first overall pick. In 1986 they selected University of Arkansas infielder Jeff King, who would go onto a solid 11-year big league career (though Greg Swindell, Matt Williams, Kevin Brown, and Gary Sheffield were taken immediately after). Ten years later that chose Clemson University ace Kris Benson, who pitched in the big leagues for nine years and tallied nearly $30,000,000 in career earnings. Then, of course, Pittsburgh used the top pick in the 2011 summer draft for UCLA ace Gerrit Cole, who needs no introduction or background. And, on the other hand, the club's been able to unearth a pair of above-average backstops in the first round as well. Jason Kendall, the 23rd overall pick in 1992, put together a borderline Hall of Fame career. Twelve years later they nabbed high school catcher-turned-big-league infielder Neil Walker with the 11th overall pick. Pittsburgh fans are hoping that Davis's name can be added to both lists. A four-year letter winner at Fox Lane High School, Davis made the move to the ACC with aplomb as he batted a rock solid .280/.345/.386 in 45 games as a true freshman in 2019. The following year the 6-foot-2, 210-pound backstop was in the midst of a *massive* breakout campaign before the COVID pandemic derailed it, slugging .372/.481/.663 with eight extra-base knocks in 14 games for the Cardinals. *Shockingly*, Davis as able to maintain that same level of production across a full season in 2021: he bashed .370/.483/.663 with nine doubles, 15 homeruns, and 10 stolen bases (in only 13 attempts). After Pittsburgh grabbed with him with the top overall pick and signed him to a deal worth $6.5 million, Davis slugged .308/.387/.808 in eight low level games. Last season, the front office sent their prized prospect straight up to High-A, but after mashing .342/.450/.585 through 22 games, he was deemed ready for the minors' most challenging level – Double-A. After just two games, though, Davis hit the disabled list for a month, made a couple brief rehab assignments, and finally found his way back to Altoona in mid-June. After a difficult 15-game stretch, the former first rounder hit the disabled list *again* for more than six weeks. He closed out the year by hitting .241/.328/.407 over his final 14 games with the Curve. Overall, Davis finished the year with an aggregate .264/.380/.472 mark with 12 doubles, one triple, 10 homeruns, and nine stolen bases. His overall production, according to *Weighted Runs Created Plus*, was 36% better than average. Davis spent fall with the Surprise Saguaros, hitting .260/.435/.440.

Snippet from The 2022 Prospect Digest Handbook: An old school throwback that refuses to wear batting gloves at the plate, Davis has always shown an advanced approach at the plate – as evidenced by his stellar peripherals. The Louisville standout starts from a modified crouch and generates plus bat speed thanks to his core and lower body. He's a perennial 20-homerun threat. Defensively, he unfurls a howitzer on potential thieves with the accuracy to match. In terms of upside think: .270/.340/.450.

Scouting Report: Davis was caught up in a bit of a hullabaloo this offseason – through no fault of his own. *MLB Pipeline* wrote an article, which was eventually removed / appended that listed Davis, the 2021 #1 overall pick, as the most overrated prospect in the game. But is that *really* the case? Let's take a look...

Pittsburgh Pirates

#1. Davis got off to a hellacious start to the year, slugging .342/.450/.585 with strong contacts rates and *zero* red flags during his first 22 games in High-A at the start of the year. His production, as measured by *Weighted Runs Created Plus*, topped the league average mark by 80% during that stretch.

#2. Pittsburgh promptly pushes him up to Double-A – *with just 30 professional games under his belt* – and he goes 1-for-2 with a dinger, a walk, and a HBP during his first game. Two days later he hits the disabled list for a month with a wrist injury.

#3. One he comes off the DL, he struggled significantly and hit the injury list two weeks after coming back with a...wrist injury. He spent *another* six weeks on the bench. Including his time in the Arizona Fall League, he batted .250/.381/.423

So, is he *really* overrated or was he just hurt? He was clearly hurt. Buy into the dip. Plus in-game power, average hit tool, average patience, and strong contact rates. Defensively, he won't win any Gold Gloves, but he does enough to remain a competent catcher. He's still tracking like a .270/.340/.450 hitter with 25-homerun thump.

Ceiling: 4.0-win player
Risk: Moderate
MLB ETA: 2023/2024

4. Michael Burrows, RHP

FB	CB	CH	Command	Overall
65	60	50	50	60

Born: 11/08/99	Age: 23	Bats: R	Top Production Comp: Luis Castillo
Height: 6-2	Weight: 195	Throws: R	

Season	Team	Age	Level	IP	TBF	K/9	K%	BB/9	BB%	K-BB%	ERA	FIP	xFIP	Pit/Bat
2021	PIT	21	A+	49.0	193	12.12	34.20%	3.67	10.36%	23.83%	2.20	3.28	4.36	4.27
2022	PIT	22	AA	52.0	213	11.94	32.39%	3.29	8.92%	23.47%	2.94	2.72	3.94	4.00
2022	PIT	22	AAA	42.1	180	8.93	23.33%	2.55	6.67%	16.67%	5.31	3.98	4.40	4.05

Background: When it comes to most organizations, Mike Burrows, a former 11th round Bonus Baby, would stand atop the list of their best prospects. In the Pirates' bountiful farm system, he's merely another name, another cog in what should become their re-emergence in the coming years. A product of Connecticut-based Waterford High School, Burrows really came into his own after a dominant showing in High-A two years ago. The 6-foot-2, 195-pound right-hander averaged an impressive 12.1 strikeouts and 3.7 walks per nine innings across 13 starts with Greensboro. The only thing that slowed him that year was an oblique injury, which knocked him out for roughly two months. Last season, Burrows kept his foot on the developmental accelerator as he breezed through 12 strong starts with Altoona and settled in nicely for another 12 appearances with Indianapolis in Triple-A. Overall, the former late round prep star struck out 111 versus just 31 walks across a career best 94.1 innings of work. He finished the year with an aggregate 4.01 ERA and a sparkling 3.29 FIP.

Snippet from The 2022 Prospect Digest Handbook: There's reliever risk here. But if the changeup comes around, he's going to be a wipe big league arm. If I were to select one pitcher that comes from an unknown, under-the-radar to reach Shane Bieber territory it would be Michael Burrows.

Scouting Report: Consider the following:

> Since 2006, here's the list of 22-year-old hurlers that posted a 30% to 34% strikeout percentage with an 8% to 10% walk percentage in any Double-A league (min. 50 IP): Josh Hader, Yordano Ventura, Mike Minor, A.J. Puk, Brayan Bello, Jose De Leon, Tony Sipp, Daniel Herrera, and – of course – Mr. 11th rounder, Mike Burrows.

Let's start with the floor: at the very least, barring any type of injury, Burrows is a light's out, James Karinchak-type reliever with an absurd fastball / curveball combination with the latter collecting awkward swings like Wall Street investors buying five-figure Ultra-Modern Baseball Cards of middle-tier prospects. Now the ceiling: there's at least mid-rotation caliber potential here. Borderline plus-plus fastball that's in the running for tops in the Buccos' system, the heater will sit in the mid-90s and touch a few ticks higher. The curveball haunts my dreams and I've never had to dig in against it. The lone thing holding Burrows back, at least for now, is his average changeup. It's workable, but if it every upticks – be careful. There's all kinds of helium collecting in this prospect balloon.

Ceiling: 4.0-win player
Risk: Moderate
MLB ETA: 2023

Pittsburgh Pirates

5. Quinn Priester, RHP

	FB	CB	SL	CH	Command	Overall
	60	60	60	55	50/55	60

Born: 09/16/00	Age: 22	Bats: R	Top Production Comp: Lance McCullers Jr.
Height: 6-3	Weight: 175	Throws: R	

Season	Team	Age	Level	IP	TBF	K/9	K%	BB/9	BB%	K-BB%	ERA	FIP	xFIP	Pit/Bat
2021	PIT	20	A+	97.2	407	9.03	24.08%	3.59	9.58%	14.50%	3.04	4.08	4.26	3.85
2022	PIT	21	AA	75.1	312	8.96	24.04%	2.63	7.05%	16.99%	2.87	3.23	3.85	3.59

Background: The 2019 draft class is shaping up to one of the deeper, more talented classes in recent memory. Adley Rutschman's already a star. Bobby Witt, Andrew Vaughn looked like above-average big league regulars. Nick Lodolo was simply brilliant during his rookie season in 2021 for the Reds of Cincinnati – as was George Kirby for the Mariners. Alek Manoah, the 11th overall pick that summer, has already established himself as the Blue Jays' ace and one of the best young hurlers in the game. And that's not including the likes of Riley Greene or Josh Jung – or top prospects like Brett Baty, Corbin Carroll, Daniel Espino, or Pittsburgh's Quinn Priester. Taken with the 18th overall pick that year, Priester made the transition from Cary-Grove High School to the minor leagues with ease. He posted a dominant 41-to-14 strikeout-to-walk ratio in 36.2 innings during his debut. After minor league baseball returned from its COVID-induced absence, the front office shipped the then-20-year-old right-hander right up to High-A at the start of 2021. And he more than held his own. Making 20 starts for the Greensboro Grasshoppers, the promising youngster averaged 9.0 strikeouts and 3.6 walks per nine innings. An oblique injury forced Priester to miss the opening couple of months last season, but after tune-up starts in Low-A and High-A, he made his way up to the fires of Double-A. He would throw 75.1 innings in the minors' toughest proving ground, posting a 75-to-22 strikeout-to-walk ratio with a 2.87 ERA. Priester capped up his year with a pair of starts with the Indianapolis Indians in Triple-A.

Snippet from The 2022 Prospect Digest Handbook: Priester handled himself like a 10-year veteran as he navigated the waters of the hitter friendly confines of First National Bank Field, home to the Grasshoppers. There's the making of a very good #3-type hurler with some added helium if everything breaks the right way.

Scouting Report: Consider the following:

> Since 2006, seven 21-year-old pitchers posted a 23% to 25% strikeout percentage with a 6% to 8% walk percentage in any Double-A league (min. 75 IP): Zach Davies, Adam Miller, Jose Garcia, Juan Pablo Oramas, Coleman Crow, Kyle Smith, and Quinn Priester.

It seems like *forever* ago that Mitch Keller seemed destined to be the Pirates ace of the future – though it was only a mere few seasons ago. While Keller turned in his best big league season to date in 2022, he's failed to live up to his consensus Top 100 prospect status. Quinn Priester won't have that problem. Four above-average or better offerings. Priester's plus heater sits in the 93- to 96-mph range and his two-seamer shows hard, boring life. His plus mid-80s slider is hellacious, late-biting. His plus curveball, which works in the shadow of his slider, is *another* plus offering. And his changeup, the worst pitch of his repertoire, would be the best offering for a lot of successful big leaguers. Priester owns above-average command, works quickly, and doesn't cower to top hitters. Bulldog mentality. He may never ascend to true ace-dom, at least on a contending team, but he's going to be a very good #2 / #3 type starting pitcher for many years.

Ceiling: 3.5-win player
Risk: Moderate
MLB ETA: 2023

6. Luis Ortiz, RHP

	FB	CB	SL	CH	Command	Overall
	65	50/55	55	50	55	55

Born: 01/27/99	Age: 24	Bats: R	Top Production Comp: Johnny Cueto
Height: 6-2	Weight: 240	Throws: R	

Season	Team	Age	Level	IP	TBF	K/9	K%	BB/9	BB%	K-BB%	ERA	FIP	xFIP	Pit/Bat
2021	PIT	22	A	87.1	376	11.65	30.05%	2.89	7.45%	22.61%	3.09	3.09	3.23	3.76
2022	PIT	23	AAA	10.0	42	10.80	28.57%	3.60	9.52%	19.05%	3.60	3.91	3.60	4.05
2022	PIT	23	AA	114.1	468	9.92	26.92%	2.68	7.26%	19.66%	4.64	4.45	3.76	3.71

Background: The Pirates signed the under-the-radar right-hander to a paltry $25,000 bonus in the fall of 2018. But the portly hurler wouldn't make his professional debut until two years later. And he looked *abysmal* during his jaunt through the Appalachian League. Squaring off against younger competition, Ortiz averaged just 6.6 strikeouts and a whopping 4.3 walks per nine innings across 11 starts. But something happened to the 6-foot-2, 240-pound righty because he morphed into a viable pitching prospect once he returned after the lost 2020 COVID season. Making 19 starts and three relief appearances with the Bradenton Marauders in Low-A two years ago, Ortiz punched out 113 and walked just 28 walks in only 87.1 innings of work. And that happened to be a harbinger of things to come in 2022. Ortiz was borderline brilliant in 24 games with the Altoona Curve, the club's Double-A affiliate. He breezed through two games in Triple-A and made four starts with

Pittsburgh Pirates

the big league club. Ortiz finished his minor league tenure in 2022 with 124.1 innings, recording 138-to-38 strikeout-to-walk ratio. He averaged an impeccable 10 strikeouts and just 2.8 walks per nine innings. And he fanned 17 and walked 10 in 16.0 innings with the Buccos.

Scouting Report: Consider the following:

> Since 2006, only three 23-year-old hurlers posted a 26% to 28% strikeout percentage with a 6.5% to 8.5% walk percentage in any Double-A league (min. 100 IP): Brandon Woodruff, Brett Kerry, and Luis Ortiz.

Built like a young Johnny Cueto. Ortiz is listed as a hefty 240 pounds, but (A) he doesn't look that heavy and (B) it's a sturdy, solid weight, not a fluffy build. Heavy mid-90s fastball that looks like hitters are hitting a concrete ball. It's particularly effective above the belt and borderline plus-plus. Ortiz is reliant on his above-average, mid-80s slider – which shows subtle, but late movement. He'll also mix in a rare curveball that will flash above-average, and a firm, 50-grade changeup. Ortiz shows a surprising amount of pitchability and game-planning to his approach to pitching given his lack of time on a professional mound. He shows impressive command of his borderline plus-plus fastball.

Ceiling: 3.0-win player
Risk: Moderate
MLB ETA: Debuted in 2022

7. Liover Peguero, SS

Hit	Power	SB	Patience	Glove	Overall
50/55	45	60	50	55	55

Born: 12/31/00	Age: 22	Bats: R	Top Production Comp: Nick Ahmed
Height: 6-1	Weight: 200	Throws: R	

Season	Team	Age	Level	PA	1B	2B	3B	HR	SB	CS	BB%	K%	AVG	OBP	SLG	ISO
2021	PIT	20	A+	417	66	19	2	14	28	6	7.91%	25.18%	0.270	0.332	0.444	0.174
2022	PIT	21	AA	521	88	22	5	10	28	6	5.57%	21.31%	0.259	0.305	0.387	0.128

Background: Signed by the Diamondbacks for $475,000 during the summer of 2017. Peguero's stint in the Arizona organization barely lasted two years before he was used as trade bait to lure Starling Marte from Pittsburgh. The Buccos acquired the twitchy, well-built shortstop, along with 2019 first rounder Brennan Malone in late January 2020. But the prospects wouldn't make their debuts in his new organization until a year, thanks to the COVID pandemic. The Pirates' brass sent the then-20-year-old Dominican prospect up to High-A at the start of 2021. And Peguero looked comfortable squaring off against the older competition, slugging .270/.332/.444 with 19 doubles, two triples, 14 homeruns, and 28 stolen bases in only 90 games. Last season, after smashing the competition with Greensboro, he was deemed ready to take on the hurlers in the ultra-competitive Double-A environment. And he escaped without too many bumps and bruises. Appearing in 121 games with the Curve of Altoona, Peguero batted a mediocre .259/.305/.387 with 22 doubles, five triples, 10 homeruns, and 28 stolen based (he was caught stealing only six times). Per *Weighted Runs Created Plus*, his overall production fell 12% *below* the league average mark. Peguero squeezed in an appearance with the Pirates as well, going 1-for-3 against the Giants in early June.

Snippet from The 2022 Prospect Digest Handbook: The power output is a bit misleading, though. The young infielder took full advantage of the Grasshoppers' incredibly hitter-friendly confines – particularly in the homerun department as he slugged 10 of his 14 dingers at home.

Scouting Report: Consider the following:

> Since 2006, only three 21-year-old hitters met the following criteria in Double-A (min. 350 PA): 83 to 93 wRC+, a 19.5% to 21.5% strikeout rate, and a 4.5% to 6.5% walk rate. Those three hitters: Cornelius Randolph, Jahmai Jones, and – of course – Liover Peguero. For those counting at home:
>> Randolph is a former early first round pick that hasn't hacked in three stints in Double-A, across two separate organizations. Jones, a 2015 second round pick, hasn't hacked in several stints in the upper minors.

Peguero had a weird 2022. The Dominican infielder started off like a consensus Top 100 prospect by slugging .292/.315/.469 across his first 54 games. Pittsburgh called him up for a game. Then he was promptly sent back down. From that point on through the rest of the year he batted .230/.297/.315. Seems like it's more than a coincidence, no? Known for his defensive wizardry, Peguero's leatherwork regressed some last season as well. Offensively, he chewed some percentage points off of his borderline concerning punch out rate from 2021. He flashed doubles power, which was expected. He's a strong bounce back candidate. The lack of on-base skills will tarnish his overall ceiling, but there's starting caliber potential here. Ceiling: .270/.320/.400 with above-average defense.

Ceiling: 3.0-win player
Risk: Moderate
MLB ETA: Debuted in 2022

Pittsburgh Pirates

8. Jared Jones, RHP

	FB	CB	SL	CH	Command	Overall
	60	55	60	50	40/45	55

Born: 08/06/01	Age: 21	Bats: L	Top Production Comp: Chris Archer
Height: 6-1	Weight: 180	Throws: R	

Season	Team	Age	Level	IP	TBF	K/9	K%	BB/9	BB%	K-BB%	ERA	FIP	xFIP	Pit/Bat
2021	PIT	19	A	66.0	302	14.05	34.11%	4.64	11.26%	22.85%	4.64	3.91	3.75	3.66
2022	PIT	20	A+	122.2	532	10.42	26.69%	3.74	9.59%	17.11%	4.62	4.85	4.27	3.85

Background: After nabbing New Mexico State star Nick Gonzales with the seventh overall pick in 2020, the front office spent the rest of their draft capital on pitching. But only one of those five picks wouldn't come from a four-year college – right-hander Jared Jones. A product of La Mirada High School, Pittsburgh signed Jones, the 44th overall player taken that summer, to a massive $2.2 million deal. The 6-foot-1, 180-pound right-hander made 18 appearances with the Marauders of Bradenton two years ago, throwing just 66.0 innings with an impressive 103 punch outs against just 34 free passes. Last season, the front office did the prudent thing and sent him up to High-A. And Jones made some important strides as he moved up the minor league ladder. Handling nearly double the workload, Jones averaged 10.4 strikeouts and 3.7 walks per nine innings across 26 starts for the Grasshoppers. He finished his sophomore professional season with a 4.62 ERA, a 4.85 FIP, and a 4.27 xFIP. For his career, he's averaging 11.7 punch outs and 4.1 walks per nine innings.

Snippet from The 2022 Prospect Digest Handbook: A really, *really* promising arm that remains incredibly underrated – despite the dominant showing in 2021. The command will likely climb into the 45-grade area in the next 12 to 24 months. The arsenal screams mid-rotation caliber arm, but he needs a more reliable third option if the command doesn't move into above-average territory.

Scouting Report: Consider the following:

> Since 2006, there have been four 20-year-old hurlers that posted a 25.5% to 27.5% strikeout percentage with an 8.5% to 10.5% walk percentage in any High-A league (min. 100 IP): Josh Hader, Caleb Ferguson, Julio Rodriguez, and – of course – Jared Jones.

Jones saw a definite uptick in velocity over the previous year as he was regularly touching 96 and sometimes as high as 97 mph. It's a *heavy* fastball with incredible life, often times allowing him to work primarily off the borderline plus-plus offering. Plus slider – a wickedly filthy mid-80s offerings with straight downward bite. Above-average curveball. And a decent, mid-80s changeup. As expected, the command improved from a 40- to 45-grade offering. There's mid-rotation caliber potential here. And Jones remains one of the more underrated hurlers in the minor leagues. He could be one of the larger breakout hurlers in 2023 – even as he moves into Double-A.

Ceiling: 3.0-win player
Risk: Moderate
MLB ETA: 2024

9. Nick Gonzales, 2B/SS

	Hit	Power	SB	Patience	Glove	Overall
	50	50	40	55	50	55

Born: 05/27/99	Age: 24	Bats: R	Top Production Comp: Josh Rojas
Height: 5-10	Weight: 195	Throws: R	

Season	Team	Age	Level	PA	1B	2B	3B	HR	SB	CS	BB%	K%	AVG	OBP	SLG	ISO
2021	PIT	22	A+	369	53	23	4	18	7	2	10.84%	27.37%	0.302	0.385	0.565	0.262
2022	PIT	23	AA	316	40	20	1	7	5	3	13.61%	28.48%	0.263	0.383	0.429	0.166

Background: The 2020 draft was *always* going to be a crapshoot – no matter how prepared, or how well a team has historically drafted. So it's not surprising that a lot of the early first round selections have either struggled or been massive disappointments. Guys like Asa Lacy or Austin Martin or Austin Hendrick. The jury, though, is still out on Nick Gonzales. The seventh overall pick that summer, Gonzales left the Aggies as career .399/.502/.747 hitters in 128 games. Pittsburgh sent the sweet-swinging infielder straight up to High-A two years ago. And he – more or less – dominated as he slugged .303/.385/.565 with 23 doubles, four triples, and 18 homeruns in only 80 games. Last season, in another abbreviated campaign, Gonzales passed the rigors of Double-A, hitting .263/.383/.429 with 20 doubles, one triple, seven homeruns, and five stolen bases. His overall production, according to *Weighted Runs Created Plus*, topped the league average mark by 27%. A heel injury put him out of commission for nearly 2.5 months midway through the year. Gonzales made his second consecutive trip to the Arizona Fall League as well, batting .279/.351/.500 in 18 games with the Surprise Saguaros.

Snippet from The 2022 Prospect Digest Handbook: Gonzales flirted with some questionable swing-and-miss numbers throughout the season – he whiffed 27.4% of his total plate appearances – but he showed steady improvement as he adjusted to minor league pitching. He whiffed in 31.2% of his plate appearances in May, June, and July, but posted a 25.1% mark in August and September.

Pittsburgh Pirates

Scouting Report: Consider the following:

Since 2006, only four 23-year-old hitters posted a 122 to 132 wRC+ with a strikeout rate between 27% and 30% in any Double-A league (min. 300 PA): Zack Collins, Corey Ray, Brian Pointer, and – of course – Nick Gonzales.

After an abysmal start to the year, Gonzales, who batted a lowly .180/.324/.292 over his first 26 games, rebounded to slug an impressive .306/.411/.506 over his remaining 48 contests (including his rehab appearances). His bloated walks rates help compensate for his questionable swing-and-miss tendencies. There's sneaky power that may peak in the 17- to 19-homer range. Average defense on either side of the keystone. One of the questions that he needs to answer is whether he can stay on the diamond for an entire year. Solid, league average starting material but he won't be a star. In terms of big league ceiling, think: .260/.340/.430.

Ceiling: 3.0-win player
Risk: Moderate
MLB ETA: 2023

10. Bubba Chandler, RHP

	FB	CB	SL	CH	Control	Overall
	70	55	60	55	30/45	60

Born: 09/14/02	Age: 20	Bats: B	Top Production Comp: N/A
Height: 6-3	Weight: 200	Throws: R	

Season	Team	Age	Level	IP	TBF	K/9	K%	BB/9	BB%	K-BB%	ERA	FIP	xFIP	Pit/Bat
2022	PIT	19	CPX	15.1	59	15.85	45.76%	5.87	16.95%	28.81%	0.00	2.26	2.98	2.37
2022	PIT	19	A	26.0	114	11.42	28.95%	6.23	15.79%	13.16%	4.15	4.79	4.39	4.04

Background: I'm sure it's happened before in history – at least a few times. But Chandler received the second largest signing bonus in Pittsburgh's 2021 draft – despite (A) the prep two-way star going in the third round *and* (B) he was the club's fourth overall selection that summer. The 72nd overall player taken two years ago, the perennial downtrodden National League Central Division franchise signed the 6-foot-3, 200-pound right-hander / shortstop to a *massive* $3 million deal – a bonus equivalent to mid-first round money. As if starring in every facet of the game for North Oconee High School wasn't enough, Chandler was ranked by some outlets as the 19th best quarterback in the country as well, earning a four-star recruit status. After signing with the club, the front office limited the Georgia-born prospect to just hitting during his abbreviated debut in the Florida Complex League two years ago. Chandler batted a lowly .167/.324/.300 in 11 games. The former Bonus Baby opened up last season back in the Complex League where he (A) dominated on the mound and (B) showed some serious thump and concerning hit tool. The front office bumped him up to Low-A in mud-July where Chandler continued to show promise on the bump, though he struggled at the plate. He finished his first full season in the minors with a lowly .196/.331/.382 with three doubles, two triples, four homeruns, and four stolen bases. He also tossed 41.1 innings, recording 60 punch outs and 28 walks with an aggregate 2.61 ERA.

Snippet from The 2022 Prospect Digest Handbook: First off, the organization intends on keeping their prized third rounder on both sides of the ball – a la Shohei Ohtani – at least at the beginning stages of his journey. But watching Chandler hit and pitch, it's immediately clear that his future's on the mound. It's not that he's a bad hitting prospect, but the swing is long – particularly from the left side and it needs a lot of seasoning. Also, it has too much of an uppercut.

Scouting Report: Hitting a baseball is the hardest task in any professional sport – period. Hitting a baseball while developing your craft as a pitcher is nearly impossible. It's exactly why Shohei Ohtani's accomplishments over the past few seasons are so remarkable and – nearly – incomprehensible. Bubba Chandler is attempting to do it, and it's *crystal clear* just how impossible the feat actually is. It's not overly surprising that the former highly touted, highly recruited prep quarterback possesses a howitzer for a right arm. His fastball sits – *consistently* – in the 95- to 97-mph range with, late, explosive life. He'll feature a wickedly unfair, plus mid- to upper-80s slider, and a surprisingly strong changeup. He'll mix in a rare, low-80s curveball as well. The command is a 30, but when he's on he's nearly unhittable. It's almost unfair. At the plate, Chandler owns plus-plus raw power, speed, and he just oozes athleticism. The argument could be made he owns some of the best power in the entire system. Great bat speed, but the hit tool is questionable. Chandler's future is on the hill, which was evident during his senior season in high school. The Pirates may continue to give him at bats, but at some point he's going to have to focus solely on pitching or he's going to turn into the great "What If?". There's mid-rotation caliber potential, maybe even as high a #2, but the command has a *LONG* ways to go.

Ceiling: 4.5-win player
Risk: Extreme
MLB ETA: 2026

Pittsburgh Pirates

11. Hunter Barco, LHP

FB	SL	CH	Command	Overall
55	60	55	55	55

Born: 12/15/00	Age: 22	Bats: L	Top Production Comp: N/A
Height: 6-4	Weight: 210	Throws: L	

Background: The Bolles School, a Jacksonville-based college preparatory and boarding school, doesn't own an extensive list of former big league alums – though it's a fairly impressive one. Former Bulldogs include: D.J. Stewart, Austin Slater, Rick Wilkins, and – easily – the most famous among the group, Chipper Jones, the top pick in the 1990 draft. Barco was a legend coming out of high school. He was a pre-season All-American according to *Perfect Game* heading into his senior season; played at the 2018 *Under Armour All-American* game at Wrigley Field, and struck out 67 in 38 innings and batted .355 to cap off his prep career. The Mets took a 24th round flier on him that year, but it wasn't enough to dissuade Barco from heading to the land of the Gators. The lanky, herky-jerky left-hander was nearly unhittable during his COVID-abbreviated freshman campaign at the University of Florida, posting a 26-to-6 strikeout-to-walk ratio in 19.1 innings of work. His production took a bit of step back the following year as he made 16 starts for the SEC powerhouse, posting a 4.01 ERA while averaging 10.2 strikeouts and 2.8 walks per nine innings. But things seemed to align themselves during his junior campaign: through his first nine starts, he struck out 69, walked just 11, and posted a 2.50 ERA across 50.1 innings of work. Unfortunately for Barco and Florida, the big lefty succumbed to Tommy John surgery – though that didn't stop the Pirates from selecting him in the second round, 44th overall, and signing him to a deal worth $1,525,000.

Scouting Report: Per the usual, my pre-draft write-up:

"Consider the following:

Since 2015, only five SEC pitchers averaged at least 12 strikeouts and fewer than 2.1 walks per nine innings in a season (min. 50 IP): Casey Mize, Kevin Kopps, Chase Dollander, Brett Kerry, and Hunter Barco.

Hides the ball exceptionally well, giving the illusion it's firing from his shoulder joint at times. Lively low- to mid-90s fastball, sitting in the 92- to 94-mph range. Hard-biting, tumbling, slicing low-80s slider, easily a plus pitch. And a sneakily good, above-average low 80s changeup. Barco has always been a consistent strike thrower, even extending back to his prep days at The Bolles school. He shows a willingness to change speeds at any point in the count. He could have been the top pitcher taken in 2022 – if not for the Tommy John surgery. It's certainly a gamble to taken an injured hurler, but Barco has some poor man's Robbie Ray vibes going on."

Ceiling: 3.0-win player
Risk: High
MLB ETA: 2025/2026

12. Ji-hwan Bae, 2B/SS/CF

Hit	Power	SB	Patience	Glove	Overall
55	40	60	50	45	50

Born: 07/26/99	Age: 23	Bats: L	Top Production Comp: Cesar Hernandez
Height: 6-1	Weight: 185	Throws: R	

Season	Team	Age	Level	PA	1B	2B	3B	HR	SB	CS	BB%	K%	AVG	OBP	SLG	ISO
2021	PIT	21	AA	365	65	12	5	7	20	8	10.41%	22.74%	0.278	0.359	0.413	0.134
2022	PIT	22	AAA	473	84	23	6	8	30	8	10.15%	16.91%	0.289	0.362	0.430	0.141

Background: Almost an Atlanta Brave prospect before the international free agency scandal went down, Pittsburgh swooped in and signed the South Korean infielder to a deal worth $1.25 million in the fall of 2017. Bae, a 6-foot-1, 185-pound second baseman/ shortstop / part-time centerfielder, has been a remarkably consistent, somewhat underrated bat throughout his minor league tenure. He spent the 2019 season in Low-A, hitting .323/.403/.430 in 86 games as a 19-year-old. Bae moved straight up to Double-A without so much as missing a beat in 2021; he hit .278/.359/.413 with 12 doubles, five triples, seven homeruns, and 20 stolen bases (in only 29 total attempts). And after a quick jaunt through the Arizona Fall League, the Pirates' brass deemed him ready to take on the final minor league level – Triple-A. Appearing in a career best 108 games with the Indians of Indianapolis, the Daegu native did what he always does – hit. He batted .289/.362/.430 with 23 doubles, six triples, eight homeruns, and 30 stolen bases (in 30 total attempts). Per *Weighted Runs Created Plus*, his overall production topped the league average mark by 12%. Pittsburgh called the then-22-year-old up for his big league debut in late September. He promptly went 11-for-33 with a trio of doubles and stolen bases in 10 games.

Snippet from The 2022 Prospect Digest Handbook: The bat is the carrying tool here. If he can consistently bat near .300 he'll be a league average starting option.

Pittsburgh Pirates

Scouting Report: Consider the following:

> Since 2006, only three 22-year-old hitters met the following criteria in any Triple-A season (min. 350 PA): 107 to 117 wRC+, an 8% to 12% walk rate, and a 15% to 19% strikeout rate. Those three hitters: Ronald Guzman, Caleb Gindl, and – of course – Ji-hwan Bae.

A batting average-driven producer with a nose for first base and little thump, Bae's been groomed to be a solid utility option as he's bounced all around the diamond over the past couple of seasons. Average-ish glove at either middle infield position. No platoon splits. Above-average hit tool. He just…doesn't hit for power. In terms of big league ceiling, think: .290/.360/.390 with 25 stolen bases.

Ceiling: 2.0-win player
Risk: Low to Moderate
MLB ETA: Debuted in 2022

13. Tom Harrington, RHP

FB	CB	SL	CH	Command	Overall
55	55	55	55	55	50

Born: 07/12/01	Age: 21	Bats: R	Top Production Comp: N/A
Height: 6-2	Weight: 185	Throws: R	

Background: Fun Fact Part I: Campbell University has produced just two players taken before the third round of the MLB Draft in its history – Seth Johnson, a supplemental first rounder taken by the Rays in 2019, and John Posey, a second round pick by the Orioles all the way back in 1986. Fun Fact Part II: despite a lack of notable early round draft selections, the Fighting Camels produced a trio of notable big leaguers – Hall of Famer and spitball extraordinaire Gaylord Perry; 1970 AL Cy Young Award winner and three-time All-Star Jim Perry, and 2021 breakout All-Star and Silver Slugger Cedric Mullins. Harrington, a 6-foot-2, 185-pound right-hander, *and* his teammate Zach Neto figure to add their names to the list of notable alums from Campbell University. A two-sport star during his days at Southern Lee High School, Harrington stepped right into the Camels' rotation as a true freshman in 2021. Making a total of 16 appearances, 14 of which coming via the start, he tossed 75.2 innings with 75 punch outs and 28 walks to go along with a 6-3 record and a 3.45 ERA. Harrington's production improved tremendously during his stellar showing in 2022: in 15 starts, the promising righty posted a phenomenal 111-to-18 strikeout-to-walk ratio with a 2.53 ERA and a 12-2 record in 92.2 innings of work. Pittsburgh selected him in the opening round, 36th overall, and signed him to a deal worth $2,047,500. He did not appear in an affiliated game.

Scouting Report: Per the usual, my pre-draft write-up:

> "Consider the following:
>
> > Since 2015, there have been 15 instances in which a Division I pitcher averaged at least 10.5 strikeouts and fewer than 1.8 walks per nine innings (min. 90 IP): David Peterson, Casey Mize, Clayton Andrews, Nick Sandlin, Frank German, Miller Hogan, Adam Scott, Dylan Dodd, Will Dion, Chad Dallas, Hunter Stanley, Parker Messick, Trey Dombroski, Tanner Hall, and – of course – Thomas Harrington.
>
> After throwing a solid amount of strikes during his freshman season, Harrington honed in on the strike zone with laser-like precision during his breakout 2022 campaign. Above-average command of four pitches – fastball, curveball, slider, and a firm, running changeup, all of which grade out as above-average. Harrington doesn't own the biggest of frames, but he's efficient with his offerings and mechanics. He has the ceiling of a #4-type arm. He could be a very quality pick in the opening of the second round."

Ceiling: 2.0-win player
Risk: Moderate
MLB ETA: 2025

Pittsburgh Pirates

14. Lonnie White Jr., CF

Hit	Power	SB	Patience	Glove	Overall
35/45	40/60	40/35	50	50	50

Born: 12/31/02	Age: 20	Bats: R	Top Production Comp: N/A
Height: 6-3	Weight: 212	Throws: R	

Season	Team	Age	Level	PA	1B	2B	3B	HR	SB	CS	BB%	K%	AVG	OBP	SLG	ISO
2021	PIT	18	CPX	33	4	2	0	2	0	0	6.06%	42.42%	0.258	0.303	0.516	0.258

Background: The Pirates chased a ton of high upside talent throughout the 2021 draft. After picking Louisville star Henry Davis with the first overall pick, Pittsburgh followed up with four consecutive high schoolers: Anthony Solometo, Lonnie White Jr., and two-way star Bubba Chandler – each of them receiving hefty seven-figure bonuses. White, the 64th overall pick that summer, signed for the smallest deal of the trio, agreeing on a pact worth $1.5 million. A product of Malvern Preparatory School, White, who was committed to play football at Penn State University, turned in a solid – though a little concerning – debut in the Complex League as he hit .258/.303/.516 but fanned 14 times in 33 plate appearances. And unfortunately for White, as well as the club, he was limited to just a pair of Complex League games last season as he dealt with a UCL issue in his elbow, as well as hamstring woes.

Scouting Report: With nothing new to report on, here's his draft scouting report:

> "As much power potential as any hitter in the club's farm system, including top overall pick Henry Davis. Plus bat speed. Incredibly fast hands. Tremendous rotation around the torso / spine. And White does it all effortlessly. He may struggle with contact – especially through the early parts of his career – and he's a bit rawer than the typical second rounder. Defensively, he's a long strider with a plus arm. There's All-Star caliber potential here, but there's a lot of risk. If White succeeds, it will be a true indictment of the club's development program."

Ceiling: 2.5-win player
Risk: High
MLB ETA: 2025

15. Malcom Nunez, 1B/3B

Hit	Power	SB	Patience	Glove	Overall
50	55/60	35/30	55	45	50

Born: 03/09/01	Age: 22	Bats: R	Top Production Comp: Jesus Aguilar
Height: 5-11	Weight: 205	Throws: R	

Season	Team	Age	Level	PA	1B	2B	3B	HR	SB	CS	BB%	K%	AVG	OBP	SLG	ISO
2021	STL	20	A+	151	24	10	2	3	5	2	7.28%	17.88%	0.285	0.351	0.453	0.168
2021	STL	20	AA	224	41	5	0	6	2	1	9.38%	19.64%	0.257	0.330	0.371	0.114
2022	STL	21	AA	350	48	11	0	17	4	2	13.71%	20.29%	0.255	0.360	0.463	0.208
2022	PIT	21	AA	126	20	5	0	5	1	0	13.49%	21.43%	0.286	0.381	0.476	0.190
2022	PIT	21	AAA	17	2	0	0	1	0	0	23.53%	29.41%	0.231	0.412	0.462	0.231

Background: Pirates GM Ben Cherington played the game perfectly, something that a small-budget franchise with tight purse strings needs to do. The club signed a downtrodden Jose Quintana to a free agent deal last offseason. But after 20 strong starts with the bottom dwelling team, the front office sent Quintana and Chris Stratton, a solid, yet replaceable reliever, to the Cardinals for power-hitting corner infielder Malcom Nunez and right-hander Johan Oviedo. Nunez, a native of La Habana, Cuba, was a tornado of destruction during his debut in the Dominican Summer League in 2018, slugging .415/.498/.774 in 44 games. But his ferocity sagged significantly the following year as he batted .229/.305/.318 in 58 games with Johnson City and Peoria. The 6-foot-1, 183-pound infielder regained some of his offensive prowess in 2021, as he mashed his way through High-A but struggled during a 54-game stint in Double-A. Last season in 119 games between both organizations, Nunez slugged .262/.367/.466 with 16 doubles and a career-high 23 dingers in 119 games. Per *Weighted Runs Created Plus*, his overall production topped the league average by 17%.

Scouting Report: Nunez has gone from an otherworldly slugger at the early onset of his career to an afterthought and now onto a potential low-end starting option for a big league – non-contending – club. He's always possessed plus-raw power, but he finally started tapping into it last season. Surprisingly strong contact rates given his thump with plus walk rates. Nunez's made some minor mechanical tweaks throughout his career, moving away from a small stride to more noticeable leg kick. Defensively, he's a designated hitter playing the infield – though it's less of a problem at first base. There's some Jesus Aguilar vibes going on. In terms of big league ceiling, think: .240/.330/.480.

Ceiling: 1.5- to 2.0-win player
Risk: Moderate
MLB ETA: 2023

Pittsburgh Pirates

16. Carmen Mlodzinski, RHP

	FB	CB	CH	Command	Overall
	60	60	55	45	45

Born: 02/19/99	Age: 24	Bats: R	Top Production Comp: Tom Koehler
Height: 6-2	Weight: 232	Throws: R	

Season	Team	Age	Level	IP	TBF	K/9	K%	BB/9	BB%	K-BB%	ERA	FIP	xFIP	Pit/Bat
2021	PIT	22	A+	50.1	213	11.44	30.05%	3.58	9.39%	20.66%	3.93	4.34	4.00	4.15
2022	PIT	23	AA	105.1	460	9.48	24.13%	3.42	8.70%	15.43%	4.78	3.77	4.55	4.01

Background: After joining the ball club as General Manager in November of 2019, veteran front office member Ben Cherington's first draft class focused heavily on pitching the following year. Cherington and Co. selected New Mexico State University star infielder Nick Gonzales with the seventh overall pitch, and then ripped off six straight hurlers as part of the five-round COVID-limited draft. The first hurler nabbed by the newly crowned GM – University of South Carolina ace right-hander Carmen Mlodzinski. Taken with the 31st overall pick and signed to a deal worth slightly more than $2 million, Mlodzinski was thrust right up to Double-A for his debut two years ago. And he held his own, despite making the leap directly from the SEC, as he averaged 11.4 strikeouts and 3.6 walks per nine innings. Last season, in a bit of a surprising move, the front office sent the former first rounder back down to Double-A for additional seasoning. Making 27 appearances with the Altoona Curve, 22 of which came via the start, Mlodzinski tossed a career high 105.1 innings with 111 punch outs and 40 free passes. He finished the year with a 4.78 ERA, 3.77 FIP, and a 4.55 xFIP.

Snippet from The 2022 Prospect Digest Handbook: A limited collegiate track record both in terms of success and health, Mlodzinski's showing in the Cape did more for his value than anything else. Efficient mechanics with a long stride, the only thing stopping Mlodzinski's plod to a #4-type rotation spot is health – maybe command, too. Very solid gamble by the Pirates two years ago.

Scouting Report: Consider the following:

> Since 2006, there have been eleven 23-year-old pitchers that posted a 23% to 25% strikeout percentage with a 7.5% to 9.5% walk percentage in any Double-A league (min. 100 IP): Austin Gomber, David Parkinson, Eli Morgan, James McDonald, Nabil Crismatt, Anthony Ranaudo, Ariel Pena, Jorge Alcala, Randy Vasquez, George Kontos, and – of course – Carmen Mlodzinski.

Mlodzinski seemed to alter his approach from his debut showing two years ago, moving away from a fastball / curveball style to a more fastball / changeup profile. Plus, mid-90s fastball, sitting consistently in the 95 mph. There are distinct movement profiles between his riding four-seamer and his darting two-seamer, which he likes to start in off the plate against lefties and let it drift back onto the black. His curveball is a big bending, 12-6'er with great shape and depth. And his changeup adds a third swing-and-miss option. The command is fringy at this point. Two years into his career and he's still tracking like a backend starter with a high leverage relief upside.

Ceiling: 1.5-win player
Risk: Moderate
MLB ETA: 2023

17. Anthony Solometo, LHP

	FB	SL	CH	Command	Overall
	50	55	50	50/55	45

Born: 12/02/02	Age: 20	Bats: L	Top Production Comp: Kodi Medeiros
Height: 6-5	Weight: 220	Throws: L	

Season	Team	Age	Level	IP	TBF	K/9	K%	BB/9	BB%	K-BB%	ERA	FIP	xFIP	Pit/Bat
2022	PIT	19	A	47.2	188	9.63	27.13%	3.59	10.11%	17.02%	2.64	2.83	3.57	3.90

Background: The Pirates opened up their 2021 draft class by selecting Henry Davis and signing him to a below-average deal, saving the club nearly $2 million. Nearly half of that went towards prep southpaw Anthony Solometo, who commanded almost $2.8 million as the 37th overall pick. A product of Bishop Eustace Preparatory School, the 6-foot-5, 220-pound lefty made his professional debut with the club's Low-A affiliate last season. Solometo made 13 brief appearances with the Bradenton Marauders, eight of which were starts, throwing just 47.2 innings of work with 51 strikeouts against just 19 free passes. He finished the season with a sparkling 2.64 ERA, a 2.83 FIP, and a 3.57 xFIP.

Snippet from The 2022 Prospect Digest Handbook: There's some Kodi Medeiros-type feeling here with Solometo. Medeiros had to move into the bullpen, despite his lofty draft status out of high school, due to his inability to get right-handers out.

Scouting Report: Didn't like the arm angle coming out of high school, and I dislike it even more as a professional. It's *brutally* long and it's a crossfire, low three-quarter slinging release. Platoon splits against right-handers are likely going to be a concern in the coming years. And he already struggles getting it in on righties. Average 89- to 92-mph fastball, above-average 83- to 84-mph slider, and a decent, moving changeup,

Pittsburgh Pirates

though he telegraphs the offering by digging in his glove more than usual. He's already death on lefties, so he'll at least be able to slide into a LOOGY / specialist role of some sort in the coming years.

Ceiling: 1.0- to 1.5-win player
Risk: Moderate
MLB ETA: 2025

18. Dariel Lopez, 2B/3B/SS

Hit	Power	SB	Patience	Glove	Overall
45	50	35	45	45	50

Born: 02/07/02	Age: 21	Bats: R	Top Production Comp: N/A
Height: 6-1	Weight: 183	Throws: R	

Season	Team	Age	Level	PA	1B	2B	3B	HR	SB	CS	BB%	K%	AVG	OBP	SLG	ISO
2021	PIT	19	A	416	65	17	1	10	1	2	9.86%	24.76%	0.258	0.341	0.393	0.136
2022	PIT	20	A+	420	77	15	1	19	6	4	5.00%	25.48%	0.286	0.329	0.476	0.189

Background: One of the club's bigger free agents on the international scene during the summer of 2018. Pittsburgh signed the Dominican infielder to a deal worth $400,000. Lopez would make his professional debut the following year, hitting a scorching .341/.404/.485 with 10 doubles, four triples, two homeruns, and five stolen bases in 47 Dominican Summer League games. Once minor league action returned from its COVID hiatus, the front office sent the 6-foot-1, 183-pound infielder up to Low-A where – as expected – his numbers declined. He finished his sophomore season with a mediocre .258/.341/.393 slash line in 98 games. Lopez continued his plod through the low levels of the minors last season as he squared off against the older competition in High-A. Appearing in 102 games with the Greensboro Grasshoppers, he mashed .286/.329/.476 with 15 doubles, one triple, a career best 19 homeruns, and six stolen bases (in 10 total attempts). His overall production, per *Weighted Runs Created Plus*, topped the league average mark by 16%.

Scouting Report: Consider the following:

> Since 2006, only two 20-year-old hitters posted a 110 to 120 wRC+ with a 4% to 7% walk rate and a 24% to 27% strikeout rate in any High-A league (min. 350 PA): Jose Tena and Dariel Lopez.

A defensive vagabond that handled the hot corner well last season, Lopez thoroughly enjoyed his time in Greensboro's hitter-friendly confines as he mashed .303/.344/.571 at home and cobbled together a mediocre .269/.314/.378 slash line away. Aggressive approach at the plate that's lead to low OBPs and concerning punch out rates. Lopez started out the year as frigid as an iceberg and flailed away at everything like a windsock; he batted .175/.224/.286 with 22 punch outs over his first 68 plate appearances. After that, though, he mashed .308/.349/.512 with a 24% K-rate over his remaining 84 games (352 PA). The swing is on the longer side, and he gets caught swinging from his feels at time. He's likely ticketed for Double-A at the start of 2023, but he should be sent back down to High-A – at least for a few months – because he's going to struggle with Altoona.

Ceiling: 1.0-win player
Risk: Moderate
MLB ETA: 2024/2025

19. Kyle Nicolas, RHP

FB	CB	SL	CH	Command	Overall
55	50	55	50	45	40

Born: 02/22/99	Age: 24	Bats: R	Top Production Comp: Kyle Funkhouser
Height: 6-4	Weight: 223	Throws: R	

Season	Team	Age	Level	IP	TBF	K/9	K%	BB/9	BB%	K-BB%	ERA	FIP	xFIP	Pit/Bat
2021	MIA	22	A+	59.2	259	12.97	33.20%	3.62	9.27%	23.94%	5.28	5.03	3.79	4.25
2021	MIA	22	AA	39.1	167	11.44	29.94%	5.72	14.97%	14.97%	2.52	3.99	5.01	3.90
2022	PIT	23	AA	90.2	390	10.03	25.90%	4.67	12.05%	13.85%	3.97	4.30	4.92	4.11

Background: Pittsburgh and Miami got together on a bit of an interesting trade right after the conclusion of the 2021 season. The specifics: the Buccos sent Gold Glove-winning catcher Jacob Stallings southward for a package of two recent high-round picks (Connor Scott and Kyle Nicolas) and a mediocre big league starting pitcher (Zach Thompson). Stallings was abysmal in his season with the Fish. Scott, the 13th overall pick in 2018, continued to trek towards minor league mediocrity. Thompson was a below replacement level hurler with the Pirates. So that leaves Nicolas as the lone "bright spot" for either time – at least comparatively speaking. Born in Massillon, Ohio, and drafted in the second round out of Ball State in 2020, the 6-foot-4, 223-pound right-hander made 24 brief appearances with the Curve of Altoona last season, his first in the Pirates' organization and his second stint at the level. He tossed just 90.2 innings, recording 101 punch outs against 47 free passes. He finished the season with a 3.97 ERA, a 4.30 FIP, and a 4.92 xFIP.

Pittsburgh Pirates

Snippet from The 2022 Prospect Digest Handbook: There's a lot of reliever risk here. And, truthfully, there's not a lot of difference between Nicolas and Kyle Funkhouser.

Scouting Report: Consider the following:

> Since 2006, only four 23-year-old hurlers posted a 25% to 27% strikeout percentage with a walk percentage north of 11% in any Double-A league (min. 75 IP): Dellin Betances, Sean Newcomb, Thomas Diamond, and Kyle Nicolas. It's an interesting group of players: Betances is a 4-time All-Star who was a light's out reliever early in his big league career; Newcomb was a decent, enigmatic backend starter early in his career; and Diamond, who was once part of the Rangers vaunted D-V-D trio of pitching prospects, was once a Top 100 prospect.

The book on Nicolas coming out of college was simple: smoke. Except he really hasn't had anywhere close to that type of velo as he's moved into the professional ranks. The big 6-foot-4, 223-pound right-hander was sitting in the 92- to 94-mph range last season, essentially above-average territory, not the once scouted plus-plus range. Average low-80s deuce. Above-average mid-80s slider. Average upper-80s changeup. Command's a 40 on a good day. He's entering his age-24 season with a backend starter's arsenal and a middle relief feel for the zone.

Ceiling: 1.0-win player
Risk: Moderate
MLB ETA: 2023

20. Jack Brannigan, 3B/RHP

	FB	CH	Control	Overall
	70	55	40/50	40

Born: 09/14/02	Age: 19	Bats: B	Top Production Comp: N/A
Height: 6-3	Weight: 200	Throws: R	

Season	Team	Age	Level	PA	1B	2B	3B	HR	SB	CS	BB%	K%	AVG	OBP	SLG	ISO
2022	PIT	21	A	112	14	3	0	3	6	3	13.39%	25.00%	0.211	0.330	0.337	0.126

Background: While the University of Notre Dame isn't a traditional hotbed, per se, it's a bit shocking that the Pirates' selection of two-way star Jack Brannigan in the third round last July marked the first time in nearly a decade since the school churned out a player taken in the opening three rounds. And it's also not surprising that the Pirates, who seemed to have an affinity for two-way players, added another into the fold. Brannigan, a 6-foot-3, 200-pound third baseman / reliever was a star at the dish and hot corner for the Fighting Irish in 2022. He slugged .291/.360/.540 with 15 doubles, one triple, 12 homeruns, and 10 stolen bases (in 15 total attempts). And he squeezed in 11 appearances on the bump as well, throwing 14.2 innings with an impressive 28-to-8 strikeout-to-walk ratio. He did allow 12 earned runs and a pair of dingers during that time frame.

Scouting Report: While Brannigan possesses above-average power potential at an infield position, the 6-foot-3, 200-pound third baseman is flawed as a hitter. He whiffed in more than 20% of his plate appearances in the ACC, which isn't exactly like the SEC. So it's not surprising that he whiffed 30 times in only 119 plate appearances during his debut. His hellacious plus-plus fastball is the key to his big league future. The heat will sit in the 96- to 97-mph range and approach triple digits. He'll also mix in an above-average changeup, though he tends to slow his body down at times when throwing it. He lacks – or appears to lack – a breaking ball. But the FB / CH repertoire is a good base.

Ceiling: 1.0-win player
Risk: Moderate
MLB ETA: 2026

San Diego Padres Top Prospects

San Diego Padres

1. Jackson Merrill, SS

Hit	Power	SB	Patience	Glove	Overall
60	40/55	50	50	55	60

Born: 04/19/03 | **Age:** 20 | **Bats:** L | **Top Production Comp:** Carlos Guillen
Height: 6-3 | **Weight:** 195 | **Throws:** R |

Season	Team	Age	Level	PA	1B	2B	3B	HR	SB	CS	BB%	K%	AVG	OBP	SLG	ISO
2021	SDP	18	CPX	120	21	7	2	0	5	1	8.33%	22.50%	0.280	0.339	0.383	0.103
2022	SDP	19	CPX	31	8	3	1	1	3	0	3.23%	6.45%	0.433	0.452	0.700	0.267
2022	SDP	19	A	219	46	10	3	5	8	5	8.68%	19.18%	0.325	0.387	0.482	0.157

Background: With the parent club in a perpetual state of "win now", the Padres' once overflowing farm system is now fairly barren – sans one Samuel Zavala and one young shortstop Enter: Jackson Merrill. Taken during the shortstop-heavy first round of the 2021 draft, Merrill was the ninth of 11 total selections at the position in the opening round. A year later, though, the Severna Park High School product is making the argument as one of the better shortstop prospects *in the entire game*. Swinging from the left side, Merrill turned in a solid debut with San Diego's Complex League affiliate two years ago, batting .280/.339/.383 with seven doubles, two triples, and five stolen bases (in six attempts). And his sophomore campaign began in similar fashion. Merrill opened the season up with Lake Elsinore, going 2-for-6 and was swinging one of the hottest bats in baseball through the first few weeks of the season (.393/.452/.518). But a freak injury – termed an avulsion fracture in his wrist – knocked him out of commission and he wouldn't pop back up with the Storm until three months later. An avulsion fracture, by the way, is described as a small piece of bone, which is attached to a tendon / ligament, breaks away from the large part of the bone. Merrill's incident happened as his wrist was caught in an opposing player's jersey. Finally healthy in late July, the former first rounder mashed an impressive .335/.397/.513 over his final 35 games. In total, Merrill batted .325/.370/.482 with 10 doubles, three triples, five homeruns, and eight stolen bases (in 13 attempts) during his time with Lake Elsinore.

Snippet from The 2020 Prospect Digest Handbook: Really love the swing. It's silky smooth with plenty of bat speed and enough natural loft to belt out 15 or so homeruns during his peak. Good opposite field power. Defensively, he's fluid and should have no issues staying at the position long term. It wouldn't be surprising to see Merrill's defense grades out as above-average.

Scouting Report: Consider the following:

> Since 2006, only two 19-year-old hitters met the following criteria in any Low-A league (min. 200 PA): 120 to 130 wRC+, an 18% to 21% strikeout rate, and a 7.5% to 9.5% walk rate. Those two hitters: Andrew McCutchen, who's closing out the tail end of his Hall of Very Good career, and – of course – Jackson Merrill.

Filling in the role that former top prospect C.J. Abrams once held: a talented, young shortstop with the potential for a plus hit tool, though Merrill offers up better power potential and glove. The lefty-swinging Merrill doesn't show any major platoon splits, as well. Slightly open stance with a picture-esque swing, the young shortstop is only beginning to tap into his above-average in-game power. There's a chance he could peak in the 20- to 25-HR range. In terms of big league ceiling, think .310/.380/.460.

Ceiling: 5.5-win player
Risk: Moderate
MLB ETA: 2024

2. Samuel Zavala, CF

Hit	Power	SB	Patience	Glove	Overall
35/55	35/55	50	50	50	60

Born: 07/15/04 | **Age:** 18 | **Bats:** L | **Top Production Comp:** George Springer
Height: 6-1 | **Weight:** 175 | **Throws:** L |

Season	Team	Age	Level	PA	1B	2B	3B	HR	SB	CS	BB%	K%	AVG	OBP	SLG	ISO
2021	SDP	16	DSL	235	33	16	6	3	11	7	13.62%	15.32%	0.297	0.400	0.487	0.190
2022	SDP	17	CPX	35	5	3	1	1	0	0	11.43%	31.43%	0.345	0.412	0.621	0.276
2022	SDP	17	A	141	16	6	2	7	5	3	13.48%	26.24%	0.254	0.355	0.508	0.254

Background: San Diego inked the then-16-year-old outfielder to a hefty $1.2 million deal in mid-January 2021. Less than two years later the dynamic Venezuelan has already earned a long look at Low-A arms. Standing at 6-foot-1 and 175 pounds, Zavala debuted with the club's Dominican Summer League affiliate just months after joining the organization, batting an impressive .297/.400/.487 with 16 doubles, six triples, three homeruns, and 11 stolen bases in only 55 games. Last season, the front office took the cautious approach – at least temporarily – and sent the young centerfielder to the Complex League. But that stint lasted just 10 games before he was shoved up to full season action for the remainder of the year. Zavala hit a scorching .345/.412/.621 during his limited time in the Complex League. He followed that up with an impressive .254/.355/.508 line with six doubles, two triples, and seven homeruns in Low-A. His production with the Storm, per *Weighted Runs Created Plus*, topped the league average mark by 18%. He finished the year with an aggregate .272/.366/.530 mark.

San Diego Padres

Snippet from The 2020 Prospect Digest Handbook: Really good looking swing with some potential to develop above-average thunder in his bat. It's short, compact, and quick to the plate. And despite his youth, Zavala showed a mature approach at the plate during his debut as well. There's a lot of intrigue here. He could shoot up several lists within in the next 12 months.

Scouting Report: Yes, the sample size is too small to be reliable but – what the hell? – let's have some fun. Consider the following:

> Since 2006, only fourteen 17-year-old hitters accrued at least 125 plate appearances in any Low-A league. Zavala's overall production, 118 wRC+, was the third best among the group – trailing only Fernando Martinez and Jose Tabata, both of whom were consensus Top 100 prospects for multiple years.

Big leg kick, a la late career Daryl Strawberry, Zavala is looking to do three things in each at bat:

> #1. Hit the ball hard.
> #2. Hit the ball in the air.
> #3. Pull the ball.

Big time power potential that easily will turn into plus in-game power. Zavala turned on an offspeed pitch from sidewinding lefty Liu Fuenmayor that was easily six inches inside and kept his hands inside enough to hit a titanic dinger in late August. Zavala battled some swing-and-miss issues during his stint in Low-A, though it's not concerning given his age and level of competition. Patient approach. Throw in some above-average defense at a premium position and it's *clear* that Zavala is primed to become a contender for Top Prospect in all of baseball (even if he will eventually move into a corner position). Big league ceiling: .280/.370/.580.

Ceiling: 4.0-win player
Risk: Moderate
MLB ETA: 2024

3. Dylan Lesko, RHP

FB	SL	CH	Command	Overall
60	55	70	55	60

Born: 09/07/03	Age: 19	Bats: R	Top Production Comp: N/A
Height: 6-2	Weight: 195	Throws: R	

Background: Buford High School is no stranger to quality big league prospects. Such luminaries like Joey Bart and Brandon Marsh, both consensus Top 100 prospects during their professional careers, have walked through the school's hallowed halls. Connor Bennett, a 34th round pick by the Reds in 2015, and Jake Burnette, a seventh-round pick by the Pirates in 2011, earned hefty six-figure bonuses as well. Dylan Lesko, a firebolt-slinging right-hander, became the earliest drafted player in school history, as well as easily surpassing Brandon Marsh's $1 million bonus too – despite undergoing Tommy John surgery in late-April. And there's good reason why. The 6-foot-2, 195-pound right-hander rocketed up into a separate stratosphere during his junior campaign, posting a barely-there 0.35 ERA with a videogame-esque 112 punch outs in only 60 innings of work. He finished the year with a perfect 11-0 record en route to capturing the Gatorade Player of the Year award, the first time a junior had done so. The big righty was committed to Pitcher University – a.k.a. Vanderbilt University. But the Padres had other plans, selecting him with the 15th overall pick last July, signing him to a massive $3.9 million deal.

Scouting Report: Per the usual, my pre-draft write-up:

> "Prior to the Tommy John surgery, Lesko owned an electric arsenal – perhaps tops in the country among amateurs. Mid-90s fastball with explosion, sitting in the 93- to 95-mph range. He'll complement the plus offering with an above-average, upper 70s curveball, though it showed some slurvy tendencies at times. His third pitch, a wickedly devastating changeup, may be the best in the country. Sitting in the low-80s with hard tumble and fade, it's a genuine swing-and-miss pitch. Lesko commands the zone well – with all three pitchers. There's #2-type potential. It wouldn't be shocking to see the Mets use one of their two first round picks on the hard-throwing, recovering teenager."

Ceiling: 4.0-win player
Risk: Moderate to High
MLB ETA: 2025

4. Robby Snelling, LHP

FB	CB	CH	Command	Overall
55	55	50	45	50

Born: 12/19/03	Age: 19	Bats: R	Top Production Comp: N/A
Height: 6-3	Weight: 210	Throws: L	

Background: An All-America boy cut from the cloth of yesteryear. Snelling, seemingly, did *everything* during his time at McQueen High School. The big southpaw left his head baseball coach Brian Nelson spewing every conceivable positive adjective, according to the Nevada SportsNet (dated 06/03/2022): "Robby Snelling's work ethic is truly amazing. His composure on the mound is very impressive. He strives to be the best and he always leads by example. He is truly wise beyond his years and I couldn't be prouder of his maturity and growth as a young man." His grades are perfect, maintaining a GPA of 4.26. An outside linebacker, Snelling captured Northern Nevada's large-class football player of the year. And he capped off his impressive prep resume in big fashion on the diamond. Snelling posted a perfect 8-0 win-loss record, tallying a tidy 0.56 ERA while fanning an unfathomable 146 strikeouts in just 62.1 innings of work – a Nevada single-season state record. For those counting at home: more than 78% of the outs while he was pitching were strikeouts. Snelling was committed to collegiate powerhouse Louisiana State University prior to the Friars selecting him with the final pick in the first round last July, signing him to a deal worth an even $3 million.

Scouting Report: Per the usual, my pre-draft write-up:

> "Big tree trunk legs, like he was crafted in the left-handed likeness of Tom Seaver. Supremely athletic, but maxed out physically. Snelling, unlike former top prospect Hunter Greene, won't be gaining much bulk in the early stages of his professional career. He already has the build of a ten-year veteran power pitcher. Bulldog mentality. Low- to mid-90s above-average fastball. His curveball can get slurvy at times, but shows some late tilt, movement. He's incredibly confident in throwing the breaking ball at any point. Average changeup. There's some Mike Hampton-type potential."

Ceiling: 2.5-win player
Risk: Moderate
MLB ETA: 2025

5. Eguy Rosario, IF

Hit	Power	SB	Patience	Glove	Overall
45	45	60	50	45	45

Born: 08/25/99	Age: 23	Bats: R	Top Production Comp: N/A
Height: 5-9	Weight: 150	Throws: R	

Season	Team	Age	Level	PA	1B	2B	3B	HR	SB	CS	BB%	K%	AVG	OBP	SLG	ISO
2021	SDP	21	AA	481	72	31	3	12	30	14	10.19%	22.66%	0.281	0.360	0.455	0.174
2022	SDP	22	AAA	564	81	34	4	22	21	8	10.46%	19.33%	0.288	0.368	0.508	0.220

Background: One of the San Diego's more slowly developing prospects. Rosario, who's been a part of the organization since 2015, had a spectacular debut showing in the Dominican Summer League a year later, mashing .346/.423/.472 in 53 games and he continued to swing a hot stick during his seven game cameo in the stateside rookie league as well. Then his bat cooled significantly over the next two seasons. The Dominican-born infielder cobbled together a disappointing .206/.296/.278 across 50 games in the Midwest League before getting demoted – though he did rebound during his stint in the Arizona Summer League (.282/.363/.422). The following season, 2018, Rosario was pushed up to High-A and, well, the results were atrocious. He hit .239/.307/.363. And, for some reason, the club bounced the struggling youngster up to Double-A for a three-game cameo; he promptly went 2-for-11 with five strikeouts. Unsurprisingly, Rosario found himself back in High-A to start the 2019 season. And – finally – his bat showed some signs of life. He hit .278/.331/.412 across 122 games with Lake Elsinore. From that point on Rosario's production has remained a steady constant. He slugged .281/.360/.455 in 114 games against the minors' challenging environment – Double-A. Last season the 5-foot-9, 150-pound infielder moved up to the final stop in the minors, posting .288/.368/.508 with career bests in doubles (34) and homeruns (22) to go along with four triples and 21 stolen bases. His overall production with the El Paso Chihuahuas, as measured by *Weighted Runs Created Plus*, topped the league average mark by 16%. Rosario also squeezed in seven games with San Diego, too, going 1-for-5.

Snippet from The 2022 Prospect Digest Handbook: Low end starting material, unless the hit tool develops better than expected.

Scouting Report: Consider the following:

> Since 2006, only four 22-year-old hitters met the following criteria in a season in Triple-A (min. 350 PA): 110 to 120 wRC+, 9.5% to 11.5% walk rate, and an 18% to 20% strikeout rate. Those four hitters: Ian Stewart, Daniel Robertson, Wladimir Balentin, and – of course – Eguy Rosario.

San Diego Padres

Thick lower half. Crouched stance, slightly open. Rosario's surge in homeruns also happens to coincide with spending half of his time planning in El Paso's bandbox of a stadium. He hit .336/.414/.594 with 13 homeruns in 66 home games. And he batted .239/.322/.416 with nine homeruns in 66 road games. San Diego's been grooming him as potential utility option, bouncing him between second base, shortstop, and third base – a trend that continued last year.

Ceiling: 1.5-win player
Risk: Moderate
MLB ETA: Debuted in 2022

6. Victor Lizarraga, RHP

FB	CB	CH	Command	Overall
55	55	50/55	50	45

Born: 11/30/03	Age: 18	Bats: R	Top Production Comp: N/A
Height: 6-3	Weight: 180	Throws: R	

Season	Team	Age	Level	IP	TBF	K/9	K%	BB/9	BB%	K-BB%	ERA	FIP	xFIP	Pit/Bat
2021	SDP	17	CPX	30.0	130	10.50	26.92%	4.50	11.54%	15.38%	5.10	6.00	5.20	1.85
2022	SDP	18	A	94.1	408	9.06	23.28%	3.24	8.33%	14.95%	3.43	4.19	4.96	3.76

Background: San Diego signed the California-born right-hander on the international free agency market early in 2021, handing the 6-foot-3, 180-pound right-hander a hefty $1 million deal. Lizarraga made his debut with the club's Complex League affiliate a few weeks later, making 11 starts while averaging 10.5 strikeouts and 4.5 walks per nine innings. Last season, the talented youngster made the move up to full season action, showing promise against the significantly older competition. Making 19 starts and one relief appearance, Lizarraga tossed 94.1 innings, recording 95 punch outs and 34 walks. He finished the year with a 3.43 ERA, a 4.19 FIP, and a 4.96 xFIP. For his career, the lanky righty is averaging 9.4 strikeouts and 3.5 walks per nine innings.

Snippet from The 2022 Prospect Digest Handbook: Lizarraga's a little soft physically and needs to get in better shape, get stronger. He looks like a low level wild card at this point.

Scouting Report: Consider the following:

> Since 2006, only twenty-six 18-year-old hurlers have thrown at least 75 innings in any Low-A league. Of those 26, only two posted a strikeout percentage between 22.5% to 24.5% and a walk percentage between 7.5% to 9.5%. Those two hurlers: Bryan Mata and Victor Lizarraga.

Significantly better than his debut showing, particularly late last season. Lizarraga's fastball seemed to grow some legs over the past year, easily blowing it by several hitters late in the game. His curveball went from flashing a 55-grade to consistently showing above-average depth and shape. And his changeup, which I didn't see in 2021, showed some promise as a potential third above-average weapon. It's firm with a little bit of arm side run, but it caught several hitters out on their front foot. Lizarraga's drifting in that quasi-starter territory, showing some traits as a potential backend arm but a lot of his success now is coming from his pitchability / guile.

Ceiling: 1.5-win player
Risk: Moderate
MLB ETA: 2024/2025

7. Adam Mazur, RHP

FB	CB	SL	CH	Command	Overall
55	50	60	50	45	45

Born: 04/20/01	Age: 22	Bats: R	Top Production Comp: N/A
Height: 6-2	Weight: 180	Throws: R	

Background: For a brief moment in time, Woodbury High School, tucked away on the outskirts of Minneapolis, had two prominent ballplayers walking through their hallowed halls. Max Meyer, a 34th round pick by the Twins in 2017, would head to the University of Minnesota and three years later become the third overall pick in the draft. And Adam Mazur, a much less heralded hurler coming out high school, spent two years at South Dakota State before transferring to Iowa and eventually becoming a second round pick in 2022. Standing a wiry 6-foot-2 and 180 pounds, Mazur was limited to just four starts during the COVID-impacted 2020 season at South Dakota State, throwing 20.1 innings with 18 strikeouts, 12 walks, and a 5.75 ERA. His sophomore campaign was much the same as well, posting an 88-to-31 strikeout-to-walk ratio in 68.0 innings across 12 starts. But things seemed to click for Mazur that summer, though, and he found his groove in the Cape Cod League. Making six – mostly dominant – starts with the Wareham Gatemen, the right-hander averaged 10.6 strikeouts and just 1.9 walks per nine innings to go along with a 1.55 ERA. And after transferring to the University of Iowa, he was able to carry that momentum into earning Big 10 Pitcher of the Year in 2022. Mazur would cap off his collegiate career by

San Diego Padres

averaging 9.4 strikeouts and 2.9 walks per nine innings in 15 starts for the Hawkeyes, winning seven and losing just three times. He signed with the Padres for $1.25 million as the 53rd overall pick.

Scouting Report: Consider the following:

> Since 2015, six Division I pitchers have averaged between 9.3 and 9.6 strikeouts and 2.75 and 3.25 walks per nine innings in a season (min. 90 IP): Kris Bubic, Konnor Pilkington, Connor Noland, Brendan White, Jared Reklaitis, and – of course – Adam Mazur.

Crafty right-hander that was able to hone in on the strike zone after two mostly disappointing seasons at South Dakota State University. Mazur features a standard four-pitch mix: fastball, curveball, slider, and changeup. The wiry right-hander's above-average fastball sits in the low 90s, touching a couple ticks higher at times. His frame size may limit his ability to consistently touch the mid-90s as he moves into the rigors of professional ball. His best secondary weapon is a genuine swing-and-miss slider, easily a plus pitch. He'll also mix in an average curveball and changeup. Mazur's more of a strike-thrower rather than a command guy. He's the type that will dominate the low levels quickly, before struggling – maybe temporarily – in the mid-levels of the minor leagues. #5-type arm. I had a late second / early third round grade on him.

Ceiling: 1.0- to 1.5-win player
Risk: Moderate
MLB ETA: 2024

8. Henry Williams, RHP

	FB	SL	CH	Command	Overall
	N/A	N/A	N/A	N/A	N/A

Born: 09/18/01	Age: 21	Bats: R	Top Production Comp: N/A
Height: 6-5	Weight: 200	Throws: R	

Background: Each team sets a level of risk that they're willing to go up to, but not surpass for every decision – free agency, trades, and – of course, the draft. And one has to wonder just how high that bar was last July when they selected talented, yet injury plagued right-hander Henry Williams in the third round, 91st overall, and signed him to an $800,000. An unheralded prospect coming out of Darien High School, Williams made just one – *disastrous* – start during his 2020 season, throwing just two-thirds of an inning, allowing one run and walking three. Then COVID cancelled the rest of the year. The 6-foot-5, 200-pound righty opened his sophomore season up as Duke's Saturday starter. And he began the year on a tear. He struck out 45, walked just 10, and tallied a 3.65 ERA across 37.0 innings of work. But an injury – termed as "tightness" – forced him out the remainder of the year. *Then* he would succumb to Tommy John surgery during the winter and miss the entirety of 2022. Still, though, the Padres saw enough and took the third round plunge.

Scouting Report: During an interview with Scott Ericson (CT Insider), Williams remarked that the Padres were one of just three teams interested in him coming out of high school – so it's not overly surprising, per se, that the Friars took the risk of drafting the little used hurler last July. According to reports, Williams was featuring a mid-90s fastball, a solid, sometimes plus slider, and a decent changeup. He's now entering nearly two full years without logging any mound time, so it'll be interesting to see what he's bringing to the party.

Ceiling: Too Soon to Tell
Risk: Too Soon to Tell
MLB ETA: N/A

9. Efrain Contreras, RHP

	FB	CB	CH	Command	Overall
	55	60	50	40/45	45

Born: 01/02/00	Age: 22	Bats: R	Top Production Comp: N/A
Height: 5-10	Weight: 225	Throws: R	

Season	Team	Age	Level	IP	TBF	K/9	K%	BB/9	BB%	K-BB%	ERA	FIP	xFIP	Pit/Bat
2022	SDP	22	A+	53.1	246	10.80	26.02%	4.22	10.16%	15.85%	5.74	4.48	4.35	3.96

Background: A solid, under-the-radar signing out of Ciudad de Juarez, Mexico, five years ago. San Diego added the talented, stout right-hander to their farm system on a $50,000 deal. Contreras wouldn't make his professional debut until the following season, 2018, but blitzed through three levels, going from foreign rookie league to the stateside rookie league, and settling in for a pair of games in the old Northwest League. Contreras continued to show promise – despite his aggressive assignments – and averaged a noteworthy 9.9 strikeouts and 2.6 walks per nine innings across 23 starts and a pair of relief outings with Fort Wayne in 2019. But his right elbow flared up during the 2020 COVID season and he eventually succumbed to Tommy John surgery and knocked him out for the entirety of 2021. Finally healthy last year, Contreras made 17 starts in High-A, throwing 53.1 innings with 64 strikeouts and 25 free passes. He finished his comeback season with a 5.74 ERA, 4.48 FIP, and a 4.35 xFIP. The 5-foot-10, 225-pound righty also made another five appearances with Peoria in the Arizona Fall League as well, averaging 7.9 strikeouts and 3.4 walks per nine innings.

San Diego Padres

Scouting Report: Portly. Contreras' waistline continues to expand. During his 2019 season the young 5-foot-10 right-hander was weighing 210 pounds. Last season, though, he was tipping the scales at a hefty 225 pounds. Contreras shows an above-average, low-90s heater, a plus curveball, and an average changeup. His curveball's particularly wicked, showing plenty *hard* downward bite. There's some backend starting potential, but he's going to prove his command will return and that he can take the ball consistently every fifth day.

Ceiling: 1.5-win player
Risk: Moderate to High
MLB ETA: 2024

10. Daniel Montesino, 1B/OF

Hit	Power	SB	Patience	Glove	Overall
30/50	45/55	50/40	50	45	45

Born: 02/12/04	Age: 19	Bats: L	Top Comp: N/A
Height: 6-0	Weight: 180	Throws: L	

Season	Team	Age	Level	PA	1B	2B	3B	HR	SB	CS	BB%	K%	AVG	OBP	SLG	ISO
2021	SDP	17	DSL	243	39	13	4	4	8	4	17.70%	21.81%	0.316	0.444	0.489	0.174

Background: One of the club's big signings on the international scene two years ago. The Padres signed Montesino to hefty seven-figure deal, making the then-16-year-old an instant millionaire. The wiry, yet strong first baseman / corner outfielder turned in a dynamic showing in the Dominican Summer League. He mashed .316/.444/.490 with 13 doubles, four triples, four homeruns, and eight stolen bases. His overall production in the foreign rookie league, according to *Weighted Runs Created Plus*, topped the league average mark by a herculean 60%. He missed the entirety of 2022 recovering from Tommy John surgery.

Scouting Report: Since Montesino missed the entirety of last season, here's his scouting report heading into 2022:

> "Montesino just looks like a future run producer at the big league level. Lean but muscular. Well-built but not stocky. The Venezuelan first baseman / corner outfielder shows almost a picture-esque left-handed stroke. Plenty of bat speed. Good natural loft. Montesino already began tapping into his above-average, maybe even plus-power potential in the Dominican Summer League. His bat and pop will have to carry him through the minor leagues, because he won't be providing any value on the defensive side of the ball."

Ceiling: 1.0- to 1.5-win player
Risk: Moderate to High
MLB ETA: 2025

11. Joshua Mears, OF

Hit	Power	SB	Patience	Glove	Overall
30/35	60	50	50	50	40

Born: 02/21/01	Age: 22	Bats: R	Top Production Comp: Jeren Kendall
Height: 6-3	Weight: 230	Throws: R	

Season	Team	Age	Level	PA	1B	2B	3B	HR	SB	CS	BB%	K%	AVG	OBP	SLG	ISO
2021	SDP	20	A	291	28	10	4	17	10	5	12.37%	39.18%	0.244	0.368	0.529	0.285
2022	SDP	21	CPX	66	5	6	1	3	2	0	12.12%	39.39%	0.268	0.364	0.571	0.304
2022	SDP	21	A+	207	16	11	0	14	1	1	7.73%	43.48%	0.223	0.304	0.511	0.288
2022	SDP	21	AA	94	7	2	0	5	1	0	10.64%	47.87%	0.169	0.266	0.373	0.205

Background: San Diego, particularly under the captainship of A.J. Preller, has been drawn to toolsy high schoolers in the early rounds of the draft. Predictably so, the results have been hit-or-miss. Three years after selecting Mears in the second round, 48th overall, it's nearly certain that the Federal Way High School product isn't going to be one of the more memorable ones. After putting together an impressive debut in the Arizona Summer League, Mears' pockmarks became readily apparent during his first taste of full season ball two years ago. Appearing in 71 games with the Lake Elsinore Storm, the 6-foot-3, 230-pound outfielder batted .244/.368/.529 with 10 doubles, four triples, 17 homeruns, and 10 stolen bases. The problem: he whiffed in nearly 40% of his plate appearances. Last season Mears' production took another step backward while his K-rate continued to climb. He batted .223/.304/.511 in 52 games with Fort Wayne after sandwiching in a lengthy stay on the disabled list due to a leg injury. Mears overall numbers, as measured by *Weighted Runs Created Plus*, still topped the league mark by 21%. He also appeared in 24 games in Double-A as well, hitting .169/.266/.373 with a 47.9% K-rate.

Snippet from The 2022 Prospect Digest Handbook: When he does make contact, though, it's some of the loudest, hardest in the entire minor leagues. And if I threw 5 mph harder in college, I would be playing baseball, not writing about it.

San Diego Padres

Scouting Report: Consider the following:

> Since 2006, only six 21-year-old hitters posted a K-rate north of 40% in any High-A league (min. 200 PA). Only Telvin Nash's 44.1% manages to top Mears' 43.5% showing.

No one's going to argue against the tools. Plus power, above-average speed, solid glove. The problem – and it's always been a problem – is the actual hit tool. Will Benson had a similar toolkit and was able to chew his swing-and-miss numbers down to a far less concerning total, though it didn't happen until his age-24 season, but it's still unknown as to whether he can repeat it or hit in the big leagues. Best case scenario is that Mears follows the same path.

Ceiling: 1.0-win player
Risk: Moderate
MLB ETA: 2024

12. Jairo Iriarte, RHP

FB	SL	CH	Command	Overall
55	55	60	40	45

Born: 12/15/01	Age: 21	Bats: R	Top Production Comp: N/A
Height: 6-2	Weight: 160	Throws: R	

Season	Team	Age	Level	IP	TBF	K/9	K%	BB/9	BB%	K-BB%	ERA	FIP	xFIP	Pit/Bat
2021	SDP	19	CPX	21.0	85	10.71	29.41%	3.00	8.24%	21.18%	4.71	3.85	4.33	1.92
2022	SDP	20	A	91.1	409	10.74	26.65%	4.14	10.27%	16.38%	5.12	5.42	5.14	3.71

Background: An under-the-radar international free agent signing out of La Guairá, Venezuela, during the summer of 2018. The wiry right-hander wouldn't make his debut until the following season, throwing 35.1 innings of work with the club's foreign rookie league affiliate. Iriarte would finish the year with a disappointing 21-to-14 strikeout-to-walk ratio. And his showing in 2021 wasn't much better. Splitting time between the Arizona Complex League and Low-A, the young right-hander averaged an impressive 10.2 strikeouts and 3.9 walks per nine innings but finished with a disastrous 11.40 ERA in 30.0 innings. Last season the front office continued to push Iriarte along the minor league ladder, sending him to Lake Elsinore for his first look at full season action. He would post a 109-to-42 strikeout-to-walk ratio in 91.1 innings of work. He finished the year with a 5.12 ERA, a 5.42 FIP, and a 5.14 xFIP.

Scouting Report: Consider the following:

> Since 2006, there have seven 20-year-old hurlers that posted a 25.5% to 27.5% strikeout percentage with a 9.5% to 11.5% walk percentage (min. 75 IP): Wade Davis, Wily Peralta, Huascar Ynoa, Darwinzon Hernandez, Matt Magill, Connor Hoehn, and Jairo Iriarte.

An interesting low level arm. Iriarte shows a starter's arsenal, featuring three above-average or better offerings. His fastball, sitting in the mid-90s, has plus velocity but is a bit more hittable than expected. His go-to offspeed offering is plus changeup showing fade and fantastic velo separation. He'll also mix in an impressive above-average slider, though he doesn't throw it nearly as frequently as he should. The command – particularly when it comes to his fastball – has ways to go. He's tracking as a potential backend starter, but may eventually work his way into a relief role unless the command upticks.

Ceiling: 1.0-win player
Risk: Moderate
MLB ETA: 2024

13. Brandon Valenzuela, C/1B

Hit	Power	SB	Patience	Glove	Overall
50	35/40	30	55	45	40

Born: 10/02/00	Age: 22	Bats: B	Top Production Comp: N/A
Height: 6-0	Weight: 170	Throws: R	

Season	Team	Age	Level	PA	1B	2B	3B	HR	SB	CS	BB%	K%	AVG	OBP	SLG	ISO
2021	SDP	20	A	378	71	21	3	6	3	2	11.64%	21.16%	0.307	0.389	0.444	0.137
2021	SDP	20	A+	65	10	1	0	1	1	0	23.08%	30.77%	0.245	0.415	0.327	0.082
2022	SDP	21	A+	413	46	14	2	10	0	1	15.25%	23.00%	0.209	0.334	0.348	0.139

Background: Valenzuela was one of the more pleasant surprises in the in the Friars' farm system two years ago. The young backstop, who signed out of Hermosillo, Mexico in 2017, struggled through two disappointing seasons in 2018 and 2019, posting OPS of .702 and .689 in the Dominican and Arizona Summer Leagues. But things seemed to click after minor league ball returned from its pandemic-induced absence in 2021. Opening the year up with the Storm of Lake Elsinore, the 6-foot, 170-pound backstop / part-time first baseman batted .307/.389/.444 with 21 doubles, three triples, six homeruns, and three stolen bases in only 82 games. He spent the final few

San Diego Padres

weeks of the season battling against the pitching in High-A – more or less holding his own. Last season, with his prospect arrow firmly pointed upwards, Valenzuela completed stumbled in his return to Fort Wayne. Appearing in a career best 99 games, Valenzuela cobbled together a lowly .209/.334/.348 with 14 doubles, two triples, and 10 homeruns. His overall production with the Tin Caps was 4% *below* the league average mark, according to *Weighted Runs Created Plus*. For his career Valenzuela's sporting a .254/.372/.364 slash line over 292 games.

Snippet from The 2022 Prospect Digest Handbook: An average defender behind the plate, though he doesn't strike fear into the opposition's base runners, Valenzuela shows a bit of offensive promise – particularly one from a premium position. Solid hit tool, above-average walk rates, decent bat-to-ball skills, and doubles power. There's likely not enough to develop into a full time starter, but there's a backup ceiling here.

Scouting Report: Consider the following:

> Since 2006, only a pair of 21-year-old hitters posted a 90 to 100 wRC+ with a 22% to 24% strikeout rate and a double-digit walk rate in High-A (min. 350 PA): D.J. Burt and Brandon Valenzuela.

All in all, it was a pretty terrible showing for Valenzuela last season. So bad, in fact, he batted .211 or below in four separate months (April, June, July, and August). And nearly all of his production at the plate was tied up into his patience as he walked in more than 15% of his plate appearances. The silver lining to his season, though, is the development behind the plate as he moved from a below-average to above-average defender. He's young enough to expect a bounce back season, a la Bo Naylor, but there's still not enough to project as a starter.

Ceiling: 1.0-win player
Risk: Moderate
MLB ETA: 2024

14. Yendry Rojas, SS

Hit	Power	SB	Patience	Glove	Overall
40/55	30/40	45/40	50	50	40

Born: 01/27/05	Age: 18	Bats: L	Top Production Comp: N/A
Height: 6-0	Weight: 185	Throws: R	

Season	Team	Age	Level	PA	1B	2B	3B	HR	SB	CS	BB%	K%	AVG	OBP	SLG	ISO
2022	SDP	17	DSL	187	35	4	4	0	14	6	13.90%	12.30%	0.279	0.373	0.357	0.078

Background: The Padres have been one of the most aggressive Major League teams when it comes to signing Cuban ballplayers. In recent years they've handed out big dollar bonuses to the likes of Adrian Morejon, Jorge Ona, Michel Baez, Elier Sanchez, Wilton Castillo, Osvaldo Hernandez, Ramses Velazquez, and Yendry Rojas – with the final two coming in 2022. San Diego signed Rojas, a lefty-swinging shortstop from Ciego De Avila, to a hefty $1.3 million in mid-January. The 6-foot, 185-pound infielder spent the summer squaring off against the foreign rookie league competition. He batted .279/.373/.357 with four doubles four triples, and 14 stolen bases. His production, per *Weighted Runs Created Plus*, topped the league average mark by just 4%.

Scouting Report: Quite raw, even given his age. Rojas has a pretty left-handed swing that's more suited for slashing doubles rather than belting long balls. Solid bat speed, but not spectacular. Simple repeatable mechanics. He's not overly big, but may end up shifting to the right side of the keystone due to lack of range. Not fast. There's just not a standout tool that's present *or* projects to be. The best bet would be if the bat peaks as an above-average weapon – which will be his sole carrying tool.

Ceiling: 1.0-win player
Risk: Moderate
MLB ETA: 2026

15. Tirso Ornelas, OF

Hit	Power	SB	Patience	Glove	Overall
50	40	40	50	50	40

Born: 03/11/00	Age: 23	Bats: L	Top Production Comp: N/A
Height: 6-3	Weight: 200	Throws: R	

Season	Team	Age	Level	PA	1B	2B	3B	HR	SB	CS	BB%	K%	AVG	OBP	SLG	ISO
2021	SDP	21	A+	445	56	31	1	7	3	1	11.69%	22.02%	0.248	0.344	0.389	0.141
2022	SDP	22	AA	492	90	28	2	7	7	2	8.74%	17.28%	0.288	0.355	0.408	0.120
2022	SDP	22	AAA	15	2	1	0	0	0	0	6.67%	13.33%	0.214	0.267	0.286	0.071

Background: On the fringes of the club's Top 20 Prospect List for the past several seasons – which speaks to the depletion of the farm due to trades, graduations, and attrition. The Padres immediately fast-tracked the young outfielder at that start of his career, sending him to the Arizona Summer League as a 17-year-old and then a year later shipping up to the old Midwest League. But despite a mediocre showing in Low-A in 2018 (.252/.341/.392), the organization continued to challenge Ornelas and sent him up to High-A as a 19-year-old. He, of course, struggled even more. The COVID 2020 season placed a pause on this aggressive development path and allowed the organization to do a reset. So they did. And sent him back down to High-A two years ago, though the production was terrible (.248/.344/.389). Last season, he – finally – showed some progress at the plate. Appearing in 112 games with San Antonio and another trio with El Paso, the 6-foot-3, 200-pound outfielder batted an aggregate .286/.353/.404 with 29 doubles, two triples, seven homeruns, and seven stolen bases. According to *Weighted Runs Created Plus*, his production was 4% *below* the league average.

Scouting Report: Consider the following:

> Since 2006, only six 22-year-old hitters met the following criteria in Double-A (min. 350 PA): 95 to 105 wRC+, a 16% to 18% strikeout rate, and a 7.5% to 9.5% walk rate. Those six hitters: Austin Romine, David Winfree, Jake Cave, Engelb Vielma, Nathan Lukes, and Tirso Ornelas.

Ten years ago Ornelas would be slated for a semi-lengthy career as a fourth or fifth outfielder, showing the aptitude to play all three outfield positions, a little bit of speed, solid hit tool. Nowadays, though, he's likely to earn a few cups of coffee and not much more. He's limited by the lack of a notable tool. The bat is average, the power – despite his 6-foot-3 and 200-pound frame – never materialized, average patience at the plate. He's just…mediocre, nothing more, nothing less.

Ceiling: 1.0-win player
Risk: Moderate
MLB ETA: 2023

16. Kevin Kopps, RHP

FB	CU	Command	Overall
50	60	45/50	40

Born: 03/02/97	Age: 25	Bats: R	Top Comp: N/A
Height: 6-0	Weight: 200	Throws: R	

Season	Team	Age	Level	IP	TBF	K/9	K%	BB/9	BB%	K-BB%	ERA	FIP	xFIP	Pit/Bat
2022	SDP	25	AA	54.1	241	9.94	24.90%	5.63	14.11%	10.79%	4.14	4.66	4.98	3.98

Background: It's a remarkable story, really. One riddled with disappointment and injury mixed with joy, determination, and a strong theme of refusing to give up. Kopps was a solid, yet unremarkable hurler coming out of George Ranch High School in 2015, so it wasn't overly surprising to see the right-hander sit out his true freshman season at the University of Arkansas – courtesy of a redshirt. He established himself as a useful swing-man option for the club in 2019, making 17 relief appearances and five starts en route to throwing 49.0 innings of solid ball. But Kopps would succumb to Tommy John surgery and miss the entirety of the 2018 season. The Texas-born hurler was sent back to the Razorbacks' bullpen upon his return in 2019, making 30 appearances while averaging 11.2 strikeouts and 3.0 walks per nine innings. But his COVID-shortened 2020 season was a *disaster*: he allowed 10 earned runs and 18 hits in only 11.0 innings of work. And at that point Kopps, entering what would be his final year in college, would quietly closeout a decent, sometimes solid, sometimes frustrating career as reliever. Then he morphed into an early career version of Mariano Rivera for the 2021 season. He threw 89.2 innings, recording an absurd 131-to-18 strikeout-to-walk ratio while surrendering just nine earned runs. Good enough for a sparkling 0.90 ERA. And Kopps capped it off by winning the Golden Spikes Award, given to the top collegiate player. San Diego selected him in the third round, 99th overall, and signed him to a below-slot deal worth $300,000 in hopes of quickly pushing him through the system. But that hasn't happened – at least it didn't in 2022. After a dominant debut two years ago, Kopps spent last year in San Antonio, squaring off against the minors' toughest level – Double-A. He appeared in 42 games, averaging 9.9 K/9 and an un-Kopps-like 5.5 BB/9 to go along with a 4.14 ERA.

Snippet from The 2022 Prospect Digest Handbook: I would love to see Kopps given the chance to develop as a starting option, though his age and reliance on two pitches almost guarantees him a reliever path. Love this guy. Love watching him pitch. He could be a throwback to a consistent multi-inning bullpen arm.

Scouting Report: The stuff remains unchanged from his Golden Spikes Award winning season. Low-90s, average fastball. Plus or better, mid-80s cutter. The difference for Kopps, though, is the lack of command last season. His impeccable ability to locate his trademark fastball / cutter combo was uncanny during his final collegiate season, but it all but dissipated in 2022. And he committed the golden sin for wannabe relievers – the walks would come in bunches. Of Kopps' 42 appearances, he walked two or more batters 10 times. History's proven that the crafty right-hander can't be counted out, so it's difficult to downgrade him much after his first professional downturn, but there's also not a lot of wiggle room as he's entering his age-26 season either.

Ceiling: 1.0-win player
Risk: Moderate to High
MLB ETA: 2023

San Diego Padres

17. Jay Groome, LHP

	FB	CB	SL	CH	Command	Overall
	60	60	50	50/55	40	45

Born: 08/23/98	Age: 24	Bats: L	Top Production Comp: N/A
Height: 6-6	Weight: 262	Throws: L	

Season	Team	Age	Level	IP	TBF	K/9	K%	BB/9	BB%	K-BB%	ERA	FIP	xFIP	Pit/Bat
2021	BOS	22	AA	15.2	64	14.94	40.63%	2.30	6.25%	34.38%	2.30	1.15	2.66	3.95
2022	BOS	23	AA	76.2	325	9.51	24.92%	4.46	11.69%	13.23%	3.52	4.89	4.64	3.91
2022	BOS	23	AAA	16.0	71	8.44	21.13%	3.94	9.86%	11.27%	3.94	4.76	4.99	3.90
2022	SDP	23	AAA	51.1	219	7.71	20.09%	3.33	8.68%	11.42%	3.16	4.50	5.69	3.96

Background: The contract was always destined to become an albatross around the organization's financial neck. Handing Eric Hosmer an eight-year deal worth $144 million just didn't make sense. He was coming off of his best professional season to date back in 2017, batting .318/.385/.498 for the Royals. It was his seventh professional season and only the third time he tallied more than 2.0 wins above replacement. Five years later, sporting a completely mediocre .265/.325/.411 slash line during his time with the team, the front office was scrambling to shed any part of Hosmer's remaining deal. They eventually packaged the veteran first baseman along with tens of millions of dollars, Max Ferguson, and Corey Rosier, and shipped him off to Beantown for Jay Groome, a one-time former top prospect trying to reclaim some past semblance of his prospect status. Taken with the 12th overall pick in the disappointing first round of the 2016 draft, Groome battled on-the-field and off-the-field issues throughout his career, but crossed the 100-inning threshold for the first time in 2022. Splitting time between Double-A and Triple-A, the hefty southpaw averaged 8.8 strikeouts and 4.0 walks per nine innings to go along with a 3.44 ERA In 144.0 innings of work.

Snippet from The 2022 Prospect Digest Handbook: But he just has the "feel" of an eventual reliever, some of it just based on his portly appearance.

Scouting Report: Every time I watch Groome, I always walk away disappointed because I was expecting more – more velocity, more command, more of that potential realized. But he's now entering his age-24 season, showing an average fastball and change with two above-average breaking ball with below-average command. Soft body, too soft. There's the potential here for a late career emergence as a solid lefty reliever, but I wouldn't bank on anything more than that. Not unless the conditioning improves.

Ceiling: 0.5 to 1.0-win player
Risk: Moderate
MLB ETA: 2023

18. Garrett Hawkins, RHP

	FB	SL	CH	Command	Overall
	55	45	55	45	40

Born: 02/10/00	Age: 21	Bats: R	Top Production Comp: N/A
Height: 6-5	Weight: 230	Throws: R	

Season	Team	Age	Level	IP	TBF	K/9	K%	BB/9	BB%	K-BB%	ERA	FIP	xFIP	Pit/Bat
2021	SDP	21	CPX	15.1	62	15.85	43.55%	1.17	3.23%	40.32%	2.35	2.38	2.37	2.26
2022	SDP	22	A	77.2	321	12.52	33.64%	2.32	6.23%	27.41%	3.94	3.65	3.54	4.17
2022	SDP	22	A+	15.1	78	7.04	15.38%	5.87	12.82%	2.56%	8.80	8.96	6.27	3.82

Background: Fun Fact: the Padres have selected the most players out of the University of British Columbia. The Friars drafted their first Thunderbird back in 2010, choosing left-hander Mark Hardy in the 43rd round. Five years later they snagged right-hander Alex Webb in 36th round. Their latest pick from the Canadian College came two years ago with the addition of righty Garrett Hawkins. The big 6-foot-5, 230-pound hurler, who signed for just $75,000 as a ninth rounder, made just seven brief appearances in the Complex League during his professional debut, posting a dominating 27-to-2 strikeout-to-walk ratio with a 2.35 ERA. Predictably, the front office sent the Saskatoon native up to Lake Elsinore to begin last season. After 17 strong starts with the Storm, Hawkins capped off his first full season in the Padres' organization with four starts with Fort Wayne. He finished the year with 120 strikeouts, just 30 free passes, and a 4.74 ERA across 93.0 innings. He averaged 11.6 strikeouts and just 2.9 walks per nine innings.

Scouting Report: Consider the following:

> Since 2006, only four 22-year-old hurlers posted a strikeout percentage north of 32% in any Low-A league (min. 75 IP): Jaime Arias-Bautista, Wilfrido Perez, Kelvin Caceres, and – of course – Garrett Hawkins.

Working full-time from the stretch, Hawkins' mechanics aren't ideal. He's too rigid, too robotic. And he leans back during his leg lift and movement towards the plate. Lively above-average fastball, particularly above the belt – which coincides where he likes to live. Below-average slider that your blind grandmother wouldn't even chase. And he features an above-average changeup. There's not enough here to project as a starting pitcher, largely due to his lack of a solid breaking ball. He's strictly an organizational guy with the potential move into the up-and-down category. Expect advanced hitters to feast in 2023. He's more of a strike-thrower than a command guy.

San Diego Padres

Ceiling: 0.5- to 1.0-win player
Risk: Moderate
MLB ETA: 2024/2025

19. Jackson Wolf, LHP

FB	CB	SL	CH	Command	Overall
50	55	60	45	45	40

Born: 04/22/99	Age: 24	Bats: L	Top Production Comp: N/A
Height: 6-7	Weight: 200	Throws: L	

Season	Team	Age	Level	IP	TBF	K/9	K%	BB/9	BB%	K-BB%	ERA	FIP	xFIP	Pit/Bat
2021	SDP	22	A	12.0	52	14.25	36.54%	4.50	11.54%	25.00%	3.75	3.90	3.77	4.10
2022	SDP	23	A+	119.0	486	10.13	27.57%	3.33	9.05%	18.52%	4.01	4.21	4.11	3.94
2022	SDP	23	AA	10.2	50	6.75	16.00%	5.06	12.00%	4.00%	8.44	5.45	6.18	3.60

Background: After nabbing a pair of high upside, toolsy prep hitters with their first two picks in the 2021 draft, the Padres ripped off 11 consecutive selections from four-year colleges, including a pair of hurlers from the Land of the Mountaineers. San Diego used the 129th pick that year on the gigantic, Ohio-born southpaw from WVU who sparkled during the COVID-shortened 2020 and remained rocksteady during his fourth year in the Big-12. Wolf, who stands an impressive 6-foot-7 and wiry 200 pounds, began his collegiate career working on the West Virginia's bullpen as a true freshman, but transitioned into a starting gig in 2019 – though the results were mediocre, at best. Throwing 69.2 innings of work, Wolf struck out 50 and walked 31 to go along with a 5.17 ERA. But after a dominant stint in the Cape Cod League that summer, Wolf reemerged in 2020 as a force to be reckoned with. He allowed just three earned runs while averaging 9.5 strikeouts and just 1.8 walks per nine innings across four starts before COVID prematurely ended the season. After going undrafted, Wolf tossed a career high 89.0 innings for the Morgantown-based college, posting a 104-to-37 strikeout ratio. He spent the majority of last season with Fort Wayne, making 23 appearances and another two final starts with San Antonio. He totaled 129.2 innings, striking out 142 and walking 50 to go along with an aggregate 4.37 ERA and a 7-10 win-loss record.

Scouting Report: Consider the following:

> Since 2006, only two 23-year-old hurlers posted a 26.5% to 28.5% strikeout percentage with a 8% to 10% walk percentage in any High-A League (min. 100 IP): Austin Love and Jackson Wolf, both achieving the feat last season.

A lot of pre-set gyrations a la Mike Clevinger. Wolf's an older-ish, quasi-interesting arm in the Padres' system. Long, long limbs and a slinging, low three-quarter release point. His fastball's fringy average, but plays up half-of-a-grade due to his size. The big lefty showcases two above-average breaking balls: a slower curveball and a sweeping slider that's unfairly hellacious on left-handed hitters. Like a lot of arms left in the Padres' system, there's just not enough here to project as even a backend starter at the big league level. He could carve out a three- to five-year career as a cheap second lefty in a pen though.

Ceiling: 0.5- to 1.0-win player
Risk: Moderate
MLB ETA: 2023/2024

20. Ryan Bergert, RHP

FB	CB	SL	CH	Command	Overall
50	50	50	50	45	40

Born: 03/08/00	Age: 23	Bats: R	Top Production Comp: N/A
Height: 6-1	Weight: 205	Throws: R	

Season	Team	Age	Level	IP	TBF	K/9	K%	BB/9	BB%	K-BB%	ERA	FIP	xFIP	Pit/Bat
2021	SDP	21	CPX	11.0	37	11.45	37.84%	0.00	0.00%	37.84%	0.00	1.92	2.74	1.76
2022	SDP	22	A+	103.1	472	11.24	27.33%	3.66	8.90%	18.43%	5.84	4.50	3.75	4.10

Background: Prior to the 2021 draft, the Padres had selected only three West Virginia Mountaineers in their history. And two of the players – Jedd Gyorko and Vince Belnome – both cracked a Major League lineup in their careers with the former in the midst of a solid eight-year career. Then in 2021 the Friars selected left-hander Jackson Wolf in the fourth round then doubled back around and grabbed right-hander Ryan Bergert two rounds later. The 190th player taken that year, San Diego handed Bergert the largest bonus in the sixth round, signing him to a deal worth $500,000. Bergert would make seven brief appearances in the Complex League during his debut, throwing 11 innings with 14 punch outs and three free passes without surrendering an earned run. Last season, his first full year in the organization, the front office gave the 6-foot-1, 205-pound right-hander an aggressive assignment and sent him directly to Fort Wayne. And despite a wonky 5.84 ERA, Bergert competed well against the High-A competition. In 24 starts for the Tin Caps, the WVU alum tossed 103.1 innings, averaging an impressive 11.7 strikeouts and 3.7 walks per nine innings. He tallied a 4.50 FIP and a 3.75 xFIP.

San Diego Padres

Scouting Report: Consider the following:

> Since 2006, only two 22-year-old hurlers posted a 26.5% to 28.5% strikeout percentage with an 8% to 10% walk percentage in any High-A league (min. 100 IP): Buddy Baumann and – of course – Ryan Bergert.

Everything about Bergert screams "vanilla". In terms of professional pitchers, he's of average height (6-foot-1) and a little on the soft/ bulky side (205 pounds). His fastball sits in the low-90s, peaking at 94 mph on occasion. His curveball is textbook definition of a 50-grade – average shape, velocity (77 mph), and depth. His slider, which is the better of the two breaking balls, has some potential and will flash above-average at times. His 84-mph change won't fool anyone, but it's not exactly terrible either. The only thing that isn't average about Bergert is his command – which is *below-average*. He's going to be an up-and-down arm for as long as he can grab the ball every fifth day and generally keep his team in the game, which is exactly an average thing to do.

Ceiling: 0.5- to 1.0-win player
Risk: Moderate
MLB ETA: 2024

San Francisco Giants Top Prospects

San Francisco Giants

1. Kyle Harrison, LHP

	FB	SL	CH	Command	Overall
	60	55	50/55	45/40	70

Born: 08/12/01	Age: 21	Bats: R	Top Production Comp: Chris Sale
Height: 6-2	Weight: 200	Throws: L	

Season	Team	Age	Level	IP	TBF	K/9	K%	BB/9	BB%	K-BB%	ERA	FIP	xFIP	Pit/Bat
2021	SFG	19	A	98.2	440	14.32	35.68%	4.74	11.82%	23.86%	3.19	3.48	4.06	3.99
2022	SFG	20	A+	29.0	118	18.31	50.00%	3.10	8.47%	41.53%	1.55	1.63	1.70	4.14
2022	SFG	20	AA	84.0	349	13.61	36.39%	4.18	11.17%	25.21%	3.11	3.74	3.32	4.13

Background: Rarely will a team completely miss on their first round pick – particularly an early first round pick – and still look back on its draft class with fond memories. But the Giants can do just that. Owning the 13th overall pick in 2020, the front office decided to go with N.C. State backstop Patrick Bailey, a stout defender with some offensive upside at a premium position. Two years later and Bailey is coming off of a disappointing .225/.342/.420 showing. But, again, the draft class has a lot to offer – despite COVID limiting it to just five rounds. Enter: Kyle Harrison. Viewed as one of the top talents in the 2020 draft class, Harrison slid until the third round due to signability issues. The front office, though, moved some monies around and convinced the De La Salle High School product to join the organization for a hefty $2,497,500 deal – roughly late first round money. And he quickly established himself as not only the Giants' top pitching prospect, but among the best young arms in all of the minor leagues. Harrison dominated Low-A West during his debut in 2021, averaging more than 14 strikeouts and 4.7 walks per nine innings. Last season he shredded the High-A competition for seven starts before the brass was convinced enough that he could handle the minors' toughest challenge: Double-A. And he did. When the dust had settled the 6-foot-2, 200-pound lefty compiled a videogame-esque 186-to-49 strikeout-to-walk ratio in only 113.0 innings of work. He finished the year with an aggregate 2.71 and a 3.20 FIP.

Snippet from The 2022 Prospect Digest Handbook: If the command ticks up to average he's a quality #2/#3 starting pitcher. He could pop in a big way in 2022. He's a bit of slinger, so platoon splits will have to be monitored (LHH batted .302/.432/.365 in 2021).

Scouting Report: Consider the following:

> Since 2006, here's the list of 20-year-old hurlers to post at least a 35% strikeout percentage in any Double-A league (min. 60 IP): Kyle Harrison. In fact, only three 20-year-olds have eclipsed the 30% K% threshold in Double-A since 2006 (min. 60 IP): Phil Hughes, Jaime Melendez, and – of course – Kyle Harrison. The Giants' young lefty, by the way, was nearly four full percentage points higher than runner-up Melendez.

Harrison led all qualified minor league arms in strikeout rate (14.81 K/9), strikeout percentage (39.8%), strikeout-to-walk percentage (29.3%), and he finished second in total strikeouts (186) – trailing Arizona's Brandon Pfaadt. Harrison fanned 32 fewer hitters despite throwing 54 innings less. Arguably the best fastball / slider combo in the minor leagues – among lefties *and* righties. Harrison's fastball sits – *comfortably* – in the 95-mph range and will touch as high as 97 mph on occasion. The slider is borderline plus-plus with nightmare-inducing sweep and tilt. The young lefty has the utmost confidence in the breaking ball, throwing it any anytime in the count. He'll also mix in an occasional above-average changeup, which he'll likely need to rely on more at the big league level. Harrison has a low three-quarter arm slot with a loose, fast arm. He has elite, true ace potential if the command upticks to average. And I think that does happen in the coming years.

Ceiling: 6.0-win player
Risk: Moderate
MLB ETA: 2023

2. Marco Luciano, SS

	Hit	Power	SB	Patience	Glove	Overall
	50/55	55/60	30	55	50	60

Born: 09/10/01	Age: 21	Bats: R	Top Production Comp: Carlos Correa
Height: 6-2	Weight: 178	Throws: R	

Season	Team	Age	Level	PA	1B	2B	3B	HR	SB	CS	BB%	K%	AVG	OBP	SLG	ISO
2021	SFG	19	A	308	39	14	3	18	5	5	12.34%	22.08%	0.278	0.373	0.556	0.278
2021	SFG	19	A+	145	22	3	2	1	1	0	6.90%	37.24%	0.217	0.283	0.295	0.078
2022	SFG	20	A+	230	34	10	0	10	0	0	9.57%	22.17%	0.263	0.339	0.459	0.195

Background: When enough time passes – and we're not quite there just yet – the 2018 International Free Agency crop could go down as one of the greatest, *if not the greatest*, in history. The class featured the likes of Diego Cartaya, who's in the conversation for the top catching prospect in the game; Noelvi Marte, a top prospect who headlined the Reds' return in the Luis Castillo deal last summer; Orelvis Martinez, a former consensus Top 100 prospect who reached – and admittedly struggled in – Double-A during his age-20 season; Francisco Alvarez, arguably the top prospect in the game after the graduation of Adley Rutschman; and – not to be overlooked – the Giants' Marco Luciano. A native of San Francisco de Macoris, Dominican Republic, Luciano inked a contract with the front office on a hefty $2.6 million contract. And it's been a bargain since his first professional swing. Luciano ripped through the Arizona Rookie League during his debut (.322/.438/.616) and spent the last two weeks in the Northwest League – as a 17-year-old. After minor league ball returned from the pandemic-

San Francisco Giants

induced absence, the young shortstop mashed through Low-A (.278/.373/.556) and spent more than a month in High-A. He also acquitted himself well enough in the Arizona Fall League as well, hitting .253/.356/.373 in 21 games with the Scottsdale Scorpions. Luciano opened his third professional season up in the Northwest League, but was limited to just 57 games as a back injury forced him to miss two months of action. The 6-foot-2, 178-pound shortstop slugged .263/.339/.459 with 10 doubles and 10 homeruns in only 57 games with the Emeralds. His overall production, per *Weighted Runs Created Plus*, topped the league average mark by 21%.

Snippet from The 2022 Prospect Digest Handbook: Luciano owns a patient approach at the plate and solid contact skills that belie his prodigious power potential. He'll swipe a handful of bags each season, but that's almost guaranteed to become a non-skill at full maturity. Defensively, he played a passable Derek Jeter version of shortstop.

Scouting Report: Consider the following:

> Since 2006, only three 20-year-old hitters posted a 115 to 125 wRC+ with a 21% to 24% strikeout rate and an 8.5% to 10.5% walk rate in any High-A league (min. 225 PA): Coby Mayo, Yu Chang, and Marco Luciano.

The overall production is good, but far from great. But there's another story to be told. Mainly: pre-injury and post-injury. Prior to hitting the disabled list with a back injury – an issue that would knock him out of action for eight weeks – Luciano slugged .288/.360/.507 through his first 40 games. His production during that time period was 39% above the league average. However, after he returned, the Giants' top prospect hit a paltry .200/.281/.350 over his final 22 contests with the Emeralds and Flying Squirrels. His production during that time period: 22% *below* the league average mark. In terms of big league ceiling, think .285/.360/.530. Luciano is due for a massive season – 2023 might be just that.

Ceiling: 5.0-win player
Risk: Moderate
MLB ETA: 2023/2024

3. Aeverson Arteaga, SS

Hit	Power	SB	Patience	Glove	Overall
40/45	45/50	50	50	60	55

Born: 03/16/03	Age: 20	Bats: R	Top Production Comp: Nick Ahmed
Height: 6-1	Weight: 170	Throws: R	

Season	Team	Age	Level	PA	1B	2B	3B	HR	SB	CS	BB%	K%	AVG	OBP	SLG	ISO
2021	SFG	18	CPX	226	36	12	1	9	8	0	10.18%	30.53%	0.294	0.367	0.503	0.208
2022	SFG	19	A	565	85	35	2	14	11	6	8.67%	27.43%	0.270	0.345	0.431	0.161

Background: Headlining the club's international free agency class – which also added players like Anthony Rodriguez, Esmerlin Vinicio, Manuel Mercedes, and Adrian Sugastey – San Francisco handed the wiry shortstop prospect $1 million during the 2019 signing period. A native of Chirgua, Venezuela, Arteaga made his affiliated debut with the organization's Complex League affiliate two years ago, hitting a solid .294/.367/.503 with 12 doubles, one triple, nine homeruns, and eight stolen bases. His overall production in the rookie league, per *Weighted Runs Created Plus*, topped the average threshold by 23%. Last season, the front office sent the infielder up to Low-A for his first extended look at full-season ball. In 122 games with San Jose, Arteaga batted .270/.345/.431 with 35 doubles, two triples, 14 homeruns, and 11 stolen bases (in 17 total attempts). His production topped the league average mark by just 1%.

Snippet from The 2022 Prospect Digest Handbook: The swing's OK, but it's not special. It needs to be cleaned up, simplified. Good bat speed, but it's chaos. And not controlled chaos.

Scouting Report: Consider the following:

> Since 2006, only five 19-year-old hitters posted a 95 to 105 wRC+ with a strikeout rate between 26% and 29% in a season in Low-A (min. 400 PA): Josh Lowe, Delvi Cid, Kevin Ahrens, Zac Shepherd, and Aeverson Arteaga.

Here's the thing about Arteaga: any value that comes from his bat is an added bonus, icing on his defensive wizardry-based cupcake. And, yes, the glove is so good that it may get him to the big leagues alone. Range, soft hands, arm – you name it on the defensive side of the ball, and he has it. But, surprisingly, Arteaga isn't a one dimensional player. Bat speed and surprising thunder. Two years ago Arteaga struggled making consistent contact, whiffing in more than 30% of his plate appearances, but he was able to chew that down to a less concerning 27.4% in 2022. Utility / backup shortstop floor with a multiple Gold Glove winning ceiling.

Ceiling: 3.0-win player
Risk: Moderate
MLB ETA: 2024/2025

San Francisco Giants

4. Luis Matos, CF

	Hit	Power	SB	Patience	Glove	Overall
	40/45	50/55	55	50	60	55

Born: 01/28/02	Age: 21	Bats: R	Top Production Comp: Starling Marte
Height: 5-11	Weight: 160	Throws: R	

Season	Team	Age	Level	PA	1B	2B	3B	HR	SB	CS	BB%	K%	AVG	OBP	SLG	ISO
2021	SFG	19	A	491	90	35	1	15	21	5	5.70%	12.42%	0.313	0.358	0.494	0.182
2022	SFG	20	A+	407	52	14	1	11	11	3	6.63%	15.97%	0.211	0.275	0.344	0.133

Background: Signed off the international free agency market for $725,000 in 2018. Matos, a native of Valera, Venezuela, entered the 2022 season coming off of back-to-back tremendous showings. The 5-foot-11, 160-pound center fielder made quick work of the foreign and stateside rookie leagues during his debut, mashing an aggregate .367/.438/.566 with 25 doubles, two triples, seven homeruns, and 21 stolen bases in only 60 games. Once minor league baseball returned to action following the lost 2020 COVID campaign, Matos had no problem with the Low-A West pitching as he slugged .313/.359/.495 with 35 doubles, one triple, 15 homeruns, and 21 stolen bases. His prospect status seemed to be reaching a crescendo as the calendar turned to 2022. Then things went kaput. Matos would appear in just 91 games with the Eugene Emeralds, hitting a lowly .211/.275/.344 with 14 doubles, one triple, 11 homeruns, and 11 stolen bases (in 14 total attempts). His overall production, per *Weighted Runs Created Plus*, was a whopping 27% *below* the league average threshold. Matos did spend the fall playing with the Scottsdale Scorpions, though the performance was similarly disappointing (.239/.278/.388).

Snippet from The 2022 Prospect Digest Handbook: Loud tools across the board. Matos is doing everything and he's doing everything well. He's making consistent, hard contact. He's hitting for plenty of power. He's fast *and* efficient on the base paths. He's an above-average defender in center field. And he did so while playing half of his games in ballpark that slants toward pitchers. Elite, elite bat speed.

Scouting Report: Matos' 2020 campaign got off on the wrong foot, hitting a disappointingly poor .149/.260/.149 over his first 19 games. Then he promptly hit the disabled for four weeks. When he returned to action in mid-June his offensive woes continued as he batted .181/.247/.341 over his next 34 games. But beginning in late July through the end of the year, Matos slugged .270/.309/.433 over his final 41 games. Beyond a poor BABIP, .226, a lot of Matos' peripheral stats were within close proximity to his career norms: average-ish walk rate and strong contact numbers. The power sagged a bit, but he spent half of his games pitcher-friendly confines of PK Park, home of the Eugene Emeralds. Matos did tweak his stance from the previous season: he hands are now much further from his torso. There's legitimate five-tool potential here, and Matos is young enough to deserve a do-over. But if he flounders in 2023, then there may be no way back to reclaiming his potential status.

Ceiling: 3.0-win player
Risk: High
MLB ETA: 2024

5. Grant McCray, CF

	Hit	Power	SB	Patience	Glove	Overall
	45	55	60	55	55	50

Born: 12/07/00	Age: 22	Bats: L	Top Production Comp: Trent Grisham
Height: 6-2	Weight: 190	Throws: L	

Season	Team	Age	Level	PA	1B	2B	3B	HR	SB	CS	BB%	K%	AVG	OBP	SLG	ISO
2021	SFG	20	CPX	65	12	3	1	1	3	1	13.85%	30.77%	0.309	0.400	0.455	0.145
2021	SFG	20	A	88	14	2	2	2	4	1	6.82%	34.09%	0.250	0.299	0.400	0.150
2022	SFG	21	A+	62	10	2	0	2	8	0	14.52%	35.48%	0.269	0.387	0.423	0.154
2022	SFG	21	A	507	76	21	9	21	35	10	11.44%	29.19%	0.291	0.383	0.525	0.234

Background: McCray's old man, Rodney, spent three *very* brief stints with the White Sox and Mets in the early 90s, totaling just 15 plate appearances. But he did manage to play alongside some of the game's better players, including: Carlton Fisk, Robin Ventura, Sammy Sosa, Frank Thomas, Tim Raines, and Eddie Murray, among others. The younger McCray is hoping for a longer stint in the big leagues, regardless of teammates. The second highest drafted player in Lakewood Ranch High School (behind Lastings Milledge, the 12th overall selection in 2003), San Francisco signed McCray to a deal worth just slightly less than $700,000 after picking him in the third round, 87th overall, four years ago. The 6-foot-2, 190-pound centerfielder turned in a solid, yet unremarkable debut in the rookie league that summer, hitting .270/.379/.335 with eight extra-base hits in 48 games. He lost significant development time due to injuries in his follow-up campaign in 2021, btting an aggregate .274/.342/.422 in 45 games between San Jose and the Complex League. Last season, though, Rodney's son quickly made up for lost time. Back in Low-A with San Jose again, McCray hit an impressive .291/.383/.525 with 21 doubles, nine triples, 21 homeruns, and 35 stolen bases (in 45 attempts). His overall production with the club was 30% better than the league average, per *Weighted Runs Created Plus*. He spent the final two weeks in High-A, hitting a solid .269/.387/.423.

Scouting Report: Consider the following:

> Since 2006, only two 21-year-old hitters met the following criteria in a season in Low-A (min. 350 PA): 125 to 135 wRC+, a strikeout rate north of 28% and a double-digit walk rate. Those two hitters: Vince Fernandez and Grant McCray.

San Francisco Giants

McCray's breakout must be viewed with some level of skepticism, for a variety of reasons, including:

#1. It came in his fourth professional season.
#2. He was in an age-appropriate level of competition.
#3. He spent part of the previous season in A-ball – however short it was.
#4. He swung and missed *a lot*. His 29.2% K-rate was the sixth highest in California League among all qualified hitters. And he didn't show any improvement in his contact rates throughout the year, either.

Similar to Heliot Ramos in that they both have an interesting foundation, but the hit tool may prove to be too much to overcome. McCray, though, has the superior toolkit. Above-average defender in centerfield. Plus speed. Above-average power. Patient approach at the plate. Again, it's going to come down to his ability to make consistent, quality contact. And he hasn't proven that over the past two seasons. Open stance, a la Russell Branyan, with great rotation and bat speed. If he can hit .240 with power, speed, and a net positive defensive value, McCray could be a solid league average regular.

Ceiling: 2.0-win player
Risk: Moderate
MLB ETA: 2024

6. Jairo Pomares, LF/RF

Hit	Power	SB	Patience	Glove	Overall
45	60	30	50	45	50

Born: 08/04/00	Age: 22	Bats: L	Top Production Comp: N/A
Height: 6-1	Weight: 185	Throws: R	

Season	Team	Age	Level	PA	1B	2B	3B	HR	SB	CS	BB%	K%	AVG	OBP	SLG	ISO
2019	SFG	18	A-	62	9	3	0	0	0	0	1.61%	27.42%	0.207	0.258	0.259	0.052
2019	SFG	18	R	167	40	10	4	3	5	3	5.99%	15.57%	0.368	0.401	0.542	0.174
2021	SFG	20	A	224	38	22	0	14	0	0	6.70%	24.11%	0.372	0.429	0.693	0.322
2021	SFG	20	A+	104	15	5	1	6	1	0	0.96%	31.73%	0.262	0.269	0.505	0.243
2022	SFG	21	A+	386	52	20	0	14	0	0	9.33%	32.90%	0.254	0.330	0.438	0.183

Background: If the Giants' 2018 international free agency class isn't the club's best in recent memory, then it's certainly near the top of the list. At least, it has the *potential* to be near the top. San Francisco rolled out the red carpet and convinced Marco Luciano, their consensus top prospect; Luis Matos, their top outfield prospect; and Jairo Pomares, another top outfield prospect, to join the fold. Hailing from Sancti Spiritus, Cuba, Pomares earned a near-seven-figure deal from the organization. And he *immediately* began paying dividends. The 6-foot-1, 185-pound corner outfielder simply overmatched the Arizona Complex League competition (.368/.401/.542) and spent the final two weeks of his 2019 debut in the Northwest League. Once minor league ball returned from its COVID-imposed hiatus, he continued his Babe Ruth impression on Low-A West, mashing .372/.429/.694 in 51 games and he looked respectable in a month of action in High-A (.262/.269/.505). Last season, Pomares found himself back in High-A for an extended look – though, the results respectable, they were far from dominant. Appearing in 95 games with the Eugene Emeralds, hit batted .254/.330/.438 with 20 doubles and 14 homeruns. His production, according to *Weighted Runs Created Plus*, topped the league average mark by 13%.

Snippet from The 2020 Prospect Digest Handbook: He's going to be a low OBP, 35-homerun threat whose overall value will fluctuate according to his batting averages.

Scouting Report: Consider the following:

Since 2006, only four 21-year-old hitters posted a 108 to 118 wRC+ mark with a strikeout rate north of 31% in a High-A season (min. 350 PA): Billy Rowell, Brandon Howlett, Jose Ramos, and Jairo Pomares.

So, there are a few things to consider here – both of which will boost opinions on Pomares' prospect stock:

#1. Typically, what's plagued lefty-swinging mashers with tremendous power and contact issues are platoon splits. A lot of times they're inept at handling southpaws. Not only is that *not* an issue with Pomares, but he hasn't shown concerning splits the past two seasons: he hit .264/.356/.460 and .275/.309/.510 against LHP in 2022 and 2021.

#2. A slow start to the year absolutely wrecked his overall numbers last season. Pomares batted a lowly .224/.297/.430 during his first 44 games. The front office sent him back down to the Complex League in mid-June and he promptly went 8-for-15 with six extra-base hits (three doubles and three homeruns). After he returned to Eugene he mashed .279/.355/.447 with 18 extra-base hits over his final 50 games. His production during that stretch was 23% better than the league average.

San Francisco Giants

Every time Pomares digs in, there's one thing he intends to do. And it's all based on ill intentions. He's an absolute monster at the plate. Massive power – perhaps the best in the minor leagues – thanks to tremendous loft and plus bat speed. He's not going to be a consistent star, but he can be a star at times. He's going to be streaky. And the bat is a 45-grade, same as the defense. But the power is game changing.

Ceiling: 2.0-win player
Risk: Moderate
MLB ETA: 2024

7. Will Bednar, RHP

FB	SL	CH	Command	Overall
55	60	50	55	45

Born: 06/13/00	Age: 23	Bats: R	Top Production Comp: N/A
Height: 6-2	Weight: 230	Throws: R	

Season	Team	Age	Level	IP	TBF	K/9	K%	BB/9	BB%	K-BB%	ERA	FIP	xFIP	Pit/Bat
2022	SFG	22	A	43.0	184	10.67	27.72%	4.60	11.96%	15.76%	4.19	6.26	5.56	3.83

Background: The year 2021 proved to be a good for the Bednar family. David Bednar established himself as one of the game's best relievers for the Pirates after failing in cups of coffee with the Padres the previous two seasons. And Will, the younger Bednar brother, burst onto the scene and declared himself one of college baseball's finest arms. After making a quartet of appearances for Mississippi State in the COVID-shortened season, the 6-foot-2, 230-pound right-hander made 19 appearances in 2021, 16 of which came via the start, throwing 92.1 innings with 139 strikeouts against just 26 free passes. He finished the year with a solid 3.12 ERA and a nearly perfect 9-1 win-loss record. Of course, though, the crescendo of his remarkable season came in historic fashion – *TWICE*. Bednar combined with Bulldogs' closer Landon Sims to set a new College World Series record, striking out 21 hitters in a win against the University of Texas. Less than two weeks later he nearly tossed a no-hitter in a blowout championship winning outing against highly touted Vanderbilt University. The win ended Mississippi State's 126-year title drought. The Giants would select Bednar in the opening round two years ago, 14th overall, and signed him to a deal worth slightly more than $3.6 million. After making four brief appearances during his pro debut, Bednar opened the 2022 season up with the San Jose Giants – a stay that *should* have been short given his collegiate success and polish. But he made just 12 starts before an undisclosed injury curtailed his season in mid-June. He would toss just 43.0 innings, posting a mediocre 51-to-22 strikeout-to-walk ratio. Bednar would pop back up in the Arizona Fall League – briefly – before a back injury ended that after 3.1 innings.

Snippet from The 2022 Prospect Digest Handbook: Put him down as a quick moving #3/#4 type arm. Love him. Very safe.

Scouting Report: A year into his professional career and the book on Bednar is still the same: fastball, slider, slider, slider, and a rare changeup. It was an up-and-down year for Bednar, who – according to reports – battled that lower back issue for the majority of the year. The command / feel for the strike zone that he showed during his final season at Mississippi State seemed to abandoned him in 2022. Above-average low-90s fastball, plus slider, and a tumbling average changeup. Bednar will tweak the break on his slider, going from a traditional lateral moving breaking ball to a more 12-6 biting one. If Bednar can recapture his 2021 magic, it wouldn't be out of the question to see him spend significant portion of 2023 in Double-A. He looks more like a #5 arm now, not a mid-rotation candidate.

Ceiling: 1.5- to 2.0-win player
Risk: Moderate
MLB ETA: 2024

8. Reggie Crawford, LHP

FB	SL	CH	Command	Overall
70	70	N/A	45	50

Born: 12/04/00	Age: 22	Bats: L	Top Production Comp: N/A
Height: 6-4	Weight: 235	Throws: L	

Background: A two-sport athlete during his career at North Schuylkill High School – though not a "traditional" two-sport star. Crawford, a hulking left-hander / first baseman, starred on the diamond for the Spartans and was a state champion swimmer in the 50-yard freestyle, setting a record time of 20.45 seconds during his junior year. But that hardly proved to be the defining moment of his prep career. After batting .482 with eight homeruns at the plate and punching out 49 in 33 innings on the mound, the Royals took a late round flier on the behemoth prospect in 2019, nabbing him in the 37th round, 1099th overall. Crawford, of course, bypassed the opportunity to join the AL Central Division squad and head to the University of Connecticut. The 6-foot-4, 235-pound first baseman / hurler got off to a scorching – albeit COVID-shortened – start to this collegiate career, batting .365/.414/.558 in 13 games and making one brief relief appearance on the mound. Crawford continued to show two-way promise during his sophomore season with the Huskies in 2021, hitting .295/.349/.543 with 11 doubles, one triple, and 13 homeruns while throwing 7.2 innings with a whopping 17 strikeouts and three free passes. He spent the ensuing summer splitting time with Team USA and the Cape Cod League. In six games with the Bourne Braves, he slugged .296/.345/.482 and tossed another pair of innings, fanning four without surrendering a hit, walk, or run. With Team USA, the big lefty went 1-for-6 as a hitter, but was practically perfect in four relief innings; he walked eight and surrendered one hit. Crawford missed the

San Francisco Giants

entirety of 2022 recovering from Tommy John surgery. The San Francisco Giants selected him in the back of the first round, 30th overall, and signed him to a slightly below-slot deal worth $2,297,500; the recommended slot-bonus was $2,486,800.

Scouting Report: With respect to his work as a hitter during his sophomore season, consider the following:

Since 2011, only three Big East hitters batted at least .290/.340/.530 with at least 10 homeruns and a strikeout rate north of 24% in a season (min. 200 PA): Ethan Stern, Steve Shelinsky, and Reggie Crawford.

As a hitter, Crawford owns (A) tremendous power potential – maybe even creeping in 70- or 80-grade territory had he not missed his junior season. The problem, of course, is that he owns average patience (at best), and full-blown red flag territory swing-and-miss concerns. Crawford whiffed in 25% of his plate appearances as a junior and 24.8% of his career plate appearances. He also posted an 8-to-1 K/BB ratio in the Cape. On the mound, well, Crawford possesses arguably the class's top fastball, sitting in the mid- to upper-90s and reportedly touching as high as 100 mph on an occasion. He'll also feature a wickedly devastating slider as well, giving the part-time reliever two plus or better offerings. The problem, of course, with Crawford as a pitcher is that he's (A) a project, (B) relied too heavily on his fastball to the point that 15 of his 17 whiffs as a sophomore were registered off the heater, and (C) lacks a third option. With that being said, he's a superior prospect as a pitcher.

Ceiling: 2.0- win player
Risk: Moderate to High
MLB ETA: 2024/2025

9. Vaun Brown, OF

Hit	Power	SB	Patience	Glove	Overall
45	55	60	50	50	50

Born: 06/23/98	Age: 25	Bats: R	Top Production Comp: N/A
Height: 6-1	Weight: 215	Throws: R	

Season	Team	Age	Level	PA	1B	2B	3B	HR	SB	CS	BB%	K%	AVG	OBP	SLG	ISO
2021	SFG	23	CPX	98	15	7	4	2	8	1	7.14%	29.59%	0.354	0.480	0.620	0.266
2022	SFG	24	A+	194	34	10	2	9	21	3	11.34%	26.80%	0.350	0.454	0.611	0.261
2022	SFG	24	A	262	46	14	5	14	23	3	9.54%	25.57%	0.346	0.427	0.636	0.289

Background: Trivia time, kiddos. There have been four notable players and one former fan favorite Giant to attend Florida Southern College. Name them. Answer: veteran "Professional Hitter" Matt Stairs, Brett Tomko, Andy McGaffigan, crazy flame-throwing reliever Rob Dibble, and San Francisco fan / cult favorite Lance Niekro. And in recent years the Lakeland, Florida-based school has turned into a little miniature hotbed of baseball talent as nine players' names were called in the draft since 2017, including three in 2021 alone. The player chosen earliest among the group: Vaun Brown, a 10th round selection by the Giants two years ago. Handed a laughably small $7,500 bonus, the sturdy outfielder shredded the Complex League competition during his 25-game debut, hitting .354/.480/.620. And he continued to mash as he moved into full season action in 2022. Splitting time between San Jose and Eugene (plus one game in Richmond), the 6-foot-1, 215-pound slugger batted an aggregate .346/.437/.623 with 24 doubles, seven triples, 23 homeruns, and a whopping 44 stolen bases (in 50 attempts). His yearly production topped the league average mark by a staggering 75%, per *Weighted Runs Created Plus*.

Scouting Report: Just how good was Brown last season? There were 609 minor league hitters to accrue at least 400 plate appearances. Here's how his numbers stacked up:

Batting Average (.346): 1st
On-Base Percentage (.437): 6th
Slugging Percentage (.623): 3rd
On-Base Plus Slugging (1.059): 1st

Total Production (175 wRC+): 1st
Stolen bases: tied for 24th
Isolated Power (.276): 15th

Everything about Brown screams fluke – his age (24), level of competition (Low-A and High-A), college pedigree, draft status, bonus, strikeout rate (26.0%). You name it and it just simply doesn't make sense that (A) it's repeatable, (B) organizations somehow let him slip through the cracks, or (C) it's actually real. And then there's his track record in college. Brown was a complementary player in 2017. He was a solid, though unremarkable hitter in 2018, 2019, and in the COVID-shortened 2020 season (though he did start driving the ball more frequently). But something clicked for him during his fifth and final season as he slugged .387/.462/.793. Here's what we do know:

#1. The above-average power is legit, even going the other way.
#2. The hit tool has some holes in it, as evidenced by his K-rate and nearly 16% swing-strike percentage.
#3. Plus speed, but average defense.

San Francisco Giants

There's a Hunter Pence vibe when watching Brown play. His stance is sandlot-esque, hands letter height and held from his body. But the swing is oh-so-short and will pepper line drives all over the field. There's little doubt he doesn't see some type of action at the big league level, which is a win in itself. And he's an absolute gamer, backed up by the tape. But he's also sporting a career BABIP in the .500 range. He doesn't make sense as a prospect. But until he faulters, he's tracking like a potential fringe average starting option. There's an Austin Hays-type ceiling here.

Ceiling: 2.0-win player
Risk: Moderate to High
MLB ETA: 2023/2024

10. Carson Whisenhunt, RHP

FB	CB	CH	Command	Overall
50	55	70	45/50	50

Born: 10/20/00	Age: 22	Bats: L	Top Production Comp: N/A
Height: 6-3	Weight: 209	Throws: L	

Background: A product of Davie County High School – home to two-time All-Star Whit Merrifield – Whisenhunt bookended his collegiate career in a spectacularly peculiar way. The big southpaw appeared on the mound for a single, solitary performance during his true freshman season, allowing one hit and three earned runs without registering an out. Good enough for a perfectly imperfect infinite ERA. His final season in 2022 was just as strange. The promising lefty, who was tabbed for the Preseason Golden Spikes Award Watch List, was popped for a banned substance and subsequently suspended for the entirety of his junior campaign. In between the two lost seasons, Whisenhunt tantalized the competition as a sophomore: in 13 starts, the 6-foot-3, 209-pound hurler struck out 79, walked 22, and posted a 3.77 ERA in 62.0 innings of work. The big left-hander made four starts in the Cape Cod League that following summer as well, posting a 21-to-6 strikeout-to-walk ratio in 16.0 innings with the Chatham Anglers. San Francisco took a calculated gamble on him in the second round, 66th overall, and signed him to an above-slot bonus worth $1.8 million, nearly $800,000 above the recommended slot.

Scouting Report: Typical smooth-throwing southpaw with seemingly effortless mechanics. Whisenhunt isn't going to overpower any hitter with his fastball. But the average offering plays up considerably thanks to his plus-plus changeup and above-average curveball. The command can waiver at times, but given his lack of collegiate experience, additional fine-tuning shouldn't be out of the question. Whisenhunt's ceiling isn't tremendously high, but he should settle in as a competent #4-type starting pitcher, league average-ish.

Ceiling: 1.5- to 2.0-win player
Risk: Moderate
MLB ETA: 2024/2025

11. Casey Schmitt, 3B/SS

Hit	Power	SB	Patience	Glove	Overall
45	50	30	50	55/60	50

Born: 03/01/99	Age: 24	Bats: R	Top Production Comp: N/A
Height: 6-2	Weight: 215	Throws: R	

Season	Team	Age	Level	PA	1B	2B	3B	HR	SB	CS	BB%	K%	AVG	OBP	SLG	ISO
2021	SFG	22	A	280	39	14	1	8	2	2	7.86%	15.71%	0.247	0.318	0.406	0.159
2022	SFG	23	A+	383	59	14	1	17	1	2	10.97%	22.45%	0.273	0.363	0.474	0.201
2022	SFG	23	AA	127	27	10	1	3	0	0	4.72%	22.83%	0.342	0.378	0.517	0.175
2022	SFG	23	AAA	16	3	1	0	1	0	0	0.00%	31.25%	0.333	0.313	0.600	0.267

Background: A two-way star at San Diego State University. Schmitt left the Mountain Conference School as a career .295/.366/.408 hitter and posted a 78-to-29 strikeout-to-walk ratio in 87.0 innings on the mound. San Francisco selected the 6-foot-2, 215-pounder in the second round three years ago, 49th overall, and signed him to a deal worth $1,147,500. The former Aztec star turned in a mediocre debut in Low-A the following season, cobbling together a .247/.318/.406 slash line in 64 games with San Jose. Last season, the shortstop / third baseman morphed into an offensive force at the dish. Opening the season up with Eugene, Schmitt bashed .273/.363/.475 with 14 doubles, one triple, and 17 homeruns in 93 games. San Francisco bounced him up to the true testing ground, Double-A, and he caught fire. He slugged .342/.378/.51 in 29 games – which earned him a late season cameo up to Sacramento to cap off the year. Schmitt batted an aggregate .293/.365/.489 with 25 doubles, two triples, 21 homeruns, and a trio of stolen bases. His overall production, per *Weighted Runs Created Plus*, was 34% above the league average mark.

Scouting Report: A solid defender at shortstop, where he appeared in 40 games last season, Schmitt's defense sparkled at the hot corner, grading out as a potential plus skill. And the bat showed significantly more promise at the plate – despite the potential for regression in 2023. The hit tool may creep into 50-grade territory, average power, below average speed, and a decent eye at the plate. There's low end starting potential with the bat, but the glove pushed him into league average territory.

San Francisco Giants

Ceiling: 1.5- to 2.0-win player
Risk: Moderate
MLB ETA: 2023

12. Mason Black, RHP

FB	SL	CH	Command	Overall
60	60	45/50	50	45

Born: 12/10/99	Age: 23	Bats: R	Top Production Comp: N/A
Height: 6-3	Weight: 230	Throws: R	

Season	Team	Age	Level	IP	TBF	K/9	K%	BB/9	BB%	K-BB%	ERA	FIP	xFIP	Pit/Bat
2022	SFG	22	A	34.1	135	11.53	32.59%	2.10	5.93%	26.67%	1.57	2.66	3.09	3.83
2022	SFG	22	A+	77.2	328	10.66	28.05%	3.24	8.54%	19.51%	3.94	4.52	4.16	3.84

Background: Lehigh University is far from a baseball hotbed. Just three players were drafted before the fourth round in school history. But Black achieved a remarkable feat: not only did he make the Cape Cod League from a non-traditional school, but he did so after his true freshman season. Black, a well-built 6-foot-3, 230-pound right-hander, tossed just 33.0 innings with 28 strikeouts and 12 walks during his first collegiate season, but he blew the doors off the competition in the Cape, averaging 9.6 strikeouts and just 2.9 walks per nine innings in five starts and three relief appearances. And he continued to miss plenty of bats during the COVID-abbreviated 2020 season (11.9 K/9). During his final season with the Mountain Hawks, Black continued to impress as he struck out 95 and walked 31 in 72.1 innings of work. San Francisco selected him in the third round, 85th overall, that summer. He made his debut last summer, ripping through the California League for eight starts and continued to impress with Eugene the rest of the year. Black finished the season with 112.0 innings, averaging 10.9 strikeouts and just 2.9 walks per nine innings. He compiled an aggregate 3.21 ERA and a 3.95 FIP.

Scouting Report: Consider the following:

> Since 2006, nine 22-year-old hurlers posted a 27% to 29% strikeout percentage with a 7.5% to 9.5% walk percentage in a season in any High-A league (min. 75 IP): Rogelio Armenteros, David Hernandez, C.C. Lee, Cody Martin, Buddy Baumann, Tanner Burns, Ryan Bergert, Victor Castaneda, and Mason Black.

Equipped with one of the better heater's in the system, Black was able to rein in his problematic control noticeably during his first full season in pro ball. His fastball reportedly touched triple-digits in shorter stints in previous seasons, but was sitting consistently in the mid-90s late in the year. The slider upticked from an above-average to plus offering. And he showed more willingness to mix in his tumbling changeup. Despite owning two plus pitches, Black isn't a lock for a rotation spot in the future. Definite reliever risk.

Ceiling: 1.5-win player
Risk: Moderate
MLB ETA: 2024

13. Patrick Bailey, C

Hit	Power	SB	Patience	Glove	Overall
40	55	30	60	60	45

Born: 05/29/99	Age: 24	Bats: R	Top Production Comp: Jacob Stallings
Height: 6-1	Weight: 210	Throws: R	

Season	Team	Age	Level	PA	1B	2B	3B	HR	SB	CS	BB%	K%	AVG	OBP	SLG	ISO
2021	SFG	22	A	207	34	16	0	7	1	1	13.53%	22.71%	0.322	0.415	0.531	0.209
2021	SFG	22	A+	155	14	9	0	2	6	0	11.61%	27.74%	0.185	0.290	0.296	0.111
2022	SFG	23	A+	325	33	14	1	12	1	1	15.08%	22.15%	0.225	0.342	0.419	0.195

Background: The Giants have burned an awful lot of draft capital into the second riskiest position over the past nine years and have little return on their investments. They selected Aramis Garcia in the second round in 2014. The former FIU backstop appeared in just 37 games with San Francisco, hitting a lowly .229/.270/.419. Equipped with the second overall pick four years later, the front office opted for Georgia Tech phenom Joey Bart, who is likely running out of chances with the ballclub after hitting .222/.294/.351 in 132 games spread across three years. Then in 2020 the club drafted N.C. State catch Patrick Bailey, a two-time Team USA alum. And – unfortunately – for all involved parties, Bailey may end up heading down a similar path. A stout middle-of-the-lineup thumper during his college days – he slugged .302/.411/.568 in 131 games with the Wolfpack – Bailey was immediately sent to High-A for his debut in 2021. And he was abysmal, hitting a putrid .185/.290/.296. The organization finally showed their former first round some mercy and demoted down to Low-A in mid-July following a brief stint on the DL. He finally regained his stroke and hit .322/.416/.531 with San Jose the remainder of the year. Last season Bailey got his second crack at High-A pitching, but the results were unchanged. Appearing in 83 games with the Eugene Emeralds, the 6-foot-1, 210-pound catcher hit .225/.342/.420 with 14 doubles, one triple, and 12 homeruns. His overall production, per *Weighted Runs Created Plus*, was 13% better than the league average threshold. He did hit well in 14 games with the Scottsdale Scorpions in the Arizona Fall League to end his season on a high note (.292/.375/.417).

San Francisco Giants

Snippet from The 2020 Prospect Digest Handbook: He's not likely going to be much more than a .250 hitter. But Bailey owns enough thump to slug 20 homeruns and post a .340 OBP. Throw in above-average defense and a strong throwing arm and he looks like a lock to be a solid caliber starting option for the Giants in a couple years.

Scouting Report: Consider the following:

> Since 2006, there have been seven 23-year-old hitters that met the following criteria in a High-A season (min. 300 PA): 108 to 118 wRC+, a 20% to 24% strikeout rate, and a walk rate north of 14%. Those seven hitters: Jacob Stallings, Antoan Richardson, Danny Payne, Anthony Aliotti, Dominic D'Anna, Anthony Seigler, and Patrick Bailey.

Just for fun:

Name	Season	Level	Age	PA	BB%	K%	AVG	OBP	SLG	OPS
Jacob Stallings	2013	A+	23	307	14.66%	20.20%	0.219	0.352	0.371	0.722
Patrick Bailey	2022	A+	23	325	15.08%	22.15%	0.225	0.342	0.419	0.761

Stallings, of course, blossomed into a late career starting option for the Pirates (though his first season in Miami left a lot to be desired). Bailey's calling card is his tremendous, plus defense behind the dish. His work on that side of the ball adds enough value that his sagging hit tool is no longer a void. 40-grade hit tool. 55-grade power. Very patient approach at the plate. There's enough here to suggest a late blooming career like Stallings. Don't expect Bailey to hit better than .235/.325/.420, though. One more thought: after a slow start to the year he did bat .242/.362/.456 over his final 67 games.

Ceiling: 1.0- to 1.5-win player
Risk: Moderate
MLB ETA: 2024

14. Eric Silva, RHP

	FB	CB	SL	CH	Command	Overall
	55	50	55/60	50	40	45

Born: 10/03/02 **Age:** 20 **Bats:** R **Top Production Comp:** N/A
Height: 6-1 **Weight:** 185 **Throws:** R

Season	Team	Age	Level	IP	TBF	K/9	K%	BB/9	BB%	K-BB%	ERA	FIP	xFIP	Pit/Bat
2022	SFG	19	A	85.2	365	10.40	27.12%	4.10	10.68%	16.44%	5.88	5.05	4.89	3.86

Background: While it's not a traditional hotbed for baseball talent, per se, JSerra Catholic High School has churned out a few notable prospects over the years. Austin Hedges, once considered a consensus Top 25 prospect, was a second round pick out of the California-based school by the Padres in 2011. Six years later the Minnesota Twins drafted shortstop Royce Lewis with the #1 overall selection. And, of course, Eric Silva, who received a hefty $1.5 million over-slot bonus from the Giants as a fourth rounder two years ago. Standing a wiry 6-foot-1 and 185-pounds, Silva starred in every facet of the game during his lone season at the school, including: authoring a no-hitter and helping capture the Division I SoCal Regional Championship. A native of Baldwin Park, California, Silva spent the 2022 season in the San Jose Giants' rotation. Making 22 starts and throwing a conservative 85.2 innings of work, the hard-throwing righty struck out 99 and walked 39 to go along with a 5.88 ERA, a 5.05 FIP, and a 4.89 xFIP.

Scouting Report: Consider the following:

> Since 2006, six 19-year-old hurlers posted a 26% to 28% strikeout percentage with a 9% to 12% walk percentage in a season in any Low-A league (min. 75 IP): Lance McCullers Jr., Lucas Sims, Trevor Cahill, Randall Delgado, Kasey Kiker, and former fourth rounder Eric Silva.

Listed at 6-foot-1 and 185-pounds, Silva looks noticeably small with little – if any – physical projection remaining. He sports an above-average low- to mid-90s heater that has a bit of giddy up when he elevates it. He'll complement it with three offspeed offerings, the best of which is an above-average slider that will flash plus on occasion. His average curveball has a similar with slower break / movement. And his 50-grade changeup has some arm side run to it. Silva missed quite a few bats in Low-A last season, but he lacks a true swing-and-miss offering – though the slider may eventually creep into that territory. Backend starting potential because of his pitchability and willingness to mix it up, but not much more. I'd be surprise if he doesn't see a precipitous decline in K-numbers in High-A next season.

Ceiling: 1.0- to 1.5-win player
Risk: Moderate
MLB ETA: 2024/2025

San Francisco Giants

15. Ryan Murphy, RHP

FB	CB	SL	CH	Command	Overall
55	55	55	55	60	45

Born: 10/08/99	Age: 23	Bats: R	Top Production Comp: Mike Leake
Height: 6-1	Weight: 190	Throws: R	

Season	Team	Age	Level	IP	TBF	K/9	K%	BB/9	BB%	K-BB%	ERA	FIP	xFIP	Pit/Bat
2021	SFG	21	A	76.0	300	13.74	38.67%	2.13	6.00%	32.67%	2.96	3.85	3.18	4.04
2021	SFG	21	A+	31.1	117	13.79	41.03%	2.30	6.84%	34.19%	1.44	2.29	3.33	4.19
2022	SFG	22	A+	31.0	125	13.65	37.60%	3.48	9.60%	28.00%	2.90	2.31	3.29	4.19

Background: Arguably the biggest riser up the Giants' prospect chart following the 2021 season. Murphy, an unheralded right-hander out of LeMoyne College, was the club's final selection in the COVID-abbreviated draft – the 144th overall player taken. His bonus: a paltry $22,500. A year later, though, it looked like the franchise had – potentially – the two *largest* steals when they snagged top prospect Kyle Harrison in the third round in combination with Murphy. The 6-foot-1, 190-pound right-hander was figuratively – and almost *literally* – unhittable during his debut season two years ago. Splitting time between San Jose and Eugene, the club's Low-A and High-A affiliates, Murphy posted an immaculate 164-to-26 strikeout-to-walk ratio in 107.1 innings of work. For those counting at home: he averaged a whopping 13.8 strikeouts and just 2.2 walks per nine innings to go with an aggregate 2.52 ERA. And with his prospect status reaching a potential crescendo his sophomore professional season was a complete dud. Murphy would miss the opening six weeks courtesy of a back issue. He finally made it to the mound in mid-May. By the early July he was back on the disabled list with elbow inflammation. He would make it back on the bump in late August for a rehab appearance and then one more start before the end of the year. Murphy ended up throwing just 42.1 innings with 57 strikeouts and 23 walks to go along with a 4.68 ERA.

Snippet from The 2020 Prospect Digest Handbook: Murphy is very reminiscent of veteran right-hander Josh Tomlin. San Francisco's right-hander won't blow his 91 mph heater past a lot bats, but he can sure as hell pitch.

Scouting Report: It was clear – *immediately* – that Murphy's fastball had upticked from the previous season. Murphy's fastball, which hovered in the 91 mph range, gained noticeable giddy up early in the season – particularly up in the zone. He has sitting 93 mph in late May. Above-average 12-6 curveball. His average slider ticked up enough that it's better than his curveball. He has an above-average changeup in his repertoire, but I didn't see it. Murphy's trademark command seemed a bit off last season, but he's a safe bet to regain it in 2023. There's enough here to be a viable #5-type starting pitcher.

Ceiling: 1.0- to 1.5-win player
Risk: Moderate
MLB ETA: 2023/2024

16. Heliot Ramos, CF

Hit	Power	SB	Patience	Glove	Overall
35	50	50	50	45	40

Born: 09/07/99	Age: 23	Bats: R	Top Production Comp: N/A
Height: 6-1	Weight: 188	Throws: R	

Season	Team	Age	Level	PA	1B	2B	3B	HR	SB	CS	BB%	K%	AVG	OBP	SLG	ISO
2019	SFG	19	A+	338	59	18	0	13	6	7	9.47%	25.15%	0.306	0.385	0.500	0.194
2019	SFG	19	AA	106	13	6	1	3	2	3	9.43%	31.13%	0.242	0.321	0.421	0.179
2021	SFG	21	AA	266	31	14	1	10	7	2	10.15%	27.44%	0.237	0.323	0.432	0.195
2021	SFG	21	AAA	229	41	11	2	4	8	2	6.55%	28.38%	0.272	0.323	0.399	0.127
2022	SFG	22	AAA	475	68	17	1	11	6	6	8.63%	23.58%	0.227	0.305	0.349	0.122

Background: The 2017 draft will likely go down as one of the more disappointing crops of Major League hopefuls – particularly after the first couple of selections. So it's important to remember that the Giants didn't swing-and-miss too badly on their selection in the opening round – given the state of the class. Taken with the 19th overall pick that year – a selection, by the way, that raised quite a few eyebrows at the time – Ramos looked like the potential steal of the draft after his remarkably dominant debut in the Arizona Rookie League as he slugged .348/.404/.645 in 35 games. Low-A proved to be a bit of an overmatch for the then-18-year-old the following season (.245/.313/.396), but Ramos would eventually regain his stroke in High-A the following year. He would hit .306/.385/.500 in 77 games with San Jose and closed out the year with a respectable month in Double-A. After minor league action returned from its COVID-induced break, Ramos struggled through half a year in Double-A, but rebounded – again – after a promotion to Triple-A. Last season, though, was another campaign mainly engulfed by disappointment – despite earning a couple brief cups of coffee in San Francisco. The 6-foot-1, 188-pound centerfielder batted a meager .227/.305/.349 in 108 games with the Sacramento River Cats. His overall production with the club's Triple-A affiliate was a staggering 36% *below the* league, per *Weighted Runs Created Plus* – easily the worst mark of his roller coaster career.

Snippet from The 2020 Prospect Digest Handbook: The tools remain in place and, yes, he's still quite young – he's only entering his age-22 season – but Ramos has never really dominated a level for an extended period – sans his explosion in High-A three years ago.

San Francisco Giants

Scouting Report: Consider the following:

> Since 2006, only seven 22-year-old hitters posted a sub-70 wRC+ total in any Triple-A league (min. 350 PA): Nick Gordon, Jeter Downs, Sergio Santos, Magneuris Sierra, Oswaldo Navarro, Javy Guerra, and Heliot Ramos.

While each member of the entire group has accrued some big league time – including Ramos – only one would go on to prove to be a competent big league bat: Gordon, at least for one season. But the production was so poor that two of them – Sergio Santos and Javy Guerra – would convert into (successful) big league relievers. Ramos' enigmatic ways continues to confound. Solid speed / power combination and improving contact numbers, but he's a fallacy in centerfield and the hit tool is proving to be a 40-grade. He's still only entering his age-23 season – which is nearly impossible to believe – so there's hope he'll make some adjustments. But as shown above, it's going to be a steep hill to climb.

Ceiling: 1.0-win player
Risk: Moderate
MLB ETA: Debuted in 2022

17. Landen Roupp, RHP

FB	CB	CH	Command	Overall
55	55	50	50	40

Born: 09/10/98	Age: 24	Bats: R	Top Production Comp: N/A
Height: 6-2	Weight: 205	Throws: R	

Season	Team	Age	Level	IP	TBF	K/9	K%	BB/9	BB%	K-BB%	ERA	FIP	xFIP	Pit/Bat
2022	SFG	23	A	48.2	197	12.76	35.03%	3.14	8.63%	26.40%	2.59	3.02	3.33	4.06
2022	SFG	23	A+	32.1	125	14.47	41.60%	2.51	7.20%	34.40%	1.67	1.68	2.23	4.03
2022	SFG	23	AA	26.1	110	10.59	28.18%	3.76	10.00%	18.18%	3.76	3.79	3.55	4.03

Background: San Francisco – perhaps unsurprisingly – hasn't unearthed a whole lot of big leaguers in the 12th round of the summer draft. In their history, the franchise has made 57 selections in the round, 10 of which eventually made the big leagues. The best of the aforementioned 10 – Kelby Tomlinson and Chris Heston. The front office is hoping that their 2021 twelfth rounder, Lander Roupp, will be among the list of big leaguers. The 356th overall pick, Roupp, who signed for a meager $75,000, was particularly effective over his final two seasons with UNC Wilmington. He made 20 appearances, only one coming out of the bullpen, throwing 128.0 innings with 148 strikeouts and 49 free passes. Two years ago, during his professional debut, Roupp upped the production in five low level appearances, throwing eight innings with 14 strikeouts against just one free pass. Last season, the 6-foot-2, 205-pound right-hander strapped a jetpack to his back and rocketed through three stops en route to tossing 107.1 innings while averaging 12.7 K/9 and 3.1 BB/9.

Scouting Report: The former late round picks own a backend starter's arsenal. His fastball sits in the low 90s and touched 94 mph several times during one of his Double-A starts late in the season. His bread-and-butter offering though is an above-average curveball with downward bite and he'll vary the velocity on it. (Note: Most scouting reports indicate a slider and curveball. Not only did I not see the former, but I didn't see his catcher signal for it either.) He'll also mix in an average-ish changeup that's workable as long as he's locating it low in the zone. Roupp is a strike-thrower, but not necessarily a consistently *quality* strike-thrower. There's a high probability he turns into a solid middle relief option with a heavy reliance on his fastball / curveball combo.

Ceiling: 1.0-win player
Risk: Moderate
MLB ETA: 2023

18. Nick Swiney, LHP

FB	CB	CH	Command	Overall
45	60	60	45	40

Born: 02/12/99	Age: 24	Bats: R	Top Production Comp: J.P. Howell
Height: 6-3	Weight: 185	Throws: L	

Season	Team	Age	Level	IP	TBF	K/9	K%	BB/9	BB%	K-BB%	ERA	FIP	xFIP	Pit/Bat
2021	SFG	22	A	24.1	102	15.53	41.18%	4.44	11.76%	29.41%	0.74	2.26	3.20	4.10
2022	SFG	23	A+	89.0	381	10.62	27.56%	4.55	11.81%	15.75%	3.84	4.11	4.79	3.76

Background: San Francisco has been fairly familiar with prospects coming out of North Carolina State University throughout the years, having selected a total of nine members of the Wolfpack. The organization, though, has selected just two players from the school before fifth round – Patrick Bailey and Nick Swiney, both joining the ball club during the 2020 draft class. A lanky 6-foot-3, 185-pound southpaw, Swiney was primarily a reliever with a penchant for handing out the free pass over his first two collegiate seasons. But things seem to click during the COVID-abbreviated 2020 campaign as he posted a stellar 42-to-6 strikeout-to-walk ratio in only 28.0 innings. The dominance – however abbreviated as it was – convinced the front office brass to draft the lefty in the second round, 67th overall, and sign him to a deal worth slightly less than $1.2 million. Swiney was absurdly good during his debut the following season, posting a 0.84 ERA with 58 strikeouts and

San Francisco Giants

18 walks in 32.1 injury-interrupted innings. Last season the Tennessee native spent the entire year in Eugene's rotation, throwing just 89.0 innings while averaging 10.6 strikeouts and 4.6 walks per nine innings. He compiled a 3.84 ERA, a 4.11 FIP, and a 4.79 xFIP.

Snippet from The 2020 Prospect Digest Handbook: It's all about the offspeed, baby.

Scouting Report: Consider the following:

> Since 2006, only two 23-year-old pitchers posted a K% between 26.5% and 28.5% with a walk percentage between 11% and 13% in High-A (min. 75 IP): Noel Vela and Nick Swiney.

Swiney's an intriguing pitching prospect, possessing two plus pitches that generate a ton of weak contact and / or swings-and-misses. But his third offering, though, is firmly in the below-average range. So what, exactly, makes Swiney so intriguing because there are dozens upon dozens of hurlers in the minor leagues that match that description? His fastball is lacking, hovering in the 90-mph range, but it's buoyed by his tremendous curveball / changeup combination. Despite some subpar command, Swiney has a simple game plan that he follows during each at bat. Try to cheat a fastball in for strike zone, throw plenty of offspeed pitches, and then elevate the heater – which does get some swing-and-misses above the beltline, despite the lack of velocity. Typically, soft-tossing lefties are supposed to command the zone exceptionally well. Swiney doesn't. And he hasn't done so for an extended period even going back to his college days. It wouldn't be surprising to see him take a J.P. Howell path at some point in his career. He needs the command to tick up to *at least* average if he's going to remain in the rotation.

Ceiling: 1.0-win player
Risk: Moderate
MLB ETA: 2023/2024

19. Matt Mikulski, LHP

FB	CB	SL	CH	Command	Overall
55	N/A	45/50	60	45	40

Born: 05/08/99	Age: 24	Bats: L	Top Production Comp: Ron Mahay
Height: 6-4	Weight: 205	Throws: L	

Season	Team	Age	Level	IP	TBF	K/9	K%	BB/9	BB%	K-BB%	ERA	FIP	xFIP	Pit/Bat
2022	SFG	23	A	79.0	367	10.94	26.16%	3.53	8.45%	17.71%	6.95	5.40	5.01	3.90

Background: Trivia Time: Name the earliest draft player in Fordham University history. The answer: 1991 All-Star Pete Harnisch, the 27th overall pick in the 1987 draft. Harnisch, by the way, turned in the seventh most productive big league career among first rounders that year, trailing Ken Griffey Jr. (#1), Craig Biggio (22nd), Kevin Appier (9th), Travis Fryman (30th), Jack McDowell (5th), and Delino DeShields (12th). Two years ago the Giants made Mikulski the second highest player draft from Fordham, taking him with the 50th overall pick and signing him to a deal worth a smidgeon under $1.2 million. As dominant a force as any during his final season with the Atlantic 10 Conference squad, the 6-foot-4, 205-pound lefty posted an incredible 124-to-27 strikeout-to-walk ratio in only 68.1 innings of work. He capped off his collegiate career with a laughably impossible 1.45 ERA. Last season, after tossing just 5.0 innings in the Complex League during his debut, Mikulski made the move up to Low-A for 22 appearances. He would toss just 79.0 innings, averaging a solid 10.9 strikeouts and 3.5 walks per nine innings. He finished with a laughably impossible 6.95 ERA.

Snippet from The 2020 Prospect Digest Handbook: Back of the rotation caliber prospect, high floor, low ceiling.

Scouting Report: It was an interesting selection at the time and remains so more than a year later – for a variety of reasons, like:

> #1. He was 22-years-old at the time of the draft.
> #2. He battled command issues throughout the majority of his collegiate career.
> #3. He's essentially a two-pitch pitcher.

Funky, extreme short-arming southpaw. Mikulski has little bit of giddy up on his low- to mid-90s fastball, making it an above-average offering. His best pitch is a plus changeup with some downward tumble thrown with phenomenal arm speed. He'll also mix in a fringy average slider. Reports indicate he'll mix in a below-average curveball, but I never saw one. So, just to recap: two pitches, 45-grade command, old. Not a recipe for future starting success. Mikulski does own several terrific pickoff moves. He's strictly a future reliever.

Ceiling: 1.0- win player
Risk: Moderate
MLB ETA: 2024

San Francisco Giants

20. William Kempner, RHP

FB	SL	CH	Command	Overall
60	60	55	35	40

Born: 06/18/01	Age: 22	Bats: R	Top Production Comp: N/A
Height: 6-0	Weight: 222	Throws: R	

Background: Playing alongside Gabriel Hughes, the 10th overall pick last July, and Trystan Vrieling, who was taken by the Yankees with the 100th pick, Kempner completed the triumvirate to become the first draft class to feature three Gonzaga University players taken before the fourth round. A stalwart in the Bulldogs' rotation during his final two seasons, the hard-throwing right-hander missed considerable time in 2022 due to a finger ligament issue. He finished his collegiate career with just 84.0 innings pitched, averaging 9.0 strikeouts and a whopping 6.3 walks per nine innings to go along with a 3.43 ERA. San Francisco selected him in the third round, 106th overall, and signed him to a deal worth $522,500. He tossed nine low level innings during his pro debut, striking out 11 and walking six to go along with a 5.00 ERA.

Scouting Report: Ignoring the arsenal, lack of command, and any potential injury issues; Kempner is 100% a future reliever. Why? Mechanics. Low, low three-quarter slot release with a winging action that he struggles to repeat with any type of consistency – hence the command issues. Plus fastball, pus slider, and an above-average changeup. The Giants may convince themselves that the organization can force him into some mechanical improvements, but it's not likely to take shape.

Ceiling: 0.5- to 1.0-win player
Risk: Moderate
MLB ETA: 2024/2025

Seattle Mariners Top Prospects

Seattle Mariners

1. Harry Ford, C

Hit	Power	SB	Patience	Glove	Overall
45/55	45/55	50/40	50/55	60	60

Born: 02/21/03 | **Age:** 20 | **Bats:** R | **Top Production Comp:** Buster Posey
Height: 5-10 | **Weight:** 200 | **Throws:** R |

Season	Team	Age	Level	PA	1B	2B	3B	HR	SB	CS	BB%	K%	AVG	OBP	SLG	ISO
2021	SEA	18	CPX	65	6	7	0	3	3	0	13.85%	21.54%	0.291	0.400	0.582	0.291
2022	SEA	19	A	499	69	23	4	11	23	5	17.64%	23.05%	0.274	0.425	0.438	0.164

Background: Seattle's been no stranger to drafting catchers in the early rounds of the midsummer draft throughout their history, taking a total of nine backstops in the first round and four in the second. And the list includes more than a few notable names, like: Jason Varitek (who was foolishly traded along with Derek Lowe for Heathcliff Slocumb), Jeff Clements (the third round pick in 2005 who was taken directly ahead of Ryan Zimmerman and Ryan Braun), Mike Zunino, Dave Valle (who spent 13 years in the big leagues), and – of course – Harry Ford, who became the club's first prep backstop taken in the opening round in 12 years. The 12th overall pick in 2021, Ford turned in a dynamic – albeit shortened – debut with the franchise's Complex League that summer, bashing .291/.400/.582 with 10 extra-base knocks in only 19 games. Unsurprisingly, the front office sent the stocky backstop straight up to Modesto for the 2022 season. And Ford mashed – especially for a catcher still learning the finer nuances of the most difficult position. In 104 games with the Nuts, the 5-foot-10, 200-pound catcher slugged .274/.425/.439 with 23 doubles, four triples, 11 homeruns, and 23 stolen bases (in only 28 total attempts). His production topped the league average mark by 32%, according to *Weighted Runs Created Plus*.

Snippet from The 2022 Prospect Digest Handbook: One of the most athletic – either college or prep – prospects in the 2021 draft class. Ford, a [catcher], shows plus bat speed and matching 60-times, as well. He was reportedly clocked in the 6.4-range in the 60-yard dash. One of my favorite prospects in the draft.

Scouting Report: Consider the following:

> Since 2006, only four 19-year-old hitters met the following criteria in a season in Low-A (min. 350 PA): 127 to 137 wRC+ with a strikeout rate between 22% and 24%. Those four hitters: Nick Castellanos, who owns a 112 wRC+ in his big league career, Oneil Cruz, Triston Casas, and – of course – the supremely underrated Harry Ford.

Ignoring Ford's offensive prowess, at least momentarily, the North Cobb High School product was nothing short of spectacular behind the dish during his first full season in the minors – regardless of the metric. Clay Davenport's numbers showed him as a +9 defender, and *Baseball Prospectus's* calculations had him as 6.8 *Fielding Runs Above Average*. And just like a cheesy infomercial host would say, "That's not all!" *Baseball Prospectus's* showed he was an above-average pitch-framer as well. Whatever Ford adds with the bat, let alone on the base paths, is simply icing on the proverbial cake. And it's *a lot*. Above-average hit tool, developing power that should peak in the 20- to 25-homerun range. Elite patience at the plate. And plus speed on the base paths. Last year he – almost predictably so – got off to a slow start with the Nuts, which isn't surprising because of the position, his age, and level of competition. He batted a lowly .209/.370/.291 over his first 29 games. After that, though, his bat caught fire and he slugged .300/.446/.496 over his final 75 games. The bat speed is off the charts. And if he wasn't so good behind the plate, he'd be a candidate to move away from the position to hasten his development. It wouldn't be shocking to see him listed as the consensus top catching prospect within a year. He looks like perennial All-Star in the making with a ceiling as a .290/.380/.460 hitter with Gold Glove winning defense.

Ceiling: 5.0-win player
Risk: Moderate
MLB ETA: 2024

2. Cole Young, 2B/SS

Hit	Power	SB	Patience	Glove	Overall
45	55	30	55	50	

Born: 07/29/03 | **Age:** 19 | **Bats:** L | **Top Production Comp:** N/A
Height: 6-0 | **Weight:** 180 | **Throws:** R |

Season	Team	Age	Level	PA	1B	2B	3B	HR	SB	CS	BB%	K%	AVG	OBP	SLG	ISO
2022	SEA	18	CPX	26	5	1	1	0	3	0	15.38%	15.38%	0.333	0.423	0.476	0.143
2022	SEA	18	A	45	13	0	0	2	1	2	8.89%	8.89%	0.385	0.422	0.538	0.154

Background: While Young doesn't have the bloodlines of the some of the other top prep hitters in the 2022 Draft Class – guys like Druw Jones or Elijah Greene or Cam Collier or Jackson Holliday – the promising lefty-swinging shortstop, nonetheless, has been a known commodity in eastern Pennsylvania for nearly a decade. Young would capture the title for MLB's Pitch, Hit, and Run competition in 2014 as a 10-year-old. And his draft stock has been on a steady climb since then. North Alleghany High School isn't exactly a known hotbed for baseball talent throughout the years, graduating just one player – right-hander Tom Carroll – to the big leagues out of six total draft picks. And their most recent draft pick, Kevin McCarthy, was a fourth rounder by the Mets all the way back in 1994, the same year the club selected Paul Wilson, Terence Long, and Jay Payton. McCarthy, by the way, also happens to be the school's high drafted player as well. Until Young heard his name. Two years ago the young middle infielder batted a scorching .437 while scoring 33 runs and driving in 23. And he continued to swing a hot stick as a senior in 2022 as well: in 21 games for North Alleghany, the 6-foot, 180-pound youngster slugged .433/.564/.800 with eight doubles, four triples, and a pair of homeruns. Young committed to Duke University following his freshman season in high school. Seattle selected the 6-foot, 180-pound middle infielder 21st overall, signing him to a deal worth $3.3 million. He batted an impressive .367/.423/.517 with one double, one triple, two homeruns, and four stolen base in the Complex League and Low-A.

Scouting Report: Per the usual, my pre-draft write-up:

> *"Young takes a well-rounded approach at the plate, showing a willingness to turn on the inside pitch and shoot outside offerings down the left line. He doesn't project to develop more than average power, but should pepper plenty of two-baggers in the gaps. Defensively, the Pennsylvania-native has the chops to stick at shortstop, showing soft hands and a quick release. Young isn't going to be a superstar, but he has the potential to turn into a fringe big league starting caliber shortstop. Low ceiling / high floor high school prospect."*

Following his blistering start, I've bumped up my original assessment.

Ceiling: 3.0-win player
Risk: Moderate
MLB ETA: 2025/2026

3. Bryce Miller, RHP

FB	SL	CH	Command	Overall
70	55	50	50	55

Born: 08/23/98	Age: 24	Bats: R	Top Production Comp: N/A
Height: 6-2	Weight: 180	Throws: R	

Season	Team	Age	Level	IP	TBF	K/9	K%	BB/9	BB%	K-BB%	ERA	FIP	xFIP	Pit/Bat
2022	SEA	23	A+	77.2	316	11.47	31.33%	2.90	7.91%	23.42%	3.24	3.48	3.50	3.74
2022	SEA	23	AA	50.2	204	10.84	29.90%	3.37	9.31%	20.59%	3.20	3.42	4.40	4.30

Background: The Mariners have really turned into one of the better pitching development organizations over the past couple of years. They may not be on the same level as, say, the Dodgers or Rays or Guardians, but they're in a tier directly below them, though. And just another example of Seattle's pitching evaluation prowess is Bryce Miller. Taken in the fourth round two years ago out of Texas A&M, Miller's collegiate career wrapped up with a multitude of ups-and-downs as he moved into the Aggies' rotation for the first time. The good: the 6-foot-2, 180-pound right-hander averaged an impressive 11.1 strikeouts per nine innings. The bad: his bloated walk rate (5.1 BB/9). But almost immediately after he donned a Seattle affiliate organization Miller honed in the strike zone with pinpoint precision during his debut as he walked just a pair of hitters in 9.1 innings of work. But no one could have expected the dominant performance awaiting the former Aggie heading into last season. Miller made 27 appearances in 2022 (all but one coming with Everett and Arkansas), throwing 133.2 innings with a whopping 163 strikeouts and just 46 walks. He finished his first full season with a tidy 3.16 ERA and a 3.49 FIP.

Scouting Report: Consider the following:

> Since 2006, seven 23-year-old hurlers posted a 29% to 31% strikeout percentage with an 8.5% to 10.5% walk percentage in any Double-A league (min. 50 IP): Dinelson Lamet, Konnor Pilkington, Alejandro Chacin, Humberto Sanchez, Travis Ott, Yerry Rodriguez, and Bryce Miller.

Slow methodical worker, like the type to lull his defense asleep if he's not careful. If you went in blind, not knowing anything about Miller or Emerson Hancock, or their draft statuses, and watched them pitch. It'd be difficult to not side with Miller. He doesn't have the repertoire depth, but his upper-90s fastball is better; his slider is similar. And he's proven to be able to handle the workload. Explosive fastball. The slider lacks consistency, but will flash above-average. He'll also show a solid-average changeup. He's not a command guy, but doesn't really need to be given the ferocity of heater. If there was one pitcher that could burst onto the scene like Spencer Strider, Miller's name would be on the list.

Ceiling: 3.0-win player
Risk: Moderate
MLB ETA: 2023

Seattle Mariners

4. Axel Sanchez, SS

Hit	Power	SB	Patience	Glove	Overall
50	50	50	50	55	55

Born: 12/10/02 **Age:** 20 **Bats:** R **Top Production Comp:** N/A
Height: 6-0 **Weight:** 170 **Throws:** R

Season	Team	Age	Level	PA	1B	2B	3B	HR	SB	CS	BB%	K%	AVG	OBP	SLG	ISO
2021	SEA	18	DSL	190	34	7	0	1	15	4	10.53%	24.21%	0.261	0.360	0.323	0.062
2022	SEA	19	CPX	99	14	5	2	2	9	2	11.11%	20.20%	0.267	0.354	0.442	0.174
2022	SEA	19	A	152	17	13	2	8	4	1	9.87%	27.63%	0.305	0.401	0.618	0.313
2022	SEA	19	A+	34	7	1	0	0	0	0	0.00%	26.47%	0.235	0.235	0.265	0.029

Background: A bit of an under-the-radar signing out of the Dominican Republic in early July 2019 – at least as much as a $290,000 signing can be under-the-radar. Sanchez, like a lot of amateurs that turned pro at that point had to wait until the 2021 season to make his affiliated debut due to the COVID pandemic. Seattle would send the then-18-year-old slick-fielding middle infielder into the Dominican Summer League. And the results were completely underwhelming as he batted a punchless .261/.360/.323 with just seven doubles and a dinger in 52 games. Last season the brass shipped Sanchez up to the Complex League, but he hardly resembled the same player – despite yo-yoing by the front office. Sanchez began the year in High-A for six games, was then sent to the Complex League before going back up to High-A briefly. He was then sent back down to the Complex League – again – in late June. A month later he has up with Modesto. In spite of the club's handling, Sanchez quietly turned in a breakout campaign as he mashed .283/.365/.510 with 19 doubles, four triples, 10 homeruns, and 13 stolen bases (in 16 attempts). Per *Weighted Runs Created Plus*, his overall production topped the league average threshold by 28% -- a 27-percentage point improvement from the previous year.

Scouting Report: Just for fun, here are Sanchez's numbers prorated for a full 162-game schedule: 45 doubles, 10 triples, 24 homeruns, and 31 stolen bases. Not bad work for a defensive wizard. Sanchez struggled driving ball during his debut in the Dominican Summer League two years ago, projecting – at that time – as a smooth-fielding backup infielder. Fast forward a year, all of sudden he's mashing *and* his defensive numbers are above-average (in an admittedly small sample size). Sanchez could very well announce his arrival as one of the top shortstop prospects in the minors as soon as 2023. Remember the name. Boom goes the dynamite.

Ceiling: 3.0-win player
Risk: Moderate to High
MLB ETA: 2025

5. Gabriel Gonzalez, RF

Hit	Power	SB	Patience	Glove	Overall
55	45/50	50/40	50	50	50

Born: 01/04/04 **Age:** 19 **Bats:** R **Top Production Comp:** Jorge Soler
Height: 5-10 **Weight:** 165 **Throws:** R

Season	Team	Age	Level	PA	1B	2B	3B	HR	SB	CS	BB%	K%	AVG	OBP	SLG	ISO
2021	SEA	17	DSL	221	28	15	4	7	9	3	9.50%	15.84%	0.287	0.371	0.521	0.234
2022	SEA	18	CPX	140	31	9	0	5	5	3	5.71%	15.00%	0.357	0.421	0.548	0.190
2022	SEA	18	A	150	28	5	1	2	4	1	8.67%	14.00%	0.286	0.400	0.389	0.103

Background: Trader Jerry Dipoto may not be the Mariners' General Manager anymore, thanks to his promotion to President of Baseball Operations, but the club's new GM, Justin Hollander, is picking up right where his predecessor left off. Hollander dealt away one of the club's top young arms, Adam Macko, as part of the package to fetch Teoscar Hernández from the Blue Jays. And that comes months after the Mariners used their prospect capital to acquire ace right-hander Luis Castillo from the Cincinnati Reds, dealing away Edwin Arroyo, Noelvi Marte, Andrew Moore, and Levi Stoudt. So Seattle's farm system cupboard is pretty barren at this point – though it's not without a handful of potential quality future big league contributors. Like Gabriel Gonzalez. Signed out of Carupano, Venezuela, in early February 2021, Gonzalez made his affiliated debut just a few months later with the club's Dominican Summer League affiliate. And he sparkled. The 5-foot-10, 165-pound corner outfielder slugged .287/.371/.521 with 15 doubles, four triples, seven homeruns, and nine stolen bases (in 12 attempts). The front office brass bumped Gonzalez stateside and into the Complex League. But after mashing .357/.421/.548 in 35 games, Gonzalez was pushed up to Low-A. And he continued to hit with Modesto (.286/.400/.389). He finished the 2020 campaign with a .321/.410/.468 with 14 doubles, one triple, seven homeruns, and nine stolen bases (in 13 total attempts). Per *Weighted Runs Created Plus*, his overall production topped the league average threshold by an impressive 39%.

Scouting Report: Gonzalez continues to fly under the radar, even in a farm system that's as thin as the Mariners'. He's not overly big, but he's lean and should add some strength to his 165-pound frame in the coming years. Good bat speed, but not elite. Gonzalez owns an above-average hit tool with 50-grade power. He's spent some time in centerfield the past two seasons, but he's better suited for a corner spot where his glove should provide net positive value. He could turn in one of the more surprising breakout campaign in 2023.

Seattle Mariners

Ceiling: 2.5-win player
Risk: Moderate
MLB ETA: 2025

6. Michael Arroyo, SS

Hit	Power	SB	Patience	Glove	Overall
45/55	40/50	40	50	50/55	55

Born: 11/03/04	Age: 18	Bats: R	Top Production Comp: N/A
Height: 5-10	Weight: 160	Throws: R	

Season	Team	Age	Level	PA	1B	2B	3B	HR	SB	CS	BB%	K%	AVG	OBP	SLG	ISO
2022	SEA	17	DSL	199	32	10	2	4	4	4	13.57%	16.58%	0.314	0.457	0.484	0.170

Background: The front office dealt away a tremendous amount of up-the-middle infield talent last season (Noelvi Marte and Edwin Arroyo), but they were able to add a notable shortstop from the international market too. Seattle signed Michael Arroyo, a 5-foot-10, 160-pound infielder, for a hefty $1.375 million in mid-January last year. A few months later the young Venezuelan was torching the Dominican Summer League to the tune of .314/.457/.484 with 10 doubles, two triples, four homeruns, and four stolen bases (in eight attempts). According to *Weighted Runs Created Plus*, his overall production topped the league average threshold by a staggering 58%.

Scouting Report: Not close to being physically mature, the baby-faced infielder is already showing an advance approach at the plate. Short, quick stroke. Fast bat / hands. Arroyo could be one the better value signings from the entire class. Only entering his-18 season, Arroyo's a near lock to square off against Low-A pitching for the majority of 2023 – if not for the entire year. Despite his slight frame and twitchy movements, it wouldn't be shocking to see his develop 15- to 20-homer thump in the coming years. He could POP in a big way in 2023.

Ceiling: 3.0-win player
Risk: High
MLB ETA: 2025

7. Emerson Hancock, RHP

FB	CB	SL	CH	Command	Overall
60	50	55	55	50	60

Born: 05/31/99	Age: 24	Bats: R	Top Production Comp: Marco Estrada
Height: 6-4	Weight: 213	Throws: R	

Season	Team	Age	Level	IP	TBF	K/9	K%	BB/9	BB%	K-BB%	ERA	FIP	xFIP	Pit/Bat
2021	SEA	22	A+	31.0	124	8.71	24.19%	3.77	10.48%	13.71%	2.32	3.91	4.15	4.25
2021	SEA	22	AA	13.2	55	8.56	23.64%	2.63	7.27%	16.36%	3.29	2.45	4.28	3.80
2022	SEA	23	AA	98.1	413	8.42	22.28%	3.48	9.20%	13.08%	3.75	5.31	5.43	4.00

Background: It may take a couple more years before it finally settles in, but the sheer level of high end talent the Mariners' farm system curated, but also sent *successfully* to the big leagues is astonishing. Perennial MVP candidate Julio Rodriguez, Logan Gilbert, and George Kirby immediately come to mind. And that doesn't count outfielder Jarred Kelenic, though hope is dwindling quickly that he can figure out big league pitching – particularly left-handers. The last of the club's Big 5 is Emerson Hancock. Taken with the sixth overall pick out of the University of Georgia two years ago, there was talk during his sophomore year with the Bulldogs that he could be a potential top pick and he narrowly missed. Hancock's 2021 season was severely interrupted to a non-structural shoulder issue, limiting him to just 44.2 innings between Everett and Arkansas. And the opening parts of last season looked like a repeat may be in order. A lat injury forced him to miss the first several weeks of year. Finally healthy, Hancock made it back to the Travelers' mound in mid-May and was able to log 21 solid starts. The hard-throwing righty just missed the 100-inning threshold, tossing 98.1 innings with the club's Double-A affiliate, fanning 92 and walking 38. He averaged 8.4 strikeouts and 3.5 walks per nine innings. He finished the year with a 3.75 ERA, 5.31 FIP, and a 5.43 xFIP.

Snippet from The 2022 Prospect Digest Handbook: Hancock doesn't quite have the ceiling that [George] Kirby does, but he's going to be a very good – sort of Robin to Kirby's Batman. Barring any significant injury, of course.

Scouting Report: Consider the following:

> Since 2006, fourteen 23-year-old hurlers posted a 21.5% to 23.5% strikeout percentage with an 8% to 10% walk percentage in any Double-A league (min. 90 IP): Jordan Montgomery, Tyler Beede, James McDonald, Ariel Pena, Esmerling Vasquez, Hansel Robles, Jerad Eickhoff, Jeremy Beasley, Jorge Alcala, Kyle Weiland, Ofreidy Gomez, Parker Bridwell, Same LeCure, and – of course – Emerson Hancock. It's worth noting that beyond Montgomery it's a list of relievers or failed starters.

Seattle Mariners

The polished approach at pitching is still in place, but Hancock no longer looks – or, more importantly, *feels* – like a special pitching prospect, one that could take that final step towards the front of a big league rotation. That's not to say he won't be a successful big leaguer, but the ceiling and expectations have to be dialed back. Plus fastball, average curveball, above-average changeup. His slider seemed to regress from plus to above-average, but it's still a serviceable weapon. The above-average, sometimes plus, command he showed during his final two seasons at Georgia seems to have taken a step back now as well. Hancock's looking like a league average arm, which is still a win as a former early first round pick.

Ceiling: 2.0-win player
Risk: Moderate
MLB ETA: 2023

8. Lazaro Montes, RF

Hit	Power	SB	Patience	Glove	Overall
35/45	60/70	30	50	50	55

Born: 10/22/04	Age: 18	Bats: L	Top Production Comp: N/A
Height: 6-3	Weight: 210	Throws: R	

Season	Team	Age	Level	PA	1B	2B	3B	HR	SB	CS	BB%	K%	AVG	OBP	SLG	ISO
2022	SEA	17	DSL	223	22	13	5	10	3	1	15.70%	33.18%	0.284	0.422	0.585	0.301

Background: Ranked as the eighth best prospect on the international market by MLB Pipeline. Seattle signed the Cuban import to a massive $2.5 million deal last January, committing nearly half of the club's allotted monies to the corner outfielder. Montes would make his affiliated debut with the organization's Dominican Summer League affiliate a few months later. He would slug .284/.422/.585 with 13 doubles, five triples, 10 homeruns, and a trio of stolen bases in 55 games. Per *Weighted Runs Created Plus*, Montes' overall production surpassed the league average threshold by an impressive 62%.

Scouting Report: A ferocious left-handed swing that aims to destroy baseballs when contact is made. But unfortunately for Montes, though, that didn't happen as nearly as much as the Mariners would have liked during his debut. Playing in the pitcher-friendly DSL, Montes whiffed in a third of his plate appearances last season. He did not strike out in only 10 of his 55 games last season. Just to put that into perspective:

> Since 2006, there have been 199 instances in which a prospect whiffed in more than 30% of his DSL appearances. Not one of them would go on to establish themselves as an adequate big league hitter.

Big time power potential, the La Habana native's thump may be the best in the entire system already. The force from his swing meeting a pitch is a *loud* audible explosion, the type that isn't heard very frequently. If Montes can chew down his whiff rate to 70% of his current total, he could develop into one of the game's best power-hitting prospects. It's something that can be done, but it hasn't happened yet.

Ceiling: 3.0-win player
Risk: Extremely High
MLB ETA: 2025

9. Jonatan Clase, CF

Hit	Power	SB	Patience	Glove	Overall
45/50	50	80	50	50/55	50

Born: 05/23/02	Age: 21	Bats: B	Top Production Comp: N/A
Height: 5-8	Weight: 150	Throws: R	

Season	Team	Age	Level	PA	1B	2B	3B	HR	SB	CS	BB%	K%	AVG	OBP	SLG	ISO
2019	SEA	17	R	286	46	12	7	2	31	10	17.83%	19.58%	0.300	0.434	0.444	0.143
2021	SEA	19	CPX	57	9	1	0	2	16	0	10.53%	26.32%	0.245	0.333	0.388	0.143
2022	SEA	20	A	499	67	22	11	13	55	10	13.03%	26.65%	0.267	0.373	0.463	0.196

Background: An oft-told story *always* comes up when Billy Wagner is the conversation. The should-be-Hall-of-Famer broke his right arm as a child, so he began to throw with his left, a move that undoubtedly change the course of his entire life as he went on to save 422 games and tally nearly $100,000,000 in career earnings. Well, Jonatan Clase has a similar story of his own. The speedster, as told by MLB.com, missed the majority of the 2021 season due to a lower leg issue. With the added time on his hands he – simply – decided to pick switch-hitting back up after shelving it as an amateur. The naturally right-handed hitter promptly went out and turned in a dynamic, breakout-esque showing in 2022, including hitting a respectable (given the circumstances) .232/.312/.438 as a lefty. Clase, who signed the Mariners during the summer of 2018, mashed .267/.374/.463 with 22 doubles, 11 triples, 13 homeruns, and 55 stolen bases (in 65 total attempts). As measured by *Weighted Runs Created Plus*, his overall production topped surpassed the league average threshold by 17%.

Seattle Mariners

Scouting Report: Consider the following:

> Since 2006, only four 20-year-old hitters met the following criteria in a Low-A season (min. 350 PA): 112 to 122 wRC+, at least an 11% walk rate, and a 25% to 28% strikeout rate. Those four hitters: Ryan Dent, Boss Moanaroa, Thomas Hickman, and Jonathan Clase.

A speed demon on the base paths that runs efficiently (85% success rate last season), Clase's power took an unexpected step forward last season – a surprise given his 5-foot-8, 150-pound frame *and* that Modesto's home ballpark is one of the more homer-suppressing environments in the minors. Despite going back to switch-hitting for the first time in a couple years, Clase performed decently as a lefty. Average defender that should improve to above-average. He could be a dynamic table-setter in a few years. Don't sleep on the new switch-hitter.

Ceiling: 1.5- to 2.0-win player
Risk: Moderate
MLB ETA: 2024

10. Tyler Locklear, 1B/3B

Hit	Power	SB	Patience	Glove	Overall
45	55	30	55	50	

Born: 11/24/00	Age: 22	Bats: R	Top Production Comp: N/A	
Height: 6-3	Weight: 210	Throws: R		

Season	Team	Age	Level	PA	1B	2B	3B	HR	SB	CS	BB%	K%	AVG	OBP	SLG	ISO
2022	SEA	21	A	133	21	5	0	7	0	0	5.26%	21.80%	0.282	0.353	0.504	0.222

Background: Locklear's entire family tree is littered with athletes: his father played baseball at St. Andrew's College, then a Division II school; his cousin, Gavin Locklear, earned a scholarship after walking onto the N.C. State football team; and his uncle, Jeff Locklear, spent five seasons in the minor leagues after the San Francisco Giants drafted him in the 54th round in 1991. An All-Star and 2018 Under Armour All-American during his high school days at Archbishop Curley, Locklear got off to a bit of a slow start during his freshman season at Virginia Common Wealth, hitting a mediocre .259/.380/.397 during the 2020 COVID-shortened season. The 6-foot-3, 210-pound corner infielder had a massive coming out party for the Rams the following season as he slugged an impressive .345/.515/.686 with 12 doubles, three triples, and 16 homeruns. The production was enough to earn him a trip to the prestigious Cape Cod League where he batted a respectable .256/.333/.504 in 34 games with the Orleans Firebirds. Last season Locklear morphed into – arguably – the most lethal college bat in the game as he mashed .402/.542/.799 with 25 doubles, two triples, 20 homeruns, and six stolen bases. Seattle selected him in the second round, 58th overall, and signed him to a deal worth $1,276,500. After a two-game cameo in the Complex League, Locklear tore through the Low-A pitching to the tune of .282/.353/.504.

Scouting Report: My pre-draft write-up:

> "Consider the following:
>
>> Since 2011, only four Division I players hit at least .400/.525/.700 in a season (min. 275 PA): Nick Gonzales, Peyton Burdick, Trenton Moses, and – of course – Tyler Locklear.
>
> The question is going to come down to the level of competition – the Atlantic 10 Conference is hardly the SEC. And, on one hand, Locklear handled himself well enough during his extended jaunt through the Cape Cod League two summers ago. But his trademark plate discipline (he walked 101 times vs. 78 punch outs in his career at VCU) had all but evaporated against the most elite competition. In 34 games with Orleans he whiffed 22% of the time against a paltry 4% walk rate. Big time power – both raw and in-game. And Locklear makes his intentions well known during his plate appearance: he shooting for extra-bases on every pitch. Huge natural uppercut on the swing as he drops his back shoulder to help elevate the ball better. He's big and slow, so he's not long for the hot corner. If he can walk at a good clip, he'll be a TTO (Three True Outcomes) hitter. Right now, he looks one dimensional."

I had a fourth round grade on Locklear heading into the draft. One more note: he walked just 5.8% and fanned a reasonable 21.8% of the time in Low-A.

Ceiling: 1.5-win player
Risk: Moderate
MLB ETA: 2024/2025

Seattle Mariners

11. Walter Ford, RHP

FB	SL	CH	Command	Overall
60	50/60	45	40/45	45

Born: 12/28/04	Age: 18	Bats: R	Top Production Comp: N/A
Height: 6-3	Weight: 198	Throws: R	

Background: One of the youngest players in the draft class last July, Ford was originally scheduled to be a member of the 2023 class but reclassified in late 2021. A product of Hoover High School, the 6-foot-3, 198-pound right-hander tossed just 29.2 innings of work two years ago, tallying a 1.85 ERA. He played for the 18U Team USA National squad that summer as well, joining the like of Termarr Johnson, Elijah Green, Jackson Holliday, Druw Jones, and Jackson Ferris. In one brief outing with the team, Ford tossed three innings, recording four punch outs and handing out a pair of free bases. Last year, which technically became his senior campaign thanks to the reclassification, the hard-throwing righty was named 6A Player of the Year and All-State after throwing 70.1 innings with a 1.00 ERA, a 10-2 win-loss record, 126 strikeouts, and 30 free passes. Seattle selected the young hurler in the second round, 74th overall, and signed him to an above-slot bonus worth $1.25 million – roughly $400,000 above the recommended slot bonus. He did not throw an affiliated pitch after joining the organization.

Scouting Report: It's easy to see why the Mariners went above-slot to sign the University of Alabama commit. He's(A) incredibly young for this draft class, (B) quite projectable thanks to his long limbs, wiry frame, and age, and (C) his arsenal packs a wallop. Ford's fastball sits in the mid-90s with added deception thanks to a bit of funk in his windup. His slider, the better of his two offspeed pitches, will flash plus at times, and his changeup – as expected – is raw. His command will waver at times as well. Seattle's pitching development program is one of the better ones in the game, so Ford landed in an ideal spot.

Ceiling: 1.5-win player
Risk: Moderate
MLB ETA: 2025

12. Michael Morales, RHP

FB	CB	SL	CH	Command	Overall
55	55	50	55	50	45

Born: 08/13/02	Age: 20	Bats: R	Top Production Comp: N/A
Height: 6-2	Weight: 205	Throws: R	

Season	Team	Age	Level	IP	TBF	K/9	K%	BB/9	BB%	K-BB%	ERA	FIP	xFIP	Pit/Bat
2022	SEA	19	A	120.1	559	9.35	22.36%	3.74	8.94%	13.42%	5.91	5.05	5.13	3.65

Background: Two years ago the Mariners opened up their draft class with three consecutive high schoolers for the first time since 2010 when they selected Taijuan Walker, Marcus Littlewood, and Ryne Stanek, who failed to sign with the team. Seattle snagged Harry Ford, Edwin Arroyo, and Morales in 2021. The 83rd overall pick, Morales, who signed for $1.5 million, left quite the impression on the front office. *Baseball America* quoted Scott Hunter, the club's scouting director, as saying: "I don't want to put this much pressure on him, but there are some comparisons from our guys that this is what Walker Buehler looked like in high school – an 88 – 92 (mph) guy with a ton of strikes, can really spin a breaking ball." Last season, after throwing just one inning in the Complex League during his debut, Morales got the bump up to Low-A. He would make 26 starts, throwing 120.1 innings with an impressive 125-to-50 strikeout-to-walk ratio. He finished the year with an incredibly unsightly 5.91 ERA, a 5.05 FIP, and a 5.13 xFIP.

Snippet from The 2022 Prospect Digest Handbook: All projection at this point. Morales still has plenty of room to fill out. He's the type of guy that could really grow in the Mariners' increasingly pitching development savvy front office.

Scouting Report: Consider the following:

> Since 2006, only six 19-year-old hurlers met the following criteria in any Low-A league (min. 100 IP): 21.5% to 23.5% strikeout percentage with an 8% to 10% walk percentage. Those six hurlers: Jose Berrios, Michael Fulmer, Travis Wood, Shaun Garceau, Andry Lara, and – of course – Michael Morales.

It seems that the Mariners only governed Morales' workload on a start-per-start basis, and not on a yearly innings cap. The 6-foot-2, 205-pound right-hander only logged five starts where he pitched more than five innings, but managed to log a surprising 120 innings on the year. No other 19-year-old eclipsed that mark in Low-A in 2022. And the last to do so was Pirates' rising star Roansy Contreras, who accomplished the feat as part of the Yankees' organization in 2019. Morales added an average slider to his solid three-pitch mix. His fastball is still sitting in the low 90s, the curveball is a promising above-average hammer, and the change shows some impressive tumble and fade. A year ago Morales offered up plenty of projection, but now, though, I'm wondering if he's going to fall into that category of Matt Sauer or Matt Tabor, former high schoolers who never took that final step forward. Still, though, as it stands Morales could grow into a #5-type hurler due to his poise, pitchability, and strike-throwing prowess. We definitely know he can take the ball every fifth day based on last year's workload.

Seattle Mariners

Ceiling: 1.0- to 1.5-win player
Risk: Moderate
MLB ETA: 2025

13. Zach DeLoach, OF

Hit	Power	SB	Patience	Glove	Overall
40/45	50	40	55	50	45

Born: 08/18/98	Age: 24	Bats: L	Top Production Comp: N/A
Height: 6-1	Weight: 205	Throws: R	

Season	Team	Age	Level	PA	1B	2B	3B	HR	SB	CS	BB%	K%	AVG	OBP	SLG	ISO
2021	SEA	22	A+	285	44	23	2	9	6	3	11.23%	22.11%	0.313	0.400	0.530	0.217
2021	SEA	22	AA	216	25	10	2	5	1	2	12.96%	26.85%	0.227	0.338	0.384	0.157
2022	SEA	23	AA	499	76	15	3	14	4	1	14.23%	23.85%	0.258	0.369	0.409	0.151

Background: DeLoach had a mostly unremarkable career at Texas A&M – sans an incredible 18-game hot stretch. The lefty-swinging Aggie stepped into a starting gig as a true freshman, hitting a solid, uninspiring .264/.355/.374 through 62 games. After a wildly dominant tour through the Northwoods League that summer, the wheels seemed to fall of the DeLoach Development Vehicle during his sophomore campaign as he batted a lowly .200/.318/.294. But, somehow, DeLoach was invited to the vaunted Cape Cod League. And he *dominated* as he mashed .353/.428/.541 with 14 extra-base hits in 37 games with the Falmouth Commodores. DeLoach was able to harness that lightning and carry it into the greatest 18-game stretch of his life: he bashed .421/.547/.490 with three doubles and six homeruns before COVID prematurely ended the 2020 season. Seattle liked what they saw and snagged him in the second round, 43rd overall, and signed him to a deal worth $1,729,800. DeLoach split his debut between Everett and Arkansas, hitting an aggregate .277/.373/.468 – though he struggled mightily during a 49-game cameo in Double-A. So, unsurprisingly, the 6-foot-1, 205-pound outfielder spent the 2022 season back with the Travelers. He batted a mediocre .258/.369/.409 with 15 doubles, three triples, 14 homeruns, and a quartet of stolen bases. Per *Weighted Runs Created Plus*, his overall production topped the league average threshold by 3%.

Snippet from The 2022 Prospect Digest Handbook: But the fact is simple: DeLoach has the basic toolkit as a lot of failed high round college outfielders, like Brad Snyder, Michael Choice, etc… And his struggles in the Arizona Fall League don't help assuage that gut feeling.

Scouting Report: Double-A will forever be the true litmus test for prospects. A natural selection process that inevitably separates the haves from the have nots, the eventual big leaguers from the future minor league vagabonds. Two years into his admittedly aggressive development schedule, and DeLoach owns a completely average, far from noteworthy .249/.359/.401 in 163 games in Double-A. 45-grade bat, the power hovers in the same neighborhood. Average glove. Great walk rates. There's just not enough here to be a meaningful big leaguer.

Ceiling: 1.0-win player
Risk: Moderate
MLB ETA: 2023

14. Taylor Dollard, RHP

FB	CB	SL	CH	Command	Overall
45	45	50	50	60	40

Born: 02/17/99	Age: 24	Bats: R	Top Production Comp: Tommy Milone
Height: 6-3	Weight: 195	Throws: R	

Season	Team	Age	Level	IP	TBF	K/9	K%	BB/9	BB%	K-BB%	ERA	FIP	xFIP	Pit/Bat
2021	SEA	22	A	37.2	162	14.10	36.42%	2.39	6.17%	30.25%	3.35	2.66	3.04	3.91
2021	SEA	22	A+	67.1	297	9.89	24.92%	1.87	4.71%	20.20%	6.15	4.99	4.49	3.73
2022	SEA	23	AA	144.0	572	8.19	22.90%	1.94	5.42%	17.48%	2.25	3.60	4.66	4.01

Background: The Mariners started their 2020 draft class off with a college arm sporting averaging more than 12 strikeouts and fewer than 2 walks per nine innings and ended with a collegiate arm that averaged more than 12 strikeouts and fewer than two walks per nine innings. The difference in bonus pay between Emerson Hancock and Taylor Dollard, though, was pretty staggering – like $5.3 million staggering. A product of Cal Poly San Luis Obispo, where he teamed with 2022 first rounder Brooks Lee, Dollard sparkled during his COVID-abbreviated junior campaign with the Mustangs, recording a 36-to-4 strikeout-to-walk ratio in only 27.0 innings of work. He split his 2021 debut season between Modesto and Everett, recording an impressive 133-to-24 strikeout-to-walk ratio in only 105.0 innings of work. Last season the former fifth rounder continued to dazzle as he breezed through 27 starts at the minors' most challenging level – Double-A. He averaged 8.2 strikeouts and 1.9 walks per nine innings. He finished the year with a 2.25 ERA, a 3.60 FIP, and a 4.66 xFIP. He won the most games for the Travelers since Don Brady in 1960.

Snippet from The 2022 Prospect Digest Handbook: I don't see a fifth round talent here. He could be a Ljay Newsome-type of arm.

Seattle Mariners

Scouting Report: Consider the following:

> Since 2006, only four 23-year-old hurlers posted a 22% to 24% strikeout percentage with a sub-6% walk percentage in any Double-A league (min. 100 IP): Tommy Milone, Logan Verrett, Slade Cecconi, and Taylor Dollard.

Dollard is still doing what Dollard's always done: limit walks and pitch backwards. In one of the starts I scouted, Dollard didn't throw a heater *until the sixth pitch of the game*. It's a below-average offering that may chip a pane of glass and – certainly – won't splinter any wooden bats. Very, very slider heavy in his approach to pitching, which is surprising because it's average and shouldn't miss many sticks, but the opposition has had trouble squaring it up. Average changeup. He'll mix in a slow, loopy curveball that looks more like an eephus pitch that Rip Sewell would be proud of. As long as the command stays at a plus level, he has a chance to throw some big league innings.

Ceiling: 1.0-win player
Risk: Low to Moderate
MLB ETA: 2023

15. Alberto Rodriguez, RF

Hit	Power	SB	Patience	Glove	Overall
45/50	50	50/40	50	55	45

Born: 10/06/00 **Age:** 22 **Bats:** L **Top Production Comp:** N/A
Height: 5-11 **Weight:** 180 **Throws:** L

Season	Team	Age	Level	PA	1B	2B	3B	HR	SB	CS	BB%	K%	AVG	OBP	SLG	ISO
2021	SEA	20	A	431	64	30	5	10	13	7	11.83%	22.04%	0.295	0.383	0.484	0.189
2021	SEA	20	A+	28	4	1	0	0	2	0	7.14%	25.00%	0.208	0.321	0.250	0.042
2022	SEA	21	A+	527	82	28	3	10	6	4	9.49%	26.19%	0.261	0.336	0.396	0.136

Background: Trader Jerry Dipoto played the game perfectly. The Mariners signed veteran righty – and former top prospect – Taijuan Walker for just $2 million during February 2020. Six-and-a-half months after rejoining the organization, the club flipped Walker and his expiring contract to the Blue Jays for a player to be named later. Seattle eventually settled on outfielder Alberto Rodriguez. Signed by Toronto out of Cotui, Dominican Republic, during the summer of 2017, Rodriguez opened some eyes during his stateside debut two years later as he batted .301/.364/.422 with 16 extra-base hits in 47 Gulf Coast League games. Once minor leaguers returned to work following the lost 2020 COVID year, Rodriguez continued to impress in Low-A with the Modesto Nuts; he mashed .295/.383/.484 with career bests in doubles (30), triples (5), and homeruns (10). Last season, Seattle sent the promising youngster up to Everett, an extremely hitter-friendly environment, but Rodriguez's production took a noticeable step back. He batted a mediocre .261/.336/.396 with 28 doubles, three triples, 10 homeruns, and six stolen bases. Per *Weighted Runs Created Plus*, his overall production was just 6% better than the league average. The Mariners sent him to the Arizona Fall League following the summer. Rodriguez hit .243/.349/.351 in 11 games with Peoria.

Snippet from The 2022 Prospect Digest Handbook: Rodriguez is reminiscent of a young Rusty Greer, a short, compact swing with some power and speed. The young outfield is adept at recognizing breaking pitches, particularly low, but he does loved elevated fastballs. No platoon splits. And he can play the hell out of right field. There may be an outside shot he reaches a low end starting production level, but he's going to have to carry a similar level of production for the next two years.

Scouting Report: Consider the following:

> Since 2006, only three 21-year-old hitters posted a 100 to 110 wRC+ with a 25% to 27% strikeout rate and an 8.5% to 10.5% walk rate in any High-A league (min. 350 PA): Tommy Pham, Kellin Deglan, and Alberto Rodriguez.

Despite spending half of his time in Everett's hitter-friendly home field, Funko Field, Rodriguez actually hit significantly better on the road last season (.281/.361/.426 vs. .239/.308/.365). The hit tool's stagnated over the past couple of years, just hovering in the 45-grade range at this point. The power, too, has plateaued. And Rodriguez isn't running as frequently as he once did either. Physically, it looks like he's put on a bit of weight, and not the good kind. Rodriguez is tracking like a fifth outfielder at this point. And unless he puts together a strong showing in Double-A in 2023, he may end up falling off of the club's Top 20 prospect list.

Ceiling: 1.0-win player
Risk: Moderate
MLB ETA: 2024

Seattle Mariners

16. Ashton Izzi, RHP

FB	SL	CH	Command	Overall
55/60	55	50	50	40

Born: 11/18/03	Age: 19	Bats: R	Top Production Comp: N/A
Height: 6-3	Weight: 165	Throws: R	

Background: Prior to 2022, Oswego East High School never had a player selected in the Major League Baseball Draft. A combination of kismet and timing had the Illinois-based school churn out not one, but *two* high profile picks last summer. Massive 6-foot-9, 220-pound southpaw Noah Schultz was selected by the White Sox in the opening round, 26th overall, and signed a deal worth $2.8 million. Exactly 100 picks later the Mariners, who became enamored with Ashton Izzi, grabbed him in the fourth round and signed him to a $1.1 million contract, the second highest bonus handed out to fourth round prospect last summer. Izzi, who's known by A.J., did not throw an affiliated pitch after joining the organization last summer.

Scouting Report: Sitting between 93- and 94-mph with his heater, Izzi has – reportedly – touched as high as 97 mph on the showcase circuit. He complements above-average offering with a 55-grade slider that figures to miss plenty of bats in the low levels of the minor leagues, showing late downward bite. Reports indicate he will mix in an average changeup, though I didn't see it. Izzi is the exact type of projectable arm that pitching savvy organizations (like the Mariners) can groom into a viable starting pitcher.

Ceiling: 1.0-win player
Risk: Moderate
MLB ETA: 2026

17. Starlin Aguilar, 3B

Hit	Power	SB	Patience	Glove	Overall
45/55	20/40	30	55	50/55	40

Born: 01/26/04	Age: 19	Bats: L	Top Production Comp: N/A
Height: 5-11	Weight: 170	Throws: R	

Season	Team	Age	Level	PA	1B	2B	3B	HR	SB	CS	BB%	K%	AVG	OBP	SLG	ISO
2021	SEA	17	DSL	220	29	13	1	2	0	2	13.18%	18.64%	0.246	0.359	0.361	0.115
2022	SEA	18	CPX	185	44	6	1	0	0	1	4.32%	22.70%	0.291	0.319	0.337	0.046

Background: One of the club's high profile free agents off the international scene. Seattle signed the lefty-swinging infielder to a substantial seven-figure deal in late January two years ago. A native of Azua, Dominican Republic, the teenage third baseman debuted with the club's Dominican Summer League affiliate just a few months later, hitting .246/.359/.361 with 13 doubles, one triple, and two dingers in 53 games. Last season, despite a bit of a disappointing showing in the foreign rookie league, the front office sent their big investment to the Complex League – and the results were pleasantly surprising, at least, sort of. In 46 games against the age-appropriate competition Aguilar batted .291/.319/.337 with six doubles and a triple. Per *Weighted Runs Created Plus*, his overall production fell short of the league average mark by 17%.

Scouting Report: Power's – typically – the last skill to fully develop. And it's also the most difficult to project. But 99 games and 405 plate appearances into his professional career, Aguilar's slugged just 19 doubles, two triples, and a pair of homeruns. The young third baseman owns a smooth left-handed stroke in the same mold as John Kruk or Mark Grace. His swing and bat path are more geared for peppering line drives from gap-to-gap. Defensively, he's shown promise and may grow into a consistent above-average glove at the hot corner.

Ceiling: 1.0-win player
Risk: Moderate
MLB ETA: 2026

18. Prelander Berroa, RHP

FB	SL	CH	Command	Overall
60	55	50	35	40

Born: 04/18/00	Age: 23	Bats: R	Top Production Comp: N/A
Height: 5-11	Weight: 170	Throws: R	

Background: It's been a busy couple of years for Berroa. Originally signed by the Twins in 2016, Minnesota shipped the hard-throwing right-hander to San Francisco three years later as part of package for Sam Dyson. Three years later – again – the Giants sent Berroa to the Mariners for infielder Donovan Walton. Berroa split last season between High-A and Low-A, throwing a career best 100.2 innings across 26 starts. He finished the year with a whopping 150 punch outs, another career high, and a concerning 63 free passes to go along with a 2.86 ERA. For his career, Berroa is averaging 11.6 strikeouts and a whopping 5.0 walks per nine innings with a surprisingly solid 3.72 ERA. Seattle added the Dominican hurler to their 40-man roster this offseason.

Seattle Mariners

Scouting Report: Watching Berroa unfurl one fastball and it becomes abundantly clear as to why teams have been so interested in acquiring him as part of trade packages. Watching Berroa throw two pitches and it's abundantly clear as to why teams haven't been reluctant to include him in trade packages. *Electric* fastball sitting *comfortably* in the mid-90s. Berroa complements the plus-offering with an above-average, hard, downward biting slider. He'll also mix in a rare – very *rare* – average-ish changeup. The problem for Berroa has never been about the *stuff*. Rather, it's been about the strike-throwing ability with the stuff. It's awful. Grading it out as a 40 would be optimistic. But because the fastball / slider combination are so strong, he continues to work himself out of jams. Strictly a reliever unless Seattle's pitching development program has some magical potion to increase his command.

Ceiling: 0.5- to 1.0-win player
Risk: Moderate
MLB ETA: 2023/2024

19. Bryan Woo, RHP

FB	SL	CH	Command	Overall
55	45	50/55	45/50	40

Born: 01/30/00	Age: 23	Bats: R	Top Production Comp: N/A
Height: 6-2	Weight: 205	Throws: R	

Season	Team	Age	Level	IP	TBF	K/9	K%	BB/9	BB%	K-BB%	ERA	FIP	xFIP	Pit/Bat
2022	SEA	22	A	20.1	85	12.84	34.12%	2.66	7.06%	27.06%	3.98	3.75	3.76	3.99
2022	SEA	22	A+	32.0	148	12.94	31.08%	4.50	10.81%	20.27%	4.78	3.47	4.15	3.93

Background: After finding success with crafty, soft-tossing, slider-heavy right-hander Taylor Dollard, the Mariners dipped back into the baseball pond at Cal Poly San Luis Obispo and selected Bryan Wood the following year. Taken in the sixth round in 2021, 174th overall, despite recovering from recent Tommy John surgery, Woo left the Big West Conference School with an unsightly 6.36 ERA while averaging 11.6 strikeouts and 4.0 walks per nine innings across 25 relief appearances and six starts. Seattle signed the hard-throwing right-hander to a deal worth $318,200. Woo made it back to the bump in early June last year, appearing in three rehab appearances in the Complex League. After that he would make six brief starts with Modesto and seven more with Everett in High-A. The 6-foot-2, 205-pound righty would finish his debut season with 84 strikeouts and just 22 free passes across 57.0 innings of work. Woo would make five mostly dominant appearances with the Peoria Javelinas in the Arizona Fall League as well, fanning 16 and walking four.

Scouting Report: Despite spending part of three seasons at Cal Poly San Luis Obispo, Woo's more of a project than expected – though some of it is certainly due to regaining feel for his repertoire following the Tommy John surgery. His 93-mph fastball is the best of his three offerings, grading out as a 55. His slider looked underwhelming, lacking both depth and movement. His changeup would flash above-average at times, showing solid velocity separation (roughly 8- to 9-mph difference) with some arm side run. The arsenal's not deep enough to support a full time starting gig, but he may be able to grow into a fastball / changeup relief arm. For now, though, Seattle seems content on stretching him out to see if things (like his slider) improve.

Ceiling: 0.5- to 1.0-win player
Risk: Moderate
MLB ETA: 2024

20. Robert Perez Jr., 1B

Hit	Power	SB	Patience	Glove	Overall
45	55	30	55	50	

Born: 06/26/00	Age: 23	Bats: R	Top Production Comp: N/A
Height: 6-1	Weight: 170	Throws: R	

Background: A native of Barquisimeto, Venezuela, the club signed the hulking slugger during the summer of 2016 – which seems like a lifetime ago at this point. Originally signed as a corner outfielder, Perez's professional career began slowly. He batted an underwhelming .226/.312/.359 in stints in the Dominican Summer League. And then he followed that up with a similar showing in the old Northwest League, hitting .233/.325/.379 in 54 games. But Perez emerged a completely different hitter following the COVID layoff as he mashed .282/.359/.456 with 21 doubles, two triples, and 15 homeruns in 98 games with Modesto. Unimpressed by the Perez's newly found offensive prowess, the club sent him back to Low-A for another look. He responded with a similar level of production: .270/.369/.501. Seattle bumped him up to Everett in early August. And he continued to mash. Perez finished the year with an aggregate .288/.398/.523 slash line with 24 doubles, two triples, 27 homeruns, and six stolen bases. Per *Weighted Runs Created Plus*, his overall production topped the league average by an impressive 40%.

Seattle Mariners

Scouting Report: Performing like the prototypical Quad-A masher. Perez's value is solely derived from his ability to hit homeruns, which he started doing in 2021. He works the count well, but the hit tool is never going to progress to average. Seattle's likely to send him back to High-A for at least half of 2023 before bumping him to the true testing ground, Double-A.

Ceiling: 0.5- to 1.0-win player
Risk: Moderate
MLB ETA: 2024

Seattle Mariners

St. Louis Cardinals

Top Prospects

St. Louis Cardinals

1. Jordan Walker, OF

	Hit	Power	SB	Patience	Glove	Overall
	45/55	50/60	55/45	50	40/50	80

Born: 05/22/02   **Age:** 21   **Bats:** R   **Top Production Comp:** Matt Holliday
Height: 6-5   **Weight:** 220   **Throws:** R

Season	Team	Age	Level	PA	1B	2B	3B	HR	SB	CS	BB%	K%	AVG	OBP	SLG	ISO
2021	STL	19	A	122	19	11	1	6	1	0	14.75%	17.21%	0.374	0.475	0.687	0.313
2021	STL	19	A+	244	41	14	3	8	13	2	6.15%	27.05%	0.292	0.344	0.487	0.195
2022	STL	20	AA	536	88	31	3	19	22	5	10.82%	21.64%	0.306	0.388	0.510	0.204

Background: Just three years removed from the 2020 draft, and it's already apparent that the first round is pockmarked with tons of disappointment and stalled development. Spencer Torkelson, the #1 overall pick that year, looked dreadful during his debut in Detroit last season. Miami's Max Meyer underwent Tommy John surgery. Asa Lacy, the fourth overall selection, lost all feel for the strike zone. Austin Martin's already been traded and has overwhelmed in Double-A. Austin Hendrick swings and missed too frequently. Patrick Bailey's hit tool has regressed. Ed Howard, Carson Tucker, and Aaron Sabato haven't hit – at all. But the Cardinals do what they seemingly always do – they didn't miss. Equipped with the 21st overall pick that year, the front office opted to take prep third baseman Jordan Walker. A product of Decatur High School, Walker, according to most reports, had the skillset in place but there were questions about his actual hit tool. A year later, once he debuted with St. Louis's Low-A affiliate, Walker answered every single question *and* established himself as one of the game's preeminent prospects. The 6-foot-5, 220-pounder, who split time between third base and the outfield, mashed .317/.388/.548 with 25 doubles, four triples, 14 homeruns, and 14 stolen bases in only 82 games two years ago between Palm Beach and Peoria. Last season the organization sent him up to the minors' most challenging level – Double-A – and Walker didn't miss a beat. Appearing in 119 games with Springfield, the budding middle-of-the-lineup thumper bashed .306/.388/.510 with 31 doubles, three triples, 19 homeruns, and 22 stolen bases (in 27 total attempts). Per *Weighted Runs Created Plus*, his overall production topped the league average mark by 28%. Walker spent the fall with the Salt River Rafters, hitting .286/.367/.558 with 11 extra-base knocks in 21 games.

Snippet from The 2022 Prospect Digest Handbook: The Cardinals' young infielder showed an incredible feel for the strike zone and strong contact skills during his abbreviated stint in Low-A at the beginning of the year. His k-rate through his first 33 games in High-A was a reasonable 24.5%. Over his final 22 contests he whiffed 31% of the time. He either (A) tired down the stretch or (B) the league figured him out. If it's the latter, I'm betting on Walker making the necessary adjustments.

Scouting Report: Consider the following:

> Since 2006, only six 20-year-old hitters posted a wRC+ total between 123 and 133 in any Double-A league (min. 350 PA): Billy Butler, Luis Urias, Nomar Mazara, Jake Bauers, Orlando Arcia, and – of course – Jordan Walker.

While Walker's defense at third base continues to improve, it's still below-average. In his limited time in the outfield last season, though, he showed Gold Glove caliber potential. Speed, power, hitting for average, defense. Walker ticks off every important checkbox on either side of the ball. The 6-foot-5, 220-pound burgeoning star hasn't full tapped into his plus-power potential, but it's coming – and quickly. Really, really good-looking swing, Walker shows an innate ability to (A) adjust mid-pitch to offspeed offerings, (B) take the pitch the other way, and (C) absolutely destroy mistakes. His numbers are a little inflated by Springfield's home ballpark, but he still mashed on the road (.283/.370/.481). Walker is a prototypical Cardinals-type player, and he's poised to step in for Paul Goldschmidt when his bat finally slows. There's the potential to become a perennial .300/.370/.550 slugger, adding 30 doubles, 35 homer, and 20 stolen bases. He's on his way to being Matt Holliday 2.0.

Ceiling: 6.5-win player
Risk: Moderate
MLB ETA: 2023

2. Tink Hence, RHP

	FB	SL	CH	Command	Overall
	65	70	70	60	60

Born: 08/06/02   **Age:** 20   **Bats:** R   **Top Production Comp:** Pedro Martinez
Height: 6-1   **Weight:** 175   **Throws:** R

Season	Team	Age	Level	IP	TBF	K/9	K%	BB/9	BB%	K-BB%	ERA	FIP	xFIP	Pit/Bat
2022	STL	19	A	52.1	195	13.93	41.54%	2.58	7.69%	33.85%	1.38	1.59	1.94	4.15

Background: It's undeniable that the organization hit a mammoth homerun with their 2020 draft just by selecting Jordan Walker in the opening round. But their draft class moved into a different stratosphere with the emergence of wiry right-hander Tink Hence (and that doesn't account for Masyn Winn either). Hence, who was taken 42 picks after Walker, turned in an intriguing, albeit short, debut in the Complex League that summer – he posted a 14-to-3 strikeout-to-walk ratio in only eight innings pitched. Then the Cardinals did the prudent thing. They unleashed the right-handed version of Godzilla onto the unsuspecting hitters in Low-A. Limited to just turning the opposition's lineup less than two times per game, the 6-foot-1, 175-pound right-hander looked like the second coming of Pedro Martinez as he tallied a sparkling 81-to-15 strikeout-to-walk ratio in only 52.1 innings of work. For those counting at

St. Louis Cardinals

home, he averaged 13.9 strikeouts and just 2.6 walks per nine innings. Hence finished the year with a 1.38 ERA, 1.59 FIP, and a laughably impossible 1.94 xFIP. He made nine additional appearances working out of the Salt River Rafters' bullpen in the Arizona Fall League as well, fanning nine and walking a quartet. He allowed just four hits and two earned runs during that time frame.

Snippet from The 2022 Prospect Digest Handbook: He's skinny and needs to pack on some serious poundage, but he's shown an intriguing mix prior to his debut. Very, very loose arm.

Scouting Report: Consider the following:

> Since 2006, there have been 333 instances in which a 19-year-old tossed at least 50 innings in the any Low-A league. Tink Hence's strikeout percentage, 41.5%, is the highest over the past 17 seasons. Subsequently, his strikeout-to-walk percentage, 33.9%, also is the highest as well – by a *wide* margin.

The argument could be made that Hence is the best pitching prospect in baseball, not Miami's Eury Perez nor Philadelphia's Andrew Painter nor Baltimore's Grayson Rodriguez nor Cleveland's Daniel Espino. *Electric* arsenal, it's the type that doesn't come along very often. And I don't think its sacrilege to say that it could be generational. Explosive, late-life mid- to upper-90s fastball that was sitting in 94- to 97-mph range and touching 98 mph against his midseason start against the Bradenton Marauders. His breaking ball, often called a curveball, is actually a slider (the backstop signals with three fingers) is so wickedly devastating. It's hard with unfair tilt and depth. And his changeup is Bugs Bunny-esque, showing tremendous velocity separation (about 12 mph difference) with arm-side fade. The sky's – literally – the limit for the former second rounder. And for the sake of baseball and baseball fans everywhere, I hope that Hence can avoid the vaunted injury nexus because he's going to special with the chance to be generational. You don't have to squint too hard to see flashes of a young Pedro Martinez. It's doubtful he transcends the game the way Martinez did, but – man – if there's any young pitcher that *could* do it, well, Hence would be my pick.

Ceiling: 5.5-win player
Risk: Moderate to High
MLB ETA: 2024

3. Masyn Winn, SS

Hit	Power	SB	Patience	Glove	Overall
40/50	35/40	60	55	60	55

Born: 03/21/02	Age: 21	Bats: R	Top Production Comp:
Height: 5-11	Weight: 180	Throws: R	

Season	Team	Age	Level	PA	1B	2B	3B	HR	SB	CS	BB%	K%	AVG	OBP	SLG	ISO
2021	STL	19	A	284	41	15	3	3	16	2	14.08%	21.13%	0.262	0.370	0.388	0.127
2021	STL	19	A+	154	23	4	2	2	16	3	3.90%	25.97%	0.209	0.240	0.304	0.095

Background: Stop me if you've heard this one before: Winn was part of the club's vaunted – and potentially historic – 2020 draft class. A product of Kingwood High School, St. Louis selected the 5-foot-11, 180-pound dynamo in the second round, 54th overall, and handed him a hefty $2.1million deal. Winn began his professional career with Palm Beach two years ago, hitting a respectable .262/.370/.388 through 61 games, and then spent the remainder of the season – mostly struggling – with Peoria. Unsurprisingly, the former Bonus Baby found his way back to High-A to begin the 2022 campaign. This time, though, the results were incredible. Winn mashed the opposition to the tune of .349/.404/.566 through 33 games and looked like a legitimate top prospect in his extended stint at the most challenging minor league level – Double-A. He finished his second full season with an aggregate .283/.364/.468 slash line with 36 doubles, eight triples, 12 homeruns, and 43 stolen bases (in only 48 attempts). Per *Weighted Runs Created Plus*, his overall production topped the league average mark by 17%. Winn was named to the 2022 Futures Game as well.

Snippet from The 2022 Prospect Digest Handbook: A lot of Winn's value is tied up into two different facets: (1) his patient approach at the plate and (2) his plus speed on the base paths. He's never going to win a gold glove, but he should have no problem manning the position. Winn also flashed an upper-90s heater as an amateur, though he tossed just one inning as pro last year.

Scouting Report: Consider the following:

> Since 2006, only two 20-year-old hitters met the following criteria in any Double-A league (min. 350 PA): 95 to 105 wRC+, a walk rate north of 10%, and a strikeout rate between 20% and 23%. Those two hitters: Wil Myers and Masyn Winn.

Winn opened a lot of eyes and garnered even more social media attention when he unfurled a 100 mph throw from shortstop during the Futures Game last summer. But as noted in the 2022 Prospect Digest Handbook, that's nothing new for the former two-way prep star. The real progress, though, was made at the dish. The offensive sparkplug developed more pop leading to a career high in extra-base hits while maintaining strong patience at the plate and consistent contact rates. Plus speed, above-average bat speed, improving hit tool, and a nose for

St. Louis Cardinals

first base. Throw in Gold Glove caliber defense and Winn has the makings of a valuable big league infielder. In terms of big league ceiling, think something along the lines of .260/.340/.415.

Ceiling: 3.5-win player
Risk: Moderate
MLB ETA: 2023/2024

4. Alec Burleson, LF/RF

Hit	Power	SB	Patience	Glove	Overall
50	55	35	50	50	50

Born: 11/25/98 **Age:** 24 **Bats:** L **Top Production Comp:** Stephen Piscotty
Height: 6-2 **Weight:** 212 **Throws:** L

Season	Team	Age	Level	PA	1B	2B	3B	HR	SB	CS	BB%	K%	AVG	OBP	SLG	ISO
2021	STL	22	A+	49	7	1	0	4	1	0	12.24%	30.61%	0.286	0.367	0.595	0.310
2021	STL	22	AA	282	51	10	0	14	2	0	6.74%	20.92%	0.288	0.333	0.488	0.200
2021	STL	22	AAA	172	25	7	0	4	0	1	9.88%	15.70%	0.234	0.310	0.357	0.123
2022	STL	23	AAA	470	97	25	1	20	4	0	6.17%	14.26%	0.331	0.372	0.532	0.201

Background: A part of what's quickly becoming one of the franchise's best draft classes in recent memory – and, perhaps, in their entire history. St. Louis selected the East Carolina University slugger in the second round three years ago, 70th overall, after a stellar sophomore and junior campaigns. Burleson's collegiate career began slowly as he batted a lowly, power-deficient .252/.325/.282 in 49 games with the Pirates. But after shredding the Cal Ripken Collegiate Baseball League competition that summer (.383/.444/.776), Burleson returned to school with a vengeance as he mashed .370/.399/.573. And he continued to slaughter the opposition during his COVID-abbreviated 2020 season too – .375/.440/.547. The former two-way star showed no signs of slowing at the plate as he moved into the professional ranks as well, hitting an aggregate .270/.329/.454 between stops in High-A, Double-A, and Triple-A in 2021. Last season he raised the bar even further during his time with Memphis, slugging .331/.372/.532 with 25 doubles, one triple, 20 homeruns, and four stolen bases. His overall production, per *Weighted Runs Created Plus*, topped the league average mark by 37%. Burleson, barely just two years removed from college, cracked the Cardinals' lineup for 16 games as well, hitting .188/.264/.271 with one double and one homerun.

Snippet from The 2022 Prospect Digest Handbook: Burleson is a typical Cardinals draft pick: he's going to pop up in the big leagues, without much fanfare, and hit .270/.335/.450 in 400 plate appearances a season for eight years.

Scouting Report: Consider the following:

> Since 2006, only six 23-year-old hitters posted a 132 to 142 wRC+ with a sub-17% strikeout rate in any Triple-A league (min. 350 PA): Chris Carter, Alberto Callaspo, Corban Joseph, L.J. Hoes, Devin Mesoraco, and Alec Burleson.

At some point Burleson has to stumble, at least once – right? Within two years he went from starring at East Carolina to briefly starting for one of the best run organizations in baseball. He's 228 games into his minor league career and he owns a .300/.350/.492 slash line with above-average power, a 55-grade hit tool, and no discernible platoon splits. Throw in average defense at either corner outfield position and Burleson has the makings of a league average starter, maybe more if he doesn't stop hitting. Reasonable baseline: .270/.335/.450.

Ceiling: 2.5- to 3.0-win player
Risk: Low to Moderate
MLB ETA: Debuted in 2022

5. Matthew Liberatore, LHP

FB	CB	SL	CH	Command	Overall
55	55	50	50	55	50

Born: 11/06/99 **Age:** 23 **Bats:** L **Top Production Comp:** Danny Duffy
Height: 6-4 **Weight:** 200 **Throws:** L

Season	Team	Age	Level	IP	TBF	K/9	K%	BB/9	BB%	K-BB%	ERA	FIP	xFIP	Pit/Bat
2021	STL	21	AAA	124.2	520	8.88	23.65%	2.38	6.35%	17.31%	4.04	4.26	4.15	3.66
2022	STL	22	AAA	115.0	495	9.08	23.43%	3.21	8.28%	15.15%	5.17	4.63	4.27	3.88

Background: It's generally bad for business to get involved with the Rays on any type of transaction because, well, they'll probably pull the wool over your eyes and you'll have no idea how they evaluated your players better than you did. But the Cardinals, who have a long track record of successful player evaluation, threw caution to the wind in early January 2002 and agreed on a four-player, two-draft pick deal with the AL East contending club. The specifics of the swap: Tampa Bay acquired outfielder Randy Arozarena, declining infielder / outfielder Jose Martinez, and a supplemental first round pick for Matthew Liberatore, minor league backstop Edgardo Rodriguez, and a supplemental second round selection. The Rays added Arizona State University infielder Alika Williams with their newly acquired supplemental pick and the Cardinals, well, the used their selection on Tink Hence, who's developing into one of the game's best

St. Louis Cardinals

prospects. So while Liberatore hasn't established himself as a viable big league option – yet – the deal still appears to be a win-win. Acquired with the 16th overall pick in 2018, Liberatore spent the past two seasons working out of the Memphis Redbirds' rotation. He's posted a 239-to-74 strikeout-to-walk ratio over 239.2 innings of work to go along with an aggregate 4.58 ERA.

Snippet from The 2020 Prospect Digest Handbook: He's not destined to become an upper echelon pitcher, but should settle in for St. Louis as a very strong mid-rotation arm.

Scouting Report: Consider the following:

> Since 2006, only six 22-year-old hurlers posted a strikeout percentage between 22.5% to 24.5% in any Triple-A league (min. 100 IP): Lucas Giolito, Gio Gonzalez, Zac Gallen, Mike Foltynewicz, Brad Hand, and – of course – former Tampa Bay Ray Matthew Liberatore. Giolito, Gonzalez, and Gallen are / were above-average starting pitchers at the game's pinnacle level. Foltynewicz was a league average arm – briefly – with one All-Star season on his resume. Hand is a three-time All-Star closer.

Liberatore was throwing significantly harder than 2021. Instead of sitting 92- to 94-mph, the big, thick-bodied southpaw was consistently sitting 94- to 95-mph and touching 96 mph on occasion. The problem, of course, is that the velocity has moved into plus territory, but it's more hittable than you'd expect, downgrading it into above-average range. His changeup is a solid-average offering but doesn't show a whole lot of velocity separation, ranging about 7- to 8-mph slower. And it appears that he slows down when he's throwing it as well. His slider didn't look as sharp as previous seasons. And his curveball, which he doesn't throw as often as he should, is his best offspeed weapon. It's hard to believe because it feels like he's been around forever, but Liberatore is only entering his age-23 season and has logged two full years in Triple-A. He's ready for the big leagues now and could grab the club's #5 gig. Danny Duffy's made over $70 million in his career as – mostly – a fringy league average arm. Liberatore's going to hover in the same neighborhood. He's likely going to average around 8 K/9 and 3.5 BB/9.

Ceiling: 2.5- to 3.0-win player
Risk: Low to Moderate
MLB ETA: Debuted in 2022

6. Leonardo Bernal, C

Hit	Power	SB	Patience	Glove	Overall
40/50	55/60	30	50	50	55

Born: 02/13/04	Age: 19	Bats: B	Top Production Comp: N/A
Height: 6-0	Weight: 200	Throws: R	

Season	Team	Age	Level	PA	1B	2B	3B	HR	SB	CS	BB%	K%	AVG	OBP	SLG	ISO
2021	STL	17	DSL	178	18	9	1	5	3	1	9.55%	15.73%	0.209	0.298	0.373	0.165
2022	STL	18	A	171	24	8	1	7	1	1	7.02%	18.71%	0.256	0.316	0.455	0.199

Background: The Cardinals are always on the hunt for the next big catching prospect – or at least that's how it *seems*. But they have a knack for developing backstops that make it to the big leagues. Carson Kelly, Andrew Knizner, and Ivan Herrera all immediately come to mind. And the latest promising youngster the club unearthed – Leonardo Bernal. Signed out of Panama for $680,000 two years ago, Bernal looked abysmal during his debut in the Dominican Summer League as he cobbled together a lowly .209/.298/.373 slash line with only 15 extra-base hits in 44 games. Last season, though, the front office took a rather unpredictable route and sent the young, unproven teenage backstop straight up to Low-A. And Bernal flourished in 45 games with Palm Beach. The 6-foot, 200-pound prospect batted a respectable .256/.316/.455 with eight doubles, one triple, seven homeruns, and a stolen base – just for good measure. His overall production, according to *Weighted Runs Created Plus*, topped the league average mark by 17%.

Scouting Report: Consider the following:

> Since 2006, only three 18-year-old hitters met the following criteria in any Low-A league (min. 150 PA): 112 to 122 wRC+ total with a K-rate between 17.5% to 20%. Those three: Justin Upton, Cheslor Cuthbert, and Leonardo Bernal.

The Cardinals clearly know their prospects well. Because there's no other reason why they would have sent a teenager coming off of a *disastrous* debut showing in the Dominican Summer League straight into full season action not expecting him to succeed. And that's *exactly* what the young switch-hitter did. Massive raw power that may translate into 25- to 30-homer territory. Very good bat-to-ball skills. There's enough glove to stick behind the plate, as well. Bernal may be primed for the biggest breakout in 2023. And it wouldn't be shocking to see him become a consensus Top 100 prospect. This will be the most aggressive ranking in the entire 2023 Prospect Digest Handbook.

Ceiling: 3.5-win player
Risk: Moderate to High
MLB ETA: 2024/2025

St. Louis Cardinals

7. Ivan Herrera, C

Hit	Power	SB	Patience	Glove	Overall
45	40/50	35	60	50	50

Born: 06/01/00   **Age:** 23   **Bats:** R   **Top Production Comp:** Tucker Barnhart
Height: 5-11   **Weight:** 220   **Throws:** R

Season	Team	Age	Level	PA	1B	2B	3B	HR	SB	CS	BB%	K%	AVG	OBP	SLG	ISO
2021	STL	21	AA	437	54	13	0	17	2	3	13.73%	21.97%	0.231	0.346	0.408	0.176
2022	STL	22	AAA	278	46	10	1	6	5	1	13.67%	18.71%	0.268	0.374	0.396	0.128

Background: For the first time in nearly two full years the Cardinals will begin a season without future Hall of Famer Yadier Molina behind the dish. The front office moved swiftly following the 2022 season, signing three-time All-Star Willson Contreras to hefty five-year, $87.5 million contract – effectively closing whatever window was opened for Ivan Herrera, the once-thought heir apparent. Signed out of Panama for $200,000 during the summer of 2016, the stocky young backstop immediately established himself on the club's Top 20 Prospect List by slugging .335/.425/.441 during his debut in the foreign rookie league. He continued to mash in his stint in the Gulf Coast League in 2018 and handled the Low-A competition at the beginning of 2019. Herrera's first true stumble at the plate didn't happen until his jaunt in Double-A two years ago as he hit a mediocre, secondary skills-driven .229/.342/.403. Last season, though, the 5-foot-11, 220-pound backstop's bat regressed towards his career norms, hitting .268/.374/.396 with 10 doubles, one triple, six homeruns, and five stolen bases (in six attempts). His overall production with Springfield, according to *Weighted Runs Created Plus*, topped the league average mark by 11%. Herrera also appeared in 11 games with St. Louis as well, hitting .111/.190/.111 in 22 plate appearances.

Snippet from The 2022 Prospect Digest Handbook: After a bit of an adjustment period, Herrera finished the year on a high note, slugging .256/.335/.518 over his final 43 games with Springfield.

Scouting Report: Consider the following:

> Since 2006, only four 22-year-old hitters met the following criteria in a Triple-A season (min. 275 PA): 105 to 115 wRC+, a double-digit walk rate, and a 17% to 20% strikeout percentage. Those four hitters: J.P. Crawford, Brice Turang, Daniel Robertson, and – of course – Ivan Herrera.

A solid defensive catcher throughout his minor league tenure, Herrera will flirt with average power at the dish but he hasn't quite tapped into it fully – or consistently. The Panamanian backstop has a nose for first base, which only increases his value, and he makes consistent contact. The swing is a bit long, which limits the projection to 45-grade territory. There's lower end starting capability here, but there's not a clear path to playing time – at least not for the next five years. In terms of big league ceiling, think .245/.330/.415.

Ceiling: 2.0- to 2.5-win player
Risk: Moderate
MLB ETA: Debuted in 2022

8. Gordon Graceffo, RHP

FB	CB	SL	CH	Command	Overall
60	55	55	50	60	50

Born: 03/17/00   **Age:** 23   **Bats:** R   **Top Production Comp:** Alex Cobb
Height: 6-4   **Weight:** 210   **Throws:** R

Season	Team	Age	Level	IP	TBF	K/9	K%	BB/9	BB%	K-BB%	ERA	FIP	xFIP	Pit/Bat
2021	STL	21	A	26.0	116	12.81	31.90%	3.12	7.76%	24.14%	1.73	2.72	3.02	3.73
2022	STL	22	A+	45.2	165	11.04	33.94%	0.79	2.42%	31.52%	0.99	1.71	2.63	3.95
2022	STL	22	AA	93.2	379	7.98	21.90%	2.31	6.33%	15.57%	3.94	5.07	4.63	3.70

Background: There may teams that consistently find talent later in the draft as well as St. Louis, but there aren't any teams that do it better or more frequently than the Cardinals. And Gordon Graceffo is just another example. A member of the Villanova's rotation for three seasons, Graceffo was particularly dominant between 2020 and 2021 for the Wildcats. He tossed 107.1 innings, recording 98-to-20 strikeout-to-walk ratio while allowing only 14 earned runs. St. Louis selected him in the fifth round two years ago, 151st overall, and handed him a $300,000 bonus to join the organization. He made 11 brief – nearly flawless – appearances with Palm Beach two years ago, posting a 37-to-9 strikeout-to-walk ratio in 26.0 innings of work. And that proved to be harbinger of things to come. Splitting time between Peoria and Springfield, the 6-foot-4, 210-pound right-hander averaged 9.0 K/9 and just 1.8 BB/9 to go along with an aggregate 2.97 ERA.

Scouting Report: Consider the following:

> Since 2006, eleven 22-year-old hurlers posted a 21% to 23% strikeout percentage and a 5.5% to 7.5% walk percentage in any Double-A league (min. 75 IP): Zack Greinke, Brady Singer, Brett Kennedy, Brock Huntzinger, Chase De Jong, Deolis Guerra, Jen-Ho Tseng, Jose Ascanio, Ricardo Sanchez, Wilfredo Boscan, and Gordon Graceffo.

St. Louis Cardinals

Built in a similar fashion as former Cardinal Lance Lynn. Graceffo looks larger than his 6-foot-4, 210-pound listing. Graceffo owns a solid four-pitch mix: his fastball will sit in the 93- to 94-mph range and will touch as high as 98 mph; his slider is above-average with a little bit of late wrinkle that helps it avoid the fat part of the bat; his upper 70s curveball is a big bending, 12-6 breaking ball; and his changeup is very solid. The entirety of Graceffo's arsenal plays up half of a grade due to his pinpoint accuracy. There's league average starting material here, maybe a touch more depending upon his defense because his pitch-to-contact approach.

Ceiling: 2.0-win player
Risk: Moderate
MLB ETA: 2023

9. Jonathan Mejia, SS

Hit	Power	SB	Patience	Glove	Overall
45/55	45/55	40	50	50	50

Born: 04/12/05	Age: 18	Bats: B	Top Production Comp: N/A
Height: 6-0	Weight: 185	Throws: R	

Season	Team	Age	Level	PA	1B	2B	3B	HR	SB	CS	BB%	K%	AVG	OBP	SLG	ISO
2022	STL	17	DSL	208	22	14	3	5	3	2	15.87%	23.08%	0.267	0.418	0.479	0.212

Background: The Cardinals made one of their trademark unexpected big splashes last January when they signed switch-hitting shortstop Jonathan Mejia to a deal in the $2 million range. Unfairly dubbed by some media outlets as the "Next Javier Baez", Mejia settled in nicely against Dominican Summer League competition just months after joining the historic organization. The La Romana, Dominican Republic native slugged a hearty .267/.418/.479 with 14 doubles, three triples, five homeruns, and a trio of stolen bases. The young middle infielder's production, according to *Weighted Runs Created Plus*, topped the league average threshold by 45%. He finished the season with a solid 48-to-33 strikeout-to-walk ratio in 208 trips to the plate.

Scouting Report: Unsurprisingly, at least for a young switch-hitter, Mejia whiffed far more frequently from the left-side than the right-side (36.7% to 19.9%). So his 23% K-rate, which raised at least an eyebrow, isn't nearly as concerning. Mejia shows fluidity and soft hands on the defensive side of the ball and should stay at the infield's most important position as he matures. Good power from the right side with a simple, easy swing that could generate 20 homeruns at full maturity. The swing from the left-side is *clearly* not his normal and looks forced, stiff, and robotic (though he did manage to bat .240/.367/.440 as a lefty).

Ceiling: 2.0-win player
Risk: Moderate
MLB ETA: 2026

10. Cooper Hjerpe, LHP

FB	CB	CH	Command	Overall
50	55	50	55	45

Born: 03/16/01	Age: 22	Bats: L	Top Production Comp: N/A
Height: 6-3	Weight: 200	Throws: L	

Background: A product of Woodland High School – home to borderline Hall of Fame second baseman Dustin Pedroia – Hjerpe committed to Pac-12 conference powerhouse Oregon State University as a sophomore. He continued to live up to those lofty expectations during the remaining two years of his prep career. The lanky left-hander posted an impeccable 0.78 ERA with a whopping 128 strikeouts in only 55.2 innings of work as a junior. And he was even better during his final campaign for the Wolves, tossing four no-hitters with 105 strikeouts in only 44 innings of work. Hjerpe struggled a bit during his COVID-abbreviated freshman campaign at Oregon State, posting a 16-to-7 strikeout-to-walk ratio in six relief outings, spanning 12 innings. The 6-foot-3, 200-pound southpaw had a bit of a coming out party during his sophomore season with the Beavers, averaging 11.5 strikeouts and 3.2 walks per nine innings to go along with a 4.21 ERA in 77.0 innings. Last season Hjerpe continued to progress as a crafty moundsmen: in a career best 18 appearances and 103.1 innings, the California native struck out a nation-leading 161 hitters while averaging 14.0 K/9 – the second best total. St. Louis selected him in the opening round, 22nd overall, and signed him to a deal worth $3,182,200. He did not appear in an affiliated game after joining the Cardinals' organization.

Scouting Report: Per the usual, my pre-draft write-up:

> "*Consider the following:*
>
> *Since 2015, here's the list of Division I pitchers to average at least 13 strikeouts per nine innings in a season (min. 100 IP): Kumar Rocker, Jack Leiter, Logan Gilbert, Ethan Small, Reid Detmers, Andrew Abbott, and – of course – Cooper Hjerpe.*

St. Louis Cardinals

Let's continue:

> *Among the aforementioned group, here's the list of hurlers to walk less than 2.5 BB/9: Logan Gilbert and Cooper Hjerpe.*

Low slot lefty gunslinger. Hjerpe attacks hitters with a low 90s fastball, an above-average, difficult to pick up curveball, and an average fading changeup. Listed generously as 6-foot-2 and 190-pounds, Hjerpe is physically maxed and shouldn't expect to see any sizeable velocity gains in the future. Back of the rotation caliber arm as long as he can take the ball every fifth day.

I had a second round grade on Hjerpe heading into the draft. He's likely going to move quickly through the low levels of the minor leagues.

Ceiling: 1.5-win player
Risk: Moderate
MLB ETA: 2024

11. Michael McGreevy, RHP

	FB	CB	SL	CH	Command	Overall
	55	50	55	50	55	45

Born: 07/08/00	Age: 22	Bats: R	Top Production Comp: N/A
Height: 6-4	Weight: 215	Throws: R	

Season	Team	Age	Level	IP	TBF	K/9	K%	BB/9	BB%	K-BB%	ERA	FIP	xFIP	Pit/Bat
2022	STL	21	A+	45.1	178	8.14	23.03%	0.79	2.25%	20.79%	2.58	2.29	3.37	3.81
2022	STL	21	AA	99.0	414	6.91	18.36%	2.36	6.28%	12.08%	4.64	4.85	4.49	3.95

Background: For the ninth time in club history, the Cardinals selected a UC Santa Barbara product in the midsummer draft two years ago. McGreevy followed in the recent footsteps of Tommy Jew, Matt Valaika, and – of course – St. Louis fan favorite Skip Schumaker. McGreevy took the usual collegiate route to the draft, beginning his career with the Gauchos in relief as a true freshman before transitioning into a full-time starting gig as a sophomore. He left the school with a career 2.33 ERA with 194 strikeouts and 31 walks in 189.1 innings of work. The Cardinals selected the 6-foot-4, 215-pound right-hander opening round, 18th overall, and signed him to a deal worth $2.75 million two years ago. Last season the California-born right-hander made eight starts with Peoria and another 20 with Springfield. He finished the season with a 3.99 ERA while averaging 7.3 strikeouts and just 1.9 walks per nine innings across 144.1 frames.

Snippet from The 2022 Prospect Digest Handbook: He's not overpowering, but gets the most out of his talent and arsenal due to his superb feel for the strike zone. He's a safe, low risk college arm that should move quickly through the minor leagues.

Scouting Report: Consider the following:

> Since 2006, twelve 21-year-old hurlers met the following criteria in a Double-A season (min. 90 IP): 17% to 20% strikeout percentage and a 5.5% to 7.5% walk percentage. Those twelve pitchers: Jair Jurrjens, Vin Mazzaro, Zach McAllister, Adalberto Mejia, Alex White, Casey Kelly, Collin Balester, Ryan Castellani, Spencer Adams, Steve Garrison, and – of course – Michael McGreevy.

A solid four-pitch mix without a true standout or genuine swing-and-miss offering, McGreevy's fastball will work in the 92- to 94- mph range and touch as high as 96 mph on occasion. It's a solid, above-average offering but it doesn't generate a lot of weak contact and / or swings-and-misses. His mid-80s slider is his best offspeed weapon, showing late movement. He'll also mix in an average 12-6 curveball and a firm, diving 87 mph changeup. McGreevy's a pitch-to-contact hurler and his command was better than expected. There's the ceiling of a fourth or fifth starter.

Ceiling: 1.5-win player
Risk: Moderate
MLB ETA: 2023/2024

St. Louis Cardinals

12. Moisés Gómez, RF

Hit	Power	SB	Patience	Glove	Overall
40	60	30	50	50	45

Born: 08/27/98	Age: 24	Bats: R	Top Production Comp: N/A
Height: 5-11	Weight: 200	Throws: R	

Season	Team	Age	Level	PA	1B	2B	3B	HR	SB	CS	BB%	K%	AVG	OBP	SLG	ISO
2021	TBR	22	AA	301	25	13	0	8	5	3	8.97%	38.21%	0.171	0.256	0.309	0.138
2022	STL	23	AA	257	32	17	0	23	7	3	10.51%	35.02%	0.321	0.401	0.705	0.384
2022	STL	23	AAA	244	32	8	2	16	3	0	10.25%	34.43%	0.266	0.340	0.541	0.275

Background: There was a point very early in his professional career that Gómez looked like perennial Top 100 prospect in the Rays' farm system. He batted .275/.328/.398 as an 18-year-old in 53 games with the club's Appalachian League team. And he really came into his own the following season, mashing .280/.328/.503 with 34 doubles, seven triples, 19 homeruns, and four stolen bases in 122 games in the old Midwest League. But things started to unravel for the Venezuelan outfielder starting in 2019. He cobbled together a lowly .220/.297/.402 slash line in High-A. And things only got worse as moved into Double-A in 2021 (.171/.256/.309). So Tampa Bay decided to cut their losses. He's was coming off of miserable showings in back-to-back seasons. He was going to be 23 and he, simply, looked to be of no use. But the Cardinals, wearing their blue and red cape, swooped in and signed Gomez to a deal before the 2022 season. And just like that, with the team's Midas Touch, he rediscovered his stroke and put together a career season. He mashed an aggregate .294/.371/.624 with 25 doubles, two triples, and 39 homeruns, more than double his previous career high.

Scouting Report: Consider the following:

> Since 2006, only two 23-year-old sluggers posted a wRC+ between 123 and 133 with a strikeout rate north of 32% in any Triple-A league (min. 240 PA): Bobby Bradley and Moisés Gómez.

St. Louis was able to unlock Gómez's past success by, simply, focusing on hitting line drives. He consistently put together line drive rates in the 25% range during his two finest seasons in Tampa Bay. But when he began to struggle that total dropped to 15% and then crept up to 21% in Double-A. Last season he was peppering the ball with a line drive rate north of 30%. The quality of contact simply got better. Plus power. Average glove in the outfield. The only question that remains is whether he can make enough contact at the big league level. St. Louis added him to their 40-man roster this offseason. He could put together a .240/.310/.460 line given enough time.

Ceiling: 1.5-win player
Risk: Moderate
MLB ETA: 2023

13. Brycen Mautz, LHP

FB	CB	CH	Command	Overall
50	55	50	55	45

Born: 07/17/01	Age: 21	Bats: L	Top Production Comp: N/A
Height: 6-3	Weight: 190	Throws: L	

Background: Coming from a family of athletes, Mautz's parents competed at the University of Wisconsin. His father, Alex, was involved in Track & Field. And his mother, Jaime, played volleyball. The left-hander bucked the family lineage and attended the University of San Diego – where his career got off to a less than stellar start. Working primarily as a reliever during the COVID-interrupted 2020 season, the then-freshman tossed 10.0 innings, recording eight strikeouts and five free passes. His split his sophomore season between the club's rotation and bullpen, making five starts and another eight relief appearances as he posted a mediocre 26-to-14 strikeout-to-walk ratio in 27.0 innings of work. Mautz spent the ensuing summer working out of the Waterloo Bucks' bullpen where he – once again – struggled with his command as he walked 15 hitters in 30.1 innings of work. Last season, though, the 6-foot-3, 190-pound southpaw was able to hone in on the strike zone for the first time in his collegiate career. Working primarily as a starter for the first time, Mautz averaged an impressive 12.8 strikeouts and just 2.2 walks per nine innings to go along with 10-2 win-loss record and a 3.87 ERA. St. Louis selected him in the second round, 59th overall, and signed him to a deal worth $1.1 million, slightly below the recommended slot of $1,246,200.

Scouting Report: Consider the following:

> Since 2015, only eight Division I arms averaged at least 12.5 whiffs and between 2.0 and 2.4 walks per nine innings in a season (min. 75 IP): Logan Gilbert, Gavin Williams, Justin Campbell, Cooper Hjerpe, Parker Messick, Ky Busch, Drew Thorpe, and Brycen Mautz.

Production befitting of an early round draft pick, however short the track record may actually be. Mautz is a three-quarter slot slinger from the left-side. His fastball generally sits in the 92 mph range and will occasionally touch 93 with some added effort. And despite an average grade,

St. Louis Cardinals

it's solid due to deception and run created from his arm slot. He'll complement it with a solid above-average slider, and rare changeup. Despite the borderline elite production, he doesn't have traditional swing-and-miss stuff. I had a late second / early third round grade on the southpaw.

Ceiling: 1.5-win player
Risk: Moderate
MLB ETA: 2024

14. Joshua Baez, CF

Hit	Power	SB	Patience	Glove	Overall
35/40	50/60	50	50	50	45

Born: 06/28/03	Age: 20	Bats: R	Top Production Comp: Joshua Mears
Height: 6-4	Weight: 220	Throws: R	

Season	Team	Age	Level	PA	1B	2B	3B	HR	SB	CS	BB%	K%	AVG	OBP	SLG	ISO
2021	STL	18	CPX	95	6	3	1	2	5	0	14.74%	29.47%	0.158	0.305	0.303	0.145
2022	STL	19	A	79	9	5	1	3	4	3	13.92%	37.97%	0.286	0.418	0.540	0.254
2022	STL	19	CPX	43	5	3	0	1	6	1	11.63%	32.56%	0.237	0.326	0.395	0.158

Background: The Cardinals used just one of their first seven picks on a prep prospect two years ago, selecting Dexter School outfielder Joshua Baez in the second round. Baez, who received nearly the same bonus as the club's first round pick, looked abysmal during his abbreviated stint in the Complex League that summer as he hit .158/.305/.303 with a bloated strikeout rate (29.5%). Baez opened up last season in Low-A, but after just one game and one plate appearance the toolsy outfielder hit the disabled list with a wrist injury, knocking him out of commission for nearly 10 weeks. The Massachusetts-born outfielder spent a couple weeks in the Complex League rehabbing before rejoining Palm Beach in mid-August. He hit a solid .286/.418/.540 with five doubles, one triple, three homeruns, and four stolen bases in only 20 games with the club's Low-A affiliate.

Snippet from The 2022 Prospect Digest Handbook: The tools are there to be an impact player. But he's raw. And he needs a lot of work to get there. It's a very atypical Cardinals type draft pick. And I wouldn't be surprised if he ends up back on the mound at some point to increase his chances at the big leagues.

Scouting Report: Just for fun, here's his production line prorated for a full 162-game season: 41 doubles, eight triples, 24 homeruns, and 32 stolen bases. It didn't take long for Baez to put his complete set of skills on full display, but that tantalizing potential continues to be plagued by a gargantuan – potentially career killing – red flag: his swing-and-miss issues. Last season, albeit in an incredibly short sample size, Baez whiffed 30 times in only 79 plate appearances, or 38% of the time. And he's sporting a career 33.2% mark through 55 games. There are a lot of similarities here to San Diego's Joshua Mears. Be careful.

Ceiling: 1.5-win player
Risk: High
MLB ETA: 2025

15. Pete Hansen, LHP

FB	CB	SL	CH	Command	Overall
45	55	55	50	55	40

Born: 07/28/00	Age: 22	Bats: R	Top Production Comp: N/A
Height: 6-2	Weight: 205	Throws: L	

Background: A product of Oak Ridge High School, home to former Expos outfielder F.P. Santangelo and knuckleballer Charlie Zink, Hansen left the California-based school crowned as the *Perfect Game World Series* Most Valuable Pitcher. Hansen, a 6-foot-2, 205-pound southpaw, sparkled during his first season at the University of Texas, throwing 17.0 innings of nearly perfect baseball before COVID-prematurely ended the year. He struck out 18 and walked only a pair to go along with perfect 0.00 ERA. *Collegiate Baseball Newspaper* named him as a Freshman All-American. Unsurprisingly, the Longhorn coaching staff moved the talented lefty into a full-time starting gig for the 2021 season. And he picked up right where he left off, throwing 91.0 innings with a 1.88 ERA while averaging 7.9 whiffs and just 2.3 walks per nine innings. The Texas-born hurler struggled during his stint in the Cape Cod League that summer, finishing his four-game cameo with Brewster with a 6.32 ERA. Last season, Hansen set career bests in K-rate (10.0 BB/9) and BB-rate (1.6 BB/9). St. Louis selected him in the third round, 97th overall, and signed him to a deal worth $629,800.

Scouting Report: Consider the following:

> Between 2017 and 2022, only two Big-12 pitchers averaged between 9 K/9 and 11/9 with a BB-rate below 2.0 in a season (min. 100 IP): Jake Bennett, who was taken by the Nationals in the second round last July, and Pete Hansen.

St. Louis Cardinals

Not a lot of mustard on the ol' heater, Hansen's fastball operates in the 87- to 89-mph range – which is practically in Jamie Moyer territory in today's high octane game. Hansen survives, often dominating, with guile and changing speeds. Above-average curveball and slider – the latter being the better option. And his 79- to 81-mph changeup is average. There's not a lot of margin for error, but Hansen's the type of prospect to get everything and then some out of his talent. He could move quickly. High floor / low ceiling.

Ceiling: 1.0-win player
Risk: Low to Moderate
MLB ETA: 2023/2024

16. Jimmy Crooks, C

Hit	Power	SB	Patience	Glove	Overall
40	50	30	50	55	40

Born: 07/19/01	Age: 21	Bats: L	Top Production Comp: N/A
Height: 6-1	Weight: 210	Throws: R	

Season	Team	Age	Level	PA	1B	2B	3B	HR	SB	CS	BB%	K%	AVG	OBP	SLG	ISO
2022	STL	20	A	96	13	3	2	3	0	0	12.50%	22.92%	0.266	0.396	0.468	0.203

Background: A decorated ballplayer coming out of Trinity High School, Crooks was a key cog in the school's run to the 2019 Connie Mack World Series title that year by batting .423 with six dingers and 30 runs driven in. The lefty-swinging backstop spent a season at McLennan Community College in 2020, slugging .319/.462/.458 with four doubles, three triples, and a pair of stolen bases. He would transfer to the University of Oklahoma following the season and immediately stepped into a starting gig for the Sooners. And Crooks slugged an impressive .287/.385/.502 with 18 doubles, 10 homeruns, and a trio of stolen bases in 54 games for the Big-12 powerhouse. Last season the Texas-born backstop raised the bar even further, mashing .305/.430/.506 with 21 doubles, one triple, nine homeruns, and 10 stolen bases. St. Louis drafted him in the fourth round, 127th overall, and signed him to a deal worth $470,300. He appeared in 23 games in Palm Beach, hitting .266/.396/.468 with three doubles, two triples, and three homeruns.

Scouting Report: A grinder. And it's never a good thing to bet against a grinder. But Crooks swing / hit tool may never creep into 45-grade territory. It's long and forcing him to get under low pitches. He can turn on elevated fastballs and give them a jolt. Average power. Good glove behind the dish. Crooks is tracking like a solid backup that will run into the occasional fastball.

Ceiling: 1.0-win player
Risk: Moderate
MLB ETA: Debuted in 2022

17. Dionys Rodriguez, RHP

FB	SL	CH	Command	Overall
60	55	50	50	40

Born: 09/03/00	Age: 22	Bats: L	Top Production Comp: N/A
Height: 6-0	Weight: 188	Throws: R	

Season	Team	Age	Level	IP	TBF	K/9	K%	BB/9	BB%	K-BB%	ERA	FIP	xFIP	Pit/Bat
2021	STL	20	A	69.2	288	11.37	30.56%	2.84	7.64%	22.92%	3.36	3.37	3.81	4.02
2022	STL	21	A+	121.2	535	8.80	22.24%	3.92	9.91%	12.34%	4.59	4.53	5.04	3.73

Background: Signed out of Pedro Brand, Dominican Republic during the summer of 2018. Rodriguez, a wiry 6-foot, 188-pound righty, went from a disappointing reliever with two stints in the foreign rookie league to emerging as a legitimate prospect following the COVID break. The young Dominican fire-baller made 12 starts and 10 relief appearances with Palm Beach two years ago, averaging an impressive 11.4 strikeouts and just 2.8 walks per nine innings to go along with a 3.36 ERA. Last season, Rodriguez continued his upward ascension on the prospect lists with another strong showing in High-A. Making a career high 27 appearances, only two coming via the bullpen, he tallied a 119-to-53 strikeout-to-walk ratio in 121.2 innings. He finished the year with a 4.59 ERA, a 4.53 FIP, and a 5.04 xFIP.

Snippet from The 2022 Prospect Digest Handbook: Rodriguez, who can really spin it, could jump up pretty quickly if he can repeat his performance in High-A in 2022. He's a potential helium guy.

Scouting Report: So the helium that looked to be forming in Rodriguez's balloon never quite took off – though he did look solid as a 21-year-old squaring off against the High-A competition. Rodriguez's heater moved from the low- to mid-90s two years ago to the mid-to upper-90s last season, touching as high as 97 mph on several occasions. His slider remains an above-average weapon. And his changeup flashed slightly above-average a few times during a start I scouted. Admittedly, Rodriguez is a long shot to crack a big league team's rotation, but there could be some use for him as a middle inning relief specialist. Consider the following:

> Since 2006, seven 21-year-old hurlers posted a 21% to 23% strikeout percentage with a 9% to 11% walk percentage in any High-A league (min. 100 IP): Zach Britton, Brett Kennedy, Kodi Medeiros, Luis Lugo, Chorye Spoone, Greg Harris, and Dionys Rodriguez.

St. Louis Cardinals

Ceiling: 1.0-win player
Risk: Moderate
MLB ETA: 2024

18. Alec Willis, RHP

	FB	CB	CH	Command	Overall
	N/A	N/A	N/A	N/A	N/A

Born: 03/30/03	Age: 20	Bats: R	Top Production Comp: N/A
Height: 6-5	Weight: 220	Throws: R	

Background: The Cardinals took the calculated, conservative path at the start of the 2021 draft, selecting UC Santa Barbara right-hander Michael McGreevy in the first round and signed him to a well-below slot deal saving the club nearly $750,000. That money, along with more, went to signing outfielder Joshua Baez. But the club saved cash with signings of Ryan Holgate, Austin Love, Zane Mills, Gordon Graceffo, Alfredo Ruiz, Mike Antico, Trent Baker, and Osvaldo Tovalin. And all that bonus money went – largely – to Mr. Alec Willis, a prep right-hander out of Regis Jesuit High School. A sturdy 6-foot-5, 220-pound hurler, Willis – famously or infamously – underwent ulnar nerve decompression surgery and his velocity popped form the mid-80s to the mid-90s. St. Louis handed Willis a massive $1 million bonus, nearly $800,000 above the recommended value. The former high school star made one appearance in the Complex League in 2021 and missed the opening couple of months due to an injury last season. Once he was back to full health he logged 11.1 innings with the team's Complex League affiliate, recording 16 punch outs and just two free passes to go along with a 1.59 ERA.

Scouting Report: Next to nothing to go off of, both in terms of data *and* available game tape. Willis showed an above-average fastball / curveball combo in high school. He also reportedly mixed in an average changeup as well. Willis, despite the loss of development time, showed a strong feel for the strike zone. He'll be one of the more intriguing prospects in the system to watch heading into 2023.

Ceiling: Too Soon to Tell
Risk: Too Soon to Tell
MLB ETA: N/A

19. Austin Love, RHP

	FB	SL	CH	Command	Overall
	55	55	45	50	40

Born: 01/26/99	Age: 24	Bats: R	Top Production Comp: N/A
Height: 6-3	Weight: 232	Throws: R	

Season	Team	Age	Level	IP	TBF	K/9	K%	BB/9	BB%	K-BB%	ERA	FIP	xFIP	Pit/Bat
2022	STL	23	A+	125.2	564	10.81	26.77%	3.72	9.22%	17.55%	5.73	4.04	3.79	3.91

Background: The Cardinals have made a semi-regular habit by picking a University of North Carolina product over the past couple of seasons, most notably selecting underrated right-hander Zac Gallen in the third round in 2016. The front office went back to the Tar Heel well two years ago and selected right-hander Austin Love in the third round, 90th overall. A full-time reliever at the beginning of his collegiate career, Love shined as starter during his final season in the ACC as he averaged 11.4 strikeouts and just 2.8 walks per nine innings across 16 starts and one relief appearance. Love made a quick tour through the Cardinals' low level affiliates after joining the organization and was sent directly up to High-A to begin 2022. He would make 25 starts and one relief appearance with Peoria, throwing 125.2 innings while recording 151 punch outs and handing out 52 free passes. He compiled a 5.73 ERA, a 4.04 FIP, and a 3.79 xFIP.

Snippet from The 2022 Prospect Digest Handbook: He's lacking a true swing-and-miss weapon, so he's likely headed for a relief role.

Scouting Report: Consider the following:

> Since 2006, six 23-year-old hurlers posted a 26% to 28% strikeout percentage with an 8% to 10% walk percentage in any High-A League (min. 100 IP): Jordan Stephens, Tim Crabbe, Jackson Wolf, Jimmy Joyce, Mitch Spence, and Austin Love.

Extreme short arm. Love seems to tap the ball on his back leg as he's moving toward the plate. Primarily a two-pitch pitcher, Love's heater seemed to have a little extra life last season than the previous year. And, likewise, his slider appeared to have a little bit of an extra bite as well. He'll also mix in a rare – very *rare* – changeup. Love always seemed destined for some type of relief role and – despite the gaudy strikeout numbers in 2022 – he's done nothing to dispel that, particularly as he continues to push his changeup to the back burner.

Ceiling: 0.5- to 1.0-win player
Risk: Moderate
MLB ETA: 2023/2024

St. Louis Cardinals

20. Inohan Paniagua, RHP

	FB	CB	CH	Command	Overall
	50	55	45/55	50	40

Born: 02/06/00	Age: 23	Bats: R	Top Production Comp: N/A
Height: 6-1	Weight: 148	Throws: R	

Season	Team	Age	Level	IP	TBF	K/9	K%	BB/9	BB%	K-BB%	ERA	FIP	xFIP	Pit/Bat
2021	STL	21	A	46.1	197	12.04	31.47%	3.69	9.64%	21.83%	3.88	3.65	3.64	3.78
2022	STL	22	A+	38.2	165	8.84	23.03%	3.72	9.70%	13.33%	4.42	5.60	4.78	3.78
2022	STL	22	A	99.0	398	9.73	26.88%	2.09	5.78%	21.11%	2.18	3.01	3.62	3.67

Background: Hailing from Bonao, Dominican Republic, Paniagua joined the St. Louis organization on a low six-figure deal in mid-December 2017. The 6-foot-1, 148-pound right-hander debuted with the club's foreign rookie league the following summer, throwing 57.1 innings with 51 strikeouts and 16 free passes to go along with a 3.77 ERA. The Cardinals brass bumped the wispy Dominican up to the Gulf Coast League and eventually onto State College – briefly. The results were, at best, mediocre. He posted a 6.38 ERA while averaging 7.9 strikeouts and 3.6 walks per nine innings. Following the return of minor league action in 2021, Paniagua emerged as a swing-man for Palm Beach, showcasing a bloated strikeout rate (12.0 K/9) and a decent feel for the strike zone (3.7 BB/9). Last season he returned to Palm Beach as a full-time starter, but eventually spent the last two months of the season with Peoria. Paniagua finished the season with a career best 137.2 innings, recording 145 punch outs and just 39 walks to go along with a sparkling 2.81 ERA.

Scouting Report: Consider the following:

> Since 2006, only seven 22-year-old hurlers posted a 26% to 28% strikeout percentage with a 5% to 7% walk percentage in Low-A (min. 75 IP): Yohan Pino, Taylor Williams, Kirk McCarty, Leovanny Rodriguez, Drew Naylor, Mason Radeke, and Inohan Paniagua.

Not too much meat on Paniagua's bones – though he's far from Triston McKenzie territory. After watching the wiry righty throw, I walked away disappointed, expecting more. His fastball was a soft 91-mph. He'll mix in a floating, above-average curveball – though he had trouble repeating it on the day I watched him. And his change would alternate between below- and above-average. Paniagua's more of a strike-thrower than a command guy. He's likely going to struggle during his foray into Double-A.

Ceiling: 0.5- to 1.0-win player
Risk: Moderate
MLB ETA: 2024

St. Louis Cardinals

Tampa Bay Rays Top Prospects

Tampa Bay Rays

1. Curtis Mead, 2B/3B

Hit	Power	SB	Patience	Glove	Overall
60	50	40	50	50	60

Born: 10/26/00	Age: 22	Bats: R	Top Production Comp: Sean Casey
Height: 6-2	Weight: 171	Throws: R	

Season	Team	Age	Level	PA	1B	2B	3B	HR	SB	CS	BB%	K%	AVG	OBP	SLG	ISO
2021	TBR	20	A	211	39	21	1	7	9	2	7.11%	14.22%	0.356	0.408	0.586	0.230
2021	TBR	20	A+	233	35	15	1	7	2	2	8.15%	16.31%	0.282	0.348	0.466	0.184
2022	TBR	21	AA	246	33	21	0	10	6	2	10.16%	18.29%	0.305	0.394	0.548	0.243
2022	TBR	21	AAA	85	11	6	0	3	1	0	12.94%	20.00%	0.278	0.376	0.486	0.208

Background: At the time, Mead's signing with the Phillies barely caused a ripple on the baseball newswire. Philly agreed to a $200,000 deal with the Australian-born infielder back in early May five years ago. Mead would make his stateside debut the following summer, appearing in 44 games with the ball club's Gulf Coast League affiliate, hitting a respectable .285/.351/.462 as an 18-year-old squaring off against similarly aged prospects. A few months after the season the Phillies worked out a deal with the Tampa Bay Rays, agreeing to send Mead southward for hard-throwing, erratic lefty Cristopher Sanchez – another transaction that hardly caused waves. Mead, a 6-foot-2, 171-pound infielder, would spend that offseason battering the Australian Baseball League competition to the tune of .309/.373/.485. COVID would crush the 2020 minor league season before it even began, so the Adelaide native would pop up again in the AUBL the following winter where he could continue to mash, putting together an impressive .347/.385/.569 in 76 plate appearances with the Adelaide Giants. Finally, more than a year-and-a-half after joining the organization, Mead would appear in a Tampa Bay affiliated game in 2021. He shredded the Low-A East pitching (.356/.408/.586), continued to perform better than expected in his promotion up to High-A East (.282/.348/.466), and he caught fire during his brief cameo with Durham at the end of the year. The smooth-swinging second / third baseman hit an aggregate .321/.378/.533 with 38 doubles, two triples, 15 homeruns, and 11 stolen bases. Last season, despite dealing with an elbow injury in the second half of the year, Mead slugged .298/.390/.532 with 27 doubles, 13 homeruns, and seven triples in 76 games between Montgomery and Durham. His overall production, as measured by *Weighted Runs Created Plus*, surpassed the league average threshold by a staggering 42%.

Snippet from The 2022 Prospect Digest Handbook: Despite spending half of his time in two pitcher-friendly ballparks, Mead put together his finest season to date. There's a chance for a plus-hit tool, 20-homerun power, and phenomenal contact rates. Throw in an overall solid approach at the plate and a good glove at the hot corner, and Mead has the makings of a quality, sometimes borderline All-Star big leaguer. In terms of big league ceiling, think: .300/.360/.470.

Scouting Report: After shooting up prospect lists during his breakout 2021 season, Mead followed it up with an even *better* campaign last year – doing most of the damage at the minors' most difficult level, Double-A. Consider the following:

> Since 2006, only two 21-year-old hitters met the following criteria in a season in Double-A (min. 225 PA): 140 to 150 wRC+, 16% to 20% strikeout rate, and an 8% to 11% walk rate. Those two hitters both happened to accomplish the feat in Tampa Bay's organization – Justin Williams and – of course – Curtis Mead.

Not only is Mead one of the purest hitters in the Rays' system, but also in the entire minor leagues. Poised to be a consistent .300 hitter at the big league level, he combines a plus-plus hit tool with developing power that should develop into a perennial 25-homerun total. Patient approach with a knack for barreling up the baseball, Mead's bat whizz's through the zone with blistering speed and plenty of natural loft. Tampa Bay had the Australian youngster spend time at both corners of the infield in 2021, but they experimented with him at the keystone in 2022 – and the results were encouraging. There's Sean Casey-like potential that plays up even more at an up-the-middle position.

Ceiling: 4.5-win player
Risk: Moderate
MLB ETA: 2023

2. Shane Baz, RHP

FB	CB	SL	CH	Command	Overall
70	50	60	50	60	60

Born: 06/17/99	Age: 24	Bats: R	Top Production Comp: Corbin Burnes
Height: 6-2	Weight: 190	Throws: R	

Season	Team	Age	Level	IP	TBF	K/9	K%	BB/9	BB%	K-BB%	ERA	FIP	xFIP	Pit/Bat
2021	TBR	22	AA	32.2	120	13.50	40.83%	0.55	1.67%	39.17%	2.48	1.96	1.86	3.94
2021	TBR	22	AAA	46.0	178	12.52	35.96%	2.15	6.18%	29.78%	1.76	3.32	2.98	3.93
2022	TBR	23	AAA	13.0	53	13.85	37.74%	2.77	7.55%	30.19%	1.38	2.58	2.73	3.89

Background: Yes, the Chris Archer deal with the Pirates is a slam dunk, no-doubt win for the Rays. But the trio of top prospects Tampa Bay acquired have battled issues over the past couple of seasons. Tyler Glasnow dealt with a wonky elbow and underwent Tommy John surgery in early 2021, forcing him to miss the remainder of the year and the overwhelming majority of the 2022 campaign. Austin Meadows, a 2019 All-Star for the Rays, batted a massively disappointing .228/.311/.440 over his final two seasons with the club and was shipped off to

Tampa Bay Rays

Detroit last April for Isaac Paredes. And Baz, who was the Player To Be Named Later in the Archer deal, had not one, but *two* surgical procedures on his precious right elbow in 2022. In late March Baz underwent the knife to remove loose bodies in joint and was shut down for a couple weeks. He made it back to a minor league mound in mid-May. But just two months later he hit the disabled list and eventually succumbed to Tommy John surgery. Originally taken by the Pirates with the 12th overall pick in the 2017 draft; Baz finished the year with a total of 13.0 innings with Durham and another 27.0 frames with the Rays. For his minor league career, he's averaging 10.8 strikeouts and 3.5 walks per nine innings. And he's averaging 10.7 strikeouts and just 2.7 walks per nine innings in his brief cups of big league coffee.

Snippet from The 2022 Prospect Digest Handbook: Baz always had the *potential* to become an elite pitching prospect. Last season, his control improved by leaps and bounds, allowing him to become one of the best in the game. The fastball / slider combo ranks as one of the best.

Scouting Report: Early in his career the question was whether Baz would be able to harness his high octane arsenal enough to capitalize on his vast potential. But after his command took several leaps forward over the past several seasons, the next question he needs to answer is whether he can consistently take the rock every fifth day for the duration of a season. He hasn't surpassed the 100-inning threshold at any point in his professional career (note: part of his 2021 season was spent on Team USA's Olympic squad, though he tossed fewer than 3.0 innings). Between both elbow procedures last season, Baz's arsenal looked as good as ever. A plus-plus fastball that sat in the 96- to 98-mph range, a plus upper 80s slider, an average low 80s curveball, and a solid-average changeup. Baz is more than the typical strike-thrower. He commands the zone well with all four of his offerings. There's true ace potential here.

Ceiling: 5.0-win player
Risk: Moderate to High
MLB ETA: Debuted in 2021

3. Taj Bradley, RHP

FB	CB	SL/CU	CH	Command	Overall
60	45	55	50	60	55

Born: 03/20/01 **Age:** 22 **Bats:** R **Top Production Comp:** Dylan Bundy
Height: 6-2 **Weight:** 190 **Throws:** R

Season	Team	Age	Level	IP	TBF	K/9	K%	BB/9	BB%	K-BB%	ERA	FIP	xFIP	Pit/Bat
2021	TBR	20	A	66.2	249	10.94	32.53%	2.70	8.03%	24.50%	1.76	3.45	3.65	3.81
2021	TBR	20	A+	36.2	148	10.31	28.38%	2.70	7.43%	20.95%	1.96	3.79	4.24	3.70
2022	TBR	21	AA	74.1	285	10.65	30.88%	2.18	6.32%	24.56%	1.70	2.72	3.75	3.89
2022	TBR	21	AAA	59.0	247	8.08	21.46%	2.29	6.07%	15.38%	3.66	4.83	4.64	3.79

Background: The Rays' 2018 draft class has already been a smashing success. The club added southpaws Matthew Liberatore (who was dealt away for Randy Arozarena) and ace Shane McClanahan in the first round. Six rounds later they selected Joe Ryan and signed him to a team-friendly deal for less than $150,000. Ryan was eventually traded as part of the package to Minnesota for Nelson Cruz and Calvin Faucher. And that's not including the potential of Taj Bradley. Taken in the fifth round, 150th overall, that year, Tampa Bay signed the Redan High School product to an above-slot bonus of nearly $750,000. The 6-foot-2, 190-pound right-hander exploded up prospect charts during his dominant breakout two years ago. He tallied a tidy 1.83 ERA while blowing the doors off the Low-A and High-A competition. And he continued his meteoric rise as he split time between Montgomery and Durham in 2022. Making a career high 28 starts, Bradley pitched 133.1 innings, recording an impressive 141-to-33 strikeout-to-walk ratio with a 2.57 ERA. For his career, he's averaged 10 strikeouts and just 2.8 walks per nine innings over parts of four years.

Snippet from The 2022 Prospect Digest Handbook: The former University of South Carolina commit showed significant progress in his ability to command the strike zone in 2021. Solid mid-rotation caliber arm with the floor of a high leverage, fastball / slider combo reliever.

Scouting Report: Consider the following:

> Since 2006, only two 21-year-old hurlers posted a 20% to 23% strikeout percentage with a 5% to 7% walk percentage in any Triple-A league (min. 50 IP): Michael Wacha and – of course – Taj Bradley. Wacha was an All-Star in 2015 and has spent parts of 10 seasons at the big league level.

Bradley seemed to be tired in his final start of the year against Charlotte Bulls. The broad-shouldered right-hander came out firing in the mid-90s with relative ease, but by the third inning he was working in the lower 90s. When he's right, he'll consistent pump mid-90s heat with an above-average slider / cutter. He was more reliant on his average-ish changeup as well. Bradley will also mix in a fringy curveball at times as well. The deuce is more of a steal-a-strike breaking ball rather than quality big league offering. The former fifth rounder commands the zone well, particularly with his fastball. Bradley should be ready to slide into a mid-rotation spot by midseason 2023.

Ceiling: 4.0-win player
Risk: Moderate
MLB ETA: 2023

Tampa Bay Rays

4. Cole Wilcox, RHP

	FB	SL	CH	Command	Overall
	60	60	55/60	60	60

Born: 07/14/99	Age: 22	Bats: R	Top Production Comp: Jake Arrieta
Height: 6-5	Weight: 232	Throws: R	

Season	Team	Age	Level	IP	TBF	K/9	K%	BB/9	BB%	K-BB%	ERA	FIP	xFIP	Pit/Bat
2021	TBR	21	A	44.1	174	10.56	29.89%	1.02	2.87%	27.01%	2.03	2.40	2.84	3.60
2022	TBR	22	A	11.0	45	12.27	33.33%	1.64	4.44%	28.89%	2.45	3.12	2.37	3.67

Background: The University of Georgia ace was one of the largest over-slot signings in the COVID-abbreviated 2020 draft class. The Padres signed the third rounder to a massive $3.3 million deal after a nearly unhittable – albeit incredibly short – campaign with the Bulldogs; he posted an unimaginable 32-to-2 strikeout-to-walk ratio while allowing only a quartet of earned runs in only 23.0 innings that spring. Before he could make his affiliated debut in the San Diego organization, the Friars sent Wilcox, along with Francisco Mejia, Luis Patino, and Blake Hunt for Cy Young-winning southpaw Blake Snell. Settling in with the Rays' pitching development program, Wilcox continued his dominant run during his professional debut in 2021, averaging 10.6 strikeouts and just 1.0 walk per nine innings. He eventually succumbed to Tommy John surgery in mid-September 2021. The 6-foot-5, 232-pound right-hander made it back to the mound in early August last season, making three appearances in the Complex League and another four starts with the Charleston RiverDogs. He tossed 16.0 innings, recording 24-to-4 strikeout-to-walk ratio to go along with a 3.94 ERA.

Snippet from The 2022 Prospect Digest Handbook: Incredibly talented and the potential to have three plus pitches *and* plus command. After watching Wilcox shred through the Low-A competition, it's abundantly clear why the Padres handed out the massive bonus two years ago, as well as why the Rays went after the burgeoning ace in the trade. Assuming there aren't any ill effects from the TJ surgery, Wilcox could be a legitimate, genuine, bonafide ace. LOVE him.

Scouting Report: The former Bulldog ace might be the only pitcher in the minor leagues that a catcher will signal for two separate fastballs. His battery mate will use one finger for a four-seamer and use two fingers for his two-seamer. Both offerings are of the plus variety. The four-seamer is straight with riding, explosive life. The two-seamer shows plus movement down-and-away from left-handed hitters. He'll complement the offerings with a pair of strong offspeed pitches: a plus, hard-biting slider and an above-average changeup that remains one of the most underrated in the minor leagues. Despite the loss of development time over the past several seasons, Wilcox has had no issues commanding the strike zone with all three pitches. Assuming there aren't any setbacks from the elbow injury, the big 6-foot-5, 232-pound right-hander is poised to become one of the biggest risers in baseball in 2023. Big, big breakout candidate. LOVE him.

Ceiling: 4.5-win player
Risk: Moderate to High
MLB ETA: 2023/2024

5. Carson Williams, SS

	Hit	Power	SB	Patience	Glove	Overall
	45/50	55	60	50	60	55

Born: 06/25/03	Age: 20	Bats: R	Top Production Comp: Jeremy Pena
Height: 6-2	Weight: 180	Throws: R	

Season	Team	Age	Level	PA	1B	2B	3B	HR	SB	CS	BB%	K%	AVG	OBP	SLG	ISO
2021	TBR	18	CPX	47	6	4	1	0	2	2	12.77%	27.66%	0.282	0.404	0.436	0.154
2022	TBR	19	A	523	63	22	10	19	28	10	10.90%	32.12%	0.252	0.347	0.471	0.219

Background: The opening round of the 2021 draft saw 11 shortstops go within the first 36 selections, including nine high school players. The second to last of those teenagers was Carson Williams, whom the Rays snagged with the 28th overall pick. A product of Torey Pines High School, Williams joined the organization after signing for a $2,347,500. He put together a solid – albeit abbreviated – debut in the Complex League that summer, hitting .282/.404/.436 with four doubles, one triple, and a pair of stolen bases. Last season the Rays sent the 6-foot-2, 180-pound shortstop up to full season action. He responded with an impressive .252/.347/.471 slash line, belting out 22 doubles, 10 triples, and 19 homeruns to go along with 28 stolen bases (in 38 attempts). His overall production, per *Weighted Runs Created Plus*, topped the league average mark by 24%.

Snippet from The 2022 Prospect Digest Handbook: Fundamentally solid on the defensive side of the ball with plenty of arm strength – of course – to make all the difficult throws. Williams may not be an elite shortstop, but he should have no issues sticking at the position.

Scouting Report: Consider the following:

> Since 2006, only four 19-year-old hitters met the following criteria in a Low-A season (min. 350 PA): 120 to 130 wRC+ total and a strikeout rate between 30% to 34%. Those four hitters: M.J. Melendez, Khalil Lee, Alex De Jesus, and Carson Williams.

Tampa Bay Rays

Williams was far more productive than expected in several facets of the game during his first full season in the minor leagues. He showed far more thump and flashed impressive leather at the infield's most important position. On the other hand, the overall hit tool wasn't as advanced as expected either as he whiffed in nearly one-third of his plate appearances. Even if the hit tool hovers somewhere between the 40- and 45-grade territory, there should be enough secondary skills to make him an above-average big league shortstop.

Ceiling: 3.5-win player
Risk: Moderate
MLB ETA: 2025

6. Kyle Manzardo, 1B

Hit	Power	SB	Patience	Glove	Overall
55	50	20	50	55	45

Born: 07/18/00	Age: 22	Bats: L	Top Production Comp: Jose Martinez
Height: 6-1	Weight: 205	Throws: R	

Season	Team	Age	Level	PA	1B	2B	3B	HR	SB	CS	BB%	K%	AVG	OBP	SLG	ISO
2021	TBR	20	CPX	50	8	5	0	2	0	0	8.00%	12.00%	0.349	0.440	0.605	0.256
2022	TBR	21	A+	275	40	16	1	17	0	0	16.36%	16.73%	0.329	0.436	0.636	0.307
2022	TBR	21	AA	122	17	10	0	5	1	1	11.48%	15.57%	0.323	0.402	0.576	0.253

Background: Viewed as a production over projection pick two years ago. The 6-foot-1, 205-pound first baseman put together a solid career at Washington State, shining brightly during his junior campaign with the Cougars as he bashed .366/.437/.640 with 19 doubles, one triple, and 11 homeruns in 47 games. Tampa Bay – in a very Tampa Bay-like move – selected the junior slugger in the second round, 63rd overall, and signed him to a deal for a smidgeon less than $750,000. The lefty-swinging Manzardo continued to mash as got his first look at minor league pitching, hitting .349/.440/.605 in 50 plate appearances in the Complex League. Last season, the front office brass pushed the advanced hitter straight up to High-A, completely bypassing a stop in Charleston. And Manzardo did what he's done for several years – hit. The Idaho native shredded the Advanced-A competition through 63 games and continued to dominate during his 30-game cameo with Montgomery. The former second rounder finished his first full season with an aggregate .327/.426/.617 slash line with 26 doubles, one triple, 22 homeruns, and one stolen base. Per *Weighted Runs Created Plus*, his production topped the league average mark by a whopping 72%.

Snippet from The 2022 Prospect Digest Handbook: In a lot of ways Manzardo's a very typical Rays-type-pick. He's not overly big, but performed well. He's maxed out physically, but does a little bit of everything. He'll flash some above-average power, mix in a handful of walks, and make consistent contact. He's not going to be a star, but he has a shot at being a low end starting option at first base.

Scouting Report: Consider the following:

> Since 2006, there have been 635 hitters that earned at least 250 plate appearances during their age-21 season in any High-A league. Of those 635 hitters, Manzardo's overall production was the fourth highest, trailing Ryan McKenna, Miles Head, and Michael Chavis.

Among all minor league hitters with at least 250 plate appearances in 2022, Manzardo's 172 wRC+ was second highest, trailing only San Francisco's Vaun Brown, who was three years older than the Rays' young power hitter. Manzardo did a little bit of everything last season: he hit for average, hit for power, walked a bunch, made consistent contact, handled lefties and righties well, and he even provided some positive value with the leather too. Short swing, but long through the zone. Manzardo is a really good offspeed hitter and shows an uncanny ability to adjust mid-pitch. The history of the minor leagues has been littered with power-hitting, lethal first baseman and very few actually produce at the big league level. Manzardo won't be one of them. He's going to continue to hit and hit well. He has a ceiling as a .310/.380/.460-type hitter.

Ceiling: 3.0-win player
Risk: Moderate
MLB ETA: 2023

7. Junior Caminero, 3B/SS

Hit	Power	SB	Patience	Glove	Overall
50	55	50/30	50	50	50

Born: 07/05/03	Age: 19	Bats: R	Top Production Comp: Sean Casey
Height: 5-11	Weight: 157	Throws: R	

Season	Team	Age	Level	PA	1B	2B	3B	HR	SB	CS	BB%	K%	AVG	OBP	SLG	ISO
2021	CLE	17	DSL	171	26	8	3	9	2	0	11.70%	16.37%	0.295	0.380	0.534	0.240
2022	TBR	18	CPX	154	32	5	1	5	7	1	9.74%	13.64%	0.326	0.403	0.492	0.167
2022	TBR	18	A	117	23	2	1	6	5	0	6.84%	18.80%	0.299	0.359	0.505	0.206

Background: If there already wasn't enough evidence to never trade with the Rays, consider this just *another* example of the risks of dealing with the organization. Following the conclusion of the 2021 season, the Guardians dealt Junior Caminero to

Tampa Bay Rays

Tampa Bay for veteran minor league hurler Tobias Myers, who was coming off of a *dominant* campaign in Double-A and Triple-A as he set career bests in strikeout rate (11.2 K/9) to go along with his consistent ability to throw strikes (2.1 BB/9). Fast forward seven months: Myers looked abysmal in Cleveland's system and he was eventually dealt to the San Francisco Giants for cash considerations. Roughly three weeks later San Francisco designated the right-hander for assignment and he was claimed by the White Sox. That stint lasted a couple months before his release. Milwaukee eventually signed him to a minor league deal. As for Caminero, well, he went from a low level lottery ticket to becoming one of the Rays' top young hitting prospects. Originally signed by the Guardians in 2019, Caminero made his professional debut two years later with the club's Dominican Summer League affiliate, hitting a robust .295/.380/.534 as a 17-year-old in the offensive-friendly confines. Last season, his first in Tampa's system, Caminero torched the Complex League and spent the last several weeks bashing the Low-A competition. He finished the year with an aggregate .314/.384/.498 slash line with seven doubles, two triples, 11 homeruns, and 12 stolen bases (in 13 total attempts). Per *Weighted Runs Created Plus*, his overall production topped the league average threshold by 42%.

Scouting Report: Caminero packs considerable wallop for a 5-foot-11, 157-pound infield prospect (though he looks at least two pounds heavier than his listed weight). Big leg kick and a vicious right-handed swing. Watching Caminero's cuts leaves the impression that he's selling out for long ball power, but he's made consistent contact in his young career. Defensively, Caminero's split time between both positions on the left side of the infield, but he's likely to gain additional girth that pushes him permanently to the hot corner. He's tracking like a league average starting option with the ceiling as a .270/.330/.460 type hitter.

Ceiling: 2.5- to 3.0-win player
Risk: Moderate
MLB ETA: 2024/2025

8. Mason Montgomery, LHP

FB	SL	CH	Command	Overall
60	50/55	55	60	50

Born: 06/17/00 | **Age:** 23 | **Bats:** L | **Top Production Comp:** Ted Lilly
Height: 6-2 | **Weight:** 195 | **Throws:** L

Season	Team	Age	Level	IP	TBF	K/9	K%	BB/9	BB%	K-BB%	ERA	FIP	xFIP	Pit/Bat
2021	TBR	21	CPX	10.2	37	16.87	54.05%	0.84	2.70%	51.35%	0.84	0.68	1.78	2.19
2022	TBR	22	A+	69.2	282	15.24	41.84%	3.49	9.57%	32.27%	1.81	2.64	2.44	4.10
2022	TBR	22	AA	54.1	218	8.78	24.31%	2.65	7.34%	16.97%	2.48	3.71	4.15	3.83

Background: The Rays had their sights set on a lot of hitters during the early stages of the 2021 draft, selecting everyday players with their first six selections. Their first hurler, Mason Montgomery, wasn't chosen until the sixth round. A highly touted prospect coming out of Leander High School, Montgomery, who was originally selected by the White Sox in the latter rounds of the 2018 draft, struggled through a disappointing freshman season at Texas Tech. He tallied a 5.14 ERA and walked (26) more than he fanned (24) in 35.0 innings of work. But things seemed to click for the 6-foot-2, 195-pound southpaw during his COVID-abbreviated 2020 season, though, as he averaged 10 punch outs and 3.5 walks per nine innings. And he continued to show flashes of brilliance during his final season with the Red Raiders as well. Throwing a career best 63.2 innings, Montgomery struck out 84 and walked 27. After Tampa Bay selected him with the 191st pick and signed him for $222,500 – roughly $20,000 below the recommended slot bonus. The Texas-born lefty put together one of the most dominant debuts in recent memory as he punched out 20 and walked just one in 10.2 innings of work in the Complex League. And Montgomery continued to impress during his first full season in pro ball. In 27 High-A and Double-A starts, the southpaw fanned 171 and walked 43.

Scouting Report: Consider the following:

> Since 2006, there have been twenty-two instances of a hurler posted a 23.5% to 25.5% strikeout percentage with a walk percentage of 6.5% to 8.5% in any Double-A league during their respective age-22 season (min. 50 IP): David Price, Alex Cobb, Alex Wood, Anibal Sanchez, Justin Masterson, Luke Jackson, Michael Fulmer, Mitch Talbot, Wade LeBlanc, Trevor Stephan, Adam Warren, Brian Moran, Brian Shaffer, Connor Seabold, Fernando Hernandez, Jackson Kowar, Javier Solano, Juan Gutierrez, Robert Dugger, Angel Zerpa, Ky Bush, and – of course – Mason Montgomery.

Producing in Double-A at the same level as a litany of current and former big leaguers, Montgomery was one of the largest surprises in the Tampa Bay system last year. The 6-foot-2, 195-pound southpaw works out of the stretch and he's an extreme short-armer, which adds deception to his average fastball. Montgomery's a peculiar pitcher. His fastball velocity is fringy in today's game, generally hovering in the 90- to 92-mph range, though it can touch the mid-90s on occasion. But hitters – very talented minor league hitters – seem to *always* be late on the offering, particularly the first time through the order which makes him an ideal "opener" candidate. His slider is average, but can be a smidge better when he's locating it down. His changeup hovers in the same territory as well, but consistency makes it the better option.

Ceiling: 2.5-win player
Risk: Moderate
MLB ETA: 2023

Tampa Bay Rays

9. Willy Vasquez, IF

Hit	Power	SB	Patience	Glove	Overall
45/50	45/55	60/40	50	55	50

Born: 09/06/01	Age: 21	Bats: R	Top Production Comp: N/A
Height: 6-0	Weight: 191	Throws: R	

Season	Team	Age	Level	PA	1B	2B	3B	HR	SB	CS	BB%	K%	AVG	OBP	SLG	ISO
2019	TBR	17	R	46	13	2	1	0	2	1	2.17%	8.70%	0.364	0.370	0.455	0.091
2021	TBR	19	CPX	173	31	6	3	2	14	6	11.56%	15.61%	0.288	0.382	0.411	0.123
2022	TBR	20	A	492	75	21	9	10	25	3	7.32%	25.61%	0.256	0.313	0.410	0.154

Background: The ball club signed the infielder out of Santo Domingo, Dominican Republic at the end of July in 2019. Vasquez made his abbreviated debut just weeks after joining the organization, batting a scorching .364/.370/.455 in 11 games in the foreign rookie league. After Minor League Baseball returned from its COVID hibernation, Vasquez made the leap up to the organization's Complex League affiliate without missing a beat; he hit a respectable .288/.382/.411 with six doubles, three triples, two homeruns, and 14 stolen bases. Last season the Dominican infielder – finally – moved into full season action, appearing in 113 games with the Charleston RiverDogs. He finished the year with a .256/.313/.410 with 21 doubles, nine triples, 10 homeruns, and 25 stolen bases (in 28 total attempts). His overall production, according to *Weighted Runs Created Plus*, was 1% *below* the league average threshold.

Scouting Report: Consider the following:

> Since 2006, only four 20-year-old hitters met the following criteria in any Low-A season (min. 350 PA): 95 to 105 wRC+, 24% to 27% strikeout rate, and a 6.5% to 8.5% walk rate. Those four hitters: Michael A. Taylor, Dylan Cozens, Aaron Whitefield, and – of course – Willy Vasquez.

Vasquez showcases above-average raw power, but he's just beginning to tap into it during games. Above-average speed. Enough leather to man third base (his likely landing spot). Last year proved to be a tale of two seasons for Vasquez: he start 2022 off hitting a lowly .202/.263/.296 over his first 58 games, but caught fired and slugged .320/.377/.537 over his remaining 59 contests. If he can maintain the second half production for the majority of 2023, Vasquez could be a consensus Top 100 prospect. I'm betting big on his final 59 contests.

Ceiling: 2.5-win player
Risk: Moderate
MLB ETA: 2024/2025

10. Mason Auer, CF

Hit	Power	SB	Patience	Glove	Overall
45	50	70	50	55	50

Born: 03/01/01	Age: 22	Bats: R	Top Production Comp: N/A
Height: 6-1	Weight: 210	Throws: R	

Season	Team	Age	Level	PA	1B	2B	3B	HR	SB	CS	BB%	K%	AVG	OBP	SLG	ISO
2021	TBR	20	CPX	41	7	2	0	0	10	1	14.63%	17.07%	0.265	0.390	0.324	0.059
2022	TBR	21	A	270	42	13	9	4	24	3	11.48%	17.78%	0.293	0.378	0.478	0.185
2022	TBR	21	A+	259	43	8	3	11	24	4	9.27%	23.94%	0.288	0.367	0.496	0.208

Background: The early returns on the club's 2021 draft class have been beyond phenomenal. Carson Williams bat has provided more power than expected and his glove-work was nothing short of extraordinary during his debut. Kyle Manzardo was one of the most lethal bats in all of the minor leagues. Left-hander Mason Montgomery is knocking – loudly – on the big league club's door. And, of course, there's Mason Auer who was taken 30 selections before Montgomery. After spending his freshman season at Missouri State University, the 6-foot-1, 210-pound centerfielder transferred to JuCo San Jacinto College where he promptly dominated by slugging .373/.524/.622 with 11 doubles, four triples, 11 homeruns, and 36 stolen bases. Auer struggled a bit during his debut in the Complex League, though, hitting a mediocre .265/.309/.324 in 11 games. Last season, the toolsy outfielder rebounded as he spent time with Charleston and Bowling Green. He slugged an aggregate .290/.372/.487 with 21 doubles, 12 triples, 15 homeruns, and 48 stolen bases (in only 55 total attempts). Per *Weighted Runs Created Plus*, his overall production topped the league average threshold by 34%.

Scouting Report: Consider the following:

> Since 2006, only three 21-year-old hitters met the following criteria in a High-A season (min. 250 PA): 128 to 138 wRC+ total, 8.5% to 11.5% walk rate, and a 23.5% to 25.5% strikeout rate. Those three hitters: Sean Rodriguez, Michael Choice, and – of course – Mason Auer.

A speedster on the base paths that's translated in additional value in centerfield, Auer breezed through the lower levels with relative ease and he's primed to spend a significant portion – if not all – of 2023 in Double-A. His swing's a bit long, so his batting average may stumble against

The 2023 Prospect Digest Handbook

more advanced pitching. But there's enough in the secondary / peripheral tank to make him a valuable asset at the big league level. Auer's the typical Tampa Bay prospect with versatility and tons of tools. He's tracking like a fourth outfielder.

Ceiling: 1.5- to 2.0-win player
Risk: Moderate
MLB ETA: 2024

11. Cooper Kinney, 2B/3B

Hit	Power	SB	Patience	Glove	Overall
50	50/55	45	50	50	50

Born: 01/27/03	Age: 20	Bats: L	Top Production Comp: N/A
Height: 6-3	Weight: 200	Throws: R	

Season	Team	Age	Level	PA	1B	2B	3B	HR	SB	CS	BB%	K%	AVG	OBP	SLG	ISO
2021	TBR	18	CPX	47	8	1	1	0	2	0	21.28%	19.15%	0.286	0.468	0.371	0.086

Background: The Rays went after a couple high profile high schoolers with their first two selections in the 2021 draft, first selecting shortstop Carson Williams with the 28th overall pick and then choosing Cooper Kinney six selections later. A product of Tennessee-based Baylor School, Kinney signed with the organization for $2,145,600 – just a smidgeon below the recommended slot bonus. The lefty-swinging infielder batted an OBP-driven .286/.468/.371 during his 11-game cameo in the Complex League during his debut. Kinney did not appear in an affiliated game last season. An injured shoulder after a dive back to a base during the spring required surgery and knocked him out for the remainder of the year.

Scouting Report: With nothing new to report on, here's my draft write-up:

> "Per the Rays' Scouting Director, Rob Metzler, the lefty-swinging infielder will work at second and third bases in the professional ranks, not shortstop. Defensively, Kinney shows soft hands and enough twitch to handle the keystone. At the plate, the young prospect does not get cheated, showcasing phenomenal bat speed with an upper cut swing. Quick hands. Smooth swing. The power has a chance to be above-average."

Shoulder injuries, particularly ones that require surgery, can be tricky and difficult to bounce back from. Hopefully, Kinney's able to regain his explosive bat speed and quick twitch movements.

Ceiling: 2.0-win player
Risk: Moderate to High
MLB ETA: 2025

12. Xavier Isaac, 1B

Hit	Power	SB	Patience	Glove	Overall
40/45	50/60	30	50	50	50

Born: 12/17/03	Age: 19	Bats: L	Top Production Comp: N/A
Height: 6-4	Weight: 240	Throws: L	

Season	Team	Age	Level	PA	1B	2B	3B	HR	SB	CS	BB%	K%	AVG	OBP	SLG	ISO
2022	TBR	18	CPX	21	1	3	0	0	0	0	9.52%	14.29%	0.211	0.286	0.368	0.158

Background: Throughout the club's 26-year history, the Rays have selected just three first basemen in the opening round of the midseason draft: Casey Gillaspie, the 20th overall pick out of Wichita State University in 2014; Brendan McKay, the former University of Louisville two-way star who was taken fourth overall three years later; and – of course – the team's most recent first round selection, Xavier Isaac – the lone prep player among the group. And just how rare is it that Tampa Bay selects a high school first baseman in any round of the draft? The last time was all the way back in 2016 – when they selected Andrew Daschbach in the 40th round. Isaac, a University of Florida commit, was unstoppable during his prep career at East Forsyth High School. A four-year letter winner, the hulking first baseman batted .354 with five doubles, one triple, and five homeruns in 26 games. He was limited to just a pair of games the following season due to the pandemic induced shutdown. Isaac was also limited just six contests during his brief junior campaign as well. Last season, though, the 6-foot-4, 240-pound slugging prospect made up for all the lost time. In 26 games for the Eagles, he mashed .578/.708/1.296 with six doubles, two triples, and 12 homeruns. Tampa Bay grabbed him with the 29th overall pick, signing him to a deal worth $2,548,900. The North Carolina native appeared in just five Complex League games, going 4-for-19 with three doubles.

Scouting Report: Physically reminiscent of a young Bobby Bradley. There are very few ballparks on the planet that can hold a smash from Isaac. Power is the true calling card for the first base-only prospect, making him a risk for one of the more risk adverse organization's in Major League Baseball. The big first baseman has a tendency to get caught hitting off his front leg. Enough strength to adjust mid-swing and shoot the ball the other way. Best raw power in the class. Isaac can flick his wrist and hit it 400 feet. The swing needs improvement. Big league future as a .250/.320/.500-type hitter. I had a second round draft grade on him, just an FYI.

Tampa Bay Rays

Ceiling: 1.5- to 2.0-win player
Risk: Moderate
MLB ETA: 2026

13. Chandler Simpson, 2B/SS/LF

Hit	Power	SB	Patience	Glove	Overall
65	30	60	55	55	50

Born: 11/18/00	Age: 22	Bats: L	Top Production Comp: N/A
Height: 6-2	Weight: 170	Throws: R	

Season	Team	Age	Level	PA	1B	2B	3B	HR	SB	CS	BB%	K%	AVG	OBP	SLG	ISO
2022	TBR	21	CPX	34	7	3	0	0	8	0	17.65%	11.76%	0.370	0.471	0.481	0.111

Background: A relatively highly touted prospect coming out of St. Pius X High School in 2019. *Perfect Game* ranked the lefty-swinging middle infielder as the 13th best shortstop and the 73rd best player in the state of Georgia. And his performance that summer only reaffirmed those rankings. Appearing in 22 games with the Brookhaven Bucks of the Sunbelt League, Simpson slashed a scorching .402/.471/.511 with two doubles, four triples, and 12 stolen bases while walking more than striking out (12-to-7). The Georgia native spent his first two collegiate seasons at the University of Alabama-Birmingham where the production never quite stacked up. In 14 pre-COVID games in 2020, the then true-freshman batted .256/.353/.279 with just one extra-base hit. His numbers as a sophomore the following season, while greatly improved, didn't scream "future early round draft pick" either. Simpson batted .288/.339/.345 with just eight extra-base hits (six doubles and two triples) to go along with 24 stolen bases. Things seemed to click for him in the Northwoods League that summer, though, as he hit an impressive .378/.429/.402 with four extra-base hits and 55 stolen bases in only 51 games with the Fond du Lac Dock Spiders. Simpson would transfer to Georgia Tech before his junior year. And, well, he morphed into one of the country's best hitters in 2022. Appearing in 47 games with the Yellow Jackets, the 6-foot-2, 170-pound second baseman / shortstop *slugged* .434/.506/.517 with eight doubles, three triples, and one homerun. He swiped 27 bags in 31 total attempts. He also finished the year with an impressive 16-to-31 strikeout-to-walk ratio. Tampa Bay – unsurprisingly – selected him in the second round, 70th overall, and signed him to a deal worth $750,000 – roughly $200,000 below the recommended slot bonus. Simpson batted a scorching .370/.471/.482 in eight Complex League games, spanning just 34 plate appearances.

Scouting Report: Consider the following:

> Since 2011, there have been 77 Division I hitters that batted at least .400 in a season (min. 200 PA). Of those aforementioned 77 hitters, only four hitter walked more than 12% of the time and posted a strikeout rate less than 7%: Luis Trevino, Chad Zurcher, Chris O'Brien, and – of course – Chandler Simpson.

One of the more intriguing prospects – if not the *most* intriguing prospect – in last year's class. Simpson is cut from the cloth of yesteryear, showcasing phenomenal, elite bat-to-ball skills, plus speed, and 30-grade power. So it's not surprising to see the Rays take a calculated gamble on his 65-grade bat and see if they can coax some added power from his lanky frame. Slashing type swing that will spray line drives around the diamond. Simpson isn't afraid to lay down a bunt or two during a game, a rarity nowadays. Patient approach. 60-grade speed. He could very well end up as a version of Jarrod Dyson. Prior to the draft, I had a third round grade on the former Yellow Jacket.

Ceiling: 1.5- to 2.0-win player
Risk: Moderate to High
MLB ETA: 2025

14. Carlos Colmenarez, SS

Hit	Power	SB	Patience	Glove	Overall
30/45	30/55	50/40	50	55	45

Born: 11/15/03	Age: 19	Bats: L	Top Production Comp: N/A
Height: 5-10	Weight: 170	Throws: R	

Season	Team	Age	Level	PA	1B	2B	3B	HR	SB	CS	BB%	K%	AVG	OBP	SLG	ISO
2021	TBR	17	DSL	114	21	2	1	0	7	6	7.02%	26.32%	0.247	0.319	0.289	0.041
2022	TBR	18	CPX	153	21	7	3	1	13	2	11.11%	26.80%	0.254	0.379	0.381	0.127

Background: Tampa Bay took a calculated gamble on the international scene two years ago, committing nearly 50% of their allotted bonus pool to Colmenarez. The Rays signed the San Felipe, Venezuela native to a deal worth $3 million in mid-January 2021. The lefty-swinging shortstop would make his affiliated debut with the club's foreign rookie league affiliate after recovering from a broken hamate bone in late-August, hitting .247/.319/.289 in 26 games. Last season, despite the disappointing production line in 2021, Colmenarez was pushed stateside to the Complex League. And the results were better, but still not stellar. Appearing in 35 games, the 5-foot-

Tampa Bay Rays

10, 170-pound shortstop batted .254/.379/.381 with seven doubles, three triples, one homerun, and 13 stolen bases (in 15 total attempts). Per *Weighted Runs Created Plus*, Colmenarez's production topped the league average production line by a surprising 20%.

Snippet from The 2022 Prospect Digest Handbook: Really good looking swing with a plenty of bat speed and a natural loft in his swing that projects for average or better power. Defensively, he's smooth with a touch of flash and should have no issues sticking at the position. It wouldn't be shocking to see the front office push the now-18-year-old up to the Complex Leagues for the 2022 season.

Scouting Report: Ferocious left-handed swing that hasn't produced a whole lot of thump yet, though some of it could be the lingering hamate issue he suffered the previous season. It's an injury that can sap a hitter's power for more than a year. Colmenarez's hit tool hasn't been as advanced as expected. The lefty-swinging Venezuelan middle infielder is also showing some concerning platoon splits as well, hitting .191/.295/.238 against lefties (vs. .263/.383/.411 against righties). Colmenarez has punched his ticket to full season action in 2023. He seems poised to put together a Carson Williams-type showing with Charleston (.252/.347/.471 with power and plenty of punch outs).

Ceiling: 1.5-win player
Risk: Moderate
MLB ETA: 2025

15. Osleivis Basabe, IF

Hit	Power	SB	Patience	Glove	Overall
50	50/55	45	50	50	50

Born: 09/13/00	Age: 22	Bats: R	Top Production Comp: N/A
Height: 6-1	Weight: 188	Throws: R	

Season	Team	Age	Level	PA	1B	2B	3B	HR	SB	CS	BB%	K%	AVG	OBP	SLG	ISO
2021	TBR	20	A	309	61	10	6	2	18	4	8.41%	12.62%	0.284	0.347	0.385	0.101
2021	TBR	20	A+	18	3	0	0	1	0	0	11.11%	33.33%	0.250	0.333	0.438	0.188
2022	TBR	21	A+	236	46	16	2	4	7	5	6.78%	14.41%	0.315	0.370	0.463	0.148
2022	TBR	21	AA	259	50	23	3	0	14	0	9.27%	9.65%	0.333	0.399	0.461	0.127

Background: While Tampa Bay generally does well in every transaction with another front office, every one of them doesn't turn out to be slam dunk wins. Take for example the club's deal with the Rangers in mid-December 2020. Texas agreed to send a trio of prospects – Heriberto Hernandez, Alexander Ovalles, and Osleivis Basabe – to the Rays in exchange for first baseman Nathaniel Lowe, minor leaguer Jake Guenther, and a Player To Be Named Later. Lowe, who was a good but not great hitter during his first three seasons in the big leagues, blossomed into a bonafide middle-of-the-lineup slugger during his breakout campaign last season, slugging .302/.358/.492 with 26 doubles, three triples, and 27 homeruns. Regardless of how the three prospects pan out, the loss of Lowe's bat was certainly felt during the 2022 season. Basabe, like the player he was traded for, turned in *his* finest season to date last year. Splitting time between Bowling Green and Montgomery, the 6-foot-1, 188-pound shortstop / second / third baseman slugged an aggregate .324/.385/.462 with 39 doubles, five triples, four homeruns, and 21 stolen bases (in 26 total attempts). His overall production, as measured by *Weighted Runs Created Plus*, topped the league average mark by 29%.

Scouting Report: Consider the following:

> Since 2006, only three 21-year-old hitters posted a 125 to 135 wRC+ total with a sub-12% strikeout rate in any Double-A league (min. 250 PA): former All-Star infielder Asdrubal Cabrera, Adrian Cardenas, and – of course – Osleivis Basabe.

An extreme contact hitter that rarely (A) swings-and-misses and (B) strikes out. Basabe actually walked more than he whiffed during his extended stay with Montgomery last season. Basabe owns solid raw power, but he hasn't come close to showcasing that in games – though he did tie for the sixth highest doubles total in the minor leagues in 2022. Defensively, the organization continues to bounce him around the infield dirt. His glove continues to grade out as at least average, if not better, as well. Basabe is a plus runner so even though he puts the ball on the ground too frequently for the power to consistently show up in games, he can still find a way on base. He's tracking like a utility / bench option.

Ceiling: 1.0- to 1.5-win player
Risk: Moderate
MLB ETA: 2023

Tampa Bay Rays

16. Brock Jones, CF

Hit	Power	SB	Patience	Glove	Overall
45	55	55	55	50	45

Born: 03/28/01	Age: 22	Bats: L	Top Production Comp: N/A
Height: 6-0	Weight: 197	Throws: L	

Season	Team	Age	Level	PA	1B	2B	3B	HR	SB	CS	BB%	K%	AVG	OBP	SLG	ISO
2022	TBR	21	CPX	24	4	0	0	0	2	2	20.83%	25.00%	0.211	0.375	0.211	0.000
2022	TBR	21	A	62	5	4	1	4	9	3	19.35%	33.87%	0.286	0.419	0.653	0.367

Background: Heading into last July's draft, Jones had a chance to become the first Stanford Cardinal to be selected in the opening round of the Major League Baseball Draft since Nico Hoerner and Kris Bubic were snagged by the Cubs and Royals in 2018 – though he would ultimately come up short. Jones, who starred on the diamond and the gridiron during his time at Buchanan High School, spent his freshman season on Stanford's baseball *and* football teams. In 16 games with the Pac-12 Conference Powerhouse, the 6-foot, 197-pound outfielder batted a paltry .228/.323/.316; he also appeared in 11 games on special teams on the football team as well. The well-built, tools-laden outfielder had a coming out party during his sophomore season, slugging an impressive .311/.453/.646 with 13 doubles, one triple, and 18 homeruns. He also swiped 14 bags in 19 total attempts. And Jones raised the bar even further during his junior campaign: in a career best 65 games, he hit .324/.451/.664 with 13 doubles, five triples, 21 homeruns, and 16 stolen bases. Tampa Bay drafted the former two-way star in the second round, 65th overall, and signed him to a deal worth $1,077,600 – the recommended slot bonus. Jones appeared in 19 games between the Complex League and Low-A, hitting .265/.407/.529 with nine extra-base knocks.

Scouting Report: Per the usual, my pre-draft write-up:

> "Consider the following:
>
> Since 2011, only two Pac-12 hitters batted .300/.450/.650 in a season (min. 300 PA): Trevor Larnach, the 20th overall player taken in the 2018 draft, and – of course – Brock Jones.
>
> Let's look closer:

Name	G	PA	2B	3B	HR	BB%	SO%	AVG	OBP	SLG	OPS
Trevor Larnach	68	315	19	1	19	15.87%	20.95%	0.348	0.463	0.652	1.115
Brock Jones	63	308	13	5	20	17.86%	24.35%	0.327	0.455	0.665	1.120

> It's readily apparent that Jones' shortcoming is his swing-and-miss tendencies. His 24.35% K-rate is highly unlikely to decrease once he enters pro ball and it likely will rise at least a few percentage points. Larnach, for example, owns a 33% k-rate in 130 big league games with the Twins. Jones is loaded with tools: above-average speed, above-average power, and the defensive chops to man center fielder. The question, of course, is will he make enough contact to allow those tools to play up?"

I had a second round grade on Jones heading into the draft.

Ceiling: 1.5-win player
Risk: Moderate
MLB ETA: 2026

17. Kameron Misner, CF

Hit	Power	SB	Patience	Glove	Overall
40	45	60	55	55	45

Born: 01/08/98	Age: 25	Bats: L	Top Production Comp: N/A
Height: 6-4	Weight: 218	Throws: L	

Season	Team	Age	Level	PA	1B	2B	3B	HR	SB	CS	BB%	K%	AVG	OBP	SLG	ISO
2021	MIA	23	A+	400	47	22	3	11	24	2	12.50%	29.75%	0.244	0.350	0.424	0.179
2021	MIA	23	AA	62	9	7	0	1	2	2	11.29%	27.42%	0.309	0.387	0.491	0.182
2022	TBR	24	AA	510	62	25	1	16	32	7	16.86%	30.39%	0.251	0.384	0.431	0.181

Background: Tampa Bay acquired the former first rounder from the Marlins for the forever on-the-move infielder Joey Wendle during the 2021 offseason. Misner, the 35th overall pick in 2019, was a dynamic, toolsy bat during his three-year career at the University of Missouri, but his production has languished near mediocrity in the professional levels. The 6-foot-4, 218-pound centerfielder hit a blasé .276/.380/.373 in 34 games in Low-A during his debut. Once minor league action returned from its COVID-induced absence, Misner was sent up to High-A and he cobbled together a decent .244/.350/.424 slash line in 88 games. Miami would eventually send their former first rounder up to Double-A for a couple weeks as well. Last season, in his first year in the Rays' system, the former SEC standout batted .251/.384/.431 with 25 doubles, one triple, 16 homeruns, and 32 stolen bases (in 39 total attempts). His overall production topped the league average mark by 20%, according to *Weighted Runs Created Plus*. For his career, Misner's sporting a .255/.373/.420 slash line in 261 games.

Scouting Report: Consider the following:

> Since 2006, only three 24-year-old hitters posted a 115 to 125 wRC+ total with a 28% to 32% strikeout rate and a walk rate north of 12% in any Double-A season (min. 350 PA): Kyle Jensen, Jarrett Parker, and Kameron Misner.

Misner's development has stagnated on a couple fronts. The hit tool, which regressed a bit during his junior campaign at Missouri, plateaued even though his K-rates have exploded. The power never took the expected step forward and now languishes in the below-average category. The 6-foot-4, 218-pound prospect can handle centerfield decently enough to stick at the position. He runs well. On a bit of silver lining, Misner did finish out the year on a high note, hitting .289/.405/.473 over his final 77 games. If he can repeat that moving forward, he could be a viable option in the outfielder, though he'll be stretched too far as a regular. Lefties seemed to give him fits as well. Platoon option.

Ceiling: 1.0- to 1.5-win player
Risk: Moderate
MLB ETA: 2023

18. Ryan Cermak, OF

Hit	Power	SB	Patience	Glove	Overall
45	55	40	50	50	45

Born: 06/02/01	Age: 22	Bats: R	Top Production Comp: N/A
Height: 6-1	Weight: 205	Throws: R	

Season	Team	Age	Level	PA	1B	2B	3B	HR	SB	CS	BB%	K%	AVG	OBP	SLG	ISO
2022	TBR	21	CPX	24	3	0	1	2	3	0	4.17%	37.50%	0.273	0.333	0.636	0.364

Background: Jeff Cermak was a baseball vagabond. Originally taken by the Minnesota Twins in the 25th round coming out of Riverside-Brookfield High School in 1992, the right-hander would eventually make his way to Mesa Community College – where he was drafted by the Florida Marlins in the 46th round three years later. But Cermak would bypass the opportunity at pro ball and transfer to powerhouse Arizona State University a year later. The Houston Astros would then take a 12th round gamble on the Sun Devil. And despite getting drafted three times, from three different schools, by three different teams, he never appeared in an affiliated game. Four years later he would pop up for 15 mostly miserable starts with the Valley Vipers in the Western League. The following year his son Ryan was born. A stout two-way player coming out of Riverside-Brookfield High School, his father's alma mater, the younger Cermak looked miserable during his COVID-abbreviated 2020 season as he hit a disappointing .208/.296/.396. Things clicked for the toolsy outfielder the following season as he batted an impressive .284/.349/.553 with 10 doubles, four triples, 11 homeruns, and three stolen bases. And Cermak raised the bar even further during his impressive junior campaign. Appearing in just 48 games for the Illinois State Redbirds, the 6-foot-1, 205-pound prospect slugged .340/.441/.696 with 12 doubles, 19 homeruns, and eight stolen bases (in nine attempts). Tampa Bay selected him in the second round, 71st overall, and signed him to a deal worth $747,500, just a smidgeon below the recommended slot bonus. He slugged .273/.333/.636 with nine punch outs in 24 plate appearances in the Complex League during his debut.

Scouting Report: Consider the following:

> Since 2011, only five Missouri Valley Conference hitters have batted at least .330/.430/.680 in a season (min. 200 PA): Casey Gillaspie, Kevin Kaczmarski, Austin Listi, Jackson Glenn, and – of course – Ryan Cermak.

The Missouri Valley Conference will never be confused with the SEC or ACC or – hell – even the Big10, so Cermak spent the overwhelming majority of his career against less-than-typical competition. And he never got the chance to face the top flight pitching in the Cape Cod League or with Team USA either. Meaning: there's some risk associated with his performance – however good it may be. Doesn't get cheated at the plate with his uppercut swing. Above-average power, but there's going to be some swing-and-miss to his game. Above-average speed. He looks like a fourth outfielder, though, the type that exceeds in Tampa Bay's system.

Ceiling: 1.0- to 1.5-win player
Risk: Moderate
MLB ETA: 2025

Tampa Bay Rays

19. Ian Seymour, LHP

	FB	SL	CH	Command	Overall
	50	55	55	45	45

Born: 12/13/98 | **Age:** 24 | **Bats:** L | **Top Production Comp:** N/A
Height: 6-0 | **Weight:** 210 | **Throws:** L |

Season	Team	Age	Level	IP	TBF	K/9	K%	BB/9	BB%	K-BB%	ERA	FIP	xFIP	Pit/Bat
2021	TBR	22	A	35.1	135	15.03	43.70%	3.31	9.63%	34.07%	2.55	3.01	3.02	4.26
2021	TBR	22	A+	10.0	42	17.10	45.24%	1.80	4.76%	40.48%	1.80	3.07	3.06	3.64
2021	TBR	22	AAA	10.0	37	8.10	24.32%	3.60	10.81%	13.51%	0.00	2.76	5.25	4.16
2022	TBR	23	AA	16.2	81	12.42	28.40%	6.48	14.81%	13.58%	8.10	4.54	4.99	4.33

Background: In the club's history, the front office has drafted just two prospects from Virginia Tech: right-hander Jesse Hahn, who was taken in the sixth round in 2010, and – of course – Ian Seymour, their second round pick three years ago. Seymour's production hit another gear during his tour through the Cape Cod League in 2019 and he continued his masterful performance during the abbreviated 2020-campaign as well. And he confounded hitters during his first season in the minor leagues two years ago as he rocketed through three separate levels en route to averaging 14.2 strikeouts and 3.1 walks per nine innings. Last season the organization sent the 6-foot, 210-pound southpaw to Montgomery, but after just five brief starts Seymour hit the disabled list and eventually succumbed to Tommy John surgery. He finished the year with 23 punch outs, 12 free passes and an 8.10 ERA in 16.2 innings of work.

Snippet from The 2022 Prospect Digest Handbook: n a lot of ways Seymour is the prototypical lefty with a little bit of funk in his windup, almost quasi-Madison Bumgarner. Solid repertoire, though it's a bit unremarkable. He features a low-90s fastball, an above-average 10-4 breaking curveball, a horizontally darting slider, and a fantastic, 55-grade changeup, easily his best overall offering. Seymour shows complete confidence in his changeup, throwing it ahead in the count, behind in the count, to lefties, to righties. He commands it better than any of his other pitches.

Scouting Report: Things seemed to be just "off" for Seymour before hitting the injury list last season. His fastball was sitting a few ticks slower and his command had regressed. Before the year Seymour looked like a potential "Opener" in a couple years, but that's been delayed at least 18 months or so.

Ceiling: 1.0- to 1.5-win player
Risk: Moderate to High
MLB ETA: 2022

20. Trevor Martin, RHP

	FB	CB	SL	CH	Command	Overall
	60	50/55	N/A	N/A	35/40	40

Born: 12/15/00 | **Age:** 22 | **Bats:** R | **Top Production Comp:** N/A
Height: 6-5 | **Weight:** 235 | **Throws:** R |

Background: The burly righty was practically unhittable during his final two seasons at Asher High School, recording 240 strikeouts in only 115.1 innings of work. The production helped him earn All-State status during his tenure at the Oklahoma-based prep school. After graduation in 2019, Martin headed to Oklahoma State University and immediately stepped in as a high octane reliever for the Big 12 powerhouse after baseball returned from its COVID absense. The 6-foot-5, 235-pound righty averaged a whopping 12.6 strikeouts and 6.0 walks per nine innings across 22 appearances. Martin earned a spot on the Big 12 All-Freshman Team as well as a trip through the celebrated Cape Cod League. He would throw another 19.1 innings with the Chatham Anglers, recording an impressive 27-to-9 strikeout-to-walk ratio. Last season Martin captured the Cowboys' closer role and saved nine games while fanning 79 and walking just 22 in 47.1 innings of work. Tampa Bay selected him in the third round, 104th overall, and signed him to a deal worth $586,200. Martin made one appearance with the club's Complex League affiliate, striking out a pair and walking one without surrendering an earned run.

Scouting Report: Plus fastball that sits in the mid-90s and will touch the upper-90s that's particularly difficult to hit above the belt. His breaking ball will flash above-average at times but lacks consistency. According to reports, he'll also mix in a slider and a below-average changeup. There's impressive life on his fastball and enough shape and tilt on the slider that if the Rays opt to keep him as a reliever he could scrap the rest of the arsenal. Tampa Bay is likely to stretch him out as a starting pitcher, at least initially.

Ceiling: 1.0-win player
Risk: Moderate
MLB ETA: 2025/2026

Texas Rangers

Top Prospects

Texas Rangers

1. Evan Carter, CF

Hit	Power	SB	Patience	Glove	Overall
55	5/550	55	60	55	60

Born: 08/29/02	Age: 20	Bats: L	Top Production Comp: George Springer
Height: 6-4	Weight: 190	Throws: R	

Season	Team	Age	Level	PA	1B	2B	3B	HR	SB	CS	BB%	K%	AVG	OBP	SLG	ISO
2021	TEX	18	A	146	14	8	1	2	12	4	23.29%	19.18%	0.236	0.438	0.387	0.151
2022	TEX	19	A+	447	69	18	10	11	26	12	13.20%	16.78%	0.287	0.388	0.476	0.189
2022	TEX	19	AA	28	5	3	0	1	2	1	17.86%	21.43%	0.429	0.536	0.714	0.286

Background: Former GM Jon Daniels helped stock the farm system thanks in part to a very strong 2020 Draft Class. It turned out to be Daniels' last draft class as the club's General Manager. Ivy League-educated former big league All-Star Chris Young was promoted to the position following the season. But under Daniels' guidance, the Rangers selected a quartet of potential big leaguers in the five-round, COVID-limited draft: Justin Foscue, Even Carter, Tekoah Roby, and Thomas Saggese, all of whom rank among the club's Top 20 prospects. Taken with the 50th overall pick that year, Carter, who signed with the club for $1.25 million, turned in a solid – albeit limited – debut showing with Down East two years ago. The 6-foot-4, 190-pound centerfielder hit .236/.438/.387 with eight doubles, one triple, two homeruns, and 12 stolen bases in only 32 games. A stress fracture in his back pushed to the disabled list in mid-June, forcing him to miss the remainder of the season. Last season, despite the limited exposure to professional pitching, the front office sent their former second round pick up to High-A. And he blossomed into one of the game's best outfield prospects. In 100 games with Hickory, Carter mashed .287/.388/.476 with 18 doubles, 10 triples, 11 homeruns, and 26 stolen bases (though he was caught stealing 12 times). His overall production with the Crawdads, according to *Weighted Runs Created Plus*, surpassed the league average threshold by 36%. Carter spent the last weeks of the year annihilating the Double-A pitching, going 9-for-21 with a trio of doubles. Carter finished the year with an aggregate .295/.397/.489 slash line.

Snippet from The 2022 Prospect Digest Handbook: Carter has a little Brandon Nimmo in him – both owning incredible patience at the plate. The Rangers' young center fielder walked in more than 23% of his plate appearances and posted a sub-20% K-rate as well. It's an aggressive statement but Carter could find his way into the Top 100 as early as 2023.

Scouting Report: Consider the following:

> Since 2006, only four 19-year-old hitters posted a wRC+ total between 130 and 140 in any High-A league (min. 350 PA): two-time All-Star and former MVP Cody Bellinger; Domingo Santana, who owns a 110 wRC+ career mark in the big leagues; Addison Russell, a former consensus Top 5 prospect; and – of course – Evan Carter. But here's the impressive part: Carter's swing-and-miss rate in High-A last season, 16.8%, was – by far – the lowest among the group. Addison Russell's 23% K-rate was the runner-up.

Carter combines one of the minors' most patient eyes at the plate with consistently strong contact numbers as well. Easy raw power. Carter hasn't fully tapped into his above-average power potential just yet, but it is coming. Above-average hit tool. Plus speed. And an above-average glove in centerfield. The lone tool keeping him from a true five-tool prospect is his average arm. In terms of big league ceiling, think: .300/.375/.500 with 25 homeruns and 25 stolen bases.

Ceiling: 5.-win player
Risk: Moderate
MLB ETA: 2023

2. Josh Jung, 3B

Hit	Power	SB	Patience	Glove	Overall
55	55	40	50	50	60

Born: 02/12/98	Age: 25	Bats: R	Top Production Comp: Ryan Zimmerman
Height: 6-2	Weight: 214	Throws: R	

Season	Team	Age	Level	PA	1B	2B	3B	HR	SB	CS	BB%	K%	AVG	OBP	SLG	ISO
2021	TEX	23	AA	186	33	8	1	10	2	2	6.99%	22.58%	0.308	0.366	0.544	0.237
2021	TEX	23	AAA	156	24	14	0	9	0	0	11.54%	21.79%	0.348	0.436	0.652	0.304
2022	TEX	24	AAA	106	14	7	0	6	1	0	3.77%	28.30%	0.273	0.321	0.525	0.253

Background: One of the most lethal college bats during his tenure at Texas Tech. Jung's achievements with the Red Raiders reads like a novella. Some of the highlights include: 15 All-American awards, named a semifinalist for the Dick Howser Trophy, which is considered the Heisman Trophy of college baseball, a semifinalist for the Golden Spikes Award, and *D1 Baseball* named him as the Big 12 Player of the Decade. A .348/.455/.577 career hitter, Jung didn't have to travel too far to join the professional ranks as the Rangers selected the Slugging Red Raider with the eighth overall pick in 2019. The 6-foot-2, 214-pound third baseman would turn in a solid debut with the Hickory Crawdads, hitting .287/.363/.389 in 40 games. After minor league action returned from its COVID-induced absence, Jung manhandled the two highest levels of the minor leagues in 2021 as he slugged .326/.398/.592 with 22 doubles, one triple, 19 homeruns, and a pair of stolen bases. The former Red Raider missed several months at the start of the year to repair of torn labrum in his left shoulder. The injury, according to the

Texas Rangers

Associated Press and ESPN, was discovered prior to the start of the minor league camp and was initially diagnosed as a strain. Jung made it back to the Complex League for a brief rehab assignment in late July. By early August he was back with Round Rock mashing Triple-A pitching. Jung spent the last several weeks with the Rangers, hitting a disappointing .204/.235/.418 in 26 games.

Snippet from The 2022 Prospect Digest Handbook: Jung got off to a late start to the year – he didn't play his first game until June – so his time at each level was exceptionally long: he appeared in just 43 games in Double-A and 35 games in Triple-A. But the production, though, remained among the best in professional baseball. Solid patience at the plate. Above-average thump combined with strong contact skills. The .280/.340/.480-type ceiling is still tracking.

Scouting Report: Jung's been hampered by injuries the past couple of years, limiting him to just 135 games since the start of 2021. But when he has been healthy, the numbers have been incredibly strong. Above-average hit tool and power. Jung starts his swing with a slow, timed leg kick that may give him problems if he's not getting his foot down in time. Jung has the potential to anchor the hot corner in Texas for the next decade, maybe more if the Rangers are still handing out mega-dollar deals. Big League ceiling: .280/.340/.480 hitter with 25 homeruns annually.

Ceiling: 4.0-win player
Risk: Moderate
MLB ETA: 2022

3. Jack Leiter, RHP

FB	CB	SL	CH	Command	Overall
60	50	60	55	40/50	60

Born: 04/21/00	Age: 23	Bats: R	Top Production Comp: N/A
Height: 6-1	Weight: 205	Throws: R	

Season	Team	Age	Level	IP	TBF	K/9	K%	BB/9	BB%	K-BB%	ERA	FIP	xFIP	Pit/Bat
2022	TEX	22	AA	92.2	425	10.59	25.65%	5.44	13.18%	12.47%	5.54	5.02	5.13	4.18

Background: The most ballyhooed pitching prospect over the past couple of decades has to be Stephen Strasburg. You would have had to live through the hoopla to full understand the level of mania that surrounded Strasburg's every movement. An unnamed scout, as quote by Tim Keown in a summer 2009 issue of ESPN The Magazine, noted: "This is my 36th draft. I've never seen anything like this." Those 36 drafts, at that time, saw the professional births of some of the most hyped pitching prospects to ever grace the game, like Ben McDonald or Todd Van Poppel or Brien Taylor or Kris Benson or Mark Prior. A little more than a decade after the Nationals grabbed Strasburg with the top overall pick, Jack Leiter began to make waves as the next great, fantastical pitching prospect – a hurler that was guaranteed to be a first round pick coming out of Delbarton School, but basically withdrew his name from the draft due to his impossibly unbreakable commitment to Vanderbilt University. And with the baseball world abuzz heading into the 2020 season, Leiter seemingly surpassed any and every single expectation during his first season at Vanderbilt. He was nearly unhittable across four appearances for the Commodores, posting a 22-to-8 strikeout-to-walk ratio in 15.2 innings. And the only thing that could slow Leiter was a pandemic. But that early collegiate success only proved to be a harbinger of things to come, a sample before the main course, a spark before the flame. The 6-foot-1, 205-pound right-hander dazzled during his only full season in the SEC, throwing 110.0 innings, recording a 179-to-45 strikeout-to-walk ratio with a 2.13 ERA and an 11-4 win-loss record. The presumed top pick heading into the draft that summer, Pittsburgh bypassed him with the first selection and the Rangers, with the influx of cash and the expectations that come along with a brand new stadium stood waiting with opened arms. Texas signed him to a $7,922,000 deal, the fourth largest handed out in Draft history. Leiter made his highly anticipated debut last year, stepping right into the fire of Double-A, the most difficult minor league level. The hard-throwing righty tossed 92.2 innings across 23 appearances, averaging 10.6 whiffs and a surprising 5.4 walks per nine innings. He tallied a 5.54 ERA, 5.02 FIP, and a 5.13 xFIP.

Snippet from The 2022 Prospect Digest Handbook: He has a chance to be a dominant ace, along the lines of a Max Scherzer, if the command ticks up. I would expect him to be in the big leagues by end of 2022 for a September cup of coffee.

Scouting Report: Consider the following:

> Since 2006, only seven 22-year-old pitchers met the following criteria in a Double-A season (min. 75 IP): 24.5% to 26.5% strikeout percentage with a walk percentage north of 12%. Those seven hurlers: Lucas Sims, Alex Torres, Carlos Pimentel, J.B. Bukauskas, Kelvin De La Cruz, Scott Nestor, and – of course – Jack Leiter.

Leiter was never a true-command guy in college, per se, but last season's collapse was completely unexpected – particularly when it came to his plus fastball. And his feel for all three offspeed pitches were even worse. Lauded for his ability to robotically repeat the same release point on each of the four offerings, Leiter's loss of the strike zone was a battle all season long. Of his 23 games last season, he walked four or more five times; he walked three or more 12 times; he walked at last two 15 times. And there were only two games in which he didn't register a free pass, one of them being a one-inning appearance. Plus fastball and slider, above-average changeup, and the curveball seemed to back up a little

Texas Rangers

bit, downgrading it to a solid average offering. Leiter still has the ceiling of a very good starting pitcher, but he's rawer than expected – particularly given his bloodlines and collegiate performance / background.

Ceiling: 4.0-win player
Risk: Moderate
MLB ETA: 2023

4. Brock Porter, RHP

FB	CB	SL	CH	Command	Overall
60	55	55	60	45	60

Born: 06/03/03	Age: 20	Bats: R	Top Production Comp: N/A
Height: 6-4	Weight: 208	Throws: R	

Background: Draft picks coming out of Orchard Lake St. Mary's have been few and far between. The Michigan-based prep school graduated just four players – Gary Ignasiak, Gary Morris, Brian Justice, and Blaise Salter – to the minor leagues. None of whom, by the way, were drafted before the 27th round coming out of high school. That quickly changed as Brock Porter, fresh off of earning Gatorade's Player of the Year award in 2021, was selected by the Rangers in the fourth round last summer. Viewed as one of the top pitching prospects in a class light on young arms, the 6-foot-4, 208-pound right-hander – Clemson University commit – was practically unhittable throughout his prep career. Porter fanned 85 to go along with a 9-2 win-loss record and a 1.20 ERA as a true freshman. After the 2020 season was lost due to COVID, he came back with a vengeance, winning 12 games without a loss to go along with 126 strikeouts and a 0.56 ERA in 62.1 innings. And heading into the state semifinals, Porter owned a perfect 9-0 record to go along with a sparkling 0.41 ERA. He tallied a whopping 115 strikeouts. He committed to Clemson University after his freshman campaign. Porter also was named Gatorade's National Player of the Year. The Rangers handed Porter a massive $3.7 million bonus, easily surpassing the previous high for a fourth rounder.

Scouting Report: Here's pre-draft analysis:

> "A deep, quality arsenal with four above-average or better pitches. Porter isn't the typical hard-throwing, blow-it-by-ya' teenage hurler. He'll regularly mix in an above-average, big bending 12-6 curveball, an even better slider, and a plus change with hard tumble. All three complement a plus fastball. Command will likely never creep into average territory, but Porter has the look and feel of a strong mid-rotation arm. There's some Ian Anderson-type potential here."

Ceiling: 4.0-win player
Risk: Moderate
MLB ETA: 2026

5. Mitch Bratt, LHP

FB	CB	SL	CH	Command	Overall
60	50	60	50	55	55

Born: 07/03/03	Age: 19	Bats: L	Top Production Comp: N/A
Height: 6-1	Weight: 190	Throws: L	

Season	Team	Age	Level	IP	TBF	K/9	K%	BB/9	BB%	K-BB%	ERA	FIP	xFIP	Pit/Bat
2022	TEX	18	A	80.2	336	11.05	29.46%	3.12	8.33%	21.13%	2.45	3.26	3.73	3.83

Background: Born in Canada and drafted out of US-based Georgia Premier Academy. The Rangers selected the 6-foot-1, 190-pound southpaw in the fifth round two years ago, signing the 134th overall pick to a hefty $850,000 deal – tied with Tanner McDougal as the second highest bonus given out in the round that year. One of the youngest members of the 2021 draft, Bratt would make four brief appearances with the Rangers' Complex League affiliate that summer, posting an impeccable 13-to-0 strikeout-to-walk ratio in only six innings of work. Unsurprisingly, given Bratt's initial dominance, the front office sent the teenage lefty straight into full-season action in 2022. And he sparkled across 18 starts and one relief appearance. Throwing 80.2 innings for the Wood Ducks, Bratt averaged 11 strikeouts and just 3.1 walks per nine innings. He finished his first full professional season with a 2.45 ERA, a 3.26 FIP, and a 3.73 xFIP.

Scouting Report: Consider the following:

> Since 2006, only two 18-year-old hurlers posted a 28.5% to 30.5% strikeout percentage with a 7% to 9% walk percentage in any Low-A league (min. 75 IP): Luis Patino, the former consensus Top 100 prospect, and Mitch Bratt, a recent fifth round selection.

A great athlete that can field his position well, Bratt's probably the best pitching prospect you've never heard of – at least not yet. The Canadian-born southpaw features a high quality four-pitch arsenal highlighted by a plus fastball. Sitting in the 92- to 96-mph range, Bratt's

Texas Rangers

heater will touch a tick or two higher on occasion as well. Easy velocity, like he's just playing catch without actually exerting himself. Wipeout, hard tilting, mid-80s slider that's one of the best in the minor leagues. Solid average curveball that shows similar break as the slider, though it's several miles-per-hour slower. Firm changeup that avoids the fat part of the bat. Bratt is a strike-throwing machine. He's destined for a #3 / #4-type role. He'll be a consensus Top 100 prospect by midseason 2023.

Ceiling: 3.0-win player
Risk: Moderate
MLB ETA: 2024/2025

6. Luisangel (Jose) Acuna, 2B/SS

Hit	Power	SB	Patience	Glove	Overall
50/55	50	60	50	50	55

Born: 03/12/02	**Age:** 21	**Bats:** R	**Top Production Comp:** Jonathan Villar
Height: 5-10	**Weight:** 181	**Throws:** R	

Season	Team	Age	Level	PA	1B	2B	3B	HR	SB	CS	BB%	K%	AVG	OBP	SLG	ISO
2021	TEX	19	A	473	80	15	3	12	44	11	10.36%	23.26%	0.266	0.345	0.404	0.138
2022	TEX	20	A+	240	47	10	0	8	28	6	14.17%	25.00%	0.317	0.417	0.483	0.166
2022	TEX	20	AA	169	23	6	2	3	12	3	10.06%	21.30%	0.224	0.302	0.349	0.125

Background: It's difficult growing up in the shadow a famous baseball playing brother. There aren't too many people that remember Chris Gwynn or Craig Griffey or Ozzie Canseco or Tommie Aaron. Luisangel Acuna, whose brother, Ronald Acuna Jr., happens to be one of the game's brightest stars, is bound and determined to make sure that *doesn't* happen to him. Acuna's younger brother, Bryan just completed his professional debut in the Twins' organization in 2022. And the Acuna brothers' father, Ronald, spent nearly a decade in the minor leagues before retiring. Luisangel, who sometimes goes by the nickname Jose, made his affiliated debut with the club's Dominican Summer League team in 2019, mashing a scorching .342/.438/.455 in 55 games. After minor league action returned from its COVID hiatus, Acuna held his own as a 19-year-old in Low-A, batting a respectable .266/.345/.404 with 15 doubles, three triples, 12 homeruns, and 44 stolen bases (in 55 attempts). Last season Acuna moved quickly through High-A as he slugged .317/.417/.483 with 10 doubles, eight homeruns, and 28 stolen bases in only 54 games. His numbers, though, took a noticeable dive following his early August promotion up to Double-A (.224/.302/.349). Acuna finished the season with an aggregate .277/.369/.425 slash line with 16 doubles, two triples, 11 homeruns, and 40 stolen bases. His overall production, according to *Weighted Runs Created Plus*, topped the league average mark by 15%. Acuna missed the opening month of the year due to a hamstring issue.

Snippet from The 2022 Prospect Digest Handbook: There's the potential for an above-average hit tool, plus speed, and 15- to 20-homerun pop from a middle infield position.

Scouting Report: Consider the following:

> Since 2006, only three 20-year-old hitters met the following criteria in a season in any High-A league (min. 225 PA): 145 to 155 wRC+, a double-digit walk rate, and a 22% to 26% strikeout rate. Those three hitters: Anthony Volpe, Andy Pages, and – of course – the supremely underrated Luisangel Acuna.

Despite the terrible numbers with Frisco, Acuna's stint in Double-A started off a solid footing as he hit .247/.314/.441 over his first 23 games with the RoughRiders. His final 18 games (.173/.271/.200) proved to be a millstone that dragged his overall numbers down. Defensively, Acuna's a man without a position, or at least not yet, but the Rangers already have hundreds of millions of dollars invested in Marcus Semien and Corey Seager at second base and shortstop. So it wouldn't be surprising to see him takes his talents / athleticism to centerfield in 2023. Plus speed, above-average hit tool, average power. There's a lot to like wrapped up in a 5-foot-10, 181-pound package. Very similar offensive profile with more power as former Ranger Delino DeShields Jr. Acuna profiles as a .280/.340/.430 hitter.

Ceiling: 3.0-win player
Risk: Moderate
MLB ETA: 2023/2024

7. Kumar Rocker, RHP

FB	CB	SL	CH	Command	Overall
60	55	70	50	50	55

Born: 11/22/99	**Age:** 23	**Bats:** R	**Top Production Comp:** N/A
Height: 6-5	**Weight:** 245	**Throws:** R	

Background: There are more than a few parallels between former University of Tennessee ace right-hander Luke Hochevar and former Vanderbilt University ace Kumar Rocker. They're both 6-foot-5, well-built, hard-throwing right-handers. Both hurlers dominated during their respective careers in college. Both players were

Texas Rangers

represented by mega-agent Scott Boras. Both players were eventual first round picks. And, of course, both players failed to come to terms with the clubs that drafted them and would eventually spend some time in the Indy Leagues as they waited for the following year's draft. Hochevar, of course, would eventually be drafted by the Kansas City Royals #1 overall and turned in a long, mostly uninspiring big league career. Rocker, on the other hand, was the third overall pick last June – one of the draft's biggest, if the biggest, surprise. The Mets found an undisclosed issue that caused some concerns in his post-2021 draft physical and (B) he had surgery, deemed a "minor scope" on his powerful right shoulder in September of 2021. Rocker has popped up with the Tri-City ValleyCats in the Frontier League, dominating – of course – the second-rate competition. Through his first four games, spanning 20.0 innings, he struck out 32 and tallied a 1.35 ERA. Texas signed Rocker to a deal worth $5.2 million last summer. He made his debut in the Arizona Fall League, throwing 14.0 innings, recording an 18-to-12 strikeout-to-walk ratio.

Scouting Report: Here's 2021's pre-draft analysis:

> *"Consider the following:*
>
> > *Between 2011 and 2020, here's the list of SEC pitchers to average at least 13 strikeouts and fewer than three walks per nine innings in a season (min. 75 IP): Ethan Small.*
>
> *Rocker's production and, of course, dwarfed that of Small's time at Mississippi State. Rocker's been project to be a top pick – if not the top pick – since bypassing the 2018 draft. Explosive fastball, arguably the best offspeed pitch in the entire class (slider), and an above-average curveball. The broad-shouldered righty will also mix in an underrated changeup, which he relied on more than normal during the season's final championship game. There was talk heading into the draft that Rocker has some reliever risk, but he's no Dillon Tate. Rocker may not develop into a bonafide ace, but he's going to be a very good, if not great major league starting pitcher."*

Prior to the 2022 draft, reports had Rocker's heater upwards of 99 mph and still flashing his plus-plus slider. He'll likely be one of the most viewed hurlers at the start of 2023.

Ceiling: 3.0-win player
Risk: High
MLB ETA: 2024

8. Thomas Saggese, 2B/3B

Hit	Power	SB	Patience	Glove	Overall
55	50	50/40	50	50	50

Born: 04/10/02	Age: 21	Bats: R	Top Production Comp: Daniel Robertson
Height: 5-11	Weight: 175	Throws: R	

Season	Team	Age	Level	PA	1B	2B	3B	HR	SB	CS	BB%	K%	AVG	OBP	SLG	ISO
2021	TEX	19	A	288	35	14	3	10	11	3	14.58%	29.51%	0.256	0.372	0.463	0.207
2022	TEX	20	A+	419	79	22	2	14	11	3	6.92%	22.43%	0.308	0.359	0.487	0.179
2022	TEX	20	AA	22	2	3	2	1	1	0	4.55%	13.64%	0.381	0.409	0.857	0.476

Background: It's going to take a few more years for things to shake out, but the Rangers' 2020 draft class may end up being one of the better ones in baseball. The front office opened up the midsummer draft by selecting Mississippi State infielder Justin Foscue. They followed it up with prep outfielder Evan Carter, who's already established himself a consensus Top 100 prospect, then they snagged a couple of high school arms in Tekoah Roby and Dylan MacLean. And they closed it out with a wiry shortstop out of Carlsbad High School – Thomas Saggese, who received the fourth highest bonus in the round that summer. No longer a shortstop with the abundance of options at the position, both in the big leagues and minors, Saggese would make his debut the following summer with the Down East Wood Ducks. He slugged an impressive .256/.372/.463 with 14 doubles, three triples, 10 homeruns, and 11 stolen bases (in only 14 attempts). Last season, unsurprisingly, the Rangers sent the infield vagabond to Hickory. And Saggese continued to shine as he raised the bar by mashing .308/.359/.487 with 22 doubles, two triples, 14 homeruns, and 11 stolen bases (in 14 attempts). His overall production, according to *Weighted Runs Created Plus*, surpassed the league average by 27%. Saggese spent the last week of the season getting his feet wet in Double-A. He just happened to go 8-for-21 with three doubles, two triples, one homeruns, and a stolen base. That's a pretty successful five-game cameo.

Snippet from The 2022 Prospect Digest Handbook: The 29% k-rate is concerning, yes, but let's take a look at his production. During the first 30 games of his 2021 season – and remember he didn't play much in high school or any in pro ball last season due to COVID – Saggese batted a lowly .217/.327/.413 with a hefty 38% punch out rate. Beginning on July 15th through the end of the year he slugged .287/.394/.509 while whiffing in just a quarter of his plate appearances. I'm betting big on the latter numbers. There's some low end starting potential here, but it's years away.

Texas Rangers

Scouting Report: Consider the following:

> Since 2006, only a pair of 20-year-old hitters posted a 122 to 132 wRC+ mark with a 21.5% to 23.5% strikeout rate and a 6% to 8% walk rate. Those two hitters: former three-time All-Star and 2010 batting title winner Carlos Gonzalez, who earned more than $80,000,000 in his career, and – of course – former fifth rounder Thomas Saggese.

Even after two strong showings to open up his career, Saggese remains incredibly underrated – even within the Rangers' improving farm system. From a defensive standpoint, the former prep shortstop has bounced between the keystone and the hot corner with average or better results with the leather. His bat, though, profiles better at second base. Above-average hit tool, average thump and a little bit of speed. There may be enough in the tank where he tops out at 20 homeruns in a season. Great looking swing with natural loft and plenty of bat speed. Don't sleep on this guy. A strong showing in Double-A could position the former Carlsbad High School star as a potential late season calling.

Ceiling: 2.5-win player
Risk: Moderate
MLB ETA: 2023/2024

9. Cole Winn, RHP

	FB	CB	SL	CH	Command	Overall
	60	55	55	60	50	60

Born: 11/25/99	Age: 23	Bats: R	Top Production Comp: Noah Syndergaard
Height: 6-2	Weight: 190	Throws: R	

Season	Team	Age	Level	IP	TBF	K/9	K%	BB/9	BB%	K-BB%	ERA	FIP	xFIP	Pit/Bat
2021	TEX	21	AA	78.0	296	11.19	32.77%	3.00	8.78%	23.99%	2.31	3.15	3.90	4.03
2022	TEX	22	AAA	121.2	573	9.10	21.47%	6.44	15.18%	6.28%	6.51	5.49	6.18	3.95

Background: It's difficult to believe, but nearly a decade ago the Rangers had a highly touted, early round draft pick that was simply annihilating the completion. This former prospect posted an incredible 120-to-27 strikeout-to-walk ratio in 96.2 innings in the old South Atlantic League. A year later, he shredded High-A to go along with a 1.31 ERA across 13 starts and posted a 3-to-1 strikeout-to-walk ratio in 69.0 innings in Double-A, the true testing ground. Then...POOF! Just like that he lost control of the strike zone and never regained it. He walked 35 guys in only 10.2 innings in 2013, another 56 in 59.2 innings the next season, and 39 in 51.0 innings. He would hang on for one season longer than wash out of the minor leagues. Cody Buckel just – inexplicably – lost it. The Rangers selected right-hander Cole Winn in the middle of the first round in 2018. A year later he was battling some minor control demons in the old South Atlantic League, averaging 5.1 walks per nine innings. But after minor league action returned from its COVID-induced absence, Winn discovered a newfound ability: throwing consistent strikes. He finished the year with a dazzling 107-to-31 strikeout-to-walk ratio in just 86.0 innings, all of which occurred in the upper minors. Last season, with his prospect status surging to an all-time high, Winn – simply – lost control of the strike zone as he walked 87 hitters in 112.2 innings of work.

Snippet from The 2022 Prospect Digest Handbook: He's still refining his command, but it's taken several leaps forward. He's going to be a #3-type guy with some potential to uptick if the command continues to improve.

Scouting Report: Consider the following:

> Since 2006, there have been 47 instances in which a 22-year-old hurler surpassed the 100-inning mark at any Triple-A level. Cole Winn's walk percentage, 15.2%, is the second worst total, trailing only former reliever Franklin Morales. Directly after Winn are several notable – successful – big league hurlers, like: Tyler Glasnow, Edinson Volquez, and Trevor Bauer.

There aren't too many 22-year-old hurlers in the upper minors that could go toe-to-toe with Winn's arsenal – both in terms of quality or depth. Plus, mid-90s fastball, plus 12-6 bending curveball, above-average downward biting slider, above-average tumbling changeup. It's the repertoire of a quality big league pitcher – and one that's likely to earn at least $75 million in his career. Last season the command was beyond atrocious – particularly with his fastball, which he was often missing high and to the third base side of the plate. Winn has the athleticism and has thrown consistent quality strikes in the past. So there's hope that he can regain his once promising career – a la Glasnow, Volquez, or Bauer.

Ceiling: 4.0-win player
Risk: Extremely High
MLB ETA: 2023

Texas Rangers

10. Justin Foscue, 2B/3B

Hit	Power	SB	Patience	Glove	Overall
50	50	40	45	50	50

Born: 03/02/99   **Age:** 24   **Bats:** R   **Top Production Comp:** Nick Solak
Height: 6-0   **Weight:** 205   **Throws:** R

Season	Team	Age	Level	PA	1B	2B	3B	HR	SB	CS	BB%	K%	AVG	OBP	SLG	ISO
2021	TEX	22	A+	150	11	11	1	14	1	1	10.67%	26.00%	0.296	0.407	0.736	0.440
2021	TEX	22	AA	104	14	7	0	2	0	1	7.69%	27.88%	0.247	0.317	0.387	0.140
2022	TEX	23	AA	460	68	31	1	15	3	4	9.78%	14.35%	0.288	0.367	0.483	0.195

Background: The Alabama native had a mediocre true freshman season for SEC powerhouse Mississippi State University, batting .241/.332/.353 as the team's main third baseman. The 6-foot, 205-pound infielder had a massive breakout during his sophomore campaign with the Bulldogs, though, slugging .331/.395/.564 with 22 doubles and 14 homeruns. And Foscue maintained that production line during his abbreviated junior campaign too, mashing .321/.464/.509 with plenty of extra-base hits before COVID prematurely ended what could have been a special season. The Rangers drafted him in the opening round that summer, 14th overall, and signed him to a deal worth $3.25 million. The former Bulldog would make his affiliated debut in 2021, spending time with Hickory and Frisco as he batted an aggregate .275/.371/.590 with 19 doubles, one triple, 17 homeruns, and a pair of stolen bases. The organization sent him to the Arizona Fall League – where he continued to hit (.257/.416/.529). Foscue spent the entirety of 2022 with the RoughRiders of Frisco, slugging a Foscue-like .288/.367/.483 with 31 doubles, one triple, 15 homeruns, and three stolen bases (in seven total attempts). His overall production, as measured by *Weighted Runs Created Plus*, topped the league average threshold by 16%.

Snippet from The 2022 Prospect Digest Handbook: Foscue is a quasi-hybrid of the Rangers' Nick Solak and Tampa Bay's Brandon Lowe. Expect Foscue to be a .270/.330/.450-type of bat.

Scouting Report: Consider the following:

> Since 2006, six 23-year-old hitters met the following criteria in a season in any Double-A league (min. 350 PA): 110 to 120 wRC+, 12% to 16% strikeout rate, and a 9% to 11% walk rate. Those six hitters: James Darnell, Justin Sellers, Pablo Reyes, Bryan Peterson, Brian Friday, and Justin Foscue.

A "professional hitter" if there ever was one. Foscue does things well, without having a true standout offensive weapon. He'll take the occasional walk and clobber the occasional dinger. He makes consistent contact. And he'll swipe a bag or three in a year. Foscue's always been a safe low ceiling / high floor guy – a professional hitter.

Ceiling: 2.0-win player
Risk: Low to Moderate
MLB ETA: 2022/2023

11. Owen White, RHP

FB	CB	SL	CH	Command	Overall
55	50	60	55	50	50

Born: 08/09/99   **Age:** 23   **Bats:** R   **Top Production Comp:** N/A
Height: 6-3   **Weight:** 199   **Throws:** R

Season	Team	Age	Level	IP	TBF	K/9	K%	BB/9	BB%	K-BB%	ERA	FIP	xFIP	Pit/Bat
2021	TEX	21	A	33.1	135	14.58	40.00%	3.24	8.89%	31.11%	3.24	2.69	2.92	3.96
2022	TEX	22	A+	58.2	243	12.43	33.33%	2.91	7.82%	25.51%	3.99	3.42	2.98	3.30
2022	TEX	22	AA	21.2	85	9.55	27.06%	1.66	4.71%	22.35%	2.49	2.93	3.77	3.80

Background: There's snake-bitten. And then there's Owen White snake-bitten, which is on a *whole* other level. After the club selected the promising right-hander in the second round out of Carson High School in 2018, White would miss all of 2019 due to Tommy John surgery. Then, of course, there was the pandemic, which knocked out the entire 2020 campaign. White would make it back to the bump in early May of 2021, but that lasted just 2.2 innings before he was shut down for several months – courtesy of a fractured hand when – you know – he slammed it on the ground after making an error. The former second round pick would make nine appearances (eight with Down East and one in the Complex League), throwing a career high 35.1 innings while recording a 56-to-12 strikeout-to-walk ratio. Then he promptly mowed down the Arizona Fall League competition by averaging 9.2 strikeouts and 4.1 walks per nine innings to go along with a tidy 1.91 ERA in six starts with the Surprise Saguaros. Last season started out normally for the 6-foot-3, 199-pound right-hander as he made 11 starts with Hickory and another four with Frisco. But he was shut down in mid-July with "forearm fatigue". White finished the year with 80.1 innings, which seems like a miracle at this point, averaging 11.7 strikeouts and just 2.6 walks per nine innings. He tallied an aggregate 3.59 ERA and a 3.29 FIP.

Snippet from The 2022 Prospect Digest Handbook: There's some reliever risk given his lack of a solid third option. It's important to remember his lack of development time. If the changeup ticks up to average White looks like a backend innings gobbler.

Texas Rangers

Scouting Report: Consider the following:

> Since 2006, only six 22-year-old hurlers posted at least a 32% strikeout percentage with a 6.5% to 8.5% walk percentage in any High-A league (min. 50 IP): Dean Kremer, Logan Allen, Brandon Bielak, Sammy Gervacio, Ben Brown, and – of course – Owen White.

The arsenal didn't seem as crisp as it was the previous season. His fastball was operating in the 91- to 93-mph range, not the 93- to 94-mph I had seen previous. It's still an above-average offering, at times, but it was not the plus offering I was expecting. All three of his offspeed offerings are in the above-average range. He's now entering his age-23 seasons with a total of 115.2 innings on his professional resume, spanning parts of five seasons. There's backend starting potential, but he seems to be made of glass.

Ceiling: 2.5-win player
Risk: Moderate to High
MLB ETA: 2023/2024

12. Tekoah Roby, RHP

FB	CB	SL	CH	Command	Overall
55	60	50	55	50	50

Born: 09/18/01	Age: 21	Bats: R	Top Production Comp: N/A
Height: 6-1	Weight: 185	Throws: R	

Season	Team	Age	Level	IP	TBF	K/9	K%	BB/9	BB%	K-BB%	ERA	FIP	xFIP	Pit/Bat
2021	TEX	19	A	22.0	90	14.32	38.89%	2.86	7.78%	31.11%	2.45	2.75	3.33	4.00
2022	TEX	20	A+	104.2	444	10.83	28.38%	3.01	7.88%	20.50%	4.64	4.79	3.91	3.79

Background: The club's third round pick out of Pine Forest High School three years ago, Roby started his professional career off with a bang during the 2021 season. The 6-foot-1, 185-pound right-hander tallied a tidy 2.45 across six starts with the Wood Ducks, averaging an impossible 14.3 strikeouts and just 2.9 walks per nine innings. But a sprained elbow knocked him out of commission in mid-June through the remainder of the year. Despite the lack of innings on his professional resume, the Rangers sent the promising right-hander to Hickory for the 2022 season. And Roby continued to impress. Making 21 starts and one relief appearance, the North Carolina-born hurler recorded a 126-to-35 strikeout-to-walk ratio in 104.2 innings. He finished his first – healthy – season with a 4.64 ERA, a 4.79 FIP, and a 3.91 xFIP.

Snippet from The 2022 Prospect Digest Handbook: He has the makings of a #5-type arm.

Scouting Report: Consider the following:

> Since 2006, only two 20-year-old hurlers posted a 27.5% to 29.5% strikeout percentage with a 7% to 10% walk percentage in any High-A league (min. 100 IP): Ian Anderson and Tekoah Roby.

Big time spin rate guy. Roby's above-average heater sits, typically, in the 92- to 94-mph range and can touch as high as 97 mph on occasion. His curveball looks significantly better than the previous year, consistently grading out as a plus offering. He'll mix in a rare average slider, and an above-average low 80s changeup. Roby throws a surprising amount of strikes, particularly with his hammer of a curveball. There's backend starting potential here. Don't be surprised if Roby continues to miss bats in Double-A and spends a month of two in Triple-A in 2023.

Ceiling: 2.0-win player
Risk: Moderate
MLB ETA: 2024

13. Aaron Zavala, RF

Hit	Power	SB	Patience	Glove	Overall
55	45	40	60	50	45

Born: 06/23/00	Age: 23	Bats: L	Top Production Comp: N/A
Height: 6-0	Weight: 193	Throws: R	

Season	Team	Age	Level	PA	1B	2B	3B	HR	SB	CS	BB%	K%	AVG	OBP	SLG	ISO
2021	TEX	21	A	67	11	4	0	1	7	0	14.93%	19.40%	0.302	0.433	0.434	0.132
2022	TEX	22	A+	375	59	10	3	11	10	5	18.13%	21.07%	0.278	0.424	0.441	0.164
2022	TEX	22	AA	139	18	8	0	5	4	1	15.11%	20.86%	0.277	0.410	0.482	0.205

Background: The Rangers have quietly put together a string of very strong draft classes over the past several seasons. Some of it is certainly due to their dreadful big league performances and their subsequent draft positions. But the front office has also found incredible value beyond the first round, like Brock Porter, their way over-slot, handsomely paid fourth rounder last summer, or Evan Carter or Tekoah Roby or Thomas Saggese or former Oregon star Aaron Zavala. Taken in the second round two years ago after a phenomenal career with the Pac-12 powerhouse, Zavala left the Ducks as a career .354/.465/.506 hitter, including nearly hitting .400 between 2020 and

Texas Rangers

2021. After signing with the club for a surprisingly low $830,000, Zavala was able to log 22 low level minor league games during his debut, hitting a Zavala-like .293/.419/.400. Last season the lefty-swinging corner outfielder appeared in 111 games between Hickory and Frisco, slugging .277/.420/.453 with 18 doubles, three triples, 16 homeruns, and 14 stolen bases (in 20 total attempts). His aggregate production surpassed the league average mark by an impressive 40%, according to *Weighted Runs Created*.

Snippet from The 2022 Prospect Digest Handbook: Zavala's a little miscast as a right fielder because he doesn't have the traditional thump, but could carve out a career as a super-utility guy. Good arm. Lightning quick bat that's geared towards line drives and plenty of doubles. There's some Adam Eaton to Zavala's game.

Scouting Report: Consider the following:

> Since 2006, only three 22-year-old hitters met the following criteria in any High-A league (min. 350 PA): 138 to 148 wRC+ with a walk rate north of 14%. Those three hitters: Rob Refsnyder, Mark Zagunis, and Aaron Zavala.

Similar to a few of the club's other top bats, Zavala's a workhorse at the plate, just grinding out at bat after at bat, forcing the opposition to throw pitch after pitch. But a large red flag popped up last season, though: he can't hit southpaws. Zavala batted an impressive .309/.454/.515 against right-handers, but struggled to the tune of .183/.318/.269 against left-handers. Plus he struck nearly twice as much against lefties as well (32.5% vs. 17.3%). That level of ineptitude is career damning unless he can turn it around. Zavala may never completely solve southpaws, but he should improve upon that poor showing thanks to his lightning quick, short swing.

Ceiling: 1.5- to 2.0-win player
Risk: Moderate
MLB ETA: 2023

14. Yeison Morrobel, OF

Hit	Power	SB	Patience	Glove	Overall
50/55	40/50	50/40	50	50	50

Born: 12/08/03	Age: 19	Bats: L	Top Production Comp: N/A
Height: 6-2	Weight: 170	Throws: L	

Season	Team	Age	Level	PA	1B	2B	3B	HR	SB	CS	BB%	K%	AVG	OBP	SLG	ISO
2021	TEX	17	DSL	229	32	11	6	1	8	4	13.10%	10.92%	0.270	0.395	0.411	0.141
2022	TEX	18	CPX	173	33	13	1	3	5	5	9.83%	19.65%	0.329	0.405	0.487	0.158
2022	TEX	18	A	29	5	1	0	0	2	1	10.34%	20.69%	0.231	0.310	0.269	0.038

Background: Signed out of Luperon, Dominican Republic, for $1.8 million during the 2020-21 offseason. Morrobel would make his affiliated debut with his home country's Summer League team just a few months later, hitting a .270/.395/.411 with 11 doubles, six triples, one homeruns, and eight stolen bases (in only 12 attempts). The Rangers' brass shipped the 6-foot-2, 170-pound outfielder to the Complex League for the start of 2022. Morrobel mashed his way through 41 contests, slugging .329/.405/.487 with 13 doubles, one triple, three homeruns, and five stolen bases (in 10 total attempts). According to *Weighted Runs Created Plus*, his production topped the league average threshold by a whopping 44%. Morrobel spent the last week or so of the season with the Wood Ducks.

Scouting Report: The tools to be an impact player are present: above-average speed, strong contact rates, average power potential, solid glove. And while Morrobel's been able to handle himself well enough in the foreign and stateside rookie leagues, the swing is still a work in progress and can be lengthy. Morrobel could be one of the bigger breakout stars in 2023.

Ceiling: 2.0-win player
Risk: Moderate to High
MLB ETA: 2025/2026

15. Dustin Harris, 1B/LF

Hit	Power	SB	Patience	Glove	Overall
50	50	50/40	50	45	45

Born: 07/08/99	Age: 23	Bats: L	Top Production Comp: N/A
Height: 6-2	Weight: 185	Throws: R	

Season	Team	Age	Level	PA	1B	2B	3B	HR	SB	CS	BB%	K%	AVG	OBP	SLG	ISO
2021	TEX	21	A	306	54	11	3	10	20	1	11.11%	15.69%	0.301	0.389	0.483	0.181
2021	TEX	21	A+	160	34	10	0	10	5	1	8.13%	15.63%	0.372	0.425	0.648	0.276
2022	TEX	22	AA	382	50	16	2	17	19	5	10.99%	19.37%	0.257	0.346	0.471	0.215

Background: Drafted by the Oakland Athletics out of St. Petersburg College during the summer of 2019. The A's eventually flipped the slugging corner infielder / outfielder along with Marcus Smith for declining veteran lefty Mike Minor in late August three years ago. The 6-foot-2, 185-pound masher has remained a consistent force at the plate during his four-year minor league career. Two years ago the former late round pick clobbered Low-A and High-A pitching to the tune of .327/.401/.542 with 21 doubles, three triples, 20 homeruns, and 25 homeruns (in only 27 total attempts). Last season, unsurprisingly, the Rangers sent Harris into the minors' most difficult level, Double-A, for the 2022 season. And the St. Petersburg alum came out bloody and bruised, but passed the test. Harris batted .257/.346/.471 with 16 doubles, two triples, 17 homeruns, and 19 stolen bases (24 total attempts). Per *Weighted Runs Created Plus*, his overall production surpassed the league average threshold by 7%. Harris is sporting a career .302/.382/.487 slash line.

Scouting Report: Consider the following:

> Since 2006, only three 22-year-old hitters met the following criteria in any Double-A league (min. 350 PA): 102 to 112 wRC+ with a 17% to 21% strikeout rate and a 10% to 12% walk rate. Those three hitters: Shane Peterson, David Cooper, and Dustin Harris.

Regardless of whatever big league value Harris may – or may not – generate, he's already exceeded every expectation placed upon an eleventh round pick. Below-average defender at first base or leftfield, the onus is placed heavily on the bat to be the sole carrying tool. Average power, hit tool, and speed. Harris lacks a true standout tool, as well as a red flag. He finished last season with the highest fly ball rate of his career in 2022 (43.8%). Combine that with Frisco's homer-depressing environment, and it wouldn't be shocking to see him slug 25 or more dingers in 2023. Harris could fake it as a low end starter on a non-contending team, but he's best suited for a bench role. Best case scenario is Kole Calhoun-type production with a .250/.320/.420 slash line.

Ceiling: 1.5-win player
Risk: Moderate
MLB ETA: 2023

16. Anthony Gutierrez, CF

Hit	Power	SB	Patience	Glove	Overall
40/45	50	40	50	50	45

Born: 11/25/04 **Age:** 18 **Bats:** R **Top Production Comp:** N/A
Height: 6-3 **Weight:** 180 **Throws:** R

Season	Team	Age	Level	PA	1B	2B	3B	HR	SB	CS	BB%	K%	AVG	OBP	SLG	ISO
2022	TEX	17	DSL	103	21	8	0	3	5	3	7.77%	17.48%	0.352	0.408	0.538	0.187
2022	TEX	17	CPX	87	13	5	2	1	6	3	3.45%	18.39%	0.259	0.299	0.407	0.148

Background: MLB Pipeline notes the interesting free agency history of Gutierrez, namely: the wiry outfielder had an agreement to sign with the Nationals during the 2023 period, but opted to sign with the Rangers a year earlier for less money. When it was all said and done, the 6-foot-3, 180-pound centerfielder agreed to a deal with Texas for just a smidgeon less than $2 million. A native of El Tocuyo, Venezuela, Gutierrez made his affiliated debut last season, splitting time between the club's foreign and rookie league affiliates. He slugged an aggregate .308/.358/.477 with 13 doubles, two triples, four homeruns, and 11 stolen bases between both stops. His overall production, according to *weighted Runs Created Plus*, topped the league average threshold by 23%.

Scouting Report: Long and wiry with plenty of room to fill out on his 6-foot-3, 180-pound frame. Gutierrez has the speed and athleticism to not only stay in centerfield, but also develop into a solid defender. The swing is a bit robotic, lacking fluidity, but he shows average power and projects for 20-homeruns. Strong bat-to-ball skills. Great bat speed. Gutierrez could be one of the more intriguing names to watch in 2023.

Ceiling: 1.5-win player
Risk: Moderate
MLB ETA: 2025/2026

17. Gleider Figuereo, 3B

Hit	Power	SB	Patience	Glove	Overall
40/45	55	50/35	50	45/50	40

Born: 06/27/04 **Age:** 19 **Bats:** L **Top Production Comp:** N/A
Height: 6-0 **Weight:** 165 **Throws:** R

Season	Team	Age	Level	PA	1B	2B	3B	HR	SB	CS	BB%	K%	AVG	OBP	SLG	ISO
2021	TEX	17	DSL	190	24	6	4	2	3	2	14.74%	16.32%	0.231	0.354	0.359	0.128
2022	TEX	18	CPX	146	16	5	5	9	7	1	10.27%	22.60%	0.280	0.363	0.616	0.336
2022	TEX	18	A	26	5	0	0	0	0	0	7.69%	30.77%	0.208	0.269	0.208	0.000

Background: A bit of an under-the-radar signing out of Las Matas de Farfan, Dominican Republic two years ago. The Rangers convinced the lefty-swinging third baseman to join the organization for just $80,000 in mid-January 2021. Figuereo, whose father player briefly in the low levels of the Rangers' system more than 20 years ago, looked a bit overmatched during his debut in the Dominican Summer League a few months after turning pro; he batted a lowly .231/.355/.359 with just 12 extra-base knocks in 48 total games. Last season, though, was a completely different story for the now-slugging infielder. Figuereo belted out five doubles, five triples, and nine

Texas Rangers

homeruns to go along with seven stolen bases (in eight attempts) en route to mashing .280/.363/.616 in only 35 games in the Complex League. Texas sent him up to Low-A for the final week of the season; he went 5-for-24.

Scouting Report: Just for fun, here are Figuereo's numbers in the Complex League pro-rated for a full 162-game season: 23 doubles, 23 triples, 42 homeruns, and 32 stolen bases. Yeah, that'll play – for sure. Figuereo went from a light-hitting, punch-less infielder into a bonafide knock-it-out-the-park third baseman in the matter of a year. Heavier than his listed weight of 165 pounds, Figuereo shows solid bat speed, though the swing is long, forcing him to get underneath the ball at times. He didn't struggle with contact issues in the Complex, at least in terms of strikeouts. But he did swing-and-miss a lot -23.9% of his swings, according to FanGraphs. Expect him to deal with some punch out issues in the coming years.

Ceiling: 1.0-win player
Risk: Moderate
MLB ETA: 2026

18. Danyer Cueva, SS

Hit	Power	SB	Patience	Glove	Overall
45/55	35/45	50	50	50	40

Born: 05/27/04	Age: 19	Bats: L	Top Production Comp: N/A
Height: 6-1	Weight: 160	Throws: R	

Season	Team	Age	Level	PA	1B	2B	3B	HR	SB	CS	BB%	K%	AVG	OBP	SLG	ISO
2021	TEX	17	DSL	232	42	11	3	1	9	4	9.48%	20.69%	0.282	0.375	0.381	0.099
2022	TEX	18	CPX	189	42	10	1	5	3	2	5.29%	21.16%	0.330	0.376	0.483	0.153
2022	TEX	18	A	18	2	0	0	0	0	0	0.00%	27.78%	0.111	0.111	0.111	0.000

Background: Another one of the club's high profile, shortstop phenoms signed off the international free agency market. Texas signed the lefty-swinging infielder to a hefty deal worth a touch over $1 million mid-January two years ago. Cueva turned in a solid, yet unremarkable, debut in the foreign rookie league as he batted .282/.375/.381 with 11 doubles, three triples, one homerun, and nine stolen bases. The Rangers bounced the teenage prospect up to the Complex League for the 2022 season. And like his counterpart Gleider Figuereo, Cueva turned in a breakout campaign. He mashed .330/.376/.483 with 10 doubles, one triple, five homeruns, and three stolen bases. Cueva spent the last week of the year with the Wood Ducks of Down East.

Scouting Report: Another one of the club's low level everyday lottery tickets. Cueva didn't provide the offensive thump that Gleider Figuereo did, but he was certainly a force among his peers. Short quick stroke that should allow for at least 45-grade power in the coming years. Cueva displayed solid patience and a decent glove. If everything breaks just the right way, the hit tool may creep into 55-grade territory.

Ceiling: 1.0-win player
Risk: Moderate
MLB ETA: 2026

19. Maximo Acosta, SS

Hit	Power	SB	Patience	Glove	Overall
40/45	40/45	60	50	50	40

Born: 10/29/02	Age: 19	Bats: R	Top Production Comp: N/A
Height: 6-1	Weight: 187	Throws: R	

Season	Team	Age	Level	PA	1B	2B	3B	HR	SB	CS	BB%	K%	AVG	OBP	SLG	ISO
2021	TEX	18	CPX	68	10	2	2	1	7	2	4.41%	22.06%	0.246	0.279	0.393	0.148
2022	TEX	19	A	456	75	26	1	4	44	17	8.77%	19.08%	0.262	0.341	0.361	0.099

Background: Like a few of the club's other notable youngsters, Acosta entered last season with little minor league experience – despite joining the club four years ago. Acosta, of course, would miss the entirety of the 2020 season courtesy of the COVID pandemic. The front office would send the former International Bonus Baby to the Complex League for the start of the 2021 campaign. But after just 17 games and 68 plate appearances, Acosta would hit the disabled list and remain there for the rest of the season. He finished his abbreviated debut with a lowly .246/.279/.393 slash line. The cause for the lengthy injury stay: thoracic outlet syndrome. Finally healthy least year, the Rangers brass continued to push the Venezuelan infielder through the low levels, shipping him up to Low-A. The 6-foot-1, 187-pound second baseman / shortstop hit a mediocre .262/.341/.361 with 26 doubles, one triple, four homeruns, and 44 stolen bases (in 61 total attempts). Per *Weighted Runs Created Plus*, his overall production surpassed the league average threshold by just 1%.

Scouting Report: Consider the following:

Texas Rangers

> Since 2006, only four 19-year-old hitters posted a 95 to 105 wRC+ with an 18% to 22% strikeout rate and an 8% to 10% walk rate in any Low-A league (min. 350 PA): Tyler Wade, Michael Siani, Roberto Campos, and Maximo Acosta.

Lauded as one of the more advanced bats in the 2019 international class, the Rangers had no qualms in handing the young Venezuelan prospect a hefty $1.65 million deal. And while his approach at the plate is sound, leading to solid peripherals, the actual results have been mediocre – at best. Big healthy cuts that haven't led to much homerun power, Acosta, instead, peppered line-drives around the outfield as he swatted 26 doubles last season. Some of those will eventually turn into long balls at some point in his career he matures and gets stronger. Beyond his plus speed, there's just not a true standout tool (present or future) that allows him to project as a big league regular. He's split time on both sides of the keystone, but his final landing spot will likely be second base.

Ceiling: 1.0-win player
Risk: Moderate
MLB ETA: 2025

20. Antoine Kelly, LHP

FB	SL	CH	Command	Overall
60	50/55	50	30	40

Born: 12/05/99	Age: 23	Bats: L	Top Production Comp: Taylor Hearn
Height: 6-6	Weight: 205	Throws: L	

Season	Team	Age	Level	IP	TBF	K/9	K%	BB/9	BB%	K-BB%	ERA	FIP	xFIP	Pit/Bat
2021	MIL	21	A	17.0	79	12.71	30.38%	8.47	20.25%	10.13%	6.88	4.15	5.59	4.24
2022	MIL	22	A+	91.0	388	11.77	30.67%	5.14	13.40%	17.27%	3.86	3.80	3.96	4.13
2022	TEX	22	AA	18.2	86	11.57	27.91%	9.16	22.09%	5.81%	7.23	4.88	6.19	4.65

Background: Originally taken by the Padres in the 13th round coming out of Maine Township High School East in 2018, Kelly bypassed the chance to join the Friars and – instead – enrolled at Wabash Valley College. After a dominant showing with the Illinois-based JuCo school, the Brewers came calling the big lefty's name in the second round, signing him to a deal worth just a smidgeon over a million dollars. Kelly would turn in a dominant, albeit abbreviated debut in 2019, and a disastrous, command-less showing in 2021 that was plagued by Thoracic Outlet Syndrome surgery. Halfway through his third season in Milwaukee's system, the front office shipped the 6-foot-6, 205-pound left-hander (as well as Mark Mathias) to Texas for veteran reliever Matt Bush, the failed #1 overall pick in the 2004 draft. As soon as Kelly joined the Rangers' system he was bumped up to the toughest minor league level, Double-A, for seven final appearances. Kelly finished his third pro season with a career best 109.2 innings, averaging 11.7 strikeouts and 5.8 walks per nine innings. He compiled an aggregate 4.43 ERA.

Snippet from The 2022 Prospect Digest Handbook: While he's only entering his age-22 season, I think he's going to head down the path to relief-dom. In order to avoid that, he needs two major transformations to occur: (1) consistently throw more quality strikes and (B) develop a legitimate secondary weapon.

Scouting Report: Consider the following:

> Since 2006, only four 22-year-old hurlers posted a 29% to 32% strikeout percentage with a walk percentage of at least 12% in any High-A league (min. 75 IP): Oliver Ortega, Blake King, Doug Nikhazy, and Antoine Kelly.

Built like a NBA-sized small forward with long limbs and tons of athleticism. Kelly bounced back from the Thoracic Outlet Syndrome surgery better than hoped / expected. Plus mid-90s fastball. The slider showed more horizontal movement than in previous years, though it's still an average offering. And the changeup looked better as well. The problem for Kelly – and it's *always* been the problem – is that he lacks any type of semblance of control. And just forget about command. He's a low-slot slinging, cross-body throwing hurler that impedes his ability to consistently throw strikes. Until that's cleaned up – and it likely won't be – Kelly will be nothing more than an erratic, hard-throwing reliever sitting at the end of the bench, to be used only in blowout games.

Ceiling: 0.5- to 1.0-win player
Risk: Moderate
MLB ETA: 2024

Toronto Blue Jays

Top Prospects

Toronto Blue Jays

1. Ricky Tiedemann, LHP

FB	SL	CH	Command	Overall
60	45/50	55	50/55	60

Born: 08/18/02	Age: 20	Bats: L	Top Production Comp: Carlos Rodon
Height: 6-4	Weight: 220	Throws: L	

Season	Team	Age	Level	IP	TBF	K/9	K%	BB/9	BB%	K-BB%	ERA	FIP	xFIP	Pit/Bat
2022	TOR	19	A	30.0	110	14.70	44.55%	3.90	11.82%	32.73%	1.80	2.09	2.29	3.83
2022	TOR	19	A+	37.2	150	12.90	36.00%	2.87	8.00%	28.00%	2.39	2.92	3.27	4.03
2022	TOR	19	AA	11.0	41	11.45	34.15%	3.27	9.76%	24.39%	2.45	2.23	3.08	4.15

Background: The former Golden West College ace has become the de facto top pick for the Blue Jays' 2021 draft class. Toronto opened up that year's midsummer selection process by netting University of Mississippi ace Gunnar Hoglund with the 19th overall pick. Less than a year later the club would package Hoglund with Zach Logue, Kevin Smith, and Kirby Sneed to acquire All-Star three-time Gold Glove winning third baseman Matt Chapman. Their second rounder was lost due to the George Springer signing. So Ricky Tiedemann, who dazzled the JuCo competition for just 38.0 innings before his selection, is the next man up. His sparkling performance last season has proven that not only is he the best prospect the club draft in 2021, but also among the best in the entire class. Toronto kept the 6-foot-4, 220-pound southpaw from making his affiliated debut two years ago, opting, instead, to hold out until 2022. Tiedemann made six dominating starts with Dunedin, allowing only 11 base hits and six earned runs in 30 innings. The front office saw enough from their surging southpaw and decided to bump him up to Vancouver in late May. Tiedemann promptly ripped off eight more dominant starts, including a stretch that saw him hold the opposition to one earned run over his first 23.2 innings of work. Toronto decision makers – once again – had seen enough and deemed the hard-throwing youngster ready for the minors' toughest challenge – Class AA. Tiedemann promptly went out and allowed only three earned runs over 11 innings. Tiedemann finished his breakout season – *and professional debut* – with 78.2 innings of work, 117 strikeouts and just 29 walks. He averaged 13.4 strikeouts and 3.3 walks per nine innings. He tallied a tidy 2.17 ERA, a 2.23 FIP, and a 3.08 xFIP.

Snippet from The 2022 Prospect Digest Handbook: Combined with Tiedemann's low slot and lack of a third pitch, I think he's looking at a life of relief-dom. Mechanically speaking, he looks like Brad Hand.

Scouting Report: Consider the following:

> Last season, there were 659 minor league hurlers that tossed 70 or more innings. Tiedemann's strikeout percentage, 38.9%, ranked second, trailing only San Francisco's Kyle Harrison.

One of the loosest arms, generating one of the easiest plus fastballs in all of the minor leagues; Tiedemann saw a noticeable uptick in velocity from his pre-draft days to last season. The lanky lefty was sitting 94- to 96-mph and peaking at 97 mph. He features two plus-plus secondary offerings: a low- to mid-80s sweeping slider that absolutely death on lefties and righties, as well as a mid-80s changeup. The intriguing part of Tiedemann's changeup is the fact that there's natural cutting motion, not the typical arm-side fade that's associated with the pitch. Throw in a surprisingly improved feel for the strike zone and Tiedemann has the makings of a bonafide ace. The lone red flag, thus far, is the fact that he rarely turned over a lineup, especially in High-A and Double-A.

Ceiling: 5.0-win player
Risk: Moderate
MLB ETA: 2023

2. Brandon Barriera, LHP

FB	CB	SL	CH	Command	Overall
70	55	55	60	45	60

Born: 03/04/04	Age: 19	Bats: L	Top Production Comp: N/A
Height: 6-2	Weight: 180	Throws: L	

Background: The New York-born Florida transplant is no stranger to playing elite age-appropriate competition. The young left-hander made a trio of appearances for Team USA's 12U squad back in 2016, throwing 5.0 innings of work, handing out five free passes and fanning a couple of hitters. He also went 1-for-4 with a dinger as well. A few years later, in 2019, the then-15-year-old hurler made a pair of starts for the Team USA's 15U club, posting a 10-to-4 strikeout-to-walk ratio in 9.1 innings of work. Last season the 6-foot-2, 180-pound lefty was limited to just 37 innings as a senior, striking out a whopping 68 and walking 11 hitters during that span. The interesting part, as Kiley McDaniel notes in a June 14th article for *ESPN*, is that Barriera made the decision to prematurely end his final amateur season in self-preservation, a way to avoid injury – namely Tommy John issues – as the draft was closing in. Toronto selected him in the opening round, 23rd overall, and signed him to a hefty $3,597,500. He did not appear in an affiliated game.

Toronto Blue Jays

Scouting Report: Per the usual, my pre-draft write-up:

> "As McDaniel notes, Barriera's long been on scouts' radars – with plenty of game tape available of a young freshman throwing in the upper 80s and lower 90s. Nowadays it's peaking in the upper 90s and it's in the conversation for one of the class's best heaters – a rarity for a southpaw. He'll complement the plus-plus offering with a strong trio of offspeed pitches: a late bending curveball, a tightly spun slider, and a tremendous changeup that's his best secondary weapon. The changeup was on display early during a 2021 Perfect Game appearance. Even though the fastball has plenty of giddy up, Barriera doesn't look anywhere close to being physically maxed out. He's tall and lanky, but strong with one of the loosest arms / deliveries around. He's battled command issues – which is nothing new for a southpaw – but there's some Cole Hamels-type potential here. He could be special, if he avoids the injury nexus."

Ceiling: 3.5-win player
Risk: High
MLB ETA: 2025/2026

3. Addison Barger, 3B/SS

Hit	Power	SB	Patience	Glove	Overall
50	60	40	50	50	55

Born: 11/12/99	Age: 23	Bats: L	Top Production Comp: Casey McGehee
Height: 6-0	Weight: 175	Throws: R	

Season	Team	Age	Level	PA	1B	2B	3B	HR	SB	CS	BB%	K%	AVG	OBP	SLG	ISO
2021	TOR	21	A	374	40	21	2	18	7	0	9.63%	32.89%	0.249	0.334	0.492	0.243
2022	TOR	22	A+	292	41	21	2	14	7	2	8.56%	26.03%	0.300	0.366	0.558	0.258
2022	TOR	22	AA	198	35	11	0	9	2	2	9.09%	25.25%	0.313	0.384	0.528	0.216

Background: It was a tough year on the club's best hitting prospects. Toronto's most promising infielder, Orelvis Martinez, struggled to hit his weight in Double-A. The front office dealt away their top overall prospect, backstop Gabriel Moreno, as well as former first rounder Jordan Groshans. But the struggles and losses were buoyed by the emergence of two under-the-radar prospects: corner outfielder Gabriel Martinez, and shortstop / third baseman Addison Barger. While there was ongoing speculation as to whether the Blue Jays could risk safely leaving Martinez off the club's 40-man roster (he was not added, nor was he taken in the Rule 5 draft), the front office did add Barger. Drafted out of C. Leon King High School in the sixth round in 2018, the lefty-swinging shortstop showed slow, steady progress through the opening seasons of his career, leading to his breakout in 2022. The former prep star looked abysmal during his lengthy debut in the Gulf Coast League that summer, hitting .194/.318/.322. He was limited to 13 games in the Appalachian League the following season – though he managed to bat .283/.345/.434. Once minor league ball returned to action after the COVID delay, Barger spent the majority of the 2021 season squaring off against the Low-A Southeast League. And he turned in a surprising production line: .249/.334/.492 with 21 doubles, two triples, 18 homeruns, and seven stolen bases – which lead to his true breakout last season. Appearing in a combined 124 games between Vancouver (69 games), New Hampshire (47), and Buffalo (8), the Washington-native mashed .308/.378/.555 with career highs in doubles (33), homeruns (26), and stolen bases (nine). Per *Weighted Runs Created Plus*, his production topped the league average mark by a whopping 51%.

Scouting Report: Consider the following:

> Since 2006, only two 22-year-old hitters met the following criteria in a High-A season (min. 275 PA): 145 to 155 wRC+, 7% to 10% walk rate, and a 24% to 28% strikeout rate. Those two hitters: future Hall of Famer Paul Goldschmidt and – of course – the quietly underrated Addison Barger.

An average defender at either shortstop or third base, the lefty-swinging Barger was a force to be reckoned with last season, showing above-average power, solid patience, and a surprisingly strong hit tool – especially given his proclivity to the punch out. Barger's a student of hitting, which helps explain his emergence. Semi-open, upright stance with a newly-found large leg kick, Barger has a ferocious swing and that creates an explosion on contact. His leg kick, by the way, is nearly equivalent – if not equal to – a pitcher's leg kick. As long as he's getting the foot down in time, though, it shouldn't be a problem. It should be noted that he improved his strikeout rate considerably since 2021. He also showed significant improvement in his ability to handle southpaws as well, slugging .291/.364/.466 last season against them. It almost sounds crazy, but there's a little Josh Donaldson to his offensive game. There's a solid chance he develops into a .280/.350/.450 type hitter. But he's got to repeat the production against lefties *and* keep his strikeout rate in check.

Ceiling: 3.0-win player
Risk: Moderate to High
MLB ETA: 2024

Toronto Blue Jays

4. Yosver Zulueta, RHP

FB	CB	SL	CH	Command	Overall
70	60	55	N/A	40	55

Born: 01/23/98 **Age:** 25 **Bats:** R **Top Production Comp:** N/A
Height: 6-1 **Weight:** 190 **Throws:** R

Season	Team	Age	Level	IP	TBF	K/9	K%	BB/9	BB%	K-BB%	ERA	FIP	xFIP	Pit/Bat
2022	TOR	24	A	12.0	51	17.25	45.10%	2.25	5.88%	39.22%	3.00	1.44	2.12	3.88
2022	TOR	24	A+	23.2	102	11.79	30.39%	4.18	10.78%	19.61%	3.80	3.37	3.82	4.23
2022	TOR	24	AA	15.1	73	14.67	34.25%	8.22	19.18%	15.07%	4.11	4.33	4.49	4.38

Background: The stocky, well-built right-hander from Remedios, Cuba, first popped up on scouts' radar several years before making the leap stateside. Zulueta made his debut in the Cuban National Series as a spry, erratic 18-year-old during the 2016-17 season. The hard-throwing hurler would make 11 appearances, including three starts, for Naranjas de Villa Clara, posting a problematic 22-to-17 strikeout-to-walk ratio in 22.0 innings of work. Zulueta spent the next two seasons working for the club, as well as half of a season with Alazanes de Granma, before joining Toronto's organization in mid-June 2019. The club handed him a million dollar deal that summer. Unfortunately, Zulueta eventually underwent Tommy John surgery to repair a barking right elbow. He would – *finally* – make his affiliated debut two years ago. But that lasted just three – THREE! – pitches before he hit the disabled list, *again*. This culprit was a torn ACL in his knee. Healthy for the start of the 2022 season, the 6-foot-1, 190-pound right-hander took off like a bat out of hell as he shredded the Low-A competition for three starts, breezed through six starts in Double-A. Halfway through his tenure with New Hampshire he hit the disabled list for a month with knee and shoulder issues. He eventually made it back to the Fisher Cats' mound in early September. He would cap his wild ride of a first full season in the minors with three brief appearances with the Bisons of Buffalo. Zulueta finished 2022 with 84 punch outs, 32 walks, and a 3.72 ERA in 55.2 innings.

Scouting Report: One of the farm system's best: fastball, curveball, and arm. And his above-average, hard-tilting slider is in the conversation for the best as well. It's easy to see why the club has remained so incredibly patient with the injury-ridden right-hander. His fastball sits in the 94- to 97-mph range and will reach as high as 99 mph. His curveball is so unfairly wicked, a snap-dragon that will haunt dreams. His slider, which he commands the worst of the three, is above-average and flashes plus at times. Zulueta reportedly throws a changeup as well, but not only did I not see one during a late season contest, but the catcher never even signaled for it either. Zulueta has the second highest ceiling among all Toronto minor league arms. Whether he can stay on the mound *and* throw consistent strikes is an entirely different question. Some of those command / control issues could just be from a lack of mound time.

Ceiling: 3.0-win player
Risk: Moderate to High
MLB ETA: 2023

5. Gabriel Martinez, LF/RF

Hit	Power	SB	Patience	Glove	Overall
N/A	N/A	N/A	N/A	N/A	N/A

Born: 07/24/02 **Age:** 20 **Bats:** R **Top Production Comp:** N/A
Height: 6-0 **Weight:** 170 **Throws:** R

Season	Team	Age	Level	PA	1B	2B	3B	HR	SB	CS	BB%	K%	AVG	OBP	SLG	ISO
2021	TOR	18	CPX	125	25	8	0	0	7	2	16.80%	14.40%	0.330	0.448	0.410	0.080
2021	TOR	18	A	13	3	1	0	0	0	1	7.69%	30.77%	0.333	0.385	0.417	0.083
2022	TOR	19	A	264	44	14	0	11	3	1	8.33%	17.05%	0.288	0.348	0.483	0.196
2022	TOR	19	A+	113	22	8	0	3	0	0	7.96%	15.04%	0.324	0.381	0.490	0.167

Background: It doesn't happen all that frequently, but Martinez is one the few prospects that debuts during their age-16 season. Signed out of Maracaibo, Venezuela, on his birthday in 2018, the 6-foot, 170-pound corner outfielder would make his affiliated debut with the Jays' foreign rookie league squad the next summer. The results were mediocre given his age and level of competition: he batted .239/.317/.347 with 13 doubles, two triples, two homeruns, and eight stolen bases. Toronto moved the teenager into the Gulf Coast League once Minor League Baseball returned from its COVID-induced vacation in 2021. This time, though, the wiry corner outfielder proved to be up to the task as he mashed .330/.448/.410 with eight doubles in 31 games. The club let him dip his toes in the proverbial waters of Low-A at the end of the year. Last season, still only 19-years-old, Martinez turned in his best offensive campaign to date. He opened the year up by slashing .288/.349/.483 in 65 games with Dunedin. And he continued to shred the competition after a promotion up to Vancouver (.324/.381/.490). The Venezuelan youngster finished the year with an aggregate .293/.355/.477 with 23 doubles, 14 homeruns, and four stolen bases – despite missing more than a month of action due to a fracture wrist that required surgery. His overall production, according to *Weighted Runs Created Plus*, topped the league average mark by 34%.

Snippet from The 2022 Prospect Digest Handbook: Patient approach at the plate with a contact oriented swing. Above-average runner. He could be very interesting to watch in 2021 as he's likely ticketed for Dunedin for a full year.

Toronto Blue Jays

Scouting Report: Consider the following:

> Since 2006, only four 19-year-old hitters met the following criteria in any Low-A league (min. 250 PA): 130 to 140 wRC+, a 15% to 19% strikeout rate, and an 8% to 12% walk rate. Those four hitters: Hao Yu Lee, Alejandro Osuna, Bryan Anderson, Gabriel Martinez.

Very fast hands that allow him to stay inside the baseball, the head of the bat crackles though the strike zone like a whip. Martinez is an intriguing prospect because he takes the toes-to-nose approach at the strike zone, but (A) consistently makes contact (a la Vladimir Guerrero), (B) walks an average amount of times, and (C) shows a willingness to shoot the ball the other way. Dunedin's one of the more homer-friendly environments in the minors, so it's not surprising to see Martinez's power surge in 2022. He's likely ticketed for another brief stint in High-A before moving on to Double-A, so it'll be interesting to see if he can continue belting dingers at the same pace. Above-average hit tool, average power, strong contact skills, and an average glove. There's starting material here, maybe more if he continues to hit like he did in 2022.

Ceiling: 2.0-win player
Risk: Moderate
MLB ETA: 2024

6. Dahian Santos, RHP

FB	SL	CH	Command	Overall
55	55/60	55	40/50	50

Born: 02/26/03 **Age:** 20 **Bats:** R **Top Production Comp:** N/A
Height: 5-11 **Weight:** 160 **Throws:** R

Season	Team	Age	Level	IP	TBF	K/9	K%	BB/9	BB%	K-BB%	ERA	FIP	xFIP	Pit/Bat
2021	TOR	18	CPX	35.1	149	13.50	35.57%	3.06	8.05%	27.52%	4.58	4.09	3.01	1.88
2022	TOR	19	A	73.1	305	14.73	39.34%	4.30	11.48%	27.87%	3.44	3.51	3.09	3.70
2022	TOR	19	A+	12.2	64	15.63	34.38%	6.39	14.06%	20.31%	10.66	5.64	3.88	4.16

Background: Toronto signed the diminutive right-hander out of Acarigua, Venezuela during the summer of 2019 – though it would be nearly two years before Santos would toe the rubber during an affiliated game. The front office sent the promising youngster to the Complex Leagues to begin his career in 2021. Santos would make 10 appearances in the stateside rookie league before earning a promotion up to Low-A to cap his professional debut. Santos tossed 40.1 innings, striking out 12.9 and walking 3.6 walks per nine innings to go along with a 5.58 ERA. Last season the Venezuelan righty spent the first four months of the year back in Dunedin before earning a late season call up to Vancouver. He would finish the 2022 campaign with an impressive 142-to-44 strikeout-to-walk ratio in only 86.0 innings of work. He compiled an aggregate 4.50 ERA and a solid enough 3.82 FIP.

Scouting Report: Consider the following:

> Since 2006, there have been 271 hurlers that tossed at least 70 innings during their age-19 season in any Low-A league. Dahian Santos' strikeout percentage, 39.34%, was the best of the bunch. For those interested, here's the Top 10 strikeout percentage for 19-year-old hurlers in Low-A (min. 70 IP):
>
> #1. Dahian Santos
> #2. Tyler Glasnow
> #3. Kyle Harrison
> #4. Joey Cantillo
> #5. Grayson Rodriguez
> #6. Jose Fernandez
> #7. Clayton Kershaw
> #8. Joey Estes
> #9. Carlos Duran

Santos possesses a windup and release point similar to potential future Hall of Famer Chris Sale – a little bit of a hunched over low-slot slinging release point. High quality arsenal that the young right-hander commands well. An above-average fastball that sits in the 93-mph range, and there may be more velo in the coming years as he continues to add strength. An above-average slider that flashes plus on occasion. And a very good, sneaky mid-80s changeup that tumbles and fades. If Santos was four inches taller he'd be a consensus Top 100 prospect. Like a lot of the club's other young arms, Santos' game day workload was highly governed; he pitched past the fourth inning just six times in his 23 appearances. There's backend potential here, maybe more if the velocity upticks another few miles-per-hour.

Ceiling: 2.0-win player
Risk: Moderate
MLB ETA: 2024/2025

Toronto Blue Jays

7. Orelvis Martinez, 3B/SS

Hit	Power	SB	Patience	Glove	Overall
30/40	60	35	50	45	55

Born: 11/19/01   **Age:** 21   **Bats:** R   **Top Production Comp:** N/A
Height: 6-1   **Weight:** 188   **Throws:** R

Season	Team	Age	Level	PA	1B	2B	3B	HR	SB	CS	BB%	K%	AVG	OBP	SLG	ISO
2021	TOR	19	A	326	36	22	2	19	4	1	10.12%	26.07%	0.279	0.369	0.572	0.293
2021	TOR	19	A+	125	11	4	0	9	0	1	8.00%	22.40%	0.214	0.282	0.491	0.277
2022	TOR	20	AA	492	43	15	0	30	6	3	8.13%	28.46%	0.203	0.286	0.446	0.242

Background: Regarded as one of the top talents available on the market during the international signing period in 2018. The front office sent their prized prospect straight into the Gulf Coast League the following season for his debut, bypassing the foreign rookie league all together. And the wiry, 6-foot-1, 188-pound third baseman / shortstop sparkled against the older competition as he mashed .275/.352/.549. After minor league action returned from its forced COVID absence, Martinez quickly shredded the Low-A competition to the tune of .279/.369/.572 in 71 games. So Toronto bumped the burgeoning star up to High-A for the remaining month – though he struggled to the tune of .214/.282/.491. Last season, despite the month-long struggle with Vancouver to close out the 2021 campaign, Martinez was deemed ready enough to take on the harsh environment of Double-A. But, once again, the Dominican infielder struggled – *significantly*. Appearing in a career best 118 games, Martinez cobbled together a lowly .203/.286/.446 slash line with 15 doubles, a career best 30 homeruns, and half-a-dozen stolen bases (in nine total attempts). Per *Weighted Runs Created Plus*, his overall production fell 4% below the league average mark. Martinez owns a career .237/.320/.503 slash line in 256 games.

Snippet from The 2022 Prospect Digest Handbook: Like Jordan Groshans, he's almost assuredly getting moved to the hot corner with Bo Bichette entrenched at shortstop. Making Martinez's numbers in Low-A all that more impressive: according to *Baseball America's* park factors, Dunedin is heavily slanted towards pitchers.

Scouting Report: Consider the following:

> Since 2006, there have been 46 instances in which a 20-year-old hitter received at least 350 plate appearances in Double-A. Only eight of them finished their respective Double-A stints with a wRC+ mark between 90 and 100: Andrew McCutchen, Jonathan Schoop, Hudson Potts, Francisco Martinez, Bryan Anderson, Dayan Viciedo, Andrew Lambo, and – of course – Orelvis Martinez.

Obviously, the big league success rate for similarly performing players is fairly small. Let's continue:

> Only two of those aforementioned hitters whiffed in more than 22% -- Potts and Martinez, both of whom whiffed in 28% of their plate appearances.

The plus power is quite evident, particularly for a 20-year-old squaring off in Double-A. The problem, of course, is the Cadillac-sized hole in his ferocious swing. Fastballs, even 80-grade heaters, aren't the problem. Badly hung breakings balls aren't an issue too. Martinez can't hit low soft-stuff, particularly changeups and sliders that bend / fade just below the zone. He doesn't walk enough to compensate either. Throw in 45-grade defense, and it's certainly not a recipe for success. Batting averages aren't entirely solid predictors of future performance (obviously), but Martinez hit .188 in April, .184 in July, and .146 in August. He cracked the Mendoza line in a full month just twice – .244 in May and .221 in June. The power is worth betting on, but the hit tool makes it a long shot.

Ceiling: 3.0-win player
Risk: Extremely High
MLB ETA: 2024

8. Kendry Rojas, LHP

FB	SL	CH	Command	Overall
50/55	60	50	45/55	50

Born: 10/12/01   **Age:** 21   **Bats:** R   **Top Production Comp:** N/A
Height: 6-1   **Weight:** 160   **Throws:** R

Season	Team	Age	Level	IP	TBF	K/9	K%	BB/9	BB%	K-BB%	ERA	FIP	xFIP	Pit/Bat
2021	TOR	18	CPX	23.2	87	14.83	44.83%	1.90	5.75%	39.08%	2.28	2.03	2.43	2.13
2022	TOR	19	A	39.2	174	9.76	24.71%	4.31	10.92%	13.79%	4.08	3.19	4.24	3.82

Background: A little more than a year after signing Cuban import Yosver Zulueta, Toronto inked fellow countryman Kendry Rojas for $215,000 in 2019. Standing 6-foot-2 and 190 pounds, the lanky left-hander made his affiliated debut two years ago as he briefly pitched for the Jays' Complex League affiliate. He tossed 23.2 innings that summer, averaging a ridiculous 14.8 strikeouts and 1.9 walks per nine innings to go along with a sparkling 2.28 ERA. Last season, despite missing roughly 2.5 months due to an undisclosed injury, Rojas tossed 39.2 innings with Dunedin, posting a 43-to-19 strikeout-to-walk ratio. He finished the stint in Low-A with a 4.08 ERA, a 3.19 FIP, and a 4.24 xFIP.

Toronto Blue Jays

Scouting Report: Textbook definition of projection. Rojas owns one of the loosest, easiest throwing arms in the minor leagues. But the wiry 6-foot-1, 160-pound southpaw is only sitting in the 89- to 91-mph range. Without a doubt, though, there's much more velo in the tank. And it wouldn't be surprising to see him sitting 93- to 94-mph in a year or two. Despite the lack of present velocity, Rojas's heater snuck up on a lot of minor league bats in 2022. Plus, mid-80s slider with phenomenal two-plane break. And his mid-80s changeup, while lacking typical velo separation, shows above-average movement and solid deception. Rojas is a cross-body thrower, but he commands the strike zone exceptionally well with all three offerings. There's backend starting potential here, maybe more if he added more velocity than expected. He could be a longshot candidate for Breakout of the Year in 2023. Really, really like this lottery ticket. And I think it's one worth betting big one.

Ceiling: 1.5- to 2.0-win player
Risk: Moderate
MLB ETA: 2024

9. Tucker Toman, 3B/SS

Hit	Power	SB	Patience	Glove	Overall
45/50	50/55	30	45	50	50

Born: 11/12/03	Age: 19	Bats: B	Top Production Comp: N/A
Height: 6-1	Weight: 190	Throws: R	

Season	Team	Age	Level	PA	1B	2B	3B	HR	SB	CS	BB%	K%	AVG	OBP	SLG	ISO
2022	TOR	18	CPX	46	8	3	0	0	0	0	15.22%	26.09%	0.289	0.391	0.368	0.079

Background: Continuing the 2022 Draft subtheme of strong bloodlines, Toman's father, Jim, is a long time collegiate coach. The elder Toman, who was a two-year team captain at N.C. State during his playing days, has spent time coaching at Florida International University, N.C. State, South Carolina, Liberty, College of Charleston, and is currently the head coach at Middle Tennessee State University. A member of Hammond's varsity baseball team since his eighth grade year, Toman batted a scorching .502 with eight dingers and 25 RBIs as a junior. And he finished his senior campaign with a .487 average with seven homeruns and 27 RBIs. He was committed to powerhouse Louisiana State University. The Jays grabbed him in the second round, 77th, and signed him a massive $2 million deal. Toman made an 11-game cameo in the Complex League, hitting .290/.391/.368 with three doubles.

Scouting Report: My pre-draft write-up:

> "A high school athlete playing shortstop but is destined to slide over to the hot corner. Toman's robotic and lacks a lot of lateral movement to stay at the infield's prime position. Offensively, the young switch-hitter shows an open stance from either side of the batter's box. Upright with plenty of natural loft, Toman hasn't begun to fully tap into his above-average power potential. His swing looks more natural as a lefty, showing impressive bat speed for his non-dominant side. There's some sneaky upside as potential second round pick."

Ceiling: 1.5- to 2.0-win player
Risk: Moderate
MLB ETA: 2025/2026

10. Cade Doughty, 2B/3B

Hit	Power	SB	Patience	Glove	Overall
50	50	35	50	50	50

Born: 03/26/01	Age: 22	Bats: R	Top Production Comp: N/A
Height: 6-1	Weight: 195	Throws: R	

Season	Team	Age	Level	PA	1B	2B	3B	HR	SB	CS	BB%	K%	AVG	OBP	SLG	ISO
2022	TOR	21	A	119	17	5	0	6	3	2	8.40%	24.37%	0.272	0.370	0.495	0.223

Background: The two most famous Denham Spring High School alums just happened to bypass a chance at professional baseball as teenagers, opting, instead, to attend SEC Conference powerhouse Louisiana State University. All the way back in 1986, the Atlanta Braves took a 27th round chance on a big, lanky, hard-throwing right-hander by the name of "Big" Ben McDonald. Three years later, of course, the Baltimore Orioles used the top pick in the draft to select the LSU ace. Like McDonald, infielder Cade Doughty was a late round gamble coming out of the Louisiana-based prep school. But the reigning Gatorade State Player of the Year had his sights set on the land of the Tigers. Doughty opened up his collegiate career by batting .278/.365/.407 in 16 games before the pandemic forced the season to a premature close. After ripping through the South Florida Collegiate Baseball League competition with the Boca Raton Blazers that summer, Doughty established himself as one of LSU's best hitters during his sophomore season. He batted .308/.368/.546 with 11 doubles, two triples, and 13 homeruns in 58 games. And the 6-foot-1, 205-pound infielder basically repeated that production line during his final season as well, slugging .298/.393/.567 with career highs in doubles (19), homeruns (15), and stolen bases (4). The Toronto Blue

Toronto Blue Jays

Jays selected Doughty in the second round, 78th overall, and signed him to a deal worth $833,600. The second / third baseman hit an impressive .272/.370/.495 with five doubles, six homeruns, and three stolen bases in 26 games with Dunedin.

Scouting Report: My pre-draft write-up:

> "Consider the following:
>
> Since 2011, only six (6) SEC Conference hitters batted between .290/.380/.550 and .300/.420/.600 in a season (min. 600 PA): Harrison Bader, Jordan Beck, Greg Deichmann, Cayden Wallace, Andre Lipcius, and – of course – Cade Doughty.
>
> Really nice looking swing. Short, quick, and packs more of a punch than his 6-foot-1, 205-pound frame would suggest. Even ignoring the loud audible "pings" from an aluminum bat, Doughty's contact regularly sounds like an explosion. 50-grade hit tool. 50-grade power. Solid defender at the keystone. Runs well, but won't steal many bases. There's some Joey Wendle-type potential."

Ceiling: 1.5- to 2.0-win player
Risk: Moderate
MLB ETA: 2024/2025

11. Adam Macko, LHP

FB	CB	SL	CH	Command	Overall
55	55	50	50	40/45	50

Born: 12/30/00 **Age:** 21 **Bats:** L **Top Production Comp:** Erik Bedard
Height: 6-0 **Weight:** 170 **Throws:** L

Season	Team	Age	Level	IP	TBF	K/9	K%	BB/9	BB%	K-BB%	ERA	FIP	xFIP	Pit/Bat
2019	SEA	18	R	21.1	94	13.08	32.98%	4.64	11.70%	21.28%	3.38	3.80	3.95	2.84
2021	SEA	20	A	33.1	155	15.12	36.13%	5.67	13.55%	22.58%	4.59	3.33	4.10	3.84
2022	SEA	21	A+	38.1	167	14.09	35.93%	4.70	11.98%	23.95%	3.99	3.77	3.21	4.17

Background: Starring at the possibility of losing 2021 All-Star and two-time Silver Slugger Teoscar Hernandez to free agency after the 2023 season, the Blue Jays decided to maximize his trade value and sent him to Seattle for a pair of diametrically opposite arms. Reliable, veteran, in-his-prime right-handed reliever Erik Swanson, who's coming off of a career year in which he tallied a tidy 1.68 ERA; and then there's Adam Macko, a promising, yet enigmatic left-hander that has potential but can't seem to harness the lightning in his arm. Taken in the seventh round out of Vauxhall High School in 2019, the Slovakian-born southpaw was a force to be reckoned with during his brief debut that summer: he posted a 32-to-12 strikeout-to-walk in 23.1 innings, most of which were spent in the Complex League. Once minor league action returned from its COVID hiatus, Macko made nine, injury-shortened starts with the Modesto Nuts in Low-A. He struck out 56 and walked 21 to go along with a 4.59 ERA in 33.1 innings of work. And, unfortunately for the promising lefty, the 2022 season was much the same as an undisclosed injury prematurely capped his season at 38.1 innings. He averaged 14.1 strikeouts and 4.7 walks per nine innings. He did make it back to the mound in the Arizona Fall League, throwing 13.1 innings with 14 strikeouts and 13 walks.

Snippet from The 2022 Prospect Digest Handbook: High ceiling southpaw, which is surprising given his draft status (seventh round, 2019) and unimpressive frame size (6-foot, 170 pounds). His command has to bump up at least to a 45. He also has to avoid the injury nexus as well.

Scouting Report: Back when Mark Shapiro was Cleveland's General Manager, the squad shipped Cy Young-winning southpaw Cliff Lee to the Phillies for a package of four prospects: Jason Donald, Lou Marson, Carlos Carrasco, and Jason Knapp. At that time Knapp, not Carrasco, was viewed as the centerpiece of the deal. A talented, sky's-the-limit right-hander who happened to have a shoulder issue. Fast forward 13 years and the Shapiro-led Blue Jays dealt away an above-average outfielder for a good reliever, who's likely to regress some, and a talented, young pitcher who missed half-of-a-year (2021) with a shoulder injury and then the majority of 2022. Macko started the year off well as he posted a 29-to-3 strikeout-to-walk ratio in only 16.0 innings. But then his command / control demons reared their ugly heads. Above-average fastball. The curveball looked loopier, but is still an above-average offering. He's added an average, laterally darting slider, and the changeup crept up to average territory. Toronto might catch lightning in a bottle and can sprinkle some of the Ricky Tiedemann dust on Macko.

Ceiling: 2.0-win player
Risk: High
MLB ETA: 2025

Toronto Blue Jays

12. Hayden Juenger, RHP

FB	SL	CH	Command	Overall
60	50	55	45	45

Born: 08/09/00	Age: 22	Bats: R	Top Production Comp: N/A
Height: 6-0	Weight: 180	Throws: R	

Season	Team	Age	Level	IP	TBF	K/9	K%	BB/9	BB%	K-BB%	ERA	FIP	xFIP	Pit/Bat
2021	TOR	20	A+	20.0	74	15.30	45.95%	1.80	5.41%	40.54%	2.70	1.33	2.43	4.55
2022	TOR	21	AA	56.0	227	10.77	29.52%	3.38	9.25%	20.26%	4.02	5.04	4.33	3.95
2022	TOR	21	AAA	32.2	134	9.09	24.63%	4.41	11.94%	12.69%	3.31	5.34	4.68	4.16

Background: Highly touted coming out of O'Fallon Township High School in 2018, *Perfect Game* ranked the wiry hurler as the third best right-handed pitching prospect and 11th best senior in the state of Illinois. The 6-foot, 180-pound right-hander put up mixed results during his debut campaign with Missouri State. Working as a multi-inning reliever / rare spot-starter, Juenger averaged 8.5 strikeouts and 4.6 walks per nine innings. The Bears' coaching staff kept the young right-hander in the bullpen during the 2020 COVID-abbreviated season, where he would strike out 13 and walk a quartet. And, once again, Juenger was relegated to only relief work during his final year in college as well, posting an impressive 31-to-6 strikeout-to-walk ratio in 21.0 innings of work. Toronto selected Juenger in the sixth round two years ago, and immediately began stretching him out in longer outings. He would make 11 brief appearances in High-A during his professional debut, throwing 20.0 innings with 34 punch outs and just six walks. And while momentum was building towards a breakout campaign in 2022, Juenger *easily surpassed* all expectations. Making 19 starts and 19 relief appearances between New Hampshire and Buffalo, the talented hurler tossed a career best 88.2 innings (including his time in college), while average 10.2 K/9 and 3.8 BB/9.

Scouting Report: The front office did a solid job governing Juenger's workload last season, limiting him to four innings of less in each of his 20 Double-A appearances and two innings or less in his 18 Triple-A games. In doing so, though, Juenger rarely got the opportunity to turn the opposing team's lineup over twice. I would expect some regression in 2022 as teams get more than one or two plate appearances per game against the former Missouri State Bear. Juenger features a mid-90s plus fastball that Double-A hitters had trouble squaring up. His go-to secondary offering if a fantastically underrated, above-average fading changeup – which will miss some bats, especially when he's locating it near the knees. He'll also mix in a solid-average slider. Juenger has the repertoire and command to grow into a backend starter, perhaps peaking as a #4. With respect to his work in Double-A last season, consider the following:

> Since 2006, only two 21-year-old hurlers posted a 28.5% to 30.5% strikeout percentage with an 8% to 11% walk percentage in any Double-A league (min. 50 IP): Gio Gonzalez and Hayden Juenger.

Ceiling: 1.5-win player
Risk: Moderate
MLB ETA: 2023

13. Alex De Jesus, 3B/SS

Hit	Power	SB	Patience	Glove	Overall
40	55	35	55	45	45

Born: 03/02/02	Age: 21	Bats: R	Top Production Comp: N/A
Height: 6-2	Weight: 170	Throws: R	

Season	Team	Age	Level	PA	1B	2B	3B	HR	SB	CS	BB%	K%	AVG	OBP	SLG	ISO
2021	LAD	19	A	422	56	25	1	12	1	0	16.35%	30.33%	0.268	0.386	0.447	0.179
2022	LAD	20	A	176	20	9	1	7	2	0	18.18%	28.41%	0.259	0.398	0.483	0.224
2022	LAD	20	A+	226	38	11	2	4	0	1	12.39%	28.76%	0.282	0.376	0.421	0.138
2022	TOR	20	A+	104	12	5	0	2	0	0	11.54%	34.62%	0.211	0.298	0.333	0.122

Background: The Blue Jays and Dodgers got together on an interesting swap in early August. The details of the two-for-two deal: Los Angeles would send former top prospect turned serviceable backend starter Mitch White and infielder Alex De Jesus in exchange for low level lottery ticket Moises Brito and flame-throwing right-hander Nick Frasso. White, of course, fell flat on his face during his cameo with the Jays down the stretch, posting an ERA north of 7.50 in 43.0 innings. As for De Jesus, well, his numbers, too, cratered once he moved into Toronto's organization. Originally signed for $500,000 out of Santo Domingo, Dominican Republic, in 2018, De Jesus had a bit of a coming out party in 2021 as he slugged .268/.386/.447 with 25 doubles, one triple, and 12 homeruns with Rancho Cucamonga. Last season the Dodgers sent the promising young infielder back down to Low-A for additional seasoning. But after hitting .259/.398/.483 through 37 games, De Jesus was moved up to High-A. And he continued to perform well against the older competition – at least, initially. He mashed .282/.376/.421 in 50 games with Great Lakes. Following the trade, though, De Jesus cobbled together a lowly .211/.298/.333 slash line in 24 games with Toronto's High-A affiliate, the Vancouver Canadians. De Jesus finished the season with an aggregate .263/.370/.433 slash line with 26 doubles, three triples, 14 homeruns, and a pair of stolen bases (in three total attempts).

Snippet from The 2022 Prospect Digest Handbook: De Jesus got off to a dreadful start to the year in 2021; he batted a rotten .179/.294/.316 with a strikeout rate of more than 38% through his first 33 games. However, beginning on June 19th through the rest of the year, De Jesus slugged a hearty .312/430/.513 with 21 doubles, one triple, and eight homeruns in only 64 games. The best part: his 26.2% swing-and-miss rate is far less concerning. Defensively, he'll never be confused with Ozzie Smith, but projects as an average shortstop.

Toronto Blue Jays

Scouting Report: The glove remains a work in progress and may actually never creep into average territory. De Jesus has had some trouble with swing-and-miss issues at numerous points in his professional career; he whiffed in a third of his plate appearances in the Arizona Summer League and posted a 30% K-rate two years ago (though, as noted above, it improved throughout the season). Last year, it hovered in the 28% range with the Dodgers' farm teams and blew up to 34.6% with Vancouver. There's an intriguing power / patience blend brewing in his 6-foot-2, 170-pound frame. The question is whether he'll hit enough to be an asset (because there's no value in his glove). He's likely ticketed for Double-A in 2023. And he's only going to be 21-years-old.

Ceiling: 1.5-win player
Risk: Moderate to High
MLB ETA: 2024

14. Dasan Brown, CF

Hit	Power	SB	Patience	Glove	Overall
45	40/50	60	50	45/55	50

Born: 09/25/01	Age: 21	Bats: R	Top Production Comp: N/A
Height: 6-0	Weight: 185	Throws: R	

Season	Team	Age	Level	PA	1B	2B	3B	HR	SB	CS	BB%	K%	AVG	OBP	SLG	ISO
2021	TOR	19	A	226	29	8	1	4	22	6	8.85%	32.74%	0.212	0.310	0.323	0.111
2022	TOR	20	A	162	25	8	2	4	11	6	10.49%	27.78%	0.279	0.369	0.450	0.171
2022	TOR	20	A+	176	32	11	0	2	11	3	7.95%	28.41%	0.298	0.392	0.411	0.113
2022	TOR	20	CPX	22	2	1	0	0	2	1	9.09%	31.82%	0.188	0.409	0.250	0.063

Background: The Blue Jays nabbed the toolsy prep star in the third round out of Abbey Park High School in 2019, signing the 88th overall pick for a smidgeon less than $800,000. And for the first couple of years Brown returned little on the club's initial investment. His hit tool looked abysmal during his 14-game debut in the old Gulf Coast League as he batted .222/.444/.356. Once minor league action returned from its forced COVID absence, Brown continued to struggle with low level pitching as he cobbled together a lowly .212/.310/.323 in 51 games with Dunedin. Needless to say, but Brown's prospects as a…prospect looked murky – at best. Things clicked for the toolsy centerfielder last season in one of the club's more pleasant surprises. In an injury-interrupted campaign, Brown slugged .279/.369/.450 in a return to Dunedin. And he continued to mash upon a second half promotion up to Vancouver. Including his six-game rehab assignment in the Complex League, the 6-foot, 185-pound outfielder bashed .283/.383/.420 with 20 doubles, two triples, six homeruns, and 24 stolen bases (in 34 total attempts). Per *Weighted Runs Created Plus*, his overall production topped the league average mark by an impressive 31%.

Scouting Report: Despite the breakout season by Brown, he remains incredibly raw but promising. There's a power-speed aspect to his approach on both sides of the ball. But, again, he still hasn't quite harnessed it yet. He's a below-average defender in centerfield presently, though he should creep up towards average as he continues to mature. Plus-plus runner. But he's not efficient on the bases or in the outfield. Presently, he was below-average power but there's enough jolt in the bat to creep into 15- to 20-homer territory. There's plenty of risk. And a WIDE range of outcomes. He could be anything for Lorenzo Cain or never figure it out in the upper minors.

Ceiling: 2.0-win player
Risk: High
MLB ETA: 2024/2025

15. Josh Kasevich, 3B/SS

Hit	Power	SB	Patience	Glove	Overall
50/55	45	35	50	50	45

Born: 01/17/01	Age: 22	Bats: R	Top Production Comp: N/A
Height: 6-2	Weight: 200	Throws: R	

Season	Team	Age	Level	PA	1B	2B	3B	HR	SB	CS	BB%	K%	AVG	OBP	SLG	ISO
2022	TOR	21	A	122	20	8	0	0	0	2	9.02%	7.38%	0.262	0.344	0.336	0.075

Background: A prominent prospect coming out of Palo Alto High School in 2019. *Perfect Game* ranked Kasevich as the 33rd best third baseman in the country and fourth in California. But his collegiate career didn't begin on such a promising note. Prematurely capped by the COVID pandemic, Kasevich batted a paltry .135/.158/.162 with one extra-base hit (double) in 14 games. The 6-foot-2, 200-pound infielder slid over to shortstop from the hot corner at the start of his sophomore season. And his production *exploded*. In 55 games with the Pac-12 powerhouse, he slugged .324/.397/.444 with 10 doubles, two triples, four homeruns, and seven stolen bases. He continued to torch the competition as he moved into the Northwoods League that summer as well, batting .374/.403/.450 with nine extra-base knocks. Last season, in a career best 61 contests, Kasevich maintained status quo for the Ducks of Oregon: he hit .310/.383/.445 with 10 doubles, one triple, and a career high seven long balls. Toronto selected him in the second round, 60th overall, and signed him to a deal worth a smidgeon below $1 million. Kasevich hit a mediocre .262/.344/.336 with eight doubles in 25 games with Dunedin during his debut.

Toronto Blue Jays

Scouting Report: My pre-draft write-up:

"Consider the following:

Since 2011, only three Pac-12 hitters met the following criteria in a season (min. 250 PA): bat between .300/.375/.430 and .325/.400/.460. Those three hitters: Beau Amaral, Coldy Shade, and Josh Kasevich – the latter two accomplishing the feat with Oregon during the 2022 season.

An extreme bat-to-ball prospect that seems to be gaining in popularity over the past year or two. Kasevich fanned just 40 times over his final 529 plate appearances – or roughly 7.6% of the time. Solid patience. Doubles power. A smattering of speed. Simple, short, quick swing. Smooth, fluid actions in the field, though he won't win any Gold Gloves. Lower tier starting material."

Ceiling: 1.5-win player
Risk: Moderate
MLB ETA: 2024/2025

16. Rainer Nunez, 1B

Hit	Power	SB	Patience	Glove	Overall
45	60	30	50	55	45

Born: 12/04/00	Age: 22	Bats: R	Top Production Comp: N/A
Height: 6-3	Weight: 180	Throws: R	

Season	Team	Age	Level	PA	1B	2B	3B	HR	SB	CS	BB%	K%	AVG	OBP	SLG	ISO
2021	TOR	19	A	226	29	8	1	4	22	6	8.85%	32.74%	0.212	0.310	0.323	0.111
2022	TOR	20	A	162	25	8	2	4	11	6	10.49%	27.78%	0.279	0.369	0.450	0.171
2022	TOR	20	A+	176	32	11	0	2	11	3	7.95%	28.41%	0.298	0.392	0.411	0.113
2022	TOR	20	CPX	22	2	1	0	0	2	1	9.09%	31.82%	0.188	0.409	0.250	0.063

Background: To call it a breakout would be a touch misleading. But it's not *really* that incorrect either. Originally signed out of Dominican Republic during the summer of 2017, Nunez was absolutely dreadful during his organizational debut in his home country the following year as he batted .247/.298/.328. And he was even *worse* as he moved stateside in 2019, cobbling together a lowly .173/.248/.286 in 30 games. But once minor league ball returned to work in 2021, Nunez began to flash some intriguing upside – though it came in the Complex League as a 20-year-old. He slugged .274/.370/.484 with 11 doubles and five homeruns in 36 games. And he looked solid in an admittedly brief, six-game cameo with Dunedin as well. And while it was a solid showing, no one could have expected him to take it to another level in 2022. Opening the year back up with Dunedin, the Dominican first baseman mashed .299/.328/.482 with 19 doubles, one triple, and 15 homeruns in 93 games. And he continued to batter the competition during his 27-game cameo with Vancouver (.321/.379/.491). Nunez finished the year with an aggregate .304/.340/.484 with 25 doubles, one triple, and 19 homers. His production, per *Weighted Runs Created Plus*, topped the average mark by 30%. At the end of the year, he was notified that he captured the batting title in the Florida State League and named the league's top first baseman.

Scouting Report: Consider the following:

Since 2006, only four 21-year-old hitters posted a 120 to 130 wRC+ total with a sub-5.0% walk rate in any Low-A league (min. 350 PA): Jose Briceno, Gustavo Nunez, Roldani Baldwin, and – of course – Rainer Nunez.

Rob Terranova noted in a January 5th 2023 article on MiLB.com that Nunez was the only prospect that appeared in a game for Dunedin that posted an exit velocity north of 110 mph. Crouched stance, bent knees with the bat resting on his shoulder. Nunez shows a big leg kick and emphatically slams his front foot down and torques his body as he whips the lumber ferociously through the air. While he set a career best in homeruns in 2022, he's just beginning to tap into his plus power potential. Average-ish walk rates, solid contact numbers. There's some Franmil Reyes-type potential here. He should provide some value with the first baseman's mitt, too.

Ceiling: 1.5-win player
Risk: Moderate
MLB ETA: 2024/2025

Toronto Blue Jays

17. Otto Lopez, 2B/SS/CF

Hit	Power	SB	Patience	Glove	Overall
55	35	60	50	50	45

Born: 10/01/98	Age: 24	Bats: R	Top Production Comp: Ryan Theriot
Height: 5-10	Weight: 160	Throws: R	

Season	Team	Age	Level	PA	1B	2B	3B	HR	SB	CS	BB%	K%	AVG	OBP	SLG	ISO
2021	TOR	22	AA	314	64	24	1	3	7	3	8.92%	19.75%	0.331	0.398	0.457	0.126
2021	TOR	22	AAA	194	37	8	3	2	15	1	6.70%	13.40%	0.289	0.347	0.405	0.116
2022	TOR	23	AAA	391	73	19	6	3	14	5	10.49%	15.60%	0.297	0.378	0.415	0.118

Background: Now entering his sixth season in the Blue Jays' organization (not including the 2020 COVID season), Lopez has been remarkably consistently throughout his career, using solid batting averages, doubles power, and above-average speed to hop, skip, and jump his way up the minor league ladder. The Dominican-born middle-infielder / centerfielder reached the top minor league rung, Triple-A, *and* cracked the Jays' lineup for one game before the end of his age-21 season. Last season, Lopez, a 5-foot-10, 160-pound budding utility man extraordinaire, appeared in 91 games with the Bisons of Buffalo. He batted an Otto Lopez-esque .297/.378/.415 with 19 doubles, six triples, three homeruns, and 14 stolen bases (in 19 attempts). His overall production in Triple-A, according to *Weighted Runs Created Plus*, topped the league average mark by 14%. Lopez appeared in an additional eight games with the Jays as well, going six for nine.

Snippet from The 2022 Prospect Digest Handbook: One step closer to his utility role in the big leagues, especially now that he's accruing some valuable time in the outfield. Lopez is a slashing speedster with modest patience and very little power.

Scouting Report: Consider the following:

> Since 2006, only three 23-year-old hitters met the following criteria in a Triple-A season (min. 350 PA): 110 to 120 wRC+, 14% to 17% strikeout rate, and a 9% to 12% walk rate. Those three hitters: Vidal Brujan, Jeff Clement, and – of course – Otto Lopez.

Otto Lopez continues to be Otto Lopez. A slashing, batting-average driven hitter that takes the occasional walk and will hit a handful of doubles and triples. Decent glove at any of the three positions. He could be a solid role player on a contending team – a la like the 2023 Toronto Blue Jays squad.

Ceiling: 1.0- to 1.5-win player
Risk: Low to Moderate
MLB ETA: Debuted in 2021

18. Sem Robberse, RHP

FB	CB	SL	CH	Command	Overall
55	55	50	50	55	45

Born: 10/12/01	Age: 21	Bats: R	Top Production Comp: N/A
Height: 6-1	Weight: 160	Throws: R	

Season	Team	Age	Level	IP	TBF	K/9	K%	BB/9	BB%	K-BB%	ERA	FIP	xFIP	Pit/Bat
2021	TOR	19	A	57.2	239	9.52	25.52%	3.12	8.37%	17.15%	3.90	3.63	3.90	3.78
2021	TOR	19	A+	31.0	150	8.42	19.33%	5.23	12.00%	7.33%	5.23	5.20	5.16	3.74
2022	TOR	20	A+	86.2	358	8.10	21.79%	2.49	6.70%	15.08%	3.12	3.85	4.12	3.47
2022	TOR	20	AA	24.2	104	6.93	18.27%	3.65	9.62%	8.65%	3.65	5.44	5.22	3.65

Background: Hailing from the Netherlands, which is home to Hall of Famer Bert Blyleven and solid MLB infielder Didi Gregorius, Toronto signed the promising, under-the-radar right-hander midsummer 2019. Since then, he's quietly improved and shown a strong aptitude for pitching. Robberse would make his affiliated stateside debut just three days after joining the organization. He would eventually throw 10.1 innings in the Gulf Coast League, posting a 9-to-1 strikeout-to-walk ratio. After life returned to normal following the lost 2020 season, Robberse mowed down the Low-A competition for 14 appearances and looked solid enough as a 19-year-old in High-A, though he did battle some control yips in his seven-game cameo with Vancouver. Last season the front office kept Robberse on a similar trajectory as he made 17 starts in High-A and capped the year off with five final starts in the minors' true proving ground – Double-A. The 6-foot-1, 160-pound righty would throw a career best 111.1 innings of work, tallying a 3.23 ERA while averaging a solid 7.8 strikeouts and just 2.7 walks per nine innings. He compiled an aggregate 4.20 FIP across both stops.

Snippet from The 2022 Prospect Digest Handbook: Robberse has the starter's kit for a solid #4 / #5 arm.

Scouting Report: Consider the following:

> Since 2006, only eight 20-year-old hurlers met the following criteria in any High-A league (min. 75 IP): 21% to 23% strikeout percentage and a 5.5% to 7.5% walk percentage. Those eight hurlers: Zach Davies, Aneury Rodriguez, Ariel Jurado, Edgar Garcia, Gaby Hernandez, Kasey Kiker, Kyle Smith, and Sem Robberse.

Toronto Blue Jays

While Robberse is still tracking like a solid, pitchability-based backend starting pitcher, the Dutch right-hander's arsenal didn't take a step forward as expected. Low-90s above-average fastball and a matching curveball. His slider and changeup are languishing in average territory. He's a low ceiling / high floor prospect with a high probability of spending at least a few seasons in the majors.

Ceiling: 1.0- to 1.5-win player
Risk: Low to Moderate
MLB ETA: 2023/2024

19. C.J. Van Eyk, RHP

FB	CB	SL	CH	Command	Overall
55	60	50/55	50	40/45	45

Born: 09/15/98	Age: 24	Bats: R	Top Production Comp: N/A
Height: 6-1	Weight: 198	Throws: R	

Season	Team	Age	Level	IP	TBF	K/9	K%	BB/9	BB%	K-BB%	ERA	FIP	xFIP	Pit/Bat
2021	TOR	22	A+	80.1	353	11.20	28.33%	4.37	11.05%	17.28%	5.83	4.55	4.58	3.89

Background: After bypassing the opportunity to join the Mets' organization as a 19th round pick coming out of high school, Van Eyk would turn in a solid, sometimes dominant three-year career at Florida State University. He dazzled as a spot-starter / relief arm as a true freshman, averaged 11.7 strikeouts and 3.7 walks per nine innings as a full-time starter during his sophomore year, and battled some command / control demons as junior, though he would finish his COVID-abbreviated final campaign with a 1.31 ERA. Toronto snatched the crafty right-hander in the second round three years ago, a part of their all-college player class. Van Eyk would make his professional debut the following summer, moving directly up to Vancouver in High-A. He would finished the year with 19 starts, spanning 80.1 innings with 100 punch outs, 39 free passes, and an unsightly 5.83 ERA. Unfortunately for the former Seminole, as well as the Jays, Van Eyk underwent Tommy John surgery in September of 2021, forcing him to miss the entirety of last season.

Scouting Report: With no new updates available because of the elbow surgery, here's his previous scouting report:

> "Very solid four-pitch repertoire highlight by a lively 93 mph fastball. Van Eyk complements the above-average heater with a plus, 12-6 downward biting curveball that falls off the table, a slider that projects to be above-average, and a firm changeup. Even going back to his collegiate days, Van Eyk's never displayed a solid grasp of the strike zone (his lowest walk rate was 3.7 BB/9, which happened during his sophomore campaign). He needs to show some type of tangible improvement in the next year or so. If that happens, he looks like a #4-type arm."

Ceiling: 1.0- to 1.5-win player
Risk: Moderate to High
MLB ETA: 2024/2025

20. Alan Roden, 1B/LF/RF

Hit	Power	SB	Patience	Glove	Overall
55/60	40/50	30	55	50	40

Born: 12/22/99	Age: 23	Bats: L	Top Production Comp: N/A
Height: 6-0	Weight: 215	Throws: R	

Season	Team	Age	Level	PA	1B	2B	3B	HR	SB	CS	BB%	K%	AVG	OBP	SLG	ISO
2022	TOR	22	A	115	16	4	0	1	5	1	14.78%	11.30%	0.233	0.374	0.311	0.078

Background: After selecting high schoolers with two of their first three selections, the Blue Jays rattled off a string of 10 straight four-year collegiate players. Following behind the selection of LSU infielder Cade Doughty, Toronto drafted Creighton slugger Alan Roden in the third round, 98th overall, last June. Roden marked the third time the franchise nabbed a Creighton Blue Jay in midsummer draft. A 6-foot, 215-pound corner outfielder / first baseman, Roden was one of college baseball's most lethal bats over his career in the Big East, leaving the school as a .383/.484/.640 with 42 doubles, two triples, and 14 homeruns in only 91 games. After signing with the Jays for slightly less than $500,000, Roden turned in a disappointing debut showing with Dunedin, batting a lowly .233/.374/.311 with just five extra-base knocks in 25 games.

Scouting Report: The eighth highest drafted Creighton Blue Jay in history, Roden became the earliest drafted player from the school since 1994. The former Big East Freshman of the year, Roden is broad-shouldered with a surprisingly short, quick swing that doesn't project for much power, but allows him to consistently make contact. He posted an almost impossible 6.5% strikeout rate in college, and that number was just 11.3% during his limited debut. There may be more thump lurking in the bat, but a swing-rework may need to happen.

Ceiling: 1.0-win player
Risk: Moderate
MLB ETA: 2024/2025

Washington Nationals Top Prospects

Washington Nationals

1. James Wood, CF

Hit	Power	SB	Patience	Glove	Overall
55	70	50	55	50	70

Born: 09/17/02 **Age:** 20 **Bats:** L **Top Production Comp:** Yordan Alvarez
Height: 6-7 **Weight:** 240 **Throws:** R

Season	Team	Age	Level	PA	1B	2B	3B	HR	SB	CS	BB%	K%	AVG	OBP	SLG	ISO
2021	SDP	18	CPX	101	24	5	0	3	10	0	12.87%	31.68%	0.372	0.465	0.535	0.163
2022	SDP	19	A	236	35	19	1	10	15	5	15.68%	17.80%	0.337	0.453	0.601	0.264
2022	WSN	19	A	93	14	8	0	2	4	0	10.75%	27.96%	0.293	0.366	0.463	0.171

Background: Faced with the possibility of losing future Hall of Famer Juan Soto to free agency in a couple seasons, the ball club did the seemingly impossible. They traded this generation's version of Ted Williams. A task that will always be viewed as a complete failure unless the front office somehow adds multiple All-Stars in the process. And they may have actually done that. Last August Washington dealt away their franchise cornerstone, the one who helped absorb the loss of countless stars like Bryce Harper and Trea Turner, to the Padres. The specifics of the deal: The Nats acquired southpaw MacKenzie Gore, first baseman Luke Voit, shortstop C.J. Abrams, outfielders Robert Hassell and James Wood, and pitcher Jarlin Susana for Soto and first baseman Josh Bell. Taken in the second round out of baseball hotbed IMG Academy two years ago, Wood immediately impressed during his 26-game tenure in the Complex League that summer, bashing .372/.465/.535 with five doubles, three homeruns, and 10 stolen bases (without getting caught). And despite a few red flags during his debut, like a whiff rate north of 30%, Wood put together a breathtakingly awesome campaign between both organizations' Low-A affiliates. Even some knee and wrist injuries, which limited to him to 76 games with Lake Elsinore and Fredericksburg, weren't enough to cool his bat. The 6-foot-7, 240-pound centerfielder mashed an aggregate .313/.420/.536 with 27 doubles, 12 homeruns, and 20 stolen bases (in 25 total attempts). Per *Weighted Runs Created Plus*, his overall production surpassed the league average mark by a whopping 50%.

Snippet from The 2022 Prospect Digest Handbook: Another of the raw, high ceiling prospects that the organization seems to focus on in recent years. Like 2019 second round pick Joshua Mears, James Wood is absolutely loaded with loud tools. If he can chew several percentage points off of his whiff rate, Wood has the potential to be a legitimate middle-of-the-order thumper.

Scouting Report: Consider the following:

> Since 2006, only three 19-year-old hitters met the following criteria in any Low-A league (min. 300 PA): 145 to 155 wRC+, a double-digit walk rate, and a strikeout rate between 18% to 24%. Those three hitters: Corey Seager, Ji-hwan Bae, and – of course – James Wood.

There aren't too many prospects that can be slapped with the true five-tool label. Wood, though, is one of them. The 6-foot-7, 240-pound prospect runs like a gazelle, belts long balls like a perennial homerun leader, showed an impressive feel for the strike zone while chewing off considerable percentage points from his K-rate, has the chops to stick in centerfield, though he may outgrow the position as he continues to fill out. And the lefty-swinging Wood was equally dominant against right-handers *and* left-handers. Plus-plus bat speed with 70-grade raw power to all fields. He's going to be a star as long as he's making consistent contact, which he showed he can in 2022. In terms of big league ceiling, think: .300/.400/.600 with 40 homeruns.

Ceiling: 6.5-win player
Risk: Moderate
MLB ETA: 2024/2025

2. Brady House, SS

Hit	Power	SB	Patience	Glove	Overall
50	50/55	30	50	50	55

Born: 06/04/03 **Age:** 20 **Bats:** R **Top Production Comp:** N/A
Height: 6-4 **Weight:** 215 **Throws:** R

Season	Team	Age	Level	PA	1B	2B	3B	HR	SB	CS	BB%	K%	AVG	OBP	SLG	ISO
2021	WSN	18	CPX	66	12	3	0	4	0	0	10.61%	19.70%	0.322	0.394	0.576	0.254
2022	WSN	19	A	203	38	8	0	3	1	0	5.91%	29.06%	0.278	0.356	0.375	0.097

Background: Going back to the days of the old Montreal Expos, the franchise has drafted just 11 shortstops in the opening round. Of those 11, ten of them were taken from the high school ranks. And the only outlier, Glen Franklin, was taken from JuCo Chipola College. The club's latest first round shortstop: Brady House, the 11th overall pick two years ago. A product of Winder-Barrow High School, House was part of the memorable first round that included 11 total shortstops, including nine prepsters. After a successful debut in the Complex League, the 6-foot-4, 215-pound middle infielder spent the 2022 season squaring off against the Carolina League competition. An undisclosed injury limited him to just 45 games. He batted .278/.356/.375 with eight doubles, three homeruns, and a stolen base – just for good measure. His overall production, as measured by *Weighted Runs Created Plus*, topped the league average mark by 8%. House owns a .289/.366/.426 career slash line through his first 61 games.

Washington Nationals

Snippet from The 2022 Prospect Digest Handbook: There are some concerns about his inability to lay off of and/or fight off offspeed pitches low in the zone – though he's shown a propensity to fight them off in high school. There's some Carlos Correa-type potential. On the mound, his fastball routinely reaches the mid-90s.

Scouting Report: The concerns about the hit tool started to come to fruition last season as his swing-and-miss rate spiked up to nearly 30%. Even more alarming are his numbers over his final 40 games: he whiffed 40 times in only 113 plate appearances. House seemed to be battling some type of injury woe over that duration. He started the year out by slugging .364/.444/.494 with just 19 punch outs across his first 90 appearances. House to poised for a solid rebound and potentially a breakout candidate.

Ceiling: 4.0-win player
Risk: Moderate
MLB ETA: 2025/2026

3. Cade Cavalli, RHP

FB	CB	SL	CH	Command	Overall
65	60	60	55	45	60

Born: 08/14/98	Age: 24	Bats: R	Top Production Comp: Dylan Cease
Height: 6-4	Weight: 240	Throws: R	

Season	Team	Age	Level	IP	TBF	K/9	K%	BB/9	BB%	K-BB%	ERA	FIP	xFIP	Pit/Bat
2021	WSN	22	A+	40.2	158	15.71	44.94%	2.66	7.59%	37.34%	1.77	1.63	2.21	4.01
2021	WSN	22	AA	58.0	243	12.41	32.92%	5.43	14.40%	18.52%	2.79	3.02	3.84	4.05
2021	WSN	22	AAA	24.2	121	8.76	19.83%	4.74	10.74%	9.09%	7.30	4.54	4.92	3.89
2022	WSN	23	AAA	97.0	401	9.65	25.94%	3.62	9.73%	16.21%	3.71	3.25	4.47	4.04

Background: The Nationals have drafted a surprising amount of pitching over the past decade or so, including: Stephen Strasburg (duh), Drew Storen, Robbie Ray, Lucas Giolito, Nick Pivetta, Jesus Luzardo, and Dane Dunning. Right-hander Cade Cavalli is poised to be the next hurler to add his name to the list (as is Cole Henry – maybe). Taken with the 22nd overall pick three years ago, Cavalli was an unhittable whirlwind during his COVID-abbreviated 2020 season at Oklahoma: 23.2 innings pitched, 37 strikeouts, and just five free passes. Cavalli, a former two-way player with the Sooners, would blitz through three levels during his professional debut two years ago, throwing 123.1 innings with a whopping 175 strikeouts and 60 free passes with Wilmington, Harrisburg, and Rochester. Last season, the 6-foot-4, 240-pound righty made 20 starts with the Red Wings of Rochester, averaging 9.6 strikeouts and 3.6 walks per nine innings to go along with a 3.71 ERA. Washington called him for his debut at the end of August. But after one disastrous starts against the Reds, Cavalli hit the disabled list with shoulder inflammation.

Snippet from The 2022 Prospect Digest Handbook: If the command upticks to average Cavalli has a chance to reach a Dylan Cease-type level.

Scouting Report: Consider the following:

> Since 2006, only three 23-year-old hurlers posted a 25% to 27% strikeout percentage with an 8.5% to 10.5% walk percentage in any Triple-A league (min. 75 IP): Reynaldo Lopez, Allen Webster, and Cade Cavalli.

An arsenal that's destined for a spot at – or, at least, near – the top of a big league rotation, the only thing that made hold Cavalli back is a spotty injury history. He dealt with a stress fracture in his precious right arm during his collegiate career, and then last season missed the last month or so with shoulder inflammation. Mid-90s fastball that hovers near plus-plus territory. Plus hammer curveball. Above-average changeup. He'll also work in an upper-80s, above-average slider. Physically, he's built like Jacob deGrom.

Ceiling: 4.0-win player
Risk: Moderate
MLB ETA: Debuted in 2022

4. Robert Hassell, CF

Hit	Power	SB	Patience	Glove	Overall
45/55	50	60	55	50	55

Born: 08/15/01	Age: 21	Bats: L	Top Production Comp: N/A
Height: 6-2	Weight: 195	Throws: L	

Season	Team	Age	Level	PA	1B	2B	3B	HR	SB	CS	BB%	K%	AVG	OBP	SLG	ISO
2021	SDP	19	A	429	77	31	3	7	31	6	13.29%	17.25%	0.323	0.415	0.482	0.159
2021	SDP	19	A+	87	9	2	1	4	3	0	10.34%	28.74%	0.205	0.287	0.410	0.205
2022	WSN	20	A+	45	7	1	0	0	3	0	13.33%	26.67%	0.211	0.311	0.237	0.026
2022	SDP	20	A+	346	61	19	1	10	20	3	10.98%	19.08%	0.299	0.379	0.467	0.168
2022	WSN	20	AA	122	18	5	0	1	1	0	10.66%	28.69%	0.222	0.311	0.296	0.074

Background: The early picks of the 2020 draft have been plagued by a *lot* of disappointment – which isn't overly surprising given the pandemic's effect on the college and high school seasons. But the Padres – seemingly – did well with their selection of Robert Hassell. The eighth overall

Washington Nationals

pick that summer, Hassell was an offensive dynamo during his debut the next year. The 6-foot-2, 195-pound Tennessee native dominated the Low-A competition to the tune of .323/.415/.482 and spent the last few weeks getting acclimated in High-A. The 2022 campaign was a tale of two seasons for the former first rounder. He slugged .299/.379/.467 with 19 doubles, one triple, 10 homeruns, and 20 stolen bases with the Fort Wayne TinCaps. But Hassell struggled considerably following his trade to Washington, hitting .211/.311/.237 in 10 High-A games and a paltry .222/.312/.296 in 27 games with Harrisburg. The young centerfielder finished his sophomore professional season with an aggregate .273/.357/.407 slash line with 25 doubles, one triple, 11 homeruns, and 24 stolen bases. Per *Weighted Runs Created Plus*, his production topped the league average mark by 14%. Washington sent Hassell to the Arizona Fall League after the season, though he squeezed in just a pair of games due to a broken hamate in his right hand – an injury that can sap a hitters' power for a while after he returns.

Snippet from The 2022 Prospect Digest Handbook: Strong contact hitter who sprays the ball from foul line to foul line, shows an advanced feel for hitting, a terrific eye at the plate, and plus speed. He's also showing the trademarks of above-average power as well.

Scouting Report: It's not overly concerning that Hassell's production cratered following his organizational move. It's likely a young player pressing to make a good impression with his new team. But there *are* some red flags that popped up last season, though. Mainly, his struggles against left-handers; he batted a lowly .235/.333/.314 against them (as compared to a .285/.364/.434 production line vs. right-handers). Even more concerning were his contact rates: he fanned in nearly 37% plate appearances against southpaws and just 17.7% time against right-handers. Hassell continues to take a spray-it-around-the-diamond approach at the plate. Above-average power to the pull side. Above-average speed and leatherwork in centerfield. There's borderline All-Star potential, but he needs to be able to hit lefties (which he did in 2021).

Ceiling: 3.5-win player
Risk: Moderate to High
MLB ETA: 2024

5. Elijah Green, CF

Hit	Power	SB	Patience	Glove	Overall
30/40	60	50	50	55	60

Born: 12/04/03	Age: 19	Bats: R	Top Production Comp: N/A
Height: 6-3	Weight: 225	Throws: R	

Season	Team	Age	Level	PA	1B	2B	3B	HR	SB	CS	BB%	K%	AVG	OBP	SLG	ISO
2022	WSN	18	CPX	52	7	4	0	2	1	0	11.54%	40.38%	0.302	0.404	0.535	0.233

Background: IMG Academy has an interesting backstory. It was originally the Nick Bollettieri Tennis Academy, which opened all the way back in 1978. Less than a decade later IMG would purchase the tennis coach's school and would slowly add athletic programs under their brand. Baseball, along with soccer, would eventually be added in 1994. From there it took another 11 seasons before the one the members would be drafted from their Florida-based campus. And, for the most part, IMG Academy had very little sway in the sport for nearly another decade – though they would eventually send the likes of Paolo Espino, Tyler Pastornicky, and John Ryan Murphy, none of whom were drafted particularly early, the big leagues. But beginning in 2015 the school has a tremendous run of talent called in the MLB draft:

> #1. 18 total players were chosen over the previous seven years.
> #2. Of those 18, ten of them received bonuses of at least $500,000.
> #3. In 2019 and 2021, the program had 10 players draft – including one first rounder (Brennan Malone), three second rounders (Rece Hinds, Kendall Williams, and James Wood), and a third round selection (Drew Gray).

Elijah Green, the explosively talented outfielder, became the highest drafted player in school history. The son of former NFL Pro Bowler Eric Green, the top prospect slugged a scorching .462/.592/1.000 with 11 doubles, two triples, nine homeruns, and 15 stolen bases. The younger Green was committed to the University of Miami. Washington selected him in the opening round, fifth overall, and signed him to a deal worth $6.5 million. Green mashed an impressive .302/.404/.535 with four doubles, two homeruns, and a stolen base in only 12 games in the Complex League. He finished the year with a poor 21-to-6 strikeout-to-walk ratio.

Scouting Report: Per the usual, here's my pre-draft scouting report:

> "Joe Mauer, a future Hall of Fame catcher, famously struck out just one time during his four-year high school career – a span that lasted 222 at bats. Paul Feiner, a digital marketer, was the pitching culprit snapped off a curveball that the Mighty Casey swung right through. Elijah Green, on the other hand, has whiffed a lot during his final two seasons. As a junior the 6-foot-3, 225-pound outfielder struck out 34 times in just 98 plate appearances – or nearly 35% of the time. Last season, he improved that horrific total to a still-concerning 20%. That seems like an awful lot for a potential top prospect.

Washington Nationals

Green faced a bevy offspeed pitches during his final season and he looked vulnerable at times, particularly to slow stuff low and away. Big time power, perhaps the best in the draft class. Toolsy oozing from every pore. Plus arm, plus speed, plus power. The question: will the bat be enough to make him a consistent threat in the professional ranks. I wouldn't be surprised to see Green slide to the latter half of the first round or second, despite having the Potential Top Pick label slapped on him."

Ceiling: 4.0-win player
Risk: High
MLB ETA: 2026

6. Jarlin Susana, RHP

FB	CB	SL	CH	Command	Overall
80	N/A	60	45	40/50	60

Born: 03/23/04	Age: 19	Bats: R	Top Production Comp: N/A
Height: 6-6	Weight: 235	Throws: R	

Season	Team	Age	Level	IP	TBF	K/9	K%	BB/9	BB%	K-BB%	ERA	FIP	xFIP	Pit/Bat
2022	SDP	18	CPX	29.1	111	13.50	39.64%	3.38	9.91%	29.73%	2.45	3.13	3.19	2.17
2022	WSN	18	A	10.1	44	11.32	29.55%	4.35	11.36%	18.18%	2.61	4.04	3.93	4.43

Background: Very few prospects had the type of whirlwind 2022 season that Susana did. San Diego signed the gargantuan right-hander to an equally large $1.7 million deal last January. Less than seven months later the Friars shipped off the teenager as a key cog in the Juan Soto mega deal. His entire stint in the Padres' farm system lasted all of eight Complex League starts. But he *clearly* made quite the impression. He tossed 29.1 innings with 44 punch outs and just 11 free passes in his eight games. Following the trade all the way across the country, Washington sent the 6-foot-6, 235-pound righty down to the Complex League for another pair of starts before pushing him up to full season action for three final games. Overall, Susana hurled 45.0 innings of work, recording 66 punch outs and 20 free passes to go along with an aggregate 2.40 ERA. For those counting at home: he averaged 13.2 strikeouts and 4.0 walks per nine innings during his debut.

Scouting Report: My new favorite pitching prospect in the minor leagues. Susana is poised to become 2023's version of Eury Pérez, who quickly became one of the game's best pitching prospects during his dominant 2022 campaign. Susana owns one of the best fastballs in the minor leagues and one of the best MiLB heaters I've seen in several years. It's a plus-plus offering sitting comfortably in the 99- to 100-mph with explosive, almost unfair late life. It touched as high as 102 mph during one of the game's I scouted and reached 103 mph during the season. It's easy, premium velocity, like watching Brusdar Graterol throw. His main offspeed weapon is an 86- to 91-mph slider that made the mortals in Low-A bend a knee in reverence. His low- to mid-90s changeup is firm and he struggled to command it. Reports indicated he'll throw a curveball as well, though I never saw it. Susana adds a little bit of Johnny Cueto / Luis Tiant funk-and-twist at times in his windup. Susana's command is solid, surprisingly so given his age, level of competition, and velocity. He needs to develop a third offering. But the ceiling is practically unlimited – as long as he can navigate his way through the injury nexus.

Ceiling: 4.5-win player
Risk: High
MLB ETA: 2024/2025

7. Jake Bennett, LHP

FB	SL	CH	Command	Overall
55	50	55	55	50

Born: 12/02/00	Age: 22	Bats: L	Top Production Comp: N/A
Height: 6-6	Weight: 234	Throws: L	

Background: Oklahoma-based Bixby High School is home to a pair of well-known ballplayers: right-hander Cade Cavalli and southpaw Jake Bennett. Their time overlapped a couple years during their respective prep careers. And, of course, Cavalli was originally drafted by the Atlanta Braves in 29th round in 2017, but would eventually head to the University of Oklahoma and become a late-round pick by the Nationals three years later. Bennett's path to professional ball was eerily similar. The big 6-foot-6, 234-pound lefty was originally selected by the – you've guessed it – the Washington Nationals in the 39th round in 2019. And after a solid three-year career at – you've guessed it – the University of Oklahoma, the Nationals came calling again in 2022, selecting him in the second round, 45th overall. Bennett was particularly dominant during final season with the Sooners last year. Making a career best 20 appearances, 19 of which came via the start, he posted an impressive 133-to-22 strikeout-to-walk ratio in 117.0 innings of work. He tallied a 10-4 win-loss record and a 3.69 ERA. For his career, he averaged 10.4 strikeouts and just 1.9 walks per nine innings to go along with a 4.30 ERA. Washington signed him to a deal worth $1,734,800. Bennett did not appear in an affiliated game.

Washington Nationals

Scouting Report: My pre-draft write-up:

> "Consider the following:
>
> Since 2015, seven Division I hurlers averaged at least 10 strikeouts and fewer than 2.0 walks per nine innings in a season (min. 105 IP): Casey Mize, Luke Heimlich, Pete Hansen, Devin Hemmerich, Miller Hogan, Tanner Hall, and – of course – Jake Bennett.
>
> The long-limbed lefty attacks hitters with a low- to mid-90s fastball that – unsurprisingly – plays up due to his frame size. The plus offering will touch as high as 96 mph when needed. Bennett complements the offering with an average slider and an above-average changeup, that he tends to use as his go-to offspeed pitch to either lefties or righties. Bennett has a long history of filling the strike zone with quality pitches, going from his high school days through his college years and into the Cape Cod League (where he posted a 30-to-3 strikeout-to-walk ratio in 28.0 innings of work). Ceiling as a #4-type arm – a la Sean Manaea with more velocity."

Ceiling: 2.5-win player
Risk: Moderate
MLB ETA: 2025

8. Cole Henry, RHP

FB	CB	CH	Command	Overall
60	60	55	50	55

Born: 07/15/99 **Age:** 23 **Bats:** R **Top Production Comp:** Rich Harden
Height: 6-4 **Weight:** 215 **Throws:** R

Season	Team	Age	Level	IP	TBF	K/9	K%	BB/9	BB%	K-BB%	ERA	FIP	xFIP	Pit/Bat
2021	WSN	21	A+	43.0	163	13.19	38.65%	2.30	6.75%	31.90%	1.88	2.86	3.32	3.91
2022	WSN	22	AA	23.2	85	10.65	32.94%	3.42	10.59%	22.35%	0.76	2.87	3.82	4.11

Background: A prized arm coming out of Alabama-based Florence High School. *Perfect Game* ranked the 6-foot-4, 215-pound righty as 79th overall prospect in the country. But his firm commitment to Louisiana State University caused him to stumble in the draft – though the Tigers snagged him in the 38th round five years ago. Henry sparkled during his freshman season at LSU, stepping into the SEC powerhouse's rotation for 11 starts (as well as three relief appearances). He recorded a dominant 72-to-18 strikeout-to-walk ratio in only 58.1 innings of work. The burgeoning ace carried that momentum into a dominant start to the 2020 season as well, averaging 10.9 strikeouts and 2.8 walks per nine innings across four starts before the year prematurely ended due to the pandemic. Henry's professional debut was interrupted by an elbow issue, but he managed to sparkle in nine appearances in High-A. Last season, yet again, he dealt with an injury – though this one forced him under the knife. Henry underwent thoracic outlet syndrome in late August. Prior to the injury, he made nine starts with Harrisburg and Rochester, throwing just 31.2 innings with 34 punch outs and 11 walks with a dazzling 1.71 ERA.

Snippet from The 2022 Prospect Digest Handbook: Henry's battled some health issues throughout his career: a wonky elbow forced him out of action for a couple months in 2021; he also battled COVID and then dealt with a stress reaction in his upper arm, as well as another elbow issue as a freshman with LSU. But when he's healthy he's…damn near brilliant. He has some #3/#4-type potential, though he needs to stay healthy.

Scouting Report: Henry ticks off a lot of the important boxes for future big league success: plus 94- to 96-mph fastball with riding life, plus 80s curveball, above-average changeup, strike-thrower, athletic. But the one thing he hasn't displayed is largely out of his control – health. Even going back to his days at LSU, Henry hasn't made it through a full season without some sort of serious ailment, from elbow woes to COVID to a stress reaction, a second elbow issue, and now thoracic outlet syndrome. Best case scenario at this point is Rich Harden. Plenty of risk. At this point Washington has to just be hoping to catch lightning in a bottle.

Ceiling: 3.0-win player
Risk: High
MLB ETA: 2024

Washington Nationals

9. Cristhian Vaquero, CF

Hit	Power	SB	Patience	Glove	Overall
30/50	30/55	60	50	50/55	50

Born: 09/13/04	Age: 18	Bats: B	Top Production Comp: N/A
Height: 6-3	Weight: 180	Throws: R	

Season	Team	Age	Level	PA	1B	2B	3B	HR	SB	CS	BB%	K%	AVG	OBP	SLG	ISO
2022	WSN	17	DSL	216	36	4	4	1	17	7	15.28%	17.59%	0.256	0.379	0.341	0.085

Background: The ball club has never shied away from spending big on the international market. The Mike Rizzo-led front office signed Dominican infielder Yasel Antuna to a massive $3.9 million during the summer of 2016. Roughly five years later the Nationals handed fellow infielder and countryman Armando Cruz the same seven-figure deal. The problem is that the organization has seen little return on their large investments. Antuna has been abysmal since moving into full-season ball in 2018. Cruz had a disappointing debut in the Dominican Summer League two years ago and batted an empty .275/.320/.362 in the Complex League in 2022. The front office is hoping that Cristhian Vaquero makes a larger splash. A native of La Habana, Cuba, Vaquero signed out the Dominican Republic last January for a *huge* $4,925,000 deal. The 6-foot-3, 180-pound switch-hitting centerfielder batted a mediocre .256/.379/.341 with just four doubles, four triples, a dinger, and 17 stolen bases (in 24 total attempts). Per *Weighted Runs Created Plus*, his overall production was just 3% better than the league average threshold.

Scouting Report: Plus speed that should allow him to develop into an adept base thief and an above-average defender in centerfield. A recent convert to switch-hitting, Vaquero's swing looks more natural, fluid from the right side than the left, which looks robotic and a bit stiff. There's above-average power potential. A lot of Vaquero's production last summer came from his bloated walk rate (15.3%). Very, very raw. The tools are there. But it looks like he's going to need quite a bit of developmental time.

Ceiling: 2.5-win player
Risk: Moderate to High
MLB ETA: 2026

10. Israel Pineda, C

Hit	Power	SB	Patience	Glove	Overall
45	45	30	50	60	45

Born: 04/03/00	Age: 23	Bats: R	Top Production Comp: Tucker Barnhart
Height: 5-11	Weight: 188	Throws: R	

Season	Team	Age	Level	PA	1B	2B	3B	HR	SB	CS	BB%	K%	AVG	OBP	SLG	ISO
2021	WSN	19	A	358	47	12	4	5	7	8	8.38%	34.08%	0.209	0.279	0.316	0.107
2022	WSN	20	A	315	57	19	2	10	26	5	11.43%	24.76%	0.315	0.394	0.505	0.190
2022	WSN	20	A+	133	17	4	1	1	13	2	9.02%	27.82%	0.195	0.273	0.271	0.076

Background: Since their first season in 2005, the Nationals have been on this perpetual search for a long term catcher. They've run out decent veterans like Brian Schneider or Matt Wieters and coaxed 155 games out of Hall of Famer Ivan Rodriguez at the end of his career. Young homegrown candidates like Jesus Flores and Wilson Ramos had have flashes of solid – and underrated – performances, but they were just that – flashes. Personally, I do think Keibert Ruiz becomes a mainstay behind plate as a batting average-driven hitter. And Israel Pineda may offer a solid Option B if Ruiz fails. A native of Maracay, Venezuela, the 5-foot-11, 188-pound backstop looked quite promising during his brief stint in the Gulf Coast League (.288/.323/.441) and his trip through the old New York-Penn League as well (.273/.341/.388). But Pineda stumbled in Low-A as a 19-year-old in 2019 and he continued to struggle in High-A two years ago (.208/.260/.389). Last season, though, the Venezuelan catcher finally found his hitting stroke again. Making stops with Wilmington, Harrisburg, and Rochester, Pineda batted .258/.325/.458 with career highs in doubles (20), homeruns (16), stolen bases (three), and he tied career high with two triples. Washington promoted Pineda up to The Show at the end of the year. He would go 1-for-13 in four games.

Scouting Report: Pineda's breakout season came with a rather large caveat of sorts: beyond his 67-game cameo in his return to High-A, his trips through Double-A, Triple-A, and the big leagues were quite abbreviated. Meaning: the league wasn't able to make any necessary adjustments. But let's take a look at his work with the Blue Rocks of Wilmington. Consider the following:

> Since 2006, only seven 22-year-old hitters met the following criteria in any High-A league (min. 250 PA): 102 to 112 wRC+, 24.5% to 26.5% strikeout rate, and a 7% to 9% walk rate. Those seven hitters: Darnell Sweeney, Anfernee Seymour, Cale Iorg, Keon Barnum, Bruce Caldwell, Dillon Persinger, and – of course – Israel Pineda.

Pineda's true calling card has always been his work with the leather behind the plate, continually grading out as an above-average, sometimes plus, defender. And according to *Baseball Prospectus'* pitch framing metrics, he's serviceable at that as well. Anything he adds with the bat is just icing on the proverbial cake – which should be sufficient enough to push him into a low-end starting gig. 45-grade hit tool and power.

Ceiling: 1.5-win player
Risk: Moderate
MLB ETA: Debuted in 2022

Washington Nationals

11. Jackson Rutledge, RHP

FB	CB	SL	CH	Command	Overall
70	50	60	55	50	50

Born: 04/01/99	Age: 24	Bats: R	Top Production Comp: N/A
Height: 6-8	Weight: 243	Throws: R	

Season	Team	Age	Level	IP	TBF	K/9	K%	BB/9	BB%	K-BB%	ERA	FIP	xFIP	Pit/Bat
2021	WSN	22	A	22.0	98	10.64	26.53%	3.68	9.18%	17.35%	5.32	3.70	4.16	3.86
2021	WSN	22	A+	10.2	58	8.44	17.24%	7.59	15.52%	1.72%	12.66	4.70	6.60	4.31
2022	WSN	23	A	97.1	423	9.15	23.40%	2.68	6.86%	16.55%	4.90	3.89	3.93	3.68

Background: The 2021 season was not kind to Jackson Rutledge. A wonky right shoulder limited the former first rounder to just 13 appearances, spread across the three lowest stateside levels, and 36.1 innings of work. And even when he was on the bump – which wasn't often – the 6-foot-8, 243-pound hurler was awful, posting a 7.68 ERA while struggling with command / control issues. And the struggles carried on over into the Arizona Fall League as well; he posted a mediocre 17-to-10 strikeout-to-walk ratio in 19.1 innings with the Surprise Saguaros. Finally healthy, at least superficially, in 2022, Rutledge made 20 brief starts with the Fredericksburg Nationals, throwing a career high 97.1 innings with 99 punch outs and just 29 free passes. He averaged 9.2 punch outs and 2.7 walks per nine innings. He finished the year with a 4.90 ERA, a 3.89 FIP, and a 3.93 xFIP.

Snippet from The 2022 Prospect Digest Handbook: If you catch him on a good game you'd swear he'd be nearly as unhittable as Bob Gibson. But those good days didn't come nearly as frequently as the club – or Rutledge, for that matter – would've liked in 2021. Rutledge, like Cole Henry, needs to prove he can take the ball every fifth day. It goes without saying that there's some reliever, two-pitch wipe out risk in play.

Scouting Report: Consider the following:

> Since 2006, twenty 23-year-old hurlers posted a 22.5% to 24.5% strikeout percentage with a 6% to 8% walk percentage in any Low-A league (min. 75 IP). Of those twenty aforementioned pitchers, the most notable is Mark Leiter Jr., who's thrown 181.2 innings in the big leagues between the Blue Jays, Cubs, and Phillies.

Not only has the repertoire and overall velocity held up through the shoulder woes and limited 2021 season, but Rutledge's changeup flashed above-average at times. A strong upgrade from the below-average one he featured two summers ago. The big right-hander will frequently touch as high as 98 mph with his plus-plus fastball. And his mid- to upper-80s slider adds a second swing-and-miss offering to his arsenal. It seems that he's completely scrapped his average-ish / fringy curveball all together. Rutledge is now entering his age-24 season with just 10.2 innings above Low-A (and that happened two years ago). So it's surprising the Nationals didn't promote him at the end of the year. He's going to have to make up for a lot of lost development time. And he's going to need to do it quickly.

Ceiling: 1.5-win player
Risk: Moderate
MLB ETA: 2024

12. T.J. White, LF/RF

Hit	Power	SB	Patience	Glove	Overall
45/50	50/55	40/30	50	45	45

Born: 06/23/03	Age: 210	Bats: B	Top Production Comp: N/A
Height: 6-2	Weight: 210	Throws: R	

Season	Team	Age	Level	PA	1B	2B	3B	HR	SB	CS	BB%	K%	AVG	OBP	SLG	ISO
2021	WSN	17	CPX	59	9	2	0	4	1	0	8.47%	23.73%	0.283	0.356	0.547	0.264
2022	WSN	18	A	382	52	20	2	11	8	1	11.52%	27.23%	0.258	0.353	0.432	0.173

Background: During the mid-1960s through the early-1970s Paul M. Dorman High School was a little bit of a baseball hotbed, producing four prospects that were taken among the first five rounds of the MLB Draft. The most prominent of those players was shortstop Terry Hughes, the #2 overall pick in the 1967 draft who went ahead of Hall of Famer Ted Simmons, lefty Jon Matlack, and Bobby Grich (who should be in the Hall of Fame). Eventually, though, the school's pipeline to the minor leagues eventually turned off and it would be nearly fifty years before the South Carolina-based high school would produce another player chosen among the top five rounds. That player: switch-hitting outfielder T.J. White, the 143rd overall pick two years ago. The 6-foot-2, 210-pound masher quietly turned in one of the better debuts that summer, slugging .283/.356/.547 with two doubles, four dingers, and a stolen base in only 15 games in the Complex League. Last season the front office sent White up to the Carolina League. And the young teenager more than held his own. Appearing in 92 games with the Fredericksburg Nationals, White batted .258/.353/.432 with 20 doubles, two triples, 11 homeruns, and eight stolen bases. Per *Weighted Runs Created Plus*, his production topped the league average mark by 18%.

Washington Nationals

Scouting Report: Consider the following:

Here's the of 18-year-old hitters that posted a 113 to 123 wRC+ in any Low-A league (min. 350 PA): Justin Upton, Rafael Devers, Ozzie Albies, Gleyber Devers, Willy Adames, Domingo Santana, Wendell Rijo, Ruddy Giron, and – of course – T.J. White.

Now the bad news…

White's strikeout rate, 27.2%, is the second worst among the group, trailing only Domingo Santana.

Arguably the most intriguing prospect in the Nationals system (read: not best, just most intriguing). The Nationals may have unearthed a potential starting caliber big leaguer in the fifth round. The ball jumps off of White's bat. There's above-average power potential, though he's just tapping into it. There's some swing-and-miss to his game and he's prone to streakiness. But there's a chance for a 50-grade bat and 55-grade power. Defensively, he plays the outfield like a future designated hitter. It seems like a long shot, but White has some very real starting potential here. He's set to spent 2023 in High-A, and potentially a portion in Double-A, as a 19-year-old. Don't sleep on him.

Ceiling: 1.5-win player
Risk: Moderate
MLB ETA: 2025/2026

13. Armando Cruz, SS

Hit	Power	SB	Patience	Glove	Overall
50	30	50	50	60	45

Born: 01/16/04 **Age:** 19 **Bats:** R **Top Production Comp:** César Izturis
Height: 5-10 **Weight:** 160 **Throws:** R

Season	Team	Age	Level	PA	1B	2B	3B	HR	SB	CS	BB%	K%	AVG	OBP	SLG	ISO
2021	WSN	17	DSL	197	31	8	1	1	11	4	8.12%	13.71%	0.232	0.292	0.305	0.073
2022	WSN	18	CPX	226	45	8	2	2	6	5	4.87%	17.26%	0.275	0.320	0.362	0.087
2022	WSN	18	A	17	3	1	0	0	0	0	11.76%	11.76%	0.267	0.353	0.333	0.067

Background: The front office rolled out the proverbial red carpet for the Dominican youngster two years ago, handing the teenager a franchise record-tying $3.9 million. The Nationals matched the deal handed to Yasel Antuna several years earlier. (Note: the franchise has since surpassed its record deal by inking Cristhian Vaquero to a deal worth more than a million dollars more.) Cruz made his debut in the foreign rookie league two years ago, hitting a lowly .232/.292/.305 with just eight doubles, one triple, and a homerun in 48 games. Last season the front office pushed the 5-foot-10, 160-pound shortstop stateside to the Complex League. He responded with a mediocre, power-deficient .275/.320/.362 with just eight doubles, two triples, and two homeruns. His production, as measured by *Weighted Runs Created Plus*, was 7% *below* the league average mark. He capped off his sophomore season with a three-game cameo in High-A.

Snippet from The 2022 Prospect Digest Handbook: Like a peacock sporting its feathers during mating season; Cruz is a flashy, silky smooth defender with the potential to earn a couple Gold Gloves in his career. Fluid movements with a strong arm and soft hands, there's no concern about his ability to handle the position as his 5-foot-10, 160-pound frame fills out. He has that certain pizzazz on the defensive side of the ball that can't be taught. It borderlines on cockiness – which I like. The swing, as expected, needs some work. He shows average bat speed and willingness to shoot the ball the other way, but he's robotic and stiff.

Scouting Report: It's still a glove-first profile, though his bat began to show a little bit of heartbeat during his sophomore season. Solid bat to ball skills without a true offensive skill standout, so the glove is going to have to carry him the rest of the way. Average bat. 30-grade power. Best case – and that's an *absolute best case scenario* – is that he becomes Omar Vizquel. But it's more likely than not he's César Izturis.

Ceiling: 1.5-win player
Risk: Moderate
MLB ETA: 2025/2026

14. Daylen Lile, OF

Hit	Power	SB	Patience	Glove	Overall
50	45	30	50	60	45

Born: 11/30/02 **Age:** 20 **Bats:** L **Top Production Comp:** N/A
Height: 6-0 **Weight:** 195 **Throws:** R

Season	Team	Age	Level	PA	1B	2B	3B	HR	SB	CS	BB%	K%	AVG	OBP	SLG	ISO
2021	WSN	18	CPX	80	12	2	0	0	2	1	18.75%	25.00%	0.219	0.363	0.250	0.031

Background: The Nationals opened up their 2021 draft class with a pair of high upside prep bats, first selecting shortstop Brady House with the 11th overall pick and then circling back around to grab Trinity High

Washington Nationals

School product Daylen Lile 36 selections later. Signed for $1.175 million, Lile appeared in 19 games with the organization's Complex League affiliate that summer, hitting a disappointing .219/.363/.250 with just a pair of doubles in 80 plate appearances. Unfortunately for the former second rounder, as well as for Washington, the young outfielder underwent Tommy John surgery last March and missed the entirety of 2022.

Scouting Report: With nothing new to report on, here's his scouting report in last year's Handbook:

> "Short, quick stroke and a natural loft that allows him to shoot balls to the gap and – perhaps – will develop into average power as his wiry frame fills out. He has trouble getting on top of pitches at the top of the zone. Very compact at the plate. And he's likely going to be slapped with the "professional hitter" label at some point in his career. There's a chance he develops into a corner outfielder with a 55- grade hit tool, solid walk rates, and slightly below average power. Average arm, nothing to write home about. Poor man's Carl Crawford."

Ceiling: 1.5-win player
Risk: Moderate
MLB ETA: 2026

15. Jeremy De La Rosa, CF

Hit	Power	SB	Patience	Glove	Overall
35/45	50	50	50	50	40

Born: 01/16/02	Age: 20	Bats: L	Top Production Comp: N/A
Height: 6-0	Weight: 199	Throws: L	

Season	Team	Age	Level	PA	1B	2B	3B	HR	SB	CS	BB%	K%	AVG	OBP	SLG	ISO
2021	WSN	19	A	358	47	12	4	5	7	8	8.38%	34.08%	0.209	0.279	0.316	0.107
2022	WSN	20	A	315	57	19	2	10	26	5	11.43%	24.76%	0.315	0.394	0.505	0.190
2022	WSN	20	A+	133	17	4	1	1	13	2	9.02%	27.82%	0.195	0.273	0.271	0.076

Background: Washington invested a decent sized sum into signing the toolsy, yet raw, centerfielder from Santo Domingo. And it looked like a sunk cost after his first two years in pro ball. De La Rosa cobbled together a putrid .232/.343/.366 slash line during his debut in the old Gulf Coast League four years ago. And that made his production in Low-A looked Ruthian. After minor league baseball returned from its COVID-imposed hiatus, the 6-foot, 199-pound outfielder batted a lowly .209/.279/.316 with just 12 doubles, four triples, five homeruns, and seven stolen bases (in 15 attempts) in 87 games with Fredericksburg. Unsurprisingly, the front office sent the young Dominican back down to Low-A and his bat – *finally* – awakened as he slugged .315/.394/.505 with 19 doubles, two triples, 10 homeruns, and 26 stolen bases (in only 31 attempts). His overall production with Fredericksburg, according to *Weighted Runs Created Plus*, was a massive 47% better than the league average mark. The organization's player development regime sent him up to High-A in mid-July. And De la Rosa's bat went limp as he hit a lowly .195/.273/.271 in 133 plate appearances.

Snippet from The 2022 Prospect Digest Handbook: The silver lining, though, is that in his last 30 games with the Low-A squad he slugged .272/.331/.412. He's probably better suited for a return trip to Low-A, but it wouldn't be surprising to see the Nationals continue to aggressively challenge him by promoting him up to High-A to start 2022.

Scouting Report: With regard to his breakout during his return trip to Fredericksburg last season, consider the following:

> Since 2006, only four 20-year-old hitters met the following criteria in any Low-A league (min. 300 PA): 142 to 152 wRC+, 24% to 26% strikeout rate, and a double-digit walk rate. Those four hitters: Nolan Jones, Isan Diaz, Eddys Leonard, and – of course – Jeremy De La Rosa.

De La Rosa's entire toolkit was on full display during his second stint with Fredericksburg last season, showcasing a solid hit tool, 55-grade power potential, and plus speed. But as soon as he was promoted up to High-A it was like a switch was turned off. Here's the bottom line: through 214 games of his minor league career, De La Rosa's been phenomenal for 69 games; the rest he's been abysmal. On more item to note: since the start of his professional career, De La Rosa's grown one inch and added 39 pounds of weight.

Ceiling: 1.0- to 1.5-win player
Risk: Moderate
MLB ETA: 2024/2025

Washington Nationals

16. Trey Lipscomb, 3B

Hit	Power	SB	Patience	Glove	Overall
50	55	30	45	50	45

Born: 06/14/00 **Age:** 23 **Bats:** R **Top Production Comp:** N/A
Height: 6-1 **Weight:** 200 **Throws:** R

Season	Team	Age	Level	PA	1B	2B	3B	HR	SB	CS	BB%	K%	AVG	OBP	SLG	ISO
2022	WSN	22	A	101	23	4	1	1	12	1	3.96%	18.81%	0.299	0.327	0.392	0.093

Background: There are numerous stories telling the tales of players betting on themselves, especially when it comes to the draft. Seemingly each year a highly touted player or two spurs the chance to enter pro ball as a high round pick for a chance to play collegiately – Brooks Lee immediately jumps to mind. But there aren't too many stories that perfectly capture the essence as Trey Lipscomb. After appearing in 12 games, but earning only 14 plate appearances, during his COVID-abbreviated freshman season, Lipscomb was caught in a numbers game over the next two seasons – thanks in large part to the vast wealth of Tennessee's talent. The 6-foot-1, 200-pound corner infielder played in just 25 contests, earning just 69 trips to the plate in 2020 and 2021. But he stuck with the Volunteers. Despite entering his final season. Despite entering his last chance at the draft as a 22-year-old. Despite being a relative unknown. And that bet paid off in a big way. In 66 games for Head Coach Tony Vitello, Lipscomb slugged a scorching .355/.428/.717 with 19 doubles, three triples, 22 homeruns, and four stolen bases (in five total attempts) for, arguably, the best team in the country. Washington selected him in the third round, 84th overall, and signed him for the recommended slot bonus – $758,900. He hit a respectable, batting average-driven .299/.327/.392 with four doubles, one triple, one homeruns, and a surprising 12 stolen bases (in 13 attempts).

Scouting Report: Per the usual, here's my pre-draft scouting report:

"Consider the following:

Since 2011, there have been just 34 Southeastern Conference hitters that batted at least .350 in a season (min. 275 PA). Of those aforementioned 34, thirty-one posted an OBP north of .420. Of those aforementioned 31, just five hitters slugged at least .700. Those five hitters are: Jonathan India, Andrew Benintendi, Brent Rooker, Wyatt Langford, and – of course – Trey Lipscomb.

Solid bat speed with a short, quick path to the plate. Lipscomb had no problem consistently barreling the SEC competition. He's likely going to be a solid batting average, lower-ish OBP, power driven player. Think along the lines of Maikel Franco's year in Kansas City when he batted .278/.321/.457."

Ceiling: 1.0- to 1.5-win player
Risk: Moderate
MLB ETA: 2025

17. Thad Ward, RHP

FB	CB	SL	CH	Command	Overall
50	50	55	55	45	40

Born: 01/16/97 **Age:** 26 **Bats:** R **Top Production Comp:** N/A
Height: 6-3 **Weight:** 192 **Throws:** R

Season	Team	Age	Level	IP	TBF	K/9	K%	BB/9	BB%	K-BB%	ERA	FIP	xFIP	Pit/Bat
2022	BOS	25	AA	33.1	139	11.07	29.50%	3.78	10.07%	19.42%	2.43	3.56	3.74	4.09

Background: There was quite a bit of hoopla surrounding this year's Rule 5 Draft. And Washington, armed with the top pick in the winter classic, snagged the best player available – right-hander Thad Ward. Originally taken by the Red Sox out of the University of Central Florida in the fifth round in 2018, Ward quickly established himself as one of the organization's most promising minor league hurlers after a tremendous 2019 campaign in which he posted a 157-to-57 strikeout-to-walk ratio in 126.1 innings between Greenville and Salem. But the surging former Knight would miss 2020 – like every other minor leaguer – and a wonky elbow limited him to just a pair of starts in 2021. Ward would eventually succumb to Tommy John surgery. He would make it back to action midway through last season. Including some tune-up / rehab starts, the 6-foot-3, 192-pound righty tossed 51.1 innings with 66 punch outs and 19 free passes to go along with a sparkling 2.28 ERA. Ward spent the fall playing for the Scottsdale Scorpions, fanning 15 against five free passes in 12.2 innings of work.

Scouting Report: Ward's always displayed a quality big league arsenal, but the wavering command / control had his final destination pointing towards a middle relief role. His stuff looked solid in the Arizona Fall League: average fastball / curveball with an above average slider and changeup. He should have no issues sliding into a medium leverage role in the middle innings of a game. Very quality pick up by Nats.

Washington Nationals

Ceiling: 1.0-win player
Risk: Moderate
MLB ETA: 2023

18. Jake Irvin, RHP

FB	CB	CH	Command	Overall
60	60	N/A	55	40

Born: 04/01/99	Age: 26	Bats: R	Top Production Comp: N/A
Height: 6-6	Weight: 225	Throws: R	

Season	Team	Age	Level	IP	TBF	K/9	K%	BB/9	BB%	K-BB%	ERA	FIP	xFIP	Pit/Bat
2022	WSN	25	A+	30.0	118	8.70	24.58%	2.40	6.78%	17.80%	1.50	2.72	3.86	3.75
2022	WSN	25	AA	73.1	306	9.57	25.49%	2.45	6.54%	18.95%	4.79	3.99	4.17	3.76

Background: Washington has made a point to scout the University of Oklahoma quite heavily over the past six years, eventually snagging a total of five former Sooners. And each of those five Oklahoma products have been drafted no later than the fourth round. The last of those picks just happens to be Jake Irvin, a member of the club's 2018 draft class who was selected with the 131st overall pick. A member of the school's rotation for his three collegiate seasons, Irvin dominated the old Gulf Coast and New York-Penn Leagues during his debut. And he remained solid, yet uninspiring, during his stint in Low-A in 2019 as he averaged 7.9 strikeouts and just 2.7 walks per nine innings. Like all minor leaguers, Irvin would lose a year of precious development time due to the pandemic. And then he would miss all of 2021 as he recovered from Tommy John surgery. Finally healthy last season, the 6-foot-6, 225-pound right-hander made 24 starts between Wilmington and Harrisburg, throwing 103.1 innings of work, recording 107 punch outs and just 28 free passes to go along with a 3.83 ERA.

Scouting Report: Consider the following:

> Since 2006, only four 25-year-olds posted a 24.5% to 26.5% strikeout percentage with a 5.5% to 7.5% walk percentage in any Double-A league (min. 70 IP): Austin Warner, Cole Johnson, Francisley Bueno, and Jake Irvin.

Almost exclusively a fastball / breaking ball pitcher. Irvin's fastball sits in the 94- to 97-mph range that he commands well to all four quadrants of the strike zone. He'll try to get hitters to chase it high when he's ahead in the count. His breaking ball is fascinating. It appears he'll throw two separate offerings, but the catcher only signals with one sign – curveball. It's almost exclusively called a slider, but it looks more like a curveball. He'll vary the break and velocity, having it range from the upper 70s all the way to the mid-80s. He's very resistant to throw the changeup, which almost guarantees him a spot in a bullpen in the coming years. Middle relief arm. Quality strike-thrower.

Ceiling: 1.0-win player
Risk: Moderate
MLB ETA: 2023

19. Andry Lara, RHP

FB	SL	CH	Command	Overall
55	55	45/50	50/55	40

Born: 01/06/03	Age: 20	Bats: R	Top Production Comp: N/A
Height: 6-4	Weight: 180	Throws: R	

Season	Team	Age	Level	IP	TBF	K/9	K%	BB/9	BB%	K-BB%	ERA	FIP	xFIP	Pit/Bat
2021	WSN	18	CPX	39.2	167	10.66	28.14%	2.95	7.78%	20.36%	4.54	4.55	4.12	1.75
2022	WSN	19	A	101.1	451	9.33	23.28%	3.91	9.76%	13.53%	5.51	4.54	4.44	3.68

Background: One of the club's big signings during the 2019 international free agency period. Washington handed the 6-foot-4, 180-pound right-hander a hefty $1.25 million bonus that summer. But unfortunately for Lara, as well as the organization, the former Bonus Baby wouldn't make his professional debut for nearly two years courtesy of the COVID pandemic. Lara would made nine appearances in the Complex League and another pair of starts in Low-A in 2021, throwing 48.1 innings with 52 strikeouts and 21 free passes to go along with a 4.66 ERA. Last season the Coro, Venezuela native made 23 starts with Fredericksburg, averaging 9.3 strikeouts and 3.9 walks per nine innings. He finished the year with a 5.51 ERA, a 4.54 FIP, and a 4.44 xFIP.

Snippet from The 2022 Prospect Digest Handbook: Unimpressive. At least during the A-Ball game I watched at the end of the year. Lara's fastball was sitting 90-91 but he could ramp it up to 94 mph when he felt like it. His above-average curveball would sit in the low 80s with promising shape and depth. And his changeup – at least the few that I saw – was, well, disappointing. Lara likely wouldn't have cracked the first round had he been in the 2021 draft, probably settling a round or three later.

Scouting Report: Consider the following:

> Since 2006, only three 19-year-old hurlers posted a 22.5% to 24.5% strikeout percentage with a 9% to 11% walk percentage in any Low-A league (min. 100 IP): Travis Wood, Paul Demny, Andry Lara.

Washington Nationals

Physically maxed before reaching his twenties. Lara looked much better during his sophomore season, showing a bit more life on his heater and a touch more bit on his breaking ball. The changeup is a bit too firm, though it does tumble. He owns two solid offerings, but he's lacking a true standout, swing-and-miss pitch that he can rely on when the opposition knows what's coming. Wavering command. But he's entering his age-20 season and should see a significant amount of time in High-A.

Ceiling: 1.0-win player
Risk: Moderate
MLB ETA: 2025

20. Gerardo Carrillo, RHP

FB	SL	CH	Command	Overall
50	55	50	40	40

Born: 09/13/98 **Age:** 23 **Bats:** R **Top Production Comp:** N/A
Height: 5-10 **Weight:** 170 **Throws:** R

Season	Team	Age	Level	IP	TBF	K/9	K%	BB/9	BB%	K-BB%	ERA	FIP	xFIP	Pit/Bat
2021	LAD	22	AA	59.1	267	10.62	26.22%	4.40	10.86%	15.36%	4.25	5.37	4.62	3.66
2021	WSN	22	AA	37.0	177	9.24	21.47%	5.11	11.86%	9.60%	5.59	5.49	5.00	3.87
2022	WSN	23	A+	10.0	43	9.00	23.26%	4.50	11.63%	11.63%	3.60	4.76	4.79	3.60
2022	WSN	23	AA	10.1	58	14.81	29.31%	6.97	13.79%	15.52%	11.32	4.87	5.11	4.14

Background: Baseball fans outside of Washington have been spoiled by the club's blockbuster deals the past couple of seasons. They received a massive haul last season in the Juan Soto selloff. Two years ago they acquired a quartet of players in the Trea Turner, Max Scherzer deal with Los Angeles. Keibert Ruiz and Josiah Gray spent the entirety of 2022 developing at the big league level with the Nationals. Minor league veteran Donavan Casey was added organizational depth. And Gerardo Carrillo, who was beginning to turn some heads prior to the trade, was limited to just 23.1 innings between the Complex League, Wilmington, and Harrisburg due to a wonky shoulder. He recorded a 28-to-13 strikeout-to-walk ratio with a 6.94 ERA.

Snippet from The 2022 Prospect Digest Handbook: Carrillo's not long for the rotation, but he has the makings – potentially – of a very useful, sometimes high leverage setup arm.

Scouting Report: Mediocre. Carrillo hardly resembled the pitcher I scouted the previous season. His once solid fastball was sitting 91- to 92-mph in short outings late in the year. His changeup had a little bit of funk to it but lacked a whole lot of velocity separation. His above-average slider, though, still looked good. He was always destined for a relief role. And it seems even more certain given the arsenal and lagging command as he's entering his age-24 season.

Ceiling: 0.5- to 1.0-win player
Risk: Moderate
MLB ETA: 2023/2024

Washington Nationals